CW00339800

STREE

Greater Manchester

Altrincham, Bolton, Bury, Oldham, Rochdale, Stockport, Wigan

First published in 1997 by

Philip's, a division of
Octopus Publishing Group Ltd
2-4 Heron Quays, London E14 4JP
An Hachette Livre UK Company

Fourth edition 2007
First impression 2007
GMADA

ISBN-10   0-540-09085-9 (pocket)
ISBN-13   978-0-540-09085-3 (pocket)

© Philip's 2007

Ordnance Survey®

This product includes mapping data licensed from
Ordnance Survey® with the permission of the
Controller of Her Majesty's Stationery Office.
© Crown copyright 2007. All rights reserved.
Licence number 100011710.

Data for the speed cameras provided by
PocketGPSWorld.com Ltd.

Ordnance Survey and the OS Symbol are
registered trademarks of Ordnance Survey, the
national mapping agency of Great Britain.

Printed by Toppan, China

Contents

II   **List of mobile speed cameras**

III   **Key to map symbols**

IV   **Key to map pages**

VI   **Route Planning**

VIII   **Administrative and Postcode boundaries**

1   **Street maps** at 2⅔ inches to 1 mile

138   **Street maps of selected areas**
at 5⅓ inches to 1 mile

172   **Index** of towns, villages, streets, hospitals, industrial
estates, railway stations, schools, shopping centres,
universities and places of interest

Digital Data

The exceptionally high-quality mapping found in this atlas is available as digital data in TIFF
format, which is easily convertible to other bitmapped (raster) image formats.

The index is also available in digital form as a standard database table. It contains all the details
found in the printed index together with the National Grid reference for the map square in which
each entry is named.

For further information and to discuss your requirements, please contact james.mann@philips-maps.co.uk

Mobile speed cameras

The vast majority of speed cameras used on Britain's roads are operated by safety camera partnerships. These comprise local authorities, the police, Her Majesty's Court Service (HMCS) and the Highways Agency.

This table lists the sites where each safety camera partnership may enforce speed limits through the use of mobile cameras or detectors. These are usually set up on the roadside or a bridge spanning the road and operated by a police or civilian enforcement officer. The speed limit at each site (if available) is shown in red type, followed by the approximate location in black type.

A6
Manchester, Stockport Rd

Salford, Manchester Rd

A34
Manchester, Birchfield Road

A49
Marus Bridge, Warrington Rd

A56
Bury, Bury New Rd

Bury, Walmersley Rd

Bury, Whalley Rd

A57
Manchester, Hyde Rd

Salford, Liverpool Rd

Tameside, Manchester Rd

A58
Bury, Bury & Bolton Rd

Bury, Rochdale Rd

A62
Manchester, Oldham Rd

Oldham, Oldham Rd

Oldham, Oldham Way

A575
Salford, Walkden Rd

A580
Salford, East Lancashire Rd

A627
Oldham, Chadderton Way

Oldham, Ashton Rd

A662
Manchester, Ashton New Rd

A663
Oldham, Broadway

A664
Manchester, Rochdale Rd

A665
Bury, New Rd

Bury, Radcliffe New Rd

A666
Bolton, Blackburn Rd

Bolton, St Peter's Way

Salford, Manchester Rd

A667
Bury, Ringley Rd West

A5103
Manchester, Princess Parkway/Road

A6010
Manchester, Alan Turing Way

A6044
Prestwich, Sheepfoot Lane

Prestwich, Hilton Lane

A6053
Radcliffe, Dumers Lane

A6104
Blackley, Victoria Avenue

B6196
Ainsworth, Church Street

Ainsworth, Cockey Moor Rd

B6213
Tottington, Turton Rd

B6214
Greenmount, Brandlesholme Rd

Holcombe, Helmshore Rd

Holcombe Brook, Longsight Rd

B6226
Horwich, Chorley Old Rd

UNCLASSIFIED
Ashton on Mersey, Ashton Lane

Bolton, Chorley Old Rd

Bolton, Hardy Mill Rd

Bolton, Hulton Lane

Bolton, Lever Park Avenue

Bolton, Plodder Lane

Bolton, Stitch Mi Lane

Bredbury, Ashton Rd

Bury, Croft Lane

Bury, Higher Lane

Bury, Stand Lane

Bury, Walshaw Rd

Manchester, Blackley New Rd

Manchester, Kingsway

Manchester, Mancunian Way

Oldham, Abbey Hills Rd

Oldham, Manchester Rd

Rochdale, Bagslate Moor Rd

Rochdale, Broad Lane

Rochdale, Bury Old Rd

Rochdale, Caldershaw Rd

Rochdale, Edenfield Rd

Rochdale, Halifax Rd

Rochdale, Heywood Old Rd

Rochdale, Hollin Lane

Rochdale, Manchester Rd

Rochdale, Queens Park Rd

Rochdale, Shawclough Rd

Rochdale, Smithybridge Rd

Rochdale, Todmorden Rd

Rochdale, Wildhouse Lane

Salford, Belvedere Rd

Salford, Langley Rd

Stockport, Birdhall Lane

Stockport, Bridge Lane

Stockport, Buxton Rd

Stockport, Chester Rd

Stockport, Councillor Lane

Stockport, Dialstone Lane

Stockport, Harrytown

Stockport, Jacksons Lane

Stockport, Kingsway

Stockport, Longhurst Lane

Stockport, Marple Rd

Stockport, Sandy Lane

Stockport, Schools Hill

Stockport, Strines Rd

Stockport, Styal Rd

Stockport, Wellington Rd North

Tameside, Mossley Rd

Tameside, Mottram Old Rd

Tameside, Mottram Rd

Tameside, Stamford Rd

Tameside, Stamford Street

Trafford, Church Rd

Trafford, Edge Lane

Trafford, Glebelands Rd

Trafford, Hope Rd

Trafford, Mosley Rd

Trafford, Norris Rd

Trafford, Park Rd

Trafford, Seymour Grove

Trafford, Warburton Lane

Trafford, Westinghouse Rd

Wigan, Almond Brook Rd

Wigan, Bickershaw Lane

Wigan, Bolton Rd

Wigan, Chaddock Lane

Wigan, Chorley Rd

Wigan, Crow Orchard Rd

Wigan, Lily Lane

Wigan, Newton Rd

Wigan, Pemberton Rd

Wigan, Scot Lane

Wigan, Victoria Street

Wigan, Wigan Rd

Motorway with junction number (22a)	**Ambulance station**
Primary route – dual/single carriageway	**Coastguard station**
A road – dual/single carriageway	**Fire station**
B road – dual/single carriageway	**Police station**
Minor road – dual/single carriageway	**Accident and Emergency entrance to hospital**
Other minor road – dual/single carriageway	**Hospital**
Road under construction	**Place of worship**
Tunnel, covered road	**Information Centre** (open all year)
Speed cameras - single, multiple	**Shopping Centre**
Rural track, private road or narrow road in urban area	**Parking, Park and Ride**
Gate or obstruction to traffic (restrictions may not apply at all times or to all vehicles)	**Post Office**
Path, bridleway, byway open to all traffic, road used as a public path	**Camping site, caravan site**
Pedestrianised area	**Golf course, picnic site**
Postcode boundaries DY7	**Important buildings, schools, colleges, universities and hospitals** Prim Sch
County and unitary authority boundaries	**Built up area**
Railway, tunnel, railway under construction	**Woods**
Tramway, tramway under construction	**Water name** River Medway
Miniature railway	**River, weir, stream**
Railway station Walsall	**Canal, lock, tunnel**
Private railway station	**Water**
Metro station South Shields	**Tidal water**
Tram stop, tram stop under construction	**Non-Roman antiquity** Church
Bus, coach station	**Roman antiquity** ROMAN FORT

	Adjoining page indicators and overlap bands The colour of the arrow and the band indicates the scale of the adjoining or overlapping page (see scales below)
87	
237	

	Railway or bus station building
	Place of interest
	Parkland

Acad	**Academy**	Inst	**Institute**	Recn Gd	**Recreation Ground**
Allot Gdns	**Allotments**	Ct	**Law Court**		
Cemy	**Cemetery**	L Ctr	**Leisure Centre**	Resr	**Reservoir**
C Ctr	**Civic Centre**	LC	**Level Crossing**	Ret Pk	**Retail Park**
CH	**Club House**	Liby	**Library**	Sch	**School**
Coll	**College**	Mkt	**Market**	Sh Ctr	**Shopping Centre**
Crem	**Crematorium**	Meml	**Memorial**	TH	**Town Hall/House**
Ent	**Enterprise**	Mon	**Monument**	Trad Est	**Trading Estate**
Ex H	**Exhibition Hall**	Mus	**Museum**	Univ	**University**
Ind Est	**Industrial Estate**	Obsy	**Observatory**	W Twr	**Water Tower**
IRB Sta	**Inshore Rescue Boat Station**	Pal	**Royal Palace**	Wks	**Works**
		PH	**Public House**	YH	**Youth Hostel**

■ The small numbers around the edges of the maps identify the 1 kilometre National Grid lines

■ The dark grey border on the inside edge of some pages indicates that the mapping does not continue onto the adjacent page

The scale of the maps on the pages numbered in blue is 4.2 cm to 1 km • 2⅔ inches to 1 mile • 1: 23810

0	¼	½	¾	1 mile
0	250m	500m	750m	1 kilometre

The scale of the maps on pages numbered in red is 8.4 cm to 1 km • 5⅓ inches to 1 mile • 1: 11900

0	220 yards	440 yards	660 yards	½ mile
0	125m	250m	375m	½ kilometre

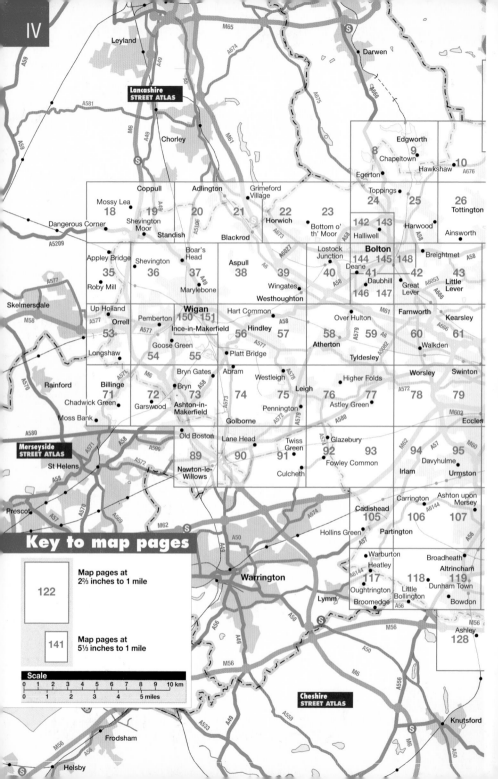

IV

Leyland

Darwen

Lancashire
STREET ATLAS

Chorley

Edgworth
8   9   Chapeltown   10
Egerton   Hawkshaw

Coppull   Adlington   Grimeford
Village   Toppings   24   25   26
Mossy Lea   Tottington
18   19   20   21   22   23   142   143   Harwood
Shevington   Horwich   Ainsworth
Moor   Standish   Blackrod   Bottom o'   Halliwell   Bolton
th' Moor   Lostock   144   145   148   Breightmet
Junction
Appley Bridge   Boar's   Aspull   Deane   41   42   43
Head   Daubhill   Great   Little
35   36   37   38   39   40   Lever   Lever
Roby Mill   Marylebone   Wingates   146   147
Shevington   Westhoughton

Up Holland   Wigan   Hart Common   Over Hulton   Farnworth   Kearsley
Orrell   Pemberton   150   151   56   57   58   59   60   61
53   Ince-in-Makerfield   Hindley   Atherton   Walkden
Longshaw   Goose Green   Platt Bridge   Tyldesley
54   55

Rainford   Billinge   Bryn Gates   Abram   Westleigh   Higher Folds   Worsley   Swinton
71   72   73   74   75   76   77   78   79
Chadwick Green   Garswood   Bryn   Leigh   Astley Green   Eccles
Moss Bank   Ashton-in-   Pennington
Makerfield   Golborne

Merseyside   Old Boston   Lane Head   Twiss   Glazebury   Davyhulme
STREET ATLAS   89   90   91   Green   92   93   94   95
St Helens   Culcheth   Fowley Common   Irlam   Urmston
Newton-le-   Partington
Willows   Carrington   Ashton upon
Prescot   Cadishead   Mersey
105   106   107
Hollins Green   Partington

Key to map pages

Warburton   Broadheath
Heatley   Altrincham
117   118   119
Oughtrington   Little   Dunham Town
Broomedge   Bollington   Bowdon
Warrington   Lymm

	Map pages at 2⅔ inches to 1 mile
122	

	Map pages at 5⅓ inches to 1 mile
141	

Ashley
128

Cheshire
STREET ATLAS

Scale
0 1 2 3 4 5 6 7 8 9 10 km
0   1   2   3   4   5 miles

Knutsford

Frodsham

Helsby

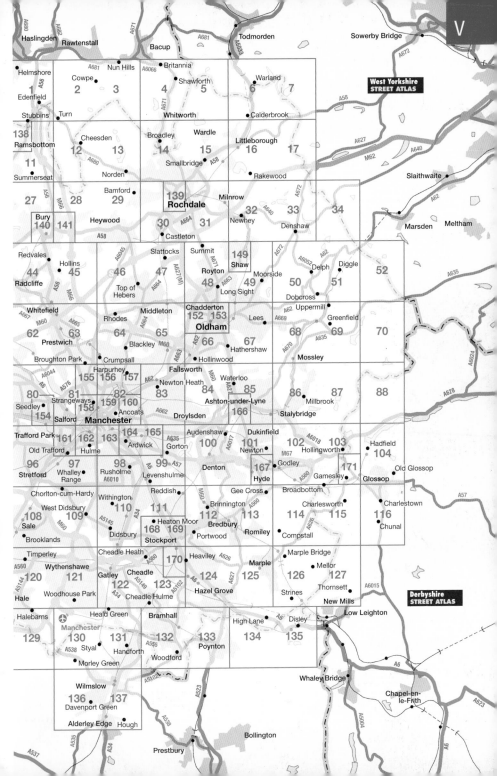

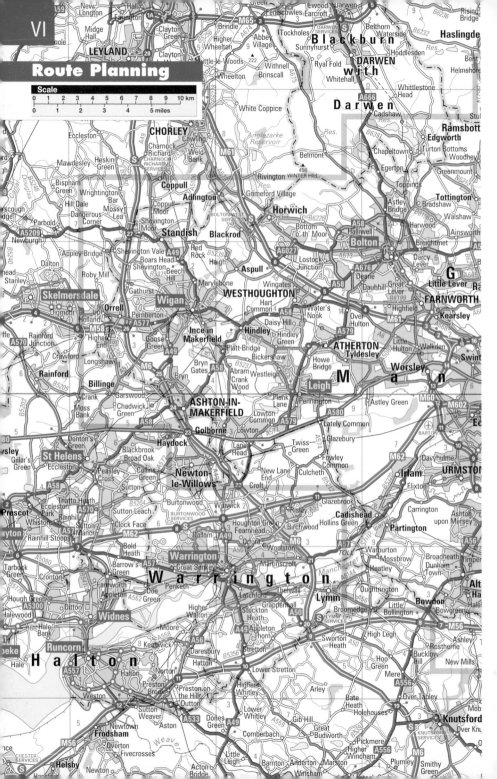

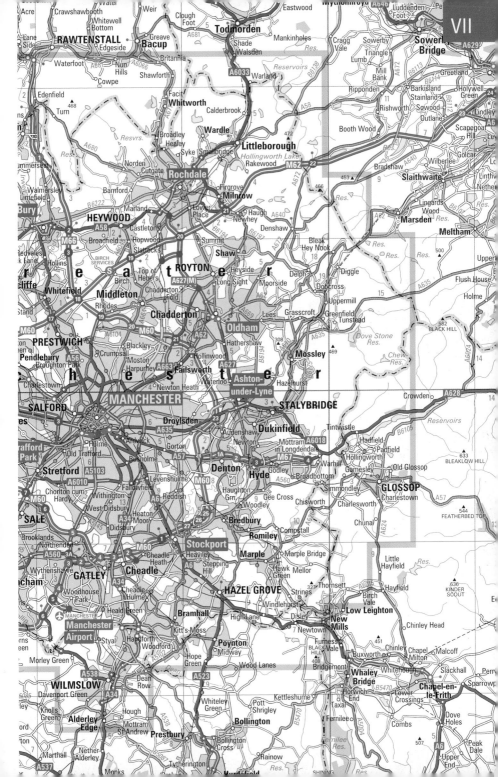

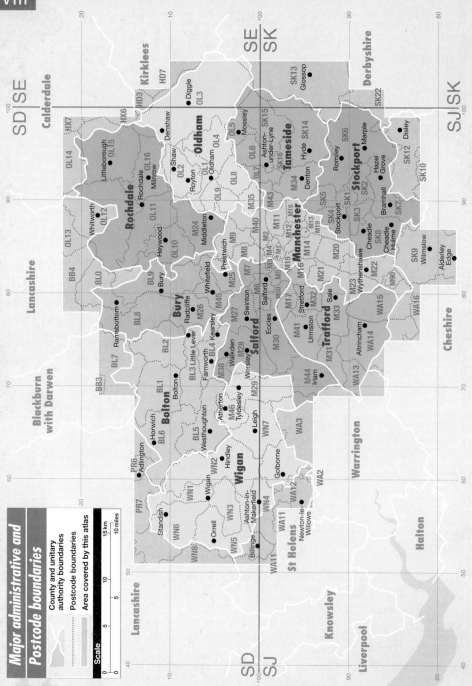

Major administrative and Postcode boundaries

County and unitary authority boundaries

Postcode boundaries

Area covered by this atlas

Scale

0   5   10   15 km

0   5   10 miles

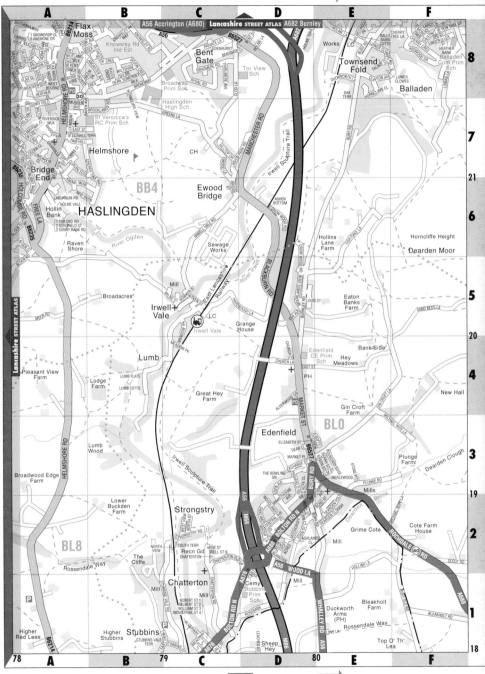

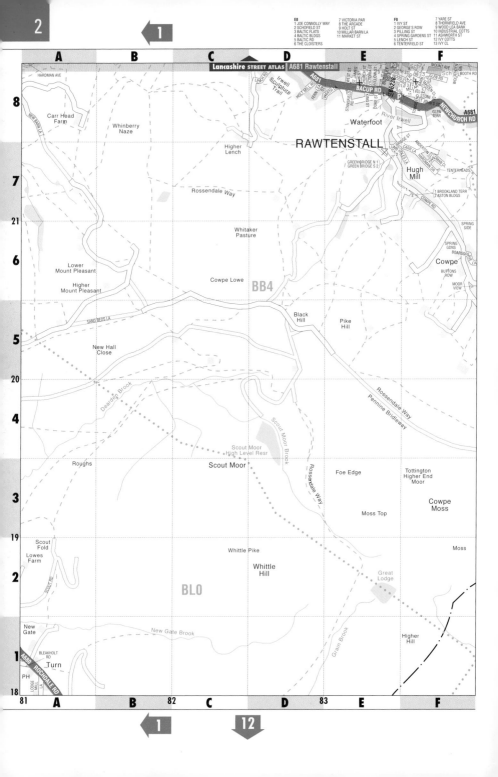

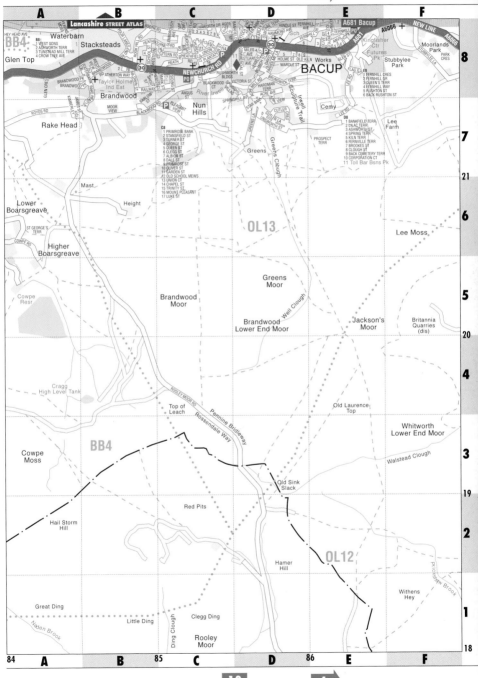

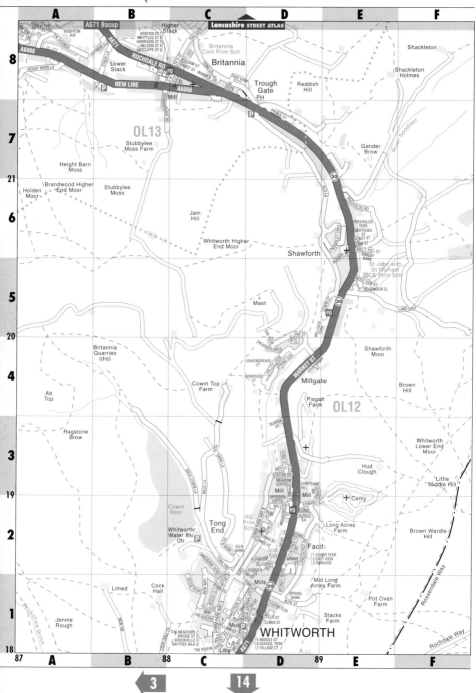

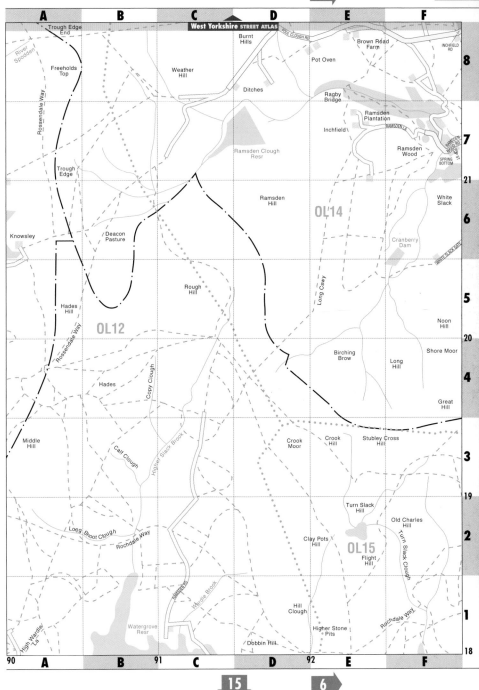

West Yorkshire STREET ATLAS

A **B** **C** **D** **E** **F**

8

7

21

6

20

5

4

19

3

2

18

1

River Spodden

Trough Edge End

Freeholds Top

Rossendale Way

Trough Edge

Knowsley

Deacon Pasture

Hades Hill

OL12

Hades

Rossendale Way

Middle Hill

Copy Clough

Calf Clough

Higher Slack Brook

Long Shoot Clough

Rochdale Way

High Wardle La

Watergrove Resr

Wardle Brook

Dobbin Hill

Weather Hill

Burnt Hills

Ditches

Ramsden Clough Resr

Rough Hill

Crook Moor

Clay Pots Hill

Hill Clough

Higher Stone Pits

POLE CLOUGH RD

Pot Oven

Ragby Bridge

Inchfield

Ramsden Hill

Long Cswy

Birching Brow

Crook Hill

Stubley Cross Hill

Turn Slack Hill

OL15

Flight Hill

Brown Road Farm

INCHFIELD RD

Ramsden Plantation

RAMSDEN LA

Ramsden Wood

RAMSDEN WOOD RD

SPRING BOTTOM

OL14

White Slack

Cranberry Dam

WHITE SLACK GATE

Long Hill

Noon Hill

Shore Moor

Great Hill

Old Charles Hill

Turn Slack Clough

Rochdale Way

90 91 C 92

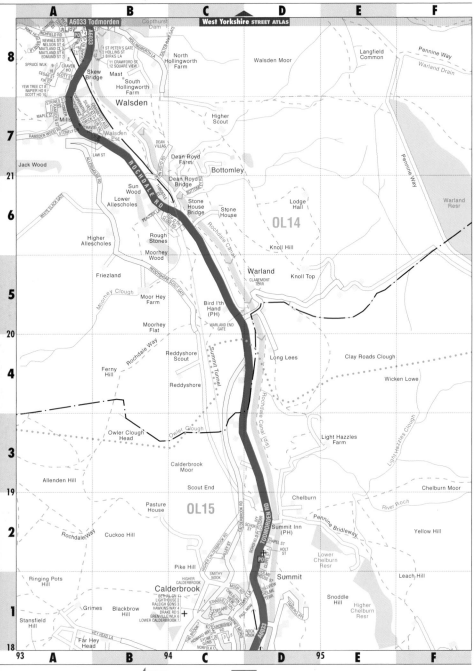

West Yorkshire STREET ATLAS

A **B** **C** **D** **E** **F**

8

Pennine Way
Warland Drain
Warland Drain
Bird Nest Hill
Turley Holes and Higher House Moor

7

HX7

Blake Moor

White Holme Drain

21

Little Dove Lowe

OL14

White Holme Moss

Round Hills

Turvin Clough

6

B6138

BLACKSTONE EDGE RD

Light Hazzles Resr

Little Moor Clough

5

Saw Gill Hollow

White Holme Resr

Little Moor

20

Round Hill

4

Captains Mark Hill

Farther Hill

Light Hazzles Edge

Chelburn Moor

Pennine Way

OL15

Toad La

Middle Hill

Soyland Moor

HX6

Knave Holes Hollow

Knave Holes Hill

3

Utley Edge

Byron Edge

Nigher Hill

TURVIN RD

Cold Laughton Drain

19

Head Drain

Black Castle Drain

Rush Bed Hill

2

Cow Head

Blackstone Edge Resr

B6138

Black Castle Hill

ROCHDALE RD

A58

Fairy Hill

1

A58 HALIFAX RD

Slate Pit Hill

18

96 **A** **B** 97 **C** **D** 98 **E** **F**

West Yorkshire STREET ATLAS

A58 Halifax

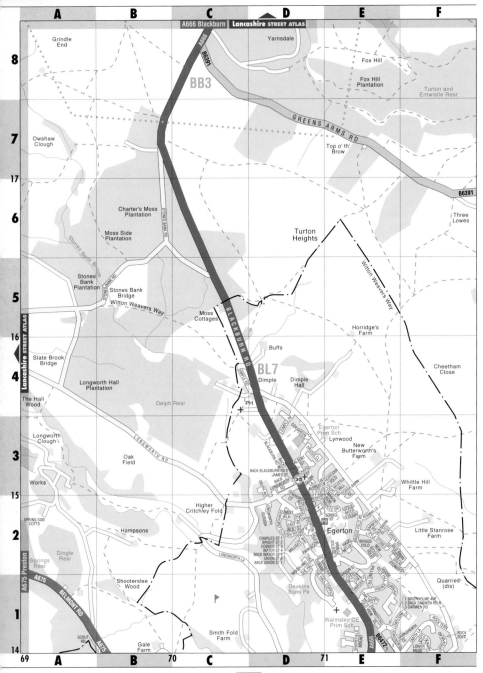

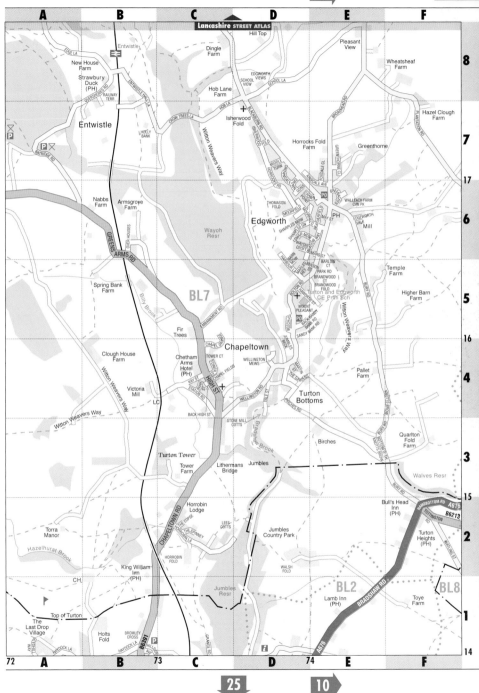

Lancashire STREET ATLAS

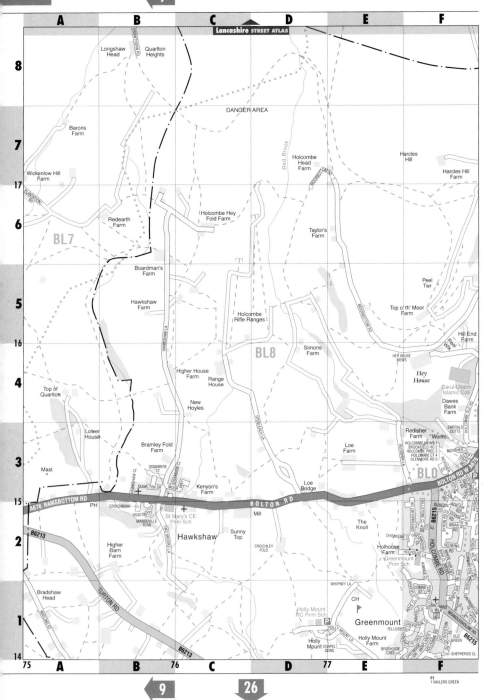

A　B　C　D　E　F

Lancashire STREET ATLAS

8

Longshaw
Head

Quarlton
Heights

DANGER AREA

7

Barons
Farm

Red Brook

Holcombe
Head
Farm

Harcles
Hill

Harcles Hill
Farm

17

Wickenlow Hill
Farm

6

BL7

Redearth
Farm

Holcombe Hey
Fold Farm

Taylor's
Farm

Boardman's
Farm

Hawkshaw
Farm

Peel
Twr

Top o' th' Moor
Farm

5

Holcombe
Rifle Ranges

BL8

Simons
Farm

Hill End
Farm

16

Higher House
Farm

Range
House

HEY HOUSE
MEWS

Hey
House

Darul-Uloom
Islamic Coll

4

Top of
Quarlton

New
Hoyles

Dawes
Bank
Farm

EMERALD
COTTS

Lower
House

Bramley Fold
Farm

STANMERE
CT

Loe
Farm

Redisher
Farm

Works

HOLCOMBE MEWS 1
BROOKFIELD HO 2
HOLCOMBE PREC 3
HOLCOMBE CT 4
GLENMORE RD 5

3

Mast

QUARLTON DR

Kenyon's
Farm

Loe
Bridge

REDISHER LA

BL0

BOLTON RD W

P

15

A676 RAMSBOTTOM RD

PH

CROCHBANK

TROUTBECK

MANDEVILLE
TERR

St Mary's CE
Prim Sch

Mill

BOLTON RD

The
Knoll

HILLSTONE

2

B6213

Higher
Barn
Farm

Hawkshaw

Sunny
Top

CROICHLEY
FOLD

Holhouse
Farm

Greenmount
Prim Sch

HOLCOMBE RD

B6215

1

Bradshaw
Head

TURTON RD

WHIPNEY LA

CH

Holly Mount
RC Prim Sch

P

Greenmount

Holly Mount
Farm

ORCHARD

B6215

14

Holly
Mount

CHAPEL
GDNS

BROOKSIDE
CRES

SHEPHERDS CL

B6213

75　A　B　76　C　D　77　E　F

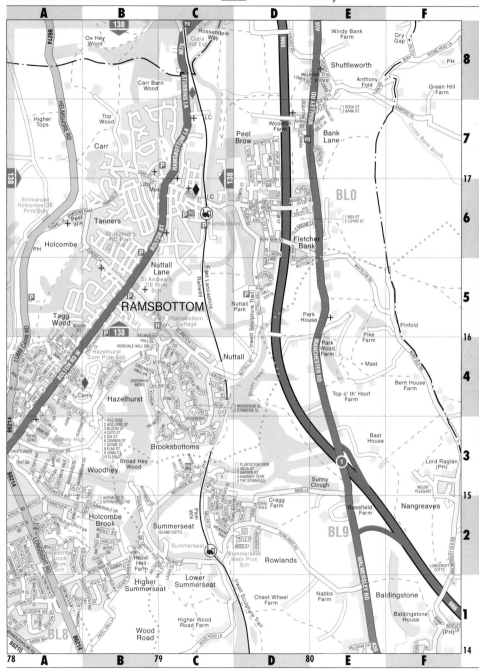

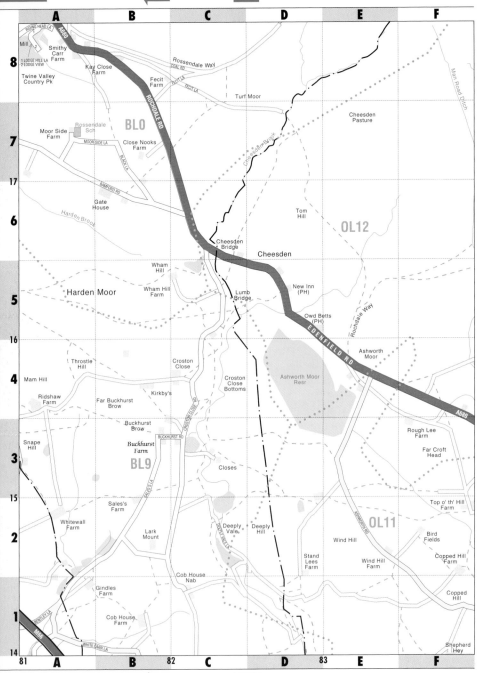

A   B   C   D   E   F

8

RIDING HEAD LA
Mill
1 LODGE HILL LA
2 LODGE VIEW
Smithy Carr Farm
Kay Close Farm
Twine Valley Country Pk
A680
Rossendale Way
COAL RD
Fecit La
FECIT LA
TECIT LA
Turf Moor

Cheesden Pasture

ROCHDALE RD
BL0

7

Moor Side Farm
Rossendale Sch
MOOR SIDE LA
Close Nooks Farm
BLACK LA

Cheesden Brook

OL12

17

BAMFORD RD
Gate House

Harden Brook

6

Tom Hill

Cheesden Bridge
Cheesden

Wham Hill

New Inn (PH)

5

Harden Moor
Wham Hill Farm
Lumb Bridge

Owd Betts (PH)

EDENFIELD RD
Rochdale Way

16

Croston Close

Ashworth Moor

4

Mam Hill
Throstle Hill
Kirkby's

Croston Close Bottoms
Ashworth Moor Resr

Ridshaw Farm
Far Buckhurst Brow

CROSTON CLOSE RD

Rough Lee Farm
Far Croft Head

Buckhurst Brow
BUCKHURST RD

Snape Hill
Buckhurst Farm
BL9
Closes

A680

3

Top o' th' Hill Farm

15

Sales's Farm
FECIT LA

OL11

Whitewall Farm
Lark Mount
Deeply Vale
Deeply Hill

Bird Fields

2

FECIT LA
Wind Hill
Copped Hill Farm

ASHWORTH RD

Stand Lees Farm
Wind Hill Farm

Copped Hill

Gindles Farm
Cob House Nab

1

M66
BENTLEY LA
Cob House Farm
WHITE CARR LA

Shepherd Hey

14

81   A   B   82   C   D   83   E   F

Man Road Ditch

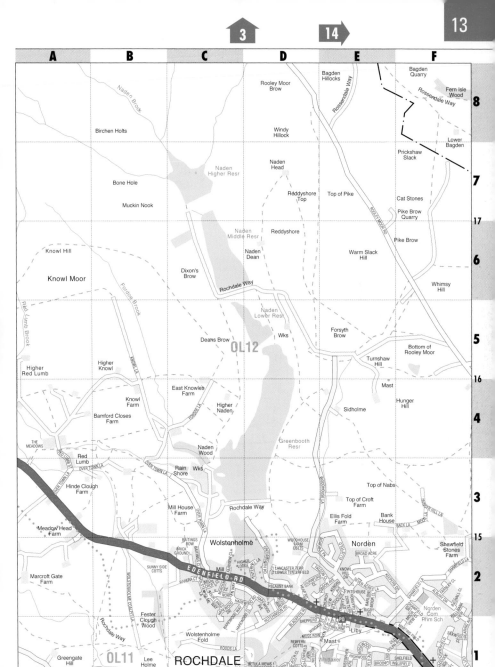

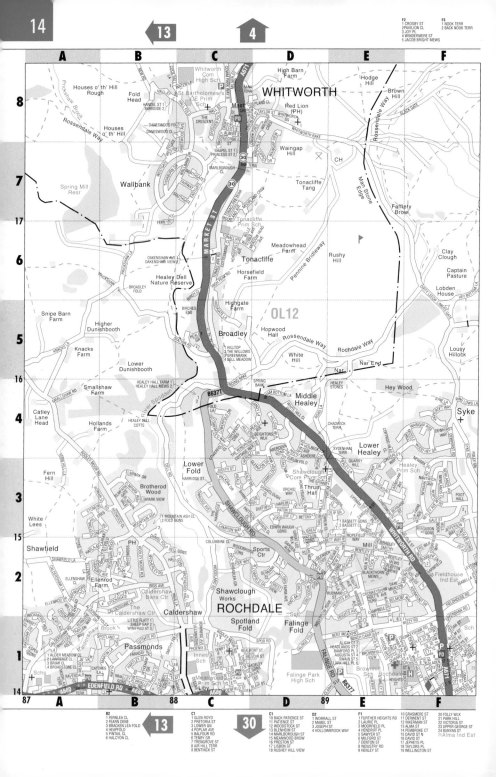

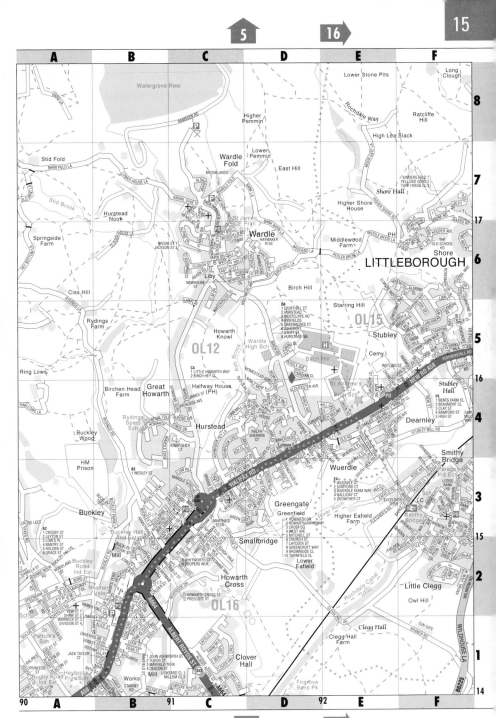

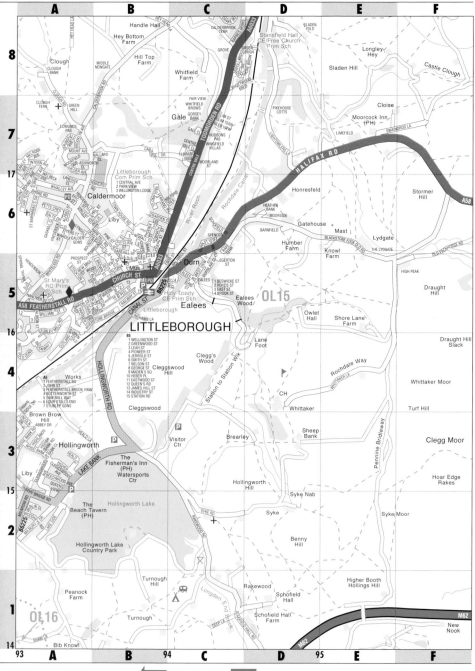

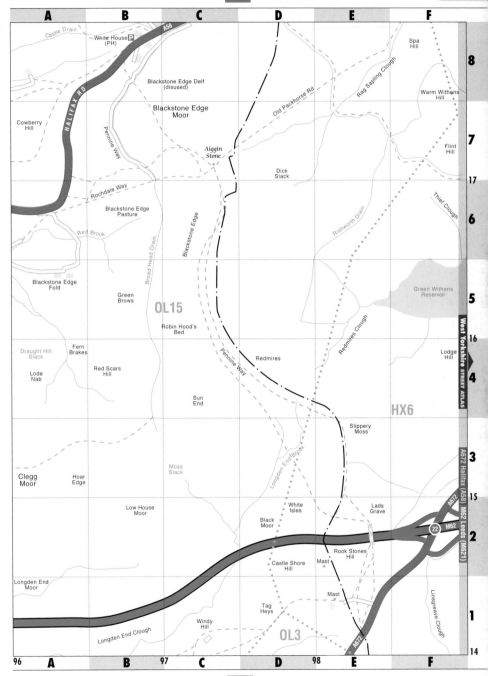

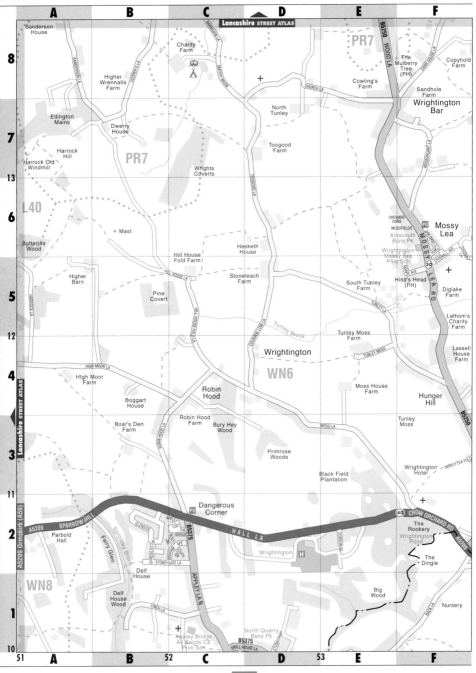

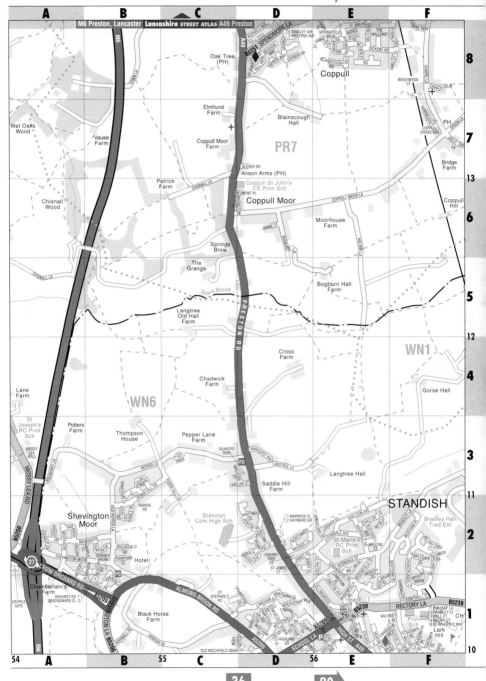

Oak Tree (PH)

Coppull

Wet Oaks Wood

Vause Farm

Elmhurst Farm

Blainscough Hall

Coppull Moor Farm

PR7

Patrick Farm

Chisnall Wood

Glover Rd

Alison Arms (PH)

Coppull St John's CE Prim Sch

Coppull Moor

Belmont Pl

Coppull Moor La

Coppull Hill

Crane St

Moorhouse Farm

Springs Brow

The Grange

Stars Brook

Bogburn Hall Farm

Langtree Old Hall Farm

WN1

Cross Farm

Chadwick Farm

Gorse Hall

Lane Farm

WN6

St Joseph's RC Prim Sch

Potters Farm

Thompson House

Pepper Lane Farm

Quakers Terr

Langtree La

Langtree Hall

Mossy Lea Fold

Pepper La

Ludlow St

Saddle Hill Farm

STANDISH

Shevington Moor

Whitwell

Standish Com High Sch

1 Marwick Cl
2 Hayward Gr

Bradley Hall Trad Est

St Marie's RC Prim Sch

Cherry Tree Ct

St James Ct

B5250

Crow Orchard Rd

Chamberlain's Farm

Ashurst Rd 1
Greensward Cl 2

Brookfield Rd

Hotel

Almond Brook Rd

St Stephen's Ct

B5239

Rectory La

Wilfrid's Pl

1 Bradley La
2 Bramley Cl
3 Well Ct
4 Moody St
5 St Wilfrid's Way

Prim Sch

CH

Cripple Gate

Shevington Rd B5206

Black Horse Farm

A5209

High St A49

School La

Lark Hill

Old Beechfield Gdns

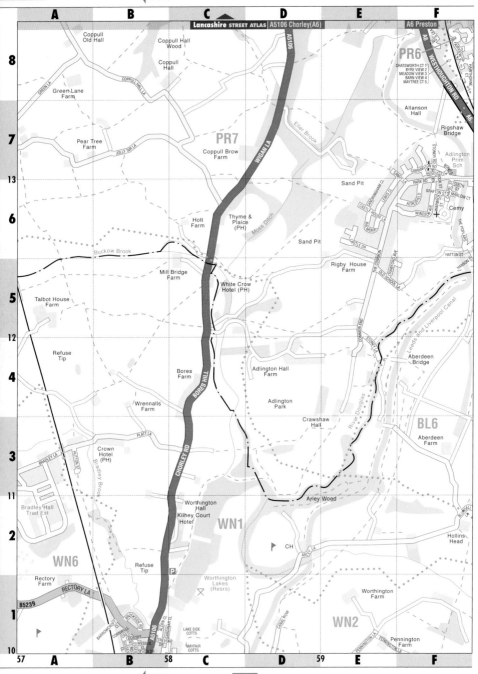

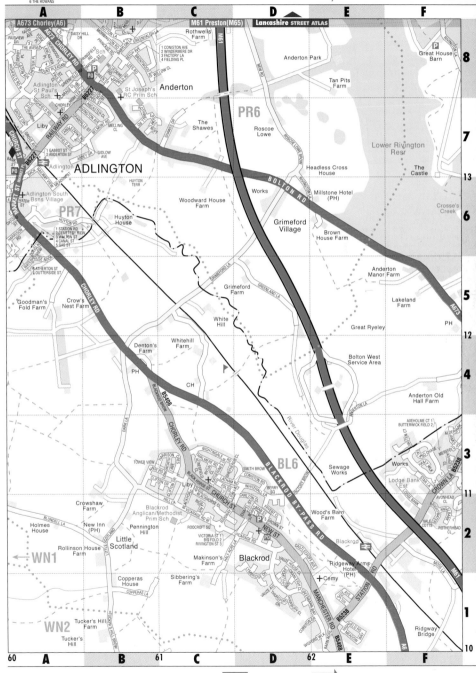

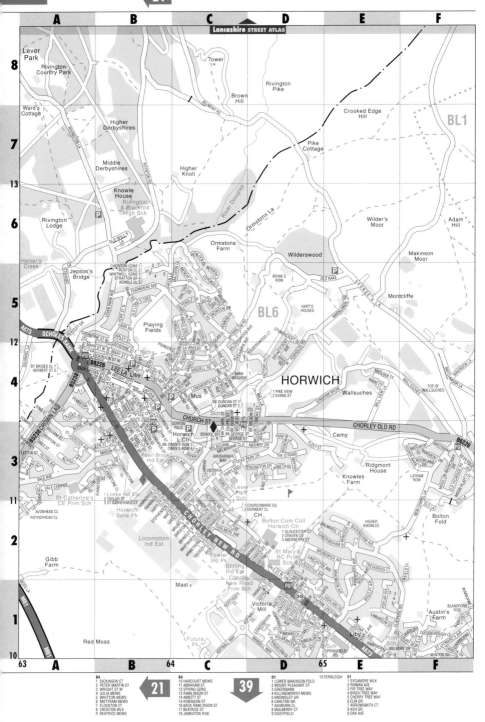

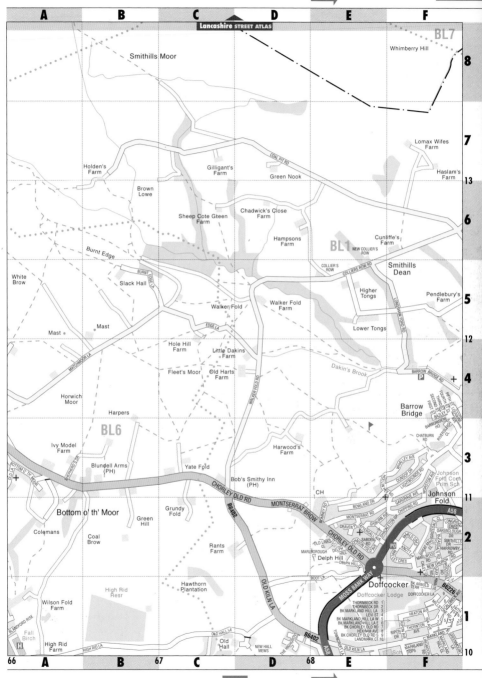

Smithills Moor

Whimberry Hill

BL7

Lomax Wifes Farm

Holden's Farm

Gilligant's Farm

Green Nook

Haslam's Farm

Brown Lowe

Sheep Cote Green Farm

Chadwick's Close Farm

Hampsons Farm

Cunliffe's Farm

BL1

NEW COLLIER'S ROW

Burnt Edge

White Brow

Slack Hall

Walker Fold

Walker Fold Farm

COLLIER'S ROW

COLLIERS ROW RD

Smithills Dean

Higher Tongs

Pendlebury's Farm

Mast

Mast

Hole Hill Farm

Little Dakins Farm

EDGE LA

Lower Tongs

Dakin's Brook

BARROW BRIDGE RD

Horwich Moor

Fleet's Moor

Old Harts Farm

Harpers

BL6

Barrow Bridge

CHATBURN RD

Ivy Model Farm

Blundell Arms (PH)

Yate Fold

Harwood's Farm

Johnson Fold Com Prim Sch

WHALLEY AVE

CH

Johnson Fold

Bob's Smithy Inn (PH)

CHORLEY OLD RD

MONTSERRAT BROW

A58

Bottom o' th' Moor

Grundy Fold

Green Hill

Colemans

Coal Brow

Rants Farm

OLD KILN LA

CHORLEY OLD RD

PO

Delph Hill

MOSS BANK WAY

Doffcocker

Doffcocker Lodge

B6226

Wilson Fold Farm

High Rid Resr

Hawthorn Plantation

THORNBECK RD   1
THORNBECK DR   2
BK MARKLAND HILL LA   3
LEVI ST   4
BK MARKLAND HILL LA W 5
BK MARKLAND HILL LA E 6
BK CHORLEY OLD RD   7
HEXHAM AVE   8
BK CHORLEY OLD RD S   9
LANDMARK CT   10

Fall Birch

High Rid Farm

Old Hall

New Hall Mews

B6402

A58

OLD KILN LA

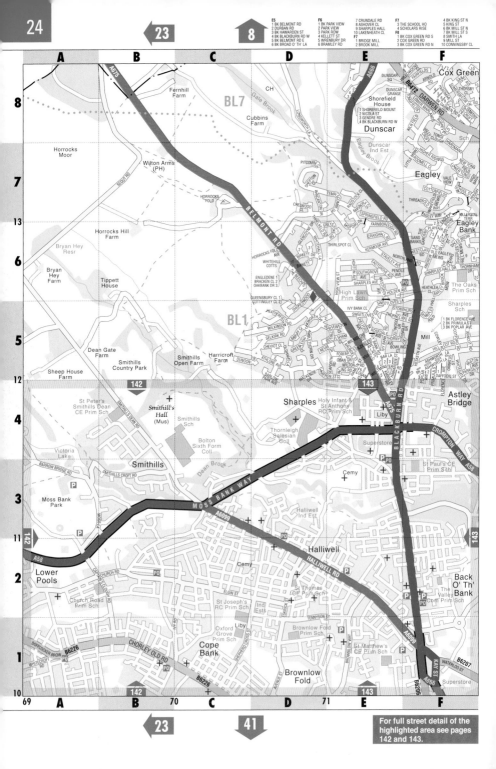

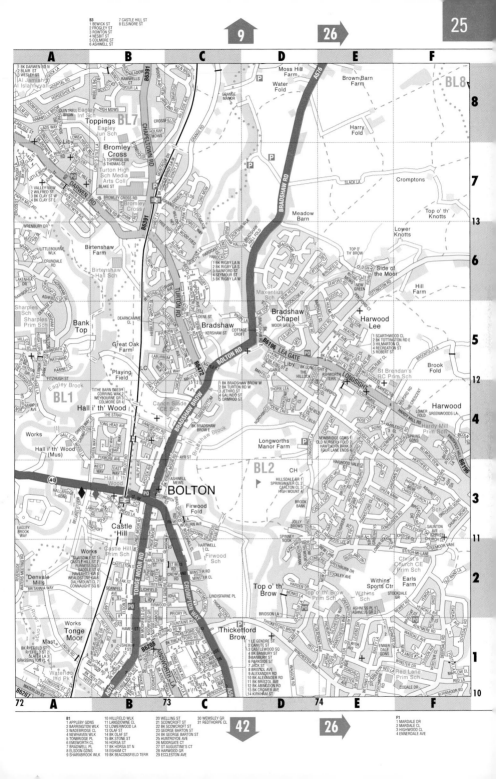

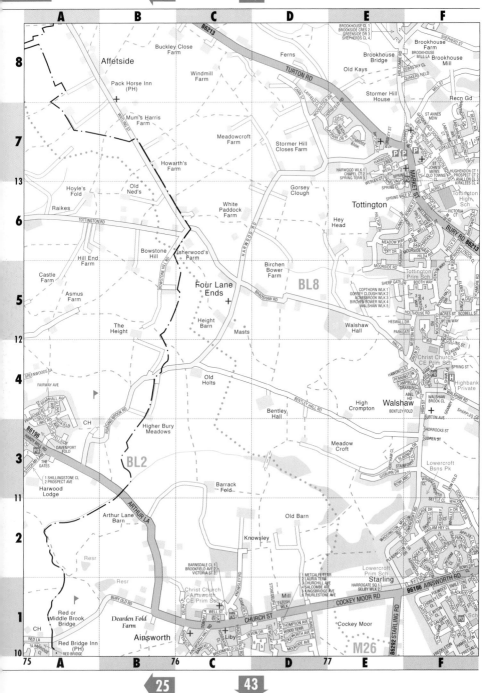

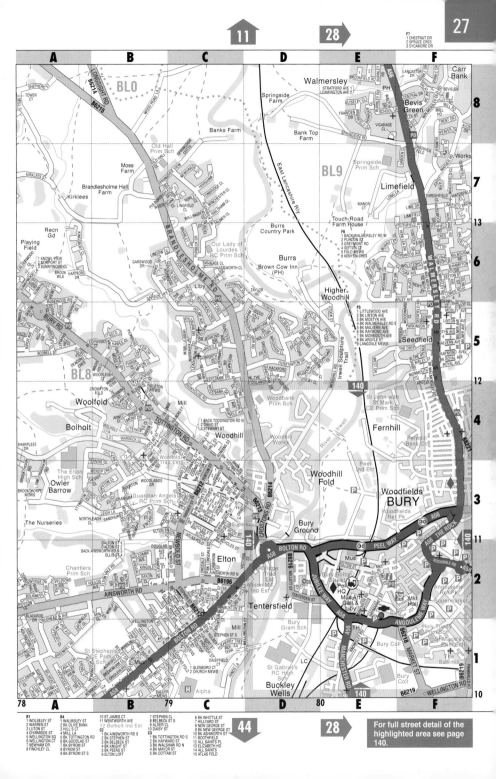

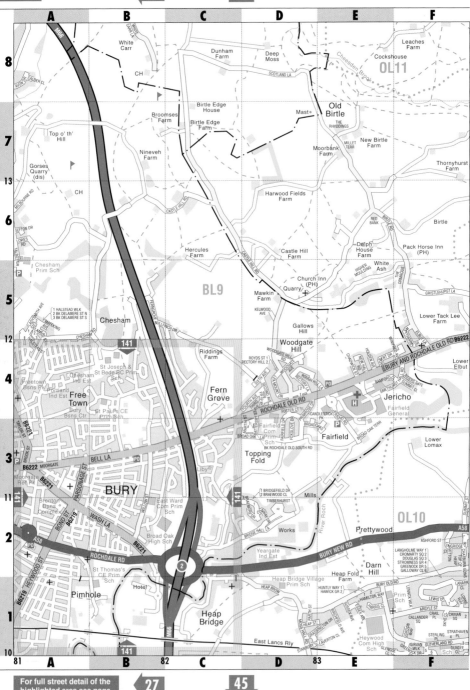

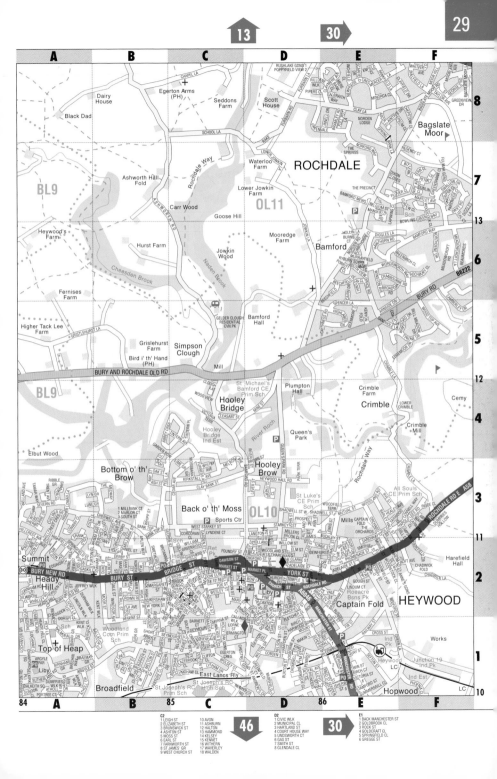

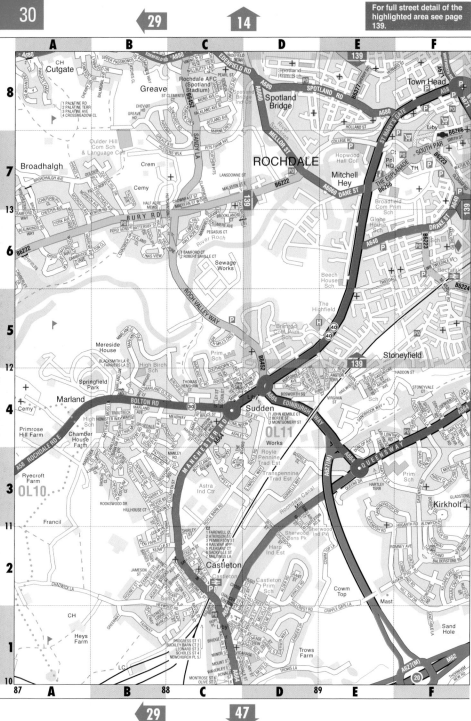

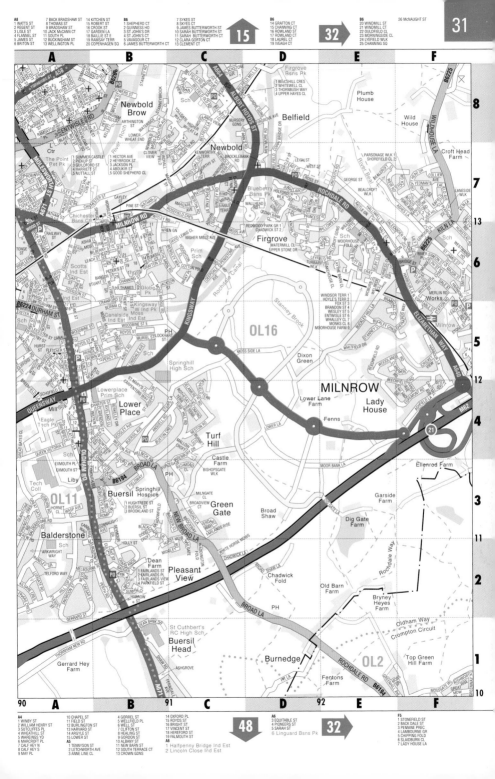

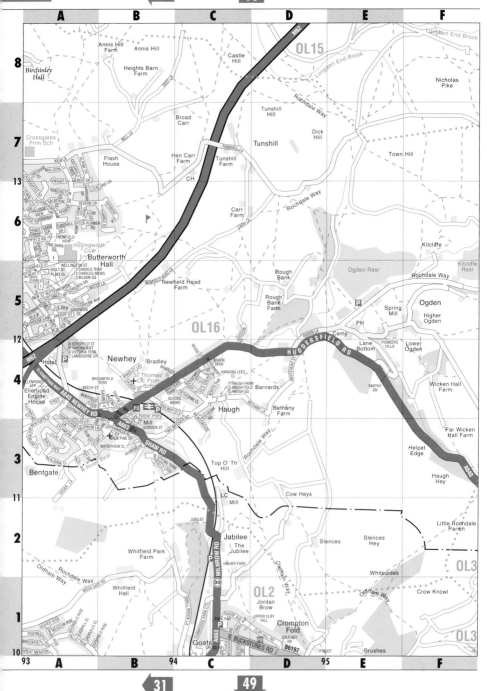

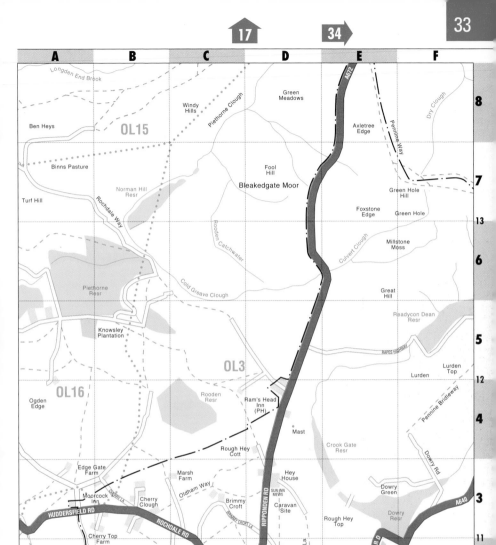

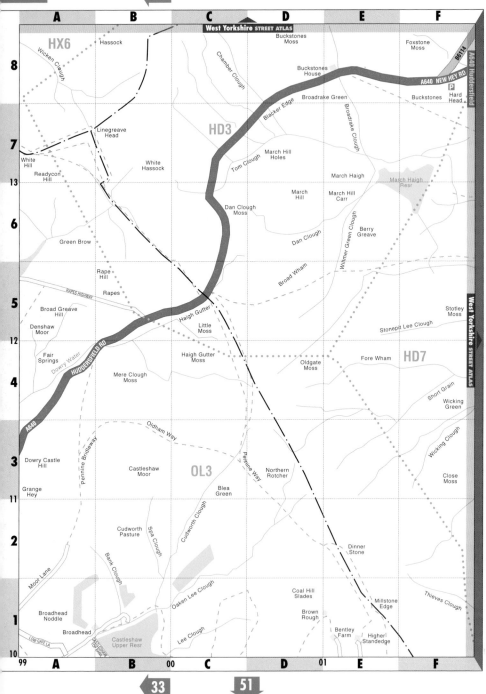

A   B   C   D   E   F

8

HX6

Hassock

Wicken Clough

Buckstones
Moss

Foxstone
Moss

Buckstones
House

A640 NEW HEY RD   A640 Huddersfield

B6114

P

Hard
Head

Buckstones

7

Linegreave
Head

HD3

Blacker Edge

Broadrake Green

Broadrake Clough

13

White
Hill

Readycon
Hill

White
Hassock

Chamber Clough

Tom Clough

March Hill
Holes

March Hill
Carr

March Haigh

March Haigh
Resr

6

Green Brow

Dan Clough
Moss

March
Hill

Willmer Green Clough

Berry
Greave

Dan Clough

5

Rape
Hill

Rapes

RAPES HIGHWAY

Broad Greave
Hill

Haigh Gutter

Little
Moss

Broad Wham

Stotley
Moss

Stonepit Lee Clough

12

Denshaw
Moor

Fair
Springs

Dowry Water

HUDDERSFIELD RD

Haigh Gutter
Moss

Oldgate
Moss

Fore Wham

HD7

4

Mere Clough
Moss

Short Grain

Wicking
Green

A640

3

Dowry Castle
Hill

Pennine Bridleway

Oldham Way

Castleshaw
Moor

OL3

Pennine Way

Northern
Rotcher

Wicking Clough

Close
Moss

11

Grange
Hey

Blea
Green

2

Cudworth
Pasture

Spa Clough

Cudworth Clough

Dinner
Stone

Moor Lane

Bank Clough

Coal Hill
Slades

Thieves Clough

1

Broadhead
Noddle

Broadhead

Oaken Lee Clough

Lee Clough

Brown
Rough

Millstone
Edge

Bentley
Farm

Higher
Standedge

Low Gate La

CASTLESHAW

Castleshaw
Upper Resr

10

99   A   B   00   C   D   01   E   F

West Yorkshire STREET ATLAS

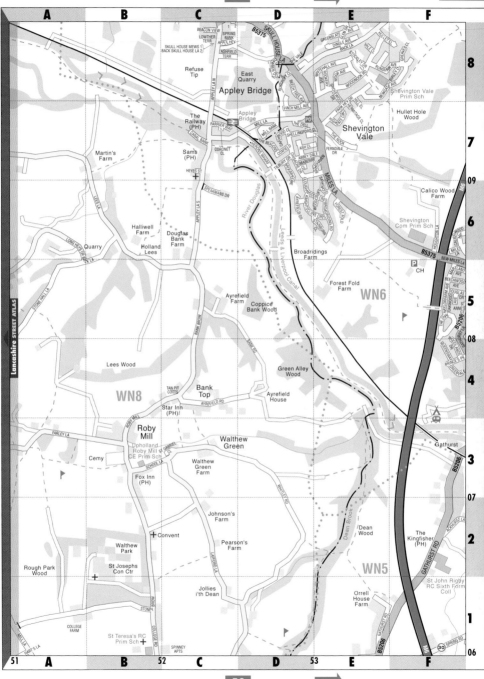

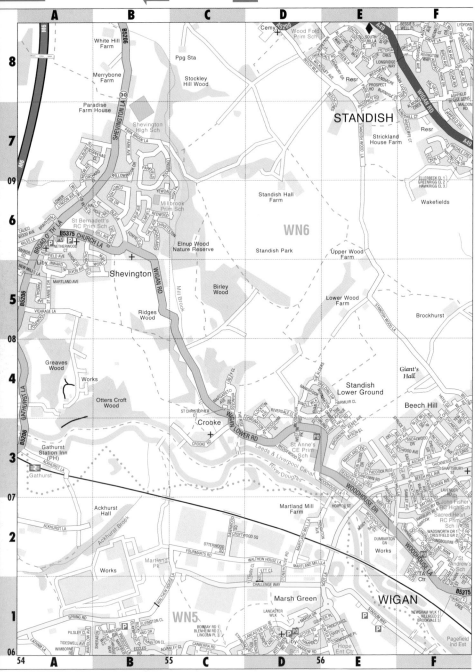

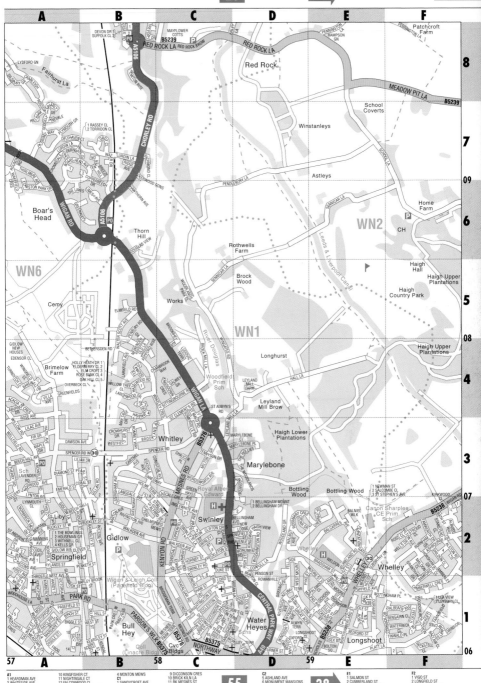

20
38
55
38

A1
1 HEARDMAN AVE
2 WHITESIDE AVE
3 WATERLOO ST
4 BROOKVALE
5 HEDGEMEAD
6 FOSTER ST
7 MEADOW CT
8 BERESFORD ST
9 GORMAN ST

10 KINGFISHER CT
11 NIGHTINGALE CT
12 FALCONWOOD CL
13 LOWER ST STEPHEN ST
14 TIERNAN LO
15 PAGEFIELD CL
B3
1 RIPON AVE
2 PATELEY SQ
3 YEWDALE CRES

B1
4 MONTON MEWS
C1
1 SANDYCROFT AVE
2 CHARLES ST
3 SCARISBRICK ST
4 CLIFTON ST
5 MAB'S CROSS HO
6 BRADSHAGH HO
7 CROSS YD
8 LITTLE LONDON

9 DICCONSON CRES
10 BRICK KILN LA
11 BK MESNES ST
12 MESNES TERR
13 POWELL ST
C2
1 INGLEWHITE CRES
2 WARNFORD ST
3 EVEREST PL

C2
5 ASHLAND AVE
6 MONUMENT MANSIONS
7 HOLME CT
8 ST MICHAEL'S CT

E1
1 SALMON ST
2 CUMBERLAND ST
3 WESTMOORLAND ST
4 PERCH ST
5 WINDERMERE ST
6 WRIGHT ST
7 SEDWYN ST

F2
1 VIGO ST
2 LONGFIELD ST
3 CHELTENHAM ST
4 MILFORD ST
5 BORDEN CL

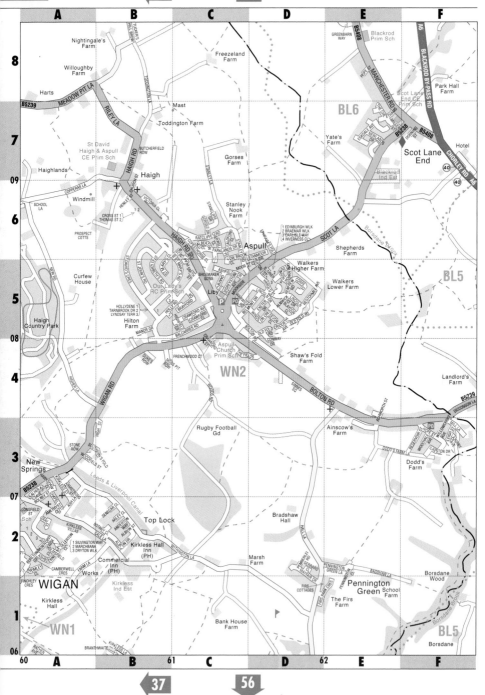

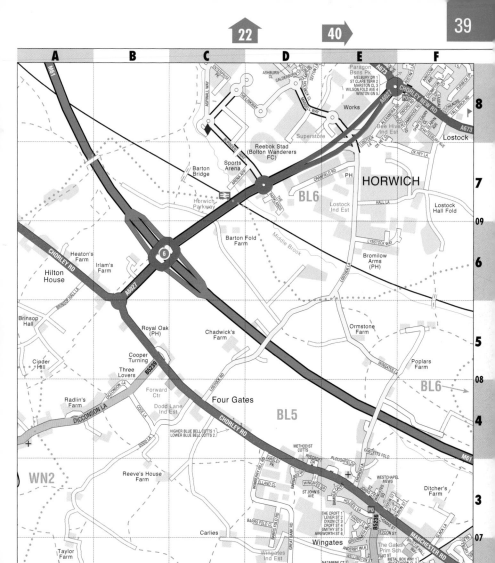

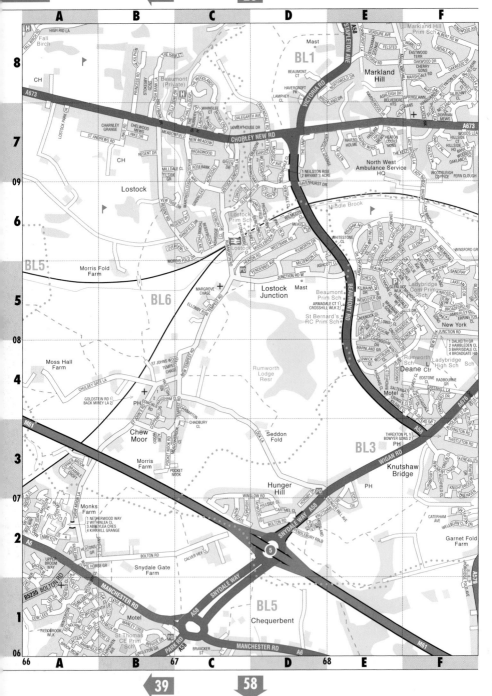

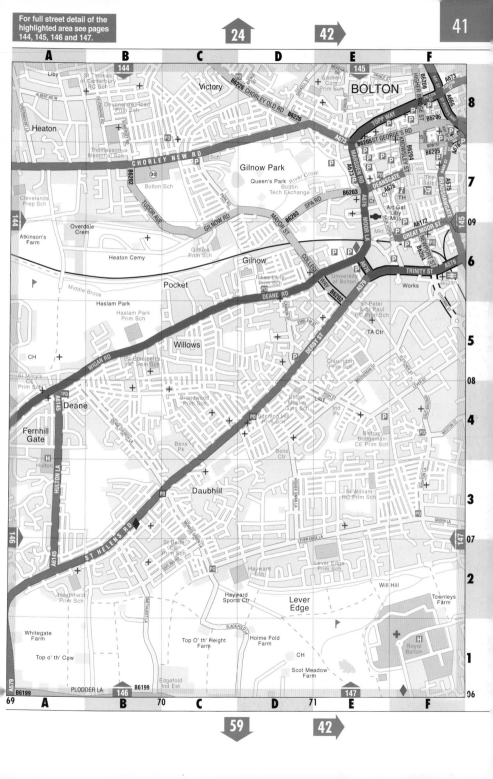

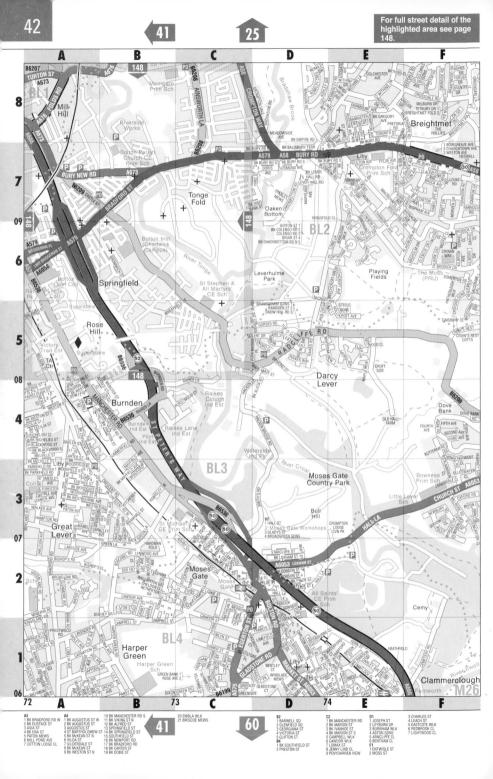

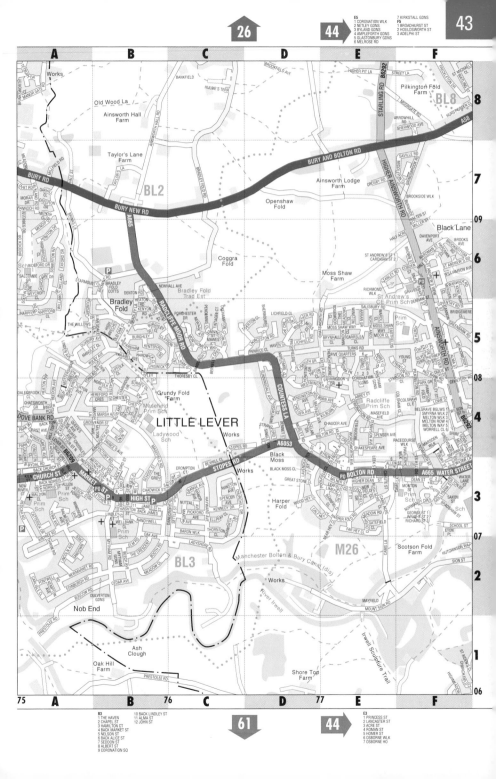

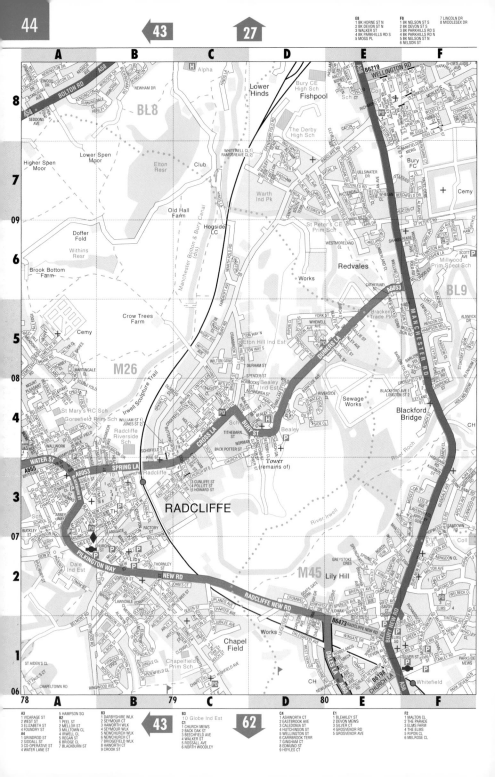

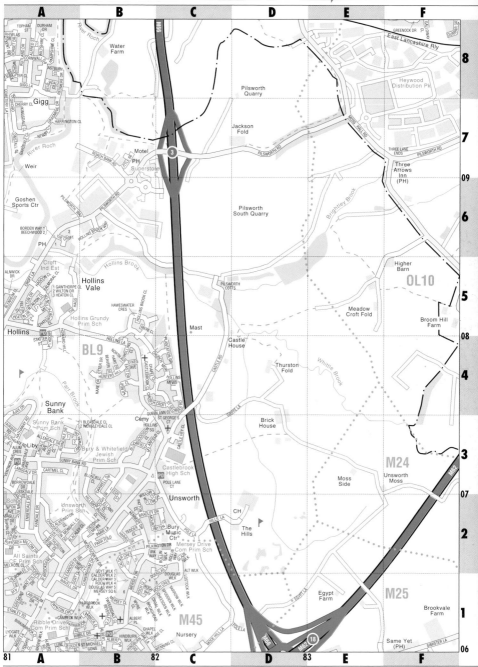

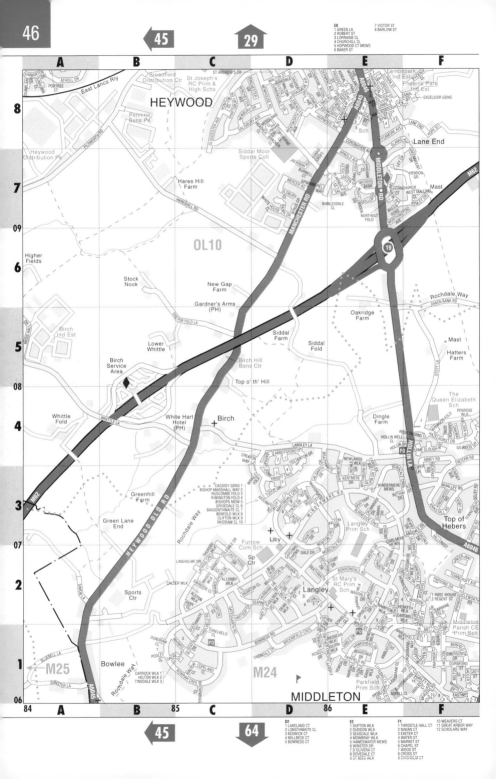

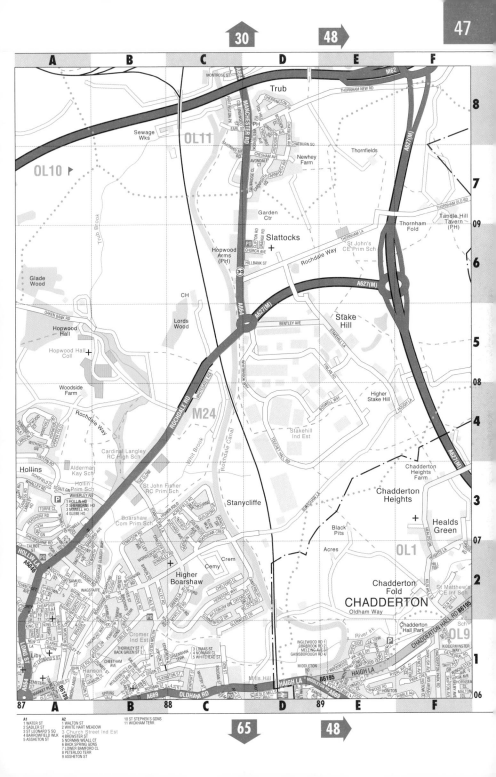

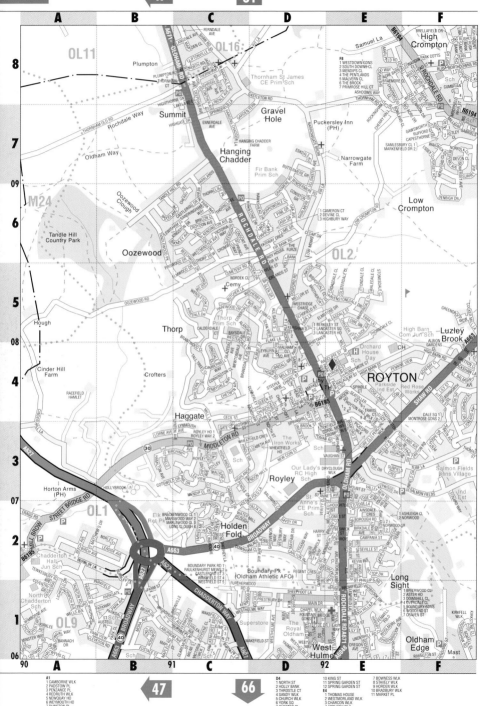

A1
1 CAMBORNE WLK
2 PADSTOW PL
3 PENZANCE PL
4 REDRUTH WLK
5 NEWQUAY HO
6 WEYMOUTH HO
7 DUNSTON PL
8 SOMERTON WLK

D4
1 NORTH ST
2 HOLLY BANK
3 THROSTLE CT
4 SANDY WLK
5 CHURCH WLK
6 YORK SQ
7 CHESTER PL
8 SPRING GDNS
9 ST PAULS HOUSE

10 KING ST
11 SPRING GARDEN ST
12 SPRING GARDEN ST
E4
1 THOMAS HOUSE
2 WESTMORLAND WLK
3 CHARCON WLK
4 APPLEBY WLK
5 TROUTBECK WLK
6 BYRON WLK

7 BOWNESS WLK
8 STAVELY WLK
9 HORDEN WLK
10 BRADBURY WLK
11 MARKET PL

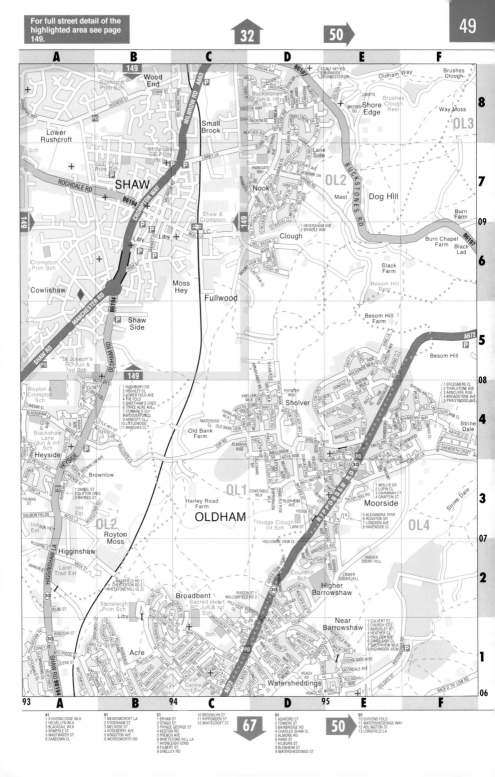

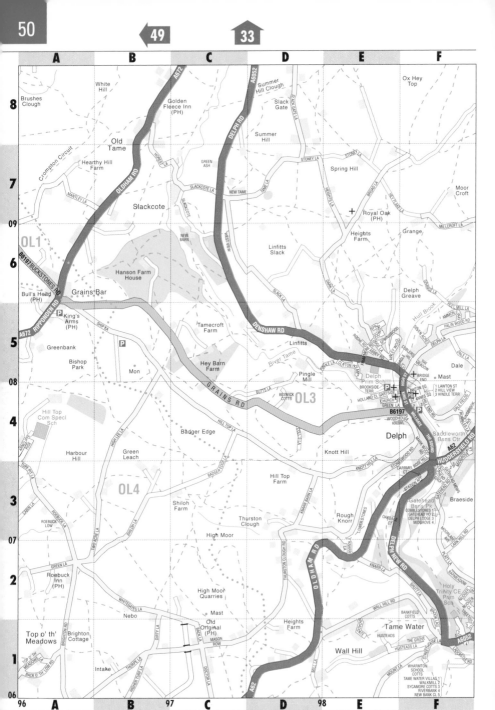

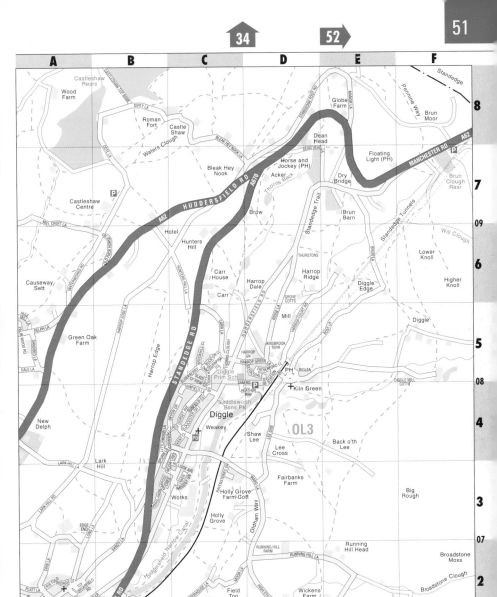

34
52
69
52

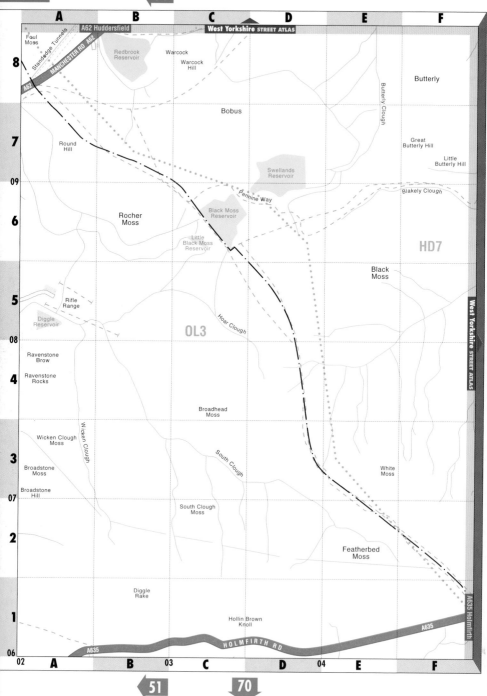

West Yorkshire STREET ATLAS

A62 Huddersfield

Foul
Moss

Standedge Tunnels

MANCHESTER RD A62

A62

Redbrook
Reservoir

Warcock

Warcock
Hill

Butterly

Butterly Clough

Bobus

Great
Butterly Hill

Little
Butterly Hill

Round
Hill

Swellands
Reservoir

Blakely Clough

Pennine Way

Rocher
Moss

Black Moss
Reservoir

Little
Black Moss
Reservoir

HD7

Black
Moss

Rifle
Range

Diggle
Reservoir

OL3

Hoar Clough

Ravenstone
Brow

Ravenstone
Rocks

Broadhead
Moss

Wicken Clough
Moss

Wicken Clough

South Clough

White
Moss

Broadstone
Moss

Broadstone
Hill

South Clough
Moss

Featherbed
Moss

Diggle
Rake

Hollin Brown
Knoll

A635

HOLMFIRTH RD

A635

A635 Holmfirth

West Yorkshire STREET ATLAS

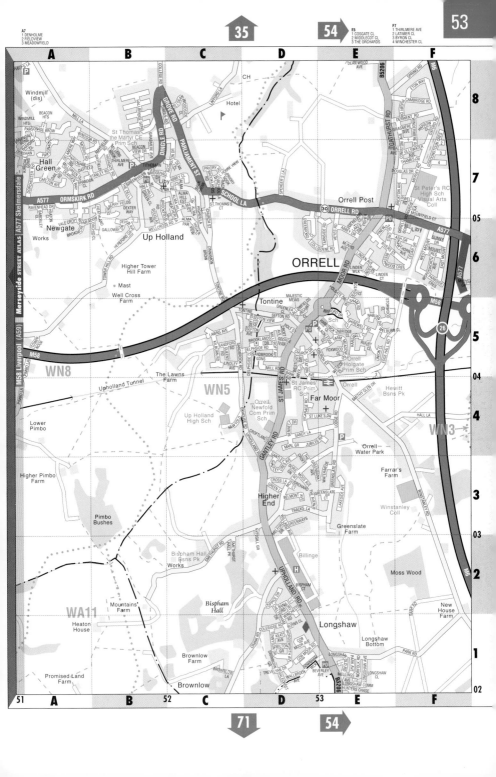

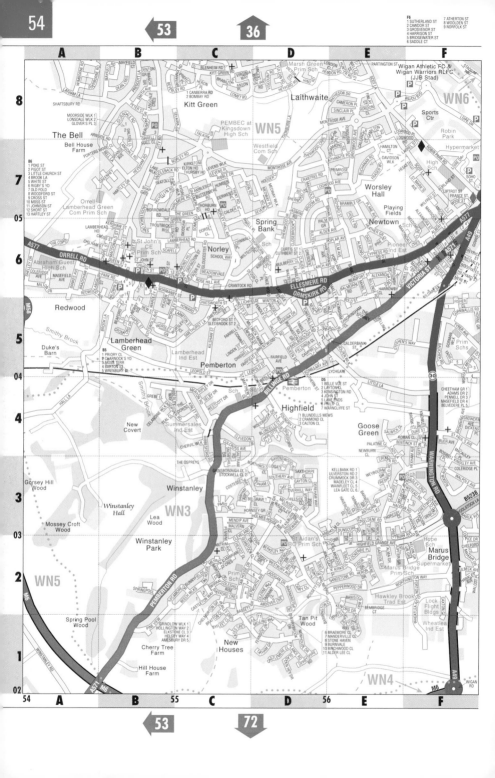

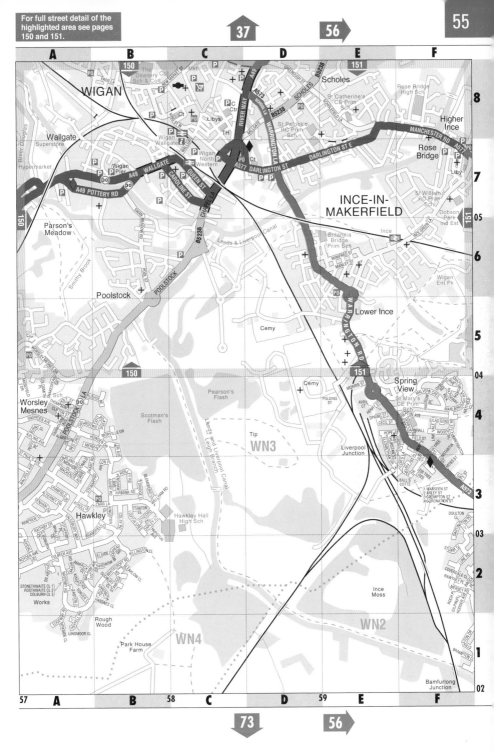

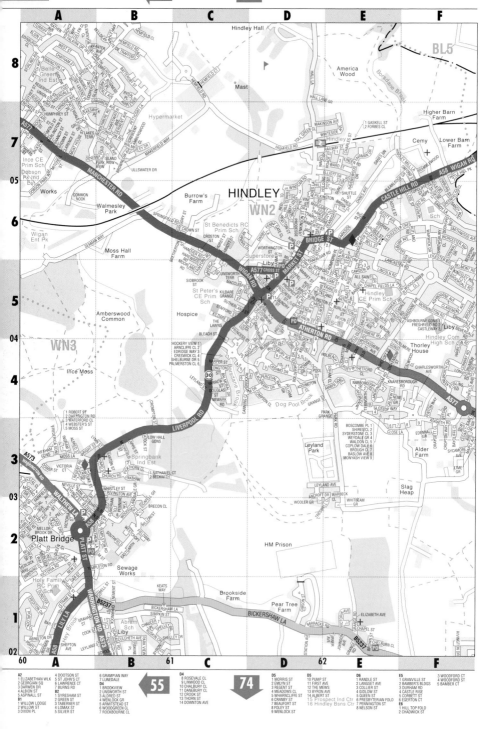

A2
1 ELIZABETHAN WLK
2 GEORGIAN SQ
3 DARWEN DR
4 ALBION ST
5 ASPINALL ST
B1
1 WILLOW LODGE
2 WILLOW ST
3 DIXON PL

4 DOOTSON ST
5 ST JOHN'S CT
6 LAWRENCE CT
7 BURNS RD
B2
1 SYRESHAM ST
2 GREEN ST
3 TABERNER ST
4 LOMAX ST
5 SILVER ST

6 GRAMPIAN WAY
7 LUNEDALE
D4
1 BROOKVIEW
2 UNSWORTH ST
3 ALDRED ST
4 WENLOCK GR
5 ARMITSTEAD ST
6 WOODGREEN CL
7 ROCKBOURNE CL

D4
8 ROSEVALE CL
9 LINWOOD CL
10 CHALBURY CL
11 DANEBURY CL
12 CROOK ST
13 THORN ST
14 DOWNTON AVE

D5
1 MORRIS ST
2 EMLYN ST
3 REGENT ST
4 MEADOWS CL
5 WHARNCLIFFE ST
6 CRANBY ST
7 BEAUFORT ST
8 FOLEY ST
9 WENLOCK ST

D5
10 PUMP ST
11 FIRST AVE
12 THE MEWS
13 BYRON AVE
14 ALBERT ST
15 Prospect Ind Ctr
16 Hindley Bsns Ctr

D6
1 RANDLE ST
2 LANGSET AVE
3 COLLIER ST
4 GIDLOW ST
5 QUEEN ST
6 PRESBYTERIAN FOLD
7 PENNINGTON ST
8 NELSON ST

E5
1 GRANVILLE ST
2 BAMBERS BLDGS
3 DURHAM RD
4 CASTLE RISE
5 CORBETT ST
6 EGERTON CT
E6
1 HILL TOP FOLD
2 CHADWICK ST

3 WOODFORD CT
4 WOODFORD ST
5 BAMBER CT

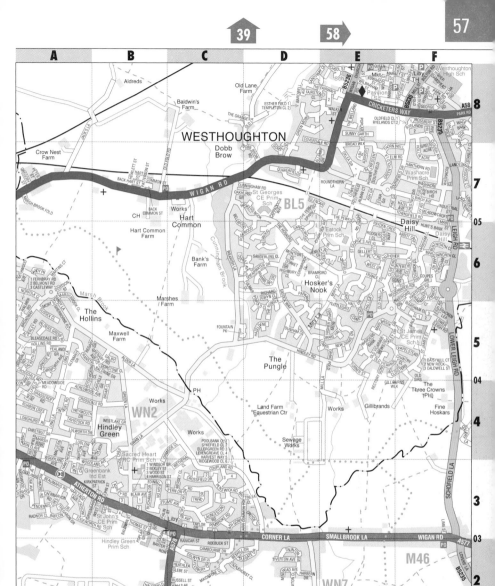

57 40

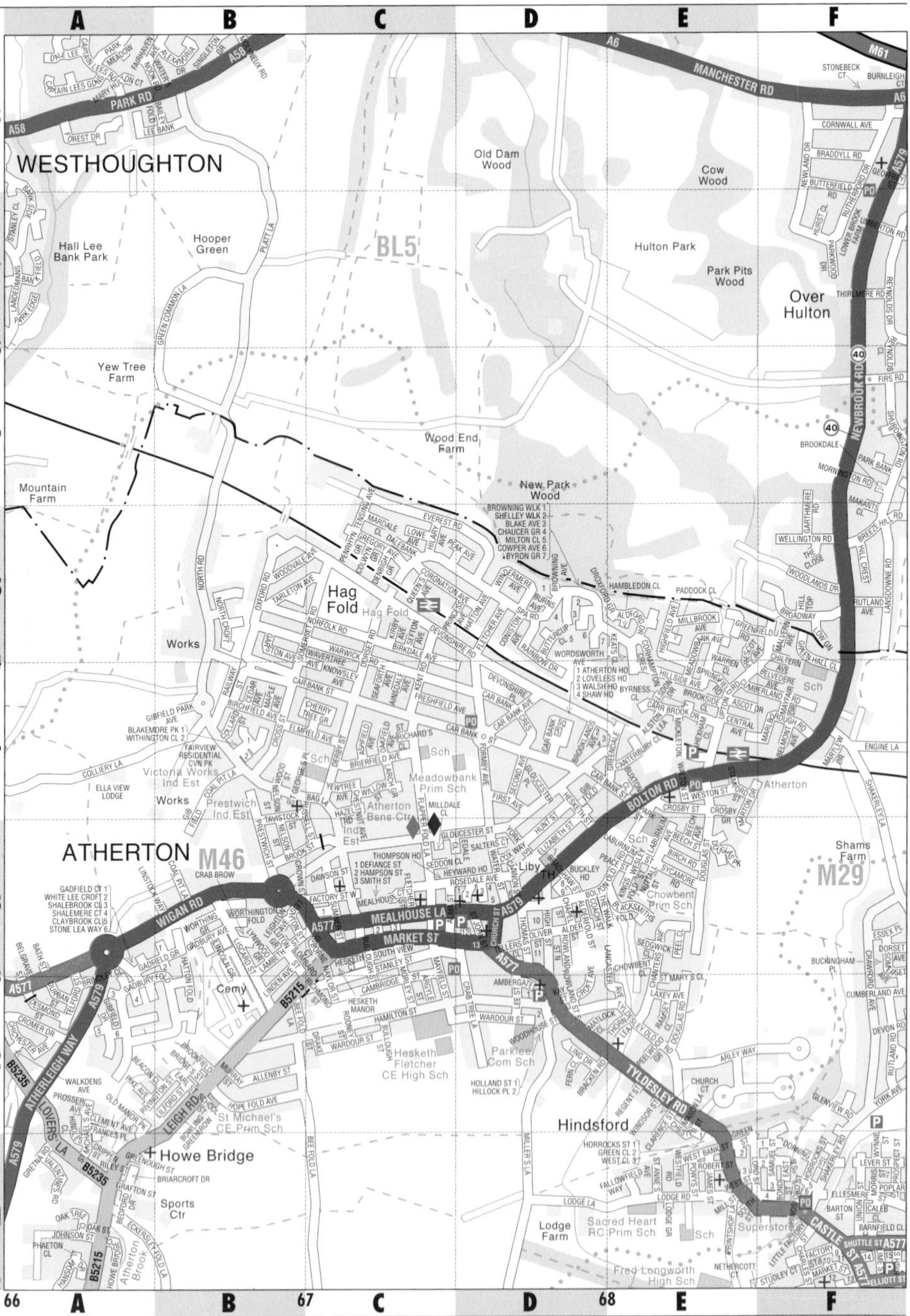
A B C D E F
8 7 6 5 4 3 2 1
05 04 03 02
66 67 68
WESTHOUGHTON
ATHERTON
Hag Fold
Over Hulton
Hindsford
Howe Bridge
BL5
M46
M29
M61
A6
A58
A579
A577
B5215
B5235
MANCHESTER RD
PARK RD
WIGAN RD
BOLTON RD
NEWBROOK RD
MEALHOUSE LA
MARKET ST
TYLDESLEY RD
LEIGH RD
ATHERLEIGH WAY
LOVERS' LA
CASTLE ST
Old Dam Wood
Cow Wood
Hulton Park
Park Pits Wood
Hall Lee Bank Park
Hooper Green
Yew Tree Farm
Wood End Farm
New Park Wood
Mountain Farm
Works
Victoria Works Ind Est
Prestwich Ind Est
Atherton Bsns Ctr
Ind Est
Meadowbank Prim Sch
Chowbent Prim Sch
Parklee Com Sch
Hesketh Fletcher CE High Sch
St Michael's CE Prim Sch
Sacred Heart RC Prim Sch
Fred Longworth High Sch
Sports Ctr
Lodge Farm
Shams Farm
Cemy
Liby
Superstore
Atherton
Sch
ELLA VIEW LODGE
FAIRVIEW RESIDENTIAL CVN PK
GADFIELD CT 1
WHITE LEE CROFT 2
SHALEBROOK CL 3
SHALEMERE CT 4
CLAYBROOK CL 5
STONE LEA WAY 6
BLAKEMORE PK 1
WITHINGTON CL 2
BROWNING WLK 1
SHELLEY WLK 2
BLAKE AVE 3
CHAUCER GR 4
MILTON CL 5
COWPER AVE 6
BYRON GR 7
1 ATHERTON HO
2 LOVELESS HO
3 WALSH HO
4 SHAW HO
1 DEFIANCE ST
2 HAMPSON ST
3 SMITH ST
HOLLAND ST 1
HILLOCK PL 2
HORROCKS ST 1
GREEN CL 2
WEST CL 3

D3
1 SPRING GDNS
2 MATHER ST
3 GEORGE ST
4 THE BEECHES
5 THE WILLOWS
6 THE HAWTHORNS
7 BLAKEBOROUGH HO
8 MARTIN ST
9 BRAMPTON ST
10 THE HOLLIES
11 SMITH'S PL
12 WARBURTON PL
13 MARKET PL

F1
1 LORD GR
2 LORD AVE
3 SHORT ST
4 BACK SHORT ST
5 TYLDESLEY PAS
6 BACK SHAKERLEY RD
7 LEVER CL
8 ELIZABETH CT
9 ALFRED ST
10 ELIZABETHAN CT
11 KINGS CT
12 GEORGIAN CT
13 CASTLETON CT
14 PETER ST
15 MARLANDS SQ

57 76

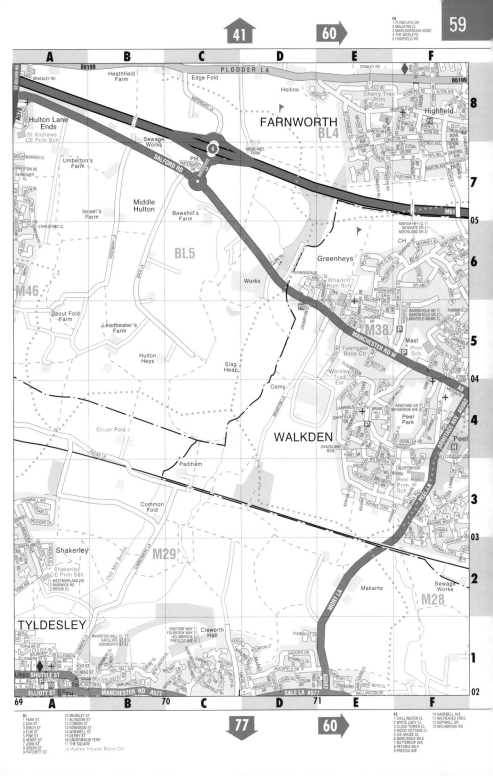

FARNWORTH
BL4

Highfield

Hulton Lane Ends

BL5

M46

Middle Hulton

Greenheys

M38

WALKDEN

Peel

Shakerley

M29

Makants

M28

TYLDESLEY

A1
1 PARK ST
2 ASH ST
3 BIRCH ST
4 ELM ST
5 PINE ST
6 HENRY ST
7 JOHN ST
8 GREEN ST
9 PATCHETT ST
10 MEANLEY ST
11 BLOSSOM ST
12 COBDEN ST
13 ROBINSON ST
14 WHEWELL ST
15 DERBY ST
16 UNDERWOOD TERR
17 THE SQUARE
18 Astley House Bsns Ctr

F3
1 SHILLINGTEN CL
2 WHITE LADY CL
3 CLOCK TOWER CL
4 WOOD COTTAGE CL
5 ICE HOUSE CL
6 NARCISSUS WLK
7 BUTTERCUP AVE
8 PETUNIA WLK
9 FREESIA AVE
10 HAREBELL AVE
11 WICHEAVES CRES
12 ASPINALL GR
13 WICHBROOK RD

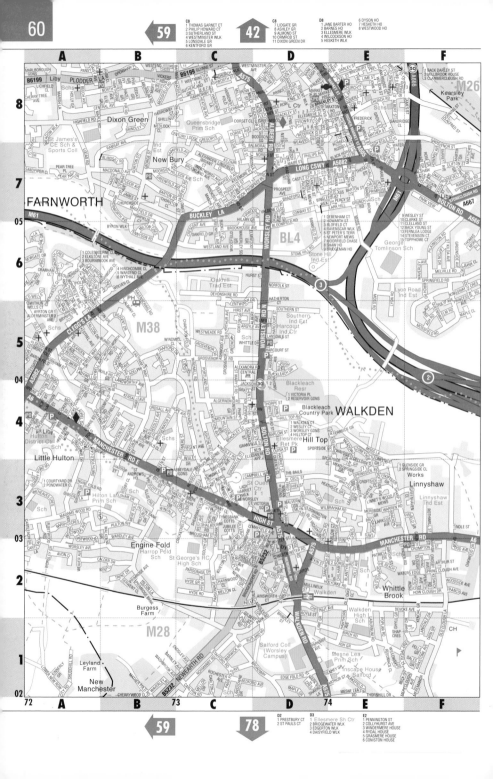

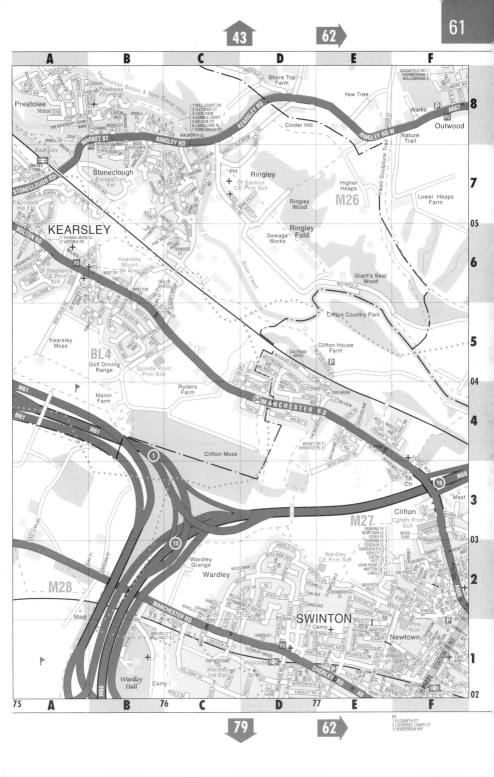

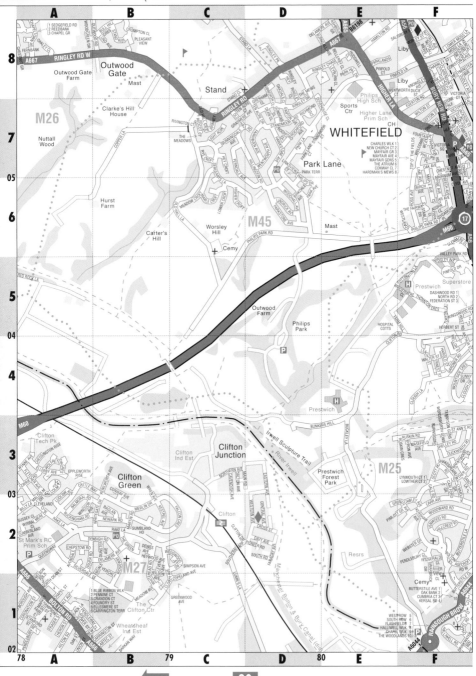

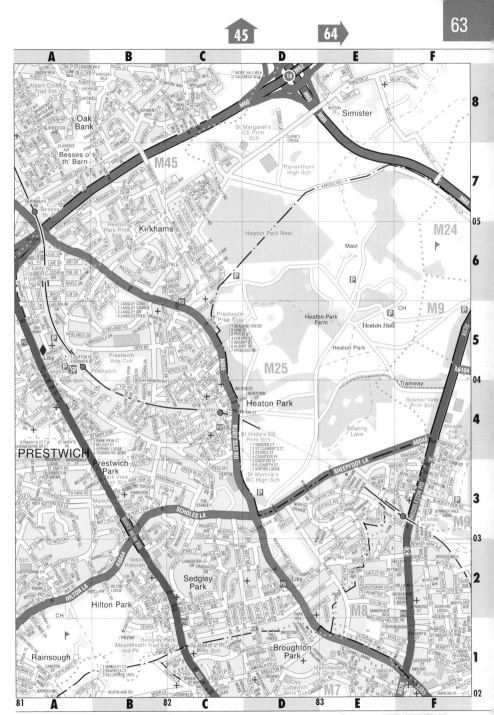

C1
1 MAYFAIR
2 KERSAL CL
3 ST PAULS CT
4 ST PAUL'S RISE
5 THE CHENIES
6 ST PAULS GDNS
7 MOORHILL CT
8 VERNON CT

E1
1 BERKELEY CT
2 BRISTOL CT
3 NORFOLK HO
4 RAVENHURST
5 MILTON CT
6 PARKLEA CT
7 CADOGAN PL
8 INGLEDENE CT
9 LANGLEY CT

10 MONTPELLIER MEWS
11 WATERPARK HALL
12 ALLANADALE CT
13 CASTLETON RD
14 LINCOLN CT
15 GAN EDEN
E2
1 WESTHORNE FOLD
2 CLAYTHORPE WLK

3 TIXALL WLK
4 SHARBROOK WLK
5 LOWER BROOKLANDS PAR

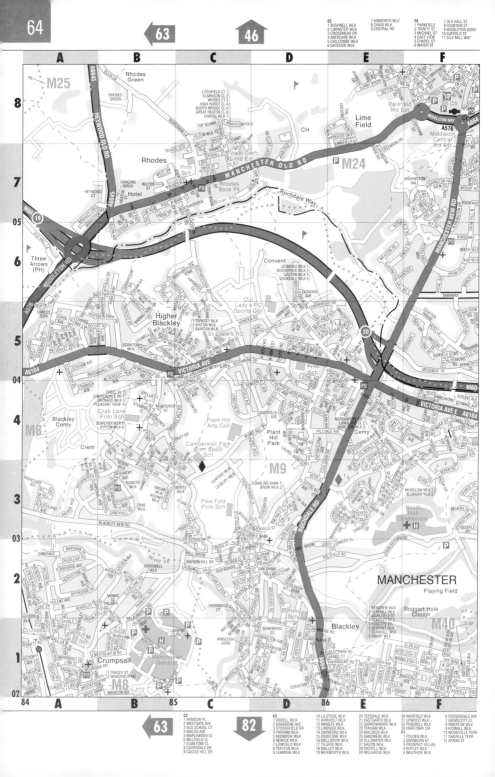

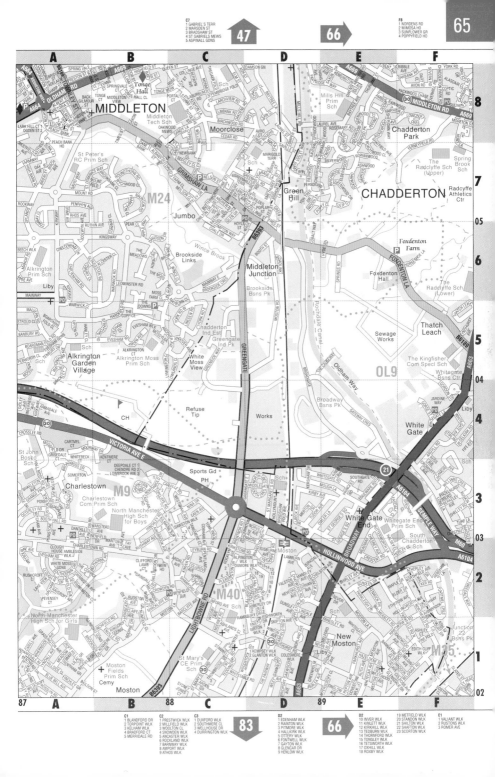

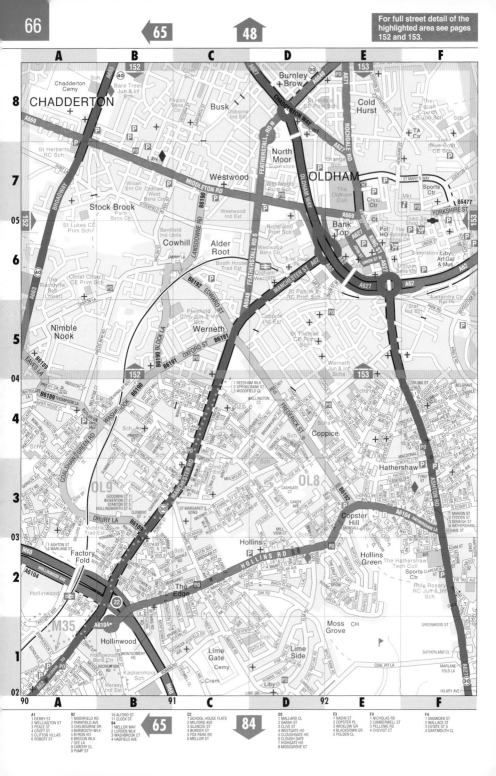

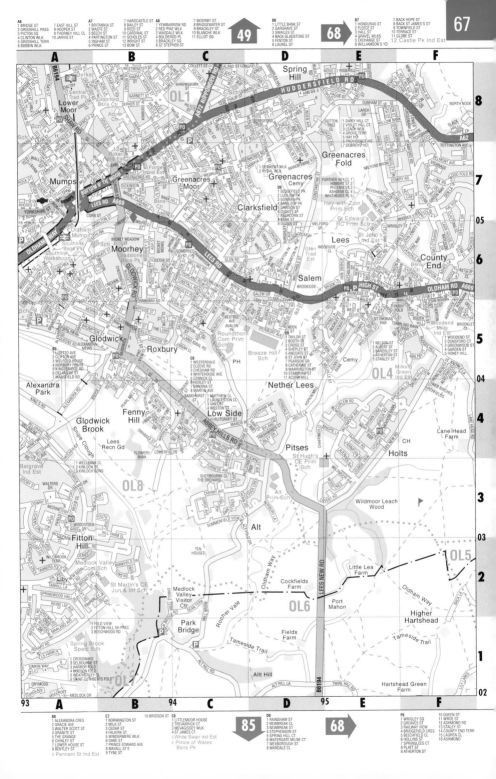

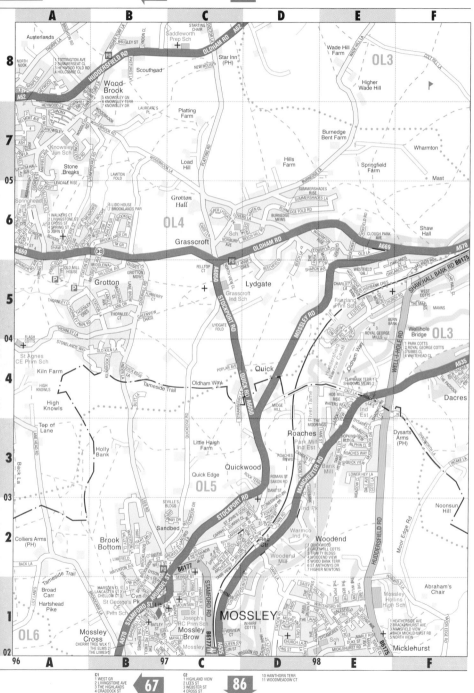

C1
1 WEST GR
2 LIVINGSTONE AVE
3 THE HIGHLANDS
4 CRADDOCK ST
5 CHAPEL CT
6 CHAPEL ST

C2
1 HIGHLAND VIEW
2 LEES ST
3 WEBSTER ST
4 CROSS ST
5 WILD'S SQ
6 BIRBECK ST
7 QUICKMERE CT
8 SPRING COTTS
9 BACK MILL LA

10 HAWTHORN TERR
11 WOODMEADOW CT

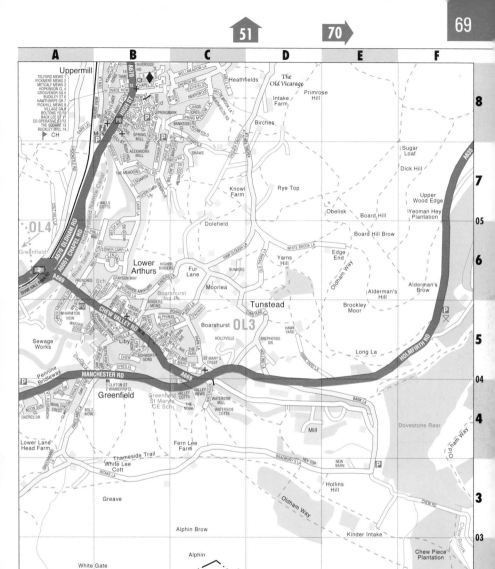

Uppermill

TELFORD MEWS 1
PICKMERE MEWS 2
METCALF MEWS 3
HOPKINSON CL 4
GROSVENOR SQ 5
BUCKLEY ST 6
HAWTHORPE GR 7
PICKHILL MEWS 8
VILLAGE GN 8
BOLTONS YD 9
BACK LEE ST 11
CO-OPERATIVE ST 12
THE SQUARE 13
BUCKLEY MILL 14
CH

Heathfields

The Old Vicarage

Intake Farm

Primrose Hill

Birches

Sugar Loaf

Dick Hill

Knowl Farm

Rye Top

Upper Wood Edge

Obelisk

Board Hill

Yeoman Hey Plantation

Dolefield

Board Hill Brow

WHITE BROOK LA

Lower Arthurs

Fur Lane

Yarns Hill

Edge End

Moorlea

Bunkers

Tunstead

Alderman's Hill

Alderman's Brow

Boarshurst

OL3

Brockley Moor

Sewage Works

Hollyville

SHEPHERDS GN

HAWK YARD

Long La

Lby

HOLMFIRTH RD

Pennine Bridleway

MANCHESTER RD

St Mary's CE Sch

Greenfield

1 CLIFTON ST
2 WIMBERRY CL

VALLEY MEWS

VALLEY COTTS

THE NOOK

Greenfield

WATERSIDE MILL

BANK LA

WATERSIDE COTTS

Mill

Dovestone Resr

Lower Lane Head Farm

Fern Lee Farm

Thameside Trail

White Lee Cott

INTAKE LA

BRADBURY'S LA

HEY TOP

NEW BARN

Oldham Way

Hollins Hill

Greave

CHEW RD

Alphin Brow

Kinder Intake

Chew Brook

White Gate

Alphin

Chew Piece Plantation

Alphin Pike

Slack Head Brow

Warlow Pike

Wimberry Stones Brow

OL5

Rams Clough

SK15

Wimberry Moss

Broken Ground

8
05
7
6
05
6
5
04
4
3
03
2
02
1

A | **B** | **C** | **D** | **E** | **F**

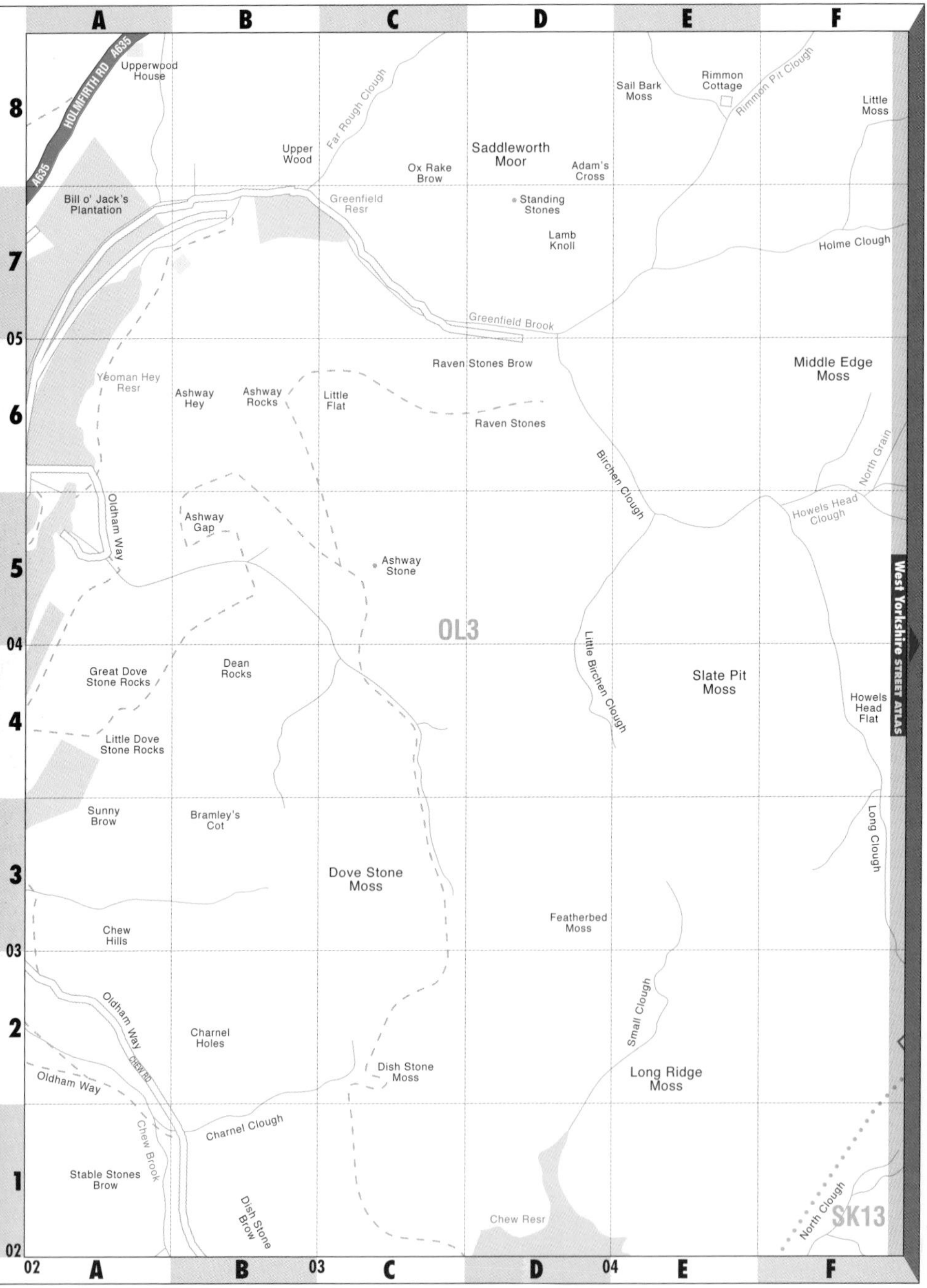

HOLMFIRTH RD A635

Upperwood House

A635

8

Saddleworth Moor

Sail Bark Moss

Rimmon Cottage

Rimmon Pit Clough

Little Moss

Upper Wood

Far Rough Clough

Ox Rake Brow

Adam's Cross

Bill o' Jack's Plantation

Greenfield Resr

Standing Stones

Lamb Knoll

Holme Clough

7

Greenfield Brook

05

Yeoman Hey Resr

Raven Stones Brow

Middle Edge Moss

Ashway Hey

Ashway Rocks

Little Flat

Raven Stones

6

Birchen Clough

North Grain

Oldham Way

Ashway Gap

Ashway Stone

Howels Head Clough

5

OL3

Little Birchen Clough

Slate Pit Moss

04

Great Dove Stone Rocks

Dean Rocks

Howels Head Flat

4

Little Dove Stone Rocks

Long Clough

Sunny Brow

Bramley's Cot

Dove Stone Moss

Long Clough

3

Chew Hills

Featherbed Moss

03

Oldham Way

Charnel Holes

Small Clough

2

Oldham Way

Chew Brook

Dish Stone Moss

Long Ridge Moss

Charnel Clough

North Clough

1

Stable Stones Brow

Dish Stone Brow

Chew Resr

North Clough

SK13

02

A | **B** | 03 | **C** | **D** | 04 | **E** | **F**

West Yorkshire STREET ATLAS

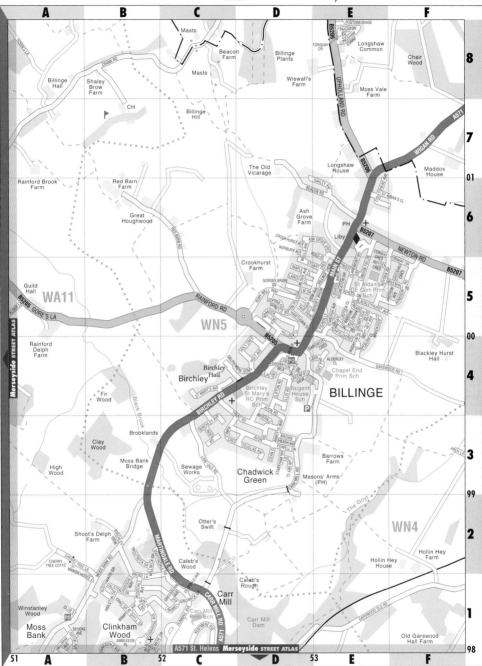

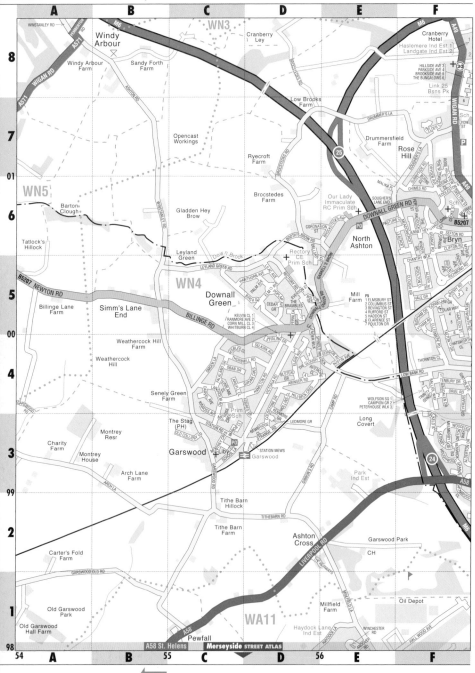

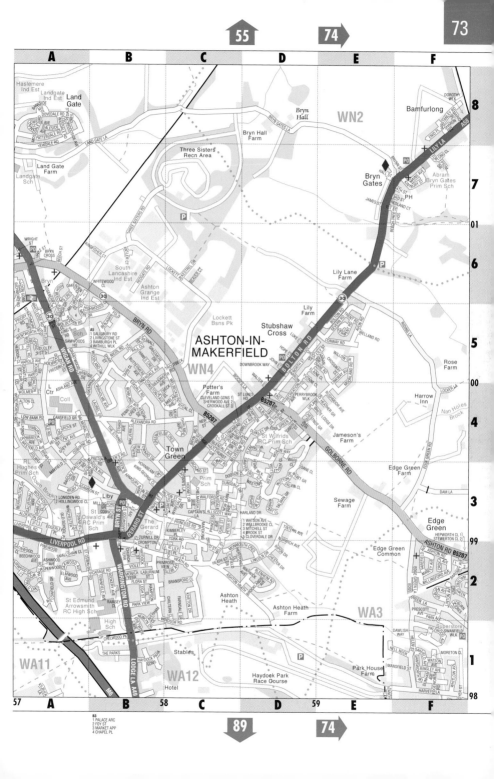

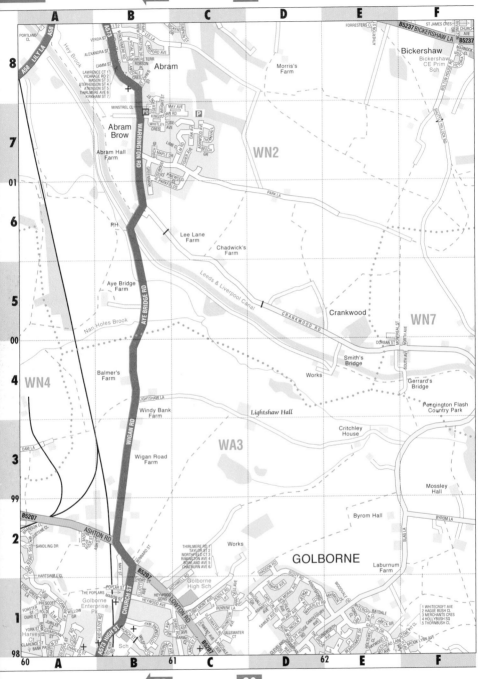

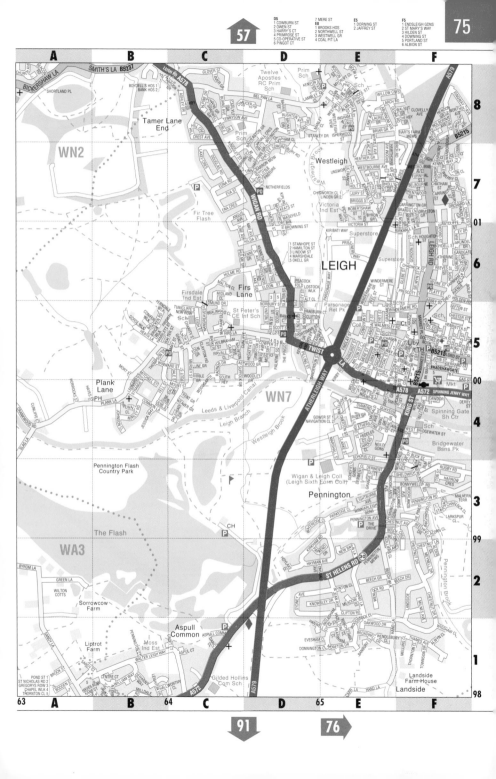

75 58

LEIGH

M46 **M29** **WN7** **WA3**

Crab Fold Farm
HANSON DR
LEIGH RD
B5215
Atherton Brook
Atherton Hall
Atherton Wood
Long Cswy
Leigh
Lilford Park
Higher Folds Prim Sch
KENILWORTH
Walmsley Farm Mast
Higher Folds Enterprise Ctr
Gin Pit
Works
Sports Gd
Bates Farm
Village Inn (PH)
Higher Folds
BLACK LA
Bedford Lodge
St Andrews Dr
Cemy
KERFOOT ST
MANCHESTER RD
Bedford
CHAPEL ST
Bedford B Dock
Bedford High Sch
Marsland Green
Marsland Green Bridge
Great Fold Bridge
A572
A580
EAST LANCASHIRE RD
Siddow Common
St Joseph's RC Prim Sch
Hooten Gardens
Regency Waltham Gdns
South Ave
Great Fold Rutland
Morley's Hall
Sewage Works
Leigh Bsns Pk
Acorn Bsns Ctr
Recn Gd
Bedford Hall Meth Prim Sch
Crompton House
WARRINGTON RD
Leigh Commerce Pk
Sandy Pool Farm
Grange Farm
Magpie's Nest
Environmental Education Centre
Hurstwood
Pennington Bridge
Bedford Bridge
Hawk Hurst Farm
Hope Carr Nature Reserve
Pennington Brook
Hotel
Grave Oak La
WA3
Lately Common
Glaze Brook
Netherbarrow Farm
Black or Moss Brook
Hope Carr La
A574
A580

A4
1 BROWN ST S
2 WHARFDALE
3 RAMSEY ST
4 EAST BRIDGEWATER ST
5 OULTON CL
6 BURWELL CL
7 SIZE HOUSE PL
8 BEDFORD CT

A5
1 BEDFORD ST
2 BROWN ST N
3 BROWN ST
4 BACK QUEEN ST
5 PRINCESS ST
6 DUKINFIELD ST
7 NOBLE ST
8 WILLIAM ST
9 SMITH ST

B4
1 WATERSIDE TRAD EST
2 VILLAGE VIEW
3 WARDS PL
4 LANCASTER CT
5 GEORGIAN CT
6 FARNWORTH ST
7 COSWORTH CL

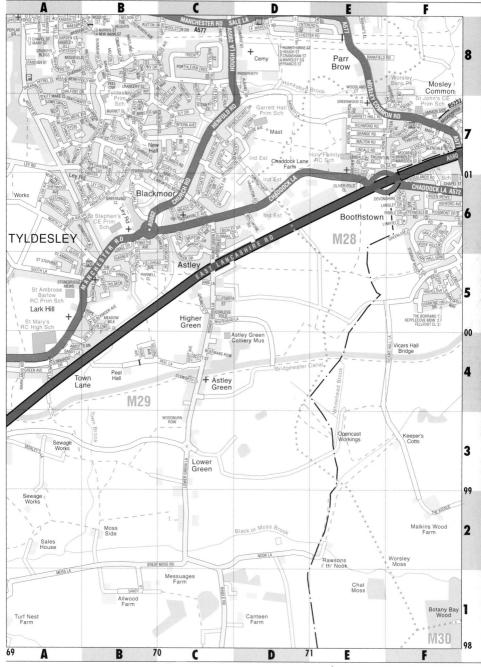

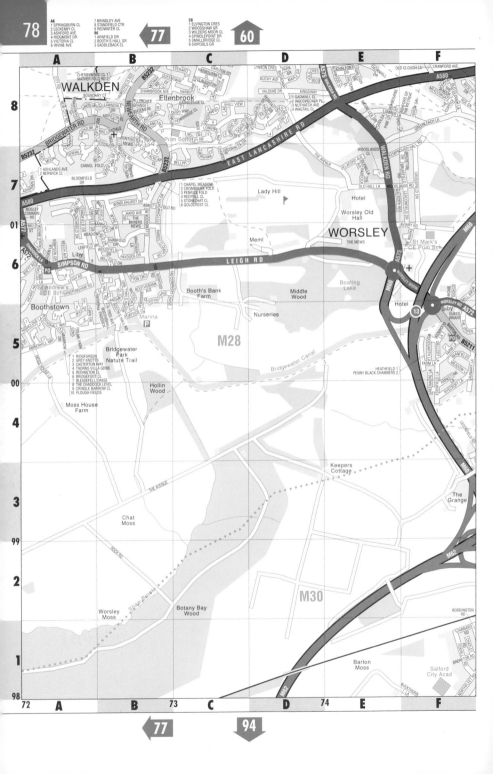

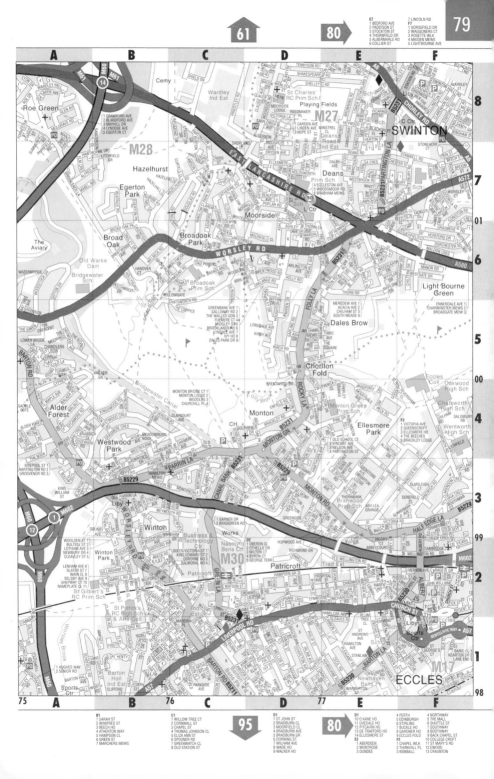

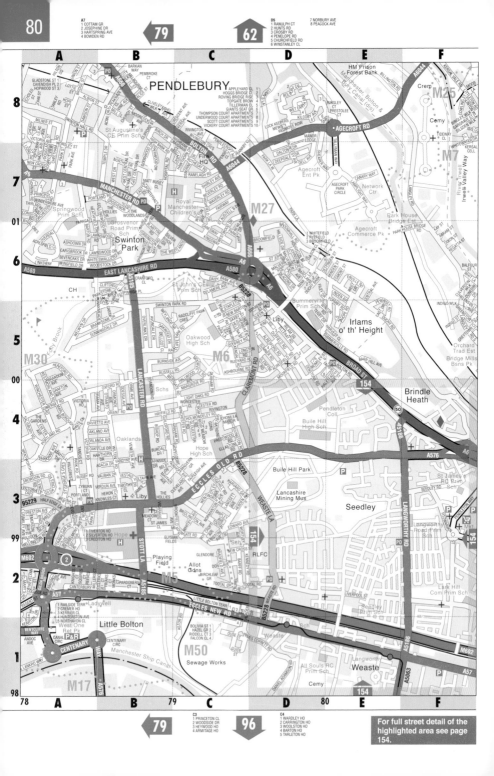

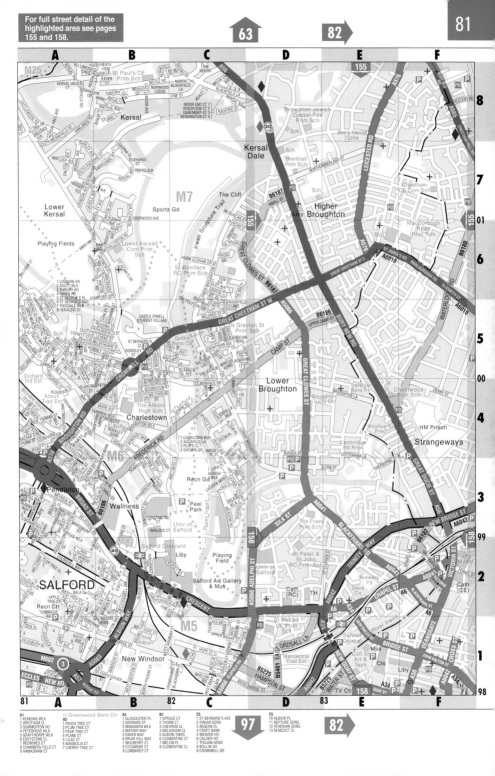

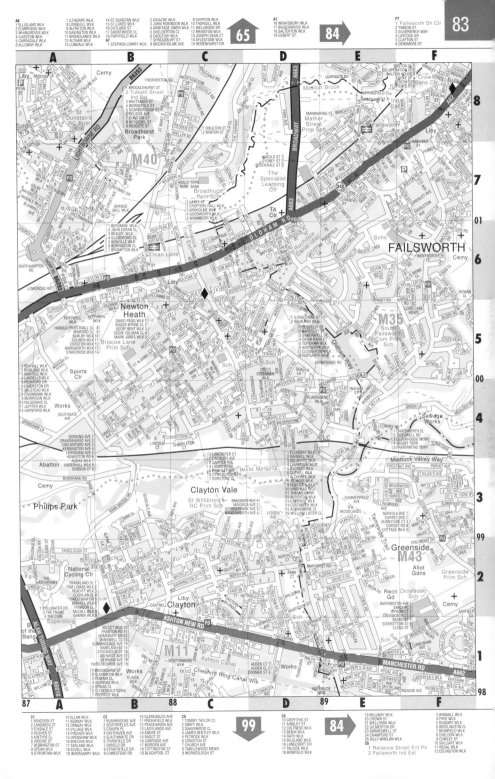

OL8

Ashton Rd

Higher
Failsworth
Prim Sch

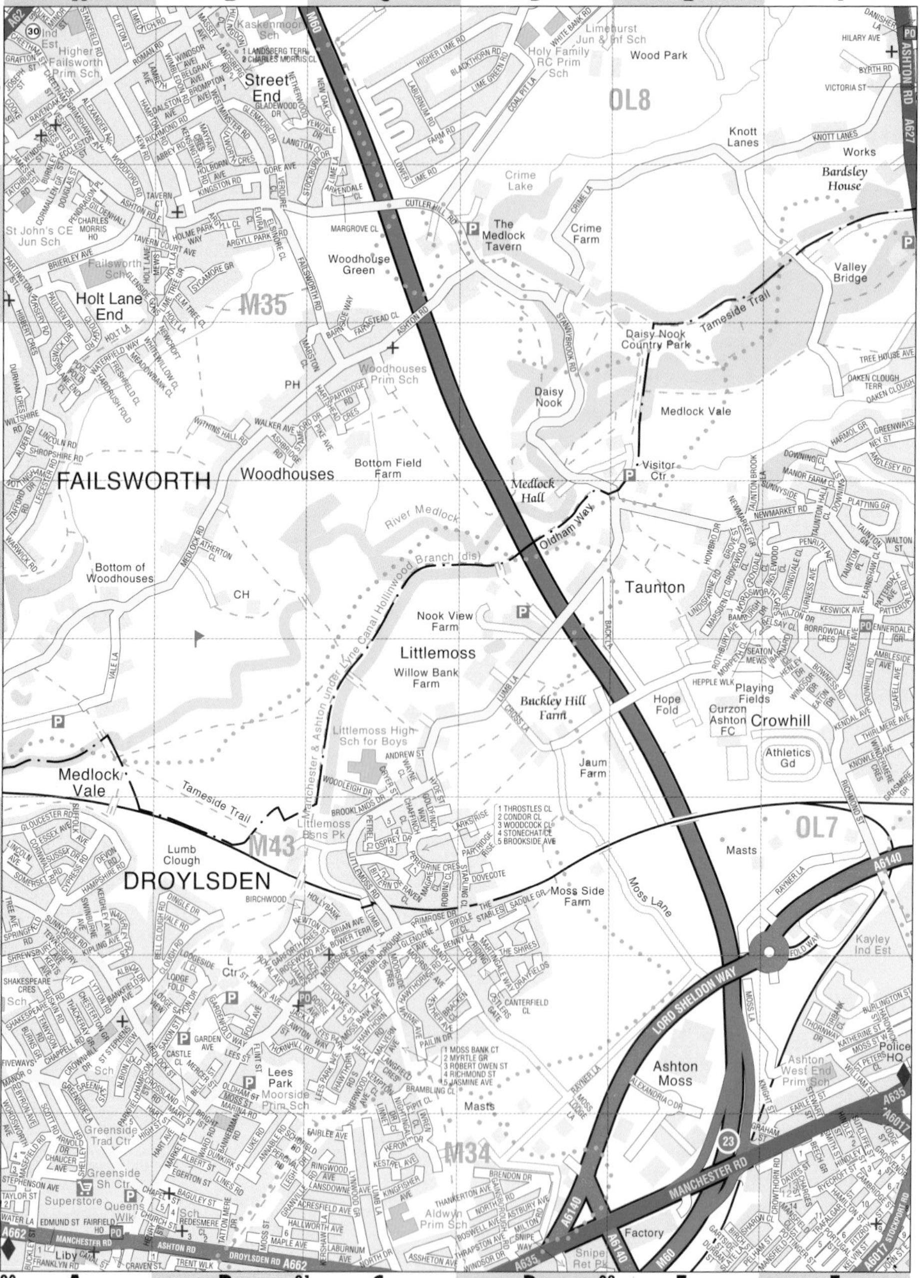

Street
End

St John's CE
Jun Sch

Holt Lane
End

M35

Woodhouse
Green

FAILSWORTH

Woodhouses

Bottom Field
Farm

Bottom of
Woodhouses

Woodhouses
Prim Sch

River Medlock

Manchester & Ashton under Lyne Canal Hollinwood Branch (dis)

Nook View
Farm

Willow Bank
Farm

Littlemoss

Littlemoss High
Sch for Boys

Medlock
Vale

Tameside Trail

Lumb
Clough

M43

DROYLSDEN

Littlemoss
Bsns Pk

Birchwood

Lees Park

Greenside
Trad Ctr

Greenside
Sch Ctr

Queens

Liby

Superstore

A662

MANCHESTER RD

DROYLSDEN   A662

M34

Aldwyn
Prim Sch

Holy Family
RC Prim
Sch

Wood Park

Crime
Lake

The Medlock
Tavern

Crime
Farm

Daisy Nook
Country Park

Daisy
Nook

Medlock Vale

Medlock
Hall

Oldham Way

Visitor
Ctr

Taunton

Buckley Hill
Farm

Hope
Fold

Jaum
Farm

Curzon
Ashton
FC

Playing
Fields

Crowhill

Athletics
Gd

OL7

Moss Side
Farm

Masts

Ashton
Moss

LORD SHELDON WAY

Kayley
Ind Est

OL7

Ashton
West End
Prim Sch

Police
HQ

23

MANCHESTER RD

Factory

Snipe
Ret Pk

Knott
Lanes

Bardsley
House

Valley
Bridge

Hilary Ave

Victoria St

Works

Tameside Trail

1 THROSTLES CL
2 CONDOR CL
3 WOODCOCK CL
4 STONECHAT CL
5 BROOKSIDE AVE

1 MOSS BANK CT
2 MYRTLE GR
3 ROBERT OWEN ST
4 RICHMOND ST
5 JASMINE AVE

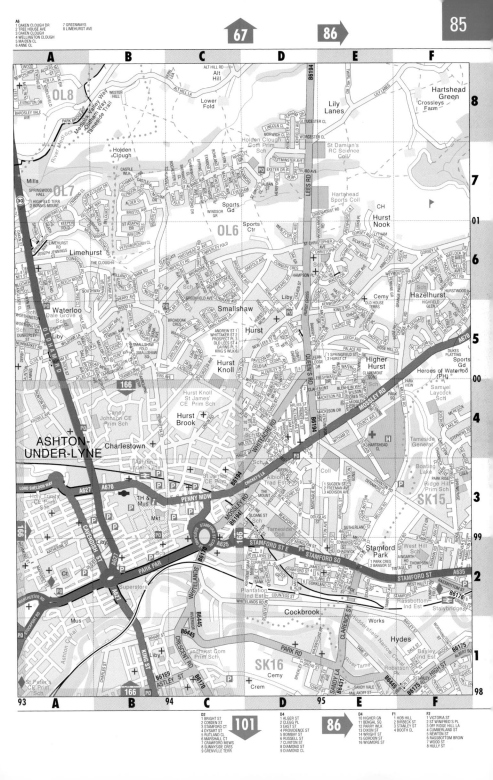

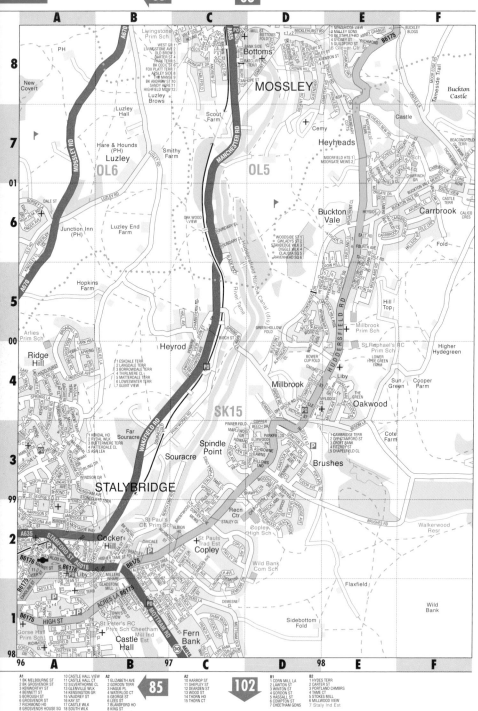

A1
1 BK MELBOURNE ST
2 BK GROSVENOR ST
3 KENWORTHY ST
4 BENNETT ST
5 BOROUGH ST
6 GROSVENOR ST
7 RICHMOND HO
8 GROSVENOR HOUSE SQ
9 GROSVENOR GDNS

10 CASTLE HALL VIEW
11 CASTLE HALL CT
12 SILVERTHORNE CL
13 GLENVILLE WLK
14 KENSINGTON GR
15 VAUDREY ST
16 KAY ST
17 CASTLE WLK
18 SOUTH WLK
19 EDGY WLK

A2
1 ELIZABETH AVE
2 GORDON TERR
3 HAGUE PL
4 WATERLOO CT
5 GEORGE ST
6 LEES ST
7 BLANDFORD HO
8 KING ST
9 CROSSLEY ST

A2
10 HARROP ST
11 SHEPLEY ST
12 DEARDEN ST
13 WOOD ST
14 THORN HO
15 THORN CT

B1
1 CORN MILL LA
2 LAWTON ST
3 WINTON ST
4 GORDON ST
5 HASSALL ST
6 COMPTON ST
7 CHEETHAM GDNS

B2
1 HYDES TERR
2 CARTER ST
3 PORTLAND CHMBRS
4 TAME CT
5 STOKES MILL
6 MILLWOOD VIEW
7 Staly Ind Est

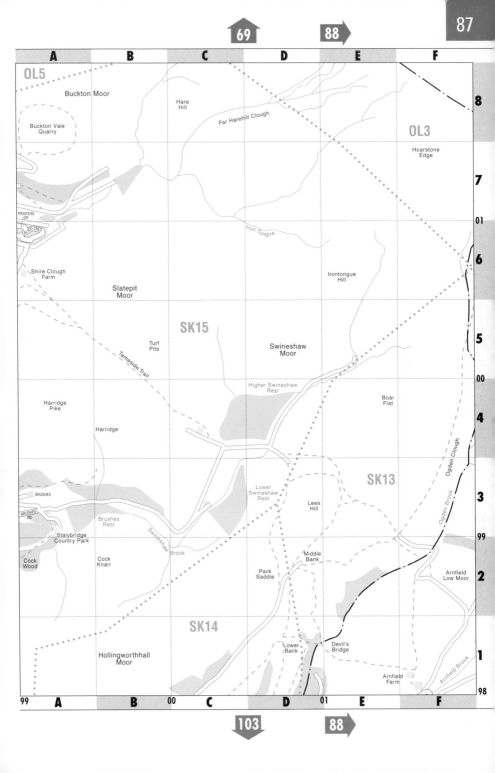

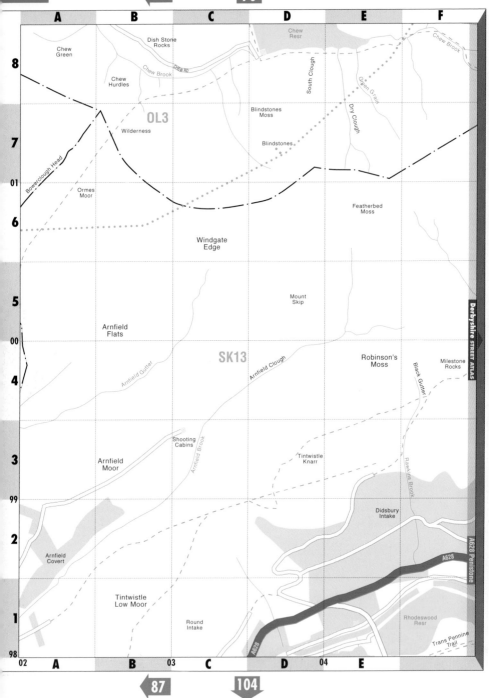

A B C D E F

8

OL3

7

01

6

5

00

4

3

99

2

1

98

02 A B 03 C D 04 E

Chew Green

Dish Stone Rocks

Chew Brook

Chew Resr

Chew Brook

Chew Hurdles

CHEW RD

South Clough

Green Grain

Wilderness

Blindstones Moss

Dry Clough

Bowerclough Head

Ormes Moor

Blindstones

Featherbed Moss

Windgate Edge

Mount Skip

Arnfield Flats

SK13

Robinson's Moss

Milestone Rocks

Arnfield Gutter

Arnfield Clough

Black Gutter

Derbyshire STREET ATLAS

Shooting Cabins

Tintwistle Knarr

Arnfield Moor

Arnfield Brook

Rawkins Brook

Didsbury Intake

Arnfield Covert

A628

A628 Penistone

Tintwistle Low Moor

Round Intake

A628

Rhodeswood Resr

Trans Pennine Trail

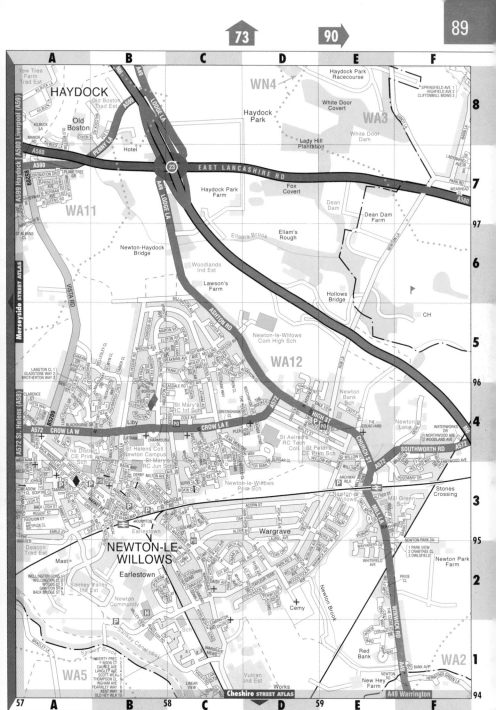

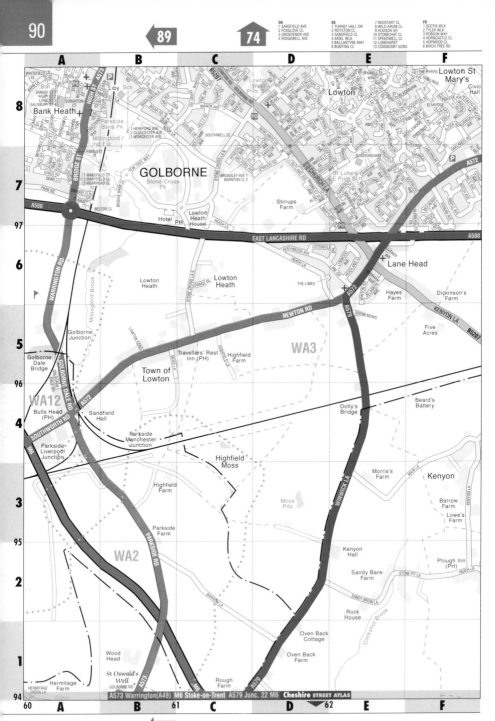

89

74

89

A B C D E F

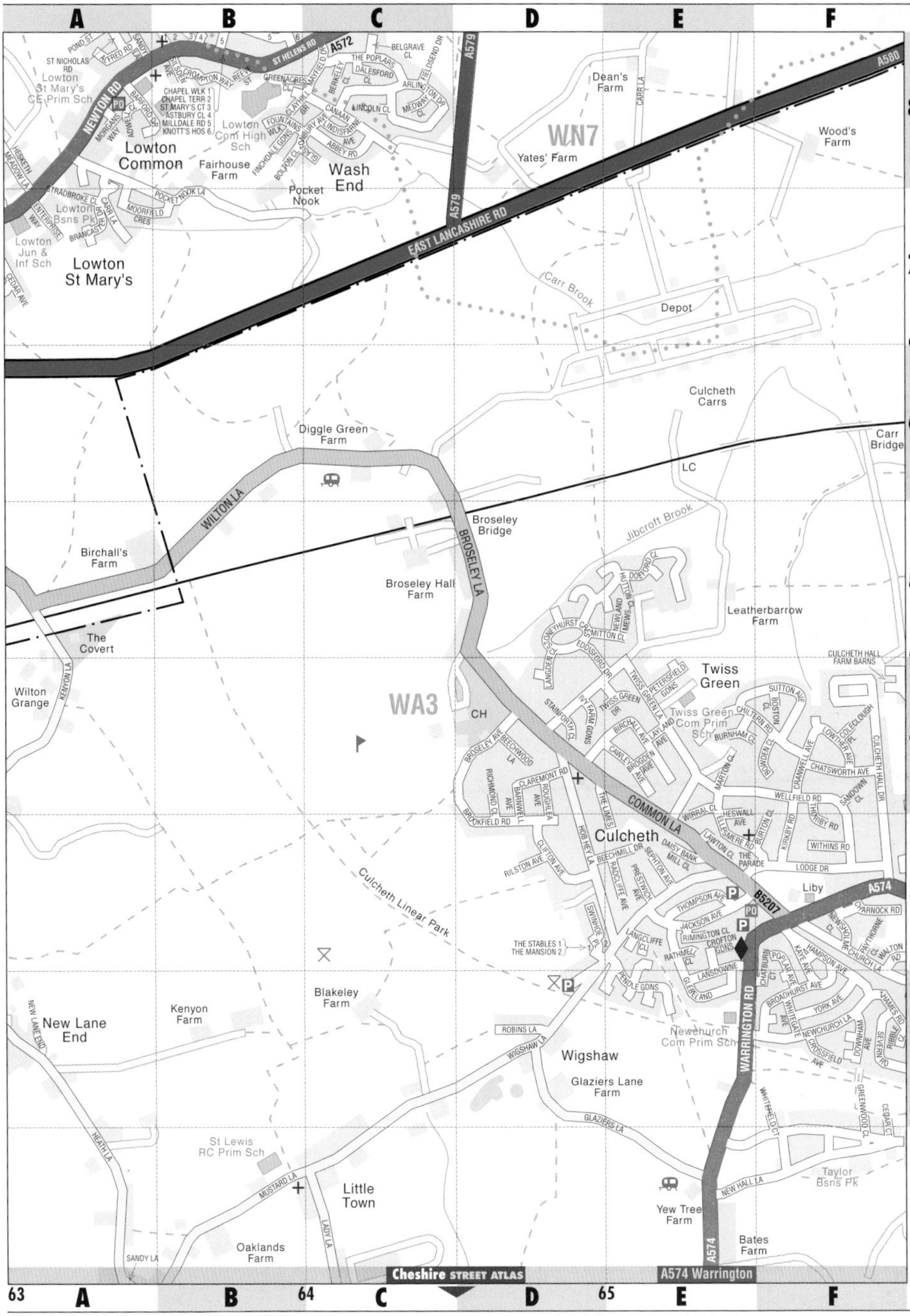

St Nicholas RD
Pond ST
NEWTON RD
Lowton St Mary's CE Prim Sch
ST HELENS RD
A572
CHAPEL WLK 1
CHAPEL TERR 2
ST MARY'S CT 3
ASTBURY CL 4
MILLDALE RD 5
KNOTT'S HOS 6
THE POPLARS
BELGRAVE CL
ARLINGTON DR
Lowton Com High Sch
Lowton Common
Fairhouse Farm
Wash End
Pocket Nook
A579
Dean's Farm
CARR RD
WN7
Yates' Farm
Wood's Farm

8

Lowton Bsns Pk
Lowton Jun & Inf Sch
Lowton St Mary's
MOORFIELD CRES

A580
EAST LANCASHIRE RD

7

Carr Brook
Depot

97

Diggle Green Farm
Culcheth Carrs
Carr Bridge

6

WILTON LA
LC

Birchall's Farm
Broseley Bridge
Broseley Hall Farm
BROSELEY LA
Jibcroft Brook
Leatherbarrow Farm

5

The Covert
Twiss Green
Culcheth Hall Farm Barns

96

Wilton Grange
WA3
CH
Twiss Green Com Prim Sch
COMMON LA
CHATSWORTH AVE

4

Culcheth
WELLFIELD RD
THE PARADE
LODGE DR

Liby
BS207
A574
PARNOCK RD

3

Culcheth Linear Park
P
P
WARRINGTON RD

95

New Lane End
Kenyon Farm
Blakeley Farm
THE STABLES 1
THE MANSION 2
P
ROBINS LA
WIGSHAW LA
Wigshaw
Newchurch Com Prim Sch

2

NEW LANE END
HEATH LA
St Lewis RC Prim Sch
MUSTARD LA
LADY LA
Little Town
GLAZIERS LA
Glaziers Lane Farm
Yew Tree Farm
NEW HALL AV
Taylor Bsns Pk

1

SANDY LA
Oaklands Farm
A574 Warrington
A574

94

63 A B 64 C D 65 E F

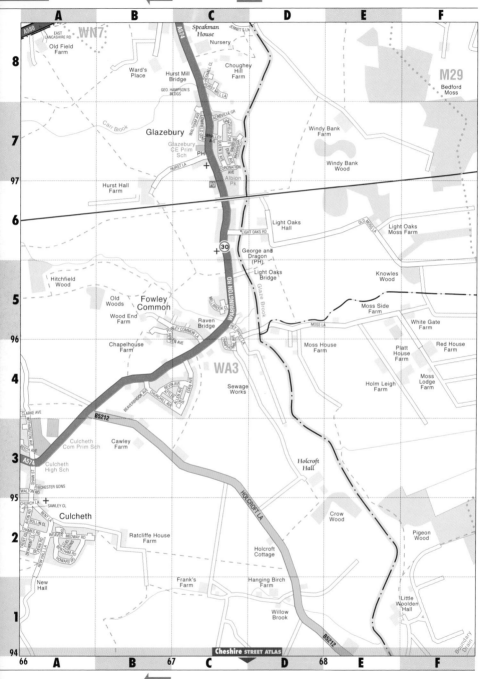

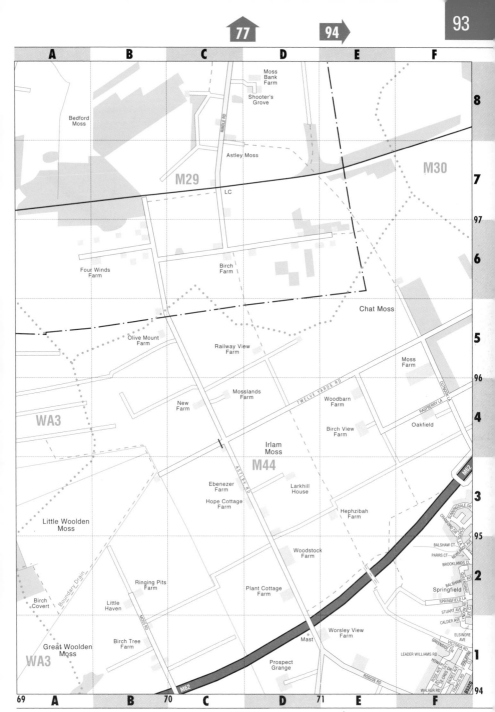

77
94

A **B** **C** **D** **E** **F**

8

Bedford
Moss

Moss
Bank
Farm

Shooter's
Grove

RIDDLE RD

Astley Moss

M29

7

LC

97

Four Winds
Farm

Birch
Farm

6

M30

Chat Moss

Olive Mount
Farm

Railway View
Farm

5

Moss
Farm

96

WA3

New
Farm

Mosslands
Farm

TWELVE YARDS RD

Woodbarn
Farm

CUTNOOK LA

RASPBERRY LA

4

Birch View
Farm

Oakfield

Irlam
Moss

M44

ASTLEY RD

Ebenezer
Farm

Larkhill
House

3

Hope Cottage
Farm

Hephzibah
Farm

M62

Little Woolden
Moss

BARTON MOSS RD

CRANFORD DR

GRINDSDALE DR

95

Woodstock
Farm

BALSHAW CT.

PARRS CT.

NORVILLE AVE

BROOKLANDS CL.

Ringing Pits
Farm

Plant Cottage
Farm

BALSHAW
AVE

Springfield

2

Boundary Drain

MOSS RD

Little
Haven

SPRINGFIELD LA

STUART AVE

CALDER AVE

Birch
Covert

Birch Tree
Farm

Mast

Worsley View
Farm

ELSINORE
AVE

GREENSIDE DR

VICTORIA RD

Great Woolden
Moss

WA3

Prospect
Grange

LEADER WILLIAMS RD

HOWARTH DR

ROSCOE RD

ROSCOE RD

FRANCIS RD

1

M62

WALKER RD

94

69 **A** **B** 70 **C** **D** **E** 71 **F**

105
94

A   B   C   D   E   F

8

Brookhouse
Sports Ctr

LC

PYRUS CL

Barton Moss
Com Prim Sch

Moulder's
Farm

Brighton
Grange

Crem

Nursery
Farm

Cemy

Manor
Farm

PROCTOR
WAY

Birch
Farm

Tunnel
Farm

Twelve Yards Rd

VANGUARD
CL

7

Barton
Aerodrome

A57

M30

97

Univ of Manchester
(Sch of Mechanical
Aerospace &
Civil Engineering)

Football
Gd

Black
Wood

Bartonmoss
Farm

Barton
Moss

Salteye Brook

TWELVE YARDS RD

6

Barton
Locks

Mast

Parkhall

Raspberry La

Davyhulme
Millennium Pk

5

Barton
Grange

Nature Reserve

CRES

96

BOOTH

Mast

M44   Gladwyn
Farm

Ferry P   Sewage
Works
(dis)

BENT LANES

Boysnope
Wharf

REDBOURNE
DR

LILBURN

Liverpool Rd

Recn
Gd

Fallows
Farm

Manchester Ship Canal

Woods
End

Calder
Bank

LINGARD

CH

M2

M41

4

B5320

EASEDALE

Com
Prim Sch

RC Prim
Sch

Boundary Rd

Bradwell Wlk 1
Woodsend Circ 2
Marbury Cl 3
Forest Ct 4

Liby

Chesham Ave

MOSS
RD

MOORSIDE RD

LINDALE

Liby

Boundary
Trad Est

Barton
Terr

Mayfield
Ind Est

Clarendon Rd
Brighton Rd

Belgrave Ave

Com Prim
Sch

Pipers Ct
Oleo Terr

BALMORAL

3

95

Queens Ct 1
Ashworth Ave 2
Bridle Cl 3
Ambuscade Cl 4

Derwent Rd

ASHLEY
AVE

LONGWORTH
AVE

Flixton Jun &
Inf Sch

IRLAM

Cadishead Way

Woodsend Park
Acre Hall
Prim Sch

WINDSOR AVE

Flixton

A2
4 Woodbine Terr
1 Olympia Ct
2 Whitestar Ct
3 Weston Rd
5 Etherley Ct

Carr Rd

2

HIGHBURY AVE

Sch

Irlam Rd
Wellacre
Tech
Coll

Grange
Ave

B5158

Flixton Rd

Towns
Gate

Delamere
Sch

Woodlands

MARLFIELD

Bosdin
Rd W

1 Roslyn Ave
2 Alexandra Ct
3 Parsonage Rd
4 Grasmere Ave
5 Hampstead Ave
6 Reade Ho
7 Brentwood
8 Stocks Ho

B5320

Grave
Yard

Boat
House (PH)

WESTERN RD

De Brook Cl

LONGWD

1

Irlam
Locks

Sewage
Works

AMBLESIDE AVE

Flixton

St Michael's CE
Prim Sch

BARNVIEW
DR

A57

The
Village

B5158   B5213

THE GROVE

FERRYMASTERS
WAY

94

72   A   B   73   C   D   74   E   F

B1
1 WOODSEAVES CL
2 BANKQUAY CT
3 STICKENS LOCK LA
B3
1 HOLLY CT
2 ST CLEMENT'S CT
3 DAIRYDALE CL
4 BUTTERMILL CL
5 PENNISTONE CL

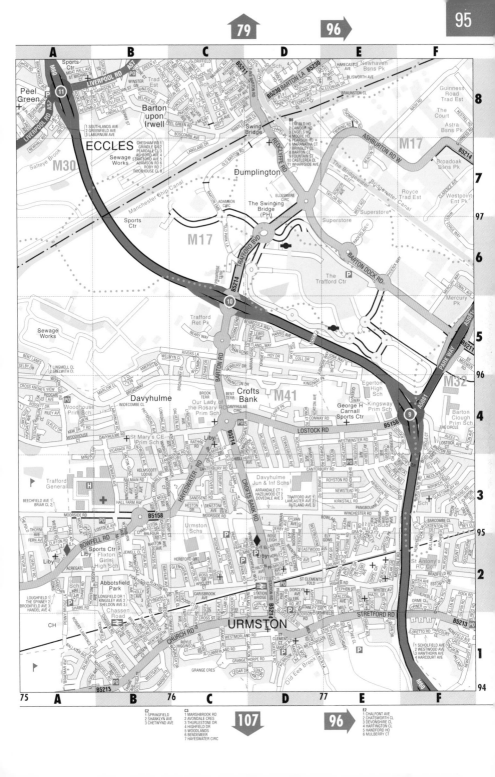

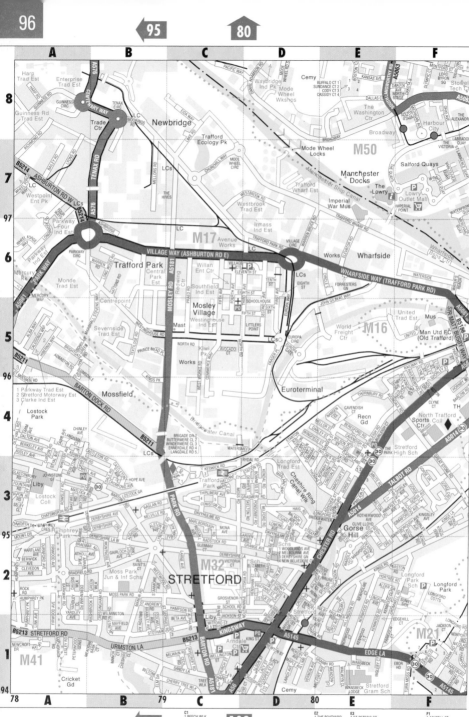

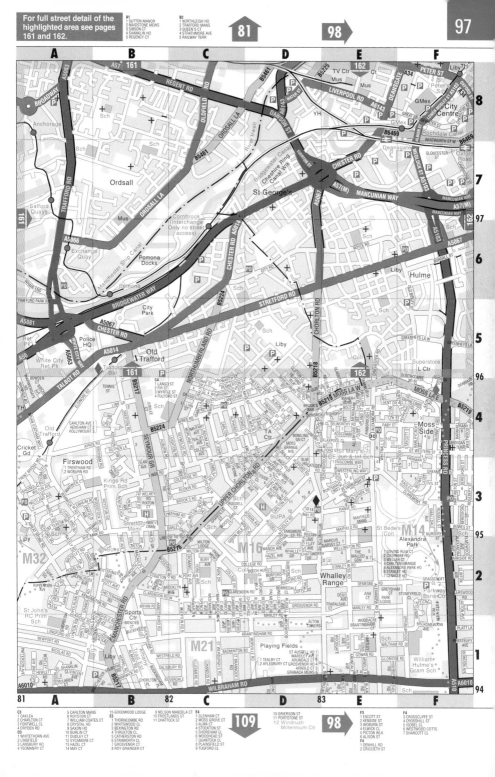

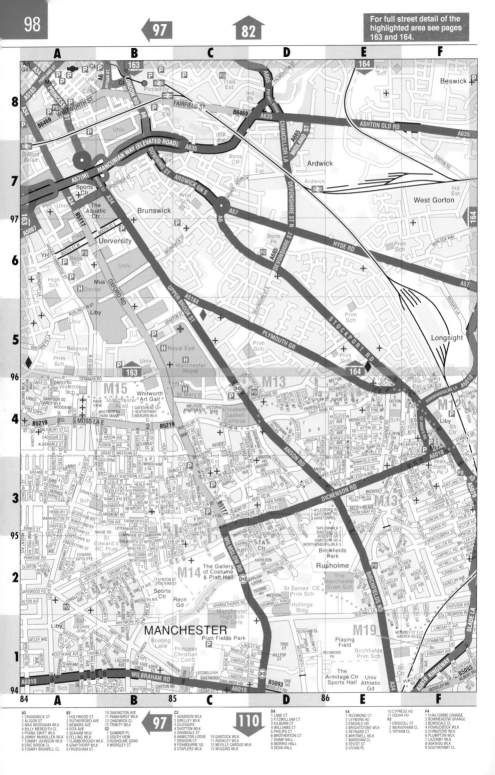

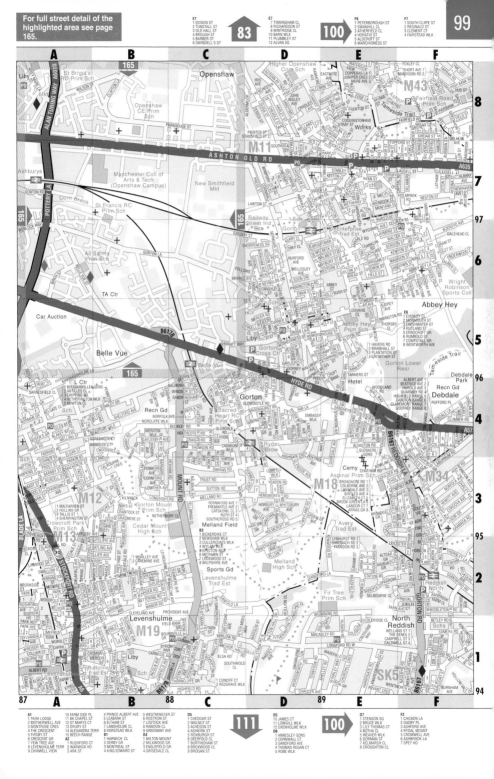

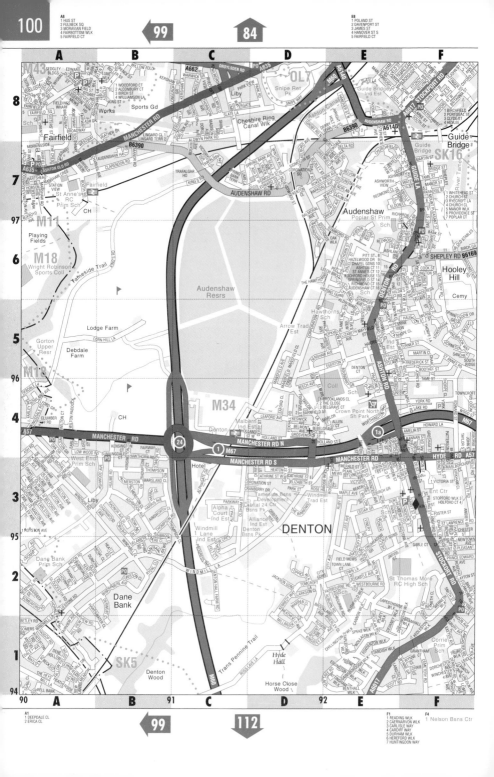

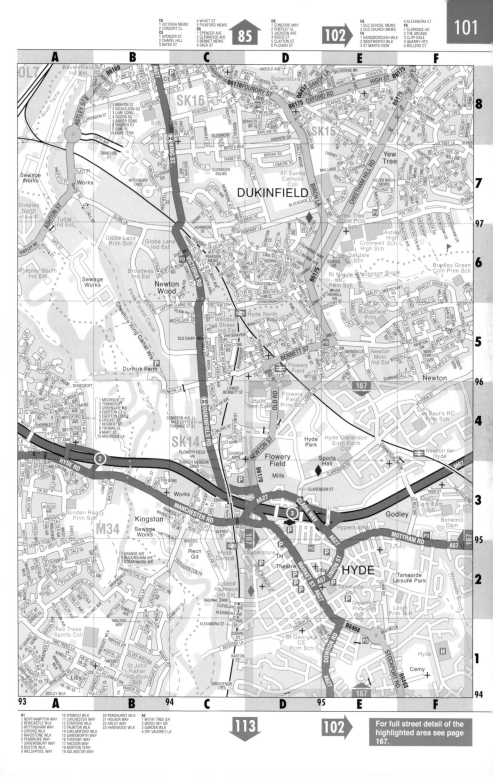

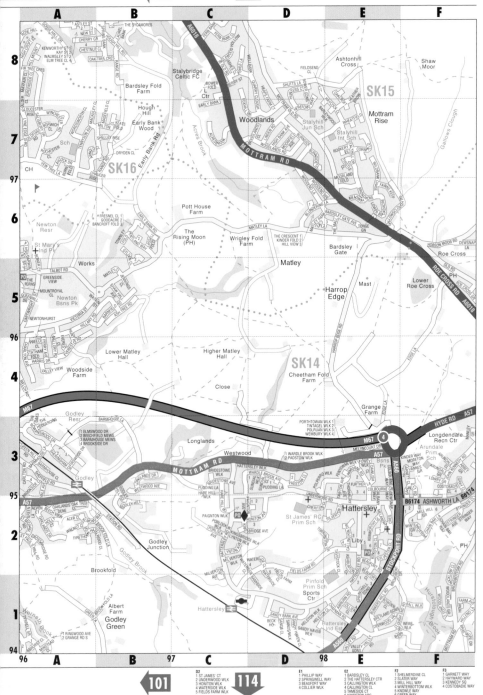

D2
1 ST JAMES CT
2 UNDERWOOD WLK
3 HONITON WLK
4 WATERSIDE WLK
5 FIELDS FARM WLK

E1
1 PHILLIP WAY
2 SPRINGWELL WAY
3 BEAUFORT WAY
4 COLLIER WLK

E2
1 BARDSLEY CL
2 THE HATTERSLEY CTR
3 CALLINGTON WLK
4 CALLINGTON CL
5 TAMESIDE CT
6 KINGSTON ARC
7 WORTHINGTON CL
8 SYLVESTER WAY

F2
1 SHELMERDINE CL
2 SLATER WAY
3 MILL HILL WAY
4 WINTERBOTTOM WLK
5 KNOWLE WAY
6 GREEN WAY
7 GREEN WLK
8 ASHWORTH WAY

F3
1 GARNETT WAY
2 HAYWARD WAY
3 KENNEDY SQ
4 COSTOBADIE WAY

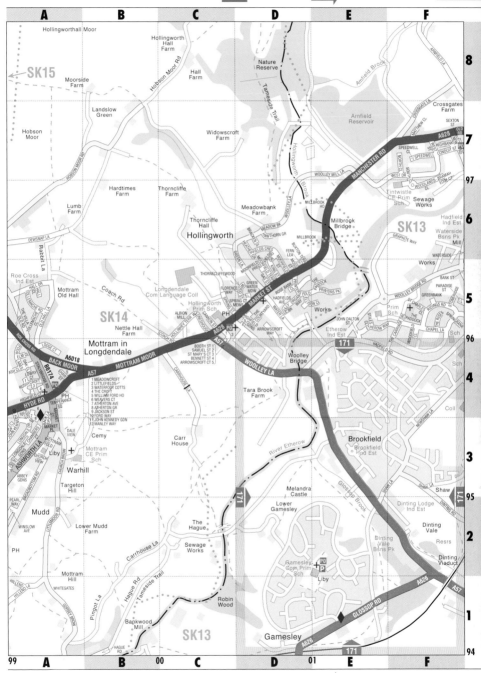

For full street detail of the highlighted area see page 171.

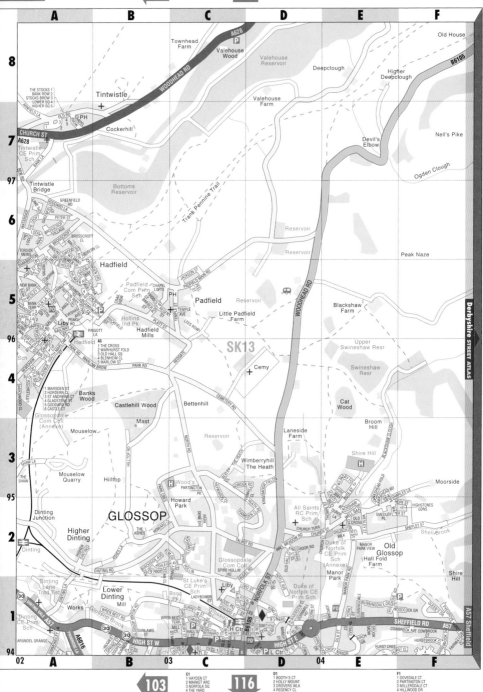

103
88

	A	B	C	D	E	F

8

Old House

Townhead Farm

Valehouse Wood

Valehouse Reservoir

Deepclough

Higher Deepclough

B6105

WOODHEAD RD

A628

Tintwistle

Valehouse Farm

Nell's Pike

Devil's Elbow

Cockerhill

7

CHURCH ST

A628

Tintwistle CE Prim Sch

Ogden Clough

97

Tintwistle Bridge

Bottoms Reservoir

Trans Pennine Trail

GREENFIELD HO

PETER ST

6

Reservoir

Reservoir

Peak Naze

Hadfield

Padfield Com Prim Sch

CHAPEL LOFTS

PH

Padfield

Reservoir

Blackshaw Farm

5

WOODHEAD RD

Little Padfield Farm

TEMPLE AVE

LEES ROW

Hollins Ind Pk

Upper Swineshaw Resr

96

Hadfield Mills

PINGOTT LA

A5
1 THE CROSS
2 WARHURST FOLD
3 OLD HALL SQ
4 BLENHEIM CL
5 MARLOW ST

SK13

Swineshaw Resr

PARK RD

Cemy

4

Banks Wood

Castlehill Wood

Bettenhill

CEMETERY RD

Cat Wood

Broom Hill

1 MARSDEN ST
2 HORDERN CL
3 ST ANDREWS VW
4 GLADSTONE ST
5 GODDARD RD
6 CASTLE CT

Mast

Laneside Farm

Shire Hill

3

Glossopdale Com Coll (Annexe)

Mouselow

Reservoir

Wimberryhill The Heath

Wood's Partington Pk

Moorside

THE SHAW

SHAW LA

Mouselow Quarry

Hilltop

Howard Park

SOWDEN RD

All Saints RC Prim Sch

Shelf Brook

HIGHSTONES GDNS

95

Dinting Junction

GLOSSOP

CHURCH TERR

Duke of Norfolk CE Prim Sch (Annexe)

MANOR PARK VIEW

SHEPLEY ST

2

Dinting

Higher Dinting

THE ASHES

TALBOT RD

KINGSMOOR RD

Old Glossop

Hall Fold Farm

Manor Park

Shire Hill

1

Dinting Lane Trad Est

Lower Dinting Mill

Works

Dinting CE Prim Sch

ARUNDEL GRANGE

A6016

HIGH ST W

DINTING RD

St Luke's CE Prim Sch

Glossopdale Com Coll

Liby

NORFOLK ST

HIGH ST E

SHEFFIELD RD

COWBROOK AVE COWBROOK CT

HURSTBROOK

Duke of Norfolk CE Prim Sch

Manor Park

A57

HURST CRES

A57 Sheffield

94

A	B	C	D	E	F

103
116

C1
1 HAYDEN CT
2 MARKET ARC
3 NORFOLK SQ
4 THE YARD
5 VICTORIA ST
6 CENTRAL STORE

D1
1 BOOTH'S CT
2 HOLLY MOUNT
3 DROVERS WLK
4 REGENCY CL

F1
1 DOVEDALE CT
2 PARTINGTON CT
3 MILLSDALE CT
4 HILLWOOD DR
5 HATHERSAGE DR

Derbyshire STREET ATLAS

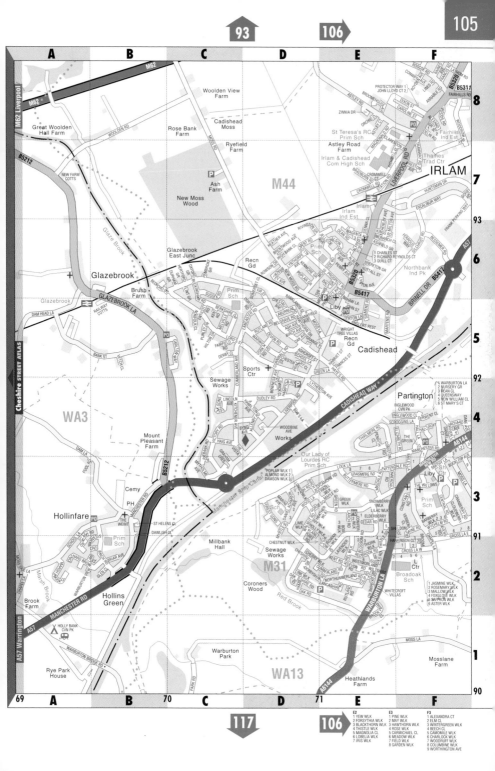

105
94

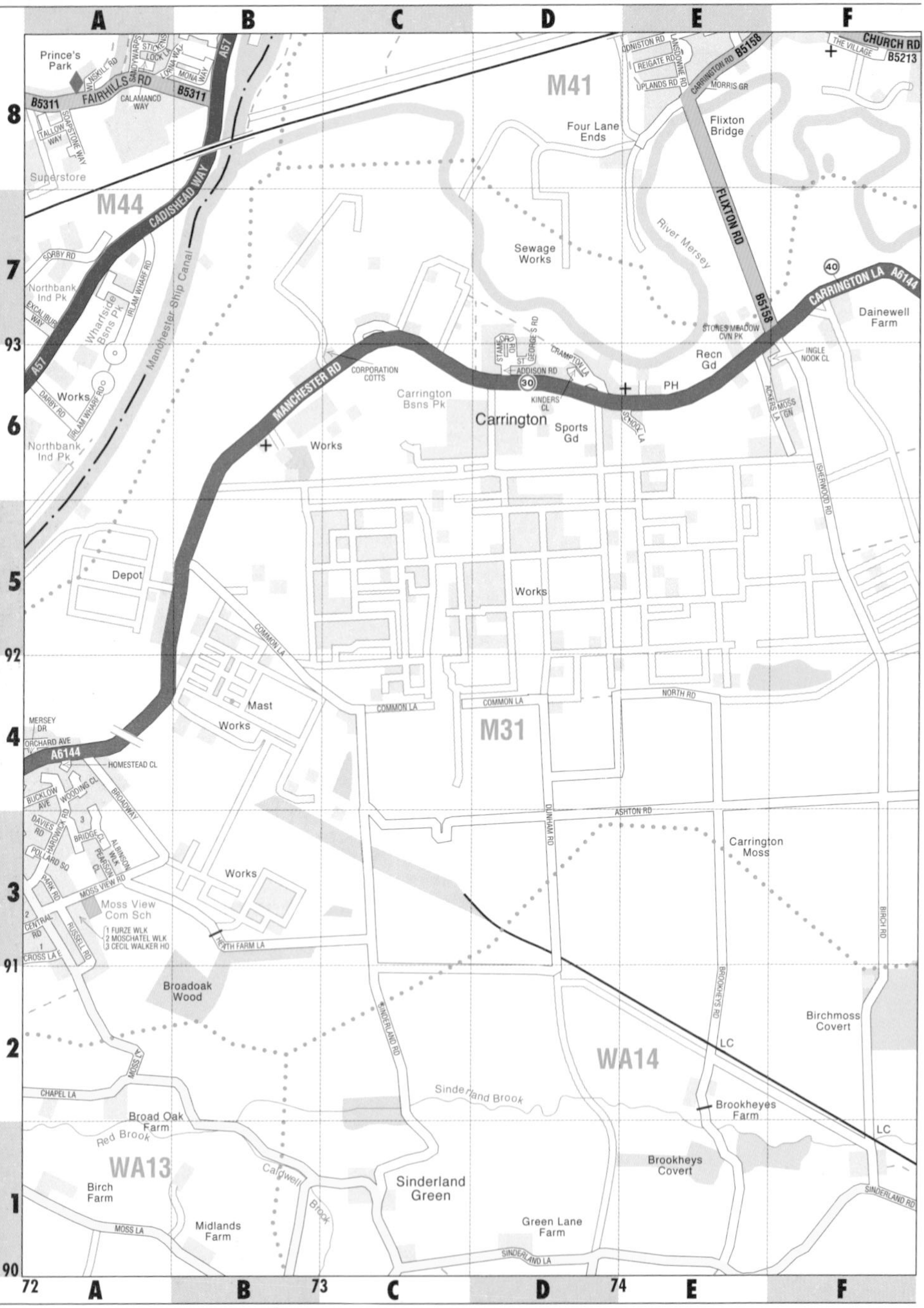

A B C D E F

8

Prince's Park
FAIRHILLS RD
B5311
CALAMANCO WAY
B5311
A57
M41
Four Lane Ends
DONISTON RD
REIGATE RD
UPLANDS RD
MORRIS GR
CARRINGTON RD
B5158
THE VILLAGE
CHURCH RD
B5213
Flixton Bridge
FLIXTON RD

7

Superstore
M44
CADISHEAD WAY
M44
CORBY RD
Northbank Ind Pk
Wharfside Bsns Pk
Manchester Ship Canal
River Mersey
Sewage Works
STONES MEADOW CVN PK
Recn Gd
CARRINGTON LA A6144
40
INGLE NOOK CL
Dainewell Farm

93

A57
DARBY RD
Works
Northbank Ind Pk
MANCHESTER RD
CORPORATION COTTS
Carrington Bsns Pk
ST HELENS RD
GEORGE'S RD
CRAMPTON LA
ADDISON RD
30
KINDERS CL
Carrington
PH
FENDCK LA
MOSS TON
SHERWOOD RD

6

Works
Sports Gd

5

Depot
COMMON LA
Works

92

Mast
Works
COMMON LA
COMMON LA
NORTH RD
M31

4

MERSEY DR
ORCHARD AVE
A6144
HOMESTEAD CL
BUCKLOW AVE
BROADWAY
DAVIES RD
BRIDGE
ALBERT RD
POLD RD
Works
Moss View Com Sch
1 FURZE WLK
2 MOSCHATEL WLK
3 CECIL WALKER HO
NTH FARM LA
DUNHAM RD
ASHTON RD
Carrington Moss
BROOKHEYS DR
BIRCH RD

3

MOSS VIEW RD
CENTRAL RD
CROSS LA
Broadoak Wood
SINDERLAND RD

91

Birchmoss Covert

2

CHAPEL LA
MOSS LA
WA14
Sinderland Brook
LC
Brookheyes Farm
LC
SINDERLAND RD

1

WA13
Birch Farm
Broad Oak Farm
Red Brook
Caldwell Brook
Sinderland Green
Brookheys Covert
Green Lane Farm
MOSS LA
Midlands Farm
SINDERLAND RD

90

72 A B 73 C D 74 E F

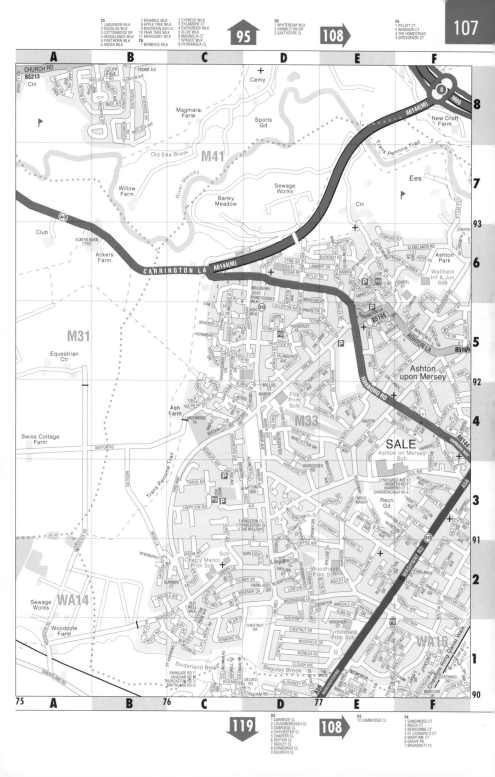

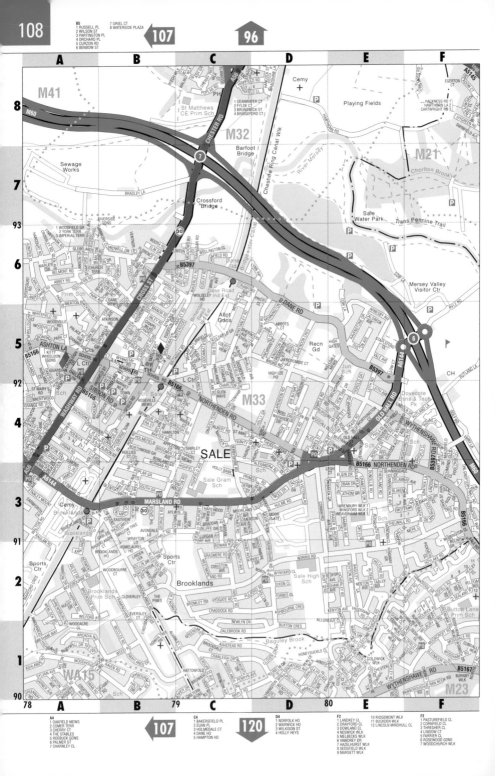

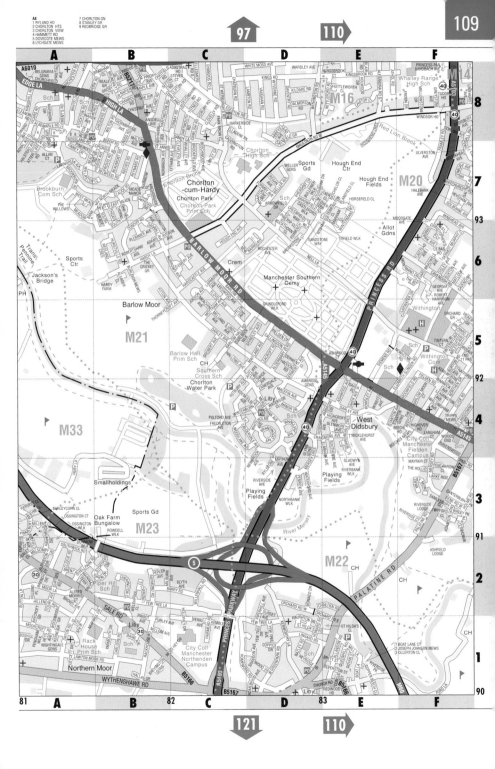

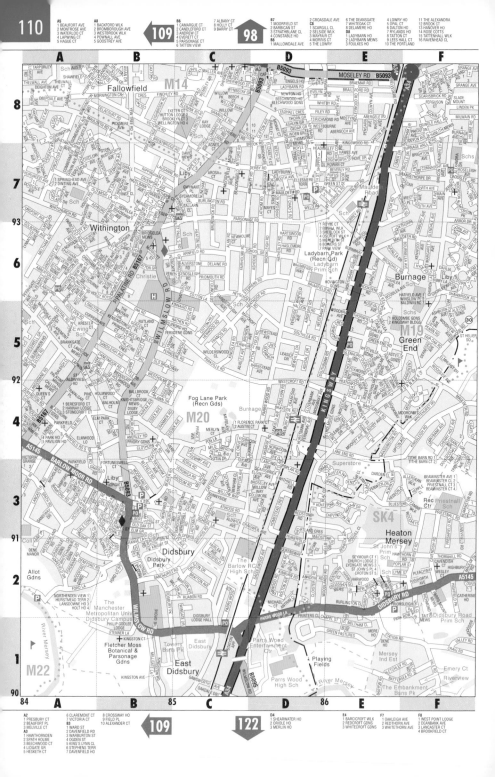

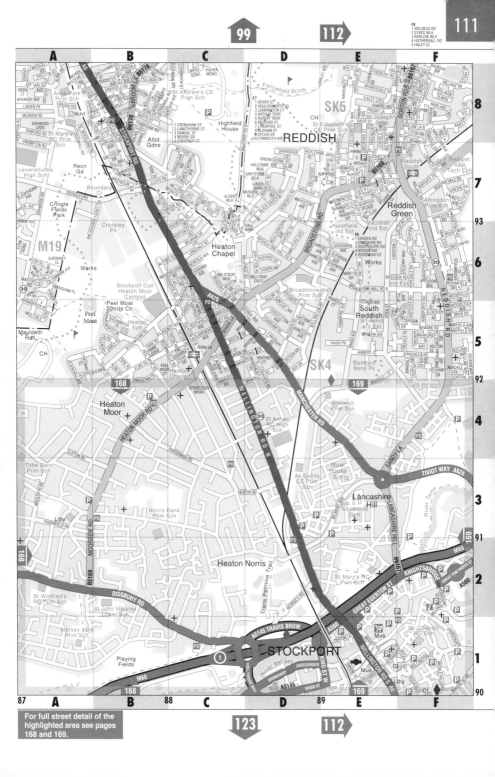

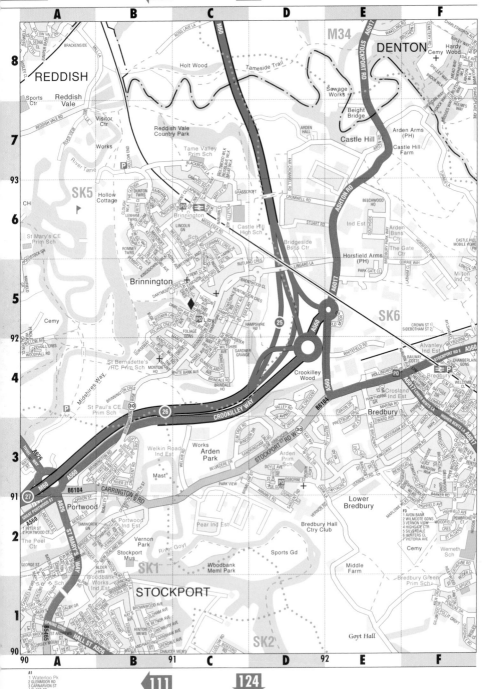

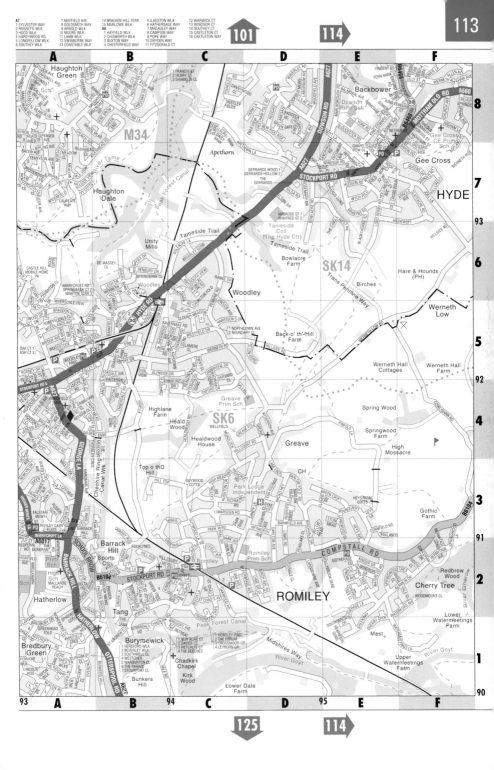

113
102

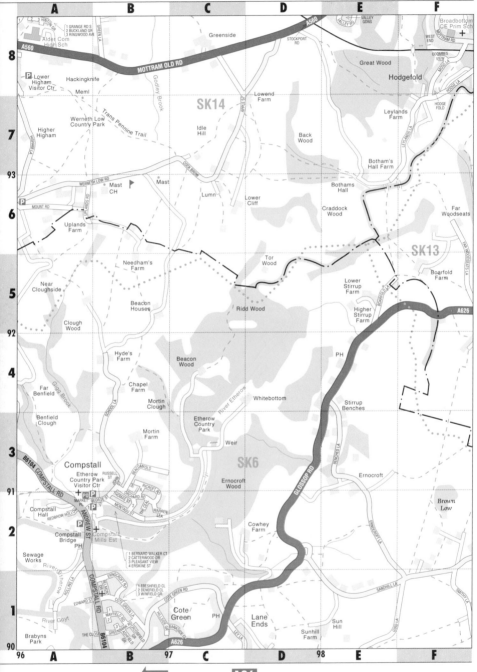

113
126

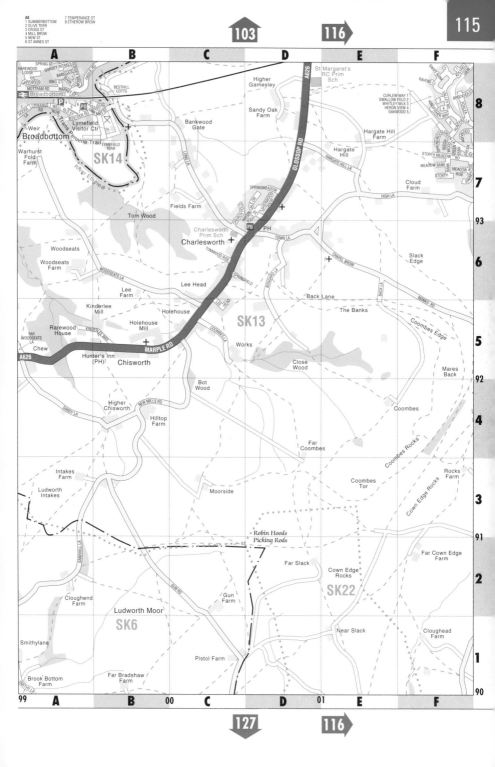

115

104

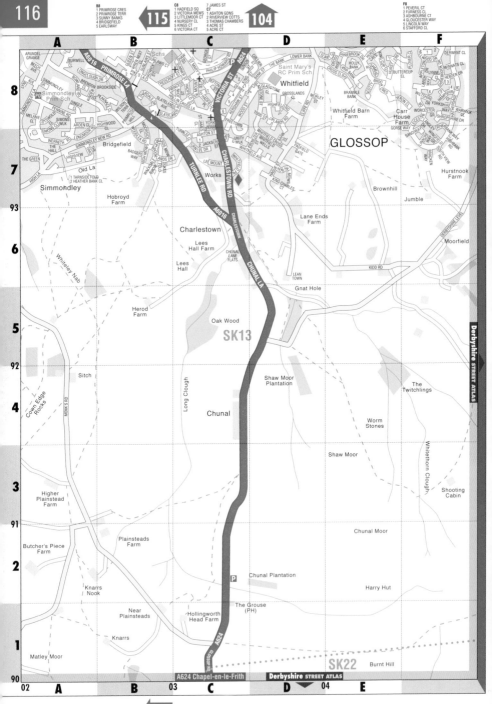

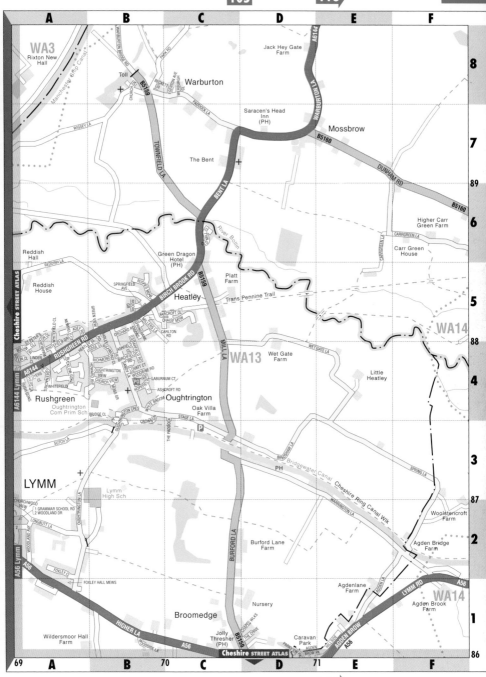

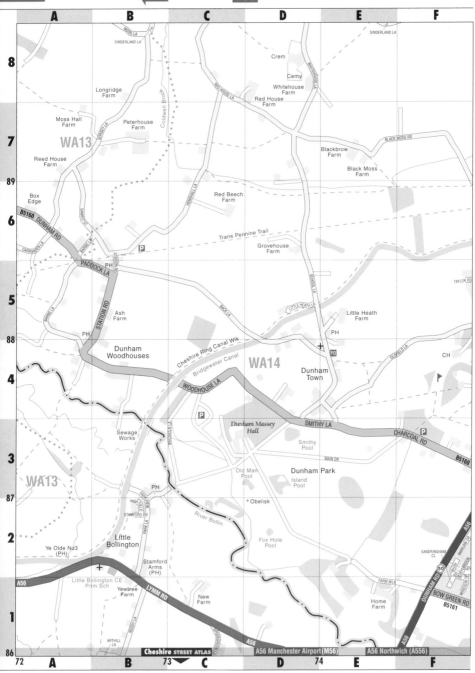

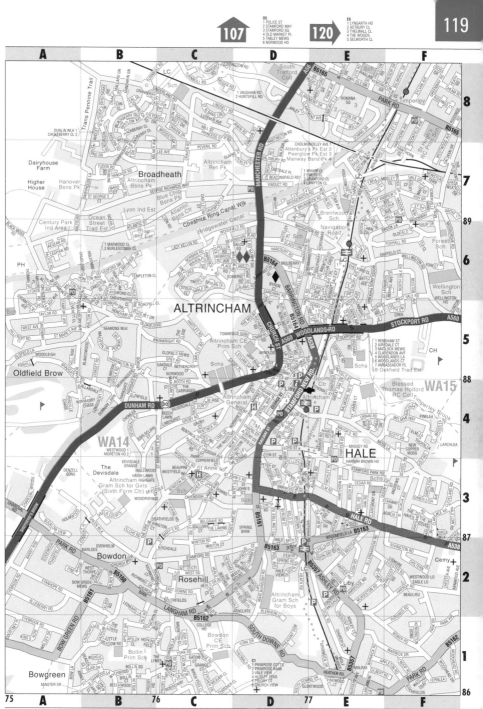

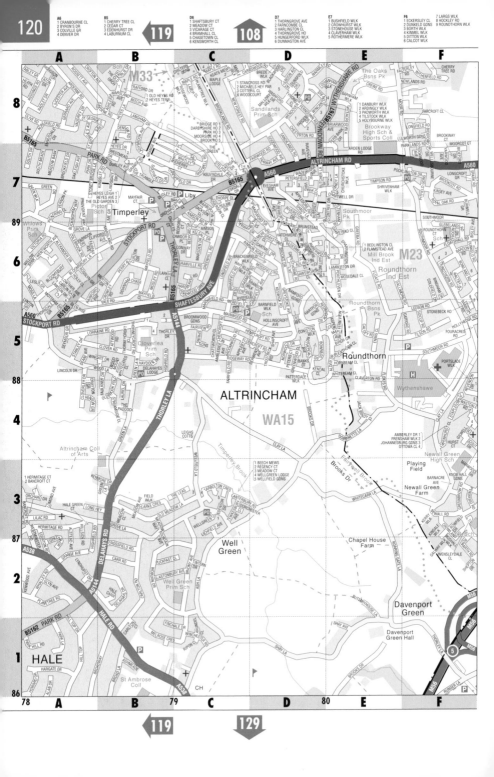

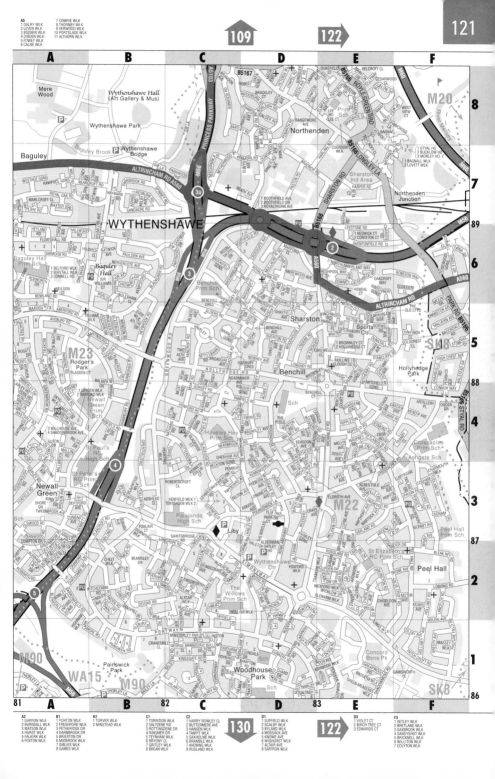

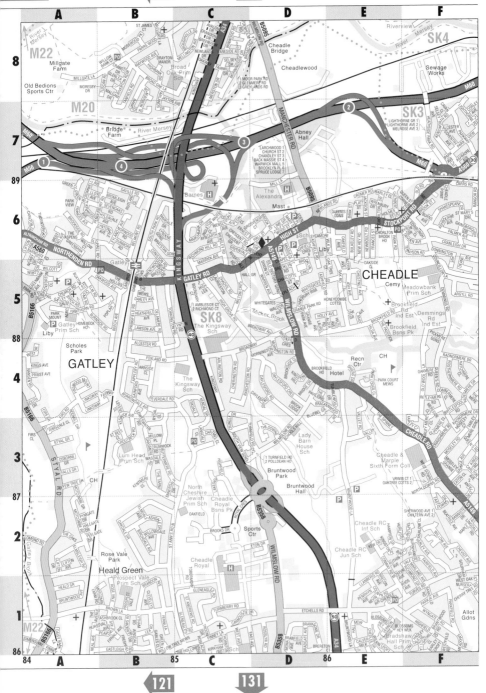

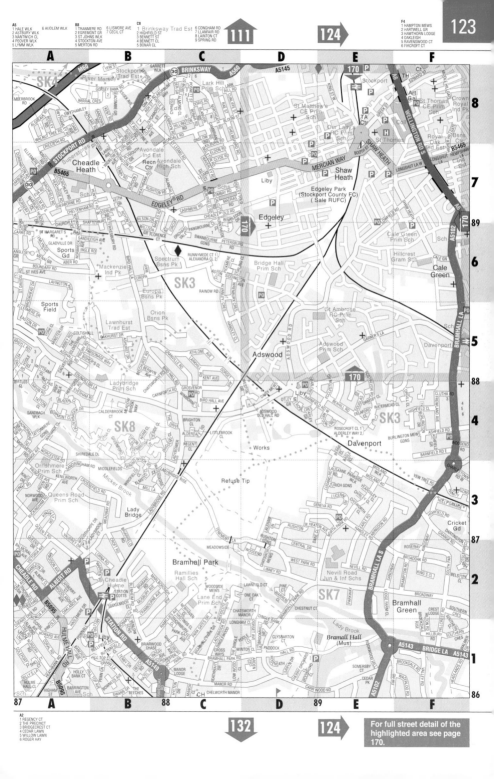

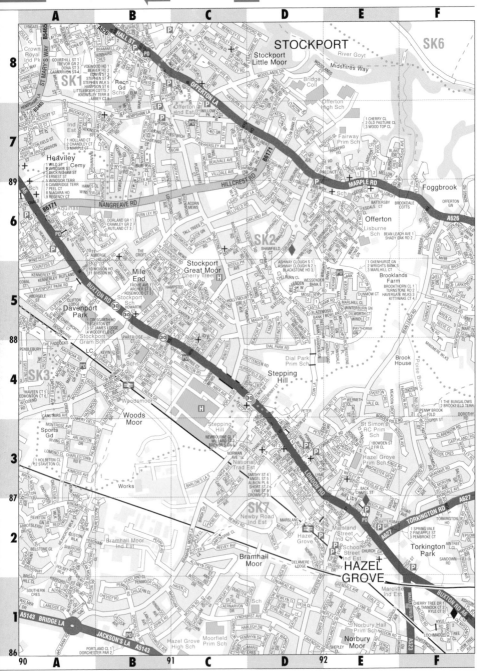

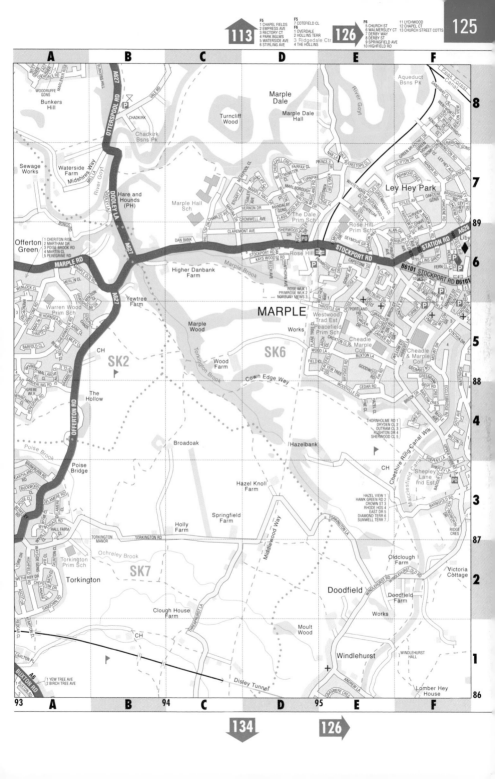

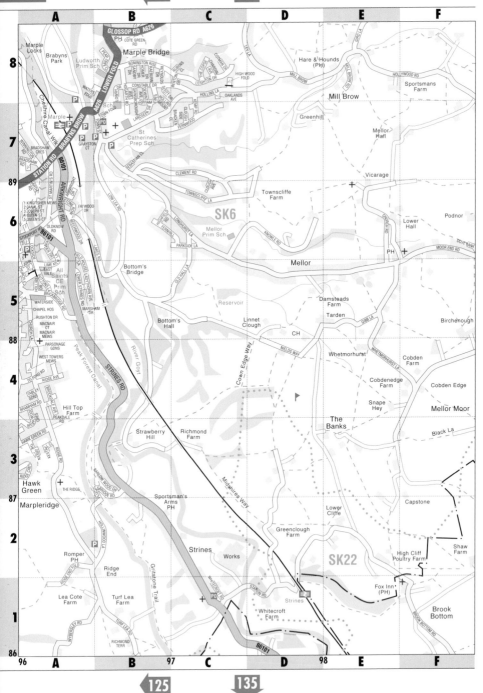

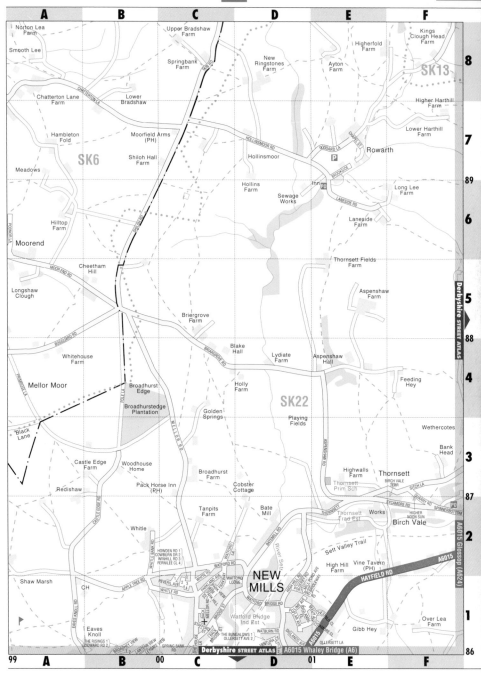

A **B** **C** **D** **E** **F**

Norton Lea Farm
Smooth Lee
Chatterton Lane Farm
Hambleton Fold
Meadows
SK6
Hilltop Farm
Moorend
Cheetham Hill
Longshaw Clough
Whitehouse Farm
Mellor Moor
Black Lane
Castle Edge Farm
Redishaw
Whitle
Shaw Marsh
CH
Eaves Knoll
THE RISINGS 1
GODWARD RD 2

Upper Bradshaw Farm
Springbank Farm
Lower Bradshaw
Moorfield Arms (PH)
Shiloh Hall Farm
Briergrove Farm
Broadhurst Edge
Broadhurstedge Plantation
Woodhouse Home
Pack Horse Inn (PH)
HOWDEN RD 1
COWBURN DR 2
WINNHILL RD 3
FERNILEE CL 4
PEVERIL AVE
APPLE TREE RD
WHITLE RD
BROADWAY VIEW
LANTERN VIEW
SPRING BANK RD

New Ringstones Farm
Hollinsmoor
HOLLINSMOOR RD
Hollins Farm
Sewage Works
Blake Hall
Holly Farm
Golden Springs
Broadhurst Farm
Cobster Cottage
Tanpits Farm
Bate Mill
WATFORD RD
WATFORD LODGE
NEW MILLS
Watford Bridge Ind Est
WATFORD BRIDGE RD
WATBURN RD
THE BUNGALOWS 1
OLLERSETT AVE 2

Ayton Farm
Higherfold Farm
Rowarth
Inn PO
Lydiate Farm
Aspenshaw Hall
SK22
Playing Fields
Highwalls Farm
Thornsett Prim Sch
Thornsett Trad Est
Thornsett Works
Sett Valley Trail
High Hill Farm
Vine Tavern (PH)
OLLERSETT LA

Kings Clough Head Farm
SK13
Higher Harthill Farm
Lower Harthill Farm
Long Lee Farm
Laneside Farm
LANESIDE RD
Thornsett Fields Farm
Aspenshaw Farm
Feeding Hey
Wethercotes
Bank Head
Thornsett
BIRCH VALE TERR
SYCAMORE RD
SPINNERBOTTOM
Birch Vale
HAYFIELD RD
A6015
Gibb Hey
Over Lea Farm

8
7
89
6
5
88
4
3
87
2
1
86

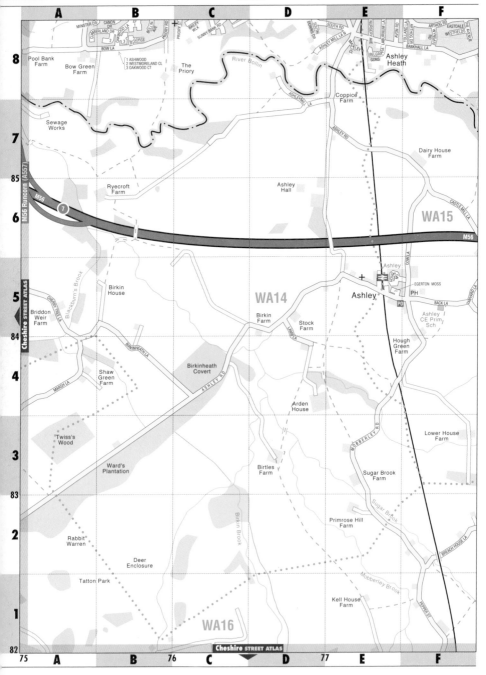

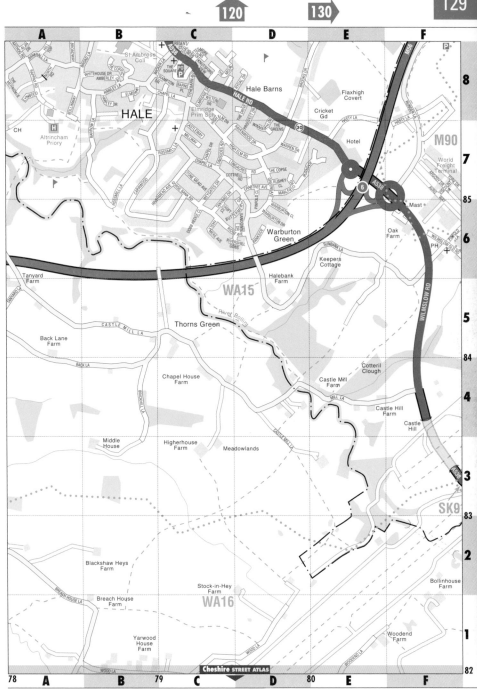

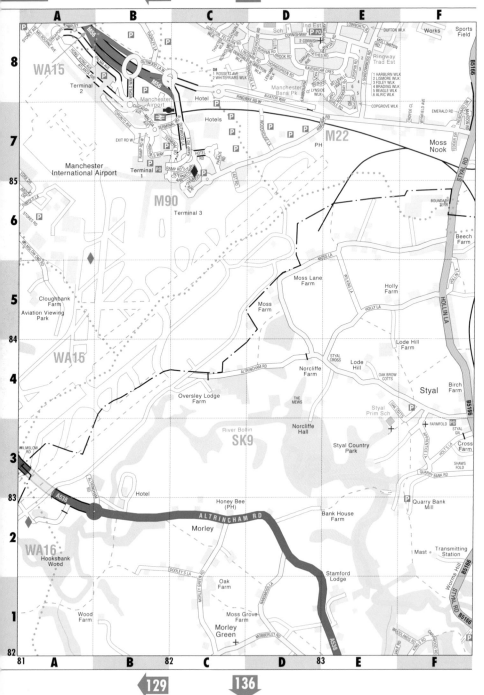

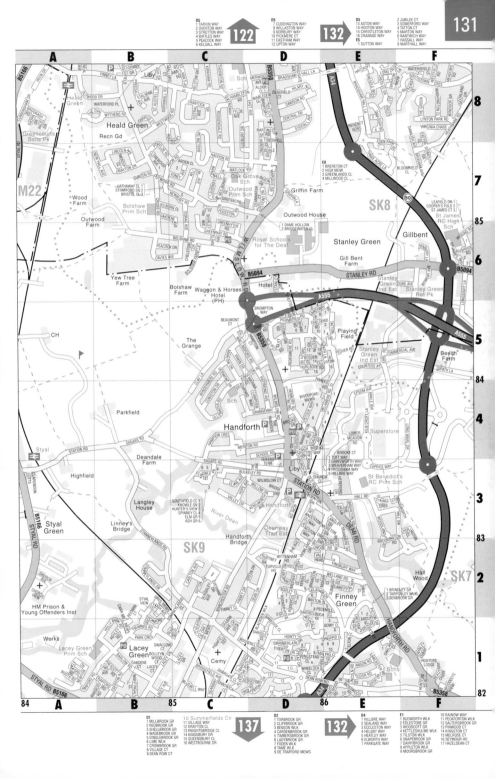

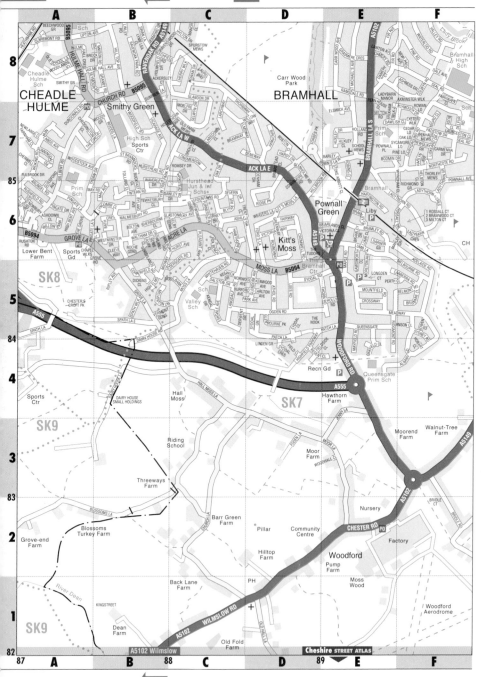

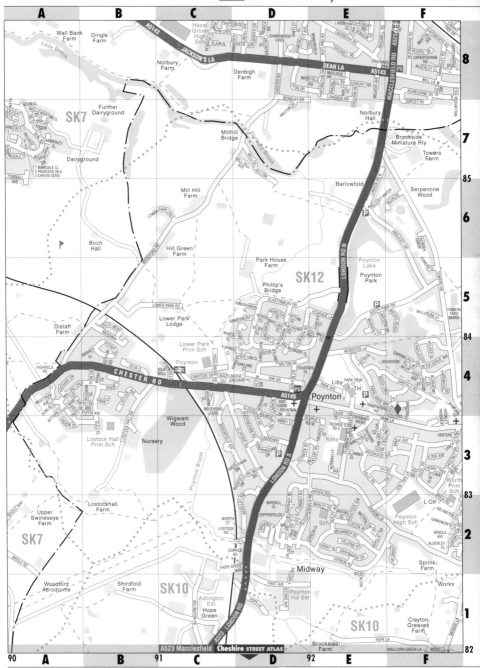

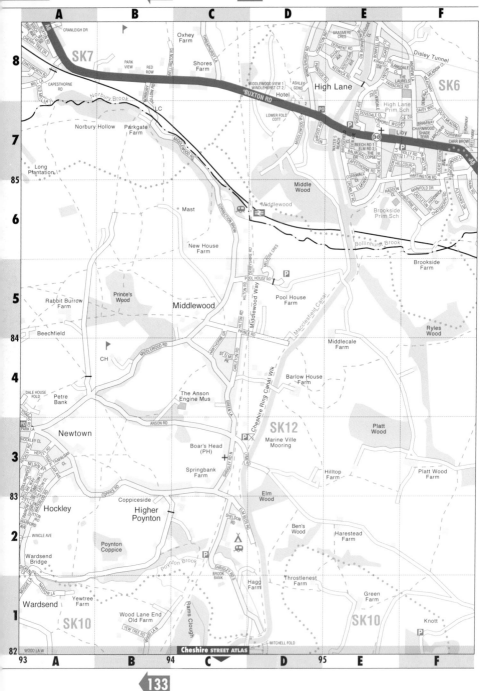

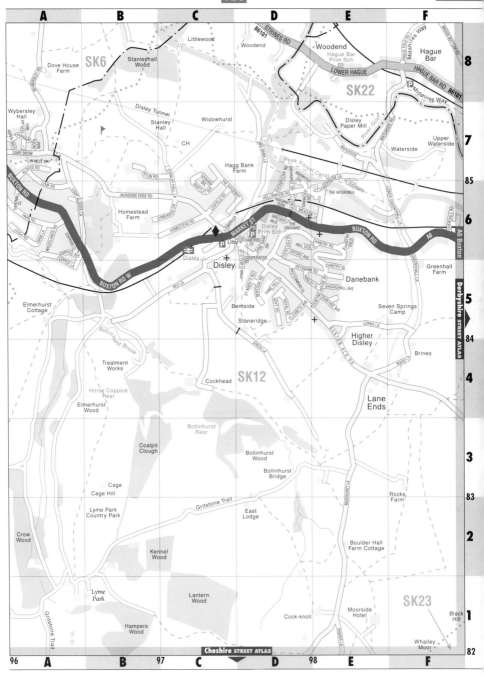

130

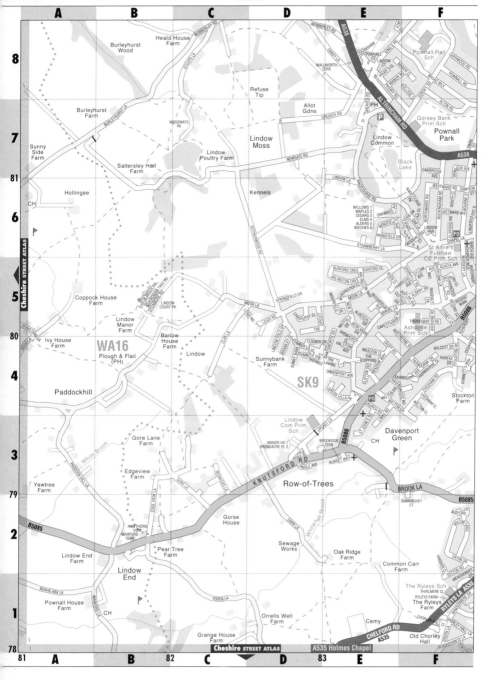

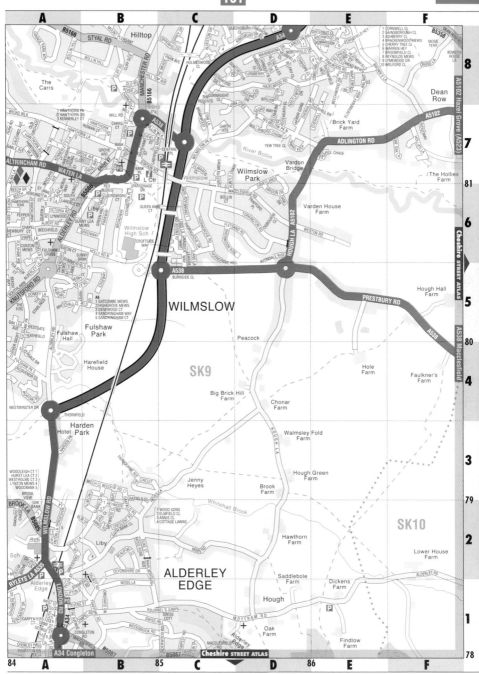

C8
1 GLADEWOOD CL
2 SANDHURST DR
3 CALVERLEY CL
4 DARESBURY CL

131

The Carrs

Hilltop

STYAL RD

B5166

MANCHESTER RD

B5166

Queensbury Cl

A34

Dean Row

A5102 Hazel Grove (A523)

A5102

Brick Yard Farm

ADLINGTON RD

The Hollies Farm

Dean Row

1 CORNWELL CL
2 GAINSBOROUGH CL
3 ASHBERRY CL
4 BRACKENWOOD MEWS
5 CHERRY TREE CL
6 WARREN HEY
7 BROOMFIELD CL
8 REYNOLDS MEWS
9 LYMEWOOD CL
10 WELFORD CL

B5358

ALTRINCHAM RD

WATER LA

B5086

KNUTSFORD RD

ALDERLEY RD

River Bollin

Wilmslow Park

Wilmslow High Sch

Croftside Way

River Bollin

Vardon Bridge

Varden House Farm

HOUGH LA

A5102

WESTON RD

PRESTBURY RD

Hough Hall Farm

A538

A538 Macclesfield

WILMSLOW

A538
BURNSIDE CL

Fulshaw Park

Fulshaw Hall

Harefield House

WESTMINSTER DR

SK9

Peacock

Big Brick Hill Farm

Chonar Farm

Hole Farm

Faulkner's Farm

Thornfield

Harden Park

Hotel Park

WILMSLOW RD

B5086

BROOK LA

Walmsley Fold Farm

WOODLEIGH CT 1
HURST LEA CT 2
WESTHOLME CT 3
LYNTON MEWS 4
WOODBANK 5

BROOK VIEW

Jenny Heyes

Hough Green Farm

Brook Farm

SK10

Whitehall Brook

HOUGH LA

1 WOOD GDNS
2 ELMFIELD CL
3 ANNIS CL
4 COTTAGE LAWNS

Liby

Hawthorn Farm

Lower House Farm

ALDERLEY EDGE

Saddlebole Farm

Hough

Dickens Farm

ALDERLEY RD

Alderley Edge

PO

LONDON RD

A34

RYLEYS LA A535

MOTTRAM RD

Oak Farm

Findlow Farm

WEST LA

B5087

CHORLEY HALL LA

A34 Congleton

B5087

A1
1 THE PARADE
2 ROYLES SQ
3 BROWN ST
4 BERESFORD CT
5 GREEN ST
6 MASSEY ST
7 CHAPEL ST
8 HUBERT WORTHINGTON HO
9 SOUTH GR
10 ARDERNE PL
11 CARLISLE ST
12 SOUTH TERR

84 85 86 78 79 80 81

A B C D E F

8 7 6 5 4 3 2 1

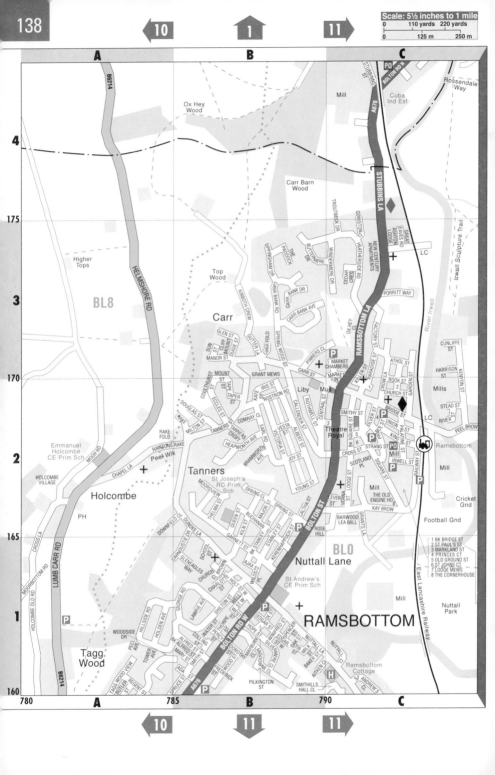

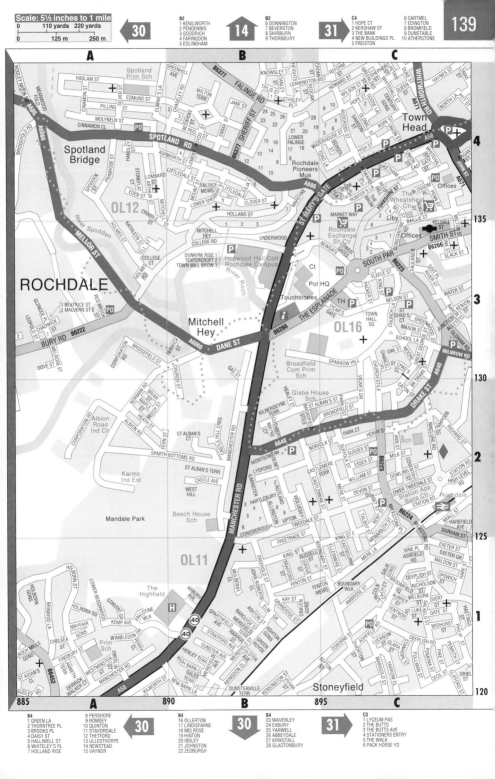

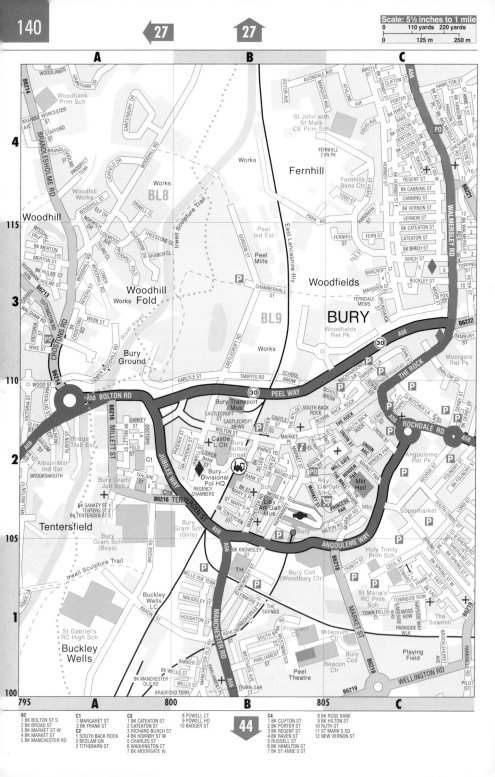

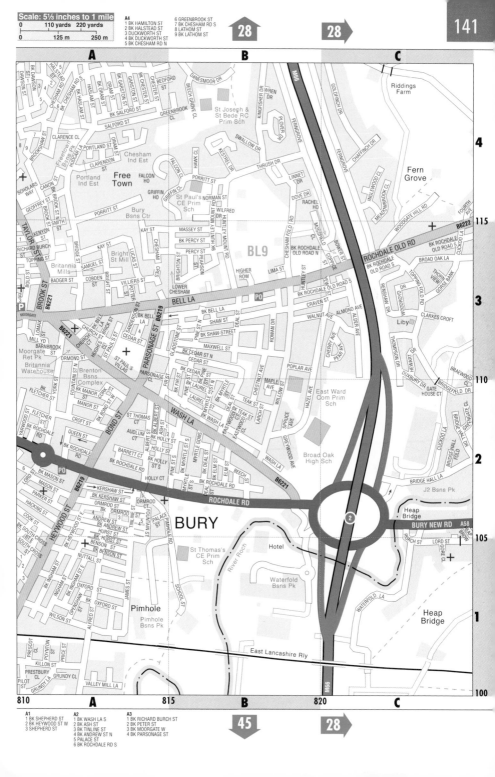

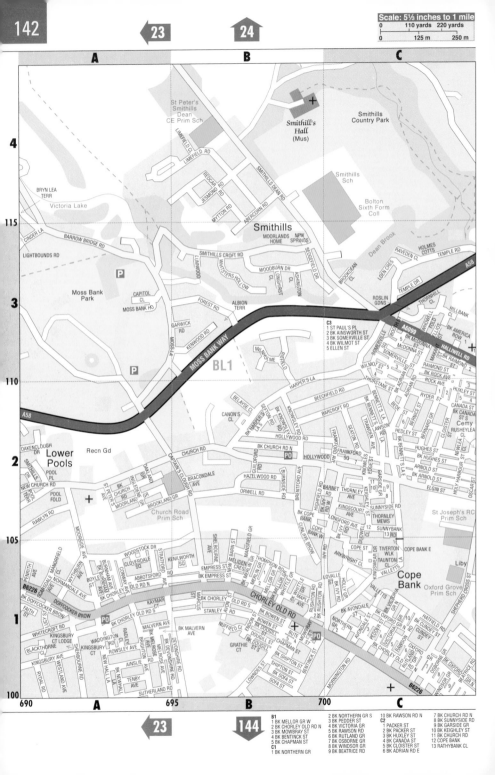

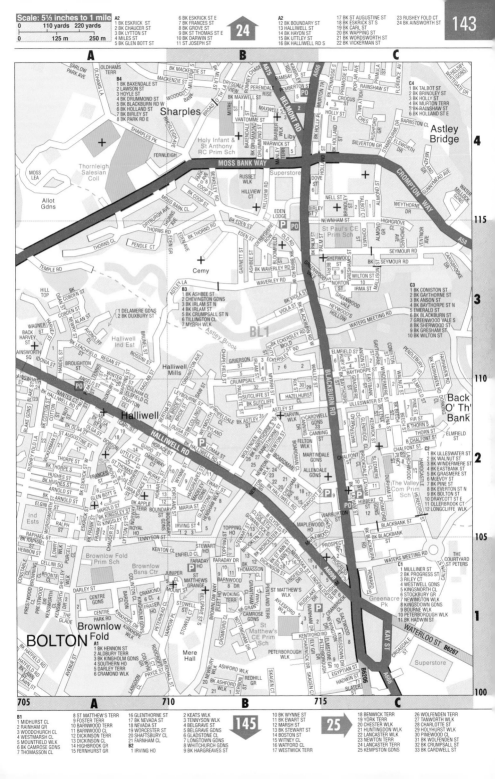

Scale: 5⅓ inches to 1 mile

| 0 | 110 yards | 220 yards |
| 0 | 125 m | 250 m |

Victory

Heaton

Clevelands Prep Sch

BL1

Atkinson's Farm

Overdale Crem

Heaton Cemy

River Croal

Middle Brook

Pocket

Haslam Park

BL3

Willows

Haslam Park Prim Sch

Gilnow Prim Sch

Lincoln Mill (Bolton Ent Ctr)

The Pocket Workshops

The Kirkhall Workshops

Bolton Sch Girls' & Boys' Division

CHORLEY NEW RD

C1
1 TORBAY CL
2 BLACKSHAW ROW
3 LANGLEY DR
4 BK DEANE RD
5 HARLESDEN CRES
6 NEASDEN GR
7 COLINDALE CL
8 CAMBRIA SQ
9 NORTHUMBRIA ST
10 BK ALICE ST
11 BK PARKINSON ST
12 BK JAUNCEY ST
13 HOVE ST N

C2
1 BK VINE ST
2 BK FERN ST E
3 WASHINGTON ST
4 RYLEY ST
5 BK GILNOW LA

C4
1 BK BATTENBERG RD
2 BATTENBERG RD
3 BK WALDECK ST
4 BK CHORLEY OLD RD N
5 MOORE'S CT
6 TURK ST
7 CAVENHAM GR
8 METFIELD PL
9 MABEL ST
10 BK VICTORY ST E
11 LONGDEN ST
12 BK LONGDEN ST
13 BK CLARKE ST
14 BK MARSH FOLD LA
15 SCORTON ST
16 BK HARTINGTON RD
17 BK COLUMBIA RD
18 BK WESTWOOD RD
19 BK ELMWOOD GR W
20 BK ELMWOOD GR
21 BK NORWOOD GR
22 BK RUSSELL ST
23 BK RUSSELL ST

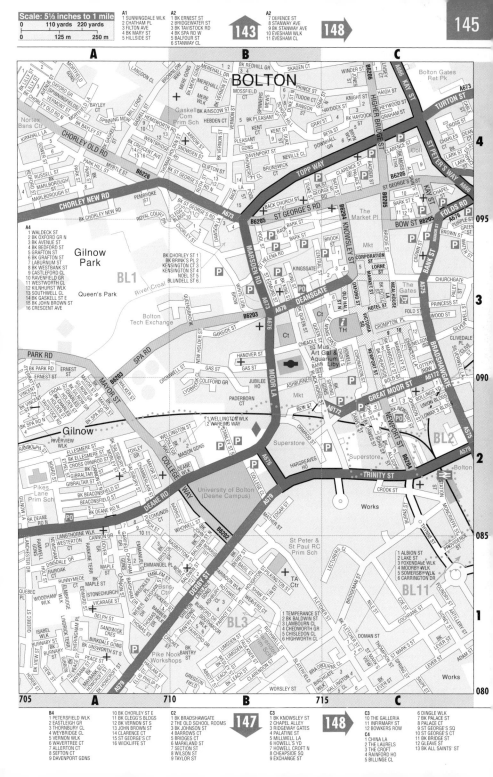

40
144

A4
1 WINDOVER ST
B4
1 BK DEANE CHURCH LA
2 BK LENORA ST
3 PENGWERN AVE

4 BK ANNIS RD
5 BK HAWTHORNE ST
6 BK HAWTHORNE ST
7 BK PENARTH RD
8 CLEVELAND ST
9 MIRIAM ST

Scale: 5⅓ inches to 1 mile
0   110 yards   220 yards
0   125 m   250 m

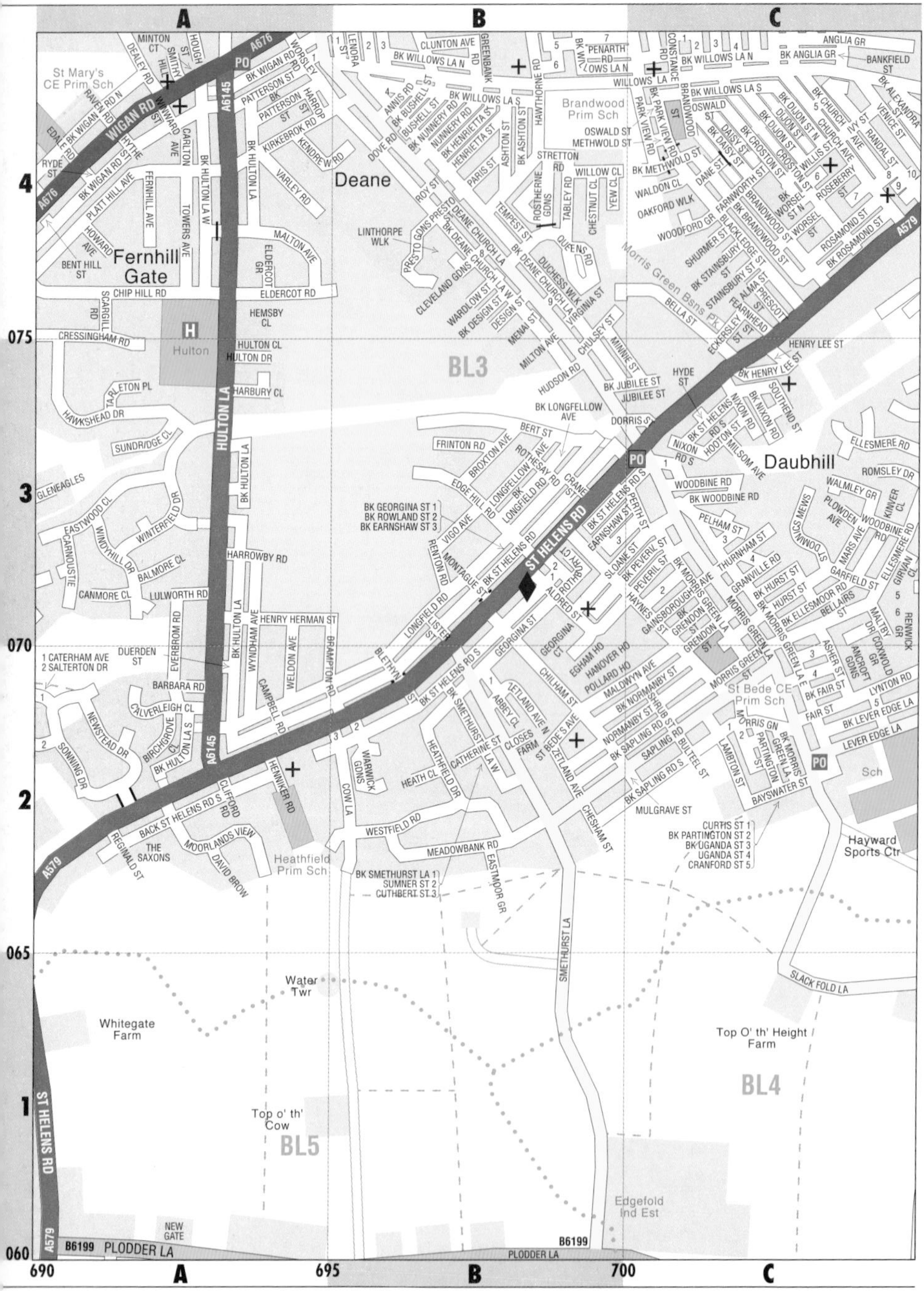

A **B** **C**

St Mary's CE Prim Sch

WIGAN RD
A676
A6145

RYDE ST

Deane

Fernhill Gate

Brandwood Prim Sch

Oswald St
Methwold St

BL3

CHIP HILL RD

Hulton

HULTON LA

Daubhill

BK GEORGINA ST 1
BK ROWLAND ST 2
BK EARNSHAW ST 3

ST HELENS RD

St Bede CE Prim Sch

Morris Green Bsns

1 CATERHAM AVE
2 SALTERTON DR

THE SAXONS

Heathfield Prim Sch

BK SMETHURST LA 1
SUMNER ST 2
CUTHBERT ST 3

Hayward Sports Ctr

CURTIS ST 1
BK PARTINGTON ST 2
BK UGANDA ST 3
UGANDA ST 4
CRANFORD ST 5

Water Twr

Whitegate Farm

Top O' th' Height Farm

BL4

ST HELENS RD
A579

Top o' th' Cow

BL5

NEW GATE

Edgefold Ind Est

A579   B6199   PLODDER LA   B6199   PLODDER LA

690   695   700

A **B** **C**

C3
1 BK WOODBINE RD N
2 BK GAINSBOROUGH AVE
3 BK THURNHAM ST
4 WORTHINGTON ST
5 EPWORTH GR
6 MALHAM GDNS

C4
1 HIGH VIEW ST
2 ROLAND RD
3 BK ROLAND RD
4 BROOMFIELD RD
5 PHOEBE ST
6 BK WILLIS ST
7 BK ROSEBERRY ST

8 BK TUDOR ST
9 TUDOR ST
10 COMO ST

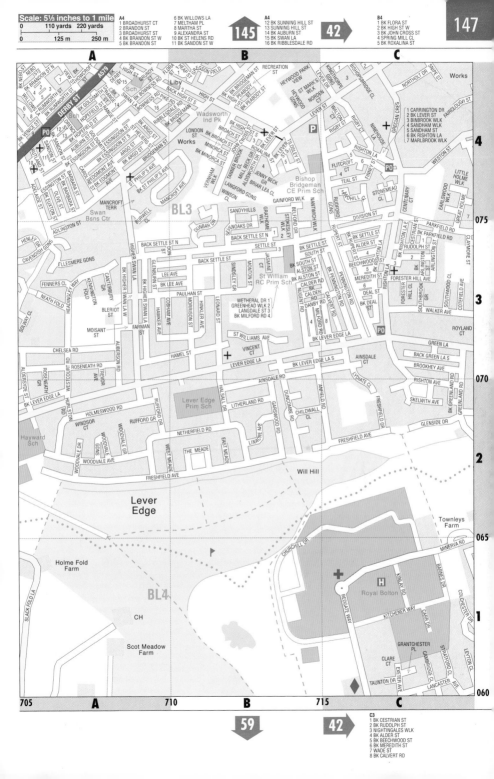

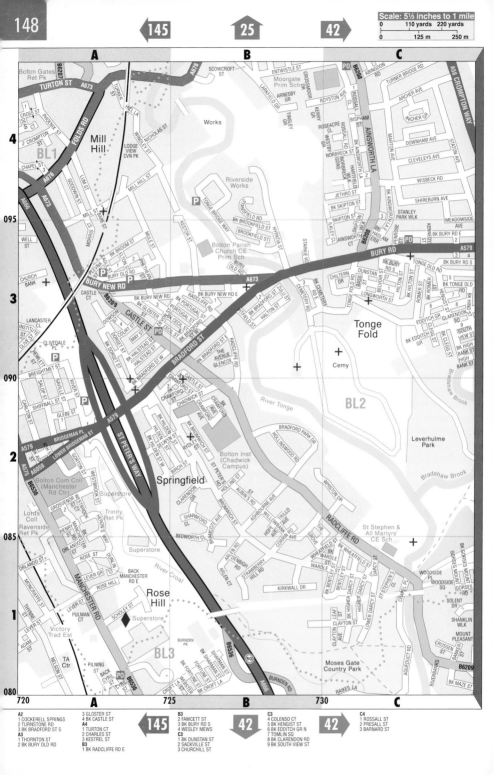

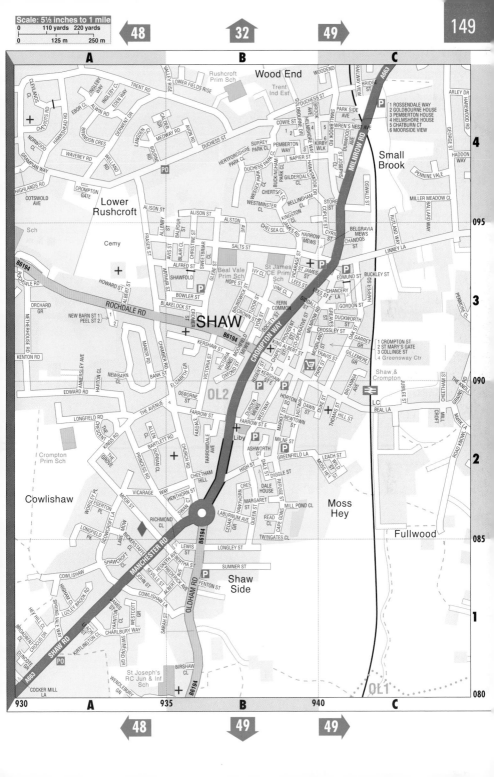

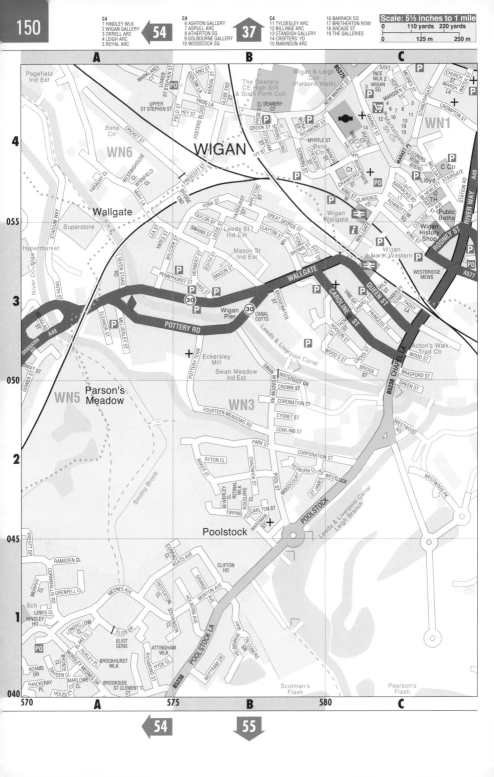

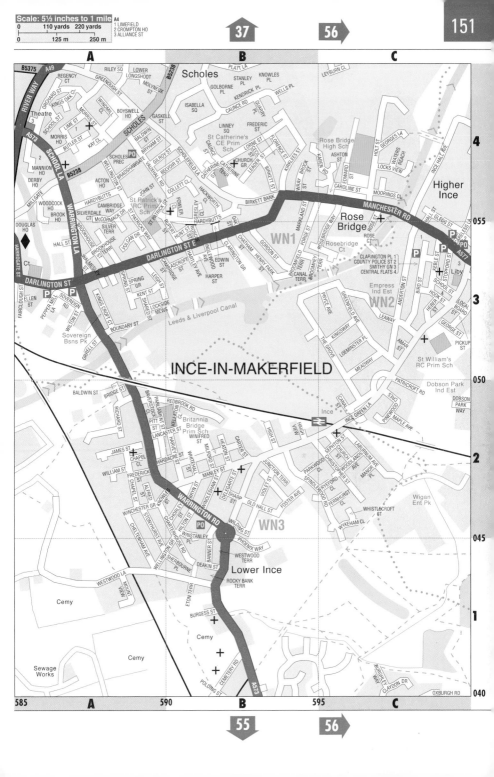

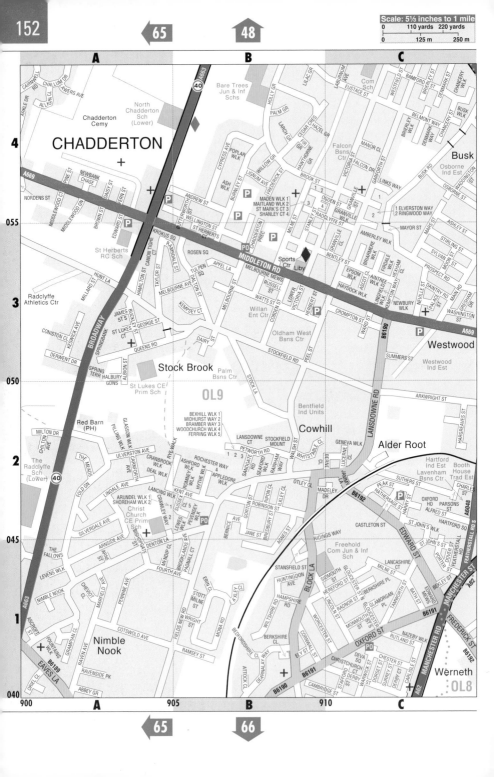

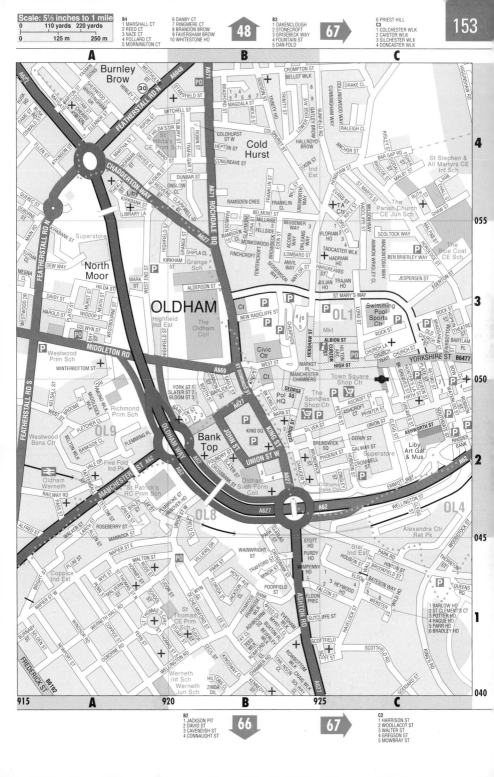

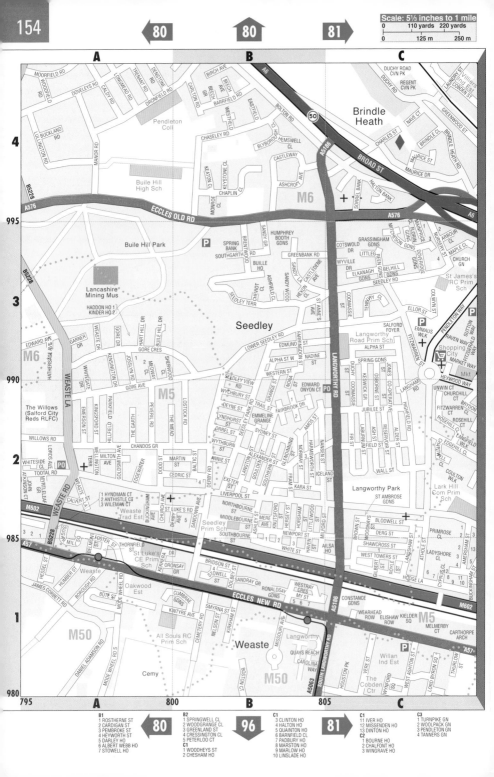

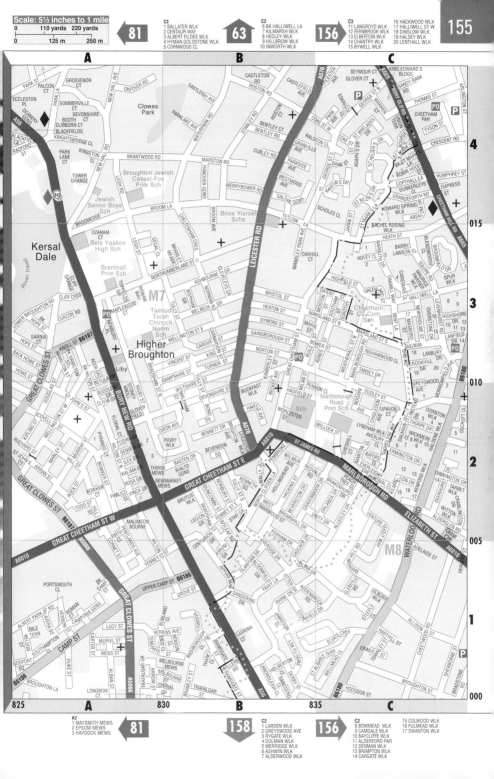

155
64

Scale: 5⅓ inches to 1 mile
0 110 yards 220 yards
0 125 m 250 m

A
B
C
4
3
2
1
015
010
005
000
840
845
850
CRAVENWOOD RD
SEFTON ST
BALFOUR ST
WELLFIELD
DOBROYD ST
HILLCROFT CL
LIMESTEAD AVE
GERALD AVE
MOSS BANK
CROMHURST ST
CRESCENT AVE
St Anne's RC Prim Sch
SEDGLEY RD
MAUREEN AVE
KINGS AVE
ASH TREE RD
ENVER RD
WELLINGTON RD
HALLWORTH RD
DUCHESS RD
PEAKDALE AVE
CHARMINSTER DR
SPRINGFIELD AVE
SADDLECOTE CL
Cemy
TURNBERRY WLK 1
BRITWELL WLK 2
TELRYN WLK 3
RONTON WLK 4
LANESFIELD WLK 5
WOODCOTE WLK 6
BILTON WLK 7
Caravan Site
PO
ETHERSTONE ST
CELIA ST
WATERLOO ST
GARTLAND WLK
STAKEFORD DR
BROOKWOOD AVE
MAWDSLEY DR
HARPURHEY RD
CRESCENT RD
City Coll Manchester Abraham Moss Campus
1 BROCKTON WLK
2 ANDOVER WLK
3 REBECCA ST
HUMPHREY ST
BALLIOL ST
PARSLOW AVE
L Ctr
Abraham Moss High Sch
CRESCENT ST
NUNTHORPE DR
COTTESMORE DR
CHATAWAY RD
St Thomas Com Prim Sch
GREENSTEAD AVE
WOOD HALT RD
GREENHILL RD
EGMONT ST
DARESBURY ST
CHISELHURST ST
ESMOND RD
HARDWOOD CL
WOODLANDS ST
WOODLANDS RD
VALE PARK WAY
BIRKDALE ST
GREENFORD RD
CHALFONT DR
THETFORD DR
RAINHAM DR
SHIRLEY RD
ANSDELL ST
SHAFTESBURY RD
Woodlands Road
AMWELL ST
HAZELBOTTOM RD
Hendham Vale Ind Pk
HODDESDON ST
Vale Park Ind Est
A665
AVONDALE ST
ABBOTSFIELD CT
WATERLOO RD
ALBYNS AVE
BECKENHAM RD
DEANERY CT
KEANE CT
KNIGHTSWOOD RD
MARTINGALE CT
MANSWOOD DR
THURLSTON CRES
WIGMORE RD
TOLWORTH DR
CARDINAL ST
DURLEY AVE
FROME DR
GLENMORE DR
JEHLUM CL
RAJA CL
TAHIR CL
HARLAND DR
BLANWOOD DR
CAMELIA RD
DALTHORPE AVE
1 WAYFORD WLK
2 HOLWAY WLK
3 CAVENHAM WLK
4 DUNMERE WLK
5 ANSFORD WLK
6 HAREFORD WLK
7 DENBURY WLK
8 FILTON WLK
B6180
ABERCARN CL
REDLYNCH WLK
HAMBRIDGE CL
ALMS HILL RD
HUMBER ST
HALEY ST
Cheetham Hill
LICHFIELD DR
SMEDLEY LA
MANNINGTON DR
River Irk
HENDHAM VALE
WESTMERE DR
ASHMILL WLK
BRIDEOAK ST
BRIDEOAK CT
DAIMLER ST
M8
SAXELBY DR
CHIME BANK
Mus & Art Gall
M9
Queens Park
BELLOTT ST
BROADOAK CT
ALDRED CL
LANGDALE CT
HANSDON CL
BRENTFIELD AVE
BIGNOR ST
HEYWOOD ST
THACKERAY CL
TARVINGTON CL 8
RUTHERGLADE CL 9
ERINDALE WLK 10
MANORDALE WLK 11
WESTMOUNT CL 12
GAYWOOD WLK 13
CRESTWOOD WLK 14
Temple Prim Sch
SMEDLEY LA
HAREDALE DR
GLOVER AVE
ROWOOD AVE
SMEDLEY AVE
SPENDER AVE
CARLYLE CL
OAKFIELD ST
ELMFIELD ST
BEECHFIELD ST
HURSTEAD CL
CHEETHAM HILL RD
SCHOOLSIDE CL
Museum of Transport
SONNING WLK
LUKE WLK
MULLION WLK
WILBY ST
1 GOSPORT WLK
2 HOGARTH WLK
3 INWOOD WLK
4 KELDAY WLK
5 DIPTON WLK
6 KENLEY WLK
7 HEDDON WLK
REDSHAW RD
PARK VIEW
TAMERTON DR
STARMOOR DR
HUXLEY AVE
FORSTON WLK
MOORDOWN CL
HAWKESHEAD RD
LECESTER RD
BUNYARD ST
ECKFORD ST
DERWENT ST
WYTHBURN AVE
A6010
TOPLEY ST
BRINSWORTH DR
KELVIN GR
SMEDLEY ST
DARELL WLK
APPLEFORD DR
TURLEY ST
CLIBRAN ST
PO
ALSHAM WLK
HEATHERDALE DR
WORDSWORTH AVE
GALSWORTHY A
FARADAY AVE
LYTTON AVE
PENROSE CL
TEMPLE SQ
BOYLE ST
HIGHSTONE DR
SMEDLEY RD
LANHILL DR
GRANSDEN DR
IRKDALE ST
BARNSTABLE DR
MILSTON WLK
HOLST AVE
QUEENS RD
SMEATON ST
BARNSDALE DR
BALMFIELD ST
FALFIELD DR
DOVE WLK
BATTY ST
ALDERGLEN RD
THORNGATE RD
St Chad's RC Prim Sch
SIGNET WLK
REDWOOD DR
HOLBORN DR
TELFORD ST
NASMYTH ST
GLENDOWER DR
FENHAM CL
SHIREGREEN AVE
1 BANKFOOT WLK
2 HILLHEAD WLK
A6010
ELIZABETH ST
SHERBORNE ST
ST DAVID'S CT
DALBURY DR
ELDOT CL
ELIZABETH ST
BRIDGAM ST
COLLYHURST RD
Saviour CE Prim Sch
RIBBLESDALE DR
PHELAN CL
Sherborne Trad Est
Manchester Fort Sh Pk
P
ETCHELL ST
EGGINGTON ST
ROCHDALE RD
M40
St Malachy's RC Prim Sch
BRADSTONE RD
BENT ST
A665
NORTH ST
FITZGEORGE ST
A664
BURGIN WLK

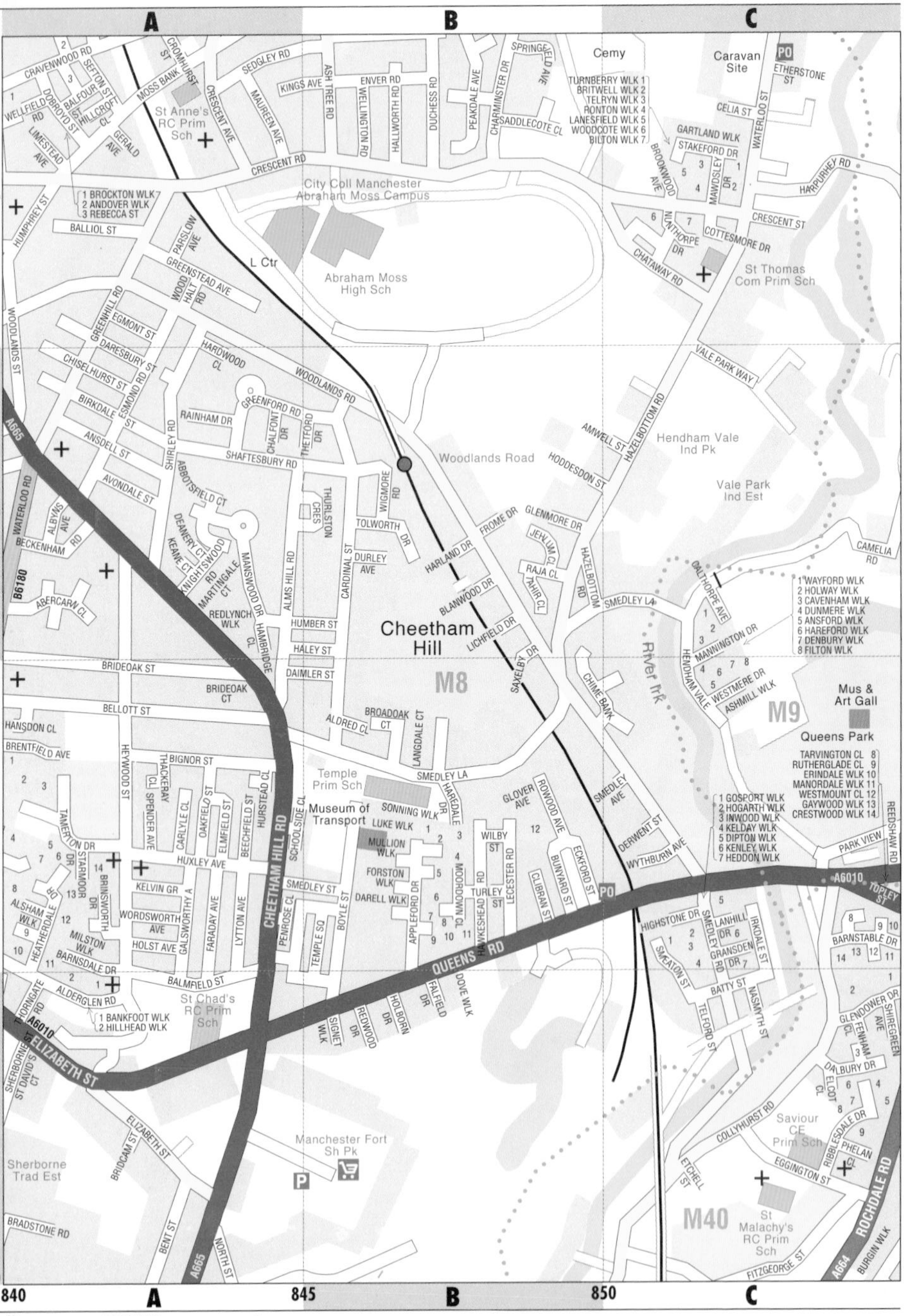

A2
1 MINSMERE CL
2 NEWMILL WLK
3 BOXGROVE WLK
4 CANTLEY WLK
5 NEWPARK WLK
6 DOWNGATE WLK
7 WELLSIDE WLK
8 OXTED WLK
9 CAWSTON WLK
10 BELTON WLK
11 LUDWELL WLK
12 MIDFORD WLK
13 MODBURY WLK
14 BENHALE WLK

155
159

B2
1 CAMLEY WLK
2 LARKHILL WLK
3 FYFIELD WLK
4 COVALL WLK
5 FOXWELL WLK
6 HAMPSHIRE WLK
7 CORBRIDGE WLK
8 BRADBURN WLK
9 BUSHNAY WLK
10 LANREATH WLK
11 GENEVA WLK
12 CARADOC AVE

C1
1 OVERCOMBE WLK
2 TYNWELL WLK
3 WILLOWDENE CL
4 ALLENBY WLK
5 KINTORE WLK
6 OVINGTON WLK
7 PURITAN WLK
8 KEDINGTON CL
9 BUSHTON WLK

A3
1 BROMWICH DR
2 CLATFORD WLK
3 OAKRIDGE WLK
4 BINDON WLK
5 WATFIELD WLK
6 HOLMFOOT WLK

7 LINSLADE WLK
8 SELWOOD WLK
9 PORTWOOD WLK
10 TREMAIN WLK
11 CALDERBROOK WLK
A4
1 MILLPOOL WLK

2 PATHFIELD WLK
3 MURROW WLK
4 DERVILLE WLK
5 SHAPWICK CL
6 HARROWDENE WLK
7 BRENLEY WLK
8 ROXWELL WLK

9 PORTAL WLK
10 HAYGROVE WLK
11 MAYBROOK WLK
B3
1 WILLOW BANK
2 ORPINGTON RD
3 OSBORNE RD

B3
4 ASHGILL WLK
5 GLENPARK WLK
6 DRYGATE WLK
7 BELSYDE WLK
8 NORBET WLK
9 PURTON WLK

B3
10 BANKHALL WLK
11 LOWREY WLK
12 DURHAM ST
13 EVANTON WLK
14 MERTON WLK
15 TRONGATE WLK

16 VIEWFIELD WLK
17 FIRDON WLK

64

83

157

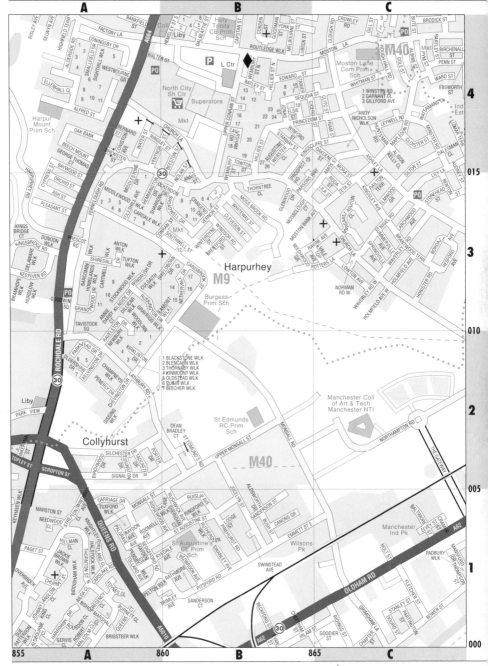

Scale: 5⅓ inches to 1 mile
0   110 yards   220 yards
0   125 m   250 m

B4
1 HERSHAM WLK
2 RADFORD DR
3 MONKWOOD DR
4 LONGDELL WLK
5 ROCKFIELD DR
6 DENESIDE WLK
7 BROWNSON WLK

8 PRIMLEY WLK
9 DARLTON WLK
10 SIMISTER ST
11 THORNSETT CT
12 KINGCOMBE WLK
13 TIPTREE WLK
14 HANSLOPE WLK
15 SWAINSTHORPE DR

B4
16 BOOKHAM WLK
17 FARNDALE WLK
18 APPRENTICE CT
19 WADCROFT WLK
20 BRAXTON WLK
21 LODDEN WLK
22 BURNTWOOD WLK

B4
23 SALTBURN WLK
24 NAUNTON WLK
25 CROCKER WLK
26 HIGHDOWN WLK
27 ROUNDHAM WLK

160

83

Scale: 5⅓ inches to 1 mile

| 0 | 110 yards | 220 yards |
| 0 | 125 m | 250 m |

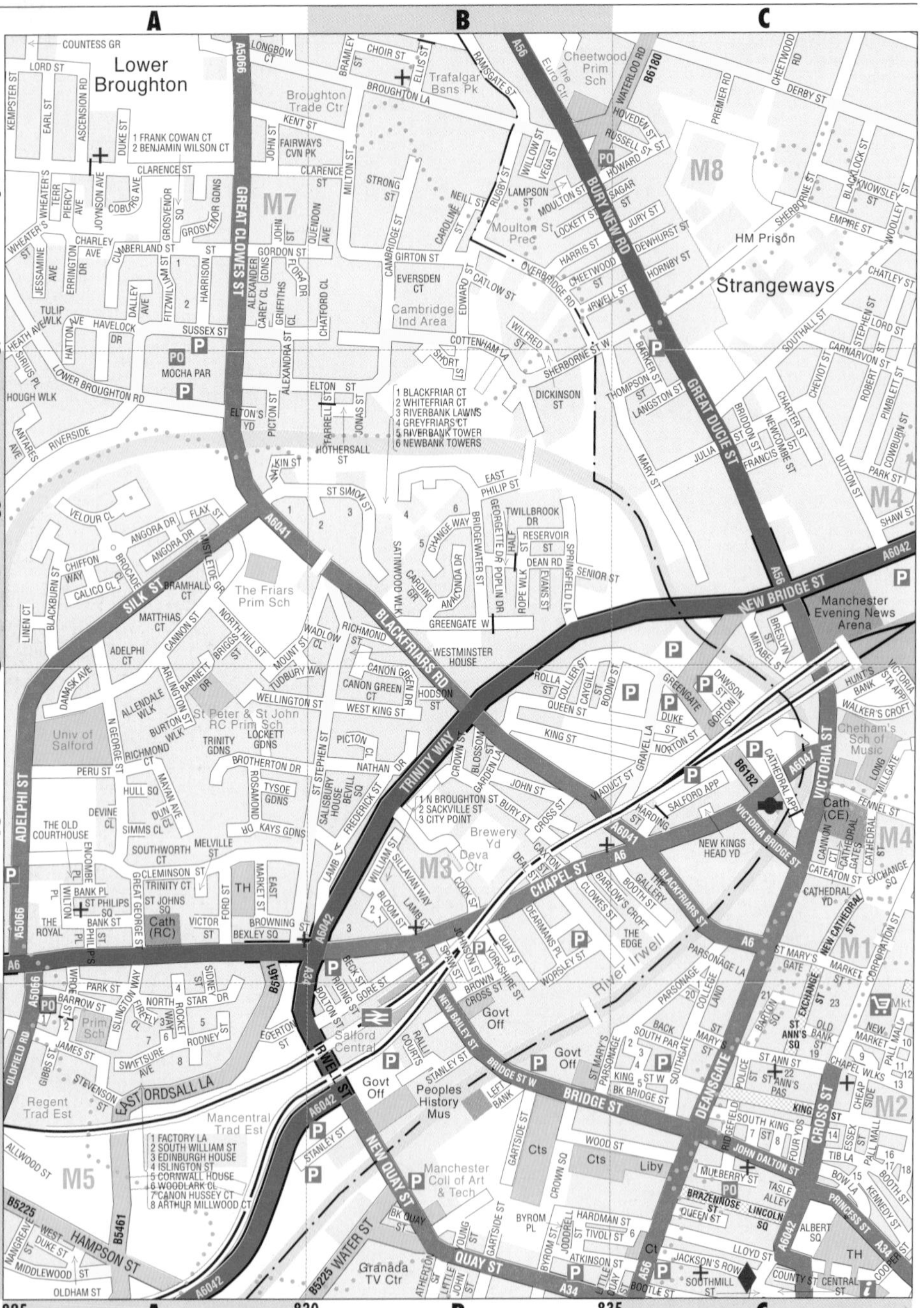

A   **B**   **C**

Lower Broughton

COUNTESS GR
LORD ST
KEMPSTER ST
EARL ST
ASCENSION ST
DUKE ST
JOHNSON AVE
CLARENCE ST
LONGBOW CT
BRANLEY
CHOIR ST
ELLIS ST
BROUGHTON LA
TRAFALGAR BSNS PK
RAMSGATE ST

1 FRANK COWAN CT
2 BENJAMIN WILSON CT

BROUGHTON TRADE CTR
KENT ST
FAIRWAYS CVN PK
CLARENCE ST
MILTON ST
WILLOW ST
LAMPSON ST
MOULTON ST
CHEETWOOD PRIM SCH
WATERLOO RD
HOVEDEN ST
PREMIER RD
DERBY ST
CHEETWOOD
B6180

WHEATER'S TERR
WHEATER'S CRES
PERCY AVE
ERRINGTON DR
JESSAMINE AVE
COBLY
GROSVENOR
GROSVENOR SQ
JOHN ST
GORDON ST
STRONG ST
NEILL ST
CAROLINE
MOULTON ST PREC
LOCKETT ST
JURY ST
HARRIS ST
CHEETWOOD
HORNBY ST
DEWHURST ST
RUSSELL ST
SAGAR ST
PO
HM Prison
Strangeways

M7
M8

CHARLEY
CUMBERLAND ST
DALLEY
FITZWILLIAM ST
HARRISON ST
SUSSEX ST
ALEXANDER
CAREY CL
GRIFFITHS ST
CHATFORD CL
GIRTON ST
CATLOW ST
EVERSDEN CT
OVERBRIDGE
ARWELL ST
CHATLEY ST
SOUTHALL ST

TULIP
HAVELOCK DR
HEATH AVE
WALK
LOWER BROUGHTON RD
PO
MOCHA PAR
P
Cambridge Ind Area
CAMBRIDGE ST
ALEXANDRA ST
CLARENDON AVE
WILFRED ST
SHERBORNE ST
COTTENHAM LA
DICKINSON ST
THOMPSON ST
LANGSTON ST
BARKER ST
CARNARVON ST
CHEVIOT ST
ROBERT ST
PIMBLETT ST
DUTTON ST

995

1 BLACKFRIAR CT
2 WHITEFRIAR CT
3 RIVERBANK LAWNS
4 GREYFRIARS CT
5 RIVERBANK TOWER
6 NEWBANK TOWERS

EAST PHILIP ST
SIMOX ST
TWILLBROOK DR
RESERVOIR
DEAN ROYD
SPRINGFIELD LA
SENIOR ST
GREAT DUCIE ST
PARK ST
SHAW ST

M4

3

VELOUR CL
ANGORA DR
FLAX ST
CHIFFON WAY
CALICO CL
BRAMHALL ST
SILK ST
CHANGE WAY
GARING
BRIDGEWATER ST
GEORGETTE DR
POPLIN DR
EVANS ST
GREENGATE W
POPLAR
NEW BRIDGE ST

The Friars Prim Sch

MATTHIAS CT
ADELPHI CT
ALLENDALE WK
BURTON ST
NORTH HILL ST
CANON ST
MOUNT ST
TUDBURY WAY
CANON ST
CANON GREEN DR
WEST KING ST
RICHMOND
HODSON ST
ROLLA ST
COLLIER ST
CAYGILL ST
BOUND ST
GREENGATE
DANTON ST
HUNT'S BANK
VICTORIA
WALKER'S CROFT

990

Univ of Salford
The Old Courthouse

PERU ST
DAMASK AVE
CLEMINSON ST
GEORGE ST
RICHMOND
HULL SQ
SIMMS CL
St Peter & St John RC Prim Sch
TRINITY GDNS
LOCKETT GDNS
BROTHERTON DR
TYSOE GDNS
KAYS GDNS
STEPHEN ST
SALISBURY ST
BEVILL SQ
FREDERICK ST
NATHAN DR
PICTON
CROWN ST
BLOSSOM ST
JOHN ST
SALFORD APP
KING ST
QUEEN ST
GRAVELL ST
NORTON ST
GORTON ST
BRISTOW
CHAPEL ST
Chetham's Sch of Music
Cath (CE)
M4

ADELPHI ST
A5066

2

THE OLD COURTHOUSE
DEVINE CL
BANK PL
ST PHILIPS ST
BANK ST
THE ROYAL
Cath (RC)
ST JOHNS
VICTOR ST
BEXLEY SQ
TRINITY CT
SOUTHWORTH ST
MELVILLE ST
EAST ST
WILLIAM ST
SELAWAN WAY
LAMB ST
M3
Brewery Yd Deva Ctr
1 N BROUGHTON ST
2 SACKVILLE ST
3 CITY POINT
CROSS ST
YORKSHIRE ST
BLOOM ST
New KINGS HEAD YD
CATEATON ST
VICTORIA BRIDGE ST
CATHEDRAL
NEW CATHEDRAL ST
M1

985

PO
PARK ST
BARLOW ST
ISLINGTON WAY
NORTH ST
Prim Sch
STAR ST
ROCKET
RODNEY ST
EGERTON ST
SWIFTSURE AVE
EAST ORDSALL LA
Salford Central
Govt Off
NEW BAILEY ST
STANLEY ST
BRIDGE ST
NEW QUAY ST
BACK SOUTH PARDE
ST MARY'S GATE
PARSONAGE
DEANSGATE
ST ANN'S SQ
ST ANN'S
CHAPEL WLKS
NEW MARKET
EXCHANGE
OLD BANK ST
KING ST
M2

B5461
RIVER IRWELL
River Irwell

1 FACTORY LA
2 SOUTH WILLIAM ST
3 EDINBURGH HOUSE
4 ISLINGTON ST
5 CORNWALL HOUSE
6 WOODLARK CL
7 CANON HUSSEY CT
8 ARTHUR MILLWOOD CT

M5

Regent Trad Est
Mancentral Trad Est
Govt Off
Peoples History Mus
Manchester Coll of Art & Tech

Granada TV Ctr

ALLWOOD ST
STEVENSON SQ
GIBBS ST
JAMES ST
WEST HAMPSON ST
DUKE ST
NANGREAVE ST
MIDDLEWOOD ST
OLDHAM ST
B5225
WATER ST
QUAY ST
ATHERTON ST
BK QUAY ST
YOUNG ST
BYROM ST
HARDMAN ST
WOOD ST
CROWN SQ
TONMAN ST
TIVOLI ST
BYROM PL
ATKINSON ST
BOOTLE ST
JACKSON'S ROW
SOUTHMILL
A56
A34
A6042
PRINCESS ST
ALBERT SQ
TH
LINCOLN SQ
BRAZENNOSE ST
JOHN DALTON ST
MULBERRY ST
TASLE ALLEY
KENNEDY ST
QUEEN ST

1

980

A   825   830   **B**   835   **C**

C1

1 BK COLLEGE LAND
2 DUNLOP ST
3 GARDEN LA
4 SMITHY LA
5 BUTTER LA
6 SIDNEY ST
7 BOW ST
8 ST JAMES'S SQ
9 BK POOL FOLD
10 NORFOLK ST
11 KENT ST
12 SUSSEX ST
13 MARSDEN ST
14 TOWN HALL LA
15 CLARENCE ST
16 CHANCERY LA
17 CHANCERY PL
18 BROWN ST
19 HALF MOON ST
20 NORTH PAR
21 BARTON ARC
22 ST ANNS CHURCHYARD
23 ROYAL EXCHANGE ARC

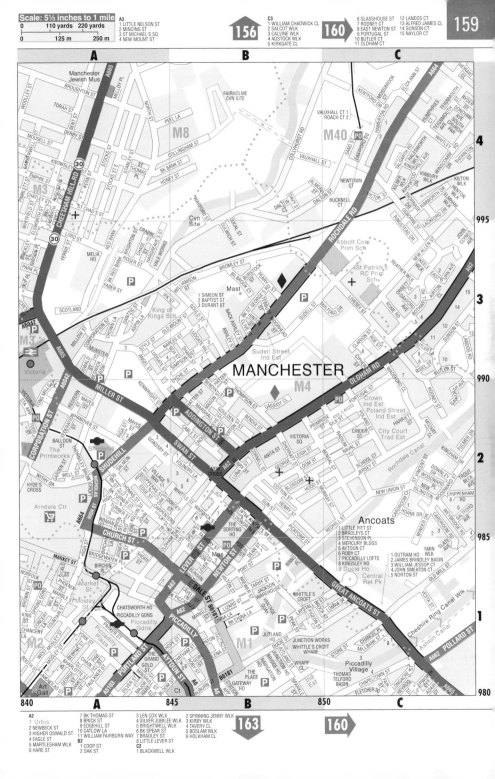

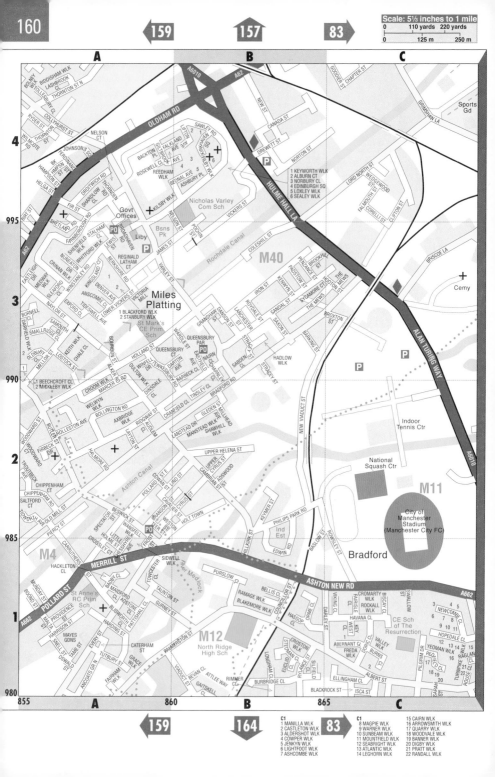

A   B   C

OLDHAM RD
A6010 A62

159 164 83

855   860   865

C1
1 MANILLA WLK
2 CASTLETON WLK
3 ALDERSHOT WLK
4 COWPER WLK
5 JENKYN WLK
6 LIGHTFOOT WLK
7 ASHCOMBE WLK

C1
8 MAGPIE WLK
9 WARNER WLK
10 SUNBEAM WLK
11 MOUNTFIELD WLK
12 SEABRIGHT WLK
13 ATLANTIC WLK
14 LEGHORN WLK

15 CAIRN WLK
16 ARROWSMITH WLK
17 QUARRY WLK
18 WOODVALE WLK
19 BANNER WLK
20 DIGBY WLK
21 PRATT WLK
22 RANDALL WLK

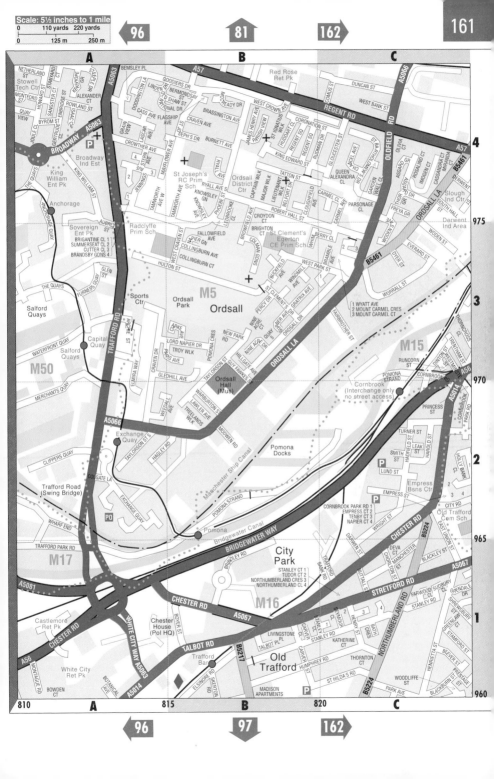

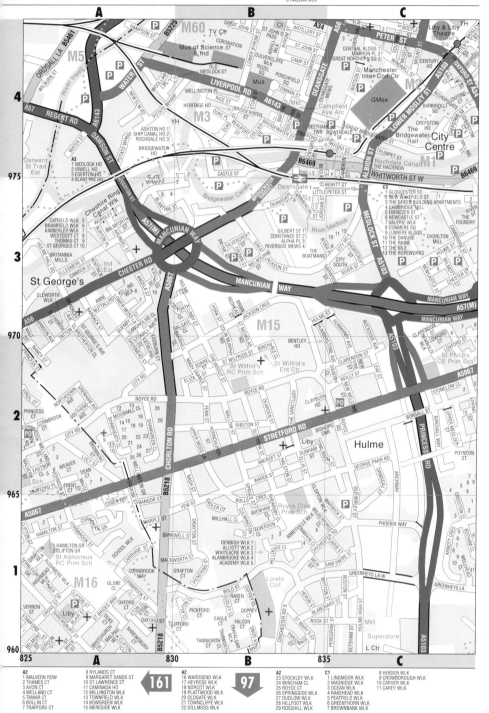

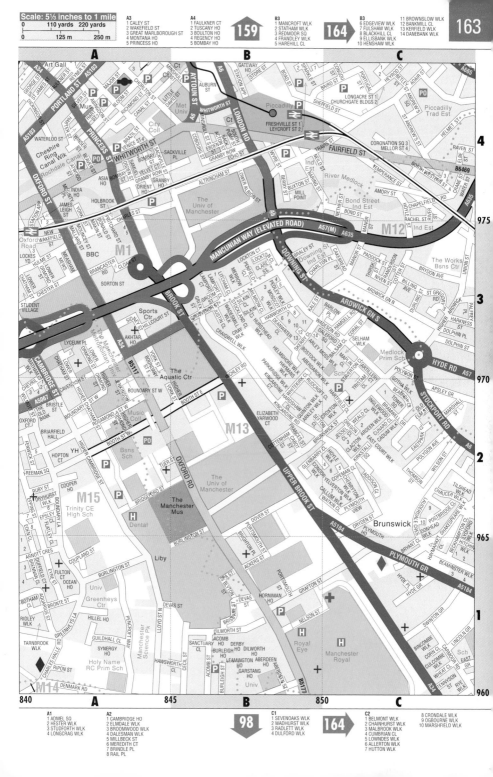

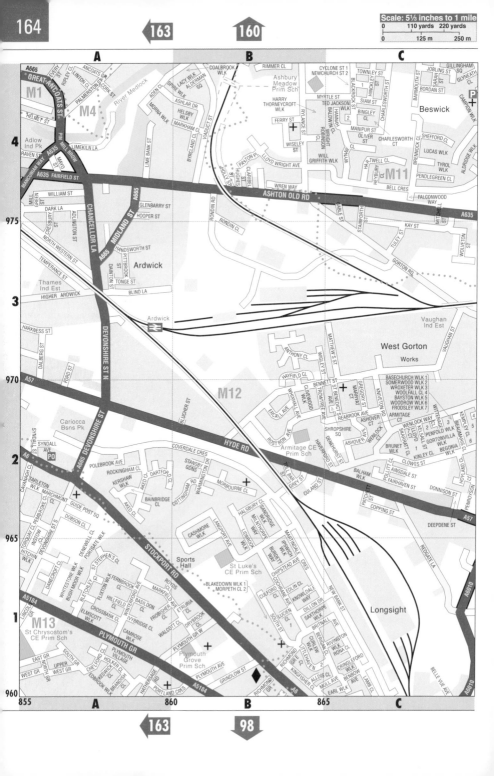

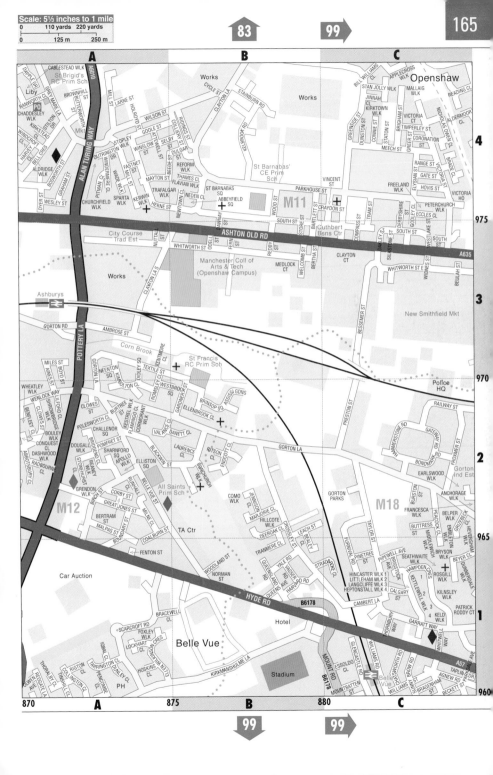

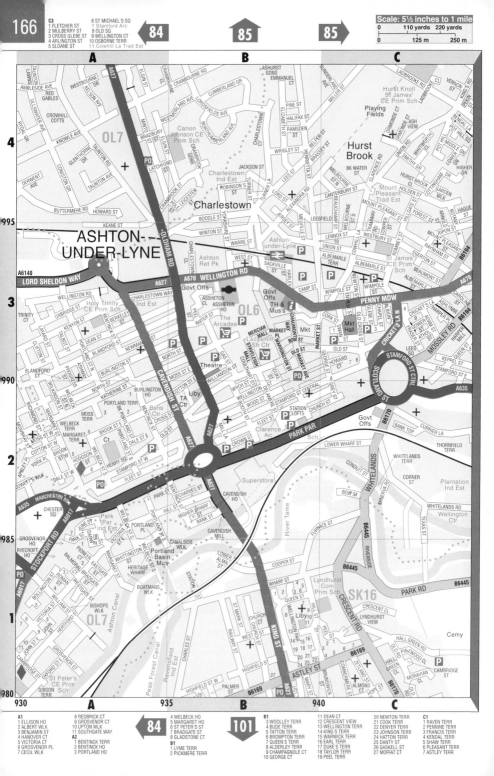

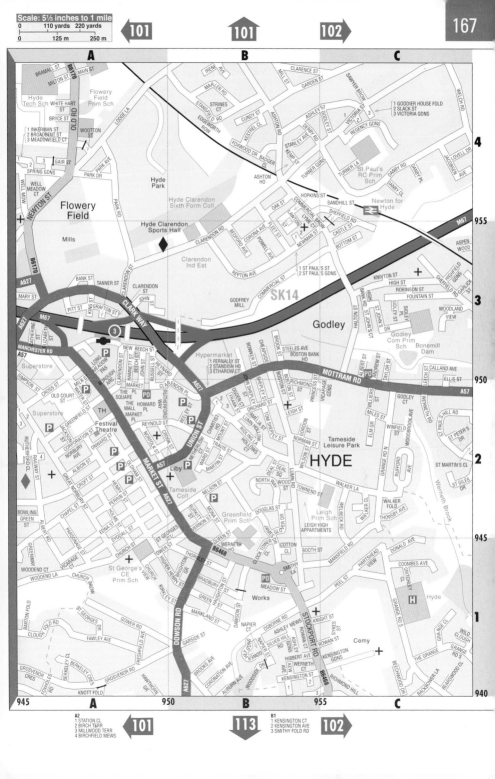

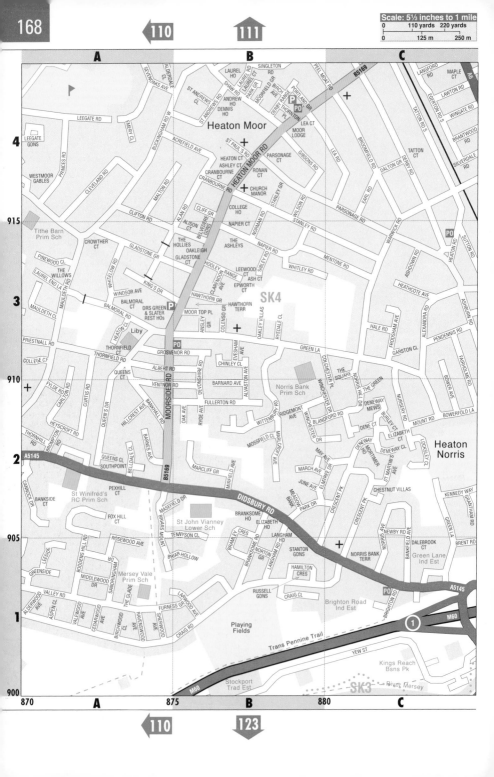

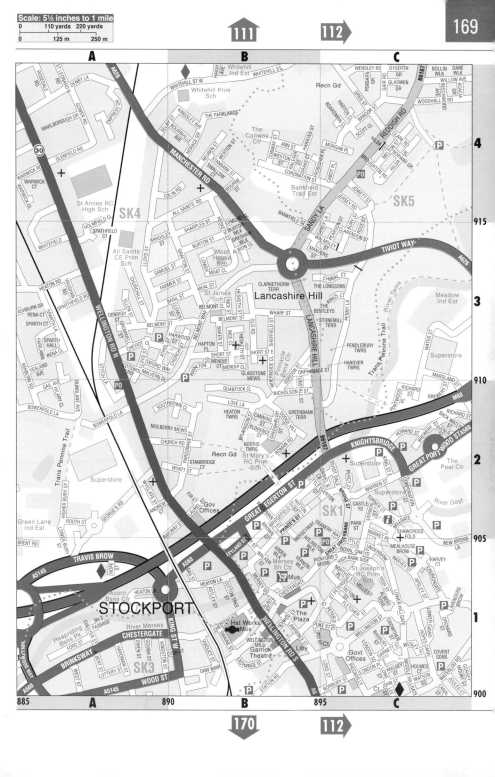

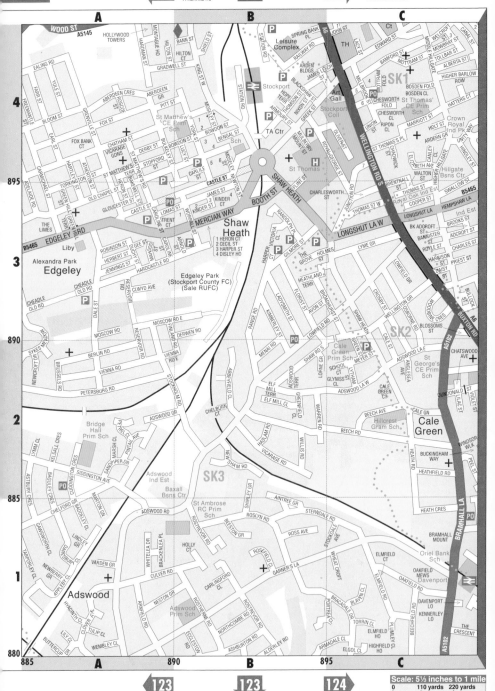

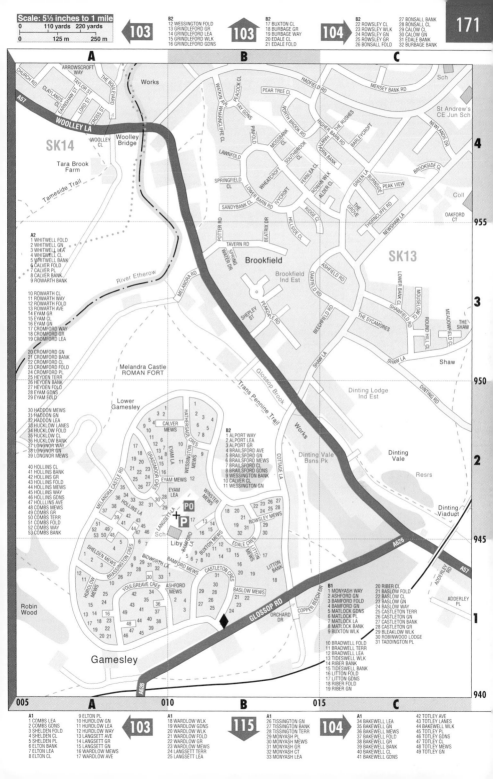

Index

Place name May be abbreviated on the map

Location number Present when a number indicates the place's position in a crowded area of mapping

Locality, town or village Shown when more than one place has the same name

Postcode district District for the indexed place

Page and grid square Page number and grid reference for the standard mapping

> **Church Rd 6** Beckenham BR2..........**53** C6

Cities, towns and villages are listed in CAPITAL LETTERS   **Public and commercial buildings** are highlighted in magenta

Places of interest are highlighted in blue with a star ★

Abbreviations used in the index

Acad	Academy	Comm	Common	Gd	Ground	L	Leisure	Prom	Promenade
App	Approach	Cott	Cottage	Gdn	Garden	La	Lane	Rd	Road
Arc	Arcade	Cres	Crescent	Gn	Green	Liby	Library	Recn	Recreation
Ave	Avenue	Cswy	Causeway	Gr	Grove	Mdw	Meadow	Ret	Retail
Bglw	Bungalow	Ct	Court	H	Hall	Meml	Memorial	Sh	Shopping
Bldg	Building	Ctr	Centre	Ho	House	Mkt	Market	Sq	Square
Bsns, Bus	Business	Ctry	Country	Hospl	Hospital	Mus	Museum	St	Street
Bvd	Boulevard	Cty	County	HQ	Headquarters	Orch	Orchard	Sta	Station
Cath	Cathedral	Dr	Drive	Hts	Heights	Pal	Palace	Terr	Terrace
Cir	Circus	Dro	Drove	Ind	Industrial	Par	Parade	TH	Town Hall
Cl	Close	Ed	Education	Inst	Institute	Pas	Passage	Univ	University
Cnr	Corner	Emb	Embankment	Int	International	Pk	Park	Wk, Wlk	Walk
Coll	College	Est	Estate	Intc	Interchange	Pl	Place	Wr	Water
Com	Community	Ex	Exhibition	Junc	Junction	Prec	Precinct	Yd	Yard

Index of towns, villages, streets, hospitals, industrial estates, railway stations, schools, shopping centres, universities and places of interest

172 1st–Acr

1st St WN2..............73 E7
3rd St WN2..............73 E7
4th St WN2..............73 F7

A

Abberley Dr M40..........65 D2
Abberley Way WN3......54 B4
Abberton Rd M20......110 A6
Abbey Cl
  Altrincham WA14.......119 B1
  Bolton BL3...........146 B2
  Radcliffe M26.........43 E5
  Up Holland WN8.......53 C7
  Urmston M32...........95 F3
Abbeycourt M30..........79 E2
Abbey Cres OL10........29 B4
Abbeycroft Cl M29.......77 C6
Abbey Ct
  Manchester M18........99 E6
  Poynton SK12.........133 D3
  Radcliffe M26.........43 E4
  Stockport SK1........124 B8
  Wigan WN5.............36 E2
Abbeydale 20 OL12.....139 B4
Abbey Dale WN6.........35 D7
Abbeydale Cl OL6........85 E6
Abbeydale Gdns M28.....60 C3
Abbeydale Rd M40.......83 C8
Abbey Dr
  Bury BL8..............27 A1
  Littleborough OL15....15 F3
  Orrell WN5............53 E6
  Swinton M27...........61 E1
Abbeyfield Cl SK3......170 E8
Abbeyfields WN6.........36 E2
Abbeyfield Sq M11.....165 B4
Abbey Gdns LS K14......103 A3
Abbey Gr
  Adlington PR6.........21 B7
  Chadderton OL9.......152 A1
  Eccles M30............79 E2
  Mottram in L SK14....102 F3
  Stockport SK1........124 B8
ABBEY HEY..............99 F5
Abbey Hey La M11, M18..99 F6
Abbey Hey Prim Sch
  M18..................99 E5

Abbey Hills Rd OL4,
  OL8..................67 C4
Abbey La WN7............57 D1
Abbey Lawn M16..........97 B3
Abbeylea Cres BL5.......40 A2
Abbeylea Dr BL5.........40 A2
Abbey Rd
  Cheadle SK8..........123 A5
  Delph OL3.............50 E5
  Droylsden M43.........83 F3
  Failsworth M35........84 B8
  Golborne WA3..........91 C8
  Middleton M24.........46 F4
  Sale M33............108 A6
  Tyldesley M29.........77 C7
Abbey Sq WN7............57 D1
Abbey St WN7............75 F6
Abbeystead Ave M21...109 D8
Abbeyville Wlk M15....162 B1
Abbey Way M40..........44 A3
Abbeyway N WA11........89 A7
Abbeyway S WA11........89 A7
Abbeywood Ave M18......99 E4
Abbingdon Way WN7......57 D1
Abbot Croft BL5........57 F6
Abbotsbury Cl
  Manchester M12......165 A2
  Poynton SK12........133 D5
Abbots Ct M33.........108 D5
Abbots Cl M33.........108 D5
Abbotsfield Cl M41.....94 D3
Abbotsfield Cl M41....156 A3
Abbot's Fold Rd M28....78 B7
Abbotsford Cl WA3......74 D1
Abbotsford Dr M24......46 D4
Abbotsford Gr WA14...119 E8
Abbotsford Prep Sch
  M41..................95 A2
Abbotsford Rd
  Bolton BL1...........142 A1
  Chadderton OL9........65 E8
  Manchester M21........97 B1
  Oldham OL1............49 B1
Abbotside Cl M16........97 D3
Abbotsleigh Dr SK7....124 B8
Abbott Com Prim Sch
  M40.................159 C3
Abbotts Gn M29.........77 A4
Abbott St
  Bolton BL3...........145 B1
  Hindley WN2...........56 C6
  14 Horwich BL6.........22 B4
  Rochdale OL11.........30 B3

Abbotts Way WN5........71 D3
Abbotts Rd M26.........44 A3
Abel Ho BL8.............26 F4
Abels La OL3............69 C8
Aber Ave SK2..........124 C4
Abercarn Cl M8.........156 A3
Abercorn Rd BL1.......142 B4
Abercorn St 7 OL4......67 D6
Abercrombie Ct M33...108 D5
Aberdare Wlk 4 M9.....64 E5
Aberdeen Wlk M13......163 B3
Aberdeen 1 M30.........79 E2
Aberdeen Cres SK3....170 A4
Aberdeen Ho M13......163 B1
Aberdeen St M13,
  M15.................163 B1
Aberford Rd M23.......121 A5
Abergele Rd M14......110 E8
Abergele St SK2.......124 A5
Aberley Fold OL15......15 F7
Abernant Cl M11......160 C1
Abernethy St BL6.......22 D2
Abernethy St BL6.......22 D2
Aber Rd SK8...........123 A6
Abersoch Ave M14.....110 E8
Abingdon Ave M45......44 F2
Abingdon Cl
  Oldham OL9...........66 B4
  Rochdale OL11.......139 B1
  Whitefield M45........44 F2
Abingdon Prim Sch
  SK5.................111 F7
Abingdon Rd
  Bolton BL2............25 E6
  Reddish SK5.........111 F7
  Stockport SK7.......123 E3
  Urmston M41...........95 E3
Abingdon St
  Ashton-u-L OL6........85 D2
  Manchester M1......163 A4
Abinger Rd WN4.........72 D4
Abinger Wlk M40........83 D4
Abington Dr WN2........56 A1
Abington Rd M33......108 C3
Abney Grange OL5......86 E8
Abney Rd
  Mossley OL5...........86 C8
  Stockport SK4.......111 C5
Aboukir St OL16........31 B8
Abraham Guest High Sch
  WN5..................54 A6

Abraham Moss High Sch
  M8..................156 B4
Abraham St 11 BL6......22 B4
ABRAM..................74 B8
ABRAM BROW............74 B7
Abram Bryn Gates Prim
  Sch WN2..............73 F7
Abram CE Prim Sch
  WN2..................56 B1
Abram Cl M14...........98 A1
Abram St M6............80 F6
Absalom Dr M8........155 C4
Abson St OL1...........48 C1
Acacia Ave
  Altrincham WA15......119 F3
  Cheadle SK8..........123 A2
  Denton M34...........101 A3
  Swinton M27...........79 E6
  Wilmslow SK9........136 F5
Acacia Cres WN6........36 F3
Acacia Dr
  Altrincham WA15......119 F3
  Salford M6............80 B3
Acacia Gr SK5.........169 C4
Acacia Rd OL8..........66 D1
Acacias Com Prim Sch
  M19.................110 F7
Academy Wlk M15......162 B1
Acer Cl
  Hyde SK14...........102 A2
  Rochdale OL11.........13 D1
Acer Gr M7............155 A3
Acheson St 3 M18......99 D5
Ackers Barn Ctyd
  M31.................107 B6
Ackers La M31.........106 F6
Ackersley Ct SK8......132 B8
Ackers St M13.........163 B1
Acker St OL16.........139 C4
Ackhurst La
  Shevington WN6........36 A3
  Wigan WN5............36 A2
Ack La E SK7..........132 D7
Ack La W SK8..........132 C7
Ackroyd Ave M18........99 F6
Ackroyd St M11.........99 E7
Ackworth Dr M23.......121 A6
Ackworth Rd OL8........61 E1
Acme Dr M27............80 B8
Acomb Ho M13.........163 B1
Acomb St
  Manchester M14........98 B4
  Manchester M15......163 B1

Acorn Ave
  Cheadle SK8..........122 E5
  Hyde SK14...........113 E8
Acorn Bsns Ctr
  Leigh WN7.............76 B4
  Stockport SK4.......169 A1
Acorn Cl
  Leigh WN7.............75 F3
  Manchester M19......110 F8
  Whitefield M45........62 F6
Acorn Ct WN7...........76 B3
Acorn Ctr OL1..........67 B8
Acorn Mews SK2.......124 C6
Acorn St 11 OL4.........67 E6
Acorn St
  Newton-le-W WA12......89 D3
  Oldham OL4............67 E6
Acorn Way OL1........153 B3
Acre Ave OL13...........3 D8
Acre Barn OL2..........48 E8
Acre Cl BL0.............1 D3
Acre Ct 5 SK13.......116 C7
Acre Field BL2.........25 D4
Acrefield M33.........108 A3
Acrefield Ave
  Stockport SK4.......168 B4
  Urmston M41...........95 F1
Acre Hall Prim Sch
  M41..................94 D2
Acre La
  Cheadle SK8..........132 C6
  Oldham OL1............49 A1
Acre Mill Rd OL13.......3 D8
Acresbrook SK15......102 C7
Acresbrook Wlk BL8.....26 F5
Acres Ct M23..........121 D4
Acresdale BL6..........40 C7
Acrefield
  Adlington PR7.........20 F6
  Tyldesley M29.........77 C7
Acrefield Ave M34......84 C1
Acrefield Cl
  Blackrod BL6..........21 C3
  Prestbury M27.........80 A6
Acrefield Rd
  Dukinfield SK14......101 F5
  Middleton M24.........47 C3
  Sale M15.............120 A8
  Salford M6............80 B5
  Walkden M38...........60 B4
Acres Fold Ave M22....121 E3

Acres La SK15 .... 86 B1
Acres Rd
Gatley SK8 .... 122 A5
Manchester M21 .... 109 B8
Acres St BL8 .... 26 F5
Acre St
Denton M34 .... 100 E3
4 Glossop SK13 .... 116 C7
Oldham OL9 .... 66 B2
3 Radcliffe M26 .... 43 E3
Whitworth OL12 .... 4 D1
Acreswood Ave WN2 .... 57 A4
Acreswood Cl PR7 .... 19 E8
Acre Top Rd M9 .... 64 B5
Acre View OL13 .... 3 D7
Acreville Gr WA3 .... 92 C7
Acre Wood BL6 .... 40 B3
'A' Ct WN4 .... 73 B2
Acton Ave M40 .... 83 B4
Acton Ho WN1 .... 151 A4
Acton Sq M5 .... 81 B2
Acton St
Oldham OL1 .... 67 B8
Rochdale OL12 .... 15 A1
Wigan WN1 .... 37 C1
Acton's Walk Trad Ctr
WN3 .... 150 C3
Acton Terr WN1 .... 37 C1
Actonville Ave M22 .... 121 D3
Adair St
Manchester M1 .... 163 C4
Rochdale OL11 .... 30 B2
Adam Cl SK8 .... 123 B4
Adams Ave M21 .... 109 B6
Adams Cl
Newton-le-W WA12 .... 89 D2
Poynton SK12 .... 133 E2
Adams Dr WN3 .... 150 A1
Adamson Circ M17 .... 95 C7
Adamson Gdns M20 .... 109 F3
Adamson Rd M30 .... 95 C8
Adamson St
Ashton-in-M WN4 .... 73 A3
Dukinfield SK16 .... 101 C6
Adamson Wlk 1 M14 .... 98 C3
Adam St
Ashton-u-L OL6 .... 166 C3
Bolton BL3 .... 148 A1
Oldham OL8 .... 66 F2
Ada St
Manchester M9 .... 64 D1
Ramsbottom BL0 .... 138 B1
Rochdale OL12 .... 15 A2
Adastral Ho M21 .... 109 C8
Adbaston Rd M32 .... 96 A5
Adcroft St SK1 .... 170 C3
Addenbrook Rd M8 .... 155 B1
Adderley Pl SK13 .... 171 C1
Adderley Rd SK13 .... 171 C1
Addingham Cl M9 .... 64 B5
Addington Cl WN2 .... 56 D4
Addington Rd BL3 .... 40 F3
Addington St M4 .... 159 B2
Addison Ave OL6 .... 85 D3
Addison Cl M13 .... 163 C2
Addison Cres M16 .... 97 B4
Addison Dr M24 .... 47 C3
Addison Rd
Altrincham WA15 .... 119 E2
Carrington M31 .... 106 D6
Irlam M44 .... 94 C4
Stretford M32 .... 96 B3
Urmston M41 .... 95 D1
Adelaide Rd
Bramhall SK7 .... 132 F5
Stockport SK3 .... 170 A3
Adelaide St E OL10 .... 29 E2
Adelaide St
5 Adlington PR6 .... 21 A8
Bolton BL3 .... 147 A4
Eccles M30 .... 79 D1
Heywood OL10 .... 29 D2
Middleton M24 .... 65 A8
Ramsbottom BL0 .... 11 A4
Salford M8 .... 155 C1
Swinton M27 .... 79 D7
Adelphi Ct M3 .... 158 A3
Adelphi Dr M38 .... 60 B5
Adelphi Gr M38 .... 60 B5
Adelphi St
3 Radcliffe M26 .... 43 F5
Salford M3 .... 158 A2
Standish WN6 .... 19 E2
Aden Cl M12 .... 164 A4
Aden St
Oldham OL4 .... 67 D5
Rochdale OL12 .... 15 A1
Adey Rd WA13 .... 117 A5
Adisham Dr BL1 .... 143 C1
ADLINGTON 21 B7
Adlington Cl
Altrincham WA15 .... 120 D6
Bury BL8 .... 27 A1
Poynton SK12 .... 133 F2
Adlington Dr M32 .... 96 F4
Adlington Est SK10 .... 133 C1
Adlington Pk SK10 .... 133 C1
Adlington Prim Sch
PR7 .... 20 F7
Adlington Rd SK9 .... 137 E7
Adlington St Paul's CE
Prim Sch PR6 .... 21 A7
Adlington South Bsns
Village PR7 .... 21 A6
Adlington St
Bolton BL3 .... 147 A3
Manchester M12 .... 164 A4
12 Oldham OL4 .... 49 D1
Adlington Sta PR6 .... 21 A7
Adlington Way 19
M34 .... 101 A1
Adlington Wlk SK1 .... 169 B1
Adlow Ind Pk M12 .... 164 A4
Admel Sq 1 M15 .... 163 A1
Adrian Rd BL1 .... 142 C2
Adrian St M40 .... 83 A7
Adrian Terr OL16 .... 31 C7
Adria Rd M20 .... 110 C3
Adscombe St M16 .... 97 E4
Adshall Rd SK8 .... 123 A5
Adshead Cl M22 .... 121 B3
Adstock Wlk 4 M40 .... 159 C3
Adstone Cl M4 .... 160 A1
ADSWOOD 170 A1
Adswood Cl OL4 .... 49 D1
Adswood Gr SK3 .... 170 A2
Adswood Ind Est SK3 .... 170 A2
Adswood La E SK2 .... 170 C2
Adswood La W SK2,
SK3 .... 170 C2
Adswood Old Hall Rd
SK8 .... 123 D4
Adswood Prim Sch
SK3 .... 170 B1
Adswood Rd SK3, SK8 .... 170 A1
Adswood St M40 .... 160 B2
Adswood Terr SK3 .... 170 B2
Adwell Cl WA3 .... 91 A8
Aegean Cl 3 M7 .... 81 C5
Aegean Rd WA14 .... 119 A6
AFFETSIDE 26 B8
Affetside Dr BL8 .... 26 E2
Affleck Ave M26 .... 61 A8
Afghan St OL1 .... 67 B8
Agden Brow WA13 .... 117 E1
Agden Brow Pk
WA13 .... 117 D1
Agden La WA13 .... 117 E1
Age Croft OL8 .... 67 C3
Agecroft Commerce Pk
M6 .... 80 E6
Agecroft Ent Pk M27 .... 80 E7
Agecroft Park Circ
M27 .... 80 E7
Agecroft Rd
Manchester M27 .... 80 E8
Romiley SK6 .... 113 A1
Agecroft Rd E M25 .... 63 A2
Agecroft Rd W M25 .... 63 A2
Ager St OL13 .... 3 C8
Agincourt St OL10 .... 29 B2
Agnes Cl OL9 .... 66 C4
Agnes Ct M14 .... 110 C7
Agnes St
Chadderton OL9 .... 152 B2
Manchester M19 .... 99 A2
Salford M7 .... 155 C3
Agnew Pl M6 .... 81 A4
Agnew Rd M18 .... 165 C1
Aigburth Gr SK5 .... 99 E2
Ailsa Cl M40 .... 157 A1
Ailsa Ho M6 .... 154 C1
Aimson Pl WA15 .... 120 C6
Aimson Road E WA15 .... 120 D6
Aimson Road W
WA15 .... 120 C7
Aines St M12 .... 165 A3
Aingarth Ho SK15 .... 85 F2
Ainley Rd M22 .... 121 D3
Ainley Wood
Delph OL3 .... 50 E5
Dukinfield SK16 .... 101 D7
Ainsbrook Ave
Delph OL3 .... 50 F4
Manchester M9 .... 65 B2
Ainsbrook Terr OL3 .... 51 D5
Ainscoughs Ct WN7 .... 75 F4
Ainscouth Bsns Pk
WN6 .... 18 F6
Ainscow Ave BL6 .... 39 F8
Ainsdale Ave
Atherton M46 .... 58 C4
Bury BL8 .... 27 B2
Edgworth BL7 .... 9 E6
Manchester M7 .... 63 D1
Ainsdale Cl
Bramhall SK7 .... 133 A7
Oldham OL8 .... 66 D4
Ainsdale Cres OL2 .... 48 E2
Ainsdale Ct BL3 .... 147 C3
Ainsdale Dr
Gatley SK8 .... 122 B1
Sale M33 .... 107 E2
Whitworth OL12 .... 14 D7
Ainsdale Gr SK5 .... 111 F8
Ainsdale Rd BL3 .... 147 B3
Ainsdale St M12 .... 164 C2
Ainse Rd BL6 .... 21 B3
Ainsford Rd M20 .... 110 D5
Ainsleigh Gdns M9 .... 64 D1
Ainsley Gr M28 .... 60 D2
Ainsley St 11 M40 .... 83 C5
Ainslie Rd BL1 .... 142 A1
Ainsty Rd M14 .... 98 A4
AINSWORTH 26 B1
Ainsworth Ave BL6 .... 22 E2
Ainsworth Cl M34 .... 100 B3
Ainsworth Ct
Bolton BL2 .... 148 C3
Walkden M28 .... 60 D2
Ainsworth Hall Rd BL2 .... 43 B8
Ainsworth La BL2 .... 148 C4
Ainsworth Rd
Bury BL8 .... 27 B2
Little Lever BL3 .... 43 B4
Radcliffe M26 .... 43 F5
Ainsworth Sq BL1 .... 143 A3
Ainsworth St
Bolton BL1 .... 142 C2
Rochdale OL16 .... 31 A6
Ainthorpe Wlk M40 .... 83 D5
Aintree Ave M33 .... 107 C3
Aintree Cl SK7 .... 124 F2
Aintree Dr OL11 .... 29 E8
Aintree Gr SK3 .... 170 B1
Aintree Rd BL3 .... 43 A3
Aintree St M11 .... 83 B1
Aintree Wlk OL9 .... 152 C3
Airedale Cl SK8 .... 122 C6
Airedale Ct WA14 .... 119 E5
Aire Dr BL2 .... 25 B5
Aireworth St BL5 .... 39 F3
Air Hill Terr 8 OL12 .... 14 C1
Airton Cl M40 .... 159 C3
Airton Pl WN3 .... 55 B3
Aitken Cl BL0 .... 138 B1
Aitken St
Haslingden BL0 .... 1 C5
Reddish M19 .... 99 C1
Ajax Dr BL9 .... 45 A4
Ajax St
Ramsbottom BL0 .... 138 B1
Rochdale OL11 .... 30 B3
Aked Cl M12 .... 164 A2
Akesmoor Dr SK2 .... 124 C6
Akhtar Ho M1 .... 163 A3
Alamein Dr SK6 .... 113 F2
Alan Ave M35 .... 83 F5
Alanbrooke Wlk M15 .... 162 B1
Alandale Ave M34 .... 100 E7
Alandale Dr OL2 .... 48 C5
Alandale Rd SK3 .... 123 C7
Alan Dr
Altrincham WA15 .... 120 A1
Marple SK6 .... 125 F6
Alan Rd
Manchester, Withington
M20 .... 110 C6
Stockport, Heaton Moor
SK4 .... 168 B4
Alan St BL1 .... 143 A3
Alan Turing Way
Droylsden M11 .... 83 A1
Manchester M11, M40 .... 160 C3
Alasdair Cl OL9 .... 65 F8
Alba Cl M30 .... 79 D1
Alban Ct
Ashton-u-L OL6 .... 85 D7
Westhoughton BL5 .... 57 E7
Alban St M7 .... 155 A1
Albany Ave M11 .... 99 F7
Albany Cl M38 .... 60 B5
Albany Ct
7 Manchester M20 .... 110 B6
Sale M33 .... 108 C5
Urmston M41 .... 95 B3
Albany Dr BL9 .... 44 F7
Albany Gr M29 .... 77 D8
Albany Rd
Bramhall SK7 .... 132 F4
Eccles M30 .... 79 B3
Manchester M21 .... 97 B1
Wilmslow SK9 .... 136 F5
Albany St
Middleton M24 .... 65 B7
Oldham OL4 .... 49 D1
10 Rochdale OL11 .... 31 A5
Albany Trad Est M21 .... 97 B1
Albany Way
Hattersley SK14 .... 102 E2
Salford M6 .... 81 A3
Alba Way M32 .... 96 A5
Albemarle Ave M20 .... 110 A6
Albemarle Rd M21 .... 109 A8
Albemarle St
Ashton-u-L OL6 .... 166 C3
Manchester M14 .... 98 A4
Albemarle Terr OL6 .... 166 C3
Alberbury Ave M23 .... 120 D7
Albermarle Rd 5 M27 .... 79 E7
Alberta St
Bolton BL3 .... 144 C1
Stockport SK1 .... 170 C4
Albert Ave
Dukinfield SK16 .... 101 C6
Manchester M25 .... 63 D1
Reddish M18 .... 99 F4
Shaw OL2 .... 149 B1
Urmston M41 .... 95 E2
Walkden M28 .... 60 C5
Albert Cl
Cheadle SK8 .... 123 A2
Whitefield M45 .... 63 A8
Albert Close Trad Est
M45 .... 63 A8
Albert Ct WA14 .... 119 D4
Albert Dr M45 .... 45 B1
Albert Fildes Wlk 3
M8 .... 155 C3
Albert Gdns M40 .... 83 D5
Albert Gr
Farnworth BL4 .... 60 D8
Manchester M12 .... 99 A4
Albert Hill St M20 .... 110 B3
Alberton Cl WN2 .... 38 C6
Albert Park Rd M7 .... 155 A1
Albert Pl
Altrincham WA14 .... 119 D5
Manchester M13 .... 98 F3
Whitefield M45 .... 45 B1
Albert Rd
8 Altrincham WA14 .... 119 D4
Bolton BL1 .... 144 B4
Cheadle SK8 .... 123 A2
Albert Rd *continued*
Eccles M30 .... 79 F2
Farnworth BL4 .... 60 D8
Hale WA15 .... 119 E3
Hyde SK14 .... 167 A2
Manchester M19 .... 99 A1
Sale M33 .... 108 C4
Stockport SK4 .... 168 A3
Whitefield M45 .... 63 A8
Wilmslow SK9 .... 137 A6
Albert Rd E WA15 .... 119 E3
Albert Rd W BL1 .... 40 F8
Albert Royds St OL12,
OL16 .... 15 B2
Albert St W M35 .... 83 D6
Albert Sq
Altrincham WA14 .... 119 D3
Manchester M2 .... 158 C1
Stalybridge SK15 .... 85 F1
Albert St
Ashton-in-M WN4 .... 73 B3
Bolton BL7 .... 8 D3
Bury BL9 .... 141 A2
Denton M34 .... 100 F3
Droylsden M43 .... 84 B1
Eccles M30 .... 79 F2
Farnworth BL4 .... 60 D7
Farnworth BL4 .... 60 E8
Glossop SK13 .... 104 A5
Hazel Grove SK7 .... 124 D3
Heywood OL10 .... 29 B2
14 Hindley WN2 .... 56 D5
Horwich BL6 .... 22 B4
Hyde SK14 .... 167 C3
Irlam M44 .... 105 E6
Littleborough OL15 .... 16 B5
8 Little Lever BL3 .... 43 B3
Manchester M11 .... 160 C1
Middleton M24 .... 65 A8
Milnrow OL16 .... 32 A5
Oldham, Factory Fold
OL9 .... 66 B3
Oldham, Hollinwood OL8 .... 66 B1
Oldham, Nether Lees
OL4 .... 67 E5
Prestwich M25 .... 63 C4
Ramsbottom BL0 .... 138 B2
Royton OL2 .... 48 D4
Shaw OL2 .... 149 A3
Stockport SK3 .... 169 A1
Whitworth OL12 .... 14 C8
Wigan WN5 .... 54 F6
Albert Street Wks 7
M34 .... 84 B1
Albert Terr SK1 .... 169 C1
Albert Webb Ho 6
M5 .... 154 B1
Albert Wlk 2 OL7 .... 166 A1
Albine St M40 .... 157 C4
Albinson Wlk M31 .... 106 A3
Albion Cl SK4 .... 169 B3
Albion Ct BL8 .... 140 A2
Albion Dr
Droylsden M43 .... 84 A2
Wigan WN2 .... 38 B2
Albion Fold M43 .... 84 A2
Albion Gardens Cl OL2 .... 48 F4
Albion Gdns SK15 .... 86 B1
Albion Gr M33 .... 108 A4
Albion High Sch The
M6 .... 81 B4
Albion Ho SK15 .... 86 C2
Albion Mill SK14 .... 103 C5
Albion Mill Ind Est
BL8 .... 140 A2
Albion Pk WA3 .... 92 C7
Albion Pl
Hazel Grove SK7 .... 124 D3
Prestwich M25 .... 63 A4
10 Salford M7 .... 81 C5
Albion Rd
Manchester M14 .... 98 C1
Rochdale OL11 .... 139 A2
Albion Road Ind Ctr
OL11 .... 139 A2
Albion St
Ashton-u-L OL6 .... 166 C3
7 Bacup OL13 .... 3 C8
Bolton BL3 .... 145 C1
Bury BL8 .... 140 A2
Chadderton OL9 .... 152 A3
Failsworth M35 .... 83 E7
Hyde SK14 .... 167 A2
Kearsley BL4 .... 61 A7
6 Leigh WN7 .... 75 F5
Littleborough OL15 .... 16 A5
Manchester, City Centre
M1 .... 162 C4
Manchester, Old Trafford
M16 .... 97 D4
Oldham OL1 .... 153 C3
Pendlebury M27 .... 80 A8
4 Platt Bridge WN2 .... 56 A2
Radcliffe M26 .... 44 B1
Rochdale OL11 .... 30 D1
Sale M33 .... 108 B4
Stalybridge SK15 .... 86 B2
Westhoughton BL5 .... 39 F3
Wigan WN2 .... 38 B2
Albion Terr BL1 .... 142 B3
Albion The M5 .... 81 B1
Albion Trad Est
Ashton-u-L OL6 .... 85 D3
Salford M6 .... 81 A4
Albion Twrs 5 M5 .... 81 B2
Albion Way M5 .... 81 B1
Alburn Ct M40 .... 160 B4
Albury Dr
Manchester M19 .... 110 D2
Rochdale OL12 .... 13 F2
Albury Way WN2 .... 37 F2
Albyns Ave M8 .... 156 A3
Alcester Ave SK3 .... 122 F7
Alcester Cl
Bury BL8 .... 27 B3
Middleton M24 .... 65 B6
Alcester Rd
Gatley SK8 .... 122 B4
Sale M33 .... 108 B2
Alcester St OL9 .... 66 A3
Alcester Wlk M9 .... 64 C5
Alconbury Ct M43 .... 100 B8
Alconbury Wlk M9 .... 64 B6
Aldborough Cl M20 .... 110 B6
Aldbourne Cl M40 .... 157 A1
Aldbury Terr 2 BL1 .... 143 A1
Aldcliffe WA3 .... 90 F8
Aldcroft St 5 M18 .... 99 F6
Alden Cl
Haslingden BB4 .... 1 A6
Standish WN1 .... 20 B1
Whitefield M45 .... 63 A8
Alden Rd BB4 .... 1 A5
Alden Rise BB4 .... 1 A6
Alden Wlk SK4 .... 111 D7
Alder Ave
Ashton-in-M WN4 .... 72 F5
Billinge WN5 .... 71 D5
Bury BL9 .... 141 C3
Poynton SK12 .... 133 F3
Wigan WN5 .... 54 D6
Alderbank
Horwich BL6 .... 21 F3
Wardle OL12 .... 15 C7
Alderbank Cl BL4 .... 60 F6
Alderbrook Rd M38 .... 59 F3
Alder Cl
Ashton-u-L OL6 .... 85 B7
9 Bury BL8 .... 27 C2
Dukinfield SK16 .... 102 A7
Gatley SK8 .... 131 D8
Glossop SK13 .... 171 C4
Leigh WN7 .... 75 F2
Alder Com High Sch
SK14 .... 114 A8
Aldercroft Ave
Bolton BL2 .... 25 D1
Wythenshawe M22 .... 121 C2
Alder Ct M8 .... 63 F1
Alderdale Cl SK4 .... 168 A4
Alderdale Dr
Droylsden M43 .... 83 E2
High Lane SK6 .... 134 E7
Manchester SK4 .... 111 A5
Alderdale Gr SK9 .... 136 E5
Alderdale Rd SK8 .... 123 C4
Alder Dr
Altrincham WA15 .... 120 E5
Stalybridge SK15 .... 86 C3
Swinton M27 .... 61 C1
Alder Edge 8 M21 .... 96 F1
Alderfield Ho 5 M21 .... 96 F1
Alderfield Rd M21 .... 96 F1
Alderfold St M46 .... 58 D3
Alderford Par 11 M8 .... 155 C2
ALDER FOREST 79 A4
Alder Forest Ave M30 .... 79 A4
Aldergate Gr OL6 .... 85 F5
Alderglen Rd M8 .... 156 A1
Alder Gr
Bolton BL7 .... 25 C6
Denton M34 .... 101 A3
Stockport SK3 .... 123 C8
Stretford M32 .... 96 E2
Alder Hts SK1 .... 112 B2
Alder La
Hindley WN2 .... 57 B5
Oldham OL8 .... 66 D2
Alder Lee Cl WN3 .... 54 D1
Alderley Ave
Bolton BL1 .... 24 E5
Golborne WA3 .... 90 D7
Alderley Cl
Billinge WN5 .... 71 E5
Hazel Grove SK7 .... 133 F8
Poynton SK12 .... 133 F2
Alderley Dr SK6 .... 112 E3
ALDERLEY EDGE 137 C2
Alderley Edge* SK9 .... 137 D1
Alderley Edge Prim Sch
SK9 .... 137 A2
Alderley Edge Sch for
Girls SK9 .... 137 A2
Alderley Edge Sta
SK9 .... 137 A2
Alderley La WN7 .... 76 B2
Alderley Lo SK9 .... 137 A5
Alderley Rd
Alderley Edge SK10,
SK9 .... 137 F2
Hindley WN2 .... 57 A5
Reddish SK5 .... 111 F5
Sale M33 .... 108 E2
Stockport SK3 .... 170 B1
Urmston M41 .... 95 A2
Wilmslow SK9 .... 137 A6
Alderley St OL6 .... 85 D5
Alderley Terr 8 SK16 .... 166 B1
Alderley Way SK3 .... 123 E4
Alderman Foley Dr
OL12 .... 14 A2

Alderman Gatley Ho
 M22 . . . . . . 121 D2
Alderman Kay Sch
 M24 . . . . . . 47 A3
Alderman Sq M12 . . . 164 B4
Aldermary Rd M21 . . . 109 D5
Aldermaston Gr M9 . . . 64 B6
Alder Meadow Cl OL12 . . 14 A1
Aldermere Cres M41 . . . 94 F3
Alderminster Ave M38 . . 60 A5
Aldermoor Cl M11 . . . 99 D8
Alderney Dr WN3 . . . 55 A3
Alder Rd
 Cheadle SK8 . . . . 122 E5
 Failsworth M35 . . . 83 F5
 Golborne WA3 . . . 90 F8
 Middleton M24 . . . 47 C2
 Rochdale OL11 . . . 30 D2
ALDER ROOT . . . 152 C2
Alders SK9 . . . . 136 F6
Alders Ave M22 . . . 121 C5
Alders Ct OL8 . . . 85 A8
Aldersgate Rd
 Cheadle SK8 . . . 132 C5
 Stockport SK2 . . . 124 B6
Alders Green Ave
 SK6 . . . . . 134 F7
Alders Green Rd WN2 . . 57 A5
Aldershot Wlk 3
 M11 . . . . . 160 C1
Alderside Rd M9 . . . 157 A4
Aldersley Ave M9 . . . 64 B5
Alderson St
 Oldham OL9 . . . 153 B3
 Salford M6 . . . 81 A4
Alders Rd
 High Lane SK12 . . . 135 A7
 Wythenshawe M22 . . 121 C5
Alder St
 Atherton M46 . . . 58 D3
 Bolton BL3 . . . 147 C3
 Eccles M30 . . . 79 A4
 Newton-le-W WA12 . . 89 C3
 Salford M6 . . . 154 C2
Alders The WN6 . . . 36 D4
Aldersyde St BL3 . . . 147 A3
Alderton Dr BL5 . . . 57 E6
Alderue Ave M22 . . . 121 D6
Alderway BL0 . . . 1 C1
Alderwood Ave M41 . . 168 A1
Alderwood Fold OL4 . . 67 F5
Alderwood Gr BL0 . . 1 D4
Alderwood Wlk 7
 M8 . . . . 155 C2
Aldfield Rd M23 . . . 108 F1
Aldford Cl M20 . . . 110 C3
Aldford Dr M46 . . . 58 E5
Aldford Gr BL2 . . . 43 B5
Aldford Pl SK9 . . . 136 F2
Aldford Way WN6 . . 36 E8
Aldham Ave M40 . . 83 C4
Aldred Cl M8 . . . 156 B2
Aldred St
 Bolton BL3 . . . 146 B3
 Eccles M30 . . . 79 C1
 Failsworth M35 . . . 83 E7
 3 Hindley WN2 . . 56 D4
 Leigh WN7 . . . 75 E8
 Salford M5 . . . 81 B2
Aldridge Cl WN3 . . . 55 B3
Aldridge Wlk M11 . . 164 C4
Aldsworth Dr
 Bolton BL3 . . . 147 B4
 Manchester M40 . . 157 B1
Aldwick Ave M20 . . . 110 C3
Aldwinians Cl M34 . . 100 E5
Aldworth Gr M33 . . 107 D3
Aldwych OL11 . . . 30 F3
Aldwych Ave M14 . . 98 B2
Aldwyn Cl
 Denton M34 . . . 100 C4
 Radcliffe M26 . . 44 B1
Aldwyn Cres SK7 . . 124 C2
Aldwyn Park Rd M34 . . 100 C8
Aldwyn Prim Sch M34 . . 84 C1
Alexander Ave M35 . . 84 A8
Alexander Briant Ct
 BL4 . . . . . 60 C7
Alexander Ct
 10 Manchester, Didsbury
  M20 . . . . 110 B3
 Manchester, Ordsall
  M5 . . . . 161 A4
Alexander Dr
 Altrincham WA15 . . 120 A6
 Milnrow OL16 . . . 31 F6
 Whitefield BL9 . . . 45 A2
Alexander Gdns M7 . . 158 E4
Alexander Rd BL2 . . 25 C1
Alexander St
 Rochdale OL11 . . . 30 B2
 Salford M6 . . . 154 B2
 Tyldesley M29 . . . 77 A8
Alexandra Ave
 Hyde SK14 . . . 101 C2
 Manchester M14 . . 97 F2
 Whitefield M45 . . . 63 A8
Alexandra Cl SK3 . . 123 C6
Alexandra Cres
 1 Oldham OL1 . . 67 B8
 Wigan WN5 . . . 54 E6
Alexandra Ct
 4 Dukinfield SK14 . . 101 F5
 1 Partington M31 . . 105 F3
 Urmston M41 . . . 94 E1

Alexandra Ctr Ret Pk
 OL4 . . . . 153 C2
Alexandra Dr M19 . . 110 F7
Alexandra Gr M44 . . 105 F8
Alexandra Hospl The
 SK8 . . . . 122 D6
Alexandra Mews OL4 . . 67 A5
Alexandra Mill OL3 . . 69 B8
ALEXANDRA PARK . . 67 A4
Alexandra Park Ho
 M16 . . . . 97 E2
Alexandra Park Inf Sch
 SK3 . . . . 123 C7
Alexandra Park Jun Sch
 SK3 . . . . 123 C7
Alexandra Park Prim Sch
 OL8 . . . . 67 A5
Alexandra Rd
 Ashton-in-M WN4 . . 73 B4
 Ashton-u-L OL6 . . 166 B4
 Denton M34 . . . 101 A4
 Eccles M30 . . . 95 C8
 Horwich BL6 . . . 39 E8
 Kearsley BL4 . . . 61 A7
 Kearsley, Prestolee M26 . 61 A8
 Manchester, Moss Side
  M16 . . . . 97 E4
 Oldham OL8 . . . 67 A4
 Sale M33 . . . 108 D3
 Stockport, Heaton Norris
  SK4 . . . . 168 C3
 Walkden M28 . . . 60 C5
Alexandra Rd S M16 . . 97 E2
Alexandra St
 Abram WN2 . . . 74 B8
 Ashton-u-L OL6 . . 85 D4
 1 Bolton BL3 . . 147 A4
 Farnworth BL4 . . . 60 D7
 Heywood OL10 . . 46 E8
 Hyde SK14 . . . 101 C1
 Oldham OL8 . . . 67 A5
 Salford M7 . . . 158 A3
 Wigan WN5 . . . 54 F6
Alexandra Terr
 14 Manchester M19 . . 99 A1
 Oldham OL4 . . . 49 E3
Alexandra The
 11 Manchester M14 . . 110 D8
 Stretford M50 . . . 96 A8
Alexandria Dr
 Ashton-u-L OL7 . . 84 E2
 Westhoughton BL5 . . 58 B8
Alford Ave M20 . . . 110 A8
Alford Cl BL2 . . . 42 F6
Alford Rd SK4 . . . 111 C6
Alford St OL9 . . . 66 B2
Alfred Ave M28 . . . 79 A7
Alfred James Cl 13
 M40 . . . . 159 C3
Alfred Morris Ct M23 . . 109 A2
Alfred Rd WA3 . . . 91 A8
Alfred St
 Ashton-u-L OL7 . . 85 D4
 Bolton, Burnden BL3 . . 42 B4
 Bolton, Egerton BL7 . . 8 D3
 Bury BL9 . . . 141 A1
 Dukinfield SK14 . . 101 C3
 Eccles M30 . . . 79 C3
 Farnworth BL4 . . . 42 D2
 Ince-in-M WN3 . . 151 A2
 Irlam M44 . . . 105 E6
 Kearsley BL4 . . . 60 F8
 Littleborough OL15 . . 16 A6
 Manchester M9 . . 157 A4
 Newton-le-W WA12 . . 89 E3
 Oldham OL9 . . . 152 C2
 Platt Bridge WN2 . . 56 A3
 Ramsbottom BL0 . . 138 B1
 Shaw OL2 . . . 149 B3
 1 Tyldesley M29 . . 58 F1
 Walkden M28 . . . 60 D3
 Whitworth OL12 . . . 4 D2
 Wigan WN1 . . . 37 B2
Alfreton Ave M34 . . 113 A8
Alfreton Rd SK2 . . 124 E5
Alfreton Wlk 9 M40 . . 83 A6
Afriston Dr M23 . . 109 A2
Alger Mews OL6 . . 85 D4
Algernon Rd M28 . . 60 C4
Algernon St
 Eccles M30 . . . 79 D3
 Hindley WN2 . . . 56 D5
 Swinton M27 . . . 79 D8
 Wigan WN3 . . . 55 A6
Alger St 1 OL6 . . 85 D4
Algreave Rd SK3 . . 123 A8
Alice Ingham RC Prim Sch
 OL16 . . . . 15 C2
Alice St
 Bolton BL3 . . . 144 C1
 Hyde SK14 . . . 113 E7
 Pendlebury M27 . . 80 B8
 Rochdale OL12 . . . 15 B1
 Sale M33 . . . 108 D4
Alicia Ct OL12 . . . 14 E1
Alicia Dr OL12 . . . 14 E1
Alick's Fold 9 BL5 . . 39 E1
Alison Ct M34 . . . 168 B3
Alison Kelly Cl M9 . . 157 C4
Alison St
 6 Manchester M14 . . 97 F3
 1 Manchester M14 . . 98 A3
 Shaw OL2 . . . 149 B4
Al Jamiah Al Islamiyyah
 BL7 . . . . 25 A8
Alker Rd M40 . . . 160 A3
Alker St WN5 . . . 54 F6
Alkrington Cl BL9 . . 45 A2

Alkrington Ct M24 . . 65 B5
ALKRINGTON GARDEN
 VILLAGE . . . 65 A5
Alkrington Gn M24 . . 64 F7
Alkrington Hall M24 . . 64 F7
Alkrington Hall Rd N
 M24 . . . . 64 F7
Alkrington Hall Rd S
 M24 . . . . 64 E6
Alkrington Moss Prim Sch
 M24 . . . . 65 B5
Alkrington Park Rd
 M24 . . . . 65 A6
Allama Iqbal Rd OL4 . . 67 C5
Allanadale Ct 12 M7 . . 63 E1
Allan Ct M21 . . . 109 A7
Allandale WA14 . . . 119 B4
Allandale Rd M19 . . 98 F1
Allan Roberts Cl M9 . . 64 D1
Allanson Rd M22 . . 109 E1
Allan St M29 . . . 76 F8
Alldis Cl M12 . . . 164 B1
Alldis St SK2 . . . 124 B5
Allen Ave
 Fowley Common WA3 . . 92 C4
 Hyde SK14 . . . 113 F8
Allenby Gr BL5 . . . 57 D7
Allenby Rd
 Irlam M44 . . . 105 C4
 Swinton M27 . . . 79 C6
Allenby St
 Atherton M46 . . . 58 B2
 Shaw OL2 . . . 149 A3
Allenby Wlk 4 M40 . . 156 C1
Allen Cl OL2 . . . 149 A2
Allen Ct M34 . . . 100 E4
Allendale Dr BL9 . . 45 A3
Allendale Gdns BL1 . . 143 B2
Allendale Wlk M3 . . 158 A2
Allen Rd M41 . . . 95 F2
Allen St
 Bury BL8 . . . 27 C3
 Little Lever BL3 . . 43 A3
 Oldham OL8 . . . 153 A2
 Radcliffe M26 . . 43 F3
Allerby Way WA3 . . 90 E8
Allerdean Wlk SK4 . . 110 F3
Allerford St M16 . . 97 F4
Allerton Cl BL5 . . 40 A1
Allerton Ct 12 BL1 . . 145 B4
Allerton Wlk 6 M13 . . 163 C2
Allescholes Rd OL14 . . 6 B7
Allesley Cl BL5 . . 40 A1
Allesley Dr M7 . . 155 C2
Allgreave Cl M33 . . 108 E1
Alliance Ind Est M4 . . 160 D3
Alliance St 3 WN1 . . 151 A4
Alligin Cl OL9 . . . 152 A4
Allingham St M13 . . 98 E4
Allington OL11 . . . 139 B2
Allington Dr M30 . . 79 E4
Alliott Wlk M15 . . 162 B1
Allison Gr M30 . . 79 B1
Allison St M8 . . . 155 C1
Allonby Wlk M24 . . 46 C2
Allotment Rd M44 . . 105 D6
Alloway Wlk 4 M40 . . 83 A6
All Saints 4 BL3 . . 27 C3
All Saints Catholic Coll
 SK16 . . . . 101 D7
All Saints CE Prim Sch
 Failsworth M40 . . 83 C5
 Marple SK6 . . . 126 A5
 Rochdale OL12 . . 15 A3
 Stockport SK4 . . 169 A3
 Whitefield M45 . . 45 A2
All Saints' CE Prim Sch
 BL4 . . . . 42 D2
All Saint's Cl OL2 . . 48 D5
All Saint's Ct M32 . . 96 B2
All Saints Gr WN2 . . 56 E5
All Saints Pl 2 BL8 . . 27 C3
All Saints Prim Sch
 M12 . . . . 165 A2
All Saints RC Prim Sch
 Glossop SK13 . . . 104 D2
 Golborne WA3 . . 90 B8
 Sale M33 . . . 107 D6
All Saints' Rd SK4 . . 169 B4
All Saints' St
 Bolton BL1 . . . 145 C4
 Failsworth M40 . . 83 C5
All Saints Terr OL12 . . 15 B2
Allscott Way WN4 . . 73 C3
Allsopp St 1 BL3 . . 145 C2
All Souls CE Prim Sch
 OL10 . . . . 29 F3
All Souls RC Prim Sch
 M5 . . . . 154 A1
Allwood St M5 . . 158 A1
Alma Cl WN8 . . 53 C7
Alma Ct
 3 Manchester M15 . . 97 E4
 Up Holland WN8 . . 53 C7
Alma Gr WN3 . . . 54 E2
Alma Hill WN8 . . 53 C7
Alma Hill Est WN8 . . 53 C7
Alma Ind Est 22 OL12 . 14 F1
Alma Par WN3 . . . 54 E2
Alma Park Prim Sch
 M19 . . . . 111 A8
Alma Rd
 Hazel Grove SK7 . . 134 A8
 Manchester, Heaton Moor
  SK4 . . . . 111 B5

Alma Rd continued
 Manchester, Levenshulme
  M19 . . . . 111 A8
 Sale M33 . . . 107 E2
 Up Holland WN8 . . 53 C7
 Westhoughton BL5 . . 57 F8
Alma St
 Atherton M46 . . . 58 C3
 Bolton BL3 . . . 146 C4
 Eccles M30 . . . 79 F1
 Kearsley BL4 . . . 61 B5
 Leigh WN7 . . . 75 E8
 11 Little Lever BL3 . . 43 B3
 Newton-le-W WA12 . . 89 B3
 Radcliffe M26 . . 43 F5
 8 Rochdale OL12 . . 14 F1
 Stalybridge SK15 . . 86 B2
 Tyldesley M29 . . 76 F8
Alminstone Cl M40 . . 83 D4
Almond Ave BL9 . . 141 C3
Almond Brook Rd
 WN6 . . . . 19 C1
Almond Cl
 Failsworth M35 . . 83 F6
 Littleborough OL15 . . 15 F6
 Salford M6 . . . 81 B2
 Stockport SK3 . . 123 C8
Almond Cres
 Rawtenstall BB4 . . 1 F8
 Standish WN6 . . . 36 F7
Almond Ct SK16 . . 166 C1
Almond Dr M33 . . 107 F6
Almond Gr
 Bolton BL1 . . . 143 C3
 Wigan WN5 . . . 54 E6
Almond Rd 6 OL4 . . 49 D1
Almond St
 Bolton BL1 . . . 143 C4
 9 Farnworth BL4 . . 60 C8
 Manchester M40 . . 159 B4
Almond Tree Rd SK8 . . 123 A1
Almond Way OL4 . . 102 A2
Almond Wlk M31 . . 105 D3
Alms Field Rd M8 . . 156 A3
Alness Rd M16 . . 97 E2
Alnwick Cl WN2 . . 38 D5
Alnwick Dr BL9 . . 45 A5
Alnwick Rd M9 . . 64 D5
Alperton Wlk M40 . . 83 A6
Alpha Court Ind Est
 M34 . . . . 100 C3
Alpha Pl M15 . . 162 B3
Alphagate Dr M34 . . 100 C3
Alpha Rd M32 . . 96 C1
Alpha St W M6 . . 154 B3
Alpha St
 Manchester M11 . . 99 E7
 Salford M6 . . . 154 C3
Alphin Cl
 Mossley OL5 . . 68 E3
 Uppermill OL3 . . 69 A4
Alphingate Cl SK15 . . 86 D4
Alphin Sq OL5 . . 68 D1
Alphonsus St M16 . . 97 C4
Alpine Dr
 Leigh WN7 . . . 75 C8
 Milnrow OL16 . . 32 A7
 Royton OL2 . . 48 C3
 Wardle OL12 . . 15 C2
Alpine Rd
 Stockport SK1 . . 112 A1
 Stockport SK1 . . 112 A2
Alpine St
 Droylsden M11 . . 83 B2
 Newton-le-W WA12 . . 89 A3
Alpington Wlk M40 . . 65 C2
Alport Ave M16 . . 97 C2
Alport Gr 3 SK13 . . 171 E2
Alport Lea 2 SK13 . . 171 E2
Alport Way 1 SK13 . . 171 B2
Alresford Rd
 Middleton M9 . . 64 F5
 Salford M6 . . . 80 D5
Alric Wlk M22 . . 130 E8
Alsager Cl M21 . . 109 B6
Alsham Wlk M8 . . 156 A2
Alsop Ave M7 . . 81 B7
Alstead Ave WA15 . . 120 A3
Alston Ave
 Sale M33 . . . 107 F3
 Shaw OL2 . . . 149 B4
 Stretford M32 . . 96 B3
Alston Cl SK7 . . 124 A1
Alstone Dr WA14 . . 119 A6
Alstone Rd SK4 . . 111 C6
Alston Gdns M19 . . 110 F5
Alston Lea M46 . . 58 E4
Alston Rd
 Manchester M18 . . 99 E5
 Wigan WN2 . . . 37 F2
Alston St
 Bolton BL3 . . . 147 B3
 Bury BL8 . . . 27 C4
Alston Wlk M24 . . 65 D8
ALT 67 D3
Altair Ave 7 M22 . . 121 D1
Altair Pl M7 . . 81 C4
Altcar Gr SK2 . . 99 E2
Altcar Wlk M22 . . 121 C2
Alt Cl WN7 . . . 75 D6
Altham Cl BL9 . . 44 D7
Altham Wlk 12 M40 . . 83 A6
Alt Hill La OL6, OL7 . . 85 C8
Alt Hill Rd OL6 . . 67 C1

Althorn Wlk 11 M23 . . 121 A5
Althorpe Wlk M40 . . 83 D4
Alt La OL8 . . . 67 C3
Alton Ave M41 . . 94 D2
Alton Cl
 Ashton-in-M WN4 . . 73 A4
 Ashton-u-L OL6 . . 85 C7
 Whitefield BL9 . . 45 A5
Alton Rd SK9 . . 136 F7
Alton Sq M11 . . 99 E7
Alton St OL8 . . 66 F3
Alton Twrs M16 . . 97 D1
Alt Prim Sch OL8 . . 67 D3
Alt Rd OL6 . . 85 B6
ALTRINCHAM . . 119 C5
Altrincham Bsns Pk
 WA14 . . . . 119 B7
Altrincham CE Prim Sch
 WA14 . . . . 119 D5
Altrincham Coll of Arts
 WA15 . . . . 120 B3
Altrincham General Hospl
 WA14 . . . . 119 D4
Altrincham Gram Sch for
 Boys WA14 . . . 119 D2
Altrincham Gram Sch for
 Girls WA14 . . . 119 C3
Altrincham Gram Sch for
 Girls (Sixth Form Ctr)
 WA14 . . . . 119 B3
Altrincham Prep Sch
 WA14 . . . . 119 D2
Altrincham Priory Hospl
 WA15 . . . . 129 A7
Altrincham Rd
 Styal SK9 . . . 130 C4
 Wilmslow SK9 . . 130 C2
 Wythenshawe M23 . . 120 E7
 Wythenshawe, Sharston
  M22 . . . . 121 E5
Altrincham Ret Pk
 WA14 . . . . 119 C7
Altrincham Sta WA15 . . 119 D4
Alt Wlk M45 . . 45 C2
Alum Cres BL9 . . 45 A3
Alvanley Cl
 Sale M33 . . . 108 C1
 Wigan WN5 . . . 36 C1
Alvanley Cres SK3 . . 123 C6
Alvanley Ind Est SK8 . . 112 F4
Alvan Sq 3 M11 . . 99 E7
Alva Rd OL4 . . 49 D2
Alvaston Ave SK4 . . 168 B2
Alvaston Rd M18 . . 99 E4
Aveley Ave M20 . . 110 C5
Alverston Rd M20 . . 110 C6
Alveston Dr SK9 . . 137 C8
Alvington Gr SK7 . . 124 A1
Alvon Ct SK14 . . 102 A2
Alwin Rd OL2 . . 149 A4
Alwinton Ave SK4 . . 110 E3
Alworth Rd M9 . . 64 D5
Alwyn Cl WN7 . . 75 F1
Alwyn Dr M13 . . 98 E4
Alwyn St WN1 . . 37 D1
Amar Terr WN1 . . 151 C3
Ambassador Pl WA15 . . 119 E5
Ambergate M46 . . 58 D2
Amber Gdns
 Dukinfield SK16 . . 101 B8
 Hindley WN2 . . 56 E4
Amber St 39 F2
Amberhill Way
 Boothstown M28 . . 77 F5
 Worsley M28 . . 78 A5
Amberley Cl
 Bolton BL3 . . 40 F5
 Wigan WN2 . . 37 F2
Amberley Dr
 Altrincham WA15 . . 129 B8
 Irlam M44 . . . 94 A1
 Wythenshawe M23 . . 121 A4
Amberley Rd M33 . . 107 E5
Amberley Wlk OL9 . . 152 C3
Amberswood Cl WN2 . . 56 B7
Amberwood OL9 . . 65 C3
Amberwood Dr M23 . . 120 D6
Amblecote Dr E M38 . . 60 A6
Amblecote Dr W M38 . . 60 A6
Ambleside
 Ince-in-M WN2 . . 56 B7
 Stalybridge SK15 . . 86 A3
 Wigan WN5 . . 54 C7
Ambleside Ave
 Ashton-u-L OL7 . . 84 F4
Ambleside Cl
 Bolton BL2 . . 25 F4
 Middleton M24 . . 46 E1
Ambleside Ct
 Cheadle SK8 . . 122 C5
 Stalybridge SK15 . . 86 A3
Ambleside Pl WA11 . . 71 B1
Ambleside Rd
 Reddish SK5 . . 111 F6
 Urmston M41 . . 94 D1
Ambleside Wlk M9 . . 65 A2
Amblethorn Dr BL1 . . 24 D5
Ambrose Ave WN7 . . 57 E1
Ambrose Cres OL3 . . 51 B3
Ambrose Dr M20 . . 109 E4
Ambrose Gdns M20 . . 109 E4
Ambrose St
 Hyde M16 . . 113 E7
 Manchester M12 . . 165 A3

Ambrose St continued
Rochdale OL11 . . . . . . 139 C1
Ambuscade Ct M41 . . . 94 E2
Ambush St M11 . . . . . . 99 F7
Amelia St
Denton M34 . . . . 100 F4
Hyde SK14 . . . . 167 B2
Amersham Cl M41 . . . . 95 B5
Amersham Pl M19 . . . 111 A6
Amersham St M5 . . . . 154 C1
Amesbury Dr WN3 . . . 54 C2
Amesbury Gr SK5 . . . 111 F5
Amesbury Rd M9 . . . . 64 E4
Amethyst Cl WN2 . . . . 38 A2
Amherst Rd M14, M20 110 D7
Amis Gr WA3 . . . . 90 E8
Amlwch Ave SK2 . . . . 124 D6
Ammon's Way OL3 . . . 50 F5
Ammon Wrigley Cl
OL1 . . . . 153 C3
Amory St M12 . . . . . . 163 C4
Amos Ave M40 . . . . . . 83 C4
Amos St
Manchester M9 . . . . . 157 C4
Salford M6 . . . . 154 B2
Ampleforth Gdns 🗌
M26 . . . . 43 E5
Ampney Cl M30 . . . . . . 79 B1
Amport Wlk 🗌 M40 . . . 65 C2
Amwell St M8 . . . . 156 C3
Amy St
Middleton M24 . . . . . . 47 B1
Rochdale OL12 . . . . . . 14 B1
Anaconda Dr M3 . . . . 158 B3
Ancaster Wlk 🗌 M40 . . 65 C2
Anchorage Quay M50 161 A4
Anchorage Rd M41 . . . 96 A1
Anchorage St M5 . . . 161 A4
Anchorage Wlk M18 . 165 C2
Anchor Cl M19 . . . . . . 99 C1
Anchor Ct M8 . . . . 63 F1
Anchor La BL4, M38 . . 59 F7
Anchorside Cl M21 . . 109 B7
Anchor St OL1 . . . . . . 153 C4
ANCOATS 159 C2
Ancoats Gr M4 . . . . . . 164 A4
Ancoats Gr N M4 . . . . 160 A1
Ancoats St 🗌 OL4 . . . . 67 E6
Ancroft Dr WN2 . . . . . 56 D3
Ancroft Gdns BL3 . . . 146 C2
Ancroft St M15 . . . . . 162 B2
Anderby Pl BL5 . . . . . . 39 E2
Anderby Wlk BL5 . . . . 39 E2
ANDERTON 21 C8
Anderton Cl
Bury BL8 . . . . 26 F1
Rawtenstall BB4 . . . . . . 2 F7
Anderton Gr OL6 . . . . . 85 E5
Anderton La BL6 . . . . . 21 E4
Anderton Prim Sch
PR6 . . . . 21 B8
Anderton St Joseph's RC
Prim Sch PR6 . . . . . . 21 B8
Anderton St
Adlington PR7 . . . . 21 A7
Ince-in-M WN2 . . . . . . 151 C3
Anderton Way
Handforth SK9 . . . . . . 131 D3
Wigan WN2 . . . . 38 B2
Andoc Ave M30 . . . . . . 80 A1
Andover Ave M24 . . . . 65 C5
Andover Cres WN3 . . . 54 D2
Andover Rd WA11 . . . . 72 E1
Andover St M30 . . . . . . 79 C1
Andover Wlk M8 . . . . . 156 A4
Andre St 🗌 M11 . . . . . . 83 C2
Andrew Ave WN5 . . . . 71 F5
Andrew Cl
Radcliffe M26 . . . . 44 C1
Ramsbottom BL8 . . . . . 10 F1
Andrew Ct 🗌 M20 . . . . 110 B6
Andrew Gr SK16 . . . . . 101 D8
Andrew Ho SK4 . . . . . 168 B4
Andrew La
Bolton BL1 . . . . 24 F6
High Lane SK6 . . . . . . 134 F8
Andrew Rd M9 . . . . 64 D7
Andrews Ave M41 . . . . 94 E3
Andrew St
Ashton-u-L OL6 . . . . . . 85 C5
Bury M9 . . . . 141 A2
Chadderton OL9 . . . . . 152 B4
Compstall SK6 . . . . . . 114 A2
Droylsden M43 . . . . . . 84 C4
Failsworth M35 . . . . . . 83 E8
Hyde SK14 . . . . 167 C3
Middleton M24 . . . . . . 65 C7
Mossley OL5 . . . . 86 C8
Stockport SK4 . . . . . . 169 A2
Andrew's Terr 🗌 BL5 . . 39 E1
Andy Nicholson Wlk
M9 . . . . 157 C4
Anemone Dr BB4 . . . . . . 1 A8
Anerley Rd M20 . . . . . 110 B4
Anfield Cl BL9 . . . . 45 B3
Anfield Rd
Bolton BL3 . . . . 147 C2
Cheadle SK8 . . . . 122 F3
Failsworth M40 . . . . . . 65 D1
Sale M33 . . . . 108 C5
Angela Ave OL1, OL2 . 48 E2
Angela St M15 . . . . . . 162 A3
Angelbank BL6 . . . . . . 21 F2
Angel Cl SK16 . . . . 101 B8
Angelica Rise OL1 . . . . 49 D3
Angelo St BL1 . . . . 143 A2
Angel St
Denton M34 . . . . 101 A4

Angel St continued
Hazel Grove SK7 . . . . . 124 D3
Manchester M4 . . . . . . 159 A3
Angier Gr M4 . . . . 100 F3
Anglers Rest M44. . . . . 105 E5
Anglesea Ave SK2 . . . . 170 C2
Anglesey Cl OL7 . . . . . . 85 A6
Anglesey Dr SK12. . . . . 133 F6
Anglesey Gr SK8 . . . . . 123 A6
Anglesey Rd OL7 . . . . . 84 F6
Anglesey Water SK12 . . 133 E6
Angleside Ave M19 . . . 110 E4
Angle St BL2 . . . . 148 C7
Aglezarke Rd PR6 . . . . 21 A7
Anglia Gr BL3 . . . . 146 C4
Angora Dr M3 . . . . 158 A3
Angouleme Ret Pk
BL9 . . . . 140 C1
Angouleme Way BL9 . . 140 C1
Angus Ave
Heywood OL10. . . . . . . 29 A1
Leigh WN7 . . . . 75 C7
Angus St OL13 . . . . 3 C8
Aniline St M11 . . . . 83 B1
Anita St M4 . . . . 159 B2
Anjou Bvd WN5 . . . . . . 54 F8
Annable Rd
Droylsden M43 . . . . . . 84 B1
Irlam M44 . . . . 105 F8
Manchester M18 . . . . . 99 E6
Romiley SK6. . . . . 112 D3
Arnald Sq M43 . . . . . . 100 A8
Annandale Gdns WN8. . 53 A7
Annan Gr WN4 . . . . 73 E5
Annan St M34 . . . . 100 F4
Anne Cl 🗌 OL7 . . . . . . 85 A6
Annecy Cl BL8. . . . . 27 B4
Anne Line Cl 🗌 OL11 . . 31 A5
Anne Nuttall Rd M15 . . 162 A3
Annersley Ave OL2 . . . 149 A2
Annesley Cres WN3 . . . 54 F3
Annesley Gdns 🗌 M18. . 99 D6
Anne St SK16 . . . . 101 D8
Annette Ave WA12 . . . . 89 A5
Annie Darby Ct M9 . . . 157 A3
Annie St
Ramsbottom BL0 . . . . . 11 A4
Salford M6. . . . . 154 B2
Annis Cl SK9 . . . . 137 B2
Annisdale Cl M30. . . . . . 79 B2
Annisfield Ave OL3 . . . . 69 C5
Annis Rd
Alderley Edge SK9 . . . 137 B2
Bolton BL3. . . . . 146 B4
Annis St M9 . . . . 157 B3
Ann La M29 . . . . 77 C5
Ann Sq OL7 . . . . 67 D8
Ann St
Ashton-u-L OL7 . . . . . 100 F8
Denton M34. . . . . 100 E3
Dukinfield SK14 . . . . . 101 C3
Farnworth BL4. . . . . . . 60 D7
Heywood OL10. . . . . . . 29 D3
Leigh WN7 . . . . 75 E8
Reddish SK5 . . . . 169 B4
Rochdale OL11 . . . . . . 139 C2
Anscombe Cl M40 . . . . 160 A3
Ansdell Ave M21 . . . . . 109 C8
Ansdell Dr M43 . . . . 83 E2
Ansdell Rd
Horwich BL6 . . . . 22 C4
Reddish SK5 . . . . 100 A1
Rochdale OL16 . . . . . . 31 B4
Wigan WN5 . . . . 54 D5
Ansdell St M8 . . . . 156 A3
Ansell Cl M18 . . . . 99 D6
Anselms Ct OL8 . . . . . . 66 C4
Ansford Ave M40 . . . . . 74 B8
Ansford Wlk M9 . . . . . 156 C2
Ansleigh Ave M8 . . . . . 64 A1
Ansley Gr SK4 . . . . 168 B3
Anslow Cl M40 . . . . 157 A1
Anson Ave M27 . . . . 79 E6
Anson Cl SK7 . . . . 132 F5
Anson Engine Mus The*
SK12 . . . . 134 C4
Anson Pl WN5 . . . . 54 C8
Anson Rd
Handforth SK9 . . . . . . 131 E1
Manchester M14 . . . . . 98 D3
Poynton SK12 . . . . . . 134 B3
Reddish M34, SK5 . . . 100 A2
Swinton M27 . . . . 79 E6
Anson St
Bolton BL1 . . . . 143 C3
Eccles M30 . . . . 79 B4
Swinton M27 . . . . 54 F7
Answell Ave M8 . . . . . . 64 A2
Antares Ave M7 . . . . . . 158 A3
Anthistle Ct M5 . . . . . . 154 A2
Anthony Cl M12 . . . . . 164 B3
Anthony St OL5 . . . . 68 B1
Anthorn Rd WN3 . . . . . 54 E3
Antilles Cl M12 . . . . . . 99 A4
Antler Ct WN4 . . . . 73 B6
Antrim Cl
Manchester M19 . . . . . 110 D2
Wigan WN3 . . . . 54 C2
Anvil Cl WN5 . . . . 53 D5
Anvil St OL13 . . . . 3 E8
Anvil Way OL1 . . . . 153 B3
Apethorn La SK14 . . . . 113 D7
Apfel La OL9 . . . . 152 B3
Apollo Ave BL9 . . . . 44 F3
Apollo Wlk M12 . . . . . . 165 A2

Apperley Grange M30. . . 79 E4
Appian Way M7 . . . . . . 155 B1
Appleby Ave
Altrincham WA15 . . . . 120 C5
Dukinfield SK14 . . . . . 101 C5
Manchester M12 . . . . . 99 A3
Appleby Cl
Bury BL8 . . . . 26 F2
Stockport SK3 . . . . . . 170 A1
Appleby Gdns
1 Bolton BL2 . . . . 25 B1
Whitefield BL9 . . . . 44 F3
Appleby Lo M14 . . . . . . 98 D2
Appleby Rd SK8 . . . . . . 122 B4
Appleby Wlk 🗌 SK12 . . 133 E6
Apple Cl OL8 . . . . 66 E3
Applecross Wlk M11 . . 165 C4
Apple Dell Ave WA3 . . . 74 C1
Appledore Dr
Bolton BL2 . . . . 25 F3
Wythenshawe M23 . . . 120 D7
Appleford Ave SK4 . . . . 169 D2
Appleford Dr M8 . . . . . 156 B2
Appleford Dr M8 . . . . . 156 B2
Apple Hey WN6 . . . . 35 C8
Apple St SK14 . . . . 114 C7
Applethwaite M27. . . . . 56 B8
Appleton Ct M33 . . . . . 108 B4
Appleton Dr SK13. . . . . 116 F8
Appleton La OL5 . . . . . 137 C2
Appleton La BL5. . . . . . . 59 F1
Appleton Rd
Altrincham WA15 . . . . 119 F1
Reddish SK4 . . . . 111 D6
Appleton St WN3 . . . . . 150 B4
Apple Tree Ct M5 . . . . . 81 A2
Apple Tree Rd SK22. . . 127 B1
Apple Tree Wlk 🗌
M33 . . . . 107 C5
Apple Way M24 . . . . 65 B6
Applewood OL9 . . . . 65 E7
Appleyard Cl M27 . . . . . 80 D8
APPLEY BRIDGE 35 E8
Appley Bridge All Saints
CE Prim Sch WN6. . . . 18 C1
Appley Bridge Sta
WN6. . . . . 35 C7
Appley Cl WN6 . . . . 18 C2
Appley La N WN6 . . . . . 18 C2
Appley La S WN6, WN8 . 35 C6
Apprentice Ct 🗌 M9 . . 157 B4
April Cl OL8 . . . . 67 C4
Apsley Cl WA14 . . . . . . 119 B1
Apsley Gr
Altrincham WA14 . . . . 119 B1
Manchester M12 . . . . . 163 C2
Apsley Pl OL6 . . . . 166 A2
Apsley Rd M34 . . . . . . 100 F4
Apsley Side OL5 . . . . . . 86 C8
Apsley St SK1 . . . . 169 C1
Aquarius La M6 . . . . 81 C4
Aquarius St M15 . . . . . 163 A1
Aqueduct Bsns Pk
SK6. . . . . 125 F8
Aqueduct Rd BL2 . . . . . 148 C1
Aquinas Coll SK2 . . . . . 124 A6
Aragon Dr OL10 . . . . . . 29 C2
Aragon Way SK6 . . . . . 125 E6
Arbor Ave M19 . . . . . . 110 F6
Arbor Dr M19 . . . . 110 F7
Arbor Gr
Droylsden M43. . . . . . . 83 F3
Walkden M38. . . . . 59 E4
Arbory Ave M40 . . . . . . 65 E7
Arbory Cl WN7 . . . . 76 C5
Arbour Cl
Bury BL9 . . . . 27 E6
Salford M6. . . . . 154 C3
Arbour La WN6 . . . . 19 E1
Arbour Rd OL4 . . . . 67 E4
Arbroath St M43. . . . . . . 83 E1
Arbory Ave
Cheadle SK3 . . . . 123 A7
Rochdale OL11 . . . . . . 139 B1
Arcade St 🗌 WN1 . . . . 150 C4
Arcades The OL6 . . . . . 166 B3
Arcade The
Brinnington SK5. . . . . . 112 C5
2 Rawtenstall BB4 . . . . 2 E8
3 Stalybridge SK15. . 101 F8
Arcadia Ave M33 . . . . . 108 A1
Archer Ave BL2. . . . . . . 148 C4
Archer Gr BL2 . . . . 148 C4
Archer Pk M24 . . . . 46 F2
Archer Pl M32. . . . . 95 F3
Archer St
Boothstown M28. . . . . . 77 E7
Droylsden M11. . . . . . . 83 A2
Leigh WN7 . . . . 76 B2
Mossley OL5 . . . . 68 C2
Stockport SK5 . . . . . . 124 C5
Archie St M5 . . . . 161 A3
Arch La WN4 . . . . 72 B3
Arch St BL1 . . . . 25 A1
Archway HD7 . . . . 168 C2
Archway Wlk WA12 . . . . 89 E3
Arcid Cl SK9 . . . . 131 E1
Arcon Cl OL16 . . . . 31 E6
Arcon Dr M16 . . . . 97 E3
Arcon Pr WA14 . . . . . . 119 A6
Ardale Ave M40 . . . . . . 65 C5
Ardcombe Ave M40 . . . 163 C4
Ardeen Wlk M13. . . . . . 163 C4
Arden Ave M40 . . . . 65 C5
Arden Bldgs SK3 . . . . . 170 B4
Arden Bsns Ctr SK6. . . 112 C6

Arden Cl
Ashton-u-L OL6 . . . . . . 85 E7
Bury BL9 . . . . 44 E8
Gatley SK8 . . . . 131 C7
Glossop SK13. . . . . . . 116 A8
Arden Ct SK2 . . . . 123 D1
Ardenfield M34 . . . . . . 113 A7
Ardenfield Cl M26 . . . . . 44 B1
Ardenfield Dr M22. . . . . 121 E3
Arden Gr M40 . . . . 65 C1
Arden Hall SK6 . . . . . . 112 D7
Arden Ho OL2 . . . . 48 E4
Arden Lodge Rd M23 . . 120 E7
ARDEN PARK 112 C3
Arden Prim Sch SK6. . . 112 D3
Arden Rd SK6 . . . . 112 E7
Ardens Cl M27 . . . . 61 D2
Arden St OL9 . . . . 66 A3
Ardent Way M25 . . . . . . 63 B1
Arden Wlk
6 Sale M33 . . . . 107 C5
Stockport SK3 . . . . . . 169 E1
Arderne Pl 🗌 SK9 . . . . 137 A1
Arderne Rd WA15. . . . . 120 A8
Ardern Gr SK1. . . . . . . 170 C4
Ardern Rd M8 . . . . 63 F2
Ardingly Wlk M23 . . . . 120 D8
Ardley Rd BL6 . . . . 22 C4
Ardmore Wlk M22 . . . . 121 E2
ARDWICK 164 A3
Ardwick Grn N M12,. . . 163 C3
Ardwick Grn S M12,
M13 . . . . 163 C3
Ardwick Sta M12 . . . . . 164 A3
Arena App SK6 . . . . 39 C7
Argo St BL3 . . . . 147 A4
Argosy Dr
Eccles M30 . . . . 94 F7
Wythenshawe M90. . . 129 F7
Argus St OL8 . . . . 66 C2
Argyle Ave
Manchester M14 . . . . . 98 E4
Walkden M28 . . . . 60 C5
Whitefield M45 . . . . . . 63 A8
Argyle Cres OL10 . . . . . 29 B1
Argyle Par OL10 . . . . . . 29 A1
Argyle St
Atherton M46 . . . . 58 C2
Bury BL9 . . . . 140 C4
5 Droylsden M43 . . . . 84 A1
Hazel Grove SK7 . . . . 124 E2
Heywood OL10. . . . . . . 29 A1
Hindley WN2 . . . . 56 E5
Manchester M18 . . . . . 99 D5
Mossley OL5 . . . . 68 C1
14 Rochdale OL16. . . . 31 A4
Swinton M27 . . . . 79 E7
Wigan WN5 . . . . 54 F6
Argyll Ave M32 . . . . 96 B2
Argyll Cl
Failsworth M35 . . . . . . 84 B7
Garswood WN4 . . . . . . 72 C4
Argyll Park Rd M35. . . . 84 B7
Argyll St
Cheadle SK8 . . . . 122 F5
Oldham OL9 . . . . 65 F4
Argyll St OL6 . . . . 85 E3
Ariel Gdns WA3 . . . . . . 92 A2
Ariel Wlk 4 M32 . . . . . 90 E8
Arkendale M35 . . . . 84 C7
Arkholme M28. . . . . 78 A8
Arkholme Wlk M40 . . . . 65 D8
Arkle Ave SK9 . . . . 131 E4
Arkle Dr OL9 . . . . 65 F8
Arkley Wlk M13 . . . . . 163 B2
Ark St 🗌 M19 . . . . 99 A2
Arkwright Dr SK6 . . . . 126 A6
Arkwright Rd SK6 . . . . 126 A6
Arkwright St
Horwich BL6 . . . . 22 C2
Oldham OL9 . . . . 152 C2
Arkwright Way OL11 . . 31 A2
Arlen Ct BL2 . . . . 148 B1
Arlen Rd BL2 . . . . 148 B1
Arley Ave
Bury BL9 . . . . 27 F6
Manchester M20 . . . . 109 F5
Arley Cl
Altrincham WA14 . . . . 119 D8
Dukinfield SK16 . . . . . 101 D6
Wigan WN2 . . . . 38 B2
Arley Dr
Sale M33 . . . . 108 A2
Shaw OL2 . . . . 49 D8
Arley Gr SK3 . . . . 123 D4
Arley Ho M23 . . . . 121 A4
Arley La WN1, WN2. . . . 22 D2
Arley Mere Cl SK8 . . . . 122 F3
Arley Moss Wlk M13 . . 163 B3
Arley St
Ince-in-M WN3 . . . . . . 55 F4
Radcliffe M26 . . . . 44 B1
Arley Way
Atherton M46 . . . . 58 C2
2 Denton M34 . . . . . . 101 A1
Arlies Cl SK15 . . . . 86 A4
Arlies La SK15 . . . . 86 B4
Arlies Prim Sch SK15. . 86 A4
Arlies St SK15 . . . . 85 D4
Arlington Ave
Denton M34 . . . . 101 A2
Manchester M25 . . . . . 63 B2
Swinton M27 . . . . 79 D6
Arlington Cl
Ramsbottom BL9 . . . . . 11 C2
Royton OL2 . . . . 48 E2

Arlington Cres SK9 . . . 136 E5
Arlington Dr
Golborne WN7. . . . . . . 91 C8
Poynton SK12 . . . . . . 133 D3
Stockport SK2 . . . . . . 124 A3
Arlington Rd
Cheadle SK8 . . . . 122 C4
Stretford M32 . . . . 96 B1
Arlington St
4 Ashton-u-L OL6 . . . 166 C3
Bolton BL3 . . . . 147 C3
Manchester M8 . . . . . 155 C4
Salford, Broughton Park
M7 . . . . 158 A2
Salford M3 . . . . 158 A2
Arlington Way SK9 . . . . 136 E5
Arliss Ave M19 . . . . 111 A8
Armadale Ave M9 . . . . . 65 A4
Armadale Cl SK3 . . . . . 170 C1
Armadale Ct BL1 . . . . . . 40 E5
Armadale Rd
Bolton BL3 . . . . 40 E5
Dukinfield SK16 . . . . . 101 D7
Armdale Rise OL4 . . . . . 49 E1
Armitage Ave M38 . . . . 59 F4
Armitage CE Prim Sch
M12 . . . . 164 B2
Armitage Cl
Hyde SK14 . . . . 113 E8
Middleton M24. . . . . . . 64 D7
Oldham OL8 . . . . 66 C3
Armitage Ct M12 . . . . . 164 C2
Armitage Gr M38 . . . . . 59 F4
Armitage Ho 4 M6 . . . . 80 C3
Armitage Owen Wlk 4
M40 . . . . 83 A7
Armitage Rd WA14 . . . 119 D3
Armitage St M30 . . . . . . 79 D1
Armit Rd OL3. . . . . 68 E5
Armitstead St 5 WN2 . . 56 D4
Armour Pl 1 M9 . . . . . . 64 C2
Armoury Bank WN4 . . . 73 B3
Armoury St SK3 . . . . . 170 B4
Arm Rd OL15 . . . . 15 E4
Armstrong Hurst Cl
OL12. . . . . 15 B2
Armstrong St
Horwich BL6 . . . . 22 C2
Wigan WN2 . . . . 38 A3
Arncliffe WA14 . . . . . . 119 D2
Arncliffe Dr
5 Farnworth BL4. . . . . 42 D1
Hindley WN2 . . . . 56 C1
Arncliffe Dr M23 . . . . . 121 A3
Arncliffe Rise OL4 . . . . . 50 A4
Arncot Rd BL1 . . . . 24 F5
Arncott Cl 🗌 OL2. . . . . . 49 A4
Arndale Ctr
Manchester M4 . . . . . 159 A2
Stretford M32 . . . . 96 C1
Arne St SK2 . . . . 125 A5
Arnesby Ave M33 . . . . 108 E5
Arnesby Gr BL2. . . . . . 148 B4
Arne St SK9 . . . . 152 A1
Arnfield Dr 1 M28 . . . . 78 B6
Arnfield La SK13. . . . . . 103 F8
Arnfield Rd
Manchester M20 . . . . 110 C6
Stockport SK3 . . . . . . 170 A1
Arnold Ave
Heywood OL10. . . . . . . 46 E7
Hyde SK14 . . . . 113 F7
Arnold Cl SK16 . . . . . . 102 A7
Arnold Ct M16 . . . . 97 E1
Arnold Dr
Droylsden M43. . . . . . . 84 A1
Middleton M24. . . . . . . 47 C3
Arnold Rd
Bolton BL7 . . . . 24 F8
Hyde SK14 . . . . 113 F7
Manchester M16 . . . . . 97 E1
Arnold St
Ashton-u-L OL6 . . . . . 166 C3
Bolton BL1 . . . . 145 F8
Oldham OL1 . . . . 67 A8
Stockport SK3 . . . . . . 170 B3
Arnold Wlk 3 M34 . . . 113 A7
Arnott Cres M15 . . . . . 162 C1
Arnside Ave
Chadderton OL9 . . . . . 65 F7
Hazel Grove SK7 . . . . 124 C2
Ince-in-M WN2 . . . . . . 56 A4
Reddish SK4 . . . . 111 E6
Arnside Cl
Gatley SK8 . . . . 122 B4
High Lane SK6 . . . . . . 134 E7
Shaw OL2. . . . . 49 D7
Arnside Dr
Dukinfield SK14 . . . . . 101 C4
Rochdale OL11. . . . . . . 29 E5
Salford M6. . . . . 80 B3
Arnside Gr
Bolton BL2 . . . . 42 E8
Sale M33 . . . . 108 B6
Arnside Ho SK7
Hindley WN2 . . . . 57 A5
Wigan WN5 . . . . 54 B8
Arnside St M13 . . . . 98 E3
Arosa Ct M20. . . . . 110 C7
Arran Ave
Oldham OL8 . . . . 66 F3
Sale M33 . . . . 108 A6
Stretford M32 . . . . 96 A2
Arran Cl BL3 . . . . 146 F4
Arrandale Ct M41. . . . . . 95 D3

Arran Gdns M41.........95 C5
Arran Gr M26.........43 E5
Arran Rd SK16.........101 C7
Arran St
  12 Manchester M40.....64 F1
  Salford M7.........155 A2
Arran Wlk OL10.........29 A1
Arras Gr M43.........99 F3
Arreton Sq M14.........98 D3
Arrivals Way M90.......130 B7
Arrowfield Dr M21.......109 D7
Arrowfield Rd M21......109 D7
Arrowhill Rd M26......43 F8
Arrowscroft Ct SK14....103 D5
Arrowscroft Way
  SK14.........171 A4
Arrowsmith Ct 7 BL6....22 E1
Arrowsmith Wlk 16
  M11.........160 C1
Arrow St
  Bolton BL1.........145 B4
  Leigh WN7.........76 B3
  Salford M7.........155 A1
Arrow Trad Est M44......100 D5
Arthill La WA14.........118 B1
Arthington St OL16......31 B8
Arthog Dr WA15.........128 F8
Arthog Rd
  Altrincham WA15......128 F8
  Manchester M20......110 C3
Arthur Ave M28.........60 C5
Arthur La BL2.........26 B2
Arthur Millvoad Ct
  M3.........158 A1
Arthur Rd M16.........97 C3
Arthurs La OL3.........69 B6
Arthur St
  Bury BL8.........27 C2
  Eccles M30.........79 C1
  Farnworth BL4.........60 D8
  Heywood OL10.........29 D2
  Hindley WN2.........56 E5
  Hyde SK14.........101 C1
  Leigh WN7.........75 E4
  Little Lever BL3.........43 B3
  Prestwich M25.........62 F4
  Reddish SK5.........111 E7
  Rochdale OL12.........139 A4
  Shaw OL2.........149 B3
  Swinton M27.........79 D2
  Walkden M28.........60 E1
  Walkden M28.........60 F2
Arthur Terr 4 SK5......111 E7
Artillery Ct M13.........163 C3
Artillery Pl M22.........121 F4
Artillery St
  Bolton BL3.........145 C1
  Manchester M3.........162 B4
Artwright Cl BL1.........142 C1
Arundale BL5.........39 F2
Arundale Ave M16........97 E1
Arundale Ct SK14........102 F3
Arundale Cl M16.........97 E1
Arundale Gr SK14......102 F3
Arundale Prim Sch
  SK14.........102 F3
Arundel Ave
  Hazel Grove SK7.......133 D8
  Prestwich M45.........63 B7
  Rochdale OL11.........30 E4
  Urmston M41.........94 C1
Arundel Cl
  Altrincham WA15......120 C1
  Bolton BL1.........24 E5
  Mossley SK15.........86 F6
Arundel Dr WN7.........75 F6
Arundel Gr SK2.........124 B4
Arundel Grange SK13...116 A8
Arundel Rd SK8.........132 A6
Arundel St
  Ashton-u-L OL6.......85 E3
  Bolton BL1.........24 E5
  Glossop SK13.........104 C1
  Hindley WN2.........56 E5
  Manchester M15......162 A3
  Mossley OL5.........68 B1
  Oldham OL4.........67 C2
  Rochdale OL11.........30 E4
  Swinton M27.........61 C1
  Wigan WN5.........54 F6
Arundel Wlk OL9........152 A2
Asby Cl M24.........46 D2
Ascension Rd M7.......158 A4
Ascot Ave
  Sale M33.........107 D3
  Stretford M32.........96 F3
Ascot Cl
  Chadderton OL9.......152 C3
  Rochdale OL11.........29 E8
Ascot Dr
  Atherton M46.........58 E4
  Hazel Grove SK7......125 A2
  Urmston M41.........94 C2
Ascot Mdws BL9.........44 E8
Ascot Par M9.........110 F6
Ascot Rd
  Failsworth M40.......83 B4
  Little Lever BL3......42 F3
Ascot Wlk M6.........81 A5
Ascroft Ave WN6.......36 F3
Ascroft St
  Chadderton OL9......152 A1
  Oldham OL1.........153 C2
  Wigan WN1.........151 B3
Asgard Dr M5.........161 C4

Asgard Gr M5.........161 C4
Ash Ave
  Altrincham WA14......119 A5
  Cheadle SK8.........122 E5
  Irlam M44.........105 D5
  Newton-le-W WA12....89 C2
Ashawe Cl M38.........59 E3
Ashawe Gr M38.........59 E3
Ashawe Terr M38.......59 E3
Ashbank Ave BL3.......40 E6
Ashbee St BL1.........143 B3
Ashberry Cl SK9.......137 D8
Ashbourne Dr BL9.....11 D2
Ashbourne Ave
  Bolton BL2.........148 B2
  Cheadle SK8.........122 F6
  Hindley WN2.........56 E5
  Middleton M24.........47 C3
  Urmston M41.........94 E2
  Wigan WN2.........38 A2
Ashbourne Cl
  Leigh WN7.........57 D1
  Wardle OL12.........15 D6
Ashbourne Cres M33...108 D2
Ashbourne Ct 3
  SK13.........116 F8
Ashbourne Dr
  Ashton-u-L OL6.......85 F6
  High Lane SK6.........134 F6
Ashbourne Gdns WN2...56 F5
Ashbourne Gr
  Salford M7.........155 B3
  Whitefield M45.........44 D1
  Worsley M28.........78 E8
Ashbourne Rd
  Denton M34.........100 E2
  Eccles M30.........79 E1
  Hazel Grove SK7......133 F8
  Salford M6.........80 C5
  Stretford M32.........96 A3
Ashbourne Sq OL8......153 B1
Ashbourne St OL11.....13 E1
Ashbridge M17.........96 B6
Ashbridge Rd M35......84 B6
Ashbrook Ave M34.....100 B3
Ashbrook Cl
  Gatley SK8.........122 B1
  Reddish M34.........100 B3
  Whitefield M45.........63 B8
Ashbrook Cres OL12....15 C4
Ashbrook Farm Cl SK5...99 F2
Ashbrook Hey La OL12...15 C4
Ashbrook La 8 SK5.....99 F2
Ashbrook Rd OL4.......67 F5
Ashbrook St M11.......100 A7
Ashburn 11 OL10.......29 C2
Ashburn Ave M19.......110 F5
Ashburn Cl 7 BL6......22 D1
Ashburne Ho M14.......98 D4
Ashburner St BL1.......148 B6
Ashburn Gr SK4.........169 A3
Ashburn Rd SK4.........169 A3
Ashburton Cl SK14.....102 E2
Ashburton Rd SK3......170 B1
Ashburton Rd W M17,
  M41.........95 D2
Ashbury Cl BL3.........145 B1
Ashbury Meadow Prim
  Sch M11.........164 B4
Ashbury Pl M40.........160 B4
Ashburys Sta M12......165 A3
Ashby Ave M19.........110 E4
Ashby Cl BL3.........42 C2
Ashby Gr
  Leigh WN7.........75 C8
  Whitefield M45.........63 B7
Ashby Rd WN3.........55 B3
Ash Cl
  Appley Bridge WN6....35 D7
  Ashton-u-L OL6.......85 D5
  Mottram in L SK14....103 A4
  Rochdale OL12.........15 C4
  Stockport SK2.........124 C5
Ashcombe Dr
  Bolton BL2.........43 A6
  Radcliffe M26.........43 D5
Ashcombe Wlk 7
  M11.........160 C1
Ashcott Ave M22.......121 D4
Ashcott Cl BL6.........40 E5
Ashcroft
  6 Rochdale OL12.....15 D4
  Wilmslow SK9.........136 F5
Ashcroft Ave M6.......154 B4
Ashcroft Ct
  Irlam M44.........105 D5
  Oldham OL1.........153 C2
Ashcroft Rd WA13.....117 B4
Ashcroft St WN2.......56 E4
Ash Ct
  Manchester, Whalley Range
    M16.........97 E2
  Romiley SK6.........113 A5
  Stockport, Heaton Moor
    SK4.........168 B3
Ashdale Ave BL3.......40 E5
Ashdale Cl
  Coppull PR7.........19 D8
  Reddish SK5.........111 F5
Ashdale Cres M43.......83 F1
Ashdale Dr
  Gatley SK8.........122 B2
  Manchester M20......110 D5
Ashdale Rd
  Hindley WN2.........57 A5
  Wigan WN3.........55 A2
Ashdene
  Ashton-u-L OL6.......85 D2

Ashdene continued
  Rochdale OL12.........14 D4
Ashdene Cl
  Chadderton OL1, OL9...48 C1
  Oldham OL4.........67 F7
Ashdene Cres BL2......25 D4
Ashdene Prim Sch
  SK9.........136 F5
Ashdene Rd
  Manchester, Heaton Mersey
    M44.........110 D2
  Manchester, Withington
    M20.........110 D6
  Wilmslow SK9.........136 F5
Ashdene Rise OL1......49 D4
Ashdown Ave
  Manchester M9.........64 D4
  Romiley SK6.........113 C5
Ashdown Cl SK8.........132 A6
Ashdown Dr
  Bolton BL2.........25 C3
  Pendlebury M27.......80 A6
  Walkden M28.........78 A7
Ashdowne Lawns SK15...86 D3
Ashdown Gr M9.........64 D4
Ashdown Rd SK4.......168 C3
Ashdown Terr M9.......64 D4
Ashdown Way OL2......48 E8
Ash Dr M27.........61 C2
Ashen Bottom BB4.......1 D6
Asher St BL3.........146 C2
Ashes Cl SK15.........102 C8
Ashes Dr BL2.........42 F8
Ashes La
  Glossop SK13.........104 B2
  Milnrow OL16.........31 F7
  Oldham OL4.........67 F6
  Stalybridge SK15.....102 C8
Ashes The SK13.........104 B2
Ashfell Ct 1 M21......96 F1
Ashfield M34.........101 A5
Ashfield Ave
  Atherton M46.........58 C4
  Hindley WN2.........56 F4
Ashfield Cl
  Lymm WA13.........117 B4
  Salford M6.........154 B3
Ashfield Cres
  Billinge WN5.........71 E4
  Cheadle SK8.........122 D6
  Oldham OL4.........67 F6
Ashfield Ct M41.......95 D1
Ashfield Dr
  Aspull WN2.........38 C5
  Failsworth M40.......83 D4
Ashfield Gr
  Bolton BL1.........25 A6
  Irlam M44.........105 E6
  Marple SK6.........114 B1
  Reddish M18.........99 F4
  Stockport SK3.........123 F4
Ashfield Ho OL11.......139 C1
Ashfield House Gdns
  WN6.........36 F8
Ashfield La OL16.......31 F4
Ashfield Lo M20.......109 F2
Ashfield Park Dr WN6...36 F8
Ashfield Rd
  Adlington PR6.........21 B8
  Altrincham WA15......119 E3
  Cheadle SK8.........122 D5
  Cheadle SK8.........122 D6
  Glossop SK13.........171 C3
  Manchester M13.......98 E3
  Rochdale OL11.........139 C1
  Sale M33.........108 B5
  Stockport SK3.........123 F4
  Urmston M41.........95 D2
Ashfield Sq M43.......83 F2
Ashfield St OL8.........66 C3
Ashfield Terr M9.......35 C8
Ashfield Valley Prim Sch
  OL11.........30 E4
Ashford M33.........107 C4
Ashford Ave
  Boothstown M28.......77 F6
  Eccles M30.........95 C8
  3 Reddish SK5.......99 F2
  Swinton M27.........79 C7
Ashford Cl
  Bolton BL2.........25 E4
  Bury BL8.........27 B1
  Handforth SK9.........131 C4
Ashford Ct OL4.........49 D1
Ashford Gn 8 SK13....171 B1
Ashford Gr M28.........78 F8
Ashford Mews SK13...171 B1
Ashford Rd
  Manchester M20......110 B7
  Reddish SK4.........111 D6
  Salford M6.........154 C1
  Wilmslow SK9.........137 A4
Ashford Rise OL1......37 B4
Ashford St OL10.......28 F7
Ashford Wlk
  Bolton BL1.........143 B1
  Chadderton OL9......152 B2
Ashgate Ave M22.......121 E4
Ashgate Specialist
  Support Prim Sch
    M22.........121 F4
Ashgill Wlk 4 M9....157 B3
Ash Gr
  Altrincham, Rosehill
    WA14.........119 C1
  Altrincham WA15......119 F7
  Bolton, Harwood BL2...25 F3
  Bolton, Victory BL1...144 B4
  Bury BL8.........27 A5

Ash Gr continued
  Droylsden M43.........100 A8
  Gatley SK8.........131 B8
  Golborne WA3.........90 B8
  Handforth SK9.........131 C3
  8 Horwich BL6.......22 C1
  Littleborough OL15....15 F5
  Manchester M14.......99 E4
  Marple SK6.........125 E5
  Newhey OL16.........32 A3
  Oldham OL4.........68 A7
  Orrell WN5.........53 F6
  Prestwich M25.........63 A6
  Ramsbottom BL0.......10 F3
  Reddish SK4.........111 D5
  Royton OL2.........48 D6
  Stalybridge SK15.....85 F3
  Standish WN6.........36 F8
  Stretford M32.........108 C8
  Swinton M27.........79 D5
  Walkden M28.........60 E1
  Westhoughton BL5.....57 E7
Ashgrove OL16.........31 B1
Ash Grove Cres WN5...71 E6
Ash Hill Dr OL5.........86 E8
Ashia Cl OL16.........31 B6
Ashill Wlk M3.........162 B4
Ashington Cl
  Bolton BL1.........142 B3
  Wigan WN5.........36 B1
Ashington Dr BL8.......26 F2
Ashkirk St 4 M18.....99 D5
Ash La
  Altrincham WA15......120 C2
  Wigan WN2.........38 A2
Ashland Ave
  Ashton-in-M WN4......73 A4
  5 Wigan WN1........37 C2
Ashlands M33.........108 A5
Ashlands Ave
  Failsworth M40.......65 C1
  Swinton M27.........79 D6
  Wigan WN6.........78 A7
Ashlands Cl BL0.......1 D2
Ashlands Dr M34.......100 E6
Ashlands Rd WA15......108 A1
Ashlar Dr M12.........164 B4
Ash Lawns BL1.........144 B3
Ash Lea SK15.........86 A3
Ashlea Gr OL4.........68 B6
Ash Lea Grange M30....79 E3
Ashleigh Ave SK13....104 B2
Ashleigh Cl OL2.......48 E2
Ashleigh Dr BL1.......40 E8
Ashleigh Rd WA15......120 B8
ASHLEY.........128 E5
Ashley Ave
  Bolton BL2.........42 D8
  Manchester M16.......97 D4
  Swinton M27.........79 D6
  Urmston M41.........94 E2
Ashley CE Prim Sch
  WA15.........128 F5
Ashley Cl OL11.........30 C4
Ashley Court Dr M40,
  OL9.........65 F1
Ashley Cres M27.......79 D7
Ashley Ct
  Altrincham WA15......119 E1
  Failsworth M40.......65 F1
  Stockport SK4.........168 B4
  Swinton M27.........61 F2
Ashley Dr
  Bramhall SK7.........132 C6
  Leigh WN7.........75 C8
  Sale M33.........107 E2
  Swinton M27.........79 D6
Ashley Gdns
  High Lane SK6........134 D8
  Hyde SK14.........167 B1
Ashley Gr 8 BL4......60 C8
Ashley Heath........128 E8
Ashley La M9.........157 C4
Ashley Mews
  3 Hyde SK14.......167 B1
  Whitefield M45.......63 B7
Ashleymill La WA14....128 D7
Ashley Mill La N
  WA14.........128 E8
Ashley Rd
  Altrincham WA14,
    WA15.........119 E2
  Ashley, Ashley Heath WA14,
    WA15.........128 E7
  Ashley WA14, WA15,
    WA16.........128 C4
  Droylsden M43.........83 E2
  Handforth SK9.........131 B1
  Hindley WN2.........57 B3
  Stockport SK2.........124 C8
Ashley St
  Hyde SK14.........167 B4
  Manchester M4.........159 B3
  Oldham OL8.........67 A8
  Salford M6.........154 B2
Ashley Sta WA15......128 E5
Ashleys The SK4.......168 B3
Ashling Ct M29.........59 D1
Ash Lo SK12.........133 D4
Ashlor St BL9.........140 B1
Ashlyn Gr M14.........110 D8
Ashlynne OL6.........166 C3
Ashmeade WA15.......119 F7
Ashmill Wlk M9.......156 C2
Ashmond 16 OL4......67 F6
Ashmond Rd 12 OL4...67 F6
Ashmoor Rd M22.......121 E1
Ashmoor Wlk M22......121 E1

Ashmore Ave SK3......122 F7
Ashmore St M29.......77 D8
Ashmount Dr OL12......14 F2
Ashness Cl BL6.........21 F3
Ashness Dr
  Bolton BL2.........25 E1
  Bramhall SK7.........132 E8
  Middleton M24.........46 D3
Ashness Gr BL2.........25 E1
Ashness Pl BL2.........25 E1
Ashover Ave M12.......164 C2
Ashover Cl 8 BL1....24 F6
Ashover Ct M32.......164 C2
Ashover St M32.........96 E3
Ash Rd
  Coppull PR7.........19 E8
  Droylsden M43.........83 F2
  Hollinfare WA3.........105 A2
  Kearsley BL4.........60 F5
  Partington M31.......105 D3
  Poynton SK12.........133 F3
  Reddish M34.........99 F3
Ashridge Cl BL6.......40 C6
Ashridge Dr
  Dukinfield SK16.......101 B7
  Eccles M30.........95 C8
Ashridge Way WN5....36 B1
Ash Sq OL4.........67 D8
Ash St
  Bolton BL2.........148 A3
  Bury BL9.........141 A2
  Denton M34.........100 D7
  Failsworth M35.......83 E8
  Golborne WA3.........74 B2
  Hazel Grove SK7......124 D3
  Heywood OL16.........29 B3
  Manchester M9.........157 A3
  Middleton M24.........65 C8
  Oldham OL4.........67 B6
  Rochdale OL11.........30 C2
  Salford M6.........154 C2
  2 Tyldesley M29......59 C3
Ashstead Rd M33......108 C1
Ashton Ave M14.......119 E6
Ashton Cres OL9.......66 A2
ASHTON CROSS.........72 D2
Ashton Ct
  Denton M34.........100 F6
  Sale M33.........107 E4
Ashton Field Dr M28...60 C4
Ashton Gallery 6
  WN1.........150 C4
Ashton Gdns
  1 Glossop SK13.....116 C7
  Rochdale OL11.........139 B1
Ashton Grange Ind Est
  WN4.........73 B6
Ashton Heath WN4.....73 C2
Ashton Hill La M43....100 A8
Ashton Ho
  Hyde SK14.........167 B4
  Manchester M15......162 B4
ASHTON-IN-MAKERFIELD
  ....73 C5
Ashton La
  Middleton M24.........65 A8
  Sale M33.........107 F6
ASHTON MOSS.........84 E2
Ashton New Rd
  Droylsden M11, M43...83 C1
  Manchester M12.......160 C1
Ashton Old Rd
  Manchester, Beswick M11,
    M12.........164 B4
  Manchester, Openshaw
    M11.........99 D7
Ashton on Mersey Sch
  M33.........107 F4
Ashton Pl SK7.........124 F1
Ashton Rd
  Brinnington SK6.......112 C6
  Carrington M31.......106 E3
  Denton M34.........100 C5
  Droylsden M43.........84 B1
  Dukinfield SK14.......101 E5
  Failsworth M35.......84 C2
  Golborne WA3.........74 A2
  Newton-le-W WA12....89 C5
  Oldham OL6, OL7......66 F3
  Windy Arbour WN5....72 B8
  Ashton Rd E M35.....83 F7
  Ashton Ret Pk OL6....166 B3
Ashton St
  Bolton BL3.........146 B4
  Chadderton OL9.......66 A3
  Dukinfield SK16.......101 A7
  Glossop SK13.........116 C7
  4 Heywood OL10.....29 C3
  Little Lever BL3......43 B3
  Rochdale OL11.........139 B1
  Romiley SK6.........113 C6
  Wigan WN1.........151 C4
ASHTON-UNDER-LYNE
  ....166 A3
Ashton-under-Lyne Sixth
  Form Coll OL6.......85 E3
Ashton-under-Lyne Sta
  ....166 B3
ASHTON UPON MERSEY
  ....107 F5
Ashton West End Prim Sch
  OL7.........84 C2
Ash Tree Ave M43......83 F2
Ash Tree Dr SK16......101 F7

Ash Tree Rd	
Dukinfield SK14	102 B5
Manchester M8	64 A1
Ashurst Ave M11	83 B2
Ashurst Cl	
Bolton BL2	25 F3
Hyde SK14	102 A1
Ashurst Dr SK3,SK8	123 B5
Ashurst Gdns OL6	166 B4
Ashurst Gr M26	44 B1
Ashurst Rd	
Shevington Moor WN6	19 B2
Wythenshawe M22	121 F3
Ash View OL6	166 C4
Ashville Terr M40	64 F1
Ashway OL6	166 A3
Ashway Clough N	
SK2,	124 D5
Ashway Clough S	
SK2,	124 D5
Ashwell Ave WA3	74 D1
Ashwell Mews BL2	25 C3
Ashwell Rd M23	121 B7
Ashwell St ❺ BL2	25 B3
Ashwin Wlk ❽ M8	155 C2
Ash Wlk	
Chadderton OL9	152 B4
Middleton M24	64 F6
Sale M33	107 D5
Ashwood	
Altrincham WA14	128 B8
Chadderton OL9	65 E7
Glossop SK13	115 F8
Kearsley M26	61 B7
Ashwood Ave	
Abram Brow WN2	74 C7
Ashton-in-M WN4	73 A2
Golborne WA3	90 D8
Manchester M20	109 E4
Ramsbottom BL0	11 D7
Reddish M34	100 B3
Sale M33	108 A3
Walkden M28	60 C5
Ashwood Cres SK6	125 F7
Ashwood Ct M20	109 E5
Ashwood Dr	
Bury BL8	27 B6
Littleborough OL15	15 F5
Royton OL2	48 C5
Ashwood Rd SK12	135 D6
Ashworth Ave	
Denton M34	100 F7
Little Lever BL3	43 C3
Urmston M41	94 E2
Ashworth Cl	
Altrincham WA14	119 B1
Littleborough OL15	16 A7
Oldham OL9	66 C4
Royton OL2	48 F4
Ashworth Ct	
❶ Radcliffe M26	44 C4
Shaw OL2,	149 B2
Ashworth Gdns OL3	69 B5
Ashworth La	
Bolton BL1	25 A5
Mottram in L SK14	103 A3
Ashworth Rd OL10,	
OL11,	13 A1
Ashworth St	
Aspull WN2	38 E4
❸ Bacup OL13	3 D8
Bury BL8	27 C3
Denton M34	100 E4
Failsworth M35	83 D6
Farnworth BL4	60 C8
Heywood OL10	46 E8
Oldham OL1	153 C2
Radcliffe M26	44 C4
❶❶ Rawtenstall BB4	2 F8
Rochdale OL12	139 B4
Ashworth Terr	
❷ Bacup OL13	3 B8
Bolton BL2	25 E4
Ashworth View M34	100 F7
Ashworth Way ❽	
SK1	102 F2
Asia Ho M1	163 A4
Asia St ❸ BL3	42 A3
Askern Ave M22	121 D3
Askett Cl M40	83 D6
Askhigg Cl M46	76 A8
Askrigg Wlk ❽ M13	98 F4
Askwith Rd WN2	56 F3
Aspell Cl M24	64 F8
Aspen Cl	
Altrincham WA15	120 E5
Stockport SK4	168 A1
Westhoughton BL5	39 F2
Aspen Gdns OL12	14 A1
Aspen Gn M34	101 A2
Aspenshaw Rd SK22	127 E3
Aspens The SK8	122 A6
Aspen Way SK6	132 D6
Aspenwood M44	73 A2
Aspen Wood SK14	167 C3
Aspenwood Cl SK6	125 E7
Aspenwood Dr	
Chadderton OL9	65 E7
Manchester M9	64 D2
Sale M33	107 C4
Aspinall Cl	
Horwich BL6	22 D1
Walkden M28	59 F3
Aspinall Cres M28	59 F2
Aspinall Ct WN5	65 C7
Aspinall Gr ❶❷ M28	59 F3
Aspinall Rd WN6	19 B1

Aspinall St	
Heywood OL10	29 E2
Horwich BL6	22 D1
Manchester M41	98 C3
❺ Middleton M24	65 C7
❻ Platt Bridge WN2	56 A2
Aspinall Way BL6	22 C1
Aspinal Prim Sch M18	99 E3
Aspin La M4	159 A3
Aspland Rd SK14	113 F8
Aspul Ct WN7	75 C1
ASPULL	38 D6
Aspull Arc ❼ WN1	150 C4
Aspull Church Prim Sch	
WN2	38 C4
Aspull Comm WN7	75 C1
ASPULL COMMON	75 C1
Aspull St OL4	67 C5
Asquith Ave SK16	101 C6
Asquith Rd M19	110 F6
Asquith St SK5	99 F1
Assheton Ave M34	84 C1
Assheton Cl	
Ashton-u-L OL6	166 B3
Newton-le-W WA12	89 B4
Assheton Cres M40	83 D4
Assheton Ho OL6	166 B3
Assheton Rd	
Failsworth M40	83 D4
Shaw OL2,	48 F7
Assheton St	
❺ Middleton M24	47 A1
❾ Middleton M24	47 A2
Assheton Way M24	65 A8
Assisi Gdns M12	165 B2
Assumption Rd M24	46 D3
Astan Ave M43	83 D2
Astbury Ave	
Droylsden M34	84 D1
Manchester M21	109 C4
Astbury Cl	
❷ Altrincham WA15	119 E6
Bury BL9	45 A8
Golborne WA3	91 B8
Oldham OL4	48 E1
Astbury Cres SK3	170 A2
Astbury St M26	44 B1
Astbury Wlk ❷ SK8	123 A5
Aster Ave BL4	42 A1
Aster Ho OL1	48 E1
Aster St OL1	48 E1
Aster Wlk M31	105 F2
ASTLEY	77 C5
ASTLEY BRIDGE	143 C4
Astley Cl OL2	48 F7
Astley Ct M44	105 E8
Astley Gdns SK16	101 B8
Astley Gr SK15	85 F3
ASTLEY GREEN	77 C4
Astley Green Colliery	
Mus *,M29	77 C4
Astley Hall Dr	
Ramsbottom BL0	11 C4
Tyldesley M29	77 B6
Astley House Bsns Ctr ❶❻	
M29	59 A1
Astley La BL1	143 B3
Astley Rd	
Bolton BL2	25 E5
Irlam M44	93 C3
Stalybridge SK15	85 F2
Astley Sports Coll & Com	
High Sch SK16	101 E6
Astley St	
Bolton BL1	143 B2
Droylsden M11	83 C1
Dukinfield SK16	101 A8
Leigh WN7	76 B4
Stalybridge SK15	102 A8
Stockport SK4	169 B1
Tyldesley M29	77 A7
Astley Terr ❼ SK16	166 C1
Aston Ave M14	98 A2
Aston Bldgs BB4	2 F7
Aston Cl SK3	123 C6
Aston Gdns ❹ BL4	42 D1
Aston Gr M29	59 C1
Aston Ho OL1	48 E1
Aston Way ❶❸ SK9	131 D5
Astor Rd	
Manchester M19	110 E7
Salford M50	80 C1
Astra Bsns Pk M17	95 F8
Astra Ind Ctr OL11	30 C3
Atcham Gr M9	64 B6
Athenaeum Art Gall The *	
M1	163 A4
Athenian Gdns ❶❷ M7	81 C5
Athens Dr M28	60 C2
Athens St SK1	124 A8
Athens Way OL4	48 E1
Atherfield BL2	25 E4
Atherfield Cl ❸ M18	99 F6
Atherleigh Way WN7	75 F7
Atherley Gr WN6,	65 F2
Atherstone ❶❾ OL12	139 C4
Atherstone Ave M8	64 A2
Atherstone Cl BL8	27 C4
ATHERTON	81 B1
Atherton Ave M14	103 A4
Atherton Bsns Ctr M46	58 C4
Atherton Cl M35	84 B5
Atherton Ct SK14	103 A4
Atherton Ho M46	58 D4
Atherton La	
Atherton WN2	56 D5
Atherton St ❸ WN1	150 C4

Atherton St	
Adlington PR7	21 A6
Bacup OL13	3 C8
Bickershaw WN2	74 E8
Eccles M30	79 B1
Manchester M3	158 B1
Oldham, County End OL4	67 F5
❾ Oldham, County End	
OL4	67 F6
Oldham, Salem OL4	67 C5
Stockport SK3	170 A4
❼ Wigan WN5	54 F6
Atherton Sta M46	58 E4
Atherton Way	
Bacup OL13	3 B8
❷ Eccles M30	79 B1
Athlone Ave	
Bolton BL1	24 D5
Bury BL9	140 C4
Cheadle SK8	123 C5
Manchester M40	83 A8
Athol Cres WN2	57 B3
Athole St M5,M6	154 C1
Athol Gr M32	96 A2
Atholl Cl BL3	40 B1
Atholl Dr OL10	46 A8
Atholl Gr WN3	55 A3
Athol Rd	
Bramhall SK7	132 D5
Manchester M16	109 E8
Athol St	
Ashton-u-L OL6	166 C3
Eccles M30	79 C1
Ramsbottom BL0	138 C3
Reddish M18	99 E3
Rochdale OL11	139 F6
Stockport SK4	169 A3
Athos Wlk ❾ M40	65 C2
Atkinson Av BL3	42 B3
Atkinson Ho M33	108 B5
Atkinson Rd	
Sale M33	108 A5
Urmston M41	95 D2
Atkinson St	
Abram WN2	74 B8
Manchester M3	158 B1
Oldham OL9	153 A4
❷ Rochdale OL11	30 C2
Stockport SK1	124 A7
Atkin St M28	60 D2
Atlanta Ave WN7	130 A8
Atlantic Bsns Ctr	
WA14	119 C7
Atlantic St M14	99 A2
Atlantic Wlk ❶❸ M11	160 C1
Atlas Fold ❶❺ BL8	27 C3
Atlas St	
Ashton-u-L OL7	85 A5
Dukinfield SK16	101 D8
Oldham OL8	153 B2
Atlow Dr M23	121 B5
Atrium The M45	62 F7
Attenbury's La WA14	119 E8
Attenbury's Pk Est	
WA14	119 E8
Attercliffe Rd M21	109 A7
Attewell St M11	111 A1
Attingham Wlk	
Denton M34	100 E1
Wigan WN3	54 A8
Attleboro Rd M40	83 A7
Attlee Ave WA3	92 B4
Attlee Way M12	160 B1
Attock Cl OL9	152 B1
Attwood Rd WA15	128 C5
Attwood St M12	99 A3
Atwood Rd M20	110 C3
Atwood St M1	163 A4
Auberge Ho SK2	124 A6
Auberson Rd BL3	147 A3
Aubrey Rd M14	110 E7
Aubrey St	
Rochdale OL11	139 C1
Salford M5	161 A3
Auburn Ave	
Hyde SK14	167 B1
Romiley SK6	112 F4
Auburn Dr M41	95 E1
Auburn Rd	
Denton M34	100 C2
Manchester M16	97 B4
Auburn St	
Bolton BL3	147 A4
Manchester M1	159 B1
Manchester M1	163 B4
Auckland Dr M6	81 A5
Auckland Rd M19	110 E6
Audax Wlk M40	83 B4
Auden Cl M11	111 A2
Auden Ct M11	83 D1
AUDENSHAW	100 C4
Audenshaw Prim Sch	
M34	100 D7
Audenshaw Rd	
Ashton-u-L M34	100 B8
Denton M34	100 C6
Audenshaw Sch M34	100 E6
Audlem Cl M40	160 A2
Audlem Wlk ❻ SK8	123 A5
Audley Ave ❸ M32	96 A2
Audley Rd M19	99 B2
Audley St	
Ashton-u-L OL6	85 E2
Mossley, Bottoms OL5	86 D8
Mossley OL5	68 D1

Audlum Ct BL9	141 A2
Audrey Ave M18	99 E5
Audrey St M9	157 C3
Aughton Cl WN5	71 E4
Aughton St WN2	56 D4
Augusta Cl OL12	14 E2
Augusta St OL12	14 E1
Augustine Webster Cl	
M9	157 B4
Augustus St	
❸ Bolton BL3	42 A4
Manchester M3,M8	159 A4
Augustus Way M15	97 E4
Auriga Wlk M7	81 C3
Austell Rd M22	121 D1
Austen Ave BL9	44 F6
Austen Rd M30	79 D1
Austen Wlk OL1	49 E4
Auster Cl M14	110 A8
Austin Ave WN4	72 E4
Austin Ct M20	110 C4
Austin Dr M20	110 C4
Austin Gr M19	110 E4
Austin's La BL6	22 F1
Austin St WN7	75 D5
Autumn St M13	98 C4
Avallon Cl BL8	26 F7
Avalon Dr M20	122 C8
Avalon Pk OL4	67 D6
Avebury Cl	
Golborne WA3	90 E8
Horwich BL6	22 F1
Salford M7	155 C2
Avebury Rd M23	121 A5
Avenham Cl M15	162 B1
Avening Wlk ❼ M22	121 C2
Avens Rd M31	105 F3
Avenue St	
Bolton BL1	143 A1
Stockport SK1	169 C2
Avenue The	
Adlington PR6	21 A8
Alderley Edge SK9	137 A1
Altrincham WA15	128 F8
Bolton BL2	148 B3
Bury BL9	27 F5
Eccles M30	79 D1
Gatley SK8	122 A1
Glossop SK13	104 A4
Leigh WN7	76 A6
Newton-le-W WA12	89 D4
Orrell WN5	53 D3
Romiley SK6	112 D4
Sale M33	107 E3
Salford M7	81 C5
Shaw OL2,	149 A2
Urmston M41	94 E2
Westhoughton BL5	39 F1
Wigan, Standish Lower	
Ground WN6	36 E4
Wigan, Swinley WN1	37 D2
Worsley M28	78 B3
Worsley M28	78 D7
Avenue Works M17	96 C6
Averham Cl WN4	73 B2
Averhill M28	44 B8
Averill St M40	83 D5
Averon Rise OL1	49 D4
Avery Trad Est SK5	99 E3
Aveson Ave M21	109 B6
Avian Cl M30	94 F7
Avian Dr M14	110 B8
Aviary Rd M28	78 F6
Aviary The *,M28	79 A6
Aviemore Cl	
Newton-le-W WA12	89 C4
Ramsbottom BL0	11 A2
Avis St OL2	149 B3
Avocado Ct M17	96 C5
Avocet Cl	
Leigh WN7	76 A6
Newton-le-W WA12	89 C4
Avocet Dr	
Altrincham WA14	119 B8
Irlam M44	94 A4
Avon ❶❶ OL10	29 C2
Avon Bank ❶ SK6	112 F3
Avonbrook Dr OL9	65 F2
Avon Cl	
Marple SK6	125 E5
Milnrow OL16	32 A6
Walkden M28	60 B6
Avoncliff Cl BL1	143 A3
Avoncourt Dr M20	110 A4
Avon Ct S M15	162 A2
Avondale M27	62 A2
Avondale Ave	
Bury BL9	140 C4
Hazel Grove SK7	124 F3
Avondale Cres ❷ M41	95 C3
Avondale Ct OL11	47 D7
Avondale Dr	
Ramsbottom BL0	10 F2
Salford M6	80 B5
Tyldesley M29	77 D3
Avondale High Sch	
SK3	123 B7
Avondale Lo M33	123 B7
Avondale Rd	

Avondale St	
Bolton BL1	142 C1
Manchester M8	156 A3
Oldham OL8	66 F4
Standish WN6	19 E2
Avon Dr BL9	28 A8
Avon Gdns M19	111 A6
Avonhead Cl BL6	21 F3
Avonlea Dr M19	110 E6
Avonlea Rd	
Droylsden M43	83 E2
Sale M33	107 D1
Avonleigh Gdns ❼	
OL9	49 C1
Avon Rd	
Altrincham WA15	128 E8
Ashton-in-M WN4	73 E5
Billinge WN5	71 D3
Chadderton OL9	65 F8
Culcheth WA3	92 A2
Gatley SK8	131 C7
Heywood OL10	29 A2
Kearsley BL4	61 B5
Manchester M19	111 A6
Shaw OL2,	149 B4
Tyldesley M29	77 C7
Wigan WN5	54 C7
Avon St	
Bolton BL1	142 B1
Leigh WN7	76 B4
Oldham OL8	66 F4
Stockport SK3	170 B3
Avril Cl SK5	111 F8
Avril Ct WN3	55 E4
Avro Cl M14	98 B1
Avro Ct M24	65 D8
Avroe Rd M90	94 F7
Avro Way M90	129 F7
Awburn Rd SK14	102 E1
Axbridge Wlk M40	160 A2
Axelholme Ct BL6	21 F3
Axford Cl M7	155 C2
Axminster Wlk SK7	132 E7
Axon Sq M16	97 F4
Aycliffe Ave M21	109 D5
Aycliffe Gr M13	98 E3
Aye Bridge Rd WA3	74 85
Aylesbury Ave	
Denton M34	100 F1
Urmston M41	95 E3
Aylesbury Cl M5	81 A1
Aylesbury Cres WN2	57 C2
Aylesbury Gr M24	65 C7
Aylesbury Rd M24	97 C1
Aylesby Ave M18	99 B4
Aylesford Rd M14	98 D3
Aylesford Wlk BL1	143 B1
Aylestone Wlk ❶❹ M40	83 A7
Aylsham Cl M29	112 F4
Aylsham Mews M27	79 C5
Aylwin Dr M33	108 C3
Ayr Ave OL8	66 F3
Ayr Cl SK7	125 A2
Ayrefield Gr WN6	35 D6
Ayrefield Rd WN8	35 C4
Ayres Rd M16	97 C4
Ayr Gr OL10	29 A1
Ayrshire Rd M7	81 B6
Ayr St BL2	25 C1
Ayrton Gr M38	60 A5
Aysgarth Ave	
Altrincham WA14	122 C6
Droylsden M18	99 E5
Romiley SK6	113 D4
Aysgarth Cl M33	107 D3
Ayshford Cl WA14	119 B6
Ayton Gr M14	98 E4
Aytoun St M1	159 B1
Aytoun St M1	159 B1
Azalea Ave M18	99 D6

B	
Babbacombe Gr M9	64 B5
Babbacombe Rd SK2	124 C6
Babylon La PR6,	21 B8
Back Abingdon Rd BL2	25 C1
Back Acton St M1	163 B4
Back Adrian Rd BL1	142 C3
Back Adrian Rd E ❻	
BL1	142 C3
Back Ainscow St BL1	145 B4
Back Ainsworth La	
BL2,	25 C1
Back Ainsworth La E ❻	
BL2,	25 C1
Back Ainsworth Rd N	
Bury BL8	27 B2
Back Ainsworth Rd S ❶	
BL8	27 C2
Back Ainsworth St	
❷ Bolton BL1	142 C3
Back Albert St BL9	141 A2
Back Albion PI BL9	140 C4
Back Alder St BL3	147 C3
BL2,	25 C1
Back Alexander Rd	
BL3,	146 C4
Back Alexandra St	
BL3,	146 C4
Back Alfred St ❶❷ BL3	42 A4

Back Alice St
[10] Bolton BL3 . . . . 144 C1
[6] Little Lever BL3 . . . . . . 43 B3
Back Alicia St BL3 . . . . 42 D5
Back All Saints' St [13]
BL1. . . . . 145 C4
Back Alston St BL3 . . . . 147 B3
Back America Row
BL1. . . . . 142 C3
Back Andrew St N [4]
BL9. . . . . 141 A2
Back Andrew St BL9. . . . . . 141 A2
Back Anglia Gr BL3 . . . . 145 A2
Back Annis Rd [4] BL3. . . . . 146 B4
Back Anson St BL3 . . . . 143 C3
Back Apple Terr BL1 . . . . . . 143 A2
Back Argo St BL3 . . . . 147 A4
Back Argyle St [8] BL9 . . . . . 27 F5
Back Arlington St
BL3. . . . . 147 C3
Back Arnold St BL1 . . . . 142 C2
Back Arnold Terr BL1 . . . . . . 23 F1
Back Ashbee St
BL3. . . . . 143 B3
Back Ashford Wlk
BL1. . . . . 143 B1
Back Ashley St M4. . . . . 159 B3
Back Ash St
[2] Bury BL9. . . . . 141 A2
Back Ashton St BL3 . . . . . . 146 B4
Back Ashworth La BL1 . . . . . 24 F5
Back Ashworth St [10]
BL8. . . . . 27 C3
Back Astley St BL1. . . . . 143 B2
Back Auburn St [14]
BL3. . . . . 147 A4
Back Augustus St W [4]
BL3. . . . . 42 A4
Back Augustus St [2]
BL3. . . . . 42 A4
Back Avenue St [3]
BL3. . . . . 145 A4
Back Avondale St
BL1. . . . . 142 C1
Back Baldwin St N
BL3. . . . . 143 B3
Back Baldwin St BL3. . . . . . . 145 B1
Back Banbury St BL2 . . . . . . 25 C1
Back Bankfield St
BL3. . . . . 144 C1
Back Bank St M8 . . . . 159 A4
Back Bantry St BL3 . . . . 147 B1
Back Barbara St BL3 . . . . . . 147 A4
Back Bark St BL1. . . . . 145 B3
Back Bashall St BL1 . . . . 144 C4
Back Battenberg Rd [1]
BL3. . . . . 147 A4
Back Baxendale St [1]
BL1. . . . . 143 B4
Back Bayley St BL1 . . . . 145 A4
Back Baythorpe St N [4]
BL1. . . . . 143 C3
Back Baythorpe St
BL1. . . . . 143 C2
Back Beaconsfield St
BL1. . . . . 145 A2
Back Beaconsfield Terr [19]
BL2. . . . . 25 B1
Back Beatrice Rd [9]
BL1. . . . . 142 C1
Back Bedford St [4]
BL1. . . . . 145 A4
Back Beech St BL1 . . . . 143 C2
Back Beechwood St [5]
BL3. . . . . 147 C3
Back Belbeck St [3]
BL8. . . . . 27 C2
Back Bell La
Bury BL9 . . . . 141 A3
Bury BL9 . . . . 141 B3
Back Belmont Rd [1]
BL1. . . . . 24 E5
Back Belmont Rd E [5]
BL3. . . . . 143 B3
Back Bennett's La
BL1. . . . . 142 C2
Back Bennett's La E
BL1. . . . . 142 C2
Back Benson St BL9 . . . . 141 A1
Back Bentinck St [4]
BL3. . . . . 143 B3
Back Bentley St BL2 . . . . . . 148 C1
Back Bertrand Rd
BL1. . . . . 144 C3
Back Beverley Rd
BL1. . . . . 144 C4
Back Birch St BL9 . . . . 140 C3
Back Birley St [7] BL1 . . . . . 143 B4
Back Blackadm St
BL1. . . . . 145 B3
Back Blackburn Rd
BL1. . . . . 143 C1
Back Blackburn Rd E
BL7. . . . . 8 D3
Back Blackburn Rd W
Bolton BL7. . . . . 8 D3
Bolton, Dunscar BL7. . . . . 24 E8
Bolton, Halliwell BL1 . . . . 143 B3
[4] Bolton, Sharples BL1 . . 24 E5
[5] Bolton, Sharples
BL1. . . . . 143 B4
Back Blackburn St [6]
BL1. . . . . 143 C1

Back Blackwood St
BL3. . . . . 42 A4
Back Bolton Rd N BL8 . . . . . 27 C1
Back Bolton Rd S
Bury BL8 . . . . 27 C1
Bury BL8 . . . . 27 C2
Back Bolton St S [1]
BL9. . . . . 140 B2
Back Bolton St [9]
BL1. . . . . 143 C2
Back Bond St W BL1 . . . . . . 141 A2
Back Boundary St [12]
BL1. . . . . 143 A2
Back Bowen St BL1. . . . . . . 142 B1
Back Bowness Rd
BL3. . . . . 147 A4
Back Bradford Rd
Bolton BL3. . . . . 42 A3
[2] Bolton BL3 . . . . 42 A4
Back Bradford Rd W [1]
BL3. . . . . 42 A3
Back Bradford St [3]
BL3. . . . . 148 B3
Back Bradford St S [3]
BL3. . . . . 148 A2
Back Bradford St W
Bolton BL2. . . . . 148 A3
Bolton BL2. . . . . 148 B3
Back Bradshaw Brow E
BL2. . . . . 25 C4
Back Bradshaw Brow W
BL2. . . . . 25 C4
Back Bradshawgate [1]
BL1. . . . . 145 C2
Back Bradshaw Rd E
BL2. . . . . 25 D5
Back Bradshaw St [7]
OL16. . . . . 31 A8
Back Brandon St N
BL3. . . . . 147 A4
Back Brandon St W [4]
BL3. . . . . 147 A4
Back Brandon St [5]
BL3. . . . . 147 A4
Back Brandwood St
BL3. . . . . 146 C4
Back Bride St BL1 . . . . 143 B2
Back Bridgeman St
BL3. . . . . 147 B4
Back Bridge St
[1] Bolton BL1 . . . . 145 C4
Manchester M3 . . . . 158 C1
New Mills SK22 . . . . 127 C1
Newton-le-W WA12 . . . . . . 89 B3
Ramsbottom BL0 . . . . 138 C2
Back Brierley St S BL0 . . . . . 44 E8
Back Brierley St BL0 . . . . . . 44 E8
Back Brindle St BL1 . . . . . . 144 C3
Back Brindley St [2]
BL1. . . . . 143 C4
Back Brink's Pl BL1 . . . . 145 B3
Back Bristol Ave BL2 . . . . . . 25 C1
Back Bristol St BL3 . . . . 145 A1
Back Broach St BL3. . . . . . . 147 B4
Back Broad o' th' La [6]
BL1. . . . . 24 E5
Back Broad St [2] BL9 . . . . 140 B2
Back Bromwich St
BL2. . . . . 148 B2
Back Brookfield St
BL3. . . . . 148 B3
Back Brook St N BL9 . . . . . 141 A4
Back Broom St BL2 . . . . 148 A3
Back Brow WN8 . . . . 53 C7
Back Burnaby St BL3 . . . . . 145 A1
Back Burnham Ave
BL2. . . . . 142 A1
Back Bury New Rd
BL2. . . . . 148 A3
Back Bury New Rd E
BL2. . . . . 148 B3
Back Bury Old Rd [2]
BL2. . . . . 148 A3
Back Bury Rd BL2 . . . . 42 E7
Back Bury Rd E BL2 . . . . . . 148 C3
Back Bury Rd S
Bolton, Breightmet BL2 . . . 42 F7
[3] Bolton, Tonge Fold
BL2. . . . . 148 B3
Bolton, Tonge Fold BL2 . . 148 C3
Back Bushell St BL3 . . . . . . 146 B4
Back Byrom St [9]
BL8. . . . . 27 B4
Back Byrom St N [7] BL8 . . . 27 B4
Back Calder Rd BL3 . . . . . . 147 B3
Back Caledonia St
BL3. . . . . 144 C1
Back Calvert Rd [6]
BL3. . . . . 147 C3
Back Cambridge St
OL7. . . . . 84 F1
Back Camp St M7 . . . . 155 A1
Back Camrose Gdns [6]
BL1. . . . . 143 B1
Back Canada St S
BL1. . . . . 142 C2
Back Canada St
[4] Bolton BL1 . . . . 142 C2
Horwich BL6 . . . . 22 B3
Back Canning St BL9 . . . . . 140 C4
Back Cardwell St [33]
BL3. . . . . 147 B3
Back Carl St [19] BL1. . . . . 143 A4
Back Carter St [18] BL3. . . . 42 A4

Back Castle St
[4] Bolton BL2 . . . . 148 A3
Bolton BL2. . . . . 148 B2
Back Cateaton St [1]
BL1. . . . . 140 C3
Back Cecilia St BL3 . . . . 42 A4
Back Cecil St BL2 . . . . 148 B3
Back Cedar St N BL9 . . . . . 141 B3
Back Cedar St BL9 . . . . 141 B3
Back Cemetery Rd E
BL2. . . . . 148 B3
Back Cemetery Terr [1]
OL13. . . . . 3 D8
Back Cestrian St [1]
BL3. . . . . 147 C3
Back Chalfont St BL1 . . . . . 143 C2
Back Chapel St
[2] Eccles M30. . . . . 79 F2
Hazel Grove SK7 . . . . 124 E3
Horwich BL6 . . . . 22 C3
Wardle OL12 . . . . 15 C7
Back Chapman St [5]
BL3. . . . . 142 B1
Back Charles Holden St
BL1. . . . . 145 A2
Back Chaucer St [2]
BL1. . . . . 143 A2
Back Cheapside BL1 . . . . . . 145 C3
Back Chesham Rd N [6]
BL9. . . . . 141 A4
Back Chesham Rd S [7]
BL9. . . . . 141 A4
Back Chester St BL1 . . . . . . 141 A4
Back China La M1 . . . . 159 B1
Back Chorley New Rd
Bolton, Gilnow Park
BL1. . . . . 145 A4
Bolton, Victory BL1 . . . . . 144 C3
Back Chorley New Rd N
Bolton BL1. . . . . 144 B3
Bolton BL1. . . . . 144 C3
Back Chorley Old Rd
BL1. . . . . 23 F1
Back Chorley Old Rd N
Bolton, Cope Bank
BL1. . . . . 142 C1
Bolton, Doffcocker BL1 . . 142 A1
[2] Bolton, Doffcocker
BL1. . . . . 142 B1
[4] Bolton, Victory BL1 . . . 144 C4
Back Chorley Old Rd S
Bolton, Doffcocker
BL1. . . . . 142 A1
Bolton, Doffcocker BL1 . . 142 B1
Bolton, Victory BL1 . . . . . 144 C4
Doffcocker BL1 . . . . 23 F1
Back Chorley St E [10]
BL1. . . . . 145 B4
Back Chorley St BL1 . . . . . . 145 B3
Back Church Ave BL3 . . . . . 146 C4
Back Church Rd
[11] Bolton, Cope Bank
BL1. . . . . 142 C2
Bolton, Doffcocker BL1 . . 142 A2
Back Church Rd N
BL1. . . . . 142 B2
[7] Bolton BL1 . . . . 142 B2
Back Church St
Bolton BL1. . . . . 145 B4
Little Lever BL3 . . . . 43 A3
Back Clarendon Rd [8]
BL2. . . . . 148 C3
Back Clarke St [13]
BL3. . . . . 144 C4
Back Clay St E BL7 . . . . 25 A7
Back Clay St W BL7. . . . . . . 25 A7
Back Clegg's Bldgs [11]
BL1. . . . . 145 B4
Back Clegg St [2] BL1 . . . . 148 C3
Back Clifton St [3]
BL9. . . . . 140 C4
Back Cloister St [5]
BL1. . . . . 142 C2
Back Clyde St BL1 . . . . 143 B2
Back Cobden St BL1. . . . . . 143 A3
Back Colenso Rd BL2 . . . . . 42 D7
Back College Land [1]
M3 . . . . 158 C1
Back College Way
BL3. . . . . 145 B2
Back Collings St BL1 . . . . . 143 B2
Back Columbia Rd [7]
BL1. . . . . 144 C4
Back Common St BL5. . . . . . 57 B7
Back Coniston St [1]
BL1. . . . . 143 C3
Back Coop St BL1 . . . . 143 B4
Back Cope Bank BL1 . . . . . 142 B2
Back Cornall St BL8 . . . . . . 27 C3
Back Corson St BL4 . . . . . . 42 D2
Back Cottam St BL1 . . . . . . 145 B3
Back Cotton St BL3 . . . . 143 A2
Back Cowm La OL12. . . . . . . 4 C3
Back Cox Green Rd N [3]
BL7. . . . . 24 F8
Back Cox Green Rd S [1]
BL7. . . . . 24 F8
Back Crawford Ave
BL2. . . . . 148 B2
Back Crescent Ave
BL2. . . . . 148 B2
Back Crescent Rd BL3 . . . . 145 A4
Back Crescent Rd W
BL3. . . . . 42 B3
Back Croft La BL3 . . . . 148 B1
Back Cromer Ave BL2. . . . . . 25 C1

Back Crosby Rd BL1 . . . . . . 144 B4
Back Cross La WA12. . . . . . . 89 B4
Back Crostons Rd
BL8. . . . . 140 A3
Back Croston St BL3. . . . . . 146 C4
Back Crown St BL6 . . . . 22 C4
Back Crumpsall St N [5]
BL3. . . . . 143 B3
Back Crumpsall St [32]
BL3. . . . . 143 B3
Back Cundey St BL1 . . . . . . 142 C1
Back Curzon Rd BL1 . . . . . . 144 C3
Back Cyril St BL3 . . . . 148 A1
Back Daisy St BL3 . . . . 146 C4
Back Dale St [2] OL16 . . . . . 31 F5
Back Darley St BL4 . . . . 60 E8
Back Darwen Rd N
Bolton, Bromley Cross
BL7. . . . . 25 B7
Bolton, Cox Green BL7. . . . . 8 E1
Bolton, Cox Green BL7. . . 24 F8
Bolton, Toppings BL7. . . . 25 A7
Back Darwen Rd S BL7 . . . . 25 A7
Back Dawes St BL1 . . . . 145 C2
Back Deal St
BL3. . . . . 147 C3
Back Deane Church La [1]
BL3. . . . . 8 E1
Back Deane Church La W
BL3. . . . . 146 B4
Back Deane Rd [4]
BL3. . . . . 144 C1
Back Deane Rd N
BL3. . . . . 144 C1
Bolton BL3. . . . . 144 C1
Back Delamere St N
BL9. . . . . 28 A5
Back Delamere St S
BL9. . . . . 28 A5
Back Denton St BL9 . . . . . . 140 C4
Back Derby St
Bolton BL3. . . . . 145 B1
Horwich BL6 . . . . 147 A4
Bury BL9 . . . . 140 C2
Back Design St BL3. . . . . . . 146 B4
Back Devon St N [2]
BL9. . . . . 44 E8
Back Devon St S [2]
BL9. . . . . 44 E8
Back Devonshire Rd
BL1. . . . . 144 C3
Back Dijon St N BL3 . . . . . . 146 A1
Back Dijon St BL3 . . . . 146 A1
Back Dobie St [11] BL3. . . . . 42 A4
Back Doffcocker Brow
BL1. . . . . 142 B1
Back Dorset St BL2 . . . . 148 A3
Back Dougill St S
BL1. . . . . 142 B1
Back Dougill St BL1 . . . . . . 142 B1
Back Drake St OL16. . . . . . 139 C3
Back Drummond St
BL1. . . . . 143 B4
Back Ducie Ave BL1 . . . . . . 144 C3
Back Duckworth St [4]
BL9. . . . . 141 A4
Back Duncan St
Horwich BL6 . . . . 22 C3
Salford M7. . . . . 81 C7
Back Dunstan St
BL2. . . . . 148 C3
Back Durham St OL11. . . . . 31 A5
Back Duxbury St BL3 . . . . . 143 A3
Back Earnshaw St
BL3. . . . . 146 B3
Back Eastbank St [4]
BL3. . . . . 143 C2
Back East St BL9 . . . . 140 C1
Back Eckersley Rd
BL1. . . . . 143 B3
Back Edditch Gr BL2 . . . . . . 148 C3
Back Edditch Gr N [6]
BL2. . . . . 148 C3
Back Eden St BL1. . . . . 143 B3
Back Edgmont Ave
BL3. . . . . 147 A4
Back Eldon St BL9 . . . . 140 C4
Back Elgin St BL1 . . . . 143 A2
Back Ellesmere Rd
BL3. . . . . 146 C3
Back Ellesmere St
BL3. . . . . 145 A2
Back Elm St BL9 . . . . 141 B2
Back Elmwood Gr [20]
BL1. . . . . 144 C4
Back Elmwood Gr W [19]
BL1. . . . . 144 C4
Back Elsworth St M3,
M4 . . . . 155 B3
Back Emmett St BL6. . . . . . . 22 B3
Back Empire Rd BL2 . . . . . . 42 D7
Back Empress St BL1 . . . . . 142 B1
Back Ena St BL3 . . . . 42 A3
Back Ernest St [1]
BL3. . . . . 145 A2
Back Eskrick St E [6]
BL3. . . . . 143 A2
Back Eskrick St S [18]
BL3. . . . . 143 A2
Back Eskrick St W
BL3. . . . . 143 A2
Back Eskrick St [1]
BL3. . . . . 143 A2
Back Essingdon St S
BL3. . . . . 147 A4

Back Essingdon St
BL3. . . . . 147 A4
Back Eustace St [2]
BL3. . . . . 42 A3
Back Euxton St BL3. . . . . . . 147 A4
Back Everton St N [6]
BL1. . . . . 143 C2
Back Ewart St [11] BL1 . . . . 143 B2
Back Fairhaven Rd
BL1. . . . . 143 C3
Back Fair St BL3 . . . . 146 C2
Back Fenton St BL8. . . . . . . 27 C3
Back Fern St E [2]
BL3. . . . . 144 C2
Back Fir St BL9. . . . . 141 B2
Back Fletcher St S
BL3. . . . . 145 C1
Back Fletcher St
Bury BL9 . . . . 141 A2
Kearsley M26. . . . . 61 B8
Back Flora St [1] BL3. . . . . . 147 A4
Back Florence Ave BL3 . . . . 24 F5
Backford Wlk [1] M20 . . . . . 110 A8
Back Fortune St BL3 . . . . . . 148 B1
Back Foundry St BL9 . . . . . 140 C2
Back Frances St [7]
BL3. . . . . 143 A2
Back Frank St
Bolton BL1. . . . . 143 A2
[2] Bury BL9. . . . . 140 C1
Back Fylde St BL4 . . . . 42 D2
Back Gainsborough Ave [4]
BL3. . . . . 146 C3
Back Garside Gr BL3
BL1. . . . . 142 C2
Back Garston St [8] BL1 . . . 141 A4
Back Gaskell St E [14]
BL1. . . . . 145 A4
Back Gaskell St [1]
BL1. . . . . 145 A4
Back Gaythorne St [2]
BL3. . . . . 143 C3
Back George Barton St [24]
BL3. . . . . 25 B1
Back George St
Bolton BL3. . . . . 42 A4
Horwich BL6 . . . . 22 C3
Manchester M1 . . . . 159 A1
Back Georgina St
BL3. . . . . 146 B3
Back Gibraltar St BL3 . . . . . 145 A2
Back Gigg La BL9. . . . . 44 F3
Back Gilmour St M24 . . . . . 65 A8
Back Gilnow Gr BL1 . . . . . . 145 A2
Back Gilnow La
BL1. . . . . 144 C2
Back Gilnow La W
BL1. . . . . 144 C2
Back Gilnow Rd BL1 . . . . . . 144 C3
Back Glade St BL1 . . . . 144 C3
Back Gladstone St [4]
OL4. . . . . 67 B6
Back Glen Ave BL3 . . . . 144 B3
Back Glenboro Ave
BL3. . . . . 27 C2
Back Glen Bott St [5]
BL3. . . . . 143 A2
Back Gloster St [2] BL3 . . . . 143 A3
Back Goldsmith St
BL3. . . . . 147 A4
Back Goodlad St [6]
BL8. . . . . 27 B4
Back Gordon Ave BL3 . . . . . 144 C1
Back Gorses Mount
BL2. . . . . 148 C1
Back Grafton St [4]
Altrincham WA14 . . . . 119 D4
[6] Bolton BL1 . . . . 145 A4
Back Grantham Cl
BL3. . . . . 143 B1
Back Grasmere St [5]
BL1. . . . . 143 C2
Back Greaves St OL1. . . . . . 153 C3
Back Greenhalgh St
BL3. . . . . 43 A3
Back Greenland Rd
BL3. . . . . 147 C2
Back Green La S BL3 . . . . . 147 C3
Back Green La M24 . . . . . . 47 B1
Back Gregory Ave BL2 . . . . . 42 E8
Back Grendon St BL3 . . . . . 146 C3
Back Gresham St [9]
BL3. . . . . 143 C3
Back Grove St [8] BL1 . . . . . 143 A2
Back Hadwin St [11]
BL3. . . . . 143 C1
Back Halliwell La [6]
M8 . . . . 155 C3
Back Halliwell Rd
BL1. . . . . 143 B2
Back Halliwell Rd S [18]
BL1. . . . . 143 A2
Back Halstead St
Bolton BL2. . . . . 148 A3
[2] Bury BL9. . . . . 141 A4
Back Hamilton St
[6] Bury BL9. . . . . 140 C4
Salford M7. . . . . 155 A3
Back Hampson St
M40. . . . . 160 A4
Back Hanson St BL9 . . . . . . 140 C4
Back Hargreaves St [9]
BL1. . . . . 143 B2
Back Harper's La S
BL1. . . . . 142 B2
Back Hartington Rd [18]
BL1. . . . . 144 C2
Back Hart St BL5 . . . . 57 B7

Back Harvey St
  Bolton BL1............... 143 A3
  Bury BL8................. 27 C3
Back Haslam St BL9 .... 141 A4
Back Haslam Terr
  BL2................. 148 C3
Back Hastings Rd
  BL1................. 144 B4
Back Hatfield Rd BL1 ... 143 A1
Back Hawarden St 3
  BL1................. 24 E5
Back Hawthorne Rd 5
  BL3................. 146 B4
Back Hawthorne Rd E
  BL3................. 144 B1
Back Hawthorne Rd W
  BL3................. 144 B1
Back Hawthorne Rd 5
  BL3................. 146 B4
Back Haydn St 14
  BL1................. 143 A2
Back Haydock St BL1.... 145 C4
Back Hayward St 2
  BL8................. 27 C3
Back Hengist St 5
  BL2................. 148 C3
Back Hennon St 1
  BL1................. 143 A1
Back Henrietta St
  BL3................. 146 B4
Back Henry Lee St
  BL3................. 146 C3
Back Hereford Rd
  BL1................. 144 B4
Back Hereford Rd W
  BL1................. 144 B4
Back Heywood St E
  BL9................. 141 A2
Back Heywood St W 2
  BL1................. 141 A1
Back High Bank St
  BL2................. 148 C3
Back Higher Darcy St
  BL3................. 148 C1
Back Higher Shady La W
  BL7................. 25 B7
Back Higher Swan La
  BL3................. 147 A3
Back Higher Swan La W
  BL3................. 147 A3
Back High St BL3.......147 B4
Back High St W 2
  BL3................. 147 B4
Back High St
  Bolton BL3........... 147 A4
  Bolton BL3........... 147 B4
  Chapeltown BL7......... 9 C4
  Heywood OL10......... 29 B2
Back Hilden St W
  BL2................. 148 A2
Back Hilden St BL2.... 148 A2
Back Hilton St
  Bolton BL2........... 148 C3
  9 Bury BL9......... 140 C4
  Salford M7........... 155 A3
Back Hind St BL2..... 148 C3
Back Holland St E 6
  BL1................. 143 C4
Back Holland St
  6 Bolton BL1......... 143 B4
  Bolton BL1........... 143 C4
Back Holly Pl BL1.... 143 B4
Back Holly St BL9 ... 141 A1
Back Holly St
  Bolton BL1........... 143 C4
  Bury BL9............. 141 A2
Back Hopefield St
  BL3................. 147 A4
Back Hope St
  7 Oldham OL1..........67 B7
  Salford M7........... 155 A3
Back Horbury St BL8...27 C2
Back Hornby St E
  BL9................. 140 C4
Back Hornby St W 4
  BL9................. 140 C3
Back Hornby St BL9 .. 140 C4
Back Horne St N 1
  BL9................. 44 E8
Back Horne St S BL9 .. 44 E8
Back Horsa St N 17
  BL2................. 25 B1
Back Horsa St BL2.... 25 B1
Back Hotel St BL1.... 145 C3
Back Hough La BL7....25 A7
Back Howcroft St
  BL3................. 147 A4
Back Howe St M7..... 155 A3
Back Hughes St BL1... 142 C2
Back Hulbert St BL8...27 C1
Back Hulme St
  Bury BL8............. 140 A3
  Salford M5........... 81 C1
Back Hulton La
  Bolton BL3........... 146 A3
  Bolton BL3........... 146 B3
Back Hulton La S BL3.. 146 A2
Back Hulton La W
  BL3................. 146 A4
Back Huntley Mount Rd
  BL9................. 141 B3
Back Hurst St
  Bolton BL3........... 146 C3
  Bury BL9............. 141 A1
Back Huxley St 3
  BL1................. 142 C1
Back Ingham St E
  BL9................. 141 A1

Back Ingham St BL9 .... 141 A1
Back Irlam St N 3
  BL1.................143 B3
Back Irlam St 4 BL1.....143 B3
Back Ivanhoe St 3
  BL3.................42 C2
Back Ivy Bank Rd BL1....24 E5
Back Ivy Rd BL1.......142 C1
Back Ivy Rd W BL1......142 B2
Back James St BL3......43 B3
Back Jauncey St 12
  BL3.................144 C1
Back John Brown St 15
  BL1.................145 A4
Back John Cross St 3
  BL3.................147 B4
Back Johnson St 3
  BL1.................145 C2
Back Jubilee St BL3....145 B2
Back Jubilee St BL3.....146 C3
Back Keighley St 10
  BL1.................142 C2
Back Kendal Rd BL1.....144 C4
Back Kershaw St BL9 ...141 A1
Back Kingholm Gdns 2
  BL1.................143 A1
Back King St N 4 BL1....24 F8
Back King St S BL2......25 D5
Back Kingsley St BL1 ..143 A2
Back King St
  Bolton BL1...........145 B3
  Oldham OL1...........153 B2
Back Kirkby Rd BL1.....144 B4
Back Knight St 4 BL8....27 C2
Back Knowsley Rd
  BL1.................142 B2
Back Knowsley St
  1 Bolton BL1.........145 C3
  Bury BL9.............140 B2
Back Kylemore Ave
  BL3.................144 B1
Back La
  Altrincham WA15.......129 B4
  Appley Bridge WN6......35 E8
  Ashton-u-L OL7........84 D5
  Bolton BL1...........24 F8
  Glossop SK13..........115 E6
  Mossley OL5, OL6.......68 A2
  Mottram in L SK14.....103 A4
  Oldham OL4............50 C1
  Over Hulton BL5........59 B6
  Partington WA14.......118 C5
  Rochdale OL12.........13 F7
  Whitworth OL12..........4 C3
Back Lark St BL1.......145 C4
Back Latham St BL1 ....143 C2
Back Lathom St 9
  BL9.................141 A4
Back Laurel St BL1.....141 B2
Back Lawn St BL1.......143 A1
Back Leachfield St
  BL1.................143 B3
Back Leach St BL3.....145 B1
Back Lee Ave BL3......147 A3
Back Lee St OL3.........69 B8
Back Legh St WA12.....89 A3
Back Lena St BL1......143 C2
Back Lenora St
  BL3.................146 B4
Back Lever Edge La
  Bolton, Daubhill BL3 ..146 C2
  Bolton, Great Lever
  BL3.................147 C3
Back Lever Edge La S
  BL3.................147 B3
Back Lever Hall Rd
  BL2.................42 D7
Back Lever St N BL3....43 A4
Back Lever St S BL3...147 B4
Back Lever St
  Bolton BL3...........145 C1
  Bolton BL3...........145 C1
Back Lightburne Ave
  BL1.................144 B3
Back Lilly St BL1.....145 A4
Back Lincoln Rd BL1...144 C4
Back Lindley St 10 BL3..43 B3
Back Linton Ave 2
  BL9.................27 F5
Back Longden St 12
  BL1.................144 C4
Back Longfellow St
  BL3.................146 B3
Back Longfield Rd
  BL3.................146 B3
Back Long La BL2......42 E7
Back Longsight N BL2...25 E5
Back Longsight S BL2...25 E5
Back Longworth Rd BL7 ..8 D3
Back Lonsdale Rd
  BL1.................144 B4
Back Lonsdale Rd N
  BL1.................144 B4
Back Lonsdale St BL8...27 C2
Back Lord St
  Bury BL9.............140 C2
  Little Lever BL3.......43 B3
Back Loxham St BL4....42 D2
Back Lumsden St BL1...145 B1
Back Luton St BL3......42 A4
Back Lytton St
  BL1.................143 A2
Back McDonna St
  BL1.................142 C3
Back McKean St N 5
  BL3.................42 A4
Back McKean St 8
  BL3.................42 A4

Back Mackenzie St
  BL1.................143 B4
Back Malvern Ave
  Bolton BL1...........142 A1
  1 Bury BL9...........27 F5
Back Manchester Old Rd
  BL9.................140 B1
Back Manchester Rd
  Bolton BL2...........148 A2
  5 Bury BL9...........140 B2
  1 Farnworth BL2......42 C2
Back Manchester Rd E
  BL2.................148 A1
Back Manchester Rd S 10
  BL3.................42 A4
Back Manchester Rd W
  BL3.................42 A4
Back Manchester St 1
  OL10.................29 E1
Back Manor St BL9.....141 A2
Back Maple St BL3.....145 A1
Back Marion St 4
  BL3.................42 C2
Back Market St W 3
  BL9.................140 B2
Back Market St
  4 Bury BL9...........140 B2
  Hindley WN2...........56 D5
  Kearsley M26...........61 B8
  4 Little Lever BL3 .....43 B3
  Newton-le-W WA12......89 A3
Back Markland Hill La
  BL1.................23 F1
Back Markland Hill La E
  BL1.................23 F1
Back Markland Hill La W
  BL1.................23 F1
Back Marlborough St
  BL1.................145 A4
Back Marsh Fold La 14
  BL1.................144 C4
Back Mary St 4 BL1....145 A1
Back Mason St BL1.....141 A2
Back Massie St SK8....122 D6
Back Mawdsley St
  BL1.................145 C3
Back Maxwell St BL3...143 B4
Back Maybank St BL3...42 B3
Back Mayfield Ave BL3...42 B3
Back Mayor St N BL1 ..145 A4
Back Mayor St
  Bolton BL1...........145 A2
  4 Bury BL8...........27 C3
Back Maze St BL3......146 C4
Back Melbourne Rd
  BL3.................144 C1
Back Mellor Gr BL1....142 B1
Back Mellor Gr W 1
  BL1.................142 B1
Back Mellor Rd SK22...127 C1
Back Melrose Ave
  BL1.................142 A1
Back Mercia St BL3....144 C1
Back Meredith St 6
  BL3.................42 A4
Back Mere Gdns BL1...145 B4
Back Merlin Gr BL1....142 B1
Back Merton St BL8....140 A3
Back Mesnes St 11
  WN1.................37 C1
Back Michelhurst Rd
  OL5.................68 E1
Back Milford Rd BL3...147 B3
Back Miller St BL1....143 B4
Back Millet St BL9....140 A2
Back Mill St N 8 BL7...24 F8
Back Mill St S BL7.....24 F8
Back Milner Ave BL3...27 F5
Back Minorca St BL3...147 B4
Back Mirey La BL8......40 B4
Back Monmouth Ave 7
  BL9.................27 F5
Back Moor SK14.......103 A3
Back Moorfield Gr BL2...25 B1
Back Moorgate W 7
  BL9.................140 C3
Back Mornington Rd
  BL1.................144 B4
Back Mornington Rd E
  BL1.................144 C3
Back Mornington Rd W
  BL1.................144 B4
Back Morris Green La
  BL3.................146 C3
Back Morris Green La E
  BL3.................146 C3
Back Moss Terr BL1....144 C3
Back Mostyn Ave 3
  BL9.................27 F5
Back Mowbray St 3
  BL1.................142 B1
Back Murton Terr 4
  BL3.................143 C4
Back Musgrave Rd
  Bolton BL1...........144 B4
  Bolton BL1...........144 C4
Back Musgrave Rd N
  BL1.................144 C4
Back Myrtle St S BL9...141 B2
Back Myrtle St BL3....147 B4
Back Nebo St BL3......147 A4

Back Nelson St N 6
  BL3.................44 F8
Back Nelson St S 1
  BL3.................44 F8
Back Nelson St BL6....22 D3
Back Nevada St 17
  BL3.................143 B1
Back Newbold St BL3...27 C2
Back New George St 9
  BL3.................27 C3
Back Newhall La BL1 ..142 A1
Back Newport Rd 16
  BL3.................42 A4
Back Newport St BL1...145 C2
Back Newton St BL1...143 B2
Back Nixon Rd BL3....146 C3
Back Nook Terr 2
  BL2.................14 F3
Back Normanby St
  BL3.................146 C2
Back Norris St BL3.....43 A4
Back Northern Gr 1
  BL1.................142 C1
Back Northern Gr S 2
  BL1.................142 C1
Back Nunnery Rd BL3..146 B4
Back Nut St BL1.......143 A2
Back Oakenbottom Rd N
  BL2.................42 D7
Back Oak St 2 M26...44 C1
Back Oldham Rd OL16...31 A6
Back Olga St N BL1....143 A2
Back Olga St BL3......143 A2
Back Olive Bank 2
  BL8.................27 B4
Back Oram St BL9.....141 A4
Back Oriel St BL3......144 C1
Back Ormrod St BL2...141 A2
Back Osborne Gr 2
  BL1.................142 C1
BACK O' TH' BANK 143 C2
Back o' th' Low Rd
  OL4.................49 F1
BACK O' TH' MOSS.....29 C3
Back Owen's Row BL6...22 C3
Back Oxford Gr N
  2 Bolton, Brownlow Fold
  BL1.................145 A4
  Bolton, Cope Bank BL1 .142 C1
Back Oxford St BL9 ...141 A1
Back Packer St 2
  BL1.................142 C2
Back Palace St 7
  BL1.................143 B3
Back Palm St BL1.....143 C4
Back Parkdale Rd BL2...25 C1
Back Parkfield Rd
  Bolton BL3...........42 A3
  Bolton BL3...........147 C3
Back Parkhills Rd N 4
  BL9.................44 F8
Back Parkhills Rd S
  4 Bury BL9...........44 F8
  3 Bury BL9...........44 F8
Back Parkinson St 11
  BL3.................144 C1
Back Park Rd
  Bolton BL1...........144 C1
  Bolton BL1...........145 A3
Back Park Rd E 8
  BL3.................143 B4
Back Park St BL1......145 A4
Back Park View 7
  BL1.................144 A6
Back Park View Rd
  BL3.................146 C4
Backparsons La BL9 ...140 C3
Back Partington St
  BL3.................146 C2
Back Patience St 10
  OL12.................14 C1
Back Patterson St
  BL3.................146 A4
Back Peabody St BL3...147 B4
Back Peace St BL3.....145 A1
Back Pedder St 3
  BL1.................142 C1
Back Peers St 5 BL8...27 C2
Back Penarth Rd 3
  BL3.................146 B4
Back Pennington Rd
  BL3.................147 C3
Back Percy St BL1.....141 B3
Back Peter St 2 BL1....141 A3
Back Peveril St BL3....146 B3
Back Phoenix St BL3...140 B2
Back Piccadilly M1....159 B1
Back Pikes La W BL3...144 C1
Back Pine St
  2 Bolton BL1.........143 C2
  Bury BL9.............141 B2
  Newhey OL16..........32 B4
Back Pleasant St BL1..145 B4
Back Pool Fold 9
  M2.................158 C2
Back Poplar Ave BL1...24 F5
Back Porter St 2
  BL9.................140 C4
Back Portugal St BL3..148 B3
Back Potter St M26....44 D4
Back Preston St BL3...42 B4
Back Primrose St
  BL3.................143 C4
Back Primula St BL1...24 F5
Back Proctor St BL3....27 C1
Back Progress St 2
  BL3.................143 C1
Back Quay St M3......158 B1

Back Quebec St BL3 .... 144 C1
Back Queensgate
  BL1.................144 C4
Back Queen St
  Bolton BL1...........145 B3
  4 Leigh WN7...........76 A5
Back Radcliffe Rd E 1
  BL2.................148 B3
Back Railway View
  PR7.................21 A7
Back Raimond St BL1...142 C3
Back Rainshaw St 5
  BL1.................143 C4
Back Rake St BL3......140 C4
Back Ramsden Rd
  OL12.................15 C7
Back Range St BL3.....147 A4
Back Raphael St BL1...143 A1
Back Rathbone St
  WA12.................89 A3
Back Raven St 4 BL9...140 C4
Back Rawlinson St 10
  BL6.................22 B4
Back Rawson Rd 6
  BL1.................142 C1
Back Rawson Rd N 10
  BL1.................142 C1
Back Rawsthorne St
  BL3.................143 B2
Back Raymond Ave 6
  BL9.................27 F5
Back Red Bank M4....159 A3
Back Redhill Gr BL1...145 B4
Back Regent St 3
  BL9.................140 C4
Back Ribblesdale Rd 16
  BL3.................147 A4
Back Richard Burch St 1
  BL3.................141 A3
Back Richelieu St BL3...42 A4
Back Rigby La N BL2...25 C6
Back Rigby La S BL2...25 C6
Back Rishton La
  BL3.................147 C3
  Bolton BL3...........147 C4
Back Rishton La E
  BL3.................147 C3
Back Rochdale Old Rd S
  BL9.................141 B3
Back Rochdale Old South
  Rd BL9..............28 B3
Back Rochdale Rd
  Bury BL9.............141 A2
  Bury BL9.............141 B2
Back Rochdale Rd S 6
  BL9.................141 A2
Back Rock Ave BL1....142 C3
Back Roland Rd 3
  BL3.................146 C4
Back Romer St BL3....148 C3
Back Rosamond St
  BL3.................146 C4
Back Roscow Ave BL2...42 E8
Back Rose Bank 8
  BL9.................140 C4
Back Roseberry St 7
  BL3.................146 C4
Back Rowena St BL3....42 C2
Back Rowland St BL3...146 B3
Back Roxalina St 5
  BL3.................147 B4
Back Royal Ave BL2....27 F5
Back Rudolph St 2
  BL3.................147 C3
Back Rumworth St
  BL3.................147 A4
Back Rupert St BL3....147 C3
Back Rushton Rd BL1..142 B1
Back Rushton St
  OL13.................3 E8
Back Russell Cl 23
  BL1.................144 C1
Back Russell St 22
  BL1.................144 C1
Back Rutland Gr 6
  BL1.................142 C1
Back Ryefield St BL1...25 A1
Back St Anne's St 7
  BL9.................140 C4
Back St Ann St BL1....143 B1
Back St Augustine St 17
  BL3.................143 A2
Back St George's Rd
  Bolton BL1...........145 B4
  Manchester M4.......159 B3
Back St George's Rd N
  BL1.................145 B4
Back St Helens Rd
  BL3.................146 B3
  10 Bolton BL3........147 A4
Back St Helens Rd S
  Bolton BL3...........146 A2
  Bolton BL3...........146 B2
  Bolton BL3...........146 B2
  Bolton BL3...........146 C3
Back St James's St 8
  OL1.................67 B7
Back St Mark's La
  M8.................155 C4
Back St Mary's Pl
  BL9.................140 B2
Back St Philip's Ave
  BL3.................147 A4
Back St Thomas St E 9
  BL1.................143 A2

Back Salford WN7 ..... 75 F5
Back Salford St BL9 ... 141 A4
Back Salisbury St
BL3 .... 145 A2
Back Salisbury Terr
BL2 ....42 D7
Back Sandon St W 11
BL3 .... 147 A4
Back Sandon St BL3 ... 147 A4
Back Sandy Bank Rd
BL7 ....9 D5
Back Sankey St BL9 .... 140 C2
Back Sapling Rd BL3 ... 146 C2
Back Sapling Rd S
BL3 .... 146 C2
Back Scholes St BL8 ... 27 C3
Back School La WN8 ... 53 C7
Back Scowcroft St 22
BL2 .... 145 A2
Back Second Ave BL1 ... 144 B3
Back Settle St BL3 .... 147 B3
Back Settle St
Bolton BL3 .... 147 B3
Bolton BL3 .... 147 C3
Back Seymour Rd
BL1 .... 143 C3
Back Shakerley Rd 6
M29 ....58 F1
Back Sharman St BL3 ... 148 B1
Back Shaw-Street
BL9 .... 141 B3
Back Shepherd St 1
BL9 .... 141 A1
Back Sherwood St 8
BL1 .... 143 C3
Back Shipton St BL1 ... 142 B1
Back Short St 41 M46 ... 58 F1
Back Shrewsbury Rd
BL1 .... 144 B4
Back Silverdale Rd
BL1 .... 144 C3
Back Silver St BL9 .... 140 B2
Back Skipton St BL2 ... 148 C4
Back Skull House La
WN6 ....35 C8
Back Smethurst La
BL3 .... 146 B2
Back Smethurst La W
BL3 .... 146 B2
Back Sofa St BL1 ..... 142 B1
Back Soho St BL3 ..... 145 C2
Back Somerset Rd
BL1 .... 144 B4
Back Somerset Rd W
BL1 .... 144 B4
Back Somerville St 3
BL1 .... 142 C3
Back South Cross St E
BL9 .... 141 A2
Back Southfield St 1
BL3 ....42 B4
Back South Par M3 .... 158 C1
Back South St BL3 .... 147 B3
Back South View St 9
BL2 .... 148 C3
Back Spa Rd BL1 ..... 145 A4
Back Spa Rd N BL1 ... 145 A4
Back Spa Rd W 4
BL1 .... 145 A4
Back Spear St 6 M1,
M4 .... 159 B2
Back Springfield St 14
BL3 ....42 A4
Back Spring Gdns
Bolton BL1 .... 145 C2
6 Middleton M24 ... 47 A2
Back Spring St E BL9 ... 140 C1
Back Spring St W
BL9 .... 140 C1
Back Square St BL0 ... 138 C2
Back Stainsbury St
BL3 .... 146 C4
Back Stanley St BL0 ... 138 B1
Back Stanway Ave 9
BL3 .... 146 C4
Back Stephen St 2
BL8 ....27 C2
Back Stewart St 13
BL1 .... 143 B2
Back Stone St 13 BL2 ... 25 B1
Back Sunlight Rd BL1 ... 144 C3
Back Sunning Hill St 12
BL3 .... 147 A4
Back Sunnyside Rd 8
BL1 .... 142 C2
Back Sutcliffe St BL1 ... 143 B2
Back Swan La 15 BL3 ... 147 A4
Back Talbot St 1
BL1 .... 143 C4
Back Tavistock Rd 3
BL1 .... 145 A2
Back Teak St BL9 ..... 141 B2
Back Tenterden St
Bury BL9 .... 140 A2
Bury BL9 .... 140 A2
Back Thicketford Rd
BL2 ....25 C1
Back Thicketford Rd W
BL2 ....25 B1
Back Thomasson Cl
BL1 .... 143 B1
Back Thomas St 7
M4 .... 159 A2
Back Thorns St BL1 ... 143 B3
Back Thorn St BL1 ... 143 C2

Back Thorpe St BL1 ... 143 A2
Back Thurnham St 3
BL3 .... 146 C3
Back Tinline St 3
BL3 .... 141 A2
Back Tonge Moor Rd
BL2 ....25 B3
Back Tonge Moor Rd E
Bolton BL2 .... 25 C3
Bolton, Castle Hill La ... 25 B2
Bolton, Tonge Moor BL2 ... 25 B1
Back Tonge Old Rd
BL2 .... 148 C3
Back Tottington Rd 5
BL8 ....27 B4
Back Tottington Rd E
BL2 ....25 E5
Back Tottington Rd N
BL8 ....27 C4
Back Tottington Rd S 1
BL8 ....27 C4
Back Tudor St 8 BL3 ... 146 C4
Back Turner St M4 .... 159 A2
Back Turton Rd E BL2 ... 25 C5
Back Turton Rd W BL2 ... 25 C4
Back Uganda St BL3 ... 146 C2
Back Ulleswater St 1
BL1 .... 143 C2
Back Union Rd BL2 ... 25 B1
Back Union Rd M 8 D2
Back Unsworth St S
BL3 .... 145 A1
Back Uttley St 18 BL1 ... 143 A2
Back Venice St BL3 ... 147 A4
Back Vernon St 1
BL1 .... 145 B4
Back Vernon St
BL1 .... 145 B4
Bury BL9 .... 140 C4
Back Vickerman St 22
BL3 .... 144 C4
Back Victoria Gr 4
BL1 .... 142 C1
Back Victoria Gr N
BL1 .... 142 C1
Back Victory St E 10
BL1 .... 144 C4
Back Viking St N 11
BL3 ....42 A4
Back Vincent St BL1 ... 145 A2
Back Vine St 1 BL1 ... 144 C2
Back Viola St BL1 ... 143 B3
Back Waldeck St 3
BL1 .... 144 C4
Back Walmersley Rd E
Bury, Fernhill BL9 ... 140 C3
Bury, Fernhill BL9 ... 140 C4
4 Bury, Seedfield BL9 ... 27 F5
Bury, Seedfield BL9 ... 27 F6
Back Walmersley Rd W
Bury, Fernhill BL9 ... 140 C4
1 Bury, Seedfield BL9 ... 27 F6
Back Walnut St 2
BL3 .... 143 C2
Back Walshaw Rd N 3
BL8 ....27 C3
Back Walshaw Rd S
BL8 ....27 C3
Back Wapping St 20
BL3 .... 143 A2
Back Wardle St BL2 ... 148 C1
Back Wash La BL9 ... 141 B2
Back Wash La S 1
BL9 .... 141 A2
Back Water St
Bolton BL7 ....8 D2
Stockport SK1 ... 169 C2
Back Waverley Rd
BL1 .... 143 B3
Back Webster St BL3 ... 148 B1
Back Wellington Rd S
BL3 ....44 F8
Back Wells St BL9 ... 140 B1
Back Westbank St
BL1 .... 145 A4
Back Westbourne Ave
BL3 ....42 A4
Back Weston St N 9
BL3 ....42 A4
Back Weston St S BL3 ... 42 A4
Back Westwood Rd 18
BL1 .... 144 C4
Back Wheatfield St
BL2 .... 148 C1
Back Whittle Gr BL1 ... 142 B1
Back Whittle St 8 BL8...27 C3
Back Wigan Rd BL3 ... 146 A4
Back Wigan Rd N
Bolton BL3 .... 145 B4
Bolton BL3 .... 146 A4
Back Wigan Rd S BL3 ... 144 B1
Back Willis St BL3 ... 146 C4
Back Willows La 6
BL3 .... 147 A4
Back Willows La N
BL3 .... 146 B4
Back Willows La S
BL3 .... 146 C4
Back Wilmot St 4
BL1 .... 142 C3
Back Wilton St 10
BL1 .... 143 C3
Back Windermere St 3
BL1 .... 143 C2

Back Windsor Gr 8
BL1 .... 142 C1
Back Wolfenden St 31
BL1 .... 143 B2
Back Woodbine Rd
BL3 .... 146 C3
Back Woodbine Rd N 1
BL3 .... 146 C3
Back Woodfield St
BL3 ....42 A3
Back Woodgate St BL3 ... 42 A3
Back Wood St
Bury BL8 ....27 C3
Horwich BL6 ....22 C3
Back Worcester St
BL3 .... 143 B1
Back Wordsworth St 21
BL1 .... 143 A2
Back Worsel St N
BL3 .... 146 C4
Back Wright St BL6 ... 22 B4
Back Wynne St 10
BL1 .... 143 B2
Back Yates St BL2 .... 25 B1
Back Young St BL4 ... 60 E7
Baclav Cl WN1 ....37 F1
Bacon Ave M34 .... 113 A7
BACUP 3 E8
Bacup & Rawtenstall Gram
Sch BB4 ....2 F8
Bacup Rd BB4, OL13 ... 2 E8
Bacup St M40 ....83 A8
Badby Cl M44 ....160 A1
Baddeley Cl SK3 ... 170 A1
Badder St BL1 ..... 145 C4
Bader Dr OL10 ....46 D7
Badger Cl
Hyde SK14 .... 167 B4
Marple SK6 .... 125 F3
Rochdale OL16 .... 31 C3
Badger Edge La OL3,
OL4 ....50 C3
Badger La OL16 ....31 B2
Badger Rd WA14 ... 119 C8
Badger St
10 Bury BL9 .... 140 C3
Bury BL9 .... 141 A3
Badgers Way SK13 ... 116 B7
Badgers Wlk M22 ... 121 E1
Badminton Rd M21 ... 97 C1
Bag La M46 ....58 C4
Bagnall Cl
Rochdale OL12 .... 13 F2
Uppermill OL3 .... 51 C1
Bagnall Ct M22 .... 121 E8
Bagnall Wlk M22 ... 121 E8
Bagot St
16 Droylsden M11 ... 83 C2
Swinton M27 ......61 C1
Bagshaw La WN2 ... 38 E2
Bagshaw St SK14 ... 101 E5
BAGSLATE MOOR ... 29 F8
Bagslate Moor La OL11 ... 29 F8
Bagslate Moor Rd
OL11 .... 29 F8
Bagstock Ave SK12 ... 133 E2
BAGULEY 121 A7
Baguley Cres
Middleton M25 .... 64 A7
Stockport SK3 .... 170 A2
Baguley Dr BL9 ......45 A2
Baguley Hall Prim Sch
M23 .... 121 A6
Baguley La M33 .... 108 E2
Baguley Rd M33 .... 108 E4
Baguley St M43 .... 84 B2
Baildon Rd OL12 .... 14 B1
Baildon St M40 .... 65 A1
Bailey Fold BL5 ......58 B8
Bailey La
Bolton BL2 ....25 E1
Partington M31 ... 105 F3
Wythenshawe M90 ... 121 B1
Bailey Rd M17 ....96 A7
Bailey's Ct WN1 .... 150 C4
Bailey St
Droylsden M43 .... 83 C1
8 Oldham OL1 .... 67 A7
Prestwich M25 .... 63 C4
Bailey Wlk WA14 ... 128 C8
Baillie St E 18 OL16 ... 31 A8
Baillie St
Radcliffe M26 .... 44 E5
Rochdale OL16 ... 31 A8
Bails The
Salford M7 ....81 C6
Walkden M28 ......60 D3
Bainbridge Ave WA3 ... 90 F8
Bainbridge Cl M12 ... 164 A2
Bainbridge Rd 3 OL4 ... 49 D1
Bainburgh Clough OL8 ... 67 A4
Baines Ave M44 .....93 F1
Baines St BL1 ..... 144 B4
Bain St M27 ....79 F7
Bainton Wlk M9 ... 64 C5
Baird St M1 .... 163 C4
Baitings Cl OL12 .... 13 C2
Baitings Row OL12 .... 13 C2
Bakers PI 1
M33 .... 108 C4
Baker St
6 Heywood OL10 ... 46 E8
Kearsley BL4 ......61 B6
Middleton M24 .... 65 B8
Ramsbottom BL0 ... 138 B1
Sale WA15 .... 120 C7
Stalybridge SK15 ... 86 B1
Stockport SK4 .... 169 B3

Baker St continued
Wigan WN3 .... 150 B2
Bakery Ct OL6 ....85 D5
Bakewell Ave
Ashton-u-l OL6 .... 85 F6
Denton M34 ...... 113 A8
Bakewell Bank 39
SK13. .... 171 A1
Bakewell Cl 40 SK13 ... 171 A1
Bakewell Dr WN6 .... 37 A4
Bakewell Fold 37
SK13. .... 171 A1
Bakewell Gdns 41
SK13. .... 171 A1
Bakewell Gn 58 SK13 ... 171 A1
Bakewell Gr 38 SK13 ... 171 A1
Bakewell Lea 54 SK13 ... 171 A1
Bakewell Mews 45
SK13. .... 171 A1
Bakewell Rd
Droylsden M43 .... 83 E2
Eccles M30 ....95 C8
Hazel Grove SK7 ... 133 C4
Stretford M32 .....96 A3
Bakewell St
Manchester M18 ... 99 C4
Stockport SK3 .... 170 A3
Bakewell Wlk 44
SK13. .... 171 A1
Bala Cl M5 ....81 A2
Balcarres Ave WN1 ... 37 E2
Balcarres Rd WN2 ... 38 C5
Balcary Gr BL1 .... 144 B4
Balcombe Cl BL8 .... 27 C7
BALDERSTONE 31 A3
Balderstone Rd OL11 ... 31 A3
Balderstone Tech Coll
OL11. ....31 A3
Baldock Rd M20 ... 110 D3
Baldrine Dr WN2 .... 57 B5
Baldwin Rd M19 ... 110 F6
Baldwins Cl OL2 .... 48 D2
Baldwin St
Bacup OL13 ....3 B8
Bolton BL3 .... 145 A1
Hindley WN2 ....57 B3
Ince-in-M WN3 .... 151 A2
Wigan, Redwood WN5 ... 54 B6
Wigan, Scholes WN1 ... 151 A1
Bale St M2 .... 162 C4
Balfern Cl 22 BL5 .... 39 E1
Balfern Fold 11 BL5 ... 39 E1
Balfour Gr SK5 .... 111 F8
Balfour Rd
Altrincham WA14 ... 119 D7
5 Rochdale OL12 ... 14 C1
Urmston M41 ....95 B3
Balfour St
Bolton BL3 .... 145 A2
Manchester M8 ... 156 A4
Oldham OL4 ....67 C7
Salford M6 ....81 A6
Shaw OL2 .... 149 B3
Balham Wlk M12 ... 164 C2
Balholm Ct M20 ... 110 B4
BALLADEN 1 F8
Balladen Com Prim Sch
BB4 ....1 F8
Ballantine St M40 ... 83 C4
Ballantyne Way 5
WA3 ....90 E8
Ballard Cl OL15 .... 16 E7
Ballard Way OL2 .... 149 C4
Ballater Ave M41 .... 95 A1
Ballater Wlk 11 M8 ... 155 C3
Ballbrook Ave M20 ... 110 B5
Ballbrook Ct M20 ... 110 B4
Balleratt St M19 .... 99 A1
Balliol Cl SK6 .... 113 C4
Balliol Ct M33 .... 107 D4
Balliol St
Manchester M8 ... 156 A4
Swinton M27 ....79 E8
Balliol Way WN1 .... 72 F4
Balloon St M4 .... 159 A2
Ball's Cotts WN3 ... 55 F3
Ball St
Rochdale OL16 .... 31 A8
Wigan WN6 ....36 E2
Ball Wlk SK14 .... 102 F1
Balmain Ave M18 ... 99 C3
Balmain Rd M41 .....95 B3
Balmer Dr M23 .... 121 B4
Balmfield St M8 ... 156 A1
Balmforth St M15 ... 162 A3
Balmoral PR7 ....20 E6
Balmoral Ave
Cheadle SK8 .... 123 A4
Denton M34 ...... 100 D7
Golborne WA3 .....74 D1
Hyde SK14 .... 113 E8
Little Lever BL3 .... 43 A3
Rochdale OL11 ... 30 B8
Royton OL2 ....48 F4
Stretford M32 .....96 C3
Urmston M41 ....95 B1
Whitefield M45 .....63 A7
Balmoral Cl
Bury BL9 ....22 E2
Milnrow OL16 ..... 32 A6
Ramsbottom BL8 ... 11 B3
Whitefield BL9 .....45 A5
Balmoral Ct
Ashton-u-L OL6 ... 166 A1
Stockport SK4 .... 168 A3

Balmoral Dr
Altrincham WA14 ... 119 F8
Heywood, Top of Heap
OL10 ....29 A1
High Lane SK6 .... 134 E7
Hindley WN2 ....56 C4
Leigh WN7 ....76 D6
Poynton SK12 .... 133 D3
Reddish M34 ...... 100 A3
Stalybridge SK15 ... 86 A3
Balmoral Gr SK7 .... 124 F3
Balmoral Grange M25 ... 63 E3
Balmoral Ho M30 .... 79 C2
Balmoral Rd
Altrincham WA15 ... 119 E6
Ashton-in-M WN4 ... 73 A4
Farnworth BL4 .....60 D7
Manchester, Burnage
M14 .... 110 D8
Stockport, Heaton Mersey
SK4 .... 168 A3
Swinton M27 ....62 A2
Urmston M41 ....95 A1
Wigan WN5 ....54 E6
Balmoral St M18 .....99 F4
Balmoral Way SK9 ... 137 A6
Balmore Cl BL3 .... 146 A3
Balm St BL0 ....11 A4
Balniel Wlk WN1 .....37 E2
Balsam Cl M13 .... 163 C3
Balshaw Ave M44 ... 93 F2
Balshaw Cl BL3 .... 144 C1
Balshaw Ct M44 .....94 A2
Baltic Bldgs 4 BB4 ... 2 E8
Baltic Flats 3 BB4 ... 2 E8
Baltic Rd
Altrincham WA14 ... 119 A6
6 Rawtenstall BB4 ... 2 E8
Baltic St M5 ..... 154 B2
Baltimore St M40 ... 157 C1
Bamber Ave M33 ... 108 E3
Bamber Croft BL5 .... 39 E3
Bamber Ct 5 WN2 ... 56 E6
Bamber's Bldgs 2
WN2 ....56 E5
Bamber St M9 ....64 D5
Bamber Wlk BL3 ... 145 A1
Bamburgh Cl M26 ... 43 C5
Bamburgh Dr OL7 ... 84 E5
Bamburgh PI 8 WN4 ... 73 A5
Bamburgh Sq BL9 ... 140 C3
BAMFORD 29 E6
Bamford Ave
Denton M34 ...... 112 F8
Middleton M24 .....47 A2
Bamford Bsns Pk SK4 ... 111 E5
Bamford Cl
Bury BL9 ....28 E4
Gatley SK8 ...... 131 D8
Bamford Ct OL11 ... 30 C6
Bamford Dr WN2 .... 37 F2
Bamford Fold 3
SK13. .... 171 B1
Bamford Gdns WA15 ... 120 D6
Bamford Gn 4 SK13 ... 171 B1
Bamford Gr
Ashton-u-L OL6 ... 85 F6
Manchester M20 ... 110 A3
Bamford La 6 SK13 ... 171 B1
Bamford Mews
Gamesley SK13 ... 171 B1
Rochdale OL11 .....29 E7
Bamford PI OL12 ... 14 E1
Bamford Prim Sch
OL11. ....29 F7
Bamford Rd
Heywood OL10 .... 29 D3
Manchester M20 ... 110 A3
Ramsbottom BL0 ... 12 B6
Bamford St
Chadderton OL9 ... 152 C4
Droylsden M11 .... 83 B2
4 Littleborough OL15 ... 15 F5
Royton OL2 ....48 E3
Stockport SK1 .... 170 C4
Bamford Way OL11 ... 29 F6
BAMFURLONG 73 F8
Bampton Ave WA11 ... 71 B1
Bampton Cl
Stockport SK2 .... 124 B7
Westhoughton BL5 ... 39 E2
Bampton Rd M22 ... 121 D1
Bampton Wlk M24 ... 46 E2
Banastre Dr WA12 ... 89 F3
Banbury Ct WN7 .....75 E1
Banbury Dr WA14 ... 119 E8
Banbury Mews M27 ... 61 D1
Banbury Rd
Failsworth M35, M40 ... 83 E4
Longshaw WN5 .....53 D2
Middleton M24 .....65 A5
Wythenshawe M23 ... 120 F5
Banbury St
Bolton BL2 ....25 C1
Stockport SK1 .... 169 C1
Bancroft Ave SK8 ... 123 A1
Bancroft Cl SK6 .... 112 E3
Bancroft Fold SK14 ... 102 A3
Bancroft Rd
Altrincham WA15 ... 120 A3
Swinton M27 ....61 E1
Banff Gr OL10 ....29 A1
Banff Rd M14 ....98 C4
Bangor Fold WN7 ... 76 C4
Bangor Rd SK8 .... 122 F6
Bangor St
Ashton-u-l OL6 ....85 E2

Bangor St *continued*
Bolton BL1 145 B4
Manchester M15 162 A1
Reddish SK5 169 C4
Rochdale OL16 31 B6
Banham Ave WN3 54 C3
Banister Way WN3 54 E2
Bank Ave WN5 53 D5
Bank Barn La OL12 15 D6
Bankbottom SK13 104 A5
Bank Bridge Rd M11,
M40 83 B3
Bankbrook WN6 36 D4
Bank Brow WN8 35 C5
Bank Cl OL15 16 A3
Banker St BL3 148 C1
Bankes Ave WN5 54 A6
Bankfield
Ainsworth BL2 43 C8
Dukinfield SK14 101 D5
Bank Field BL5 58 A7
Bankfield Ave
Droylsden M43 84 A2
Irlam M44 105 D5
Manchester M13 98 E3
Stockport SK4 168 C1
Bankfield Cl BL2 26 C1
Bankfield Cotts OL3 50 F2
Bankfield Dr
Oldham OL8 67 B2
Worsley M28 78 B7
Bankfield La OL11 29 E8
Bankfield Mews BL9 44 F7
Bankfield Rd
Cheadle SK8 122 F1
Farnworth BL4 60 D6
Romiley SK6 113 B5
Sale M33 107 E6
Tyldesley M29 77 E8
Bankfield St
Bacup OL13 3 D8
Bolton BL3 144 C1
Bolton BL3 146 C4
Manchester M9 157 A4
Reddish SK4 169 B3
Bank Field St M26 61 D7
Bankfield Terr 1 OL13 3 D8
Bankfield Trad Est
SK5 169 B4
Bankfoot Wlk M8 156 A1
Bankgate SK14 115 A8
Bank Gr M38 59 F6
Bank Hall BL8 27 A2
Bankhall Cl WN2 57 B1
Bankhall La WA14,
WA15 128 F8
Bankhall Rd SK4 168 A2
Bankhall Wlk 10 M9 157 B3
BANK HEATH 90 A8
Bank Hey BL5 39 F1
Bank Hill St OL4 67 C7
Bankhirst Cl M8 64 A1
Bank Hos WN2 75 B8
Bank House Cl M29 59 E1
Bankhouse Rd BL8 27 C4
Bank House Rd M9 64 C4
Bank La
Glossop SK13 104 A7
Pendlebury M6, M27 80 D6
Uppermill OL3 69 E4
Walkden M38 59 F6
Wardle OL12 15 D7
Banklands Cl M44 105 D5
BANK LANE 11 E7
Bankley St M19 99 A1
Bank Mdw BL6 22 C4
Bank Mill OL5 68 E3
Bankmill Cl 12 M13 163 B3
Bank Pas WA3 74 A1
Bank Pl
Bury BL8 27 C3
Salford M3 158 A2
Wilmslow SK9 137 B7
Bankquay Ct 2 M44 94 B1
Bank Rd
Manchester M8 64 A1
Mossley SK15 86 E6
Romiley SK6 113 A3
Up Holland WN8 35 D4
Bank Row SK13 104 A7
Banks Croft OL10 46 D7
Banks Ct
Altrincham WA15 120 D5
Leigh WN7 75 D5
Bankside
Altrincham WA15 129 D6
Hattersley SK14 102 D1
Bank Side
Mossley OL5 86 C8
Westhoughton BL5 58 A7
Bankside Ave
Ashton-in-M WN4 73 A8
Radcliffe M26 44 D4
Uppermill OL3 69 C7
Bankside Cl
Handforth SK9 131 D1
Marple SK6 114 C1
Oldham OL9 153 A2
Uppermill OL3 69 C8
Bankside Ct
Manchester M12 99 A4
Stockport SK4 168 A2
Bankside Rd M20 122 B7
Banks La SK1 124 B8
Banks Lane Inf Sch
SK1 124 B8
Banks Lane Jun Sch
SK1 124 B8
Bank Sq SK9 137 B7
Bank St
Adlington PR7 21 A7
Ashton-u-L OL6 166 B2
Bolton BL1 145 C3
Broadbottom SK14 115 A8
Bury BL9 140 B2
Bury, Walshaw BL8 26 F4
Chapeltown BL7 9 C4
Cheadle SK8 122 E6
Denton, Haughton Green
M34 113 B8
Denton, Hooley Hill
M34 100 F6
Droylsden, Clayton M11 83 B2
Droylsden, Fairfield M43 99 F8
Failsworth M40 83 A3
Farnworth BL4 60 D8
Glossop SK13 116 D8
Golborne WA3 74 A1
Hadfield SK13 104 A5
Heywood OL10 29 B2
Hollinfare WA3 105 B5
Hyde SK14 167 A3
8 Oldham OL4 67 D6
Platt Bridge WN2 56 A3
Radcliffe M26 44 B2
Ramsbottom BL0 11 E7
Rochdale OL11 31 A4
Romiley SK6 113 B5
Sale M33 108 C5
Salford, Broughton Park
M7 155 C4
Salford M3 158 A2
Shaw OL2 149 A3
Whitefield M45 44 E1
Wigan WN5 54 E6
Bankswood Cl SK13 104 A4
Bank Terr
Glossop SK13 104 A5
Whitworth OL12 14 C8
Bank The
Glossop SK13 116 D8
3 Rochdale OL16 139 C4
Bank Top OL6 166 C2
BANK TOP 25 A5
Bank Top
Bury BL9 11 F1
Heywood OL10 29 B3
BANK TOP
Oldham 153 B2
Skelmersdale 35 C4
Bank Top Gr BL1 25 A5
Bank Top Pk 4 OL4 67 D6
Bank Top St OL10 29 B3
Bankwell St M15 162 B1
Bankwood WN6 35 E6
Bank Wood BL1 40 F7
Bankwood Ct M9 64 D1
Banky La M33 107 D6
Bannach Dr OL9 48 A1
Bannatyne Cl M40 65 E1
Banner Dale Cl M13 98 F4
Bannerman Ave M25 63 C3
Bannerman Rd M43 84 B1
Banner St
Hindley WN2 56 E5
Ince-in-M WN3 151 B1
Banner Wlk 19 M11 160 C1
Bannister Dr SK8 122 F2
Bannister St
Bolton BL2 42 E8
Stockport SK1 170 C3
Bann St SK3 170 B4
Banstead Ave M22 121 D7
Bantry Ave M9 64 B3
Bantry St
Bolton BL3 145 B1
4 Rochdale OL12 15 A2
Baptist St M4 159 B3
Barathea Cl OL11 30 B3
Barbara Rd BL3 146 A2
Barbara St BL3 147 A4
Barbeck Cl M40 160 B3
Barberry Bank BL7 8 E2
Barberry Cl WA14 119 B7
Barberry Wlk M31 105 F3
Barber St
5 Droylsden M11 99 E7
Glossop SK13 104 B5
Barber Wlk BL1 143 B4
Barbican St 2 M20 110 B7
Barbirolli Sq M2 162 C4
Barbrook Cl WN6 19 B2
Barbury Cl WN7 75 F7
Barchester Ave BL2 25 E1
Barcheston Rd SK8 122 C4
Barcicroft Rd M19,
SK4 110 E4
Barcicroft Wlk 1
M19 110 E4
Barclay Dr M30 79 E3
Barclay Rd SK12 133 E2
Barclays Ave M6 80 D6
Barcliffe Ave M40 65 C2
Barclyde St OL11 139 B1
Barcombe Cl
Oldham OL4 49 D2
Urmston M32 95 F3
Barcombe Wlk M9 157 A3
Barcroft Rd BL1 142 C2
Barcroft St BL9 140 C3
Bardale Gr WN4 73 A3
Bardell Cl SK12 133 D2
Bardney Ave WA3 73 F2
Bardon Cl BL1 143 A1
Bardon Rd M23 120 F6
Bardsea Ave M22 121 D1
Bardsley Ave M35 83 F7
Bardsley Cl
Bolton BL2 25 D5
1 Hattersley SK14 102 E2
Up Holland WN8 53 A7
Bardsley Gate Ave
SK15 102 E6
Bardsley St
Failsworth M40 83 D5
Middleton M24 47 A1
Oldham, Salem OL4 67 E5
Oldham, Watersheddings
OL4 49 E1
Oldham, White Gate OL9 65 F3
Stockport SK4 169 A3
Bardsley Vale Ave OL8 85 A8
Bardwell Ave BL5 57 D8
Barehill St OL15 16 B6
Bare St BL1 148 A4
Bare Trees Jun & Inf Schs
OL9 152 B4
Barff Rd M5 80 C2
Barfold Cl SK2 125 A5
Barford Cl WN8 53 A7
Barford Dr
Golborne WA3 91 A8
Handforth SK9 131 C1
Barford Gr BL6 22 F1
Barford Wlk M23 121 A4
Bar Gap Rd OL1 153 C4
Baric Cl M30 79 F1
Baring St M1, M12 163 B4
Baring Street Ind Est
M1 163 B4
Barkan Way M27 80 B8
Barker Rd SK6 112 F2
Barker's La M33 107 F4
Barker St
Bury BL9 140 B1
Heywood OL10 29 B1
Leigh WN7 75 C5
Manchester M3 158 C3
Barke St OL15 15 F3
Barking St M40 160 B3
Bark St E BL1 145 C4
Bark St
Bolton BL1 145 B3
Kearsley BL4 61 B5
Barkway Rd M32 96 A2
Barkwell La OL5 68 B1
Barkworth Wlk M40 83 B6
Bar La BL1 24 E5
Barlborough Rd WN5 54 D5
Barlby Wlk M40 83 B6
Barlea Ave M40 65 D1
Barley Brook Mdw BL1 24 F6
Barley Brook St WN6 37 B1
Barleycorn Cl M33 109 A3
Barleycroft SK13 171 C4
Barley Croft SK8 122 F1
Barley Croft Rd SK14 101 E6
Barleycroft St M16 97 F4
Barley Dr SK7 132 E7
Barleyfield Wlk M24 46 F1
Barley Hall St OL10 29 E3
Barleywood Wlk
SK15 102 E7
Barlow Cl BL9 27 F5
Barlow Cres SK6 125 F4
Barlow Ct
Edgworth BL7 9 E5
Walkden M28 60 E3
Barlow Fold
Bury BL9 44 F5
Romiley SK6 113 D3
Barlow Fold Cl BL9 44 F5
Barlow Fold Rd
Reddish SK5 111 F8
Romiley SK6 113 D3
Barlow Hall Prim Sch
M21 109 C5
Barlow Hall Rd M21 109 C5
Barlow Ho OL8 153 C1
Barlow La M30 79 C2
Barlow La N SK5 111 F8
BARLOW MOOR 109 B5
Barlow Moor Cl OL12 13 E2
Barlow Moor Ct M20 109 F4
Barlow Moor Rd M21 109 C6
Barlow Park Ave BL1 24 D5
Barlow Pl M13 163 C3
Barlow RC High Sch &
Specialist Science Coll
The M20 110 C2
Barlow Rd
Altrincham WA14 119 B7
Dukinfield SK16 101 D8
Handforth SK9 131 B1
Reddish M19 99 C1
Salford M5 81 C1
Stretford M16, M32 96 F4
Barlow's Croft M3 158 B2
Barlow's La S SK7 124 C3
Barlow St
Bacup OL13 3 B7
Bury BL9 140 C3
Eccles M30 79 D1
8 Heywood OL10 46 E8
Horwich BL6 22 C2
Oldham OL4 67 A6
Radcliffe M26 44 B3
Rochdale OL16 31 A7
Walkden M28 60 D4
Barlow Terr M21 109 C6
Barlow Wlk 3 SK5 111 F8
Barlow Wood Dr SK6 126 B3
Barmeadow OL3 50 F2
Barmhouse Cl SK14 102 A3
Barmhouse La SK14 102 B3
Barmhouse Mews
SK14 102 A3
Barmouth St M11 164 C4
Barmouth Wlk 4 OL8 66 B2
Barmskin La WN6 18 C8
Barnaby Rd SK12 133 D2
Barnabys Rd BL5 39 D3
Barn Acre BL6 21 E1
Barnacre Ave
Bolton BL2 42 F7
Wythenshawe M23 120 F3
Barnard Ave
Prestwich M45 63 B7
Stockport SK4 168 B2
Barnard Cl OL7 84 F4
Barnard Rd M18 99 B3
Barnard St 3 BL2 148 C4
Barnbrook St BL9 141 A3
Barnby St M12 99 A3
Barn Cl
Glossop SK13 116 D7
Urmston M41 94 C2
Barnclose Rd M22 121 D1
Barncroft Dr BL6 22 F3
Barncroft Gdns M22 121 C5
Barncroft Rd BL4 60 D8
Barnes Ave SK4 168 A2
Barnes Cl
Farnworth BL4 60 D8
Ramsbottom BL0 11 A3
Barnes Dr BL4 147 C1
Barnes Ho 2 BL4 60 D8
Barnes Hospl SK8 122 C6
Barnes Mdws OL15 6 C1
Barnes St BL4 60 B8
Barnes Terr BL4 61 A7
Barneswell St 23 M40 83 C5
Barnet Rd BL1 142 C2
Barnett Ave M20 110 B6
Barnett Ct OL10 29 C1
Barnett Dr M3 158 A2
Barnfield
Littleborough OL15 16 D6
Urmston M41 95 B1
Barnfield Ave SK6 113 D3
Barnfield Cl
Bolton BL7 8 E2
Radcliffe M26 43 E3
6 Salford M5 154 C1
Tyldesley M29 58 F1
Barnfield Cres M33 107 F6
Barnfield Dr
Westhoughton BL5 40 A1
Worsley M28 78 B6
Barn Field La OL12 15 A7
Barnfield Rd
Dukinfield SK14 102 B5
Manchester M19 110 E4
Swinton M27 61 D2
Barnfield Rd E SK3 123 F4
Barnfield Rd W SK3 123 D4
Barnfield Rise OL2 32 A1
Barnfield St
Denton M34 100 D4
Heywood OL10 29 E2
Rochdale OL12 14 F2
Barnfield Wlk WA15 120 C5
Barn Fold OL4 67 E5
Barngate Dr OL5 86 C8
Barngate Rd SK8 122 A6
Barngill Gr WN3 54 E3
Barn Gr M34 100 E7
Barnham Cl WA3 90 A8
Barnham Wlk M23 120 E8
Barn Hill 8 BL5 39 E1
Barnhill Ave M25 63 B2
Barnhill Dr M25 63 B2
Barnhill Rd M25 63 B3
Barnhill St M14 97 F4
Barn Hill Terr 7 BL5 39 E1
Barn La WA3 89 F8
Barnley Cl M44 94 B3
Barn Mdw BL7 9 D5
Barnsdale Cl BL2 26 C1
Barnsdale Dr M8 156 A2
Barnsfold Ave M14 110 C8
Barnsfold Rd SK6 125 F3
Barnside OL12 14 B8
Barnside Ave M28 60 E3
Barnside Cl BL9 27 E8
Barnside Way M35 84 C6
Barns La
Partington WA14 118 A5
Partington WA14 118 A6
Barnsley St
Stockport SK1 124 B8
Wigan WN6 37 B2
Barns Pl WA15 129 C8
Barn St
Bolton BL1 145 B3
Oldham OL1 153 B2
Whitefield M45 62 F7
Barnstable Dr M40 156 C2
Barnstead Ave M20 110 D5
Barnston Ave M14 98 B2
Barnston Cl BL1 143 C4
Barnton Cl WA3 90 D7
Barn View PR6 20 F8
Barnview Dr M44 94 A1
Barn Way WA12 89 B3
Barnway Wlk 7 M40 65 C2
Barnwell Ave WA3 91 D4
Barnwell Cl M34 100 E5
Barn Wlk 10 M11 99 E7
Barnwood Cl 11 BL1 143 B1
Barnwood Dr BL1 143 B1
Barnwood Rd M23 121 A3
Barnwood Terr 10
BL1 143 B1
Baroness Gr M7 81 C4
Baron Fold M38 60 A5
Baron Fold Cres M38 59 F5
Baron Fold Gr M38 59 F5
Baron Fold Rd M38 59 F5
Baron Gn SK8 131 D7
Baron Rd SK14 113 F7
Barons Ct M35 83 D6
Baron St
Bury BL9 140 A1
Rochdale OL16 139 C3
Baron Wlk BL3 43 C3
BARRACK HILL 113 B2
Barrack Hill SK6 113 A2
Barrack Hill Cl SK6 113 A3
Barracks OL3 33 C1
Barrack Sq 16 WN1 150 C4
Barracks Rd WN2 56 D1
Barrack St M15 162 A3
Barracks Yd WN1 150 C4
Barra Dr M41 95 D5
Barrass St M11 99 D7
Barratt Gdns M24 46 D4
Barrett Ave BL4 60 F7
Barrett Ct BL9 141 A2
Barrett St OL4 67 B5
Barrfield Rd M6 154 B4
Barr Hill Ave M6 80 E5
Barrhill Cl M15 162 B2
Barrie St WN7 75 D8
Barrie Way BL1 25 B4
Barrington Ave
Cheadle SK8 123 A1
Droylsden M43 83 F1
Barrington Cl
Altrincham WA14 119 D6
Wigan WN3 54 D2
Barrington Rd WA14 119 D5
Barrington St M11 83 C2
Barrington Wlk 2 BL2 25 B1
Barrisdale Cl BL3 40 F5
Barron Mdw WN7 75 D7
BARROW BRIDGE 23 F4
Barrow Bridge Rd
BL1 142 A3
Barrowcroft Cl WN1 20 B1
Barrowdale Rd WA3 90 B8
Barrowdene Ho BL1 23 F4
Barrowfield Rd M22 121 A2
Barrowfields M24 47 A2
Barrowfield Wlk 4
M24 47 A1
Barrow Hill Rd M8 155 C1
Barrow La
Altrincham WA15 129 B7
Golborne WA2, WA3 90 C2
Barrow Mdw SK8 131 E8
Barrows Ct 4 BL1 145 C2
Barrowshaw Cl M28 60 C2
Barrow St
Ashton-in-M WN4 73 D5
Salford M3, M5 158 A1
Barrs Fold Cl BL5 39 D3
Barrs Fold Rd BL5 39 D3
Barrule Ave SK7 124 E1
Barry Cres M28 60 A3
Barry Ct 9 M20 110 B6
Barry Lawson Cl M8 155 C3
Barry Rd
Reddish SK5 111 F5
Wythenshawe M23 109 C2
Barry Rise WA14 119 A2
Barry St OL1 67 B8
Barsham Dr BL3 145 A1
Bar St WN2 56 A1
Bar Terr OL12 14 C7
Bartlam Pl OL1 153 C3
Bartlemore St OL1 49 B1
Bartlett Rd OL2 149 A2
Bartlett St M11 165 B4
Bartley Rd M22 121 C8
Barton Arc 21 M2 158 C1
Barton Ave
Urmston M41 95 B2
Wigan WN1 37 B2
Barton Bsns Pk M30 79 C1
Barton Cl SK9 131 D2
Barton Clough WN5 71 E5
Barton Clough Prim Sch
M32 95 F4
Barton Ct
8 Eccles M30 95 D8
Hyde SK14 101 C1
Barton Dock Rd
Stretford M32 96 B4
Urmston M41 95 E6
Barton Emb M17 95 C7
Barton Fold SK14 167 A1
Barton Hall Ave M30 79 A1
Barton Hall Ind Est
M30 79 B1
Barton Ho 4 M6 80 C4
Barton La M30 79 E1
Barton Moss Com Prim
Sch M30 94 F8
Barton Moss Rd M30 94 D7
Barton Rd
Dukinfield SK14,
SK16 101 C6
Eccles, Alder Forest M28 78 F5
Eccles M30 79 C1
Farnworth BL4 60 B7
Manchester SK4 110 E1

Barton Rd continued
Middleton M24. . . . . .64 F8
Pendlebury M27 . . . . .80 A6
Stretford M32 . . . . .96 B3
Stretford M32 . . . . .96 C1
Urmston M41. . . . . .95 C5
Barton Sq M2 . . . . .158 C1
Barton St
Farnworth BL4. . . . . .60 E7
Golborne WA3 . . . . .74 A1
Manchester M3 . . . . .162 B4
Oldham OL1. . . . . .153 A4
Platt Bridge WN2. . . . . .56 B3
Tyldesley M29 . . . . .58 F1
4 Wigan WN5 . . . . .54 B5
Barton Terr M44 . . . . . . .94 C3
BARTON UPON IRWELL
. . . . .95 B8
Barway Rd M21. . . . . . . .96 F1
Barwell Cl
Golborne WA3 . . . . .74 C1
Reddish SK5 . . . . .112 A8
Barwell Rd M43 . . . . . . .107 E5
Barwell Sq 1 BL4 . . . . . .42 B2
Barwick Pl M33 . . . . . . .108 A4
Barwood Lea Mill
BL0. . . . . .138 C2
Basechurch Wlk M12 . . . .164 C2
Basford Rd M16 . . . . .97 B3
Bashall St BL1. . . . . .144 C4
Basil Ct OL16. . . . . .31 B6
Basildon Cl M13 . . . . . . .164 A1
Basil St
Bolton BL3. . . . . .145 B1
Manchester M14 . . . . .98 C3
Rochdale OL16. . . . . .31 B6
Stockport SK4 . . . . .169 B3
Basle Cl SK7 . . . . .123 E4
Baslow Ave
Hindley WN2 . . . . .56 F3
Manchester M19 . . . . .99 C2
Baslow Cl 2 SK13 . . . . . . .171 B1
Baslow Dr
Gatley SK8. . . . . .131 C8
Hazel Grove SK7. . . . . .133 F8
Baslow Fold 21 SK13. . . . . .171 B1
Baslow Gn 22 SK13 . . . . . .171 B1
Baslow Gr SK5 . . . . .111 F5
Baslow Mews SK13 . . . . . .171 B1
Baslow Rd
Denton M34. . . . . .112 F8
Droylsden M43. . . . . .83 E3
Stretford M32 . . . . .96 A3
Baslow Way 24 SK13 . . . . .171 B1
Bassenthwaite Cl M24 . . . .46 D3
Basset Ave M40 . . . . .81 C5
Bassett Cl OL12. . . . . .14 E3
Bassett Gdns OL12. . . . . . . .14 E3
Bassett Gr WN3 . . . . .54 C2
Bassett Way OL12. . . . . . . .14 E2
Bass La BL9 . . . . .11 D3
Bass St
Bolton BL2. . . . . .148 C3
Dukinfield SK16. . . . . .101 B8
Basswood Gn WN2 . . . . . . .57 A3
Basten Dr M7 . . . . .155 B2
Batchelor Cl M21 . . . . .109 E7
Bateman St BL6 . . . . .22 D2
Batemill Rd SK22 . . . . . . .127 D2
Bates Cl OL11 . . . . .30 D1
Bateson Dr OL4 . . . . .67 F6
Bateson St OL1. . . . . .112 A2
Bateson Way OL8. . . . . . . .153 C1
Bates St
3 Dukinfield SK16 . . . . . .101 C8
Manchester M13 . . . . .98 F4
Bath Cl SK7 . . . . .125 A2
Bath Cres
Cheadle SK8 . . . . .132 B6
Manchester M16 . . . . .161 C1
Batheaston Gr WN7. . . . . . .75 D8
Bath Pl WA14. . . . . .119 D2
Bath St
Altrincham WA14. . . . . . . .119 D2
Atherton M46 . . . . .58 A3
Bolton BL1. . . . . .145 C4
Oldham OL9 . . . . .152 C1
Rochdale OL16. . . . . .15 B1
Wigan WN2 . . . . .37 F2
Batley St
Manchester M9 . . . . .157 B4
Mossley OL5 . . . . .68 B1
Batridge Rd BL7 . . . . .9 A7
Batsmans Dr M27. . . . . . . .61 E4
Battenberg Rd 2
BL1. . . . . .144 C4
Battersbay Gr SK14 . . . . . .124 E2
Battersby St SK2 . . . . .124 E6
Battersby St
Bury BL9 . . . . .28 D3
Droylsden M11. . . . . .99 E7
Ince-in-M WN2 . . . . .56 B8
Leigh WN7 . . . . .76 B4
Rochdale OL11. . . . . .30 B6
Battersea Rd SK4. . . . . . . .110 F1
Batty St M8 . . . . .156 C1
Baucher Rd WN3 . . . . .54 F5
Baum The OL16 . . . . .139 C4
Baverstock Cl WN1 . . . . . .151 A2
Baxall Bsns Ctr SK3. . . . . .170 B2
Baxendale St BL1. . . . . . . .143 B4
Baxter Gdns M23 . . . . .121 A4
Baxter Rd M33 . . . . .108 B4
Baxter's Row WN2. . . . . . . .57 C2

Baxter St
Oldham OL8. . . . . .66 B2
Standish WN6 . . . . .19 F1
Baybutt St M26. . . . . .44 C3
Baycliffe Cl WN2 . . . . .56 F3
Baycliffe Wlk 10 M8 . . . . .155 C2
Baycroft Gr M23. . . . . .109 A1
Baydon Ave M7 . . . . .155 C2
Bayfield Gr M40 . . . . .65 A1
Bayley Cl SK14 . . . . .101 E5
Bayley Ct BL1 . . . . .145 A4
Bayley Ind Est SK15. . . . . . .85 F1
Bayley St SK15 . . . . .85 F1
Baynard Wlk M9. . . . . .64 B4
Baysdale Ave BL3. . . . . . . .40 F4
Baysdale Dr OL2. . . . . .48 C5
Bay St
Heywood OL10. . . . . .29 B3
Oldham OL9 . . . . .153 A3
Rochdale OL12. . . . . .15 A1
Bayston Wlk M12 . . . . .164 C2
Bayswater Ave M40 . . . . . .83 C4
Bayswater St BL3. . . . . . . .146 C2
Baythorpe St BL1. . . . . . . .143 C3
Baytree Ave
Chadderton OL9. . . . . .65 E8
Denton M34. . . . . .101 A4
Bay Tree Ave M28. . . . . . . .79 A5
Baytree Dr SK6. . . . . .112 F4
Baytree Gr BL0 . . . . .11 B2
Baytree La M46 . . . . .65 D8
Baytree Rd WN6. . . . . .36 F2
Baytree Wlk OL12. . . . . .4 C1
Baywood St M9 . . . . .157 A4
Bazaar St M6. . . . . .81 A4
Bazley Rd M22 . . . . .109 D1
Bazley St BL1. . . . . .23 F4
Beacomfold SK6. . . . . .114 B3
Beacon Cl M46 . . . . .58 B2
Beacon Dr M23. . . . . .121 A2
Beacon Gr OL8 . . . . .67 C4
Beacon Hts WN8 . . . . .53 A8
Beacon Rd
Billinge WN5 . . . . .71 E6
Leigh WN7 . . . . .75 A8
Romiley SK6. . . . . .113 A1
Shevington Moor WN6. . . . . .19 B2
Urmston M17. . . . . .95 E7
Beaconsfield M14 . . . . .110 C7
Beaconsfield Rd
WA14. . . . . .119 D7
Beaconsfield St BL3 . . . . . .145 A2
Beaconsfield Terr
SK15. . . . . .86 F7
Beacons The WN6 . . . . .35 D7
Beacon View
Appley Bridge WN6 . . . . . . .35 C8
Marple SK6. . . . . .125 F8
Standish WN6 . . . . .19 E1
Beacon View Dr WN8 . . . . .53 B7
Beadham Dr M9 . . . . .64 A5
Beadle Ave OL12. . . . . .15 D5
Beaford Cl WN5. . . . . .54 B5
Beagle Wlk M22. . . . . .130 E8
Bealbank Cl OL16. . . . . .32 A3
Beal Cl SK4 . . . . .110 D3
Beal Cres OL16 . . . . .15 C1
Bealcroft Cl OL16. . . . . .31 E7
Bealcroft Wlk OL16 . . . . . . .31 E7
Beal Dr WN2 . . . . .56 A2
Beale Gr M21 . . . . .109 B8
Bealey Ave M26 . . . . .44 E5
Bealey Cl
Manchester M18 . . . . .165 B1
Radcliffe M26 . . . . .44 D4
Bealey Dr BL9 . . . . .44 D7
Bealey Hospl M26 . . . . .44 D4
Bealey Ind Est M26 . . . . . . .44 D4
Bealey Row M26. . . . . .44 C4
Beal La OL2 . . . . .149 C2
Beal Vale Prim Sch
OL2. . . . . .149 B3
Beal Wlk M45 . . . . .63 C8
Beaminster Ave SK4 . . . . . .110 F3
Beaminster Cl SK4. . . . . . .110 F3
Beaminster Rd SK4. . . . . . .110 F3
Beaminster Wlk M13 . . . . .163 C1
Beamish Cl M12, M13 . . . .163 C2
Beamsley Dr M22. . . . . . . .121 B2
Beanfields M28. . . . . .78 F5
Bean Leach Ave SK2. . . . . .124 F6
Bean Leach Dr SK2. . . . . . .124 F6
Bean Leach Rd SK2,
SK7. . . . . .124 F5
Beard Rd M18. . . . . .99 C4
Beardsmore Dr WA3 . . . . . .74 E1
Beard St
Droylsden M43. . . . . .83 F1
Royton OL2 . . . . .48 E3
Beardwood Rd M9 . . . . . . .64 D4
Bearswood Cl M14. . . . . . .167 C1
Beathwaite Dr SK7 . . . . . . .123 C1
Beatrice Ave
Cheadle SK8 . . . . .122 F2
Reddish M18 . . . . .99 F4
Beatrice Mews 9 BL6 . . . .22 B4
Beatrice Rd
Bolton BL1. . . . . .142 C1
Swinton M28 . . . . .79 B7
Beatrice St
Denton M34. . . . . .100 E3
Farnworth BL4. . . . . .60 C8
7 Horwich BL6. . . . . .22 B4
Rochdale OL11. . . . . .139 A3
Swinton M27 . . . . .61 D1
Beatrice Wignall St
M43 . . . . .100 A8

Beatrix Dr SK13. . . . . .171 B3
Beattock St M15. . . . . .162 A3
Beatty Dr BL5 . . . . .39 E1
Beauchamp St OL6 . . . . . .166 C4
Beaufort Dr OL4. . . . . .67 C5
Beaufort Ave
1 Manchester M20 . . . . . .110 A5
Sale M33 . . . . .108 C2
Swinton M27 . . . . .79 D7
Beaufort Chase SK9 . . . . . .131 F1
Beaufort Cl
Alderley Edge SK9. . . . . . . .137 B2
Hattersley SK14. . . . . .102 E2
Beaufort Pl 2 M20 . . . . . .110 A2
Beaufort Rd
Ashton-u-L OL6 . . . . .85 D3
Hattersley SK14. . . . . .102 E2
Sale M33 . . . . .108 C3
Stockport SK2 . . . . .124 D5
Beaufort St
Eccles M30 . . . . .79 B3
7 Hindley WN2 . . . . .56 D5
Manchester M3 . . . . .162 B4
Prestwich M25. . . . . .63 C4
Rochdale OL12. . . . . .14 C1
Wigan WN5 . . . . .54 E6
Beaufort Way 3
SK14. . . . . .102 E1
Beaulieu WA15 . . . . .119 F2
Beauly Cl BL0 . . . . .11 A2
Beaumaris Cl
Leigh WN7 . . . . .75 C5
Manchester M12 . . . . .164 C2
Beaumaris Cres SK7 . . . . .124 C1
Beaumonds Way M41 . . . . .95 C4
Beaumont Ave BL6 . . . . . . .22 C4
Beaumont Chase BL3 . . . . .40 F3
Beaumont Cl 2 OL15 . . . . .15 F5
Beaumont Ct
Bolton BL1. . . . . .40 D8
Handforth SK9 . . . . .131 C5
Beaumont Dr BL3. . . . . .40 E5
Beaumont Gr WN5. . . . . . . .54 B8
Beaumont Hospl (Private)
BL6. . . . . .40 C8
Beaumont Prim Sch
BL3. . . . . .40 E5
Beaumont Rd
Bolton BL1, BL3, BL6. . . . . . .40 E5
Horwich BL6. . . . . .22 C4
Manchester M21 . . . . .109 B7
Worsley M28 . . . . .78 A6
Beaumont St OL6 . . . . . . .166 C3
Beaupre WA14. . . . . .119 C3
Beauvale Ave SK2 . . . . . . .124 C7
Beaverbrook Ave WA3 . . . .92 B4
Beaver Ct WN4 . . . . .73 C6
Beaver Dr BL9 . . . . .45 B4
Beaver Ho SK16 . . . . .124 B8
Beaver Rd M20 . . . . .110 B3
Beaver Road Prim Sch
M20 . . . . .110 B3
Beaver St M1. . . . . .163 A4
Bebbington Cl M33 . . . . . .108 F3
Bebbington St 7 M11 . . . . .83 C1
Beccles Rd M33 . . . . .108 B1
Beckenham Cl BL8. . . . . . . .27 B1
Beckenham Rd M8 . . . . . . .156 A3
Becket Ave M7 . . . . .155 B2
Becket Mdws St
OL4. . . . . .67 B6
Beckett Dr WA13 . . . . .117 B8
Beckett St
Manchester M18 . . . . .165 C1
2 Sale M33. . . . . .107 F4
Oldham OL4 . . . . .81 A3
Beckfield Rd M23. . . . . . . .121 A5
Beckfoot Dr M13 . . . . .98 E3
Beckford St M40. . . . . .157 B1
Beck Gr
Shaw OL2. . . . . .49 D8
Walkden M38. . . . . .60 F1
Beckhampton Cl M13. . . . .163 C2
Beck Ho SK14 . . . . .102 D1
Beckley Ave M21. . . . . .63 A2
Beckley Cl OL2 . . . . .49 B4
Beckside
Reddish SK5 . . . . .100 A1
Tyldesley M29 . . . . .76 E8
Beck St
Droylsden M11. . . . . .99 E7
Manchester M18 . . . . .158 B1
Beckton Gdns M22 . . . . . .121 C3
Beckwith WN2. . . . . .56 B3
Becontree Ave M34. . . . . . .101 A4
Becontree Dr M23 . . . . . . .120 E7
Bedells La SK9 . . . . .137 A6
Bede St M11 . . . . .142 C2
Bedfont Wlk M9 . . . . .64 E1
BEDFORD 76 C4
Bedford Ave
Hyde SK14. . . . . .167 B3
Manchester M16 . . . . .97 D2
Sale M33 . . . . .108 D2
Shaw OL2. . . . . .48 F7
1 Swinton M27 . . . . .79 E7
Walkden M38. . . . . .60 C1
Bedford Ct
Altrincham WA15. . . . . . . .120 C6
3 Leigh WN7 . . . . .76 A4
Bedford Dr
Altrincham WA15. . . . . . . .120 C6
Atherton M46 . . . . .58 A1
Bedford Gdns WN2 . . . . . . .56 F6
Bedford Hall Meth Prim
Sch WN7 . . . . .76 C3

Bedford High Sch
WN7. . . . . .76 D4
Bedford Pl WN4 . . . . .73 A5
Bedford Rd
Eccles M30 . . . . .79 E3
Manchester M16 . . . . .97 A3
Urmston M41. . . . . .95 C4
Bedford St
Bolton BL1. . . . . .145 A4
Bolton, Egerton BL7. . . . . . . .8 D2
Bury BL9 . . . . .141 A4
Heywood OL10. . . . . .29 E2
1 Leigh WN7 . . . . .76 A5
Prestwich M25. . . . . .63 C5
6 Reddish SK5 . . . . .111 E7
Wigan, Longshoot WN1. . . . .37 E1
Wigan, Norley WN5 . . . . . . .54 C5
Bedford Terr BB4 . . . . .1 A8
Bedlam Gn 2 BL9 . . . . . .140 C2
Bedlington Cl M23. . . . . . . .120 E6
Bednal Ave M40 . . . . .160 B4
Bedwell St M16 . . . . .97 F3
Bedworth Cl BL2 . . . . .148 B3
Beechacre BL0 . . . . .11 D5
Beech Ave
Adlington PR6 . . . . .21 B8
Atherton M46 . . . . .58 E3
Chadderton OL1, OL9. . . . . .48 A3
Culcheth WA3 . . . . .92 A3
Denton M34. . . . . .100 D4
Droylsden M43. . . . . .83 F1
Farnworth BL4. . . . . .60 A8
Gatley SK8 . . . . .122 B5
Glossop SK13. . . . . .116 A8
Golborne WA3 . . . . .90 F7
Hazel Grove SK7. . . . . .124 E2
Horwich BL6. . . . . .22 E1
Irlam M44 . . . . .94 C3
Kearsley BL4. . . . . .61 B5
Little Lever BL3. . . . . .43 B2
Marple SK6 . . . . .125 D6
New Mills SK22 . . . . .127 F8
Oldham OL4 . . . . .67 D8
Radcliffe M26 . . . . .61 F8
Sale WA15 . . . . .120 B8
Salford M6. . . . . .154 B4
Stockport SK2, SK3 . . . . . .170 C2
Uppermill OL3 . . . . .69 B6
Urmston M41. . . . . .95 C2
Whitefield M45 . . . . .62 F6
Worsley M28 . . . . .78 A6
Wythenshawe M22 . . . . . . .121 D8
Beech Cl
Alderley Edge SK9. . . . . . . .137 B3
Bolton BL2. . . . . .25 C6
Newton-le-W WA12. . . . . . . .89 C2
4 Partington M31 . . . . . . .105 F3
Prestwich M25. . . . . .63 C3
Whitworth OL12. . . . . .4 C1
Beech Cres
Leigh WN7 . . . . .75 F3
Poynton SK12 . . . . .133 E4
Standish WN6. . . . . .36 E8
Beechcroft M25 . . . . .63 C3
Beechcroft Ave BL2. . . . . . .42 G6
Beechcroft Cl M40. . . . . . . .160 A3
Beechcroft Gr BL2 . . . . .42 E6
Beech Ct
Manchester, Crumpsall
M8 . . . . .63 F1
Manchester, Fallowfield
M14 . . . . .110 C8
9 Manchester M21. . . . . . .96 F1
2 Sale M33 . . . . .107 F4
Stockport SK3 . . . . .81 A3
Beechcroft Cl WA13 . . . . . .117 B8
Beecher Wlk M9 . . . . .157 A2
Beeches SK9 . . . . .136 F4
Beeches Mews M20. . . . . . .109 F4
Beeches The
Altrincham WA14. . . . . . . .119 C3
4 Atherton M46. . . . . .58 D3
Bolton BL1. . . . . .24 D6
Cheadle SK8 . . . . .123 B1
4 Eccles M30 . . . . .79 F3
Manchester M20 . . . . .109 F4
Mossley OL5 . . . . .68 C2
Romiley SK6. . . . . .113 B2
Beechfield
Altrincham WA14. . . . . . . .119 C3
Rochdale OL11. . . . . .29 F6
Sale M33 . . . . .108 A2
Uppermill OL4 . . . . .68 D5
Wilmslow SK9 . . . . .137 A6
Beechfield Ave
Hindley WN2 . . . . .57 A4
3 Radcliffe M26. . . . . .44 C1
Urmston M41. . . . . .95 A3
Walkden M38. . . . . .60 A5
Wilmslow SK9 . . . . .136 E5
Beechfield Cl
5 Oldham OL4. . . . . .67 F6
Rochdale OL16. . . . . .29 E6
Beechfield Dr
Bury BL9 . . . . .27 F3
Leigh WN7 . . . . .75 F3
Beechfield Mews
SK14. . . . . .102 A3
Beechfield Rd
Bolton BL1. . . . . .142 C2
Cheadle SK8 . . . . .132 B8
Glossop SK13. . . . . .171 C3
Milnrow OL16. . . . . .31 F4
Stockport SK3 . . . . .170 C1
Swinton M27 . . . . .79 D5

Beechfield St M8 . . . . .156 A2
Beech Gr
Abram Brow WN2 . . . . .74 C7
Ashton-u-L OL7 . . . . .84 F1
Leigh WN7 . . . . .75 E2
Manchester M14 . . . . .110 D7
Ramsbottom BL8. . . . . .11 A1
Sale M33 . . . . .107 F4
Salford M6. . . . . .154 B4
Stalybridge SK15. . . . . . . .101 F8
Walkden M38. . . . . .59 E5
Wigan WN6 . . . . .36 E3
Wilmslow SK9 . . . . .137 A6
Beech Grove Cl BL9 . . . . . .141 B4
Beechhead Ave M33 . . . . . .37 A2
BEECH HILL 36 F4
Beech Hill Ave WN6 . . . . . .37 A2
BEECH HILL 36 F4
Beech Hill Com Prim Sch
WN6. . . . . .37 A3
Beech Hill La WN6. . . . . . . .36 E3
Beech Hill Rd OL4 . . . . .68 D6
Beech Ho
3 Eccles M30. . . . . .79 B1
Manchester M20 . . . . .109 F4
Beech Holme Gr SK2 . . . . .124 C8
Beech House Sch
OL11. . . . . .139 B2
Beech Hurst Cl M16 . . . . . . .97 D3
Beech La
Romiley SK6. . . . . .113 C2
Uppermill OL4 . . . . .68 D5
Wilmslow SK9 . . . . .137 A6
Beech Lawn M14 . . . . .119 C4
Beech Mews
Altrincham WA15. . . . . . . .120 C3
Manchester M21 . . . . .109 A8
Stockport SK2 . . . . .124 A5
Beechmill Dr WA3. . . . . .91 E3
Beech Mount
Altrincham WA14. . . . . . . .119 D2
Ashton-u-L OL7 . . . . .85 A4
Manchester M9 . . . . .157 A4
Beechpark Ave M22 . . . . . .121 C7
Beech Range 15 M19 . . . . .99 A1
Beech Rd
Alderley Edge SK9. . . . . . . .137 B3
Altrincham WA15. . . . . . . .119 E3
Cheadle SK8 . . . . .123 B1
Golborne WA3 . . . . .74 A1
High Lane SK6. . . . . .134 F7
Hyde SK14. . . . . .167 A3
Paddockhill WA16. . . . . . . .136 B5
Sale M33 . . . . .108 C4
Stockport SK2, SK3 . . . . . .170 C2
Beech St
Ashton-u-M WN4 . . . . .73 A4
Atherton M46 . . . . .58 E3
Bolton BL1. . . . . .143 C2
Bury BL9 . . . . .141 B2
Droylsden M43. . . . . .83 E8
Edgworth BL7 . . . . .9 D5
Failsworth M35. . . . . .83 E8
Hyde SK14. . . . . .167 A3
Middleton M24. . . . . .64 F8
Newhey OL16. . . . . .32 B4
3 Oldham OL1. . . . . .67 A7
Radcliffe M26 . . . . .44 C1
Ramsbottom BL9. . . . . .11 C3
Rochdale OL11. . . . . .139 E6
Swinton M27 . . . . .79 F7
Beech Street Com Prim
Sch M30 . . . . .79 B1
Beech Tree Ave WN6. . . . . .35 D8
Beech Tree Hos WN6. . . . . .73 F7
Beechurst Rd SK8 . . . . . . .123 B5
Beech View SK14 . . . . .102 A2
Beechway
High Lane SK6. . . . . .134 F7
Wilmslow SK9 . . . . .136 F5
Beech Wlk
Leigh WN7 . . . . .75 E2
Middleton M24. . . . . .65 A6
Standish WN6 . . . . .36 D8
1 Stretford M32. . . . . .96 C1
Beech Wlks WN3 . . . . .54 C2
Beechwood
Altrincham WA14. . . . . . . .119 B1
Glossop SK13. . . . . .115 F7
Shaw OL2. . . . . .49 D8
Whitefield BL9 . . . . .45 A6
Beechwood Ave
Ashton-in-M WN4 . . . . .73 A2
Littleborough OL15 . . . . . . .16 A3
Manchester M21 . . . . .109 C7
Newton-le-W WA12. . . . . . . .89 D4
Ramsbottom BL0. . . . . .11 D6
Reddish SK5 . . . . .169 C4
Romiley SK6. . . . . .113 D2
Shevington WN6 . . . . .35 F5
Stalybridge SK15. . . . . .86 C4
Urmston M41. . . . . .94 E3
Beechwood Cres
Orrell WN5. . . . . .53 E6
Tyldesley M29 . . . . .77 A4
Beechwood Ct
Bury BL8. . . . . .27 A5
Coppull PR7 . . . . .19 F8
3 Manchester M20 . . . . . .110 A3
Beechwood Dr
Hyde SK14. . . . . .167 C1
Marple SK6 . . . . .126 A6
Mossley OL5 . . . . .68 C2
Royton OL2 . . . . .48 C6
Sale M33 . . . . .107 C4
Swinton M28 . . . . .79 B6
Wilmslow SK9 . . . . .137 B8
Beechwood Gdns
M14 . . . . .110 D8

Beechwood Gr
Cheadle SK8 132 A8
Manchester M9 157 B3
Beechwood Ho
Brinnington SK6 112 E6
Manchester M14 110 D8
Beechwood La
Culcheth WA3 91 D4
Stalybridge SK15 86 C4
Beechwood Rd
Manchester M25 63 D3
Oldham OL8 66 F2
Beechwood St BL3 147 C3
Beechy Sq OL1 67 A7
Beede St M11 165 B4
Beedon Ave BL3 43 A4
Bee Fold La M46 58 C1
Beeford Dr WN5 53 E5
Beehive Gn BL5 40 B1
Bee Hive Ind Est BL6 39 E8
Beehive St OL8 66 F3
Beeley St
Hyde SK14 167 B2
Salford M6 81 B5
Beenham Cl M33 107 C3
Beeston Ave
Altrincham WA15 119 F6
Salford M7 81 B6
Beeston Cl BL1 25 A6
Beeston Gr
Leigh WN7 76 D7
Prestwich M45 63 B7
Stockport SK3 170 B1
Beeston Rd
Handforth SK9 131 D5
Sale M33 107 F4
Beeston St M9 157 B4
Beetham Twr M3 162 B4
Beeth St M11 99 D7
Beeton Gr M13 98 E4
Beever Prim Sch OL1 67 A8
Beever St
Manchester M16 161 C1
Oldham OL1 67 A7
Begley Cl SK6 112 F1
Begonia Ave BL4 42 B1
Begonia Wlk M12 164 C2
Beightons Wlk OL12 14 D4
Beis Rochel Girls' Sch
M8 63 F1
Beis Yaakov High Sch
M7 155 A3
Belayse Cl BL1 142 B2
Belbeck St S 8 BL8 27 C2
Belbeck St BL8 27 C2
Belcroft Cl M22 121 E8
Belcroft Dr M38 59 E6
Belcroft Gr M38 59 E5
Belding Ave M40 65 F1
Beldon Rd M9 64 B4
Belfairs Cl OL7 85 B7
BELFIELD 31 D8
Belfield Cl OL16 31 C8
Belfield Com Sch OL16 31 C8
Belfield La
Milnrow OL16 31 D7
Rochdale OL16 31 C8
Belfield Mill La OL16 31 D8
Belfield Old Rd OL16 31 C8
Belfield Rd
Manchester, Didsbury
M20 110 B3
Manchester, Sedgley Park
M25 63 E2
Reddish SK5 99 F3
Rochdale OL16 31 C8
Belford Ave M34 100 A3
Belford Coll OL8 66 C4
Belford Dr BL3 147 B3
Belford Rd M32 96 D3
Belford Wlk M23 121 A6
Belfort Dr M5 161 B4
Belfry Cl SK9 137 D8
Belfry Cres WN6 19 F2
Belgate Cl M12 99 A4
Belgium St OL11 29 E7
Belgrave Ave
Failsworth M35 84 B8
Manchester M14 98 E3
Marple SK6 125 F6
Oldham OL8 67 A4
Urmston M41 94 E3
Belgrave Bglws M26 43 F4
Belgrave Cl
Golborne WN7 91 C8
Radcliffe M26 44 A4
Wigan WN3 54 D3
Belgrave Cres
Eccles M30 79 F2
Horwich BL6 22 D3
Stockport SK2 124 B4
Belgrave Ct
Denton M34 100 D4
Oldham OL8 66 F4
Belgrave Dr M26 44 A4
Belgrave Gdns 5 BL1 143 B2
Belgrave Ind Est OL8 67 A3
Belgrave Rd
Altrincham WA14 119 C3
Failsworth M40 65 F1
Irlam M44 105 D5
Oldham OL8 66 F4
Sale M33 108 A4
Belgrave St S BL1 143 B1
Belgrave St
Atherton M46 58 A2
4 Bolton BL1 143 B2
Denton M34 100 D4
Belgrave St *continued*
Heywood OL10 29 C1
Radcliffe M26 44 A4
Rochdale OL12 14 D1
Belgravia Gdns
Altrincham WA15 128 E8
Manchester M21 109 A8
Belgravia Ho 4
WA14 119 D3
Belgravia Mews OL2 149 C3
Belhaven Rd M8 63 F2
Belhill Gdns M6 154 C3
Bellairs St BL3 146 C3
Bellam Ct M27 61 C1
Bellamy Dr WN7 76 B5
Bella St BL3 146 C4
Bell Clough Rd M43 84 B3
Bell Cres M11 164 C4
Belldale Cl SK4 168 A2
Belldean WN2 56 B8
Belle Green Ind Est
WN2 56 A8
Belle Green La WN2 56 A8
Belle Isle Ave OL12 14 C6
Bellerby Cl M45 62 E8
Belleville Ave M22 130 E8
BELLE VUE 165 B1
Belle Vue Ave M12 164 C1
Belle Vue St
Manchester M12 165 A2
1 Wigan WN5 54 D5
Belle Vue Sta M18 165 C1
Belle Vue Terr BL9 140 B1
Bellfield Ave
Cheadle SK8 123 B1
Oldham OL8 66 F2
Bellfield Cl 6 M9 64 C2
Bellfield View BL1 25 A3
Bellingham Ave WN1 37 C2
Bellingham Cl
Bury BL8 26 F2
Shaw OL2 149 B4
Bellingham Dr WN1 37 D2
Bellingham Mount
WN1 37 D2
Bellis Cl M12 160 B1
Bell La
Bury BL9 141 B3
Milnrow OL16 32 B7
Wigan WN5 54 B7
Bell Meadow Dr OL11 29 F5
Bellott St M8 156 A2
Bellot Wlk OL1 153 B4
Bellpit Cl M28 78 C7
Bells Croft Ave M40 83 B7
Bellshill Cres OL16 15 C1
Bell St
Droylsden M43 84 B2
Hindley WN2 56 E6
Leigh WN7 57 D1
Oldham OL1 67 A7
Rochdale OL16 139 C4
Bell Terr M30 95 C8
Bellwood BL5 57 C6
Belmont Ave
Atherton M46 58 F4
Denton M34 100 D4
Golborne WA3 74 C1
Leigh WN2 57 A1
Oldham OL4 67 F7
Orrell WN5 53 D3
Salford M6 80 A2
Swinton M27 61 D5
Belmont Cl SK4 169 B3
Belmont Dr
Aspull WN2 38 D5
Bury BL8 27 A1
Marple SK6 114 B1
Belmont Pl PR7 19 D6
Belmont Rd
Adlington PR6 21 B7
Altrincham WA15 119 E2
Bolton BL1, BL7 24 D6
Bramhall SK7 132 F5
Gatley SK8 122 B6
Hindley WN2 56 F5
Horwich BL6 22 C7
Radcliffe M26 44 A1
Sale M33 108 A6
Belmont St
Eccles M30 79 D3
Manchester M16 162 A1
Oldham, Cold Hurst
OL1 153 B4
Oldham, Nether Lees
OL4 67 E5
Salford M5 154 A1
Stockport SK4 169 A3
Belmont View BL2 25 F4
Belmont Way
Chadderton OL9 152 C4
Rochdale OL12 14 E2
Stockport SK4 169 B3
Belmont Wlk 1 M13 163 C2
Belmore Ave M8 63 F1
Belper Rd
Eccles M30 95 B8
Manchester SK4 110 F1
Belper St OL6 166 B4
Belper Way M34 113 A8
Belper Wlk M18 165 C2
Belroy Ct M25 63 B3
Belsay Cl OL7 84 F5
Belsay Dr M23 121 A4
Belstone Ave M23 121 A3
Belstone Cl SK7 123 F2
Belsyde Wlk 7 M9 157 B3
Belthorne Ave M9 65 B2
Belton Ave OL16 15 C1
Belton Cl WA3 90 A7
Beltone Cl M32 96 B1
Belton Wlk
10 Manchester M8 156 A2
Oldham OL9 153 A2
Belvedere Ave
Atherton M46 58 F4
Ramsbottom BL8 11 A1
Reddish SK5 99 F2
Belvedere Cl WN7 76 D7
Belvedere Ct M25 63 A3
Belvedere Dr
Dukinfield SK15,
SK16 101 E8
Romiley SK6 112 C3
Belvedere Gdns SK4 168 B3
Belvedere Hts BL1 40 E8
Belvedere Pl WN3 54 F5
Belvedere Rd
Adlington PR6 21 B8
Ashton-in-M WN4 73 C4
Manchester M14 110 E8
Newton-le-W WA12 89 B5
Salford M6 81 A3
Belvedere Rise OL1 49 D3
Belvedere Sq M22 121 F3
Belvoir Ave
Hazel Grove SK7 133 E8
Manchester M19 99 A2
Belvoir Mdws OL16 15 E4
Belvoir St
Bolton BL2 148 C3
Rochdale OL12 14 C1
Wigan WN1 151 B4
Belvor Ave M34 100 E7
Belwood Rd M21 109 B7
Bembridge Cl M14 98 C3
Bembridge Ct WN3 54 E2
Bembridge Dr BL3 42 D5
Bembridge Rd M34 113 B8
Bempton Cl SK2 125 A5
Bemrose Ave WA14 119 C6
Bemsley Pl M5 161 A4
Benbecula Way M41 95 D5
Benbow Ave M12 164 C1
Benbow St 6 M33 108 B5
Ben Brierley Way
OL1 153 C3
Benbrook Gr SK9 131 E2
Bench Carr OL12 14 E1
Benches La SK6 114 E3
BENCHILL 121 D5
Benchill Ave M22 121 D5
Benchill Court Rd
M22 121 E4
Benchill Cres M22 121 C5
Benchill Ct M22 121 E4
Benchill Dr M22 121 D5
Benchill Prim Sch
M22 121 C6
Benchill Rd M22 121 D5
Bendall St M11 99 E8
Bendemeer 6 M41 95 C3
Bendix St M4 159 B2
Benedict Cl 13 M7 81 C5
Benedict Dr SK16 101 D6
Benfield Ave M40 65 C2
Benfield St OL10 29 D1
Benfleet Cl M12 165 A2
Benfold Wlk M24 46 D3
Bengairn Cl WN1 37 F1
Bengal La OL6 166 C4
Bengal Sq 11 OL6 85 D4
Bengal St
Leigh WN7 75 F5
Manchester M4 159 C2
Stockport SK3 170 B4
Benhale Wlk 14 M8 156 A2
Benham Cl M20 110 C3
Benin Wlk 13 M40 83 C5
Benjamin Fold WN4 73 B5
Benjamin St 3 OL7 166 A1
Benjamin Wilson Ct
M7 158 A4
Benmore Cl OL10 29 A1
Benmore Rd M9 64 F3
Bennet Mews 3
SK14 101 D5
Bennet St M26 43 D4
Bennett Cl 4 SK3 123 C8
Bennett Dr
Orrell WN5 53 D4
Salford M7 155 B2
Bennett Rd M8 63 F1
Bennett's La BL1 142 C2
Bennett St
6 Ashton-u-L OL7 84 F1
Dukinfield SK14 101 D5
Hollingworth SK14 103 D5
Manchester M12 164 B2
4 Stalybridge SK15 86 A1
3 Stockport SK3 123 C8
Stretford M32 96 C1
Benny La M43 84 D3
Benson Cl M7 155 B1
Benson St
Bury BL9 141 A1
Edgworth BL7 9 E5
Benson Wlk 3 SK9 131 D2
Ben St M11 83 B2
Bentcliffe Way M30 80 A1
Bentfield Cres OL16 32 A4
Bentfield Ind Units
OL9 152 B2
Bent Fold Dr BL9 45 A1
BENTGATE 32 A3
BENT GATE 1 C8
Bentgate Cl
Haslingden BB4 1 D8
Newhey OL16 32 A4
Bentgate St OL16 32 A3
Benthall Wlk M34 100 E1
Bentham Cl
Bury BL8 26 E3
6 Farnworth BL4 42 D1
Bentham Pl WN6 19 F2
Bentham Rd
Culcheth WA3 92 A2
Standish WN6 19 F2
Bent Hill St BL3 146 A4
Bentinck Bsns Ctr
OL6 166 A2
Bentinck Cl WA14 119 C4
Bentinck Ho 2 OL6 166 A2
Bentinck Ind Est M15 162 A3
Bentinck Rd WA14 119 C4
Bentinck St
Ashton-u-L OL6 166 A2
Bolton BL1 142 B1
Farnworth BL4 42 C1
Manchester M15 162 A3
Oldham OL8 66 F4
9 Rochdale OL12 14 C1
Wigan WN3 54 F4
Bentinck Terr 1 OL6 166 A2
Bent La
Culcheth WA3 92 A2
Lymm WA13 117 C6
Prestwich M25 63 C4
Salford M8 155 C3
Bent Lanes M41 94 F5
Bentley Ave M24 47 D5
Bentley Cl M26 44 D4
Bentley Ct
Farnworth BL4 42 D1
Salford M7 155 B4
Bentley Fold BL8 26 F4
Bentley Hall Rd BL2,
BL8 26 D4
Bentley Ho M15 162 B2
Bentley La BL9 12 A1
Bentley Mews OL12 14 E2
Bentley Rd
Denton M34 100 F3
Manchester M21 97 A1
Salford M7 155 B4
Bentley St
Bolton BL2 148 C1
Chadderton OL9 152 C3
Farnworth BL4 42 D1
8 Oldham OL1 67 B8
Rochdale OL12 14 E2
Bentleys The SK5 169 C3
Bentmeadows OL12 14 E1
Benton Dr SK6 126 C8
Benton St M9 157 C3
Bents Ave
Romiley SK6 112 F3
Urmston M41 94 F1
Bents Farm Cl 1 OL12 15 F5
Bentside Rd SK12 135 D5
Bent Spur Rd BL4 61 A5
Bent St
Farnworth BL4 60 E7
Haslingden BB4 1 D8
Manchester M3, M8 159 A4
Bent Terr M41 95 C4
Bentworth Cl BL5 57 F6
Benville Wlk M40 83 B6
Benwick Terr 18 BL1 143 B2
Benyon St OL4 67 E6
Berberis Wlk 1 M33 107 C6
Beresford Ave BL3 144 C1
Beresford Cres
Oldham OL4 67 D8
Reddish SK5 99 E3
Beresford Ct
4 Alderley Edge SK9 137 A1
Manchester M20 110 A4
Beresford Rd
Manchester M13 98 F3
Stretford M32 96 E4
Beresford St
Failsworth M35 83 E7
Manchester M14 97 F3
Newhey OL16 32 B4
Oldham OL4 67 D8
8 Wigan WN6 37 A1
Bergman Wlk M40 83 B6
Berigan Cl M12 164 B1
Berisford Cl WA15 119 E7
Berkeley Ave
Manchester M14 98 E4
Oldham OL9 65 F3
Stretford M32 96 A4
Wigan WN3 54 D2
Berkeley Cl
Golborne WN7 91 C8
Hyde SK14 167 A1
Stockport SK2 124 C8
Berkeley Cres
Hyde SK14 167 A1
Little Lever M26 43 C5
Berkeley Ct 1 M7 63 E1
Berkeley Dr
Rochdale OL16 31 B4
Royton OL2 48 D2
Berkeley Rd
Bolton BL1 143 B4
Hazel Grove SK7 124 F3
Berkeley St
Ashton-u-L OL6 166 A3
Royton OL2 48 D5
Berkley Ave M19 99 A1
Berkley Ho BL1 144 C3
Berkley Wlk OL15 15 F5
Berkshire Cl OL9 152 B1
Berkshire Ct BL9 44 F7
Berkshire Dr M44 105 C5
Berkshire Pl OL9 152 C1
Berkshire Rd M40 160 A3
Berlin Rd SK3 170 A2
Berlin St BL3 144 C2
Bermondsay St M5 161 B4
Bernard Gr BL1 142 C2
Bernard St
Glossop SK13 104 C1
Manchester M9 157 A4
Rochdale OL12 14 E3
Bernard Walker Ct
SK6 114 B2
Berne Ave BL6 22 A3
Berne Cl
Chadderton OL9 152 C2
Stockport SK7 123 E4
Bernice Ave OL9 152 B2
Bernice St BL1 142 C2
Berriedale Cl M16 97 D2
Berrie Gr M19 111 B8
Berrington Gr WN4 73 A3
Berry Brow
Failsworth M40 83 D4
Uppermill OL3 69 B5
Berry Cl SK9 137 A5
Berrycroft La SK6 113 A3
Berryfold Way M29 77 B8
Berry Sq BL6 21 D3
Berry St
Eccles M30 95 B8
Manchester M1 163 B4
Stalybridge SK15 102 C8
Swinton M27 61 F2
Uppermill OL3 69 B5
Bertha Rd OL16 31 C7
Bertha St
Bolton BL1 143 A2
Manchester M11 165 B3
Shaw OL2 149 B1
Bertie St OL11 30 D4
Bertram St
Manchester M12 165 A2
Newton-le-W WA12 89 A4
Sale M33 108 E4
Bertrand Rd BL1 144 C3
Bert St BL3 146 B3
Berwick Ave
Manchester SK4 110 E2
Stretford M41 96 A2
Whitefield M45 63 A7
Berwick Cl
Boothstown M28 77 F7
Heywood OL10 29 A1
Berwick Pl WN1 37 E1
Berwick St OL16 31 B6
Berwyn Ave
Cheadle SK8 123 B5
Manchester M9 64 C5
Middleton M24 65 C8
Berwyn Cl
Horwich BL6 22 C5
Oldham OL8 66 E3
Beryl Ave BL8 26 F7
Beryl St BL1 143 C3
Besom La SK15 86 E3
Bessemer Rd M44 105 F6
Bessemer St M11,
M18 165 C3
Bessemer Way OL1 153 B3
BESSES O' TH' BARN 63 A7
Besses o' th' Barn Sta
M45 63 A7
Bessie's Well Pl WN6 36 F8
Bessybrook Cl BL6 40 C6
Besthill Cotts SK14 115 B8
BESWICK 164 C4
Beswick Cotts OL3 50 D4
Beswick Dr M35 84 A6
Beswicke Royds St
OL16 15 C1
Beswicke St
Littleborough OL15 16 C5
Rochdale OL12 139 B4
Beswick Row M4 159 A3
Beswicks La SK9 136 C3
Beswick St
5 Droylsden M43 84 B1
Manchester M4 160 A2
Royton OL2 48 E2
Walsden OL14 6 A7
Beta Ave M32 96 C1
Beta Ct M22 121 E7
Beta St BL1 145 C4
Bethal Gn OL15 6 C1
Bethany La OL16 32 D4
Bethel Ave M35 83 E7
Bethel St OL10 29 C2
Bethersden Rd WN1 37 B4
Bethesda St OL8 66 F4
Bethnall Dr M14 110 B8
Betjeman Pl OL2 49 D8
Betleymere Rd SK8 122 F4
Betley Rd SK5 99 F1
Betley St
Heywood OL10 29 C1
Manchester M1 163 C4
Radcliffe M26 44 C4
Betnor Ave SK1 112 B1
Betony Cl OL12 14 D3
Betsham St M15 162 C1
Bettison Ave WN7 76 C3

Bettwood Dr M8. . . . . .63 F2
Betty Nuppy's La OL16. . . .31 C5
Betula Gr M7. . . . . .155 A3
Betula Mews OL11. . . . . . . .13 D1
Beulah Ave WN5. . . . . .71 D4
Beulah St M18. . . . . .165 C3
Bevan Cl M7. . . . . .160 B1
Bevendon Sq M7 . . . . .155 B2
Beveridge St M14 . . . . .98 A3
Beverley Ave
  Denton M34. . . . . .101 A2
  Leigh WN7. . . . . .76 A6
  Longshaw WN5 . . . . .53 E1
  Urmston M41. . . . . .95 E3
Beverley Cl M45. . . . . .45 B1
Beverley Pl OL16 . . . . .31 A8
Beverley Rd
  Bolton BL1. . . . . .144 C4
  Little Lever BL3 . . . . .42 F3
  Pendlebury M27 . . . . .80 C7
  Stockport SK2 . . . . .124 C8
  Wigan WN5 . . . . .54 B8
Beverley St M9 . . . . .64 E1
Beverley Wlk
  Oldham OL8. . . . . .153 B1
  Romiley SK6. . . . . .113 A1
Beverly Cl OL6 . . . . .85 B7
Beverly Rd M14 . . . . .110 E7
Beverston Dr M7. . . . . . . .155 B2
Bevill Sq M3 . . . . .158 E2
Bevin Ave WA3 . . . . .92 B4
Bevington St 8 WN4 . . . . .72 F5
Bevis Dr M27 . . . . .27 F8
BEVIS GREEN 27 F8
Bewerley Cl WN3 . . . . .150 B2
Bewick St 1 BL2 . . . . .25 B3
Bewley Gr WN7. . . . . .76 A6
Bewley St OL8. . . . . .66 D2
Bewley Wlk M40. . . . . .83 A6
Bexhill Ave WA15. . . . . . . .119 F6
Bexhill Cl BL3 . . . . .43 C3
Bexhill Dr
  Hindley WN7 . . . . .57 C2
  Manchester M13 . . . . .98 F3
Bexhill Rd SK3 . . . . .123 E4
Bexhill Wlk OL9 . . . . .152 B2
Bexington Rd 8 M16 . . . . .97 E3
Bexley Cl
  Glossop SK13. . . . . .104 C3
  Urmston M41. . . . . .95 B4
Bexley Dr
  Bury BL8 . . . . .27 B1
  Walkden M38. . . . . .60 C4
Bexley Sq M3 . . . . .158 A2
Bexley St
  Hindley WN2 . . . . .57 B3
  Oldham OL9. . . . . .152 C1
Bexley Wlk M40 . . . . .83 B6
Beyer Cl M18 . . . . .165 C1
Bibby La M19. . . . . .110 F6
Bibby St
  Bury BL9 . . . . .44 F5
  Dukinfield SK14 . . . . .101 D5
Bibury Ave M22. . . . . .121 B3
Bickerdike Ave M12. . . . . . .99 B3
Bickerdike Ct 1 M12 . . . . .99 B3
Bickershaw 74 F8
Bickershaw CE Prim Sch
  WN2. . . . . .74 F8
Bickershaw Dr M28. . . . . . .60 C2
Bickershaw La
  Bickershaw WN2 . . . . .74 F8
  Leigh WN2. . . . . .56 D1
Bickerstaffe Cl OL2. . . . . .149 A1
Bickerton Cl OL9 . . . . .66 B3
Bickerton Dr SK7 . . . . . . .124 A1
Bickerton Rd WA14 . . . . .119 B6
Bickley Gr M29. . . . . .77 C6
Biddall Dr M23. . . . . .121 B6
Biddisham Wlk
  Manchester M40 . . . . . . .157 A1
  Manchester M40 . . . . . . .160 A4
Biddulph Ave SK2 . . . . . . .124 C5
Bideford Dr
  Bolton BL2. . . . . .43 A6
  Wythenshawe M23 . . . . . .120 F8
Bideford Rd
  Rochdale OL11. . . . . .30 B3
  Stockport SK2 . . . . .124 C8
Bidford Cl M29 . . . . .59 C1
Bidston Ave M14 . . . . .98 B2
Bidston Cl
  Bury BL8 . . . . .27 A2
  Shaw OL2. . . . . .49 D6
Bidston Dr SK9 . . . . .131 E2
Bidworth La SK13. . . . . . . .171 A1
Big Fold BL6. . . . . .21 D2
Biggenwood Wlk 17
  M40 . . . . .83 A7
Biggin Gdns OL10. . . . . . . .46 E7
Bignor St M8. . . . . .156 A2
Bilbao St BL1. . . . . .144 C4
Bilberry St
  Rochdale OL16. . . . . .31 A6
  Rochdale OL16. . . . . .31 B6
Bilbrook St M4. . . . . .159 B3
Billberry Cl M45. . . . . .63 B8
Billing Ave M12. . . . . .163 C3
BILLINGE 71 E4
Billinge Arc 12 WN1 . . . . .150 C4
Billinge Cl 5 BL1. . . . . . . .145 D8
Billinge Hospl WN5. . . . . . .53 D2
Billinge Rd
  Garswood WN4 . . . . .72 C5

Billinge Rd continued
  Wigan, Pemberton WN3,
  WN5 . . . . .54 D4
  Wigan, Worsley Hall
  WN5 . . . . .54 E6
Billington Ave WA12 . . . . . .89 C5
Billington Rd M27 . . . . . . .80 E8
Bill La M45. . . . . .62 F8
Bill Williams Cl M11. . . . . .165 C4
Billy La M27. . . . . .62 A2
Billy Meredith Cl 4
  M14 . . . . .98 A3
Billy's La SK8 . . . . .123 A1
Billy Whelan Wlk 25
  M40 . . . . .83 C5
Bilsland Wlk 18 M40. . . . . .83 C5
Bilson Dr SK3 . . . . .123 B7
Bilson Sq OL16. . . . . .32 A5
Bilton Wlk M8. . . . . .156 C4
Binbrook Wlk BL3 . . . . . . .147 C4
Bincombe Wlk M13. . . . . .163 C1
Bindloss Ave M30. . . . . . . .80 A3
Bindon Wlk 4 M9 . . . . . . .157 A3
Bingham Dr M23 . . . . .120 F6
Bingham St M27 . . . . .79 F8
Bingley Cl M11. . . . . .164 C4
Bingley Dr M41. . . . . .94 F4
Bingley Rd OL16. . . . . .31 C7
Bingley Sq OL16 . . . . .31 C7
Bingley Terr OL16. . . . . . . .31 C7
Bingley Wlk
  Farnworth BL4. . . . . .60 D7
  Manchester M7 . . . . .80 F8
Binns Nook Rd OL12. . . . . .15 A2
Binns Pl M4. . . . . .159 B1
Binns St SK15 . . . . .85 E1
Binsley Cl M44 . . . . .94 A1
Binstead Cl M14. . . . . .98 E3
Birch Rd
  Abram Brow M42. . . . . . . .74 B7
  Atherton M46. . . . . .58 E3
  Carrington M31, WA14 . . .106 F3
  Coppull PR7 . . . . .19 E8
  Gatley SK8 . . . . .122 A5
  Hollinfare WA3 . . . . .105 B2
  Kearsley BL4 . . . . .60 F6
  Leigh WN7. . . . . .75 F7
  Manchester M8. . . . . .64 B1
  Middleton M24. . . . . .107 A3
  Partington M31. . . . . .105 D3
  Poynton SK12 . . . . .133 F2
  Rochdale OL12. . . . . .15 D5
  Swinton M27 . . . . .79 D5
  Uppermill OL3 . . . . .69 C7
  Walkden M28. . . . . .60 E1
Birch St
  Ashton-u-L OL7 . . . . .84 E1
  Ashton-u-L OL7 . . . . .100 F8
  Bolton BL2. . . . . .148 B2
  Bury BL9 . . . . .140 C3
  Droylsden M43. . . . . .100 B8
  Heywood OL10. . . . . .29 D1
  Hindley WN2 . . . . .56 D5
  Manchester M12 . . . . .165 A2
  Radcliffe M26 . . . . .44 F4
  Stalybridge SK15. . . . . . . .86 C5
  3 Tyldesley M29 . . . . .59 A1
  Wardle OL12 . . . . .15 C6
  Wigan WN6 . . . . .37 A1
Birch Terr 2 SK14 . . . . . . .167 A2
Birch Tree Ave SK7 . . . . . .134 A8
Birch Tree Cl WA14 . . . . . .119 C1
Birch Tree Ct M22 . . . . . . .121 D3
Birch Tree Dr M22 . . . . . . .121 D3
Birch Tree Rd BL3 . . . . . . .90 F8
Birch Tree Way 4 BL6. . . . .22 E1
BIRCH VALE 127 F2
Birchvale Cl
  Manchester M15. . . . . . . .162 B2
  Poynton SK12 . . . . .133 E3
Birchvale Dr SK6 . . . . .113 D3
Birch Vale Terr SK22 . . . . .127 F3
Birchway
  Bramhall SK7. . . . . .132 D7
  High Lane SK6. . . . . .134 F7
Birchwood
  Chadderton OL9. . . . . .65 E7
  Droylsden M43. . . . . .84 B3
Birchwood Cl
  Leigh WN7. . . . . .75 F3
  Stockport SK4 . . . . .168 A1
  Wigan WN3 . . . . .54 D1
Birchwood Dr
  Manchester M40 . . . . . . .157 A2
  Wilmslow SK9 . . . . .137 D8
Birchwood Rd M24 . . . . . . .65 C8
Birchwood Way SK16 . . . . .101 D6
Bird Hall Ave SK8 . . . . . . .123 C4
Birdhall Gr M19 . . . . .111 A8
Bird Hall La SK3 . . . . .123 B6
Bird Hall Rd SK8 . . . . .123 C5
Birdlip Dr M23 . . . . .121 A3
Bird St M12 . . . . .151 C3
Birkby Dr M24. . . . . .46 E2
Birkdale Ave
  Atherton M46 . . . . .58 C5
  Royton OL2 . . . . .48 E2
  Whitefield M45 . . . . .62 D6
Birkdale Cl
  Bramhall SK7. . . . . .133 A7
  Dukinfield SK16 . . . . .101 F5
  Heywood OL10. . . . . .46 D8
Birkdale Dr
  Bury BL8 . . . . .27 B2
  Sale M33 . . . . .107 E2
Birkdale Gdns BL3. . . . . . .145 A1

Birch Gr continued
  Denton, Hooley Hill
  M34 . . . . .100 F6
  Denton M34. . . . . .100 E3
  Downall Green WN4 . . . . . .72 D5
  Manchester M14 . . . . .98 D3
  Prestwich M25. . . . . .63 A6
  Ramsbottom BL0 . . . . .11 A3
Birchgrove Cl BL3 . . . . . . .146 A3
Birch Hall Cl OL4 . . . . .67 F4
Birch Hall La M13 . . . . . . .98 E3
Birch Hey Cl 2 OL12. . . . . .15 C4
Birch Hill Bsns Ctr
  OL10. . . . . .46 C5
Birch Hill Cres OL12 . . . . . .15 E4
Birch Hill Hospl OL12 . . . . .15 E5
Birch Hill La OL12 . . . . . . .15 D6
Birch Hill Wlk OL15 . . . . . .15 F5
Birch Ho BL5. . . . . .57 F7
Birch Ind Est OL10. . . . . . .46 A5
Birchington Rd M14,
  M20 . . . . .110 A8
Birchin La M4. . . . . .159 A1
Birchinlee Ave OL2 . . . . . . .48 C3
Birchin La M4. . . . . .159 A1
Birch La
  Dukinfield SK16. . . . . . . .101 D7
  Manchester M13 . . . . .98 F4
Birchlea WA15. . . . . .119 F4
Birchleaf Gr M5 . . . . .80 C2
Birch-Lea Cl BL9 . . . . .44 F7
Birchleaf Gr M5 . . . . .80 C2
Birling Dr M23 . . . . .121 B4
Birnham Gr OL10 . . . . .29 A1
Birshaw Cl OL2 . . . . .149 B1
Birstall Wlk M23. . . . . . . .121 A6
Birtenshaw Cres BL7. . . . . .25 B7
Birtenshaw Hall Sch
  BL7. . . . . .25 B6
Birtle Dr M29. . . . . .77 C7
Birtle Rd BL9 . . . . .28 E6
Birtles Ave SK5. . . . . .99 F3
Birtles Cl
  Cheadle SK8 . . . . .123 A5
  Dukinfield SK16. . . . . . . .102 A8
Birtlespool Rd SK8 . . . . . .122 F4
Birtles The M22 . . . . .121 B2
Birtles Way 4 SK9. . . . . . .131 D5
Birtle View Sch OL10. . . . . .29 C2
Birt St M40 . . . . .160 A4
Birwood Rd M8. . . . . .64 B2
Biscay Cl M11 . . . . .160 C1
Bishop Bilsborrow Meml
  RC Prim Sch M14 . . . . . . .97 F3
Bishopbridge Cl BL3. . . . . .147 C4
Bishop Bridgeman CE
  Prim Sch BL3 . . . . .147 B4
Bishop Cl M16. . . . . .97 E4
Bishopdale Cl OL2 . . . . . . .48 D5
Bishopgate WN1. . . . . . . .150 C4
Bishopgate St OL9. . . . . . .152 A1
Bishop Marshall CE
  Prim Sch M40 . . . . .157 A1
Bishop Marshall Way
  M24 . . . . .46 D4
Bishop Rd
  Salford M6. . . . . .80 B8
  Urmston M41. . . . . .94 D2
Bishops Cl
  Altrincham WA14. . . . . . .119 B1
  Ashton-u-L OL7 . . . . .85 A5
Bishop's Cl
  Bolton BL3. . . . . .42 A2
  Cheadle SK8 . . . . .123 A5
Bishops Cnr M15. . . . . . . .162 C2
Bishopsgate M2 . . . . .162 C4
Bishopsgate Wlk OL16 . . . .31 C4
Bishops Mdw M24 . . . . . . .46 D3
Bishops Mews M33. . . . . .107 E6
Bishops Rd M25. . . . . .63 C2
Bishop's Rd BL3 . . . . .42 A2
Bishop St
  Middleton M24. . . . . .65 D7
  Rochdale OL16. . . . . .15 B1
  Stockport SK1 . . . . .112 A1
Bishops Wlk OL7. . . . . . . .106 A8
Bishopton Cl M19 . . . . . . .99 C1
Bisley Ave M23. . . . . .120 F6
Bisley St OL8. . . . . .153 A2
Bismarck St OL4 . . . . .67 B5
Bispham Ave
  Bolton BL2. . . . . .42 F7
  Reddish SK5 . . . . .99 F3
Bispham Cl BL8 . . . . .26 F1
Bispham Ct WN5. . . . . .53 D2
Bispham Dr WN4 . . . . .72 F5
Bispham Gr M7. . . . . .155 B3
Bispham Hall Bsns Pk
  WN5 . . . . .53 C2
Bispham St BL2 . . . . .148 C4
Bittern Cl
  Poynton SK12 . . . . .133 A4
  Rochdale OL11 . . . . .29 F3
Bittern Dr M43 . . . . .84 C3
Bk Adcroft St SK1 . . . . . . .170 C3
Bk Alfred St BL0. . . . . . . .138 B1
Bk Andrew St OL5 . . . . . . .86 C8
Bk Cecil St OL5. . . . . .86 C8
Bk Chapel St
  Bury BL8 . . . . .27 A2
  11 Manchester M19 . . . . .99 A1
Bk Cheshire St OL6. . . . . . .85 B7
Bk Deane Church La
  BL3. . . . . .146 B4
Bk Grosvenor St 2
  SK15. . . . . .86 A1
Bk Knowl St SK15. . . . . . . .86 B2
Bk Melbourne St 1
  SK15. . . . . .86 A1

Birkdale Gr
  Eccles M30 . . . . .79 F2
  Reddish SK5. . . . . .111 F5
Birkdale Rd
  Reddish SK5. . . . . .111 F5
  Rochdale OL16. . . . . .31 C4
Birkdale St M8 . . . . .156 A3
Birkenhills Dr BL3 . . . . . . .40 E5
Birkett Bank WN1 . . . . . . .151 B4
Birkett Dr BL1 . . . . .24 D6
Birkett Dr BL1 . . . . .24 D6
Birkett St WN1 . . . . .151 B4
Birkinbrook Cl M45. . . . . . .45 A1
Birkinheath La WA14 . . . . .128 A4
Birkleigh Wlk BL2 . . . . .42 E6
Birks Av OL4 . . . . .67 F8
Birks Dr BL8 . . . . .27 B6
Birkside Cl WN3 . . . . .55 A1
Birks La OL14 . . . . .6 B8
Birkworth Ct SK2 . . . . . . .124 D6
Birley Cl
  Altrincham WA15. . . . . . .119 F7
  Appley Bridge WN6 . . . . . .35 F8
Birley Pk M20 . . . . .109 F3
Birley St
  Bolton BL1. . . . . .143 B4
  Bury BL9 . . . . .27 F5
  Leigh WN7. . . . . .76 A6
  Newton-le-W WA12. . . . . .89 D4
  Rochdale OL12. . . . . .15 A1
  Salford M3. . . . . .158 A3
Blackcap Cl M28 . . . . .78 B7
Blackcarr Rd M23 . . . . . . .121 B6
Blackchapel Dr OL16 . . . . . .31 B3
Blackcroft Cl M27 . . . . .79 E8
Blackden Wlk SK9 . . . . . . .131 D1
Blackdown Gr 8 OL8 . . . . .66 E3
Blackfield La M7 . . . . .81 C8
Blackfields M7 . . . . .155 A4
Blackford Ave BL9 . . . . . . .44 F4
BLACKFORD BRIDGE 44 F4
Blackford Rd M19 . . . . . . .111 B7
Blackford Wlk M40 . . . . . .160 A3
Blackfriar St M3. . . . . .158 A3
Blackfriars Rd M3 . . . . . . .158 B2
Blackfriars St M3 . . . . . . .158 C2
Blackhill Cl 8 M13 . . . . . .163 B3
Blackhorse Ave BL6. . . . . . .21 C2
Blackhorse St BL6. . . . . . . .21 C3
Black Horse St
  Blackrod BL6. . . . . .21 C3
  Bolton BL1. . . . . .145 B2
  Farnworth BL4. . . . . .60 E7
Black La
  Leigh WN7. . . . . .76 D5
  Ramsbottom BL0. . . . . . . .12 B7
BLACK LANE 43 F6
Blackleach Ctry Pk*
  M28 . . . . .60 D4
Blackleach Dr M28 . . . . . . .60 D5
Blackledge Cl WN5 . . . . . . .53 E5
Blackledge St BL3 . . . . . . .146 C4
BLACKLEY 64 B5
Blackley Cl BL9 . . . . .45 A2
Blackleyhurst Ave
  WN5. . . . . .71 E5
Blackley New Rd M9,
  M25 . . . . .64 C5
Blackley St
  Manchester M16 . . . . . . .161 C1
  Middleton M24. . . . . .64 B7
Blacklock St M3, M8. . . . .158 C4
Blackmoor Ave M29 . . . . . .77 B6
Black Moss Cl M26 . . . . . . .43 D3
Black Moss Rd WA14 . . . . .118 F7
Blackpits Rd OL11 . . . . .13 C2
Blackpool St 8 M11. . . . . . .83 C2
Blackrock OL5. . . . . .86 C6
Blackrock St M11 . . . . .164 C4
BLACKROD 21 D2
Blackrod Anglican/
  Methodist Prim Sch
  BL6. . . . . .21 C2
Blackrod Brow BL6. . . . . . . .21 D1
Blackrod By-Pass Rd
  BL6. . . . . .21 D2
Blackrod Dr BL8 . . . . .26 F1
Blackrod Ind Est BL6 . . . . .38 E7
Blackrod Prim Sch
  BL6. . . . . .38 E8
Blackrod Sta BL6 . . . . .21 D2
Blacksail Wlk 8 OL1 . . . . . .49 A1
Blackshaw Ho BL3 . . . . . . .144 C2
Blackshaw La
  Alderley Edge SK9. . . . . . .136 F1
  Bolton BL3. . . . . .144 C2
  Royton OL2. . . . . .49 A4
Blackshaw Lane Jun & Inf
  Sch OL2. . . . . .49 A4
Blackshaw Prim Sch
  BL2. . . . . .42 E4
Blackshaw St SK13 . . . . . .171 D3
Blackshaw St 3 SK3. . . . . .170 B4
Blackshaw Row 2
  BL3. . . . . .144 C1
Blackshaw St SK3. . . . . . . .170 B4
Blacksmith La OL11. . . . . . .30 B4
Blacksmiths Fold M46 . . . .58 E2
Blackstock St M13. . . . . . . .98 C4
Blackstone Ave OL16. . . . . .31 B8
Blackstone Edge Old Rd
  OL15. . . . . .16 E6
Blackstone Edge Rd
  HX7 . . . . .7 F5
Blackstone Ho SK2 . . . . . .124 D5
Blackstone Rd SK2 . . . . . .124 D5
Blackstone Wlk M9 . . . . . .157 A2

Bk Parsonage St 4
  BL9. . . . . .141 A3
Bk Portland St OL6 . . . . . .166 A2
Bk Rochdale Old Road N
  BL9. . . . . .141 C3
Bk Stayley Rd OL5 . . . . . . .86 D8
Bk Water St OL6 . . . . .166 B2
Blackbank St BL1 . . . . .143 C2
Blackberry Cl WA14. . . . . .119 B8
Blackberry Cl WN2. . . . . . .56 C4
Blackberry La SK5 . . . . . . .112 C7
Black Brook Rd SK4 . . . . . .111 D7
Blackburn Cl WA3. . . . . . . .90 E8
Blackburn Gdns M20. . . . .110 A4
Blackburn Pl M5 . . . . .81 C1
Blackburn Rd
  Bolton, Back O' Th' Bank
  BL1. . . . . .143 C2
  Bolton, Egerton BL7 . . . . . . .8 C4
  Edenfield BL0, BB4 . . . . . . .1 D5
  Edgworth BL7 . . . . .9 D7
Blackburn St
  Manchester M16 . . . . .161 C1
  Prestwich M25. . . . . .63 C4
  Radcliffe M26 . . . . .44 A3
  7 Radcliffe M26. . . . . .44 B2
  Salford M3. . . . . .158 A3
Black Horse St

Blackthorn Ave
Manchester M19 . . . . 111 A7
Wigan WN6 . . . . 36 F3
Blackthorn Cl OL12 . . . . . . 14 E2
Blackthorne CT BL1 . . . . . 142 A1
Blackthorne Dr M33 . . . . . 107 D2
Blackthorne St SK14 . . . . 113 E7
Blackthorn Mews OL12 . . 14 E2
Blackthorn Rd OL8 . . . . . . 84 C8
Blackthorn Wlk **3**
M31 . . . . 105 E2
Blackwin St M12 . . . . 165 A2
Blackwood Ct OL13 . . . . . . 3 C8
Blackwood Dr M23 . . . . . 120 D8
Blackwood Rd OL13 . . . . . . 3 B7
Blackwood St BL3 . . . . 42 A4
Bladen Cl SK8 . . . . 123 A4
Blainscough Rd PR7 . . . . . 19 E8
Blair Ave
Hindley WN2 . . . . 57 B3
Urmston M41 . . . . 94 E2
Walkden M38 . . . . 60 B4
Blair Cl
Hazel Grove SK7 . . . . 133 C8
Sale M33 . . . . 107 C1
Shaw OL2 . . . . 149 B3
Blairhall Ave M40 . . . . 83 A7
Blair La BL2 . . . . 25 D1
Blairmore Dr BL3 . . . . 40 E5
Blair Rd M16 . . . . 97 E1
Blair St
Bolton BL7 . . . . 25 A8
Kearsley BL4 . . . . 61 B6
Manchester M16 . . . . 162 A1
Rochdale OL12 . . . . 14 D1
Blake Ave M46 . . . . 58 D5
Blakeborough Ho **8**
M46 . . . . 58 D3
Blake Dr M31 . . . . 150 A1
Blakedown Wlk M12 . . . . 164 B1
Blake Dr SK2 . . . . 124 E2
Blakefield Dr M28 . . . . 60 E1
Blake Gdns BL1 . . . . 143 A2
Blakelock St OL2 . . . . 149 B3
Blakemere Ave M33 . . . . 108 E3
Blakemore Pk M46 . . . . . . 58 B4
Blakemore Wlk M12 . . . . 160 B1
Blake St
Bolton, Bromley Cross
BL7 . . . . 25 A7
Bolton, Halliwell BL1 . . . . 143 A2
Rochdale OL11 . . . . 31 A8
Blakeswell Cl M41 . . . . 94 D3
Blakey Cl BL3 . . . . 40 F4
Blakey St M12 . . . . 164 A4
Blanchard St M15 . . . . . . 162 B1
Blanche St OL12 . . . . 15 A2
Blanche Wlk **10** OL1 . . . . 67 A8
Bland Cl M35 . . . . 83 E7
Blandford Ave M28 . . . . . . 79 A8
Blandford Cl
Bury BL8 . . . . 27 D5
Tyldesley M29 . . . . 59 A1
Blandford Ct
Ashton-u-L OL6 . . . . 166 A3
Stalybridge SK15 . . . . 86 A2
Blandford Dr **1** M40 . . . . . 65 C1
Blandford Ho **7** SK15 . . . 86 A2
Blandford Rd
Eccles M30 . . . . 79 B2
Salford M6 . . . . 81 B4
Stockport SK4 . . . . 168 C2
Blandford Rise BL6 . . . . . . 22 F1
Blandford St
Ashton-u-L OL6 . . . . 166 A3
Stalybridge SK15 . . . . 86 A2
Bland St M25 . . . . 63 B2
Bland St M16 . . . . 97 E4
Blanefield Cl M21 . . . . . . 109 E7
Blantyre Ave M28 . . . . 60 E2
Blantyre Ho **4** M15 . . . . . 162 A3
Blantyre Rd M27 . . . . 80 B6
Blantyre St
Eccles M30 . . . . 79 A3
Hindley WN2 . . . . 56 E6
Manchester M15 . . . . 162 A3
Swinton M27 . . . . 61 D1
Blanwood Dr M8 . . . . 156 B3
Blaven Cl SK3 . . . . 170 E8
Blaydon Cl WN2 . . . . 38 D5
Blazemoss Bank SK2 . . . 124 D5
Bleach St WN2 . . . . 56 C4
Bleackley St BL8 . . . . 27 C4
Bleadale Cl SK9 . . . . 131 D1
Bleak Hey Nook La
OL3 . . . . 51 C8
Bleak Hey Rd M22 . . . . . . 121 F2
Bleakholt Rd BL0 . . . . 1 F1
Bleakledge Gr WN2 . . . . . . 56 F7
Bleakley St **1** M45 . . . . . . 44 E1
Bleaklow WN3 . . . . 55 B2
Bleaklow Wlk **29**
SK13 . . . . 171 B1
Bleak St BL2 . . . . 25 B2
Bleasby St OL4 . . . . 67 C7
Bleasdale Cl
Horwich BL6 . . . . 39 F8
Whitefield BL9 . . . . 45 A3
Bleasdale Rd
Bolton BL1 . . . . 23 F2
Newton-le-W M22 . . . . 89 C4
Wythenshawe M22 . . . . . 121 A2
Bleasdale Rd WN2 . . . . 57 A5
Bleasefell Chase M28 . . . . 78 A5
Bleatarn Rd SK1 . . . . 124 B7

Bledlow Cl M30 . . . . 79 E3
Blencarn Wlk M9 . . . . 157 A2
Blendworth Cl M8 . . . . . . 155 C3
Blenheim Ave M16 . . . . . . 97 D2
Blenheim Cl
Altrincham WA14 . . . . . . 119 D2
4 Glossop SK13 . . . . . . 104 A5
Heywood OL10 . . . . 29 E2
Poynton SK12 . . . . 133 F4
Whitefield BL9 . . . . 45 A5
Wilmslow SK9 . . . . 137 D7
Blenheim Dr WN7 . . . . 76 E7
Blenheim Rd
Ashton-in-M WN4 . . . . 73 D2
Bolton BL2 . . . . 42 E6
Cheadle SK8 . . . . 123 B2
Manchester M16 . . . . 97 A3
Wigan WN5 . . . . 54 C8
Blenheim St
8 Oldham OL4 . . . . 49 D1
13 Rochdale OL12 . . . . . 14 C1
Tyldesley M29 . . . . 76 F8
Blenheim Wlk OL6 . . . . . . 85 E4
Blenheim Ave OL1 . . . . . . 49 D3
Blenmar Cl M26 . . . . 44 C5
Bleriot St BL3 . . . . 147 A3
Blessed Thomas Holford
RC Coll WA15 . . . . 119 E4
Bletchley Cl M13 . . . . 164 A1
Bletchley Rd SK4 . . . . 110 E1
Blethyn St BL3 . . . . 146 B2
Blewberry Cl WN7 . . . . 75 F7
Bligh Rd **15** BL5 . . . . 39 E1
Blinco Rd M41 . . . . 95 F1
Blind La M12 . . . . 164 A3
Blindsill Rd BL4 . . . . 60 B7
Blissford Cl WN2 . . . . 56 D4
Blisworth Ave **3** M30 . . . 95 E8
Blisworth Cl M4 . . . . 160 A1
Blithfield Wlk M40 . . . . . 100 E2
Block La OL9 . . . . 152 B1
Blocksage St SK16 . . . . . 101 D7
Blodwell St M6, M5 . . . . . 154 C2
Blofield Ct BL4 . . . . 60 D7
Blomley St OL4 . . . . 30 C2
Bloomfield Ct SK8 . . . . . . 131 E7
Bloomfield Dr
Salford M8 . . . . 155 B1
Whitefield BL9 . . . . 45 B3
Worsley M28 . . . . 78 A7
Bloomfield Rd BL4 . . . . 60 D6
Bloomfield St BL1 . . . . . . 145 B8
Bloomsbury Gr WA15 . . . 120 A6
Bloomsbury La WA15 . . . 120 A6
Bloom St
Manchester M1 . . . . 163 A4
Oldham OL9 . . . . 153 B2
Ramsbottom BL0 . . . . 11 A4
Salford M3 . . . . 158 D2
Stockport SK3 . . . . 170 A4
Blossom Pl OL16 . . . . 139 C4
Blossom Rd M31 . . . . 105 E2
Blossoms Hey SK8 . . . . . . 122 E1
Blossoms Hey Wlk
SK8 . . . . 122 E1
Blossoms La SK7 . . . . 132 B2
Blossoms St SK7 . . . . 170 C3
Blossom St
Manchester M4 . . . . 159 B2
Salford M3 . . . . 158 B2
11 Tyldesley M29 . . . . . . 59 A1
Bloxham Wlk M9 . . . . 64 F3
Blucher St
Ashton-u-L OL7 . . . . 85 A6
Manchester M12 . . . . 164 B2
Salford M5 . . . . 81 C1
Bluebell Ave
Manchester M40 . . . . 65 A1
Wigan WN6 . . . . 36 F4
Bluebell Cl SK14 . . . . 101 F5
Bluebell Dr OL13 . . . . 3 B3
Bluebell Gr SK8 . . . . 122 D4
Bluebell La M24, M25 . . . . 46 A1
Bluebell Way SK9 . . . . . . 131 C1
Blueberry Ave M40 . . . . . . 65 D2
Blueberry Bsns Pk
OL16 . . . . 31 D7
Blueberry Dr OL2 . . . . 49 D7
Blueberry Rd WA14 . . . . . 119 A2
Blue Chip Bsns Pk
WA14 . . . . 119 C7
Blue Coat CE Sch The
OL1 . . . . 153 C3
Bluefields OL2 . . . . 49 D8
Blue Ribbon Wlk M27 . . . . 62 A1
Bluestone Dr SK4 . . . . . . 110 E3
Bluestone Rd
M40 . . . . 83 A8
Reddish M34 . . . . 100 A2
Blundell Cl BL9 . . . . 45 B3
Blundell La BL6 . . . . 21 A2
Blundells Ct WN3 . . . . 54 D4
Blundells Mews WN3 . . . . 54 D4
Blundell St BL1 . . . . 145 B3
Blundering La SK15 . . . . . 102 D6
Blunn St OL8 . . . . 66 F4
Blyborough Cl M6 . . . . . . 154 A4
Blyth Ave
Littleborough OL15 . . . . . . 15 F3
Wythenshawe M23 . . . . . 109 C2
Blyth Cl WA15 . . . . 120 D6
Blythe Ave SK7 . . . . 132 C6
Blyton St M15 . . . . 163 B1
Blyton Way M34 . . . . 113 B7
Bnos Yisroel Schs
M7 . . . . 155 B4
Boad St M1 . . . . 163 B4

Boardale Dr M24 . . . . 46 E1
Boardman Cl
Bolton BL1 . . . . 143 B2
Reddish SK5 . . . . 169 C4
Boardman Fold Cl
M24 . . . . 65 A5
Boardman Fold Rd
M24 . . . . 65 A5
Boardman La M24 . . . . 64 C8
Boardman Rd M8 . . . . 63 F2
Boardman St
Blackrod BL6 . . . . 21 D2
Bolton BL1 . . . . 143 B2
Eccles M30 . . . . 79 E1
Hyde SK14 . . . . 167 A2
Board St
Ashton-u-L OL6 . . . . 85 D4
Bolton BL3 . . . . 145 A2
Boarfold La SK13,
SK14 . . . . 114 C5
Boar Green Cl M40 . . . . . . 83 C7
Boarsgreave La B84 . . . . . . 2 D5
Boarshaw Clough M24 . . . 47 B2
Boarshaw Clough Way
M24 . . . . 47 A2
Boarshaw Com Prim Sch
M24 . . . . 47 B2
Boarshaw Cres M24 . . . . . 47 C3
Boarshaw La M24 . . . . 47 D3
Boarshaw Rd M24 . . . . 47 B2
BOAR'S HEAD 37 A6
Boars Head Ave WN6 . . . . 37 A7
Boarshurst Ind Pk OL3 . . . 69 B6
Boarshurst La OL3 . . . . 69 C5
Boat La
Diggle M44 . . . . 51 E5
Irlam M44 . . . . 94 B2
Wythenshawe M22 . . . . . 109 E1
Boat Lane Ct M22 . . . . . . 109 F1
Boatman's Row M29 . . . . . 77 C4
Boatmans The M15 . . . . . 162 B3
Boatmans Wlk OL7 . . . . . 166 A1
Boatyard The **1** M32 . . . . 96 E2
Bobbin Wlk **6** OL1 . . . . . 49 B1
Bob Massey Cl M11 . . . . . 83 C1
Bob's La M44 . . . . 105 D4
Boddens Hill Rd SK4 . . . . 168 A1
Bodden St WA3 . . . . 75 A1
Boddington Rd M40 . . . . . 79 A1
Bodiam Rd BL8 . . . . 10 F2
Bodley St M11 . . . . 83 C2
Bodmin Cl OL2 . . . . 49 A3
Bodmin Cres SK5 . . . . . . 112 B5
Bodmin Dr
Bramhall SK7 . . . . 132 E7
Platt Bridge WN2 . . . . 56 A1
Bodmin Rd
Sale M33 . . . . 107 D5
Tyldesley M29 . . . . 77 C8
Bodmin Wlk **3** M23 . . . . 121 A5
Bodney Wlk M9 . . . . 64 B3
Bogburn La PR7 . . . . 19 C6
Boggard La SK13 . . . . 115 D6
Bogguard Rd SK6 . . . . . . 127 A4
Bognor Rd SK3 . . . . 123 E4
BOHOLT 27 A4
Bolam Cl M23 . . . . 108 F1
Boland Dr M14 . . . . 110 D8
Bolbury Cres M27 . . . . 80 D8
Bolderod Pl OL1 . . . . 67 A8
Bolderstone Pl SK2 . . . . . 124 E4
Bolderwood Dr M12 . . . . 165 A5
Bold St
Altrincham WA14 . . . . . . 119 D3
Bolton BL1 . . . . 145 C2
Bury BL9 . . . . 141 A3
Leigh WN7 . . . . 75 F5
Leigh WN7 . . . . 75 F6
Manchester, Moss Side
M16 . . . . 97 C4
Manchester, Old Trafford
M15 . . . . 162 B1
Swinton M27 . . . . 61 F2
Wigan WN5 . . . . 54 E5
Bolesworth Cl M21 . . . . . 108 F8
Boleyn Ct OL10 . . . . 29 C1
BOLHOLT 27 A4
Bolholt Ind Est **12** BL8 . . . 27 B4
Bolholt Terr BL8 . . . . 27 B4
Bolivia St M5 . . . . 154 A1
Bollen Wood Ct SK9 . . . . 131 B1
Bollin Ave WA14 . . . . 119 B5
Bollin Cl
Culcheth WA3 . . . . 92 A2
Kearsley BL4 . . . . 61 B6
Lymm WA13 . . . . 117 A4
Bollin Ct
Altrincham WA14 . . . . . . 119 B1
6 Manchester M15 . . . . 162 A2
Wilmslow SK9 . . . . 137 C6
Bollin Dr
Altrincham WA14 . . . . . . 119 A1
Lymm WA13 . . . . 117 A4
Sale M33 . . . . 108 B2
Bollings Yd BL1 . . . . 145 C2
Bollington Rd
Manchester M40 . . . . 160 A2
Stockport SK4 . . . . 111 D5
Bollington St OL7 . . . . 166 A4
Bollin Hill SK9 . . . . 137 B8
Bollin Ho **8** M7 . . . . 81 C5
Bollin Prim Sch
WA14 . . . . 119 D1
Bollin Sq WA14 . . . . 119 B1
Bollinway WA15 . . . . 129 A8
Bollin Way M45 . . . . 45 C2
Bollin Wlk
Reddish SK5 . . . . 169 C4

Bollin Wlk continued
Whitefield M45 . . . . 45 C2
Wilmslow SK9 . . . . 137 C7
Bollinwood Chase
SK9 . . . . 137 D7
Bolney St WN2 . . . . 38 A3
Bolney Wlk M40 . . . . 160 A4
Bolshaw Farm La
SK8 . . . . 131 C6
Bolshaw Prim Sch
SK8 . . . . 131 C6
Bolshaw Rd SK8 . . . . 131 C6
Bolt Mdw OL3 . . . . 69 A4
BOLTON 145 B4
Bolton Ave
Cheadle SK8 . . . . 132 B6
Manchester M19 . . . . 110 D2
Bolton Boys' Division Jun
Dept BL1 . . . . 144 C3
Bolton Cl
Golborne WA3 . . . . 91 B8
Poynton SK12 . . . . 133 D4
Prestwich M25 . . . . 62 F2
Bolton Com Coll (Clarence
St Ctr) BL1 . . . . 145 C4
Bolton Com Coll, Horwich
Ctr BL6 . . . . 22 D2
Bolton Com Coll
(Manchester Rd Ctr)
BL2 . . . . 148 A2
Bolton Gates Ret Pk
BL1 . . . . 145 C4
Bolton House Rd WN2 . . . 74 F8
Bolton Inst (Chadwick
Campus) BL2 . . . . 148 B2
Bolton Mus, Art Gal &
Aquarium *** BL1 . . . . . 145 C3
Bolton Muslim Girls Sch
BL3 . . . . 147 A4
Bolton Old Rd M46 . . . . . . 58 E3
Bolton Parish Church CE
Prim Sch BL2 . . . . 148 B3
Bolton Rd
Adlington BL6, PR6 . . . . . . 21 D6
Ashton-in-M WN2, WN4 . . 73 D5
Aspull WN2 . . . . 38 D4
Atherton M46 . . . . 58 E4
Blackrod BL2 . . . . 38 A8
Bolton, Hunger Hill BL3 . . 40 D2
Bury BL8, BL9 . . . . 27 C1
Edgworth BL7 . . . . 9 D5
Farnworth BL4 . . . . 42 D2
Kearsley BL4 . . . . 60 F7
Pendlebury M27 . . . . 80 C7
Radcliffe M26 . . . . 43 E3
Ramsbottom BL8 . . . . 10 D7
Rochdale OL11 . . . . 30 B4
Salford M6 . . . . 80 E5
Swinton M27 . . . . 62 A1
Walkden M28 . . . . 60 D4
Westhoughton BL5 . . . . . . 39 F1
Bolton Rd N BL0 . . . . 1 D2
Bolton Rd W BL0 . . . . 11 A4
Bolton Road Ind Est
BL5 . . . . 39 F1
Bolton St
Bolton Girls' & Boys'
Division BL1 . . . . 144 B3
Bolton Sixth Form Coll
BL1 . . . . 122 C4
Bolton Sq WN1 . . . . 37 E1
Bolton St
Bury BL9 . . . . 140 B2
Downall Green WN4 . . . . . 72 D5
Oldham OL4 . . . . 153 B8
Oldham OL4 . . . . 67 B6
Radcliffe M26 . . . . 43 F3
Ramsbottom BL0 . . . . 11 A4
Reddish SK5 . . . . 111 E7
Bolton St SK3 . . . . 145 C2
Boltons Yd OL3 . . . . 69 B8
Bolton Tech Exchange
BL1 . . . . 145 A3
Bombay Ho **5** M1 . . . . . . 163 A4
Bombay Rd
Stockport SK3 . . . . 123 C7
Wigan WN5 . . . . 36 C1
Bombay St
5 Ashton-u-L OL6 . . . . . 85 D4
Manchester M1 . . . . 163 A4
Bonar Cl **5** SK3 . . . . 123 C8
Bonar Rd SK3 . . . . 123 C8
Boncarn Dr M23 . . . . 121 A4
Bonchurch Wlk M18 . . . . 165 B2
Bond Cl BL6 . . . . 22 C3
Bondmark Rd M18 . . . . . . 165 C2
Bond's La PR7 . . . . 20 F7
Bond St M7 . . . . 155 B2
Bond St
Bury BL9 . . . . 141 A2
Denton M34 . . . . 100 F3
Edenfield BL0 . . . . 1 E2
Leigh WN7 . . . . 75 F1
Manchester M12 . . . . 163 C4
Rochdale OL12 . . . . 15 A2
Stalybridge SK15 . . . . 86 A3
Tyldesley M46 . . . . 58 F1
Bond Street Ind Est
M12 . . . . 163 C4
Bongs Rd SK2 . . . . 124 F6
Bonhill Wlk M11 . . . . 83 B2
Bonington Rise SK6 . . . . . 126 B8
Bonis Cres SK2 . . . . 124 C4
Bonny Brow St M24 . . . . . 64 B7
Bonnyfields SK6 . . . . 113 B2
Bonnywell Rd WN7 . . . . . . 75 F3
Bonsall Bank **3** SK13 . . 171 B2
Bonsall Fold **26** SK13 . . 171 B2

Bonsall St M15 . . . . 162 C2
Bonscale Cres M24 . . . . . . 46 E3
Bonville Chase WA14 . . . 119 A4
Bonville Rd WA14 . . . . . . 119 A4
Boodle St OL6 . . . . 166 B4
Bookham Wlk **16** M9 . . . 157 B4
Boond St
Manchester M4 . . . . 160 A1
Salford M3 . . . . 158 B2
Boonfields BL7 . . . . 25 A8
Booth Ave M14 . . . . 110 D7
Booth Bridge Cl M24 . . . . 64 C7
Boothby Rd M27 . . . . 61 E1
Boothby St SK2 . . . . 124 C4
Booth Cl
Bury BL8 . . . . 27 A5
4 Stalybridge SK15 . . . . 85 F1
Booth Clibborn Ct
M7 . . . . 155 A4
Boothcote M34 . . . . 100 D6
Booth Dr M41 . . . . 94 F5
Boothfield
11 Bury BL8 . . . . 27 C3
Eccles M30 . . . . 79 C2
Boothfield Ave M22 . . . . 121 D6
Boothfield Dr M22 . . . . . . 121 D6
Boothfield Rd M22 . . . . . . 121 D6
Booth Hall Dr BL8 . . . . 27 A5
Booth Hall Hospl M9 . . . . . 64 F3
Booth Hall Rd M9 . . . . 65 A3
Booth Hill La OL1 . . . . 48 E1
Booth House Trad Est
OL9 . . . . 152 C2
Boothman Ct M30 . . . . 79 F3
Booth Rd
Altrincham WA14 . . . . . . 119 C4
Bacup OL13 . . . . 3 B8
Droylsden M34 . . . . 100 A7
Handforth SK9 . . . . 131 A1
Little Lever BL3 . . . . 43 B2
Manchester M16 . . . . 97 C3
Sale M33 . . . . 108 B6
Boothroyden Cl M24 . . . . . 64 C7
Boothroyden Rd
Manchester M24, M9 . . . . 64 C6
Middleton M24 . . . . 64 C7
Boothroyden Terr M9 . . . . 64 C6
Booth St E M13 . . . . 163 B2
Booth St W M13, M15 . . . 163 A2
Boothsbank Ave M28 . . . . 78 B6
Booth's Brow Rd WN4 . . . . 72 D6
Booth's Ct **1** SK13 . . . . . 104 D1
Booth's Hall **2** 78 B5
Booth's Hall Rd M28 . . . . . 78 B5
Boothshall Paddock
M28 . . . . 78 B5
Booth's Hall Way M28 . . . . 78 B6
Booth St
Ashton-u-L OL6 . . . . 166 B2
Bolton BL1 . . . . 142 C3
Bury BL8 . . . . 26 F5
Denton M34 . . . . 100 F5
Failsworth M35 . . . . 83 E7
Hollingworth SK14 . . . . . 103 C5
Hyde SK14 . . . . 167 B1
Manchester M3 . . . . 158 C2
Middleton M24 . . . . 64 F5
Oldham, Bank Top OL9 . . 153 B2
2 Oldham, Lees OL4 . . . 67 E6
Rawtenstall B84 . . . . 2 E8
Stalybridge SK15 . . . . 170 B3
Stockport SK3 . . . . 170 B3
BOOTHSTOWN 78 A5
Boothstown Dr M28 . . . . . 78 A5
Boothstown Meth Prim
Sch M28 . . . . 77 F6
Boothway **8** M30 . . . . 79 F2
Booth Way BL8 . . . . 26 F5
Boot La BL1 . . . . 23 E1
Bootle St M2 . . . . 162 C4
Bor Ave WN3 . . . . 55 B4
Bordale Ave M9 . . . . 157 C3
Bordan St M1 . . . . 164 C4
Borden Cl **5** WN2 . . . . . . 37 F2
Border Brook La M28 . . . . 78 A6
Bordesley Ave M38 . . . . . . 60 A6
Bordley Wlk M23 . . . . . . 121 A5
Bordon Rd SK3 . . . . 123 B7
Bores Hill WN1 . . . . 20 C4
Boringdon Cl M40 . . . . 83 B6
Borland Ave M40 . . . . 65 D1
Borough Arc SK14 . . . . . 167 A2
Borough Ave
Radcliffe M26 . . . . 44 D5
Swinton M27 . . . . 62 A1
Borough Rd
Altrincham WA15 . . . . . . 119 E4
Salford M50 . . . . 154 A1
Borough St **5** SK15 . . . . . 86 A1
Borrans The M28 . . . . 77 F7
Borron St WA12 . . . . 89 B4
Borron St WN5 . . . . 89 B5
Borrowdale Ave
Bolton BL1 . . . . 144 A4
Gatley SK8 . . . . 122 B4
Borrowdale Cres
Ashton-u-L OL7 . . . . 84 F4
Manchester M20 . . . . 109 E4
Borrowdale Dr
Rochdale OL11 . . . . 30 C4

Borrowdale Dr *continued*
Whitefield BL9 45 A3
Borrowdale Rd
Middleton M24 46 E2
Stockport SK2 124 B6
Wigan WN5 54 B7
Borrowdale Terr SK15 86 A4
Borsdane Ave WN2 56 F5
Borsden St M27 61 D2
Borth Ave SK2 124 C7
Borth Wlk 3 M23 120 F6
Borwell St M18 99 D5
Boscobel Rd, BL4 BL3 42 B2
Boscombe Ave M30 95 C8
Boscombe Dr SK7 124 C1
Boscombe Pl WN2 56 E4
Boscombe St
Manchester M14 98 B2
Reddish SK5 99 F2
Boscow Rd BL3 43 A2
Bosden Ave SK7 124 F3
Bosden Cl
Handforth SK9 131 D5
Stockport SK1 170 C4
Bosden Fold SK1 170 C4
Bosden Fold Rd SK7 124 E3
Bosden Hall Rd SK7 124 E3
Bosdin Rd E M41 94 E1
Bosdin Rd W M41 94 E1
Boslam Wlk 5 M4 159 C2
Bosley Ave M20 110 A8
Bosley Cl SK9 131 D2
Bosley Dr SK12 134 A3
Bosley Rd SK3 123 A8
Bossall Ave M9 64 E4
Bossington Cl SK2 124 C8
Bostock Rd SK14 115 A8
Bostock Wlk M13 163 B3
Boston Bank Ho SK14 167 B3
Boston Cl
Bramhall SK7 132 D7
Culcheth WA3 91 F4
Failsworth M35 83 F8
Boston Ct
Hyde SK14 167 B3
Salford M50 96 E8
Boston Gr WN7 75 E8
Boston St
14 Bolton BL1 143 B2
Hyde SK14 167 B2
Manchester M15 162 C1
Oldham OL8 66 F4
Boston Wlk 8 M34 101 A1
Boswell Ave M34 84 D1
Boswell Pl WN3 54 F3
Boswell Way M24 47 E4
Bosworth Cl M45 63 C8
Bosworth Sq OL11 30 D4
Bosworth St
Horwich BL6 22 B4
Manchester M11 165 A4
Rochdale OL11 30 D4
Botanical Ave M16 161 A1
Botany Cl
Heywood OL10 29 B2
Wigan WN2 38 B2
Botany La OL6 166 C3
Botany Rd
Eccles M30 79 A4
Romiley SK6 113 A6
Botesworth Cl WN2 57 A4
Botesworth Gn OL16 32 A5
Botha Cl 4 M11 99 D7
Botham Cl M15 162 C1
Bothwell Rd M40 159 C3
Bottesford Ave M20 109 F5
Bottomfield Cl OL1 49 A1
BOTTOMLEY 6 C7
Bottomley Rd OL14 6 C6
Bottomley Side M9 64 C2
BOTTOM O' TH' BROW
29 B3
Bottom o' th' Knotts Brow
BL7 9 E3
Bottom O'Th Moor
BL2 25 D2
BOTTOM O' TH' MOOR
23 A2
Bottom o' th' Moor
Horwich BL6 23 A3
Oldham OL1, OL4 67 B7
BOTTOMS 86 D8
Bottoms Fold OL5 86 D8
Bottom St SK14 167 C3
Bougainvillea Gdns
M12 99 A4
Boughey St WN7 75 E5
Boulden Dr BL8 27 C5
Boulder Dr M23 121 A2
Boulderstone Rd SK15 86 A4
Boulevard The
Hazel Grove SK7 124 E2
Hollingworth SK14 171 A4
Manchester M20 109 F6
Bouley Wlk M12 165 A2
Boulton Ho 3 M1 163 A4
Boundary Cl
Mossley OL5 86 C6
Romiley SK6 113 C5
Boundary Cotts SK15 86 E7
Boundary Ct SK8 122 C5
Boundary Ct SK4 111 A7
Boundary Ct M28 78 B8
Boundary Dr BL2 43 A5
Boundary Edge BL0 1 E3
Boundary Gdns
Bolton BL1 143 B2
Oldham OL1 48 E1
Boundary Gn M34 100 E4
Boundary Gr M33 108 F2
Boundary La
Manchester M15 163 A2
Shevington Moor WN6 19 A3
Boundary Park Rd OL1 48 C1
Boundary Pk (Oldham Athletic AFC) OL1 48 D2
Boundary Rd
Cheadle SK8 123 A6
Irlam M44 94 C3
Swinton M27 61 F1
Boundary St E M1, M13 163 A3
Boundary St W M15 163 A2
Boundary St
Bolton BL1 143 A2
Leigh WN7 76 B4
Littleborough OL15 16 B6
Manchester M12 165 A2
Rochdale OL11 139 C1
Tyldesley M29 59 A1
Wigan WN1 151 A3
Boundary Terr SK9 130 F6
Boundary The M27 61 E4
Boundary Trad Pk M44 94 C3
Boundary Wlk OL11 139 B1
Bourdon St M40 160 A3
Bourget St M7 155 C4
Bournbrook Ave M38 60 A6
Bourne Ave
Golborne WA3 90 D8
Swinton M27 79 F7
Bourne Dr M40 65 B1
Bourne Ho 1 M6 154 C2
Bournelea Ave M19 110 F6
Bourne Rd OL2 149 A4
Bourne St
Oldham OL9 66 B2
Stockport SK4 169 B4
Wilmslow SK9 136 F6
Bourneville Dr BL8 27 A2
Bourne Wlk 9 BL1 143 C1
Bournville Ave SK4 169 B4
Bournville Gr M19 99 C1
Bourton Cl BL8 27 B3
Bourton Ct M29 59 D1
Bourton Dr M18 99 B4
Bowden Cl
Culcheth WA3 91 F4
Hattersley SK14 102 E1
Leigh WN7 76 C2
Trub OL11 47 D8
Bowden Ct M16 97 A4
Bowden House La
SK9 137 F8
Bowden La SK6 125 E7
Bowden Rd
Glossop SK13 104 C3
4 Pendlebury M27 80 A7
Bowden St
Denton M34 100 E3
Hazel Grove SK7 124 E3
BOWDON 119 B2
Bowdon Ave M14 97 F1
Bowdon CE Prim Sch WA14 119 C1
Bowdon Ho 2 SK3 170 B4
Bowdon Prep Sch WA14 119 C2
Bowdon Rd WA14 119 C3
Bowdon Rise WA14 119 D2
Bowdon St SK3 170 B4
Bowen Cl SK7 132 F5
Bowen St BL1 142 B1
Bower Ave
Hazel Grove SK7 124 D1
Rochdale OL12 15 D4
Stockport SK4 168 C2
Bower Ct SK14 102 A5
Bower Cup Fold SK15 86 E4
Bowerfield Ave SK7 133 D8
Bowerfield Cres SK7 133 E8
Bower Fold SK15 102 C8
Bowerfold La SK4 169 A2
Bower Gdns SK15 102 D8
Bower Gr SK15 86 C2
Bower Rd WA15 119 F1
Bowers Ave M41 95 B3
Bowers St M14 110 E7
Bower St
Bury BL9 141 C3
Failsworth M40 83 A5
Oldham OL1 67 B8
Reddish SK5 99 F2
Salford M7 155 C3
Bower Terr M43 84 C3
Bowery Ave SK8 131 F6
Bowes Cl BL8 27 B5
Bowes St M14 97 F3
Bowfell Dr SK6 134 E8
Bowfell Gr M9 64 B4
Bowfell Rd M41 95 B2
Bowfield Wlk 18 M40 83 C5
Bowgreave Ave BL2 42 F7
BOWGREEN 119 A1
Bow Green Mews
WA14 119 B2
Bow Green Rd WA14 119 A1
Bowgreen Wlk 14
M15 162 A2
Bowker Ave M34 113 B8
Bowker Bank Ave M8 63 F2
Bowker Cl OL11 13 E1
Bowker Ct M7 155 A2
Bowkers Row 12 BL1 145 C3
Bowker St
Haslingden BL0 1 C5
Hyde SK14 167 B3
Radcliffe M26 44 A3
Salford M7 155 A2
Walkden M28 60 B3
Bowker Vale Gdns M9 63 F3
Bowker Vale Prim Sch M8 63 F4
Bowker Vale Sta M8 63 F3
Bow La
Altrincham WA14 128 B8
Heywood OL10 29 D2
Manchester M2 158 C1
Bowlacre Rd SK14 113 D7
Bowland Ave
Ashton-in-M WN4 73 B4
Golborne WA3 74 C1
Reddish M18 100 A4
Bowland Cl
Ashton-u-L OL6 85 C7
Bury BL8 26 F3
Shaw OL2 48 E7
Stockport SK2 124 E5
Bowland Ct M33 108 B4
Bowland Dr BL1 23 E2
Bowland Gr OL16 31 F4
Bowland Rd
Glossop SK13 116 A8
Reddish M34 100 B3
Romiley SK6 113 B5
Wythenshawe M23 121 A6
BOWLEE 46 B1
Bowlee Cl BL9 45 A2
Bowler St
Manchester M19 111 B8
Shaw OL2 149 B3
Bowlers Wlk OL12 14 F2
Bowley Ave M22 121 A2
Bowling Ct BL1 24 E5
Bowling Gn Ct M16 97 D4
Bowling Gn The BL0 1 D3
Bowling Green Cl OL9 66 A4
Bowling Green Row
M46 58 B2
Bowling Green St
Heywood OL10 29 D2
Hyde SK14 167 A2
Bowling Green Way
OL11 29 F7
Bowling Rd M18 99 E3
Bowling St OL9 66 B2
Bowlings The WN6 37 A2
Bowman Cres OL6 85 D3
Bowmeadow Grange 2
M12 98 F4
Bowmead Wlk 8 M8 155 C2
Bowmont Cl SK8 123 A4
Bowness Ave
Cheadle SK8 123 B1
Irlam M44 105 D4
Reddish SK4 111 E6
Rochdale OL12 14 C1
Bowness Ct 5 M24 46 D2
Bowness Dr M33 107 F5
Bowness Pl WN2 56 B8
Bowness Prim Sch BL3 42 F3
Bowness Rd
Altrincham WA15 120 D5
Ashton-u-L OL7 84 F4
Bolton BL3 147 A4
Little Lever BL3 42 F4
Middleton M24 46 D1
Bowness St
Droylsden M11 99 F7
Stretford M32 96 D3
Bowness Wlk 7 OL2 48 E4
Bow Rd WN7 76 B3
Bowring St M7 81 C5
Bowscale Cl 3 M13 98 F4
Bow St
Ashton-u-L OL6 166 B3
Bolton BL1 145 C3
Dukinfield OL6, SK16 166 C2
7 Manchester M2 158 C1
Oldham OL1 153 C3
Rochdale OL11 30 D3
Stockport SK3 123 C8
Bowstone Hill Rd BL2,
BL8 26 B5
Bowyer Gdns BL3 40 F3
Boxgrove Rd M33 107 F5
Boxgrove Wlk 3 M8 156 A2
Boxhill Dr M23 109 A1
Box St
Littleborough OL15 16 A5
Ramsbottom BL0 11 D6
Boxtree Ave M18 99 D4
Box Wlk M31 105 E3
Boyd Cl WN6 19 F1
Boydell's Hos WN2 75 B8
Boydell St WN7 75 F6
Boyd St M12 165 A3
Boyd's Wlk SK16 101 C7
Boyer St M16 161 B1
Boyle St
Bolton BL1 142 A1
Manchester M8 156 B2
Boysnope Cres M30 94 C4
Boysnope Wharf M30 94 D4
Boyswell Ho WN1 151 A4
Brabant Rd SK8 123 B2
Brabazon Pl WN5 54 C8
Brabham Cl M21 109 B8
Brabham Mews M27 79 D7
Brabyns Ave SK6 113 D3
Brabyns Brow SK6 126 A7
Brabyns Rd SK14 113 E7
Bracadale Dr SK3 170 C1
Bracewell Cl M12 165 B1
Bracken Ave M28 60 E3
Bracken Cl
Bolton BL1 24 D6
Droylsden M43 84 D2
Heywood OL10 46 D8
Hollingworth SK14 103 D6
Marple SK6 126 C7
Oldham OL4 67 F6
Sale M33 107 C5
Bracken Dr M23 121 B5
Brackenfield Wlk
WA15 120 D6
Bracken Gr BB4 1 A8
Bracken Hill Terr 14
M34 113 A7
Brackenhurst Ave OL5 68 E1
Bracken Lea BL5 57 F5
Brackenlea Dr M9 64 C2
Bracken Lea Fold 3
OL12 14 B2
Brackenlea Pl SK3 170 A1
Bracken Rd
Atherton M46 58 D2
Leigh WN7 75 B5
Brackenside SK5 112 A8
Bracken Trade Pk M26 44 E5
Bracken Way SK13 116 F7
Brackenwood Cl OL2 48 C2
Brackenwood Dr SK8 122 E4
Brackenwood Mews
SK9 137 E8
Brackley Ave
Irlam M44 105 D6
Manchester M15 162 A3
Tyldesley M29 59 B1
Brackley Ct M22 121 D8
Brackley Dr M24 65 A5
Brackley Lo 5 M30 79 F3
Brackley Rd
Eccles M30 79 D4
Over Hulton BL5 59 A8
Reddish SK4 111 D5
Brackley Sq 5 OL1 67 A8
Brackley St
Farnworth BL4 60 D8
9 Oldham OL1 67 A8
Walkden M28 60 C4
Bracondale Ave BL1 142 B2
Bradbourne Cl BL3 145 C1
Bradburn Ave 4 M30 79 D1
Bradburn Cl 2 M30 79 D1
Bradburn Gr 5 M30 79 D1
Bradburn Rd M44 105 E7
Bradburn St M30 79 D1
Bradburn Wlk 8 M8 156 B2
Bradbury Ave WA14 119 A5
Bradbury's La OL3 69 D3
Bradbury St
Ashton-u-L OL7 166 A4
Hyde SK14 167 B1
Radcliffe M26 44 A2
Bradbury Wlk 10 OL2 48 E4
Bradda Mount SK7 124 A2
Braddan Ave M33 108 C3
Bradden Cl M5 81 A1
Braddocks Cl OL12 15 D4
Braddon Ave M41 95 D2
Braddon Rd SK6 113 A5
Braddon St 1 M11 83 C1
Braddyll Rd BL5 58 F8
Brade Cl M11 165 C4
Bradfield Ave M6 80 C2
Bradfield Cl SK5 99 E2
Bradfield Rd M32, M41 96 A2
BRADFORD 160 C1
Bradford Ave BL3 42 B3
Bradford Ct 4 M40 65 C1
Bradford Park Dr BL2 148 B2
Bradford Rd
Bolton BL3, BL4 42 A2
Eccles M30 79 E4
Manchester M40 160 B2
Bradford St
Bolton BL2 148 B3
Farnworth BL4 60 D7
Oldham OL1 153 B4
Wigan WN3 150 C3
Bradford Terr BL9 140 B1
Bradgate Ave SK8 122 D1
Bradgate Cl M22 121 E8
Bradgate Rd
Altrincham WA14 119 A5
Sale M33 108 B2
Bradgate St
Ashton-u-L OL7 166 A1
7 Ashton-u-L OL7 166 A2
Bradgreen Rd M30 79 C3
Brading Wlk M22 130 E8
Bradlegh Rd WA12 89 B1
Bradley Ave M7 81 B7
Bradley Cl WA15 119 E7
Bradley Dr BL9 45 B2
BRADLEY FOLD 43 B5
Bradley Fold SK15 86 B2
Bradley Fold Cotts BL2 43 B6
Bradley Fold Rd BL2 43 C7
Bradley Fold Trad Est BL2 43 C6
Bradley Green Com Prim Sch SK14 101 F6
Bradley Green Rd
SK14 101 F6
Bradley Hall Trad Est WN6 20 A2
Bradley Ho OL8 153 C1
Bradley La
Little Lever BL2, M26 43 B5
Newhey OL16 32 B4
Newton-le-W WA5, WA12 89 A1
Sale M32, M33 108 B7
Standish WN6 19 F2
Bradleys Ct M1 159 B1
Bradley Smithy Cl
OL12 14 E2
Bradley St
7 Manchester M1 159 B2
Newhey OL16 32 B4
Bradney Cl M9 64 B4
Bradnor Rd M22 121 D7
Bradshaigh Ho 6
WN1 37 C1
BRADSHAW 25 C5
Bradshaw Ave
Failsworth M35 83 E5
Manchester M20 110 B7
Whitefield M45 44 E2
Bradshaw Brow BL2 25 C4
BRADSHAW CHAPEL 25 D5
Bradshaw Cl WN6 19 D1
Bradshaw Cres SK6 126 A7
Bradshaw Fold Ave
M40 65 D3
Bradshawgate
Bolton BL1, BL3 145 C3
Leigh WN7 75 F5
Wigan WN1 151 A4
Bradshaw Hall Dr BL2 25 C6
Bradshaw Hall Fold
BL2 25 D6
Bradshaw Hall La
Cheadle SK8 131 E8
Gatley SK8 131 D8
Bradshaw Hall Prim Sch SK8 122 E1
Bradshaw La
Lymm WA13 117 D3
Stretford M32 108 D8
Bradshaw Mdws BL2 25 D6
Bradshaw Rd
Bolton BL2 25 D7
Bury BL8 26 D5
Marple SK6 125 F7
Bradshaw St N M7 155 A3
Bradshaw St
Atherton M46 58 D3
Farnworth BL4 60 D7
Heywood OL10 29 E2
3 Middleton M24 65 C7
Oldham OL1 153 C3
Radcliffe M26 43 F3
9 Rochdale OL16 31 A8
Salford M7 155 B2
Wigan, Redwood WN5 54 A6
Wigan, Whelley WN1 37 E2
Bradstock Rd M16 97 E3
Bradstone Rd M8 156 A1
Bradwell Ave
Manchester M20 109 F6
Stretford M32 96 A3
Bradwell Dr SK8 131 C7
Bradwell Fold 10
SK13 171 B1
Bradwell Lea 12 SK13 171 B1
Bradwell Pl 7 BL2 25 B1
Bradwell Rd
Golborne WA3 90 E7
Hazel Grove SK7 133 E8
Bradwell Terr 11
SK13 171 B1
Bradwell Wlk M41 94 D3
Bradwen Ave M8 64 A1
Bradwen Cl M34 101 A1
Brady St BL6 22 A4
Braeburn Ct WN7 75 D5
Braemar Ave
Stretford M32 96 A2
Urmston M41 95 A1
Braemar Dr M33 107 C2
Braemar Gdns BL3 40 E5
Braemar Gr OL10 29 A1
Braemar La M28 78 B6
Braemar Rd
Hazel Grove SK7 124 F3
Manchester M14 110 E8
Braemar Wlk WN2 38 D5
Braemore Cl
Shaw OL2 48 E8
Wigan WN3 54 D2
Braemore Dr
Broadbottom SK14 102 F1
Bury BL9 28 D2
Brae Side OL8 66 E2
Braeside Cl SK2 124 F6
Braeside Cres WN5 71 D5
Braeside Gr BL3 40 F5
Braewood Cl BL9 28 D2
Bragenham St M18 165 C1
Braidhaven WN6 35 E7
Brailsford Ave 4
SK13 171 B2
Brailsford Cl 7 SK13 171 B2
Brailsford Gdns 8
SK13 171 B2
Brailsford Gn 5 SK13 171 B2
Brailsford Mews 6
SK13 171 B2
Brailsford Rd
Bolton BL2 25 C3
Manchester M14 110 E8
Braintree Rd M22 130 E8
Braithwaite WN6 36 A6

Braithwaite Rd
Golborne WA3 ... 90 D8
Middleton M24 ... 46 D4
Brakehouse Cl OL16 ... 31 E6
Brakenhurst Dr M7 ... 155 C2
Brakesmere Gr M28 ... 60 A4
Braley St M12 ... 163 B3
Bramah Edge Ct SK13 ... 103 F7
Bramall Cl BL9 ... 45 B2
Bramall Hall (Mus)* SK7 ... 123 E1
Bramall St SK14 ... 167 A4
Bramber Way OL9 ... 152 B2
Bramble Ave
Oldham OL4 ... 49 D1
Salford M5 ... 161 C3
Bramble Bank SK13 ... 116 E8
Bramble Cl OL15 ... 15 F5
Bramble Croft BL6 ... 40 A3
Bramble Gr WN5 ... 54 E7
Brambles The WN4 ... 72 D5
Bramble Wlk
7 Sale M33 ... 107 C5
6 Wythenshawe M22 ... 121 C2
Bramblewood
Chadderton OL9 ... 65 E8
Hindley WN2 ... 56 F7
Brambling Cl
Droylsden M34 ... 84 C2
Hazel Grove SK2 ... 125 A5
Brambling Dr BL5 ... 57 D6
Brambling Way WA3 ... 90 E7
Bramcote Ave
Bolton BL2 ... 148 B2
Wythenshawe M23 ... 121 B6
Bramdean Ave BL2 ... 25 E5
Bramfield Wlk M15 ... 162 A3
Bramford Cl BL5 ... 57 E6
BRAMHALL ... 132 D8
Bramhall Ave BL2 ... 26 A4
Bramhall Cl
4 Altrincham WA15 ... 120 D6
Dukinfield SK16 ... 101 D6
Milnrow OL16 ... 31 E5
Sale M33 ... 108 E3
Bramhall Ct M3 ... 158 A3
Bramhall Ctr The SK7 ... 132 E6
BRAMHALL GREEN ... 123 F2
Bramhall High Sch SK7 ... 132 F8
Bramhall La SK2, SK3 ... 170 C1
Bramhall La S
Bramhall SK7 ... 132 E7
Stockport SK3, SK7 ... 123 E2
BRAMHALL MOOR ... 124 D2
Bramhall Moor Ind Est SK7 ... 124 B2
Bramhall Moor La SK7 ... 124 C2
Bramhall Mount SK2 ... 170 C1
BRAMHALL PARK ... 123 C2
Bramhall Park Gr SK7 ... 123 C1
Bramhall Park Rd SK7, SK8 ... 123 D2
Bramhall St
Bolton BL3 ... 42 B3
Manchester M18 ... 99 E5
Bramhall Sta SK7 ... 132 E6
Bramhall Wlk M34 ... 100 F1
Bramham Rd SK6 ... 126 A4
Bramhope Wlk M9 ... 157 A3
Bramley Ave
Manchester M19 ... 111 A8
Stretford M32 ... 96 B1
Bramley Cl
Bramhall SK7 ... 132 E6
Swinton M27 ... 79 C6
Wilmslow SK9 ... 136 D4
Bramley Cres SK4 ... 168 B1
Bramley Ct WN6 ... 19 E1
Bramley Dr
Bramhall SK7 ... 132 E6
Bury BL8 ... 27 C6
Bramley Meade M7 ... 155 B3
Bramley Rd
Bolton BL1 ... 25 A6
Bramhall SK7 ... 132 E6
Rochdale OL11 ... 29 E8
Bramley St M7 ... 155 B1
Brammay Dr BL8 ... 26 E6
Brampton Cl WN2 ... 55 F1
Brampton Rd
Bolton BL3 ... 146 A2
Stockport SK7 ... 123 F2
Brampton St 9 M46 ... 58 D3
Brampton Wlk M40 ... 83 B6
Bramway
Bramhall SK7 ... 132 C7
High Lane SK6 ... 134 F7
Bramwell Dr M13 ... 163 C2
Bramwell St SK1 ... 124 B8
Bramwood Ct SK7 ... 132 E6
Bramworth Ave BL0 ... 138 B2
Brancaster Dr WA3 ... 91 A7
Brancaster Rd M1 ... 163 A3
Branch Cl BL8 ... 140 A3
Branch Rd OL15 ... 15 F1
Branch St
Bacup OL13 ... 3 D8
Ince-in-M WN2 ... 56 A7
Brancker St BL5 ... 40 C1
Brandish Cl M13 ... 164 A1
Brandle Ave BL8 ... 27 C4
Brandlehow Dr M24 ... 46 C2
Brandlesholme Cl BL8 ... 140 A4
Brandlesholme Rd BL8 ... 27 C6
Brandon Ave
Gatley SK8 ... 122 B1
Reddish M34 ... 99 F3
Salford M30 ... 80 A5
Wythenshawe M22 ... 121 C8
Brandon Brow 8 OL1 ... 153 B4
Brandon Cl
Bury BL8 ... 27 D5
Handforth SK9 ... 131 D2
Up Holland WN8 ... 53 A7
Brandon Cres OL2 ... 149 A4
Brandon Rd M6 ... 80 B5
Brandon St
2 Bolton BL3 ... 147 A4
Milnrow OL16 ... 31 E6
Brandram Rd M25 ... 63 C4
Brandreth Pl WN6 ... 19 F1
Brandsby Gdns M5 ... 161 A4
BRANDWOOD ... 3 B8
Brandwood OL1 ... 47 E1
Brandwood Ave M21 ... 109 D4
Brandwood Cl M28 ... 78 A8
Brandwood Ct BL7 ... 9 E5
Brandwood Fold BL7 ... 9 E5
Brandwood Pk OL13 ... 3 B8
Brandwood Prim Sch BL3 ... 146 C4
Brandwood Rd OL13 ... 3 B8
Brandwood St BL3 ... 146 C4
Branfield Ave SK8 ... 122 D1
Brankgate Ct M20 ... 110 A5
Branksome Ave M25 ... 63 B4
Branksome Dr
Cheadle SK8 ... 122 D1
Manchester M9 ... 64 B6
Salford M6 ... 80 B5
Branksome Ho SK4 ... 168 B2
Branksome Rd SK4 ... 168 B1
Bransby Ave M9 ... 64 E4
Branscombe Dr M33 ... 107 C5
Branscombe Gdns BL3 ... 42 D5
Bransdale Ave OL2 ... 48 C4
Bransdale Cl BL3 ... 40 F4
Bransdale Dr WN4 ... 73 D3
Bransfield Cl WN3 ... 55 B3
Bransford Cl WN4 ... 73 C2
Bransford Rd
Droylsden M11 ... 99 E8
Urmston M41 ... 95 C3
Branson Cl WA3 ... 74 A2
Branson St M4, M40 ... 160 A2
Branson Wlk WA15 ... 120 C6
Branston Rd M40 ... 65 D2
Brantfell Gr BL2 ... 42 F8
Branthwaite WN2 ... 38 B1
Brantingham Ct M16 ... 97 E1
Brantingham Rd M16, M21 ... 97 D1
Brantwood Cl OL2 ... 48 C4
Brantwood Dr BL2 ... 42 F8
Brantwood Rd
Cheadle SK8 ... 122 F1
Salford M7 ... 155 A4
Stockport SK4 ... 168 C4
Brantwood Terr M9 ... 157 C3
Branwood Prep Sch M30 ... 79 E3
Braodlands Rd M9 ... 65 A3
Brassey St
Ashton-u-L OL6 ... 166 B4
Middleton M24 ... 47 A1
Brassica Cl M30 ... 79 A4
Brassington Ave
Manchester M21 ... 109 B7
Salford M5 ... 161 B4
Brassington Cres SK13 ... 171 A1
Brassington Rd SK4 ... 110 E4
Brathay Cl
Bolton BL2 ... 25 F2
Prestwich M45 ... 63 C8
Bratton Cl WN3 ... 54 C2
Brattray Dr M24 ... 46 E3
Braunston Cl M30 ... 95 E8
Braxton Wlk 20 M9 ... 157 B4
Bray Ave M30 ... 79 B3
Braybrook Dr BL1 ... 40 D7
Bray Cl SK8 ... 122 E2
Brayford Dr WN2 ... 38 C5
Brayford Rd M22 ... 121 D1
Brayshaw Cl OL10 ... 29 C1
Brayside Rd M19, M20 ... 110 D4
Braystan Gdns SK8 ... 122 B6
Brayston Fold M24 ... 64 C8
Brayton Ave
Manchester M20 ... 110 C2
Sale M33 ... 107 D5
Brayton Ct WN2 ... 56 D6
Brazennose St M2 ... 158 C1
Brazil St M1 ... 163 A4
Brazley Ave
Bolton BL3 ... 42 B3
Horwich BL6 ... 22 E1
Breach House La WA16 ... 129 A1
Bread St M18 ... 99 E6
Breaktemper BL5 ... 39 E1
Brean Wlk 8 M22 ... 121 C1
Brearley St OL13 ... 3 D8
Breaston Ave WN7 ... 76 C3
Brechin Way OL10 ... 29 A1
Brechin Wlk 16 M11 ... 83 C1
Breckland Cl SK15 ... 86 D2
Breckland Dr BL1 ... 40 D8
Breckles Pl BL3 ... 145 A1
Breck Rd M30 ... 79 B2
Brecon Ave
Cheadle SK8 ... 122 E1
Brecon Ave *continued*
Denton M34 ... 100 F1
Manchester M19 ... 110 F7
Urmston M41 ... 94 D3
Brecon Cl
Platt Bridge WN2 ... 56 B2
Poynton SK12 ... 133 F4
Royton OL2 ... 48 C6
Brecon Cres OL6 ... 85 B6
Brecon Dr
Bury BL9 ... 44 E7
Hindley WN2 ... 57 A3
Brecon Wlk 6 OL8 ... 66 B2
BREDBURY ... 112 E4
Bredbury Dr BL4 ... 60 E8
Bredbury Gn SK6 ... 113 A1
BREDBURY GREEN ... 113 A1
Bredbury Green Prim Sch SK6 ... 112 F1
Bredbury Park Way SK6 ... 112 E6
Bredbury Rd M14 ... 98 B2
Bredbury St
Chadderton OL9 ... 152 B2
Dukinfield SK14 ... 101 D5
Bredbury Sta SK6 ... 112 F4
Brede Wlk M23 ... 120 D8
Bredon Way OL8 ... 66 E3
Breeze Hill WN6 ... 37 B7
Breeze Hill Rd
Oldham OL4 ... 67 D5
Over Hulton M46 ... 58 F5
Breeze Hill Sch OL4 ... 67 D5
Breeze Mount M25 ... 63 C3
BREIGHTMET ... 42 F8
Breightmet Dr BL2 ... 42 E7
Breightmet Fold La BL2 ... 42 F8
Breightmet St BL2 ... 148 A3
Brellafield Dr OL2 ... 48 F8
Brenbar Cres OL12 ... 4 D1
Brenchley Dr M23 ... 109 A2
Brencon Ave M23 ... 108 C1
Brendall Cl SK2 ... 125 A5
Brendon Ave
Manchester M40 ... 83 A7
Reddish SK5 ... 111 F6
Brendon Cl SK13 ... 116 A8
Brendon Dr M34 ... 84 D1
Brendon Hills OL2 ... 48 D3
Brenley Wlk 7 M9 ... 157 A4
Brennan Cl M15 ... 163 A1
Brennan Ct OL8 ... 66 C2
Brennock Cl M11 ... 164 C4
Brentbridge Rd M14 ... 110 B8
Brent Cl
Little Lever BL2 ... 43 B5
Poynton SK12 ... 133 B4
Brentfield Ave M8 ... 156 A2
Brentford Ave BL1 ... 142 B2
Brentford Rd SK5 ... 111 F6
Brentford St M9 ... 157 B3
Brent Moor Rd SK7 ... 124 A3
Brentnall Prim Sch M7 ... 155 A3
Brentnall St SK1 ... 170 C3
Brentnor Rd M40 ... 65 C3
Brenton Ave M33 ... 108 A4
Brenton Bsns Complex BL9 ... 141 A2
Brent Rd
Stockport SK4 ... 168 C1
Wythenshawe M23 ... 109 A2
Brentwood
Sale M33 ... 108 A4
Salford M6 ... 154 B3
Urmston M41 ... 94 F1
Wigan WN5 ... 54 D5
Brentwood Ave
Altrincham WA14 ... 119 E7
Irlam M44 ... 105 D6
Swinton M28 ... 79 B6
Urmston M41 ... 95 D2
Brentwood Cl
Brinnington SK5 ... 112 D5
Littleborough OL15 ... 15 F3
Stalybridge SK15 ... 86 C2
Brentwood Cres WA14 ... 119 E6
Brentwood Ct M25 ... 62 F3
Brentwood Dr
Eccles M30 ... 79 D4
Farnworth BL3, BL4 ... 42 C2
Gatley SK8 ... 122 B5
Brentwood Gr WN7 ... 75 F7
Brentwood Rd
Adlington PR6 ... 21 B8
Swinton M27 ... 79 D6
Brentwood Sch WA14 ... 119 E7
Brentwood St M16 ... 97 F3
Brereton Cl WA14 ... 119 C1
Brereton Ct SK8 ... 122 E1
Brereton Dr M28 ... 78 F7
Brereton Gr M44 ... 105 E6
Brereton Rd
Eccles M30 ... 78 F1
Handforth SK9 ... 131 E3
Breslyn St M3 ... 158 C3
Bretherton Row 17 WN1 ... 150 C4
Bretherton St WN2 ... 56 C6
Brethren's Ct M43 ... 100 A8
Bretland Gdns SK14 ... 102 E1
Bretland Wlk 2 M22 ... 121 F3
Breton Ho SK2 ... 124 A6
Brettargh St M6 ... 81 A4
Bretton Ct BL4 ... 61 B6
Bretton Wlk M22 ... 130 D8
Brett Rd M28 ... 77 F6
Brett St M22 ... 109 E1
Brewer's Gn SK7 ... 124 D3
Brewer St M1 ... 159 B1
Brewerton Rd OL4 ... 67 C6
Brewery La WN7 ... 76 A5
Brewery St
5 Altrincham WA14 ... 119 D4
Stockport SK1 ... 169 C2
Brewery Yd M3 ... 158 B2
Brewster St
Manchester M9 ... 157 A4
4 Middleton M24 ... 47 A2
Brian Ave M43 ... 84 C3
Brian Farrell Dr SK16 ... 101 D6
Brian Rd BL4 ... 42 A1
Brian Redhead Ct M15 ... 162 B3
Brian St OL11 ... 30 B2
Brian Statham Way M16 ... 97 A4
Briar Ave
Hazel Grove SK7 ... 124 F2
Hollinfare WA3 ... 105 B2
Oldham OL4 ... 49 D1
Briar Cl
Ashton-in-M WN4 ... 73 A4
Hindley WN2 ... 57 B4
Rochdale OL12 ... 14 A1
Sale M33 ... 107 C4
Urmston M41 ... 95 A3
Briar Cres M22 ... 121 E5
Briarcroft Dr M46 ... 58 A1
Briardene M34 ... 101 A4
Briardene Gdns M22 ... 121 E4
Briarfield BL7 ... 8 D2
Briarfield Hall M1 ... 163 A2
Briarfield Rd
Altrincham WA15 ... 120 C6
Cheadle SK8 ... 123 B3
Farnworth BL4 ... 42 A1
Manchester M19, M20 ... 110 D6
Reddish SK4 ... 111 E6
Uppermill OL3 ... 51 A2
Worsley M28 ... 78 F7
Briar Gr
Chadderton OL9 ... 48 B1
Leigh WN7 ... 75 E8
Romiley SK6 ... 113 A5
Briargrove Rd SK22 ... 127 C4
Briar Hill Ave M38 ... 59 E4
Briar Hill Cl M38 ... 59 E4
Briar Hill Gr M38 ... 59 E4
Briar Hill Way 6 M6 ... 81 A3
Briar Hollow SK4 ... 168 B1
Briarlands Ave M33 ... 107 F2
Briarlands Cl SK7 ... 132 D6
Briar Lea Cl BL3 ... 147 B4
Briarlea Gdns M19 ... 110 E5
Briarley Gdns SK6 ... 113 C6
Briarly WN6 ... 37 A7
Briarmere Wlk OL9 ... 152 C3
Briar Rd
Golborne WA3 ... 90 B8
Wigan WN5 ... 54 E7
Briars Mount SK4 ... 168 A2
Briars Pk SK7 ... 123 C1
Briar St
Bolton BL2 ... 42 D7
Rochdale OL11 ... 139 A2
Briarstead Cl SK7 ... 132 D7
Briar Wlk WA3 ... 90 B8
Briarwood
Bolton BL2 ... 25 B1
Wilmslow SK9 ... 137 C7
Briarwood Ave
Droylsden M43 ... 83 F3
Wythenshawe M23 ... 120 E8
Briarwood Chase SK8 ... 123 B1
Briarwood Cres SK6 ... 126 A3
Briary Dr M29 ... 77 B8
Brice St SK16 ... 101 B8
Brickbridge Rd SK6 ... 126 A5
Brickfield St
Glossop SK13 ... 104 B5
Rochdale OL16 ... 15 B2
Brick Ground OL12 ... 13 C2
Brickhill La WA15 ... 129 B4
Brickkiln La WA14 ... 118 C3
Brick Kiln La 10 WN1 ... 37 C1
Brickkiln Row WA14 ... 119 C1
Brickley St M3, M4 ... 159 A3
Bricknell Wlk 5 M22 ... 121 F3
Brick St
Bury BL9 ... 141 A3
8 Manchester M4 ... 159 A2
Bridcam St M8 ... 156 A1
Briddon St M3 ... 158 C3
Brideoak Ct M8 ... 156 A2
Brideoake St WN7 ... 76 B4
Brideoak St
Manchester M8 ... 156 A2
Oldham OL4 ... 67 E8
Bride St BL1 ... 143 B2
Bridestowe Ave SK14 ... 102 C3
Bridestowe Wlk SK14 ... 102 C3
Bridge Ave SK6 ... 113 A5
Bridge Bank Cl WA3 ... 90 B7
Bridge Bank Rd OL15 ... 16 A3
Bridge Cl
Lymm WA13 ... 117 B4
Partington M31 ... 106 A3
6 Radcliffe M26 ... 44 B2
Bridge Coll SK2 ... 124 D8
Bridgecrest Ct 3 SK8 ... 123 A2
Bridge Dr
Cheadle SK8 ... 122 D4
Bridge Dr *continued*
Handforth SK9 ... 131 D3
BRIDGE END ... 1 A7
Bridge End
Delph OL3 ... 50 F4
Wigan WN3 ... 150 B4
Bridge End Cl BB4 ... 1 A7
Bridgefield 4 SK13 ... 116 B8
Bridgefield Ave SK9 ... 131 C1
Bridgefield Cl SK6 ... 134 E7
Bridgefield Cres 4 OL4 ... 67 F6
Bridgefield Dr BL9 ... 28 D2
Bridgefield St
Radcliffe M26 ... 44 B3
Rochdale OL11 ... 139 A3
Stockport SK1 ... 169 B2
Bridgefield Wlk 7 M26 ... 44 B3
Bridgefold Rd OL11 ... 139 A4
Bridgefoot Cl M28 ... 78 A5
Bridgeford Ct M32 ... 108 D8
Bridgeford St M13, M15 ... 163 A2
Bridge Gr WA15 ... 119 F7
Bridgehall Dr WN8 ... 53 B7
Bridge Hall Dr BL9 ... 141 C2
Bridge Hall Fold BL9 ... 141 C2
Bridge Hall La BL9 ... 28 D2
Bridge Hall Prim Sch SK3 ... 170 A2
Bridge Ho M1 ... 159 B1
Bridge La SK7 ... 123 F1
Bridgelea Mews M20 ... 110 B6
Bridgelea Rd M20 ... 110 B6
Bridgeman Ho BL4 ... 60 D7
Bridgeman Pl BL2 ... 148 A2
Bridgeman St
Bolton BL3 ... 145 C1
Farnworth BL4 ... 42 D1
Bridgeman Terr WN1 ... 37 C1
Bridgemere Cl M26 ... 43 F5
Bridge Mill 1 BL7 ... 24 F7
Bridge Mills Bsns Pk M6 ... 80 F5
Bridgend Cl
Cheadle SK8 ... 123 C4
Manchester M12 ... 165 A2
Bridgenorth Ave M41 ... 95 F2
Bridgenorth Dr OL15 ... 15 F3
Bridge Rd
Bury BL9 ... 140 A1
Sale M23 ... 120 C7
Bridge St W M3 ... 158 B1
Bridges Ave BL9 ... 44 F6
Bridges Ct 5 BL3 ... 145 C2
Bridgeside Bsns Ctr SK6 ... 112 D6
Bridge's St M46 ... 58 B2
Bridge St
Bolton BL1 ... 145 C3
Bury BL9 ... 141 A3
Denton, Guide Bridge M34 ... 100 F7
Droylsden M43 ... 99 E8
Dukinfield SK16 ... 101 A6
Farnworth BL4 ... 42 E1
Golborne WA3 ... 90 A7
Haslingden BB4 ... 1 C6
Heywood OL10 ... 29 C2
Hindley WN2 ... 56 E6
Horwich BL6 ... 22 C4
Ince-in-M WN3 ... 151 A2
Kearsley M26 ... 61 B8
Manchester M3 ... 158 B1
Middleton M24 ... 65 A8
Milnrow OL16 ... 31 F6
New Mills SK22 ... 127 C1
Newton-le-W WA12 ... 89 B3
Oldham, County End OL4 ... 67 F6
1 Oldham, Lower Moor OL1 ... 67 A6
Oldham, West Hulme OL1 ... 48 D1
Pendlebury M27 ... 80 A8
Ramsbottom BL0 ... 138 C2
Rawtenstall BB4 ... 2 E7
Rochdale, Castleton OL11 ... 30 C1
Rochdale, Hurstead OL12 ... 15 C3
Shaw OL2 ... 149 C4
Stalybridge SK15 ... 85 F1
Stockport SK1 ... 169 C2
Uppermill OL3 ... 69 B7
Whitworth OL12 ... 4 C1
Wigan WN3 ... 150 C3
Bridges Way M34 ... 112 F7
Bridge Trad Est BL8 ... 140 A2
Bridgewater Bsns Pk WN7 ... 75 F4
Bridgewater Cl SK8 ... 131 D7
Bridgewater Ct M32 ... 96 E3
Bridgewater Ctr The M41 ... 95 E7
Bridgewater Ho M15 ... 162 A4
Bridgewater Park Nature Trail* M28 ... 78 B5
Bridgewater Pl M4 ... 159 A1
Bridgewater Prim Sch M38 ... 60 B4
Bridgewater Rd
Altrincham WA14 ... 119 D7
Pendlebury M27 ... 80 B7

Bridgewater Rd continued
Walkden, Ellenbrook
M28 . . . . .78 A8
Walkden, Engine Fold
M28 . . . . .60 D2
Bridgewater Sch M28 . . . .79 A6
Bridgewater St
2 Bolton BL1 . . . . .145 A2
Eccles M30 . . . . .79 B2
Farnworth BL4 . . . . .60 E8
Hindley WN2 . . . . .56 E6
Manchester M3 . . . . . . .162 B4
8 Oldham OL1 . . . . . . .67 A8
Sale M33 . . . . .108 B5
Salford M3 . . . . .158 B3
Stretford M32 . . . . .96 E2
Walkden M38 . . . . .60 B4
Wigan WN3 . . . . .150 B3
5 Wigan, Worsley Hall
WN5 . . . . .54 F6
Bridgewater Viaduct M15,
M3 . . . . .162 B3
Bridgewater Way M15,
M16 . . . . .161 B1
Bridgewater Wlk 3
M28 . . . . .60 D3
Bridgnorth Rd M9 . . . . . .64 A3
Bridle Cl
Droylsden M43 . . . . .84 C3
Manchester M41 . . . . . . .94 E2
Bridle Ct SK7 . . . . .132 F2
Bridle Fold M26 . . . . .44 A4
Bridle Rd
Prestwich M25 . . . . .63 E7
Woodford SK7 . . . . .132 F2
Bridleway SK22 . . . . . . .127 D1
Bridle Way SK7 . . . . . . .133 A2
Bridlington Ave M6 . . . . .80 C3
Bridlington Cl **6** M40 . . .83 C6
Bridport Ave M40 . . . . . .83 D8
Bridson La BL2 . . . . .25 D2
Bridson St
10 Oldham OL4 . . . . . . .67 C7
Salford M5 . . . . .154 B1
Brief St BL2 . . . . .25 C1
Brien Ave WA14 . . . . . . .119 E7
Briercliffe M18 . . . . .99 D6
Briercliffe Rd BL3 . . . . .144 C1
Brierfield Ave M46 . . . . . .58 C4
Brierfield Dr BL9 . . . . . . .27 E8
Brierholme Ave BL7 . . . . . .8 E1
Brierley Cl
Ashton-u-L OL6 . . . . .86 A6
Denton M34 . . . . .100 E1
Brierley Dr M24 . . . . .65 A7
Brierley Rd E M27 . . . . . .61 E1
Brierley Rd W M27 . . . . . .61 E1
Brierley St
Bury BL9 . . . . .44 E8
Chadderton OL9 . . . . . .152 C4
Heywood OL10 . . . . .29 D2
Oldham OL8 . . . . .66 F3
Stalybridge SK16 . . . . . .85 D1
Brierley Wlk **6** M9 . . . .152 C4
Brierton Dr **5** M22 . . . .121 B1
Brierwood Cl OL1 . . . . . .48 E1
Briery Ave BL2 . . . . .25 D6
Brigade Dr M32 . . . . .96 C3
Brigade St BL1 . . . . . . .144 C3
Brigadier Cl M20 . . . . . .110 B6
Brigantine Cl M5 . . . . . .161 A4
Briggs Cl M33 . . . . .107 C1
Briggs Fold BL7 . . . . .8 E2
Briggs Fold Cl BL7 . . . . . .8 E2
Briggs Fold Rd BL7 . . . . .8 E2
Briggs Rd M32 . . . . .96 F4
Briggs St
Leigh WN7 . . . . .75 E7
Manchester M3 . . . . . . .158 A3
Brigham St M11 . . . . . . .165 C4
Brightgate Way M32 . . . .96 A5
Brightman St M18 . . . . . .99 E6
Brighton Ave
Bolton BL1 . . . . .142 A1
Manchester M19 . . . . . .110 F7
Reddish SK5 . . . . .99 F2
Salford M7 . . . . .155 B2
Urmston M41 . . . . .94 E3
Brighton Cl SK8 . . . . . . .123 C4
Brighton Ct
Manchester M14 . . . . . . .98 D2
Salford M5 . . . . .161 B3
Brighton Gr
Hyde SK14 . . . . .167 B1
Manchester M14 . . . . . . .98 D2
Sale M33 . . . . .108 B5
Urmston M41 . . . . .94 E3
Brighton Pl M13 . . . . . . .163 B2
Brighton Range M18 . . . .99 F4
Brighton Rd
Oldham OL4 . . . . .50 A1
Stockport SK4 . . . . .168 C1
Brighton Road Ind Est
SK4 . . . . .168 C1
Brighton St
Bury BL9 . . . . .141 B3
Manchester M4 . . . . . . .159 A3
Bright Rd M30 . . . . .79 E2
Bright St Mill BL9 . . . . . .141 A3
Bright St
1 Ashton-u-L OL6 . . . . .85 D2
Bolton BL7 . . . . .8 D2

Bright St continued
Bury BL9 . . . . .141 A3
Chadderton OL9 . . . . . . .66 A4
Droylsden M43 . . . . .84 B1
Leigh WN7 . . . . .75 E7
Oldham OL8 . . . . .153 A1
Radcliffe M26 . . . . .44 C4
7 Rochdale OL16 . . . . . .31 A5
Brightstone Wlk 4
M13 . . . . .98 E4
Brightwater Ho BL3 . . . . .21 F2
Brightwater Cl M45 . . . . .63 A8
Brightwell Wlk **4** M8 . . .156 B2
Brignall Gr WA3 . . . . . . .74 D1
Brigsteer Wlk M40 . . . . .157 A1
Brigstock Ave M18 . . . . .165 C1
Briksdal Way BL6 . . . . . .40 C7
Brimelow St SK6 . . . . . .112 D3
Brimfield Ave M29 . . . . . .59 C1
Brimfield Wlk **7** M40 . . . .83 C6
Brimmy Croft La OL3 . . . .33 C3
Brimpton Wlk **7** M9 . . . .157 D8
Brimrod Com Prim Sch
OL11 . . . . .139 A1
Brimrod La OL11 . . . . . .139 A1
Brimscombe Ave
M22 . . . . .121 C2
Brindale Ho SK5 . . . . . . .112 C4
Brindale Rd SK5 . . . . . . .112 C4
Brindle Cl M6 . . . . .154 C4
BRINDLE HEATH 154 C4
Brindle Heath Ind Est
M6 . . . . .81 A4
Brindle Heath Rd M6 . . .154 C4
Brindlehurst Dr M29 . . . .77 D7
Brindle Pl **7** M15 . . . . .163 A2
Brindle St
Hindley WN2 . . . . .56 F6
Tyldesley M29 . . . . .59 A1
Brindle Way OL2 . . . . . . .49 D7
Brindley Ave
Manchester M9 . . . . .64 B5
Marple SK6 . . . . .125 F5
Sale M33 . . . . .108 C6
7 Worsley M28 . . . . . . .78 A6
Brindley Cl
Atherton M46 . . . . .58 A2
7 Eccles M30 . . . . .95 D8
Farnworth BL4 . . . . .60 B8
Brindley Gr SK9 . . . . . . .131 E2
Brindley Rd M16 . . . . . . .161 B1
Brindley St
Bolton BL1 . . . . .143 C4
Boothstown M28 . . . . . . .77 F6
Eccles M30 . . . . .79 B3
Horwich BL6 . . . . .22 C2
Swinton M27 . . . . .61 F2
Walkden M28 . . . . .54 C5
Wigan WN5 . . . . .54 C5
Brinell Dr M44 . . . . .105 F6
Brinkburn Rd SK7 . . . . .125 A3
Brinklow Cl M11 . . . . . . .99 E7
Brinkshaw Ave M22 . . . .121 E2
Brinks La BL2 . . . . .43 A6
Brink's Row BL6 . . . . . . .22 D5
Brinksway
Bolton BL1 . . . . .40 D7
Stockport SK3 . . . . .123 C8
Brinksway Trad Est 1
SK3 . . . . .123 C8
Brinksworth Cl BL2 . . . . .43 A8
BRINNINGTON 112 B5
Brinnington Cres SK5 . . .112 B4
Brinnington Rd
Brinnington SK5 . . . . . . .112 C4
Stockport SK5 . . . . .112 B3
Brinnington Rise SK1,
SK5 . . . . .112 B4
Brinnington Sta SK5 . . . .112 B5
Brinsop Hall La BL5 . . . . .39 A6
Brinsop Sq M12 . . . . . . .165 C6
Brinston Wlk **12** M40 . . . .83 A7
Brinsworth Dr M8 . . . . . .156 A2
Briony Ave WA15 . . . . . .120 C2
Briony Cl OL2 . . . . .48 E2
Brisbane Cl SK7 . . . . . . .132 F5
Brisbane St M13, M15 . . .163 B1
Briscoe La M40 . . . . .83 B4
Briscoe Lane Prim Sch
M40 . . . . .83 B5
Briscoe Mews **21** BL3 . . .42 A4
Briscoe St OL1 . . . . .153 C4
Briscoe Wlk M24 . . . . . . .46 C2
Bristle Hall Way BL5 . . . .39 F2
Bristle St M1 . . . . .163 A2
Bristol Ave
Ashton-u-L OL6 . . . . .85 B7
Bolton BL2 . . . . .25 C1
Manchester M19 . . . . . .111 B8
Bristol Cl SK8 . . . . .131 C7
Bristol Ct **2** M7 . . . . . . .63 E1
Bristol St M7 . . . . .155 B3
Bristowe St M11, M43 . . . .83 D3
Britain St BL9 . . . . .44 F5
BRITANNIA 4 C8
Britannia Ave OL12 . . . . .149 C2
Britannia Bridge Prim Sch
WN3 . . . . .151 B2
Britannia Cl M26 . . . . . . .44 A3
Britannia Com Prim Sch
OL13 . . . . .4 C8
Britannia Mill Ind Est
OL10 . . . . .29 C2
Britannia Mills BL9 . . . . .141 A3
Britannia Mills M15 . . .162 B3
Britannia Rd
Sale M33 . . . . .108 C5
Wigan WN5 . . . . .54 B8

Britannia Road Ind Est
M33 . . . . .108 C5
Britannia St
Ashton-u-L OL7 . . . . . . .100 F8
Heywood OL10 . . . . .29 B2
1 Oldham OL1 . . . . .67 A7
Salford M6 . . . . .81 A5
Britannia Warehouse
BL9 . . . . .141 A3
Britannia Way
Bolton BL1 . . . . .25 A2
Haslingden BB4 . . . . .1 A8
Britnall Ave M12 . . . . . . .164 C1
Briton St
6 Rochdale OL16 . . . . . .31 A8
Royton OL2 . . . . .48 E2
Britwell Wlk M8 . . . . . . .156 C4
Brixham Ave SK8 . . . . . .131 F7
Brixham Dr M33 . . . . . . .107 D6
Brixham Rd M16 . . . . . . .97 B4
Brixham Wlk M13 . . . . . .132 E7
Brixton Ave M20 . . . . . . .110 A6
Brixworth Wlk **19** M9 . . .64 E3
Broach St BL3 . . . . .147 B4
Broadacre
Shevington Moor WN6 . . .19 B2
Stalybridge SK15 . . . . . .102 C6
Up Holland WN8 . . . . . . .53 A6
Broad Acre OL12 . . . . . . .13 E2
Broadacre Pl SK9 . . . . . .136 D3
Broadacre Rd M18 . . . . . .99 E3
BROADBENT 49 C2
Broadbent Ave
Ashton-u-L OL6 . . . . .85 C6
Dukinfield SK16 . . . . . . .101 D8
Broadbent Cl
Mossley SK15 . . . . .86 E6
Royton OL2 . . . . .149 A1
Broadbent Dr BL9 . . . . . .28 E4
Broadbent Fold Prim Sch
SK16 . . . . .102 A7
Broadbent Gr SK14 . . . . .102 E1
Broadbent Rd OL1 . . . . . .49 C1
Broadbent St
Hyde SK14 . . . . .167 A4
Swinton M27 . . . . .79 D7
BROADBOTTOM 115 A8
Broadbottom CE Prim Sch
SK14 . . . . .114 F8
Broadbottom Rd
SK14 . . . . .103 A3
Broadbottom Sta
SK14 . . . . .115 A8
Broadcarr La OL5 . . . . . .68 B1
BROADFIELD 29 B1
Broadfield Cl M34 . . . . . .101 A2
Broadfield Com Prim Sch
OL16 . . . . .139 B3
Broadfield Distribution Ctr
OL10 . . . . .46 B8
Broadfield Dr OL15 . . . . . .15 F3
Broadfield Gr SK5 . . . . . .99 E3
Broadfield Prim Sch
OL8 . . . . .66 F4
Broadfield Rd
Manchester M14 . . . . . . .98 A3
Reddish SK5 . . . . .99 E3
Broadfield St
Heywood OL10 . . . . .29 B1
Rochdale OL16 . . . . . . .139 C2
Broadfield Stile OL16 . . .139 B2
Broadford Rd BL3 . . . . . .40 F5
Broadgate
Bolton BL3 . . . . .40 F5
Middleton M24, OL9 . . . . .65 D5
Uppermill OL3 . . . . .50 E1
Broadgate Ho BL3 . . . . . .40 F5
Broadgate Mdw M27 . . . .79 F6
Broadgreen Gdns 4
BL4 . . . . .42 D2
BROADHALGH 30 A7
Broadhalgh Ave OL11 . . . .30 A7
Broadhalgh Rd OL11 . . . . .30 A6
Broadhead Rd BL7 . . . . . . .9 E7
Broadhead Rd M34 . . . . .160 A3
Broadhead Rd BL7 . . . . . . .9 E7
BROADHEATH 119 C7
Broadheath Cl BL5 . . . . . .40 A1
Broadheath Prim Sch
WA14 . . . . .119 C8
Broadhey View SK22 . . .127 B1
Broad Hill Cl SK7 . . . . . .124 A2
Broadhill Rd
Manchester M19 . . . . . .110 E6
Stalybridge SK15 . . . . . . .86 A5
Broadhurst M34 . . . . . .101 A5
Broadhurst Ave
Chadderton OL1 . . . . .48 C1
Culcheth WA3 . . . . .91 F2
Swinton M27 . . . . .79 D6
Broadhurst Ct 1 BL3 . . .147 A4
Broadhurst Gr OL6 . . . . . .85 C6
Broadhurst La WN6 . . . . .18 F7
Broadhurst Prim Sch
M40 . . . . .83 C7
Broadhurst St
3 Bolton BL3 . . . . .147 A4
1 Radcliffe M26 . . . . . . .43 F5
Stockport SK3 . . . . .170 C3
Broad Ing OL12 . . . . .14 C1
Broad La
Altrincham WA15 . . . . . .120 B1
Billinge WA11 . . . . .71 B1
Delph OL3 . . . . .50 E7
Rochdale, Buersil OL16 . . .31 B3
Rochdale, Burnedge
OL16 . . . . .31 D2

Broadlands WN6 . . . . .36 B6
Broadlands Rd M28 . . . . .79 C6
Broadlands Wlk 11
M40 . . . . .83 A6
Broad Lea M41 . . . . .95 C3
Broadlea Gr OL12 . . . . . . .14 C2
Broadlea Rd M19 . . . . . .110 E5
BROADLEY 14 C5
Broadley Ave
Golborne WA3 . . . . .90 C7
Wythenshawe M22 . . . . .121 D4
Broadley Fold OL12 . . . . .14 B6
Broadlink M24 . . . . .65 D6
Broadmeadow BL7 . . . . . .25 B8
Broadmeadow Ave
M16 . . . . .97 F1
Broadmoss Dr M9 . . . . . .65 A3
Broadmoss Rd M9 . . . . . .65 A3
BROAD OAK 79 B6
Broadoak Ave
Boothstown M28 . . . . . . .77 F7
Wythenshawe M22 . . . . .121 C5
Broadoak Bsns Pk M17 . .95 F7
Broad Oak Cl **4** PR6 . . . .21 A8
Broadoak Cres OL8 . . . . .67 A2
Broadoak Ct M8 . . . . . . .156 B2
Broadoak Dr M22 . . . . . .121 D5
Broad Oak High Sch
BL9 . . . . .141 B2
Broad Oak La
Bury BL9 . . . . .28 D3
Manchester M20 . . . . . .122 B8
Manchester M20 . . . . . .122 C8
BROADOAK PARK 79 C6
Broad Oak Pk
Eccles M30 . . . . .79 D4
Swinton M28 . . . . .79 B6
Broadoak Prim Sch
Ashton-u-L OL6 . . . . .85 C6
Swinton M27 . . . . .79 C6
Broad Oak Prim Sch
M20 . . . . .122 C8
Broadoak Rd
Ashton-u-L OL6 . . . . .85 C6
Rochdale OL11 . . . . .29 E6
Stockport SK7 . . . . .123 F2
Wythenshawe M22 . . . . .121 C5
Wythenshawe M22 . . . . .121 C5
Broad Oak Rd BL3 . . . . . .42 A2
Broadoaks BL9 . . . . .28 D3
Broadoak Sch M31 . . . .105 F2
Broadoaks Rd
Sale M33 . . . . .108 A4
Urmston M41 . . . . .95 B1
Broad Oak Terr BL9 . . . . .28 E3
Broad o' th' La
Shevington WN6 . . . . . . .36 A6
Broad Rd M33 . . . . .108 D5
Broadriding Rd WN6 . . . .35 C4
Broad Shaw La
Rochdale, Burnedge
OL16 . . . . .31 D2
Rochdale, Green Gate
OL16 . . . . .31 D3
Broad St
Bury BL9 . . . . .140 B2
Middleton M24 . . . . .64 C7
Salford M6 . . . . .154 C4
Broadstone Ave OL4 . . . .49 F4
Broadstone Cl
Prestwich M25 . . . . .63 A3
Rochdale OL12 . . . . .14 A1
Broadstone Hall Prim Sch
SK4 . . . . .111 D6
Broadstone Hall Rd N
SK4 . . . . .111 D6
Broadstone Hall Rd S SK4,
SK5 . . . . .111 C6
Broadstone Rd
Bolton BL2 . . . . .25 D5
Reddish SK4, SK5 . . . . .111 D6
Broadview Ct OL16 . . . . . .31 C3
Broadway
Altrincham WA15 . . . . . .120 B1
Chadderton, Stock Brook
OL9 . . . . .152 A3
Chadderton, White Gate End
M40, OL9 . . . . .65 E2
Cheadle SK8 . . . . .122 C4
Droylsden M43 . . . . . . .100 A8
Dukinfield SK14, SK16 . .101 B5
Failsworth M35, M40 . . . .83 D8
Farnworth BL4 . . . . .42 A1
Haslingden BB4 . . . . .1 B8
Hindley WN2 . . . . .57 A5
Horwich BL6 . . . . .22 D3
Irlam M44 . . . . .94 A1
Manchester M19 . . . . . . .99 B2
Reddish SK4 . . . . .111 D5
Sale M33 . . . . .149 B4
Swinton M27 . . . . .79 F7
Uppermill OL3 . . . . .69 C8
Broadway Bsns Pk OL9 . .65 E4
Broadway Cl M30 . . . . . . .79 B2
Broadway Cl M41 . . . . . . .95 C5
Broadway Cres BB4 . . . . . .1 A8
Broadway Ind Est
Dukinfield SK16 . . . . . . .101 B6
Salford M50 . . . . .161 A4
Broadway N M43 . . . . . .100 A8

Broadway Prim Sch
BB4 . . . . .1 C8
Broadway St OL8 . . . . . . .66 F4
Broadway Sta SK6 . . . . . .96 F8
Broadway The SK6 . . . . .112 E3
Broadwell Dr
Leigh WN7 . . . . .75 E1
Manchester M9 . . . . . . .157 B3
Broad Wlk
Salford M6 . . . . .81 A3
Westhoughton BL5 . . . . . .57 E7
Wilmslow SK9 . . . . .136 F8
Broadwood BL6 . . . . .40 C7
Broadwood Cl SK6 . . . . .134 F7
Brocade Cl M3 . . . . .158 A3
Broche Cl OL11 . . . . .30 B3
Brock Ave BL2 . . . . .42 F7
Brock Cl M11 . . . . .99 D7
Brock Dr SK8 . . . . .132 B8
Brockenhurst Dr BL2 . . . .25 F3
Brockford Dr M9 . . . . . . .64 E5
Brockholes SK13 . . . . . .115 F8
Brockhurst Wlk M17 . . . .150 A1
Brocklebank Rd
Manchester M14 . . . . . .110 C8
Rochdale OL16 . . . . .31 D7
Brocklehurst Ave BL9 . . .140 C1
Brocklehurst St M9,
M40 . . . . .83 A8
Brockley Ave M14 . . . . . . .98 B2
Brock Pl WA1 WN1 . . . . . .37 C4
Brock Pl WN2 . . . . .55 F2
Brock St
Manchester M1 . . . . . . .159 B1
Wigan WN1 . . . . .151 B4
Brockstedes Ave WN4 . . .72 E6
Brock The **6** OL2 . . . . . .48 F8
Brockton Wlk M8 . . . . . .156 A4
Brockway WA3 . . . . .111 C3
Brocstedes Rd WN4 . . . . .72 D7
Brocton Cl M7 . . . . .63 D1
Brodick Dr BL2 . . . . .42 F6
Brodick St M40 . . . . .157 C4
Brodie Cl M30 . . . . .79 B2
Brogan St **8** M18 . . . . . .99 D5
Brogden Ave WA3 . . . . . .91 E4
Brogden Dr SK8 . . . . . . .122 B5
Brogden Gr M33 . . . . . . .108 A3
Brogden Terr M33 . . . . . .108 A3
Bromborough Ave 2
M20 . . . . .110 A8
Bromfield **8** OL12 . . . . .139 C4
Bromfield Ave M9 . . . . . . .64 D1
Bromleigh Ave SK8 . . . . .122 B6
Bromley Ave
Golborne WA3 . . . . .90 D7
Royton OL2 . . . . .48 C6
Urmston M41 . . . . .94 E1
Bromley Cl WN2 . . . . .38 A2
Bromley Cres OL6 . . . . . .85 B6
BROMLEY CROSS 25 B7
Bromley Cross Rd BL7 . . .25 B7
Bromley Cross Sta BL7 . .25 B7
Bromley Dr WN7 . . . . . . .75 D8
Bromley Rd M33 . . . . . . .108 C2
Bromley St
Chadderton OL9 . . . . .66 A3
Denton M34 . . . . .100 F3
Manchester M4, M40 . . .159 B3
Bromlow St M11 . . . . . . .83 C1
Brompton Ave M35 . . . . .84 B8
Brompton Rd
Manchester M14 . . . . . . .98 B2
Stockport SK4 . . . . .168 A2
Urmston M32 . . . . .95 F3
Brompton St M10 . . . . . . .67 A5
Brompton Terr 6
SK16 . . . . .166 B1
Brompton Way SK9 . . . . .131 C5
Bromsgrove Ave M30 . . . .79 B2
Bromshill Dr M7 . . . . . . .155 B2
Bromwich Dr **11** M9 . . . .157 A3
Bromwich St BL2 . . . . . .148 B2
Bromington Cl M27 . . . . .121 E2
Bronte Ave BL9 . . . . .44 F4
Bronte Cl
Bolton BL1 . . . . .143 A1
Oldham OL1 . . . . .49 D4
Rochdale OL12 . . . . .14 A1
Wigan WN3 . . . . .163 A1
Bronte St M15 . . . . .163 A1
Bronville Cl OL1 . . . . .49 C1
Brookash Rd M22 . . . . . .131 A8
Brook Ave
Altrincham WA15 . . . . . .119 E6
Droylsden M43 . . . . .83 E1
Handforth SK9 . . . . .131 D4
Manchester M19 . . . . . . .99 B2
Reddish SK4 . . . . .111 D5
Sale M33 . . . . .149 B4
Swinton M27 . . . . .79 F7
Uppermill OL3 . . . . .69 C8
Brook Bank
Bolton BL2 . . . . .25 D3
Poynton SK12 . . . . .134 C2
Brookbank Cl M24 . . . . . .65 B7
BROOK BOTTOM
Mossley 68 B2
Whitfield 126 F1
Brookbottom Rd M26 . . . .43 F6
Brook Bottom Rd SK6 . . .126 F1
BROOKBOTTOMS 11 C3
Brookburn Com Sch
M21 . . . . .109 A7
Brookburn Rd M21 . . . . .109 A7
Brook Cl
Altrincham WA15 . . . . . .119 E6

Brook Cl *continued*
Tyldesley M29 59 A2
Whitefield M45 63 B8
Brookcot Rd M23 120 F7
Brookcroft Ave M22 121 D5
Brookcroft Rd M22 121 D5
Brook Ct
12 Manchester M14 110 D8
Prestwich M7 63 C1
Brookdale
Over Hulton M46 58 F6
Rochdale OL12 14 E3
Brookdale Ave
Denton, Audenshaw M34 100 E7
Denton M34 101 B2
Failsworth M40 83 D4
Marple SK6 126 A4
Brookdale Cl
Bolton BL1 143 C2
Romiley SK6 112 F3
Brookdale Cotts SK2 124 F6
Brookdale Ct M33 108 C1
Brookdale Rd
Bramhall SK7 123 F1
Hindley WN2 56 F5
Wythenshawe SK8 121 F5
Brookdale Rise SK7 123 F1
Brookdale St M35 83 E7
Brookdean Cl BL1 142 C3
Brookdene Rd
Manchester M19 110 E6
Whitefield BL9 45 A2
Brook Dr
Marple SK6 125 F4
Tyldesley M29 77 C5
Whitefield M45 63 B8
Brooke Ct SK9 131 E4
Brooke Dr SK9 131 D4
Brookes St
7 Bacup OL13 3 D8
Middleton M24 47 B2
Brooke Way SK9 131 D4
Brook Farm Cl M31 105 E2
BROOKFIELD 171 B3
Brookfield
Atherton M46 58 B2
Prestwich M25 63 B4
Shaw OL2 32 A1
Brookfield Ave
Ainsworth BL2 26 C1
Ainsworth BL2 43 D8
Altrincham WA15 119 F8
Manchester M21 109 C7
Poynton SK12 133 C3
Romiley SK6 113 A4
Royton OL2 48 D3
Salford M6 80 C3
Stockport SK1 124 A7
Urmston M41 95 A2
Brookfield Bsns Pk SK8 122 E5
Brookfield Cl
Prestwich M25 63 B4
Stockport SK1 124 A7
Brookfield Cres SK8 122 D4
Brookfield Ct 4 M19 110 F8
Brookfield Dr
Altrincham WA15 120 A7
Boothstown M28 77 F6
Littleborough OL15 15 F6
Swinton M27 61 E1
Brookfield Gdns M22 121 C6
Brookfield Gr OL6 85 D2
Brookfield Ho
Cheadle SK8 122 D4
Ramsbottom BL0 10 F3
Brookfield Ind Est SK13 171 B3
Brookfield Rd
Bury BL9 27 E8
Cheadle SK8 122 E5
Culcheth WA3 91 D3
Eccles M30 79 B4
Manchester M8 64 A1
Shevington Moor WN6 19 B2
Up Holland WN8 53 B7
Brookfield Rd Ind Est SK8 122 F5
Brookfield St
Bolton BL2 148 B3
Leigh WN7 76 A6
Newton-le-W WA12 89 B3
Oldham OL8 153 C1
Brookfield Terr SK7 124 F4
Brookfold M35 83 E8
Brookfold La BL2 25 F5
Brook Fold La SK14 102 B2
Brookfold Rd SK4 111 D6
Brook Gdns
Bolton BL2 25 E4
Heywood OL10 29 C2
Brook Gr M44 94 A2
Brook Green La M34 99 F3
Brookhead Ave M20 109 F7
Brookhead Dr SK8 123 A6
Brookhey SK14 101 B3
Brookhey Ave BL3 147 C3
Brook Hey Cl OL12 15 D4
Brookheys Rd M31, WA14 106 E2
Brookhill Cl OL3 51 C5
Brookhill St M40 160 B3
Brook Ho
Sale WA15 120 C7
Wigan WN1 151 A4
Brookhouse Ave
Eccles M30 95 A8

Brookhouse Ave *continued*
Farnworth BL4 60 C6
Brookhouse Cl BL8 26 E8
Brook House Cl BL2 25 E3
Brookhouse Mill La BL8 26 F8
Brookhouse Sports Ctr M30 94 F8
Brookhouse St WN1 151 A3
Brookhouse Terr WN1 151 A3
Brookhurst La M38 59 E6
Brookhurst Rd M18 99 D4
Brook La
Alderley Edge SK9 136 F3
Altrincham WA15 119 F6
Oldham, Alexandra Park OL8 67 B4
Oldham, Salem OL4 67 E6
Rochdale OL16 31 B3
Uppermill OL3 50 F2
Whitefield BL9 45 A4
Wigan WN5 54 B5
Brookland Ave
Denton M34 100 D2
Farnworth BL4 60 C7
Hindley WN2 56 D5
Brookland Gr BL1 142 A2
Brookland Rd WN1 37 B3
BROOKLANDS 108 C2
Brooklands
Horwich BL6 22 C3
Wardle OL12 15 C7
Brooklands Ave
Ashton-in-M WN4 73 D2
Atherton M46 58 D4
Chadderton OL9 152 B1
Haslingden BB4 1 B7
Leigh WN7 75 E3
Manchester M20 110 A6
Brooklands Cl
Denton M34 100 D4
Irlam M44 93 F2
Mossley OL5 68 B2
Reddish SK4 111 D5
Brooklands Cres M33 108 B3
Brooklands Ct
Manchester M8 63 F2
Rochdale OL11 30 C6
Sale M33 108 B3
Brooklands Dr
Droylsden M43 84 C3
Glossop SK13 116 B7
Oldham OL4 68 B6
Orrell WN5 53 D5
Brooklands Ho M33 108 B2
Brooklands Par OL4 68 B6
Brooklands Pl M33 108 A3
Brooklands Prim Sch M33 108 A2
Brooklands Rd
Hazel Grove SK7 124 E1
Manchester M25, M8 63 E2
Ramsbottom BL0 11 A2
Reddish SK5 99 E2
Sale M23, M33 108 B2
Swinton M27 79 D6
Up Holland WN8 53 C7
Brooklands St
Middleton M24 47 A1
Royton OL2 48 D5
Brooklands Sta M33 108 A3
Brooklands Station App M33 108 A3
Brookland St OL16 31 B3
Brookland Terr BB4 2 F7
Brooklawn Dr
Manchester M20 110 B4
Prestwich M25 63 C6
Brookleigh Rd M20 110 D6
Brooklet Cl OL4 67 F5
Brook Lo SK8 122 D4
Brooklyn Ave
Littleborough OL15 16 A7
Manchester M16 97 C2
Rochdale OL16 15 E4
Urmston M41 94 E2
Brooklyn Cres SK8 122 D5
Brooklyn Ct M20 110 C7
Brook Lynn Ave WA3 74 F1
Brooklyn Pl SK8 122 D6
Brooklyn Rd
Cheadle SK8 122 D5
Stockport SK2 124 C6
Brooklyn St
Bolton BL1 143 B1
10 Oldham OL1 49 C1
Brook Mdw
Glossop SK13 104 E1
Westhoughton BL5 40 A1
Brook Mill 2 BL7 24 F7
Brook Rd
Cheadle SK8 122 D6
Manchester M14 110 D7
Reddish SK4 111 C5
Urmston M41 95 A2
Brook St E OL6 166 A2
Brook St Ind Est SK1 170 C3
Brook St W OL6 166 A2
Brooks Ave
Hazel Grove SK7 124 D3
Hyde SK14 167 B1
Radcliffe M26 43 F6
Brook's Bar M16 97 D4
Brooksbottom Cl BL0 11 C4
Brooks Dr
Altrincham, Halebarns WA15 129 D8

Brooks Dr *continued*
Altrincham M23, WA15 120 D6
Failsworth M35 83 E6
Gatley SK8 122 C2
Brooks End OL11 13 E1
Brookshaw St
Bury BL9 141 A4
Droylsden M11 83 A1
Brooks Hos 1 WN7 75 E8
Brookside
Glossop SK13 116 B8
Mossley OL5 68 B2
New Mills SK22 127 E7
Oldham OL4 67 D6
Wigan WN3 150 A1
Brookside Ave
Ashton-in-M WN4 72 F8
Droylsden M43 84 C3
Farnworth BL4 60 C7
Oldham OL4 68 B6
Poynton SK12 133 E3
Stockport SK2 124 F7
Brookside Bsns Pk M24 65 D6
Brookside Cl
Atherton M46 58 E4
Billinge WN5 71 E5
Bolton BL2 25 D5
Cheadle SK8 122 D4
Glossop SK13 171 C4
Hyde SK14 102 A3
Ramsbottom BL0 11 A3
Brookside Cres
Bury BL8 26 E8
Middleton M24 65 C6
Ramsbottom BL8 10 E1
Walkden M28 60 E3
Brookside Ct M19 99 A2
Brookside Dr
Hyde SK14 102 A3
Manchester M7 63 D1
Brookside La SK6 134 E7
Brookside Miniature Rly* SK12 133 F7
Brookside Prim Sch SK6 134 E6
Brookside Rd
Bolton BL2 42 D8
Gatley SK8 122 A6
Manchester M40 65 A1
Sale M33 108 A2
Standish WN1 20 B1
Brookside Terr
Delph OL3 50 E4
Wilmslow SK9 136 E3
Brookside Wlk M26 43 F7
Brooksmouth BL8 140 A2
Brook's Pl 3 OL12 139 B4
Brook's Rd M16 97 C3
Brooks St SK1 170 C3
Brook St
Ashton-in-M WN4 73 C2
Atherton M46 58 B3
Bank Heath WA3 90 A8
Bolton BL1 145 C3
Bury BL9 141 A3
Chadderton OL9 152 B4
Cheadle SK8 122 F6
Failsworth M35 83 D6
Farnworth BL4 42 E1
Glossop SK13 104 C1
Golborne, Aspull Common WA3 75 A1
Hazel Grove SK7 124 E2
Hyde SK14 167 B3
Ince-in-M WN2 56 A7
Kearsley M26 61 A7
Littleborough OL15 16 C5
Manchester M1 163 A3
Oldham OL1 67 A7
Radcliffe M26 44 B3
Royton OL2 48 D3
Sale M33 108 C5
Swinton M27 79 D8
Wardle OL12 15 C6
Westhoughton BL5 39 F1
Wigan WN3 54 F4
Brookstone Cl M21 109 D6
Brook Terr
Manchester M13 98 F3
Newhey OL16 32 C4
Urmston M41 95 C4
Brook The OL15 6 C1
Brookthorn Cl SK2 124 F5
Brookthorpe Ave M19 110 E6
Brookthorpe Mdws BL8 27 A3
Brookthorpe Rd BL8 27 A3
Brookvale 4 WN6 37 A1
Brookview 1 WN2 56 D4
Brook View SK9 137 A3
Brookville OL12 4 C1
Brookwater Cl BL8 26 F6
Brookway
Altrincham WA15 119 F7
Littleborough OL15 16 A4
Oldham OL4 67 E5
Uppermill OL4 68 E6
Brookway Cl M19 110 E4
Brookway Ct M23 120 F7
Brookway High Sch & Sports Coll M23 120 E7
Brook Wlk
Bury BL8 27 A6
Denton M34 112 F8
Brookwood Ave
Manchester M8 156 C4

Brookwood Ave *continued*
Sale M33 107 E3
Brookwood Cl M34 113 A7
Broom Ave
Leigh WN7 75 E7
Manchester M19 111 B8
4 Reddish SK5 111 F6
Salford M7 155 B4
BROOMEDGE 117 C1
Broomedge M7 155 A4
Broome Gr M35 83 F6
Broomehouse Ave M44 105 E8
Broome St OL9 153 A2
Broomfield M6 80 D6
Broomfield Cl
Ainsworth BL2 26 C1
Reddish SK5 111 F6
Wilmslow SK9 137 E8
Broomfield Cres
Middleton M24 46 D1
Stockport SK2 124 A4
Broomfield Dr
Reddish SK5 111 F6
Salford M8 155 C3
Broomfield La WA15 119 E3
Broomfield Pl WN6 19 E1
Broomfield Rd
4 Bolton BL3 146 C4
Standish WN6 19 E2
Stockport SK4 168 C4
Broomfields M34 101 A5
Broomfield Sq OL11 139 C1
Broomfield Terr
Newhey OL16 32 B4
Wigan WN1 151 B3
Broomflat Cl WN6 19 E1
Broomgrove La M34 101 A4
Broomhall Rd
Manchester M9 64 B5
Pendlebury M27 80 D6
Broomhey Ave WN1 37 C4
Broomhey Terr WN1 151 B3
Broomhill Dr SK7 123 D1
Broomholme WN6 35 D7
Broomhurst Ave OL8 66 D4
Broom La
Manchester M19 111 B8
Salford M7 155 A4
Broom Rd
Altrincham WA15 119 E3
Partington M31 105 F2
Wigan WN5 54 D7
Broom St
Bury BL8 140 A2
Newhey OL16 32 B4
Swinton M27 79 F7
Broomstair Rd M34 100 F6
Broomville Ave M33 108 B4
Broom Way BL5 40 A2
Broomwood Gdns WA15 120 C5
Broomwood Prim Sch WA15 120 D5
Broomwood Rd WA15 120 C5
Broomwood Wlk 3 M15 163 A2
Broseley Ave
Culcheth WA3 91 D4
Manchester M20 110 D3
Broseley La WA3 91 D5
Broseley Rd M16 97 A2
Brosscroft SK13 104 A6
Brosscroft Cl SK13 104 A6
Brosscroft Village SK13 104 A6
Brotherdale Cl OL2 48 D5
Brotherod Hall Rd OL12 14 C2
Brotherton Cl M15 162 A2
Brotherton Ct 6 M14 98 D4
Brotherton Dr M3 158 A2
Brotherton Way WA12 89 B4
Brougham St M28 60 C3
Brough Cl WN2 56 E3
Brough St 4 M11 99 E7
Broughton Ave
Golborne WA3 90 D7
Walkden M38 60 B4
Broughton Cl M24 46 D2
Broughton Jewish Cassel-Fox Prim Sch M7 155 A4
Broughton La
Salford M7 155 A1
Salford M7, M8 158 B4
BROUGHTON PARK 63 D1
Broughton Rd
Reddish SK5 169 C4
Salford M6 81 A4
Broughton Rd E M6 81 B4
Broughton St
Bolton BL1 143 A2
Manchester M8 159 A4
Salford M8 155 C1
Broughton Trade Ctr M7 158 B4
Broughville Dr M20 122 C8
Brow Ave M24 65 C6
Browbeck OL1 153 B3
Browfield Ave M5 161 B4
Browfield Way OL1 48 E1
Browmere Dr M20 110 A4
Brownacre St M20 110 B6
Brown Bank Rd OL15 15 F3
Brownbank Wlk 7 M15 162 C1
Browncross St M3 158 B1

Brown Edge Rd OL4 67 E4
Brown Heath Ave WN5 71 D3
Brownhill Countryside Ctr* OL3 51 B1
Brownhill Dr OL4 68 A7
Brownhill La OL3 51 B1
Brownhill Sch OL12 14 E1
Brownhills Cl BL8 27 A5
Brownhill St M11 165 A4
Brownhill View OL12 14 E1
Browning Ave
Atherton M46 58 D5
2 Droylsden M43 84 A1
Wigan WN3 54 F4
Browning Cl BL1 143 A1
Browning Gr WN6 36 E3
Browning Rd
Middleton M24 47 B2
Oldham OL1 49 B1
Reddish SK5 99 E2
Swinton M27 79 E8
Browning St
Leigh WN7 75 D6
Manchester M15 162 A2
Salford M3 158 A2
Browning Wlk M46 58 D5
Brown La SK8 122 B1
Brownlea Ave SK16 101 C7
Brownley Court Rd M22 121 D5
Brownley Ct M22 121 E5
Brownley Rd M22 121 E4
Brown Lodge Dr OL15 15 F3
Brown Lodge St OL15 15 F3
BROWNLOW 53 C1
Brownlow Ave
Ince-in-M WN2 56 B7
Royton OL2 49 A3
Brownlow Bsns Ctr BL1 143 A1
Brownlow Cl SK12 133 E2
BROWNLOW FOLD 143 A1
Brownlow Fold Prim Sch BL1 143 A1
Brownlow La WN5 53 C1
Brownlow Rd BL6 22 C5
Brownlow Way BL1 143 B1
Brownmere WN6 36 F2
Brownrigg Cl M24 46 C1
Brown St N 2 WN7 76 A5
Brown St S 1 WN7 76 A4
Brownside Cl OL16 15 C3
Brown's La SK9 137 E8
Brownslow Wlk 11 M13 163 B3
Brownson Wlk 7 M9 157 B4
Browns Rd BL2 43 B6
Brown St
3 Alderley Edge SK9 137 A1
Altrincham WA14 119 D3
Bickershaw WN2 56 E1
Blackrod BL6 21 D2
Bolton BL1 145 C3
Chadderton OL9 152 A4
Failsworth M35 83 E7
Heywood OL10 29 D3
Ince-in-M WN2 56 A7
3 Leigh WN7 76 A5
Littleborough OL15 16 B5
Manchester M2 159 A1
Middleton M24 47 A2
Oldham OL1 67 A7
Radcliffe M26 43 F6
Ramsbottom BL0 138 B1
Salford M6 154 C1
Stockport SK1 169 B2
Tyldesley M29 76 F7
Wigan WN3 150 B3
Brownsville Rd SK4 111 C5
Brownville Gr SK16 101 E7
Brownwood Ave SK1 112 B1
Brownwood Cl M33 108 C1
Brows Ave M23 109 A2
Browsholm Ho BL1 144 C3
Brow St OL11 31 A4
Brow Wlk M9 64 D3
Broxton Ave
Bolton BL3 146 B3
Orrell WN5 53 F7
Broxton St M40 160 C3
Broxwood Cl 8 M18 99 D5
Bruce St OL11 30 C4
Bruce Wlk 2 M11 99 D7
Brundage Rd M22 121 D2
Brundrett Pl 7 M33 107 F4
Brundrett's Rd M21 109 B8
Brundrett St SK1 124 A8
Brunel Ave M5 81 B1
Brunel Cl M32 96 E2
Brunel St
Bolton BL1 143 A3
Horwich BL6 22 C2
Brunet Wlk M12 164 C2
Brun La OL3 51 E6
Brunstead Cl M23 120 D6
BRUNSWICK 163 C2
Brunswick Ave BL6 22 E2
Brunswick Ct BL1 145 B4
Brunswick Rd
Altrincham WA14 119 D7
Manchester M20 110 C7
Brunswick Sq OL1 153 C2
Brunswick St
Bury BL9 140 C3
Dukinfield SK16 101 C8

Brunswick St *continued*
Heywood OL10 29 C2
3 Heywood OL10 29 C2
Leigh WN7 76 A4
Manchester M13 163 B2
Mossley OL5 86 D8
Oldham OL1 153 B2
Rochdale OL16 31 A8
Shaw OL2 149 B3
Stretford M32 108 D8
Brunswick Terr OL13 3 D8
Brunton Rd SK5 111 F6
Brunt St M14 98 B3
Bruntwood Ave SK8 122 A1
Bruntwood La
Cheadle Hulme SK8 122 E2
Cheadle SK8 122 E1
BRUSHES 86 D3
Brushes SK15 87 A3
Brushes Ave SK15 86 D3
Brushes Rd
Hollingworth SK15 87 A3
Stalybridge SK15 86 E2
Brussels Rd SK3 170 A2
Bruton Ave M32 96 B1
Brutus Wlk M7 155 B2
Bryan Rd M21 97 B2
Bryan St 1 OL4 49 C1
Bryant Cl M13 163 C1
Bryant's Acre BL1 40 D7
Bryantsfield BL1 40 D6
Bryce St SK14 167 A4
Brydges Rd SK6 125 E5
Brydon Ave M12 163 C3
Brydon Cl M6 154 C2
Bryham St WN1 151 A4
BRYN 72 F6
Bryn Cross WN4 73 A6
Bryndale Gr M33 107 F1
Brynden Ave M20 110 C5
Bryn Dr SK5 111 F5
Brynford Ave M9 64 A5
BRYN GATES 73 E7
Bryn Gates La WN2 73 D8
Bryngs Dr BL2 25 F4
Brynhall Cl M26 43 E5
Brynheys Cl M38 60 A5
Bryn Lea Terr BL1 142 A4
Brynn St WN2 73 F7
Brynorme Rd M8 64 A2
Bryn Rd WN4 73 B5
Bryn Rd S WN4 73 C4
Bryn St Peter's CE Prim Sch WN4 72 F6
Bryn St
Ashton-in-M WN4 73 B3
Ince-in-M WN3 151 B2
Bryn Sta WN4 73 A6
Brynton Rd M13 98 E2
Bryn Wlk BL1 145 C4
Bryone Dr SK2 124 B5
Bryony Cl
Orrell WN5 53 D5
Walkden M28 60 D5
6 Wythenshawe M22 121 C1
Bryson Wlk M18 165 C1
Buchanan Dr WN2 57 B3
Buchanan Rd WN5 54 E7
Buchanan St
Leigh WN7 75 E5
Ramsbottom BL0 138 B1
Swinton M27 61 F1
Buchan St M11 83 B2
Buckden Rd SK4 111 D7
Buckden Wlk 11 M23 108 F2
Buckfast Ave
Haydock WA11 89 A7
Oldham OL8 67 D3
Buckfast Cl
Altrincham WA15 120 B2
Cheadle SK8 132 B6
Manchester M21 97 B1
Poynton SK12 133 D5
Buckfast Rd
Middleton M24 46 F3
Sale M33 107 E6
Buckfast Wlk M7 155 B2
Buckfield Ave M5 161 B3
Buckhurst Rd
Manchester M19 99 A1
Ramsbottom BL9 12 C3
Buckingham Ave
Denton M34 101 B2
Horwich BL6 22 E2
Salford M6 154 A2
Whitefield M45 63 A7
Buckingham Cl WN5 54 E5
Buckingham Dr
Bury BL8 44 B8
Dukinfield SK16 101 F7
Buckingham Park Cl OL2 149 B4
Buckingham Pl
Manchester M21 97 B1
Tyldesley M29 58 F3
Buckingham Rd
Cheadle SK8 123 A3
Droylsden M43 83 E1
Irlam M44 105 C6
Manchester, Heaton Chapel SK4 111 C6
Manchester, Heaton Moor SK4 111 B5
Manchester, Hilton Park M25 63 C2

Buckingham Rd *continued*
Manchester M21 97 B1
Poynton SK12 133 D3
Sale WA14 107 F1
Stalybridge SK15 86 A3
Stretford M32 96 F4
Swinton M27 62 A2
Wilmslow SK9 136 F6
Buckingham Rd W SK4 168 A4
Buckingham St
12 Rochdale OL16 31 A8
Salford M5 154 C1
Stockport SK2 124 A6
Buckingham Way
Altrincham WA15 120 A7
Stockport SK2 170 C2
Buck La M33 107 E6
Buckland Ave M9 64 A3
Buckland Dr WN5 36 B1
Buckland Gr SK14 114 A8
Buckland Rd M6 154 A4
Buckle Ho 7 M30 79 E2
BUCKLEY 15 A3
Buckley Ave M18 99 C4
Buckley Barn Ct OL11 30 C1
Buckley Bldgs OL5 86 E8
Buckley Brook St OL12 15 B2
Buckley Chase OL16 31 E5
Buckley Cl SK14 113 E7
Buckley Dr
Denshaw OL3 33 C1
Romiley SK6 113 A1
Buckley Farm La OL12 15 B3
Buckley Fields OL12 15 A2
Buckley Hall Ind Est OL12 15 B3
Buckley Hill La OL16 31 E5
Buckley Ho M46 58 D3
Buckley La
Farnworth BL4 60 C7
Prestwich M25 62 E3
Rochdale OL12 15 B3
Buckley Mill 14 OL3 69 B8
Buckley Rd
Manchester M18 99 C4
Oldham OL4 67 D8
Rochdale OL12 15 B2
Buckley Road Ind Est OL12 15 A2
Buckley St W WN6 37 A2
Buckley Sq BL4 60 C6
Buckley St
Bury BL9 140 C3
Chadderton OL9 152 A3
Denton M34 100 D7
Droylsden M43 84 A1
Heywood OL10 29 E3
Manchester M11 99 E7
Oldham OL4 67 E5
Radcliffe M26 44 A3
Reddish SK5 99 E2
Rochdale OL16 31 A8
Shaw OL2 149 C3
Stalybridge SK15 101 F8
Uppermill OL3 69 B8
Wigan WN6 37 B2
Buckley Terr OL12 15 B3
Buckley View OL12 15 B3
BUCKLEY WELLS 140 A1
Bucklow Ave
Manchester M14 98 B1
Partington M31 105 F3
Bucklow Cl
Broadbottom SK14 102 F1
Oldham OL4 49 E4
Bucklow Dr M22 121 E8
Bucklow Gdns WA13 117 A4
Bucklow Ho M22 121 F7
Bucklow View WA14 119 A3
Bucknell Ct M40 159 C4
Buck St WN7 75 F4
Buckstones Jun & Inf Sch OL2 49 D8
Buckstones Rd OL1, OL2 49 E7
Buckthorn Cl
Altrincham WA15 120 E5
Manchester M21 109 D6
Westhoughton BL5 39 F2
Buckthorn La M30 94 F8
Buckton Cl OL3 51 C5
Buckton Dr SK15 86 E5
BUCKTON VALE 86 E6
Buckton Vale Mews SK15 86 F7
Buckton Vale Prim Sch SK15 86 F7
Buckton Vale Rd
Mossley, Carrbrook SK15 86 F6
Mossley, Millbrook SK15 86 D4
Buckwood Cl SK7 125 A3
Buddleia Gr M7 155 A2
Bude Ave
Brinnington SK5 112 B5
Tyldesley M29 77 C8
Urmston M41 107 B8
Bude Cl SK7 132 F7
Bude Terr 4 SK16 166 B1
Bude Wlk M23 121 B5
Budsworth Ave M20 110 B7
Budworth Gdns 2 M43 84 B1
Budworth Rd M33 108 E3
Budworth Wlk 1 SK9 131 E1
Buer Ave WN3 54 F4
BUERSIL 31 B3

Buersil Ave OL16 31 B4
BUERSIL HEAD 31 C1
Buersil St OL16 31 B3
Buerton Ave M9 64 A5
Buffalo Ct M50 96 E8
Buffoline Trad Est M19 99 B1
Bugle St M1 162 B4
Buile Dr M9 64 F4
Buile Hill Ave M38 60 B5
Buile Hill Dr M5 154 A3
Buile Hill Gr M38 60 B5
Buile Hill High Sch M6 154 A4
Buile St M7 155 B3
Buille Ho M6 154 B3
Bulford Ave M22 121 B2
Bulkeley Rd
Cheadle SK8 122 E6
Handforth SK9 131 D3
Poynton SK12 133 E3
Bulkeley St SK3 170 A4
Bullcote Gn OL2 49 B4
Bullcote La OL1, OL2 49 B4
Bullcroft Dr M29 77 C6
Buller Mews BL8 27 B1
Buller Rd M13 98 F2
Buller St
Bury BL8 27 C1
Droylsden M43 100 B8
Farnworth BL3 42 C2
Oldham OL4 67 D8
Bullfinch Dr BL9 28 B5
Bullfinch Wlk M21 109 D7
BULL HEY 37 B1
Bull Hill Cres M26 62 B8
Bullock St SK1 170 C3
Bullough St
Atherton M46 58 C2
Atherton M46 58 C3
Bullows Rd M38 59 F6
Bullrush Cl M28 60 D5
Bulteel St
Bolton BL3 146 C2
Boothstown M28 77 E7
Eccles M30 79 B3
Wigan WN5 54 D6
Bulwer St OL16 31 A8
Bungalow Rd WA12 89 E1
Bungalows The
Ashton-in-M WN4 72 F7
Hazel Grove SK7 124 F4
New Mills SK22 127 D1
Bunkers OL3 69 C6
Bunkers Hill
Romiley SK6 113 B1
Swinton M45 62 D3
Bunkers Hill Rd SK14 102 E1
Bunsen St M1 159 B1
Bunting Cl 6 WA3 90 E8
Bunting Mews M28 78 B8
Bunyan Cl OL1 49 E4
Bunyan St 24 OL12 14 F1
Bunyard St M8 156 B2
BUPA Hospl Manchester M16 97 D3
Burbage Bank 32 SK13 171 B2
Burbage Gr 18 SK13 171 B2
Burbage Rd M23 121 A2
Burbage Way 19 SK13 171 B2
Burbridge Cl M11 160 B1
Burchall Field OL16 31 B7
Burdale Dr M6 80 B4
Burdale Wlk M23 108 F1
Burder St 4 OL8 66 C2
Burdett Ave OL12 13 F1
Burdett Way M12 164 B1
Burdith Ave M14 98 A2
Burdon Ave M22 121 E3
Burford Ave
Bramhall SK7 132 D5
Manchester M16 97 D2
Urmston M41 95 E4
Burford Cl SK9 136 E5
Burford Cres SK9 136 E5
Burford Dr
Bolton BL3 145 B1
Manchester M16 97 D2
Swinton M27 61 E2
Burford Gr M33 107 E1
Burford La WA13 117 C2
Burford Rd M16 97 D2
Burford Wlk M16 97 D2
Burgess Ave OL6 85 C5
Burgess Dr M35 83 F7
Burgess Prim Sch M9 157 B3
Burgess St WN3 151 B1
Burghley Ave OL4 67 D6
Burghley Cl
Little Lever M26 43 B5
Stalybridge SK15 86 A2
Burghley Dr M26 43 B5
Burghley Way WN3 151 C1
Burgin Wlk M40 156 C1
Burgundy Dr BL8 26 F7
Burke St BL1 143 A2
Burkhardt Dr WA12 89 E3
Burkitt St SK14 167 B2
Burland Cl M7 155 A1
Burland St WN5 54 F7
Burleigh Cl SK7 124 A1
Burleigh Ct M32 96 E4
Burleigh Ho M13 163 B1
Burleigh Mews M21 109 B6
Burleigh Rd M32 96 E4
Burleigh St M15 163 B1

Burlescombe Cl WA14 119 B6
Burley Ave WA3 74 D1
Burley Cres WN3 54 C2
Burley Ct SK4 168 C2
Burleyhurst La SK9, WA16 136 B7
Burlin Ct 9 M16 97 D3
Burlington Ave OL8 66 E4
Burlington Cl SK4 110 E2
Burlington Ct WA14 119 D5
Burlington Dr SK3 123 F4
Burlington Gdns SK3 123 F4
Burlington Ho OL6 166 A3
Burlington Mews Gdns SK3 123 F4
Burlington Rd
Altrincham WA14 119 D5
Eccles M30 79 E4
Manchester M20 110 C7
Burlington St
Ashton-u-L OL6, OL7 166 A3
Hindley WN2 56 D5
Hindley WN2 56 E5
Manchester M13, M15 163 B1
Manchester M15 163 A1
12 Rochdale OL11 31 A4
Burlton Gr WN2 38 A2
Burman St M11, M43 99 F7
Burnaby St
Bolton BL3 145 A1
Oldham OL8 153 A1
Rochdale OL11 30 C4
BURNAGE 110 F6
Burnage Ave M19 110 F8
Burnage Hall Rd M19 110 F7
Burnage High Sch M19 110 E5
Burnage La M19 110 F4
Burnage Range M19 99 A1
Burnage Sta M20 110 D4
Burnaston Gr WN5 54 D5
Burn Bank OL3 68 F5
Burnbray Ave M19 110 E6
Burnby Wlk M23 108 F1
Burndale Dr BL9 45 A3
BURNDEN 42 B4
Burnden Ind Est BL3 42 B4
Burnden Pk BL3 148 B1
Burnden Rd BL3 148 B1
Burnden Way BL6 39 C7
BURNEDGE 31 D1
Burnedge Cl OL12 4 D2
Burnedge Fold Rd OL4 68 D6
Burnedge La OL4 68 D7
Burnedge Mews OL4 68 D6
Burnell Cl M40 160 A3
Burnell Ct OL10 46 D7
Burneside Cres M24 46 E3
Burnet Cl
Rochdale OL16 31 C4
Tyldesley M29 77 B7
Burnett Ave M5 161 B4
Burnett Cl M40 157 A1
Burnfell WA3 90 E7
Burnfield Rd
Manchester M18 99 D3
Reddish SK5 99 F3
Burnham Ave
Bolton BL1 142 A1
Reddish SK5 99 F1
Burnham Cl
Cheadle SK8 122 F2
Culcheth WA3 91 E4
Burnham Dr
Manchester M19 110 F8
Urmston M41 95 C3
Burnham Gr WN2 37 F2
Burnham Rd M34 100 A3
Burnham Wlk 3 BL4 42 D1
Burnhill Ct WN6 36 E8
Burnleigh Ct BL5 58 F8
BURNLEY BROW 153 A4
Burnley Brow Com Sch OL9 152 C4
Burnley La
Chadderton, Busk OL9 48 C1
Chadderton OL1, OL9 48 A2
Burnley Rd
Bury BL9 27 E8
Edenfield BL0 1 D5
Burnley Rd E BB4 2 E8
Burnley St
Chadderton OL9 152 B4
Failsworth M35 84 A8
Burnmoor Rd BL2 42 F8
Burnsall Ave
Golborne WA3 90 F8
Whitefield M45 62 D8
Burnsall Gr OL2 48 D4
Burnsall Wlk 2 M22 121 A2
Burns Ave
Atherton M46 58 D5
Bury BL9 44 F6
Cheadle SK8 122 F6
Leigh WN7 75 C8
Swinton M27 61 D1
Burns Cl
Ashton-in-M WN4 72 F6
Longshaw WN5 53 D1
Manchester M11 160 C1
Oldham OL1 49 E5
Wigan WN3 55 A4
Burns Cres SK2 124 E7
Burns Ct OL11 29 E6
Burns Fold SK16 102 A7
Burns Gdns M25 62 F3
Burns Gr M43 84 A2

Burnside
Altrincham WA15 129 D7
Edenfield BL0 1 D2
Glossop SK13 171 C4
Shaw OL2 49 D8
Stalybridge SK15 102 D7
Burnside Ave
Reddish SK4 111 E6
Salford M6 80 B5
Burnside Cl
Heywood OL10 29 D1
Radcliffe M26 43 F7
Romiley SK6 112 F3
Stalybridge SK15 102 D7
Tyldesley M29 77 B7
Wilmslow SK9 137 C6
Burnside Dr M19 110 F7
Burnside Rd
Bolton BL1 142 B2
Gatley SK8 122 B5
Rochdale OL16 31 C6
Burns Rd
7 Abram WN2 56 B1
Denton M34 113 A7
Walkden M38 60 B5
Burns St
Bolton BL3 145 C2
Heywood OL10 29 E1
Burnt Edge La BL6 23 B5
Burnthorp Ave M9 64 B3
Burnthorpe Cl OL11 29 E6
Burntwood Wlk 22 M9 157 B4
Burnvale WN3 54 D2
Burran Rd M22 130 D8
Burrington Dr WN7 75 D7
Burrows Ave M21 109 C6
BURRS 27 D6
Burrs Cl BL8 27 C6
Burrs Ctry Pk BL8 27 D6
Burrs Lea Cl BL9 27 E6
Burrswood Ave BL9 27 F6
Bursar Cl WA12 89 D4
Burslem Ave M20 110 A8
Burstead St M18 99 E7
Burstock St M4 159 B3
Burston St M18 165 C2
Burtinshaw St 7 M18 99 D5
Burton Ave
Bury BL8 26 F4
Manchester M20 110 B6
Sale WA15 108 A1
Burton Cl WA3 91 F3
Burton Dr SK12 133 D4
Burton Gr M28 79 C8
Burton Pl M15 162 A3
Burton Rd M20 110 A6
Burton St
Middleton M24 64 F8
Oldham OL4 67 E5
Stockport SK4 169 B3
Burton Wlk
Salford M3 158 A2
Stockport SK4 169 B3
Burtonwood Ct M24 46 F1
Burtree St M12 165 A2
Burwell Ave PR7 19 D8
Burwell Cl
Bolton BL3 147 A4
Glossop SK13 116 A8
6 Leigh WN7 76 A4
Rochdale OL12 14 D4
Burwell Gr M23 120 F7
BURY 140 C3
Bury Art Gall & Mus* BL9 140 B2
Bury Ave M16 97 C2
Bury & Bolton Rd M26 43 E7
Bury Bolton Street Sta* BL9 140 B2
Bury Bsns Ctr BL9 141 A4
Bury CE High Sch BL9 44 D8
Bury Coll (Beacon Ctr) BL9 140 C1
Bury Coll (Millenium Ctr) BL9 140 C1
Bury Coll (Peel Theatre) BL9 140 B1
Bury Coll (Prospect Ctr) BL9 140 B1
Bury Coll (Woodbury Ctr) BL9 140 B1
Bury FC (Gigg La) BL9 44 F7
Bury Gram Jun Sch (Boys) BL9 140 A2
Bury Gram Sch (Boys) BL9 140 A2
Bury Gram Sch (Girls) BL9 140 B2
BURY GROUND 140 A3
Bury Intc BL9 140 B2
BURYMEWICK 113 B1
Bury Mkt Hall* BL9 140 C2
Bury New Rd
Ainsworth BL2, M26 43 B7
Bolton BL1, BL2 148 A3
Bury BL9 141 C2
Heywood BL9, OL10 28 E2
Prestwich M25 63 B3
Ramsbottom BL0 11 D6
Salford M7, M8, M25 155 B1
Whitefield M45 62 F7
Bury Old Rd
Ainsworth BL2 26 B1
Bolton BL2 148 A3
Bolton BL2 148 B3
Edenfield BL0 1 F1
Heywood BL9, OL10 28 E1

Bury Old Rd *continued*
Prestwich M25, M45, M7,
M8 ....63 C4
Ramsbottom BL9 .... 11 F4
Salford M8 .... 155 C4
Bury Pl M11 ....83 C2
Bury RC Prep Sch BL9 ..44 E8
Bury Rd
Bolton BL2 ....42 D7
Bury BL8 ....27 A5
Edenfield BL0 .... 1 D3
Edgworth BL7 .... 9 E5
Radcliffe BL9, M26 ....44 C5
Rawtenstall BB4 .... 1 E7
Rochdale OL11 ....30 B6
Bury & Rochdale Old Rd
BL9, OL10 ....29 B5
Bury Sch of Arts & Crafts
BL9 ....140 B2
Bury St
Heywood OL10 ....29 B2
Mossley OL5 ....86 C8
Radcliffe M26 ....44 D4
Reddish SK5 ....169 C3
Salford M3 ....158 B2
Bury Sta BL9 ....140 B2
Bury Transport Mus*
BL9 ....140 B2
Bury & Whitefield Jewish
Prim Sch BL9 ....45 B3
Bushell St BL3 ....146 B4
Bushey Dr M23 ....121 A5
Busheyfield Cl SK14 ...101 D5
Bushfield Wlk 1 M23 ..120 E7
Bushgrove Wlk M9 .....64 D5
Bush Moor Wlk M13 ...164 A1
Bushnay Wlk 9 M8 ....156 B2
Bushnell Wlk 1 M9 ....64 D5
Bush St M40 ....157 B1
Bushton Wlk 9 M40 ...156 C1
Business & Technology
Ctr M30 ....79 C2
BUSK 152 C4
Busk Rd OL9 ....152 C4
Busk Wlk OL9 ....152 C4
Butcherfield Row WN2 ..38 B7
Butcher La
Bury BL9 ....140 C2
Royton OL2 ....48 C5
Wythenshawe M23 ......120 D7
Butchers La WN4 ......73 B3
Bute Ave OL8 ....66 F3
Bute St
Bolton BL1 ....142 B1
Glossop SK13 ....104 E3
Manchester M40 ....157 C4
Salford M5, M50 ......154 A1
Butler Ct 10 M40 ......159 C3
Butler Gn OL9 ....66 A4
Butler La M4, M40 .....159 C3
Butler St
Manchester M4, M40 ...160 A2
Ramsbottom BL0 ....138 A1
Wigan WN1 ....151 A4
Butley St SK7 ....124 E4
Butman St M18 ....99 F6
Buttercup Ave 7 M28 ..59 F3
Buttercup Cl
Atherton M46 ....58 C5
Glossop SK13 ....116 E8
Buttercup Dr
Oldham OL4 ....49 D2
Rochdale OL11 ....30 B3
Stockport SK3 ....170 A1
Butterfield Cl SK8 ....123 B1
Butterfield Rd PR6 .....58 F8
Butterhouse La OL3 ....51 C2
Butter La 5 M3 ....158 C1
Butterley Cl SK16 .....101 F7
Buttermere Ave
Ashton-in-M WN4 ......73 B5
Oldham OL1 ....46 D8
Swinton M27 ....79 F6
Buttermere Cl
Little Lever BL3 ....42 F4
Stretford M32 ....96 C3
Buttermere Dr
Altrincham WA15 ......129 D6
Middleton M24 ....46 E2
Ramsbottom BL0 ....138 B3
Buttermere Gr OL2 .....48 D7
Buttermere Rd
Ashton-u-L OL7 ....166 A4
Farnworth BL4 ....59 E8
Gatley SK8 ....122 B3
Oldham OL4 ....67 D8
Partington M31 ....105 E3
Wigan WN5 ....54 C7
Buttermere Terr SK15 ..86 A3
Buttermill Cl 4 M44 ...94 B3
Butterstile Ave M25 ...62 F1
Butterstile Cl M25 .....62 F1
Butterstile La M25 .....63 A3
Butterstile Prim Sch
M25 ....63 A2
Butterworth Cl M12 ....99 B3
Butterworth Fold BL6 ...21 B1
BUTTERWORTH HALL ...32 B6
Butterworth Hall OL16 ..32 A5
Butterworth La M40,
OL9 ....65 C2
Butterworth St
Chadderton OL9 ......152 B4
4 Littleborough OL15 ..16 A5
Manchester M11 ......165 A4
Middleton M24 ....65 C7
Radcliffe M26 ....44 B4

Butterworth Way OL3 ...69 B5
Butteryhouse La
WA15 ....120 E2
Butt Hill Ave M25 .....63 B3
Butt Hill Cl M25 ....63 B3
Butt Hill Dr M25 ....63 B3
Butt Hill Rd M25 ....63 B3
Butt La OL4 ....68 B4
Button Hole OL2 ....49 D7
Button La M23 ....109 A2
Button La Prim Sch
M23 ....108 F2
Buttons Row BB4 ....2 F6
Buttress St M18 ....165 C2
Butts Ave WN7 ....76 C3
Butts Ave The 3
OL16 ....139 C3
Butts St WN7 ....76 A4
Butts La OL3 ....50 D4
Butts St WN7 ....76 B3
Butts The 2 OL16 .....139 C3
Buxted Rd OL1 ....49 B1
Buxton Ave
Ashton-u-L OL6 ....85 F6
Manchester M20 ......109 F6
Buxton Cl
Atherton M46 ....58 E4
17 Gamesley SK13 ....171 E2
Buxton Cres
Rochdale OL16 ....31 B4
Sale M33 ....108 D1
Buxton La
Droylsden M43 ....83 C1
Marple SK6 ....125 E5
Buxton Mews SK13 ....171 B2
Buxton Old Rd SK12 ...135 C4
Buxton Pl OL8 ....153 B1
Buxton Rd
High Lane SK6, SK7,
SK12 ....134 D8
Stockport SK2 ....124 B5
Stretford M32 ....96 A3
Buxton Rd W SK12 ....135 B5
Buxton St
Bury BL8 ....27 C2
Hadfield SK14 ....122 A5
Hazel Grove SK7 ......124 D3
Heywood OL10 ....29 D1
Manchester M1 ....163 B4
Whitworth OL12 .... 4 D3
Buxton Terr SK14 .....103 D5
Buxton Way 3 M34 ...113 A8
Buxton Wlk 9 SK13 ...171 B1
Bycroft Wlk M40 ....83 D2
Bye Rd BL0 ....11 E8
Bye St M11 ....99 C2
Byfield Rd M22 ....121 C4
Byfleet Cl WN3 ....54 C1
Byland Ave
Cheadle SK8 ....132 B6
Oldham OL4 ....67 D4
Byland Cl BL1 ....143 B2
Byland Gdns 3 M26 ...43 F3
Bylands Cl SK12 ......133 D4
Bylands Fold SK16 ....101 D6
Byland Wlk 3 M22 ....121 D1
Byley Rise WN6 ....36 E8
Byng Ave M44 ....105 D4
Byng St
Farnworth BL4 ....60 D8
Heywood OL10 ....46 E8
Byrchall High Sch The
WN4 ....73 B1
Byrcland Cl M12 ......164 B4
Byre Cl M23 ....109 A3
Byre View PR6 ....20 F8
Byrness Cl M46 ....58 E4
Byrom Ave M19 ....99 C1
Byrom Ct M43 ....83 F1
Byrom La M43 ....74 F2
Byrom Par M19 ....99 C1
Byrom Pl 1 M3 ....158 B1
Byrom St
Altrincham WA14 .....119 D8
8 Bury BL8 ....27 B4
Manchester M3 ....158 B1
Manchester M3 ....162 B4
Manchester, Old Trafford
M16 ....97 D4
Salford M5 ....161 A4
Byron Ave
Droylsden M43 ....84 A2
13 Hindley WN2 ......56 D5
Prestwich M25 ....62 F3
Radcliffe M26 ....43 E4
Swinton M27 ....79 E8
Byron Cl
Abram WN2 ....56 B1
3 Orrell WN5 ....53 F7
Wigan WN6 ....36 E3
Byron Cres PR7 ....19 F8
Byron Ct
Altrincham WA14 .....119 D6
4 Eccles M30 ....79 D2
Byron Dr SK8 ....122 F6
Byron Gr
Atherton M46 ....58 D5
Heywood OL10 ....117 F7
Reddish SK5 ....99 E1
Byron Ho 5 OL8 ....66 B2
Byron Rd
Denton M34 ....112 F8
Middleton M24 ....47 B2
Ramsbottom BL8 ......10 F2
Stretford M32 ....96 F3
Byron's Dr 2 WA15 ...120 A6
Byron St
Eccles M30 ....79 D2

Byron St *continued*
Leigh WN7 ....75 F7
Oldham OL8 ....66 B2
Royton OL2 ....48 E4
Byron Street Inf Sch
OL2 ....48 E4
Byron Wlk
Farnworth BL4 ....60 B6
6 Royton OL2 ....48 E4
Byrth Rd OL8 ....84 F8
Bywell Wlk 15 M8 ....155 C3

C

Cabin La OL4 ....50 A3
Cable St
Bolton BL1 ....145 C4
Manchester M4 ....159 B2
Cablestead Wlk M11 ...165 A4
Cabot Pl SK5 ....169 C4
Cabot St M13 ....163 C1
Caddington Rd M21 ...109 C8
CADISHEAD 105 E5
Cadishead Prim Sch
M44 ....105 E6
Cadishead Way M41,
M44 ....94 C2
Cadleigh Wlk 6 M40 ...83 A7
Cadman Gr WN2 ....56 D4
Cadmium Wlk M18 .....99 C4
Cadnam Dr M22 ....121 F3
Cadogan Dr WN3 ....54 D2
Cadogan Pl 7 M7 ......63 E1
Cadogan St M14 ....98 A4
Cadum Wlk M13 ....163 C2
Caen Ave M40 ....65 C3
Caernarvon Cl BL8 .....10 F1
Caernarvon Dr SK7 ....124 C1
Caernarvon Rd WN2 ....57 A3
Caernarvon Way 2
M34 ....100 F1
Caesar St OL11 ....31 A2
Cairn Dr
Rochdale OL11 ....29 E6
Salford M6 ....81 C5
Cairngorm Dr BL3 ......40 E5
Cairns Pl OL6 ....85 D5
Cairnwell Rd OL9 ......65 F8
Cairn Wlk 15 M11 ....160 C1
Caister Ave M45 ....63 A7
Caister Cl M41 ....94 C1
Caistor Cl M16 ....109 E8
Caistor St SK4 ....112 B3
Caistor Wlk 2 OL1 ....153 C3
Caithness Cl M23 .....121 A4
Caithness Dr BL3 ......40 E6
Caithness Rd OL11 .....29 E5
Cakebread St M12 .....163 C3
Calamanco Way M44 ...106 A8
Calbourne Cres M12 ....99 B3
Calcot Wlk 6 M23 ....120 F6
Calcutta Rd SK3 ....123 C7
Caldbeck Ave
Bolton BL1 ....23 F1
Sale M33 ....108 A5
Caldbeck Cl WN4 ....73 B4
Caldbeck Dr
Farnworth BL4 ....59 E7
Middleton M24 ....46 E2
Caldecott Rd M9 ....64 A5
Calder Ave
Hindley WN2 ....57 C3
Irlam M44 ....93 F1
Littleborough OL15 .....16 A7
Wythenshawe M22 ....121 D8
CALDER BANK 94 F4
Calderbank Ave M41 ...94 E4
Calderbank St WN5 ....54 E5
Calderbank Way M22 ..121 E6
CALDERBROOK 6 C1
Calderbrook Ct SK8 ...123 B4
Calderbrook Rd OL15 ...6 C1
Calderbrook Terr OL15 ..16 C8
Calderbrook Way OL4 ..67 A8
Calderbrook Wlk 11
M9 ....157 A3
Caldercourt Cl BL6 .....39 D8
Calder Cl
Bury BL9 ....28 A8
Poynton SK12 ....133 D2
Reddish SK5 ....112 A4
Caldercourt 94 E4
Calder Cres M45 ....45 B2
Calderdale Ct OL2 ......48 C5
Calder Dr
Kearsley BL4 ....61 B5
Platt Bridge WN2 ......56 A1
Swinton M27 ....61 E1
Walkden M28 ....60 B2
Calder Gdns OL15 .....16 A6
Calder Gr OL2 ....149 B4
Calder Ho 8 M7 ....65 B1
CALDERMOOR 16 B6
Calder Pl WN5 ....54 C7
Calder Rd BL3 ....147 B3
CALDERSHAW 14 C2
Caldershaw Bsns Ctr
OL12 ....14 B2
Caldershaw Ctr The
OL12 ....14 B2
Caldershaw Prim Sch
OL12 ....14 A1
Caldershaw Rd OL11,
OL12 ....14 A1

Calder St OL16 ....15 B2
Caldervale Ave M21 ...109 C4
Calder Way M45 ....45 B2
Calder Wlk
Middleton M24 ....46 C2
Whitefield M45 ....45 B2
Calderwood Cl BL8 .....27 A6
Caldew Cl WN2 ....56 E4
Caldey Rd M23 ....120 C5
Caldford Cl WN2 ....58 A4
Caldon Cl WN3 ....95 D8
Caldwell Ave M29 ......77 B4
Caldwell Cl M29 ....77 B5
Caldwell St
Reddish SK5 ....99 F1
Westhoughton BL5 ......57 F5
Caldy Dr BL0 ....11 A3
Caldy Rd
Handforth SK9 ....131 D3
Salford M6 ....154 A4
Caleb Cl M29 ....58 F1
Caledon Ave M40 ......83 A8
Caledonian Dr M30 .....95 E8
Caledonia St
Bolton BL3 ....144 C1
3 Radcliffe M26 ....44 C4
Caledonia Way M32 ....96 A5
Cale Gn OL2 ....170 C2
CALE GREEN 170 C2
Cale Green Ct SK2 ....170 C3
Cale Green Prim Sch
SK3 ....170 C2
Cale La WN2 ....38 B2
Cale St SK2 ....170 C2
Caley St
Bolton BL1 ....23 F2
1 Manchester M1 ....163 A3
Calf Hey OL15 ....15 F6
Calf Hey Cl M26 ....43 D3
Calf Hey N 7 OL11 ....31 A4
Calf Hey Rd OL2 ....49 D8
Calf Hey S 8 OL11 ....31 A4
Calf La OL3, OL5 ....68 E4
Calgarth Dr M24 ....46 D3
Calgary St M18 ....165 C1
Calico Cl M3 ....158 A3
Calico Cres
Hollingworth SK15 ......87 A6
Mossley SK15 ....86 F6
Calico Wood Ave WN6 ..35 F6
Callaghan Wlk OL10 ...29 C1
Calland Ave SK14 .....167 C3
Callander Sq WN5 .....54 E8
Callander Sq OL10 .....28 F1
Callender St BL0 ......138 B2
Callingdon Rd M21 ...109 C6
Callington Cl 4 SK14 ..102 E2
Callington Dr SK14 ...102 E2
Callington Wlk 3
SK14 ....102 E2
Callis Rd BL3 ....144 C1
Callum Wlk M13 ......163 C2
Calluna Mews M20 ....110 A4
Calne Wlk 6 M23 .....121 A5
Calow Cl WN7 ....76 C3
Calow 29 SK13 ....171 E2
Calow Gn 30 SK13 ...171 B2
Caltha St BL0 ....138 B2
Calthorpe Ave M9 .....156 C3
Calton Ave M7 ....81 A7
Calve Croft Rd M22 ...121 F2
Calvedon Rd M40 ....83 C7
Calver Ave BL3 ....147 C3
Calver Pl 32 SK13 ....171 A2
Calverleigh Cl BL3 ....146 A2
Calverley Ave M19 ....110 F7
Calverley Cl 3 SK9 ...137 C8
Calverley Way OL12 ....14 E4
Calverly Rd SK8 ......123 A5
Calver Mews SK13 ....171 B2
Calverton Dr M40 ......83 C7
Calvert Rd BL3 ....147 C3
Calvert St M5 ....154 A2
Calver Wlk
Cheadle SK8 ....122 E1
Denton M34 ....113 A8
3 Calvin St BL1 ......143 C1
Camargue Cl M12 .....110 B6
Cambeck Cl M45 ....45 B1
Cambeck Wlk M45 .....45 A1
Cambell Rd M30 ....79 B2
Camberley Cl
Bramhall SK7 ....133 A7
Bury BL8 ....27 A5
Camberley Dr OL11 ....29 F5
Cambert La
Manchester, Belle Vue
M18 ....165 C1
Manchester M18 ......165 C1
2 Manchester M18 ...165 C1
Camberwell Cres WN2 ..37 F1
Camberwell Dr OL6 .....85 A3
Camberwell Park Com
Specl Sch M9 ....64 C4
Camberwell St
Manchester M3, M8 ...159 A4
2 Oldham OL8 ....66 C2
Camberwell Way OL2 ...48 C4
Camborne Rd SK14 ...102 E3
Camborne St M14 ......98 B3

Bur–Cam `191`

Camborne Wlk 1 OL9 ..48 A1
Cambourne Dr
Bolton BL3 ....144 A1
Hindley WN2 ....57 C2
Cambo Wlk SK4 ....110 F3
Cambrai Cres M30 ......79 A4
Cambrian Cres WN3 ....54 C2
Cambrian Dr
Milnrow OL16 ....32 A6
Royton OL2 ....48 D7
Cambrian Rd SK3 .....123 C8
Cambrian St M11,
M40 ....160 B2
Cambria Sq BL3 ....144 C1
Cambria St
Bolton BL3 ....144 C1
Oldham OL1 ....67 D7
Cambridge Ave
Manchester M16 ....97 C2
Rochdale OL11 ....30 A6
Wilmslow SK9 ....136 F7
Cambridge Cl
Sale M33 ....147 C1
10 Sale M33 ....107 D3
Cambridge Dr
Little Lever BL3 ....43 B4
Reddish M34 ....100 A3
Romiley SK6 ....113 C5
Cambridge Gr
Eccles M30 ....79 F2
Whitefield M45 ....63 A7
Cambridge Ho 4 M1 ...1 B1
Cambridge Ind Area
M7 ....158 B4
Cambridge Mill 4
M1 ....162 C3
Cambridge Rd
Altrincham WA15 .....119 E2
Droylsden M43 ....83 F3
Failsworth M35 ....83 F5
Gatley SK8 ....122 B5
Horwich BL6 ....39 F8
Manchester M9 ....64 D1
Orrell WN5 ....53 F8
Reddish SK4 ....111 C5
Urmston M41 ....95 B1
Cambridge St
Ashton-u-L OL7 ....84 F1
Atherton M46 ....58 C2
Dukinfield SK16 ......166 C1
Manchester M1, M15 ..162 C3
Oldham OL9 ....66 C4
Salford M7 ....158 B4
Stalybridge SK15 ......86 A2
Stockport SK2 ....124 A6
Wigan WN1 ....151 A3
Cambridge Terr
Stalybridge SK15 ......86 A2
Stockport SK2 ....124 A6
Cambridge Way WN1 ..151 A4
Camdale Wlk 9 M8 ...155 C2
Camden Ave M40 ......83 C4
Camden Cl BL2 ....26 C1
Camden St OL5 ....68 D3
Camelia Rd M9 ....156 C3
Camelia Cl BL1 ....144 B8
Cameron Ct OL2 ....48 D6
Cameron Pl WN5 ....54 B3
Cameron St
Bolton BL1 ....143 A4
Bolton, Sharples BL1 ...24 C5
Bury BL8 ....27 C2
Leigh WN7 ....75 D7
Manchester M1 15 ...162 A2
Caminada Ho 11 M15 ..162 A2
Camley Wlk M8 ....156 B2
Camm St WN2 ....74 B8
Camms View BB4 .... 1 A8
Camomile Wlk 5
M31 ....105 F3
Campania St OL2 ....48 E2
Campbell Cl BL8 ....26 F4
Campbell Ct BL4 ....42 C2
Campbell Rd
Bolton BL3 ....146 A2
Manchester M13 ....98 F2
Sale M33 ....107 F3
Swinton M27 ....79 E6
Campbell St
Farnworth BL4 ....42 B1
Reddish SK5 ....99 F1
Rochdale OL11 ....14 E2
Wigan WN5 ....54 D5
Campbell Way 2 M28 ..60 D3
Campbell Wlk 5 BL4 ...42 C2
Campden Way SK9 ....131 D4
Campfield Ave Arc
M3 ....162 B4
Campion Dr BB4 .... 1 A8
Campion Gr WN4 ....72 F4
Campion Way
1 Denton M34 ....113 A8
Rochdale OL12 ....14 C3
Campion Wlk M11 ....164 C1
Camponia Gdns M7 ...155 A1
Camp St M46 ....44 A4 ...72 E4
Camp St
Ashton-u-L OL6 ......166 B3
Bury BL8 ....27 C3
Manchester M3 ....162 B4
Salford M7 ....155 A1
Camrose Gdns BL1 ....143 B1
Camrose Wlk M13 ....164 A1
Cams Acre Cl M26 .....43 E3
Cams La M26 ....43 E2

Cams Lane Prim Sch
  M26 . . . . .43 F3
Canaan WA3 . . . . .91 C8
Canada St
  Bolton BL3 . . . . 142 C2
  Horwich BL6 . . . . .22 B3
  Manchester M40 . . . . 160 B4
  Stockport SK2 . . . . 124 A6
Canal Bank
  Appley Bridge WN6 . . . . . .35 C7
  Eccles M30 . . . . .79 C3
Canal Circ M50 . . . . .80 A1
Canal Cotts WN3 . . . . . . .150 B3
Canal Rd WA14 . . . . .119 E8
Canal Row WN2 . . . . .20 D1
Canal Side M30 . . . . .79 C3
Canalside Ind Est OL16 . . .31 B5
Canalside Wlk OL7 . . . . . .166 B3
Canal St
  Adlington PR7 . . . . .21 A6
  Droylsden M43 . . . . .84 A1
  Dukinfield SK14 . . . . 101 C3
  Heywood OL10 . . . . .46 F8
  Ince-in-M WN2 . . . . .151 C2
  Leigh WN7 . . . . .75 F4
  Littleborough OL15 . . . . . . .16 B5
  Manchester M1 . . . . 163 E8
  Marple SK6 . . . . .126 A6
  Oldham OL9 . . . . .66 B3
  Rochdale OL11 . . . . .31 A5
  Salford M5 . . . . .81 C1
  Stalybridge SK15 . . . . .86 A1
  Stockport SK1 . . . . .170 C4
  Wigan WN6 . . . . .36 F2
Canal Terr WN1 . . . . .151 B3
Canary Way M27 . . . . .80 E7
Canberra Rd
  Bramhall SK7 . . . . 132 F5
  Wigan WN5 . . . . .36 C1
Canberra St M11 . . . . .83 C2
Canberra Way OL11 . . . . . .31 A3
Candahar St BL3 . . . . .42 A3
Candleford Ct 2 M20 . . . .110 B6
Candleford Pl SK2 . . . . . . 124 E4
Candleford Rd M20 . . . . . .110 B6
Candlestick Pk BL9 . . . . . .28 D4
Canisp Cl OL9 . . . . .48 A1
Canley Cl SK1 . . . . 170 C4
Cannore Cl BL3 . . . . 146 A3
Cannel Fold M28 . . . . .78 B7
Canning Cl WN2 . . . . .56 C4
Canning Dr BL1 . . . . .143 B2
Canning St
  Bolton BL3 . . . . .143 C2
  Bury BL9 . . . . .140 C4
  Stockport SK4 . . . . .169 B2
Cannock Dr SK4 . . . . .168 A2
Cannon Cl M4 . . . . .158 C2
Cannon Gr BL3 . . . . .145 A1
Cannon St N BL3 . . . . 145 A2
Cannon St
  Atherton M46 . . . . .58 D3
  Bolton BL3 . . . . .145 A1
  Eccles M30 . . . . .79 E1
  Hollingworth SK14 . . . . . . 103 C5
  Oldham OL9 . . . . 153 B3
  Radcliffe M26 . . . . .43 F5
  Ramsbottom BL0 . . . . 11 A4
  Salford M3 . . . . .158 A3
Cannon Wlk M34 . . . . 100 E2
Cann St BL8 . . . . .26 D8
Canon Burrows CE Prim
  Sch OL7 . . . . .85 A5
Canon Cl WN6 . . . . .19 F2
Canon Dr WA14 . . . . .119 E8
Canon Flynn Ct OL16 . . . .31 C7
Canon Green Ct M3 . . . . .158 B2
Canon Green Dr M3 . . . . .158 B2
Canon Hussey Ct M3 . . . .158 A1
Canon Johnson CE Prim
  Sch OL7 . . . . .166 B4
Canon's Cl BL1 . . . . .142 B2
Canons Gr M40 . . . . .157 B1
Canon Sharples CE Prim
  Sch WN1 . . . . .37 E2
Canon Slade CE Sch
  BL2 . . . . .25 C4
Canonsleigh Cl M8 . . . . . .155 E1
Canon St
  Bury BL9 . . . . .141 A4
  Rochdale OL16 . . . . .15 B2
Canonsway M27 . . . . .79 E8
Canon Tighe Ct OL6 . . . . .152 A3
Cansfield Ct BL4 . . . . .61 A6
Cansfield Gr WN4 . . . . .73 A4
Cansfield High Specialist
  Language Coll WA4 . . . . . . .73 A4
Canterbury Ave WA3 . . . . .74 D1
Canterbury Cl
  Atherton M46 . . . . .58 E4
  Dukinfield SK16 . . . . 101 D6
  Rochdale OL11 . . . . .30 A7
Canterbury Cres M24 . . . . .47 D2
Canterbury Dr
  Bury BL8 . . . . .140 A4
  Manchester M25 . . . . .63 C2
Canterbury Gdns M5 . . . . .80 A2
Canterbury Gr BL3 . . . . . .147 A3
Canterbury Pk M20 . . . . . .109 F3
Canterbury Rd
  Altrincham WA15 . . . . 120 C3
  Stockport SK1 . . . . .112 B1
  Urmston M41 . . . . .95 D3
Canterbury St OL6 . . . . . .166 C4
Canterfield Cl M43 . . . . . . .84 D2

Cantley Wlk 4 M8 . . . . . .156 A2
Cantrell St M11 . . . . .83 B2
Canute Ct 3 M32 . . . . .96 E3
Canute Rd M32 . . . . .96 E3
Canute St
  Bolton BL2 . . . . .25 C1
  Radcliffe M26 . . . . .43 E3
Cape Gdns OL2 . . . . .149 B2
Capella Wlk M7 . . . . .81 C4
Capenhurst Cl
  Poynton SK12 . . . . .133 F4
  Wythenshawe M23 . . . . . . 120 F4
Cape St M20 . . . . .110 C7
Capesthorne Cl SK7 . . . . .133 F8
Capesthorne Dr OL2 . . . . . .48 F7
Capesthorne Rd
  Altrincham WA15 . . . . 120 D6
  Dukinfield SK16 . . . . 101 D6
  Hazel Grove SK7 . . . . .133 F8
  High Lane SK6 . . . . .134 E7
  Wilmslow SK9 . . . . .136 E5
Capesthorne Wlk
  M34 . . . . 100 E2
Capital Quay M50 . . . . . . .161 A3
Capital Rd M11 . . . . .99 F7
Capitol Cl BL1 . . . . .142 A3
Cappadocia Way BL5 . . . . .57 D7
Capri St WN2 . . . . .56 B3
Capricorn Rd M9 . . . . .65 B3
Capricorn Way M6 . . . . . . .81 C4
Capstan St M9 . . . . .157 B4
Capstone Dr SK6 . . . . .125 E6
Captain Clarke Rd
  SK14 . . . . 101 C5
CAPTAIN FOLD 29 E2
Captain Fold OL10 . . . . . . .29 E2
Captain Fold Rd M38 . . . . .59 F6
Captain Lees Gdns
  BL5 . . . . .58 A8
Captain Lees Rd BL5 . . . . .40 A1
Captain's Clough Rd
  BL1 . . . . .142 B2
Captain's La WN4 . . . . .73 C3
Captain St SK16 . . . . .22 B4
Captain Wlk M5 . . . . .161 B4
Capton Cl SK7 . . . . .124 A2
Caradoc Ave 12 M8 . . . . .156 B2
Carawood Cl M46 . . . . .35 D7
Car Bank Ave M46 . . . . . . .58 D4
Car Bank Cres M46 . . . . . .58 D4
Car Bank Sq M46 . . . . .58 D4
Car Bank St M46 . . . . .58 D4
Carberry Ct SK8 . . . . .123 A2
Carberry Rd M18 . . . . .99 D5
Cardale Wlk M9 . . . . .157 A3
Carden Ave
  Swinton M27 . . . . .79 D7
  Urmston M41 . . . . .95 A3
Cardenbrook Gr 4
  SK9 . . . . .131 D2
Carder Ct M27 . . . . .79 F7
Carders Cl WN7 . . . . .75 E4
Cardew Ave M22 . . . . .121 F4
Cardiff Cl 8 OL8 . . . . .66 B2
Cardiff St M7 . . . . .155 B3
Cardiff Wlk 4 M34 . . . . . .100 F1
Cardigan Dr BL9 . . . . .44 E7
Cardigan Rd OL8 . . . . .66 B2
Cardigan St
  Radcliffe M26 . . . . .43 F6
  Rochdale OL12 . . . . .14 E3
  Royton OL2 . . . . .48 E4
  3 Salford M6 . . . . .154 B1
Cardinal Terr M14 . . . . . . .97 F4
Cardinal Langley RC High
  Sch M24 . . . . .47 B4
Cardinal Mews M24 . . . . . .46 D2
Cardinal St
  Manchester M8 . . . . .156 B3
  10 Oldham OL1 . . . . .67 A7
Carding Gr M3 . . . . .158 B3
Cardroom Cl M4 . . . . .159 C2
Cardroom Rd M4 . . . . .159 C2
Cardus St M19 . . . . .99 A1
Cardwell Gdns BL1 . . . . . .143 B2
Cardwell Rd M30 . . . . .79 A1
Cardwell St OL8 . . . . .66 F3
Careless La WN2 . . . . .151 C3
Caremine Ave M19 . . . . . . .99 B2
Carey Cl
  Salford M7 . . . . .158 A4
  Wigan WN3 . . . . .54 D2
Carey Wlk 11 M15 . . . . . .162 C1
Carfax Fold OL12 . . . . .14 B2
Carfax St M18 . . . . .99 D5
Cargate Wlk 8 M8 . . . . . .155 F7
Carib St M15 . . . . .162 C1
Carill Ave M40 . . . . .65 A1
Carill Dr M14 . . . . .110 D8
Carina Pl M7 . . . . .81 C4
Cariocca Bsns Pk
  Manchester, Ardwick
  M12 . . . . .164 A2
  Manchester, Miles Platting
  M40 . . . . .160 A3
Carisbrook Ave
  Prestwich M25, M45 . . . . . .63 A6
  Urmston M41 . . . . .95 C2
Carisbrook Dr M27 . . . . . . .80 A6
Carisbrooke Ave SK4 . . . .124 D1
Carisbrooke Dr BL1 . . . . . .143 C3
Carisbrooke Rd WN7 . . . . .76 D6
Carisbrook St M9 . . . . . . .157 A3
Carlburn St M11 . . . . .83 D2
Carleton Rd SK12 . . . . . . .134 C4
Carley Gr M9 . . . . .64 B4
Carlford Gr M25 . . . . .62 F3
Carlile St SK3 . . . . .170 B4

Carlin Gate WA15 . . . . . . .120 A6
Carling Dr M22 . . . . .121 E2
Carlingford Cl SK3 . . . . . .170 B1
Carlisle Cl
  Little Lever BL3 . . . . .43 A2
  Prestwich M45 . . . . .63 B7
  Romiley SK6 . . . . .113 A1
Carlisle Cres OL6 . . . . .85 C7
Carlisle Ave
  Altrincham WA14 . . . . .119 E8
  Irlam M44 . . . . .94 A2
Carlisle Pl 3 PR6 . . . . . . .21 A8
Carlisle St
  11 Alderley Edge SK9 . . . .137 A1
  Bolton BL7 . . . . .25 A8
  Hindley WN2 . . . . .56 E6
  Oldham OL9 . . . . .66 C4
  Oldham OL9 . . . . 152 C1
  Rochdale OL12 . . . . .14 E3
  Swinton M27 . . . . .61 F2
  Wigan WN5 . . . . .54 D6
Carlisle Way
  Aspull WN2 . . . . .38 D5
  3 Denton M34 . . . . .100 F1
Carloon Rd M23 . . . . .109 B1
Carlow Dr M22 . . . . .121 E2
Carl St BL1 . . . . .143 A2
Carlton Ave
  Bolton BL3 . . . . .146 A4
  Bramhall SK7 . . . . 132 D5
  Cheadle SK8 . . . . 122 F3
  Handforth SK9 . . . . .131 C2
  Manchester M14 . . . . .98 B3
  Manchester, Old Trafford
  M16 . . . . .97 B4
  Oldham OL4 . . . . .49 D1
  Prestwich M45 . . . . .63 E2
  Romiley SK6 . . . . .113 D2
  Up Holland WN8 . . . . .53 A7
  Whitefield M45 . . . . .44 D1
Carlton Cl
  Ashton-in-M WN4 . . . . .73 A5
  Blackrod BL6 . . . . .21 D2
  Bolton BL2 . . . . .25 E3
  Walkden M28 . . . . .60 C1
Carlton Cres
  Stockport SK1 . . . . .112 A2
  Urmston M41 . . . . .95 D1
Carlton Ct
  Altrincham WA15 . . . . 120 B1
  Manchester M25 . . . . .63 A1
Carlton Dr
  Gatley SK8 . . . . .122 A6
  Manchester M25 . . . . .63 E2
Carlton Gdns BL4 . . . . .42 D1
Carlton Gr
  Hindley WN2 . . . . .56 F4
  6 Horwich BL6 . . . . .22 D1
Carlton Grange M16 . . . . . .97 E2
Carlton Mans 4 M16 . . . . .97 D3
Carlton Pl
  Farnworth BL4 . . . . .42 D1
  Hazel Grove SK7 . . . . .125 A1
Carlton Range M18 . . . . . . .99 F4
Carlton Rd
  Altrincham WA15 . . . . 120 B2
  Ashton-u-L OL6 . . . . .85 C5
  Bolton BL3 . . . . .144 A4
  Golborne WA3 . . . . .74 D1
  Hyde SK14 . . . . .102 A3
  Lymm WA13 . . . . .117 B5
  Manchester, Whalley Range
  M16 . . . . .97 D3
  Sale M33 . . . . .108 A6
  Salford M6 . . . . .154 B4
  Stockport, Heaton Moor
  SK4 . . . . .168 A2
  Urmston M41 . . . . .95 D1
  Walkden M28 . . . . .60 C1
Carlton St
  Bolton BL2 . . . . .148 A2
  Bury BL9 . . . . .44 F8
  Eccles M30 . . . . .79 D3
  Farnworth BL4 . . . . .42 D1
  Manchester M16 . . . . .97 C4
  Wigan WN3 . . . . .150 B2
Carlton Way
  Irlam M44 . . . . 105 C5
  Royton OL1, OL2 . . . . .48 D2
Carlyle Cl M8 . . . . .156 A2
Carlyle Gr WN7 . . . . .75 C8
Carlyle St BL9 . . . . .140 B2
Carlyn Ave M33 . . . . .108 D4
Carmel Ave M5 . . . . .161 C4
Carmel Cl M5 . . . . .161 C4
Carmel Ct M9 . . . . .64 E1
Carmenna Dr SK7 . . . . . . .132 F7
Carmichael Cl 6
  M31 . . . . 105 E3
Carmichael St SK3 . . . . . .170 A4
Carmine Fold M24 . . . . . . .46 F2
Carmona Dr M25 . . . . .63 A4
Carmona Gdns M7 . . . . . . .63 C1
Carmoor Rd M13 . . . . .163 C1
Carna Rd SK5 . . . . .99 C2
Carnarvon St
  Manchester M3 . . . . .158 C3
  Oldham OL8 . . . . .66 B2
  Salford M7 . . . . .158 A4
  3 Stockport SK1 . . . . .112 A1
Carnation Rd
  Farnworth BL4 . . . . .42 A1
  Oldham OL4 . . . . .67 E4
Carnegie Ave M19 . . . . . . .99 B1
Carnegie Cl 1 M33 . . . . .107 D3
Carnegie Dr WN4 . . . . .73 A3

Carnforth Ave
  Chadderton OL9 . . . . .152 A2
  Hindley WN2 . . . . .57 A5
  Trub OL11 . . . . .47 D7
Carnforth Dr
  Ramsbottom BL0, BL8 . . . . . 11 A2
  Sale M33 . . . . .108 A3
Carnforth Rd
  Cheadle SK8 . . . . 123 C4
  Reddish SK4 . . . . .111 D7
Carnforth Sq OL11 . . . . . . .47 D7
Carnforth St M14 . . . . .98 B3
Carnoustie BL3 . . . . .146 A3
Carnoustie Cl
  Failsworth M40 . . . . .83 C7
  Wilmslow SK9 . . . . .137 D8
Carnoustie Dr
  Gatley SK8 . . . . .122 C1
  Ramsbottom BL0 . . . . 138 B1
Carnwood Cl M40 . . . . .83 D4
Carolina Way M50 . . . . . . .154 E1
Caroline St
  Ashton-u-L OL6 . . . . .166 C3
  Bolton BL3 . . . . .147 A4
  Irlam M44 . . . . 105 F8
  Salford M7 . . . . .158 B4
  Stalybridge SK15 . . . . .86 A1
  Stockport SK3 . . . . .170 A3
Carpenters Ct SK9 . . . . . .137 A1
Carpenters La M4 . . . . . . .159 A2
Carpenters Way OL16 . . . .31 B4
Carpenter's Wlk M43 . . . . .83 F1
CARR 127 F5
Carradale Dr M33 . . . . . . .107 C5
Carradale Wlk 5 M40 . . . .83 A6
Carradon Dr WN6 . . . . .19 E1
Carr Ave M25 . . . . .62 F2
CARR BANK 27 F8
Carr Bank SK13 . . . . .116 E8
Carr Bank Ave
  Manchester M9 . . . . .63 F3
  Ramsbottom BL0 . . . . .138 B3
Carr Bank Dr BL0 . . . . . . .138 B3
Carr Bank Rd BL0 . . . . . . .138 B3
CARRBROOK 86 F6
Carrbrook Cl SK15 . . . . . . .86 E6
Carrbrook Cres SK15 . . . . .86 F6
Carrbrook Dr OL1 . . . . .48 E1
Carr Brook Dr M46 . . . . . . .58 E4
Carrbrook Rd SK15 . . . . . . .86 F6
Carrbrook Terr 6 M26 . . . .44 C7
Carr Brow SK6 . . . . .135 A7
Carr Cl SK1 . . . . .124 B8
Carr Common Rd WN2 . . . .57 D3
Carr Dr BL4 . . . . .147 C1
Carrfield Ave
  Altrincham WA15 . . . . 120 D6
  Stockport SK3 . . . . .124 A4
  Walkden M38 . . . . .59 E4
Carrfield Cl M38 . . . . .59 E4
Carrfield Gr M38 . . . . .59 E4
Carr Fold BL0 . . . . .138 B3
Carr Gr OL16 . . . . .32 A6
Carrgate Rd M34 . . . . .101 B1
Carrgreen Cl M19 . . . . . . .110 F5
Carrgreen La WA13 . . . . . .117 A3
Carrhill Quarry Cl OL5 . . . .68 C2
Carrhill Rd OL5 . . . . .68 C2
Carrhouse La SK14 . . . . . .103 C4
Carr House La WN6 . . . . . . .18 F8
Carr House Rd OL4 . . . . . . .67 E6
Carriage Dr
  Littleborough OL15 . . . . . . .16 B7
  Manchester M40 . . . . .157 A1
Carriage Dr The SK13 . . . .103 F5
Carriage St M16 . . . . .162 A1
Carriages The WA14 . . . . .119 C2
Carrick CI WN1 . . . . .37 C2
Carrick Gdns
  Middleton M24 . . . . .46 F4
  Wythenshawe M22 . . . . . . 121 D4
Carrie St BL1 . . . . .144 B4
Carrigart M25 . . . . .63 B3
Carrill Gr M19 . . . . .99 A1
Carrill Gr E M19 . . . . .99 A1
CARRINGTON 106 C6
Carrington Bsns Pk
  M31 . . . . 106 C6
Carrington Cl OL16 . . . . . . .15 D3
Carrington Dr BL3 . . . . . . .145 C1
Carrington Field St
  SK1 . . . . .124 A7
Carrington La
  Carrington M31, M33 . . . . .107 E1
  Sale M33 . . . . .107 E5
Carrington Rd
  Adlington PR7 . . . . .20 F7
  Flixton M41 . . . . .106 E8
  Manchester M14 . . . . .98 C1
  Stockport SK1 . . . . .112 B3
Carrington St
  Leigh WN7 . . . . .75 F7
  Oldham OL9 . . . . .66 B1
  Swinton M27 . . . . .62 B1
Carrington Terr OL7 . . . . . .62 A1
Carr La
  Alderley Edge SK9 . . . . . . .136 D2
  Diggle OL3 . . . . .51 C5
  Golborne WA3 . . . . .91 A7
  Leigh WN7 . . . . .91 E8
  Milnrow OL16 . . . . .32 C6
  Mossley SK15 . . . . .86 F7
  Rawtenstall BB4 . . . . .2 F7

Carr La continued
  Uppermill OL3 . . . . .69 B7
  Wigan WN3 . . . . .55 B3
Carr Lea OL4 . . . . .68 C6
Carmel Ct OL3 . . . . .50 F3
Carr Mill Cres WN5 . . . . . .71 E4
Carr Mill Mews SK9 . . . . .131 B1
Carr Mill Prim Sch
  WA11 . . . . .71 C1
Carr Mill Rd WA11,
  WN5 . . . . .71 D3
Carrock Wlk M24 . . . . .46 B1
Carron Ave M9 . . . . .64 F1
Carron Gr BL2 . . . . .42 F7
Carr Rd
  Altrincham WA15 . . . . 120 B2
  Horwich BL6 . . . . .22 B5
  Irlam M44 . . . . .94 B2
Carr Rise SK15 . . . . .86 F7
Carr Sk WN5, SK8 . . . . . . .123 A6
Carrs Ct SK9 . . . . .137 B7
Carrsdale Dr 8 M9 . . . . . .64 C2
Carrsfield Rd M22 . . . . . . .121 E6
Carrslea Cl M26 . . . . .43 E5
Carr St
  Ashton-u-L OL6 . . . . .85 D5
  Hindley WN2 . . . . .56 D6
  Leigh WN7 . . . . .75 C5
  Ramsbottom BL0 . . . . .138 B3
  Swinton M27 . . . . .79 D7
Carrsvale Ave M41 . . . . . . .95 B3
Carrswood Rd M23 . . . . . .120 D8
Carruthers Cl OL10 . . . . . .29 F3
Carruthers St M4 . . . . .160 A1
Carwood Ave 129 B7
Carr Wood Ave SK7 . . . . . .132 E8
Carrwood Hey BL0 . . . . 11 A4
Carrwood Rd SK9 . . . . . . .136 F8
Carr Wood Rd SK7 . . . . . .123 E1
Carsdale Rd M22 . . . . .130 E8
Carslake Ave BL1 . . . . . . .144 C4
Carslake Rd M40 . . . . .157 A1
Carson Rd M19 . . . . .111 A8
Car St WN2 . . . . .56 A2
Carstairs Ave SK2 . . . . . . .124 A3
Carstairs Cl M8 . . . . .155 C3
Carswell Cl M29 . . . . .59 C1
Carter Cl M34 . . . . .100 F2
Carter Pl SK14 . . . . .101 D5
Carter St
  Bolton BL3 . . . . .42 A4
  Dukinfield SK14 . . . . 101 D5
  Farnworth BL4 . . . . .60 E7
  Ince-in-M WN3 . . . . .151 B2
  Mossley SK15 . . . . .86 C8
  Salford, Lower Broughton
  M7 . . . . .155 A1
  Salford, Weaste M50 . . . . . .80 C1
  2 Stalybridge SK15 . . . . . .86 B2
Carthage St OL8 . . . . .66 F4
Carthorpe Arch M5 . . . . . .154 C1
Cartleach La WA3 . . . . .90 A3
Cartleach Ln M28 . . . . .60 A2
Cartmel OL12 . . . . .139 C4
Cartmel Ave
  Milnrow OL16 . . . . .31 F4
  Reddish SK4 . . . . .111 E6
  Wigan WN1 . . . . .37 B3
Cartmel Cl
  Bolton BL3 . . . . .40 D2
  Gatley SK8 . . . . .122 C3
  Hazel Grove SK7 . . . . .124 C3
  Oldham OL8 . . . . .66 D3
  Whitefield BL9 . . . . .45 A3
Cartmel Cres
  Bolton BL2 . . . . .25 C2
  Failsworth OL9 . . . . .65 F2
Cartmel Ct WN7 . . . . .65 A4
Cartmel Wlk M24 . . . . . . .120 D6
Cartmel Gr M28 . . . . .79 B7
Cartmel Wlk
  Manchester M9 . . . . .157 A3
  Middleton M24 . . . . .46 F2
Cartridge Cl M22 . . . . .121 F3
Cartridge St OL10 . . . . . . .29 C2
Cartwright Gr WN7 . . . . . . .57 D1
Cartwright Rd M21 . . . . . .108 F8
Cartwright St
  Denton M34 . . . . .100 F6
  Dukinfield SK14 . . . . 102 A5
Carver Ave M25 . . . . .63 C5
Carver Cl M16 . . . . .161 B1
Carver Dr SK6 . . . . .125 E5
Carver Rd
  Altrincham WA15 . . . . .119 E2
  Marple SK6 . . . . .125 E5
Carver St M16 . . . . .161 B1
Carver Wlk 10 M15 . . . . .162 C1
Carville Gr WN2 . . . . .57 B4
Carville Rd M9 . . . . .65 B3
Carwood Gr BL6 . . . . .22 D1
Cascade Dr M7 . . . . .155 B1
Cashel Ct M27 . . . . .61 C1
Cashgate Ct OL8 . . . . .66 D3
Cashmere Rd SK3 . . . . . . .123 C2
Cashmore Dr WN2 . . . . . . .56 D4
Cashmore Wlk M12 . . . . . .164 B2
Caspian Rd
  Altrincham WA14 . . . . .119 A6
  Manchester M9 . . . . .65 B3
Cassandra Ct M5 . . . . .161 C4
Cass Ave M5 . . . . .161 A4
Cassidy Cl M4 . . . . .159 B2
Cassidy Cl M50 . . . . .96 E8
Cassidy Gdns M24 . . . . . . .46 D2
Casson Gate OL12 . . . . . . .14 E1
Casson St M35 . . . . .83 F7

Casterton Way M28.......78 A5
Castle Ave
　Denton M34........100 E2
　Rochdale OL11........139 B2
Castlebrook Cl BL9 .....45 B4
Castlebrook High Sch
　BL9........45 C3
Castle Cl M43........84 B2
Castle Cres BL6........22 C5
Castle Croft BL2........25 E3
Castlecroft Ave BL6....21 D2
Castle Dr BL9 ......140 B2
Castlecroft Mews
　BL9........140 B2
Castlecroft Rd BL9...140 B3
Castle Ct
　Ashton-u-L OL6 ......85 B7
　Bolton BL2........148 A3
　Glossop SK13........104 A4
Castledene Ave M6 ....154 B3
Castle Dr PR7 ....20 E6
Castle Edge Rd SK22..127 B2
Castle Farm Dr SK2....124 B5
Castle Farm La SK2....124 C5
Castlefield Ave M7...155 B4
Castleford Cl 9 BL1...145 A4
Castleford St OL1........48 C1
Castleford Wlk M21...109 D7
Castle Gr
　Leigh WN7........76 D6
　Ramsbottom BL0 ......11 A2
CASTLE HALL........86 B1
Castle Hall Cl SK15 ....86 B3
Castle Hall Ct 11 SK15 ..86 A1
Castle Hall View 10
　SK15........86 A1
Castle Hey Cl BL9......45 C3
CASTLE HILL........25 B3
Castle Hill
　Glossop SK13........104 C2
　Newton-le-W WA12....89 C4
CASTLE HILL........112 C7
Castle Hill Cres OL11 ...139 B2
Castle Hill Dr 9 M9 ...64 C2
Castle Hill High Sch
　SK5........112 C6
Castle Hill Mobile Home
　Pk SK6........113 A6
Castle Hill Pk WN2 ....56 F7
Castle Hill Prim Sch
　BL2........25 B2
Castle Hill Rd
　Bury BL9........28 D5
　Hindley WN2........56 E6
　Manchester M25........63 D7
Castle Hill SH Philip's CE
　Prim Sch WN2........56 F6
Castle Hill St
　7 Bolton BL2........25 B3
　Bolton, Castle Hill BL2...25 B2
Castle House La PR7...20 E6
Castle Irwell Student
　Village M7........81 B5
Castle La OL5, SK15....86 F8
Castle L Ctr * BL9......140 B2
Castlemere Cl WN3.....54 D1
Castlemere Dr OL2........49 D8
Castlemere Rd M9........64 C3
Castlemere St OL11....139 B2
Castlemere Terr
　OL11........139 C2
Castle Mews BL4........60 D7
Castle Mill La WA15....129 B5
Castlemill St OL1........67 B7
Castlemoor Ave M7....81 B8
Castlemore Ret Pk
　M16........161 A1
Castle Pk Ind Est 12
　OL1........67 B7
Castlerea Cl 11 M30 ...95 D8
Castlerigg Cl SK4......111 D7
Castlerigg Dr
　Middleton M24........46 C2
　Royton OL2........48 C6
Castle Rise 4 WN2 ....56 E5
Castle Shaw Rd SK2...124 E5
Castleshaw Top Bank
　Delph OL3........51 B8
　Denshaw OL3........34 B1
Castle St
　Bolton BL2........148 A3
　Bury BL9........140 B2
　Eccles M30........79 F2
　Farnworth BL4........60 D7
　Glossop SK13........104 A4
　Hindley WN2........56 E6
　Manchester M3........162 B4
　Middleton M24........65 D7
　Ramsbottom BL0 ......11 D2
　Stalybridge SK15........86 A1
　Stockport SK3........170 B4
　Tyldesley M29........58 F1
Castle Terr SK15........86 F6
CASTLETON........30 C2
Castleton Bank 27
　SK13........171 B1
Castleton Ct
　15 Denton M34........113 A8
　13 Tyldesley M29........58 F1
Castleton Gn 28 SK13...171 B1
Castleton Dr
　Ashton-u-L OL6........85 F6
　28 Gamesley SK13 ....171 B1

Castleton Prim Sch
　OL11........30 D2
Castleton Rd
　Hazel Grove SK7 ....124 E1
　13 Manchester M7 ....63 E1
　Royton OL2, OL16 .....48 D8
　Salford M7........155 B4
　Stretford M32........96 B4
Castleton Rd S OL11...30 D3
Castleton St
　Altrincham WA14......119 C7
　Bolton BL2........25 B2
　Oldham OL9........152 C2
Castleton Sta OL11....30 C2
Castleton Terr 25
　SK13........171 B1
Castleton Way
　16 Denton M34........113 A8
　Wigan WN3........54 C2
Castleton Wlk 2
　M11........160 C1
Castleway
　Altrincham WA15......129 C7
　Hindley WN2........57 A5
　Rochdale OL11........30 B1
　Salford M6........154 B4
Castle Way M27........62 A3
Castle Wlk
　Ashton-u-L OL6........85 B7
　17 Stalybridge SK15....86 A1
Castlewood Gdns
　SK2........124 C5
Castlewood Rd M7......81 A8
Castlewood Sq BL2.....25 C1
Castle Yd SK1........169 C2
Catchdale Cl M9........64 C5
Catches Cl OL11........30 B8
Catches La OL11........14 B1
Cateaton St
　2 Bury BL9........140 C3
　Manchester M3........158 C2
Caterham Ave BL3....146 A4
Caterham St M4........160 A1
Catesby Rd M16........97 D3
Catfield Wlk M15......162 A3
Catford Rd M23........120 F5
Cathedral App M3......158 C2
Cathedral Cl SK16....101 D6
Cathedral Gates M4...158 C2
Cathedral Rd OL9.......48 A1
Cathedral Yd M3........158 C2
Catherine Ho SK4.....110 F2
Catherine Rd
　Altrincham WA14......119 C3
　Manchester M7, M8 ....63 C1
　Romiley SK6........112 F2
　Swinton M27........79 C7
Catherine St E BL6 ....22 B4
Catherine St W BL6....22 B5
Catherine St
　Bolton BL3........146 B2
　Bury BL9........44 E6
　Eccles M30........79 B3
　Hazel Grove SK7 ....124 E3
　Hyde SK14........167 A3
　Leigh WN7........75 F6
　Manchester M11........99 F7
　8 Oldham OL4........67 E6
　Wigan WN1........151 B4
Catherine Terr WN1...151 B4
Catherine Way M12....89 B2
Catherston Rd 8 M16..97 E3
Cathrine St E M34......100 D3
Cathrine St W M34....100 D3
Catlow La 10 M4........159 A2
Catlow St M7........158 B4
Caton Cl BL9........44 E8
Caton Dr M46........76 A8
Caton St OL16........139 C2
Cato St M8........11 A4
Catskowl Cl M18........99 D3
Catterall Cres BL2.....25 C6
Catterick Ave
　Manchester M20......110 C3
　Sale M33........107 C2
Catterick Dr BL3........43 A3
Catterick Rd M20......110 C3
Catterwood Dr SK6....114 B2
Cattlin Way OL8........66 C2
Caunce Ave
　Golborne WA3........90 A7
　Newton-le-W WA12....89 C1
Caunce Rd WN1........151 B4
Caunce St WN1........151 B4
Causeway Head BB4....1 A8
Causeway The
　8 Altrincham WA14....119 D4
　Oldham OL9........65 E5
Causewood Cl OL4.....49 E4
Causey Dr M24........46 B3
Cavalier St M40........160 A2
Cavanagh Cl M13......164 A2
Cavan Cl SK3........122 F7
Cavannah Ct OL1......49 E3
Cavell St M1........159 B1
Cavell Way M5........81 A1
Cavendish Ave
　Manchester M11......109 F6
　Swinton M27........62 C3
Cavendish Ct
　Manchester, Broughton Park
　　M7........63 D1
　Manchester, Heaton Mersey
　　SK4........110 F2
　Stretford M32........96 B4
Cavendish Dr WN3.....54 D2
Cavendish Gdns BL3...147 A3

Cavendish Gr M30......79 E3
Cavendish Ho OL7....166 B2
Cavendish Ind Est
　OL6........166 A3
Cavendish Mews SK9 ..137 A6
Cavendish Mill OL6....166 B2
Cavendish Pl
　Droylsden M11........83 A2
　Pendlebury M27........80 A8
Cavendish Rd
　Altrincham WA14......119 C3
　Eccles M30........79 E4
　Hazel Grove SK7 ....133 E8
　Manchester, Broughton Park
　　M7........63 D1
　Manchester, Heaton Mersey
　　SK4........110 F2
　Manchester, Withington
　　M20........109 F6
　Rochdale OL11........30 B1
　Stretford M32........96 B4
　Swinton M28........79 B6
　Urmston M41........95 C2
Cavendish St
　Ashton-u-L OL6 ......166 A2
　Leigh WN7........75 F7
　Manchester M15......163 A2
　8 Oldham OL8........153 B2
Cavendish Way OL2....48 F8
Cavenham Gr 7 BL1...144 C4
Cavenham Wlk M9.....156 F2
Caversham Dr M9.....157 B4
Cawdor Ave BL4........42 B2
Cawdor Ct BL4........42 B2
Cawdor Ho 8 M30......95 D8
Cawdor Pl WA15......120 C6
Cawdor Rd M14........98 C1
Cawdor St
　Eccles M30........79 C1
　Farnworth BL4........42 B2
　Hindley WN2........56 E5
　Leigh WN7........75 F4
　Manchester M15......162 A3
　Swinton M27........79 D8
　Walkden BL4........60 E2
　2 Wigan WN5........54 F6
Cawdor Wlk 6 BL4.....42 C2
Cawley Ave
　Culcheth WA3........91 E4
　Prestwich M25........62 F2
Cawley Terr M9........64 A5
Cawston Wlk 8 M8....156 A2
Caxton Cl WN3........54 F2
Caxton Rd M14........110 B8
Caxton St
　Heywood OL10........29 D2
　Rochdale OL11........30 C1
　Salford M3........158 B2
Caygill St M3........158 B2
Cayley St OL16........31 B7
Caythorpe St M14......98 A3
Cayton St M12........99 A3
'C' Ct WN4........73 B2
Ceal The SK6........114 B2
Cecil Ave
　Sale M33........107 F3
　Wigan WN5........37 A2
Cecil Ct 52 SK3......123 B8
Cecil Dr M41........94 E2
Cecil Gr M18........99 C5
Cecilia St BL3........42 A4
Cecil Rd
　Altrincham WA15......119 E2
　Eccles M30........79 E1
　Manchester M9........64 D5
　Stretford M32........96 B1
Cecil St
　8 Ashton-u-L OL7......84 F1
　Bolton BL2........148 B3
　Bury BL9........140 C1
　Dukinfield SK14......101 C8
　Ince-in-M WN3........55 E4
　Leigh WN7........76 A4
　Littleborough OL15....15 F5
　Manchester M15......163 B1
　Mossley OL5........86 C8
　Oldham OL8........153 B1
　Rochdale OL11........139 C1
　Royton OL2........48 C4
　Stalybridge SK15........86 B1
　Stockport SK3........170 B3
　Walkden BL4........60 E2
Cecil Walker Ho M31..106 A3
Cecil Wlk 7 OL7......166 A1
Cedar Ave
　Altrincham WA14......119 C4
　Ashton-u-L OL6........85 D5
　Atherton M46........58 B4
　Golborne WA3........90 F7
　Hazel Grove SK7 ....124 E2
　Heywood OL10........29 C3
　Hindley WN2........56 F3
　Horwich BL6........22 B4
　Little Lever BL3........43 B2
　Stalybridge SK15........86 A3
　Standish WN6........36 F8
　Whitefield M45........62 F6
Cedar Bank Cl OL16....31 D7
Cedar Cres
　Chadderton OL9......152 B4

Cedar Cres *continued*
　Newton-le-W WA12....89 D2
　Ramsbottom BL0 ....138 C3
Cedar Ct
　2 Altrincham WA15...120 B5
　Culcheth WA3........91 F1
　Manchester M14........98 C1
Cedar Dr
　Swinton M27........61 D4
　Urmston M41........95 C1
　Wigan WN1........37 D2
Cedarfield Rd WA13...117 B4
Cedar Gr
　Denton M34........100 C3
　Downall Green WN4 ...72 D5
　Farnworth BL4........60 B8
　Manchester, Heaton Chapel
　　SK4........111 C5
　Manchester M14......110 D8
　Orrell WN5........53 F6
　Prestwich M25........63 A6
　Royton OL2........48 D6
　Shaw OL2........149 B2
　Stalybridge SK16......101 F8
　Westhoughton BL5......57 C7
Cedar Ho 11 M14......98 E4
Cedar La
　Holcombe WN6........32 A3
　Uppermill OL4........68 D6
Cedar Lawn 4 SK8....123 A2
Cedar Lo SK7........132 F7
Cedar Mews OL7........85 B5
Cedar Mount High Sch
　M18........99 C3
Cedar Pk SK7........123 C1
Cedar Pl M7........81 C4
Cedar Rd
　Altrincham WA15......119 E3
　Failsworth M35........83 F6
　Gatley SK8........122 A5
　Leigh WN7........75 E8
　Marple SK6........125 E4
　Middleton M24........65 C8
　Partington M31......105 D5
　Stockport SK2........124 B4
Cedars The
　Manchester SK4........111 C5
　Salford M5........154 B1
Cedarway SK9........136 F5
Cedarwood Ave WA14..168 A1
Cedarwood Ct M22....121 E8
Cedric Rd
　Manchester M8........63 C2
　Oldham OL4........67 C7
Cedric St M5........154 B2
Celandine Cl OL15......15 F6
Celandine Wlk WN3....54 B4
Celia St M8........156 C4
Cellini Sq BL1........143 A1
Celtic St SK1........124 A8
Cemetery La WN4......45 A7
Cemetery Rd
　Bolton, Clammerclough
　　BL4........42 F1
　Bolton, Tonge Fold BL2...148 A3
　Denton, Hooley Hill
　　M34........100 F6
　Droylsden M43........83 F1
　Failsworth M35........83 F6
　Glossop SK13........104 C4
　Ince-in-M WN3........151 B1
　Mossley OL5........86 E8
　Radcliffe M26........43 F4
　Ramsbottom BL0 ......11 A4
　Royton OL2........48 C5
　Salford M5........154 B1
Cemetery Rd N M27....61 E1
Cemetery Rd S M27....61 E1
Cemetery St
　Middleton M24........47 A1
　2 Westhoughton BL5...39 E1
Cemetery View PR7....21 A6
Cenacle Ho M16........97 E2
Cennick Cl 3 OL4......67 C6
Centaur Cl M27........61 F2
Centaur Way 2 M8 ....155 C3
Centenary Circ M50....80 B1
Centenary Ct BL3......147 C4
Centenary Way
　Eccles M17........96 B8
　Salford M17, M50......80 A1
Central Ave
　Atherton M46........58 E4
　Buckley WN2........44 D7
　Edenfield BL0........1 D5
　Farnworth BL4........60 B8
　Leigh WN7........76 A6
　Littleborough OL15....16 B6
　Manchester M19........99 A1
　Pendlebury M6........158 D8
　Royton OL2........107 D1
　Swinton M27........62 C8
　Uppermill OL3........69 B5
　Walkden BL4........60 B8
Central Bldgs M2......162 C4

Central Dr
　Bury BL9........27 F8
　Gatley SK8........131 D8
　Manchester M8........64 B1
　Pendlebury M27........80 B7
　Reddish SK5........111 F5
　Romiley SK6........113 C3
　Shevington WN6........36 B6
　Stockport SK7........123 D2
　Urmston M41........95 F2
　Westhoughton BL5......39 F1
Central Flats WN1.....151 C3
Central Ho 9 M9........64 C5
Central Park Est M17 ..96 B6
Central Park Way
　WN1........37 C1
Central Pl SK9........137 B7
Central Rd
　Manchester M20......110 A5
　Partington M31......105 F3
Central Ret Pk M4....159 C1
Central St
　Bolton BL1........145 B3
　Manchester M2........158 C1
　Rochdale BL0........138 C2
Central Store 6
　SK13........104 C1
Central Trad Pk OL1...67 A8
Central Way
　Altrincham WA15......119 D4
　Newton-le-W WA12....110 B5
Centre Ct WN7........76 C6
Centre Gdns BL1......143 A1
Centre Park Rd BL3...143 A1
Centrepoint M17........96 B5
Centre The WN7........76 E6
Centre Vale OL15........16 C7
Centre Vale Cl OL15....16 C7
Centurion Gr M7......155 B2
Century Gdns OL12....139 C4
Century Ho M2........162 C4
Century Lo M2........60 C8
Century Mill Ind Est
　BL4........60 B7
Century Park Ind Area
　WA14........119 A4
Century St M3........162 B4
CE Sch of the
　Resurrection M11.....160 C1
Cestrian St BL3........147 C3
Ceylon St
　Failsworth M40........83 A6
　Oldham OL4........67 D5
Chadbury Cl BL6........40 C7
CHADDERTON
　66 A8
　152 A4
Chadderton Dr BL9.....45 A2
CHADDERTON FOLD....47 F2
Chadderton Hall Jun Sch
　OL9........48 A2
Chadderton Hall Rd OL1,
　OL9........47 F1
CHADDERTON HEIGHTS
　........47 F3
Chadderton Ind Est
　M24........65 C5
CHADDERTON PARK....65 F8
Chadderton Park Rd
　OL9........47 F1
Chadderton Prec OL9..152 B3
Chadderton St M4....159 B2
Chadderton Way
　Oldham, Burnley Brow OL1,
　　OL9........153 A4
　Oldham, Holden Fold OL9,
　　OL9........48 C1
Chaddesley Wlk M11..165 A4
Chaddock La
　Boothstown M28........77 F6
　Tyldesley M28, M29....77 D6
Chaddock Level The
　M28........78 A5
Chaddock Rd SK6.....125 B8
Chadkirk Bsns Pk
　SK6........125 B8
Chadkirk Chapel *
　SK6........113 C1
Chadkirk Rd SK6......113 B1
Chadvil Rd SK8........122 C5
Chadwell Rd SK2......124 E7
Chadwick Cl
　8 Manchester M14.....98 B3
　Milnrow OL16........32 A5
　Stalybridge SK15........85 F3
Chadwick Fold
　Bury BL9........27 F7
　Heywood OL10........29 F2
CHADWICK GREEN.....71 D3
Chadwick Hall Rd
　OL11........30 B6
Chadwick La
　Rochdale, Castleton OL10,
　　OL11........30 A2
　Rochdale, Pleasant View
　　OL16........31 C2
Chadwick Rd
　Eccles M30........79 E2
　Urmston M41........95 F2
Chadwick St
　Ashton-u-L OL6........85 E2
　Bolton BL2........148 B2
　Bury BL9........28 E4
　Glossop SK13........116 B8

Chadwick St continued
[2] Hindley WN2 ....56 E6
Leigh WN7 ....75 F6
Little Lever BL3 ....43 B3
Marple SK6 ....125 F5
Milnrow OL16 ....31 D7
Rochdale OL11 ....139 A3
Stockport SK1 ....170 C4
Swinton M27 ....79 F8
Wigan WN3 ....150 B2
Chadwick Terr OL12 ....14 D4
Chadwick Wlk M27 ....79 F8
Chaffinch Cl
Droylsden M43 ....84 C3
Oldham OL4 ....67 D4
Wythenshawe M22 ....121 F5
Chaffinch Dr BL9 .....141 C4
Chaffinch Gr SK15 ....86 E7
Chain Bar La M14 .....102 F2
Chain Bar Way SK14 ...102 F2
Chainhurst Wlk [2]
M13 ....163 C2
Chain Rd M9 ....64 D5
Chain St M1 ....159 A1
Chain Wlk [8] M9 .....64 E5
Chaise Mdw WA13 ....117 C5
Chalbury Cl [10] WN2 ...56 D4
Chalcombe Grange [1]
M12 ....98 F4
Chale Cl M40 ....160 A3
Chale Dr M24 ....65 C6
Chale Gn BL2 ....25 E3
Chalfont Ave [1] M41 ...95 E2
Chalfont Cl OL18 ......67 B4
Chalfont Dr
Manchester M8 ....156 A3
Tyldesley M29 ....77 A8
Walkden M28 ....78 E8
Chalfont Ho [2] M6 ....54 C2
Chalfont St BL1 ....143 C2
Chalford Rd M23 .....121 A4
Challenge Way WN5 ...36 D1
Challenor Sq M12 ....165 A2
Challum Dr OL9 ......152 A4
Chamber Hall Cl OL8 ...66 D4
Chamberhall St BL9 ...140 B3
Chamber House Dr
OL11.................30 B3
Chamberlain Dr SK9 ...131 D1
Chamberlain Gdns
SK6..................112 F4
Chamberlain Rd SK15 ..86 C5
Chamberlain St BL3 ...145 A2
Chamber Rd
Oldham OL8 ....66 D4
Shaw OL2 ....149 A3
Chambers Ct SK14 ....103 A3
Chambers Field Ct [8]
M5 ....81 A1
Chambers The M33 ...108 A5
Champagnole Ct [8]
SK16.................166 B1
Champneys Wlk M9 ...157 A2
Chancel Ave M5 ......161 C4
Chancel Cl SK16 ......101 C6
Chancel La SK9........137 B8
Chancellor La M12 ....164 A3
Chancel Mews SK1 ....112 A1
Chancel Pl
Manchester M1 ....159 C1
Rochdale OL16 ....139 C3
Chancery Cl M29 .....77 B8
Chancery La
Bolton BL1 ....145 C3
[16] Manchester M3 ....158 C1
Shaw OL2 ....149 C3
Uppermill OL3 ....51 A2
Chancery Pl [17] M3 ...158 C1
Chancery St
Chadderton OL9 ......152 C4
Oldham OL4 ....67 C6
Chancery Wlk OL9 ....152 C4
Chandlers Mews M22 ..109 E1
Chandlers Row M28 ...79 A5
Chandler Way WA3 ...90 E8
Chandley St SK1 ......124 A7
Chandley St SK8.......122 D6
Chandos Gr M5........154 A2
Chandos Rd
Manchester, Heaton Chapel
SK4 ....111 C6
Manchester, Hilton Park
M25 ....63 B2
Manchester M21 ......97 C1
Chandos Rd S M21....109 C8
Chandos St OL12 .....149 C3
Change Way M3.......158 B3
Channing Cl OL16 ....31 B6
Channing Sq [25] OL16 ..31 B6
Channing St OL16 ....31 B6
Chanters Ave M46 ....58 E3
Chanters The M28 ....78 C7
Chanters Ave BL8 ....27 A1
Chantlers Prim Sch
BL8..................27 A2
Chantry Cl
Disley SK12 ....135 E5
Reddish SK5 ....111 E7
Westhoughton BL5 ...57 F5
Chantry Fold SK12....135 E6
Chantry Rd SK12......135 E6
Chantry Wlk
Ashton-in-M WN4 ....72 F5
[14] Salford M8 ....155 C3
Chapel Alley [2] BL1...145 C3

Chapel Brow
Broadbottom SK13 ....115 E6
Glossop SK13.........104 A7
Chapel Cl
Dukinfield SK16.......101 D8
Ince-in-M WN3 ....151 A2
Whitefield BL9........45 B4
Chapel Croft OL2 .....48 D4
Chapel Ct
Altrincham WA14......119 D4
Bury BL8 ....26 E7
Hyde SK14 ....105 A3
[12] Marple SK6 ....125 F6
[5] Mossley OL5 ......68 C1
Sale M33 ....107 E6
Wilmslow SK9 ....137 A6
Chapel Dr
Altrincham WA15......129 C7
Ashton-u-L OL6 ......85 E5
Chapel End Prim Sch
WN5..................71 E4
Chapelfield M26 ......44 C1
CHAPEL FIELD 44 C1
Chapelfield Cl SK15...86 D4
Chapelfield Dr M38 ...60 B3
Chapelfield Prim Sch
M26 ....44 C1
Chapelfield Rd M12...163 B7
Chapel Field Rd M34 ..100 F3
Chapel Fields
Chapeltown BL7 ......9 C4
[1] Marple SK6 ....125 F5
Chapel Fields La WN2 ..56 E5
Chapelfield St BL1.....143 B3
Chapel Gate OL16 ....31 F6
Chapel Gdns
Denton M34 ....100 F6
Ramsbottom BL8 .....10 C1
Chapel Gn M34 ....100 F3
Chapel Gr
Radcliffe M26 ....62 A8
Urmston M41 ....95 C2
Chapel Grange BL7 ...9 C4
Chapel Green Rd WN2 ..56 E5
Chapel Hill
[2] Dukinfield SK16 ...101 C8
Littleborough OL15 ...16 B5
Chapelhill Dr M9 .....64 C3
Chapel Ho SK5 ....111 E8
Chapel Houses SK6 ...126 A5
Chapel La
Altrincham WA15......129 C7
Coppull PR7 ....19 E8
Glossop SK13.........103 F5
Hollinfare WA3 ....105 A2
Manchester M9 ....64 C3
Partington M31 ....105 F2
Ramsbottom BL8 .....138 A2
Rochdale OL11 ....29 C8
Royton OL2 ....48 D4
Sale M33 ....107 E6
Stretford M32 ....96 C1
Wigan WN1, WN3 ....150 C3
Wilmslow SK9 ....137 A6
Chapel Lofts SK13 ....100 B5
Chapel Mdw M28 .....78 B7
Chapel Pl
[4] Ashton-in-M WN4 ..73 B3
Bolton BL2, BL3.......148 C1
Urmston M41 ....95 D8
Chapel Rd
Alderley Edge SK9 ....137 A1
Irlam M44 ....94 A2
[1] Manchester M25 ...63 A1
Oldham OL8 ....66 C2
Swinton M27 ....79 C7
Uppermill OL3 ....69 A6
Wythenshawe M22 ...121 D8
Chapel St
Adlington PR7 ....20 F6
[4] Alderley Edge SK9 ..137 A1
Ashton-in-M WN4 ....73 B3
Ashton-u-L OL6 ......166 C3
Atherton M46 ....58 D3
[14] Bacup OL13 ......3 C8
Bickershaw WN2 .....56 E1
Blackrod BL6 ....21 D2
Bolton BL1 ....145 C4
Bolton, Egerton BL7...8 D3
Boothstown M28 .....77 F6
Bury BL9 ....140 C2
Bury, Tottington BL8...26 F7
Calderbrook OL15 ....6 D2
Cheadle SK8 ....122 D5
Denton M34 ....100 F6
Droylsden M43 ....84 B1
Dukinfield SK16 ......101 B8
[3] Eccles M30........79 C1
[1] Farnworth BL4 .....60 E8
Glossop SK13.........104 C1
Hazel Grove SK7 ....124 E3
Heywood OL10 ....29 D2
Hindley WN2 ....56 D5
Horwich BL6 ....22 C3
Hyde SK14 ....167 A2
Ince-in-M WN3 ....151 A2
Kearsley M26.........61 B8
Leigh WN7 ....76 B4
[2] Little Lever BL3....43 B3
Manchester, Heaton Mersey
SK4 ....110 E1
Manchester, Levenshulme
M19 ....99 B1
[6] Middleton M24 ....46 F1
[8] Mossley OL5 ......68 C1
New Mills, Rowarth
SK22 ....127 E7
Newton-le-W WA12...89 B3

Chapel St continued
Oldham OL4 ....67 E6
Platt Bridge WN2 .....56 B2
Prestwich M25........63 A4
[10] Rochdale OL11 ...31 A4
Romiley SK6 ....113 B5
Royton OL2 ....48 D4
Salford M3 ....158 B2
Shaw OL2 ....149 B3
Stalybridge SK15 .....86 A2
Swinton M27 ....62 A1
Tyldesley M29 ....77 A8
Uppermill OL3 ....69 B8
Wardle OL12 ....15 C7
Whitworth OL12.......14 C8
Wigan, Lamberhead Green
WN5 ....54 B5
Wigan, Lamberhead Green
WN5 ....54 B6
Wigan, Whelley WN2 ..38 A2
Wigan WN3 ....150 C3
Chapelstead BL5 .....57 F5
Chapel Street Prim Sch
M19 ....99 B1
Chapel Terr WA3 .....91 B8
CHAPELTOWN 9 C4
Chapeltown Rd
Chapeltown BL7 ......9 C2
Radcliffe M26 ....62 A8
Chapeltown St M1....159 C1
Chapel View SK16 ....101 C8
Chapel View Cl SK14 ..113 E7
Chapel Way PR7 ......19 F8
Chapelway Gdns OL2 ..48 D6
Chapel Wlk
[1] Eccles M30 ....79 F2
Golborne WA3 ....91 B8
Middleton M24 ....64 D7
Oldham OL1 ....48 D1
Prestwich M25........62 F1
Whitefield M45 ....45 B1
Chapel Wlks
Broomedge WA13 ....117 D1
Cheadle SK8 ....132 B6
Manchester M2 ....158 C1
Manchester M3 ....158 B3
Chaplin Cl M6 ....108 B5
Chapman Mews M18 ..99 D5
Chapman Rd SK14 ....102 E1
Chapman St
Bolton BL1 ....142 B1
Manchester M18 ......99 D5
Chappell Rd M43 .....84 A2
Chapter St M40 ......160 C4
Charcoal Rd WA14 ...118 F3
Charcoal Woods
WA14 ....119 A3
Charcon Wlk [3] OL2 ..48 E4
Chard Dr M22 ....121 D1
Chardin Ave SK6 .....126 C8
Chard St M26 ....44 A3
Charges St OL7 ......84 F1
Chariot St M11 ....99 D8
Charity St WN7 ....75 C5
Charlbury Ave
Manchester M25 .....63 E3
Reddish SK5 ....111 F6
Charlbury Way OL2 ...149 A1
Charlecote Rd SK12 ..133 F4
Charles Ave
Droylsden M34........100 A7
Marple SK6 ....125 C7
Charles Cl
Altrincham WA15......120 B6
Bolton BL1 ....145 C4
Charles Halle Rd M15..163 A1
Charles Holden St
BL1..................145 A2
Charles La
Glossop SK13.........104 E3
Milnrow OL16 ....32 A5
Charles Mews OL16 ...32 A5
Charles Morris Cl M35..84 B8
Charles Morris Ho
M35 ....84 A7
Charles Shaw Cl [4]
OL4..................49 D1
Charles St
Altrincham WA15......120 B6
Bolton BL1 ....145 C4
Bolton, Egerton BL7...8 D3
Bolton, Egerton BL7...8 D2
[2] Bolton, Mill Hill BL1..148 A4
[5] Bury BL9 ....140 C3
Denton M34 ....100 F5
Droylsden M43 ....83 C1
Dukinfield SK16 ......166 B1
[3] Farnworth BL4 ....42 E1
Glossop SK13.........104 C1
Golborne WA3 ....74 A1
Hazel Grove SK7 ....124 D3
Heywood OL10 ....46 E8
Hindley WN2 ....56 E7
Ince-in-M WN2 ....56 A7
Irlam M44 ....105 E6
Leigh WN7 ....75 F7
Littleborough OL15 ...16 A5
Manchester M1 ....163 A4
Oldham OL9 ....152 C2
Royton OL2 ....48 D4
Salford M6............154 F2
Stockport SK1 ....124 A7
Swinton M27 ....61 D2
Whitefield M29 ....62 F7
[2] Wigan WN1 ....37 C1

Charleston Cl M33....107 D2
Charleston St M29 ....76 F8
Charleston Sq M41 ...95 B3
Charleston St OL8 ....66 F4
CHARLESTOWN
Ashton-under-Lyne ...166 B4
Glossop 116 C6
Charlestown SK13 ....116 C6
CHARLESTOWN
Manchester 65 A3
Salford...............65 B1
Charlestown Cl OL6 ...166 B3
Charlestown Com Prim
Sch
Manchester M9 ....65 B3
Salford M6............81 B4
Charlestown Ind Est
OL6..................166 B4
Charlestown Rd
Glossop SK13.........116 C7
Manchester M9 ....64 E2
Charlestown Rd E
SK2..................124 A3
Charlestown Rd W
SK3..................123 F3
Charlestown Way
OL6..................166 A3
Charles Whittaker St [2]
OL12.................13 F1
Charles Wlk M45 .....62 F7
CHARLESWORTH 115 C6
Charlesworth Ave
Bolton BL3 ....42 B3
Denton M34 ....112 F8
Hindley WN2 ....56 F4
Charlesworth Ct M11 ..164 C4
Charlesworth Prim Sch
SK13.................115 C6
Charlesworth St
Manchester M11 .....164 C4
Stockport SK1, SK3 ...170 C3
Charley Ave M7 ......158 A4
Charlock Ave BL5.....57 E6
Charlock Sq WA14 ...119 B8
Charlock Wlk M31....105 E3
Charlotte La OL4 .....68 E5
Charlotte Pl WA15 ....119 F3
Charlotte St
[28] Bolton BL1 ....143 B2
[2] Cheadle SK8 ......122 D5
Manchester M1, M2 ..159 A1
Ramsbottom BL0 .....138 B1
Rochdale OL16........31 B3
Stockport SK1 ....112 B3
Charlton Ave
Dukinfield SK14 ......102 A4
Eccles M30 ....79 D1
Prestwich M25........63 B3
Charlton Ct M25......63 B3
Charlton Dr
Sale M33 ....108 C4
Swinton M27 ....79 F6
Charlton Fold M28 ...60 C5
Charlton Pl M12 ......163 B3
Charlton Rd M19 .....99 B1
Charminster Dr M8 ...156 B4
Charminster Mews
M27 ....79 F6
Charmouth Cl WA12 ..89 B4
Charmouth Wlk M22 ..121 F3
Charnley Cl
Manchester M40 .....160 B3
[7] Sale M33 ....108 A4
Charnley Grange BL6 ..40 B7
Charnley St M45 .....62 F8
Charnock Dr BL1 .....143 B1
Charnock Rd WA3 ...91 F3
Charnock St WN2 ....56 B6
Charnock's Yd [2] WN5..54 B5
Charnville Rd SK8 ....121 F5
Charnwood Ave M34..103 B1
Charnwood Cl
Ashton-u-L OL6 ......85 C7
Shaw OL2 ....48 E8
Tyldesley M29 ....77 B8
Walkden M28 ....60 C2
Charnwood Cres SK7 ..133 D8
Charnwood Rd
Manchester M9 ....64 D5
Romiley SK6 ....113 C5
Charter Ave M26 .....44 C2
Charter Cl [5] M33 ...107 D3
Charter Ho M30 ......79 F1
Charterhouse Rd
Wigan 151 B2
Charter Rd WA15 ....119 E4
Charter St
Manchester M3 ....158 C3
Oldham OL1 ....67 A8
Rochdale OL16........31 B4
Chartist Ho SK14 ....167 B2
Chartwell Cl M5, M6 ..154 C2
Chartwell Dr M23 ....120 E7
Chaseley Rd
Rochdale OL12 ....139 B4
Salford M6............154 E4
Chase St M4 ....159 A3
Chase The M29 ......79 A5
Chasetown Cl [5] M23..120 D6
Chassen Ave M41 ....95 B1
Chassen Ct M41 .....95 B1
Chassen Rd
Bolton BL3 ....144 B3
Urmston M41.........95 B1

Chassen Road Sta M41 ..95 B1
Chataway Rd M8 .....156 C4
Chatburn Ave
Golborne WA3 ....74 C1
Trub OL11............47 D8
Chatburn Ct
Culcheth WA3 ....91 F2
Shaw OL2.............149 C4
Chatburn Gdns OL10 ..28 F2
Chatburn Rd
Bolton BL1 ....23 F3
Manchester M21 .....109 C8
Chatburn Sq OL11 ...47 D8
Chatcombe Rd M22 ..121 A2
Chatford Rd M21 ....109 B8
Chatford Cl M7.......158 B4
Chatham Ct M20 .....110 A6
Chatham Gdns BL3 ...145 A1
Chatham Gr M20 .....110 A6
Chatham Ho [3] SK3 ..170 B4
Chatham Pl [2] BL3 ...145 A1
Chatham Rd
Manchester M16 .....97 C3
Reddish M18 ....99 E3
Chatham St
Hyde SK14 ....113 C7
Ince-in-M WN3 ....56 A8
Leigh WN7 ....75 F7
Manchester M1 ....159 B1
Stockport SK3 ....170 A4
Wigan WN1 ....151 B3
Chatley Rd M30 ......78 F1
Chatley St M3, M4 ...159 A4
Chatswood Ave SK2...170 C2
Chatsworth Ave
Culcheth WA3 ....91 F4
Ince-in-M WN3 ....55 F4
Prestwich M25........63 B4
Chatsworth Cl
Altrincham WA15......120 C5
Ashton-in-M WN4 ....72 F4
Droylsden M43 ....83 E3
Shaw OL2.............49 D8
[2] Urmston M41 .....95 E2
Whitefield BL9........45 A5
Chatsworth Cres M32 ..95 F3
Chatsworth Ct
Altrincham PR6 ......20 F8
Stockport SK2 ....124 A5
Chatsworth Dr
Leigh WN7 ....76 D7
Leigh WN7 ....76 F7
Chatsworth Gr
Little Lever BL3.......43 A4
Manchester M16 .....97 D2
Chatsworth High Sch
M30 ....79 F4
Chatsworth Ho M1 ...159 A1
Chatsworth Manor
SK7..................123 C2
Chatsworth Mews
SK7..................123 D2
Chatsworth Rd
Cheadle SK8 ....123 B5
Droylsden M43 ....83 E2
Eccles M30 ....79 F4
Hazel Grove SK7 ....133 F8
High Lane SK6 ....134 F6
Manchester M18 .....165 C1
Radcliffe M26 ....43 D5
Stretford M32 ....96 A3
Swinton M28 ....79 C5
Wilmslow SK9 ....136 E4
Chatsworth St
Oldham OL4 ....67 C5
Rochdale OL12........14 E3
Wigan WN5 ....54 C5
Chatteris Cl WN2 ....56 E4
CHATTERTON 1 C1
Chatterton BL0 ....1 C2
Chatterton Cl M20 ...110 C6
Chatterton La SK6 ...127 B8
Chatterton Old La BL0 ..1 C2
Chatterton Rd BL0 ...1 C1
Chattock St [11] M16 ..97 E3
Chatton Cl BL8 ....26 F2
Chatwell Cl OL16 ....32 C4
Chatwood Rd M40 ...65 D2
Chaucer Ave
Denton M34 ....113 A7
Droylsden M43 ....84 A1
Radcliffe M26 ....43 E4
Reddish SK5 ....99 D1
Chaucer Gr
Atherton M46 ....58 D5
Leigh WN7 ....75 D8
Chaucer Mews SK1 ...112 B1
Chaucer Pl
Abram WN2 ....56 B1
Wigan WN1 ....37 C3
Chaucer Rd M24 .....47 B2
Chaucer Rise SK16 ...102 A3
Chaucer St
Bolton BL1 ....143 A2
Oldham OL1 ....153 B2
Rochdale OL11........30 C2
Royton OL2 ....48 E5
Chaucer Wlk M13 ....163 C2
Chaumont Way OL6 ..166 B3
Chauncy Rd M40 .....83 E8
Chaytor Ave M40 ....83 B7
CHEADLE 122 E5
Cheadle Ave M7......81 A4
Cheadle Cl SK8.......122 E1
CHEADLE HEATH 123 A4
Cheadle Heath Prim Sch
SK3..................123 A7
CHEADLE HULME 132 A8

Cheadle Hulme High Sch
SK8.................132 B7
Cheadle Hulme Sch
SK8.............. 132 A8
Cheadle Hulme Sta
SK8.................123 B2
Cheadle & Marple Sixth
Form Coll
Cheadle SK8 ....122 F3
Marple SK6 ....125 E5
Marple SK6 ....125 F5
Cheadle Old Rd SK3 ..123 C7
Cheadle Point SK8 ....122 F6
Cheadle Prim Sch
SK8.................122 D6
Cheadle RC Inf Sch
SK8.................122 E2
Cheadle RC Jun Sch
SK8.................122 E2
Cheadle Rd SK8 ....122 F3
Cheadle Royal Bsns Pk
SK8.................122 C2
Cheadle Royal Hospl
SK8.................122 C2
Cheadle Sq BL1 ....145 B3
Cheadle St M11 ....99 D8
Cheadle Wood SK8 ....131 E8
Cheam Rd WA15........119 F8
Cheapside
Hyde SK14.............167 B3
Manchester M2 ....158 C1
Middleton M24..........47 A2
Oldham OL1...........153 B3
Cheapside Sq 8 BL1...145 C3
Cheddar St 1 M18 ......99 D5
Cheddington Cl SK8 ...132 A7
Chedlee Dr SK8 ....131 E8
Chedlin Dr M23 ....121 A4
Chedworth Cres M38 ...60 A6
Chedworth Dr M23 ....121 B6
Chedworth Gr BL3 ....145 B1
Cheeryble St M11, M43 ..99 F7
CHEESDEN 12 D6
Cheesden Wlk M45 ....45 C1
Cheetham Ave M24 .....47 B1
Cheetham CE Com Sch
M8.................155 C3
Cheetham Fold Rd
SK14.................113 D8
Cheetham Gdns 7
SK15.................86 B1
Cheetham Gr WN3 .....54 F5
CHEETHAM HILL 156 B3
Cheetham Hill
Shaw OL2............149 B2
Whitworth OL12.........4 D3
Cheetham Hill Rd
Dukinfield SK15,
SK16.................101 C8
Manchester, Cheetham Hill
M8.................156 A2
Cheetham Mill Ind Est
SK15.................86 B1
Cheetham Par M8 .....155 C4
Cheetham Pl SK6 .....112 F4
Cheetham Rd M27 .....80 A7
Cheetham's Cres OL2 ..49 A4
Cheetham St
Failsworth M35 ....84 A8
Manchester M40 ......157 B1
Middleton M24.........64 F8
Oldham OL1...........44 C4
Rochdale M26 ....139 C4
Shaw OL2............149 C2
Cheethams The BL6 ....38 E7
Cheetwood Prim Sch
M8.................158 A4
Cheetwood Rd M8 ....155 C1
Cheetwood St M8 ....158 B4
Chelbourne Dr 3 OL8 ..66 B2
Chelburn Cl
Leigh WN7 ....56 E1
Stockport SK2 ....124 D5
Chelburn St SK3......170 B2
Cheldon Wlk 8 M40....83 C6
Chelford Ave
Bolton BL1 ....24 E5
Golborne WA3 ....90 D8
Chelford Cl
Altrincham WA15......119 E6
Manchester M13 ......164 A1
Middleton M24.........47 C2
Wigan WN3 ....54 F2
Chelford Dr
Swinton M27 ....61 E2
Wigan WN7 ....77 C6
Chelford Gr SK3 ......170 A1
Chelford Rd
Alderley Edge SK9 ....136 E1
Handforth SK9 ....131 D5
Manchester M16 ....97 C3
Sale M33.............108 C2
Chellow Cl OL5 ....68 B1
Chellow Dene M44 ....98 A8
Chell St M13 ....98 F4
Chelmarsh Ave WN4 ...73 C3
Chelmer Cl BL5.........40 A1
Chelmer Gr OL10 ......29 A3
Chelmsford Ave M40 ...83 B4
Chelmsford Dr WN3 ...55 A4
Chelmsford Gdns
WN1.................37 C2
Chelmsford Rd SK3 ..123 C8
Chelmsford St OL8....153 B1

Chelmsford Wlk 14
M34 ....101 A1
Chelsea Ave M26 ....43 D4
Chelsea Cl OL2 ....149 B3
Chelsea Rd
Bolton BL3 ....147 A3
Failsworth M40 ....83 C5
Urmston M41..........94 C1
Chelsea St
Bury BL9 ....44 F4
Rochdale OL11........139 A1
Chelsfield Gr M21 ....109 D8
Chelston Ave M40 .....65 D2
Chelston Dr
Gatley SK8...........131 C6
Haslingden BB4 ....1 A7
Cheltenham Ave
WN3.................151 A1
Cheltenham Cres M7 ..155 B3
Cheltenham Dr
Longshaw WN5 ....53 D2
Newton-le-W WA12.....89 C5
Sale M33.............108 C4
Cheltenham Gdn M24 ..65 A6
Cheltenham Rd
Cheadle SK8 ....123 A7
Manchester M21 ....97 B2
Middleton M24.........65 A6
Cheltenham St
Oldham OL1...........49 B1
Rochdale OL11.........30 D4
Salford M6............81 A4
3 Wigan WN2 ....37 F2
Chelt Wlk M22 ....121 B2
Chelwood Cl BL1 ......24 D7
Chelwood Dr M43 ......83 F2
Chelwood Mews BL6 ...40 B7
Chelwood Pk WA12 ....73 B1
Chelworth Manor
SK7.................123 C1
Chemical St WA12 .....89 B3
Chendre Cl M27 ....61 F2
Chendre Rd M9 ....65 B3
Cheney Cl M11 ....99 D7
Chenies The 5 M7 .....63 C1
Chepstow Ave M33 ...107 C3
Chepstow Cl OL11 .....29 F8
Chepstow Dr
Hazel Grove SK7 .....125 A2
Oldham OL1...........49 B1
Chepstow Gr WN7 .....76 E7
Chepstow Ho M1 .....162 C4
Chepstow Rd
Manchester M21 ....97 A1
Swinton M27 ....62 A2
Chepstow St M1, M2 ..162 C4
Chepstow St M1, M2 ..162 C4
CHEQUERBENT 40 D1
Chequers Rd M21 ....109 B8
Chequers St WN1 ....150 B4
Cherington Cl
Handforth SK9 ....131 F3
Wythenshawe M23 ...109 B2
Cherington Dr M29 ....59 C1
Cherington Rd SK8 ...122 C4
Cheriton Ave M33 ....108 C5
Cheriton Cl SK14 ....102 D2
Cheriton Dr BL2 ....42 E6
Cheriton Rd M41 ......94 D3
Cheriton Rise SK2 ....125 A6
Cherrington Dr OL11 ...47 D8
Cherry Ave
Ashton-u-L OL6 ....85 B6
Bury BL9 ....141 C3
Oldham OL8............67 C3
Cherrybrook Dr WN3 ...54 D1
Cherry Cl
Bury BL9 ....45 A7
Cherry Crocs BB4 ......1 F8
Cherry Croft SK6 .....113 E1
Cherry Ct
3 Sale, Ashton u M
M33 ....108 A4
Sale, Timperley WA15 ..120 C7
Cherry Dr M27 ....80 A8
Cherry Gdns BL1 ......40 F8
Cherry Gr
Leigh WN7 ....75 F8
Rochdale OL11.........30 A8
Royton OL2 ....48 C6
Stalybridge SK15 .....102 A8
Wigan WN6 ....36 F3
Cherry Hall Dr OL2 ....48 E7
Cherry Hinton OL1 ....153 A4
Cherry Holt Ave SK4 ..110 F4
Cherry La
Denshaw OL16, OL3 ...33 B3
Sale M33.............107 C2
Cherry Manor Prim Sch
M33 ....107 C2
Cherry Orchard Cl
SK7.................123 D1
Cherry St SK15 ....63 C5
Cherryton Wlk M13 ...163 C2
CHERRY TREE
Cherry Tree Ave
Farnworth BL4 ....60 A8
Poynton SK12 ....133 F3
Cherry Tree Cl
1 Altrincham WA15 ..120 B5
Romiley SK6..........113 E2
Wilmslow SK9 ....137 E8
Cherry Tree Cotts
WA11 ....71 A2
Cherry Tree Ct
7 Salford M6 ....81 A2

Cherry Tree Ct continued
Standish WN6 ....19 D2
Stockport SK2 ....124 C4
Cherry Tree Dr SK7 ...134 A8
Cherry Tree Gr
Atherton M46 ....58 C4
Leigh WN7 ....75 D6
Cherry Tree Hospl
SK2.................124 C5
Cherry Tree La
Ashley WA14 ....128 A5
Billinge WA11 ....71 A2
Bury BL8 ....27 C1
Ravenstall BB4 ....1 F8
Romiley SK6..........113 E2
Stockport SK2 ....124 C5
Cherry Tree Prim Sch
BL4.................59 B8
Cherry Tree Rd
Cheadle SK8 ....123 A1
Manchester WA3 ......90 F8
Wythenshawe M23 ...108 F1
Cherry Tree Way
Bolton BL2 ....25 C5
Haslingden BB4 ....1 B7
5 Horwich BL6.........22 E1
Cherry Tree Wlk
Mossley OL5 ....68 B1
Stretford M32 ....96 C1
Cherry Wlk
Cheadle SK8 ....132 C8
Partington M31 ......105 D2
Cherrywood OL9 ....65 D7
Cherrywood Ave BL5 ...59 A7
Cherrywood Cl M28....60 B1
Chertsey Cl
Droylsden M18.........99 E5
Shaw OL2............149 B4
Chervil Cl M14 ....110 C8
Chervil Wlk WN3 ....54 C4
Cherwell Ave OL10.....29 B3
Cherwell Cl
Aspull WN2 ....38 C6
Cheadle SK8 ....132 A7
Oldham OL8............66 C1
Whitefield M45 ....63 A8
Cherwell Rd BL5 ....39 F2
CHESHAM 28 B5
Chesham Ave
Bolton BL7 ....143 B2
Trub OL11 ....47 D7
Urmston M41..........94 E3
Wythenshawe M22 ...121 C4
Chesham Cl
Hadfield SK13 ....104 A5
Wilmslow SK9 ....136 F4
Chesham Cres BL9 ...141 A3
Chesham Fold Rd
BL9.................141 B4
Chesham Ho 2 M5 ...154 F1
Chesham Ind Est BL9 ..141 A4
Chesham Pl WA14 ...119 C2
Chesham Prim Sch
BL9.................28 A5
Chesham Rd
Bury BL9 ....28 A5
Eccles M30 ....95 C8
Wilmslow SK9 ....136 F4
Chesham St BL3 .....146 B2
Cheshill Ct M7 ....155 C2
Cheshire Cl
Newton-le-W WA12.....89 E3
Stretford M32 ....96 B1
Cheshire Ct BL0 ....11 D6
Cheshire Gdns M14 ...98 A1
Cheshire Rd
Mossley SK15 ....86 E5
Partington M31 ......105 D2
Cheshire St SK15 ......86 D8
Cheshires The OL5 .....68 D1
Chesney Ave OL9 ......65 E2
Chesshyre Ave M4 ...160 A1
Chessington Rise M27 ..62 A3
Chester Ave
Altrincham WA15 ....119 F2
Dukinfield SK16 ....101 E7
Golborne WA3 ....90 D8
Little Lever BL3 ....43 B4
Rochdale OL11.........30 A6
Sale M33.............107 B1
Stalybridge SK15 ......86 D3
Urmston M41..........95 E3
Whitefield M45 ....63 A7
Chester Cl
Handforth SK9 ....131 E2
Ramsbottom BL0 ......11 A4
Little Lever BL3 ....43 B4
Chester Cres BB4 ......1 B8
Chester Dr
Ashton-in-M WN4 .....73 D2
Ramsbottom BL0 ......11 A4
Chesterfield Gr OL6....85 D3
Chesterfield St OL4 ....67 D1
Chesterfield Way 4
M34 ....113 A8
Chestergate SK1, SK3,
SK4.................169 B1
Chester Pl
Adlington PR6 ....21 A3
7 Royton OL2..........48 D4
Chester Rd
Hazel Grove SK7 .....124 D1
Manchester, City Park M15,
M16 ....161 B1
Manchester, St George's
M15 ....162 A3

Chester Rd continued
Poynton SK12 ....133 B4
Stretford M16, M32.....96 F5
Tyldesley M29 ....77 D8
Woodford SK7........132 E2
Chester's Croft Pk
SK8.................132 A5
Chester Sq OL7 ......166 A2
Chester St
Bury BL9 ....141 A4
Denton M34 ....100 F2
Leigh WN7 ....75 F5
Manchester M1 ....163 A3
Oldham OL9..........152 C1
Prestwich M25.........63 A5
Stockport SK3 ....169 A1
Swinton M27 ....79 F7
Tyldesley M46 ....58 E1
Chesterton Cl WN3 ...150 A1
Chesterton Dr BL3.....40 E5
Chesterton Gr M43 ....84 A2
Chesterton Rd
Oldham OL1...........49 B2
Wythenshawe M23 ...120 D8
Chester Wlk 20 BL1 ...143 B2
Chester Wlks SK6 ....113 A1
Chestnut Ave
Atherton M46 ....58 C4
Bury BL9 ....141 B2
Bury, Tottington BL8.....27 A5
Cheadle SK8 ....122 E5
Droylsden M43 ....83 E3
Irlam M44 ....105 D5
Leigh WN7 ....75 F3
Manchester M21 ......109 B8
Walkden M28..........60 D2
Whitefield M45 ....62 F7
Chestnut Cl
Bolton BL3 ....146 B4
New Mills SK22 ......127 E1
Oldham OL4............67 D8
Stalybridge SK15 .....102 A8
Wilmslow SK9 ....137 E8
Chestnut Cres OL8.....67 A2
Chestnut Ct
Manchester M19 ......111 B8
Stockport SK7 ....123 D2
Chestnut Dr
1 Bury BL9............27 F7
Leigh WN7 ....75 F2
Poynton SK12 ....133 F3
Rawtenstall BB4 ....1 F8
Sale M33.............107 D1
Westhoughton BL5 .....57 F7
Chestnut Dr S WN7 ...75 F2
Chestnut Fold M26 ....44 A4
Chestnut Gdns
Denton M34 ....100 C2
Heywood OL10.........29 C1
Chestnut Gr
Ashton-in-M WN4 .....73 D4
Golborne WA3 ....90 F8
Hindley WN2 ....57 A4
Radcliffe M26 ....62 A8
Chestnut La WN7 ......75 F2
Chestnut Rd
Eccles M30 ....79 A4
Wigan WN1 ....37 E2
Chestnut St OL9 ....66 A3
Chestnut Villas SK4 ..168 C2
Chestnut Way OL15 ....6 C1
Chestnut Wlk M31 ...105 D2
Chesworth Cl SK1 ...170 C4
Chesworth Ct M43 .....83 F1
Chesworth Fold SK1 ..170 C4
Chetham's Sch of Music
M3.................158 C2
Chetton Ave WN4 ......73 B1
Chetwyn Ave
Bolton BL7 ....25 A7
Royton OL2 ....48 C4
Cheviot Cl
Bolton BL1 ....24 D5
Chadderton OL9.......152 A1
Horwich BL6 ....22 C5
Middleton M24.........65 D8
Milnrow OL16 ....32 A7
Ramsbottom BL0 ......11 C4
Salford M6............169 A3
Wigan WN4 ....54 C2
Cheviot Ct 4 OL8 ......66 E4
Cheviot Ho OL11 ......30 B8
Cheviot Rd SK7 ......124 B1
Cheviots Rd OL2 .....149 A4
Cheviot St M3 ....158 C3
Chevithorne Cl WA14 .119 B5
Chevril Cl M15 ....163 A2
Chevron Cl
Rochdale OL11.........30 B3
3 Salford M6..........81 B2

Chevron Pl WA14 .....119 D7
Chew Brook Dr OL3.....69 B5
CHEW MOOR 40 B3
Chew Moor La BL5, BL6 ..40 A2
Chew Rd
Glossop OL3 ....88 C8
Oldham OL3............70 A2
Chew Vale
Dukinfield SK16 ....101 F7
Uppermill OL3 ....69 B5
Chew Valley Rd OL3 ...69 B5
Chicago Ave M90 ....130 B7
Chichester Ave M46 ...58 A2
Chichester Bsns Ctr
OL16.................31 A7
Chichester Cl
Littleborough OL15 ....15 F3
4 Sale M33 ....107 D3
Chichester Cres OL9....48 A1
Chichester Rd
Manchester M15 ......162 C1
Romiley SK6..........113 C2
Chichester Rd S M15 .162 B1
Chichester St OL16.....31 B7
Chichester Way 11
M3.................161 A1
Chicken La 1 SK5 ......99 F2
Chidlow Ave M20 .....110 A7
Chidwall Rd M22 .....121 B2
Chief St OL4............67 A6
Chiffon Way M3 ......158 A3
Chigwell Cl M22 .....121 E5
Chilcombe Wlk 8 M9 ...64 E5
Childe Ave M33 ......107 E4
Childwall Cl BL3 .....147 B2
Chilgrove Ave BL6 .....21 D1
Chilham Rd
Eccles M30 ....79 F4
Walkden M28..........60 E2
Chilham St
Bolton BL3 ....146 B2
Swinton M27 ....79 E6
Swinton M46 ....54 B6
Chillingham Dr WN7 ...76 C4
Chillington Wlk M34 ..100 E1
Chilmark Dr M23 .....121 A6
Chiltern Ave
Atherton M46 ....58 F5
Cheadle SK8 ....122 F5
Urmston M41..........94 F3
Chiltern Cl
Ashton-in-M WN4 .....73 C2
Horwich BL6 ....22 C5
Ramsbottom BL0 ......11 C4
Shaw OL2.............48 F8
Stockport SK7 ....124 B1
Walkden M28..........78 E8
Chiltern Dr
Altrincham WA15......119 F2
Bolton BL2 ....148 C3
Bury BL8 ....27 B4
Royton OL2 ....48 C4
Stockport SK2 ....124 B4
Swinton M27 ....79 F6
Wigan WN3 ....54 D2
Chiltern Gdns M33....108 C1
Chiltern Rd
Culcheth WA3 ....91 E4
Ramsbottom BL0 ......11 C4
Chiltern Way M29 ......77 B8
Chilton Ave OL9 .....152 A2
Chilton Cl WN7 ....75 F7
Chilton Dr M24 ....65 C7
Chilworth St M14 ......98 B2
Chime Bank M8 ......156 B2
Chimes Cl OL4 ....68 B5
Chimes Rd WN4 ....72 F6
China La
1 Bolton BL1 ....145 C4
Manchester M1 ......159 B1
Chingford Wlk 5 M13 ..98 F4
Chinley Ave
Manchester M40 ......83 A8
Stretford M32 ....96 A4
Chinley Cl
Sale M33.............108 D3
Stockport, Davenport
SK7.................123 E3
Stockport, Heaton Norris
SK4.................168 B3
Chinley St
6 Oldham OL1........67 B8
Salford M6............81 B5
Chinnor Cl WN7 ....75 F7
Chinwell View 3 M19 ..99 A1
Chip Hill Rd BL3 .....146 A4
Chippendale Pl OL6 ...85 E5
Chippenham Ave SK2 .124 D7
Chippenham Ct M4 ...160 A2
Chippenham Rd M4 ..160 A2
Chipping Fold 5 OL16 ..31 F5
Chipping Rd BL1 ....24 A5
Chipping Sq M12 ....99 A4
Chipstead Ave M12 ..164 B1
Chirmside St BB4 ......27 B1
Chirton Wlk 9 M40.....83 A7
Chisacre Dr WN6 ......35 D7
Chiseldon Ave M22 ..121 E2
Chiselhurst St M8 ....156 A3
Chisholm Cl WN6 ......19 B2
Chisholm Ct M24 ......65 C7
Chisholme Cl BL6 ......10 F2
Chisholm St M11 ......99 D7
Chisledon Ave M7 ....155 C2
Chisledon Cl BL3 .....145 B1

Chislehurst Ave M41......95 D3
Chislehurst Cl BL8......27 B1
Chisnall Ave WN6......18 F6
Chisnall La
　Coppull PR7............19 C6
　Wrightington Bar WN6 ...19 A5
Chiswell St WN5......54 C5
Chiswick Dr M26......43 B5
Chiswick Rd M20......110 C3
CHISWORTH............115 B5
Chisworth Cl
　Leigh WN7.............75 E7
　Stockport SK7..........123 E3
Chisworth St BL2......25 B3
Chisworth Wlk 2
　M34..................113 A8
Choir St M7............158 B4
Chokeberry Cl WA14 ...119 B8
Cholmley Dr WA12......89 E2
Cholmondeley Ave
　WA14.................119 E8
Cholmondeley Rd M6...80 C4
Cholmlea WA14.........119 B4
Chomlea Manor M6 ....80 C4
Choral Gr M7...........155 A1
Chorley Cl BL8..........26 F1
Chorley Hall Cl SK9...136 F1
Chorley Hall La SK9 ...137 A1
Chorley New Rd
　Bolton BL1, BL6........40 C7
　Horwich BL6...........22 C2
Chorley New Road Prim
　Sch BL6...............22 D2
Chorley Old Rd
　Bolton, Cope Bank
　BL1..................142 B1
　Doffcocker BL1, BL6 ...23 C3
Chorley Rd
　Adlington PR6.........21 A8
　Blackrod BL6, PR7 .....21 B5
　Four Gates BL5, BL6 ...39 C4
　Sale M33..............108 E2
　Standish WN1..........20 C3
　Swinton M27...........79 F8
Chorley St
　Adlington PR6.........21 B8
　Bolton BL1............145 B3
　Ince-in-M WN3.........151 B2
　Stretford M32..........96 F5
Chorley Wood Ave
　M19..................110 F6
Chorlton Brook Ho
　SK8..................122 E6
Chorlton CE Prim Sch
　M21..................109 A8
Chorlton Ct 2 M16....97 C3
CHORLTON-CUM-HARDY
　...................109 C7
Chorlton Dr SK8.......122 E6
CHORLTON FOLD.......79 D5
Chorlton Fold
　Eccles M30............79 D4
　Romiley SK6..........113 C5
Chorlton Gn 7 M21 ...109 A8
Chorlton Gr SK1.......124 B7
Chorlton High Sch
　M21..................109 D7
Chorlton Hts 2 M21 ...109 A8
Chorlton Mill M1......162 C3
Chorlton Park Prim Sch
　M21..................109 A8
Chorlton Pl M21........97 B1
Chorlton Rd M15, M16...162 A2
Chorlton St
　Manchester M1........163 A4
　Manchester, Old Trafford
　M16.................161 C1
Chorlton View 3
　M21..................109 A8
Chorlton Water Pk
　M21..................109 C4
Chowbent Cl M46......58 E3
Chowbent Prim Sch
　M46..................58 E3
Chretien Rd M22......109 E2
Christ Church Ainsworth
　CE Prim Sch BL2.....26 C1
Christchurch Ave M5 ...81 B2
Christ Church CE Prim
　Sch
　Bury BL8..............26 F4
　Chadderton OL9........152 A2
　Denshaw OL3...........33 D1
　Eccles M30............79 D2
　Leigh WN7.............75 F4
Christ Church Cl BL2 ...25 F2
Christchurch Ct OL9 ...152 C1
Christ Church La BL2 ...25 F3
Christchurch Rd M33 ...107 C5
Christie Hospl & Holt
　Radium Inst M20.....110 B6
Christie Rd M32........96 E2
Christie Road Ind Est
　SK1..................124 A7
Christie St SK1.......124 A7
Christine St OL2......149 B3
Christleton WN6.......36 B6
Christleton Ave SK4 ...111 D5
Christleton Way 15
　SK9..................131 D5
Christopher Acre OL11...13 E1
Christopher St
　Failsworth M40........83 D4
　Ince-in-M WN3........151 C2
　Salford M5.............81 B1

Christ's Church CE Prim
　Sch BL2...............25 F2
Christ the King RC Prim
　Sch
　Failsworth M40........83 C5
　Walkden M28..........60 E2
Chronnell Dr BL2......42 E8
Chudleigh Cl
　Altrincham WA14......119 B6
　Stockport SK7.........124 A3
Chudleigh Rd M8......64 A2
Chulsey Gate La BL6...40 A4
Chulsey St BL3........146 B4
CHUNAL...............116 C4
Chunal La SK13.......116 D6
Chunal Lane Flats
　SK13.................116 C6
Church Ave
　Bickershaw WN2.......74 F8
　Bolton BL3............146 C4
　Denton M34...........113 A8
　7 Failsworth M40.....83 C5
　Handforth SK9........131 A2
　Hyde SK14............113 F8
　Leigh WN2.............75 A8
　Salford M6...........154 A2
　Slattocks OL11........47 D6
Churchbank SK15.......86 D2
Church Bank
　Altrincham WA14......119 B2
　Bolton BL1............148 A3
Church Brow
　Altrincham WA14......119 B2
　Hyde SK14............167 A1
　Mottram in L SK14.....103 A3
Church Cl
　Denton M34...........100 F7
　Glossop SK13.........104 E2
　Handforth SK9........131 D3
　Kearsley M26..........61 B8
　Ramsbottom BL0......138 B1
Church Croft BL8......45 C4
Church Ct
　Altrincham WA15......119 E1
　Bury BL9.............141 A3
　Dukinfield SK16.......166 B1
　Edenfield BL0..........1 D4
　Tyldesley M46.........58 E2
Churchdale Rd M9......64 B4
Church Dr
　Newton-le-W WA12.....89 C1
　Orrell WN5............53 D5
　Prestwich M25........63 A4
Churchfield
　Manchester M21......109 A8
　Shevington WN6.......36 A5
Church Field Cl M26...43 F1
Churchfield Rd 5 M6...80 D5
Churchfields
　Altrincham WA14......119 B1
　Denton M34...........100 E7
　Sale M33.............107 D6
Church Fields OL3.....51 A2
Churchfield Wlk M11 ...165 A4
Church Fold
　Broadbottom SK13....115 C7
　Coppull PR7...........19 F8
Churchgate
　Bolton BL1............145 C3
　Stockport SK1.........169 C1
Churchgate Bldgs
　M1..................163 C4
Church Gn
　Lymm WA13...........117 B8
　Radcliffe M26..........44 D4
　Salford M6...........154 C3
Church Gr
　Hazel Grove SK7.....124 E2
　Wigan WN1............151 B4
Churchill Ave
　Ainsworth BL2.........26 D1
　Fowley Common WA3 ...92 B4
　Manchester M16.......97 D2
Churchill Cl 4 OL10 ...46 E8
Churchill Cres
　Marple SK6...........125 D7
　Sale SK8..............99 E1
Churchill Ct M6......154 C2
Churchill Dr
　Bolton BL4............147 B1
　Little Lever BL3........43 C3
Churchill Pl M30......79 C4
Churchill Rd WA14....119 D7
Churchill St E OL4......67 A6
Churchill St
　3 Bolton BL2.........148 C3
　Oldham OL4............67 A6
　Rochdale, Greave OL11...30 C8
　Rochdale, Spotland Fold OL11,
　OL12.................14 C1
　Stockport SK4........169 A3
Churchill Way
　Salford M5, M6........81 A2
　Stretford M17.........96 C7
Church La
　Alderley Edge SK9....137 A2
　Bramhall SK7.........132 C2
　Culcheth WA3..........91 F3
　Edenfield BL0..........1 D4
　Golborne WA3.........90 D7
　Manchester, Broughton Park
　M7..................63 C1
　Manchester, Burnage
　M19..................110 F6
　Manchester, Harpurhey
　M9..................157 B4

Church La continued
　Manchester, Harpurhey M40,
　M9..................157 C3
　Marple SK6...........125 F5
　Mossley OL5...........68 D1
　Oldham OL1...........153 C3
　Prestwich M25.........63 A4
　Rochdale OL16........139 C3
　Romiley SK6..........113 C2
　Sale M33.............107 E6
　Shevington WN6.......36 A6
　Uppermill OL3.........51 D1
　Westhoughton BL5.....39 E3
　Whitefield M45........44 E1
　Wrightington Bar WN6 ...18 D8
Churchlands La WN6 ...19 F2
Churchley Cl SK3.....123 A6
Churchley Rd SK3.....123 A7
Church Lo SK4........110 E2
Church Manor SK4 ...168 B4
Church Mdw
　Dukinfield SK14........101 C3
　Whitefield BL9.........45 C4
Church Mdws
　Bolton BL2............25 F3
　Uppermill OL3.........68 E5
Church Meadow Gdns
　SK14.................101 C3
Church Mews
　Bury BL8..............27 C1
　Denton M34...........100 E3
　1 Radcliffe M26........44 C1
Church Pl OL10........29 D2
Church Rd
　Bolton BL1............142 B2
　Cheadle SK8..........132 B8
　Eccles M30............79 F2
　Farnworth BL4.........60 E8
　Gatley SK8...........122 A5
　Handforth SK9........131 D3
　Hollingworth SK14.....171 A4
　Kearsley M26..........61 A8
　Marple SK6...........126 E6
　Middleton M24........65 D7
　Platt Bridge WN2......56 B3
　Ramsbottom BL0.......11 E8
　Rochdale OL16.........31 B6
　Sale M33.............108 D4
　Shaw OL2.............149 B2
　Stockport SK4........169 B2
　Tyldesley M29.........77 C6
　Uppermill, Lydgate OL3 ...68 E5
　Uppermill OL3.........51 A2
　Urmston M41...........95 C1
　Walkden M28..........60 D3
　Wilmslow SK9........136 E4
　Wythenshawe M22.....109 E1
Church Rd E M33.....108 D4
Church Rd W M33.....108 D4
Church Road Prim Sch
　BL1..................142 B2
Church St E
　Oldham OL4...........67 E8
　Radcliffe M26..........44 C3
Church St S SK3.....104 E2
Church St W M26......44 B3
Churchside BL4........60 B7
Churchside Cl M9.....64 D2
Church St
　Adlington PR7.........21 A7
　Ashton-u-L M26.......26 D1
　Altrincham WA14......119 D5
　Ashton-u-L OL6......166 B2
　Aspull WN2............38 B6
　Atherton M46..........58 D3
　Bacup OL13............3 C8
　Blackrod BL6..........21 C2
　Bolton BL2.............25 D5
　Bury BL9.............141 A3
　Bury, Walshaw BL8.....26 F5
　Cheadle SK8..........122 D6
　Delph OL3.............50 E4
　Denton M34...........100 F7
　Droylsden M43.........84 B1
　Dukinfield SK16.......166 B1
　Eccles M30............79 F2
　Farnworth BL4.........60 E8
　Glossop SK13.........104 D2
　Golborne WA3.........74 B1
　Hadfield SK13.........104 A4
　Heywood OL10.........29 D2
　Hindley WN2...........56 D5
　Horwich BL6...........22 C3
　Hyde SK14............167 A1
　Ince-in-M WN3........151 C2
　Leigh WN7.............75 F5
　Littleborough OL15.....16 B5
　Little Lever BL3........42 F3
　Manchester M4.......159 A2
　5 Marple SK6.........125 F6
　Marple SK6...........126 A5
　Middleton M24.........47 A2
　Newhey OL16..........32 A5
　Newton-le-W WA12.....89 E4
　Oldham OL1...........153 C3
　Oldham, Salem OL4 ....67 E5
　Orrell WN5............53 E5
　Pendlebury M27........80 B8
　Radcliffe M26..........44 B2
　Rawtenstall BB4........2 E8
　Rochdale, Greengate
　OL16.................15 D3
　Rochdale, Mitchel Hey
　OL12.................139 B3
　Romiley SK6..........113 A5
　Royton OL2............48 D4

Church St continued
　Stalybridge SK15.......86 A2
　Standish WN6..........19 E1
　Stockport SK4........169 B3
　Stretford M32..........96 C1
　Swinton M27...........79 E8
　Tintwistle SK13.......104 A7
　Up Holland WN8.......53 C7
　Westhoughton BL5.....39 E2
　Whitworth OL12.......14 C8
　Wigan, Norley WN5.....54 B6
　Wigan WN1...........150 C4
　Wilmslow SK9........137 B7
Church Stile OL16.....139 C3
Churchstoke Wlk
　M23..................120 E7
Churchston Ave SK7 ...124 A2
Church Street Cotts 13
　SK6..................125 F6
Church Street Ind Est 8
　M24..................47 A2
Church Terr
　Ashton-in-M WN4......73 B2
　Glossop SK13.........104 D2
　Handforth SK9........131 D4
　Milnrow OL16.........32 A5
　Oldham OL1...........153 C3
Churchtown Ave BL2...42 F7
Church View
　6 Altrincham WA14 ...119 C1
　Handforth SK9........131 A2
　Hyde SK14............167 A1
　Irlam M44.............94 A2
　Lymm WA13...........117 B4
　Mottram in L SK14.....103 A3
　Rochdale OL12.........13 E2
　Whitefield M45........44 D3
Church Wlk
　Farnworth BL4.........60 C8
　Glossop SK13.........104 E2
　5 Royton OL2.........48 D4
　Stalybridge SK15.......86 A3
　Swinton M27...........61 F4
　Wilmslow SK9........136 F6
Churchwood Rd M20...110 B3
Churchwood View
　WA13.................117 A2
Churnet St M40......157 A1
Churnett Cl BL5........39 F2
Churning Terr M44.....94 B3
Churston Ave M9......64 E4
Churton Ave
　Manchester M14.......98 B2
　Sale M33.............107 F3
Churton Gr WN6........19 B2
Churton Rd M18........99 C3
Churwell Ave SK4.....110 F4
Cicero St
　Manchester M9.......157 C4
　Oldham OL12..........49 A1
Cinder Hill La M24, OL1,
　OL2..................48 A3
Cinder La BL2........142 A3
Cinder St M4.........159 C2
Cinnabar Dr M24.......46 F2
Cinnamon Ave WN2.....57 A4
Cinnamon Brow WN8 ...53 C6
Cinnamon Cl
　Rochdale OL12.........139 A4
　Wythenshawe M22....121 E8
Cipher St M4.........159 C3
Circle Ct M32..........95 F4
Circle S M17...........96 E6
Circle The M32........95 F4
Circuit The
　Alderley Edge SK9....132 A7
　Cheadle SK8..........132 A7
　Manchester M20.......110 B5
　Stockport SK3........123 C6
　Wilmslow SK9........136 D5
Circular Rd
　Denton M34...........100 E1
　Manchester, Hilton Park
　M25.................63 B2
　Manchester, Withington
　M20..................110 B5
Cirencester Cl M38....60 A6
Ciss La M41............95 E2
Citrus Way M6.........81 A2
City Ave M34.........100 E2
CITY CENTRE.........162 C4
City Coll (City Campus)
　M1..................163 A4
City Coll Manchester
　Abraham Moss Campus
　M8..................156 B4
City Coll Manchester
　Fielden Campus
　M20.................109 F4
City Coll Manchester
　Northenden Campus
　M23..................109 C1
City Course Trad Est
　M11..................165 A3
City Court Trad Est
　M4..................159 C2
City Gdns M34.........100 D2
City of Manchester
　Stadium (Manchester
　City FC) M11.........160 C2
CITY PARK............161 B1
City Point M13........158 B2
City Rd
　Manchester M15......162 A4
　Walkden M28..........78 A8
　Wigan WN5............54 B7

City Rd E M15........162 C3
City S M15...........162 C3
City Wlk M27...........80 B8
Civic Wlk 1 OL10......29 D2
Clacton Wlk M13......163 C3
Clague St M11.........83 A2
Claife Ave M40.........65 B2
CLAMMERCLOUGH......42 F1
Clandon Ave M30......79 B1
Clanwood Cl WN3......54 E2
Clapgate SK6.........112 F1
Clap Gate La WN3.....54 E3
Clapgate Rd 3 OL11 ...13 E1
Clapham St M40.......83 C8
Clara Gorton Ct 12
　OL16.................31 B6
Clara St
　Oldham OL9............66 C4
　Rochdale OL11.......139 C1
　Whitworth OL12........4 D1
Clare Ave SK9........131 C3
Clarebank BL1.........40 F7
Clare Cl BL8............27 D5
Clare Ct
　Farnworth BL4.......147 C1
　4 Stockport SK1......112 A1
Claremont Ave
　Altrincham WA14......119 E8
　Hindley WN2...........56 F5
　Manchester, Heaton Chapel
　SK4..................111 C5
　Manchester, Withington
　M20..................110 A5
　Marple SK6...........125 C6
Claremont Ct 6 M20...110 A3
Claremont Dr
　Altrincham WA14......119 E8
　Walkden M38..........60 B5
Claremont Gdns OL6...85 E5
Claremont Gr
　Altrincham WA15......119 E3
　Manchester M20.......110 A3
Claremont Prim Sch
　M14..................98 A3
Claremont Range M18 ...99 F4
Claremont Rd
　Billinge WN5...........71 E5
　Cheadle SK8.........132 A8
　Culcheth WA3.........91 D4
　Manchester M14.......98 B3
　Manchester M16.......97 F3
　Milnrow OL16.........31 F5
　Rochdale OL11.........30 C7
　Sale M33.............108 B5
　Salford M6............80 D5
　Stockport SK4........124 B4
Claremont St
　Ashton-u-L OL6........85 D4
　Chadderton OL9........48 C1
　Failsworth M35........83 F8
　Oldham OL8............66 F2
Clarence Arc OL6.....166 B2
Clarence Ave
　Oldham OL8............66 D4
　Urmston M17..........95 F7
　Whitefield M45.........63 A7
Clarence Cl BL9......141 A4
Clarence Ct
　14 Bolton BL1........145 B4
　Newton-le-W WA12.....89 A4
　Wilmslow SK9.........137 A6
Clarence Ho 1 SK15 ...101 F8
Clarence Rd
　Altrincham WA15......119 F3
　Ashton-u-L OL6......166 C4
　Manchester, Heaton Chapel
　SK4..................111 C5
　Manchester, Longsight
　M13..................98 E4
　Swinton M27...........79 C7
Clarence St
　6 Ashton-in-M WN4 ...72 F5
　Bolton BL1............145 C4
　Farnworth BL4.........42 E1
　Golborne WA3.........74 A1
　Hyde SK14............167 B4
　Ince-in-M WN2.........56 A3
　Leigh WN7.............76 B4
　19 Manchester M3 ...158 C1
　Rochdale OL12.........14 D2
　Royton OL2............49 A3
　Salford M7............158 A4
　Salford M7............158 B4
　Stalybridge SK15, SK16...85 C1
　Tyldesley M46.........58 E2
　Clarence Yd WN1.....150 C4
Clarendon Ave
　Altrincham WA15......119 E5
　Stockport SK4........168 B3
Clarendon Cottage Sch
　M30..................79 F3
Clarendon Cotts SK9 ...131 A3
Clarendon Cres
　Eccles M30............79 F3
　Sale M33.............108 D5
Clarendon Fields Prim Sch
　SK16.................101 B8
Clarendon Gr BL2.....148 B2
Clarendon Ind Est
　SK14.................167 B3
Clarendon PI SK14.....167 B2
Clarendon Prim Sch
　BL3..................145 B1
Clarendon Rd
　Bolton BL3............148 C3
　Denton M34...........101 B2
　Droylsden M34........100 B7

Clarendon Rd *continued*
Eccles M30 . . . . .79 F3
Hazel Grove SK7 . . . . .124 F3
Hyde SK14 . . . . .167 B3
Irlam M44 . . . . .105 F7
Manchester M16 . . . . .97 D2
Sale M33 . . . . .79 F8
Urmston M41 . . . . .94 E3
Clarendon Rd W M21 . . .97 B2
Clarendon Recn Ctr
  M5 . . . . .81 A2
Clarendon Road Com Prim
  Sch M30 . . . . .79 F3
Clarendon St
Bolton BL3 . . . . .145 B1
Bury BL9 . . . . .141 A4
Dukinfield SK16 . . . . .101 A8
Dukinfield SK16 . . . . .101 B8
Hyde SK14 . . . . .167 A3
Manchester M15 . . . . .162 C3
Mossley OL5 . . . . .86 D8
Reddish SK5 . . . . .169 C3
Rochdale OL16 . . . . .31 B4
Whitefield M45 . . . . .62 F8
Clare Rd
Manchester M19 . . . . .111 A8
Reddish SK5 . . . . .169 C4
Clare St
Denton M34 . . . . .100 E4
Manchester M1 . . . . .163 B3
Salford M5 . . . . .81 C1
Claribel St M11 . . . . .164 B4
Claridge Rd M21 . . . . .97 A1
Clarington Gr WN1 . . . . .151 B3
Clarington Pl WN2 . . . . .151 C3
Clarion St M4 . . . . .159 C3
Clark Ave M18 . . . . .99 E5
Clarke Ave
Culcheth WA3 . . . . .92 A4
Salford M5 . . . . .161 B3
Clarke Brow M24 . . . . .47 A1
Clarke Cres
Altrincham WA15 . . . . .120 B3
Walkden M38 . . . . .59 E6
Clarke Ind Est M32 . . . . . .96 A5
Clarkes Croft BL9 . . . . . .141 C3
Clarke's La OL12 . . . . .139 A4
Clarke St
Altrincham WA14 . . . . .119 D7
Ashton-u-L OL7 . . . . .100 F8
Bolton BL1 . . . . .144 C4
Farnworth BL4 . . . . .60 E7
Heywood OL10 . . . . .29 D2
Leigh WN7 . . . . .75 E4
Rochdale OL16 . . . . .15 B2
Clarkethorn Terr SK5 . . .169 B3
Clark's Cross SK5 . . . . . .63 D8
CLARKSFIELD 67 D7
Clarksfield Prim Sch
  OL4 . . . . .67 C6
Clarksfield Rd OL4 . . . . . .67 C6
Clarksfield St OL4 . . . . . .67 C6
Clarkson Cl
Denton M34 . . . . .100 D2
Middleton M24 . . . . .64 C7
Clark Way SK14 . . . . .167 A3
Clarkwell Cl OL1 . . . . . . .153 B4
Clatford Wlk 2 M9 . . . . .157 A3
Claude Ave M27 . . . . .79 D8
Claude Rd M21 . . . . .109 B7
Claude St
Eccles M30 . . . . .79 B3
Manchester M8 . . . . .64 A1
Swinton M27 . . . . .79 D8
Wigan WN5 . . . . .54 D6
Claudia Sq SK15 . . . . .86 E5
Claughton Ave
Bolton BL2 . . . . .42 F7
Walkden M28 . . . . .78 C8
Claughton Rd BL8 . . . . . . .26 F5
Claverham Wlk 4
  M23 . . . . .120 E7
Claverton Rd M23 . . . . . .120 E5
Claxton Ave M9 . . . . .64 D3
Clay Bank M43 . . . . .83 F1
Claybank Dr BL8 . . . . .26 E7
Claybank St OL10 . . . . . . .29 C3
Claybank Terr OL5 . . . . . .68 E4
Claybar Dr M30 . . . . .79 E3
Claybarn Mews M44 . . . . .94 B2
Claybridge Cl WN5 . . . . . .36 B1
Claybrook Cl M46 . . . . . . .58 A2
Claybrook Wlk M11 . . . . . .83 A1
Clayburn Rd M15 . . . . . . .162 B2
Claycourt Ave M30 . . . . . .79 B4
Claydon Dr
Ince-in-M WN3 . . . . .151 C1
Little Lever M26 . . . . .43 C3
Clayfield Dr OL11 . . . . .29 F8
Claygate Dr M9 . . . . .64 D5
Clayhill Gr WA3 . . . . .91 B8
Clayhill Wlk M9 . . . . .64 E1
Clay La
Altrincham WA15 . . . . .120 D4
Handforth SK9 . . . . .131 C5
Rochdale OL11 . . . . .29 E8
Wilmslow SK9 . . . . .136 C4
Wythenshawe M23 . . . . . . .120 F4
Claylands Cl SK14 . . . . . .171 A4
Claymere Ave OL11 . . . . . .29 E8
Claymore OL1 . . . . .153 B3
Claymore St
Bolton BL3 . . . . .147 C3
Droylsden M18 . . . . .99 E6
Claypool Prim Sch BL6 . .22 F1
Claypool Rd BL6 . . . . .22 E1

Clay St
Bolton BL7 . . . . .25 A7
  3 Littleborough OL15 . . .15 F5
Oldham OL8 . . . . .66 E4
Claythorpe Wlk 2 M8 . .63 E2
CLAYTON 83 C2
Clayton Ave
Bolton BL3 . . . . .148 C1
Golborne WA3 . . . . .90 E8
Manchester M20 . . . . .110 B4
Rawtenstall BB4 . . . . .1 E8
Claytonbrook Rd M11 . . .83 D1
Clayton Cl
Bury BL8 . . . . .26 F1
Manchester M15 . . . . .162 B1
Clayton Ct M11 . . . . .165 C3
Clayton Hall Rd M11 . . . .83 C2
Clayton Ho WN7 . . . . .75 C5
Clayton La M11 . . . . .83 B1
  M12 . . . . .165 A3
Clayton La S M11,
  M12 . . . . .165 A3
Claytons Cl OL4 . . . . .67 F7
Clayton St
Bolton BL3 . . . . .148 C1
Chadderton OL9 . . . . .66 A3
Denton M34 . . . . .100 F2
Droylsden M43 . . . . .83 B2
  5 Dukinfield SK16 . . . . . .101 D8
  5 Failsworth M35 . . . . . . .83 F7
Rochdale OL12 . . . . .15 B2
Wigan WN3 . . . . .150 B3
CLAYTON VALE 83 C2
Cleabarrow Dr M28 . . . . . .78 A5
Cleadon Ave M18 . . . . .99 C4
Cleadon Dr S BL8 . . . . . . .27 C5
Clearwater Dr M20 . . . . .109 F5
Cleavley St M30 . . . . .79 B2
Clee Ave M13 . . . . .98 F2
Cleethorpes Ave M9 . . . . .64 B3
Cleeve Rd
Oldham OL4 . . . . .67 C6
Wythenshawe M23 . . . . . . .109 A2
Cleeve Way SK8 . . . . .132 B6
Clegg Hall Rd OL15,
  OL16 . . . . .15 E1
Clegg Pl 2 OL6 . . . . .85 D4
Clegg's Bldgs BL1 . . . . . .145 B4
Clegg's Ct OL12 . . . . .4 C2
Clegg's La M38 . . . . .60 A5
Clegg St
  5 Bacup OL13 . . . . .3 C8
Bolton BL2 . . . . .148 C3
Droylsden M43 . . . . .83 F1
Littleborough OL15 . . . . . . .15 F7
Milnrow OL16 . . . . .32 A5
Oldham, Grotton OL4 . . . . . .68 A6
Oldham OL4 . . . . .67 B8
Romiley SK6 . . . . .112 F3
Tyldesley M29 . . . . .77 A5
Whitefield M45 . . . . .62 F7
Whitworth OL12 . . . . .4 C2
Cleggswood Ave OL15 . . .16 A3
Clelland St BL4 . . . . .60 E7
Clematis Wlk M27 . . . . . . .61 E2
Clement Ave M46 . . . . .58 A2
Clement Ct
  3 Droylsden M11 . . . . . . .99 F7
  6 Rochdale OL16 . . . . .31 B6
Clementina St OL12 . . . . . .14 F1
Clementine Cl 8 M6 . . . .81 B2
Clementine Ct 8 M6 . . . .81 B2
Clement Rd SK6 . . . . .126 C7
Clement Royds St
  OL12 . . . . .139 B4
Clement St
Oldham OL9 . . . . .66 B3
Stockport SK4 . . . . .169 B3
Clement Stott Cl M9 . . . . .64 F4
Cleminson St M3 . . . . . . .158 A2
Clemshaw Cl OL10 . . . . . . .29 C1
Clerewood Ave SK8 . . . . .131 B7
Clerke St BL9 . . . . .140 C2
Clerks Ct M5 . . . . .80 B2
Clevedon Ave M41 . . . . . . .96 A2
Clevedon Dr WN3 . . . . . . .54 D4
Clevedon Rd OL9 . . . . .48 B1
Clevedon St M9 . . . . .157 B3
Cleveland Ave
Hyde SK14 . . . . .101 C2
Manchester M19 . . . . .99 B2
Salford M6 . . . . .80 C3
Wigan WN3 . . . . .54 C3
Cleveland Cl
Ashton-in-M WN4 . . . . .73 C4
Bolton BL3 . . . . .146 B4
Cleveland Gr OL2 . . . . .48 C3
Cleveland Rd
Altrincham WA15 . . . . .119 F3
Manchester, Crumpsall
  M8 . . . . .64 B2
Stockport SK4 . . . . .168 A4
Clevelands Prep Sch
Bolton BL1 . . . . .40 E7
Bolton BL1 . . . . .144 A3
Cleveland St 8 BL3 . . . . .146 B4
Cleveleys Ave
Bolton BL3 . . . . .148 C4
Bury BL9 . . . . .44 E7
Gatley SK8 . . . . .122 B1
Manchester M21 . . . . .109 C7
Rochdale OL16 . . . . .31 B3

Cleveleys Gr M7 . . . . .155 B3
Cleves Ct OL10 . . . . .29 C1
Clevlands Cl OL2 . . . . . . .149 A4
Cleworth Cl M29 . . . . .77 C4
Cleworth Rd M24 . . . . .46 F2
Cleworth St M15 . . . . . . .162 A3
Cleworth Wlk M15 . . . . . .162 A3
Clibran St M8 . . . . .156 B2
Cliffdale Dr M22 . . . . .121 E2
Cliff Ave
Ramsbottom BL9 . . . . .11 C2
Salford M7 . . . . .81 C6
Cliffbrook Gr 2 SK9 . . . .131 D2
Cliff Cres M7 . . . . .155 A3
Cliff Dale 3 SK15 . . . . . .101 F8
Cliffdale Dr M8 . . . . .64 A1
Cliffe Rd SK13 . . . . .116 D8
Cliffe St OL15 . . . . .6 D2
Cliff Gr SK4 . . . . .168 B4
Cliff Grange M7 . . . . .155 A3
Cliff Hill Rd OL2 . . . . .32 D1
Cliffmere Cl SK8 . . . . .122 F3
Cliff Mount BL0 . . . . .138 B3
Clifford Ave
Altrincham WA15 . . . . .120 B6
Denton M34 . . . . .100 E5
Clifford Ct M15 . . . . .162 B1
Clifford Ho M20 . . . . .110 B5
Clifford Lamb Ct M9 . . . . .65 B2
Clifford Rd
Bolton BL3 . . . . .146 A2
Poynton SK12 . . . . .133 D3
Wilmslow SK9 . . . . .136 F6
Clifford St
Eccles M30 . . . . .95 B4
Leigh WN7 . . . . .76 B4
Pendlebury M27 . . . . .80 B8
Rochdale OL11 . . . . .139 C1
Cliff Rd
Bury BL9 . . . . .44 F5
Wilmslow SK9 . . . . .137 B8
Cliff Side SK9 . . . . .137 B8
Cliff St OL16 . . . . .15 B1
CLIFTON 61 F3
Clifton Ave
Altrincham WA15 . . . . .119 E5
Culcheth WA3 . . . . .91 D3
Eccles M30 . . . . .79 D3
Salford M6 . . . . .80 B3
Manchester M14 . . . . .110 D8
  2 Oldham OL4 . . . . .67 B5
Tyldesley M29 . . . . .77 C4
Clifton Cl
Heywood OL10 . . . . .29 C1
Manchester M16 . . . . .97 D4
Oldham OL4 . . . . .67 B5
Clifton Cres
Royton OL2 . . . . .49 A3
Wigan WN1 . . . . .37 C2
Clifton Ct
  5 Farnworth BL4 . . . . . . .42 B2
Swinton M27 . . . . .61 B2
Clifton Ctr Pk* M27 . . . . . .62 C2
Clifton Ctry Pk*
  M26&M27 . . . . .61 E5
Clifton Dr
Blackrod BL6 . . . . .21 C3
Gatley, Heald Green
  SK8 . . . . .122 B4
Gatley SK8 . . . . .122 A6
Marple SK6 . . . . .125 F7
Swinton, Clifton Junction
  M27 . . . . .62 C2
Swinton M27 . . . . .61 D2
Wilmslow SK9 . . . . .136 E4
Clifton Gr
Manchester M16 . . . . .162 A1
Swinton M27 . . . . .61 D2
CLIFTON GREEN 62 B3
Clifton Ho WN3 . . . . .150 B1
Clifton Holmes OL3 . . . . . .50 E5
Clifton House Rd M27 . . . .62 A4
Clifton Ind Est* M27 . . . . . .62 C3
CLIFTON JUNCTION 62 C3
Clifton Lo SK2 . . . . .124 A5
Cliftonmill Mdw WA3 . . . .89 F8
Clifton Park Rd SK2 . . . .124 A5
Clifton Pl M25 . . . . .63 A5
Clifton Prim Sch M27 . . . . .61 F3
Clifton Rd
Ashton-in-M WN4 . . . . .72 F6
Blackrod WN5 . . . . .71 D4
Eccles M30 . . . . .79 D3
Leigh WN7 . . . . .75 E2
Manchester, Chorlton-cum-
  Hardy M21 . . . . .109 C8
Prestwich M25 . . . . .62 E4
Sale M33 . . . . .108 B3
Slattocks OL11 . . . . .47 D4
Stockport, Heaton Moor
  SK4 . . . . .168 A4
Urmston M41 . . . . .95 A2
Clifton St
Alderley Edge SK9 . . . . . . .137 A1
Ashton-u-L OL6 . . . . .166 A3
Bolton BL1 . . . . .145 B4
Bury BL9 . . . . .140 C4
Failsworth M35 . . . . .83 F7
Farnworth BL4 . . . . .42 B2
Kearsley BL4 . . . . .60 F7
Leigh WN7 . . . . .75 D5
Manchester, Old Trafford
  M16 . . . . .162 A1
Manchester, Philips Park
  M40 . . . . .160 C4
Milnrow OL16 . . . . .31 F6
  7 Rochdale OL11 . . . . . . .31 A5
Tyldesley M29 . . . . .77 E8

Clifton St *continued*
  1 Uppermill OL3 . . . . . . .69 B5
  4 Wigan, Water Heyes
  WN1 . . . . .37 C1
Wigan, Worsley Mesnes
  WN3 . . . . .55 A4
Clifton Sta M27 . . . . .62 C2
Clifton View M27 . . . . .61 E4
Clifton Villas 5 M35 . . . . .66 A1
Cliftonville Dr M6, M27 . . .80 B6
Cliftonville Rd OL16 . . . . . .48 C8
Clinton Ave M14 . . . . .46 D3
Clinton Gdns M14 . . . . .98 A2
Clinton Ho 3 M5 . . . . . . .154 C1
Clinton St 7 OL6 . . . . .85 D4
Clinton Wlk 4 OL4 . . . . . . .67 A6
Clippers Quay M50 . . . . . .161 A2
Clipsley Cres OL4 . . . . . . .49 F4
Cliston Wlk SK7 . . . . .124 A2
Clitheroe Cl OL10 . . . . .46 A1
Clitheroe Dr BL8 . . . . .26 F2
Clitheroe Rd M13 . . . . .98 F3
Clito St WN5 . . . . .157 C4
Clive Ave
Whitefield M45 . . . . .44 E1
Clivedale Pl BL1 . . . . .145 C3
Cliveley Wlk M27 . . . . .80 B8
Clive Lloyd Ct M32 . . . . . . .96 E3
Clively Ave M27 . . . . .62 C1
Clive Rd
Failsworth M35 . . . . .83 E6
Westhoughton BL5 . . . . .57 E6
Clive St
Ashton-u-L OL7 . . . . .85 A5
Bolton BL2 . . . . .148 A3
Manchester M4 . . . . .159 B3
  3 Oldham OL8 . . . . .66 D2
Clivewood Wlk M12 . . . . . .164 B2
Clivia Gr M7 . . . . .155 A2
Cloak St M1 . . . . .163 A3
Clock House Ave M43 . . . .83 E3
Clockhouse Mews M43 . . .83 E3
Clock St 11 OL9 . . . . .66 B2
Clock Tower Cl
Hyde SK14 . . . . .167 B1
Manchester M8 . . . . .59 F3
Clod La BB4 . . . . .1 C8
Cloister Ave WN7 . . . . .57 D1
Cloister Cl SK16 . . . . .101 C6
Cloister Rd SK4 . . . . .110 D2
Cloister St
Bolton BL1 . . . . .142 C2
Manchester M9 . . . . .157 C4
Cloisters The
Cheadle SK8 . . . . .123 A5
  8 Rawtenstall BB4 . . . . . . .1 A7
Sale M33 . . . . .108 D4
Westhoughton BL5 . . . . .57 E5
Clondberry Ct M29 . . . . . . .59 E1
Clopton Wlk M15 . . . . . . .162 B1
Closebrook Rd WN5 . . . . . .54 D6
Close La
Hindley WN2 . . . . .56 E3
Leigh WN2 . . . . .57 B1
Closes Farm BL3 . . . . . . .146 B2
Close St WN2 . . . . .56 F6
Close The
Altrincham WA14 . . . . .119 C5
Bolton BL2 . . . . .25 B3
Bury BL8 . . . . .27 A3
Denton M34 . . . . .100 D4
Middleton M24 . . . . .114 B1
Newton-le-W WA12 . . . . . . .89 C1
Over Hulton M46 . . . . .58 F5
Stalybridge SK15 . . . . .85 F4
Clothorn Rd M20 . . . . .110 B4
Cloudberry Wlk M31 . . . . .105 F3
Cloudstock Gr M38 . . . . . .59 E5
CLOUGH 49 D6
Clough Ave
Handforth SK9 . . . . .131 B2
Marple SK6 . . . . .126 C6
Sale M33 . . . . .107 D1
Westhoughton BL5 . . . . .57 F7
Cloughbank M26 . . . . .61 C7
Clough Bank
Littleborough OL15 . . . . . . .16 A8
Manchester M9 . . . . .64 D2
Clough Cl OL4 . . . . .68 E6
Clough Dr M25 . . . . .62 E4
Clough End Rd SK14 . . . .102 F1
Cloughfield Ave M5 . . . . .161 B4
Clough Fold
Kearsley M26 . . . . .61 A7
Westhoughton BL5 . . . . .57 F8
Clough Gate
Hyde SK14 . . . . .113 F8
  6 Oldham OL8 . . . . .66 D2
Cloughgate Ho 5 OL8 . . .66 D2
Clough Gr
Ashton-in-M WN4 . . . . .72 F5
Whitefield M45 . . . . .44 D2
Clough Ho M9 . . . . .65 A2
Clough House Dr WN7 . . . .76 B5
Clough House La OL12 . . . .15 B6
Clough La
Heywood OL10 . . . . .29 C4
Prestwich M25 . . . . .62 F4
Uppermill OL3 . . . . .69 B5
Clough Mdw
Bolton BL1 . . . . .23 F3
Romiley SK6 . . . . .113 C5
Clough Meadow Rd
  M26 . . . . .43 E3

Clough Park Ave OL4 . . . . .68 E6
Clough Rd
Droylsden M43 . . . . .84 B2
Failsworth M35 . . . . .84 A6
Littleborough OL15 . . . . . . .16 A7
Manchester M9 . . . . .64 F1
Middleton M24 . . . . .47 A2
Shaw OL2 . . . . .49 D6
Cloughs Ave OL9 . . . . .65 D8
Cloughside SK12 . . . . .135 E6
Clough Side
Manchester M9 . . . . .64 F1
Marple SK6 . . . . .126 C7
Clough St
  8 Bacup OL13 . . . . .3 D8
Failsworth M40 . . . . .83 C4
Kearsley BL4 . . . . .60 F7
Middleton M24 . . . . .47 B2
Radcliffe M26 . . . . .44 C2
Wardle OL12 . . . . .15 C6
Clough Terr OL15 . . . . .16 A7
Clough The
Ashton-u-L OL7 . . . . .85 B6
Brinnington SK5 . . . . .112 B6
Garswood WN4 . . . . .72 D4
Cloughton Wlk M40 . . . . . .83 D5
Clough Top Rd M9 . . . . . . .65 A2
Clough Wlk SK5 . . . . .112 B6
Cloughwood Cres
  WN6 . . . . .35 D6
Clovelly Ave
Leigh WN7 . . . . .75 F8
Oldham OL6 . . . . .66 C2
Clovelly Rd
Manchester M21 . . . . .109 C8
Stockport SK2 . . . . .124 C8
Swinton M27 . . . . .79 C6
Clovelly St
Failsworth M40 . . . . .83 D5
Rochdale OL11 . . . . .30 B3
Clover Ave SK3 . . . . .170 A1
Cloverbank Ave M19 . . . .110 D4
Clover Cres OL8 . . . . .67 C3
Clover Croft M33 . . . . . . .108 D1
Cloverdale Dr WN4 . . . . . .73 C2
Cloverdale Sq BL1 . . . . . .142 A1
Cloverfield Wlk 6
  M28 . . . . .60 D3
CLOVER HALL 15 C1
Clover Hall Cres OL16 . . . .15 C1
Cloverlea Prim Sch
  WA15 . . . . .120 B5
Cloverley OL3 . . . . .108 B2
Cloverley Dr WA15 . . . . . .120 A4
Clover Rd
Altrincham WA15 . . . . .120 B5
Romiley SK6 . . . . .113 C3
Clover St
Rochdale OL12 . . . . .139 B4
Wigan WN6 . . . . .37 B2
Clover View OL16 . . . . .31 C7
Clowes St
Manchester M12 . . . . .164 C3
Oldham OL9 . . . . .66 B2
Salford M3 . . . . .158 B2
Club St
Billinge WA11 . . . . .71 A1
Droylsden M11 . . . . .99 F7
Clumber Cl SK12 . . . . .133 E3
Clumber Rd
Poynton SK12 . . . . .133 E3
Reddish M18 . . . . .99 F4
Clunton Ave BL3 . . . . .146 B4
Clutha Rd SK3 . . . . .123 F4
Clwyd Ave SK3 . . . . .170 A3
Clyde Ave M45 . . . . .62 F6
Clyde Ct OL16 . . . . .31 B6
Clyde Rd
Manchester M20 . . . . .110 A5
Radcliffe M26 . . . . .43 F5
Stockport SK3 . . . . .123 C7
Tyldesley M29 . . . . .77 C7
Clydesdale Gdns M11 . . . .83 A1
Clydesdale Rise OL3 . . . . .51 D5
Clydesdale St OL8 . . . . . . .66 E4
Clyde St
Ashton-u-L OL7 . . . . .100 F8
Bolton BL1 . . . . .143 B2
Leigh WN7 . . . . .76 B4
Oldham OL1 . . . . .49 C1
Clyde Terr M26 . . . . .43 F5
Clyne St M32 . . . . .96 F4
Clyne St M32 . . . . .96 F5
Clysbarton Ct SK7 . . . . . .123 D1
Coach House Dr WN6 . . . . .36 B6
Coach Rd
Hollingworth SK14 . . . . . . .103 C5
Tyldesley M29 . . . . .77 C6
Coach St M46 . . . . .58 D3
Coalbrook Wlk M12 . . . . .164 B4
Coalburn St M12 . . . . .165 A2
Coal Pit La
Atherton M46 . . . . .58 B3
Atherton M46 . . . . .58 B4
Leigh, Tamer Lane End
  WN2 . . . . .57 B1
  4 Leigh, Westleigh
  WN7 . . . . .75 E8
Oldham OL8 . . . . .66 E1
Coal Pit Rd BL1 . . . . .23 D7
Coal Rd BL0 . . . . .12 C8
Coalshaw Green Rd
  OL9 . . . . .66 A3
Coatbridge St M11 . . . . . .83 C1

Cobalt Ct SK2 . . . . 124 A5
Cobalt Ave M41 . . . . 95 F6
Cobalt Way M24 . . . . 65 D6
Cobb Cl M8 . . . . 63 E3
Cobbett's Way SK9 . . . . 136 F4
Cobble Bank M9 . . . . 64 D3
Cobblestones OL3 . . . . 50 F3
Cobden Ctr The M50 . . . . 154 C1
Cobden St
 2 Ashton-u-L OL6 . . . . 85 D2
 Bolton, Egerton BL7 . . . . 8 D2
 Bolton, Halliwell BL1 . . . . 143 A3
 Britannia OL13. . . . . . . 4 B8
 Bury BL9 . . . . 141 A3
 Chadderton OL9. . . . . . . 152 B3
 Heywood OL10. . . . . . . 29 D1
 Manchester M9 . . . . 64 E1
 Newton-le-W WA12. . . . . . . 89 D4
 Oldham OL4. . . . . . . 49 D1
 Radcliffe M26 . . . . 43 F6
 Salford M6 . . . . 81 A4
 12 Tyldesley M29 . . . . 59 C7
Coberley Ave M41 . . . . 94 F4
Cob Hall Rd 6 M32. . . . . . . 96 C1
Cobham Ave
 Bolton BL3 . . . . 147 A3
 Manchester M40 . . . . 65 C2
Cob Kiln La M41. . . . . . . 95 D1
Coblers Hill OL3. . . . . . . 50 F5
Cob Moor Rd WN5. . . . . . . 53 D1
Cobourg St M1. . . . . . . 163 B4
Coburg Ave M7 . . . . 158 A4
Cochrane Ave M12. . . . . . . 164 B1
Cochrane St BL3 . . . . 145 C1
COCKBROOK 85 D2
Cock Brow SK14 . . . . 114 C7
Cock Clod St M26 . . . . 44 C1
Cockcroft Rd M5 . . . . 81 B2
Cockcroft St M9 . . . . 64 D1
Cockerell Springs 1
 BL2. . . . . . . 148 A2
COCKER HILL 86 B2
Cocker Hill SK15. . . . . . . 86 B2
Cocker Mill La OL2 . . . . 48 F5
Cocker St M38 . . . . 60 A4
Cockey Moor Rd BL2,
 BL8. . . . . . . 26 E1
Cockhall La OL12 . . . . 4 C1
Cock Hall La OL12 . . . . 14 C8
Coconut Gr M6 . . . . 81 B2
Codale Dr BL2. . . . . . . 25 F1
Coddington Ave M11. . . . . . . 99 E8
Code La BL5. . . . . . . 57 A6
Cody Ct M50 . . . . 96 E8
Coe St BL3 . . . . 145 C1
Coghlan Cl M11 . . . . 83 B2
Coin St OL2 . . . . 48 E4
Cojeton Ho M9 . . . . 64 F5
Coke St W M7 . . . . 155 C4
Coke St M7 . . . . 155 C4
Colborne Ave
 Eccles M30 . . . . 79 B2
 Reddish SK5 . . . . 99 F3
 Romiley SK6 . . . . 113 C2
Colbourne Ave M8. . . . . . . 63 F1
Colbourne Gr SK14 . . . . 102 E3
Colbourne Way SK14. . . . . . . 102 E3
Colby Rd WN3 . . . . 55 A2
Colby Wlk M40 . . . . 83 A7
Colchester Ave
 Bolton BL2. . . . . . . 42 E8
 Manchester M25 . . . . 63 C2
Colchester Cl M23 . . . . 108 C1
Colchester Dr BL4 . . . . 42 A1
Colchester Pl SK4 . . . . 168 C3
Colchester Wlk 1
 OL1. . . . . . . 153 C3
Colclough Cl M40 . . . . 83 B6
Coldalhurst La M29. . . . . . . 77 B5
Coldfield Dr M23 . . . . 120 F6
Cold Greave Cl OL16. . . . . . . 32 C4
COLD HURST 153 B4
Coldhurst St W OL1. . . . . . . 153 B4
Coldhurst St OL1 . . . . 153 B4
Coldstone Dr WN4. . . . . . . 72 D4
Coldstream Ave M9 . . . . 64 D4
Cole Ave WA12 . . . . 89 C4
Colebrook Dr M40. . . . . . . 83 A6
Colebrook Rd WA15 . . . . 120 A6
Coleby Ave
 Manchester M16 . . . . 97 C4
 Wythenshawe M22 . . . . 121 F1
Coleclough Pl WA3 . . . . 91 F4
Coledale Dr M24 . . . . 46 C2
Coleford Gr BL1 . . . . 145 B2
Colemore Ave M20 . . . . 110 D3
Colenso Ct 2 BL2 . . . . 148 C3
Colenso Gr SK4 . . . . 168 B3
Colenso Rd BL2 . . . . 42 D7
Colenso St OL8. . . . . . . 66 D3
Coleport Cl SK8 . . . . 123 A1
Coleridge Ave
 Middleton M24. . . . . . . 47 C3
 Radcliffe M26 . . . . 43 E4
 Wigan WN5 . . . . 54 A6
Coleridge Cl SK5 . . . . 99 E1
Coleridge Pl WN3 . . . . 54 F3
Coleridge Rd
 Littleborough OL15 . . . . 15 F2
 Manchester M16 . . . . 97 C3
 Oldham OL1. . . . . . . 49 D1
 Ramsbottom BL8 . . . . 10 F2

Coleridge Rd continued
 Reddish SK5 . . . . 99 E1
Coleridge Way SK5 . . . . 99 E1
Colerne Way WN2 . . . . 54 D2
Colesbourne Cl M38 . . . . 60 A6
Coleshill Rise WN3 . . . . 54 C2
Coleshill St M40. . . . . . . 160 B3
Colesmere Wlk M40 . . . . 65 D1
Cole St M40. . . . . . . 157 C4
Colgate Cres M14 . . . . 110 B8
Colgate La M5. . . . . . . 161 A2
Colgrove Ave M40 . . . . 65 C2
Colina Dr M7. . . . . . . 155 B1
Colindale Ave M9. . . . . . . 64 E4
Colindale Cl 7 BL3. . . . . . . 144 C1
Colin Murphy Rd M15. . . . . . . 162 B2
Colin Rd SK4. . . . . . . 169 B4
Colin St WN1. . . . . . . 37 C1
Colinton Cl BL1. . . . . . . 143 A1
Collard Cl OL9 . . . . 44 F3
Collard St M46 . . . . 58 B4
Coll Dr M41. . . . . . . 95 D5
College Ave
 Droylsden M43. . . . . . . 99 F8
 Oldham OL8. . . . . . . 66 D3
 Wigan WN1 . . . . 150 C4
College Bsns Ctr
 Bolton BL3 . . . . 145 B2
 Stockport SK2 . . . . 124 A6
 Wilmslow SK9 . . . . 136 F8
College Croft 10 M30 . . . . 79 F2
College Ct
 Rochdale OL12. . . . . . . 139 A3
 Stockport SK4 . . . . 168 A3
College Dr M16. . . . . . . 97 C2
College Farm M9 . . . . 35 A1
College Ho
 Altrincham WA14 . . . . 119 C1
 Stockport SK4. . . . . . . 168 B4
College Land M33 . . . . 158 C1
College Rd
 Manchester M16 . . . . 97 D2
 Oldham OL8 . . . . 66 E4
 Rochdale OL12. . . . . . . 139 B3
 Salford M30 . . . . 80 A2
 Up Holland WN8 . . . . 53 B8
College Way BL3 . . . . 145 B2
Collegiate Way M27 . . . . 61 F3
Collen Cres BL8 . . . . 27 C6
Collett Cl WN1 . . . . 151 B4
Collett St OL1 . . . . 67 C8
Colley St
 Rochdale OL16. . . . . . . 15 B1
 Stretford M32 . . . . 96 F5
Collie Ave M6 . . . . 81 C5
Collier Ave M46 . . . . 31 F7
Collier Brook Ind Est
 M46 . . . . 58 C3
Collier Cl SK14 . . . . 102 E1
Collier Ct M19. . . . . . . 99 A1
Collier Hill OL8. . . . . . . 66 D3
Collier Hill Ave OL8. . . . . . . 66 C3
Colliers Cl WN7 . . . . 75 E2
Collier's Row BL1 . . . . 23 E5
Colliers Row Rd BL1 . . . . 23 E5
Collier St
 Glossop SK13. . . . . . . 116 D8
 3 Hindley WN2 . . . . 56 D6
 Manchester, City Centre
  M3 . . . . 162 B4
 Salford M3. . . . . . . 158 B2
 4 Swinton M27 . . . . 79 F7
Collier Wlk 4 SK14. . . . . . . 102 E1
Colliery La M46. . . . . . . 58 A4
Colliery St
 Droylsden M11. . . . . . . 83 A1
 Manchester M11. . . . . . . 165 B4
Collin Ave M18 . . . . 99 C4
Collingburn Ave M5 . . . . 161 B3
Collingburn Ct M5. . . . . . . 161 B3
Colling Cl M44 . . . . 94 A1
Collingham St M8. . . . . . . 65 C8
Collinge St
 Bury BL8. . . . . . . 27 B4
 Heywood OL10. . . . . . . 29 C2
 Middleton M24. . . . . . . 65 D7
 Platt Bridge WN2. . . . . . . 56 A2
 Shaw OL2. . . . . . . 149 B3
Collingham Rd WA14. . . . . . . 107 C3
Collingham St M8 . . . . 159 B4
Collings St BL1. . . . . . . 143 B2
Collington Cl M12 . . . . 165 A1
Collingwood Ave M43. . . . . . . 83 C3
Collingwood Cl SK12. . . . . . . 134 A3
Collingwood Dr M27. . . . . . . 80 B7
Collingwood Rd
 Manchester M19 . . . . 98 F1
 Newton-le-W WA12. . . . . . . 89 B3
Collingwood St
 Standish WN6 . . . . 19 E1
 Trub OL11. . . . . . . 47 D8
Collingwood Way
 Oldham OL1. . . . . . . 153 C4
 Westhoughton BL5 . . . . 39 E1
Collins La BL5 . . . . 57 F6
Collins St BL3 . . . . 26 F4
Collisdene Rd WN5. . . . . . . 53 E6
Collop Dr OL10 . . . . 46 E7
Coll's La OL3 . . . . 50 D4
COLLYHURST 157 A2
Collyhurst Ave 2 M28. . . . . . . 60 E2
Collyhurst Rd M40. . . . . . . 156 C1
Collyhurst St M40. . . . . . . 160 A4
Coman Gdns M5 . . . . 161 B3
Colmore Dr M9. . . . . . . 65 A4
Colmore Gr BL2 . . . . 25 B4

Colmore St 5 BL2. . . . . . . 25 B3
Colnbrook WN6 . . . . 19 B1
Colne St OL11 . . . . 30 D1
Colonial Rd SK2 . . . . 124 C5
Colshaw Cl 8 M26 . . . . 43 F4
Colshaw Cl S M26 . . . . 43 F4
Colshaw Dr SK9 . . . . 131 D2
Colshaw Rd M23. . . . . . . 121 A4
Colson Dr M24 . . . . 64 F7
Colsterdale Cl OL2. . . . . . . 48 E5
Colt Hill La
 Uppermill OL3 . . . . 68 F8
 Uppermill OL3 . . . . 69 A6
Coltishall Ho SK8 . . . . 123 A5
Coltness Wlk 12 M40. . . . . . . 83 C5
Coltsfoot Cl WN7 . . . . 76 B5
Coltsfoot Dr WA14. . . . . . . 119 B8
Columbia Ave M18. . . . . . . 99 F4
Columbia Rd BL1. . . . . . . 144 C4
Columbia St OL8 . . . . 66 F4
Columbine Cl OL12 . . . . 14 C3
Columbine St M11. . . . . . . 99 D7
Columbine Wlk 8
 M31. . . . . . . 105 F3
Columbus St 2 WN4 . . . . 72 F5
Colville Dr BL8 . . . . 27 B1
Colville Gr
 3 Altrincham WA15 . . . . 120 A6
 Sale M33 . . . . 107 E1
Colville Rd OL1. . . . . . . 48 D1
Colwell Ave M32. . . . . . . 96 B1
Colwell Wlk M9 . . . . 64 B5
Colwick Ave WA14 . . . . 119 E6
Colwith Ave BL2 . . . . 25 E1
Colwood Wlk 15 M8 . . . . 155 C2
Colwyn Ave
 Manchester M14 . . . . 110 B8
 Middleton M24. . . . . . . 65 A6
Colwyn Cres SK5 . . . . 111 F5
Colwyn Dr WN2 . . . . 57 C2
Colwyn Gr
 Atherton M46 . . . . 58 C5
 Bolton BL1. . . . . . . 143 A1
Colwyn Rd
 Bramhall SK7 . . . . 132 F8
 Cheadle SK8 . . . . 122 C1
 Swinton M27 . . . . 79 C6
Colwyn St
 Ashton-u-L OL7 . . . . 85 A6
 Oldham OL9 . . . . 153 A3
 Rochdale OL11. . . . . . . 30 B2
 Salford M6. . . . . . . 154 C3
Colyton Wlk 7 M22 . . . . 121 F3
Combe Cl M11. . . . . . . 83 B3
Combermere Ave
 M20 . . . . 110 A7
Combermere Cl
 Cheadle SK8 . . . . 122 F4
 Tyldesley M29 . . . . 59 B1
Combermere St SK16 . . . . 166 C1
Combs Bank BL3 . . . . 171 A2
Combs Fold 51 SK13. . . . . . . 171 A2
Combs Gdns 2 SK13. . . . . . . 171 A1
Combs Lea 3 SK13. . . . . . . 171 A1
Combs Mews 4 SK13 . . . . 171 A2
Combs Terr 50 SK13. . . . . . . 171 A2
Combs Way 52 SK13. . . . . . . 171 A2
Comer Terr 3 M33 . . . . 108 A4
Comet Rd WN5. . . . . . . 54 C8
Commerce Way M17. . . . . . . 96 C5
Commercial Ave SK8. . . . . . . 131 F5
Commercial Brow
 SK14. . . . . . . 167 B4
Commercial Rd SK7 . . . . 124 E3
Commercial St
 Bacup OL13 . . . . 3 D8
 Hyde SK14. . . . . . . 167 B3
 Manchester M15 . . . . 162 B3
Commodore Pl WN5 . . . . 36 E1
Common End PR7 . . . . 20 E5
Common La
 Culcheth WA3. . . . . . . 91 E4
 Leigh WN7 . . . . 75 B4
 Partington M31 . . . . 106 B5
 Partington M31 . . . . 106 D4
 Tyldesley M29 . . . . 59 A1
Common Nook WN2. . . . . . . 56 A6
Common Side Rd M28 . . . . 77 F7
Common St BL5 . . . . 57 B7
Common The PR7. . . . . . . 20 E5
Commonwealth Cl
 WN7. . . . . . . 76 B3
Community St 4 OL7. . . . . . . 84 F1
Como St 10 BL3 . . . . 146 C4
Como Wlk M18. . . . . . . 165 B2
Compass St M11. . . . . . . 165 C3
COMPSTALL 114 A3
Compstall Ave M14 . . . . 98 B1
Compstall Gr 7 M18. . . . . . . 99 E6
Compstall Mills Est
 SK6. . . . . . . 114 B2
Compstall Rd
 Compstall SK6 . . . . 114 A3
 Marple SK6 . . . . 114 A2
 Romiley SK6. . . . . . . 113 E2
Compton Cl
 Hindley WN2 . . . . 56 D4
 Urmston M41. . . . . . . 94 C1
Compton Dr M23 . . . . 121 A2
Compton Fold 5 SK15. . . . . . . 86 B1
Compton Way M24 . . . . 65 C6
Comrie Wlk 7 M23. . . . . . . 121 A5
Comus St M5. . . . . . . 161 C4
Concert La M2 . . . . 159 A1
Concord Ave WN3 . . . . 55 B3
Concord Bsns Pk
 M22. . . . . . . 121 E1

Concord Pl M6. . . . . . . 81 A5
Concord Way 1
 SK16. . . . . . . 101 D8
Condor Cl M43 . . . . 84 C3
Condor Pl M6. . . . . . . 81 A5
Condor Wlk M43 . . . . 163 B2
Conduit St
 Ashton-u-L OL6 . . . . 166 C2
 Oldham OL1. . . . . . . 49 E3
 Tintwistle SK13 . . . . 103 F1
Coney Gr M23 . . . . 121 A7
Coneymead SK15 . . . . 86 A4
Congham Rd 6 SK3 . . . . 123 C8
Congleton Ave M14. . . . . . . 98 A2
Congleton Rd SK9 . . . . 137 A1
Congou St M11. . . . . . . 163 C4
Congreave St OL1 . . . . 153 B4
Congresbury Rd WN7. . . . . . . 75 D7
Conifer Wlk
 Leigh WN7 . . . . 75 B5
 Partington M31 . . . . 105 E3
Coningsby Dr M9. . . . . . . 157 A4
Coningsby Gdns 4
 WA3. . . . . . . 90 E8
Conisber Cl BL7 . . . . 8 E1
Conisborough OL11. . . . . . . 139 B2
Conisborough Pl M45. . . . . . . 63 B7
Coniston Ave
 Adlington PR6 . . . . 21 B8
 Ashton-in-M WN4 . . . . 73 B4
 Atherton M46 . . . . 58 D5
 Dukinfield SK14 . . . . 101 C4
 Farnworth BL4. . . . . . . 59 F8
 Ince-in-M WN2 . . . . 56 A2
 Manchester M9 . . . . 157 A4
 Oldham OL8. . . . . . . 66 C4
 Orrell WN5. . . . . . . 53 F7
 Sale M33 . . . . 108 C2
 Walkden M38. . . . . . . 60 A4
 Whitefield M45 . . . . 62 F8
 Wigan WN1 . . . . 37 C3
Coniston Cl
 Chadderton OL9. . . . . . . 152 A3
 Little Lever BL3 . . . . 43 A4
 Ramsbottom BL0 . . . . 138 C3
 Reddish M34 . . . . 100 B3
 Coniston M22. . . . . . . 121 E6
Coniston Dr
 Abram WN2 . . . . 74 B8
 Bury BL9 . . . . 44 E7
 Handforth SK9. . . . . . . 131 C4
 Middleton M24. . . . . . . 46 F2
 Stalybridge SK15. . . . . . . 86 A3
Coniston Gr
 Ashton-u-L OL7 . . . . 166 A4
 Heywood OL10. . . . . . . 46 D8
 Royton OL2 . . . . 48 D6
 Walkden M38. . . . . . . 60 A4
Coniston Ho 5 M28 . . . . 60 E2
Coniston Park Dr WN6. . . . . . . 37 A6
Coniston Rd
 Blackrod BL6 . . . . 21 D3
 Flixton M41 . . . . 106 E8
 Gatley SK8. . . . . . . 122 B5
 High Lane SK6. . . . . . . 134 D8
 Hindley WN2 . . . . 56 E4
 Partington M31 . . . . 105 E4
 Reddish SK5 . . . . 111 F6
 Stretford M32 . . . . 96 C3
 Swinton M27 . . . . 79 F7
 Tyldesley M29 . . . . 77 A7
Coniston St
 Bolton BL1. . . . . . . 143 C3
 8 Failsworth M40 . . . . 83 C5
 Leigh WN7 . . . . 75 E5
 Salford M6 . . . . 81 B4
Coniston Wlk WA15. . . . . . . 120 D5
Conival Way OL9 . . . . 48 A1
Conmere Sq 8 M15. . . . . . . 162 E3
Connaught Ave
 Manchester M19 . . . . 110 F7
 Rochdale OL16. . . . . . . 31 B3
 Whitefield M45 . . . . 63 A7
Connaught Cl SK9 . . . . 137 C8
Connaught Dr WA12. . . . . . . 89 C2
Connaught Sq BL2. . . . . . . 25 B2
Connaught St
 Bury BL8. . . . . . . 27 B1
 4 Oldham OL8. . . . . . . 153 B2
Connell Rd M23 . . . . 121 A6
Connell Way OL10 . . . . 29 F3
Connery Cres OL6 . . . . 85 D6
Connie St M11. . . . . . . 165 C4
Conningsby Cl 10 BL7. . . . . . . 24 F8
Connington Ave M9. . . . . . . 64 D1
Connington Cl OL2 . . . . 48 C4
Connor Way SK8. . . . . . . 121 F4
Conquest Cl M12 . . . . 165 A6
Conrad Cl
 Oldham OL1. . . . . . . 49 E4
 Wigan WN3 . . . . 150 A1
Conran St M9. . . . . . . 157 B3
Consett Ave M23 . . . . 121 A6
Consort Ave OL2. . . . . . . 48 C6
Consort Cl 3 SK16. . . . . . . 101 C6
Consort Pl WA14 . . . . 119 B3
Constable Cl BL1 . . . . 143 A1
Constable Dr
 Marple SK6 . . . . 126 B8
 Wilmslow SK9 . . . . 137 A8
Constable Ho 4 M20. . . . . . . 110 B7
Constable St M18. . . . . . . 99 E6
Constable Wlk
 13 Denton M34. . . . . . . 113 A7
 Oldham OL1. . . . . . . 49 D3
Constance Gdns M5 . . . . 154 C1

Constance Rd
 Bolton BL3. . . . . . . 146 C4
 Partington M31 . . . . 105 F3
Constance St M15 . . . . 162 B3
Constantia St WN3. . . . . . . 151 B3
Constantine Ct M6. . . . . . . 81 B3
Constantine Rd OL16. . . . . . . 139 C3
Constantine St OL4 . . . . 67 D7
Consul St M22. . . . . . . 121 E1
Convamore Rd SK7 . . . . 132 D7
Convent Gr OL11 . . . . 139 A1
Convent St OL8. . . . . . . 67 C4
Conway Ave
 Bolton BL1. . . . . . . 142 A1
 Irlam M44 . . . . 105 F8
 Swinton M27 . . . . 62 B3
 Whitefield M45 . . . . 62 F7
Conway Cl
 Heywood OL10. . . . . . . 29 A3
 Leigh WN7 . . . . 76 F7
 Manchester M16 . . . . 97 A3
 Middleton M24. . . . . . . 65 A7
 Ramsbottom BL0 . . . . 138 B2
 Whitefield M45 . . . . 62 F7
Conway Cres
 Billinge WN5 . . . . 71 E6
 Ramsbottom BL8 . . . . 10 F2
Conway Ctr The SK5. . . . . . . 169 B4
Conway Dr
 Altrincham WA15. . . . . . . 120 C6
 Bury, Walshaw WN2 . . . . 38 D5
 Billinge WN5 . . . . 71 F5
 Bury BL9 . . . . 28 D2
 Hazel Grove SK7 . . . . 124 C1
 Newton-le-W WA12. . . . . . . 89 E3
 Stalybridge SK15. . . . . . . 86 A3
Conway Gr OL9. . . . . . . 47 F1
Conway Rd
 Ashton-in-M WN4 . . . . 73 E5
 Cheadle SK8 . . . . 122 E2
 Sale M33 . . . . 56 F4
 Sale M33 . . . . 108 C3
 Urmston M41. . . . . . . 95 D4
Conway St
 Farnworth BL4. . . . . . . 60 D7
 Reddish SK5 . . . . 169 B4
 Wigan WN5 . . . . 54 C5
Conynghan Rd M14 . . . . 98 D3
Cooke St
 Ashton-in-M WN4 . . . . 72 F6
 Denton M34. . . . . . . 100 F4
 Dukinfield SK14. . . . . . . 101 F5
 Failsworth M35 . . . . 83 F8
 Farnworth BL4. . . . . . . 60 E7
 Hazel Grove SK7 . . . . 124 D3
 Hyde SK14. . . . . . . 22 D4
Cook St
 Abram WN2 . . . . 56 B1
 Bury BL9 . . . . 141 A2
 Denton M34. . . . . . . 100 F6
 Eccles M30 . . . . 79 C2
 Leigh WN7 . . . . 75 F5
 Oldham OL4. . . . . . . 67 C7
 Rochdale OL16. . . . . . . 15 B1
 Salford M3. . . . . . . 158 B2
 Stockport SK3 . . . . 169 B1
Cook Terr
 21 Dukinfield SK16. . . . . . . 166 B1
 Rochdale OL16. . . . . . . 15 B1
Cooling La M29, M27. . . . . . . 76 E8
Coomassie St
 Heywood OL10. . . . . . . 29 C1
 Radcliffe M26 . . . . 44 A3
 Salford M6. . . . . . . 154 C3
Coombe Cl M29 . . . . 77 B8
Coombes Ave
 Hyde SK14 . . . . 167 C1
 Marple SK6 . . . . 125 F6
Coombes La SK13 . . . . 115 C5
Coombes St SK2. . . . . . . 124 B5
Coombes View SK14 . . . . 114 F8
Co-operation St M35 . . . . 83 F8
Cooperative St OL14. . . . . . . 6 A7
Co-operative St
 Disley SK12 . . . . 135 D4
 Hazel Grove SK7 . . . . 124 E3
 5 Leigh WN7 . . . . 75 D5
 Oldham OL4. . . . . . . 67 F5
 3 Radcliffe M26. . . . . . . 44 A4
 Shaw OL2. . . . . . . 154 C2
 Uppermill OL3 . . . . 69 B8
 Walkden M38. . . . . . . 59 E5
Cooper Fold M24 . . . . 47 A4
Cooper Ho M15 . . . . 163 A2
Cooper La
 Manchester M9 . . . . 64 D5
 Middleton M24. . . . . . . 46 F3
Cooper's Fold SK8 . . . . 131 F6
Coopers Glen M46. . . . . . . 58 B4
Cooper's La PR7. . . . . . . 18 A8
Coopers Row WN1. . . . . . . 150 C4
Cooper St
 Bury BL9 . . . . 140 B2
 Dukinfield SK16. . . . . . . 166 B1
 Glossop SK13. . . . . . . 104 B1
 Hazel Grove SK7 . . . . 124 E3
 Horwich BL6. . . . . . . 22 B4
 Manchester M2. . . . . . . 158 C1
 Oldham OL4. . . . . . . 68 A7
 Rochdale OL12. . . . . . . 15 D4
 Stockport SK1 . . . . 170 C3
 Stretford M32 . . . . 96 D1
Coopers Wlk OL16 . . . . 15 C2
Coops Foyer & Coops Bsns
 Ctr WN1. . . . . . . 150 B4
Coop St
 Bolton BL1. . . . . . . 143 B4

Coop St *continued*
1 Manchester M4 ....**159** B2
Wigan WN1 ....**37** D1
Copage Dr SK6 ....**113** A4
COPE BANK **142** C1
Cope Bank B BL1 ....**142** C2
Cope Bank E BL1 ....**142** C1
Cope Bank W BL1 ......**142** B2
Cope Cl M11 ....**99** E7
Copeland Ave M27 ....**62** C1
Copeland Cl M24 .....**46** C1
Copeland Dr WN6 .....**19** F2
Copeland Mews BL1 ..**144** A3
Copeland St SK14 ....**101** D5
Copeman Cl M13 .....**163** C2
Copenhagen Sq 20
  ....**31** A8
Copenhagen St
  Failsworth M40 ......**83** A6
  Rochdale OL16 ......**31** A8
Cope St BL1............**145** C7
Copesthorne Cl WN2 ..**38** C6
Copgrove Rd M21 .....**109** B7
Copgrove Wlk M22 ...**130** E7
COPLEY **86** C2
Copley Ave SK15 ......**86** C2
Copley High Sch SK15 .**86** D2
Copley Park Mews
  SK15 ....**86** C2
Copley Rd M21 ....**97** A2
Copley St OL2 ....**149** C4
Coplow Dale WN2 .....**56** E3
Copperas Cl WN6 .....**36** B7
Copperas La
  Aspull WN2 ....**38** A6
  Blackrod BL6 ....**21** B1
  Droylsden M43 ....**99** E8
Copperas St M4 .....**159** A2
Copper Beech Cl M22 .**109** E1
Copperbeech Dr WN6 ..**37** B7
Copper Beech Dr
  Gamesley SK13 ......**171** B1
  Stalybridge SK15 .....**86** D3
Copperfield WN1 ......**37** C2
Copperfield Ct WA14 ..**119** C3
Copperfield Rd
  Cheadle SK8 ....**132** B5
  Poynton SK12 ....**133** D2
Copperfields
  Bolton BL6 ....**40** B3
  Poynton SK12 ....**133** D2
  Wilmslow SK9 ....**137** C8
Copper La M45 ....**62** B7
Copperways M20 ....**110** B5
COPPICE **66** E4
Coppice Ave
  High Lane SK12 .....**135** A6
  Sale M33 ....**107** D2
Coppice Cl
  High Lane SK12 .....**135** A6
  Romiley SK6 ....**113** A4
Coppice Ct SK8 .....**131** B8
Coppice Dr
  Longshaw WN5 ......**53** D2
  Whitworth OL12 .....**14** D7
  Wigan WN1 ....**54** F2
  Wythenshawe M22 ...**109** D1
Coppice Ho SK12 ....**133** D2
Coppice Ind Est OL8 .**153** A1
Coppice Inf Sch OL8 ..**66** E4
Coppice Jun Sch OL8 .**66** E4
Coppice La SK12 .....**135** A5
Coppice Rd SK12 ....**134** B3
Coppice St
  Bury BL9 ....**141** C3
  Oldham OL8 ....**66** E4
Coppice The
  Altrincham WA15 ....**129** B8
  Bolton BL2 ....**25** D5
  Manchester M9 ......**65** A2
  Middleton M24 ......**65** B5
  Prestwich M25 ....**63** A4
  Ramsbottom BL0 .....**13** A4
  Swinton M28 ....**79** C5
  Worsley M28 ....**78** F8
Coppice Way SK9 ....**131** E3
Copping St M12 .....**164** C2
Coppingford Cl OL12 ..**14** A2
Coppleridge Dr M8 ....**64** A2
Copplestone Ct M27 ..**61** C1
Copplestone Dr M33 ..**107** C5
Coppull Cross Rds PR7 .**19** F7
Coppull Hall La PR7 ...**20** B8
Coppull La WN1 ......**37** D2
COPPULL MOOR **19** E6
Coppull Moor La PR7 ..**19** C6
Coppull St John's CE Prim
  Sch PR7 ....**20** D6
Coppy Bridge Dr OL16 .**31** D8
Cop Rd OL1 ....**49** C4
Copse Ave M22 .....**121** E3
Copse Dr BL9 ....**27** F6
Copse The
  Altrincham WA15 ....**129** D7
  Chapeltown BL7 ......**9** C2
  High Lane SK6 ....**135** A6
  Marple SK6 ....**126** C8
  Newton-le-W WA12 ...**89** B4
  Wigan WN5 ....**54** A6
Copse Wlk OL15 ......**15** C5
Copson St M20 ......**110** B7
Copster Ave OL8 .....**66** E3
COPSTER HILL **66** E3
Copster Hill Rd OL8 ...**66** E4
Copster Pl 2 OL8 .....**66** E3
Copthall La M8 ......**155** C4

Copthorne Cl OL10 ....**46** D8
Copthorne Cres M13 ...**98** E3
Copthorne Dr BL2 .....**42** E6
Copthorne Wlk BL8 ....**26** F5
Coptic Rd OL9 ....**65** F8
Coptrod Head Cl OL12 .**14** E4
Coral Ave SK8 ....**123** A1
Coral Gr WN7 ....**75** E4
Coralin Way WN4 .....**72** F7
Coral Mews OL2 ......**48** E3
Coral Rd SK8 ....**123** A1
Coral St
  Manchester M13 .....**163** C3
  Wigan WN6 ....**37** A3
Coram St M18 ....**99** F6
Corbar Rd SK2 ....**124** B5
Corbett Ct 5 M22 .....**56** E5
Corbett St
  Droylsden M11........**83** A1
  Rochdale OL16 ....**31** B8
Corbett Way OL3 ......**33** C1
Corby St M12 ....**165** A2
Corcoran Cl OL10 .....**29** C3
Corcoran Dr SK6 .....**113** F2
Corda Ave M22 ......**121** D8
Corday La M25 ....**63** D8
Cordingley Ave M43 ...**99** F8
Cordova Ave M34 .....**99** F4
Corelli St M40 ....**160** C4
Corfe Cl
  Aspull WN2 ....**38** D5
  Urmston M41.........**94** C1
Corfe Cres SK7 ......**124** D1
Corhampton Cres M46 .**58** C5
Corinthian Ave M7 ....**81** C5
Corinth Wlk M28 ......**60** D2
Corkland Cl OL6 ....**85** E2
Corkland Rd M21 ....**109** C8
Corkland St OL6 ......**85** E2
Corks La SK12 ....**135** C5
Cork St
  Ashton-u-L OL6 .....**166** C3
  Bury BL9 ....**141** A2
  Manchester M12 ....**164** A4
Corless Fold M29 .....**77** C5
Corley Ave SK3 ......**122** F7
Cormallen Gr M35 ....**84** A7
Cormorant Cl M28 ....**60** C3
Cormorant Wlk M12 ..**165** A2
Cornall St BL8 ....**27** C3
Cornbrook Cl
  Wardle OL12 ....**15** C6
  Westhoughton BL5 ....**57** D6
Cornbrook Ct M15 ...**162** A2
Cornbrook Gr M16 ...**162** A1
Cornbrook Park Rd
  M15 ....**161** C2
Cornbrook Rd M15 ...**161** C2
Cornbrook St M16 ...**162** A1
Cornbrook Sta
  (Interchange only no
  street access) M15 ...**161** C2
Cornbrook Way M16 ..**162** A1
Corn Cl M13 ....**163** C1
Cornelian Gr M4 ......**159** B2
Cornell St M4 ....**159** B2
Corner Brook BL6 .....**40** A3
Corner Croft SK9 ....**137** A4
Corner Ct SK8 ....**122** F6
Cornergate BL5 ....**57** E5
Cornerhouse The
  BL0 ....**138** C2
Corner La WN7 ....**57** D3
Corner St OL6 ....**166** C2
Cornet St M7 ....**155** A1
Cornfield SK15 ......**102** E7
Cornfield Cl
  Bury BL9 ....**27** F7
  2 Sale M33 ....**108** F3
Cornfield Dr M22 ....**121** C3
Cornfield Rd SK6 ....**113** E3
Cornfield St OL16 .....**32** A5
Cornford Ave M18 ....**99** B3
Corn Hey Rd M33 ....**107** C2
Cornhill Ave M41 .....**95** B3
Corn Hill La M34 ....**100** B5
Cornhill Rd M41 .....**95** B3
Cornhill St OL1 ....**49** D2
Cornish Cl M22 ......**121** D3
Cornish Way M29 ....**130** D8
Cornish Way OL2 .....**49** A4
Cornishway Ind Est
  M22 ....**130** D8
Cornlea Dr M28 ......**78** C7
Corn Mill Cl
  Garswood WN4 ......**72** D4
  Rochdale OL12 ......**15** D4
Cornmill Ho SK13 ....**104** D1
Corn Mill La 1 SK15 ..**86** B1
Corn St
  Failsworth M35 ......**83** C6
  Glossop SK13 ....**104** D1
  Leigh WN7 ....**76** A4
  Oldham OL4 ....**67** A7
Cornwall Ave
  Manchester M19 ....**111** B8
  Over Hulton BL5 ......**58** F8
  Tyldesley M29 ....**59** A3
Cornwall Cl SK6 .....**134** E7
Cornwall Cres
  Brinnington SK5 .....**112** C6
  Diggle WN1 ....**51** B4
  Standish WN1 ....**20** B1
Cornwall Dr
  Bury BL9 ....**45** A8
  Hindley WN2 ....**56** F6

Cornwall Ho M3 .....**158** A1
Cornwallis Rd WN3 ...**150** A1
Cornwall Pl WN5 ......**54** C6
Cornwall Rd
  Droylsden M43........**84** A3
  Gatley SK8 ....**131** B8
  Irlam M44 ....**105** D5
Cornwall St
  2 Eccles M30 ....**79** C1
  Manchester M11, M18 ..**99** D7
  Oldham OL9 ....**152** B1
Cornwell Cl SK9 .....**137** D8
Cornwood Cl 8 M8 ..**155** C3
Corona Ave
  Hyde SK14 ....**167** B3
  Oldham OL8 ....**66** F3
Coronation Ave
  Atherton M46 ....**58** C5
  Dukinfield SK16 .....**101** F6
  Glazebury WA3 ....**92** C7
  Heywood OL10 ....**46** E8
  Hyde SK14 ....**167** B1
Coronation Dr
  Haydock WA11 ....**89** A7
  Leigh WN7 ....**76** E6
  Newton-le-W WA12 ....**89** E1
Coronation Gdns M26 ..**43** E4
Coronation Rd
  Ashton-u-L OL6 ....**85** C6
  Droylsden M43 ....**83** F6
  Failsworth M35 ......**83** E6
  Radcliffe M26 ....**43** E4
  Wigan WN6 ....**36** D3
Coronation Sq
  Denton M34 ....**100** D7
  9 Little Lever BL3 ....**43** A3
  Manchester M1, M12 ..**163** C4
Coronation St
  Bolton BL1 ....**145** C3
  Denton M34 ....**100** D3
  Downall Green WN4 ...**72** D6
  Ince-in-M WN3 ....**55** F3
  Manchester M11 .....**160** F1
  Oldham, Mumps OL4 ...**67** A7
  Reddish SK5 ....**169** B4
  Salford M5 ....**161** B4
  Swinton M27 ....**62** A1
  Wigan WN2 ....**150** B2
Coronation Wlk
  Billinge WN5 ....**71** D4
  1 Radcliffe M26 .....**43** E4
Coronet Cl WN6 ......**35** C7
Corporation Cotts
  M31 ....**106** C6
Corporation Ct 10 OL13 .**3** D8
Corporation Rd
  Denton M34 ....**100** D5
  Eccles M30 ....**79** F1
  Rochdale OL11 ......**139** A2
  Rochdale OL11 ......**139** A3
Corporation St
  Bolton BL1 ....**145** C3
  Hyde SK14 ....**167** A2
  Manchester M4 ......**159** A2
  Middleton M24 ....**65** A8
  Stalybridge SK15 .....**86** C1
  Stockport SK1 ......**169** C2
  Wigan WN3 ....**150** B2
Corpus Christ RC Prim
  Sch OL9 ....**66** B4
Corran Cl M30 ....**79** B2
Corranstone Cl BL6 ...**22** B3
Correction Brow
  SK12 ....**134** C6
Corrie Cl M34 ....**100** F1
Corrie Cres BL4 ......**61** D4
Corrie Dr BL4 ....**61** D4
Corrie Prim Sch M34 .**100** F1
Corrie Rd M27 ....**62** A3
Corrie St M38 ....**60** A4
Corrigan St M18 ......**99** E6
Corringham Rd M19 ..**111** C7
Corring Way BL1 .....**24** E6
Corrin Rd BL2 ....**148** B1
Corris Ave M9 ....**64** A5
Corry St OL10 ....**29** E2
Corsey Rd WN2 ....**56** E4
Corsock Dr WN1 ......**37** E1
Corson St BL4 ....**42** D2
Corston Gr BL6 ....**21** D1
Corston Wlk M40 .....**83** B6
Corwen Cl OL8 ....**66** D3
Cosgate Cl 1 WN5 ....**53** E5
Cosgrove Cres M35 ...**83** E5
Cosgrove Rd M35 .....**83** E5
Cosham Rd M22 .....**121** F3
Costabeck Wlk M40 ...**83** D4
Costessey Way WN3 ...**54** D2
Costobadie Cl SK14 ..**102** F3
Costobadie Way 4
  SK14 ....**102** F3
Cosworth Cl 7 WN7 ...**76** B4
Cotaline Cl OL11 ......**30** B3
Cotefield Ave BL3 ....**147** C3
Cotefield Cl 7 SK6 ...**125** F5
Cotefield Rd M22 ....**121** C2
COTE GREEN **114** C1
Cote Green La SK6 ...**114** C1
Cote Green Rd SK6 ..**114** C1
Cote La
  Delph OL3 ....**51** B7
  Littleborough OL15 ...**15** F4
  Mossley OL5 ....**68** E3
Cotford Rd BL1 ....**24** E6
Cotman Cl OL13 ....**4** B7
Cotman Dr SK6 ......**126** C8

Cotswold Ave
  Chadderton OL9......**152** A1
  Golborne WA3 ....**90** D2
  Hazel Grove SK7 ....**124** B1
  Shaw, High Crompton
   OL2 ....**48** F8
  Shaw, Lower Rushcroft
   OL2 ....**149** A4
Cotswold Cl
  Glossop SK13 ....**116** A8
  Prestwich M25 ....**63** C5
  Ramsbottom BL0 .....**11** C4
Cotswold Cres
  Bury BL8 ....**27** B3
  Milnrow OL16 ....**32** A7
Cotswold Dr
  Horwich BL6 ....**22** C5
  Royton OL2 ....**48** B3
  Salford M6 ....**154** C3
Cotswold Rd SK4 ....**169** A3
Cottage Croft BL2 ....**25** D5
Cottage Gdns SK6 ...**112** D3
Cottage Gr SK9 .....**136** F5
Cottage La SK13 ....**171** B2
Cottage Lawns SK9 ..**137** B2
Cottage Wlk
  Droylsden M43........**83** F3
  Rochdale OL12 ....**14** C4
Cottam Cres SK6 .....**126** B7
Cottam Gr 1 M27 .....**80** A7
Cottam St
  Bury BL8 ....**27** C3
  Oldham OL1 ....**153** A4
Cottenham La M7 ....**158** B4
Cottenham St M13 ...**163** B2
Cotterdale Cl M16 .....**97** D2
Cotterill Cl M23 ......**120** C8
Cotterill St M6 ....**81** B2
Cotter St M12 ....**163** C3
Cottesmore Cl OL12 ...**14** C6
Cottesmore Dr M8 ...**156** C4
Cottesmore Gdns
  WA15 ....**129** C8
Cottesmore Way WA3 ..**74** B1
Cottingham Dr OL6 ...**166** C4
Cottingham Rd M12 ..**164** B2
Cottingley Cl BL1 .....**24** D5
Cotton Cl SK14 ......**167** B1
Cotton Fold OL16 .....**31** C6
Cotton Hill M20 .....**110** C5
Cotton La M20 ......**110** C6
Cotton Lodge Ct 7
  BL3 ....**42** A3
Cotton Mill Cres OL9 ..**66** B4
Cotton St E OL6 .....**166** B2
Cotton St W OL6 ....**166** A2
Cotton St
  Bolton BL1 ....**143** A2
  Leigh WN7 ....**75** D5
  Manchester M4 ......**159** B2
  Old Trafford M16 .....**97** B4
  Radcliffe M26 ....**44** D3
Cotton Tree Cl OL4 ...**67** D8
Cotton Tree St SK4 ..**169** B1
Cottonwood Dr 3
  M33 ....**107** C5
Cottrell Rd WA15 ....**129** D7
Coucill Sq BL4 ....**60** E8
Coulsden Dr M9 ......**64** D3
Coulthart St BL0 .....**138** B2
Coulton Cl OL1 ....**67** A8
Coulton Wlk M5 .....**154** C2
Coultshead Ave WN5 ..**71** E6
Council Ave WN4 ......**73** B3
Councillor La SK8 ....**123** A4
Councillor St M12 ....**160** B1
Countess Ave SK8 ....**131** E5
Countess Gr M7 ......**155** D7
Countess La M26 .....**43** D4
Countess Pl M25 ......**63** C4
Countess Rd M20 ....**110** B3
Countess St
  Ashton-u-L OL6 ....**85** D2
  Stockport SK2 ....**124** A7
Counthill Dr M8 ......**63** E2
Counthill Rd OL4 .....**49** D1
Counthill Sch OL4 ....**49** D2
Counting House Rd
  SK12 ....**135** E5
Countess Sch SK12 ...**135** E5
County Ave OL6 ....**85** E4
COUNTY END **67** F6
County End Bsns Ctr
  OL4 ....**67** F6
County End Terr 14
  OL4 ....**67** F6
County Police St
  WN2 ....**151** C3
County Rd M28 ....**60** A4
County St
  Manchester M2 .....**158** C1
  Oldham OL8 ....**66** C2
Coupes Gn BL5 ....**57** F6
Coupland Cl
  Oldham OL4 ....**49** F4
  Whitworth OL12 .....**14** C6
Coupland Rd WN2 ....**57** C3
Coupland St M15 ....**163** A1
Courage Low La WN6 ..**18** C5
Courier Pl WN5 ....**36** E1
Courier St M18 ....**99** F6
Court Dr M40 ....**83** E4
Courtfield Ave M9 ....**64** D4
Courthill St SK1 .....**124** A8

Court House Way 4
  OL10 ....**29** D2
Courtney Gn SK9 ....**131** D2
Courtney Pl WA14 ...**119** A1
Court St
  Bolton BL2 ....**148** A3
  Uppermill OL3 ....**69** B8
Courts View M33 ....**108** C5
Court The M17 ....**95** F8
Courtyard Dr M28 ....**60** A3
Courtyard St Peters The
  BL1 ....**143** C1
Courtyard The
  Hollingworth SK14 ...**103** D5
  Newton-le-W WA12 ...**89** E4
Cousin Fields BL7 ....**25** C7
Covall Wlk 4 M8 ....**156** B2
Covell Rd SK12 ......**133** D5
Covent Gdns SK1 ....**169** C1
Coventry Ave SK3 ...**122** F7
Coventry Gr OL9 .....**48** A1
Coventry Rd M26 ......**43** F5
Coventry St OL11 ....**139** C2
Covent The WN7 ......**76** A4
Coverdale Ave
  Bolton BL1 ....**144** A4
  Royton OL2 ....**48** C5
Coverdale Cl
  Heywood OL16 ....**29** C1
  Platt Bridge WN2 .....**55** F2
Coverdale Cres M12 .**164** B2
Coverdale Rd BL5 ....**57** D8
Coverham Ave OL4 ...**67** D4
Coverhill Rd OL4 .....**68** B5
Covert The
  Oldham OL4 ....**67** D3
  Wythenshawe M22 ...**121** E6
Coverts The WN6 .....**36** F2
Covington Pl SK9 ...**137** B6
Cowan St M40 ....**160** A2
Cowbrook Ave SK13 ..**104** F1
Cowbrook Ct SK13 ...**104** F1
Cowburn Dr M26 ....**127** C1
Cowburn St
  Heywood OL10 ....**29** E1
  Hindley WN2 ....**56** F6
  1 Leigh WN7 ....**75** D5
  Manchester M3 .....**158** C3
Cowdals Rd BL6 ....**40** B4
Cowesby St M14 ......**98** A3
COWHILL **152** B2
Cowhill La Trad Est 11
  OL6 ....**166** C3
Cowie St OL2 ....**149** B4
Cow La
  Ashley WA15 ....**128** F6
  Bolton BL3 ....**146** B2
  Failsworth M35 ....**83** E7
  Oldham OL4 ....**67** C7
  Sale M33 ....**108** E5
  Salford M5 ....**81** C1
  Stockport SK2, SK7 ..**124** D4
  Wilmslow SK9 ....**137** C7
Cow Lees BL5 ....**40** A1
Cowley Rd BL1 ....**24** F5
Cowley St 9 M40 .....**83** C6
Cowling St
  Manchester M7 ......**80** F8
  Oldham OL8 ....**66** F4
  Wigan WN3 ....**150** A4
COWLISHAW **149** A2
Cowlishaw OL2 ......**149** A2
Cowlishaw La OL2 ...**149** A1
Cowlishaw Rd SK6,
  SK6 ....**113** F4
Cowm Park Way N OL12 .**4** D2
Cowm Park Way S OL12 .**4** C1
Cowm St OL12 ....**4** E5
Cowm Top La OL11 ....**30** E2
COWPE **2** F6
Cowper Ave M46 .....**58** C5
Cowpe Rd BB4 ....**2** F7
Cowper St
  Ashton-u-L OL6 .....**166** C3
  Leigh WN7 ....**75** D5
  Middleton M24 ....**65** D8
Cowper Wlk 4 M11 ..**160** C1
Coxfield Wlk WN6 ....**35** D7
COX GREEN **24** F8
Cox Green Cl BL7 ......**8** D3
Cox Green Rd
  2 Bolton, Cox Green
  BL7 ....**24** F8
  Bolton, Egerton BL7 ..**8** E2
Coxton Rd M22 ......**121** E1
Cox Way M46 ....**58** D3
Coxwold Gr BL3 .....**146** F4
Crabbe St M4 ....**159** A3
Crab Brow M46 ......**58** B3
Crab La M9 ....**64** B4
Crab Lane Prim Sch
  M9 ....**64** B4
Crabtree Ave
  Altrincham WA15 ....**129** D7
  Disley SK12 ....**135** E5
Crabtree Ct WA12 .....**89** E3
Crabtree La SK13 ....**135** D6
Crabtree La M11 .....**83** D1
Crab Tree La M46 ....**58** D2
Crabtree Rd
  Oldham OL1 ....**67** B8
  Wigan WN5 ....**54** D7
Craddock Rd M33 ...**108** C2

Craddock St **4** OL5 . . . . .68 C1
Cradley Ave M11 . . . . .99 D8
Crag Ave BL9 . . . . .11 D2
Crag Fold BL9 . . . . .11 D2
Crag Gr WA11 . . . . .71 B1
Cragg Rd OL1 . . . . .48 A2
Cragie St M8 . . . . .155 C1
Crag La BL9 . . . . .11 D2
Cragside Way SK9 . . . . .137 C6
Craig Ave
  Bury BL8 . . . . .27 B1
  Urmston M41 . . . . .95 A3
Craig Ct SK4 . . . . .168 B1
Craigend Dr M9 . . . . .157 B3
Craighall Ave M19 . . . . . . .110 F8
Craighall Rd BL1 . . . . .24 E6
Craiglands OL16 . . . . .31 B2
Craigmore Ave M20 . . . . . .109 E4
Craignair Ct M27 . . . . .80 C7
Craig Rd
  Manchester M18 . . . . .99 C4
  Stockport SK4 . . . . .168 B1
Craigslands Ave M40 . . . . . .83 A6
Craigweil Ave M20 . . . . . . .110 D3
Craigwell Rd M25 . . . . .63 E2
Craigwell Wlk M13 . . . . . . .163 B3
Craig Wlk OL8 . . . . .153 B1
Crail Pl OL10 . . . . .28 F1
Cramer St M40 . . . . .157 C1
Crammond Cl M40 . . . . .83 D6
Cramond Cl BL1 . . . . .143 A1
Cramond Wlk **6** BL1 . . . .143 A1
Crampton Dr WA15 . . . . . . .129 C8
Crampton La M31 . . . . .106 D6
Cranage Rd M19 . . . . .111 B8
Cranage Way **10** SK9 . . .131 D5
Cranark Cl BL1 . . . . .144 A3
Cranberry Ave
  Walsden OL14 . . . . .6 B7
  Wigan WN4 . . . . .36 F3
Cranberry Cl WA14 . . . . . . .119 B8
Cranberry Dr
  Bolton BL3 . . . . .40 F4
  Denton M34 . . . . .100 D3
Cranberry Rd M31 . . . . . . .105 F3
Cranberry St OL4 . . . . .67 B6
Cranborne Cl
  Horwich BL6 . . . . .22 F1
  Standish WN6 . . . . .19 D1
Cranbourne Ave SK8 . . . . . .123 B8
Cranbourne Cl
  1 Altrincham WA15 . . . .120 A6
  Ashton-u-L OL7 . . . . .166 B4
Cranbourne Ct SK4 . . . . . . .168 B4
Cranbourne Rd
  Ashton-u-L OL7 . . . . .166 B4
  Manchester, Chorlton-cum-
    Hardy M21 . . . . .109 B8
  Manchester, Old Trafford
    M16 . . . . .97 C4
  Rochdale OL11 . . . . .29 E6
  Stockport, Heaton Moor
    SK4 . . . . .168 B4
Cranbourne St M5 . . . . .81 C1
Cranbourne Terr OL6 . . . . . .85 B5
Cranbrook Ave WN4 . . . . . . .73 A4
Cranbrook Cl BL1 . . . . .143 C1
Cranbrook Dr M25 . . . . .63 C2
Cranbrook Gdns OL7 . . . . . .166 B4
Cranbrook Rd OL4 . . . . .67 C6
Cranbrook Rd
  Eccles M30 . . . . .79 B4
  Reddish M18 . . . . .99 F3
Cranbrook St
  Ashton-u-L OL7 . . . . .166 B4
  Oldham OL4 . . . . .67 C6
  Radcliffe M26 . . . . .44 C5
Cranbrook Way WN1 . . . . . . .37 B4
Cranbrook Wlk OL9 . . . . . . .152 A4
Crandon St **9** WN2 . . . . . .56 D5
Crandon Ct M47 . . . . .62 A1
Crandon Dr M20 . . . . .122 C8
Cranesbill Cl M22 . . . . .121 C1
Crane St
  Bolton BL3 . . . . .146 B3
  Coppull PR7 . . . . .19 D6
  Manchester M12 . . . . .163 C4
Cranfield Cl M40 . . . . .160 A2
Cranfield Rd
  Horwich BL6 . . . . .39 E7
  Wigan WN3 . . . . .55 A3
Cranford Ave
  Manchester M20 . . . . .110 D4
  Sale M33 . . . . .108 C6
  Stretford M32 . . . . .96 F3
  Whitefield M45 . . . . .44 E2
Cranford Cl
  Salford M27 . . . . .80 B6
  Whitefield M45 . . . . .44 E2
Cranford Dr M44 . . . . .93 F3
Cranford Gdns
  Marple SK6 . . . . .125 F8
  Urmston M41 . . . . .94 E3
Cranford Ho M30 . . . . .79 F3
Cranford Rd
  Handforth SK9 . . . . .131 A1
  Urmston M41 . . . . .94 E3
Cranford St BL3 . . . . .146 A3
Cranham Ave WA3 . . . . .90 E7
Cranham Cl
  Bury BL8 . . . . .27 B3
  Walkden M38 . . . . .60 A6
Cranham Rd M22 . . . . .121 A2
Crank Rd WA11, WN5 . . . . . .71 B8
CRANKWOOD 74 E5

Crankwood Rd WN2,
  WN7 . . . . .74 D5
Cranleigh WN6 . . . . .37 B8
Cranleigh Ave SK4 . . . . . . .110 F4
Cranleigh Cl
  Blackrod BL6 . . . . .21 D1
  Oldham OL4 . . . . .49 E1
Cranleigh Dr
  Cheadle SK8 . . . . .122 F6
  Hazel Grove SK7 . . . . .134 A8
  Sale M33 . . . . .108 A5
  Tyldesley M29 . . . . .77 B8
  Walkden M28 . . . . .78 E8
  Wythenshawe M23,
    M33 . . . . .108 C3
Cramlington Dr M8 . . . . . . .155 C2
Cranmer Ct OL10 . . . . .29 C1
Cranmere Ave M19 . . . . .99 C2
Cranmere Dr M33 . . . . .107 D2
Cranmer Rd M20 . . . . .110 B4
Cranshaw St M29 . . . . .77 D8
Cranstal Dr M40 . . . . .57 A5
Cranston Dr
  Manchester M20 . . . . .122 B8
  Sale M33 . . . . .108 C3
Cranston Gr SK8 . . . . .121 F5
Cranswick St **1** M14 . . . . .98 A3
Crantock Dr
  Gatley SK8 . . . . .131 C8
  Stalybridge SK15 . . . . .86 D3
Crantock St WN5 . . . . .54 C6
Crantock Rd M12 . . . . .99 B3
Cranwell Ave WA3 . . . . .91 F4
Cranwell Dr M19 . . . . .110 E4
Cranworth Ave M29 . . . . . . .77 A6
Cranworth St SK15 . . . . .86 B1
Craston Rd M13 . . . . .98 E2
Craunton **13** M30 . . . . . . .79 F2
Craven Ave
  Golborne WA3 . . . . .90 E7
  Salford M5 . . . . .161 B4
Craven Ct SK8 . . . . .22 D2
Craven Dr
  Altrincham WA14 . . . . .119 C8
  Salford M5 . . . . .161 A3
Craven Gdns OL11 . . . . . . .139 B1
Craven Ho OL14 . . . . .6 B5
Cavenhurst Ave M40 . . . . . . .83 B4
Craven Pl
  Bolton BL1 . . . . .23 E2
  3 Droylsden M11 . . . . . .83 C2
Craven Rd
  Altrincham WA14 . . . . .119 C7
  1 Reddish SK5 . . . . . . .111 F6
Craven St E BL6 . . . . .22 D2
Craven St
  Ashton-u-L OL6 . . . . .85 D5
  Bury BL9 . . . . .141 C3
  Droylsden M43 . . . . .84 A1
  Oldham OL1 . . . . .48 E1
  Salford M5 . . . . .81 C1
Craven Terr M33 . . . . .108 C4
Cravenwood OL5 . . . . .68 B4
Cravenwood Com Prim
  Sch M8 . . . . .64 A1
Cravenwood Rd M8 . . . . . . .156 A4
Crawford Ave
  Adlington PR7 . . . . .20 E5
  Aspull WN2 . . . . .38 C5
  Bolton BL2 . . . . .148 B2
  Tyldesley M29 . . . . .58 F2
  Worsley M28 . . . . .79 A8
Crawford Cl WN2 . . . . .38 C5
Crawford Mews **7**
  OL6 . . . . .85 D2
Crawford Sq OL10 . . . . .29 A1
Crawford St
  Ashton-u-L OL6 . . . . .85 D2
  Aspull WN2 . . . . .38 C4
  Bolton BL2 . . . . .148 B2
  Eccles M30 . . . . .79 D3
  Rochdale OL16 . . . . .31 B6
  Walkden OL14 . . . . .6 B8
  Wigan WN1 . . . . .150 C4
Crawley Ave
  Salford M30 . . . . .80 A3
  Wythenshawe M22 . . . . . . .121 E3
Crawley Cl M29 . . . . .59 C1
Crawley Gr SK2 . . . . .124 B6
Crawley Way OL9 . . . . .152 A7
Craydon St M11 . . . . .165 C4
Crayfield Rd M19 . . . . .111 B8
Crayford Rd M40 . . . . .83 B4
Cray The OL16 . . . . .31 E6
Cray Wlk M13 . . . . .163 B3
Creaton Way M24 . . . . .46 D4
Creden Ave M22 . . . . .121 F3
Crediton Cl
  Altrincham WA14 . . . . .119 B6
  Manchester M15 . . . . .162 C1
Crediton Dr
  Bolton BL2 . . . . .43 A7
  Platt Bridge WN2 . . . . .56 A1
Crediton Ho M6 . . . . .80 A3
Creel Cl M9 . . . . .64 B4
Cremer Ho M30 . . . . .80 A2
Cresbury St M12 . . . . .164 A4
Crescent M5 . . . . .81 C2
Crescent Ave
  3 Ashton-in-M WN4 . . . .73 A4
  8 Bolton BL1 . . . . .145 A4
  Farnworth BL4 . . . . .60 C6
  Manchester, Crumpsall
    M8 . . . . .156 A4
  Manchester, Hilton Park
    M25 . . . . .63 B2
  Over Hulton BL5 . . . . .59 A8

Crescent Ave continued
  Pendlebury M27 . . . . .80 B8
Crescent Cl
  Dukinfield SK16 . . . . .166 C1
  Stockport SK3 . . . . .124 A5
Crescent Ct
  6 Manchester M21 . . . . .96 F1
  Sale M33 . . . . .108 B3
Crescent Dr
  Manchester M8 . . . . .64 B1
  Walkden M38 . . . . .60 B5
Crescent Gr
  Cheadle SK8 . . . . .122 C6
  Manchester, Hilton Park
    M25 . . . . .63 B2
  6 Manchester, Levenshulme
    M19 . . . . .99 A1
Crescent Pk SK4 . . . . .168 C2
Crescent Range M14 . . . . . . .98 C3
Crescent Rd
  Alderley Edge SK9 . . . . . . .137 B2
  Altrincham, Ashley Heath
    WA15 . . . . .119 C1
  Altrincham, Oldfield Brow
    WA14 . . . . .119 A6
  Bolton BL3 . . . . .42 B3
  Cheadle SK8 . . . . .122 C6
  Dukinfield SK16 . . . . .166 C1
  Failsworth OL9 . . . . .65 E2
  Kearsley BL4 . . . . .60 F6
  Manchester M8 . . . . .156 A4
  Rochdale OL11 . . . . .30 B4
  Salford M6 . . . . .155 C4
  Stockport SK1 . . . . .112 B3
  Stockport M8 . . . . .156 C4
Crescent The
  Altrincham, Oldfield Brow
    WA14 . . . . .119 A5
  Altrincham, Timperley
    WA15 . . . . .119 F7
  Bolton, Bromley Cross
    BL7 . . . . .25 A7
  Bolton, Harwood BL2 . . . . . .25 F4
  Cheadle SK8 . . . . .122 D6
  Droylsden M43 . . . . .83 F1
  Horwich BL6 . . . . .22 E1
  Ince-in-M WN2 . . . . .56 B7
  Irlam M44 . . . . .93 F3
  Little Lever BL3 . . . . .43 B2
  4 Manchester M19 . . . . .99 A1
  Middleton M24 . . . . .64 E8
  Mossley OL5 . . . . .68 B1
  Prestwich M25 . . . . .63 B4
  Radcliffe M26 . . . . .43 D5
  Romiley SK6 . . . . .112 D4
  Shaw OL2 . . . . .149 A2
  Stalybridge SK15 . . . . .102 D6
  Stockport SK3 . . . . .124 A4
  Urmston M41 . . . . .94 F3
  Westhoughton BL5 . . . . .57 E7
  Whitworth OL12 . . . . .14 C8
  Wigan WN5 . . . . .54 D6
  Worsley M28 . . . . .79 A5
Crescent View **12**
  SK16 . . . . .166 B1
Crescent Way SK3 . . . . .124 A5
Cresgarth Ho SK3 . . . . .124 A4
Cressell Pk WN5 . . . . .19 B1
Cressfield Way M21 . . . . . . .109 D7
Cressingham Rd
  Bolton BL3 . . . . .146 A4
  Stretford M32 . . . . .96 B2
Cressington Cl **4** M5 . . . .154 B2
Cresswell Gr M20 . . . . .110 A5
Crestfield Gr WN6 . . . . .36 F2
Crestfold M38 . . . . .60 A4
Crest Lo SK7 . . . . .123 F2
Crest St M4 . . . . .159 A3
Crestwood Ave WN3 . . . . . . .54 F3
Crestwood Wlk M40 . . . . . .156 C2
Creswick Cl WN2 . . . . .56 C4
Crete St OL8 . . . . .66 F4
Crewe Rd M23 . . . . .120 E8
Crib Fold OL3 . . . . .51 A2
Crib La OL3 . . . . .51 A2
Criccieth Ave WN2 . . . . .38 D5
Criccieth Rd SK3 . . . . .123 A7
Criccieth St **2** M16 . . . . . .97 F4
Cricketers Fold SK7 . . . . . . .57 F8
Cricketfield La M26 . . . . . . .60 D3
Cricket Gr The M21 . . . . . . .109 B6
Cricket's La OL6 . . . . .85 D3
Cricket's La N OL6 . . . . . . .166 C3
Cricket St
  Bolton BL3 . . . . .145 A1
  Denton M34 . . . . .101 A4
  Wigan WN6 . . . . .150 A4
Cricket Street Bsns Ctr
  WN6 . . . . .150 A4
Cricket View OL6 . . . . .31 F5
Cricklewood Rd M22 . . . . . .121 C2
CRIMBLE 29 E4
Crimble La OL10, OL11 . . . . .29 F3
Crimble St OL12 . . . . .139 A4
Crime La OL8 . . . . .84 D7
Crimsworth Ave M16 . . . . . . .97 B2
Crinan Sq OL10 . . . . .28 F1
Crinan Way BL2 . . . . .42 F6
Crinan Wlk M40 . . . . .160 A3
Cringle Barrow Cl M28 . . . . .78 A5
Cringle Cl BL3 . . . . .40 F4
Cringle Dr SK8 . . . . .122 C3
Cringleford Wlk M12 . . . . . .164 C1
Cringle Hall Rd M19 . . . . . .110 F8
Cringle Rd M19 . . . . .111 C7
Crippen St M46 . . . . .58 A1

Cripple Gate WN6 . . . . .19 A2
Cripple Gate La OL11 . . . . . .30 E1
Crispin Rd M22 . . . . .130 E8
Critchley Cl SK14 . . . . .167 C1
Criterion St SK5 . . . . .99 F2
Croal Ave WN2 . . . . .56 A2
Croal St BL1 . . . . .145 A2
Croal Wlk M45 . . . . .45 B1
Croasdale Ave **2**
  M14 . . . . .110 B8
Croasdale Cl OL2 . . . . .48 E5
Croasdale St BL1 . . . . .143 C1
Crocker Wlk **23** M9 . . . . .157 B4
Crocus Dr OL2 . . . . .149 A1
Crocus St BL1 . . . . .143 C1
Crocus Wlk M7 . . . . .155 A2
Croft Acres BL0 . . . . .1 D2
Croft Ave
  Atherton M46 . . . . .58 D2
  Golborne WA3 . . . . .73 F2
  Middleton M25 . . . . .63 F8
  Orrell WN5 . . . . .53 D5
Croft Bank
  Manchester M18 . . . . .99 E5
  4 Salford M7 . . . . .81 C5
  Stalybridge SK15 . . . . .86 D4
Croft Brow OL8 . . . . .66 E2
Croft Cl WA15 . . . . .129 C6
Croft Ct WN7 . . . . .75 C1
Croft Dr BL8 . . . . .26 E6
Croft Edge OL3 . . . . .69 A5
Crofters Brook M26 . . . . . . .44 C4
Crofters Gn SK9 . . . . .136 F6
Crofters Hall Wlk M40 . . . . .83 B7
Crofters The M33 . . . . .108 F3
Crofters Wlk BL2 . . . . .25 C6
Crofters' Yd **14** WN1 . . . .150 C4
Croft Gate BL2 . . . . .25 C4
Croft Gates Rd M24 . . . . . . .64 D7
Croft Gr M38 . . . . .59 E5
Croft Head Dr OL16 . . . . . . .48 D4
Croft Head Dr OL16 . . . . . . .31 F7
Crofthill Ct **1** OL12 . . . . . .15 D4
Croft Hill Rd M40 . . . . .65 A1
Croft Ind Est BL9 . . . . .45 A5
Croft La
  Bolton BL3 . . . . .148 B1
  Radcliffe M26 . . . . .44 C4
  Whitefield BL9 . . . . .45 A5
Croftlands
  Orrell WN5 . . . . .53 D4
  Ramsbottom BL0 . . . . .11 A3
Croftlands Rd M22 . . . . . . .121 E4
Croftleigh Cl M45 . . . . .44 E2
Croft Manor SK13 . . . . .104 E1
Crofton Ave WA15 . . . . .120 A8
Crofton Gdns WA3 . . . . .91 E3
Crofton St
  Manchester M14 . . . . .98 B3
  Oldham OL8 . . . . .66 F3
  Whitefield BL9 . . . . .45 A6
Croftside Ave M28 . . . . .60 E5
Croftside Cl M28 . . . . .60 E3
Croftside Gr M28 . . . . .60 E3
Croftside Way SK9 . . . . . . .137 C6
Croft Sq OL12 . . . . .15 C3
Croft St
  Bolton BL3 . . . . .42 B4
  Bury BL9 . . . . .141 A2
  Droylsden M11 . . . . .83 A8
  4 Failsworth M35 . . . . . .66 A1
  Golborne WA3 . . . . .90 A8
  Hyde SK14 . . . . .167 A2
  Rochdale OL12 . . . . .15 C3
  Salford M7 . . . . .81 C5
  Stalybridge SK15 . . . . .86 B2
  Walkden M38 . . . . .59 F5
  Westhoughton BL5 . . . . .39 E3
Croftwood Sq WN5 . . . . .36 C2
Croichbank BL8 . . . . .10 D2
Croichley Fold BL8 . . . . .10 D2
Cromar Rd SK7 . . . . .124 F3
Cromarty Ave OL9 . . . . .65 F3
Cromarty Sq OL10 . . . . .28 F1
Cromarty Wlk M11 . . . . . . .160 C1
Crombie Ave M22 . . . . .121 D7
Crombouke Dr WN7 . . . . . . .57 E1
Crombouke Fold M28 . . . . . .78 B2
Cromdale Ave
  Bolton BL1 . . . . .144 B4
  Hazel Grove SK7 . . . . .124 F3
Cromedale Cres WN6 . . . . . .37 A7
Cromer Ave
  Bolton BL2 . . . . .25 C1
  Manchester M20 . . . . .110 B6
  Reddish M34 . . . . .100 A3
Cromer Dr M46 . . . . .58 A2
Cromer Ind Est M24 . . . . . . .47 B1

Cromer Rd
  Bury BL9 . . . . .27 D5
  Cheadle SK8 . . . . .122 E6
  Sale M33 . . . . .108 C3
  Wigan WN3 . . . . .54 E3
Cromer St
  Droylsden M11 . . . . .83 D1
  Middleton M24 . . . . .47 B1
  Rochdale OL12 . . . . .139 B4
  Shaw OL2 . . . . .149 B3
  Stockport SK1 . . . . .112 A2
Cromford Ave M32 . . . . .96 B3
Cromford Bank **21**
  SK13 . . . . .171 A2
Cromford Bsns Ctr
  OL1 . . . . .67 B8
Cromford Cl
  Bolton BL1 . . . . .143 B1
  22 Gamesley SK13 . . . .171 A2
Cromford Dr WN5 . . . . .54 B5
Cromford Fold **23**
  SK13 . . . . .171 A2
Cromford Gdns BL1 . . . . . . .143 C2
Cromford Grn **20** SK13 . . .171 A2
Cromford Gr **18** SK13 . . . .171 A2
Cromford Lea **19**
  SK13 . . . . .171 A2
Cromford Pl **24** SK13 . . . .171 A2
Cromford St OL1 . . . . .67 A8
Cromford Way **17**
  SK13 . . . . .171 A2
Cromhurst St M8 . . . . .156 A4
Cromley Rd
  High Lane SK6 . . . . .134 E6
  Stockport SK2 . . . . .124 A3
Crompton Ave
  Bolton BL2 . . . . .42 E8
  Rochdale OL16 . . . . .31 B3
Crompton Cl
  Bolton BL2 . . . . .25 A4
  Marple SK6 . . . . .125 F7
  Radcliffe M26 . . . . .43 C6
Crompton Ct
  Ashton-in-M WN4 . . . . .73 B2
  Little Lever BL3 . . . . .43 C3
CROMPTON FOLD 32 D1
Crompton Fold BL8 . . . . .27 B4
Crompton Gate OL2 . . . . . . .149 A4
Crompton Ho **2** WN1 . . . . .151 E8
Crompton House CE Sch
  OL2 . . . . .48 F7
Crompton Lodge Cvn Pk
  BL3 . . . . .42 E3
Crompton Pl
  Bolton BL1 . . . . .145 C3
  Radcliffe M26 . . . . .44 B3
Crompton Prim Sch
  OL2 . . . . .149 A2
Crompton Rd
  Horwich BL6 . . . . .39 F8
  Kearsley M26 . . . . .61 A8
  Manchester M19 . . . . .111 A7
Crompton St
  Ashton-u-L OL6 . . . . .85 E4
  Bolton BL1 . . . . .148 A4
  Bury BL9 . . . . .140 B2
  Chadderton OL9 . . . . .152 C3
  Farnworth BL4 . . . . .60 E7
  Ince-in-M WN3 . . . . .55 F3
  Oldham OL1 . . . . .153 B4
  Platt Bridge WN2 . . . . .56 B3
  Royton OL2 . . . . .48 E3
  Shaw OL2 . . . . .149 B3
  Swinton M27 . . . . .79 E8
  Walkden, Greenheys
    M38 . . . . .59 D5
  Walkden, Whittle Brook
    M28 . . . . .60 F2
  Wigan WN1 . . . . .150 C4
Crompton Vale BL2 . . . . .42 D8
Crompton Way
  Bolton BL2 . . . . .25 C2
  Golborne WA3 . . . . .91 B8
  Shaw OL2 . . . . .149 B3
Cromwell Ave
  Gatley SK8 . . . . .122 A6
  Manchester M16 . . . . .97 C2
  Marple SK6 . . . . .125 D7
  Reddish SK5 . . . . .100 A3
Cromwell Cl WA12 . . . . .89 A4
Cromwell Ct M44 . . . . .105 F7
Cromwell Gr
  Manchester M19 . . . . .99 B1
  9 Salford M7 . . . . .81 C5
Cromwell High Sch
  SK16 . . . . .101 C6
Cromwell Range M14 . . . . . .98 C2
Cromwell Rd
  Bramhall SK7 . . . . .132 D6
  Brinnington SK6 . . . . .112 C6
  Eccles M30 . . . . .79 D2
  Irlam M44 . . . . .105 E7
  Prestwich M25 . . . . .63 C4
  Royton OL2 . . . . .48 C6
  Salford M6 . . . . .81 B5
  Stretford M32 . . . . .96 F1
  Swinton M27 . . . . .61 E1
  Whitefield M45 . . . . .44 D2
Cromwell St
  Bolton BL1 . . . . .145 B3
  Heywood OL10 . . . . .29 D1
  Oldham OL1 . . . . .153 C2
  Stockport SK4 . . . . .168 C1
Crondale Wlk **8** M13 . . . .163 C2
Crondall St M14 . . . . .98 A3
Cronkeyshaw Ave
  OL12 . . . . .14 E2
Cronkeyshaw Rd OL12 . . . . .14 F1

Cronshaw St M19....111 B8
Crookall St WN4....73 C4
CROOKE....36 C3
Crooke Rd WN6....36 C3
Crookhill Dr M8....155 C3
Crookhurst Ave WN5....71 D6
Crookilley Way SK1,
SK6....112 C4
Crook St
Adlington PR7....20 F7
Bolton BL3....145 C2
12 Hindley WN2....56 D4
Hyde SK14....167 B2
9 Radcliffe M26....44 B3
16 Rochdale OL16....31 A8
Wigan WN1....150 B4
Croom Wlk M40....160 A2
Cropton Way WN2....56 F3
Crosby Ave M28....60 F2
Crosby Gr M46....58 E4
Crosby Rd
Bolton BL1....144 B4
Failsworth M40....83 D5
Radcliffe M26....43 E7
3 Salford M6....80 D5
Crosby St
Atherton M46....58 E4
1 Rochdale OL12....15 A2
Stockport SK2....170 C3
Crosfield Ave BL9....11 C2
Crosfield Gr M18....99 D4
Crosland Ind Est SK6....112 E4
Crossacres Prim Sch
M22....121 F4
Crossacres Rd M22....121 E3
Cross Ave M25....63 A4
Crossbank Av OL4....67 F7
Crossbank Cl M13....164 A1
Crossbank St
Oldham, Bank Top
OL8....153 B2
Oldham OL8....153 B1
Crossbank Way M24....46 F1
Crossbridge Rd SK14....102 A2
Crossbrook Way OL16....32 A5
Crossby Cl M9....64 F5
Cross Cliffe
Glossop SK13....116 E8
Hyde SK14....113 C8
Crosscliffe St 3 M16....97 F4
Crossdale Rd
Bolton BL2....42 F8
Manchester M9....57 A5
Manchester M9....64 F4
Crossdale Way WA11....71 B1
Crossefield Rd SK8....123 A3
Crossen St BL3....148 C1
Crossfell Ave M9....64 B5
Crossfield Ave WA3....91 F2
Crossfield Cl
Denton M34....101 A2
Stalybridge SK15....86 A1
Wardle OL12....15 C6
Crossfield Dr
Hindley WN2....57 C3
Radcliffe M26....43 E3
Swinton M27....61 E1
Worsley M28....78 F7
Crossfield Gr
Marple SK6....114 B1
Stockport SK2....124 B4
Crossfield Pl OL11....31 A5
Crossfield Rd
Altrincham WA15....120 B2
Handforth SK9....131 D4
Irlam M30....94 C4
Wardle OL12....15 C6
Crossfields BL7....25 C8
Crossfield St BL9....44 F4
Crossford Dr BL3....40 E4
Crossford St M32....96 D1
Crossgate Ave M22....121 D6
Crossgate La SK13....103 F7
Crossgate Mews SK4....110 E2
Crossgates Prim Sch
OL16....32 A7
Crossgates Rd OL16....32 A6
Crossgill M29....77 B5
Cross Glebe St 3
OL6....166 C3
Cross Gr WA15....119 F8
Crosshill St 4 M16....97 F4
Crosshill Wlk BL3....40 E5
Crossings The WA12....89 C3
Cross Keys St M4....159 B2
Cross Knowle View
M41....95 A4
Cross La
Droylsden M43....84 D4
Manchester M18....99 D5
Marple SK6....125 E5
Newton-le-W WA12....89 B4
Orrell WN5....53 D3
Radcliffe M26....44 C4
Ramsbottom BL8....138 A2
Salford M5, M6....81 B2
Wilmslow SK9....137 F8
Cross La E M31....105 F3
Crossland Rd
Droylsden M43....84 B2
Manchester M21....109 A8
Crosslands M25....43 A3
Crosslands Cl M13....116 D8
Crosslands Rd M28....77 F6
Cross La W M31....105 F2
Crosslee Com Prim Sch
M9....64 F4

Crosslee Rd M9....65 A4
Cross Lees OL12....15 A3
Crossley Cres OL6....85 E6
Crossley St M44....160 A1
Crossley Pk SK4....111 B6
Crossley Rd
Manchester M19,
SK4....111 A7
Sale M33....108 A6
Crossley St
Little Lever BL3....43 A3
Manchester M18....165 B2
Milnrow OL16....31 E6
Royton OL2....48 E2
Shaw OL2....149 C3
Stalybridge SK15....85 F2
Crossmead Dr 3 M9....64 E5
Crossmeadow Cl OL11....30 A8
Crossmoor Cres SK6....113 C1
Crossmoor Dr BL2....148 B4
Crossmoor Gr SK6....113 C2
Cross Ormrod St BL3....145 A2
Cross Rd
Gatley SK8....131 B7
Manchester M21....109 B8
Cross Rise SK15....85 F2
Cross St
4 Altrincham WA14....119 D4
Ashton-u-L OL6....166 A2
Aspull WN2....38 B6
Atherton M46....58 B4
Bolton BL1....145 C4
Bolton, Eagley BL7....25 A7
3 Broadbottom SK14....115 A8
Bury BL9....140 C2
Denton M34....100 E5
Farnworth BL4....60 D8
Glossop SK13....104 C1
Golborne WA3....90 A7
Hadfield SK13....104 A5
Heywood OL10....29 E1
Hindley WN2....56 D5
Hollingworth SK14....171 A4
Hyde SK14....167 A2
Ince-in-M WN3....55 E4
Kearsley BL4....61 B6
Leigh WN7....76 A4
Little Lever BL3....43 B3
Manchester M2....158 C1
Manchester, Old Trafford
M16....162 A1
8 Middleton M24....46 F1
Middleton M24....47 B8
Milnrow OL16....31 D7
4 Mossley OL5....68 C2
Oldham, County End OL4....68 A6
Oldham, Mumps OL4....67 B7
3 Oldham, Salem OL4....67 B7
Radcliffe M26....44 B3
Ramsbottom BL0....138 C2
Rochdale OL11....30 C2
Sale M33....108 B6
Salford M3....158 B2
Stalybridge SK15....86 D4
Standish WN6....19 E1
Stretford M32....96 D2
Swinton, Clifton Junction
M27....62 D2
Swinton, Hazelhurst M28....79 C7
Tyldesley M29....58 F2
Urmston M41....95 C1
Whitefield M45....144 E1
9 Wigan, Lamberhead Green
WN5....54 B6
Wigan WN3....150 C3
Cross The 1 SK13....104 A1
Crosswaite Rd SK2....124 E6
Crossway
Bramhall SK7....132 E5
Droylsden M43....100 A4
Manchester M20....110 B3
Stockport SK2....124 A4
Crossway Cl 9 M4....73 E5
Crossway Ho 8 M20....110 B3
Crossway Rd M23....107 F1
Crossways
Bramhall SK7....123 C1
Oldham OL8....67 A1
Cross Yd 7 WN1....37 C1
Croston Ave PR6....21 A8
Croston Cl SK9....137 C1
Croston Close Rd BL9,
OL12....12 C4
Crostons Rd BL8....140 A3
Croston St
Bolton BL3....146 C4
Hindley WN2....56 C6
Croston Wlk M11....160 B1
Croton St SK4....110 E2
Croughton Cl 8 M11....99 D7
Crowbank Wlk M40....83 A5
Crowborough Cl BL6....22 F1
Crowborough Wlk 9
M15....162 C1
Crowbrook Gr 9 SK9....131 D1
Crowcroft Park Prim Sch
M12....99 A3
Crowcroft Rd M12, M13....99 A3
Crowden Dr SK13....104 B5
Crowden Rd M40....65 B2
CROWHILL....84 F4
Crow Hill SK15....86 B1
Crowhill Cotts OL7....166 A4
Crow Hill N M24....46 F7
Crowhill Rd OL7....84 F4
Crow Hill S M24....46 F6
Crow Hill View OL4....67 F5
Crowhurst Dr WN1....37 B3

Crowhurst Wlk 2
M23....120 E7
Crow La BL0....138 C2
Crow La E WA12....89 C4
Crowland Gdns SK8....132 B6
Crowland Rd
Bolton BL2....25 C2
Wythenshawe M23....120 F3
Crow La W WA12....89 A4
Crowley La OL4....49 D1
Crowley Rd
Altrincham WA15....120 B6
Manchester M9....157 C4
Crown Bsns Ctr M35....83 F8
Crown Ct SK7....124 D3
Crowndale BL7....9 D7
Crowneast St OL11....30 C7
Crown Fields Cl WA12....89 B5
Crown Gdns
Edgworth BL7....9 D5
Newton-le-W WA12....89 B4
13 Rochdale OL16....31 A5
Crown Gn WA13....117 B4
Crown Gr WN7....76 D6
Crowngreen Rd M30....79 E1
Crown Hill OL5....86 D8
Crownhill Dr M43....84 A2
Crown Ind Est
Altrincham WA14....119 E7
Manchester M4....159 C2
Crown La
Horwich BL6....22 A4
Manchester M4....159 A3
Crown Mews SK2....124 C4
Crown Pk WA2....89 B5
Crown Pasages WA15....119 E2
Crown Point BL7....9 D6
Crown Point Ave M40....83 C5
Crown Point North Sh Pk
M34....100 E4
Crown Rd OL10....29 B2
Crown Royal Ind Pk
Stockport SK2....124 A8
Stockport SK1....170 C4
Crown Sq M3....158 B1
Crown St
Ashton-u-L OL6....166 B2
Atherton M46....58 B3
Bolton BL1....145 C3
Denton M34....100 E4
Failsworth M35....83 C5
20 Failsworth, Newton Heath
M40....83 C5
Hindley WN2....56 C6
Manchester M15....162 B3
Newton-le-W WA12....89 A3
Rochdale OL16....31 B5
Romiley SK6....112 F4
Salford M3....158 B2
Shaw OL2....150 B2
Crow Orchard Rd WN6....19 A1
Crowsdale Pl SK2....124 E4
Crowshaw Dr OL12....14 E3
Crow's Nest BL3....42 F5
Crow's Nest Cotts BL3....42 F5
Crosswood Dr SK15....86 D5
Crowther Ave M5....161 A4
Crowther Ct
Bochdale OL15....15 E4
Stockport SK4....168 A3
Crowther Dr WN3....54 E1
Crowther St
Littleborough OL15....15 E4
Manchester M18....99 E5
Rochdale OL16....31 B4
Stockport SK1....169 C1
Crowthorn Dr M23....121 A2
Crowthorn Rd
Ashton-u-L OL7....84 F1
Edgworth BL7....10 B8
Reddish SK4....111 D7
Crowton Ave M33....107 D2
Crow Tree Ave 4 OL13....3 B8
Crow Trees La BL7....9 C7
Crow Wood Rd
Edenfield BB4....1 D6
Golborne WA3....74 D1
Croxdale Cl OL7....84 E5
Croxdale Wlk M9....64 D5
Croxton Ave OL16....31 B8
Croxton Cl
Marple SK6....126 B5
Sale M33....107 D2
Croxton Wlk
8 Horwich BL6....22 B4
Manchester M13....163 C2
Croyde Cl
Bolton BL2....25 F3
Hindley WN2....57 D3
Wythenshawe M22....130 F7
Croydon Ave
Leigh WN7....75 F8
Rochdale OL12....48 C6
Truб OL11....47 D8
Croydon Ct M5....161 B4
Croydon Dr M40....83 C4
Croydon Sq OL11....47 D8
Crummock Cl BL3....42 F3
Crummock Dr
Middleton M24....46 E3
Wigan WN1....37 A1
Crummock Rd
Farnworth BL4....59 E7
Gatley SK8....122 B3
CRUMPSALL....64 B1
Crumpsall La M8....64 A1

Crumpsall Lane Prim Sch
M8....64 A1
Crumpsall St BL1....143 B8
Crumpsall Sta M8....64 A1
Crumpsall Vale M9....64 C2
Crumpsall Way M8....64 B1
Crundale Rd 7 BL1....24 F6
Cruttenden Rd SK2....124 D4
Cryer St M40....83 C2
Crystal Cl WN2....56 A3
Crystal Ho 18 M60....97 D3
Cuba Ind Est BL0....138 C4
Cube The M11....83 A2
Cubley Rd M7....155 B4
Cuckoo Gr M25....63 B6
Cuckoo La
Bury, Fern Grove BL9....141 C3
Bury, Heap Bridge BL9....141 C2
Prestwich M25....63 B6
Cuddington Ave M20....110 A8
Cuddington Cres SK3....170 A2
13 Rochdale OL16....31 A5
Cuddington Way 7
SK9....131 D5
Cudworth Rd M9....64 A5
Cuerdon Wlk M22....121 E8
Culand St M12....164 B2
Culbert Ave M20....110 C1
Culcheth Ave WN2....56 B1
Culcheth Com Prim Sch
WA3....92 A3
Culcheth Hall Dr WA3....91 F4
Culcheth Hall Farm Barns
WA14....119 D3
Culcheth Hall Sch
WA14....119 D3
Culcheth La M40....83 C4
Culcheth Rd WA14....119 D3
Culcombe Wlk M13....163 C1
Culcross Ave WN3....54 C4
Culford Cl M12....164 E6
Culgaith Wlk M9....157 A3
Culham Cl BL1....143 A2
Cullen Cl WN2....56 A8
Cullen Gr M9....64 F3
Cullercoats Wlk 3
M12....99 B3
Culmere Rd M22....121 D1
Culmington Cl M15....162 B1
Culross Ave
Bolton BL3....40 E6
Failsworth M40....65 E1
Culvercliffe Wlk M3....162 B4
Culverdon Wlk M6....80 F6
Culver Rd SK3....170 A1
Culvert St
Oldham OL4....67 E8
Rochdale OL16....31 B2
Wigan WN6....37 A3
Culverwell Dr M5....81 B2
Culzean Cl WN7....76 C4
Cumberbatch Pl WN3....55 F4
Cumber Cl SK9....136 D4
Cumber Dr SK9....136 D4
Cumber La SK9....136 D4
Cumberland Ave
Brimington SK5....112 C4
Dukinfield SK16....101 E8
Heywood OL10....29 A2
Irlam M44....105 C5
Swinton M27....61 F2
Tyldesley M29....58 F2
Cumberland Cl BL9....44 E6
Cumberland Dr
Altrincham WA14....128 B8
Royton OL1, OL2....48 D2
Cumberland Gr OL7....166 B4
Cumberland Rd
Atherton M46....58 F4
Manchester M9....64 D1
Partington M31....105 E2
Rochdale OL11....30 F2
Sale M33....108 C2
Urmston M41....95 C1
Cumberland St
Salford M7....158 A4
3 Stalybridge SK15....85 F2
2 Wigan WN1....37 E1
Cumbermere La M29....59 B2
Cumbrae Gdns M5....154 B1
Cumbrae Rd M19....99 C1
Cumbria Ct M25....62 F1
Cumbrian Cl
Manchester M13....163 C2
Platt Bridge WN2....56 B2
Shaw OL2....48 E8
Cumbria Wlk M6....81 B4
Cummings St OL8....66 C2
Cunard Cl M13....163 C2
Cundall Wlk M23....108 F1
Cundey St BL1....144 C8
Cundiff Ct M19....99 C1
Cundiff Rd M21....109 B6
Cundy St SK14....167 B4
Cunliffe Ave
Newton-le-W WA12....89 B5
Ramsbottom BL0....11 A4
Cunliffe Brow BL1....142 B1
Cunliffe Ct WN7....75 A4
Cunliffe Dr
Sale M33....108 C3
Shaw OL2....149 D7
Cunliffe St
Dukinfield SK14....101 C4
Leigh WN7....75 C5

Cunliffe St continued
Radcliffe M26....44 C3
Ramsbottom BL0....138 C3
Stockport SK3....123 C8
Cunningham Dr
Gatley M22....131 A8
Whitefield BL9....45 B2
Cunningham Rd BL5....57 D7
Cunningham Way
OL1....153 C4
Curate Ct SK1....112 A1
Curate St SK1....112 A1
Curlew Cl OL11....29 F7
Curlew Dr M44....94 A4
Curlew Rd OL4....67 E4
Curlew Way SK13....115 F8
Curlew Wlk M12....164 B1
Currier La OL6....85 D2
Curteis St BL6....22 D8
Curtels Cl M28....79 C7
Curtis Gr SK13....104 A5
Curtis Rd
Reddish M19....99 C1
Stockport SK4....168 A2
Curtis St
Bolton BL3....146 C2
Wigan WN5....54 D6
Curven Edge BB4....1 A7
Curzon Ave M14....98 E4
Curzon Dr WA15....120 B6
Curzon Gn SK2....124 D7
Curzon Mews SK9....137 A5
Curzon Rd
Ashton-u-L OL6....85 D4
Bolton BL1....144 C3
Gatley SK8....131 B7
Poynton SK12....133 E2
Rochdale OL11....30 F2
5 Sale M33....108 B5
Salford M7....155 A3
Stockport SK2....124 D7
Stretford M32....96 A4
Curzon St
Mossley OL5....68 C1
Oldham OL1....153 C3
Cutacre Cl M29....59 B1
Cutacre La BL5....59 D6
CUTGATE....30 A8
Cutgate Cl M23....108 E1
Cutgate Rd OL12....14 B1
Cuthbert Ave M19....99 B2
Cuthbert Bsns Ctr
M11....165 C3
Cuthbert Ho M16....97 E2
Cuthbert Mayne Ct
OL16....139 B2
Cuthbert Rd SK8....122 E6
Cuthbert St
Bolton BL3....146 B2
Wigan WN5....54 D6
Cuthill Wlk M40....83 D4
Cut La OL12....13 F1
Cutland St M40....83 A6
Cutland Way OL15....16 A4
Cutler Cres OL13....3 D7
Cutler Hill Rd M35....84 C7
Cutler La OL13....3 D7
Cunook La M44....94 A3
Cutter Cl M5....161 A4
Cycle St M11....165 B4
Cyclone St M11....164 C4
Cygnet St WN3....150 B2
Cygnus Ave M7....81 C3
Cymbal Ct SK5....169 C3
Cynthia Dr SK6....125 F5
Cypress Ave OL9....152 B4
Cypress Cl SK3....123 C8
Cypress Gdns OL16....31 C3
Cypress Gr
Denton M34....101 A3
Kearsley BL4....60 F7
Cypress Ho 10 M14....98 E4
Cypress Oaks SK15....86 D3
Cypress Rd
Droylsden M43....84 A3
Eccles M30....79 A4
Oldham OL4....67 E4
Wigan WN5....54 E6
Cypress St
Manchester M9....157 A3
Middleton M24....46 B1
Cypress Way SK6....135 A7
Cypress Wlk 2 M33....107 C6
Cyprus Cl
Oldham OL4....67 D6
Salford M5....154 F1
Cyprus St M32....96 D2
Cyril St
Bolton BL3....148 A1
Manchester M14....98 B3
Shaw OL2....149 C3
Cyrus St M40....160 B2

D

Daccamill Dr M27....79 F6
Dacre Ave M16....97 B2
Dacre Cl M24....46 B1
Dacre Rd OL11....30 F4
DACRES....68 F4
Dacres Ave OL3....68 F4
Dacres Dr OL3....68 F4
Dacres Rd OL3....68 F4

Daffodil Cl
Haslingden BB4 . . . . . 1 A8
Rochdale OL12 . . . . . 14 E3
Daffodil Rd BL4 . . . . . 42 A1
Daffodil St BL1 . . . . . 24 F5
Dagenham Rd M14 . . . . . 98 C4
Dagenham Road Ind Est
M14 . . . . . 98 C3
Dagmar St M28 . . . . . 60 C4
Dagnall Ave M21 . . . . . 109 B6
Dahlia Cl
Manchester M19 . . . . . 110 F6
Rochdale OL12 . . . . . 14 D3
Dailton Rd WN8 . . . . . 53 A7
Daimler St M8 . . . . . 156 B2
Dain Cl SK16 . . . . . 101 D8
Daine Ave M23 . . . . . 109 B1
Dainton St M12 . . . . . 164 A3
Daintry Cl M15 . . . . . 162 C2
Daintry Rd OL9 . . . . . 152 C3
Dairybrook Gr 7 SK9 . . . . 131 E1
Dairydale Cl 3 M44 . . . . . 94 B3
Dairyground Rd SK7 . . . . . 132 F7
Dairyhouse La WA14 . . . . . 119 B7
Dairy House La SK7 . . . . . 132 B4
Dairy House Rd SK7 . . . . . 132 B5
Dairy House Small Holdings SK7 . . . . . 132 B4
Dairy St OL9 . . . . . 152 B3
Daisy Ave
Farnworth BL4 . . . . . 42 A1
Manchester M13 . . . . . 98 E4
Newton-le-W WA12 . . . . . 89 C2
Daisy Bank
Failsworth M40 . . . . . 83 D5
Hyde SK14 . . . . . 113 C8
Daisy Bank Ave M27 . . . . . 80 C6
Daisybank Cl WN2 . . . . . 56 D5
Daisy Bank Ct M40 . . . . . 83 D5
Daisy Bank La SK8 . . . . . 122 A1
Daisy Bank Mill Cl
WA3 . . . . . 91 E3
Daisy Bank Rd M14 . . . . . 98 D4
Daisybank Villas M14 . . . . . 98 D4
Daisyfield 9 BL6 . . . . . 22 D1
Daisyfield Cl M22 . . . . . 121 C1
Daisyfield Ct BL8 . . . . . 27 C1
Daisyfield Wlk 5 M28 . . . . 60 C3
Daisy Hall Dr BL5 . . . . . 57 E5
DAISY HILL 57 F6
Daisyhill Cl M33 . . . . . 108 E4
Daisyhill Ct BL5 . . . . . 57 F5
Daisy Hill Ct OL4 . . . . . 67 E8
Daisy Hill Dr PR6 . . . . . 21 A8
Daisy Hill Rd OL5 . . . . . 68 D1
Daisy Hill Sta BL5 . . . . . 57 F6
Daisy Mews SK3 . . . . . 123 D4
Daisy Nook Ctry Pk*
OL8 . . . . . 84 E6
Daisy Rd WN5 . . . . . 54 E6
Daisy St
Bolton BL3 . . . . . 146 C4
10 Bury BL8 . . . . . 27 C2
Chadderton OL9 . . . . . 152 A4
Oldham OL9 . . . . . 153 A3
4 Rochdale OL12 . . . . . 139 B4
Stockport SK1, SK2 . . . . . 170 C3
Daisy Way SK6 . . . . . 134 F7
Dakerwood Cl 3 M40 . . . . 83 C5
Dakins Rd WN7 . . . . . 76 B3
Dakley St M11 . . . . . 165 C3
Dakota Ave M50 . . . . . 96 F8
Dakota S M50 . . . . . 96 F8
Dalbeatie Rise WN1 . . . . . 37 F1
Dalbeattie St M9 . . . . . 64 E1
Dalberg St M12 . . . . . 164 A3
Dalbury Dr M40 . . . . . 156 C1
Dalby Ave M27 . . . . . 79 E7
Dalby Gr SK1 . . . . . 112 A1
Dalby Rd WN2 . . . . . 57 B5
Dale Ave
Bramhall SK7 . . . . . 132 F8
Eccles M30 . . . . . 79 C3
Mossley OL5 . . . . . 68 E3
Dalebank M46 . . . . . 58 C5
Dalebank Mews M27 . . . . . 61 D5
Dalebeck Cl M45 . . . . . 63 C8
Dalebeck Wlk M45 . . . . . 63 C8
Dale Brook Ave SK16 . . . . 101 D6
Dalebrook Ct SK4 . . . . . 168 C1
Dalebrook Rd M33 . . . . . 108 C1
Dalecrest WN5 . . . . . 53 D1
Dale Fields OL3 . . . . . 50 F4
Daleford Sq M13 . . . . . 163 C3
Dalegarth Ave BL1 . . . . . 40 C7
Dale Gr
Altrincham WA15 . . . . . 119 F7
Ashton-u-L OL7 . . . . . 85 A5
Irlam M44 . . . . . 105 E6
Leigh WN7 . . . . . 75 C4
Dale Grove Sch OL7 . . . . . 85 A5
Dalehead Cl M18 . . . . . 99 F6
Dalehead Dr OL2 . . . . . 49 D7
Dalehead Gr WN7 . . . . . 75 C4
Dalehead Pl WA11 . . . . . 71 B1
Dale Ho OL2 . . . . . 149 B2
Dale House Fold
SK12 . . . . . 134 A4
Dale Ind Est M26 . . . . . 44 A2
Dale La OL3 . . . . . 50 F5
Dale Lee BL5 . . . . . 58 A8
Dale Prim Sch The
SK6 . . . . . 125 D7
Dale Rd
Golborne WA3 . . . . . 90 A7
Dale Rd *continued*
Marple SK6 . . . . . 125 E7
Middleton M24 . . . . . 47 B2
Dale St E
Ashton-u-L OL6 . . . . . 166 A2
Horwich BL6 . . . . . 22 D2
Dale St W
Ashton-u-L OL6 . . . . . 166 A2
Horwich BL6 . . . . . 22 D2
Dales Ave
Manchester M8 . . . . . 63 F2
Whitefield M45 . . . . . 44 D1
Dalesbrook Cl BL3 . . . . . 43 A4
DALES BROW 79 E5
Dales Brow
Bolton BL1 . . . . . 24 F6
Swinton M27 . . . . . 79 E6
Dales Brow Ave OL7 . . . . . 85 A5
Dalesfield Cres OL5 . . . . . 68 E1
Dalesford Cl WN7 . . . . . 91 C8
Dales Gr M28 . . . . . 60 F1
Daleside Ave WN4 . . . . . 73 A8
Dales La M45 . . . . . 44 E1
Dalesman Cl M9 . . . . . 157 C4
Dalesman Dr OL1 . . . . . 49 D4
Dalesman Wlk 4
M15 . . . . . 163 A2
Dales Park Dr M27 . . . . . 79 D6
Dale Sq OL2 . . . . . 48 F4
Dale St
Ashton-u-L OL6 . . . . . 86 A6
8 Bacup OL13 . . . . . 3 C8
Bury BL8 . . . . . 27 C4
Farnworth BL4 . . . . . 42 E1
Ince-in-M WN3 . . . . . 55 F3
Leigh WN7 . . . . . 75 C5
Manchester M1 . . . . . 159 B1
Middleton M24 . . . . . 65 B7
Milnrow OL16 . . . . . 31 F6
Ramsbottom BL0 . . . . . 1 C1
Rochdale OL16 . . . . . 31 C7
Shaw OL2 . . . . . 149 B2
Stalybridge SK15 . . . . . 85 F1
Stockport SK3 . . . . . 170 A3
Swinton M27 . . . . . 79 E6
Westhoughton BL5 . . . . . 57 F5
Whitefield M45 . . . . . 44 E1
Daleswood Ave M45 . . . . . 44 D1
Dale View
Denton M34 . . . . . 113 A7
Hyde SK14 . . . . . 113 D8
Littleborough OL15 . . . . . 15 F2
Mottram in L SK14 . . . . . 103 A3
Newton-le-W WA12 . . . . . 89 E4
Dalham Ave M9 . . . . . 65 A2
Dalkeith Ave SK5 . . . . . 111 F7
Dalkeith Gr BL3 . . . . . 40 F5
Dalkeith Rd
Hindley WN2 . . . . . 57 A5
Reddish SK5 . . . . . 111 F7
Dalkeith Sq OL10 . . . . . 29 A1
Dallas Ct M50 . . . . . 96 E8
Dalley Ave M7 . . . . . 158 A4
Dallimore Rd M23 . . . . . 120 E6
Dalmahoy Cl M40 . . . . . 83 C8
Dalmain Cl M8 . . . . . 155 C2
Dalmeny Terr OL11 . . . . . 30 F4
Dalmorton Rd M21 . . . . . 109 D8
Dalny St M19 . . . . . 99 B1
Dalry Wlk 1 M23 . . . . . 121 A5
Dalston Ave M35 . . . . . 84 B8
Dalston Dr
Billinge WA11 . . . . . 71 B1
Bramhall SK7 . . . . . 132 C5
Manchester M20 . . . . . 110 C2
Dalston Gr WN3 . . . . . 54 D3
Dalton Ave
Manchester M14 . . . . . 98 A2
Milnrow OL16 . . . . . 31 D7
Stretford M32 . . . . . 96 A4
Swinton M27 . . . . . 62 C3
Whitefield M45 . . . . . 63 A7
Dalton Cl
Milnrow OL16 . . . . . 31 D7
Ramsbottom BL0 . . . . . 11 A4
Wigan WN5 . . . . . 54 B7
Dalton Ct M40 . . . . . 159 B4
Dalton Dr
Pendlebury M27 . . . . . 80 D7
Wigan WN3 . . . . . 54 E2
Dalton Fold BL5 . . . . . 57 F8
Dalton Gdns M41 . . . . . 95 B3
Dalton Gr
Ashton-in-M WN4 . . . . . 73 A4
Stockport SK4 . . . . . 168 C4
Dalton Ho 6 M14 . . . . . 110 D8
Dalton Rd
Manchester M9 . . . . . 64 D5
Middleton M24 . . . . . 64 B7
Dalton St
Bury BL8 . . . . . 27 B2
Chadderton OL9 . . . . . 152 B3
Eccles M30 . . . . . 79 D3
Failsworth M35 . . . . . 83 E8
Manchester M4, M40 . . . . . 159 B4
Oldham OL1 . . . . . 67 B7
Sale M33 . . . . . 108 C6
Daltry St OL1 . . . . . 67 A8
Dalveen Ave M41 . . . . . 95 C4
Dalveen Dr WA15 . . . . . 119 F7
Dalwood Cl WN2 . . . . . 56 F4
Dalymount Cl BL2 . . . . . 25 B2
Damask Ave M3 . . . . . 158 A2
Dame Hollow SK8 . . . . . 131 D7
Damery Ct SK7 . . . . . 132 E8
Damery Rd SK7 . . . . . 132 E8
Dame St OL9 . . . . . 153 A4
Dam Head Dr M9 . . . . . 64 E3
Dam Head La WA3 . . . . . 105 A5
Damian Dr WA12 . . . . . 89 A5
Damien St M12 . . . . . 99 B2
Dam La
Ashton-in-M WN4 . . . . . 73 F3
Hollinfare WA3 . . . . . 105 A4
Dams Head Fold BL5 . . . . . 39 F1
Damson Gn M24 . . . . . 65 D8
Damson Wlk M31 . . . . . 105 D3
Dan Bank SK6 . . . . . 125 C6
Danbury Wlk M23 . . . . . 120 D8
Danby Cl SK14 . . . . . 167 C4
Danby Ct 6 OL1 . . . . . 153 B4
Danby Pl SK14 . . . . . 167 C4
Danby Rd
Bolton BL3 . . . . . 147 B3
Hyde SK14 . . . . . 167 C4
Danby Wlk M9 . . . . . 64 E1
Dane Ave
Cheadle SK3 . . . . . 123 A8
Partington M31 . . . . . 105 F4
DANEBANK 135 E5
DANE BANK 100 B2
Dane Bank M24 . . . . . 65 B7
Dane Bank Dr SK12 . . . . . 135 D6
Danebank Mews M34 . . . . 100 B2
Dane Bank Prim Sch
SK5 . . . . . 100 A2
Danebank Wlk 14
M13 . . . . . 163 B3
Danebridge Cl BL4 . . . . . 60 E8
Danebury Cl 11 WN2 . . . . . 56 D4
Dane Cl SK7 . . . . . 123 D3
Danecroft BL3 . . . . . 43 C3
Danecroft Cl M13 . . . . . 164 A1
Dane Dr SK9 . . . . . 137 D6
Danefield Ct SK8 . . . . . 131 D8
Danefield Rd M33 . . . . . 108 C6
Dane Hill Cl SK12 . . . . . 135 D5
Dane Ho 4 M33 . . . . . 108 C4
Daneholme Rd M19 . . . . . 110 E5
Dane Mews M33 . . . . . 108 B4
Dane Rd
Reddish M34 . . . . . 100 A2
Sale M33 . . . . . 108 D5
Dane Road Ind Est
M33 . . . . . 108 C6
Dane Road Sta M33 . . . . . 108 C6
Danes Ave WN2 . . . . . 56 E6
Danes Brook Cl WN2 . . . . . 56 E6
Danesbury Cl WN5 . . . . . 71 E4
Danesbury Rd BL2 . . . . . 25 B4
Danesbury Rise SK8 . . . . . 122 D5
Danes Gn WN2 . . . . . 56 E7
Daneshill M25 . . . . . 63 B6
Danesmoor Dr BL9 . . . . . 141 B4
Danesmoor Rd M20 . . . . . 110 B5
Danes Rd M14 . . . . . 98 D2
Dane St
Bolton BL3 . . . . . 146 C4
Manchester M11 . . . . . 99 E7
Mossley OL5 . . . . . 68 D3
6 Oldham OL4 . . . . . 67 C7
Rochdale OL11 . . . . . 139 B3
Danesway
Adlington PR7 . . . . . 20 F8
Manchester M25 . . . . . 63 D2
Pendlebury M27 . . . . . 80 C6
Wigan WN1 . . . . . 37 B3
Danesway Ct BL1 . . . . . 143 A2
Daneswood Ave
Manchester M9 . . . . . 64 F4
Whitworth OL12 . . . . . 14 C8
Daneswood Cl OL12 . . . . . 14 C8
Daneswood Fold OL12 . . . . 14 C8
Danett Cl M12 . . . . . 165 B2
Dane Wlk SK5 . . . . . 169 C4
Dan Fold 5 OL1 . . . . . 153 B3
Danforth Gr M19 . . . . . 111 B8
DANGEROUS CORNER
Hindley 57 D2
Standish 18 C2
Daniel Adamson Ave
M31 . . . . . 105 D3
Daniel Adamson Rd
Salford M50 . . . . . 154 A1
Stretford M50 . . . . . 96 D8
Daniel Ct M31 . . . . . 105 F4
Daniel Fold OL12 . . . . . 14 B2
Daniel's La SK1 . . . . . 169 C2
Daniel St
Hazel Grove SK7 . . . . . 124 E2
Heywood OL10 . . . . . 29 B2
Oldham OL1 . . . . . 67 C8
Royton OL2 . . . . . 49 A3
Whitworth OL12 . . . . . 4 D2
Daniel Street Ind Est
OL12 . . . . . 4 D2
Danisher La OL8 . . . . . 84 F8
Dannywood Cl SK14 . . . . . 113 C8
Danson St M40 . . . . . 160 B3
Dantall Ave M9 . . . . . 65 A3
Dante Cl M6, M30 . . . . . 80 A4
Danty St 28 SK16 . . . . . 166 B1
Dantzic St M4 . . . . . 159 A3
Danube The 10 M15 . . . . . 162 C3
Danwood Cl M34 . . . . . 101 B1
Dapple Gr M11 . . . . . 165 A4
Darbishire St BL1 . . . . . 25 A1
Darby La WN2 . . . . . 56 D6
Darby Rd M44 . . . . . 106 A6
Darbyshire Cl BL1 . . . . . 144 C4
Darbyshire Ho WA15 . . . . . 120 C7
Darbyshire St M26 . . . . . 44 A3
Darbyshire Wlk 1
M26 . . . . . 44 B3
DARCY LEVER 42 D5
Darcy St BL2 . . . . . 148 C1
Darcy Wlk M14 . . . . . 98 A4
Darden Cl SK4 . . . . . 110 E3
Darell Wlk M8 . . . . . 156 B2
Daresbury Ave
Altrincham WA15 . . . . . 119 E5
Urmston M41 . . . . . 94 E4
Daresbury Cl
Sale M33 . . . . . 108 F3
Stockport SK3 . . . . . 170 A1
4 Wilmslow SK9 . . . . . 137 C8
Daresbury Rd M21 . . . . . 96 F1
Daresbury St M8 . . . . . 156 A3
Darfield Wlk M40 . . . . . 160 A3
Dargai St M11 . . . . . 83 D1
Dargle Rd M33 . . . . . 108 B6
Darian Ave M22 . . . . . 130 D8
Daric Cl WN7 . . . . . 75 C1
Dark La
Blackrod BL6 . . . . . 21 B3
Delph OL3 . . . . . 50 E6
Manchester M12 . . . . . 164 A4
Mossley OL5 . . . . . 68 D2
Romiley SK6 . . . . . 112 D3
Uppermill OL3 . . . . . 69 A8
Darlbeck Wlk M21 . . . . . 109 C5
Darley Ave
Eccles M30 . . . . . 95 C8
Farnworth BL4 . . . . . 42 E1
Gatley SK8 . . . . . 122 B5
Manchester M21 . . . . . 109 C5
Darley Gr BL4 . . . . . 42 E1
Darley Ho 5 M5 . . . . . 154 B1
Darley Rd
Hazel Grove SK7 . . . . . 133 F7
Manchester M16 . . . . . 97 C3
Rochdale OL11 . . . . . 30 F4
Wigan WN3 . . . . . 55 B3
Darley St
Bolton BL1 . . . . . 143 A1
Farnworth BL4 . . . . . 60 E8
Horwich BL6 . . . . . 22 B5
Manchester M11 . . . . . 160 C1
Sale M33 . . . . . 108 B4
Stretford M32 . . . . . 96 E4
Darley Terr 5 BL1 . . . . . 143 A1
Darlington Cl BL8 . . . . . 27 B5
Darlington Rd
Manchester M20 . . . . . 110 A6
Rochdale OL11 . . . . . 30 F3
Darlington St E
Tyldesley M29 . . . . . 59 B1
Wigan WN1 . . . . . 151 B3
Darlington St
Ince-in-M WN2 . . . . . 56 A7
Tyldesley M29 . . . . . 59 A1
Wigan WN1 . . . . . 151 A3
Darliston Ave M9 . . . . . 64 A5
Darlton Wlk 9 M9 . . . . . 157 B4
Darnall Ave M20 . . . . . 110 A8
Darnbrook Dr 4 M22 . . . . 121 B1
Darncombe Cl M16 . . . . . 97 F4
Darnhall St WN3 . . . . . 55 F4
DARN HILL 28 E2
Darnhill Com Sch OL10 . . . 28 F1
Darnley Ave M28 . . . . . 60 C1
Darnley St M16 . . . . . 97 D4
Darnton Gdns OL6 . . . . . 85 E3
Darnton Rd OL6, SK15 . . . . 85 E3
Darran Ave WN3 . . . . . 54 F3
Darras Rd M18 . . . . . 99 C3
Dart Cl OL9 . . . . . 65 F8
Dartford Ave
Brinnington SK5 . . . . . 112 B6
Eccles M30 . . . . . 79 B2
Dartford Cl M12 . . . . . 164 A2
Dartford Rd M41 . . . . . 95 C1
Dartington Cl
Altrincham M23 . . . . . 120 D6
Stockport SK7 . . . . . 123 F2
Dartington Rd WN2 . . . . . 55 F3
Dartmouth Cl 4 OL8 . . . . . 66 F4
Dartmouth Cres SK5 . . . . 112 C5
Dartmouth Rd
Manchester M21 . . . . . 109 C8
Whitefield M45 . . . . . 63 A7
Dartnall Cl SK12 . . . . . 135 A6
Darton Ave M40 . . . . . 160 B3
Darul-Uloom Islamic Coll
BL8 . . . . . 10 F4
Darvel Ave WN4 . . . . . 72 C4
Darvel Cl BL2 . . . . . 42 F6
Darwell Ave M30 . . . . . 95 C8
Darwen Dr 3 WN2 . . . . . 56 A2
Darwen Rd BL7 . . . . . 25 A7
Darwen St M16 . . . . . 161 C1
Darwin Gr SK7 . . . . . 132 E6
Darwin St
Ashton-u-L OL7 . . . . . 166 A2
Bolton BL1 . . . . . 143 A2
Dukinfield SK14 . . . . . 102 A5
Oldham OL4 . . . . . 67 C5
Dashwood Rd M25 . . . . . 62 F5
Dashwood Wlk M12 . . . . . 165 A2
Datchett Terr OL11 . . . . . 30 F4
DAUBHILL 146 C3
Dauntesy Ave M27 . . . . . 80 D7
Davehall Ave SK9 . . . . . 137 A7
Davenfield Gr M20 . . . . . 110 B3
Davenfield Ho 7
M20 . . . . . 110 B3
Davenfield Rd 2 M20 . . . . 110 B3
Davenham Rd
Handforth SK9 . . . . . 131 D4
Reddish SK5 . . . . . 99 F2
Sale M33 . . . . . 107 F6
Davenhill Rd M19 . . . . . 111 A8
DAVENPORT 123 E4
Davenport Ave
Manchester M20 . . . . . 110 B7
Radcliffe M26 . . . . . 43 F6
Wilmslow SK9 . . . . . 136 E4
Davenport Dr SK6 . . . . . 113 B6
Davenport Fold BL2 . . . . . 26 A3
Davenport Fold Rd
BL2 . . . . . 26 A4
Davenport Gdns 9
BL1 . . . . . 145 B4
DAVENPORT GREEN
Hale 120 F2
Wilmslow 136 F3
Davenport La WA14 . . . . . 119 C7
Davenport Lo SK3 . . . . . 170 C1
DAVENPORT PARK 124 A5
Davenport Park Rd
SK2 . . . . . 124 A5
Davenport Rd SK7 . . . . . 124 D2
Davenport St
2 Ashton-u-L M34 . . . . . 100 E8
Bolton BL1 . . . . . 145 B4
Droylsden M43 . . . . . 83 E1
Davenport Sta SK3 . . . . . 170 C1
Daventry Rd
Manchester M21 . . . . . 109 D8
Rochdale OL11 . . . . . 30 F3
Daveyhulme St OL12 . . . . . 15 B1
Davey La SK9 . . . . . 137 B2
Daveylands
Urmston M41 . . . . . 94 F5
Wilmslow SK9 . . . . . 137 D7
David Brow BL3 . . . . . 146 A2
David Cl M34 . . . . . 101 A1
David Lewis Cl OL16 . . . . . 31 C6
David Mews M14 . . . . . 110 C7
David Pegg Wlk M40 . . . . . 83 B5
David St N 15 OL12 . . . . . 14 F1
David's Farm Cl M24 . . . . . 65 C7
Davids La OL4 . . . . . 67 F7
Davidson Dr M24 . . . . . 65 B6
Davidson Wlk WN5 . . . . . 54 E7
David's Rd M43 . . . . . 83 E2
David St
Bacup OL13 . . . . . 3 D8
Bury BL8 . . . . . 27 C4
Denton M34 . . . . . 101 A2
2 Oldham OL1 . . . . . 153 B2
Reddish SK5 . . . . . 111 E8
16 Rochdale OL12 . . . . . 14 F1
Davies Ave
Gatley SK8 . . . . . 131 B6
Newton-le-W WA12 . . . . . 89 C4
Davies Ct SK6 . . . . . 113 B2
Davies Rd
Partington M31 . . . . . 106 A3
Romiley SK6 . . . . . 112 D3
Davies Sq M14 . . . . . 98 A4
Davies St
Ashton-u-L OL7 . . . . . 84 F1
Kearsley BL4 . . . . . 61 A7
Oldham OL1 . . . . . 153 A4
Platt Bridge WN2 . . . . . 56 A2
Davis St M30 . . . . . 79 F1
Davy Ave M27 . . . . . 62 D2
DAVYHULME 95 B4
Davyhulme Circ M41 . . . . . 95 C4
Davyhulme Jun & Inf Schs
M41 . . . . . 95 D3
Davyhulme Rd
Stretford M32 . . . . . 96 C3
Urmston, Calder Bank
M41 . . . . . 94 F4
Urmston, Davyhulme
M41 . . . . . 95 B4
Davyhulme Rd E M32 . . . . . 96 D3
Davy St M40 . . . . . 159 B4
Daw Bank SK3 . . . . . 169 B1
Dawber Delph WN6 . . . . . 35 D8
Dawber St WN4 . . . . . 73 D4
Dawes St BL3 . . . . . 145 C2
Dawley Cl
Ashton-in-M WN4 . . . . . 73 A3
Bolton BL3 . . . . . 144 C2
Dawlish Ave
Brinnington SK5 . . . . . 112 C5
Chadderton OL9 . . . . . 47 F1
Cheadle SK8 . . . . . 131 F7
Droylsden M43 . . . . . 83 E1
Dawlish Cl
Bramhall SK7 . . . . . 132 E7
Hattersley SK14 . . . . . 102 E3
Hollinfare WA3 . . . . . 105 B3
Dawlish Rd
Manchester M21 . . . . . 109 C8
Sale M33 . . . . . 107 E5
Dawlish Way WA3 . . . . . 73 F1
Dawnay St M11 . . . . . 165 B3
Dawn St OL2 . . . . . 149 B2
Dawnwood Sq WN5 . . . . . 36 C2
Dawson Ave WN6 . . . . . 37 A3
Dawson La BL1 . . . . . 145 B3
Dawson Rd
Altrincham WA14 . . . . . 119 D8
Gatley SK8 . . . . . 131 D8
Dawson St
Atherton M46 . . . . . 58 C3
Bury BL9 . . . . . 141 A4
Heywood OL10 . . . . . 29 C2
Hyde SK14 . . . . . 167 B1
Mancheste M3 . . . . . 158 C2
Manchesterr, St George's M3,
M15 . . . . . 162 A4
5 Oldham, Clarksfield
OL4 . . . . . 67 D6
Oldham, Salem OL4 . . . . . 67 E5
Pendlebury M27 . . . . . 80 A8
Rochdale OL12 . . . . . 139 C4

Dawson St continued
Stockport SK1 . . . . .112 B3
Day Dr M35 . . . . .83 F6
Dayfield M8 . . . . .53 B7
Day Gr SK14 . . . . .103 A3
Daylesford Cl SK8 . . . . .122 D4
Daylesford Cres SK8 . . . . . .122 D4
Daylesford Rd SK8 . . . . .122 D4
Deacon Ave M27 . . . . .61 E1
Deacon Cl WA14 . . . . .119 B1
Deacons Cl SK1 . . . . .112 A1
Deacons Cres BL8 . . . . .27 A5
Deacons Dr M6 . . . . .80 D6
Deacon St OL16 . . . . .15 B1
Deacon Trad Est WA12 . . . . .89 A2
Deakins Bsns Pk BL7 . . . . . . .8 D1
Deakin St M12 . . . . .151 B1
Deal Ave SK5 . . . . .112 B6
Deal Cl M40 . . . . .83 D5
Dealey Rd BL3 . . . . .146 A4
Deal Sq SK14 . . . . .167 B2
Deal St
 Bolton BL3 . . . . .147 C3
 Bury BL9 . . . . .141 B2
 Hyde SK14 . . . . .167 B2
 Salford M3 . . . . .158 B2
Deal Wlk OL9 . . . . .152 A2
Dean Ave
 Failsworth M40 . . . . .83 B6
 Manchester M16 . . . . .97 B3
Deanbank Ave ⬛
 M19 . . . . .110 F8
Dean Bank Dr OL16 . . . . .31 B1
Dean Bradley Pl M40 . . . . . .157 B2
Dean Brook Cl M40 . . . . .83 B7
Dean Cl
 Billinge WN5 . . . . .71 D3
 Edenfield BL0 . . . . .1 D3
 Farnworth BL4 . . . . .59 F8
 Handforth SK9 . . . . .131 C1
 Partington M31 . . . . .105 F4
 Up Holland WN8 . . . . .53 C7
 Whitefield M45 . . . . .62 D7
Dean Cres WN5 . . . . .54 B8
Dean Ct
 Bolton BL1 . . . . .148 A4
 ⬛ Dukinfield SK16 . . . . . . .166 B1
 Golborne WA3 . . . . .90 A7
 Manchester M15 . . . . .162 A2
 Rochdale OL11 . . . . .30 F4
Dean Dr
 Altrincham WA14 . . . . .119 B1
 Handforth SK9 . . . . .131 D2
DEANE 40 F4
Deane Ave
 Altrincham WA15 . . . . .120 A5
 Bolton BL3 . . . . .144 B1
 Cheadle SK8 . . . . .122 F5
Deane Church La BL3 . . . . . .146 B4
Deane Rd BL3 . . . . .145 A2
Deanery CE High Sch &
 Sixth Form Coll The
 WN1 . . . . .150 B4
Deanery Ct
 Manchester M8 . . . . .156 A3
 Wigan WN1 . . . . .150 B4
Deanery Gdns M7 . . . . .155 A4
Deanery Way SK1 . . . . .169 C2
Deane Wlk BL3 . . . . .145 B2
Dean Hall ⬛ M14 . . . . .98 D4
Dean Head La OL3 . . . . .51 D7
Dean La
 Failsworth M40 . . . . .83 B6
 Hazel Grove SK7 . . . . .133 E8
Dean Mdw WA12 . . . . .89 C4
Dean Moor Rd SK7 . . . . .124 A1
Dean Rd
 Golborne WA3 . . . . .90 A7
 Handforth SK9 . . . . .131 E3
 Haslingden BB4 . . . . .1 B8
 Irlam M44 . . . . .105 E6
 Reddish M18 . . . . .99 E4
 Salford M3 . . . . .158 B3
DEAN ROW 137 F8
Dean Row Ct ⬛ SK9 . . . . . .131 D1
Dean Row Jun Sch
 SK9 . . . . .131 E1
Dean Row Rd SK9 . . . . .137 F8
Deanroyd Rd OL14 . . . . .6 B7
DEANS 79 E7
Deanscourt Ave M27 . . . . . . .79 E8
Deansgate
 Bolton BL1 . . . . .145 B3
 Hindley WN2 . . . . .56 E6
 Manchester M2, M3 . . . . . . .158 C1
 Manchester M3 . . . . .162 B3
 Radcliffe M26 . . . . .44 B3
Deansgate La WA14,
 WA15 . . . . .119 E7
Deansgate Mews M3 . . . . . .162 B4
Deansgate Sta M3 . . . . .162 B4
Deansgate The ⬛
 M14 . . . . .110 C8
Deansgreave Rd OL13 . . . . . .4 B7
Deanshut Rd OL8 . . . . .67 A2
Deans Prim Sch The
 M27 .79 E8
Deans Rd M27 . . . . .79 E7
Deans Road Ind Est
 M27 .79 E7
Dean St
 Ashton-u-L OL6 . . . . .166 A3
 Failsworth M35 . . . . .83 E7
 Mossley OL5 . . . . .68 B1
 Radcliffe M26 . . . . .43 F3
 Rochdale OL16 . . . . .15 B1

Dean St continued
 Stalybridge SK15 . . . . .86 A1
Deansway M27 . . . . .79 E8
Deanswood Dr M9 . . . . .64 A5
Dean Terr OL6 . . . . .67 C2
Dean Villas OL14 . . . . .6 B7
Deanwater Cl M13 . . . . .163 B3
Deanwater Ct
 Gatley SK8 . . . . .131 D7
 Stretford M32 . . . . .108 C8
Deanway
 Handforth SK9 . . . . .131 C1
 Manchester M40 . . . . .83 A8
 Urmston M41 . . . . .94 D2
Deanway Trad Est
 SK9 . . . . .131 D3
Dean Wlk M24 . . . . .46 D2
Dean Wood Ave WN5 . . . . . .53 E8
Dearden Ave M38 . . . . .60 A5
Dearden Clough BL0 . . . . .1 E2
Dearden Fold BL0 . . . . .1 E2
Deardens Fold BL8 . . . . .27 C1
Deardens St BL8 . . . . .27 C1
Dearden St
 Littleborough OL15 . . . . .16 B6
 Little Lever BL3 . . . . .43 A4
 Manchester M15 . . . . .162 B2
 ⬛ Stalybridge SK15 . . . . . . .86 A2
Dearden Way M38 . . . . .53 A7
Dearmans Pl M3 . . . . .158 B2
Dearnalay Way
 Chadderton OL9 . . . . .152 B1
 Oldham OL9 . . . . .66 B4
Dearncamme Cl BL2 . . . . . . .25 B5
Dearne Dr M32 . . . . .96 E2
DEARNLEY 15 F4
Dearnley Cl OL15 . . . . .15 E4
DEBDALE 99 F4
Debdale Ave M18 . . . . .99 F4
Debdale La
 Reddish M18 . . . . .99 F4
 Tyldesley M29 . . . . .76 F4
Deben Cl WN7 . . . . .76 C3
Debenham Ave M40 . . . . . . .83 C4
Debenham Ct BL4 . . . . .60 D7
Debenham Rd M32 . . . . .96 A3
De Brook Cl M41 . . . . .94 E1
Dee Ave WA15 . . . . .120 D5
Dee Dr BL4 . . . . .61 B5
Deepcar St M19 . . . . .99 A2
Deepdale
 Leigh WN7 . . . . .76 C3
 Oldham OL4 . . . . .67 D6
Deepdale Ave
 Billinge WA11 . . . . .71 C1
 Manchester M20 . . . . .110 A8
 Rochdale OL16 . . . . .31 C6
 Royton OL2 . . . . .48 C8
Deepdale Cl ⬛ SK5 . . . . . . .100 A1
Deepdale Ct M9 . . . . .65 B3
Deepdale Dr M27 . . . . .80 D7
Deepdale Rd BL2 . . . . .25 F1
Deepdene St M12 . . . . .164 C2
Deep La
 Littleborough OL15 . . . . .16 C1
 Milnrow OL15, OL16 . . . . . . .32 B8
Deeplish Com Prim Sch
 OL11 . . . . .31 A5
Deeplish Rd OL11 . . . . .139 C1
Deeplish St OL11 . . . . .139 C1
Deeply Vale La BL9,
 OL11 . . . . .12 C2
Deeracre Ave SK2 . . . . .124 C6
Dee Rd M29 . . . . .77 C7
Deerfold Cl ⬛ M18 . . . . .99 D5
Deerhurst Dr M8 . . . . .155 C2
Deeroak Cl M18 . . . . .165 B2
Deerpark Rd M16 . . . . .97 E3
Deerwood Gdns WN1 . . . . . .37 B7
Deerwood Vale SK14 . . . . . .102 E1
Defence St ⬛ BL3 . . . . .145 A2
Defiance St M46 . . . . .58 C3
Degamwy Gr SK5 . . . . .111 F5
Degas Cl M7 . . . . .81 B8
Deighton Ave M20 . . . . .110 A8
Deighton Cl WN5 . . . . .53 E6
Delacourt Rd M14 . . . . .110 B8
Delafield Ave M12 . . . . .99 A2
Delaford Ave M28 . . . . .78 E7
Delaford Cl SK3 . . . . .123 E4
Delaford Wlk M40 . . . . .83 D4
Delahays Lo WA15 . . . . .120 B5
Delahays Dr WA15 . . . . .120 B5
Delahays Range M18 . . . . . . .99 F4
Delahays Rd WA15 . . . . .120 B5
Delaine Rd M20 . . . . .110 C6
Delamere Ave
 Golborne WA3 . . . . .90 E6
 Sale M33 . . . . .108 E3
 Salford M6 . . . . .80 C6
 Shaw OL2 . . . . .49 D8
 Stretford M32 . . . . .96 E2
 Swinton M27 . . . . .79 D7
 Whitefield M45 . . . . .62 E8
Delamere Cl
 Hazel Grove SK7 . . . . .125 A3
 Mossley SK15 . . . . .86 E6
 Romiley SK6 . . . . .113 C5
Delamere Gdns BL1 . . . . . . .143 A3
Delamere Ho ⬛ M14 . . . . . .110 C8
Delamere Lo SK7 . . . . .124 D2
Delamere Rd
 Gatley SK8 . . . . .122 B5
 Handforth SK9 . . . . .131 E4
 Hazel Grove SK7 . . . . .125 A3
 Manchester M19 . . . . .99 B1
 Reddish M34 . . . . .100 D3

Delamere Rd continued
 Rochdale OL16 . . . . .31 C4
 Stockport SK2 . . . . .124 B4
 Urmston M41 . . . . .94 F2
Delamere Sch M41 . . . . .94 D2
Delamere St
 Ashton-u-L OL6 . . . . .166 B2
 Bury BL9 . . . . .28 A5
 Droylsden M11 . . . . .99 F7
 ⬛ Oldham OL8 . . . . .67 B5
Delamere Way M8 . . . . .53 A7
Delamer Rd WA14 . . . . .119 C3
Delaunays Rd
 Manchester M8 . . . . .64 B2
 Sale M33 . . . . .107 F4
Delaware Wlk M9 . . . . .157 A3
Delbooth Ave M41 . . . . .94 E4
Delegate St WN3 . . . . .151 B2
Delfhaven Ct WN6 . . . . .37 A7
Delft Wlk M6 . . . . .81 A5
Delfur Rd SK7 . . . . .132 F7
Delhi Rd M44 . . . . .105 F8
Deliar St OL12 . . . . .14 C1
Dell Ave
 Pendlebury M27 . . . . .80 D7
 Wigan WN6 . . . . .36 E3
Dellcot Cl
 Manchester M25 . . . . .63 D2
 Salford M6 . . . . .80 B5
Dellcot La M28 . . . . .78 F5
Dellhide Cl OL4 . . . . .68 A6
Dell Mdw OL12 . . . . .14 C5
Dell Rd OL12 . . . . .14 B3
Dell Side Way OL12 . . . . .14 C2
Dell St BL2 . . . . .25 C5
Dell The
 Appley Bridge WN6 . . . . .35 D7
 Bolton BL2 . . . . .25 C5
 Up Holland WN8 . . . . .53 B7
Delph Ave BL7 . . . . .8 D3
Delph Brook Way BL7 . . . . . . .8 D2
Delph Gr WN7 . . . . .57 D5
Delph Hill BL1 . . . . .23 E2
Delph Hill Cl BL1 . . . . .23 E2
Delphi Ave M28 . . . . .60 D2
Delph La
 Ainsworth BL2 . . . . .26 C1
 Delph OL3 . . . . .50 F5
 Delph Lo OL3 . . . . .50 E5
 Delph Mdw Gdns WN5 . . . . .71 D4
 Delph New Rd OL3 . . . . .50 E5
 Delph Prim Sch OL3 . . . . . . .50 E5
 Delph Rd OL3 . . . . .50 E5
Delphside Cl WN5 . . . . .53 D5
Delphside Rd WN5 . . . . .53 D5
Delph St
 Bolton BL3 . . . . .145 A1
 Milnrow OL16 . . . . .31 F6
 Wigan WN6 . . . . .37 B1
Delside Ave M40 . . . . .83 A8
Delta Cl OL2 . . . . .48 D2
Delta Ho SK6 . . . . .113 A2
Delta Rd M34 . . . . .100 E7
Delta Wlk M40 . . . . .83 A7
Delves Rd WA14 . . . . .107 D1
Delwood Wlk M14 . . . . .98 A4
Delwood Gdns M22 . . . . . . .121 D3
De-Massey Cl SK6 . . . . .113 B6
Dempsey Dr BL9 . . . . .45 B2
Denbigh Cl SK7 . . . . .133 C8
Denbigh Dr OL2 . . . . .48 E5
Denbigh Gr M46 . . . . .58 C5
Denbigh Pl M5 . . . . .81 A2
Denbigh Rd
 Bolton BL2 . . . . .148 B1
 Denton M34 . . . . .100 F1
 Swinton M27 . . . . .79 E7
Denbigh St
 Oldham OL8 . . . . .66 D8
 Stockport SK4 . . . . .169 A3
Denbigh Wlk M15 . . . . .162 B1
Denbury Dr WA14 . . . . .119 B5
Denbury Gn SK7 . . . . .124 A1
Denbury Wlk M9 . . . . .156 C2
Denbydale Way OL2 . . . . .48 C4
Denby Rd SK16 . . . . .101 C7
Dencombe St M12, M13 . . . . .98 F4
Dene Bank BL2 . . . . .25 E1
Dene Brow M34 . . . . .113 B8
Dene Ct SK4 . . . . .168 C2
Dene Dr M24 . . . . .46 D2
Denefield Cl SK6 . . . . .114 B1
Denefield Pl M30 . . . . .79 F3
Deneford Rd M20 . . . . .110 A3
Dene Gr WN7 . . . . .75 B4
Dene Ho SK4 . . . . .110 E1
Dene Hollow SK5 . . . . .100 A1
Denehurst Rd M12 . . . . .164 C2
Dene Manor M20 . . . . .110 A2
Dene Pk M20 . . . . .110 A3
Dene Rd M20 . . . . .110 A2
Dene Rd W M20 . . . . .109 F3

Deneside Cres SK7 . . . . .124 F3
Deneside Wlk ⬛ M9 . . . . . . .157 B4
Dene St
 Bolton BL2 . . . . .25 C5
 Leigh WN7 . . . . .75 D5
Denes The SK5 . . . . .99 F1
Denesway M33 . . . . .107 E3
Deneway
 Bramhall SK7 . . . . .132 D7
 High Lane SK6 . . . . .134 F8
 Stockport SK4 . . . . .168 C2
Deneway Cl SK4 . . . . .168 C2
Deneway Mews SK4 . . . . . . .168 C2
Denewell Cl M13 . . . . .164 A5
Denewood Ct ⬛ SK9 . . . . . .137 A6
Denford Cl WN3 . . . . .54 F3
Denham Cl BL1 . . . . .25 A5
Denham Dr
 Bramhall SK7 . . . . .132 D7
 Irlam M44 . . . . .94 A1
 Wigan WN3 . . . . .55 A3
Denham St
 Manchester M13 . . . . .98 D4
 Radcliffe M26 . . . . .43 F6
Den Hill Dr OL4 . . . . .67 F6
Denhill Rd ⬛ M15 . . . . .97 F4
Denholme ⬛ M6 . . . . .81 A3
Denholme Rd OL11 . . . . .30 F4
Denholm Rd M20 . . . . .122 C8
Denhurst Rd OL15 . . . . .16 B6
Denis Ave M16 . . . . .97 E2
Denison Ct ⬛ M14 . . . . .98 C3
Denison Rd M14 . . . . .98 C3
Deniston Rd SK4 . . . . .111 B5
Den La
 Oldham OL4 . . . . .67 F7
 Uppermill OL3 . . . . .69 B8
Denman Wlk ⬛ M8 . . . . . . .155 C2
Denmark Rd
 Manchester M14, M15 . . . . . .98 A4
 Sale M33 . . . . .108 B6
Denmark St
 Altrincham WA14 . . . . .119 D4
 Chadderton OL9 . . . . .152 C4
 Oldham OL4 . . . . .67 B8
 Rochdale OL11 . . . . .31 A8
Denmark Way OL9 . . . . .152 C4
Denmore Rd M40 . . . . .65 D3
Denning Pl M27 . . . . .61 F2
Dennington Dr M41 . . . . .95 C4
Dennis Ho M14 . . . . .168 B4
Dennison Ave M20 . . . . .110 B7
Dennison Rd SK8 . . . . .132 B8
DENSHAW 33 D3
Denshaw Ave M34 . . . . .100 D1
Denshaw Cl M19 . . . . .110 E3
Denshaw Rd OL3 . . . . .50 D5
Densmore St M35 . . . . .83 F7
Denson Rd WA15 . . . . .120 B8
Denstone Ave
 Eccles M30 . . . . .79 E3
 Sale M33 . . . . .107 E3
 Urmston M41 . . . . .95 C3
Denstone Cres BL2 . . . . .25 D2
Denstone Rd
 Reddish SK5 . . . . .99 F1
 Salford M6 . . . . .80 D5
 Urmston M41 . . . . .95 C3
Denstone Wlk ⬛ M9 . . . . . . .64 E3
Dental Hospl M13,
 M15 . . . . .163 A2
Dent Cl SK5 . . . . .112 C6
Dentdale Cl BL1 . . . . .40 D6
Dentdale Wlk M22 . . . . .130 C8
DENTON 100 D3
Denton Bsns Pk M34 . . . . . .100 D3
Denton Ct M34 . . . . .100 E5
Denton Gr WN5 . . . . .54 B8
Denton La OL9 . . . . .152 A1
Denton Rd
 Bolton BL2 . . . . .25 C1
 ⬛ Rochdale OL12 . . . . .14 F1
 Sale M34 . . . . .100 C4
Denton West End Prim
 Sch M34 . . . . .100 A3
Denver Ave M40 . . . . .160 A3
Denver Dr ⬛ WA15 . . . . . . .120 A6
Denver Rd OL11 . . . . .30 F4
Denville Cres M22 . . . . .121 E3
Denyer Terr ⬛ SK16 . . . . . .166 B1
Denzell Gdns WA14 . . . . . . .119 A3
Depleach Rd SK8 . . . . .122 B5
Deptford Ave M23 . . . . .121 A3
De Quincey Cl WA14 . . . . . .107 D1
De Quincey Rd WA14 . . . . . .107 D1
Deramore Cl OL6 . . . . .85 C3
Deramore St M14 . . . . .98 B3
Derby Ave M5 . . . . .154 B2
Derby Cl
 Irlam M44 . . . . .105 C5
 Newton-le-W WA12 . . . . .89 B3
Derby Ct
 Oldham OL9 . . . . .152 C1
 Sale M33 . . . . .108 C3
Derby Gr ⬛ M19 . . . . .99 B1
Derby High Sch The
 BL9 .44 D8
Derby Ho
 Manchester M13 . . . . .163 B1
 Wigan WN1 . . . . .151 A4

Derby Pl PR6 . . . . .21 A8
Derby Range SK4 . . . . .168 B4
Derby Rd
 Ashton-u-L OL6 . . . . .85 D3
 Golborne WA3 . . . . .90 C8
 Hyde SK14 . . . . .167 B4
 Kearsley M26 . . . . .61 A8
 Manchester M14, M20 . . . . .110 D7
 New Mills SK22 . . . . .127 D1
 Prestwich M25, M45 . . . . . . .63 A6
 Sale M33 . . . . .107 E6
 Salford M5 . . . . .154 B2
 Stockport, Heaton Moor
 SK4 . . . . .168 C4
 Urmston M41 . . . . .95 D3
Derbyshire Ave M32 . . . . .96 B3
Derbyshire Cres M32 . . . . . . .96 B3
Derbyshire Gn M32 . . . . .96 D2
Derbyshire Gr M32 . . . . .96 B3
Derbyshire La M32 . . . . .96 C2
Derbyshire La W M32 . . . . . . .96 B2
Derbyshire Level
 SK13 . . . . .116 F6
Derbyshire Rd
 Failsworth M40 . . . . .83 D4
 Partington M31 . . . . .105 E2
 Poynton SK12 . . . . .134 D5
 Sale M33 . . . . .108 C4
 Wigan WN3 . . . . .54 D1
Derbyshire Rd S M33 . . . . . .108 D2
Derbyshire Row BL1 . . . . . . .143 E2
Derbyshire St M11 . . . . .165 C3
Derby St
 Altrincham WA14 . . . . .119 E5
 Ashton-u-L OL7 . . . . .85 A5
 Atherton M46 . . . . .58 A3
 Bolton BL3 . . . . .145 B1
 Bury BL9 . . . . .140 C2
 Denton M34 . . . . .100 D3
 Denton M34 . . . . .100 D4
 ⬛ Failsworth M35 . . . . .66 A1
 Glossop SK13 . . . . .116 C8
 Heywood OL10 . . . . .29 B2
 Horwich BL6 . . . . .22 D1
 Ince-in-M WN3 . . . . .55 F4
 Leigh WN7 . . . . .76 A4
 Manchester M8 . . . . .158 C4
 ⬛ Marple SK6 . . . . .125 F6
 Mossley OL5 . . . . .68 B2
 Newton-le-W WA12 . . . . .89 B3
 Oldham, Factory Fold
 OL9 . . . . .66 B4
 Oldham OL11 . . . . .31 A5
 Oldham, Werneth OL9 . . . . .152 C1
 Prestwich M25 . . . . .63 A4
 Ramsbottom BL0 . . . . .11 D6
 Rochdale OL11 . . . . .31 A5
 Stockport SK3 . . . . .170 A4
 ⬛ Tyldesley M29 . . . . .59 A1
 Westhoughton BL5 . . . . .39 F1
Derby Terr M34 . . . . .100 E8
Derby Way ⬛ SK6 . . . . .125 F6
Dereham Cl BL8 . . . . .27 D5
Dereham Way WN4 . . . . .54 D3
Derg St M6 . . . . .154 C1
Derker St OL1 . . . . .67 B8
Derker Sta OL1 . . . . .67 B8
Dermot Murphy Cl
 M20 . . . . .109 F6
Dernford Ave M19 . . . . .110 F5
Derngate Dr WN3 . . . . .37 A7
Derrick Walker Ct
 OL11 . . . . .139 A1
Derry Ave M22 . . . . .121 E4
Derville Wlk ⬛ M9 . . . . .157 A4
Derwen Rd SK3 . . . . .170 B3
Derwent Ave
 Altrincham WA15 . . . . .120 D5
 Ashton-u-L OL7 . . . . .166 A4
 Droylsden M43 . . . . .83 E1
 Golborne WA3 . . . . .74 C1
 Heywood OL10 . . . . .46 D8
 Ince-in-M WN3 . . . . .56 B7
 Manchester M21 . . . . .109 D5
 Milnrow OL16 . . . . .32 B6
 Whitefield M45 . . . . .63 C8
Derwent Cl
 Culcheth WA3 . . . . .92 A2
 Horwich BL6 . . . . .22 C2
 Leigh WN7 . . . . .75 E3
 Little Lever BL3 . . . . .42 F4
 Manchester M21 . . . . .109 D5
 Partington M31 . . . . .105 F4
 Reddish M34 . . . . .100 B3
 Walkden M28 . . . . .60 B2
 Whitefield M45 . . . . .63 C8
Derwent Dr
 Bramhall SK7 . . . . .132 C5
 Bury BL9 . . . . .44 D7
 Chadderton OL9 . . . . .152 A3
 Handforth SK9 . . . . .131 C5
 Kearsley BL4 . . . . .61 B5
 Littleborough OL15 . . . . .15 F2
 Sale M33 . . . . .108 A2
 Shaw OL2 . . . . .149 A4
Derwent Pl WN5 . . . . .54 C7
Derwent Rd
 Ashton-in-M WN4 . . . . .73 E5
 Farnworth BL4 . . . . .59 F7
 High Lane SK6 . . . . .134 E8
 Hindley WN2 . . . . .56 E5
 Middleton M24 . . . . .46 E3
 Orrell WN5 . . . . .53 E8
 Stretford M32 . . . . .96 D3

Derwent Rd continued
Urmston M41...............**94** E2
Derwent St Trad Est
M5....................**162** A4
Derwent St
Droylsden M43............**83** D1
Leigh WN7................**75** E3
Manchester M8............**156** C2
11 Rochdale OL12........**14** F1
Salford M5...............**161** C4
Tyldesley M29............**77** A7
Derwent Terr SK15.......**86** A4
Derwent Way WN7.......**75** B1
Derwent Wlk
Oldham OL4..............**67** D7
Whitefield M45...........**63** B8
Desford Ave M16, M21...**97** C1
Design St BL3...........**146** B4
Desmond Rd M22........**121** E4
Desmond St M46.........**58** A2
De Trafford Dr WN2......**56** B8
De Trafford Ho 13
M30....................**79** D1
De Trafford Mews 9
SK9....................**131** D2
De Traffords The M44....**94** B3
Dettingen St M6.........**80** D6
Deva Cl
Hazel Grove SK7..........**124** D1
Poynton SK12............**133** B4
Deva Ct M16.............**161** C1
Deva Ct SK3.............**158** B2
Devaney Wlk M34.......**100** E1
Deva Sq OL9.............**152** C1
Devas St M13, M15.......**163** B1
Deverill Ave M18........**99** F4
Devine Cl
Royton OL2..............**48** D6
Salford M3...............**158** A2
Devisdale Ct WA14.......**119** C3
Devisdale Grange
WA14...................**119** B3
Devisdale Rd WA14.......**119** B4
Devoke Ave
Billinge WA11............**71** A1
Walkden M28.............**60** F2
Devoke Gr BL4...........**59** E8
Devoke Rd M22..........**121** B2
Devon Ave
Manchester M19..........**110** F8
Up Holland WN8..........**53** B6
Whitefield M45...........**44** E1
Devon Cl
Aspull WN2..............**38** D5
Brinnington SK5..........**112** C4
Little Lever BL3..........**43** B4
Shaw OL2................**80** A3
Wigan WN5..............**54** C6
Devon Cres BB4..........**1** B8
Devon Dr
Ainsworth BL2...........**26** D1
Diggle OL3...............**51** C4
Standish WN1............**20** B1
Devon Mews 2 M45......**44** E1
Devonport Cres OL2......**48** F4
Devon Rd
Droylsden M43...........**84** A3
Failsworth M35..........**83** E6
Irlam M44...............**105** D5
Partington M31..........**105** E2
Tyldesley M29...........**59** A2
Urmston M41.............**94** E1
Devonshire Cl
Horwich OL10............**29** A1
3 Urmston M41.........**95** E2
Devonshire Ct
Bolton BL1..............**144** B3
Salford M7..............**155** A4
Stockport SK2...........**124** A5
Devonshire Dr
Alderley Edge SK9.......**137** B2
Boothstown M28.........**77** F6
Devonshire Gdns
WA12...................**89** C2
Devonshire Park Rd
SK2....................**124** A5
Devonshire Pl
Atherton M46............**58** D4
Prestwich M25...........**63** A5
Devonshire Rd
Altrincham WA14.........**119** D6
Atherton M46............**58** C5
Bolton BL1..............**144** B4
Eccles M30..............**79** E2
Hazel Grove SK7.........**133** F8
Manchester, Chorlton-cum-
Hardy M21.............**109** C8
Rochdale OL11...........**30** F2
Salford M6..............**80** A3
Stockport, Heaton Norris
SK4...................**168** B3
Walkden M28............**60** C6
Devonshire Road Prim Sch
BL1....................**144** B4
Devonshire St E M35.....**83** E5
Devonshire St N M12.....**164** A3
Devonshire St S M13.....**164** A1
Devonshire St
Manchester M12..........**164** A2
Salford M7..............**155** B2
Devon St
Bolton BL2..............**148** A3
Bury BL9................**44** F8
Farnworth BL4...........**42** D2

Devon St continued
Hindley WN2.............**56** E5
Leigh WN7...............**76** E4
Oldham OL9..............**66** C4
Rochdale OL11...........**139** C2
Swinton M27.............**61** F2
Devon Way OL8..........**66** C2
Dewar Cl M11...........**83** A1
Dewberry Cl
Swinton M27.............**61** E2
Tyldesley M29...........**59** E1
Dewberry Fields WN8....**53** B7
Dewes Ave M27..........**62** B2
Dewey St M11...........**99** D7
Dewham Cl BL5..........**39** F1
Dewhirst Rd OL12.......**14** F4
Dewhirst Way OL12.......**14** F4
Dewhurst Clough Rd
BL7....................**8** D2
Dewhurst Ct BL7.........**8** D3
Dewhurst Rd BL2........**25** E3
Dewhurst St
Heywood OL10...........**29** E2
Manchester M8...........**158** C4
Dew Meadow Cl OL12...**14** F2
Dewsnap Cl SK16.......**101** C6
Dewsnap La
Dukinfield SK16.........**101** D6
Mottram in L SK14.......**103** A6
Dewsnap Way SK14......**102** E2
Dew Way OL9...........**153** A3
Dexter Rd M9...........**64** A5
Dexter Way WN8.........**53** B6
Deyne Ave
Manchester M14..........**98** C4
Prestwich M25...........**63** B4
Deyne St M6............**154** B2
Dial Cl BL4.............**60** D8
Dial Park Prim Sch
SK2....................**124** C4
Dial Park Rd SK4........**124** D4
Dial Rd
Altrincham WA15.........**129** C8
Stockport SK2...........**124** C5
Dialstone La SK2.........**124** C6
Diamond Cl 9 OL6.......**85** D4
Diamond St
8 Ashton-u-L OL6.......**85** D4
Leigh WN7...............**75** E4
Stockport SK2...........**124** A6
Wigan WN6..............**37** A3
Diamond Terr SK6........**125** F3
Diane Rd WN4...........**73** E5
Dibden Wlk 4 M23......**121** A5
Dicconson Cres 9
WN1....................**37** C1
Dicconson La BL5,
WN2...................**39** A4
Dicconson St WN1.......**37** C1
Dicconson Terr WN1.....**37** C1
Dicken Gn OL11.........**30** F4
Dicken Green La OL11...**30** F4
Dickens Cl SK8..........**132** B5
Dickens Dr WN2.........**74** C8
Dickens La SK12........**133** E2
Dickenson Rd M13,
M14...................**98** E3
Dickens St WN3.........**56** E4
Dickens Pl WN3.........**54** F4
Dickens Rd
Coppull PR7.............**19** E8
Eccles M30..............**79** D1
Dickens St
Heywood OL10...........**29** B2
Oldham OL1.............**49** B4
Dickinson Ct 13 BL1.....**143** B1
Dickinson Ct 11 BL6.....**22** B4
Dickinson St W BL6......**22** B4
Dickinson St
Bolton BL1..............**143** B1
Manchester M1...........**163** A4
Oldham OL4..............**67** B7
Salford M3..............**158** B3
Dickinson Terr 12
BL1....................**143** B1
Dickson St W BL6........**22** A4
Didcot Rd M22..........**121** C1
Didley Sq M12..........**165** A3
DIDSBURY..............**110** C2
Didsbury CE Prim Sch
M20...................**110** B3
Didsbury Gr WN2.........**56** D5
Didsbury Lodge Hall
M20...................**110** B3
Didsbury Pk M20........**110** B2
Didsbury Rd SK4........**168** B2
Didsbury Road Prim Sch
SK4...................**110** F2
Digby Lo M20...........**110** B4
Digby Rd OL11..........**30** F4
Digby Wlk 20 M11......**160** C1
Dig Gate La OL11.......**13** F5
DIGGLE................**51** C4
Diggle Mill Cotts OL3...**51** F5
Diggle Prim Sch OL3....**51** C5
Diggles La OL11.........**29** E6
Diggle St
Shaw OL2...............**149** B2
Wigan WN6..............**37** A1
Diggle Wlk SK15.........**86** E6
Diglands Ave SK22.......**127** D1
Diglands Cl SK22........**127** D1
Diglea OL3.............**51** D5
Dijon St BL3............**146** C4
Dilham Ct BL1...........**144** C4
Dillicar Wlk M9.........**157** A3
Dillmoss Wlk 22 M15...**162** A2

Dillon Dr M12...........**164** B1
Dilworth Cl OL10.........**29** A2
Dilworth Ct SK2.........**124** E5
Dilworth Ho M13........**163** B1
Dilworth St M13, M15....**163** B1
Dimple Pk BL7...........**8** D3
Dimple Rd BL7...........**8** C4
Dingle Ave
Appley Bridge WN6......**35** E8
Denton M34.............**101** B2
Row-of-Trees SK9........**136** D3
Shaw OL2...............**32** C1
Up Holland WN8.........**53** C8
Dingle Bank Rd SK7.....**123** D1
Dinglebrook Gr 5
SK9....................**131** D1
Dingle Cl
Glossop SK13............**116** A8
Radcliffe M26............**44** B1
Romiley SK6.............**113** D2
Dingle Dr M43...........**84** B3
Dingle Rd
Middleton M24..........**64** F6
Up Holland WN8.........**53** B7
Dingle Terr OL6.........**67** B2
Dingle The
Bramhall SK7............**123** C1
Hyde SK14..............**113** E7
Dingle Wlk
6 Bolton BL1...........**145** C4
Wigan WN6..............**36** D4
Dinglewood SK7.........**123** C1
Dinmore Ct SK2..........**124** D5
Dinmor Rd M22..........**121** D1
Dinnington Dr M8.......**155** C2
Dinorwic Cl M8..........**64** A2
Dinsdale Cl M40.........**160** A2
Dinsdale Dr BL3.........**145** A1
Dinslow Wlk 18 M8.....**155** C3
Dinting Ave M20........**110** A7
Dinting CE Prim Sch
SK13..................**104** A1
Dinting La SK13.........**104** A1
Dinting Lane Trad Est
SK13..................**104** A1
Dinting Lodge Ind Est
SK13..................**171** C2
Dinting Rd SK13.........**104** B2
Dinting Sta SK13.........**104** A2
Dinting Vale SK13.......**104** A1
Dinting Vale Bsns Pk
SK13..................**171** C2
Dinton Ho 6 M5.........**154** C1
Dinton St M15..........**161** C3
Dipton Wlk M8..........**156** C2
Dirty La
Delph OL3..............**51** B8
Oldham OL4.............**50** B1
Dirty Leech OL12.........**14** F6
DISLEY................**135** C5
Disley Ave M20..........**109** F6
Disley Ho SK3...........**170** B3
Disley Prim Sch SK12....**135** D6
Disley St OL11...........**30** C4
Disley Sta SK12..........**135** C6
Disley Wlk M34..........**101** A1
Distaff Rd SK12.........**133** B4
District CE Prim Sch The
WA12..................**89** A3
Ditton Brook BL5........**39** F1
Ditton Mead Cl OL12....**15** B2
Ditton Wlk 5 M23.......**120** F6
Division St
Bolton BL3..............**147** C4
Rochdale OL12...........**15** B2
Dixey St BL6............**22** A3
Dixon Ave
Newton-le-W WA12.......**89** C5
Shevington WN6.........**36** A5
Dixon Cl
Haydock WA11..........**89** A8
Sale M33...............**108** D2
Dixon Closes OL11.......**29** E7
Dixon Ct
Cheadle SK8............**122** D5
Westhoughton BL5........**39** E3
Dixon Dr
Shevington WN6.........**36** A5
Swinton M27.............**61** E4
DIXON GREEN.........**146** D3
Dixon Green Dr 11 BL4..**60** C8
Dixon Pl 3 WN2.........**56** B1
Dixon Rd M34...........**101** B1
Dixon St
18 Ashton-u-L OL6.......**85** D4
Failsworth M40..........**83** B6
Horwich BL6.............**22** B3
Irlam M44...............**105** F8
Manchester M6..........**80** F6
Middleton M24..........**47** A2
Oldham, Cold Hurst
OL1...................**153** B4
Oldham, Greenacres Fold
OL4...................**67** E8
Rochdale OL11...........**30** D4
Westhoughton BL5........**39** E3
DOBB BROW..........**57** C7
Dobb Brow Rd BL5......**57** C7
Dobb Hedge Cl WA15...**129** C6
Dobbinetts La M23,
WA15..................**120** E4
Dob Brook Cl M35, M40..**83** F5
DOBCROSS............**51** A4
Dobcross Cl M13........**99** A2
Dobcross New Rd OL3...**51** A1

Dobhill St BL4...........**60** D8
Dobroyd Ho OL4.........**67** E8
Dobroyd St M8..........**156** A4
Dobson Cl
Appley Bridge WN6......**18** E2
Manchester M13.........**164** A2
Dobson Ct M40..........**83** B4
Dobson Park Ind Est
M44...................**151** C2
Dobson Park Way
WN2....................**56** A6
Dobson Pk Ind Est
SK9....................**56** A6
Doctor Fold La OL10......**46** C5
Doctor La OL4...........**50** C1
Doctors La BL9..........**140** A2
Doctors Nook WN7.......**75** F5
Dodd Croft OL16.........**31** B3
Doddington La M5.......**161** A4
Doddington Wlk M34...**100** E1
Dodd La BL5............**39** B4
Dodd Lane Ind Est BL5..**39** C4
Dodd's Farm La WN2....**38** E3
Dodge Fold SK2..........**124** E6
Dodge Hill SK4..........**169** B2
Dodgson St OL16........**31** A6
Dodhurst Rd WN2........**56** F6
Dodson St M40..........**83** B4
Dodworth Wlk M40......**83** B6
Dodson Cl WN4..........**73** C3
Doe Brow M27..........**61** E4
Doefield Ave M28........**78** C8
Doeford Cl WA3.........**91** E5
Doe Hey Gr BL4.........**42** B2
Doe Hey Rd BL3.........**42** B2
DOFFCOCKER..........**23** E1
Doffcocker Brow BL1....**142** A1
Doffcocker La BL1........**23** F2
Dogford Rd OL2.........**48** D5
DOG HILL..............**49** E7
Dolbey St M5...........**154** B1
D'Olivera Ct 7 M24......**46** E2
Dolling St M40..........**160** D4
Dolman Wlk 4 M8......**155** C2
Dolphin Pl M12..........**163** C3
Dolphin St M12..........**163** C3
Dolwen Wlk M40........**83** B6
Doman St BL3...........**145** C1
Dombey Rd SK12........**133** D2
Domestic App M90......**130** C6
Dome The 6 WA14......**119** D4
Domett St M9...........**64** C2
Dominic Cl M23.........**108** E1
Donald Ave SK14........**167** C1
Donald St M1...........**163** A3
Dona St SK1............**124** A8
Don Ave M6.............**80** C2
Doncaster Ave M20......**110** A7
Doncaster Cl BL3.........**42** F3
Doncasters Cl OL1.......**49** D3
Doncaster Wlk 4
OL1....................**153** C3
Donhead Wlk M13......**163** C2
Donington Gdns M28...**60** D3
Donkey La SK9..........**137** A5
Donleigh St M40........**83** D6
Donnington 6 OL11....**139** B2
Donnington Ave SK8....**122** F6
Donnington Cl WN7.....**75** E1
Donnington Rd
Droylsden M18..........**99** E5
Little Lever M26.........**43** C5
Donnison St M12........**164** C2
Donovan Ave M40......**159** C4
Don St
Bolton BL3..............**147** A3
Middleton M24..........**47** C1
DOODFIELD............**125** E2
Doodfield Prim Sch
SK6....................**125** F2
Doodson Ave M44.......**94** A2
Doodson Sq BL4.........**60** D8
Dooley La SK2, SK6.....**125** B7
Dooley's La SK9.........**130** C2
Dootson St
4 Abram WN2..........**56** B1
Hindley WN2............**57** A6
Dorac Ave SK8..........**131** C7
Dora St BL0.............**11** A4
Dorchester Ave
Bolton BL2..............**25** F1
Denton M34.............**100** F1
Manchester M25.........**63** C2
Urmston M41............**95** F3
Dorchester Cl
Altrincham WA15........**120** C3
Wilmslow SK9...........**137** D8
Dorchester Ct
Bramhall SK8............**123** B1
Sale M33...............**108** B2
Dorchester Dr
Royton OL2.............**48** E2
Sale M23...............**108** E1
Dorchester Gr OL4.......**46** D8
Dorchester Par SK7.....**124** B1
Dorchester Rd
Hazel Grove SK7........**124** B1
Swinton M27............**79** F6
Up Holland WN8.........**53** C7
Dorclyn Ave M41........**95** D2
Dorfield Cl SK6.........**112** C4
Doric Ave SK6..........**112** D2
Doric Cl M11...........**160** C1
Doric St M11...........**99** D7
Doris Ave BL2...........**42** D7
Doris Rd SK3...........**123** C8
Doris St M24...........**47** A2

Dorket Gr BL5...........**57** D6
Dorking Ave M40........**83** B4
Dorking Cl
Bolton BL1..............**143** C2
Stockport SK1...........**124** B7
Dorlan Ave M18.........**99** F4
Dorland Gr SK2.........**124** B7
Dorman St 8 M11.......**99** D7
Dorney St M18..........**99** D5
Dorning Rd M27.........**80** A7
Dorning St
Bury BL8................**27** B4
6 Eccles M30..........**79** D1
Kearsley BL4............**60** F8
1 Leigh WN7...........**75** E5
Scot Lane End BL6.......**38** F7
Tyldesley M29...........**59** B1
Wigan WN1.............**150** B4
Dornton Wlk M8.........**155** C2
Dorothy Gr WN7........**75** E4
Dorothy Rd SK7.........**124** F3
Dorothy St
Ramsbottom BL0.........**138** B1
Salford M7.............**155** C3
Dorrian Mews BL1.......**40** F7
Dorrington Rd
Cheadle SK3............**123** A7
Sale M33...............**107** E4
Dorris St
Bolton BL3..............**146** C3
Manchester M19.........**111** B8
Dorrit Cl SK12..........**133** E2
Dorset Ave
Bramhall SK7............**123** D1
Brinnington SK5.........**112** C5
Cheadle SK8............**123** C5
Diggle OL3.............**51** C4
Droylsden M34..........**100** C8
Farnworth BL4...........**60** C8
Manchester M14.........**98** A2
Shaw OL2...............**48** F7
Tyldesley M29...........**59** A3
Dorset Cl
Farnworth BL4...........**60** C8
Heywood OL10..........**29** A1
Wigan WN5.............**54** C6
Dorset Dr
Bury BL9...............**45** A8
Haslingden BB4..........**1** A8
Dorset Rd
Altrincham WA14........**119** B5
Atherton M46............**58** C5
Droylsden M43..........**83** F3
Failsworth M35..........**83** F6
Irlam M44...............**105** D5
Reddish M19............**99** C1
Standish WN1...........**20** B1
Dorset St
Ashton-u-L OL6.........**85** D2
Bolton BL2.............**148** A3
Hindley WN2............**56** E6
Leigh WN7...............**76** D4
Oldham OL9.............**152** C1
Rochdale OL11..........**139** C2
Stretford M32...........**96** D1
Swinton M27............**61** F2
Wigan WN1.............**159** B2
Dorstone Cl
Failsworth M40..........**83** C4
Hindley WN2............**57** B5
Dorwood Ave M9........**64** C5
Dotterel Cl WN7........**76** A6
Dougall Wlk M12........**165** A2
Doughty Ave M30........**79** F3
Dougill St BL1..........**142** B1
Douglas Ave
Billinge WN5............**71** D3
Bury BL8................**27** B2
Horwich BL6............**22** C5
Stretford M32...........**96** D3
Up Holland WN8.........**53** B7
Douglas Bank Dr WN6...**36** F7
Douglas Cl
Horwich BL6............**22** C5
Whitefield M45..........**45** C2
Douglas Dr
Orrell WN5.............**53** F7
Shevington WN6.........**35** F5
Douglas Gn M6.........**81** A5
Douglas Ho WN1.......**151** A3
Douglas Pk M46.........**58** E3
Douglas Rd
Atherton M46............**58** E2
Hazel Grove SK7........**124** E3
1 Leigh WN7...........**75** C7
Shevington Moor WN6....**19** B2
Stockport SK3...........**123** E4
Swinton M28............**79** C7
Wigan WN1.............**37** C1
Douglas Sq OL10........**28** F1
Douglas St
2 Ashton-u-L OL6.......**85** D3
Atherton M46............**58** E3
Bolton BL1.............**145** F8
Failsworth M35..........**84** A7
Hindley WN2............**56** C4
Hyde SK14..............**167** B2
Manchester M40.........**160** D4
Oldham OL1.............**67** A8
Pendlebury M27.........**80** A7
Ramsbottom BL0.........**138** B2
Salford M7.............**155** A3
Wigan WN5.............**150** A3
Douglas View
Adlington PR7...........**21** A6
Standish WN1...........**37** B6

Douglas Way M45 ....45 C1
Douglas Wlk
2 Sale M33 .... 107 C5
Whitefield M45 ....45 C2
Doulton Cl WN2 ....55 F3
Doulton St M40............83 C8
Dounby Ave M30 ....79 B3
Douro St M40 .... 157 C1
Douthwaite Dr SK6 ......113 E1
Dove Bank Rd BL3.........43 A4
Dove Bk SK6 ....126 F6
Dovebrook Cl SK15 ....86 E7
Dovecote M43.............84 D3
Dovecote Bsns & Tech Pk
M33 ....108 F4
Dovecote Cl BL7...........25 B8
Dovecote La
Oldham OL4..............67 F8
Walkden M38.............59 E3
Dovecote Mews 5
M21 .... 109 A8
Dovedale Ave
Droylsden M43............83 E2
Eccles M30 ....79 E3
Manchester, Sedgley Park
M25 ....63 E3
Manchester, Withington
M20 .... 110 A7
Urmston M41.............95 D3
Dovedale Cl SK6.........134 E7
Dovedale Cres WN4 ......73 A8
Dovedale Ct
1 Glossop SK13.........104 F1
8 Middleton M24.........46 E2
Dovedale Dr
Standish WN6 ....19 E2
Wardle OL12 ....15 D6
Dovedale Rd
Ashton-in-M WN4 ....73 A8
Bolton BL2................25 F1
Stockport SK2 .... 124 D7
Dovedale St M35 ....83 E7
Dove Dr
Bury BL9 ....141 B4
Irlam M44 ....94 A3
Dovehouse Cl M45........62 D7
Doveleys Rd M6 .... 154 A4
Dovenby Fold WN2 ....56 B7
Dover Cl BL8..............11 A1
Dovercourt Ave SK4 .....110 F4
Dove Rd BL3 ....146 B4
Dover Gr BL3............. 145 A1
Doveridge Gdns M6 .... 154 C3
Dover Pk M41 ....95 D4
Dover Rd M27 ....62 A2
Dover St
Eccles M30 ....79 B2
Farnworth BL4............42 D2
Manchester M13 ....163 B2
Oldham OL9............ 152 C1
1 Reddish SK5..........111 E7
Rochdale OL16............15 B2
Dove St
Bolton BL1..............143 B4
Golborne WA3 ....74 A2
Oldham OL4..............67 C6
Rochdale OL11.......... 139 A3
Dovestone Cres SK16 ....101 F7
Dovestone Wlk M40 ......65 E1
Doveston Rd M33........108 B6
Dove Wlk
Farnworth BL4............59 F8
Manchester M8 ....156 B1
Dovey Cl M29 ....77 C7
Dower St WN2 ....56 A3
Dow Fold BL8 ....26 F3
Dow La BL8 ....26 F3
Dowland Cl 3 M23 ....108 F2
Dowling Cl WN6...........36 D3
Dowling St OL11........ 139 C2
DOWNALL GREEN 72 C5
Downall Green Rd
WN4.......................72 E6
Downbrook Way WN4.....73 D5
Downesway SK9..........136 F1
Downes Way M22.........121 E6
Downfield Cl BL0.........138 B2
Downfields SK5 .... 100 A1
Downgate Wlk 6 M8.... 156 A2
Downgreen Rd BL2 ....25 E3
Downhall Gn BL1....... 145 C4
Downham Ave
Bolton BL2............. 148 C4
Culcheth WA3 ....91 F2
Downham Chase
WA15......................120 B6
Downham Cl OL1..........48 D2
Downham Cres M25 ......63 E3
Downham Gdns M25.......63 E3
Downham Gr M25 ....63 E3
Downham Rd
Heywood OL10.............29 A2
Reddish SK4 .... 111 D5
Downham Wlk
Longshaw WN5 ....53 D1
Wythenshawe M23 ......120 E8
Downhill Cl OL1 ....48 E1
Downing Cl
Ashton-u-L OL7 ....84 F6
Platt Bridge WN2..........56 A2
Downing St
Ashton-u-L OL7 ....84 F5
5 Leigh WN7 ....75 F5
Manchester M1, M12,
M13 ....163 B3
Downing Street Ind Est
M12 ....163 B3
Downley Cl OL12 ....14 B2
Downley Dr M4......... 159 C2
Downs Dr WA14 ....119 E8
Downshaw Rd OL7........85 A6
Downs The
Altrincham WA14........ 119 D3
Cheadle SK8 .... 122 D3
Middleton M24............65 B5
Prestwich M25............63 A2
Wigan WN3 ....54 C4
Downton Ave 14 WN2 .....56 D4
Dowry Rd OL4.............67 F7
Dowry St OL8 ....67 A3
Dowson Prim Sch
SK14.......................113 E8
Dowson Rd SK14 ....113 E8
Dowson St BL2......... 148 A3
Dow St SK14 .... 101 D5
Doyle Ave SK6......... 112 D3
Doyle Cl OL1 ....49 E4
Doyle Rd BL3..............40 E2
Drake Ave
Farnworth BL4............60 D7
Irlam M44 ....105 E6
Wythenshawe M22 ....121 B2
Drake Cl OL1 .... 153 C4
Drake Ct SK5............169 B4
Drake Hall BL5 ....57 E5
Drake Rd
Altrincham WA14.........119 B8
Calderbrook OL15 ....6 C1
Drake St
Atherton M46 ....58 C2
Rochdale OL11, OL16 .... 139 C2
Draycote Ho M13.........98 E3
Draycott Cl WN2..........56 F3
Draycott St E 10 BL1.... 143 C2
Draycott St BL1 ....143 B2
Drayfields M43 ....84 D2
Drayford Cl 2 M23 ......108 F2
Drayton Cl
Bolton BL1............. 143 A2
12 Handforth SK9 .... 131 D1
Sale M33 .... 107 D2
Drayton Dr SK8..........131 B7
Drayton Gr WA15....... 120 A5
Drayton Manor M20 .....122 B8
Drayton St M15..........162 B1
Drayton Wlk M16........ 162 A1
Dresden St M40 ....83 C8
Drewett St M40..........160 B4
Dreyfus Ave M11 ....83 C2
Driffield St
Eccles M30 ....95 C8
Manchester M14 ....98 A3
Drinkwater Rd M25........62 F1
Driscoll St 1 M13 ....98 F3
Drive The
Altrincham WA15........ 129 D8
Brinnington SK5......... 112 C4
Broomedge WA13 .... 117 D1
Bury BL9 ....27 F5
Cheadle SK8 .... 123 C4
Edenfield BL0...............1 D3
Leigh WN7 ....75 F3
Manchester, Broughton Park
M7 ....63 C1
Manchester, Didsbury
M20 .... 110 C4
Marple SK6 ....125 E6
Prestwich M25............63 B4
Romiley SK6............ 112 D3
Sale M33 ....107 E1
Droitwich Rd M40 ...... 160 A4
Dronfield Rd
Salford M6............. 154 A4
Wythenshawe M22 ...... 121 D8
Droughts La M25 ....63 E8
Drovers Wlk 3 SK13.... 104 D1
Droxford Ct SK9 ....137 B6
Droxford Gr M46 ....58 E5
DROYLSDEN 84 B3
Droylsden Rd
Droylsden M34.......... 100 C8
Failsworth M40 ....83 D5
Droylsden Sch M43 ....83 F2
Drs Green & Slater Rest
Hos SK4 .... 168 A3
Druids Cl BL7 ....8 D3
Druid St WN4 ....73 C2
Drummer's La WN4........72 E7
Drummond Sq WN5 ....54 E7
Drummond St BL1.......143 B4
Drummond Way WN7 .....76 B5
Drury La OL9..............66 B3
Drury St 13 M19 ....99 A1
Dryad Cl M27..............61 F2
Drybrook Cl M13 ....164 B1
Dryburgh Ave BL1 ...... 143 A4
Dryclough Wlk OL2 ....48 E3
Dryden Ave
Ashton-in-M WN4 ....72 F6
Cheadle SK8 ....122 F6
Swinton M27 ....79 D7
Dryden Cl
Dukinfield SK16..........102 B7
Marple SK6 ....125 F4
Wigan WN3 .... 150 A1
Dryden Rd 4 M16 ....97 C3
Dryden St M13 .... 163 C2
Dryden Way 10 M34..... 113 A8
Dryfield La BL6............22 A5
Drygate Wlk 6 M9 ...... 157 B3
Dryhurst Dr SK12....... 135 D6
Dryhurst La SK12....... 135 D6
Dryhurst Wlk M15 ...... 163 A2
Drymoss OL8..............67 A1
Drysdale View BL1 ....143 B4
Dryton Wlk WN2...........38 A2
Drywood Ave M28 ....79 A5
Ducal St M4.............159 B4
Duchess Park Cl OL2 ....149 B4
Duchess Rd M8 ....156 B4
Duchess St OL2 ....149 B4
Duchess Wlk BL3........146 B4
Duchy Ave
Over Hulton BL5 ....59 A8
Walkden M28.............78 D8
Duchy Bank M6 ....80 D6
Duchy Rd M6..............80 E5
Duchy Road Cvn Pk
M6 .... 154 C4
Duchy St
Salford M6............. 154 C3
Stockport SK3 .... 170 A3
Ducie Ave BL1.......... 144 C3
Ducie Ho M1............159 B1
Ducie St
Manchester M1 ....159 B1
Oldham OL8..............66 F2
Radcliffe M26 ....43 F5
Whitefield M45 ....62 F8
Duckshaw La BL4.........60 D8
Duckworth La BB4..........1 E8
Duckworth Rd M25 ....62 F3
Duckworth St
3 Bury BL9............ 141 A4
Shaw OL2.............. 149 C3
Duddon Ave BL2..........25 F1
Duddon Cl
Standish WN6 ....36 F7
Whitefield M45 ....63 C8
Duddon Wlk 2 M24 ......46 E2
Dudley Ave
Bolton BL2...............25 C1
Whitefield M45 ....62 F8
Dudley Cl M15...........162 B1
Dudley Ct 10 M16.........97 D3
Dudley Rd
Irlam M44 .... 105 D4
Manchester M16 ....97 D3
Sale M33 .... 108 C6
Sale, Timperley WA15 .....120 B7
Swinton M27 ....61 F1
Dudley St
Ashton-in-M WN4 ....73 A5
Eccles M30 ....79 C1
6 Oldham OL4 ....67 D6
Salford M7............. 155 C2
Dudlow Wlk 27 M15 ..... 162 A2
Dudwell Cl BL1......... 142 C2
Duerden St BL3 .... 146 A2
Duffield Ct M15 .... 163 A1
Duffield Gdns M9.........64 F5
Duffield Rd
Middleton M9.............64 F5
Salford M6...............80 D5
Duffins Cl OL12...........14 D3
Dufton Wlk
1 Middleton M24.........46 E2
Wythenshawe M22 ....130 E8
Dugdale Ave M9..........64 E4
Dugie St BL0 ....138 B3
Duke Ave
Cheadle SK8 ....131 F6
Glazebury WA3 ....92 C7
Duke Ct M16 .... 162 A1
Dukefield St M22 ....121 E8
Duke of Norfolk CE Prim
Sch SK13 .... 104 D1
Duke of Norfolk CE Prim
Sch (Annexe) SK13.....104 E2
Duke Pl M3 ....162 B4
Duke Rd
Ainsworth BL2............26 C1
Dukinfield SK14..........101 F5
Duke St N BL1...........145 B4
Dukes Ave BL3 ....43 A4
Dukes Fold SK13 ....116 B7
Dukesgate Prim Sch
M38 ....60 A5
Dukes Platting OL6 ....85 F5
Duke's Row WN2 ....38 B4
Dukes St SK13.......... 116 C8
Duke St
Alderley Edge SK9........137 B2
Ashton-in-M WN4 ....73 C3
Ashton-u-L OL6 ....166 B3
Bolton BL1..............145 B4
Denton M34..............100 E3
Eccles M30 ....79 C4
Failsworth M35 ....84 A8
Golborne WA3 ....74 A1
Heywood OL10.............29 B2
Leigh WN7 ....76 A4
Littleborough OL15 ....16 A5
Manchester M3 .... 158 C2
Manchester M3 ....162 B4
Mossley OL5 ....68 E1
Newton-le-W WA12.........89 B3
Platt Bridge WN2..........56 A3
Radcliffe M26 ....44 B2
Ramsbottom BL0...........11 A4
Rawtenstall BB4 ....2 E8
Rochdale OL12............14 F1
Salford, Lower Broughton
M7 .... 155 A1
Salford, Lower Broughton
M7 .... 158 A4
Shaw OL2.............. 149 C2
Stalybridge SK15..........85 F1
Stockport SK1 .... 169 C1
Tyldesley M29 ....77 C6
Walkden, Linnyshaw
M28 ....61 A2
Walkden M38.............60 A5
Duke St *continued*
Wigan, Goose Green
WN3 ....54 F4
Wigan, Swinley WN1.......37 C2
Duke's Terr 17 SK16......166 B1
Dukes Wharf M28 ....78 F5
Dukes Wlk WA15 ....119 F3
DUKINFIELD 101 D7
Dukinfield Rd SK14 ..... 101 C4
Dukinfield St 6 WN7 .....76 A5
Dulford Wlk 4 M13..... 163 C1
Dulgar St M11...........165 B4
Dulverton Gdns BL3 ......43 B2
Dulverton St M40.........83 B6
Dulwich Cl 9 M33...... 107 D3
Dulwich St M4 ....159 B3
Dumbarton Cl SK5.......111 F6
Dumbarton Dr OL10 ......46 A8
Dumbarton Gn WN6 ......36 E2
Dumbarton Rd
Heywood OL10............29 A1
Reddish SK5 ....111 F6
Dumbell St M27 ....61 F2
Dumber La M33 ....107 F6
Dumers Cl M26...........44 D4
Dumers La BL9, M26 ......44 E5
Dumfries Ave OL3 ....33 C2
Dumfries Dr OL3 ....33 C2
Dumfries Hollow OL10....29 F3
Dumfries Wlk OL10.......29 A1
DUMPLINGTON 95 D7
Dunbar Ave M23........ 121 A3
Dunbar Dr BL3 ....147 B3
Dunbar Gr OL10 ....45 F8
Dunbar St OL1 ....153 B4
Dunblane Ave
Bolton BL3...............40 E5
Stockport SK4 .... 169 A2
Dunblane Cl WN4.........72 C4
Dunblane Gr OL10 ....46 A8
Duncan Ave WA12 ....89 C5
Duncan Pl WN5 ....54 E7
Duncan Rd M13 ....98 F3
Duncan St
Dukinfield SK16......... 101 C6
Horwich BL6 ....22 C3
Salford, Higher Broughton
M7 ....81 C6
Salford, New Windsor
M5 .... 161 C4
Dunchurch Cl BL6 ....40 D6
Dunchurch Rd M33 ......107 E4
Dun Cl M3 .... 158 A2
Duncombe Cl SK7 ...... 124 A3
Duncombe Dr M40 ....83 B7
Duncombe Rd BL3.......147 B2
Duncombe St M7........155 B2
Duncote Gr OL2 .... 149 A1
Dundee 3 M30............79 E2
Dundee Cl OL10 ....28 F1
Dundee La BL0 ....138 B2
Dundonald Rd
Cheadle SK8 .... 132 A7
Manchester M20 .... 110 C3
Dundonald St SK2 ...... 170 C2
Dundraw Cl M24..........46 B1
Dundrennan Cl SK12.... 133 D5
Dunecroft M34 .... 101 A4
Dunedin Dr M6............80 F6
Dunedin Rd BL8 ....10 F2
Dunelm Dr M33 .... 108 D1
Dunham Ave WA3 ....73 F1
Dunham Cl BL5............57 D5
Dunham Gr WN7 ....76 C2
Dunham Lawn WA14.....119 B4
Dunham Massey Hall*
WA14.................... 118 D3
Dunham Pk* WA14...... 118 D3
Dunham Rd
Altrincham, Bowgreen
WA14 ....118 F1
Altrincham WA14........119 B4
Carrington M31......... 106 D3
Dukinfield SK16......... 101 D6
Handforth SK9.......... 131 D5
Mossbrow WA13 ....117 E7
Dunham Rise WA14..... 119 C4
Dunham St
Manchester M15 ....162 B2
Oldham OL4..............67 E8
Dunkeld Gdns 2 M23....120 F6
Dunkeld Rd M23.........120 F6
Dunkerley Ave M35 ....83 F7
Dunkerleys Cl M8....... 155 C4
Dunkerley St
Ashton-u-L OL7 ....85 A5
Oldham OL4..............67 C7
Royton OL2 ....48 D4
Dunkery Rd M22........ 121 D1
Dunkirk Cl M34......... 100 A2
Dunkirk La SK14.........101 B4
Dunkirk Rd M45 ....44 F1
Dunkirk Rise OL12.......139 B3
Dunkirk St M43...........84 B1
Dunley Cl M12.......... 165 A1
Dunlin Ave WA12 ....89 C4
Dunlin Cl
Bolton BL2............. 148 A1
Hazel Grove SK2 .... 125 A5
Poynton SK12 .... 133 A4
Rochdale OL11............29 F7
Dunlin Dr M44............94 A3
Dunlin Gr WN7 ....76 B5
Dunlin Wlk WA14........119 B8
Dunlop Ave OL11 ....30 E4
Dunlop St 2 M3 .... 158 C1
Dunmail Ave WA11 ....71 C1
Dunmail Cl M29 ....77 C6
Dunmail Dr M24...........46 E3
Dunmaston Ave 6
M23 .... 120 D7
Dunmere Wlk M9....... 156 C2
Dunmore Rd SK8 ....122 B6
Dunmow Ct SK2 ....124 E5
Dunmow Wlk M23 ...... 109 A2
Dunne La SK13 ....104 E2
Dunnerdale Wlk M18 ... 165 C1
Dunnisher Rd M23.......121 B5
Dunnock Cl SK2 ....124 F5
Dunollie Rd M33 ....108 E3
Dunoon Cl OL10...........29 A1
Dunoon Dr BL1............24 C5
Dunoon Rd
Aspull WN2 ....38 D5
Reddish SK5 ....111 F7
Dunoon Wlk M9......... 157 A3
Dunrobin Cl OL10.........46 A8
DUNSCAR 24 E8
Dunscar Cl M45 ....62 D7
Dunscar Grange BL7......24 F8
Dunscar Ind Est BL7......24 E7
Dunscar Sq BL7 ....24 F8
Dunscore Rd WN3 ....54 E3
Dunsdale Dr WN4 ....73 C3
Dunsfold Dr M23 .... 120 D8
Dunsford Ct OL4..........67 F5
Dunsley Ave M40 ....65 D2
Dunsmore Cl M16 ....97 E4
Dunsop Dr BL1 ....23 F3
Dunstable 9 OL12...... 139 C4
Dunstable St M19 ....99 B1
Dunstall Rd M22.........121 E5
Dunstan Ct M40 ....83 A8
Dunstan St BL2......... 148 C3
Dunstar Ave M34 ....100 E7
Dunster Ave
Brinnington SK5......... 112 C5
Manchester M9 ....64 E4
Rochdale OL11...........139 B1
Swinton M27 ....62 B2
Dunster Cl
Hazel Grove SK7 .... 124 C1
Platt Bridge WN2..........56 A1
Dunster Dr M41 ....94 C1
Dunster Pl M28...........77 F7
Dunster Rd M28 ....77 F7
Dunsters Ave BL8.........27 C5
Dunsterville Terr
OL11.......................139 B1
Dunston Pl 7 OL9 ....48 A1
Dunston St M11 .... 165 C4
Dunton Gn SK5...........112 B6
Dunton Twrs SK5 ....112 B6
Dunvegan Rd SK7 ....124 F1
Dunwood Ave OL2...... 149 C4
Dunwoods Park Courts
OL2.......................32 C1
Dunworth St M14..........98 B3
Durant St M4............159 B3
Durban Cl OL2.......... 149 A2
Durban Rd 2 BL1 ....24 E5
Durban St
Ashton-u-L OL7 ....84 E1
Atherton M46 ....58 A2
Golborne WN2, WN7 ......74 E4
Oldham OL8..............66 C3
Rochdale OL11............30 C2
Durden Mews OL2.......149 B2
Durham Ave M41 ....95 E3
Durham Cl
Dukinfield SK16......... 101 D6
Little Lever BL3...........43 B4
Romiley SK6............ 113 A1
Swinton M27 ....61 F2
Tyldesley M29 ....59 A3
Durham Cres M35 ....84 A6
Durham Dr
Ashton-u-L OL6 ....85 D8
Bury BL9 ....45 A8
Ramsbottom BL0...........11 B3
Durham Gr M44 .... 105 C6
Durham Ho 6 SK3 ......170 B4
Durham Rd
3 Hindley WN2 ....56 E5
Salford M6...............80 C4
Durham St
Bolton BL1............. 143 C2
Droylsden M43.......... 100 A8
12 Manchester M9 ....157 B3
Oldham OL9..............66 C4
Radcliffe M26 ....44 C5
Reddish SK5 ....99 E2
Rochdale OL11............31 A5
Wigan WN1 ....37 E1
Durham Wlk
5 Denton M34...........100 F1
Heywood OL10............29 A2
Durley Ave
Manchester M8 ....156 B3
Sale WA15...............120 B7
Durling St M12 .... 163 C3
DURN 16 C5
Durnford Ave M41 ....96 A2
Durnford Cl OL12 ....13 D2
Durnford St M24 ....46 F1
Durnford Wlk M22.......121 B3
Durnlaw Cl OL15..........16 C5
Durn St OL15..............16 C6
Durrell Way WA3 ....90 E8
Durrington Wlk 4
M40 ....65 C3
Dursley Dr WN4 ....73 D4
Dutton Gr WN7............76 C2

Dutton St M3. . . . . .158 C3
Duty St BL1. . . . . .143 B3
Duxbury Ave
 Bolton BL2. . . . . .25 E5
 Little Lever BL3 . . . . .43 A5
Duxbury Dr BL9 . . . . .141 C2
Duxbury St BL1. . . . . .143 A2
Duxford Lo M8 . . . . .63 F2
Duxford Wlk **1** M40 . . . . . .65 C3
Dyche St M4 . . . . .159 B3
Dyehouse La OL16 . . . . .15 C3
Dye House La SK22 . . . . . .127 C5
Dye La SK6. . . . . .113 B2
Dyers Cl WA13 . . . . .117 A4
Dyers Ct OL15 . . . . .16 A6
Dyers La WA13 . . . . .117 A4
Dyer St
 Golborne WA3. . . . . .73 F1
 Manchester M11. . . . . . . .165 A4
 Salford M5. . . . . .161 C3
Dymchurch Ave M26. . . . . . .61 C7
Dymchurch St M40 . . . . . . .83 C4
Dysarts Cl OL5 . . . . .68 E3
Dysart St
 4 Ashton-u-L OL6 . . . . . . .85 D2
 Stockport SK2. . . . . .124 B5
Dyserth Gr SK5. . . . . .169 C4
Dyson Cl BL4. . . . . .60 D8
Dyson Gr OL4 . . . . .67 F8
Dyson Ho **8** BL4 . . . . .60 D8
Dyson St
 Farnworth BL4. . . . . .60 D7
 Mossley OL5 . . . . .68 B2
Dystelegh Rd SK12 . . . . . . .135 D6

E

Eades St M6 . . . . .81 A3
Eadington St M8 . . . . .64 A1
Eafield Ave OL16. . . . . .31 F7
Eafield Cl OL16 . . . . .31 F7
Eafield Rd
 Littleborough OL15 . . . . . . .15 E3
 Rochdale OL16. . . . . .15 C1
Eagar St M40 . . . . .83 C6
Eagle Cl
 Delph OL3 . . . . .50 F5
 Salford M15. . . . . .162 B1
Eagle Dr M6. . . . . .81 A5
Eagle Lo M46 . . . . .119 F2
Eagles Nest M25. . . . . .63 A3
Eagle St
 Bolton BL2. . . . . .148 A3
 4 Manchester M4 . . . . . .159 A2
 Oldham OL9 . . . . .153 B2
 Rochdale OL16. . . . . .31 A6
Eagle Tech Pk OL11. . . . . . .31 A4
EAGLEY 24 F7
EAGLEY BANK 24 F6
Eagley Bank OL12 . . . . .4 E6
Eagley Brook Way BL1. . . . . .25 A3
Eagley Br BL1 . . . . .24 F7
Eagley Dr BL8. . . . . .27 A1
Eagley Inf Sch BL7. . . . . . . .25 A8
Eagley Jun Sch BL7. . . . . . . .25 B8
Eagley View BL8 . . . . .27 A1
Eagley Way BL1, BL7 . . . . . .24 F7
Ealand Chase BL6. . . . . .21 F3
EALEES 16 C5
Ealees OL15 . . . . .16 C5
Ealees Rd OL15. . . . . .16 C5
Ealing Ave M14 . . . . .98 C2
Ealinger Way M27 . . . . .61 F2
Ealing Pl M19 . . . . .111 A6
Ealing Rd SK3 . . . . .170 A4
Eames Ave M26 . . . . .61 A8
Eamont Wlk M9 . . . . .157 A3
Earby Gr M9 . . . . .64 F3
Earle Rd SK7 . . . . .123 E3
Earlesdon Cres M38 . . . . . . .60 A5
Earlesfield Cl M33 . . . . .107 D2
Earle St
 Ashton-u-L OL7 . . . . .84 F2
 Newton-le-W WA12. . . . . . .89 A3
EARLESTOWN 89 B2
Earlestown Sta WA12. . . . . . .89 B3
Earl Rd
 Handforth SK8, SK9. . . . . . .131 E5
 Ramsbottom BL0 . . . . .138 B2
 Stockport SK4 . . . . .168 C4
Earlscliffe Ct WA14 . . . . . . .119 B4
Earl's Lo M35. . . . . .83 D6
Earl St
 Atherton M46 . . . . .58 B2
 Bury BL9 . . . . .140 C2
 6 Heywood OL10. . . . . . .29 C2
 Ince-in-M WN2 . . . . .56 A7
 Leigh WN7 . . . . .76 A4
 Mossley OL5 . . . . .68 B1
 Prestwich M25. . . . . .63 C4
 Ramsbottom BL0 . . . . .11 D6
 Reddish M34. . . . . .100 A4
 Salford M7. . . . . .158 A4
 Stockport SK3 . . . . .170 A4
 Trub OL11 . . . . .47 D8
 Wigan WN1 . . . . .37 C1
Earlston Ave M34. . . . . . . .100 A3
Earlsway **5** SK13 . . . . . . .116 B8
Earls Way M35. . . . . .83 D6
Earlswood Rd OL8 . . . . .66 E3
Earlswood Wlk
 Bolton BL1. . . . . .147 C4
 Manchester M18. . . . . . . .165 C2
Earl Terr **18** SK16 . . . . . . .166 B1

Earl Wlk M12. . . . . .164 C1
Early Bank SK15. . . . . .102 C7
Early Bank Rd SK14, SK15,
 SK16. . . . . .102 B6
Earnshaw Ave
 Rochdale OL12. . . . . .14 E3
 Stockport SK1 . . . . .112 B1
Earnshaw Cl OL7 . . . . .84 F5
Earnshaw St
 Bolton BL3. . . . . .146 B3
 Hollingworth SK14. . . . . . .171 A4
Easby Cl
 Cheadle SK8 . . . . .132 B6
 Poynton SK12 . . . . .133 D4
Easby Rd M24 . . . . .46 F3
Easedale Cl M41. . . . . .94 F3
Easedale Rd
 Bolton BL1. . . . . .144 A4
 Failsworth M40 . . . . .83 C8
Easington Wlk **10** M40 . . . .83 A6
Easingwold **2** WA14 . . . . .119 C4
East Ave
 Clifton M27 . . . . .79 E6
 Gatley SK8 . . . . .131 D8
 Golborne WA3 . . . . .74 C1
 Leigh WN7 . . . . .76 C3
 Manchester M19 . . . . .110 F7
 Stalybridge SK15. . . . . .86 A3
 Whitefield M45 . . . . .44 E2
Eastbank St BL1 . . . . .143 C2
East Bond St WN4. . . . . . . .150 B5
Eastbourne Gr BL1 . . . . . . .144 A4
Eastbourne St
 Oldham OL8 . . . . .67 B4
 Rochdale OL11. . . . . .139 C1
East Bridgewater St **4**
 WN7. . . . . .76 A4
Eastbrook Ave **2** M26 . . . .44 C4
Eastburn Ave M40 . . . . . . .159 C3
East Central Dr M27 . . . . . . .80 B7
Eastchurch Cl BL4 . . . . .60 D7
Eastcombe Ave M7 . . . . .81 B7
Eastcote Ave M11 . . . . .99 E8
Eastcote Rd SK5. . . . . .111 F5
Eastcote Wlk **5** BL4 . . . . . .42 E1
East Court Wlk M13 . . . . . .163 C2
East Cres M24. . . . . .64 F7
East Crompton St
 George's CE Sch OL2. . . . . .49 D7
East Crompton St James
 CE Prim Sch OL2. . . . . . . .149 B3
Eastdale M15 . . . . .128 F8
Eastdale Pl WA14. . . . . .119 D7
EAST DIDSBURY 110 C1
East Didsbury Sta
 M20 . . . . .110 C1
East Downs Rd
 Altrincham WA14. . . . . . . .119 C2
 Cheadle SK8 . . . . .122 F2
East Dr
 Marple SK6. . . . . .125 F3
 Pendlebury M27 . . . . .80 B7
 Salford M6. . . . . .80 E5
 Whitefield BL9 . . . . .45 B4
Easterdale OL4 . . . . .67 C6
Eastern Ave M27 . . . . .62 D3
Eastern By-Pass M11 . . . . . .83 C2
Eastern By Pass M11 . . . . . . .99 D8
Eastern Circ M19 . . . . .111 A6
Eastfield M6 . . . . .154 B4
Eastfield Ave
 Manchester M40. . . . . . . .160 B3
 Middleton M24. . . . . .65 A7
Eastfields M26 . . . . .43 E5
Eastford Sq M40. . . . . .159 C4
Eastgarth WN2 . . . . .56 B2
Eastgarth Wlk **8** M19 . . . . .64 E3
Eastgate OL12 . . . . .14 C7
Eastgate St OL7 . . . . .166 A1
East Gate St OL16 . . . . . . .139 C4
East Gr M11 . . . . .164 A1
East Grange M11. . . . . .83 C3
Eastgrove Ave BL1. . . . . . . .24 E6
Eastham Ave
 Bury BL9 . . . . .27 F6
 Manchester M14. . . . . .98 B1
Eastham Way
 11 Handforth SK9. . . . . . .131 D5
 Walkden M38. . . . . .60 B5
Easthaven Ave **4** M11 . . . . .83 C2
East Hill St **7** OL1. . . . . . . .67 A6
Eastholme Dr M19. . . . . . . .111 B7
Eastleigh M20 . . . . .110 B7
East Lancashire Rd
 Haydock WA11, WA12,
 WA3. . . . . .89 C7
 Leigh WA3, WN7, M29. . . . .76 D2
 Pendlebury M27 . . . . .80 B6
 Swinton M27, M28. . . . . . . .79 D7
 Tyldesley M28, M29. . . . . . .77 C5
 Worsley M28. . . . . .79 D7
East Lancashire Rly *b*B84,
 BL0. . . . . .1 C5
East Lancs Rly *b*
 Bury BL8 . . . . .27 D7
 Heywood OL10. . . . . .29 C1
East Lea M34. . . . . .101 A2
Eastleigh Ave M7 . . . . .155 B4
Eastleigh Cres WN7. . . . . . .76 B3
Eastleigh Dr M40 . . . . .160 A3
Eastleigh Gr **2** BL1 . . . . . .145 B4
Eastleigh Rd
 Gatley SK8. . . . . .122 B1
 Manchester M25 . . . . .63 E3
East Lynn Dr M26. . . . . .61 A3
East Market St M3. . . . . . . .158 A2
East Meade
 Bolton BL3. . . . . .147 B2

East Meade *continued*
 Manchester, Chorlton-cum-
 Hardy M21. . . . . .109 B7
 Manchester, Sedgley Park
 M25 . . . . .63 D2
 Swinton M27 . . . . .79 E6
East Moor M28 . . . . .78 A7
Eastmoor Dr M40. . . . . .83 D4
Eastmoor Gr BL3 . . . . .146 B2
East Mount WN5 . . . . .53 F6
East Newton St **8**
 M4 . . . . .159 C3
Eastnor Cl M15. . . . . .162 A2
Easton Cl
 Middleton M24. . . . . .65 C7
 Wigan WN2 . . . . .55 A2
Easton Dr SK8. . . . . .123 A5
Easton Rd M43 . . . . .83 E1
East Ordsall La M3,
 M5 . . . . .158 A1
East Over WN5 . . . . .125 A8
Eastpark Cl M13. . . . . .163 C2
East Park Cl M13 . . . . .163 C2
East Philip St M3. . . . . .158 B3
East Rd
 Manchester M12. . . . . .99 A3
 Manchester M18. . . . . .99 B4
 Mossley SK15 . . . . .86 E6
 Wythenshawe M90 . . . . . .130 C7
Eastry Ave SK5 . . . . .112 B6
East St
 Ashton-in-M WN4 . . . . .73 D4
 3 Ashton-u-L OL6 . . . . . .85 D4
 Bury BL9 . . . . .140 C1
 Denton M34. . . . . .100 F7
 Edenfield BL0. . . . . .1 D4
 Haslingden BB4. . . . . .1 A7
 Hindley WN2 . . . . .57 B3
 Littleborough OL15 . . . . . . .16 C5
 Milnrow OL16 . . . . .31 D7
 Radcliffe M26 . . . . .44 B3
 Rochdale OL16. . . . . .31 A8
 Tyldesley M46 . . . . .58 F1
 Wardle OL12. . . . . .15 C6
East Union St M16. . . . . . . .161 C2
East Vale SK6. . . . . .126 A5
Eastview M33 . . . . .108 B3
East View
 4 Middleton M24. . . . . . .64 F8
 Ramsbottom, Brooksbottoms
 BL9 . . . . .11 C3
 Ramsbottom, Chatterton
 BL0. . . . . .1 C1
 Whitworth OL12. . . . . .4 D2
Eastville Gdns M19 . . . . . . .110 E5
Eastward Ave SK9. . . . . . . .136 F6
East Ward Com Prim Sch
 BL9. . . . . .141 B2
Eastway
 Middleton M24. . . . . .46 F1
 Sale M33 . . . . .107 F1
 Shaw OL2. . . . . .149 B2
 Urmston M41. . . . . .94 E3
East Way
 Bolton BL1. . . . . .25 B3
 Chadd OL1. . . . . .48 E1
 Leigh WN7 . . . . .76 C4
 Stretford M32. . . . . .96 B3
 Urmston M41. . . . . .94 E3
East Wlk BL7 . . . . .8 C2
Eastwood M14. . . . . .98 C1
Eastwood Ave
 Droylsden M43. . . . . .83 E1
 Failsworth M40 . . . . .65 F1
 Newton-le-W WA12. . . . . . .89 F3
 Urmston M41. . . . . .95 D2
 Walkden M28. . . . . .60 A2
Eastwood Cl
 Bolton BL3. . . . . .146 A3
 Bury BL9 . . . . .141 B2
Eastwood Ct BL9 . . . . .141 B2
Eastwood Gr WN7 . . . . .75 D5
Eastwood Rd M40 . . . . .65 E1
Eastwood St
 Denton M34. . . . . .100 D7
 11 Littleborough OL15. . . .16 B5
Eastwood Terr BL1. . . . . . . .40 E8
Eatock Prim Sch BL5 . . . . . .57 E6
Eatock St WN1 . . . . .56 B3
Eatock Way BL5 . . . . .57 D6
Eaton Cl
 Cheadle SK8 . . . . .122 F3
 Dukinfield SK16 . . . . .101 C6
 Poynton SK12 . . . . .134 A3
 Swinton M27 . . . . .61 F2
Eaton Ct
 Altrincham WA14 . . . . .119 C1
 Wilmslow SK9 . . . . .137 A6
Eaton Dr
 Alderley Edge SK9. . . . . . .136 F2
 Ashton-u-L OL7 . . . . .84 F4
 Sale WA15 . . . . .120 A8
Eaton Rd
 Altrincham WA14 . . . . .119 C1
 Manchester M8 . . . . .63 F1
 Sale M33 . . . . .108 A4
 Sale M33 . . . . .109 A6
Eaves Knoll Rd SK22. . . . . .127 A1
Eaves La OL9 . . . . .152 C2
Ebbdale Cl SK1. . . . . .124 A8
Ebberstone St M14 . . . . .98 A2
Ebden St M13 . . . . .163 B4
Ebenezer St
 Glossop SK13. . . . . .116 D7
 5 Manchester M15 . . . . . .162 C3
Ebnall Wlk M14 . . . . .110 D7
Ebor Cl OL2. . . . . .149 A4
Ebor Ho M21. . . . . .96 F1

Ebor Rd M22 . . . . .121 E4
Ebor St OL15 . . . . .16 B5
Ebsworth St M40 . . . . .157 C4
Ebury St M26. . . . . .43 F3
ECCLES 79 F1
Ecclesbridge Rd SK6. . . . . .125 F4
Eccles CI M11. . . . . .165 C4
Eccles Coll M30 . . . . .79 F4
Eccles Fold **9** M30 . . . . . . .79 E2
Eccleshall St M11 . . . . .83 C1
Eccles New Rd M5,
 M50. . . . . .80 C2
Eccles Old Rd M6, M30. . . . .80 C3
Eccles Rd
 Swinton M27 . . . . .79 F6
 Wigan WN5 . . . . .36 B1
Eccles Sixth Form Coll
 M30 . . . . .79 F2
Eccleston Ave
 20 Bolton BL2. . . . . .25 B1
 Manchester M14. . . . . .98 B1
 Swinton M27 . . . . .79 D7
Eccleston Cl BL8 . . . . .27 A1
Eccleston Pl M7 . . . . .155 A4
Eccleston Rd SK3. . . . . . . .123 E4
Eccleston St
 Failsworth M35 . . . . .84 A8
 Wigan WN1 . . . . .37 C1
Eccles Way **8**
 SK9. . . . . .131 D4
Eccups La SK9. . . . . .136 C8
Echo St M1. . . . . .163 B4
Eckersley Cl **1** M23 . . . . .120 F6
Eckersley Fold La M46. . . . . .58 A1
Eckersley Mill WN3. . . . . . .150 B3
Eckersley Rd BL1 . . . . .143 B3
Eckersley St
 Bolton BL3. . . . . .146 C4
 Wigan WN1 . . . . .37 C1
Eckford St M8. . . . . .156 B2
Eclipse Cl OL16. . . . . .31 C7
Edale Ave
 Denton, Audenshaw
 M34. . . . . .100 D7
 Denton, Haughton Green
 M34. . . . . .112 F8
 Manchester M40. . . . . .83 A8
 Reddish SK5 . . . . .100 A1
 Urmston M41. . . . . .95 B1
Edale Bank **51** SK13. . . . . .171 B2
Edale Cl
 Altrincham WA14 . . . . .119 C1
 Atherton M46 . . . . .58 C3
 20 Gamesley SK13. . . . . .171 B2
 Gatley SK8 . . . . .131 D7
 Hazel Grove SK7 . . . . .124 E1
 Irlam M44 . . . . .94 A1
Edale Cres SK13 . . . . .171 B1
Edale Dr WN6 . . . . .19 E2
Edale Fold **21** SK13 . . . . . .171 B2
Edale Gr
 Ashton-u-L OL6 . . . . .86 A6
 Sale M33 . . . . .107 E2
Edale Rd
 Bolton BL3. . . . . .146 A4
 Farnworth BL4. . . . . .60 C7
 Leigh WN7 . . . . .76 C4
 Stretford M32. . . . . .96 B3
Edale St M5. . . . . .81 B5
Edbrook Wlk M13 . . . . .164 A1
Edburton Ct WA3 . . . . .90 A8
Eddie Colman Cl M40. . . . . . .83 B5
Eddisbury Ave
 Manchester M20. . . . . . . .109 F8
 Urmston M41. . . . . .94 D4
Eddisford Dr WA3 . . . . .91 D4
Edditch Gr BL2. . . . . .148 C3
Eddleston St WN4 . . . . .72 F6
Eddystone Cl **6** M5 . . . . . . .81 A1
Eden Ave
 Bolton BL1. . . . . .143 B3
 Edenfield BL0. . . . . .1 D3
 Fowley Common WA3 . . . . . .92 C4
 High Lane SK6 . . . . .134 E7
 Eden Bank WN7 . . . . .76 B6
Edenbridge Dr M26. . . . . . . .61 B7
Edenbridge Rd
 Cheadle SK8 . . . . .123 B4
 Failsworth M40 . . . . .83 B4
Eden Cl
 Heywood OL10. . . . . .29 A3
 Manchester M15 . . . . .163 A2
 Stockport SK1 . . . . .124 A8
 Wilmslow SK9 . . . . .136 E5
Eden Ct
 Edenfield BL0. . . . . .1 D2
 Manchester, Fallowfield
 M14 . . . . .98 B1
 Manchester, Levenshulme
 M19 . . . . .111 A8
Edendale Dr M22 . . . . .121 D1
EDENFIELD 1 D3
Edenfield Ave M21 . . . . . . .109 D4
Edenfield CE Prim Sch
 BL0. . . . . .1 D4
Edenfield La M28. . . . . .78 F4
Edenfield Rd
 Manchester M25 . . . . .63 E2
 Rochdale OL11, OL12 . . . . .13 C2
Edenfield St OL11,
 OL12. . . . . .14 C1
Eden Gr
 Bolton BL1. . . . . .143 B3
 Leigh WN7 . . . . .75 C5
Edenhall Ave M19 . . . . .110 F8
Edenhall Gr WN2. . . . . .56 F3
Edenham Wlk **1** M40. . . . . .65 D2
Edenhurst BB4 . . . . .1 D8

Edenhurst Dr **8**
 WA15. . . . . .120 B5
Edenhurst Rd SK2 . . . . . . .124 B6
Eden Lo BL1. . . . . .143 B3
Eden Park Rd SK8 . . . . . . .131 E8
Eden Pl SK8. . . . . .122 D6
Edensor Cl WN4. . . . . .73 A4
Edensor Dr WA15. . . . . . . .120 C3
Eden St
 Bolton BL1. . . . . .143 B3
 Bury BL9 . . . . .140 C2
 Edenfield BL0. . . . . .1 D2
 Oldham OL1 . . . . .153 B3
 Rochdale OL12. . . . . .139 A4
Edenvale M28 . . . . .78 A7
Eden Way OL2. . . . . .149 A4
Edgar St W BL0 . . . . .138 B1
Edgar St
 Bolton BL3. . . . . .145 B2
 Ramsbottom BL0. . . . . . . .138 B1
 Rochdale OL16. . . . . .31 A8
Edgbaston Dr M16. . . . . . . .97 A3
Edgecote Cl M22 . . . . .121 F6
Edgedale Ave M19 . . . . . . .110 E5
Edge End OL3. . . . . .51 A3
Edgefield Ave M9. . . . . .64 E4
Edge Fold Cres M28 . . . . . . .78 D8
Edgefold Ind Est BL4 . . . . .146 B1
Edge Fold Rd M28. . . . . . . .60 D1
Edge Gn M28. . . . . .78 C8
EDGE GREEN 73 F3
Edge Green La WA3 . . . . . . .73 F2
Edge Green Rd WN4. . . . . . .73 F4
Edge Green St WN4 . . . . . . .73 D4
Edge Hall Rd WN5. . . . . . . .53 E5
Edge Hill Ave OL2 . . . . .48 E3
Edgehill Chase SK9 . . . . . . .137 E7
Edgehill Cl M5 . . . . .154 C2
Edgehill Ct M32 . . . . .96 E1
Edgehill Rd M6. . . . . .80 C3
Edge Hill Rd
 Bolton BL3. . . . . .146 B3
 Royton OL2 . . . . .48 E3
Edgehill St **9** M4 . . . . .159 A2
Edge La
 Bolton BL1, BL0. . . . . .23 C5
 Britannia OL13. . . . . .4 C8
 Droylsden M11, M43 . . . . . .83 D2
 Entwistle BL7 . . . . .9 A8
 Mottram in L SK14. . . . . . .102 F4
 Stretford M21, M32 . . . . . . .96 E1
Edge Lane Rd OL11. . . . . . . .67 A8
Edge Lane St OL12 . . . . .48 E4
EDGELEY 170 B3
Edgeley Fold SK3. . . . . . . .123 C7
Edgeley Park (Stockport
 County FC) (Sale RUFC)
 SK3. . . . . .170 B3
Edgeley Rd
 Stockport SK3 . . . . .123 B7
 Urmston M41. . . . . .107 A4
Edgemoor WA14. . . . . .119 A2
Edgemoor Cl
 Oldham OL4 . . . . .49 D1
 Radcliffe M26 . . . . .43 E5
Edgemoor Dr OL11 . . . . .29 F5
Edgerton Rd WA3. . . . . .90 F8
Edgerton Wlk **4** M28. . . . . .60 D3
Edge St M4 . . . . .159 A2
Edge The M3 . . . . .158 C2
Edge View OL1 . . . . .47 E1
Edge View La WN3 . . . . . . .136 B2
Edgeview Wlk **13** M13. . . . .163 B3
Edgeware Ave M25 . . . . .63 F4
Edgeware Gr WN3 . . . . .54 C3
Edgeware Rd
 Eccles M30 . . . . .79 A4
 Failsworth OL9 . . . . .65 E3
Edgewater M5. . . . . .154 A2
Edgeway SK9. . . . . .137 B5
Edgeway Rd WN3. . . . . .55 A1
Edgewood WN6 . . . . .36 A5
Edgeworth Ave BL2. . . . . . . .26 D1
Edgeworth Dr
 Bury BL8 . . . . .27 A1
 Manchester M14. . . . . . . .110 E7
Edgeworth Rd
 Golborne WA3 . . . . .73 F1
 Hindley WN2 . . . . .57 C3
Edgeworth Row SK14 . . . . .167 B4
Edgeworth Vale BL7 . . . . . . .9 E6
Edgmont Ave BL3. . . . . . . .147 A4
Edgware Rd M40 . . . . .83 B4
EDGWORTH 9 D6
Edgworth Cl OL10 . . . . .29 A2
Edgworth Views BL7 . . . . . . .9 D8
Edgy Wlk **19** SK15. . . . . . .86 A1
Edilom Rd M8. . . . . .63 E2
Edinburgh **8** M30 . . . . .79 E2
Edinburgh Cl
 Cheadle SK8 . . . . .122 F6
 Ince-in-M WN2 . . . . .56 A1
 5 Sale M33 . . . . .107 D3
Edinburgh Dr
 Hindley WN2 . . . . .57 B3
 Romiley SK6. . . . . .113 C4
 Wigan WN5 . . . . .53 D3
Edinburgh Ho M3. . . . . . . .158 A1
Edinburgh Rd BL3 . . . . .43 A2
Edinburgh Sq M40 . . . . . . .160 B4
Edinburgh Way OL11. . . . . . .30 D4
Edington **7** OL12 . . . . . . .139 C4
Edison Rd M30 . . . . .95 C8
Edison St **1** M11. . . . . .99 F7
Edith Ave M14. . . . . .98 A3

Edith Cavell Cl M11........83 C1
Edith Cliff Wlk M40....65 F1
Edith St
 Bolton BL1.........144 C2
 Farnworth BL4........60 D7
 Oldham OL8..........66 F3
 Ramsbottom BL0......11 E8
 Wigan WN3.........150 B3
Edlestone Gr 2 SK9..131 E1
Edlin Cl M12..........164 B1
Edlingham 5 OL11....139 B2
Edlington Wlk 12 M40..83 C6
Edmonds St M24......47 B1
Edmonton Ct SK2....124 A4
Edmonton Rd
 Failsworth M40........83 A4
 Stockport SK2.......124 A4
Edmund Cl SK4......169 B4
Edmund Dr WN7......75 C5
Edmunds Ct BL3.....145 A2
Edmunds Fold OL15...15 F6
Edmund St
 Droylsden M43.......84 A1
 Failsworth M35.......83 F8
 Milnrow OL16........31 F6
 8 Radcliffe M26.....44 C4
 Rochdale OL12......139 A4
 Salford M6.........149 C3
 Shaw OL2..........149 C3
 Walsden OL14.........6 A8
Edna Rd WN7........75 C7
Edna St SK14.......167 A2
Edridge Way WN2....56 C4
Edson Rd M9.........63 F3
Edstone Cl BL3.......40 F4
Edward Ave
 Littleborough OL15....15 F3
 Manchester M21.....109 A8
 Romiley SK6........112 E3
 Salford M6..........80 C3
Edward Charlton Rd M16,
 M21..............97 A2
Edward Ct WA14....119 B7
Edward Dr WN4......73 B4
Edward Mews OL9...152 C1
Edward Onyon Ct M6..154 B2
Edward Rd
 Manchester M9.......64 D5
 Shaw OL2..........149 A2
Edwards Cl SK6.....125 E5
Edwards Ct M22.....121 D3
Edwards Dr M45......63 B8
Edward St
 Ashton-u-l OL6.......85 E2
 Bolton BL3.........145 A1
 Bury BL9..........140 C1
 Chadderton OL9.....152 A4
 Denton, Audenshaw
  M34..............100 D7
 Denton M34.........100 F4
 Droylsden M43.......100 A8
 Dukinfield SK16.....101 C6
 Farnworth BL4........82 B2
 Glossop SK13.......104 C1
 Horwich BL6.........22 A3
 Hyde SK14.........101 C3
 Kearsley M26........61 B8
 Leigh WN7..........76 A4
 Manchester M9.....157 B4
 Marple SK6........114 B1
 Middleton M24.......47 A1
 Oldham OL9.........152 C1
 Prestwich M25.......63 A5
 Radcliffe M26........44 C4
 Rochdale, Newbold Brow
  OL16.............31 A8
 Rochdale, Wuerdle OL12...15 D4
 Sale M33..........108 E4
 Salford M7.........158 D4
 Stockport SK3......170 C4
 Westhoughton BL5....57 E8
 Whitworth OL12.......4 D2
 Wigan, Rose Bridge
  WN1.............151 C4
 Wigan, Swinley WN1...37 C2
Edward Sutcliffe Cl
 M14..............98 A2
Edwards Way SK6....125 E5
Edwin Rd M11.......160 B1
Edwin St
 Bury BL9..........140 B2
 Stockport SK1......124 B8
 Wigan WN1.........151 B3
Edwin Waugh Gdns
 OL12..............14 D3
Eeztell Wlk 18 M11....83 C1
Eeasbrook M41.......95 D1
EES.............107 F7
Egbert St 10 M40......83 A7
EGERTON...........8 E2
Egerton Ave M13....117 C8
Egerton Cl OL10......29 D1
Egerton Cres
 Heywood OL10.......29 C1
 Manchester M20....110 B7
Egerton Ct
 Denton M34.........101 A4
 6 Hindley WN2......56 E5
 Manchester M14......98 C4
 Stockport SK3......124 A4
 Stretford M21......108 F8
 Worsley M28.........79 A8
Egerton Dr
 Altrincham WA15....120 A3
 Sale M33..........108 B5
Egerton Gr M28......60 D3
Egerton High Sch M41...95 E4
Egerton Ho 3 M15....162 A3

Egerton Lo
 Bolton BL7..........8 E1
 Denton M34.........101 A4
Egerton Mews M43...100 A8
Egerton Moss WA15..128 E5
EGERTON PARK......79 B7
Egerton Park Arts Coll
 M34..............100 E4
Egerton Pk M28.......79 B7
Egerton Pl OL2......149 A2
Egerton Prim Sch BL7...8 D3
Egerton Rd
 Altrincham WA15....120 A2
 Eccles M30..........79 D4
 Handforth SK9......131 B1
 Manchester M14.....110 D8
 Stockport SK3......124 A4
 Walkden M28.........60 D3
 Whitefield M45......62 F7
Egerton Rd N
 Manchester, Heaton Chapel
  SK4.............111 C5
 Manchester M16, M21..97 C1
Egerton Rd S
 Manchester, Chorlton-cum-
  Hardy M21.......109 C8
 Stockport, Heaton Moor
  SK4.............168 C4
Egerton St
 Abram Brow WN2.....74 B7
 Ashton-u-l OL6......166 C3
 Denton M34.........100 E5
 Droylsden M43.......84 B1
 Eccles M30..........79 B2
 Farnworth BL4.......42 C1
 Heywood OL10........29 C1
 Littleborough OL15....16 C5
 Manchester M15.....162 A3
 Middleton M24.......64 C7
 Mossley OL5.........68 C2
 Oldham OL1.........67 A8
 Prestwich M25.......63 C4
 Salford M3.........158 A1
Egerton Terr M14....110 D7
Egerton Vale BL7......8 D2
Eggar Cl M29........77 B7
Eggington St M40....156 C1
Egham Ct 18 BL2.....25 B1
Egham Ho BL3.......146 B2
Egmont St
 Manchester M8......156 A4
 Mossley OL5.........86 D8
 Pendlebury M6.......80 E6
Egremont Ave M20...110 A7
Egremont Cl M45......45 A1
Egremont Ct M7......81 C8
Egremont Gr 2 SK3..123 B8
Egremont Rd OL16....31 F4
Egret Dr M44.........94 A3
Egyptian St BL1.....143 C1
Egypt La M25........45 D1
Ehlinger Ave SK13...104 A5
Eida Way M17........96 C8
Eight Acre M45.......62 C7
Eighth Ave OL8.......66 D1
Eighth St M17........96 D6
Eileen Gr M14........98 C2
Eileen Gr W M14.....98 B2
Elaine Ave M9........65 B2
Elaine Cl WN4........73 D5
Elbain Wlk M40.......83 C5
Elberton Wlk 18 M8..155 C3
Elbe St M12........163 C4
Elbow St M19........99 A1
Elbut La BL9........28 F5
Elcho Rd WA14......119 B3
Elcombe Ave WA3.....90 E7
Elcot Cl M40........156 C1
Elderberry Cl
 Diggle OL3..........51 C5
 Wigan WN1..........37 B4
Elderberry Way SK9..137 E8
Elderberry Wlk M31..105 E3
Elder Cl
 Bury BL8...........26 F5
 Stockport SK2......124 D8
Eldercot Gr BL3.....146 A4
Eldercot Rd BL3.....146 A4
Eldercroft Rd WA15..120 D5
Elder Dr BL3.........42 E5
Elderfield Dr SK6....112 F4
Elder Gr M40.........65 F2
Eldermount Rd M9....64 D2
Elder Rd OL4........67 E6
Elder St OL16........31 B5
Elderwood OL9.......65 E7
Eldon Cl M34.......100 E7
Eldon Gdns WN4......73 A6
Eldon Pl M30........79 C1
Eldon Prec OL8.....153 B1
Eldon Rd
 Irlam M44...........94 A2
 Stockport SK3......123 C7
Eldon St
 Bolton BL2..........25 B2
 Bury BL9..........140 C4
 Leigh WN7..........75 D6
 Oldham OL8........153 C1
Eldridge Dr M40......83 A5
Eldroth Ave M22....121 D3
Eleanor Rd
 Manchester M21....109 A8
 Royton OL2..........48 E3
Eleanor St
 Bolton BL1..........25 A5
 Oldham OL1........153 A4
 Wigan WN3.........150 A3
Electo St M11........99 E7

Elevator Rd M17......96 E6
Eleventh St M17......96 D6
Elf Mill Cl SK3......170 B2
Elf Mill Terr SK3....170 B2
Elford Gr M18.......100 A4
Elgar St M12.........99 A4
Elgin Ave
 Garswood WN4.......72 D4
 Manchester M20....110 D3
Elgin Cl WN2.........56 A8
Elgin Dr M33........108 E3
Elgin Rd
 Dukinfield SK16.....101 C6
 Oldham OL4..........67 C5
Elgin St
 Ashton-u-l OL7.....166 A4
 Bolton BL1.........142 C2
 Stalybridge SK15.....86 B1
Elgol Cl SK3........170 C1
Elgol Dr BL3.........40 E6
Elham Cl M26........61 C7
Elim St OL15.........16 C7
Eliot Dr WN3.......150 A1
Eliot Gdns WN3......16 C7
Eliot Rd M30........79 D1
Eliot Wlk M24........47 C3
Elishaw Row M5.....154 C1
Eli St OL9...........66 A3
Eliza Ann St
 5 Eccles M30.......79 C1
 Manchester M40....159 C4
Elizabethan Ct 10 M29..58 F1
Elizabethan Dr WN3...55 E4
Elizabethan Way OL16...31 F5
Elizabethan Wlk 1
 WN2..............56 A2
Elizabeth Ave
 Chadderton OL9......66 A3
 Denton M34.........100 C5
 Disley SK12........135 D5
 Leigh WN2..........56 E1
 1 Stalybridge SK15...86 A2
 Stockport SK1......170 C4
Elizabeth Cl M32.....96 D2
Elizabeth Ct
 Manchester M14.....110 D7
 Reddish M19.........99 F3
 Stockport SK4......168 C2
 8 Tyldesley M29.....58 F1
Elizabeth Gr BB4......1 A8
Elizabeth Gr OL2....149 B3
Elizabeth Ho
 13 Bolton BL8.......27 C3
 Stockport SK4......168 B2
Elizabeth Rd M31....105 F4
Elizabeth Slinger Rd
 M20..............109 F5
Elizabeth St
 Ashton-u-l OL6......166 B4
 Atherton M46........58 D3
 Denton M34.........100 E5
 Edenfield BL0.........1 D3
 2 Heywood OL10.....29 C2
 Hyde SK14.........167 A3
 Ince-in-M WN2.......56 B8
 Leigh WN7..........76 A3
 Manchester M8.....156 A1
 Prestwich M25.......63 C4
 3 Radcliffe M26......44 A3
 Rochdale OL11.......30 C3
 1 Swinton M27.......61 F1
 Whitefield M45......62 F7
Elizabeth Yarwood Ct
 M13..............163 B2
Eliza St
 Manchester M15.....162 B2
 Ramsbottom BL0......11 D6
Elkanagh Gdns M6...154 C3
Elk Ret Pk OL1.......48 B2
Elkstone Ave M38.....60 A6
Elkstone Cl WN3......54 C2
Elkwood Cl WN1.......37 B4
Elladene Pk M21....109 C8
Ellanby Cl M14........98 B3
Elland Cl
 Westhoughton BL5....39 D3
 Whitefield BL9.......44 F8
Ellan Wlk 10 M11.....83 C1
Ellaston Dr M41......95 D2
Ellastone Rd M6......80 C4
Ella View Lo M46.....58 A4
Ellenbrook Cl M11...165 B2
Ellenbrook Com Prim Sch
 M28..............78 C8
Ellenbrook Rd M28...78 B7
Ellen Brook Rd M22..130 D8
Ellendale Grange M28...78 B8
Ellen Gr BL4.........61 C5
Ellen Wilkinson High Sch
 M27..............77 C7
Ellenroad App OL16...32 A4
Ellenroad Engine Ho*
 OL16.............32 A4
Ellenroad St OL16....32 A4
Ellenrod Dr OL12....14 A2
Ellenrod La OL12.....14 A2
Ellenshaw Cl OL12....14 A2

Ellen Wilkinson Cres
 M12..............165 A1
Elleray Cl BL3........43 C3
Elleray Rd
 Middleton M9........64 F5
 Salford M6..........80 D5
Ellerbeck Cl
 Bolton BL2..........25 C5
 Standish M29........36 F7
Ellerbeck Cres M28...78 C8
Ellerby Ave M27.......62 A3
Ellergreen Rd WN2....57 C3
Ellerslie Ct M14.......98 C4
Ellesmere Ave
 Ashton-u-l OL6.......85 C7
 Eccles M30..........79 E2
 Marple SK6.........125 F6
 Walkden M28.........60 C7
Ellesmere Circ M41...95 D7
Ellesmere Cl SK16...101 E8
Ellesmere Dr SK8....123 A5
Ellesmere Gdns BL3..147 A3
Ellesmere Gn M30.....79 E3
Ellesmere Ho 3 M30..79 F3
ELLESMERE PARK....79 E4
Ellesmere Rd
 Altrincham WA14....119 E6
 Ashton-in-M WN4.....72 F4
 Bolton BL3.........146 C3
 Cheadle SK3........123 A7
 Culcheth WA3........91 E3
 Eccles M30..........79 E3
 Manchester M21......97 C1
 Swinton M27.........54 D6
Ellesmere Rd N SK4..111 C5
Ellesmere Rd S M29..128 D8
Ellesmere Ret Pk M28..60 D4
Ellesmere Sh Ctr 2
 M28..............60 D3
Ellesmere St
 Bolton BL3.........145 A2
 14 Eccles M30.......79 F3
 Failsworth M35.......83 F8
 Farnworth BL4........60 D8
 Leigh WN7..........75 F4
 Manchester M15.....162 A3
 Rochdale OL11......139 C1
 Swinton, Clifton Green
  M27..............62 A1
 Swinton, Deans M27...79 D7
 Tyldesley, Higher Green
  M29..............77 C5
 Tyldesley M29........59 A1
 Walkden M28.........60 C4
Ellesmere Terr M14..110 D7
Ellesmere Wlk 3 BL4...60 D8
Ellingham Cl M11....160 C1
Elliot Sq 11 OL1......67 A8
Elliot St
 Bolton BL1.........142 C3
 Oldham OL4..........67 C6
Elliott Ave
 Dukinfield SK14.....101 D5
 Golborne WA3........74 B1
Elliott Dr
 Hindley WN2.........56 E7
 Sale M33..........107 E4
Elliott St
 Farnworth BL4........60 C7
 Rochdale OL12.......31 A8
 Tyldesley M29........76 F8
Ellisbank Wlk 9 M13..163 B3
Ellis Cres M28........60 B3
Ellis Dr M8..........64 B1
Ellis Fold OL12.......13 E2
Ellis La M24..........64 B8
Ellisland Wlk 1 M40....83 A6
Ellison Cl SK14.....103 D5
Ellison Ho 1 OL7....166 A1
Ellison St SK13......104 D1
Ellis St
 Bolton BL3.........145 A1
 Bury BL8...........27 B2
 Hyde SK14.........167 C2
 Manchester M15.....162 A3
 Salford M8.........158 B4
 Wigan WN1..........37 E1
Elliston Sq M12.....165 A2
Ellonby Rise BL6.....40 C5
Ellor St
 Salford M5..........81 B2
 Salford, Seedley M6..154 C3
 Salford SK5 M11.....81 B2
Ellwood Rd SK1......112 B1
Elm Ave
 Downall Green WN4...72 D5
 Golborne WA3........74 A1
 Newton-le-W WA12....89 C2
 Radcliffe M26........61 F8
 Standish WN6........36 F8
 Wigan WN5..........54 E6
Elmbank Ave M20....109 C4
Elmbank Rd M24......65 C8
Elm Beds Rd SK12...134 C2
Elmbridge Wlk
 Bolton BL3.........145 A1
 2 Manchester M40....83 A6
Elm Cl
 Mottram in L SK14...103 A4
 2 Partington M31....105 F3
 Poynton SK12.......133 F3
Elm Cres
 Alderley Edge SK9...137 B3
 Worsley M28.........79 A7
Elm Croft WN1........37 B4
Elm Ct SK1.........124 B8
Elmdale Ave SK8....122 B2
Elmdale Wlk 2 M15..163 A2

Elm Dr
 Billinge WN5........71 D5
 Denton M34.........100 D4
 Stretford M32......108 C8
Elmfield Wlk WN6.....36 B6
Elmfield Ave
 Atherton M46........58 C4
 Wythenshawe M22...121 E8
Elmfield Cl SK9.....137 B2
Elmfield Ct SK3.....170 C1
Elmfield Dr SK6.....125 E6
Elmfield Ho SK3.....170 C1
Elmfield St
 Bolton, Back O' Th' Bank
  BL1.............143 C2
 Bolton BL1.........143 C3
 Manchester M8.....156 A2
Elmgate Gr M19......99 A1
Elm Gr
 Alderley Edge SK9...137 B2
 Ashton-u-l OL6.......85 C5
 Bolton BL7..........25 A8
 Denton M34.........100 D5
 Droylsden M43.......83 D2
 Farnworth BL4........60 A8
 Glossop SK13.......104 C2
 Handforth SK9......131 C3
 Hyde SK14.........167 C2
 Manchester M20....110 B3
 Newhey OL16........32 A3
 Oldham OL4..........68 B6
 Prestwich M25.......63 A6
 Rochdale OL11......139 C3
 Sale M33..........108 B6
 Swinton M27.........61 B2
 Urmston M41.........95 C2
 Wardle OL12.........15 C6
Elmham Wlk M40....159 C4
Elm Ho M16..........97 D3
Elmhow Gr WN3......55 A2
Elmhurst Dr M19....110 F5
Elmira Way M5......161 A3
Elmlea Wlk5.........119 F4
Elmley Cl SK2......125 A5
Elmore Wood OL15....15 E6
Elm Park Ct M20....110 B4
Elmpark Gate OL12...14 B3
Elmpark Gr OL12.....14 B3
Elmpark Vale OL12...14 B3
Elmpark View OL12...14 B3
Elmpark Way OL12...14 B3
Elm Rd
 Abram Brow WN2.....74 C7
 Altrincham WA15....119 E3
 Gatley SK8.........122 A5
 High Lane SK6......134 F7
 Hollinfare WA3......105 A2
 Kearsley BL4.........60 A8
 Little Lever BL3......43 B2
 Manchester M20....110 A4
 Oldham OL8..........66 D2
 Westhoughton BL5....57 F7
Elm Rd S SK3........123 A7
Elmridge WN7........76 B6
Elmridge Ct WA3......90 F8
Elmridge Dr WA15...129 C8
Elmridge Prim Sch
 WA15.............129 C8
Elms SK9...........136 F6
Elms Bank Specialist Arts
 Coll M45...........44 F2
Elmsbury St 1 WN4...72 F5
Elms Cl M45..........44 F2
Elmscott Wlk M13....164 A1
Elmsdale Ave M9.....64 D5
Elms Farm 3 M45.....44 F2
Elmsfield Ave OL12...13 E1
Elmsleigh Ct M30.....79 F3
Elmsleigh Rd SK8....122 A2
Elmsmere Rd M20....110 D4
Elms Rd
 Manchester SK4.....111 B5
 Stalybridge SK15.....86 D3
 Whitefield M45......44 F1
Elms Sq M45.........44 F1
Elm St
 Bury BL9..........141 B2
 Eccles M30..........79 D1
 Edenfield BL0.........1 E3
 Failsworth M35.......83 F8
 Farnworth BL4........60 A8
 Heywood OL10........29 D2
 Leigh WN7..........75 F3
 Middleton M24.......65 C8
 Platt Bridge WN2.....56 A2
 Ramsbottom BL0......11 D6
 Rochdale OL12.......14 F1
 Romiley SK6........112 F4
 Swinton M27.........61 E1
Elmstead Ave M20...110 A6
Elmsted Cl SK8.....123 B3
Elms The
 Golborne WA3........90 F7
 Mossley OL5.........68 B1
 Rochdale OL16.......15 E4
 4 Whitefield M45.....44 F2

Elmstone Cl **7** M9 . . . . .64 C2
Elmstone Dr OL2 . . . . .48 E5
Elmstone St BL1 . . . . .143 C1
Elmsway
  Altrincham WA15. . . . . . . .129 B8
  Bramhall SK7. . . . . .132 C2
  High Lane SK6 . . . . .134 E6
Elmswood Ave M14 . . . . .97 F2
Elmswood Dr SK14 . . . . . . .102 A3
Elmsworth Ave M19. . . . . . . .99 B1
Elmton Rd M9. . . . . .64 E3
Elm Tree Cl
  Failsworth M35 . . . . .84 B7
  Stalybridge SK15. . . . . . . .102 A8
Elm Tree Dr SK4. . . . . .168 C2
Elm Tree Dr
  Dukinfield SK16 . . . . .101 F7
  Wythenshawe M22 . . . . . .121 D3
Elm Tree Rd
  Golborne WA3 . . . . .90 F8
  Romiley SK6. . . . . .112 C3
Elmwood M33 . . . . .107 C4
Elmwood Ave WN4 . . . . .73 A2
Elmwood Cl BL5. . . . . .59 A6
Elmwood Ct M32 . . . . .108 C8
Elmwood Dr OL2 . . . . .48 C5
Elmwood Gr
  Bolton BL1. . . . . .144 C4
  Farnworth BL4. . . . . .60 C6
  Manchester M9 . . . . .157 C3
Elmwood Lodge M20 . . . . . .110 A4
Elmwood Pk SK15 . . . . .86 D3
Elm Wood Prim Sch
  M24 . . . . .65 C8
Elnup Ave WN6 . . . . .36 B6
Elnup Wood Nature
  Reserve * WN6. . . . . .36 C6
Elrick Wlk M11 . . . . .83 B1
Elsa Rd M19. . . . . .99 C1
Elsdon Dr
  Atherton M46 . . . . .58 E4
  Manchester M18 . . . . .99 D6
Elsdon Gdns **8** BL2. . . . . . .25 B1
Elsdon Rd M13 . . . . .98 F2
Elsfield Cl BL1. . . . . .143 A2
Elsham Cl BL1. . . . . .24 E5
Elsham Dr M28. . . . . .60 B3
Elsham Gdns M18 . . . . .99 A4
Elsie St
  Farnworth BL4. . . . . .60 C7
  Manchester M9 . . . . .157 B4
  Ramsbottom BL0. . . . . .11 A4
Elsinore Ave M44 . . . . .94 A1
Elsinore Cl M35 . . . . .84 B7
Elsinore Rd M16. . . . . .97 A4
Elsinore St **8** BL2. . . . . . . .25 B3
Elsma Rd M40. . . . . .83 E4
Elsmore Rd M14 . . . . .110 A8
Elson Dr SK14 . . . . .113 D7
Elson St BL3 . . . . .27 B4
Elstead Gr WN4 . . . . .72 D4
Elstead Wlk M9 . . . . .64 A3
Elsted Rd OL3. . . . . .68 E5
Elston Ave WA12 . . . . .89 C5
Elstree Ave M40 . . . . .83 B4
Elstree Ct M41 . . . . .95 D2
Elswick Ave
  Bolton BL3. . . . . .144 B1
  Bramhall SK7. . . . . .132 E7
  Manchester M21. . . . . . . .109 D4
Elsworth Cl M26. . . . . .44 B1
Elsworth Dr BL1 . . . . .143 C4
Elsworth St M3. . . . . .159 A4
Elterwater Cl BL8. . . . . .27 B4
Elterwater Rd BL4 . . . . .59 E7
Eltham Ave SK2 . . . . .124 C5
Eltham Cl WN4 . . . . .73 D3
Eltham Dr M41. . . . . .95 C5
Eltham St **6** M19. . . . . . . .99 A2
ELTON 27 C2
Elton Ave
  Farnworth BL4. . . . . .59 F8
  Manchester M19 . . . . .111 A8
Elton Bank **5** SK13 . . . . .171 A1
Elton Brook Cl BL8 . . . . .27 C3
Elton Cl
  8 Gamesley SK13 . . . . . .171 A1
  Golborne WA3 . . . . .90 E7
  Handforth SK9. . . . . .131 E1
  Whitefield M45. . . . . .63 A8
Elton Com Prim Sch
  BL8. . . . . .27 C4
Elton Dr SK7 . . . . .133 D8
Elton High Sch Specialist
  Arts Coll The BL8. . . . . . . .27 A4
Elton Ho WN5 . . . . .54 C7
Elton Lea **7** SK13 . . . . . .171 A1
Elton Loft **6** BL8 . . . . .27 C2
Elton Pl **9** SK13 . . . . . . .171 A1
Elton Rd M33. . . . . .107 C2
Elton St
  Bolton BL2. . . . . .148 A3
  Rochdale OL11. . . . . .30 C1
  Salford M7. . . . . .158 B3
  Stretford M32 . . . . .96 F5
Elton's Yd M7 . . . . .158 A3
Elton Vale Rd BL8. . . . . .27 B2
Elvate Cres M4 . . . . .155 C1
Elverdon Cl M15. . . . . .162 B1
Elverston St M22 . . . . .109 E1
Elverston Way OL9. . . . . . .152 C4
Elvey St M40 . . . . .157 C5
Elvington Cl WN5 . . . . .36 B1
Elvington Cres **1** M28 . . . .78 C8
Elvira Cl M35. . . . . .84 B7

Elway Rd WN4 . . . . .73 C4
Elwick Cl M16 . . . . .97 F3
Elworth Way **6** SK9 . . . . .131 D4
Elworthy Gr WN1 . . . . .37 E2
Elwyn Ave M22 . . . . .121 D7
Ely Ave M32. . . . . .95 F3
Ely Cl M28 . . . . .78 B8
Ely Cres M35 . . . . .83 F5
Ely Dr
  Bury BL8 . . . . .140 A4
  Tyldesley M29 . . . . .77 C7
Ely Gdns M41. . . . . .95 E2
Ely Gr BL1. . . . . .143 B1
Elysian Fields M6. . . . . .80 C3
Elysian St M11 . . . . .165 C4
Ely St OL9. . . . . .152 B1
Embankment Bsns Pk The
  SK4. . . . . .110 F1
Embankment Rd BL7 . . . . .9 C5
Embassy Wlk M18 . . . . .99 D4
Ember St M11 . . . . .83 D2
Embla Wlk **20** BL3 . . . . . .42 A4
Emblem St BL3. . . . . .145 A1
Embleton Cl BL2. . . . . .25 E1
Embleton Wlk M18 . . . . . . .165 C2
Embsay Cl BL1. . . . . .24 D5
Emerald Ave WN7 . . . . .75 E4
Emerald Cotts BL8. . . . . .10 F3
Emerald Dr OL1 . . . . .49 E3
Emerald Rd M22. . . . . .130 F7
Emerald St
  6 Bolton BL1 . . . . .143 C3
  Denton M34. . . . . .100 E3
  Wigan WN6 . . . . .37 A3
Emerson Ave M30 . . . . .80 A3
Emerson Dr M24 . . . . .46 F1
Emerson St M5. . . . . .154 A2
Emery Ave M21 . . . . .109 C6
Emery Cl
  Altrincham WA14. . . . . . . .119 D7
  Stockport SK4 . . . . .168 A4
Emery Ct SK4 . . . . .110 F1
Emily Beavan Cl M11 . . . . . .83 B1
Emily Cl M35. . . . . .66 A1
Emily Pl M43 . . . . .83 F1
Emley St M19 . . . . .99 B1
Emlyn Gr SK8 . . . . .123 A6
Emlyn St
  Farnworth BL4. . . . . .42 C1
  2 Hindley WN2 . . . . . . .56 D5
  Swinton M27 . . . . .79 D8
  Walkden M28. . . . . .60 D3
Emmanuel Christian Sch
  OL12. . . . . .14 D2
Emmanuel Cl BL3. . . . . . . .145 A1
Emmanuel Cl OL6 . . . . .166 B4
Emmanuel Holcombe CE
  Prim Sch BL8 . . . . .138 A2
Emmanuel Pl BL3. . . . . . . .145 A1
Emma St
  Oldham OL8. . . . . .66 F3
  Rochdale OL12. . . . . .139 B4
Emmaus Wlk M6 . . . . .154 C3
Emmeline Grange
  M6 . . . . .154 B2
Emmerson St M27 . . . . .61 F1
Emmett St E M40. . . . . . . .157 B1
Emmett St B 22 B3
  Swinton M27 . . . . .61 D1
Emmott Way OL1 . . . . .153 C2
Empire Rd
  Bolton BL2. . . . . .42 E7
  Dukinfield SK16 . . . . .101 C6
Empire St M3, M8. . . . . . . .158 C4
Empress Ave **2** SK6. . . . .125 F5
Empress Bsns Ctr
  M16. . . . . .161 C2
Empress Ct SK15. . . . . . . .161 C2
Empress Dr
  Leigh WN7 . . . . .76 E6
  Reddish SK4 . . . . .169 A4
Empress Ind Est WN2. . . . .151 C3
Empress St
  Bolton BL1. . . . . .142 B1
  Manchester, City Park
    M16. . . . . .161 C2
  Salford M8. . . . . .155 C4
Emsworth Cl **8** BL2. . . . . .25 B1
Emsworth Dr M33 . . . . .108 C1
Ena Cres WN7 . . . . .75 C7
Ena St
  Bolton BL3. . . . . .42 A3
  Oldham OL1. . . . . .49 C1
Enbridge St M5 . . . . .161 A4
Encombe Pl M3 . . . . .158 B2
Endcott Cl M18 . . . . .165 B2
Enderby Rd M40 . . . . .65 C1
Ending Rake OL12 . . . . .14 C4
Endon Dr M21. . . . . .109 F8
Endon St BL1. . . . . .142 B1
Endsleigh Gdns **1**
  WN7. . . . . .75 F5
Endsleigh Rd M20 . . . . .110 C6
Endsley Ave M28 . . . . .60 C1
Enfield Ave
  Manchester M19 . . . . .111 A6
  Oldham OL8. . . . . .66 E3
Enfield Cl
  Bolton BL1. . . . . .143 B1
  Bury BL9 . . . . .44 F5
  Eccles M30. . . . . .95 D8
  3 Rochdale OL11. . . . . . .31 A6
Enfield Dr **7** M11 . . . . . . .83 C2
Enfield Gr WN7. . . . . .76 B6
Enfield Ho **1** M30 . . . . . . .95 D8
Enfield Rd
  Eccles M30 . . . . .79 D4
  Swinton M27 . . . . .79 E6

Enfield St
  Hyde SK14. . . . . .113 E7
  Walkden M28. . . . . .60 D5
  Wigan WN5 . . . . .54 C5
Enford Ave M22 . . . . .121 A2
Engell Cl M18 . . . . .99 D5
Engels Ho
  3 Eccles M30. . . . . .95 D8
  Manchester M14 . . . . .110 D8
Engineer St WN2 . . . . .56 A7
ENGINE FOLD 60 B2
Engine Fold Rd M28 . . . . . . .60 A3
Engine La M29 . . . . .59 B4
Engine St OL9 . . . . .66 B4
Engledene BL1 . . . . .24 D6
Englefield Gr **3** M18 . . . . .99 D4
English Martyrs' RC Prim
  Sch M41. . . . . .95 C2
English St WN7 . . . . .76 A4
Enid Cl M7 . . . . .155 A1
Enid Pl WN2. . . . . .73 F8
Ennerdale Ave
  Ashton-in-M WN4 . . . . .73 B5
  Billinge WA11 . . . . .71 B1
  4 Bolton BL2 . . . . .25 F1
  Manchester M21 . . . . .109 D4
  Royton OL2 . . . . .48 C7
  Swinton M27 . . . . .79 F6
Ennerdale Cl BL3 . . . . .42 F3
Ennerdale Dr
  Gatley SK8 . . . . .122 B3
  Sale, Ashton upon Mersey
    M33 . . . . .107 C5
  Sale, Timperley WA15 . . . . .120 A8
  Whitefield BL9 . . . . .45 A2
Ennerdale Gdns BL2 . . . . . . .25 E1
Ennerdale Gr
  Ashton-u-L OL7 . . . . .84 F5
  Farnworth BL4. . . . . .59 E8
Ennerdale Pl WN2 . . . . .56 B8
Ennerdale Rd
  Hindley WN2. . . . . .56 E5
  Leigh WN7 . . . . .76 C4
  Middleton M24. . . . . .46 F2
  Partington M31 . . . . .105 E3
  Rochdale OL11. . . . . .30 B4
  Romiley SK6. . . . . .113 B4
  Stockport SK1 . . . . .124 B7
  Stretford M32 . . . . .96 C3
  Tyldesley M29 . . . . .77 B7
Ennerdale Terr SK15 . . . . . . .86 A3
Ennis Cl M23 . . . . .120 E5
Ennismore Ave M5,
  M30 . . . . .80 A2
Enstone Dr M40 . . . . .65 D1
Enstone Way M29 . . . . .59 C1
Enterprise Pk BL6 . . . . .39 C8
Enterprise Trad Est
  M18. . . . . .99 E6
Enterprise Way WA3 . . . . . . .91 A7
Enticott Rd M44 . . . . .105 C5
Entwisle Ave M41. . . . . .95 B4
Entwisle Rd OL16. . . . . .31 A8
Entwisle Row BL4 . . . . .60 D8
Entwisle St
  1 Farnworth BL4. . . . . . .42 E1
  Milnrow OL16. . . . . .31 E6
  Swinton M27 . . . . .61 D1
ENTWISTLE 9 B7
Entwistle Gr WN7 . . . . .76 C3
Entwistle Hall La BL7. . . . . . .9 B8
Entwistle St BL2. . . . . .148 B4
Entwistle Sta BL7. . . . . .9 B8
Enver Rd M8 . . . . .156 B4
Enville Rd
  Altrincham WA14 . . . . .119 C3
  Manchester M40. . . . . .65 B1
  Pendlebury M6 . . . . .80 E6
Enville St
  Ashton-u-L OL6 . . . . .166 C3
  Denton M34. . . . . .100 F7
  Manchester M9 . . . . .64 D3
Envoy Cl WN5 . . . . .36 E1
Enys Wlk M6 . . . . .81 A5
Ephraim's Fold WN2. . . . . . .38 D6
Epping Cl
  Ashton-u-L OL6 . . . . .85 C7
  Chadderton OL9. . . . . .65 E8
Epping Dr M33 . . . . .107 C5
Epping St M15 . . . . .163 A2
Eppleworth Rise M27 . . . . . .62 A3
Epsley Cl M15 . . . . .163 A2
Epsom Ave
  Handforth SK8, SK9. . . . . .131 E4
  Manchester M19 . . . . .110 F6
  Sale M33 . . . . .107 C2
Epsom Cl
  Hazel Grove SK7 . . . . .124 F2
  Rochdale OL11. . . . . .29 F8
Epsom Croft PR6 . . . . .21 B7
Epsom Dr WN2 . . . . .73 F7
Epsom Mews **23** M7 . . . .155 A2
Epsom Wlk OL9 . . . . .152 C3
Epworth Ct SK4 . . . . .168 B3
Epworth Gr **8** BL3. . . . . .146 C3
Epworth St M4 . . . . .159 C1
Equitable St
  Milnrow OL16. . . . . .31 F5
  Oldham OL4. . . . . .67 D8
  3 Rochdale OL16. . . . . . .31 A6
Era St
  Bolton BL2. . . . . .42 E7
  Sale M33 . . . . .108 B4
Ercall Ave M12. . . . . .164 B2
Erica Ave OL4 . . . . .49 F4
Erica Cl **2** SK5 . . . . .100 A1

Erica Dr M19. . . . . .110 E4
Erica Wlk M7 . . . . .75 B5
Eric Brook Cl **8** M14 . . . . .98 A3
Eric Bullows Cl M22 . . . . . .121 C1
Eric St
  Littleborough OL15 . . . . . . .16 A6
  Oldham OL4. . . . . .67 C6
Erin Cl OL9. . . . . .152 B1
Erindale Wlk M40 . . . . .156 C2
Erin St M11 . . . . .99 E7
Erith Cl SK5. . . . . .112 B6
Erith Rd OL4. . . . . .67 C6
Erlesmere Ave M34 . . . . . . .101 A4
Erlesmere Cl OL4 . . . . .49 F4
Erlington Ave M16. . . . . .97 B2
Ermen Rd M30 . . . . .95 C8
Ermington Ct OL10 . . . . .29 C1
Ermington Dr M8. . . . . .155 C2
Erneley Cl M12 . . . . .99 B3
Ernest St
  Bolton BL1. . . . . .145 A3
  Britannia OL13. . . . . .4 C8
  Cheadle SK8 . . . . .122 C6
  Prestwich M25. . . . . .62 F4
  Stockport SK2 . . . . .124 A6
Ernest Terr OL12. . . . . .15 B1
Ernlouen Ave BL1. . . . . .144 A4
Ernocroft Gr **5** M18 . . . . . .99 E6
Ernocroft La SK6 . . . . .114 E2
Ernocroft Rd SK6 . . . . .114 B1
Erradale Cres WN3 . . . . .54 D2
Erringdon Cl SK2 . . . . .124 E6
Errington Cl BL3. . . . . .40 F5
Errington Dr M7. . . . . .158 A4
Errol Ave
  Failsworth M40 . . . . .65 C4
  Wythenshawe M23 . . . . . .108 E2
Erskine Cl BL3. . . . . .40 E5
Erskine Pl WN2. . . . . .56 B1
Erskine Rd
  Manchester M9 . . . . .64 E5
  Partington M31 . . . . .105 F3
Erskine St
  Compstall SK6 . . . . .114 B3
  Manchester M15 . . . . .162 A2
Erwin St M40 . . . . .83 B6
Eryngo St SK1 . . . . .112 A1
Escott St M16 . . . . .97 F3
Esher Dr M23, M33 . . . . . . .108 C1
Esk Ave BL0 . . . . .1 D5
Esk Cl M41. . . . . .95 A4
Eskdale SK8 . . . . .122 C4
Eskdale Ave
  Bolton BL2. . . . . .25 F2
  Bramhall SK7. . . . . .132 C5
  Manchester M20 . . . . .110 A7
  Oldham OL8. . . . . .66 D4
  Rochdale OL11. . . . . .30 B6
  Romiley SK6. . . . . .113 B4
  Royton OL2 . . . . .48 D7
  Scot Lane End BL6. . . . . . .38 E7
  Uppermill OL3 . . . . .69 B5
  Wigan WN1 . . . . .37 B3
Eskdale Cl BL9 . . . . .45 A3
Eskdale Dr
  Altrincham WA15. . . . . . . .120 C7
  Middleton M24. . . . . .46 F3
Eskdale Gr BL4. . . . . .59 F8
Eskdale Ho **3** M13 . . . . . .98 E4
Eskdale Mews OL3. . . . . . . .69 B5
Eskdale Rd
  Ashton-in-M WN4 . . . . .73 B4
  Hindley WN2 . . . . .56 E5
Eskdale Terr SK15 . . . . .86 A4
Eskrick St BL1. . . . . .143 A2
Eskrigge Cl M7 . . . . .155 C4
Esmond Rd M8. . . . . .156 A3
Esmont Dr M24 . . . . .46 E3
Esplanade The OL16 . . . . . .139 B3
Essex Ave
  Droylsden M43. . . . . .84 A3
  Heywood OL10. . . . . .28 E1
  Manchester M20 . . . . .110 B4
  Stockport SK3 . . . . .123 B8
Essex Cl
  Failsworth M35 . . . . .83 F5
  Shaw OL2. . . . . .48 F7
Essex Dr BL9 . . . . .45 A8
Essex Gdns M44 . . . . .105 C4
Essex Pl
  Swinton M27 . . . . .61 F2
  Tyldesley M29 . . . . .58 F3
Essex Rd
  Brinnington SK5. . . . . . . .112 C5
  Reddish M18 . . . . .99 F4
  Standish WN1 . . . . .37 B8
Essex St
  Horwich BL6 . . . . .22 D1
  Manchester M2 . . . . .158 C1
  Rochdale OL11. . . . . .139 C2
  Wigan WN1 . . . . .37 E1
Essex Way M15, M16 . . . . . .162 A1
Essingdon St BL3. . . . . . . .147 A4
Essington Dr M40 . . . . .157 A2
Essington Wlk M34 . . . . . . .100 E1
Essoldo Cl M18. . . . . .165 C1
Estate St S **3** OL8. . . . . . .66 F4
Estate St OL8. . . . . .66 F4
Est Bank Rd BL0. . . . . .11 A3
Estcourt Prep Sch for
  Girls OL8 . . . . .66 D4
Esther Fold BL5 . . . . .57 E8
Esther St OL4 . . . . .67 D7
Esthwaite Dr M29 . . . . .77 A7
Estonfield Dr M41. . . . . .95 D4
Eston St M13 . . . . .98 D4
Eswick St M11. . . . . .83 C1

Etchells Prim Sch
  SK8. . . . . .122 C1
Etchells Rd SK8 . . . . .122 D1
Etchells St SK1. . . . . .169 C1
Etchell St M40. . . . . .156 C1
Etharow Ct SK14. . . . . .167 B2
Ethel Ave
  Manchester M9 . . . . .64 D5
  Pendlebury M27 . . . . .80 B8
Ethel Ct OL16. . . . . .31 B6
Ethel St
  Bolton BL3. . . . . .145 A2
  Oldham OL6. . . . . .66 F3
  Rochdale OL16. . . . . .31 B6
  Whitworth OL12. . . . . .4 D2
Ethel Terr M19. . . . . .99 A1
Etherley Cl **5** M44. . . . . . .94 A2
Etherow Ave
  Failsworth M40 . . . . .65 C2
  Romiley SK6. . . . . .113 E2
Etherow Brow **8**
  SK14. . . . . .115 A8
Etherow Ctry Pk *
  SK6 . . . . .114 C3
Etherow Ctry Pk Visitor
  Ctr * SK6 . . . . .114 B2
Etherow Ind Est SK13 . . . . .103 E5
Etherstone St
  Leigh WN7 . . . . .75 E4
  Manchester M8 . . . . .156 C4
Eton Ave OL8. . . . . .66 E3
Eton Cl
  Manchester M16 . . . . .162 A1
  Rochdale OL11. . . . . .30 B6
Eton Ct M16. . . . . .162 A1
Eton Dr SK8 . . . . .122 D2
Eton Hill Ind Est M26 . . . . . .44 C5
Eton Hill Rd M26 . . . . .44 C5
Eton Pl M26. . . . . .43 F3
Eton St WN7 . . . . .75 F3
Eton Terr WN3. . . . . .151 B1
Eton Way N M26 . . . . .44 C5
Eton Way S M26 . . . . .44 C5
Etruria Cl M13. . . . . .164 B1
Ettington Cl BL8. . . . . .27 A3
Ettrick Cl M11 . . . . .99 D7
Euan Pl **2** M33 . . . . .108 C4
Euclid Cl M11 . . . . .160 B1
Euro Ctr The M8. . . . . .158 B4
Europa Bsns Pk SK3. . . . . .123 B6
Europa Circ M17 . . . . .96 C5
Europa Gate M17 . . . . .96 C5
Europa Trad Est M26 . . . . . .61 B7
Europa Way
  Cheadle SK8 . . . . .123 B6
  Kearsley M26. . . . . .61 B7
  Stretford M17 . . . . .96 D5
Eustace St
  Bolton BL3. . . . . .42 A3
  Chadderton OL9. . . . . . . .152 C4
Euston Ave M9 . . . . .65 A3
Euxton Cl BL8 . . . . .27 A1
Evan Cl WN6 . . . . .36 D4
Evans Cl M20. . . . . .110 A3
Evans Rd M30 . . . . .79 A1
Evans St
  Ashton-u-L OL6 . . . . .85 C4
  Horwich BL6 . . . . .22 D4
  Leigh WN7 . . . . .75 F5
  Middleton M24. . . . . .65 B8
  Oldham OL1. . . . . .153 C4
  Salford M3. . . . . .158 B3
Evan St M40. . . . . .157 B1
Evanstone Cl BL6. . . . . .22 B3
Evanton Wlk **13** M9 . . . . .157 B3
Eva Rd SK3. . . . . .123 A7
Eva St
  Leigh WN7 . . . . .75 C7
  Manchester M14 . . . . .98 C3
  Rochdale OL12. . . . . .15 C1
Evelyn St
  Manchester M14 . . . . .110 D8
  Oldham OL1. . . . . .49 B1
Evenholme WA14 . . . . .119 B2
Evening St M35. . . . . .83 F8
Evenley Cl **1** M18 . . . . . . .99 E6
Everard Cl M28 . . . . .78 C8
Everard St M5. . . . . .161 C3
Everbrom Rd BL3. . . . . . . .146 A3
Everdingen Wlk OL1 . . . . . . .49 D3
Everest Ave OL7. . . . . .85 B5
Everest Cl SK14. . . . . .102 A4
Everest Pl **4** WN1 . . . . . . .37 C2
Everest Rd
  Atherton M46 . . . . .58 C5
  Dukinfield SK14 . . . . .102 A4
Everest St OL11. . . . . .31 A2
Everett Ct **4** M20. . . . . . .110 B6
Everett Rd M20. . . . . .110 B6
Everglade OL8. . . . . .67 A1
Evergreen Wlk **4**
  M33 . . . . .107 C6
Everleigh Cl BL2. . . . . .25 C5
Everleigh Dr M7 . . . . .155 C2
Eversden Ct M7 . . . . .158 B4
Everside Dr M8. . . . . .155 B1
Eversley Ct M33 . . . . .108 B2
Eversley Rd M20. . . . . .110 A3
Everton Rd
  Oldham OL5. . . . . .66 D3
  Reddish SK5 . . . . .99 F2
Everton St
  Downall Green WN4 . . . . . .72 D5
  Swinton M27 . . . . .79 E8
Every St
  Bury BL9 . . . . .140 C4

Every St *continued*
Manchester M4 . . . . **160** A1
Ramsbottom BL0 . . . .**11** D6
Evesham Ave
Glossop SK13 . . . . **104** A5
Stockport SK4 . . . . **168** B3
Wythenshawe M23 . . . . . **120** D7
Evesham Cl
1 Bolton BL3 . . . . **145** A2
Leigh WN7 . . . . **75** E1
Middleton M24 . . . .**65** B5
Evesham Dr
Farnworth BL3, BL4 . . . . . . **42** B2
Handforth SK9 . . . . **131** C2
Evesham Gdns M24 . . . . . .**65** A5
Evesham Gr
Ashton-u-L OL6 . . . . **85** C7
Sale M33 . . . . **108** E4
Evesham Rd
Cheadle SK8 . . . . **123** A4
Manchester M9 . . . .**65** A2
Middleton M24 . . . .**65** B5
Evesham Wlk
10 Bolton BL3 . . . . **145** A2
Middleton M24 . . . .**65** B5
Oldham OL8 . . . . **153** B1
Eveside Cl SK8 . . . . **123** B4
Eve St OL8 . . . .**66** F2
Evington Ave M11 . . . . . . **100** A7
Ewan St M18 . . . .**99** D6
Ewart Ave M5 . . . .**81** A1
Ewart St BL1 . . . . **143** B2
Ewhurst Ave M27 . . . .**79** D6
Ewing Cl M8 . . . .**64** A1
Ewing Sch M20 . . . . **110** A5
Ewood
12 Eccles M30 . . . .**79** F2
Oldham OL8 . . . .**85** A8
EWOOD BRIDGE **1** C6
Ewood Dr BL8 . . . .**44** A8
Ewood La BB4 . . . .**1** C7
Exbourne Rd M22 . . . . . . **121** C1
Exbridge Wlk M40 . . . .**83** D4
Exbury **20** OL12 . . . . **139** B4
Exbury St M14 . . . . **110** D7
Excalibur Way M44 . . . . . **105** F7
Excelsior Gdns OL10 . . . . . .**46** F8
Excelsior Terr OL15 . . . . . . **15** F3
Exchange Quay M5 . . . . . **161** A2
Exchange Quay Sta
M5 . . . . **161** A2
Exchange Sq M4 . . . . **158** C2
Exchange St
9 Bolton BL1 . . . . **145** C3
Edenfield BL0 . . . .**1** D3
Manchester M2 . . . . **158** C1
5 Oldham OL4 . . . .**67** B7
Stockport SK3 . . . . **169** B1
Exeter Ave
Bolton BL2 . . . .**25** B2
Denton M34 . . . . **100** F1
Farnworth BL4 . . . .**59** F8
Radcliffe M26 . . . .**43** E5
Salford M30 . . . .**80** A4
Exeter Cl
Cheadle SK8 . . . . **131** F8
Dukinfield SK16 . . . . **101** D6
Exeter Ct
Manchester M20 . . . . **110** C7
3 Middleton M24 . . . .**46** F1
Exeter Dr
Ashton-u-L OL6 . . . . **85** D7
Aspull WN2 . . . .**38** D5
Irlam M44 . . . .**94** B2
Exeter Gr OL11 . . . . **139** C1
Exeter Rd
Brinnington SK5 . . . . **112** C5
Hindley WN2 . . . .**56** E5
Urmston M41 . . . .**95** D4
Exeter St
Rochdale OL11 . . . . **139** C1
Salford M6 . . . . **154** B2
Exeter Wlk SK7 . . . . **132** F7
Exford Ave WN3 . . . .**55** B4
Exford Cl
Manchester M40 . . . . **160** A3
Reddish SK5 . . . . **111** F6
Exford Dr BL2 . . . .**43** A6
Exhall Cl M38 . . . .**60** A6
Exit Rd W M90 . . . . **130** B7
Exmoor Cl OL6 . . . .**85** C7
Exmouth Ave SK5 . . . . **112** C5
Exmouth Pl OL16 . . . .**31** A3
Exmouth Rd M33 . . . . **107** D5
Exmouth Sq OL16 . . . .**31** A3
Exmouth St OL16 . . . .**31** A3
Eyam Cl **18** SK13 . . . . **171** A2
Eyam Fold **22** SK13 . . . . . **171** A2
Eyam Gdns **28** SK13 . . . . . **171** A2
Eyam Gn **16** SK13 . . . . **171** A2
Eyam Gr
14 Gamesley SK13 . . . . **171** A2
Stockport SK2 . . . . **124** D5
Eyam La SK13 . . . . **171** B2
Eyam Lea SK13 . . . . **171** B2
Eyam Mews SK13 . . . . **171** A2
Eyam Rd SK7 . . . . **124** C1
Eycott Dr M24 . . . .**46** D1
Eyebrook Rd WA14 . . . . . . **119** A2
Eyet St WN7 . . . .**75** E5
Eynford Ave SK5 . . . . **112** B6
Eyre St M15 . . . . **163** A1

F

Faber St M4 . . . . **159** A3
FACIT **4** D2
Factory Brow
Blackrod BL6 . . . .**21** D3
Middleton M24 . . . .**64** C7
FACTORY FOLD **66** A2
Factory Hill BL6 . . . .**22** D4
Factory La
Adlington PR6 . . . .**21** B8
Manchester M9 . . . .**64** D1
Salford M3 . . . . **158** A1
Factory St W M46 . . . .**58** C3
Factory St
Middleton M24 . . . .**64** F8
Radcliffe M26 . . . .**44** B3
Ramsbottom BL0 . . . . **138** C3
Tyldesley M29 . . . .**58** F1
Faggy La WN3 . . . . **150** C3
FAILSWORTH **83** F6
Failsworth Ind Est 2
M40 . . . .**83** C6
Failsworth Rd M35 . . . .**84** C7
Failsworth Sch M35 . . . .**84** A7
Failsworth Sch (Lower)
M35 . . . .**83** F7
Failsworth Sh Ctr 1
M35 . . . .**83** F7
Failsworth Sta M35 . . . .**83** E8
Fairacres WN6 . . . .**19** E1
Fair Acres BL2 . . . .**25** E3
Fairacres Rd SK6 . . . . **134** E8
Fairbairn St BL6 . . . .**22** B3
Fairbank M43 . . . .**99** F8
Fairbank Ave M14 . . . .**98** B4
Fairbottom Dr M24 . . . .**46** D2
Fairbottom St OL1 . . . . **153** C3
Fairbottom Wlk **4**
M43 . . . . **100** A8
Fairbourne Ave
Alderley Edge SK9 . . . . **137** B3
Wigan WN3 . . . .**55** A4
Wilmslow SK9 . . . . **136** F4
Fairbourne Cl SK9 . . . . **136** F4
Fairbourne Dr
Sale WA15 . . . . **108** B1
Wilmslow SK9 . . . . **136** F4
Fairbourne Rd
Denton M34 . . . . **100** C2
Reddish M19 . . . .**99** C1
Fairbrook Dr M6 . . . . **154** B2
Fairbrother St M5 . . . . **161** C3
Fairburn Cl M41 . . . .**95** A4
Fairclough St
Bolton BL3 . . . .**42** A4
Droylsden M11 . . . .**83** A2
Hindley WN2 . . . .**56** D6
Newton-le-W WA12 . . . .**89** B3
Wigan WN1 . . . . **151** A3
Faircroft WN5 . . . .**71** E3
Fairfax Ave
Altrincham WA15 . . . . **120** A6
Manchester M20 . . . . **110** B4
Fairfax Cl SK6 . . . . **125** D7
Fairfax Dr
Littleborough OL15 . . . . **15** F3
Wilmslow SK9 . . . . **136** F4
Fairfax Rd M25 . . . .**63** A5
FAIRFIELD
Bury **28** E3
Droylsden **100** A8
Fairfield Ave
Cheadle SK8 . . . . **122** F2
Droylsden M43 . . . . **100** A7
Platt Bridge WN2 . . . .**56** A3
Romiley SK6 . . . . **113** A4
Wigan WN5 . . . .**54** D5
Fairfield Com Prim Sch
BL9 . . . .**28** D3
Fairfield Ct
5 Droylsden M43 . . . . . . **100** A8
Manchester M14 . . . .**98** D4
Fairfield Dr BL9 . . . .**28** D3
Fairfield General Hospl
BL9 . . . .**28** E4
Fairfield High Sch for
Girls M43 . . . . **100** A8
Fairfield Ho M43 . . . .**84** A1
Fairfield Rd
Altrincham WA15 . . . . **120** C5
Droylsden M43 . . . .**99** F8
Farnworth BL4 . . . .**42** C1
Irlam M44 . . . . **105** C5
Middleton M24 . . . .**46** E1
Fairfield Road Prim Sch
M43 . . . .**99** F8
Fairfields
Bolton BL7 . . . .**24** F8
Oldham OL8 . . . .**66** E2
Fairfield St
Manchester M1, M12 . . . . **163** C4
Salford M6 . . . .**80** C5
Wigan WN5 . . . .**54** D5
Fairfield Sta M34 . . . . **100** A7
Fairfield View M34 . . . . **100** A7
Fairford Cl SK5 . . . . **111** F5
Fairford Dr BL3 . . . . **145** B1
Fairford Way
Reddish SK5 . . . . **111** F5
Wilmslow SK9 . . . . **137** D2
Fairham Wlk M12 . . . . **160** A1
Fairhaven Ave
Manchester M21 . . . . **109** B8
Westhoughton BL5 . . . .**58** B8
Whitefield M45 . . . .**62** D7
Fairhaven Cl SK7 . . . . **132** F8

Fairhaven Cvn Pk
SK14 . . . . **101** C2
Fairhaven Rd BL1 . . . . **143** C3
Fairhaven St M12 . . . . **164** C2
Fair Hill BB4 . . . .**1** A7
Fairhills Ind Est M44 . . . . . **105** F8
Fairhills Rd M44 . . . . **106** A8
Fairhill Terr BB4 . . . .**1** A7
Fairholme Ave
Ashton-in-M WN4 . . . .**73** B4
Urmston M41 . . . .**95** C1
Fairholme Cvn Site
M4 . . . . **159** B4
Fairholme Rd
Manchester, Withington
M20 . . . . **110** C6
Stockport, Heaton Norris
SK4 . . . . **168** C3
Fairhope Ave M6 . . . .**80** C3
Fairhurst Ave M6 . . . .**19** D3
Fairhurst Dr M28 . . . .**59** F2
Fairhurst St
Leigh WN7 . . . .**75** E5
Wigan WN3 . . . . **150** M4
Fairisle Cl M11 . . . . **160** C1
Fairlands Pl OL11 . . . .**31** B2
Fairlands Rd
Bury BL9 . . . .**27** F6
Sale M33 . . . . **107** F2
Fairlands St OL11 . . . .**31** B2
Fairlands View OL11 . . . .**31** B2
Fairlawn BL1 . . . . **169** A3
Fairlawn Cl M14 . . . .**98** A4
Fairlea M34 . . . . **101** A2
Fairlea Ave M20 . . . . **110** C2
Fairlee Ave M34 . . . .**84** C1
Fairleigh Ave M6 . . . .**80** C3
Fairless Rd M30 . . . .**79** D1
Fairlie Ave BL3 . . . .**40** A7
Fairlie Dr WA15 . . . . **120** B8
Fairlyn Cl BL5 . . . .**59** A7
Fairlyn Dr BL5 . . . .**59** A7
Fairman Dr WN2 . . . .**56** E7
Fairman St M16 . . . .**97** F3
Fairmead Rd M23 . . . . **109** C1
Fairmile Dr M20 . . . . **122** C8
Fairmount Ave BL2 . . . .**42** E8
Fairmount Rd M27 . . . .**79** C6
Fair Oak Rd M19 . . . . **110** F5
Fair St
Bolton BL3 . . . . **146** C2
Manchester M1 . . . . **159** C1
Swinton M27 . . . .**62** B1
Fairstead Cl BL5 . . . .**57** D8
Fairstead Wlk **4** M11 . . . . .**99** F7
Fairthorne Grange 7
OL7 . . . .**84** F1
Fair View
Billinge WN5 . . . .**71** D5
Britannia OL13 . . . .**4** C8
Littleborough OL15 . . . . **16** C7
Fairview Ave
Manchester M19 . . . .**98** F2
Reddish M34 . . . . **100** A1
Fair View Ave WN5 . . . .**71** D5
Fairview Cl
Ashton-in-M WN4 . . . .**73** B4
Chadderton OL9 . . . .**65** F8
Marple SK6 . . . . **125** F7
Rochdale OL12 . . . .**13** C2
Fairview Dr
Adlington PR6, PR7 . . . .**20** F8
Marple SK6 . . . . **125** F7
Fairview Rd
Altrincham WA15 . . . . **120** C5
Reddish M34 . . . . **100** A1
Fairview Residential Cvn
Pk M46 . . . .**58** B4
Fairway
Bramhall SK7 . . . . **132** D6
Droylsden M43 . . . . **100** A8
Gatley SK8 . . . . **122** B4
Manchester M25 . . . .**63** D2
Milnrow OL16 . . . .**32** A6
Pendlebury M27 . . . .**80** C7
Rochdale OL11 . . . .**30** B1
Whitworth OL12 . . . .**14** C6
Fairway Ave
Bolton BL2 . . . .**26** A4
Wythenshawe M23 . . . . . . **120** D7
Fairway Cres OL2 . . . .**48** D6
Fairway Ct M34 . . . . **100** B4
Fairway Dr M33 . . . . **107** E2
Fairway Prim Sch
SK2 . . . . **124** E7
Fairway Rd
Oldham OL4 . . . .**67** E4
Whitefield BL9 . . . .**45** A3
Fairways BL6 . . . .**22** C3
Fairways SK13 . . . . **104** F1
Fairways Cvn Pk M7 . . . . . **158** A4
Fairways The
Garswood WN4 . . . .**72** D2
Westhoughton BL5 . . . .**57** E8
Whitefield M45 . . . .**62** D7
Fairway The
Failsworth M40 . . . .**83** C8
Stockport SK2 . . . . **124** D7
Fairwood Rd M23 . . . . **120** D7
Fairy La
Salford M8 . . . . **155** B1
Wythenshawe M23 . . . . . . **109** A3
Fairy St BL8 . . . .**27** C2
Fairywell Cl SK9 . . . . **131** D1
Fairywell Dr M33 . . . . **108** A1
Fairywell Rd WA15 . . . . . . **120** C7

Faith St
Bolton BL1 . . . . **142** A1
Leigh WN7 . . . .**75** C5
Falcon Ave M41 . . . .**95** E2
Falcon Bsns Ctr OL9 . . . . . **152** C4
Falcon Cl
Bury BL9 . . . . **141** B4
Leigh WN7 . . . .**76** B5
Rochdale OL12 . . . .**13** E2
Salford M50 . . . .**80** C1
Falcon Cres M27 . . . .**62** C2
Falcon Ct
Manchester M15 . . . . **162** B1
Salford M7 . . . . **155** A4
Falcon Dr
Chadderton OL9 . . . . **152** C4
Irlam M44 . . . .**94** B4
Middleton M24 . . . .**46** E3
Walkden M38 . . . .**60** A5
Falcons Gn WN3 . . . . **150** B1
Falconers Gn WN3 . . . . . . **141** A4
Falcon Ho BL9 . . . . **141** A4
Falcon St OL8 . . . . **153** C1
Falconwood Chase
M28 . . . .**78** C6
Falconwood Cl **12**
WN6 . . . .**37** A1
Falconwood Way
M11 . . . . **164** C4
Falfield Dr M8 . . . . **156** B1
FALINGE FOLD **14** D1
Falinge Fold OL12 . . . .**14** D1
Falinge Mews OL12 . . . . . **139** B4
Falinge Park High Sch
OL12 . . . .**14** D1
Falinge Rd OL12 . . . .**14** E1
Falkirk Dr
Bolton BL2 . . . .**42** F6
Ince-in-M WN2 . . . .**56** A8
Falkirk Gr WN5 . . . .**54** C8
Falkirk St **4** OL4 . . . .**67** C7
Falkirk Wlk **5** M23 . . . . . **121** A2
Falkland Ave
Manchester M40 . . . . **160** A4
Rochdale OL11 . . . .**30** C8
Falkland Cl OL4 . . . .**49** E4
Falkland Dr WN4 . . . .**72** C4
Falkland Rd BL2 . . . .**43** A8
Fall Bank SK4 . . . . **111** D6
Fall Birch Hospl BL6 . . . .**23** A1
Fall Birch Rd BL6 . . . .**39** F8
Fallons Rd M28 . . . .**61** C1
Fallow Ave M18 . . . .**99** D2
Fallow Cl BL5 . . . .**39** E2
FALLOWFIELD **110** B8
Fallowfield Ave M5 . . . . **161** B3
Fallowfield Dr OL12 . . . .**14** D2
Fallow Fields Dr SK5 . . . . . **100** A1
Fallowfield Sh Ctr M14 . . . . .**98** E1
Fallowfield Way M46 . . . .**58** E1
Fallows The OL9 . . . . **152** A1
Falls Gr SK8 . . . . **122** A3
Falmer Cl
Bury BL8 . . . .**27** C6
Droylsden M18 . . . .**99** F6
Falmer Dr M22 . . . . **121** D1
Falmouth Ave
Sale M33 . . . . **107** D5
Urmston M41 . . . .**94** E3
Falmouth Cres SK5 . . . . . . **112** C5
Falmouth Rd M44 . . . .**94** B2
Falmouth St
Manchester M40 . . . . **160** C4
Oldham OL8 . . . .**66** F4
6 Rochdale OL16 . . . .**31** A5
Falsgrave Cl M40 . . . .**83** A5
Falshaw Dr BL9 . . . .**11** E1
Falside Wlk **17** M40 . . . .**83** C5
Falstaff Mews SK6 . . . . . . **113** A3
Falston Ave M40 . . . .**65** D2
Falstone Ave BL0 . . . .**11** C4
Falstone Cl WN3 . . . .**54** E2
Fancroft Rd M23 . . . . **120** E8
Fancroft Rd M22 . . . . **121** C5
Fane Wlk M9 . . . .**64** B3
Faraday Ave
Manchester M8 . . . . **156** A2
Swinton M27 . . . .**62** D2
Faraday Cl WN6 . . . . **150** A4
Faraday Dr BL1 . . . . **143** B1
Faraday Ho OL12 . . . .**14** B1
Faraday Rise OL12 . . . .**14** B1
Faraday St M1 . . . . **159** B1
Farcroft Ave M26 . . . .**44** C6
Farcroft Cl
Lymm WA13 . . . . **117** C5
Stockport SK2 . . . . **124** E7
Wythenshawe M23 . . . . . . **120** E8
Far Cromwell Rd SK6 . . . . **112** D7
Fardale OL2 . . . .**149** B2
Farden Dr M23 . . . . **120** D8
Fardon Cl WN3 . . . .**54** F3
Farefield Ave WA3 . . . .**73** F2
Farewell Cl **1** OL11 . . . .**30** C2
Far Hey Cl M26 . . . .**43** E3
Farholme OL2 . . . .**48** C2
Farington Cl OL11 . . . . **139** B2
Farington Wlk BL3 . . . . **145** B1
Far La M18 . . . .**99** D4
Farland Pl BL3 . . . .**40** F5
Farlands Dr M20 . . . . **122** B7
Farlands Rise OL16 . . . .**31** C3
Farleigh Cl BL5 . . . .**40** A2
Farley Ave M18 . . . . **100** A4
Farley Ct SK8 . . . . **122** F3
Farley La WN8 . . . .**35** A3
Farley Rd M33 . . . . **108** C2
Farley Way SK5 . . . .**99** E1

Farman St BL3 . . . . **147** A3
Farm Ave
Adlington PR6 . . . .**21** A8
Stretford M32 . . . .**96** A4
Farm Cl
Bury BL8 . . . .**26** F6
Reddish SK4 . . . . **111** C6
Farmers Cl M33 . . . . **109** A3
Farmer St SK4 . . . . **169** B3
Farmfield M33 . . . . **107** E6
Farmfold SK9 . . . . **130** F3
Farm Hill M25 . . . .**62** F5
Farm La
Eccles M28 . . . .**78** F5
High Lane SK12 . . . . **135** A6
Hyde SK14 . . . . **113** D8
Middleton M25 . . . .**63** E8
Wigan WN2 . . . .**38** A2
Farmlands Wlk OL1 . . . .**49** C4
Farm Meadow Rd WN5 . . . . .**53** E5
FAR MOOR **53** D4
Farm Rd OL8 . . . .**84** C8
Farmside Ave M44 . . . .**94** A3
Farm Side Pl **19** M19 . . . . . .**99** A1
Farm St
Chadderton OL1, OL9 . . . . . .**48** B1
Failsworth M35 . . . .**83** E6
Heywood OL10 . . . .**46** B8
Farmstead Cl M35 . . . .**84** C6
Farmway M24 . . . .**65** A7
Farm Way WA12 . . . .**89** E1
Farm Wlk
Altrincham WA14 . . . . **118** C1
Littleborough OL15 . . . . **15** F5
Rochdale OL16 . . . . **15** C1
Farm Yd M19 . . . .**99** A1
Farn Ave SK5 . . . .**99** F2
Farnborough Ave OL4 . . . . . .**67** D6
Farnborough Rd
Bolton BL1 . . . .**24** E6
Manchester M40 . . . . **160** A3
Farncombe Cl **2**
M23 . . . . **120** D7
Farndale Gr WN4 . . . .**73** C2
Farndale Sq M38 . . . .**60** C3
Farndale Wlk **17** M9 . . . . . **157** B4
Farndon Ave SK7 . . . . **124** F4
Farndon Cl M33 . . . . **108** C3
Farndon Dr WA15 . . . . **120** A6
Farndon Rd SK5 . . . .**99** E2
Farnham Ave M9 . . . .**64** D5
Farnham Cl
2 Bolton BL1 . . . . **143** B1
Cheadle SK8 . . . . **132** A7
Leigh WN7 . . . .**75** F6
Farnham Dr M44 . . . .**94** B1
Farnhill Wlk M23 . . . . **108** C1
Farnley Cl OL12 . . . .**13** F2
Farnsfield WN1 . . . .**37** F1
Farnsworth Ave OL7 . . . .**85** B5
Farnsworth Cl OL7 . . . .**85** B5
FARNWORTH **60** A7
Farnworth Ave M14 . . . .**98** C2
Farnworth St
Bolton BL3 . . . . **146** C4
7 Heywood OL10 . . . .**29** C2
6 Leigh WN7 . . . .**76** B4
Farrand Rd OL8 . . . .**66** B2
Farrant Rd M12 . . . .**99** A4
Farrar Rd M43 . . . .**99** E8
Farr Cl WN3 . . . .**54** F5
Farrell St
Salford M7 . . . . **158** B3
Wigan WN5 . . . .**54** C5
Farrer Rd M13 . . . .**98** F3
Far Ridings SK6 . . . . **113** D3
Farrier Cl **3** M33 . . . . **108** F3
Farrier's Croft WN6 . . . .**36** E3
Farriers La OL11 . . . .**30** B4
Farrier Way WN6 . . . .**35** C7
Farringdon Dr M26 . . . .**43** E4
Farringdon St M6 . . . . **154** B3
Farrington Ave M20 . . . . . . **110** A7
Farrowdale Ave OL2 . . . . . **149** B2
Farrow St E OL2 . . . . **149** B2
Farrow St OL2 . . . . **149** B2
Farr St SK3 . . . . **170** A4
Farsley Pk BL5 . . . .**39** D4
Farwood Cl M16 . . . . **161** C1
Far Woodseats La
SK13 . . . . **114** F5
Fastnet St M11 . . . . **165** A4
Fatherford Cl OL3 . . . .**51** D5
Faulkenhurst Mews
OL1 . . . .**48** C1
Faulkenhurst St OL1,
OL9 . . . .**48** C1
Faulkner Cl **1** M11 . . . . . . **163** A4
Faulkner Dr WA15 . . . . **120** B5
Faulkner Rd M32 . . . .**96** E2
Faulkner St
Bolton BL3 . . . . **145** B1
Manchester M1 . . . . **163** A4
Rochdale OL16 . . . . **139** C3
Fauvel Pl SK13 . . . . **104** C1
Fauvel Rd SK13 . . . . **104** C1
Faversham Brow 9
OL1 . . . . **153** B4
Faversham St M40 . . . .**83** B7
Fawborough Rd M23 . . . . . **108** F1
Fawcetts Fold BL5 . . . .**59** E4
Fawcett St B BL2 . . . . **148** B3
Fawley Ave SK14 . . . . **167** A1
Fawley Gr M22 . . . . **121** D4

Fawns Keep
Stalybridge SK15........102 E6
Wilmslow SK9.........137 D7
Fay Ave M9............65 B2
Fay Gdns SK13........171 B4
Faywood Dr SK16.....126 A6
Fearn Dene **2** OL12....14 B2
Fearney Side BL3......42 F3
Fearnham Cl WN7......75 E1
Fearnhead Ave BL6....22 B5
Fearnhead Cl BL4......60 E8
Fearnhead St BL3....146 C4
Fearnley Way WA12...89 C1
Fearns Moss OL13......3 A8
Fearn St OL11.........29 C2
Featherstall Brook View
3 OL15.............16 A5
Featherstall Ho OL9...152 C1
Featherstall Rd OL15..16 A5
Featherstall Rd N OL1,
OL9................153 A4
Featherstall Rd S
OL9................153 A2
Featherstall Sq **1**
OL15...............16 A5
Fecit La BL0...........12 C8
Federation St
Manchester M4......159 A2
Prestwich M25........62 F5
Feldom Rd M23.......108 F2
Fellbridge Cl BL5......40 B1
Fellbrigg Cl M18......99 C3
Fellfoot Cl M28.......77 F5
Fell Foot Mdw BL5....40 A2
Felling Wlk **6** M14....98 B3
Fellpark Rd M13.....109 A2
Fells Gr M28...........60 F1
Fellside
Bolton BL2...........26 A3
Oldham OL1.........153 B3
Wigan WN1...........37 D2
Fellside Cl BL8........10 F1
Fellside Gdns OL15...15 F7
Fellside Gn SK15......86 A3
Fell St
Bury BL8.............27 C2
Leigh WN7............75 B4
Felltop Ct OL4.........68 C5
Felltop Dr SK5........112 A8
Felsham Cl BL4........42 C1
Felskirk Rd M22......130 C8
Felsted BL1............40 E8
Felt Ct M34...........100 C2
Felthorpe Dr M8......155 C2
Felton Ave M22.......121 D3
Felton Cl BL9..........45 A5
Felton Wlk BL1.......143 B2
Fencegate Ave SK4....111 D5
Fence St SK2..........124 D4
Fenchurch Ave M40....83 C4
Fencot Dr M12.........99 A4
Fenella St M13.........98 E4
Fenham Cl M40.......156 C1
Fenmore Ave M18.....99 B3
Fennel St M4.........158 C2
Fenners Cl BL3.......147 A3
Fenney St E M7......155 B2
Fenney St M7........155 A1
Fenn St M15..........162 B2
FENNY HILL...........67 B4
Fenside Rd M22.......121 E5
Fenstock Wlk M40.....83 D4
Fenton Ave SK14.....102 E3
Fenton Ave SK7......124 D4
Fenton Mews OL11...139 C1
Fenton St
Bury BL8.............27 C3
Manchester M12.....165 A1
5 Oldham OL4.......67 B6
Rochdale OL11.......139 B1
Shaw OL2...........149 B1
Fenton Way WN7.....56 F4
Fenwick Cl BL5.......57 F6
Fenwick Dr
Manchester SK4......110 E3
Middleton M24........46 D1
Fenwick St
Manchester M15.....163 A2
Rochdale OL12.......139 B3
Ferdinand St M40.....83 C4
Fereday St M28........60 D4
Ferguson Ct M19.....110 F8
Ferguson Gdns OL12...14 F3
Ferguson Rise WN5....54 E8
Ferguson Way OL4.....49 D1
Fernacre M33.........108 C5
Fernally St SK14......167 B2
Fern Ave
Newton-le-W WA12...89 D2
Urmston M41.........95 A2
Fernbank M26..........62 A3
FERN BANK...........86 C1
Fern Bank
Failsworth M40........83 C7
Stalybridge SK15......86 C1
Fern Bank Cl SK15...102 C8
Fern Bank Dr M23....120 E8
Fern Bank St SK14...113 E8
Fernbray Ave M19....110 D4
Fernbray Rd WN2......57 A5
Fernbrook Cl M13....164 A1
Fernbrook Wlk **12**
M8.................155 C2
Fern Cl
Atherton M46.........58 D2

Fern Cl continued
Marple SK6..........125 F6
Middleton M24........65 D8
Oldham OL4...........67 F6
Shevington WN6.......36 A6
Fern Clough BL1.......40 F7
Fernclough Rd M9....157 A3
Fern Comm OL2......149 B3
Fern Cres SK15........86 C1
Ferndale Ave
Royton OL16..........48 C8
Stockport SK2.......124 B4
Whitefield M45........62 C7
Ferndale Cl OL4........67 D4
Ferndale Dr WN6......35 E7
Ferndale Gdns M19...110 C8
Ferndale Mews BL9...140 C3
Ferndale Rd M33.....108 B2
Ferndale Wlk WN7.....75 B5
Ferndene Gdns M20..110 B5
Ferndene Rd
Manchester M20.....110 B5
Prestwich M25, M45...63 C7
Ferndown Ave
Chadderton OL9.......65 E7
Hazel Grove SK7.....124 C1
Ferndown Dr M44.....94 A3
Ferndown Rd
Bolton BL3...........25 E3
Wythenshawe M23...120 D8
Ferneyfield Rd OL9....65 F7
Ferngate Dr M20.....110 B6
Ferngrove BL9.........28 B5
FERN GROVE.........141 C4
FERNHILL...........140 B4
Fernhill SK6..........126 B6
Fernhill Ave
Bacup OL13...........3 E8
Bolton BL3..........146 A4
Fernhill Cl
Bacup OL13...........3 E8
Glossop SK13.........104 D3
Fernhill Cres **1** OL13...3 E8
Fernhill Cvn Pk BL9...140 C4
Fernhill Dr
Bacup OL13...........3 E8
Manchester M18.......99 B4
FERNHILL GATE.....146 A4
Fernhill Gr **2** OL13...3 E8
Fern Hill La OL12.....14 A3
Fernhill Pk OL13.......3 E8
Fernhills BL7..........8 E2
Fernhills Bsns Ctr
BL9................140 C4
Fernhill St BL9.......140 C3
Fernhill Way **4** OL13...3 E8
Fern Ho M23.........121 A4
Fernholme Ct OL8.....66 C4
Fernhurst Cl WN3....151 C2
Fernhurst Gr **8** BL1...143 B1
Fernhurst Rd M20....110 C5
Fernie St M4.........159 A3
Fernilee Cl SK22.....127 C1
Fern Isle Cl OL12......14 B6
Fernlea
Altrincham WA15....119 F1
Gatley SK8..........122 B1
Manchester M14.....111 C5
Fern Lea
Ashton-u-L OL6.......85 C8
Hollingworth SK14...103 D6
Fernlea Ave OL1......48 C1
Fernlea Cl
Glossop SK13........171 B4
1 Rochdale OL12......14 B2
Fernlea Cres M27......77 F3
Fernleaf St M14........98 A4
Fernlea Gr WN4........72 D5
Fernlea Gr M38........59 F4
Fernlea Lo BL4........60 E7
Fern Lea St BB4........2 D8
Fernleigh
Bolton BL1...........143 B4
8 Horwich BL6........22 D1
Fernleigh Ave M19.....99 C1
Fernleigh Dr M16....162 A1
Fernley Ave M34.....101 A2
Fernley Rd SK2......124 B6
Fern Lodge Dr OL6....85 D5
Ferns Gr BL1.........144 B3
Fernside Ave M20....110 D5
Fernside Gr WN3......54 D1
Fernside Way OL12....14 A1
Fern St
Bolton BL3...........144 C2
Bury BL9............140 C3
Chadderton OL9.....152 A4
Farnworth BL4........42 E1
Manchester M4, M8..159 A4
Manchester, Openshaw
M11................165 B3
Oldham OL8..........153 A1
Ramsbottom BL0......11 D7
Rochdale OL11.......139 A2
Wardle OL12..........15 C6
Fernstead BL3........144 C2
Ferns The
Britannia OL13........4 A8
Dukinfield SK14.....102 A5
Fernstone Cl BL6......22 A3
Fernthorpe Ave OL3...51 C1
Fern View OL15.......120 E5
Fernview Dr BL0.......11 A1

Fernville Terr **6** OL13...3 D8
Fernwood SK6.........126 C7
Fernwood Ave M18....99 D3
Fernwood Gr SK9....137 C8
Ferrand Lo OL15.......16 C7
Ferrand Rd OL15......16 B6
Ferrer St WN4.........72 F6
Ferring Wlk OL9.....152 B2
Ferris St M11..........99 D4
Ferrous Way M44....105 F6
Ferryhill Rd M44......94 A2
Ferrymasters Way
M44................94 A1
Ferry Rd M44..........94 B2
Ferry St M11.........164 B4
Festival Theatre*
SK14...............167 A2
Fettler Cl M27.........77 F7
Feversham Cl M30.....79 F4
Fewston Cl BL1........24 E5
Fiddlers La M44.......94 B4
Fiddlers Lane Com Prim
Sch M44............94 B3
Field Bank Gr M19.....99 C1
Fieldbrook Wlk BL5....40 A1
Field Cl
Bramhall SK7........132 D4
Marple SK6..........125 D5
Fieldcroft OL11........30 B7
Fielden Ave M21.....109 D5
Fielden Ct M21......109 D5
Fielden St OL15.......15 E2
Fielders Way M27.....61 E4
Fieldfare Ave M40.....83 B4
Fieldfare Way OL7....85 B7
Fieldhead Ave
Bury BL8.............27 A2
Rochdale OL11........30 B7
Tyldesley M29........77 B5
Fieldhead Mews SK9..137 E8
Fieldhead Rd SK9....137 E8
Fieldhouse Ind Est
OL12...............14 F2
Field House La SK6...126 A6
Fieldhouse Rd OL12...14 F2
Fielding Ave SK12....133 E2
Fielding Pl PR6........21 B8
Fieldings Cl WN5.....54 D5
Fielding St
Eccles M30...........79 C1
Middleton M24........47 A2
Fieldings Wharf M43..100 A8
Field La OL6...........85 D5
Field Mews M34......100 E2
Field Pl **9** M20.......110 B3
Field Rd
Milnrow OL16.........31 D7
Sale M33............107 E6
Fields Cres SK14.....103 D6
Fieldsend Cl SK15...102 D8
Fieldsend Dr WN7.....91 C8
Fields End Fold M30...94 C4
Fields Farm Cl SK14..102 D1
Fields Farm Rd SK14..102 D2
Fields Farm Wlk 5
SK14...............102 D2
Fields Gr SK14.......103 D5
Fieldside Cl SK7.....132 D4
Fields New Rd OL9....152 B1
Field St
Droylsden M43........99 F8
Dukinfield SK14.....101 D5
Failsworth M35........83 E7
Hindley WN2.........56 E4
Ince-in-M WN3........55 F4
Manchester M18......99 E6
Rochdale OL11........31 A4
Romiley SK6.........113 A3
Salford M6...........154 C2
Wigan WN6..........150 B4
Fields The
Aspull WN2...........38 C4
Standish WN6.........36 F8
Fields Way BL8........66 E2
Field Vale Dr SK5....100 A1
Fieldvale Rd M33.....108 C1
Fieldview **7** WN6.......53 A7
Field View Wlk M16...97 F2
Fieldway
Platt Bridge WN2......56 B2
Rochdale OL16........31 B3
Field Wlk
Altrincham WA15....120 B3
7 Partington M31....105 E3
Fife Ave OL9..........66 A4
Fifield Cl OL8.........67 A3
Fifth Ave
Bolton BL1..........144 B3
Bury BL9.............28 D4
Droylsden M11........83 C2
Dukinfield SK16.....101 B8
Little Lever BL3.......42 F4
Oldham OL8..........66 C2
Stretford M17.........96 C6
Fifth St
Bolton BL1..........143 C2
Trafford Park M17....96 C5
Filbert St **8** OL11.....49 C1
Filby Wlk M40.......160 B4
Fildes St M24.........65 D7
Filey Ave
Manchester M16......97 D2
Urmston M41.........95 A4
Filey Dr M6...........80 D6
Filey Rd
Manchester M14.....110 D8
Stockport SK2.......124 C7

Filey St OL16.........15 C3
Filton Ave **3** BL3....145 A1
Filton St WN9........156 C2
Finance St OL15.......15 F4
Finborough Cl M16....97 E4
Finchale Dr WA15....120 C1
Finch Ave BL4........59 F7
Finchcroft OL1.......153 A6
Finchdale Gdns WA3...91 B8
Finch La WN6.........18 B1
Finchley Ave M40.....83 C4
Finchley Cres WN2....38 A2
Finchley Gr M40......65 A1
Finchley Rd
Altrincham WA15....119 E3
Manchester M14.....110 B8
Finch Mill Ave WN6....35 D7
Finchwood Rd M22...121 E5
Findlay Cl WA12.......89 C2
Findlay St WN7........75 E5
Findon Rd M23.......121 A6
Finger Post BL3........43 A4
Finghall Rd M41.......95 B2
Finland Rd SK3......170 A3
Finlan Rd M24.........47 E5
Finlay St WN5.........54 E8
Finlay St BL4.........60 D8
Finney Cl SK9........131 C2
Finney Dr
Handforth SK9.......131 C2
Manchester M21.....109 A7
FINNEY GREEN......131 E2
Finney La SK8........122 C1
Finney St BL3........147 C4
Finningley Rd M9......64 B5
Finny Bank Rd M33...108 A6
Finsbury Ave M40.....83 C4
Finsbury Cl OL8.......67 B4
Finsbury Rd SK5.....111 E8
Finsbury St OL11.....139 A1
Finsbury Way SK9...131 E2
Finstock Cl M30.......79 B1
Fintry Gr M30.........79 D1
Fir Ave SK7...........132 E8
Firbank Cl OL7.........84 F2
Fir Bank Prim Sch OL2..48 D7
Firbank Rd
Wigan WN3...........55 B3
Wythenshawe M23...121 B4
Fir Bank Rd OL2.......48 D6
Firbarn Cl OL16........31 D7
Firbeck Dr M4........160 A2
Fir Cl
Hazel Grove SK7....124 E3
Poynton SK12........133 F3
Fircroft WN6...........19 A2
Fircroft Cl **6** SK3....123 F4
Fircroft Rd OL8........67 A2
Firdale Ave M40.......65 E1
Firdale Wlk OL9......152 C3
Firdon Wlk **7** M9....157 B3
Firecrest Cl M28......78 B8
Firefly Cl M3.........158 A1
Fire Station Sq M5....81 C2
Firethorn Ave M19...110 F6
Firethorn Cl BL5......39 F2
Firethorn Dr SK14...102 A2
Firethorn Wlk **5** M33...107 C5
Firfield Gr M28........60 F3
Fir Gr
Chadderton OL9.....152 B4
Manchester M19......99 A1
FIRGROVE...........31 D6
Firgrove Ave OL16....31 D8
Firgrove Bsns Pk OL16...31 D8
Firgrove Gdns OL16...31 D8
Fir La OL2............48 D6
Fir Rd
Bramhall SK7........132 E8
Denton M34..........101 A3
Farnworth BL4........60 B8
Marple SK6..........125 D5
Swinton M27.........79 E6
Firs Ave
Ashton-u-L OL6.......85 B5
Failsworth M35........83 E7
Manchester M16......97 E2
Firsby Ave SK6.......112 F4
Firsby St **8** M19.......99 A1
Firs Cl SK8...........122 A3
Firs Cotts WN2........38 C1
Firs La WN4...........72 C3
Firs La WN7...........75 C6
FIRS LANE...........75 D6
Firs Park Cres WN2....38 D1
Firs Prim Sch M33...107 D4
Firs Rd
Gatley SK8...........122 A4
Over Hulton BL5......59 A6
Sale M33............107 D4
First St
Bolton BL1..........143 C2
Bury BL9............141 A2
Eccles M30...........79 D1
Failsworth M35........83 C7
Heywood OL10........29 E1
Irlam M44...........105 D8
Manchester, Miles Platting
M40................160 A4
2 Manchester, Old Trafford
M16................97 C4
Radcliffe M26.........44 B2
Ramsbottom BL0......11 D7
Royton OL2...........48 D5
Salford M6...........154 C2

Fir St continued
Stockport SK4.......169 B2
Walsden OL14..........6 A8
First Ave
Atherton M46.........58 D4
Bury BL8.............26 F6
Droylsden M11........83 D2
11 Heywood OL10.....56 D5
Little Lever BL3.......43 A4
Mossley SK15.........86 E5
Oldham OL8...........65 A5
Poynton SK12.......133 D1
Stretford M17.........96 D6
Swinton M27.........79 D5
Tyldesley M29.........77 C4
Wigan WN6...........37 A2
Firs The
Altrincham WA14....119 B3
Wilmslow SK9........137 A5
First St BL1...........23 F4
Firsway WN7..........75 B5
Firs Way M33........107 C3
FIRSWOOD..........97 A3
Firswood Dr
Hyde SK14..........102 A3
Royton OL2...........48 C6
Swinton M27.........79 E6
Firswood Mount SK8..23 A8
Firth Cl M7..........155 A2
Firth St OL1.........153 C2
Firtree Ave M33.....107 C4
Fir Tree Ave
Golborne WA3........90 F8
Oldham OL8..........67 A2
Worsley M28.........78 B5
Fir Tree Cl SK16.....101 F8
Fir Tree Cres
Ince-in-M WN3........55 F3
Stalybridge SK16....101 F8
Fir Tree Dr
Dukinfield SK14.....101 C6
Ince-in-M WN3........55 F3
Fir Tree La SK16....101 F8
Fir Tree Prim Sch SK5...99 E2
Fir Tree St WN1.......55 F4
Fir Tree Way **3** BL6....22 C1
Fir Tree Wlk WA3......90 F8
Firvale Ave SK8......122 B1
Firvale Cl WN7........75 C5
Firwood Ave
Farnworth BL4........60 C7
Stretford M41........96 A1
Firwood Cl SK2......124 C8
Firwood Cres M26....44 B1
Firwood Gr
Ashton-in-M WN4.....73 A2
Bolton BL2...........25 B2
Firwood La BL2........25 C3
Firwood Manor Prep Sch
OL9................48 B1
Firwood Pk OL9.......65 E8
Firwood Sch BL2......25 C2
Firwood Stables BL2...25 C3
Fishbourne Sq **8** M14...97 A3
Fishbrook Ind Est BL4...61 A7
Fisher Ave WN2.......74 C7
Fisher Cl WN3.........54 F5
Fisher Dr WN5.........53 E7
Fisherfield OL12.......13 F1
Fishermore Rd M41....94 F2
Fisher St OL1........153 C4
Fish Lake La BL0, BB4...1 E6
Fishwick St OL16......31 A6
Fistral Ave SK8......131 C8
Fistral Cres SK15.....86 D3
Fitchfield Wlk **7** M28...60 D3
Fitton Ave M21......109 B6
Fitton Cres M27........61 F3
FITTON HILL.........67 A3
Fitton Hill Rd OL8.....67 A3
Fitton Hill Sh Prec
OL8................67 A2
Fitton St
Rochdale OL16........31 A8
Royton OL2...........48 F4
Shaw OL2............48 F4
Fitzadam St WN1.....150 B4
Fitzalan St SK13......104 C1
Fitzgeorge St M40...156 C1
Fitzgerald Cl M25.....62 F2
Fitzgerald Ct **11** M34..113 A8
Fitzgerald Way M6....154 C3
Fitzhugh St BL1........25 A5
Fitzroy St
Ashton-u-L OL7......100 F8
Droylsden M43......100 B8
Stalybridge SK15.....86 D4
Fitzwarren Ct M6....154 C2
Fitzwarren St M6.....154 C3
Fitzwilliam Ct **2** M14...98 D4
Fitzwilliam St M7....158 A4
Five Fold Ind Pk OL9..153 A2
Five Quarters M26....84 A2
Fiveways BL4..........61 A7
Fiveways Par SK7....133 E8
Flagcroft Dr M23.....121 B5
Flagg Wood Ave SK5..125 D7
Flagship Ave M5......161 B4
Flag St OL13...........3 E8
Flake La OL2...........48 D6
Flamborough Wlk 7
M14................98 B3
Flamingo Cl M12.....165 A2
Flamingo Villas M44...94 A3
Flamstead Ave M23...120 E6
Flannel St **4** OL12.....31 A8

Flapper Fold La M46.....58 C3
Flash Cotts OL4.....68 A4
Flashfields M25.....62 F1
Flash St M40.....83 C6
Flatley Cl M15.....163 A1
Flavian Wlk M11.....165 B4
Flax Cl BB4.....1 A8
Flaxcroft Rd M22.....121 B3
Flaxfield Ave SK15.....86 D2
Flaxman Rise OL1.....49 C4
FLAX MOSS.....1 A8
Flax Moss Cl BB4.....1 A8
Flaxpool Cl M16.....97 E4
Flax St
  Ramsbottom BL0.....11 A4
  Salford M3.....158 A3
Flaxwood Wlk M22.....121 B3
Fleece St
  2 Oldham OL4.....67 B7
  Rochdale OL16.....139 C3
Fleeson St M14.....98 C3
Fleet Ho BL1.....143 B1
Fleet St
  Ashton-u-L OL6.....166 B2
  Droylsden M18.....99 F6
  Horwich BL6.....22 D3
  Hyde SK14.....167 B3
  Oldham OL4.....67 C7
  Wigan WN5.....54 B6
Fleetwood Dr WA12.....89 B4
Fleetwood Rd M28.....60 A3
Fleming Cl OL12.....15 D5
Fleming Dr WN4.....73 D4
Fleming Rd M22.....121 D2
Flemish Rd M34.....101 B2
Flemming Pl OL9.....153 A2
Fletcher Ave
  Atherton M46.....58 D5
  Swinton M27.....62 A3
FLETCHER BANK.....11 D6
Fletcher Cl
  Heywood OL10.....29 D2
  Oldham OL9.....153 A2
Fletcher Ct M26.....61 B8
Fletcher Dr
  Altrincham WA14.....119 C1
  High Lane SK12.....134 F6
Fletcher Fold Rd BL9.....44 F6
Fletcher Moss Botanical & Parsonage Gdns*
  M20.....110 B1
Fletcher Sq M1.....159 C1
Fletcher's Rd OL15.....15 E3
Fletcher St
  1 Ashton-u-L OL6.....166 C3
  Atherton M46.....58 C3
  Bolton BL3.....145 B1
  Bury BL9.....141 A2
  Farnworth BL4.....60 D8
  Little Lever BL3.....43 B3
  Manchester M40.....157 C1
  Radcliffe M26.....44 C4
  Rochdale OL11.....31 A5
  Stockport SK1.....169 C1
Fletsand Rd SK9.....137 D6
Fletton Cl OL12.....14 E2
Fletton Mews OL12.....14 E2
Flexbury Wlk M40.....83 D4
Flint Cl
  Droylsden M11.....83 B2
  Hazel Grove SK7.....124 C1
Flint Gr M44.....105 C6
Flint St
  Droylsden M43.....84 B2
  Oldham OL1.....67 C8
  Stockport SK3.....170 B3
Flitcroft Ct BL3.....147 C4
Flitcroft St OL8.....67 C4
FLIXTON.....94 F2
Flixton Girls' High Sch
  M41.....95 A2
Flixton Inf Sch M41.....94 F3
Flixton Jun Sch M41.....94 F2
Flixton Rd
  Carrington M31.....106 E7
  Flixton M41.....94 F1
  Urmston M41.....95 B2
Flixton Sta M41.....94 F1
Flixton Wlk M13.....164 A1
Floatshall Rd M23.....121 A6
Floats Rd
  Wythenshawe M23.....120 E4
  Wythenshawe M23.....120 E6
Flockton Ave WN6.....36 D4
Flockton Ct 7 BL6.....22 B4
Flora Dr M7.....158 A4
Floral Ct M7.....155 A2
Flora St
  Ashton-in-M WN4.....73 B2
  Bolton BL3.....147 B4
  Manchester M9.....64 C3
  Oldham OL1.....153 B3
Florence Ave BL1.....24 F5
Florence Ct SK3.....123 B6
Florence Park Ct
  M20.....110 C4
Florence St
  Bolton BL3.....147 A4
  Droylsden M43.....100 B8
  Eccles M30.....79 B1
  Failsworth M35.....83 F8
  Sale M33.....108 B6
  Stockport SK4.....169 B2
  Wigan WN1.....151 B4
Florence Way SK14.....103 D5
Florian Ho OL12.....153 C3
Florida St OL8.....153 B1
Florist St SK3.....170 B3

Florin Gdns M6.....154 C3
Flowery Bank OL8.....67 B4
FLOWERY FIELD.....167 A4
Flowery Field Gn
  SK14.....101 C4
Flowery Field Ind Pk
  SK14.....101 D5
Flowery Field Prim Sch
  SK14.....167 A4
Flowery Field Sta
  SK14.....101 D5
Floyd Ave M21.....109 C5
Floyer Rd M9.....64 E5
Foden La
  Alderley Edge SK9.....136 C1
  Bramhall SK7.....132 D3
Foden Wlk 7 SK9.....131 D2
FOGGBROOK.....124 F6
Fog La M19, M20.....110 C4
Fold Ave M43.....84 B2
Fold Cotts OL3.....51 A2
Fold Cres SK15.....86 F6
Fold Gdns OL12.....14 B3
Fold Gn OL9.....152 A2
Fold La OL12.....14 C4
Fold Mews
  5 Bury BL9.....27 F6
  Hazel Grove SK7.....124 E3
Fold Rd M26.....61 C7
Folds Rd BL1, BL2.....148 A4
Fold St
  Bolton BL1.....145 C3
  Bury BL9.....140 A2
  Golborne WA3.....74 A1
  Heywood OL10.....29 E3
  Manchester M40.....83 A8
Fold The
  Manchester M9.....64 D3
  Royton OL2.....49 A4
  Urmston M41.....95 A3
Fold View
  Bolton BL7.....8 E1
  Oldham OL8.....67 A2
Fold Way OL7.....84 F3
Foleshill Ave M9.....157 A3
Foley Gdns OL10.....46 E7
Foley St 8 WN2.....56 D5
Foley Wlk M22.....130 E8
Foliage Cres SK5.....112 B5
Foliage Gdns SK5.....112 C5
Folkestone Rd M11.....83 C2
Folkestone Rd E M11.....83 D2
Folkestone Rd W M11.....83 C2
Follows St M18.....99 D6
Folly La M27.....79 D6
Folly Wlk 20 OL12.....14 F1
Fonthill Gr SK13.....107 F1
Fontwell Cl
  5 Manchester M16.....97 C3
  Standish WN6.....19 F1
Fontwell La OL1.....49 A1
Fontwell Rd BL3.....43 A2
Fontwell Wlk 6 M40.....65 D2
Footman St M29.....77 B7
Foot Mill Cres OL12.....14 D2
Foot Wood Cres OL12.....14 D2
Forber Cres M18.....99 D3
Forbes Cl
  Hindley WN2.....56 E7
  Sale M33.....108 D2
  Stockport SK1.....124 B8
Forbes Pk SK7.....132 D7
Forbes Rd SK1.....112 B1
Forbes St SK6.....112 F4
Fordbank Rd M20.....110 A2
Ford Gdns OL11.....30 B6
Ford Gr SK14.....103 A4
Fordham Gr BL1.....144 C4
Ford La
  Manchester M20.....110 A2
  Salford M6.....81 A4
Fordland Cl WA3.....74 E1
Ford Lo M20.....110 B2
Fordoe La OL12.....13 C4
Ford's La SK7.....132 D3
Ford St
  Dukinfield SK16.....101 C6
  Kearsley M26.....61 A8
  Manchester M12.....164 A3
  Salford M3.....158 A2
  Stockport SK3.....169 A1
Ford Way SK14.....103 A4
Fordyce Way WN2.....56 A8
Foreland Cl M40.....157 A1
Forest Ave WN6.....36 F3
Forest Cl SK16.....101 C6
Forest Ct M41.....94 D3
Forest Dr
  Altrincham WA15.....119 F6
  Sale M33.....107 E2
  Shevington Moor WN6.....19 A2
  Westhoughton BL5.....58 A8
Forester Dr SK15.....86 A1
Forester Hill Ave
  Bolton BL3.....147 C3
  Bolton, Great Lever BL3.....147 C3
Forester Hill Cl BL3.....147 C3
Forest Fold Wlk.....35 E6
Forest Gate Com Prim Sch
  M31.....105 D3
Forest Gdns M31.....105 D3
Forest Park Sch M33.....108 A4
Forest Range M19.....99 A1

Forest Rd BL1.....142 B3
Forest Sch WA15.....119 F6
Forest St
  Ashton-u-L OL6.....166 C4
  Eccles M30.....79 A4
  Oldham OL6.....66 F2
Forest View OL12.....14 D2
Forest Way BL7.....25 C6
Forfar St BL1.....24 E5
Forge Ind Est OL4.....67 B7
Forge St
  Oldham OL4.....67 B7
  Wigan WN1.....151 B3
Formby Ave
  Atherton M46.....58 D4
  Manchester M21.....109 D7
Formby Dr SK8.....131 B8
Formby Rd M6.....80 E5
Forres Gr WN4.....72 D4
Forrester Dr OL2.....49 D8
Forresters Cl WN2.....74 E8
Forresters Gn M17.....96 E6
Forrester St M28.....79 A8
Forrest Rd M34.....99 F6
Forshaw Ave M18.....99 F6
Forshaw St M34.....100 D4
Forster St M43.....74 A1
Forston Wlk M8.....156 B2
Forsythia Wlk 2 M31.....105 E2
Forsyth St OL12.....13 E2
Fortescue Rd SK2.....124 D7
Forth Pl M26.....43 F5
Forth Rd M26.....43 F5
Forth St WN7.....76 C4
Forton Ave BL2.....42 E7
Forton Rd WN3.....54 F2
Fortran Cl M5.....81 A1
Fort Rd M25.....63 D2
Fortrose Ave M9.....64 B3
Fortuna Gr M19.....110 F8
Fortune St BL3.....148 B1
Fortuneswell Ct M20.....110 B3
Fortyacre Sch M40.....65 C6
Forum Gr M7.....155 B1
Forum The SK6.....113 C2
Forward Ctr BL5.....39 B4
Fosbrook Ave M20.....110 C4
Foscarn Dr M23.....121 B5
Fossgill Ave BL2.....25 C5
Foster Ave WN3.....54 E5
Foster Ct BL9.....28 D4
Foster La BL2.....25 F1
Fosters Bldgs WN6.....150 B4
Foster St
  Denton M34.....100 F3
  Oldham OL4.....67 C7
  Radcliffe M26.....43 F3
  Salford M5.....154 A1
  6 Wigan WN6.....37 A1
Foster Terr 2 BL1.....143 B1
Fotherby Dr M9.....64 D3
Fotherby Pl WN3.....55 A3
Foul Clough Rd OL14.....5 D8
Foulds Ave BL8.....27 B2
Foulkes Ho 3 M14.....110 D8
Foundry La
  Manchester M4.....159 B2
  Wigan WN3.....54 D4
Foundry St
  Bolton BL3.....145 C1
  Bury BL9.....140 C2
  Dukinfield SK16.....101 D8
  Heywood OL10.....29 C2
  Hindley WN2.....56 D5
  Leigh WN7.....76 B4
  Little Lever BL3.....43 A3
  Newton-le-W WA12.....89 B3
  Oldham OL8.....153 B2
  4 Radcliffe M26.....44 A3
  Swinton M27.....62 A1
Fountain Ave WA15.....120 B2
Fountain Cl SK12.....133 D4
Fountain Gdns OL1.....48 D1
Fountain Pk BL5.....57 C5
Fountain Pl
  Poynton SK12.....133 D4
  Whitefield M45.....62 F7
Fountain St N BL5.....141 A3
Fountains Ave BL2.....25 C1
Fountains Cl M29.....77 C7
Fountain Sq SK12.....135 D6
Fountain St
  Cheadle SK8.....132 C6
  Urmston M32.....95 F3
Fountain St
  Ashton-u-L OL6.....85 E4
  Bury, Elton BL9.....27 C2
  Bury, Pimhole BL9.....141 A2
  8 Eccles M30.....95 D8
  Hyde SK14.....167 C3
  Manchester M2.....159 A1
  Middleton M24.....65 A8
  4 Oldham OL1.....153 B3
Fountains Wlk
  Chadderton OL9.....152 A1
  Dukinfield SK16.....101 C6
  Golborne WA3.....91 B8
Fouracres Rd M23.....121 A5
FOUR GATES.....39 C4
FOUR LANE ENDS.....26 C5
Four Lane Ends BL2.....25 E4
Four Lanes La OL3.....103 A4
Four Lanes End Rd
  OL13.....3 B8
Four Lanes Way OL11.....13 C2
Fourmarts Rd WN5.....36 C2
Four Stalls End 6
  OL15.....16 A5

Fourteen Meadows Rd
  WN3.....150 B2
Fourth Ave
  Bolton BL1.....144 B3
  Bury BL9.....28 D4
  Chadderton OL9.....152 A1
  Droylsden M11.....83 C2
  Little Lever BL3.....42 F4
  Mossley SK15.....86 E6
  Oldham OL8.....66 C1
  Stretford M17.....96 C6
  Swinton M27.....79 D5
Fourth St BL1.....23 F4
Fourways M17.....96 A7
Four Yards M2.....158 C1
Fowey Wlk
  Hattersley SK14.....102 E3
  6 Wythenshawe M23.....121 A5
Fowler Ave M18.....99 F7
Fowler Cl WN1.....151 B4
Fowler Ind Pk BL6.....22 C2
Fowler St OL8.....66 C3
FOWLEY COMMON.....92 B5
Fowley Common La
  WA3.....92 C5
Fownhope Ave M33.....107 F3
Fownhope Rd M33.....107 F3
Foxall Cl M24.....64 C7
Foxall St M24.....64 C7
Fox Bank Ct SK3.....170 A4
Foxbank St M13.....98 E4
Fox Bench Cl SK7.....132 C6
Foxbench Wlk M21.....109 D6
Fox Cl WA15.....119 F6
Foxcroft St OL15.....15 F5
Foxdale Cl BL7.....9 E7
Foxdale St 3 M11.....83 C1
Foxdene Gr WN3.....54 E2
Foxdenton Dr M32.....95 F3
Foxdenton Hall* M24.....65 E6
Foxdenton La M24, OL9.....65 F6
Foxdenton Wlk M34.....100 E1
Foxendale Wlk BL3.....145 C1
Foxfield Cl BL8.....27 B5
Foxfield Dr OL8.....66 F1
Foxfield Gr WN6.....36 B6
Foxfield Rd M23.....121 A3
Foxfold Cl M28.....77 F7
Foxford Wlk M22.....121 E2
Foxglove Cl
  8 Golborne WA3.....90 D8
  Standish WN6.....19 D2
Foxglove Ct OL12.....14 D3
Foxglove Dr
  Altrincham WA14.....119 C8
  Bury BL9.....28 D3
Foxglove La SK15.....86 A3
Foxglove Wlk M31.....105 F2
Foxhall Rd
  Altrincham WA14.....119 F6
  Denton M34.....100 D4
Foxham Dr M7.....155 B2
Foxhill
  Altrincham WA14.....119 A5
  Shaw OL2.....48 E8
Foxhill Chase SK2.....125 A5
Fox Hill Ct SK4.....168 A2
Foxhill Dr SK15.....102 C4
Foxhill Rd M30.....78 F1
Fox Hill Rd OL11.....47 D8
Foxholes Cl OL12.....15 A1
Foxholes Rd
  Horwich BL6.....22 D4
  Hyde SK14.....113 C8
  Rochdale OL12.....121 B3
Foxlair Ct M22.....121 A3
Foxlair Rd M22.....121 A3
Foxland Rd SK8.....122 B4
Foxlea SK13.....115 F8
Foxley Cl
  Droylsden M43.....99 E8
  Lymm WA13.....117 A2
Foxley Gr BL3.....145 A2
Foxley Hall Mews
  WA13.....117 A1
Foxley Wlk M12.....165 A1
Fox Park Rd 5 OL8.....66 C2
Fox Platt Rd OL5.....68 B1
Fox Platt Terr OL5.....86 C8
Fox St
  Bury BL9.....140 C3
  Eccles M30.....79 F2
  Heywood OL10.....29 C2
  Horwich BL6.....22 C2
  Milnrow OL16.....31 E6
  Oldham OL8.....66 C1
  Stockport SK3.....170 A4
Foxton St M24.....65 A8
Foxton Wlk 8 M23.....121 A2
Foxwell Wlk 8 M8.....156 B2
Foxwood Cl WN5.....53 E5
Foxwood Dr
  Hyde SK14.....167 B4
  Mossley OL5.....68 D2
Foxwood Gdns M19.....110 E5
Foynes Cl M40.....157 A1
Foy St 3 WN4.....73 B3
Frame The M11.....83 A2
Framingham Rd M33.....108 B2
Framley Rd M20, M21.....109 F7
Frampton Cl M25.....63 B7
Fram St
  Manchester M9.....157 C4
  Salford M6.....154 E2
Frances Ave SK8.....122 A6
Francesca Wlk M18.....165 C2
Frances Pl M46.....58 A2

Frances St W SK14.....101 C3
Frances St
  Bolton BL1.....143 B2
  Cheadle SK8.....122 E6
  Dukinfield SK14.....101 C3
  Irlam M44.....105 E5
  Manchester M13.....163 B2
  Oldham OL1.....49 B1
  Rochdale OL16.....15 D4
  7 Stockport SK1, SK3.....170 B4
France St
  Hindley WN2.....56 D6
  Westhoughton BL5.....57 E6
  Wigan WN5.....54 F7
Francis Ave
  Eccles M30.....79 E2
  Walkden M28.....60 F2
Francis Rd
  Irlam M44.....93 F1
  Manchester M20.....110 C5
Francis St
  Denton M34.....113 B8
  Eccles M30.....79 D3
  Failsworth M35.....83 F7
  Farnworth BL4.....42 D1
  Hindley WN2.....56 E5
  Leigh WN7.....75 E2
  Manchester M3.....158 C3
  Tyldesley M29.....77 D8
Francis Terr 3 SK16.....166 C1
Frandley Wlk 4 M13.....163 B3
Frankby Cl M27.....80 C7
Frank Cowan Ct M7.....158 A4
Frank Fold OL10.....29 A2
Frankford Ave BL1.....142 C2
Frankford Sq BL1.....142 C2
Frankland Cl M11.....83 B2
Franklin Cl OL1.....153 B4
Franklin St
  Eccles M30.....79 D2
  Oldham OL1.....153 B4
  Rochdale OL16.....31 B5
Franklyn Ave M41.....94 E2
Franklyn Cl M34.....100 A2
Frank St
  Bolton BL1.....143 A2
  Bury BL9.....140 C1
  Failsworth M35.....83 F7
  Hyde SK14.....167 B2
  Salford M6.....81 A4
Frank Swift Wlk 5
  M14.....98 A3
Frankton Rd M45.....62 F7
Franton Rd M11.....83 B2
Fraser Ave M33.....108 E3
Fraser Ho BL1.....143 A1
Fraser Pl M17.....96 D5
Fraser Rd
  Manchester M8.....63 F1
  Wigan WN5.....54 E7
Fraser St
  Ashton-u-L OL6.....166 C3
  Rochdale OL16.....31 B4
  Shaw OL2.....149 A3
  Swinton M27.....62 A1
Fraternitas Terr M43.....83 E3
Frawley Ave WA12.....89 C5
Frecheville St BL9.....140 B1
Freckleton Ave M21.....109 C4
Freckleton Dr BL8.....43 F8
Freckleton St WN1.....37 C2
Freda Wlk M11.....160 C1
Frederica Gdns WN2.....56 A3
Frederick Ave OL2.....149 A1
Frederick Ct BL4.....60 E8
Frederick Rd M6, M7.....81 B4
Frederick St
  Ashton-in-M WN4.....73 A5
  Ashton-u-L OL6.....85 C2
  Chadderton OL9.....152 B4
  Denton M34.....60 D8
  Farnworth BL4.....56 D5
  Ince-in-M WN3.....151 A2
  Littleborough OL16.....16 A6
  Oldham OL8.....66 D4
  Ramsbottom BL0.....138 B1
  Salford M3.....158 B2
Frederic St WN7.....58 E1
Fred St M24.....65 D6
Fred Tilson Cl M14.....98 A3
Freehold Com Jun & Inf
  Sch OL9.....152 C1
Freeholds Rd OL12.....4 E6
Freeholds Terr OL12.....4 E6
Free La BB4.....1 A6
Freeland Wlk M11.....165 C4
Freeman Ave OL6.....85 D3
Freeman Rd SK16.....101 C2
Freeman Sq M15.....163 A2
Freemantle St SK3.....170 A4
Freesia Ave 8 M28.....59 F3
Freestone Cl BL8.....140 A3
Freetown SK13.....116 C8
FREE TOWN.....141 A4

Freetown Bsns Pk
BL9 ....141 A4
Freetown Cl M14 ....98 A4
Freetrade St OL11 ....139 B2
Freiston 5 OL12 ....139 C4
Fremantle Ave M18 ....99 D3
French Ave
 5 Oldham OL1 ....49 C1
 Stalybridge SK15 ....86 C1
French Barn La M9 ....64 C3
Frenches Ct OL3 ....69 A6
French Gr BL3 ....42 D5
French St
 Ashton-u-l OL6 ....85 D4
 Stalybridge SK15 ....86 C1
Frenchwood Ct WN2 ....38 C4
Frensham Wlk M23 ....120 F4
Fresca Rd OL1 ....49 D4
Fresh Ct SK13 ....115 F7
Freshfield SK8 ....131 B8
Freshfield Ave
 Atherton M46 ....58 C4
 Bolton BL3 ....147 A2
 Bolton BL3 ....147 C2
 Hyde SK14 ....167 A1
 Prestwich M25 ....63 C6
Freshfield Cl
 Failsworth M35 ....84 A6
 Marple SK6 ....114 B1
Freshfield Gr BL3 ....147 C2
Freshfield Rd
 Hindley WN2 ....56 F5
 Manchester SK4 ....110 F3
 Wigan WN3 ....54 E3
Freshfields M23 ....43 D5
Freshfield Wlk 11 M11 ...83 C2
Freshford Wlk
 M22 ....121 B1
Freshpool Way M22 ....121 E6
Freshwater Dr
 Ashton-u-l OL6 ....85 E5
 Denton M34 ....113 B8
Freshwater St 3 M18 ......99 E6
Freshwinds Ct OL4 ....67 D4
Fressel Cl SK14 ....102 B6
Freva Ho M9 ....65 B2
Frewland Ave SK3 ....123 F4
Freya Gr M5 ....161 C4
Friarmere Rd OL3 ....50 E5
Friars Cl
 Altrincham WA14 ....119 B1
 Tyldesley M29 ....59 D1
Friar's Cl SK9 ....136 E8
Friars Cres OL11 ....30 F2
Friars Ct M5 ....80 B2
Friars Prim Sch The
 M3 ....158 A3
Friar's Rd M33 ....108 B4
Friendship Ave M18 ....99 E4
Frieston Rd WA14 ....119 E8
Friezland Cl SK15 ....86 E6
Friezland La OL3 ....69 A4
Friezland Prim Sch
 OL3 ....68 E5
Frimley Gdns M22 ....121 D3
Frinton Ave M40 ....65 D3
Frinton Cl M33 ....107 F1
Frinton Rd BL3 ....146 B3
Frith Rd M20 ....110 C5
Frith St WN5 ....150 A3
Frobisher Cl M13 ....164 A1
Frobisher Pl SK5 ....169 B4
Frobisher Rd OL15 ....6 C1
Frodsham Ave SK4 ....168 C3
Frodsham Cl WN6 ....36 D3
Frodsham Rd M33 ....108 E2
Frodsham St 9 M14 ....98 B3
Frodsham Way SK9 ....131 E4
Frodsley Wlk M12 ....164 C2
Frogbrook Cl SK2 ....124 F6
Frog La WN6, WN6 ....150 B4
Frogley St 2 BL2 ....25 B3
Frogmore Ave SK14 ....113 F7
Frome Ave
 Stockport SK2 ....124 C5
 Urmston M41 ....95 B1
Frome Ct M29 ....77 C6
Frome Dr M8 ....156 B3
Frome St OL4 ....67 C6
Frostlands St 10 M16 ....97 E3
Frost St
 Manchester M4 ....160 A1
 Oldham OL8 ....66 E4
Froxmer St M18 ....165 C2
Fryent Cl BL6 ....21 D2
Fulbeck Ave WN3 ....55 A2
Fulbrook Dr SK8 ....132 A6
Fulbrook Way M29 ....59 C1
Fulford St 4 M16 ....97 C4
Fulham Ave M40 ....83 B5
Fulham St OL4 ....67 C6
Fullerton Rd SK4 ....168 B2
Full Pot La OL11 ....29 E8
FULLWOOD 149 C2
Fulmar Cl
 Poynton SK12 ....133 A4
 Westhoughton BL5 ....57 D6
Fulmar Dr
 Hazel Grove SK2 ....124 F5
 Sale M33 ....107 C2
Fulmards Cl SK9 ....137 C7
Fulmar Gdns OL11 ....29 F7
Fulmead Wlk 16 M8 ....155 C2
Fulmer Dr M4 ....159 C2
Fulmere Ct M27 ....79 D6

Fulneck Sq 2 M43 ....100 A8
Fulshaw Ave SK9 ....137 A6
Fulshaw Cross SK9 ....137 A5
Fulshaw Ct SK9 ....137 A5
FULSHAW PARK 137 B5
Fulshaw Pk SK9 ....137 A5
Fulshaw Pk S SK9 ....137 A4
Fulshaw Wlk 7 M13 ....163 B3
Fulstone Mews SK2 ....124 B6
Fulton Ct M15 ....163 A1
Fulwell Ave M46 ....76 E8
Fulwood Ave M9 ....64 F4
Fulwood Cl BL8 ....26 F1
Fulwood Rd WA3 ....90 E7
Furbarn La OL11 ....29 D8
Furbarn Rd OL11 ....29 D8
Furberry Ct OL4 ....68 B5
Furlong Cl M24 ....73 F7
Furlong Rd M22 ....121 B3
Furnace St
 Dukinfield SK16 ....166 B2
 Hyde SK14 ....101 C4
Furness Ave
 Ashton-u-l OL7 ....84 F5
 Bolton BL2 ....25 B2
 Heywood OL10 ....29 C3
 Littleborough OL15 ....16 A6
 Oldham OL8 ....67 C3
 Whitefield M45 ....63 A8
Furness Cl
 2 Glossop SK13 ....116 F8
 Milnrow OL16 ....31 E6
 Poynton SK12 ....133 D4
Furness Cres WN7 ....57 D1
Furness Gr SK4 ....168 A1
Furness Quay M50 ....161 A3
Furness Rd
 Bolton BL1 ....144 B3
 Cheadle SK8 ....132 C6
 Manchester M14 ....98 C1
 Middleton M24 ....112 A6
 Urmston M41 ....95 D3
Furness Sq BL2 ....25 B2
Furnival Cl M34 ....100 A2
Furnival Rd M18 ....165 C1
Furnival St
 Leigh WN7 ....75 F7
 Reddish SK5 ....99 F2
Furrow Com Sch M24 ....46 D2
Furrow Dr M30 ....79 B4
Further Field OL11 ....13 D1
Further Heights Rd 1
 OL12 ....14 F1
Further Hey Cl OL4 ....67 E2
Further La SK14 ....102 E3
Further Pits OL11 ....30 C7
Furtherwood Rd OL11 ....48 C1
Furze Ave BL5 ....57 F7
Furzegate OL16 ....31 C3
Furze La OL4 ....49 D1
Furze The OL2 ....48 D6
Furze Wlk M31 ....106 A3
Fushia Gr M7 ....155 A2
Futura Pk BL6 ....22 C1
Futures Pk OL13 ....3 E8
Fyfield Wlk 3 M8 ....156 B2
Fylde Ave
 Bolton BL2 ....42 E7
 Gatley SK8 ....131 C8
Fylde Cl M12 ....108 C8
Fylde Rd SK4 ....168 A2
Fylde St E BL4 ....42 D2
Fylde St BL4 ....42 D2

G

Gabbot St PR7 ....21 A7
Gable Ave SK9 ....137 A7
Gable Ct M34 ....100 F2
Gable Dr M24 ....46 E1
Gable St
 Bolton BL2 ....25 D5
 Manchester M11 ....164 C4
 Newton-le-W WA12 ....89 B3
Gables The M33 ....108 B3
Gabriel's Terr 1 M24 ......65 C7
Gabriels The OL2 ....48 F7
Gadbury Ave M46 ....58 B3
Gadbury Fold M46 ....58 A2
Gaddum Rd
 Altrincham WA14 ....119 B1
 Manchester M20 ....110 C3
Gadfield Ct M46 ....58 B3
Gadfield Gr M46 ....58 A3
Gadwall Cl M28 ....78 D8
Gail Ave SK4 ....169 A2
Gail Cl
 Alderley Edge SK9 ....137 B2
 Failsworth M35 ....83 E5
Gainford Ave SK8 ....122 B4
Gainford Gdns M40 ....65 B1
Gainford Rd SK5 ....99 F1
Gainford Wlk BL3 ....147 B4
Gainsborough Ave
 Bolton BL3 ....146 C3
 Manchester M20 ....110 C5
 Marple SK6 ....126 B8
 Oldham OL8 ....66 E4
 Stretford M32 ....96 F3
Gainsborough Cl
 Wigan WN3 ....54 D3
 Wilmslow SK9 ....137 D8
Gainsborough Dr
 Cheadle SK8 ....122 F6
 Rochdale OL11 ....30 E3
Gainsborough Ho
 M33 ....107 F3

Gainsborough Rd
 Chadderton OL9 ....47 E1
 Droylsden M34 ....84 D1
 Ramsbottom BL0 ....11 B1
Gainsborough St M7 ....155 B3
Gainsborough Wlk
 Denton M34 ....100 E1
 1 Dukinfield SK14 ....101 F5
Gairloch Ave M32 ....96 B2
Gair Rd SK5 ....169 C4
Gair St SK14 ....167 A4
Gaitskell Cl M12 ....160 B1
Galbraith Rd M20 ....110 C3
Galbraith Way OL11 ....29 E8
GALE 16 C7
Gale Cl OL15 ....16 C7
Gale Dr M24 ....46 D2
Gale Rd M25 ....62 F3
Gale St
 Heywood OL10 ....29 B2
 Rochdale OL12 ....14 F3
Gales Terr OL11 ....139 B1
Galgate Cl
 Bury BL8 ....26 F1
 Manchester M15 ....162 B3
Galindo St BL2 ....25 C4
Galland St OL4 ....67 D7
Galleria The 10 BL1 ....145 C3
Galleries The 10 WN1 ....150 C4
**Gallery of Costume & Platt
 Hall The** *M14 ....98 C2
Gallery Oldham *
 OL1 ....153 C2
Gallery The M3 ....158 C2
Galloway Cl
 Bolton BL3 ....40 E5
 Heywood OL10 ....45 F8
Galloway Dr
 Swinton M27 ....61 F4
 Up Holland WN8 ....53 B6
Galloway Rd M27 ....79 D6
Gallowsclough Rd
 SK15 ....102 E6
Galsworthy Ave M8 ....156 A2
Galvin Rd M9 ....64 B3
Galway St OL1 ....153 C2
Galway Wlk M23 ....120 F2
Galwey Gr WN1 ....37 C4
Gambleside Cl M28 ....78 B8
Gambrel Bank Rd OL6 ......85 B6
Gambrel Gr OL6 ....85 B6
GAMESLEY 171 A1
Gamesley Com Prim Sch
 SK13 ....171 B2
Game St OL4 ....67 C5
Games Wlk 8 M22 ....121 B1
Gamma Wlk M11 ....83 B2
Gandy La OL12 ....19 A6
Gan Eden 18 M7 ....63 E1
Gantley Ave WN5 ....53 D3
Gantley Cres WN5 ....53 D3
Gantley Rd WN5 ....53 D3
Gantock Wlk 10 M14 ....98 C3
Ganton Ave M45 ....62 D7
Garbrook Ave M9 ....64 C5
Garden Ave
 Droylsden M43 ....84 B2
 Stretford M32 ....96 D3
Garden City BL0 ....11 A2
Garden Cl OL15 ....15 F2
Garden Ct OL6 ....31 C8
Gardenfold Way M43 ....84 B2
Garden La
 Altrincham WA14 ....119 D5
 3 Manchester M3 ....158 C1
 10 Rochdale OL16 ....31 A8
 Salford M3 ....158 B2
 Worsley M28 ....78 A6
Garden Row
 Heywood OL10 ....29 B4
 Rochdale OL12 ....14 D2
Garden St
 11 Bacup OL13 ....3 C8
 Bury BL8 ....26 F7
 Denton M34 ....100 F6
 Eccles M30 ....79 E1
 Farnworth BL4 ....60 E8
 Heywood OL10 ....29 C2
 Hyde SK14 ....167 B4
 Manchester M4 ....159 A2
 Newhey OL16 ....32 B4
 Oldham, County End OL4 ....67 F5
 Oldham, Mumps OL1 ....153 C2
 Ramsbottom, Brooksbottoms
  BL9 ....11 C3
 Stockport SK2 ....124 C5
 Tyldesley M29 ....77 B5
Gardens The
 Bolton BL1 ....24 F6
 Edgworth BL7 ....9 D4
 Salford M30 ....80 A4
Garden Terr OL2 ....48 C7
Garden Wall Cl M5 ....161 C4
Garden Way OL15 ....15 F2
Garden Wlk
 Ashton-u-l OL6 ....166 C4
 3 Denton M34 ....101 A2
 12 Partington M31 ....105 E3
Gardiner Cl WN1 ....20 B7
Gardner Grange SK5 ....112 C4
Gardner Ho 8 M30 ....79 E2
Gardner Rd M25 ....62 F4
Gardner St
 Manchester M12 ....165 B2
 Salford M6 ....81 A3
Garfield Ave M19 ....99 B1

Garfield Cl OL11 ....13 E1
Garfield Gr BL3 ....145 A1
Garfield St BL3 ....146 C3
Garforth Ave M4 ....159 C2
Garforth Cres M43 ....84 C3
Garforth Rise BL1 ....144 A3
Garforth St OL9 ....152 C4
Gargrave Ave BL1 ....23 F2
Gargrave St
 Manchester M7 ....80 F8
 2 Oldham OL4 ....67 B6
Garland Rd M22 ....121 E3
Garlick St
 Hyde SK14 ....167 C3
 Manchester M18 ....99 D5
 Oldham OL9 ....153 B2
Garnet Cl M9 ....157 C4
Garner Ave WN5 ....108 A1
Garner Cl WA14 ....119 D2
Garner Dr
 Eccles M30 ....79 C3
 Salford M5 ....154 A3
 Tyldesley M29 ....77 B5
Garner's La SK3 ....170 B1
Garnett Cl SK14 ....102 F3
Garnett Rd SK14 ....102 F3
Garnett St
 Bolton BL3 ....143 B3
 Oldham OL1 ....67 B8
 Ramsbottom BL0 ....138 B1
 Stockport SK1 ....169 C1
Garnett Way 1 SK14 ....102 F3
Garratt Way M18 ....165 C1
Garret Gr OL2 ....149 C3
Garrett Hall Rd M28 ....77 E7
Garrett La M28, M29 ....77 D7
Garrett Wlk SK3 ....123 C8
Garrick Theatre *
 SK1 ....169 B1
Garron Wlk 1 M22 ....121 A2
Garrowmore Wlk 22
 M9 ....64 E3
Garsdale Cl BL8 ....45 A7
Garsdale La BL1 ....40 D7
Garside Ave WA3 ....90 D7
Garside Gr
 Bolton BL1 ....142 C2
 Wigan WN3 ....54 E2
Garside Hey Rd BL8 ....27 B6
Garside St
 Bolton BL1 ....145 B3
 Denton M34 ....100 F2
 Hyde SK14 ....167 B1
Garstang Ave BL2 ....42 F7
Garstang Dr BL8 ....26 F1
Garstang Ho M13 ....163 B1
Garston Ave M46 ....58 B5
Garston Cl
 Leigh WN7 ....57 E1
 Stockport SK4 ....168 C3
Garston St BL9 ....141 A4
GARSWOOD 72 C3
Garswood Cres WN5 ....71 E4
Garswood Dr BL8 ....27 B6
Garswood Old Rd WA11,
 WN4 ....71 E1
Garswood Prim Sch
 WN4 ....72 C4
Garswood Rd
 Billinge WN5 ....71 F4
 Bolton BL3 ....147 B2
 Garswood WA11, WN4 ....72 C2
 Manchester M14 ....98 A2
Garswood St WN4 ....73 B3
Garswood Sta WN4 ....72 D3
Garth Ave WA15 ....119 E6
Garth Hts SK9 ....137 C7
Garthland Rd SK7 ....124 F3
Garthmere Rd M46 ....58 F5
Garthorne Cl M16 ....97 D4
Garthorp Rd M23 ....108 E1
Garth Rd
 Marple SK6 ....126 A6
 Stockport SK2 ....124 C7
 Wythenshawe M22 ....121 D4
Garth The M5 ....154 A2
Gartland Wlk M8 ....156 C4
Garton Dr WA3 ....74 E1
Gartside Cl
 Ashton-u-l OL7 ....84 E1
 Dobl OL3 ....50 E4
 Manchester M3 ....158 B2
 Oldham OL4 ....67 B5
Garwick Rd BL1 ....142 B3
Garwood St M15 ....162 C3
Gascoyne St M14 ....98 B3
Gaskell Cl OL15 ....16 A6
Gaskell Com Prim Sch
 BL1 ....145 B4
Gaskell Rd
 Altrincham WA14 ....119 D6
 Eccles M30 ....79 E1
Gaskell St
 Bolton BL1 ....145 B4
 Eccles M30 ....79 E1
 Wigan WN5 ....49 E5
Gaskell's Brow WN4 ....72 E5
Gaskell St
 Bolton BL1 ....145 A4
 26 Dukinfield SK16 ....166 B1
 Failsworth M40 ....83 D6
 Oldham OL4 ....67 B5
 Swinton M27 ....61 F2
 Wigan WN1 ....151 A4
Gaskill St OL10 ....29 A2
Gas St
 Adlington PR7 ....21 A6
 Ashton-u-l OL6 ....166 B3

Gas St continued
 Bolton BL1 ....145 A3
 Farnworth BL4 ....60 D8
 6 Heywood OL10 ....29 D2
 Hollingworth SK14 ....103 D5
 Leigh WN7 ....75 F5
 Platt Bridge WN2 ....56 B2
 Rochdale OL11 ....139 B3
 Stockport SK4 ....169 B1
Gaston Wlk M9 ....64 D5
Gatcombe Mews 1
 SK9 ....137 A6
Gatcombe Sq M14 ....98 D3
Gateacre Wlk M23 ....120 E8
Gate Ctr The SK6 ....112 E6
Gatefield Cl M26 ....43 E3
Gategill Gr WN5 ....53 D3
Gatehead Bsns Pk OL3 .....50 F3
Gatehead Croft OL3 ....50 F3
Gatehead Mews OL3 ....50 F3
Gatehead Rd OL3 ....50 F3
Gate House Ct BL9 ....141 C2
Gatehouse Rd M28 ....60 A4
Gate Keeper Fold OL7 ......85 A7
Gatemere Cl M28 ....78 B8
Gatesgarth Rd M24 ....46 C2
Gateshead Cl M14 ....98 B4
Gateside Wlk M9 ....64 E5
Gates Prim Sch The
 BL5 ....39 F2
Gates Sh Ctr The BL1 .....145 C3
Gate St
 Dukinfield SK16 ....101 A6
 Manchester M11 ....165 C4
 Rochdale OL11 ....139 C1
Gates The BL2 ....26 A3
Gateway Cres OL9 ....65 E4
Gateway Ho M1 ....159 B1
Gateway Ind Est M1 ....159 B1
Gateway Rd M18 ....165 C2
Gateways The M27 ....61 F1
Gateway The M40 ....157 C2
Gathill Cl SK8 ....122 F1
Gathurst La WN5, WN6 ......36 A4
Gathurst Rd WN5 ....53 E8
Gathurst St M18 ....99 E6
Gathurst Sta WN6 ....36 A3
GATLEY 122 A4
Gatley Ave M14 ....98 A1
Gatley Brow OL1 ....153 B4
Gatley Cl M29 ....59 B1
Gatley Gr SK8 ....122 A5
Gatley Prim Sch SK8 ......122 A5
Gatley Rd
 Cheadle SK8 ....122 C6
 Sale M33 ....108 E3
 Gatley Sta SK8 ....122 B5
Gatling Ave M12 ....99 B2
Gatwick Ave M23 ....121 B6
Gavel Wlk M24 ....46 E1
Gavin Ave M5 ....81 A1
Gawsworth Ave M20 ....110 C1
Gawsworth Cl
 Altrincham WA15 ....120 D6
 Bramhall SK7 ....132 E6
 Glossop SK13 ....104 A5
 Poynton SK12 ....133 F2
 Shaw OL2 ....48 F7
 Stockport SK3 ....170 A1
Gawsworth Mews
 SK8 ....122 B5
Gawsworth Pl M22 ....121 F1
Gawsworth Rd
 Golborne WN3 ....73 F1
 Sale M33 ....108 E1
Gawsworth Way
 18 Denton M34 ....101 A1
 Handforth SK9 ....131 E4
Gawthorne Cl SK7 ....124 C2
Gawthorpe Cl BL9 ....45 A5
Gaydon Rd M33 ....107 D4
Gaythorne St BL1 ....143 C3
Gaythorn St M5 ....81 C1
Gayton Cl WN3 ....54 D3
Gayton Wlk 7 M40 ....65 D2
Gaywood Wlk M40 ....156 C2
Geddington Rd WA14 ......119 C8
GEE CROSS 113 F7
Gee Cross Fold SK14 ......113 E7
**Gee Cross Holy Trinity CE
 Prim Sch** SK14 ....113 F8
Gee La
 Eccles M30 ....79 B3
 7 Oldham OL8 ....66 B2
Gee St SK3 ....170 A3
**Gelder Clough Residential
 Cvn Pk** OL10 ....29 C5
Gellert Pl BL5 ....57 E6
Gellert Rd BL5 ....57 E6
Gellfield La OL3 ....51 D1
Gemini Rd M6 ....81 C4
Gendre Rd BL7 ....24 E8
Gene Rd SK7 ....123 E3
Geneva Terr OL11 ....30 C8
Geneva Wlk
 Chadderton OL9 ....152 C2
 11 Manchester M8 ....156 B2
Genista Gr M7 ....155 A2
Geoff Bent Wlk M40 ....83 B5
Geoffrey St
 Bury BL9 ....141 A4
 Horwich BL5 ....58 F8
 Ramsbottom BL0 ....11 A4
Geo Hampson's Bidgs
 WA3 ....92 C8
George Barton St 22
 BL2 ....25 B1

George Ct 10 SK16 166 B1
George H Carnall Sports Ctr M41 95 E4
George La SK6 113 A4
George Leigh St M4 159 B2
George Mann Cl M22 121 C1
George Parr Rd M15 162 C2
George Rd BL0 138 B1
George Richards Way WA14 119 C7
George St E SK1 124 B8
George St N M7 155 C4
George St S M7 155 C4
George St W SK1 124 B8
George's Cl SK12 133 E3
Georges La WN1 151 C4
George's La BL6 22 E5
George Sq OL1 153 B2
George's Rd
Sale M33 108 B3
Stockport SK4 169 A2
George's Rd E SK12 133 E3
George's Rd W SK12 133 E3
George's Row 2 BB4 2 F8
George St
Alderley Edge SK9 137 A1
Altrincham WA14 119 D4
Ashton-in-M WN4 73 C4
Ashton-u-L OL6 166 C3
3 Atherton M46 58 D3
4 Bacup OL13 3 C8
Bury BL9 140 C2
Chadderton OL9 152 A3
Compstall SK6 114 B2
Denton M34 101 A3
Eccles M30 79 C1
Failsworth M35 83 F8
Farnworth BL4 60 B7
Glossop SK13 116 C8
Heywood OL10 29 B3
Hindley WN2 56 E5
Horwich BL6 22 C3
Ince-in-M WN2 151 C3
Irlam M44 94 B3
8 Littleborough OL15 16 B5
Manchester, City Centre M1 163 A4
Manchester, Hilton Park M25 63 B1
Milnrow OL16 31 E7
Mossley OL5 68 C1
Newton-le-W WA12 89 A4
Oldham OL1 153 B2
Radcliffe M26 43 F3
Rochdale, Greengate OL16 15 D3
Rochdale, Newbold Brow OL16 31 A8
Shaw OL2 149 C4
5 Stalybridge SK15 86 A2
Stockport SK1 112 A2
Urmston M41 95 E2
Westhoughton BL5 57 F8
Whitefield M45 44 E1
Whitworth OL12 14 C8
George Terr
5 Eccles M30 79 D2
Orrell WN5 53 D5
George Thomas Ct M9 157 A4
George Tomlinson Sch BL4 60 E6
Georgette Dr M3 158 B3
Georgia Ave M20 109 F6
Georgiana St 3 BL4 42 B2
Georgian Ct
5 Leigh WN7 76 B4
12 Tyldesley M29 58 F1
Georgian Sq 2 WN2 56 A2
Georgina Ct BL3 146 B3
Georgina St BL3 146 B3
Gerald Ave M8 156 A4
Gerald Rd M6 81 B5
Gerard Ctr The WN4 73 B3
Gerard St WN4 73 B3
Germain Cl M9 64 C5
Gerrard Ave WA15 120 A8
Gerrard Cl WN2 38 D2
Gerrard Rd WN5 71 E5
Gerrards Cl M44 94 A2
Gerrards Gdns SK14 113 E7
Gerrards Hollow SK14 113 D7
Gerrard St
Farnworth BL4 60 E8
Leigh WN7 75 F5
Rochdale OL11 31 A2
2 Salford M6 81 A3
Stalybridge SK15 86 B1
5 Westhoughton BL5 39 E1
Gerrards The SK14 113 D7
Gerrards Wood SK14 113 D7
Gertrude Cl M5 161 A4
Gertrude St OL12 4 E6
Gervis Cl M40 157 A1
Ghyll Gr
Billinge WA11 71 B1
Walkden M28 60 E2
Giants Hall Rd WN6 36 E3
Giants Seat Gr M27 80 D8
Gibb La SK6 126 E5
Gibbon Ave M22 121 D2
Gibbon's Rd WN4 72 D3
Gibbon St
Bolton BL3 145 A1
Droylsden M11 83 A2
Gibb Rd M28 79 B7
Gibbs Cl OL3 68 E5
Gibbs St M5 158 A1
Gib Field M46 58 B4
Gibfield Dr M46 58 A2
Gibfield Park Ave M46 58 B4
Gib Fold M46 58 D4
Gib La M23 121 B7
Gibraltar La M34 113 B8
Gibraltar St
Bolton BL3 145 A2
Oldham OL4 67 D5
Gibsmere Cl M23, WA15 120 D6
Gibson Ave M18 99 F6
Gibson Gr M28 60 A3
Gibson La M28 60 A3
Gibson Pl M4 159 A3
Gibsons Rd SK4 168 B4
Gibson St
Bolton BL2 25 C1
Leigh WN2 56 D1
Oldham OL4 67 C6
Rochdale OL16 31 C8
Gibson Terr OL7 166 A1
Gibson Way WA14 119 C8
Gibwood Rd M22 121 C8
GIDLOW 37 B2
Gidlow Ave
Adlington PR6 21 A7
Wigan WN6 37 A2
Gidlow La
Wigan, Springfield WN6 37 A2
Wigan WN6 150 B4
Gidlow New Hos WN6 37 A4
Gidlow St
4 Hindley WN2 56 D6
Manchester M18 99 E6
Giffard Wlk SK7 124 A2
Gifford Ave M9 64 F4
Gifford Pl WN2 56 F4
GIGG 45 A7
Gigg La BL9 44 F8
Gilbert Bank SK6 113 B4
Gilbert Rd WA15 119 E1
Gilbert St
Eccles M30 95 B8
Hindley WN2 56 D5
Manchester M15 162 B3
Ramsbottom BL0 1 C1
Salford M6 154 C1
Walkden M28 60 D1
Gilbrook Way OL16 31 B2
Gilchrist Rd M44 105 F6
Gilda Brook Rd M30 80 A2
Gilda Cres Rd M30 80 A3
Gilda Rd M28 77 F7
Gilded Hollins Com Sch WN7 75 C1
Gildenhall M35 84 A7
Gilderdale Cl OL2 149 B4
Gilderdale St 7 BL3 42 A4
Gildersdale Dr M9 64 C6
Gildridge Rd M16 97 E1
Gilesgate 3 M14 98 C3
Giles St M12 99 A4
Gillan Rd WN6 37 B3
Gill Ave WN6 36 B6
GILLBENT 131 F6
Gillbent Rd SK8 132 A7
Gillbrook Rd M20 110 B2
Gillbrow Cres WN1 37 F1
Gillemere Gr OL2 149 C3
Gillers Gn M28 60 C3
Gillford Ave M9 157 C4
Gilliburns Wlk BL5 57 F5
Gillingham Rd M30 79 B2
Gillingham Sq M11 164 C4
Gill St
Manchester M9 64 F1
Stockport SK1 112 B3
Gillwood Dr SK6 112 F1
Gilman Cl M9 64 C2
Gilman St M9 64 C2
Gilmerton Dr 22 M40 83 C5
Gilmore Dr M25 63 B5
Gilmore St SK3 170 B3
Gilmour St M24 65 A8
Gilmour Terr M9 64 F1
GILNOW 145 A2
Gilnow Gdns BL1 144 C2
Gilnow Gr BL1 145 A2
Gilnow La BL3 145 A2
GILNOW PARK 145 A3
Gilnow Prim Sch BL1 144 C2
Gilnow Rd BL1 144 C2
Gilpin Pl WN2 55 F2
Gilpin Rd M41 95 F2
Gilpin Wlk M24 46 E1
Gilroy St WN1 151 A4
Giltbrook Ave M40 160 A4
Gilwell Dr M23 120 F4
Gilwood Gr M24 46 F4
Gin Croft La BL0 1 E4
Gingham Brow BL6 22 E4
Gingham Ct 7 M26 44 C4
Gingham Pk M26 43 E5
GIN PIT 76 F6
Gipsy La SK2 124 C6
Gird La SK6 114 E1
Girton Ave WN4 72 F4
Girton St
Bolton BL2 42 D7
Salford M7 158 B4
Girton Wlk M40 65 D1
Girvan Ave M40 65 D2
Girvan Cl BL3 146 C3
Girvan Cres WN4 72 D4
Girvan Wlk OL10 28 F1
Gisborn Dr M6 81 A5
Gisburn Ave
Bolton BL1 23 E2
Golborne WA3 73 F2
Gisburn Dr BL8 26 E3
Gisburne Ave M40 65 D2
Gisburn Rd OL11 31 A3
Gissing Wlk M9 157 A2
Givendale Dr M8 64 A2
Givvons Fold 10 OL4 49 D1
Glabyn Ave BL6 39 F8
Gladden Hey Dr WN3 54 D1
Glade Brow OL4 68 A6
Gladeside Ct M22 121 C4
Gladeside Rd M22 121 C4
Glade St BL1 144 C3
Glade The
Bolton BL1 143 A1
Shevington WN6 36 B6
Stockport SK4 168 A1
Gladewood Cl 1 SK9 137 C8
Gladewood Dr M35 84 B8
Gladstone Bsns Pk OL4 67 B6
Gladstone Cl
6 Bolton BL1 143 B2
Glossop SK13 116 D8
Gladstone Cres OL11 31 A3
Gladstone Ct
8 Ashton-u-L OL7 166 A2
Farnworth BL4 42 C1
Manchester, Old Trafford M15 97 E4
Stockport, Heaton Moor SK4 168 B3
Gladstone Gr SK4 168 A3
Gladstone Mews SK4 169 B3
Gladstone Mill SK15 86 B1
Gladstone Pl BL4 42 C1
Gladstone Rd
Altrincham WA14 119 D6
Eccles M30 79 E2
Farnworth BL4 42 D1
Urmston M41 95 E2
Gladstone St
Bolton BL1 143 B2
Bury BL9 141 B3
Glossop SK13 116 D8
Hadfield SK13 104 A4
Oldham OL4 67 B6
Pendlebury M27 80 B8
Stockport SK2 124 C4
Westhoughton BL5 39 E1
Gladstone Terrace Rd OL3 69 A4
Gladstone Way WA12 89 B4
Gladville Dr SK8 123 A6
Gladwyn Ave M20 109 E4
Gladys St
3 Farnworth BL3 42 D2
Manchester M16 97 C4
Glaisdale OL4 67 D6
Glaisdale Cl
Ashton-in-M WN4 73 C3
Bolton BL2 25 B2
Glaisdale St BL2 25 B2
Glaister La BL2 25 D1
Glamis Ave
Droylsden M11 83 B3
Heywood OL10 46 F8
Stretford M32 96 A2
Glamis Cl WN7 76 D6
Glamorgan Pl OL9 152 C1
Glandon Dr SK8 132 C8
Glanford Ave M9 64 A3
Glanton Wlk M40 65 D1
Glanvor Rd SK3 123 C8
Glassbrook St WN6 37 A1
Glasshouse St 6 M4 159 C3
Glasson Wlk OL9 152 A2
Glass St BL4 60 E7
Glastonbury 28 OL12 139 B4
Glastonbury Ave
Altrincham WA15 120 B2
Cheadle SK8 132 C6
Golborne WA3 91 C8
Glastonbury Dr SK12 133 D5
Glastonbury Gdns 5 M26 43 E5
Glastonbury Rd
Tyldesley M29 77 B7
Urmston M32 95 F3
Glaswen Gr SK5 169 C4
GLAZEBROOK 105 B6
Glazebrook Cl OL10 29 C1
Glazebrook La WA3 105 B5
Glazebrook Sta WA3 105 A5
GLAZEBURY 92 B7
Glazebury CE Prim Sch WA3 92 C7
Glazebury Dr
Westhoughton BL5 39 F2
Wythenshawe M23 121 B5
Glazedale Ave OL2 48 C5
Glaze Wlk M45 45 C2
Glaziers La WA3 91 D2
Gleaves Ave BL2 26 A4
Gleaves Rd M30 79 E1
Gleave St
12 Bolton BL1 145 C4
Sale M33 108 B6
Glebe Ave WN4 73 C2
Glebe Cl WN6 19 F1
Glebe End St WN6 150 B4
Glebe Ho M24 47 A2
Glebe House Sch OL16 139 B2
Glebe La OL1 49 E4
Glebeland WA3 91 E2
Glebeland Rd BL3 144 B1
Glebelands Rd
Prestwich M25 63 B5
Sale M33 108 A6
Wythenshawe M23 120 F6
Glebe Rd
Standish WN6 19 F1
Urmston M41 95 D2
Glebe St
Ashton-u-L OL6 166 C3
Bolton BL2 148 A2
Chadderton OL9 66 A3
Hindley WN2 57 C2
Leigh WN7 75 F6
Radcliffe M26 44 B3
Shaw OL2 149 B3
Stockport SK1 112 A1
Westhoughton BL5 39 E1
Gleden St M40 160 B2
Gledhall St SK15 86 A2
Gledhill Ave M5 161 B3
Gledhill Cl OL2 32 A1
Gledhill St M20 110 B7
Gledhill Way BL7 9 A1
Glegg St WN2 151 C4
Glemsford Cl
Failsworth M40 83 B6
Wigan WN3 55 B3
Glenacre Gdns M18 99 E3
Glenarm Wlk M22 121 E2
Glenart M30 79 E3
Glen Ave
Bolton BL3 144 B1
Kearsley BL4 61 B6
Manchester M9 64 F1
Sale M33 108 A6
Swinton M27 79 D8
Worsley M28 79 A8
Glenavon Dr
Rochdale OL12 14 D3
Shaw OL2 48 F8
Glenbarry Cl M13 163 B2
Glenbarry St M12 164 A4
Glenbeck Cl BL6 22 D1
Glenbeck Rd M45 44 E1
Glenboro Ave BL8 27 C2
Glenboro Ct BL8 27 C1
Glenborough Ave OL13 3 C8
Glen Bott St BL1 143 A2
Glenbourne Pk SK7 132 D5
Glenbranter Ave WN2 56 A8
Glenbrook Gdns BL4 42 D2
Glenbrook Hill SK13 104 C2
Glenbrook Rd M9 64 A5
Glenburn St BL3 147 A3
Glenby Ave M22 121 F3
Glencar BL5 57 D7
Glencar Dr 8 M40 65 D2
Glencastle Rd
Manchester, Gorton M18 99 D4
Manchester M18 99 C4
Glen Cl WA3 105 B2
Glencoe BL2 148 B3
Glencoe Cl OL10 28 F1
Glencoe Dr
Bolton BL2 42 F6
Sale M33 107 C2
Glencoe Pl OL11 139 A3
Glencoe St 3 OL8 66 C2
Glencoyne Dr BL1 24 D6
Glen Cres OL13 3 A8
Glencross Ave M21 97 A2
Glendale M27 62 B2
Glendale Ave
Ashton-in-M WN4 73 C4
Manchester M19 110 F6
Whitefield BL9 44 F3
Glendale Cl
Boothstown M28 77 F7
8 Heywood OL10 29 D2
Glendale Ct OL8 66 F4
Glendale Dr BL3 40 F6
Glendale Rd
Boothstown M28 77 F7
Manchester M18 99 C4
Salford M30 80 A3
Glendene Ave
Bramhall SK7 132 D5
Droylsden M43 84 C3
Glenden Foot OL12 14 D2
Glendevon Cl
Bolton BL3 40 F5
Ince-in-M WN2 56 A8
Glendevon Pl M45 63 B7
Glendinning St M6 154 B2
Glendon Cres OL6 85 B7
Glendon Ct OL1 49 E4
Glendore M5 80 C2
Glendower Dr M40 156 C1
Glen Dr WN6 35 E8
Gleneagles BL3 40 F3
Gleneagles Ave
10 Droylsden M11 83 C2
Heywood OL10 46 D8
Gleneagles Cl
Bramhall SK7 133 A7
Golborne WA3 90 F7
Wilmslow SK9 137 D8
Gleneagles Rd
Gatley SK8 122 C1
Urmston M41 94 F3
Gleneagles Way BL0 138 B1
Glenfield WA14 119 B4
Glenfield Cl OL4 67 D6
Glenfield Dr SK12 133 D3
Glenfield Rd SK4 169 A4
Glenfield Sq 2 BL4 42 B2
Glenfyne Rd M6 80 D5
Glengarth OL3 69 B7
Glengarth Dr BL1, BL6 40 C6
Glen Gdns OL12 14 F2
Glen Gr
Middleton M24 65 C7
Royton OL2 48 D5
Glenham Ct 1 M15 97 E4
Glenhaven Ave M41 95 C2
Glenhaven Ho M20 110 A5
Glenholme Rd SK7 132 D7
Glenhurst Rd M19 110 E5
Glenilla Ave M28 78 E7
Glenlea Dr M20 122 B8
Glenluce Wlk BL3 40 E5
Glenmay Ct M32 96 C2
Glen Maye M33 108 C4
Glenmaye Gr WN2 57 A5
Glenmere Cl M25 62 F6
Glenmere Rd M20 122 C8
Glenmoor Rd 2 SK1 112 A1
Glenmore Ave
Farnworth BL3, BL4 42 A2
Manchester M20 109 E4
Glenmore Bglws SK16 101 C7
Glenmore Cl
Bolton BL3 40 E5
Rochdale OL11 29 E5
Glenmore Dr
Failsworth M35 84 B8
Manchester M8 156 B3
Glenmore Gr SK16 101 C8
Glenmore Rd BL0 10 F2
Glenmore St BL9 140 B1
Glenmuir Cl M44 94 A2
Glenolden St M11 83 D2
Glenpark WN7 76 B6
Glenpark Wlk 5 M9 157 B3
Glen Rd
Oldham OL4 67 C6
Rawtenstall BB4 2 F8
Glenridding Cl OL1 49 A1
Glenridge Cl BL1 143 C2
Glen Rise WA15 120 A5
Glen Royd 1 OL12 14 C1
Glensdale Dr M40 65 E1
Glenshee Dr BL3 40 F5
Glenside WN6 18 B2
Glenside Ave M18 99 D3
Glenside Dr
Bolton BL3 147 C2
Romiley SK6 113 B5
Wilmslow SK9 137 C6
Glenside Gdns M35 84 B7
Glenside Gr M28 60 E3
Glen St
Bacup OL13 3 E8
Ramsbottom BL0 138 B3
Salford M50 161 A3
Glen Terr BB4 2 F8
Glen The
Bolton BL1 40 E7
Middleton M24 65 B6
Glenthorn Ave M9 64 D6
Glenthorne Dr OL7 166 A4
Glenthorne St 16 BL1 143 B1
Glenthorn Gr M33 108 B3
GLEN TOP 3 A8
Glen Trad Est OL4 67 D6
Glentress Mews BL1 144 A4
Glentrool Mews BL1 144 A3
Glent View SK15 86 A4
Glentwood WA14 119 E1
Glenvale Cl M26 44 B3
Glen View
Littleborough OL15 16 C7
Royton OL2 48 D5
Glenview Rd M29 58 F2
Glenville Rd M8 155 C1
Glenville Way M34 101 A2
Glenville Wlk 13 SK15 86 A1
Glenwood Ave 2 SK14 101 D5
Glenwood Cl M26 44 B2
Glenwood Dr
Manchester M9 157 B3
Middleton M24 47 C1
Glenwood Gr SK2 124 B4
Glenwyn Ave M9 64 E4
Globe Cl M16 162 A1
Globe Ind Est 10 M26 44 B3
Globe La
Bolton BL7 8 D3
Dukinfield SK16 101 B7
Globe Lane Ind Est SK16 101 B6
Globe Lane Prim Sch SK16 101 B6
Globe Pk OL16 31 B6
Globe Sq SK16 101 A7
Globe St 11 OL1 67 B7
GLODWICK 67 B5
Glodwick OL4 67 B5
GLODWICK BROOK 67 A4
Glodwick Inf Sch OL4 67 B5
Glodwick Rd OL4 67 B6
GLOSSOP 104 B2
Glossopbrook Bsns Pk SK13 104 C1
Glossop Brook Rd SK13 104 B1
Glossop Central Sta SK13 104 C1

Glossopdale Com Coll SK13 104 C2
Glossopdale Com Coll (Annexe) SK13 104 A4
Glossop Heritage Ctr* SK13 104 C1
Glossop Rd
Broadbottom SK13 115 D7
Gamesley SK13 171 B1
Marple SK6 114 D3
Glossop Way WN2 56 E4
Gloster St 3 BL2 148 A3
Gloucester Ave
Golborne WA3 90 B8
Heywood OL10 46 C8
Horwich BL6 22 D2
Manchester M19 111 B8
Marple SK6 125 F6
Rochdale OL12 15 D4
Whitefield M45 63 A8
Gloucester Cl OL6 85 D8
Gloucester Cres WN2 56 E6
Gloucester Ct BL6 22 D2
Gloucester Dr
Diggle OL3 51 C4
Sale M33 107 D4
Gloucester Pl
Atherton M46 58 D4
1 Salford M6 81 A3
Gloucester Rd
Droylsden M43 84 A3
Gatley SK8 131 C7
Hyde SK14 113 E8
Middleton M24 65 B6
Poynton SK12 133 D4
Reddish M34 100 A2
Salford M6 80 C4
Urmston M41 95 D1
Wigan WN5 54 C6
Gloucester Rise SK16 102 A7
Gloucester St N OL9 152 C1
Gloucester St S OL9 152 C1
Gloucester St
Atherton M46 58 D3
1 Manchester M1 162 C3
Salford, Ordsall M5 161 C4
Salford, Pendleton M6 81 A4
Stockport SK3 170 A3
Gloucester Way 4 SK13 116 F8
Glover Ave M8 156 B2
Glover Ct M7 155 C4
Glover Ctr OL5 86 D8
Glover Dr SK14 167 B2
Glover Field M7 155 A2
Glover Rd PR7 19 D7
Glover's Pl WN5 54 B8
Glover St
Horwich BL6 22 B4
Leigh WN7 75 C8
Newton-le-W WA12 89 C3
Glyn Ave WA15 120 A2
Glyneath Cl M11 164 C4
Glyniss Cl SK3 170 C2
Glynne St BL4 60 C8
Glynn Gdns M20 109 D4
Glynrene Dr M27 61 C1
Glynwood Pk BL4 42 C1
G M B National Coll M16 97 D2
GMex Sta M1 162 C4
Goadsby St M4 159 A2
GOATS 32 C1
Goats Gate Terr M45 44 D2
Godbert Ave M21 109 C5
Goddard La
Glossop SK13 104 A6
New Mills SK22 127 E7
Goddard Rd SK13 104 A4
Goddard St OL8 66 F4
Godfrey Ave M43 83 D3
Godfrey Ermen Meml CE Prim Sch M30 95 C8
Godfrey Mill SK14 167 B3
Godfrey Range M18 99 F4
Godfrey Rd M6 80 C5
Godlee Dr M27 79 E7
GODLEY 167 C3
Godley Cl M11 165 C4
Godley Com Prim Sch SK14 167 C3
Godley Ct SK14 167 C2
GODLEY GREEN 102 B1
Godley Hill SK14 102 B2
Godley Hill Rd SK14 102 B3
Godley St SK14 167 C4
Godley Sta SK14 102 A3
Godmond Hall Dr M28 77 F5
Godolphin Cl M30 79 E4
Godson St OL1 48 E1
Godward Rd SK22 127 B1
Godwin St M18 99 E6
Goit Pl OL16 139 C3
GOLBORNE 90 B7
Golborne Ave M20 109 F7
Golborne Com Prim Sch WA3 90 A8
Golborne Dale Rd WA3, WA12 90 A5
Golborne Enterprise Pk WA3 74 A1
Golborne Gallery 9 WN1 150 C4
Golborne Pl WN1 151 B4
Golborne Rd
Ashton-in-M WN4 73 E4
Golborne WA3 90 C8
Golborne St WA12 89 E4
Golbourne High Sch WA3 74 C1
Goldborne Ho OL2 149 B4
Goldbourne Dr OL2 149 B4
Goldbrook Cl 2 OL10 29 E1
Goldcraft Cl 4 OL10 29 E1
Goldcrest Cl
Walkden M28 78 B7
Wythenshawe M22 121 F5
Goldenhill Ave M11 83 C3
Golden St
Eccles M30 79 D1
Shaw OL2 49 E8
Goldenways WN1 37 C2
Goldfinch Dr BL9 141 C4
Goldfinch Way M43 84 C3
Goldie Ave M22 121 F2
Goldrill Ave BL2 42 F8
Goldrill Gdns BL2 42 F8
Goldsmith Ave
Oldham OL1 49 E4
Salford M5 154 A2
Goldsmith Pl WN3 55 A4
Goldsmith Rd SK5 99 E1
Goldsmith St BL3 147 A4
Goldsmith Way 8 M34 113 A7
Gold St M1 159 A1
Goldstein Rd BL6 40 B4
Goldsworth Rd OL1 49 E3
Goldsworthy Rd M41 94 E2
Goldwick Wlk M23 108 E1
Golf Rd
Altrincham WA15 119 F3
Sale M33 108 F4
Golfview Dr M30 79 D4
Gooch Dr WA12 89 D2
Gooch St BL6 22 C2
Goodacre SK14 102 B6
Gooden St OL10 29 E1
Goodier House Fold SK14 167 C4
Goodiers Dr M5 161 B4
Goodier St
Manchester M40 160 C4
Sale M33 108 A4
Goodier View SK14 101 F5
Goodison Cl BL9 45 B3
Goodlad St BL8 27 B4
Goodman St M9 64 E1
Goodrich 3 OL11 139 B2
Goodridge Ave M22 121 C1
Goodrington Rd SK9 131 E3
Goodshaw Rd M28 78 C8
Good Shepherd Cl OL16 31 B8
Goodwill Cl M27 79 F7
Goodwin Ct OL9 66 C3
Goodwin Sq M9 157 A3
Goodwin St BL1 148 A4
Goodwood Ave
Sale M33 107 C4
Wythenshawe M23 120 D7
Goodwood Cl BL3 42 F3
Goodwood Cres WA15 120 C6
Goodwood Dr
Oldham OL1 49 B1
Pendlebury M27 80 B7
Goodwood Lo 14 M16 97 D3
Goodwood Rd SK6 125 E5
Goodworth Wlk M40 83 B7
Goole St M11 165 A4
Goose Cote Hill BL7 8 E1
Goose Gn WA14 119 D4
GOOSE GREEN 54 E4
Goose La OL12 139 C4
Goosetrey Cl SK9 131 E1
Goostrey Ave 5 M20 110 A8
Gordon Ave
Bolton BL3 144 C1
Chadderton OL9 66 A3
Garswood WN4 72 E4
Hazel Grove SK7 124 D3
Manchester M19 111 B8
Oldham OL4 67 C6
Sale M33 108 B6
Gordon Cl WN5 54 E8
Gordon Pl M20 110 B5
Gordon Rd
Eccles M30 79 D3
Swinton M27 79 C6
Gordon St
15 Ashton-u-L OL6 85 D4
Bury BL9 140 B3
Droylsden M18 99 E6
Hyde SK14 167 B2
Leigh WN7 75 F6
Manchester M16 162 A1
Newhey OL16 32 B3
Oldham, County End OL4 68 A6
Oldham, White Gate OL9 65 F4
9 Rochdale OL11 31 A5
Salford M7 158 A4
Shaw OL2 149 C3
4 Stalybridge SK15 86 B1
Stockport SK4 169 B3
Wigan WN1 151 B3
Gordonstoun Cres WN5 53 F7
Gordon Terr 2 SK15 86 A2
Gordon Way OL10 28 F1
Gore Ave
Failsworth M35 84 B7
Gore Ave *continued*
Salford M5 154 A2
Gorebrook Ct M12 99 A4
Gore Cl BL9 141 C1
Gore Cres M5 154 A3
Goredale Ave M18 99 E4
Gore Dr M5 154 A3
Gore La SK9 136 C3
Gorelan Rd M18 99 D5
Gore's La WA11 71 A5
Gore St
Manchester M1 159 B1
Manchester M3 158 B1
Salford, Pendleton M6 81 A3
Wigan WN5 54 B6
Goring Ave M18 99 D6
Gorman St 9 WN6 37 A1
Gorman Wlk WN3 54 F5
Gorrells Way OL11 30 D3
Gorrels Cl OL11 30 D3
Gorrel St 4 OL11 31 A5
Gorse Ave
Droylsden M43 84 C2
Marple SK6 125 E6
Mossley OL5 68 E1
Oldham OL8 67 C3
Stretford M32 96 F3
Gorse Bank BL9 141 C3
Gorse Bank Rd WA15 129 C7
Gorse Cres M32 96 F3
Gorse Dr
Stretford M32 96 F3
Walkden M38 59 F6
Gorsefield Cl M26 44 A4
Gorsefield Dr 1 M27 79 F7
Gorsefield Hey SK9 137 E8
Gorsefield Prim Sch M26 44 A4
Gorse Gr BB4 1 A8
Gorse Hall Cl SK16 101 F7
Gorse Hall Dr SK15 85 F1
Gorse Hall Prim Sch SK15 86 A1
Gorse Hall Rd SK16 101 F7
GORSE HILL 96 E3
Gorse Hill Prim Sch M32 96 E4
Gorse La M32 96 F3
Gorselands SK8 132 B5
Gorse Rd
Milnrow OL16 32 A6
Swinton M27 79 E6
Walkden M28 60 E2
Gorses Dr WN2 38 C6
Gorses Mount BL2 148 C1
Gorse Sq M31 105 D3
Gorses Rd BL2, BL3 42 D5
Gorse St
Oldham OL9 65 F4
Stretford M32 96 E3
Gorse The WA14 128 B8
Gorseway SK5 112 B4
Gorse Way SK13 116 F7
Gorse Wlk WN7 75 B5
Gorsey Ave M22 121 C4
Gorsey Bank Prim Sch SK9 136 F7
Gorsey Bank Rd SK3 123 B8
Gorsey Brow
Billinge WN5 71 E5
Mottram in L SK14 103 A1
Romiley SK6 113 A2
Shevington Moor WN6 19 B2
Stockport SK1 112 A1
Gorsey Brow Cl WN5 71 D5
Gorsey Clough Wlk BL8 26 F5
Gorsey Dr M22 121 C4
Gorseyfields M43 100 A8
Gorsey Gr BL5 57 D7
Gorsey Hey BL5 57 E7
Gorsey Hill St OL10 29 D1
Gorsey Intakes SK14 115 A8
Gorsey La
Altrincham WA14 119 B5
Ashton-u-L OL6 85 F6
Partington WA13 118 B7
Gorsey Mount St SK1 112 A1
Gorsey Rd
Wilmslow SK9 136 F8
Wythenshawe M22 121 C4
Gorsey Way OL6 85 E6
Gorsley Bank OL15 16 C7
Gorston Wlk M22 130 C8
Gort Cl BL9 45 A1
GORTON 99 D4
Gorton Cres M34 100 C2
Gorton Cross Ctr M18 99 D5
Gorton Fold BL6 22 C3
Gorton Gr M28 60 C5
Gorton Ind Est M18 165 C2
Gorton La M12, M18 165 B2
Gorton Mount Prim Sch M18 99 C3
Gorton Parks M18 165 C2
Gorton Rd
Manchester M11, M12 164 C3
Reddish SK5 99 F2
Gorton St
11 Ashton-u-L OL7 84 F1
Bolton BL2 148 A2
Chadderton OL9 152 B2
Eccles M30 79 B1
Farnworth BL4 60 B7
Heywood OL10 29 E2
Manchester M3 158 C2
Gorton Sta M18 99 D6
Gortonvilla Wlk M12 164 C2
Gosforth Cl
Bury BL8 27 C5
Oldham OL1 49 A1
Gosforth Wlk M23 108 F1
Goshen La BL9 44 F6
Gosport Sq M7 155 A1
Gosport Wlk M8 156 C2
Goss Hall St OL4 67 C6
Gotha Wlk M13, M13 163 C2
Gotherage Cl SK6 113 E2
Gotherage La SK6 113 E2
Gothic Cl SK6 113 F2
Gough St
Heywood OL10 29 E2
Stockport SK3 169 A1
Goulden Rd M20 110 A5
Goulden St
Manchester M4 159 B2
Salford M6 154 B2
Goulder Rd M18 99 E3
Gould St
Denton M34 100 E3
Manchester M4 159 B3
Oldham OL1 67 B8
Gourham Dr SK8 122 F2
Govan St M22 109 E1
Govind Ruia Ct M16 97 E2
Gowan Dr M24 46 D1
Gowanlock's St BL1 143 B2
Gowan Rd M16 97 E1
Gower Ave SK7 124 C3
Gower Ct SK14 113 E8
Gowerdale Rd SK5 112 C5
Gower Hey Gdns SK14 167 B1
Gower Rd
Hyde SK14 167 A1
Reddish SK4 169 A4
Gowers St OL16 31 B8
Gower St
Ashton-u-L OL6 166 C3
Bolton BL1 145 A4
Farnworth BL4 42 C1
Leigh WN7 75 E4
Oldham OL1 67 A7
Swinton M27 62 A1
Wigan WN5 150 A3
Gowran Pk 3 OL4 67 D6
Gowy Cl SK9 131 E1
Goya Rise OL1 49 D4
Goyt Ave SK6 125 F4
Goyt Cres
Romiley SK6 112 F3
Stockport SK1 112 B3
Goyt Hey Ave WN5 71 E5
Goyt Rd
Disley SK12 135 D5
Marple SK6 125 F4
Stockport SK1 112 B3
Goyt Valley Rd SK6 112 F3
Goyt Valley Wlk SK6 112 F3
Goyt Wlk M45 45 B2
Grace St
Horwich BL6 22 B3
Leigh WN7 75 C5
6 Rochdale OL12 15 A2
Grace Wlk M4 160 A1
Gracie Ave 2 OL1 67 B8
Gradwell St SK3 170 A4
Grafton Ave M30 80 A4
Grafton Ct
Manchester M15 162 B1
14 Rochdale OL16 31 B6
Grafton House Prep Sch OL6 166 B2
Grafton St
Adlington PR7 20 F6
Altrincham WA14 119 D4
Ashton-u-L OL6 85 D2
Atherton M46 58 A1
5 Bolton BL1 145 A4
Bury BL9 44 F8
Failsworth M35 84 A8
Hyde SK14 167 A3
Manchester M13 163 B1
Newton-le-W WA12 89 B3
Oldham OL1 49 E4
Rochdale OL16 31 B6
Stalybridge SK15 86 D3
Stockport SK4 169 B3
Graham Ave WN6 18 C2
Graham Cres M44 105 C3
Graham Dr SK12 135 C6
Graham Rd
Salford M6 80 C4
Stockport SK1 124 C8
Graham St
Ashton-u-L OL7 84 F1
Bolton BL1 145 C4
Manchester M11 165 A4
Platt Bridge WN2 56 A1
Grainger Ave M12 99 A3
GRAINS BAR 50 A6
Grains Rd
Delph OL3, OL4 50 C4
Shaw OL1, OL2 49 D7
Grain View M5 161 A4
Gralam Cl M33 108 E1
Grammar School Rd
Lymm WA13 117 A2
Oldham OL8 66 B2
Grampian Cl OL9 152 A1
Grampian Way
Golborne WA3 74 D1
6 Platt Bridge WN2 56 B2
Shaw OL2 149 A4
Granada Mews M16 97 E1
Granada Rd M34 100 A3
Granada TV Ctr M3 158 B1
Granary La M28 78 F5
Granary Mews SK12 133 E3
Granary Way M33 107 F2
Granby Ho M1 163 A4
Granby Rd
Cheadle SK8 132 B8
Sale WA15 108 A1
Stockport SK2 124 B5
Stretford M32 96 E1
Swinton M27 79 C7
Granby Row M1 163 A4
Granby St
Bury BL8 26 F4
Chadderton OL9 66 A3
Grandale St 5 M14 98 C3
Grandidge St OL11 139 B1
Grand The M1 159 A1
Grand Union Way M30 95 D8
Granford Cl WA14 119 D7
Grange PR7 19 D8
Grange Ave
Altrincham WA15 120 A2
Cheadle SK8 122 F3
Denton M34 101 B2
Eccles M30 79 D4
Little Lever BL3 43 C3
Manchester M19 110 F8
Milnrow OL16 31 F4
Oldham OL8 66 C4
Reddish SK4 111 D5
Sale WA15 120 B7
Stretford M32 96 D2
Swinton M27 61 D2
Urmston M41 94 E2
Wigan, Poolstock WN3 150 B1
Wigan, The Bell WN5 54 B7
Grange Cl
Golborne WA3 90 C6
Hyde SK14 167 C1
Grange Cres M41 95 C1
Grange Ct
Altrincham WA14 119 C1
Oldham OL8 66 D4
Grange Dr
Coppull PR7 19 D8
Eccles M30 79 D4
Manchester M9 64 F3
Grangeforth Rd M8 155 C4
Grange Gr M45 62 F8
Grange La
Delph OL3 50 F6
Manchester M20 110 B2
Grange Manor BL7 25 C8
Grange Mill Wlk M40 83 B7
Grange Park Ave
Ashton-u-L OL6 85 F6
Cheadle SK8 122 D5
Wilmslow SK9 137 A8
Grange Park Rd
Bolton BL7 25 C7
Cheadle SK8 122 D5
Manchester M9 65 A3
Grange Pl M44 105 E5
Grange Rd
Altrincham WA14 119 C1
Ashton-in-M WN4 72 F6
Bolton, Bromley Cross BL7 25 C8
Bolton, Deane BL3 144 B1
Boothstown M28 77 E7
Bury BL8 27 B2
Eccles M30 79 A4
Farnworth BL4 42 A1
Leigh WN2 56 E1
Manchester M21 97 A2
Sale M33 108 A4
Sale, Timperley WA15 120 B7
Slattocks OL11 47 D6
Stockport SK7 123 F3
Urmston M41 95 C1
Whitworth OL12 4 D3
Grange Rd N SK14 167 C2
Grange Rd S
Compstall SK14 114 A8
Hyde SK14 102 A1
Grange Sch
Manchester M14 98 D3
Oldham OL9 153 B3
Grange St
Failsworth M35 83 D6
Hindley WN2 56 D4
Leigh WN7 75 E3
Oldham OL9 153 B3
Salford M6 154 B2
Grange The
Hyde SK14 167 C1
Manchester M14 98 C2
5 Oldham OL1 67 B8
Westhoughton BL5 57 D8
Grangethorpe Dr M19 110 F7
Grangethorpe Rd
Manchester M14 98 C2
Urmston M41 95 D1
Grangeway SK9 131 D4
Grange Wlk M24 46 E2
Grangewood BL7 25 C7
Grangewood Dr M9 157 A3
Granite St 4 OL1 67 B8
Gransden Dr M8 156 C2
Gransmoor Ave M11 99 F7
Gransmoor Rd M11, M43 99 F7
Grantchester Pl BL4 147 C1
Grantchester Way BL2 25 E1
Grant Cl M9 64 D2

Grantham Cl BL1 . . . . .143 B1
Grantham Ct M34 . . . . .100 F1
Grantham Dr BL8 . . . . .140 A4
Grantham Gr WN2 . . . . .37 F2
Grantham Rd SK4 . . . . .168 C2
Grantham St
  Manchester M14 . . . . .98 B3
  Oldham OL4 . . . . .67 A5
Grantley St WN4 . . . . .73 A5
Grant Mews BL0 . . . . .138 B3
Grant Rd WN3 . . . . .55 A3
Grants La BL0 . . . . .138 C2
Grant St
  Farnworth BL4 . . . . .42 B2
  Rochdale OL11 . . . . .30 D2
Grantwood WN4 . . . . .73 A5
Granville Ave
  Manchester M16 . . . . .97 C2
  Salford M7 . . . . .155 B4
Granville Cl OL9 . . . . .152 C3
Granville Ct
  Manchester M16 . . . . .97 C3
  Newhey OL16 . . . . .32 B3
Granville Gdns M20 . . . . . . .110 A2
Granville Rd
  Altrincham WA15 . . . . .120 C6
  Bolton BL3 . . . . .146 C3
  Cheadle SK3, SK8 . . . . . . .123 C5
  Droylsden M34 . . . . .84 B1
  Manchester M14 . . . . .110 C8
  Urmston M41 . . . . .95 E3
  Wilmslow SK9 . . . . .136 F5
Granville St
  Adlington PR6 . . . . .21 A7
  Ashton-u-L OL6 . . . . .85 D2
  Chadderton OL9 . . . . .152 C4
  Eccles M30 . . . . .79 D3
  Farnworth BL4 . . . . .42 D2
  Haslingden BB4 . . . . .1 A7
  1 Heywood WN2 . . . . .6 E5
  Leigh WN7 . . . . .75 F7
  Oldham OL1 . . . . .48 E1
  Swinton M27 . . . . .79 F8
  Walkden M28 . . . . .60 D4
Granville Wlk OL9 . . . . .152 C4
Graphite Way SK13 . . . . . . .103 F6
Grasdene Ave **2** M9 . . . . . .64 E3
Grasmere Ave
  Farnworth BL4 . . . . .59 F7
  Heywood OL10 . . . . .46 D8
  Hindley WN2 . . . . .56 E4
  Ince-in-M WN2 . . . . .56 B7
  Little Lever BL3 . . . . .43 A4
  Orrell WN5 . . . . .53 F8
  Reddish SK4 . . . . .111 E6
  Swinton M27 . . . . .61 C2
  Up Holland WN8 . . . . .53 B7
  Urmston M41 . . . . .94 E1
  Whitefield M45 . . . . .62 C7
Grasmere Cl SK15 . . . . .86 A4
Grasmere Cres
  Bramhall SK7 . . . . .132 E8
  Eccles M30 . . . . .79 B4
  High Lane SK6 . . . . .125 E1
Grasmere Dr
  Ashton-in-M WN4 . . . . .73 B5
  Bury BL9 . . . . .45 A7
Grasmere Gr OL7 . . . . .84 F4
Grasmere Ho **5** M28 . . . . . .60 E2
Grasmere Rd
  Alderley Edge SK9 . . . . . . .137 A1
  Altrincham WA15 . . . . .120 C6
  Gatley SK8 . . . . .122 B3
  Haslingden BB4 . . . . .1 C8
  Oldham OL4 . . . . .67 C7
  Partington M31 . . . . .105 E3
  Royton OL2 . . . . .48 D6
  Sale M33 . . . . .108 C2
  Stretford M32 . . . . .96 B3
  Swinton M27 . . . . .79 F6
  Wigan WN5 . . . . .54 C7
Grasmere St
  Bolton BL1 . . . . .143 C2
  Leigh WN7 . . . . .75 E5
  Manchester M12 . . . . .99 B3
  10 Rochdale OL12 . . . . . . .14 F1
Grasmere Terr WN2 . . . . . . .74 B8
Grasmere Wlk M24 . . . . .46 F2
Grason Ave WN1 . . . . .131 C1
GRASSCROFT 68 C6
Grasscroft SK5 . . . . .112 C6
Grasscroft Cl M14 . . . . .97 F2
Grasscroft Ind Est
  OL4 . . . . .68 C5
Grasscroft Rd
  Hindley WN2 . . . . .57 A4
  Stalybridge SK15 . . . . .86 A1
Grassfield Ave M7 . . . . .81 C6
Grassholme Dr SK2 . . . . . . .125 A5
Grassingham Gdns
  M6 . . . . .154 C3
Grassington Ave M40 . . . . . . .65 A1
Grassington Ct BL8 . . . . .26 F4
Grassington Dr BL9 . . . . .28 D1
Grassington Pl BL2 . . . . .25 A1
Grassland Rise M38 . . . . .59 E4
Grassmoor Cres SK13 . . . . .171 A2
Grathie Cl BL1 . . . . .142 B1
Grathome Wlk BL3 . . . . .147 B3
Gratrix Ave M5 . . . . .161 B3
Gratrix La M33 . . . . .108 F3
Gratrix St M18 . . . . .99 E4
Gratten Ct M28 . . . . .60 C4
Gravel Bank Rd SK6 . . . . . .113 B6
GRAVEL HOLE 48 D7
Gravel La
  Manchester M3 . . . . .158 C2

Gravel La *continued*
  Wilmslow SK9 . . . . .136 E5
Gravel Wlks **4** OL4 . . . . . . .67 B7
Gravenmoor Dr M7 . . . . . . .155 B2
Grave Oak La WN7 . . . . .76 B1
Gray La
  Failsworth M40 . . . . .83 D5
  Failsworth M40 . . . . .83 E4
Graves St M26 . . . . .43 F6
Graveyard La WA16 . . . . . . .136 A5
Gray Cl
  Mottram in L SK14 . . . . . . .102 F3
  Wigan WN2 . . . . .38 A2
Graymar Rd M38 . . . . .60 A4
Graymarsh Dr SK12 . . . . . . .133 E2
Grayrigg Wlk WN9 . . . . .157 A3
Gray St N BL1 . . . . .145 B4
Graysands Rd WA15 . . . . . . .119 F3
Grayson Ave M45 . . . . .63 B8
Grayson Rd M38 . . . . .60 B4
Grayson's Cl WN1 . . . . .37 C1
Grayson Way OL3 . . . . .69 B6
Gray St BL1 . . . . .145 B4
Grayston Ct SK6 . . . . .126 B7
Graystones Cl WN1 . . . . . . .120 D6
Graythorpe Wlk **5** M5 . . . . .81 A1
Graythorp Wlk M14 . . . . .98 B3
Graythwaite Rd BL1 . . . . .23 F2
Grazing Dr M44 . . . . .94 A3
Greame St M14, M16 . . . . . . .98 A3
Great Acre WN1 . . . . .37 D1
Great Ancoats St M1,
  M4 . . . . .159 C1
Great Arbor Way **11**
  M24 . . . . .46 F1
Great Bank Rd BL5 . . . . .39 D3
Great Bent Cl OL12 . . . . .15 D4
Great Boys Cl M29 . . . . .59 E1
Great Bridgewater St M1,
  M3 . . . . .162 C4
Great Cheetham St E
  M7 . . . . .155 B3
Great Cheetham St W
  M7 . . . . .81 C5
Great Clowes St M7 . . . . . . .155 A1
Great Ducie St M3 . . . . .158 C3
Great Eaves Rd BL0 . . . . . . .138 C3
Great Egerton St SK1,
  SK4 . . . . .169 B2
Greater Manchester Exhib
  Ctr (GMex) ★ M2,
  M3 . . . . .162 C4
Greater Manchester
  Police Mus ★ M1 . . . . . . .159 B1
Greatfield Rd M22 . . . . .121 B4
Great Flatt OL12 . . . . .14 B1
Great Gable Cl OL11 . . . . . . .67 A8
Great Gates Cl OL11 . . . . . . .31 A4
Great Gates Rd OL11 . . . . . . .31 A3
Great George St
  Rochdale OL16 . . . . .139 C3
  Salford M3 . . . . .158 A2
  Wigan WN3 . . . . .150 B3
Great Hall Cl M26 . . . . .44 A4
Great Heaton Cl M24 . . . . . . .64 C7
Great Holme BL3 . . . . .147 C4
  BL6 . . . . .21 F8
Great House Barn ★ 21 F8
GREAT HOWARTH 15 B4
Great Howarth OL12 . . . . . . .15 B4
Great Jackson St
  M15 . . . . .162 B3
Great John St M3 . . . . .162 B4
Great Jones St M12 . . . . . . .165 A2
Great Lee OL12 . . . . .14 D3
Great Lee Wlk OL12 . . . . .14 D2
GREAT LEVER 42 A3
Great Marlborough St 3
  M1 . . . . .163 A3
Great Marld Cl BL1 . . . . .23 F2
Great Mdw OL2 . . . . .31 F1
Great Moor Inf Sch
  SK2 . . . . .124 B4
Great Moor Jun Sch
  SK2 . . . . .124 B4
Great Moor St
  Bolton BL1 . . . . .145 C2
  Stockport SK2 . . . . .124 B5
Great Moss Rd M29 . . . . .77 C2
Great Newton St M40 . . . . . . .83 C5
Great Norbury St
  SK14 . . . . .167 A2
Great Northern Sq
  M2 . . . . .162 C4
Great Oak Dr WA15 . . . . . . .119 F4
Great Portwood St
  SK1 . . . . .169 C2
Great Southern St M14 . . . . . .98 B3
Greatstone Apartments 2
  M22 . . . . .96 E3
Great Stone Cl M26 . . . . .43 D3
Great Stone Rd
  Manchester M16, M21,
  M32 . . . . .97 A3
  Stretford M16, M32 . . . . . . .96 F3
Great Stones Cl BL7 . . . . .8 E2
Great Underbank SK1 . . . . . .169 C1
Great Western St M14 . . . . . . .98 B4
GREAVE
  Rochdale 30 B8
  Romiley 113 D4
Greave SK6 . . . . .113 D4
Greave Ave OL11 . . . . .30 B7
Greave Fold SK6 . . . . .113 D4
Greave Ho OL11 . . . . .30 B8
Greave Prim Sch SK6 . . . . .113 D4
Greave Rd SK1, SK2 . . . . . . .124 C8

Greaves Ave M35 . . . . .83 E6
Greaves Cl WN6 . . . . .35 F8
Greaves Rd SK9 . . . . .136 E7
Greaves St
  Mossley OL5 . . . . .68 C2
  2 Oldham, County End
  OL4 . . . . .67 F6
  Oldham OL1 . . . . .153 C2
  Shaw OL2 . . . . .149 C3
Grebe Cl
  Poynton SK12 . . . . .133 B4
  Wigan WN3 . . . . .54 B4
Grebe Wlk SK2 . . . . .125 A4
Grecian Cres BL3 . . . . .147 C4
Grecian St N M7 . . . . .81 C5
Grecian St M7 . . . . .81 C5
Grecian Terr M7 . . . . .81 C5
Gredle Cl M41 . . . . .95 F2
Greeba Rd M23 . . . . .120 E6
Greek St
  Manchester M1 . . . . .163 B3
  Stockport SK1, SK3 . . . . . .170 B4
Greenacre
  Gatley SK8 . . . . .131 C7
  Wigan WN1 . . . . .37 D1
Greenacre Cl BL0 . . . . .11 E7
Greenacre La M28 . . . . .78 F4
Greenacre Pk BL1 . . . . . . .143 C1
GREENACRES 67 D7
Greenacres BL7 . . . . .9 E6
Greenacres Cl M46 . . . . .58 A3
Greenacres Ct **5** OL12 . . . . .15 A4
Greenacres Dr M19 . . . . . . .110 E4
GREENACRES FOLD 67 E7
Greenacres Jun & Inf Sch
  OL4 . . . . .67 C7
GREENACRES MOOR 67 D7
Greenacres Rd OL4 . . . . .67 D7
Greenacres The
  WA13 . . . . .117 A4
Greenall St WN4 . . . . .73 B5
Green Ash OL3 . . . . .50 C7
Green Ave
  Bolton BL3 . . . . .42 B3
  Swinton M27 . . . . .79 F7
  Tyldesley M29 . . . . .77 A4
  Tyldesley M29 . . . . .59 E5
Greenbank
  Abram Brow WN2 . . . . .74 B7
  Hindley WN2 . . . . .57 B3
  Hollingworth SK14 . . . . . . .103 F5
  3 Horwich BL6 . . . . .22 D1
  Whitworth OL12 . . . . .14 C5
Green Bank
  Bacup OL13 . . . . .3 D8
  Bolton BL2 . . . . .25 E3
  Farnworth BL4 . . . . .42 C1
  Glossop SK13 . . . . .115 F7
  Reddish SK4 . . . . .111 D7
Greenbank Ave
  Gatley SK8 . . . . .122 A5
  Manchester SK4 . . . . .110 E2
  Orrell WN5 . . . . .53 D3
  Swinton M27 . . . . .79 D6
  Uppermill OL3 . . . . .51 C1
Greenbank Cres SK6 . . . . . .125 F5
Greenbank Dr OL15 . . . . .15 F3
Greenbank Ind Est
  WN2 . . . . .57 B3
Greenbank Prim Sch
  OL11 . . . . .14 F1
Greenbank Rd
  Bolton BL3 . . . . .144 B1
  Bolton BL3 . . . . .146 B4
  Gatley SK8 . . . . .122 A6
  Marple SK6 . . . . .114 B1
  Radcliffe M26 . . . . .44 A5
  Rochdale OL11 . . . . .14 F1
  Rochdale OL12 . . . . .15 A2
  Sale M33 . . . . .107 E5
  Salford M6 . . . . .154 B3
Greenbank Sch SK8 . . . . . .123 A1
Greenbank Terr
  Middleton M24 . . . . .47 C1
  Stockport SK4 . . . . .169 B2
Greenbarn Way BL6 . . . . .21 D1
Greenbeech Cl SK6 . . . . . . .125 E7
Greenbooth Cl SK16 . . . . . . .101 F7
Greenbooth Rd OL11,
  OL12 . . . . .13 D4
Green Bridge Cl OL11 . . . . . . .30 F4
Greenbridge La OL3 . . . . .69 B5
Green Bridge N BB4 . . . . .2 E7
Green Bridge S BB4 . . . . .2 E7
Greenbrook Cl BL9 . . . . .141 A4
Greenbrook St 6
  BL9 . . . . .141 A4
Greenbrow Inf Sch
  M23 . . . . .120 F3
Greenbrow Rd M23 . . . . . . .121 A4
Green Building
  Apartments The 3
  M1 . . . . .162 C3
Greenburn Ave WA11 . . . . . . .71 C1
Greenburn Dr BL2 . . . . .25 E2
Green Cl
  Gatley SK8 . . . . .122 A6
  Tyldesley M46 . . . . .58 E1
Green Clough OL15 . . . . .16 B8
Green Common La BL5 . . . . . .58 B7
Greencourt Dr M38 . . . . .59 F3
Green Courts WA14 . . . . . . .119 B4
Greencourts Bsns Pk
  M22 . . . . .131 A8
Green Croft SK6 . . . . .113 D5
Greencroft Mdw OL2 . . . . . . .48 F5
Greencroft Rd M30 . . . . .79 B4

Greencroft Way OL12 . . . . . . .15 D3
Green Ct WN7 . . . . .75 B1
Grendale M46 . . . . .58 E4
Greendale Cres WN7 . . . . . . .76 C4
Greendale Dr
  Manchester M9 . . . . .64 E3
  Radcliffe M26 . . . . .44 B1
Greendale Gr M34 . . . . .113 B8
Green Dr
  Altrincham WA15 . . . . .120 A7
  Bolton BL6 . . . . .40 C7
  Handforth SK9 . . . . .131 D2
  Manchester M19 . . . . .98 F1
GREEN END 110 F5
Green End M34 . . . . .113 B8
Green End Prim Sch
  M19 . . . . .110 F5
Green End Rd M19 . . . . .110 F5
Greenfield Prim Sch
  OL3 . . . . .69 B6
GREENFIELD 69 B4
Greenfield Ave
  Ashton-u-L OL6 . . . . .85 C6
  Eccles M30 . . . . .95 A8
  Ince-in-M WN2 . . . . .151 C3
  Urmston M41 . . . . .95 D2
Greenfield Cl
  Altrincham WA15 . . . . .120 C6
  Bury BL8 . . . . .27 A1
  Newton-le-W WA12 . . . . . . .89 C4
  Stockport SK2 . . . . .170 B2
  Westhoughton BL5 . . . . .40 A1
Greenfield Ct OL10 . . . . .29 D1
Greenfield Ho SK13 . . . . . . .104 A6
Greenfield La
  Rochdale, Greengate
  OL16 . . . . .15 D3
  Rochdale, Lower Place
  OL11 . . . . .31 A4
  Shaw OL2 . . . . .149 B2
Greenfield Prim Sch
  SK14 . . . . .167 B2
Greenfield Rd
  Adlington PR6 . . . . .21 A8
  Atherton M46 . . . . .58 E5
  Walkden M38 . . . . .60 A4
Greenfields WN6 . . . . .37 A4
Greenfield St Mary's CE
  Sch OL3 . . . . .69 C4
Greenfields Cl M27 . . . . .56 F6
Greenfields Cres WN4 . . . . . .73 B4
Greenfield St
  Denton M34 . . . . .100 D7
  Glossop SK13 . . . . .104 A6
  Hyde SK14 . . . . .167 A2
  Rochdale OL11 . . . . .31 A4
  Rochdale Sta OL3 . . . . .69 A6
Greenfield View WN5 . . . . . . .71 D4
Green Fold M18 . . . . .99 F6
Greenfold Ave BL4 . . . . .60 B7
Green Fold La BL5 . . . . .57 E7
Green Fold St BL4 . . . . .59 F8
Greenford Cl
  Cheadle SK8 . . . . .123 B4
  Orrell WN5 . . . . .53 D6
Greenford Rd M8 . . . . .156 A3
Green Gables Cl SK8 . . . . . .122 B1
GREENGATE 15 D3
Greengate
  Altrincham WA15 . . . . .129 D7
  Manchester M3 . . . . .158 C2
  Middleton OL9, M24,
  M40 . . . . .65 C5
GREEN GATE 31 C3
Green Gate SK14 . . . . .113 D8
Greengate Cl
  Bury BL9 . . . . .141 C2
  Rochdale OL12 . . . . .15 D3
Greengate E M40 . . . . .65 D3
Greengate Ind Pk M24 . . . . .65 C5
Greengate La
  Bolton BL2 . . . . .42 F8
  Prestwich M25 . . . . .63 A4
Greengate Rd M34 . . . . .101 A4
Greengate St OL4 . . . . .67 B6
Greengate W M3 . . . . .158 B3
Green Grove Bank
  OL16 . . . . .15 D3
Greenhalgh La PR6 . . . . .21 B8
Greenhalgh Moss La
  BL8 . . . . .27 B5
Greenhalgh St
  Failsworth M35 . . . . .83 C6
  Stockport SK4 . . . . .169 B2
Green Hall Cl M46 . . . . .58 F1
Green Hall Mews SK9 . . . . . .137 B6
Greenham Rd M23 . . . . .108 F2
Greenhaven WN8 . . . . .53 B7
Greenhaven Cl M28 . . . . .60 E3
Greenhead Fold SK6 . . . . . . .113 A1
Greenhead Wlk BL3 . . . . . . .147 B3
Greenhey WN5 . . . . .54 B7
GREENHEYS 59 E6
Greenheys
  Bolton BL2 . . . . .25 E3
  Droylsden M43 . . . . .84 A2
Greenheys Cres BL8 . . . . .10 F1
Greenheys Ctr M15 . . . . . . .163 A1
Greenheys La M15 . . . . .163 A1
Greenheys La W M15 . . . . . .162 C1
Greenheys Rd M38 . . . . .59 E6
GREEN HILL 139 A3
Green Hill OL16 . . . . .15 A7
Greenhill Ave
  Bolton BL3 . . . . .144 B1

Greenhill Ave *continued*
  Farnworth BL4 . . . . .60 C5
  Rochdale OL12 . . . . .139 B4
  Sale M33 . . . . .108 A6
  Shaw OL2 . . . . .31 E1
Greenhill Cotts OL5 . . . . .68 C2
Greenhill Cres WN5 . . . . .71 F5
Greenhill La BL3 . . . . .40 F4
Greenhill Pass **2** OL1 . . . . . .67 A6
Greenhill Prim Sch
  Bury BL8 . . . . .26 F1
  Oldham OL4 . . . . .67 A5
Greenhill Rd
  Altrincham WA15 . . . . .120 C6
  Billinge WN5 . . . . .71 F5
  Bury BL8 . . . . .27 A1
  Manchester M8 . . . . .156 A4
  Middleton M24 . . . . .65 D7
Green Hill Rd SK14 . . . . .102 A3
Green Hill St SK3 . . . . .170 A3
Greenhill Terr
  Middleton M24 . . . . .65 C7
  5 Oldham OL1 . . . . .67 A6
Green Hill Terr SK3 . . . . .170 A3
Greenhill Wlk SK12 . . . . . . .135 D6
Green Hollow Fold
  SK15 . . . . .86 D5
Greenholm Cl M40 . . . . .65 D1
Greenhow St M43 . . . . .99 F8
Greenhurst Cres OL8 . . . . . . .67 A2
Greenhurst La OL6 . . . . .85 E6
Greenhurst Rd OL6 . . . . .85 D7
Greenhythe Rd SK8 . . . . . . .131 C6
Greening Rd M19 . . . . .99 B2
Green La
  Alderley Edge SK9 . . . . . . .136 F1
  Altrincham WA15 . . . . .120 B4
  Ashton-u-L OL6 . . . . .85 B5
  Bolton BL3 . . . . .42 B2
  Compstall SK14 . . . . .114 B8
  Coppull PR7 . . . . .20 A8
  Delph OL3 . . . . .50 E4
  Disley SK12 . . . . .135 D4
  Eccles M30 . . . . .79 C2
  Failsworth M35 . . . . .83 F4
  Glossop, Brookfield
  SK13 . . . . .171 C4
  Glossop SK13 . . . . .115 F3
  Golborne WA3 . . . . .75 A2
  Hazel Grove SK7 . . . . .124 D3
  Heywood OL10 . . . . .29 F1
  Hindley WN2 . . . . .57 B4
  Hollingworth SK14 . . . . . . .103 D6
  Horwich BL6 . . . . .22 B5
  Hyde, Godley Green
  SK14 . . . . .102 A2
  Hyde, Godley SK14 . . . . . .102 A4
  Irlam M44 . . . . .105 E5
  Kearsley BL4 . . . . .61 A7
  Leigh WN7 . . . . .76 C6
  Manchester, Gorton M18 . . .99 D6
  Middleton, Green Hill
  M24 . . . . .65 D7
  Middleton, Higher Boarshaw
  M24 . . . . .47 C2
  Oldham, Moss Grove OL8 . . .66 E2
  Oldham, Top o' th' Meadows
  OL4 . . . . .50 A2
  Orrell WN5 . . . . .53 D3
  Poynton SK12 . . . . .134 C4
  1 Rochdale OL12 . . . . . .139 B4
  Romiley SK6 . . . . .113 B2
  Sale M33 . . . . .107 E6
  Standish WN6 . . . . .36 E8
  Stockport, Heaton Norris
  SK4 . . . . .168 B3
  Stockport SK4 . . . . .168 C2
  Whitefield M45 . . . . .44 F1
  Wilmslow SK9 . . . . .137 B7
Green La N WA15 . . . . .120 B5
Greenland Ave WN6 . . . . .19 E1
Greenland Cl M29 . . . . .77 B6
Greenland La PR6 . . . . .21 D5
Greenland Rd
  Bolton BL3 . . . . .147 C2
  Farnworth BL3, BL4 . . . . . . .42 A2
  Tyldesley M29 . . . . .77 B6
Greenlands Cl **3** SK8 . . . . .131 E8
Greenland St
  Salford, Cheetham Hill
  M8 . . . . .155 C3
  3 Salford, Seedley M6 . . .154 B2
Green Lane Ind Est
  SK4 . . . . .168 C1
Greenlaw St M16 . . . . .161 C1
Greenlea Ave M18 . . . . .99 D3
Greenleach La WN4 . . . . .79 A7
Greenlea Cl WN5 . . . . .53 D5
Greenleaf Cl M28 . . . . .77 F6
Greenleas BL6 . . . . .40 C6
Greenlees St OL12 . . . . .139 C4
Greenleigh Cl BL1 . . . . .24 D5
Greenmans La OL3 . . . . .69 A3
Green Mdw OL12 . . . . .15 D4
Green Mdws
  Golborne WA3 . . . . .90 E5
  Marple SK6 . . . . .126 A3
  Westhoughton BL5 . . . . .57 D8
Green Meadows Dr
  SK6 . . . . .125 F8
Green Meadows Wlk
  M22 . . . . .121 E1
GREENMOUNT 10 E1
Greenmount Cl BL8 . . . . .10 F2
Greenmount Ct BL1 . . . . . . .144 A4

Greenmount Dr
Heywood OL10 . . . . .46 F7
Ramsbottom BL8 . . . . .10 F2
Greenmount La BL1 . . . . 144 A4
Greenmount Pk BL4 . . . . .61 A7
Greenmount Prim Sch
BL8 . . . . .61 C6
Greenoak M26 . . . . .61 C6
Greenoak Dr
Sale M33 . . . . .108 C1
Walkden M28 . . . . .60 C5
Greenock Cl BL3 . . . . .40 E5
Greenock Dr OL10 . . . . .28 F1
Greenough St
Atherton M46 . . . . .58 A1
Wigan WN1 . . . . .151 A4
Greenpark Cl BL8 . . . . .10 F2
Greenpark Rd M22 . . . . . . .109 D1
Green Park View OL1 . . . .49 D2
Green Pastures SK4 . . . . .110 E1
Green Rd M31 . . . . .105 E3
Greenrigg Cl WN6 . . . . .36 F1
Greenroyd Ave BL2 . . . . . . .25 E2
Green Royde OL11 . . . . . . .139 B1
Greens Arms Rd BB3,
BL7 . . . . .8 E7
Greensbridge Gdns
BL5 . . . . .59 E8
Greenshall La SK12 . . . . . .135 F5
Greenshank Cl
Leigh WN7 . . . . .76 B5
Newton-le-W WA12 . . . . .89 C4
Rochdale OL11 . . . . .29 F7
GREENSIDE 83 F2
Greenside
Ainsworth BL2 . . . . .26 C1
Farnworth BL4 . . . . .42 C1
Stockport SK4 . . . . .168 A1
Worsley M28 . . . . .79 A5
Greenside Ave
Kearsley BL4 . . . . .60 F6
Oldham OL4 . . . . .49 E2
Greenside Cl
Dukinfield SK16 . . . . .102 A8
Hawkshaw BL8 . . . . .10 B3
Greenside Cres M43 . . . . . .83 F2
Greenside Ct M30 . . . . .79 D3
Greenside Dr
Altrincham WA14 . . . . .119 E1
Bury BL8 . . . . .28 F8
Irlam M44 . . . . .93 F1
Greenside La M43 . . . . .83 F3
Greenside Pl M43 . . . . .113 B8
Greenside Prim Sch
M43 . . . . .84 A1
Greenside Sh Ctr M43 . . . .84 A1
Greenside St M11 . . . . . . .165 C4
Greenside Trad Ctr
M43 . . . . .84 A1
Greenside View WA14 . . .102 A5
Greenside Way M24 . . . . . .65 C5
Greens La
Bacup OL13 . . . . .3 D7
Haslingden BB4 . . . . .1 C7
Greenslate Ave WN6 . . . . .35 E8
Greenslate Ct WN5 . . . . . . .53 E3
Greenslate Rd WN5 . . . . . . .53 E3
Greensmith Way BL5 . . . . .39 E3
Greenson Dr M24 . . . . .64 E7
Green St
Adlington PR6 . . . . .21 B8
5 **Alderley Edge** SK9 . . . .137 A1
Bolton BL1 . . . . .145 C3
Bury, Walshaw BL8 . . . . .26 F4
Bury, Woolfold BL8 . . . . .27 B4
Eccles M30 . . . . .95 B8
Edenfield BL0 . . . . .1 E3
Farnworth BL4 . . . . .42 C1
Hyde SK14 . . . . .167 B1
Manchester M14 . . . . .110 E7
Middleton M24 . . . . .47 B1
Oldham OL8 . . . . .153 A2
2 **Platt Bridge** WN2 . . . . . .56 B2
Radcliffe M26 . . . . .44 A3
Stockport SK3 . . . . .170 C2
Stretford M32 . . . . .108 C8
Tyldesley, Hindsford
M46 . . . . .58 E1
8 **Tyldesley** M29 . . . . .59 A1
Wigan WN3 . . . . .150 C2
Greenstead Ave M8 . . . . .156 A4
Greens The
Altrincham WA15 . . . . .129 D7
Whitworth OL12 . . . . .4 C1
Greenstone Ave BL6 . . . . .22 B3
Greenstone Dr M6 . . . . .80 F5
Greensward WN6 . . . . .19 B1
Greensway OL2 . . . . .149 B3
Green The
Cheadle SK8 . . . . .131 F8
Glossop SK13 . . . . .116 A7
Handforth SK9 . . . . .131 E3
Marple SK6 . . . . .126 A3
Oldham OL8 . . . . .67 A3
Partington M31 . . . . .105 F4
Ramsbottom BL8 . . . . .10 F1
Rochdale OL11 . . . . .120 C7
Sale WA15 . . . . .120 C2
Stalybridge SK15 . . . . .86 E4
Stockport SK4 . . . . .168 C2
Swinton M27 . . . . .62 B2
Wigan WN5 . . . . .54 B6
Wigan WN5 . . . . .54 C7
Worsley M28 . . . . .78 F5
Greenthorne Ave SK4 . . .111 D7

Greenthorne Cl BL7 . . . . .9 E7
Greenthorn Wlk 6
M15 . . . . .162 C1
Green Tree Gdns SK6 . . .113 B2
Greenvale
Rochdale OL11 . . . . .29 D8
Shevington WN6 . . . . .35 F4
Greenvale Dr SK8 . . . . .122 C6
Green View WA13 . . . . .117 B5
Greenview Chase OL4 . . . .68 B5
Greenview Dr
Manchester M20 . . . . .122 C8
Rochdale OL11 . . . . .30 A8
Green Villa Pk SK9 . . . . . .136 E4
Greenwatch Ct 7 M30 . . . .79 C1
Green Water Mdw
SK14 . . . . .103 D5
Greenway
Altrincham WA14 . . . . .119 A5
Ashton-in-M WN4 . . . . .73 A4
Bramhall SK7 . . . . .132 D6
Horwich BL6 . . . . .22 F3
Hyde SK14 . . . . .167 A1
Middleton M9 . . . . .64 F5
Rochdale OL11 . . . . .30 B1
Romiley SK6 . . . . .113 E1
Shaw OL2 . . . . .31 F1
Wilmslow SK9 . . . . .137 B6
Wythenshawe M22 . . . . .121 E8
Green Way
Bolton BL1 . . . . .25 B4
6 **Mottram in L** SK14 . . . .102 F2
Greenway Ave 9 M19 . . . . .99 B1
Greenway Cl
Bury BL8 . . . . .27 A8
Sale M33 . . . . .107 E3
Green Way Cl BL1 . . . . .25 B4
Greenway Dr OL5 . . . . .68 C2
Greenway Mews BL0 . . . . .11 C4
Greenway Rd
Altrincham WA15 . . . . .119 F8
Gatley SK8 . . . . .131 C6
Greenways
7 **Ashton-u-L** OL7 . . . . .85 A6
Failsworth M40 . . . . .65 D1
Leigh WN7 . . . . .76 B6
Orrell WN5 . . . . .53 D3
Standish WN6 . . . . .37 A6
Greenwich Cl
Failsworth M40 . . . . .83 D4
Rochdale OL11 . . . . .29 F6
Green Wlk
Altrincham, Bowdon
WA14 .119 B3
Altrincham, Timperley
WA15 .120 A7
Gatley SK8 . . . . .122 A6
Manchester M16 . . . . .97 C2
7 **Mottram in L** SK14 . . . .102 F2
Partington M31 . . . . .105 E3
Stretford M32 . . . . .96 B2
Green Wlks M25 . . . . .63 C3
Greenwood Ave
Ashton-u-L OL6 . . . . .85 C6
Horwich BL6 . . . . .22 D1
Stockport SK2 . . . . .124 C6
Swinton M27 . . . . .62 B1
Walkden M28 . . . . .60 C3
Wigan WN5 . . . . .53 D5
Greenwood Bsns Ctr 10
M5 . . . . .81 A1
Greenwood Cl
Altrincham WA15 . . . . .120 D5
Boothstown M28 . . . . .77 E7
Culcheth WA3 . . . . .91 F1
Greenwood Dr
Newton-le-W WA12 . . . . .89 D2
Wilmslow SK9 . . . . .137 D8
Greenwood Gdns SK6 . . .112 F3
Greenwood Rd
Standish WN6 . . . . .19 E2
Wythenshawe M22 . . . . .121 C5
Greenwoods La BL2 . . . . . .25 F4
Greenwood St
2 **Altrincham** WA14 . . . . . .119 D4
Farnworth BL4 . . . . .60 D8
2 **Littleborough** OL15 . . . .16 B5
Oldham, County End OL4 . . .67 F5
Oldham, Fitton Hill OL8 . . . . .66 F1
Oldham, Greenacres OL4 . . .67 C8
Rochdale OL16 . . . . .139 C3
Salford M6 . . . . .81 A4
Greenwood Vale BL1 . . . . .143 B3
Greenwood Vale S 7
BL1 . . . . .143 C3
Greer St M11 . . . . .165 C4
Greetland Dr M9 . . . . .64 F4
Gregge St
6 **Heywood**, Hopwood
OL10 . . . . .29 E1
Heywood, Lane End OL10 . . .46 B8
Greg Mews SK4 . . . . .131 B2
Gregory Ave
Atherton M46 . . . . .58 C5
Bolton BL2 . . . . .42 E8
Romiley SK6 . . . . .113 C1
Gregory Fold BB4 . . . . .1 A7
Gregorys Row WA3 . . . . . . .75 A1
Gregory St
Dukinfield SK14 . . . . .101 E5
Hindley WN2 . . . . .56 C6
Leigh WN7 . . . . .75 E4
Manchester M12 . . . . .164 C2
Oldham OL8 . . . . .66 C3
Westhoughton BL5 . . . . .57 A7
Gregory Way SK5 . . . . .111 F6
Gregson Field SK3 . . . . . .147 B4
Gregson Rd SK5 . . . . .111 E6

Gregson St 4 OL1 . . . . . . .153 C2
Greg St SK5 . . . . .111 E5
Gretley Wlk 2 M14 . . . . . . .98 C3
Grenaby Ave WN2 . . . . .57 B5
Grendale Ave
Hazel Grove SK7 . . . . .124 E1
Stockport SK1 . . . . .112 B1
Grendon Ave OL8 . . . . .66 E4
Grendon St BL3 . . . . .146 C3
Grendon Wlk M12 . . . . .165 A2
Grenfell Cl WN3 . . . . .150 A1
Grenfell Rd M20 . . . . .110 B3
Grenham Ave M15 . . . . . . .162 A2
Grenville Rd SK7 . . . . .124 D3
Grenville St
Dukinfield SK16 . . . . .101 C8
Stalybridge SK15 . . . . .86 D4
Stockport SK3 . . . . .170 A4
Grenville Terr 9 OL6 . . . . .85 D2
Grenville Wlk OL15 . . . . .6 C1
Gresford Cl M21 . . . . .109 A8
Gresham Cl M45 . . . . .62 D7
Gresham Dr OL9 . . . . .152 C3
Gresham St
Bolton BL1 . . . . .143 C3
Denton M34 . . . . .100 F4
Gresham Way M33 . . . . . . .108 A1
Gresham Wlk SK4 . . . . .169 B3
Gresley Ave BL6 . . . . .22 B3
Gresley Cl WN1 . . . . .151 B4
Gresty Ave M22 . . . . .121 F1
Greswell Prim Sch
M34 . . . . .100 E2
Greswell St M34 . . . . .100 F4
Greta Ave SK8 . . . . .131 C6
Gretna Rd M46 . . . . .58 A1
Greton Cl M13 . . . . .98 C3
Gretton Cl OL2 . . . . .48 F4
Greville St M13 . . . . .98 E4
Grey Cl SK6 . . . . .113 A4
Greyfriars WN4 . . . . .72 F4
Greyfriars Rd M22 . . . . . . .121 B2
Greyfriars Wlk M40 . . . . . . .83 B6
Grey Knotts M28 . . . . .78 A5
Greylag Cres M28 . . . . .78 D8
Greylands Rd M20 . . . . . . .122 C8
Greylands Rd M20 . . . . . . .110 B3
Grey Mare La M11 . . . . .83 A1
Greymont Rd 3 BL9 . . . . . . .27 F6
Grey Rd
Altrincham WA14 . . . . .119 C5
Ashton-in-M WN4 . . . . .73 A4
Greysham Ct M16 . . . . .97 E2
Grey St
Ashton-u-L OL6 . . . . .166 C2
Denton M34 . . . . .100 D3
Manchester M12 . . . . .164 B2
Middleton M24 . . . . .46 F1
Prestwich M25 . . . . .63 C4
Radcliffe M26 . . . . .44 B3
Stalybridge SK15 . . . . .86 C1
Greystoke Ave
Altrincham WA15 . . . . .120 D5
Reddish M19 . . . . .99 C1
Sale M33 . . . . .108 B3
Greystoke Dr
Alderley Edge SK9 . . . . .137 A2
Bolton BL1 . . . . .24 E6
Middleton M24 . . . . .46 D2
Greystoke La M35 . . . . .83 D6
Greystoke St SK1 . . . . .112 A1
Greystone Ave
Aspull WN2 . . . . .38 C5
Manchester M21 . . . . .109 F8
Greystone Wlk SK4 . . . . . .111 D7
Greyswood Ave 2
M8 . . . . .155 C2
Greytown Cl M6 . . . . .80 F5
Greywood Ave BL9 . . . . . . .141 B2
Grierson St
Bolton BL1 . . . . .143 B3
10 **Manchester** M16 . . . . . .97 E4
Griffe La BL9 . . . . .45 D4
Griffin Bsns Ctr M7 . . . . . . .81 C5
Griffin Cl BL9 . . . . .141 A1
Griffin Gr M19 . . . . .111 A8
Griffin Ho BL9 . . . . .141 A4
Griffin La SK8 . . . . .131 D7
Griffin Rd M35 . . . . .83 D6
Griffiths Cl M7 . . . . .81 C6
Griffiths St 15 M40 . . . . . . .83 C5
Grimeford La BL6, PR6 . . .21 C5
GRIMEFORD VILLAGE 21 D6
Grimes Cotts 4 OL12 . . . . .13 F1
Grime St BL0 . . . . .11 A4
Grimscott Cl 7 M9 . . . . .64 F1
Grimshaw Ave M35 . . . . .84 A8
Grimshaw Cl SK6 . . . . .113 A4
Grimshaw La
Manchester M40 . . . . .160 C4
Middleton M24 . . . . .65 C7
Grimshaw St
Failsworth M35 . . . . .83 E8
Golborne WA3 . . . . .74 A1
Stockport SK1 . . . . .112 A1
Grimstead Cl M23 . . . . .120 E6
Grindall Ave M40 . . . . .65 B2
Grindleford Gdns 16
SK13 . . . . .171 B2
Grindleford Gr 13
SK13 . . . . .171 B2
Grindleford Lea 14
SK13 . . . . .171 B2

Grindleford Wlk
15 **Gamesley** SK13 . . . . . .171 B2
Grindle Gn M30 . . . . .95 C8
Grindley Ave M21 . . . . .109 D5
Grindlow St M13 . . . . .164 B1
Grindlow Wlk WN3 . . . . .54 C2
Grindon Ave M7 . . . . .81 A7
Grindrod St 1 M43 . . . . .99 E8
Grindsbrook Rd M26 . . . . . .43 F7
Grindsbrook Rd M26 . . . . . .43 F7
Grisdale Ave M22 . . . . .44 A4
Grisdale Dr M24 . . . . .46 E2
Grisdale Rd BL3 . . . . .144 C1
Grisbeck Way 3
OL1 . . . . .153 B3
Grisedale Ave OL4 . . . . .48 C8
Grisedale Cl
4 **Manchester** M18 . . . . . . .99 D4
Middleton M24 . . . . .46 D3
Grisedale Ct M9 . . . . .65 A4
Grisedale Rd OL11 . . . . .30 B4
Gristlehurst La BL9,
OL10 . . . . .29 A5
Gritley Wlk 7 M22 . . . . .121 C1
Grizebeck Cl M18 . . . . .165 C2
Grizedale Cl
Bolton BL1 . . . . .23 F2
Mossley SK15 . . . . .86 F7
Grizedale Dr WN2 . . . . .56 A7
Grizedale Rd SK6 . . . . .113 B4
Groby Ct WA14 . . . . .119 C4
Groby Pl WA14 . . . . .119 D5
Groby Rd
Altrincham WA14 . . . . .119 C4
Denton M34 . . . . .100 E7
Manchester M21 . . . . .109 B8
Groby Rd N M34 . . . . .100 D8
Groby St
Oldham OL8 . . . . .67 A3
Stalybridge SK15 . . . . .86 C1
Groom St M1 . . . . .163 B3
Grosvenor Ave
2 **Golborne** WA3 . . . . .90 D8
5 **Whitefield** M45 . . . . .44 E1
Grosvenor Cl
Walkden M28 . . . . .60 C5
Wilmslow SK9 . . . . .137 A4
Grosvenor Ct SK14 . . . . . .101 C1
Grosvenor Ct
5 **Ashton-u-L** OL7 . . . . . . .166 A1
Cheadle SK8 . . . . .122 D6
7 **Manchester** M16 . . . . . . .97 E3
4 **Sale** M33 . . . . .107 F5
Manchester M7 . . . . .155 A4
Grosvenor Dr
Poynton SK12 . . . . .133 D3
Walkden M28 . . . . .60 C5
Grosvenor Gdns
Newton-le-W WA12 . . . . .89 C2
Salford M7 . . . . .158 A4
9 **Stalybridge** SK15 . . . . . .86 A1
Wythenshawe M22 . . . . .121 E6
Grosvenor Ho
Ashton-u-L OL7 . . . . .84 F1
Manchester M16 . . . . .97 E1
Grosvenor House Mews
M8 . . . . .63 F2
Grosvenor House Sq 8
SK15 . . . . .86 A1
Grosvenor Pl 6 OL7 . . . . .166 A1
Grosvenor Rd
Altrincham WA14 . . . . .119 E5
Cheadle SK8 . . . . .123 C4
Eccles M30 . . . . .79 A3
Hyde SK14 . . . . .167 A1
Leigh WN7 . . . . .75 D6
Manchester, Whalley Range
M16 . . . . .97 D2
Marple SK6 . . . . .125 F7
Pendlebury M27 . . . . .80 B7
Sale M33 . . . . .107 F6
Stockport, Heaton Moor
SK4 . . . . .168 B3
Urmston M41 . . . . .95 C2
Walkden M28 . . . . .60 C5
4 **Whitefield** M45 . . . . .44 E1
Grosvenor Road Prim Sch
M22 . . . . .121 E6
Grosvenor Sq
Sale M33 . . . . .108 A4
Salford M7 . . . . .158 A4
Uppermill OL3 . . . . .69 B8
Grosvenor St
Ashton-u-L OL7 . . . . .84 F1
Ashton-u-L OL7 . . . . .166 A1
Bolton BL2 . . . . .148 A2
Bury BL9 . . . . .44 F8
Denton M34 . . . . .100 D4
Hazel Grove SK7 . . . . .124 D3
Heywood OL10 . . . . .29 D2
Hindley WN2 . . . . .56 D5
Kearsley BL4 . . . . .61 A8
Little Lever BL3 . . . . .43 B4
Manchester M1 . . . . .163 B3
Prestwich M25 . . . . .63 C4
Radcliffe M26 . . . . .43 F4
Rochdale OL16 . . . . .31 C1
6 **Stalybridge** SK15 . . . . . .86 A1
7 **Stockport** SK1 . . . . .170 C4
Stretford M32 . . . . .96 D2
Swinton M27 . . . . .79 C4
3 **Wigan** WN5 . . . . .54 F6
Grosvenor Way
Horwich BL6 . . . . .22 C3
Royton OL1, OL2 . . . . .48 D2
GROTTON 68 B5
Grotton Hollow OL4 . . . . . . .68 A6

Grotton Mdws OL4 . . . . .68 B5
Grouse St OL12 . . . . .14 F1
Grove OL15 . . . . .16 C8
Grove Arc SK9 . . . . .137 A2
Grove Ave
Adlington PR6 . . . . .21 A7
Failsworth M35 . . . . .83 E5
Wilmslow SK9 . . . . .137 B7
Grove Bank OL4 . . . . .68 C5
Grove Cl M14 . . . . .98 C2
Grove Cotts OL3 . . . . .51 D6
Grove Cres PR6 . . . . .21 A7
Grove Ct M33 . . . . .108 D4
Grove Hill M28 . . . . .77 F6
Grove Ho SK8 . . . . .132 B6
Grovehurst M27 . . . . .79 C6
Grove La
Altrincham, Timperley
WA15 .120 A6
Altrincham, Well Green
WA15 .120 B3
Cheadle SK8 . . . . .132 A6
Manchester M20 . . . . .110 B3
Standish WN6 . . . . .36 F8
Grove Pk 6 M33 . . . . .107 F4
Grove Pl WN6 . . . . .36 F8
Grove Rd
Altrincham WA15 . . . . .119 E3
Middleton M24 . . . . .47 B2
Stalybridge SK15 . . . . .86 D4
Up Holland WN8 . . . . .53 C8
Uppermill OL3 . . . . .69 B7
Grove St
Ashton-in-M WN4 . . . . .73 A4
Ashton-u-L OL7 . . . . .84 E5
Bolton BL1 . . . . .143 A2
Droylsden M43 . . . . .99 F8
Farnworth BL4 . . . . .60 E8
Hazel Grove SK7 . . . . .124 E3
Heywood OL10 . . . . .29 E2
Leigh WN7 . . . . .76 B4
Oldham OL1 . . . . .67 B7
Rochdale OL11 . . . . .139 E1
Salford M7 . . . . .155 B1
Stalybridge SK16 . . . . .85 D1
Uppermill OL3 . . . . .69 B5
Wilmslow SK9 . . . . .137 B7
Grove Terr OL4 . . . . .67 E8
Grove The
Appley Bridge WN6 . . . . .18 C2
Bolton BL2 . . . . .148 B1
Cheadle SK8 . . . . .132 A6
Eccles M30 . . . . .79 F1
Glossop SK13 . . . . .171 C4
Golborne WA3 . . . . .74 C1
Ince-in-M WN2 . . . . .151 C3
Little Lever BL3 . . . . .43 B3
Manchester M20 . . . . .110 B1
Sale M33 . . . . .108 B3
Shaw OL2 . . . . .149 A2
Stockport SK2 . . . . .170 B3
Uppermill OL3 . . . . .50 F1
Urmston M41 . . . . .94 F1
Grove View SK9 . . . . .137 B7
Grovewood Cl OL7 . . . . .85 A5
Grovewood Dr WN6 . . . . . . .35 E8
Grundey St SK7 . . . . .124 E2
Grundy Ave M25 . . . . .62 F2
Grundy Cl BL9 . . . . .141 A1
Grundy La BL9 . . . . .141 A1
Grundy Rd BL4 . . . . .60 E7
Grundys Bldgs M29 . . . . . . .77 A8
Grundy's Cl M29 . . . . .77 C5
Grundy St
Bolton BL3 . . . . .147 A4
Golborne WA3 . . . . .90 A7
Heywood OL10 . . . . .46 E8
Manchester SK4 . . . . .110 E2
Walkden M28 . . . . .60 F2
Westhoughton BL5 . . . . .39 E1
Gt Western St M14,
M16 . . . . .97 F4
Guardian Angels RC Prim
Sch BL8 . . . . .27 B3
Guardian Cl OL12 . . . . .15 D5
Guardian St M33 . . . . .108 A5
Guernsey Cl M19 . . . . .111 A6
Guest Rd M25 . . . . .63 A6
Guest St M7 . . . . .76 B5
GUIDE BRIDGE 100 F8
Guide Bridge Ind Est
OL7 . . . . .100 F8
Guide Bridge Sta
M34 . . . . .100 F8
Guide La M34 . . . . .100 F7
Guide Post Sq M13 . . . . . . .164 A2
Guide St M50 . . . . .80 C1
Guildo St
Bolton BL1 . . . . .143 B2
Failsworth M35 . . . . .83 F7
Guild Ave M28 . . . . .60 D2
Guildford Ave SK8 . . . . .132 A6
Guildford Cl SK1 . . . . .124 B7
Guildford Cres WN6 . . . . . . .36 F3
Guildford Dr OL6 . . . . .85 C7
Guildford Gr M24 . . . . .47 C3
Guildford Rd
Bolton BL1 . . . . .142 B2
Dukinfield SK14 . . . . .102 A7
Manchester M19 . . . . .99 B2
Salford M6 . . . . .80 B4
Urmston M41 . . . . .95 E4
Guildford St
Mossley OL5 . . . . .86 D8
Rochdale OL16 . . . . .31 A7
Guildhall Cl M15 . . . . .163 A1
Guild St BL7 . . . . .25 B7
Guilford Rd M30 . . . . .79 B1

Guinness Circ M17 . . . . . . .96 A8
Guinness Ho **2** OL16 . . .31 B6
Guinness Rd M17 . . . . . . .96 A8
Guinness Road Trad Est
 M17 . . . . .95 F8
Guiseley St BL9 . . . . .27 E8
Guilane Cl M40 . . . . .83 C7
Gull Cl SK12 . . . . .133 B3
Gulvain Pl OL9 . . . . .65 F8
Gun Rd SK6 . . . . .115 C2
Gunson Ct M40 . . . . .159 C3
Gunson St M40 . . . . .159 C3
Gun St M4 . . . . .159 B2
Gunters Ave BL5 . . . . .57 F6
Gurner Ave M5 . . . . .161 B3
Gurney St M4 . . . . .160 A1
Gutter End BL9 . . . . .140 C2
Gutter La BL0 . . . . .138 B3
Guy Fawkes St M5 . . . . .161 B3
Guywood Cotts SK6 . . . .113 C3
Guywood La SK6 . . . . . . .113 C3
Gwelo St M11 . . . . .83 A2
Gwenbury Ave SK1 . . . . .112 B1
Gwendor Ave M8 . . . . . . .63 F2
Gwladys St SK5 . . . . .86 E6
Gwynant Pl M20 . . . . . . .110 C7
Gylden Cl SK14 . . . . .102 B5
Gypsy La OL11 . . . . .30 C3
Gypsy Wlk SK2 . . . . .124 C6
Gyte's La M19 . . . . .99 C2

H

Habergham Cl M28 . . . . . .78 C7
Hacienda The M1 . . . . . .162 C4
Hackberry Cl WA14 . . . . .119 B8
Hacken Bridge Rd BL3 . .42 D4
Hacken La BL3 . . . . .42 C4
Hackford Cl
 Bolton BL1 . . . . .144 C4
 Bury BL8 . . . . .27 D5
Hacking St
 Bury BL9 . . . . .141 A2
 Prestwich M25 . . . . .63 A4
 Salford M7 . . . . .155 B2
Hackle St M11 . . . . .83 C2
Hackleton Cl M4 . . . . . . .160 A1
Hackness Rd M21 . . . . . .108 F8
Hackney Ave M40 . . . . . . .65 D3
Hackney Cl M26 . . . . .44 A5
Hackwood Wlk **16**
 M8 . . . . .155 C3
Hackworth Cl WN1 . . . .151 B4
Hadbutt La M29 . . . . .76 F4
Haddington Dr M9 . . . . . .64 E3
Haddon Ave M40 . . . . . . .65 F1
Haddon Cl
 Alderley Edge SK9 . . . . .136 F2
 High Lane SK6 . . . . .134 E6
 Whitefield BL9 . . . . .45 A5
Haddon Gn **31** SK13 . . .171 A2
Haddon Gr
 Altrincham WA15 . . . . . .119 F7
 Reddish SK5 . . . . .111 E7
 Sale M33 . . . . .108 A4
Haddon Hall Rd M43 . . . .83 E2
Haddon Ho M5 . . . . .154 A3
Haddon Lea **32** SK13 . .171 A2
Haddon Mews **30**
 SK13 . . . . .171 A2
Haddon Rd
 Eccles M30 . . . . .95 C8
 Gatley SK8 . . . . .131 C7
 Golborne WA3 . . . . .74 D2
 Hazel Grove SK7 . . . . . .124 E1
 Manchester M21 . . . . . .109 D5
 Swinton M28 . . . . .79 C6
 Wigan WN3 . . . . .54 E3
Haddon St
 5 Ashton-in-M WN4 . .72 F5
 Rochdale OL11 . . . . .30 E4
 Salford M6 . . . . .81 B5
 Stretford M32 . . . . .96 D4
Haddon Way
 17 Denton M34 . . . . . .101 A1
 Shaw OL2 . . . . .149 C4
HADFIELD 104 B5
Hadfield Ave **4** OL9 . . .66 B4
Hadfield Cl M14 . . . . .98 D3
Hadfield Cres OL6 . . . . . . .85 E5
Hadfield Ind Est SK13 . . .103 F6
Hadfield Inf Sch SK13 . . . .103 F6
Hadfield Pl SK13 . . . . . . .116 C8
Hadfield Rd
 Glossop SK13 . . . . .171 B4
 Hadfield SK13 . . . . .104 A5
Hadfield Sq **1** SK13 . . .116 C8
Hadfield St
 Dukinfield SK14 . . . . . . .101 A7
 Glossop SK13 . . . . .116 C8
 Manchester M16 . . . . . .161 C2
 Oldham OL8 . . . . .66 F3
 Salford M7 . . . . .155 B2
Hadfield Sta SK13 . . . . . .104 A5
Hadleigh Cl BL1 . . . . .25 A6
Hadley Ave M13 . . . . .98 E2
Hadley Cl SK8 . . . . .122 F1
Hadley St M6 . . . . .81 B5
Hadlow Gn SK5 . . . . .112 B6
Hadlow Wlk M40 . . . . . . .160 B3
Hadrian Ho M1 . . . . .153 C3
Hadwin St BL1 . . . . .143 C1
Hafton Rd M7 . . . . .81 B6
Hag Mark La SK12 . . . . .135 D7
HAG FOLD 58 C5

Hag Fold Sta M46 . . . . . . .58 C5
HAGGATE 48 C4
Haggate OL2 . . . . .48 C3
Haggate Cres OL2 . . . . . . .48 C3
Hagley Rd M5 . . . . .161 A2
Hags The BL9 . . . . .45 A5
HAGUE BAR 135 F8
Hague Bar Prim Sch
 SK22 . . . . .135 E8
Hague Bush Cl WA3 . . . . .74 E1
Hague Ct **5** M20 . . . . . .110 A5
Hague Fold Rd SK22 . . . .135 F8
Hague Ho OL8 . . . . .153 C1
Hague Pl **8** SK15 . . . . . .86 A2
Hague Rd
 Broadbottom SK14 . . . . .115 A8
 Manchester M20 . . . . . .110 A5
Hague St
 Ashton-u-L OL6 . . . . .85 D4
 Glossop SK13 . . . . .116 D7
 Oldham OL4 . . . . .67 E8
Haig Ave M44 . . . . .105 C4
Haig Ct BL8 . . . . .27 B1
HAIGH 38 B7
Haigh Ave SK4 . . . . .111 E5
Haigh Ctry Pk*W2 . . . . .37 F5
Haigh Hall Cl BL0 . . . . . . .11 B4
Haigh La M24, OL9 . . . . . .47 E1
Haigh Lawn WA14 . . . . . .119 B3
Haigh Pk SK4 . . . . .111 E5
Haigh Rd WN2 . . . . .38 C6
Haigh St
 Bolton BL1 . . . . .145 C4
 Rochdale OL11 . . . . .31 A6
Haigh View
 Ince-in-M WN3 . . . . . . .151 B2
 Wigan WN1 . . . . .37 D2
Haig Rd
 Aspull WN2 . . . . .38 B7
 Bury BL8 . . . . .27 B1
 Stretford M32 . . . . .96 D3
Haig St WN3 . . . . .150 B3
Haile Dr M28 . . . . .77 F6
Hailsham Cl BL8 . . . . .27 C7
Hail St BL0 . . . . .11 A4
Hailwood St OL11 . . . . . . .30 E4
Halbury Gdns OL9 . . . . . .152 A3
Halcyon Cl **6** OL12 . . . .14 B2
Haldene Wlk M8 . . . . . . .155 C2
Haldon Rd M20 . . . . .110 D5
HALE 120 A1
Hale Ave SK12 . . . . .133 D2
Hale Bank BL5 . . . . .39 F1
Halebank Ave M20 . . . . . .109 F7
HALE BARNS 128 E8
Hale Carr WA15 . . . . .120 B2
Hale Cl WN7 . . . . .76 B2
Hale Ct WA14 . . . . .119 D2
Hale Gr WA14 . . . . .72 F5
Hale Green Ct WA15 . . . .120 A3
Hale La M35, M40 . . . . . . .83 E8
Hale Low Rd WA15 . . . . .119 F3
Hale Prep Sch WA15 . . . .119 E3
Hale Rd
 Altrincham WA15 . . . . . .120 B1
 Stockport SK4 . . . . .168 C3
Hales Cl M43 . . . . .83 F3
Halesden Rd SK4 . . . . . . .111 D5
Halesfield WN2 . . . . .57 B2
Hale Sta WA14 . . . . .119 D2
Haletop M22 . . . . .121 D2
Hale View WA14 . . . . . . .119 D2
Hale Wlk **1** SK8 . . . . . .123 A5
Halewood Ave WA3 . . . . . .73 F1
Haley Cl **6** SK5 . . . . . . .111 F8
Haley St M8 . . . . .156 B3
Half Acre M26 . . . . .43 F6
Half Acre Dr OL11 . . . . . . .30 C6
Half Acre La
 Blackrod BL6 . . . . .21 C2
 Rochdale OL11 . . . . .30 B6
Half Acre Mews OL11 . . . .30 B6
Halfacre Rd M22 . . . . . . .121 C4
Half Acre Rd OL11 . . . . . . .30 B6
Half Edge La M30 . . . . . . .79 F3
Half Moon La SK2 . . . . . .124 E6
Half Moon St **19** M2 . . .158 C1
Halford Dr M40 . . . . .83 C8
Halfpenny Bridge Ind Est
 3 OL11 . . . . .31 A6
Half St M3 . . . . .158 B3
Halifax Rd
 Littleborough OL15 . . . . .16 D7
 Rochdale OL12 . . . . .15 C3
Halifax St OL6 . . . . .166 B4
Haliwell St OL15 . . . . .16 C5
Hallam Rd M40 . . . . .83 B5
Hallam St
 Radcliffe M26 . . . . .44 D4
 Stockport SK2 . . . . .124 A6
Hallas Gr M23 . . . . .109 B1
Hall Ave
 Altrincham WA15 . . . . . .119 F7
 Manchester M14 . . . . . . .98 D3
 Sale M33 . . . . .107 C6
 Stalybridge SK15 . . . . . .86 C5
Hall Bank M30 . . . . .79 C2
Hallbottom St SK14 . . . . .101 F5
Hallbridge Gdns
 Bolton BL1 . . . . .25 A3
 Up Holland WN8 . . . . . . .53 B8
Hall Cl
 Mottram in L SK14 . . . . .103 A5
 Shevington WN6 . . . . . . .36 B6
Hall Coppice The BL7 . . . . .8 E1
Hallcroft OL11 . . . . .105 F4
Hallcroft Gdns OL16 . . . . .31 E6

Hall Dr
 Middleton M24 . . . . .64 F7
 Mottram in L SK14 . . . . .103 A5
Hall Farm Ave M41 . . . . . .95 B3
Hall Farm Cl SK7 . . . . . . .125 A3
Hall Fold OL12 . . . . .14 C8
Hallgate
 Westhoughton BL5 . . . . . .57 E5
 Wigan WN1 . . . . .150 C4
Hallgate Dr SK8 . . . . .122 A2
Hallgate Rd SK1 . . . . .124 B8
Hall Gdns OL12 . . . . .14 C2
Hall Grn Wlk M8 . . . . .53 B7
Hall Gr
 Cheadle SK8 . . . . .122 C6
 Manchester M14 . . . . . . .98 D3
HALL GREEN 53 A7
Hall Green Cl
 Dukinfield SK16 . . . . . . .166 C1
 18 Hyde SK14 . . . . . . .53 B7
Hall Green Rd SK16 . . . . .166 C1
Hall House La WN7 . . . . . .76 C4
Halliday Ct **4** OL15 . . . . .15 E4
Halliday Rd M40 . . . . .83 B4
Hallifard Rd M40 . . . . .83 A6
Hallington Cl BL3 . . . . . . .145 C1
Hall i' th' Wood La
 Bolton, Castle Hill BL1,
 BL2 . . . . .25 B3
 Bolton, Hall i' th' Wood
 BL2 . . . . .25 A4
Hall i'th'Wood (Mus)* . . . . . .
 BL2 . . . . .25 A4
HALLIWELL 143 A2
Halliwell Ave OL8 . . . . . . .66 E3
Halliwell Ind Est BL1 . . . .143 A3
Halliwell La M8 . . . . .155 C3
Halliwell Rd
 Bolton BL1 . . . . .143 A2
 Prestwich M25 . . . . .62 F1
Halliwell St W **17** M8 . . .155 C3
Halliwell St
 1 Bolton BL1 . . . . . . .143 A2
 Milnrow OL16 . . . . .31 E7
 Oldham OL9 . . . . .66 A2
 5 Rochdale OL12 . . . .139 B4
Halliwell Wlk M40 . . . . . . .65 D2
Hallkirk Wlk **4** M40 . . . .65 D2
Hall La
 Appley Bridge WN6 . . . . .18 C3
 Bolton BL3, BL4 . . . . . . .42 E3
 Farnworth BL4 . . . . .42 E3
 Horwich BL6 . . . . .39 E7
 Orrell WN5 . . . . .53 F4
 Partington M31 . . . . . . .105 F4
 Pennington Green WN2 . .38 B2
 Romiley SK6 . . . . .113 B6
 Wigan, Lamberhead Green
 WN3, WN5 . . . . .54 A4
 Wigan, Marylebone WN1 . .37 D4
 Wythenshawe M23 . . . . .121 B6
Hall Lane Gr WN7 . . . . . . .56 D8
Hall Le Dr BL5 . . . . .40 A1
Hall Mdw SK8 . . . . .122 E1
Hall Moss Cl SK14 . . . . . .132 C4
Hall Moss Rd M9 . . . . .65 A3
Hall Moss Rd SK7 . . . . . .109 C5
Hallows Farm Ave
 OL12 . . . . .14 D2
Hall Pool Dr SK2 . . . . . . .124 E7
Hall Rd
 Altrincham WA14 . . . . . .119 C1
 Ashton-u-L OL6 . . . . .85 C5
 Bramhall SK7 . . . . .123 D1
 Handforth SK9 . . . . .131 D3
 Manchester M14 . . . . . . .98 D3
 Wilmslow SK9 . . . . .137 A7
Hallroyd Brow OL1 . . . . .153 B4
Halls Cotts OL3 . . . . .69 B7
Hall's Ct SK13 . . . . .104 C1
Hall St
 Ashton-in-M WN2 . . . . . . .73 E7
 Ashton-u-L OL6 . . . . .85 B2
 1 Shaw BL4 . . . . .26 E4
 Bury, Woodhill BL8 . . . . .27 C4
 Cheadle SK8 . . . . .122 D6
 Denton SK14 . . . . .101 B3
 Failsworth M35 . . . . .83 D6
 1 Farnworth BL4 . . . . . .42 D2
 Heywood OL10 . . . . .29 E1
 Ince-in-M WN2 . . . . . . .151 C4
 Oldham OL4 . . . . .67 B7
 Radcliffe M26 . . . . .43 F6
 Ramsbottom BL9 . . . . . . .11 C2
 Royton OL2 . . . . .48 D4
 Stockport SK1 . . . . .112 A1
 Swinton M27 . . . . .61 F2
 Whitworth OL12 . . . . . . .14 D8
 Whitworth OL12 . . . . . . .14 C8
 Wigan WN1 . . . . .151 A3
Hallstead Ave M38 . . . . . . .59 E4
Hallstead Gr M38 . . . . .59 E4
Hallsville Rd M19 . . . . . . .99 C1
Halls Way OL3 . . . . .69 B6
Hallsworth Rd M30 . . . . . .79 A1
Hall The SK13 . . . . .116 A7
Hallview Way M28 . . . . . . .59 F3
Hallwood Ave M6 . . . . . . .80 C5
Hall Wood Ave WA11 . . . . .72 F1
Hallwood Rd
 Handforth SK9 . . . . .131 D2
 Wythenshawe M23 . . . . .121 A6

Hallworth Ave M34 . . . . . .84 C1
Hallworth Rd M8 . . . . . . .156 B4
Hallworthy Cl WN7 . . . . . .75 B1
Halmore Rd M40 . . . . . . .160 A2
Halsall Cl BL9 . . . . .27 F6
Halsall Rd BL3 . . . . .147 B2
Halsbury Cl M12 . . . . . . .164 B2
Halsey Cl OL9 . . . . .65 E2
Halsey Wlk **16** M8 . . . . .155 C3
Halshaw La BL4 . . . . .60 F7
Halsmere Dr M9 . . . . .64 E3
Halstead Ave
 Manchester M21 . . . . . .109 A7
 Salford M6 . . . . .80 E5
Halstead Dr M44 . . . . .94 B1
Halstead Gr
 Leigh WN7 . . . . .76 B5
 Wythenshawe SK8 . . . . .121 F5
Halstead St
 Bolton BL2 . . . . .148 A3
 Bury BL9 . . . . .141 A4
Halstead Wlk BL9 . . . . . . .28 A5
Halstock Wlk M40 . . . . . .157 A1
Halstone Ave SK9 . . . . . .136 E4
Halston St M15 . . . . .162 B2
Halter Cl M26 . . . . .44 A5
Halton **12** OL10 . . . . .29 D2
Halton Bank M6 . . . . .154 C4
Halton Dr WA15 . . . . .108 B1
Halton Ho **4** M5 . . . . . .154 C1
Halton Rd M11 . . . . .83 C2
Halton St
 Bolton BL2 . . . . .148 B3
 Hyde SK14 . . . . .167 C3
Halvard Ave BL9 . . . . .27 F6
Halvard Ct BL9 . . . . .27 F6
Halvis Gr M16 . . . . .97 B3
Hamble Croft M26 . . . . . . .61 B8
Hambleden Cl BL3 . . . . . . .40 F5
Hambledon Cl M46 . . . . . .58 E5
Hambleton Cl BL8 . . . . . . .26 F1
Hambleton Dr **2**
 M33 . . . . .107 D5
Hambleton Rd SK8 . . . . . .131 C8
Hambridge Cl M8 . . . . . . .156 A3
Hamel St
 Bolton BL2 . . . . .148 D3
 Heywood OL10 . . . . .29 B2
 Radcliffe M26 . . . . .44 C4
 Ramsbottom BL0 . . . . . . .11 B2
Hamerton Rd M40 . . . . . .159 C4
Hamer Vale OL12 . . . . . . .15 B2
Hamilcar Ave M30 . . . . . . .79 C2
Hamilton Ave
 Eccles M30 . . . . .79 E1
 Irlam M44 . . . . .105 D4
 Royton OL2 . . . . .48 B3
Hamilton Cl
 Bury BL8 . . . . .27 B3
 Prestwich M25 . . . . .63 A3
Hamilton Cres SK4 . . . . . .168 B1
Hamilton Ct
 3 Little Lever BL3 . . . . .43 B3
 Sale M33 . . . . .108 A4
 Wigan WN5 . . . . .54 E8
Hamilton Gr M16 . . . . . . .162 A1
Hamilton Lo **6** M14 . . . . .98 C3
Hamilton Mews
 Eccles M30 . . . . .79 B3
 Prestwich M25 . . . . .63 A3
Hamilton Rd
 Garswood WN4 . . . . .72 D4
 Hindley WN2 . . . . .56 F4
 Manchester M13 . . . . . . .98 F3
 Prestwich M25 . . . . .63 A3
 Tyldesley M29 . . . . .77 D6
 Whitefield M45 . . . . .62 E8
Hamilton Sq
 Stockport SK4 . . . . .169 B3
 Wigan WN5 . . . . .54 E8
Hamilton St
 Ashton-u-L OL6 . . . . .84 F1
 Atherton M46 . . . . .58 C2
 Bolton BL1 . . . . .24 E5
 Bury BL9 . . . . .140 F4
 Chadderton OL9 . . . . . . .152 A3
 Eccles M30 . . . . .79 B3
 Leigh WN7 . . . . .75 D6
 Manchester M16 . . . . . .162 A1
 Oldham OL4 . . . . .67 B7
 Salford M7 . . . . .155 A3
 Stalybridge SK15 . . . . . .85 F2
 Swinton M27 . . . . .61 F1
Hamilton Way OL10 . . . . . .28 E1
Hamlet Dr M33 . . . . .107 E6
Hamlet The BL6 . . . . .40 B8
Hammerstone Rd
 M18 . . . . .165 C2
Hammer Terr BL9 . . . . . . .11 C3
Hammett Rd **4** M21 . . .109 A8
Hammond **13** OL10 . . . . .29 C2
Hammond Ave
 Bacup OL13 . . . . .3 D8
 Reddish SK4 . . . . .111 E5
Hamnet Cl BL1 . . . . .25 A5
Hamnett St
 Droylsden M11, M43 . . . .83 D1
 Hyde SK14 . . . . .167 A3

Gui–Han **217**

Hamon Rd WA15 . . . . . . .119 E4
Hampden Cres M18 . . . . .165 C1
Hampden Gr M30 . . . . . . .79 D2
Hampden Pl WN5 . . . . . . .36 D1
Hampden Rd
 Prestwich M25 . . . . .63 C4
 Sale M33 . . . . .108 A3
 Shaw OL2 . . . . .49 D6
Hampden St
 Heywood OL10 . . . . .29 D1
 Rochdale OL11 . . . . . . .139 C2
Hampshire Cl
 Brinnington SK5 . . . . . . .112 C5
 Bury BL9 . . . . .45 A8
 Glossop SK13 . . . . .116 F8
Hampshire Ho SK5 . . . . .112 C5
Hampshire Rd
 Brinnington SK5 . . . . . . .112 C5
 Chadderton OL9 . . . . . .152 B1
 Droylsden M43 . . . . .84 A1
 Partington M31 . . . . . . .105 D2
Hampshire St M7 . . . . . . .155 E5
Hampshire Wlk **6**
 M8 . . . . .156 B2
Hampson Ave WA3 . . . . . .91 F3
Hampson Cl
 Ashton-in-M WN4 . . . . . .73 B2
 5 Eccles M30 . . . . .79 B1
Hampson Cres SK9 . . . . .131 C4
Hampson Gn M20 . . . . . . .37 E8
Hampson Mill La BL9 . . . .44 F5
Hampson Pl OL6 . . . . .85 E6
Hampson Rd
 Ashton-u-L OL6 . . . . .85 E6
 Stretford M32 . . . . .96 C2
Hampson Sq **5** M26 . . . .44 A4
Hampson St
 Atherton M46 . . . . .58 C3
 Droylsden M43 . . . . .84 A2
 Eccles M30 . . . . .79 B1
 Horwich BL6 . . . . .22 B4
 Manchester M5 . . . . . . .162 A4
 Manchester, Miles Platting
 M40 . . . . .160 A4
 Radcliffe M26 . . . . .44 A3
 Sale M33 . . . . .108 D4
 Salford M3, M5 . . . . . . .158 A1
 Stockport SK1 . . . . .124 B8
 Swinton M27 . . . . .62 A1
Hampstead Ave M41 . . . . .94 E1
Hampstead Dr
 Stockport SK2 . . . . .124 C5
 Whitefield M45 . . . . .44 E1
Hampstead La SK2 . . . . .124 C5
Hampstead Rd WN6 . . . . .19 D1
Hampsted Ho SK2 . . . . . .124 C5
Hampton Ct SK9 . . . . . . .131 D5
Hampton Gr
 Bury BL9 . . . . .27 F6
 Cheadle SK8 . . . . .122 E2
 Leigh WN7 . . . . .76 E7
 Sale WA14 . . . . .107 F1
Hampton Ho **5** M33 . . .108 C4
Hampton Mews **1**
 SK3 . . . . .123 F4
Hampton Rd
 Bolton BL3 . . . . .42 A3
 Failsworth M35 . . . . .84 B8
 Irlam M44 . . . . .105 D4
 Stretford M21 . . . . .96 F1
 Urmston M41 . . . . .95 D2
Hampton St OL8 . . . . .66 B3
Hamsell Rd M13 . . . . . . .163 C3
Hanborough Cl M29 . . . . . .76 F8
Hancock Cl M14 . . . . .98 B3
Hancock St M32 . . . . . . .108 D8
Handel Ave M41 . . . . .95 A2
Handel Mews M31 . . . . . .108 C4
Handel St
 Bolton BL1 . . . . .143 A3
 Whitworth OL12 . . . . . . .14 C8
Handforth Ho **8** M41 . . . .95 E2
HANDFORTH 131 C4
Handforth Gr M13 . . . . . . .98 E2
Handforth Rd
 Handforth SK9 . . . . .131 E1
 Reddish SK5 . . . . .111 F5
Handforth Sta SK9 . . . . . .131 D3
Hand La WN7 . . . . .75 E2
Handley Ave M14 . . . . . . .98 B1
Handley Cl SK3 . . . . .123 C5
Handley Gdns BL1 . . . . . .144 A3
Handley Rd SK7 . . . . .123 E3
Handley St
 Bury BL9 . . . . .44 B7
 Rochdale OL12 . . . . .139 A4
Hands La OL11 . . . . .30 A7
Handsworth St M12 . . . . .164 A3
Hanging Birch M24 . . . . . .64 B7
Hanging Chadder 48 C7
Hanging Chadder Farm
 OL2 . . . . .48 C7
Hanging Chadder La
 .48 C7
Hanging Lees Cl OL16 . . . .32 C4
Hani Ct M8 . . . . .63 F1
Hani Wells Bsns Pk
 M19 . . . . .111 B7
Hankinson Cl M31 . . . . . .105 E2
Hankinson Way M6 . . . . . .81 A3
Hanley Cl
 Disley SK12 . . . . .135 D5
 Middleton M24 . . . . .65 A5
Hanlith Mews M19 . . . . . .110 F8

Hanlon St M8 . . . . .63 F1
Hanmer St WN2 . . . . .56 D5
Hannah Baldwin Cl
 M11 . . . . .164 C4
Hannah Brown Ho
 WA15 . . . . .119 E3
Hannah Lo M20 . . . . .110 A4
Hannah St M12 . . . . .99 A2
Hannerton Rd OL2 . . . . .49 D7
Hannet Rd M22 . . . . .121 D2
Hanover Bsns Pk
 WA14 . . . . .119 B7
Hanover Cres WA14 . . . . . .98 D4
Hanover Ct
 4 Ashton-u-L OL7 . . . . . .166 A1
 Bolton BL3 . . . . .144 B1
 Swinton M28 . . . . .79 B6
Hanover Gdns M7 . . . . . . .155 B4
Hanover Ho
 Bolton BL3 . . . . .146 B2
 13 Manchester M14 . . . .110 D8
 Oldham OL8 . . . . .153 A2
Hanover Rd
 Altrincham WA14 . . . . . . .119 B7
 Hindley WN2 . . . . .56 C6
Hanover St N M4 . . . . . . .100 E8
Hanover St S **4** M34 . . . .100 E8
Hanover St
 Bolton BL1 . . . . .145 B3
 Leigh WN7 . . . . .76 A6
 Littleborough OL15 . . . . . . .16 A5
 Manchester M4 . . . . .159 A2
 Mossley OL5 . . . . .68 C1
 Rochdale OL11 . . . . .30 C2
 Stalybridge SK15 . . . . .85 F2
Hanover Twrs SK5 . . . . . .169 C3
Hansby Cl OL1 . . . . .48 E1
Hansdon Cl M8 . . . . .156 A2
Hansen Wlk **3** M22 . . . . .121 C2
Hanslope Wlk **14** M9 . . .157 B4
Hansom Dr M46 . . . . .58 A1
Hanson Cl M24 . . . . .47 A1
Hanson Dr M46 . . . . .76 A8
Hanson Mews SK1 . . . . . .112 B2
Hanson Pk M24 . . . . .47 A1
Hanson Rd M40 . . . . .83 B7
Hanson St
 Adlington PR7 . . . . .20 F5
 Bury BL9 . . . . .140 C4
 Middleton M24 . . . . .47 A1
 Oldham OL4 . . . . .67 C7
Hanstock Cl WN5 . . . . .53 E5
Hanwell Cl WN7 . . . . .75 E1
Hanworth Cl M13 . . . . . . .163 B3
Hapsford Wlk M40 . . . . . . .83 A5
Hapton Ave M32 . . . . .96 D1
Hapton Pl SK4 . . . . .169 B3
Hapton St M19 . . . . .99 A1
Harbern Cl M30 . . . . .79 D4
Harbern Dr WN7 . . . . .57 D2
Harbord St M24 . . . . .65 A8
Harboro Cl M33 . . . . .107 F3
Harboro Gr M33 . . . . .107 F4
Harboro Rd M33 . . . . .107 E4
Harboro Way M33 . . . . . . .107 F4
Harbour City Sta M50 . . . .96 F8
Harbour Farm Rd
 SK14 . . . . .101 E5
Harbour La
 Edgworth BL7 . . . . .9 D5
 Milnrow OL16 . . . . .31 F5
Harbour La N OL16 . . . . . . .31 F6
Harbourne Ave M28 . . . . . .78 C8
Harbourne Cl M28 . . . . .78 C8
Harbrook Gr WN2, WN7 . . .75 C8
Harburn Wlk M22 . . . . . . .130 E8
Harbury Cl
 Bolton BL3 . . . . .146 A3
 Wigan WN6 . . . . .36 D5
Harbury Cres M22 . . . . . . .121 C5
Harbury Wlk WN6 . . . . .36 F2
Harcles Dr BL0 . . . . .11 B2
Harcombe Rd M20 . . . . . . .110 C6
Harcourt Ave M41 . . . . .95 F1
Harcourt Cl M41 . . . . .95 F1
Harcourt Ind Ctr M28 . . . . .60 D5
Harcourt Mews **10** BL6 . . .22 B4
Harcourt Rd
 Altrincham WA14 . . . . . . .119 D6
 Sale M33 . . . . .108 A6
Harcourt St
 Oldham OL1 . . . . .67 B8
 Reddish SK5 . . . . .111 F8
 Stretford M32 . . . . .96 E3
 Walkden M28 . . . . .60 D5
Hardacre St WN3 . . . . .151 A2
Hardberry Pl SK2 . . . . .124 E6
Hardcastle Ave M21 . . . . .109 C6
Hardcastle Cl BL2 . . . . .25 C6
Hardcastle Gdns BL2 . . . . .25 C6
Hardcastle Rd SK3 . . . . . .170 A3
Hardcastle St
 Bolton BL1 . . . . .143 C2
 7 Oldham, Mumps OL1 . .67 A7
Harden Dr BL2 . . . . .25 D2
Harden Hills OL2 . . . . .49 D8
HARDEN PARK 137 A3
Harden Pk SK9 . . . . .137 A3
Hardfield Rd M24 . . . . .65 B5
Hardfield St OL10 . . . . .29 D2
Hardicker St M19 . . . . .111 B7
Hardie Ave M43 . . . . .84 A2
Harding St
 Adlington PR6 . . . . .21 B8
 Dukinfield SK14 . . . . .101 D5

Harding St continued
 Manchester, Bradford
 M4 . . . . .160 A1
 Manchester M3 . . . . .158 C2
 Salford, Pendleton M6 . . . . .81 A4
 Stockport SK1 . . . . .112 B1
Hard La OL12 . . . . .15 A8
Hardman Ave
 Manchester M25 . . . . .63 D2
 Rawtenstall BB4 . . . . .2 A8
 Romiley SK6 . . . . .113 A3
Hardman Cl
 Radcliffe M26 . . . . .43 F6
 Rawtenstall BB4 . . . . .2 F7
Hardman Dr BB4 . . . . .2 F7
Hardman Fold BL3 . . . . .42 B2
Hardman La M35 . . . . .83 E8
Hardman Rd SK5 . . . . .111 F8
Hardmans BL7 . . . . .24 F7
Hardman's La BL7 . . . . .24 F8
Hardman's Mews M45 . . . .62 F6
Hardman's Rd M45 . . . . . . .62 F6
Hardman St
 Bury BL9 . . . . .140 C4
 Failsworth M35 . . . . .83 D7
 Farnworth BL4 . . . . .60 E7
 Heywood OL10 . . . . .29 D2
 Manchester M3 . . . . .158 B1
 Milnrow OL16 . . . . .32 A5
 Oldham OL9 . . . . .66 B3
 Radcliffe M26 . . . . .43 F6
 Stockport SK3 . . . . .169 A1
 Stockport SK3 . . . . .170 A4
 Wigan WN3 . . . . .150 B2
Hardman Terr OL13 . . . . .3 D8
Hardon Gr M13 . . . . .98 F2
Hardrow Cl WN3 . . . . .55 B2
Hardrush Fold M35 . . . . . . .84 A6
Hardshaw Cl M13 . . . . . . .163 B2
Hardsough La BL0 . . . . .1 D5
Hardwick Cl
 High Lane SK6 . . . . .134 F6
 Little Lever M26 . . . . .43 B5
Hardwicke Rd SK12 . . . . . .133 F4
Hardwicke St OL11 . . . . . . .30 E4
Hardwick Rd
 Ashton-in-M WN4 . . . . .73 A5
 Partington M31 . . . . .106 A3
Hardwick St OL7 . . . . .84 F7
Hardwood Cl M8 . . . . .156 A3
Hardy Ave M21 . . . . .109 A8
Hardybutts
 Wigan WN1 . . . . .151 A4
 Wigan WN1 . . . . .151 B4
Hardy Cl
 Rochdale OL11 . . . . .30 F3
 Westhoughton BL5 . . . . . . .39 E3
Hardy Dr
 Altrincham WA15 . . . . . . .119 F7
 Bramhall SK7 . . . . .132 D7
Hardy Farm M21 . . . . .109 B6
Hardy Gr
 Swinton M27 . . . . .79 D5
 Worsley M28 . . . . .78 F8
Hardy La M21 . . . . .109 A6
Hardy Mill Prim Sch
 BL2 .25 F4
Hardy Mill Rd
 Bolton BL2 . . . . .25 F4
 Bolton BL2 . . . . .26 A3
Hardy St
 Ashton-u-L OL6 . . . . .85 E6
 Eccles M30 . . . . .79 B1
 Oldham OL4 . . . . .67 A6
 Wigan WN6 . . . . .37 A1
Hardyoard Rd **4**
 M34 . . . . .113 A7
Harebell Ave **10** M8 . . . . .59 F3
Harebell Cl OL12 . . . . .14 D3
Harecastle Ave M30 . . . . . .95 E8
Haredale Dr M8 . . . . .156 B2
Hare Dr BL9 . . . . .45 B4
Harefield Ave OL11 . . . . . .139 C1
Harefield Dr
 Heywood OL10 . . . . .29 F2
 Manchester M20 . . . . .110 A2
 Wilmslow SK9 . . . . .137 B5
Harefield Rd SK9 . . . . .131 E4
Hareford Wlk M9 . . . . .156 C2
Harehill Cl **5** M13 . . . . . .163 B3
Hare Hill Ct
 Hattersley SK14 . . . . .102 C2
 Littleborough OL15 . . . . . . .16 B6
Hare Hill Wlk SK14 . . . . . .102 C3
Hareshill Rd OL10 . . . . .46 C7
Hare St
 6 Manchester M4 . . . . .159 A2
 Rochdale OL11 . . . . .31 A6
 Rochdale OL11 . . . . .139 C1
Harewood St SK14 . . . . . .115 A8
Harewood Ave
 Rochdale OL11 . . . . .13 D2
 Sale M33 . . . . .107 D3
Harewood Cl OL11 . . . . . . .13 D2
Harewood Ct M33 . . . . . . .108 C3
Harewood Dr
 Rochdale OL11 . . . . .13 C2
 Royton OL2 . . . . .48 C5
Harewood Gr SK5 . . . . . . .111 E8
Harewood Lo SK14 . . . . . .115 A8
Harewood Rd
 Hindley WN2 . . . . .56 C5
 Irlam M44 . . . . .94 B2
 Rochdale OL11 . . . . .13 D2
 Shaw OL2 . . . . .49 D8
Harewood Way
 Rochdale OL11 . . . . .13 C2
 Swinton M27 . . . . .61 F2

Harewood Wlk **23**
Harford Cl SK7 . . . . .124 A1
Hargate Ave OL12 . . . . .14 A2
Hargate Dr
 Altrincham WA15 . . . . . . .120 A1
 Irlam M44 . . . . .94 A3
Hargate Hill La SK13 . . . .115 E7
Hargrave Cl M9 . . . . .64 C6
Hargreaves Ho BL3 . . . . .145 B2
Hargreaves Rd WA15 . . . .120 C6
Hargreaves St
 Bolton BL1 . . . . .143 B2
 Oldham, Alder Root
 OL9 . . . . .152 C2
 Oldham OL1 . . . . .153 C3
 Rochdale OL11 . . . . .30 C4
Hargreave's St M4 . . . . . . .159 A3
Harkerside Cl M21 . . . . . . .109 C8
Harkness St M12 . . . . .164 A3
Harland Dr
 Ashton-in-M WN4 . . . . .73 C3
 Manchester M8 . . . . .156 B3
Harland Way OL12 . . . . .14 B2
Harlea Ave M22 . . . . .57 A3
Harlech Ave
 Hindley WN2 . . . . .57 B4
 Prestwich M25, M45 . . . . . .63 B7
Harlech Dr SK7 . . . . .124 D1
Harlech St WN4 . . . . .72 F5
Harleen Gr SK2 . . . . .124 D7
Harlesden Cres **5**
 BL3 . . . . .144 C1
Harley Ave
 Ainsworth BL2 . . . . .26 D1
 Bolton BL2 . . . . .25 E3
 Manchester M14 . . . . .98 E3
Harley Ct M24 . . . . .46 F1
Harley Rd
 Middleton M24 . . . . .46 F1
 Sale M33 . . . . .108 C5
Harley St
 Ashton-u-L OL6 . . . . .166 B3
 Manchester M11 . . . . .99 D8
Harling Rd M22 . . . . .121 F7
Harlington Cl **3** M23 . . . .120 D7
Harlock St M6 . . . . .81 B3
Harlow Dr M18 . . . . .99 D3
Harlyn Ave SK7 . . . . .132 F7
Harmer Cl M40 . . . . .83 B5
Harmol Gr OL7 . . . . .84 F6
Harmony St
 Milnrow OL16 . . . . .31 F6
 Oldham OL4 . . . . .67 A6
Harmsworth Dr SK4 . . . . .111 B5
Harmsworth St M6 . . . . . .154 B2
Harmuir Cl M46 . . . . .36 E4
Harold Ave
 Ashton-in-M WN4 . . . . .73 A5
 Dukinfield SK16 . . . . .101 D8
 Reddish M18 . . . . .99 F4
Haroldene St BL2 . . . . .25 B2
Harold Lees Rd OL10 . . . . .29 F3
Harold Priestnall Cl
 M40 . . . . .83 B6
Harold St
 Aspull WN2 . . . . .38 D5
 Bolton BL1 . . . . .143 A2
 Failsworth M35 . . . . .83 E7
 Manchester M16 . . . . .161 C2
 Middleton M24 . . . . .46 E1
 Oldham OL9 . . . . .153 A3
 Prestwich M25 . . . . .62 C6
 Rochdale OL16 . . . . .15 C2
 Stockport SK3 . . . . .170 B3
 Wigan WN1 . . . . .151 B3
Harper Cl SK3 . . . . .170 B3
Harper Fold Rd M26 . . . . . .43 E3
HARPER GREEN 60 C7
Harper Green Rd BL3,
 BL4 .42 B1
Harper Green Sch BL4 . . . .42 B3
Harper Ho M19 . . . . .98 F1
Harper Pl OL6 . . . . .166 C3
Harper Rd M22 . . . . .121 E7
Harper's La BL1 . . . . .142 B2
Harper Sq OL2 . . . . .149 C3
Harper St
 Farnworth BL4 . . . . .42 B2
 Hindley WN2 . . . . .56 C4
 Oldham OL8 . . . . .66 E4
 Rochdale OL11 . . . . .139 B1
 Stockport SK3 . . . . .170 B3
 Wigan WN1 . . . . .151 B3
Harpford Cl BL2 . . . . .43 A5
Harpford Dr BL2 . . . . .43 A5
Harp Ind Est OL11 . . . . .30 D2
Harp Rd M17 . . . . .96 A8
Harp St M11 . . . . .99 D8
Harp Trad Est M17 . . . . .96 A8
Harptree Gr WN7 . . . . .75 D7
HARPURHEY 157 B3
Harpurhey Rd M8, M9 . . .157 A4
Harpur Mount Prim Sch
 M9 .157 A4
Harridge Ave
 Rochdale OL12 . . . . .14 C3
 Stalybridge SK15 . . . . .86 D2
Harridge St OL12 . . . . .14 C3
Harridge The OL12 . . . . . . .14 C3
Harrier Cl
 Leigh WN7 . . . . .76 B5
 Walkden M28 . . . . .78 D8
 Wythenshawe M22 . . . . . .121 E5
Harriet St
 Irlam M44 . . . . .105 E5
 Walkden M28 . . . . .60 D3

Harriett St
 Manchester M4 . . . . .159 C2
 Rochdale OL16 . . . . .31 A7
Harringay Rd M40 . . . . .83 B5
Harrington Cl BL9 . . . . .45 A7
Harrington Rd WA14 . . . . .119 B5
Harrington St M18 . . . . .99 E5
Harris Ave
 Reddish M34 . . . . .100 B3
 Urmston M41 . . . . .95 D5
Harris Cl
 Heywood OL10 . . . . .28 E1
 Reddish M34 . . . . .100 B3
Harris Dr
 Dukinfield SK14 . . . . .102 A4
 Whitefield BL9 . . . . .45 B2
Harrison Ave M19 . . . . .99 B2
Harrison Cl **4** OL12 . . . . .13 F1
Harrison Cres BL6 . . . . .21 C3
Harrison Rd PR7 . . . . .21 A6
Harrison's Dr SK6 . . . . . . .113 C5
Harrison St
 Britannia OL13 . . . . .4 B8
 Eccles M30 . . . . .95 B8
 Hindley WN2 . . . . .57 B3
 Horwich BL6 . . . . .22 B4
 Hyde SK14 . . . . .113 F8
 Manchester M4 . . . . .160 A1
 1 Oldham OL1 . . . . .153 C2
 Ramsbottom BL0 . . . . .138 C3
 Salford M7 . . . . .158 A4
 Stalybridge SK15 . . . . .86 A2
 Stockport SK1, SK2 . . . . . .170 C3
 Walkden M38 . . . . .60 A4
 4 Wigan WN5 . . . . .54 F6
Harrison Way WA12 . . . . . .89 C4
Harris Rd WN6 . . . . .19 B3
Harris St
 Bolton BL3 . . . . .145 B2
 Manchester M8 . . . . .158 B4
Harrock La WN6 . . . . .18 A5
Harrogate Ave M25 . . . . . . .63 D2
Harrogate Cl M11 . . . . .99 E7
Harrogate Dr SK5 . . . . .111 E8
Harrogate Rd SK5 . . . . .99 E1
Harrogate Sq BL8 . . . . .26 F1
Harrogate St WN1 . . . . . . .151 A3
Harrop Court Rd OL3 . . . . .51 D5
HARROP EDGE 102 E5
Harrop Edge La OL3 . . . . . .51 B5
Harrop Edge Rd SK14,
 SK15 . . . . .102 E4
Harrop Fold OL8 . . . . .67 A1
Harrop Fold Sch M28 . . . . .60 B3
Harrop Fold Sch
 (Longshaw Site) M28 . . . . .60 B3
Harrop Gn OL3 . . . . .51 D5
Harrop Green La OL3 . . . . .51 D5
Harrop Rd WA15 . . . . .119 F2
Harrop St
 Bolton BL3 . . . . .146 A4
 Droylsden M18 . . . . .99 F6
 10 Stalybridge SK15 . . . .86 A2
 Stockport SK1 . . . . .124 A7
 Walkden M28 . . . . .60 D1
Harrow Ave
 Manchester M19 . . . . .111 A6
 Oldham OL8 . . . . .66 E3
 Rochdale OL11 . . . . .30 A6
Harrowby Cl WN5 . . . . .54 E6
Harrowby Ct BL4 . . . . .60 B8
Harrowby Dr M40 . . . . .157 A1
Harrowby Fold BL4 . . . . . . .60 C8
Harrowby La BL4 . . . . .60 C8
Harrowby Rd
 Bolton, Fernhill Gate
 BL3 . . . . .146 A3
 Doffcocker BL1 . . . . .23 F2
 Swinton M27 . . . . .79 E7
Harrowby St
 Farnworth BL4 . . . . .60 C8
 Wigan WN5 . . . . .54 E6
Harrow Cl
 Bury BL9 . . . . .44 F5
 Orrell WN5 . . . . .53 F8
 Wilmslow SK9 . . . . .137 D8
Harrow Cres WN7 . . . . .75 F3
Harrowdene Wlk **6**
 M9 .157 A4
Harrow Dr M33 . . . . .108 A2
Harrow Mews OL2 . . . . . . .149 B3
Harrow Pl WN3 . . . . .55 F4
Harrow Rd
 Bolton BL1 . . . . .144 B4
 Sale M33 . . . . .108 A2
 Wigan WN5 . . . . .36 D1
Harrow St
 Manchester M8 . . . . .64 B1
 Rochdale OL11 . . . . .30 A6
Harrycroft Rd SK6 . . . . . . .113 B5
Harry Hall Gdns M7 . . . . . .81 C3
Harry Rd SK5 . . . . .111 F8
Harry Rowley Cl **1**
 M22 . . . . .121 C2
Harry's Ct **3** WN7 . . . . . . .75 D5
Harry St
 Oldham OL9 . . . . .152 C2
 Rochdale OL11 . . . . .30 A6
 Royton OL2 . . . . .48 E2
Harry Thorneycroft Wlk
 M11 . . . . .164 B4
Harrytown Sch SK6 . . . . . .113 A2
Harrytown RC High Sch
 SK6 . . . . .113 A2
Harswell Cl WN5 . . . . .53 E5
Hart Ave
 Droylsden M43 . . . . .84 B1
 Sale M33 . . . . .108 F3

Hart Cl OL5 . . . . .68 B2
Hart Dr BL9 . . . . .45 B4
Harter St M1 . . . . .163 A4
Hartfield Cl M13 . . . . .163 C2
Hartfield Wlk BL2 . . . . .148 C4
Hartford Ave
 Heywood OL10 . . . . .29 B3
 Reddish SK4 . . . . .111 D6
 Wilmslow SK9 . . . . .136 F5
Hartford Cl OL10 . . . . .29 B3
Hartford Dr BL8 . . . . .27 A6
Hartford Gdns WA15 . . . .120 D5
Hartford Gn BL5 . . . . .57 F6
Hartford Ind Est OL9 . . . . .152 C2
Hartford Rd
 Sale M33 . . . . .107 D2
 Urmston M41 . . . . .95 E4
 Westhoughton BL5 . . . . . . .57 F6
Hartford Sq OL9 . . . . .152 C2
Hartford St M34 . . . . .100 E5
Hart Hill Dr M5 . . . . .154 A3
Harthill St M8 . . . . .155 C1
Hartington Cl **4** M41 . . . . .95 E2
Hartington Ct OL2 . . . . .48 E4
Hartington Dr
 Droylsden M11 . . . . .83 B3
 Hazel Grove SK7 . . . . .133 C8
 Standish WN6 . . . . .36 F7
Hartington Rd
 Altrincham WA14 . . . . . . .119 D8
 Bolton BL1 . . . . .144 C4
 Bramhall SK7 . . . . .132 E6
 Eccles M30 . . . . .79 A3
 Gatley SK8 . . . . .131 D8
 High Lane SK12, SK6 . . . .134 F7
 Manchester M21 . . . . .109 B8
 Stockport SK3 . . . . .124 D5
Hartington St M14 . . . . .97 F3
Hartis Ave M7 . . . . .155 B2
Hartland Ave M41 . . . . .96 A2
Hartland Cl
 Poynton SK12 . . . . .133 D5
 Stockport SK2 . . . . .124 C8
 Tyldesley M29 . . . . .77 B8
Hartland St **3** OL10 . . . . . .29 D2
Hartlebury OL11 . . . . .139 B2
Hartlepool Cl M14 . . . . .98 B3
Hartley Ave
 Manchester M25 . . . . .63 D3
 Wigan WN1 . . . . .151 B3
Hartley Gr
 Irlam M44 . . . . .94 B4
 Wigan WN5 . . . . .54 B7
Hartley Hall Gdns M16 . . . .97 E1
Hartley La OL11 . . . . .30 E3
Hartley Rd
 Altrincham WA14 . . . . . . .119 C5
 Manchester M21 . . . . .97 A1
Hartley St
 Heywood OL10 . . . . .29 D2
 Horwich BL6 . . . . .22 B3
 Littleborough OL15 . . . . . . .16 A5
 Manchester M40 . . . . .157 C4
 Milnrow OL16 . . . . .31 D7
 Rochdale OL12 . . . . .14 B1
 Stalybridge SK15 . . . . .86 D3
 Stockport SK3 . . . . .170 A4
 Wardle OL12 . . . . .15 C6
 13 Wigan WN5 . . . . .54 B6
Hartley Terr
 Rochdale OL11 . . . . .30 E3
 Wigan WN3 . . . . .150 C3
Hart Mill Cl OL5 . . . . .68 B2
Harton Ave M18 . . . . .99 C3
Hart Rd M14 . . . . .98 B1
Hartridge Cl BL5 . . . . .57 F6
Harts Farm Mews WN7 . . .75 F7
Hartshead Ave
 Ashton-u-L OL6 . . . . .85 C6
 Stalybridge SK15 . . . . .86 A3
Hartshead Cl
 Ashton-u-L OL6 . . . . .85 E4
 Droylsden M11 . . . . .100 A7
Hartshead Cres M35 . . . . .84 C6
HARTSHEAD GREEN 85 F8
Hartshead Rd OL6 . . . . .85 C6
Hartshead Sports Coll
 OL6 .85 E7
Hartshead St OL4 . . . . .67 F5
Hartshead View SK14 . . . .167 C1
Hart's Houses BL6 . . . . . . .22 D5
Hartsop Dr M24 . . . . .46 C2
Hartspring Ave **3** M27 . . .80 A7
Hart St
 Altrincham WA14 . . . . . . .119 E5
 Droylsden M43 . . . . .84 B1
 Manchester M1 . . . . .159 A1
 Tyldesley M29 . . . . .77 C8
 Westhoughton BL5 . . . . . . .57 B7
Hartswell Cl WA3 . . . . .74 A2
Hartswood Cl M34 . . . . . . .100 D6
Hartswood Rd M20 . . . . . .110 D6
Hartwell Cl
 Bolton BL2 . . . . .25 C3
 Manchester M11 . . . . .164 C4
Hartwell Gr **2** SK3 . . . . .123 F4
Harty Ho M30 . . . . .79 E2
Harvard Cl M6 . . . . .113 C5
Harvard Gr M6 . . . . .160 D2
Harvard Rd M18 . . . . .165 B1
Harvard St **13** OL11 . . . . .31 A4
Harvest Cl
 Salford M6 . . . . .80 E5
 Wythenshawe M33 . . . . . .109 A3
Harvest Pk BL1 . . . . .144 C4
Harvest Way WN2 . . . . .57 C3

Harvey Cl M11	165 A4
Harvey Ct WA3	74 A1
Harvey Ct	
Golborne WN7	75 B1
Stockport SK1	169 C1
Harvey La WA3	73 F1
Harvey St	
Bolton BL1	143 A3
Bury BL8	27 C3
Ince-in-M WN3	151 B2
Rochdale OL12	15 B2
Stockport SK1	169 C1
Harvin Gr M34	101 A2
Harwell Rd WA14	107 C1
Harwich Cl	
Brinnington SK5	112 C6
■ Manchester M19	99 B1
Harwin Cl OL12	14 D3
HARWOOD	25 F4
Harwood Cres BL8	26 E7
Harwood Ct	
Manchester SK4	110 E2
Salford M6	81 B4
Harwood Dr BL8	27 A1
Harwood Gdns OL10	29 D1
Harwood Gr 28 BL2	25 B1
HARWOOD LEE	25 E5
Harwood Mdw BL2	25 F3
Harwood Meadows Prim Sch BL2	25 F3
Harwood Park Prim Sch OL10	29 D1
Harwood Rd	
Bury BL2, BL8	26 C6
Manchester, Burnage M19	110 E6
Manchester, Heaton Mersey SK4	110 E2
Harwood St	
Littleborough OL15	15 F5
Stockport SK4	169 B3
Harwood Vale BL2	25 E3
Harwood Vale Ct BL2	25 E3
Harwood Wlk BL8	26 E7
Haseldine St WN4	72 F6
Haseley Cl	
Little Lever M26	43 B5
Poynton SK12	133 E5
Tyldesley M29	77 A8
Hasguard Cl BL1	40 F8
Haskoll St BL6	22 D1
Haslam Brow BL9	44 E8
Haslam Ct	
Bolton BL3	144 B1
Manchester M7	63 D1
Haslam Hall Mews BL1	40 F2
Haslam Hey Cl BL8	26 F2
Haslam Park Prim Sch BL3	144 B1
Haslam Rd SK3	170 B2
Haslam St	
Bolton BL3	145 A1
Bury BL9	141 A4
Middleton M24	65 C7
Rochdale OL12	139 A4
Haslemere Ave WA15	129 C6
Haslemere Dr SK8	123 A1
Haslemere Ind Est WN4	73 A8
Haslemere Rd M20	110 C6
Urmston M41	95 B1
HASLINGDEN	1 B6
Haslingden High Sch BB4	1 B6
Haslington Rd M22	121 E2
Haspper Ave M20	110 A7
Hassall Ave M20	109 F7
Hassall St SK5	86 B1
Hassall Way 7 SK9	131 E5
Hassal St M26	44 E5
Hassnes Cl WN3	55 B2
Hassop Ave M7	81 A7
Hassop Cl M11	160 B1
Hassop Rd SK5	100 A1
Hastings Ave	
Manchester M21	109 A8
Prestwich M45	63 B7
Hastings Cl	
Bramhall SK8	123 C2
Prestwich M45	63 B7
Stockport SK1	124 B7
Hastings Dr M41	94 E3
Hastings Rd	
Bolton BL1	144 B4
Eccles M30	79 A4
Prestwich M25	63 C5
Hastings St OL11	139 C1
Haston Cl SK5	169 C4
Hasty La	
Altrincham WA15	129 E8
Hale WA15	129 E8
Wythenshawe WA15	129 F8
Hatchett Rd M22	121 E1
Hatchmere Cl	
Altrincham WA15	120 D6
Cheadle SK8	122 F4
Hatfield Ave M19	110 F6
Hatfield Cl WN3	55 F4
Hatfield Rd BL1	142 C1
Hatford Cl WN2	59 C1
Hathaway Cl SK8	131 B7
Hathaway Ct M7	76 B6
Hathaway Dr BL1	25 A5
Hathaway Gdns BL7	9 B2
Hathaway Rd BL9	45 A3
Hathaway Wlk WN3	55 F4
Hatherleigh Wlk BL2	42 F6

Hatherley Rd M20	110 D6
HATHERLOW	113 A2
Hatherlow SK6	113 A1
Hatherlow Hts SK6	113 A1
Hatherlow La SK7	124 D2
Hatherop Cl M30	79 B1
Hathersage Ave M5, M6	154 A3
Hathersage Cres SK13	171 B2
Hathersage Dr SK13	116 F8
Hathersage Rd M13	98 D4
Hathersage St OL9	152 C2
Hathersage Way 6 M34	113 A8
Hatherton Ct M28	60 D5
Hatro Ct M28	96 A1
Hatters Ct SK1	170 C4
HATTERSLEY	102 E2
Hattersley Ctr The 2 SK14	102 E2
Hattersley Ind Est SK14	102 E1
Hattersley Rd E SK14	102 E2
Hattersley Rd W SK14	102 C2
Hattersley Sta SK14	102 C1
Hattersley Wlk SK14	102 C3
Hatter St M4	159 B2
Hatton Ave	
Bolton BL3	146 A3
Middleton M24	46 E1
Royton OL2	48 D6
Hatton Fold M46	58 D5
Hatton Gr BL1	23 A5
Hatton Ct M32	96 C3
Hattons Rd M17	96 B6
Hatton St	
Adlington PR7	20 F6
Manchester M12	99 A3
Stockport SK1	169 B2
Hatton Terr 24 SK16	166 B1
Hat Works Mus 15 SK4	169 B1
HAUGH	32 C4
Haugh Farm OL16	32 C4
Haugh Fold OL16	32 C4
Haugh Hill Rd OL4	49 E3
Haugh La OL16	32 C4
Haugh Sq OL16	32 C4
Haughton Cl SK6	113 A6
HAUGHTON DALE	113 B7
Haughton Dr M22	109 D1
HAUGHTON GREEN	113 A8
Haughton Green Rd M34	113 B8
Haughton Hall Rd M34	101 A3
Haughton St	
Denton M34	100 F5
Hyde SK14	167 B1
Havana Cl M11	160 C1
Have Ct M6	154 C4
Haveley Hey Prim Sch M22	121 C4
Haveley Rd M22	121 C5
Havelock Dr M7	158 A4
Havelock St OL8	153 C1
Havenbrook Gr BL0	11 A3
Haven Cl	
Hazel Grove SK7	124 C1
Radcliffe M26	43 D5
Uppermill OL3	68 D6
Haven Dr M43	83 E2
Haven La OL4	49 E3
Havenscroft Ave M30	95 D8
Havenside Cl OL4	49 E3
Haven St M6	154 B1
Haven The	
Altrincham WA15	119 F3
■ Little Lever BL3	43 B3
Havenwood Rd WN1	37 B4
Havercroft Cl WN3	54 E3
Havercroft Pk BL1	40 D8
Haverfield Rd M9	64 E3
Haverford St M12	164 D7
Havergate Wlks SK1	124 F5
Haverhill Gr BL2	25 B2
Haversham Rd M8	63 E2
Havers Rd M18	99 E5
Haverty Prec WA12	89 B1
Havisham Cl BL6	40 B4
Hawarde Cl WA12	89 A4
Hawarden Ave M16	97 C2
Hawarden Rd WA14	119 D6
Hawarden St BL1	24 E5
Haw Clough La OL3	69 C6
Hawdraw Gn SK2	124 E6
Hawes Ave	
Farnworth BL4	59 E8
Manchester M14	110 E7
Swinton M27	79 F6
Hawes Cl	
Bury BL8	27 B5
Stockport SK2	124 A6
Hawes Cres WN4	73 B5
Haweswater Ave	
Ince-in-M WN2	56 B7
Tyldesley M29	77 B7
Haweswater Cl M34	100 A2
Haweswater Cres BL9	45 B5
Haweswater Dr M24	46 E2
Haweswater Mews 5 M24	46 E2

Hawfinch Gr M28	78 D8
Hawick Gr OL10	28 E1
Hawk Cl BL9	141 B4
Hawker Ave BL3	147 A3
Hawkeshead Rd M8	156 B2
Hawke St SK15	86 C1
HAWK GREEN	126 A3
Hawk Green Rd SK6	126 A3
Hawkhurst Ct M7	76 B5
Hawkhurst Pk WN7	76 B5
Hawkhurst Rd M13	98 F3
Hawkhurst St	
Leigh WN7	76 B4
Leigh WN7	76 C5
Hawkins St SK5	169 B4
Hawkins Way OL15	6 C1
HAWKLEY	55 A3
Hawkley Ave WN3	54 F2
Hawkley Brook Trad Est WN3	55 C3
Hawkley Hall High Sch WN3	55 C3
Hawk Rd M44	94 A3
Hawkridge Cl BL5	57 F6
Hawkridge Dr M23	108 F2
Hawkrigg Cl WN6	36 F7
HAWKSHAW	10 C2
Hawkshaw Cl	
Hawkshaw BL8	10 B3
Wigan WN2	38 A3
Hawkshaw La 9 M5	81 A1
Hawkshaw La BL8	10 B3
Hawkshaw St BL6	22 B3
Hawkshead Dr	
Bolton BL3	146 A3
Middleton M24	46 E1
Royton OL2	48 D6
Hawkshead Fold SK13	104 C3
Hawkshead Rd	
Glossop SK13	104 E3
Shaw OL2	149 A4
Hawksheath Cl BL7	8 E1
Hawksley Ind Est OL8	66 C3
Hawksley St	
Horwich BL6	22 D2
Oldham OL8	66 C3
Hawksmoor Dr OL2	149 B4
Hawkstone Ave	
Droylsden M43	83 E3
Whitefield M45	62 D7
Hawkstone Cl BL2	25 E3
Hawksworth Dr M23	109 A2
Hawkworth M20	77 B5
Hawk Yard La OL3	69 D5
Hawley Dr WA15	129 B8
Hawley Gn OL12	14 D2
Hawley La WA15	129 B8
Hawley St M19	111 B8
Haworth Ave BL0	11 A2
Haworth Cl BL9	44 F6
Haworth Ct 8 M26	44 B3
Haworth Dr	
Bacup OL13	3 C8
Stretford M32	96 A3
Haworth Rd M18	99 D4
Haworth St	
Bury BL8	26 F4
Edgworth BL7	9 D5
Hindley WN2	56 D6
Oldham OL1	48 E1
Radcliffe M26	44 B3
Haworth Wlk 3 M26	44 B3
Hawsworth M15	163 B1
Hawthorn Ave	
Altrincham WA15	119 F8
Bury BL8	27 C4
Downall Green WN4	72 D5
Eccles M30	79 D3
Edenfield BL0	1 D2
Irlam M44	105 D7
Marple SK6	125 D6
Newton-le-W WA12	89 D3
Orrell WN5	53 F6
Radcliffe M26	44 B1
Ramsbottom BL0	11 A2
Standish WN1	37 B6
Urmston M41	95 F1
Walkden M28	60 E1
Wigan WN5	54 B6
Wilmslow SK9	137 A7
Hawthorn Bank	
Bolton BL2	25 E4
Glossop SK13	171 C4
Hawthorn Cl	
Altrincham WA15	119 F7
Billinge WN5	71 D5
Tyldesley M29	59 D1
Hawthorn Cres	
Bury BL8	26 F7
Oldham OL8	66 F4
Shaw OL2	149 B2
Hawthorn Ct SK8	122 F3
Hawthornden 1 M20	110 A3
Hawthorn Dr	
Irlam M44	105 D5
Manchester M19	110 F7
Pendlebury M27	80 C7
Salford M6	80 B4
Stalybridge SK15	101 F8
Hawthorne Ave	
Farnworth BL4	60 B7
Fowley Common WA3	92 C4
Horwich BL6	22 C4
Hawthorne Ct M28	20 F8
Hawthorne Dr M28	79 A7

Hawthorne Gr	
■ Ashton-u-L OL7	84 F1
Chadderton OL9	152 B4
Leigh WN7	75 E7
Poynton SK12	134 C4
Romiley SK6	112 E4
Hawthorne La OL16	32 A3
Hawthorne Rd BL3	146 B4
Hawthorne St BL3	144 C1
Hawthorn Gn SK9	137 A7
Hawthorn Gr	
Bramhall SK7	132 C6
Hollingworth SK14	103 D6
Hyde SK14	167 A1
Stockport SK4	168 B3
Wilmslow SK9	137 B7
Hawthorn La	
Sale M33	107 D6
Stretford M21	108 F8
Wilmslow SK9	137 A7
Hawthorn Lo SK3	123 F4
Hawthorn Pk SK9	137 A7
Hawthorn Rd	
Altrincham WA15	119 E3
Droylsden M43	84 C2
Failsworth M40	65 F1
Gatley SK8	122 A5
Kearsley BL4	61 B5
Manchester SK4	110 F2
Reddish M34	100 B4
Rochdale OL11	29 E6
Stretford M21, M32	108 E8
Westhoughton BL5	57 F7
Hawthorn Rd S M43	84 C2
Hawthorns Com Sch M34	100 E5
Hawthorn St	
Denton M34	100 E6
Manchester M18	99 E5
Wilmslow SK9	137 A6
Hawthorns The	
6 Atherton M46	58 D3
Denton M34	100 D6
Hawthorn Terr	
10 Mossley OL5	68 C2
Stockport SK4	168 B3
Wilmslow SK9	137 A6
Hawthorn View	
Lindow End WA16	136 B2
Wilmslow SK9	137 A7
Hawthorn Wlk	
Littleborough OL15	15 F5
3 Partington M31	105 E3
Hawthorpe Gr OL3	69 B8
Haxby Rd M18	99 D3
Haxey Wlk BL6	21 F3
Hayburn Rd M23	121 B7
Hayburn Rd SK2	124 C8
Haycock Cl SK15	102 E7
Haycroft SK8	131 E6
Hayden Ct	
■ Glossop SK13	104 C1
Manchester M40	157 A1
Haydn Ave M14	98 B4
Haydn Fold SK13	115 D7
HAYDOCK	89 A8
Haydock Ave M33	107 B2
Haydock Cl M32	96 F4
Haydock Dr	
Altrincham WA15	120 B5
Hazel Grove SK7	124 F2
Worsley M28	78 B6
Haydock La	
Ashton-in-M WA11	72 E1
Bolton BL7	25 A8
Haydock Lane Ind Est WA11	72 F1
Haydock Mews 3 M7	155 A2
Haydock Park Gdns WA12	73 B1
Haydock Park Race Course WA12	73 D1
Haydock St	
Ashton-in-M WN4	73 B2
Bolton BL1	145 C4
Newton-le-W WA12	89 C3
Haydock Wlk OL9	152 C3
Haye's Rd M44	105 E5
Hayes Row WN4	75 A1
Hayes St	
Leigh, Plank Lane WN7	75 A4
Leigh, Westleigh WN7	75 B4
Hayeswater Circ 7 M41	95 C3
Hayeswater Rd M41	95 C3
Hayfield Rd WN3	55 A1
Hayfield Ave	
Romiley SK6	113 A4
Tyldesley M29	77 C6
Hayfield Cl	
Manchester M12	164 B3
Middleton M24	47 C3
Oldham OL4	49 F4
Ramsbottom BL8	10 F1
Hayfield Rd	
New Mills SK22	127 E2
Romiley SK6	113 A4
Salford M6	80 D4
Hayfield St M33	108 B5
Hayfield Wlk	
Altrincham WA15	120 C6
Denton M34	113 A8
Haygrove Wlk 10 M9	157 A4
Hay Ho OL4	67 E8
Hayle Rd OL1	49 D4

Hayley St M12, M13	98 E4
Hayling Cl BL8	27 C6
Hayling Rd M33	107 E5
Haymaker Rise OL12	15 D6
Hayman Ave WN7	75 D2
Haymans Wlk M13	163 B3
Haymarket Cl M13	163 C1
Haymarket St BL9	140 F2
Haymill Ave M38	60 A6
Haymond Cl M6	81 A5
Haynes St	
Bolton BL3	146 C3
Rochdale OL12	139 C4
Haysbrook Ave M28	60 A4
Haysbrook Cl OL7	85 A7
Hayside Way BL9	140 C1
Haythorp Ave M22	121 E1
Hayward Ave BL3	43 C3
Hayward Gr WN6	19 D2
Hayward St BL8	147 A2
Haywards Cl SK13	104 C3
Hayward St BL8	27 C3
Hayward Way 2 SK14	102 F3
Haywood Cl WA3	74 E1
Hazel Ave	
Ashton-u-L OL6	85 E6
Bury BL9	141 B2
Bury, Tottington BL8	27 A5
Cheadle SK8	122 E5
Kearsley M26	61 A8
Manchester M16	97 D2
Newhey OL16	32 A3
Pendlebury M27	80 A7
Ramsbottom BL0	11 B1
Romiley SK6	113 D2
Sale M33	108 B3
Walkden M38	59 E5
Westhoughton BL5	57 F7
Wigan WN6	37 A3
Hazelbadge Cl SK12	133 C4
Hazelbadge Rd SK12	133 C4
Hazelbank Ave M20	110 B7
Hazelbottom Rd M8	156 C3
Hazel Cl	
Droylsden M43	84 C2
Marple SK6	125 E4
Hazel Cl 12 M16	97 D3
Hazeldean Ct 17 SK9	131 E1
Hazeldene SK5	57 D5
Hazel-Dene Cl BL9	44 F7
Hazeldene Rd M40	65 E1
Hazel Dr	
Gatley M22	131 A8
Poynton SK12	133 F3
Stockport SK2	124 D6
Hazelfields M28	79 C7
Hazel Gr	
Chadderton OL9	152 B4
Farnworth BL4	60 B8
Golborne WA3	90 B8
Leigh WN7	75 E7
Radcliffe M26	61 F8
Salford M5	80 C2
Urmston M41	95 E2
HAZEL GROVE	124 E2
Hazel Grove High Sch SK7	133 C8
Hazel Grove Prim Sch SK7	124 E3
Hazel Grove Sta SK7	124 D2
Hazelhall Cl M28	79 B7
HAZELHURST	
Ashton-under-Lyne	85 F6
Ramsbottom	11 B4
Swinton	79 B7
Hazelhurst Cl	
Bolton BL1	143 B2
Ramsbottom BL0	11 B4
Hazelhurst Com Prim Sch BL0	11 A4
Hazelhurst Dr M28	46 F4
Hazelhurst Fold M28	79 C7
Hazelhurst Mews OL9	65 F3
Hazelhurst Rd	
Ashton-u-L OL6	85 F6
Stalybridge SK15	86 A4
Swinton M27, M28	79 C7
Hazelhurst Wlk 7 M23	108 F2
Hazel La OL8	66 D2
Hazelmere Ave M30	79 C4
Hazelmere Gdns WN2	56 E4
Hazel Mount BL7	8 E2
Hazel Rd	
Altrincham WA14	119 D6
Atherton M46	58 C4
Cheadle SK8	123 B1
Middleton M24	47 B2
Stalybridge SK15	86 C3
Whitefield M45	63 B8
Hazel St	
Denton M34	100 E6
Hazel Grove SK7	124 E3
Ramsbottom BL0	11 A4
Hazelton Cl WN7	75 E1
Hazel View SK6	125 F3
Hazelwell M33	108 C3
Hazel Wlk M31	105 E3
Hazelwood OL9	65 E8
Hazelwood Ave BL2	25 E3
Hazelwood Cl SK14	102 A2
Hazelwood Ct M41	95 D3

Hazelwood Dr
Bury BL9 . . . .**27** F7
Denton M34. . . . .**100** F6
Hazelwood Rd
Altrincham WA15. . . . .**119** E2
Bolton BL1. . . . .**142** B2
Hazel Grove SK7 . . . .**124** F3
Stockport SK2 . . . .**124** A4
Wigan WN1 . . . .**37** B4
Wilmslow SK9 . . . .**137** D8
Wythenshawe M22 . . . .**130** D8
Hazlehurst Gr WN4 . . . . . .**73** C4
Hazlemere BL4 . . . .**61** A7
Headen Ave WN5. . . . .**54** B5
Headingley Dr M16 . . . .**97** A3
Headingley Rd **110** D7
Headingley Way BL3. . . . . .**147** A3
Headland Cl WA3. . . . .**90** E6
Headlands Dr M25. . . . .**63** A1
Headlands Rd SK7. . . . .**123** F1
Headlands St OL12 . . . .**14** C1
HEADY HILL. **29** A2
Heady Hill Cl OL10. . . . . . .**29** A1
Heady Hill Ct OL10. . . . . . .**29** A2
Heady Hill Rd OL10. . . . . . .**29** A2
Heald Ave M14 . . . .**98** B3
Heald Cl
Altrincham WA14. . . . .**119** C2
Littleborough OL15 . . . .**16** A3
Rochdale OL12. . . . .**14** C3
Heald Dr
Altrincham WA14. . . . .**119** C2
Rochdale OL12. . . . .**14** C3
Heald Gr
Gatley SK8 . . . .**122** A1
Manchester M14 . . . .**98** B4
HEALD GREEN **131** B8
Heald Green Sta M22 . . . .**131** A8
Heald La OL15 . . . .**16** A3
Heald Pl M14. . . . .**98** B3
Heald Place Prim Sch
M14 . . . .**98** B3
Heald Rd WA14 . . . .**119** C2
Healds Gn OL1 . . . .**47** F3
HEALDS GREEN **47** F3
Healdwood Rd SK6 . . . . . .**113** C4
Healey Ave
Heywood OL10. . . . .**29** E3
Rochdale OL12. . . . .**14** D4
Healey Cl
Salford M7 . . . .**81** C8
Wythenshawe M23 . . . . . .**108** A2
Wythenshawe M23 . . . . . .**109** A2
Healey Dell Cotts OL12. . .**14** B4
Healey Dell Nature
Reserve* OL12. . . . .**14** B6
Healey Gr OL12. . . . .**14** C5
Healey Hall Farm OL12. . . .**14** C4
Healey Hall Mews
OL12. . . . .**14** C4
Healey La OL12 . . . .**14** E3
Healey Prim Sch OL12 . . . .**14** E3
Healey St OL16 . . . .**139** B2
Healey Stones OL12. . . . . .**14** E4
Healing St BL9 OL11 . . . . . .**31** A5
Heanor Ave M34. . . . .**113** A8
HEAP BRIDGE **141** C1
Heap Bridge Village Prim
Sch BL9 . . . .**28** D1
Heap Brow BL9. . . . .**28** D1
Heape St OL11 . . . .**30** C1
Heapfold OL12 . . . .**14** B2
Heaplands BL8 . . . .**10** F1
Heap Rd OL12 . . . .**13** D2
Heap St
Bolton BL3. . . . .**147** B4
Heywood BL9. . . . .**28** D1
Oldham OL4 . . . .**67** C7
Radcliffe M26 . . . .**44** B3
Whitefield M45 . . . .**62** F7
Heapworth Ave BL0. . . . . .**138** B2
Heapy Cl BL8. . . . .**26** F1
Heardman Ave 1 WN6. . . .**37** A1
Heath Ave
Ramsbottom BL0. . . . .**11** B1
Salford M7 . . . .**81** C4
Urmston M41. . . . .**95** E3
Heathbank Rd
Cheadle SK8 . . . .**131** F8
Manchester M9 . . . .**64** C5
Stockport SK3 . . . .**123** B7
Heathbourne Rd OL13 . . . .**3** C8
Heath Cl BL3 . . . .**146** B2
Heathcote Ave SK4 . . . . . .**168** C3
Heathcote Cotts SK6. . . .**113** C11
Heathcote Rd M18. . . . .**99** C4
Heath Cres SK2 . . . .**170** C1
Heather Ave
Droylsden M43. . . . .**84** C2
Irlam M44 . . . .**105** D6
Shaw OL2. . . . .**49** D8
Heather Bank
Bury BL8 . . . .**26** E7
Littleborough OL15 . . . .**16** D6
Rawtenstall BB4 . . . .**1** F8
Heather Bank Cl
SK13. . . . .**116** A7
Heather Brae WA12. . . . . . .**89** A4
Heather Brow SK15. . . . . .**102** E2
Heather Cl
Haslingden BB4 . . . .**1** A8
Heywood OL10. . . . .**46** D8

Heather Cl *continued*
Horwich BL6 . . . .**22** B4
Oldham OL4 . . . .**49** E1
Heather Ct SK4 . . . .**111** D5
Heatherdale Dr M8 . . . . . .**156** A2
Heatherfield
Bolton BL1. . . . .**24** D5
Edgworth BL7 . . . .**9** E6
Heatherfield Ct SK9 . . . . .**137** E8
Heather Gr
Ashton-in-M WN4 . . . .**73** E4
Droylsden M43. . . . .**100** B8
Hollingworth SK14. . . . . . .**103** D6
Leigh WN7 . . . .**75** E7
Wigan WN5 . . . .**54** E6
Heatherlands OL12 . . . .**4** D4
Heather Lea M34 . . . .**101** A2
Heatherlea Cl WN8 . . . .**53** C7
Heather Rd WA14,
WA15 . . . .**119** E1
Heatherside
Reddish SK5 . . . .**100** A1
Stalybridge SK15. . . . .**86** D2
Heatherside Ave OL6 . . . . .**68** E1
Heatherside Rd BL0 . . . . .**138** C3
Heather St M11 . . . .**83** B2
Heather The SK2. . . . .**124** B4
Heatherway
Manchester M14 . . . .**98** B4
Sale M33 . . . .**107** D5
Heather Way
Diggle OL3. . . . .**51** C4
Marple SK6 . . . .**125** E6
Heather Wlk M31. . . . .**105** E3
Heath Farm La M31. . . . . .**106** B3
Heathfield
Bolton BL2. . . . .**25** F3
Eccles M28 . . . .**78** F5
Farnworth BL4. . . . .**42** E1
Wilmslow SK9 . . . .**137** A5
Heathfield Ave
Bacup OL13 . . . .**3** C8
Denton M34. . . . .**100** D1
Gatley SK8 . . . .**122** B5
Manchester SK4 . . . .**111** C5
Heathfield Cl M33 . . . . . .**108** F4
Heathfield Dr
Bolton BL2. . . . .**146** B2
Pendlebury M27 . . . .**80** A7
Tyldesley M29 . . . .**59** D1
Heathfield Prim Sch
BL3. . . . .**146** A2
Heathfield Rd
Bacup OL13 . . . .**3** C8
Stockport SK2 . . . .**170** C2
Whitefield BL9, M45 . . . . . .**44** F3
Heathfields
Altrincham WA14. . . . .**119** C3
Uppermill OL3 . . . .**69** C8
Heathfields Sq OL3 . . . . . .**69** C8
Heathfield St M40 . . . .**83** C5
Heath Gdns WN2 . . . .**57** C3
Heath Hill Dr OL13. . . . .**3** C8
Heath La
Culcheth WA3 . . . .**91** A1
Golborne WA3 . . . .**90** F2
Leigh WN7 . . . .**75** B5
Heathland
Whitwell M8. . . . .**53** B7
Heathland Rd M7, M25 . . . .**81** B8
Heathlands Dr M25. . . . . . .**63** A1
Heathland Terr SK3 . . . . .**170** B3
Heathlea WN2 . . . .**57** C2
Heathlea Cl BL1 . . . .**24** E6
Heathmoor Ave WA3. . . . . .**90** D6
Heath Rd
Altrincham, Rosehill
WA14 . . . .**119** D2
Altrincham, Timperley
WA15 . . . .**119** F8
Ashton-in-M WN4 . . . .**73** C2
Glossop SK13. . . . .**104** D2
Stockport SK2, SK3 . . . . . .**170** C2
Wardle OL12 . . . .**15** C6
Heathside Gr M28 . . . .**60** E3
Heathside Park Rd
SK3. . . . .**122** F7
Heathside Rd
Cheadle SK3 . . . .**123** A7
Manchester M20 . . . .**110** D6
Heath St
Ashton-in-M WN4 . . . .**73** C2
Golborne WA3 . . . .**90** A8
Rochdale OL11. . . . .**139** A2
Salford M8 . . . .**155** C3
Heath The
Ashton-u-L OL7 . . . .**85** A7
Glossop SK13. . . . .**104** C3
Middleton M24 . . . .**65** B6
Heath View M7. . . . .**81** A8
Heathway Ave M11 . . . .**83** D2
Heathwood OL3 . . . .**69** C8
Heathwood Rd M19. . . . . . .**110** E4
HEATLEY **117** C5
Heatley Cl
Lymm WA13. . . . .**117** A4
Reddish M34 . . . .**100** B2
Heatley Rd OL16. . . . .**31** D6
Heatley Way 5 SK9. . . . . .**131** D4
HEATON. **144** A4
Heaton Ave
Bolton, Harwood Lee
BL2. . . . .**25** E5
Doffocker BL1. . . . .**23** F1
Farnworth BL4. . . . .**60** C8
Little Lever BL3. . . . .**43** A4
Stockport SK7 . . . .**123** E3
HEATON CHAPEL **111** C6

Heaton Chapel Sta
SK4. . . . .**111** C5
Heaton Cl
Stockport SK4 . . . .**168** A3
Up Holland WN8 . . . .**53** A7
Whitefield BL9. . . . .**45** A5
Heaton Court Gdns
BL1. . . . .**40** E7
Heaton Ct
Bury BL9 . . . .**44** E7
Prestwich M25. . . . .**63** C3
Stockport SK4 . . . .**168** B4
Heaton Dr BL9 . . . .**45** A5
Heaton Fold BL9. . . . .**44** E8
Heaton Grange Dr
BL1. . . . .**144** A3
Heaton Hall* M25. . . . .**63** E5
Heaton La SK4 . . . .**169** B1
HEATON MERSEY **110** E2
HEATON MOOR **168** B4
Heaton Moor Rd SK4 . . . .**168** B4
HEATON NORRIS **168** C2
HEATON PARK **63** D6
Heaton Park Prim Sch
M45 . . . .**63** B6
Heaton Park Rd M9 . . . . . .**64** A5
Heaton Park Rd W M9 . . . .**64** A5
Heaton Park Sta **63** C4
Heaton Park Pk* M25 . . . . .**63** E5
Heaton Rd
Bolton BL6. . . . .**40** D6
Little Lever BL2. . . . .**43** B5
Manchester, Withington
M20 . . . .**110** C6
Stockport, Heaton Norris
SK4. . . . .**168** C3
Stockport SK4 . . . .**169** A3
Heaton Sch SK4 . . . .**111** B5
Heatons Gr BL5. . . . .**40** A2
Heaton St
Aspull WN2 . . . .**38** D5
Denton M34. . . . .**100** D3
Ince-in-M WN3 . . . .**151** B2
Middleton M24 . . . .**64** F8
Milnrow OL16. . . . .**32** A5
Prestwich M25. . . . .**63** C4
Salford M7 . . . .**155** B3
Standish WN6 . . . .**19** E1
Wigan WN1 . . . .**37** C2
Heaton Twrs SK4 . . . .**169** B2
HEAVILEY **124** A7
Heaviley Gr
Horwich BL6 . . . .**22** A5
Stockport SK2 . . . .**124** A6
Hebble Butt Cl OL16 . . . . . .**31** E6
Hebble Cl BL2 . . . .**25** B5
Hebburn Dr BL8 . . . .**27** C5
Hebden Ave
Fowley Common WA3 . . . . . .**92** B5
Romiley SK6. . . . .**113** A4
Salford M5, M6. . . . .**80** C3
Hebden Cl BL1 . . . .**145** B4
Hebden Dr SK13. . . . .**116** F8
Hebden Wlk 8 M15 . . . . . .**162** C1
Hebdon Cl WN4 . . . .**73** A5
Heber Pl 10 OL15 . . . .**16** B5
Heber St
Ince-in-M WN2 . . . .**151** C3
Radcliffe M26 . . . .**44** A3
Hebron St OL2 . . . .**49** A3
Hector Ave OL16 . . . .**31** B8
Hector Rd
Manchester M13 . . . .**98** F3
Wigan WN5 . . . .**36** D1
Heddles Ct WN7. . . . .**75** E4
Heddon Cl SK4 . . . .**110** E3
Heddon Wlk M8 . . . .**156** C2
Hedgelands Wlk 4
M33 . . . .**107** C5
Hedgemead 6 WN6 . . . . . .**37** A1
Hedge Rows OL12 . . . .**4** C1
Hedgerows The SK14 . . . .**102** A3
Hedges St M35. . . . .**84** A8
Hedley St BL1 . . . .**142** C2
Hedley Wlk 8 M8 . . . .**155** C3
Heeley St WN1 . . . .**37** B2
Height Barn La OL13. . . . . . .**4** A8
Heights Ave OL12 . . . .**14** E2
Heights Cl OL12 . . . .**14** E2
Heights Ct OL12 . . . .**14** E1
Heights La
Chadderton OL1. . . . .**47** F2
Delph OL3. . . . .**50** E7
Rochdale OL12. . . . .**14** E1
Heights The
Horwich BL6 . . . .**22** D1
Tyldesley M29 . . . .**77** B8
Helena St M6 . . . .**80** C5
Helen St
Ashton-in-M WN4 . . . .**73** A4
Eccles M30 . . . .**95** B8
Farnworth BL4. . . . .**60** D7
Golborne WA3 . . . .**73** A5
Salford M7 . . . .**81** C5
Helensville Ave M6 . . . .**80** F5
Helga St M40. . . . .**160** A4
Helias Cl M28 . . . .**59** F3
Hell Nook WA3 . . . .**73** F1
Helmclough Way M28. . . . .**78** B8
Helmet St M1, M12. . . . . . .**163** C4
Helmsdale M28 . . . .**60** C2
Helmsdale Ave BL3 . . . .**40** F6
Helmsdale Cl BL0. . . . .**11** A4
HELMSHORE **1** B7
Helmshore Ave OL4. . . . . . .**49** E3
Helmshore Ho OL2 . . . . . .**149** B4

Helmshore Prim Sch
BB4 . . . .**1** A7
Helmshore Rd
Haslingden BB4 . . . .**1** A7
Ramsbottom BL0, BL8,
BB4. . . . .**1** A3
Helmshore Way OL2 . . . .**149** B4
Helmshore Wlk M13 . . . . .**163** B3
Helmsman Way WN3. . . . .**150** B1
Helsby Cl OL4 . . . .**68** A6
Helsby Gdns BL3 . . . .**143** C4
Helsby Rd M33 . . . .**108** E2
Helsby Way
4 Handforth SK9 . . . .**131** D4
Wigan WN3 . . . .**54** C2
Helsby Wlk M12. . . . .**164** B4
Helston Cl
Bramhall SK7. . . . .**132** F7
Hattersley SK14. . . . .**102** D1
Irlam M44 . . . .**94** B2
Helston Dr OL2 . . . .**48** F4
Helston Gr SK8 . . . .**131** C8
Helston Way M29 . . . .**77** C8
Helston Wlk SK14. . . . .**102** D1
Helton Wlk M24. . . . .**46** C1
Helvellyn Dr M24. . . . .**46** D2
Helvellyn Rd WN5 . . . .**54** B7
Helvellyn Wlk 2 OL1 . . . . .**49** A1
Hembury Ave M19 . . . .**110** F6
Hembury Cl M24 . . . .**47** B2
Hemfield Cl WN2 . . . .**56** B8
Hemfield Ct WN2 . . . .**56** C8
Hemfield Rd WN2 . . . .**56** B8
Hemley Cl BL5. . . . .**57** E6
Hemlock Ave OL8. . . . .**66** E3
Hemming Dr M30. . . . .**79** E1
Hemmington Dr M9 . . . . . .**157** A3
Hemmons Rd M12 . . . .**99** B3
Hempcroft Rd WA15 . . . . .**120** D5
Hempshaw La SK1,
SK2. . . . .**124** B7
Hemsby Cl BL3 . . . .**146** A4
Hemsley St S M9 . . . .**64** E1
Hemsley St M9 . . . .**64** E1
Hemswell Cl M6. . . . .**154** B4
Hemsworth Rd
Bolton BL1. . . . .**145** A4
Manchester M18 . . . .**99** D3
Henbury Dr SK6 . . . .**113** B6
Henbury La SK8 . . . .**131** F6
Henbury St
Manchester M14 . . . .**98** A3
Stockport SK2 . . . .**124** C4
Henderson Ave 3 M27. . . .**61** F1
Henderson St
Littleborough OL15 . . . .**16** A5
Manchester M19 . . . .**111** B8
Rochdale OL12. . . . .**15** B2
Henderville St OL15. . . . . . .**16** A6
Hendham Cl SK7 . . . .**124** A2
Hendham Dr WA14 . . . . . .**119** B5
Hendham Vale M9 . . . .**156** C2
Hendham Vale Ind Pk
M8 . . . .**156** C3
Hendon Dr
Bury BL9 . . . .**44** F5
Cheadle SK3 . . . .**123** A7
Hendon Gr
Heywood OL10. . . . .**46** E7
Leigh WN7 . . . .**75** F8
Hendon Rd
Manchester M9 . . . .**64** D4
Wigan WN5 . . . .**54** E8
Hendon St WN7 . . . .**75** F8
Hendriff Pl 4 OL12 . . . .**14** F1
Henfield Wlk M22 . . . .**121** C3
Henfold Rd M29 . . . .**77** C7
Hengist St
Bolton BL2. . . . .**148** C3
Manchester M18 . . . .**99** D4
Henley Ave
Cheadle SK8 . . . .**122** F2
Irlam M44 . . . .**105** E6
Manchester M16 . . . .**97** B3
Henley Cl BL8 . . . .**44** B8
Henley Dr
Altrincham WA15. . . . .**119** F7
Ashton-u-L OL7 . . . .**84** F4
Henley Gr BL3. . . . .**147** A3
Henley Pl M19 . . . .**111** A6
Henley St
Aspull WN2 . . . .**38** B6
Chadderton OL9. . . . .**66** A4
Oldham OL1 . . . .**153** A4
1 Rochdale OL12 . . . .**14** F1
Henley Terr OL11. . . . .**139** B1
Henlow Wlk 9 M40. . . . . . .**65** D2
Henniker Rd BL3 . . . .**146** A4
Henniker St M27 . . . .**79** E6
Hennon St BL1 . . . .**143** A1
Henrietta St
Ashton-u-L OL6 . . . .**166** B4
Bolton BL3. . . . .**146** B4
Leigh WN7 . . . .**75** E5
Manchester M16 . . . .**161** C1
Henry Herman St BL3. . . . .**146** F3
Henry Lee St BL3 . . . .**146** C4
Henry Park St WN1 . . . . . .**151** B3
Henry Sq OL6 . . . .**166** B3
Henry St
Bolton BL2. . . . .**148** A2
Denton M34. . . . .**113** B8
Droylsden M43. . . . .**83** A1
Eccles M30 . . . .**79** C1
Failsworth M35 . . . .**83** F7
Glossop SK13. . . . .**104** C1
Hyde SK14. . . . .**167** A2

Henry St *continued*
Ince-in-M WN3 . . . .**55** E4
Leigh WN7 . . . .**76** A3
Leigh WN7 . . . .**75** F8
Littleborough OL15 . . . .**15** F3
Manchester M4 . . . .**159** B2
Manchester, Old Trafford
M16 . . . .**161** C1
Middleton M24. . . . .**64** F8
Prestwich M25. . . . .**63** C5
Ramsbottom BL0 . . . .**11** D7
Rochdale OL11. . . . .**139** C2
Stockport SK1 . . . .**124** B8
6 Tyldesley M29 . . . .**59** A1
Wardle OL12 . . . .**15** C7
14 Westhoughton BL5. . . . .**39** E1
Henshall La WA14 . . . .**118** C6
Henshaw Ct M16 . . . .**97** B4
Henshaw La OL9. . . . .**65** F2
Henshaw St
Oldham OL1 . . . .**153** B3
Oldham OL1 . . . .**153** C4
Stretford M32 . . . .**96** D2
Henshaw Wlk
Bolton, Halliwell BL1 . . . . .**143** B2
10 Manchester M13 . . . . .**163** B3
Henson Gr WA15 . . . .**120** A4
Henthorn St OL2 . . . .**149** B2
Henton Wlk M40 . . . .**159** C4
Henwick Hall Ave BL0 . . . . .**11** A4
Henwood Rd M20. . . . .**110** C5
Hepley Rd SK12 . . . .**134** A3
Hepple Cl SK4. . . . .**110** F3
Heppleton Rd M40. . . . .**65** D2
Hepple Wlk OL7 . . . .**84** E5
Hepton St OL2. . . . .**153** B4
Heptonstall Wlk M18 . . . .**165** C1
Hepworth Cl WN3 . . . .**73** F2
Hepworth St SK14 . . . .**113** E7
HERALD GREEN **122** B2
Heraldic Ct M6 . . . .**81** A5
Herbert St
Bacup OL13 . . . .**3** D8
Chadderton OL9. . . . .**152** B3
Denton M34. . . . .**101** A4
Droylsden M43. . . . .**83** F1
Horwich BL6 . . . .**22** B4
Little Lever BL3. . . . .**43** B3
Oldham OL4 . . . .**49** D1
Prestwich M25. . . . .**63** F4
Radcliffe M26 . . . .**43** F5
Salford M6. . . . .**155** C1
Stockport SK3 . . . .**170** D3
Stretford M32 . . . .**96** D2
Westhoughton BL5 . . . .**39** E2
Wigan WN3 . . . .**150** B3
Hereford Ave WA3. . . . .**90** B8
Hereford Cl
Ashton-in-M WN4 . . . .**73** C2
Ashton-u-L OL6 . . . .**85** D7
Shaw OL2. . . . .**48** F7
Hereford Cres BL3. . . . .**43** A4
Hereford Dr
Bury BL9 . . . .**44** F8
Handforth SK9 . . . .**131** E3
Manchester M25. . . . .**63** C2
Swinton M27 . . . .**79** F6
Hereford Gr
Up Holland WN8 . . . .**53** B6
Urmston M41. . . . .**95** C2
Hereford Rd
Bolton BL1. . . . .**144** B4
Brinnington SK5. . . . .**112** C5
Cheadle SK8 . . . .**123** A4
Hindley WN2 . . . .**56** F6
Salford M30. . . . .**80** A5
Hereford St
Bolton BL1. . . . .**143** C2
Oldham OL9. . . . .**152** C1
16 Rochdale OL11. . . . .**31** A5
Sale M33 . . . .**108** B4
Hereford Way
Middleton M24. . . . .**47** C2
Stalybridge SK15. . . . .**102** D7
Hereford Wlk
6 Denton M34. . . . .**100** F1
Romiley SK6. . . . .**113** A1
Herevale Grange M28. . . . .**78** B7
Herevale Hall Dr BL0 . . . . . .**11** B4
Heristone Ave M34 . . . . . .**100** F3
Heritage Gdns M20 . . . . . .**110** B2
Heritage Ho M3 . . . .**162** B4
Heritage Wharf OL7 . . . . .**166** A1
Herle Dr M22. . . . .**121** C1
Hermitage Ave SK6 . . . . . .**113** F2
Hermitage Cl WN6 . . . .**35** E7
Hermitage Ct WA15 . . . . . .**120** A3
Hermitage Gdns SK6. . . . .**113** F2
Hermitage Green La WA2,
WA12 . . . .**89** C1
Hermitage Rd
Altrincham WA15. . . . .**120** A3
Manchester M8 . . . .**64** A1
Oldham OL4 . . . .**66** E4
Herne St M11 . . . .**165** A4
Heron Ave
Dukinfield SK16 . . . .**101** E7
Farnworth BL4. . . . .**59** F7
Heron Cl SK13. . . . .**116** F8
Heron Ct
Salford M6. . . . .**80** B3
Stockport SK3 . . . .**170** B3
Heron Ct Cl M40 . . . .**83** B5
Heron Dr
Droylsden M34. . . . .**84** C1
Irlam M44 . . . .**94** A3
Poynton SK12 . . . .**133** A3

Heron Dr *continued*
Wigan WN3 . . . .**54** E2
Heron La OL5 . . . .**68** D3
Heron Pl WN5 . . . .**54** C8
Heron St
Manchester M15 . . . .**162** B1
Oldham OL8 . . . .**66** D3
Stockport SK3 . . . .**170** A3
Swinton M27 . . . .**62** A1
Heron's Way BL2 . . . . **148** A2
Herons Wharf WN6 . . . .**35** D7
Heron View SK13 . . . .**115** F8
Herries St OL6 . . . .**85** D4
Herristone Rd M8 . . . .**64** A2
Herrod Ave SK4 . . . .**111** E5
Herschel St M40 . . . .**83** A8
Hersey St M6 . . . .**154** B2
Hersham Wlk ■ M9 . . . . . .**157** B4
Hertford Dr M20 . . . .**59** A3
Hertford Gr M44 . . . .**105** C6
Hertford Rd M9 . . . .**64** D1
Hertfordshire Park Cl
OL2 . . . .**149** B4
Hertford St OL7 . . . .**166** A1
Hesford Ave M9 . . . .**157** C3
Hesketh Ave
Bolton BL1 . . . .**24** F5
Manchester M20 . . . .**110** A3
Shaw OL2 . . . .**149** B1
Hesketh Ct
Atherton M46 . . . .**58** C3
■ Manchester M20 . . . . . .**110** A3
Hesketh Dr WN6 . . . .**19** A2
Hesketh Fletcher CE High
Sch M46 . . . .**58** C2
Hesketh Ho ■ BL4 . . . .**60** D8
Hesketh Manor M46 . . . .**58** C3
Hesketh Meadow La
WA3 . . . .**90** F8
Hesketh Rd
Rochdale OL16 . . . .**31** C7
Sale M33 . . . .**107** F3
Hesketh St
Atherton M46 . . . .**58** D4
Leigh WN7 . . . .**75** D5
Stockport SK4 . . . .**169** B3
Wigan WN5 . . . .**54** F7
Hesketh Wlk
■ Farnworth BL4 . . . .**60** D8
Middleton M24 . . . .**46** E2
Hesnall Cl WA3 . . . .**92** C8
Hessel St M50 . . . .**154** A1
Hester Wlk ■ M15 . . . .**163** A1
Heston Ave M13 . . . .**98** F2
Heston Dr M41 . . . .**95** C3
Heswall Ave
Culcheth WA3 . . . .**91** E4
Manchester M20 . . . .**110** B7
Heswall Dr BL8 . . . .**26** F5
Heswall Rd SK5 . . . .**99** F7
Heswall St BL2 . . . .**42** F7
Hetherington Wlk M12 . . . .**99** A4
Hethorn St M40 . . . .**83** C5
Hetton Ave M13 . . . .**98** E2
Heversham Ave OL2 . . . . . .**49** D7
Heversham Wlk M18 . . . . . .**165** C2
Hewart Cl M40 . . . .**159** C4
Hewart Dr BL9 . . . .**141** C2
Hewitt Ave M34 . . . .**99** F3
Hewitt Busns Pk WN5 . . . . .**53** E4
Hewitt St M15 . . . .**162** C3
Hewlett Rd M21 . . . .**97** A1
Hewlett St
Bolton BL2 . . . .**148** A3
Westhoughton BL5 . . . .**57** B7
Wigan WN1 . . . .**150** C4
Hexham Ave
Bolton BL1 . . . .**23** F1
Wigan WN3 . . . .**54** F4
Hexham Cl
Atherton M46 . . . .**58** E4
Chadderton OL9 . . . .**152** C3
Sale M33 . . . .**107** D3
Stockport SK2 . . . .**124** E5
Hexham Rd M18 . . . .**99** C3
Hexon Cl M6 . . . .**154** B3
Hexworth Wlk SK7 . . . .**124** A2
Hey Bottom La OL12 . . . .**15** A6
Heybrook Cl M45 . . . .**63** C8
Heybrook Prim Sch
OL12 . . . .**15** A1
Heybrook Rd M23 . . . .**121** B5
Heybrook St OL16 . . . .**31** B8
Heybrook Wlk M45 . . . .**63** C8
Heybury Cl M11 . . . .**164** C8
Hey Cres OL4 . . . .**67** F7
Hey Croft M45 . . . .**62** C7
Heycrofts View BL0 . . . .**1** E3
Heyden Bank 26 SK13 . . . .**171** A2
Heyden Fold 27 SK13 . . . . .**171** A2
Heyden Terr 25 SK13 . . . . .**171** A2
Heyes Ave WA15 . . . .**120** B7
Heyes Dr WA15 . . . .**120** B7
Heyes La
Alderley Edge SK9 . . . .**137** B3
Sale WA15 . . . .**120** B7
Heyes Lane Jun & Inf Schs
WA15 . . . .**120** B8
Heyes Leigh WA15 . . . .**120** B7
Heyes Rd WN5 . . . .**53** E6
Heyes St WN6 . . . .**35** C3
Heyes Terr WA15 . . . .**120** B8
Hey Flake La OL3 . . . .**50** E3
Heyford Ave M40 . . . .**65** D2
Hey Head Ave BB4 . . . .**3** A8
Hey Head La OL15 . . . .**6** B1
HEYHEADS **86** E7

Heyheads New Rd
SK15 . . . .**86** E7
Hey Hill Cl OL2 . . . .**149** A1
Hey House Mews BL8 . . . . . .**10** F4
Heyland Rd M23 . . . .**121** B6
Heylee OL7 . . . .**100** F8
Heyridge Dr M22 . . . .**109** D1
HEYROD **86** C4
Heyrod St
Manchester M1 . . . .**163** C4
Mossley SK15 . . . .**86** D5
Heyrose Wlk 17 M15 . . . . .**162** A2
Heys Ave
Romiley SK6 . . . .**113** E3
Swinton M27 . . . .**61** D2
Wythenshawe M23 . . . .**109** A1
Heysbank Rd SK12 . . . .**135** D5
Heys Cl N M27 . . . .**61** C2
Heyscroft Rd
Manchester, Withington
M20 . . . .**110** C6
Stockport, Heaton Mersey
SK4 . . . .**168** A2
Heys Farm Cotts SK6 . . . . .**113** E3
Heysham Ave M20 . . . .**109** F7
Heysham Rd WN5 . . . .**54** B7
Heyshaw Wlk M23 . . . .**108** F1
Hey Shoot La WA3 . . . .**92** C5
HEYSIDE **49** A4
Heyside OL2 . . . .**49** A3
Heyside Ave OL2 . . . .**49** A3
Heyside Cl SK15 . . . .**86** E6
Heys La
Heywood OL10 . . . .**29** A1
Romiley SK6 . . . .**113** E3
Heys Prim Sch The
OL6 . . . .**85** D3
Heys Rd
Ashton-u-L OL6 . . . .**85** D3
Prestwich M25 . . . .**63** B5
Heys St BL8 . . . .**140** A2
Hey St
Ince-in-M WN3 . . . .**55** F3
Rochdale OL16 . . . .**31** B8
Wigan WN6 . . . .**150** B4
Heys The
Ashton-u-L OL6 . . . .**85** D3
Prestwich M25 . . . .**63** B5
Reddish SK5 . . . .**100** A1
Heys View M25 . . . .**63** B3
Heythrop Cl M45 . . . .**44** E1
Hey Top OL3 . . . .**69** D3
Heyward Ho M46 . . . .**58** C3
Hey-with-Zion Prim Sch
OL4 . . . .**67** E7
HEYWOOD **29** F2
Heywood Ave
Golborne WA3 . . . .**74** B1
Oldham OL4 . . . .**68** A8
Heywood Cl SK9 . . . .**137** B2
Heywood Com High Sch
OL10 . . . .**28** E1
Heywood Ct M25 . . . .**64** A7
Heywood Distribution Pk
BL9, OL10 . . . .**45** F8
Heywood Fold Rd OL4 . . . . . .**67** F7
Heywood Gdns
Bolton BL3 . . . .**147** B4
Golborne WA3 . . . .**74** B1
Prestwich M25 . . . .**63** B4
Heywood Gr M33 . . . .**108** B6
Heywood Hall Rd OL10 . . . . .**29** D3
Heywood Ho
Oldham OL8 . . . .**153** C1
■ Salford M6 . . . .**80** C3
Heywood La OL4 . . . .**68** A7
Heywood Old Rd M24,
OL10 . . . .**46** B3
Heywood Park View
BL3 . . . .**147** B4
Heywood Rd
Alderley Edge SK9 . . . .**137** B2
Prestwich M25 . . . .**63** C7
Rochdale OL11 . . . .**30** C1
Sale M33 . . . .**108** B3
Heywood's Hollow
BL1 . . . .**143** C3
Heywood St
Bury BL9 . . . .**145** C4
Bury BL9 . . . .**141** A2
Failsworth M35 . . . .**83** D7
Little Lever BL3 . . . .**43** B3
Oldham OL4 . . . .**67** E8
Swinton M27 . . . .**79** E8
Heywood Sta ● OL10 . . . . . .**29** E1
Heywood Way M6 . . . .**154** C3
Heyworth Ave SK6 . . . .**113** D3
Heyworth St ◀ M5 . . . .**154** B1
Hibbert Ave
Denton M34 . . . .**100** E5
Hyde SK14 . . . .**167** B1
Hibbert Cres M35 . . . .**84** A6
Hibbert La SK6 . . . .**125** F5
Hibbert St
Bolton BL1 . . . .**143** C2
Manchester M14 . . . .**98** C3
Oldham OL4 . . . .**67** E7
Reddish SK4, SK5 . . . .**99** E3
Hibernia St BL3 . . . .**144** C1
Hibernia Way M32 . . . .**96** A5
Hibson Ave OL12 . . . .**13** E2
Hibson Cl OL12 . . . .**15** C6
Hic Bibi La PR7 . . . .**19** E6
Hickenfield Rd SK14 . . . . . .**101** F5
Hicken Pl SK14 . . . .**101** F5
Hickton Dr WA14 . . . .**119** B6

Hieland Rd WN1 . . . .**37** E2
HIGGINSHAW **49** A2
Higginshaw La OL2 . . . .**49** A2
Higginshaw Rd OL1 . . . .**67** A8
Higginson Rd SK5 . . . .**111** E8
Higginson St WN7 . . . .**76** A5
Higgs Cl OL4 . . . .**67** D7
Higham La OL2 . . . .**149** A1
Higham La SK14 . . . .**114** A7
Higham St SK8 . . . .**123** A1
Higham View M6 . . . .**81** A3
High Ash Gr M34 . . . .**100** D7
High Bank BL2 . . . .**42** E7
High Bank SK13 . . . .**103** F7
High Bank
Altrincham WA14 . . . .**119** D5
Bolton BL7 . . . .**24** F7
Manchester M18 . . . .**99** E5
Over Hulton M46 . . . .**59** A6
High Bank Ave SK15 . . . . . .**102** D7
High Bank Cl M44 . . . .**105** D6
High Bank Cres M25 . . . .**63** C1
Highbank Dr M20 . . . .**122** B8
High Bank Gr M25 . . . .**63** C3
High Bank La BL6 . . . .**40** B8
Highbank Private Hospl
BL8 . . . .**26** F4
Highbank Rd
Glossop SK13 . . . .**116** F7
Newhey OL16 . . . .**32** C4
Whitefield BL9 . . . .**44** F3
High Bank Rd
Droylsden M43 . . . .**99** F8
Hyde SK14 . . . .**167** C3
Pendlebury M27 . . . .**80** B7
High Bank Side SK1 . . . . . .**169** C1
High Bank St BL2 . . . .**148** C3
High Barn Cl OL11 . . . .**139** B1
High Barn Com Jun Sch
OL2 . . . .**48** E4
High Barn Rd
Middleton M24 . . . .**65** A7
Royton OL2 . . . .**48** E4
High Barn St OL2 . . . .**48** E4
High Beeches BL2 . . . .**43** B5
High Beeches Cres
WN4 . . . .**73** A6
High Bent Ave SK8 . . . .**132** A6
High Birch Sch OL11 . . . .**30** B4
Highbridge Cl BL2 . . . .**43** A6
Highbrook Gr 14 BL1 . . . . .**143** B1
Highbury SK4 . . . .**110** F2
Highbury Ave
Irlam M44 . . . .**94** A1
Urmston M41 . . . .**94** E2
Highbury Cl BL5 . . . .**57** D6
Highbury Rd
Manchester M16 . . . .**97** E1
Reddish SK4 . . . .**111** C6
Highbury Way OL2 . . . .**48** D5
Highclere Ave M7, M8 . . . . .**155** C2
Highclere Rd M8 . . . .**63** F2
Highcliffe St WN6 . . . .**36** F7
Highcliffe Rd M9 . . . .**64** A3
Highclove La M28 . . . .**77** F5
High Crest Ave SK8 . . . .**121** F5
Highcrest Gr M29 . . . .**59** D1
Highcroft
Bolton BL2 . . . .**25** A3
Hyde SK14 . . . .**113** F6
Highcroft Ave M20 . . . .**109** E4
High Croft Cl SK16 . . . .**102** A8
Highcroft Way OL12 . . . .**14** F4
Highdown Wlk 28 M9 . . . . .**157** B4
High Elm Dr WA15 . . . .**129** C8
High Elm Rd WA15 . . . .**129** D7
High Elms SK8 . . . .**132** B5
Higher Ainsworth Rd
M26 . . . .**43** E7
Higher Ardwick M12 . . . . . .**163** C3
Higher Arthurs OL3 . . . .**69** B6
Higher Bank Rd OL15 . . . . . .**16** A3
Higher Barlow Row
SK1 . . . .**170** C4
Higher Barn BL6 . . . .**22** F3
Higher Barn St SK13 . . . . . .**171** C4
HIGHER BARROWSHAW
. . . .**49** D2
Higher Bents La SK6 . . . . . .**113** A3
HIGHER BLACKLEY **64** B5
Higher Blue Bell Cotts
BL5 . . . .**39** C4
HIGHER BOARSGREAVE
. . . .**3** A6
HIGHER BOARSHAW **47** C2
Higher Bridge St BL1 . . . . .**145** C4
Higherbrook Cl BL6 . . . .**22** D1
HIGHER BROUGHTON **155** A3
Higher Bury St SK4 . . . .**169** A2
Higher Calderbrook
OL15 . . . .**6** C1
Higher Calderbrook Rd
OL15 . . . .**6** C2
Higher Cambridge St
M15 . . . .**163** A2
Higher Carr La OL3 . . . .**69** B7
Higher Chatham St
M15 . . . .**163** A2
Higher Cleggswood Ave
OL15 . . . .**16** A3
Higher Count Hill OL4 . . . . . .**49** E2

Higher Croft
Eccles M30 . . . .**95** C8
Whitefield M45 . . . .**62** C6
Higher Crossbank OL4 . . . . .**67** F8
Higher Cross La OL3 . . . .**69** C8
Higher Damshead BL5 . . . . .**57** F8
Higher Darcy St BL2 . . . . . .**148** C1
Higher Dean St M26 . . . .**43** E3
HIGHER DINTING **104** A2
Higher Dinting SK13 . . . . . .**104** A2
HIGHER DISLEY **135** E4
Higher Downs WA14 . . . . . .**119** C3
Higher Drake Mdw
BL5 . . . .**57** E5
Higher Dunscar St BL7 . . . . . .**8** E1
HIGHER END **53** D3
Higher Failsworth Prim
Sch M35 . . . .**84** A8
Higher Fold M24 . . . .**47** B3
Higher Fold La BL0 . . . .**11** E7
HIGHER FOLDS **76** E6
Higher Folds Enterprise
Ctr WN7 . . . .**76** E6
Higher Folds Prim Sch
WN7 . . . .**76** D7
Higher Fullwood OL1 . . . .**49** D4
Higher Gn OL6 . . . .**166** C4
HIGHER GREEN **77** C5
Higher Green La M29 . . . .**77** C6
HIGHER HARTSHEAD **67** F2
Higher Henry St SK14 . . . . .**167** B1
Higher Hillgate SK1,
SK2 . . . .**170** C4
Higher House Cl OL9 . . . .**66** A4
HIGHER HURST **85** E5
HIGHER INCE **151** C4
Higher Kinders OL3 . . . .**69** C6
Higher Knowles BL6 . . . .**22** E2
Higher La
Aspull WN2 . . . .**38** A4
Disley SK12 . . . .**135** E1
Lymm WA13 . . . .**117** B1
Up Holland WN8 . . . .**53** C7
Whitefield M45 . . . .**62** E8
Higher Lane Prim Sch
M45 . . . .**62** F7
Higher Lime Rd OL8 . . . .**84** C8
Higher Lo OL11 . . . .**13** D2
Higher Lomax La OL10 . . . . . .**29** A3
Higher La
OL4 . . . .**68** C6
Higher Market St BL4 . . . .**60** E8
Higher Mdws M19 . . . .**111** C8
Higher Moulding BL9 . . . .**28** E5
Higher Newtons OL5 . . . .**68** D2
Higher Noon Sun
SK22 . . . .**127** F2
Higher Openshaw Com
Sch M11 . . . .**99** D8
Higher Ormond St M13,
M15 . . . .**163** A2
Higher Oswald St ●
M4 . . . .**159** A2
Higher Pit La M26 . . . .**43** E8
Higher Poynton SK12 . . . .**32** C2
Higher POYNTON **134** B2
Higher Rd M41 . . . .**95** E2
Higher Ridings BL7 . . . .**24** F7
Higher Rise OL2 . . . .**32** A1
Higher Row BL9 . . . .**141** B3
Higher Shady La BL7 . . . .**25** C7
Higher Shore Rd OL15 . . . . . .**15** C7
Higher Southfield OL15 . . . . .**57** C7
Higher Sq SK15 . . . .**102** C8
HIGHER SUMMERSEAT
. . . .**11** B1
Higher Summerseat
BL0 . . . .**11** B2
Higher Swan La BL3 . . . .**147** A3
Higher Tame St SK15 . . . .**86** B2
Higher Turf La OL4 . . . .**50** B1
Higher Turf Pk OL2 . . . .**48** E3
Higher View WN6 . . . .**53** C6
Higher Wharf St OL6,
OL7 . . . .**166** B2
Higher Wheat La OL16 . . . . . .**31** C8
HIGHER WOODHILL **27** E6
Higher Wood St M24 . . . .**46** F1
Higher York St M13 . . . .**163** B2
HIGHFIELD **59** F8
Highfield
Gatley SK8 . . . .**122** C3
Sale M33 . . . .**108** C3
HIGHFIELD **54** D4
Highfield WN3 . . . .**54** D4
High Field WA14 . . . .**118** B2
Highfield Ave
Atherton M46 . . . .**58** E5
Bolton BL2 . . . .**26** A3
Boothstown M28 . . . .**77** F7
Golborne WA3 . . . .**89** F8
Heywood OL10 . . . .**29** A2
Leigh WN7 . . . .**76** C3
Radcliffe M26 . . . .**112** F2
Romiley SK6 . . . .**112** F2
Sale M33 . . . .**108** C3
Shevington WN6 . . . .**36** A6
Wigan WN1 . . . .**37** E1
Highfield Cl
Adlington PR6 . . . .**21** A7
Dukinfield SK14 . . . .**101** F6
Stockport SK3 . . . .**123** F4
Stretford M32 . . . .**108** C8
Highfield Cres SK9 . . . .**131** C1
Highfield Ct
Farnworth BL4 . . . .**60** B7
Mottram in L SK14 . . . .**103** A4

Highfield Dr
Eccles M30 . . . .**79** D3
Farnworth BL4 . . . .**60** A7
Middleton M24 . . . .**64** F7
Mossley OL5 . . . .**86** C8
Pendlebury M27 . . . .**80** C7
Royton OL2 . . . .**48** E2
Standish WN6 . . . .**36** F7
4 Urmston M41 . . . .**95** C3
Highfield Est SK9 . . . .**131** C1
Highfield Gdns
Hollingworth SK14 . . . .**103** D5
Hyde SK14 . . . .**167** C3
Highfield Glen OL6 . . . .**85** F5
Highfield Gr WN2 . . . .**38** C5
Highfield Grange Ave
WN3 . . . .**54** E2
Highfield Ho
5 Farnworth BL4 . . . .**59** F8
Stockport SK3 . . . .**170** C1
Highfield Hospl The
OL11 . . . .**139** B1
Highfield Ind Est SK13 . . . .**153** A3
Highfield La
Town of Lowton WA3 . . . .**90** C5
Whitefield M45 . . . .**44** F3
Highfield Mdw OL5 . . . .**86** C8
Highfield Park Rd
SK6 . . . .**112** F3
Highfield Parkway
SK7 . . . .**132** D4
Highfield Pk SK4 . . . .**110** F2
Highfield Pl
Prestwich M25 . . . .**63** A5
Reddish M18 . . . .**99** F4
Highfield Prim Sch
Farnworth BL4 . . . .**60** A8
Urmston M41 . . . .**95** F2
Highfield Range M18 . . . .**99** F4
Highfield Rd
Adlington PR6 . . . .**21** A7
Altrincham WA15 . . . .**120** B5
Altrincham, Well Green
WA15 . . . .**120** A3
Blackrod BL6 . . . .**21** E1
Bolton BL1 . . . .**142** B2
Cheadle SK8 . . . .**122** F1
Eccles M30 . . . .**79** D4
Edenfield BL0 . . . .**1** D3
Farnworth BL4 . . . .**60** A8
Glossop SK13 . . . .**116** D8
Hazel Grove SK7 . . . .**125** A2
Hindley WN2 . . . .**56** D7
10 Marple SK6 . . . .**125** F6
Mellor SK6 . . . .**126** B6
Milnrow OL16 . . . .**32** A6
Poynton SK12 . . . .**133** A4
Prestwich M25 . . . .**63** A5
Reddish M19 . . . .**99** C1
Rochdale OL11 . . . .**13** E1
Salford M6 . . . .**154** C2
Stockport SK7 . . . .**123** F3
Stretford M32 . . . .**108** C8
Walkden M38 . . . .**59** F5
Highfield Rd N PR6 . . . .**21** A8
Highfield St Matthews CE
Prim Sch WN2 . . . .**57** A3
Highfield St W SK16 . . . . . .**166** B1
Highfield St
Denton M34 . . . .**100** E5
Denton M34 . . . .**100** F6
Dukinfield SK16 . . . .**166** B1
Kearsley BL4 . . . .**61** A6
Oldham OL9 . . . .**153** A3
Salford M7, M8 . . . .**155** C3
2 Stockport SK3 . . . .**123** C8
Highfield Terr
Ashton-u-L OL7 . . . .**85** A7
Manchester M9 . . . .**157** A4
Highgate
Altrincham WA14 . . . .**119** B3
Bolton BL3 . . . .**40** C2
Highgate Ave M41 . . . .**95** A4
Highgate Cres
Appley Bridge WN6 . . . .**35** E7
Reddish M18 . . . .**99** D3
Highgate Ctr 21 SK6 . . . . . .**112** F3
Highgate Dr
Royton OL2 . . . .**48** C7
Walkden M38 . . . .**59** E5
Highgate Ho 7 OL8 . . . .**66** D2
Highgate La
Dukinfield SK14 . . . .**101** F5
Whitworth OL12 . . . .**14** C5
Highgate Rd
Altrincham WA14 . . . .**119** B4
Up Holland WN8 . . . .**53** B7
High Gates M33 . . . .**108** E5
Highgrove WA15 . . . .**108** A1
Highgrove Cl BL1 . . . .**143** C3
Highgrove Mews 2
SK9 . . . .**137** A6
High Grove Rd
Cheadle SK8 . . . .**122** C5
Uppermill OL4 . . . .**68** E5
Highgrove The BL1 . . . .**23** D1
High Hill Rd SK22 . . . .**127** D1
High Hurst Cl M24 . . . .**64** C7
High Knowls OL4 . . . .**68** A4
High La
Manchester SK13 . . . .**115** E7
Manchester M21 . . . .**109** B8
Romiley SK6 . . . .**113** B4
Highland Ave SK6 . . . .**113** A2

Highland Lo WN6........19 D1
Highland Rd
  Bolton BL7..........25 C8
  Horwich BL6.........22 E1
Highlands
  Littleborough OL15.....16 A3
  Royton OL2.........48 C3
Highlands Dr SK2.......124 F6
Highlands Rd
  Hazel Grove SK2......124 F6
  Rochdale OL11........29 E5
  Royton OL2.........48 C3
  Shaw OL2..........149 A4
Highlands The **3** OL5...68 C1
Highland View **1** OL5...68 C2
Highland Wlk M35......83 D6
HIGH LANE.........134 E8
High Lane Prim Sch
  SK6............134 F8
High Lawn Prim Sch
  BL1...........24 E6
High Lea
  Adlington PR6........21 A8
  Cheadle SK8........122 C5
High Lee Ho M33......108 D4
High Lee La OL4.......50 B4
High Legh Rd M11......99 D8
High Level Rd OL11.....31 A6
Highmarsh Cres WA12...89 B4
High Mdw **2** SK8......131 E8
High Mdws
  Bolton BL7..........25 B8
  Glossop SK13........116 B7
  Romiley SK6.........113 C3
Highmeadow
  Radcliffe M26........43 F1
  Up Holland WN8......53 A6
Highmead St M18......99 D5
Highmead Wlk M16.....162 A1
High Moor Cres OL4....49 E1
High Moor La WN6.....18 B4
Highmoor View OL4....49 E1
Highmore Dr M9......64 E3
High Mount BL2......25 E3
Highnam Wlk M22.....121 A1
Highover Ho M20......109 F4
High Peak OL15......16 F5
High Peak Rd
  Ashton-u-L OL6......86 A6
  Whitworth OL12......14 C6
High Peak St M40.....83 B6
High Pk WN6.........36 C6
High Rid La BL6......23 B1
High St E SK13.......104 D1
High St W SK13.......104 B1
Highshore Dr M8......155 C3
High St
  Altrincham WA14......119 D4
  Atherton M46........58 D3
  Bolton BL3.........147 B4
  Bury BL8..........26 F4
  Chapeltown BL7.......9 C4
  Cheadle SK8.........122 D6
  Delph OL3.........50 F5
  Droylsden M43.......84 B1
  Golborne WA3........90 A8
  Hazel Grove SK7......124 F2
  Heywood OL10.......29 B2
  Horwich BL6.........22 B4
  Hyde SK14.........167 C3
  Ince-in-M WN3.......151 B2
  Leigh WN7.........76 A5
  5 Littleborough OL15...15 F5
  Little Lever BL3......43 B3
  Manchester M1, M4.....159 A1
  Middleton M24.......47 A1
  Middleton M24.......47 A2
  Mossley OL5.........68 D2
  Newton-le-W WA12.....89 D4
  Oldham, Lees OL4.....67 E6
  Oldham OL1.........153 C3
  Rochdale OL12........139 C4
  Royton OL2.........48 D4
  Shaw OL2..........149 B2
  Stalybridge SK15......85 F1
  Stalybridge SK15......86 A1
  Standish WN6........19 E1
  Stockport SK1.......169 C1
  Tyldesley, Lark Hill M29..77 F5
  Tyldesley M29.......58 F1
  Uppermill OL3.......69 B8
  Walkden M28........60 D3
  Wigan, New Springs
    WN2............38 B3
  Wigan, Swinley WN1....37 D2
High Stile La SK15....51 D2
High Stile St BL4.....60 E7
Highstone Dr M8.....156 C2
Highstones Gdns
  SK13...........104 F2
Highthorne Gn OL2....48 C8
Highview SK13........116 A7
High View St
  Bolton, Sharples BL1....24 E6
  1 Bolton, Willows BL3...146 C4
Highview Wlk M9......63 E4
Highwood OL11.......13 E1
Highwood Cl
  3 Bolton BL2.........25 F1
  Glossop SK13........116 B8
High Wood Fold SK6...126 C8
Highwoods Cl WN4....73 B5
Highworth Cl M13.....145 B1
Highworth Dr M40.....65 D2

Higson Ave
  Eccles M30.........95 C8
  Manchester M21......109 B7
  Romiley SK6.........112 F2
Hilary Ave
  Atherton M46........58 C5
  Gatley SK8.........131 D8
  Golborne WA3........74 D1
  Oldham OL8.........84 F8
Hilary Cl SK4.......169 A2
Hilary Gr BL4.......60 D7
Hilary Rd M22.......121 C1
Hilary St OL11......30 D1
Hilberry Ho OL5......68 E3
Hilbre Ave OL1......48 D2
Hilbre Rd M19.......110 F8
Hilbury Ave M9......64 D1
Hilda Ave
  Bury BL8..........26 F6
  Cheadle SK8.........122 E5
Hilda Gr SK5.......169 C4
Hilda St SK14.......113 D7
Hilda St
  6 Bolton BL3........42 A4
  Heywood OL10.......29 D3
  Leigh WN7.........75 D6
  Oldham OL9.........153 A3
  Reddish SK5.........169 C4
Hilden Ct M16.......97 D4
Hilden St
  Bolton BL2.........148 A2
  4 Leigh WN7........75 F5
Hilditch Cl M23......121 B6
Hildyard St WN5......54 F6
Hiley Rd M30.......79 A1
Hilgay Cl WN3.......54 D3
Hill Cl M41.........95 F1
Hillary Ave
  Ashton-u-L OL7......85 B5
  Wigan WN5.........54 D5
Hillary Rd SK14......102 A5
Hillbank WN6........37 A7
Hillbank Cl BL1......142 C3
Hill Bank Cl SK15.....86 D5
Hillbank St OL11.....47 D6
Hillbeck Cres WN4....72 D4
Hillbrae Ave WA11....71 A1
Hillbre Way **1** SK9....131 D4
Hillbrook Ave M40....65 B2
Hillbrook Rd
  Bramhall SK7........132 D6
  Stockport SK1.......124 C8
1 Hilbrow Wlk **8** M8...155 C3
Hillbury Rd SK7......132 D4
Hill Cl WN6.........35 E8
Hillcote Wlk M18.....165 B2
Hill Cot Rd BL1......24 F5
Hill Court Mews SK6...113 B2
Hillcourt
  High Lane SK6.......134 F7
  Romiley SK6.........113 C4
Hillcourt St M1.......163 A3
Hill Cres
  Leigh WN7.........75 C8
  Manchester M9.......64 A3
Hillcrest
  Hyde SK14.........113 F7
  Middleton M24.......46 F3
  Platt Bridge WN2.....56 B2
  Salford M6.........80 A3
Hill Crest M46.......58 F5
Hillcrest Ave
  Heywood OL10.......29 A3
  Stockport SK4.......168 A2
Hill Crest Ave WN7....75 C8
Hillcrest Cres OL10....29 A3
Hillcrest Dr
  Denton M34.........101 B1
  Reddish M19........111 C7
Hillcrest Gram Sch
  SK3...........170 C2
Hillcrest Rd
  Prestwich M25......62 F2
  Rochdale OL11.......30 D2
  Stockport, Bramhall Green
    SK7...........123 F1
  Stockport, Stockport Great
    Moor SK2.........124 C7
  Tyldesley M29.......77 D8
Hillcroft
  Oldham OL8.........67 A1
  Stockport SK2.......124 E6
Hillcroft Cl M8......156 A4
Hillcroft Rd WA14....119 A5
Hilldale Ave M9......64 E4
Hilldean WN8........58 D3
Hill Dr SK9.........131 E3
Hillel Ho M15.......163 A1
Hillend La SK14......103 A1
Hillend PI M23......109 A2
Hillend Rd M23......109 A2
Hill End Rd OL3.......50 F4
Hill Farm Cl OL8.....67 B3
Hillfield M5.........154 A2
Hillfield Cl M13......164 A1
Hillfield Dr
  Bolton BL2.........25 B1
  Worsley M28........78 A7
Hillfield Wlk **10** BL2...25 B1
Hillfoot Wlk **20** M15...162 A2
Hillgate Ave M5......161 B3
Hillgate Bsns Ctr SK1..170 C4
Hillgate St OL6......166 C4
Hillhead Wlk M8......156 A1
Hillhouse Ct OL12....30 B3
Hill House Fold La
  WN6...........18 C5

Hill House La WN6.....18 C5
Hillier St N M9......157 B4
Hillier St M9.......157 B4
Hillingdon Cl OL8.....84 B8
Hillingdon Dr M9.....65 B2
Hillingdon Rd
  Stretford M32.......96 E2
  Whitefield M45......62 D7
Hillington Rd
  Sale M33.........107 F5
  Stockport SK3.......123 C8
Hillkirk Dr OL12......14 C3
Hillkirk St M11......160 B1
Hill La
  Blackrod BL6.......21 C2
  Bolton BL2.........148 A4
  Manchester M9.......64 D4
Hillman Cl M40......157 A1
Hill Mount M16......102 A8
Hillock The
  Bolton BL2.........25 D5
  Tyldesley M29.......77 B5
Hill Pond Ave SK22...127 D1
Hillreed WN6........36 F1
Hill Rise
  Altrincham WA14......119 A5
  Ramsbottom BL0......11 A4
  Romiley SK6.........113 B2
Hillsborough Dr BL9...45 B2
Hill's Ct **5** BL8......27 B4
Hillsdale Gr BL2......25 E3
Hillside WA13.......117 E1
Hill Side BL1........40 F7
Hillside Ave
  Ashton-in-M WN4.....72 F8
  Atherton M46........58 E4
  Blackrod BL6.......21 C2
  Bolton BL7.........25 C8
  Diggle OL3.........51 C3
  Farnworth BL4.......60 C7
  Horwich BL6........22 C4
  Hyde SK14.........113 F6
  Mossley SK15.......86 F6
  Oldham, Clarksfield OL4..67 C7
  Oldham, Grotton OL4..68 C5
  Royton OL2.........48 E5
  Salford M7.........81 A8
  Shaw OL2..........49 D8
  Walkden M28........60 C4
  Whitefield M45......44 E2
Hillside Cl
  Billinge WN5.......71 D5
  Bolton, Harwood Lee BL2..25 E5
  Bolton, Hunger Hill BL3..40 D2
  Bramhall SK7.......133 A7
  Disley SK12........135 E6
  Glossop SK13........171 B3
  Manchester M40......65 A1
  Wigan WN3.........54 D3
Hillside Cres
  Ashton-u-L OL6......85 F5
  Bury BL9..........27 F6
  Horwich BL6........22 C4
Hillside Ct **8** BL1.....40 F7
Hillside Dr
  Middleton M24.......47 B1
  Pendlebury M27......80 D6
Hillside Gr SK6......114 B1
Hillside Ho BL1......40 F7
Hillside Rd
  Altrincham WA15......120 A3
  Hyde SK14, SK6......113 D5
  Ramsbottom BL0......138 A1
  Stockport SK2.......124 D7
Hillside St **8** BL3.....145 A1
Hillside View
  Denton M34.........113 A7
  Milnrow OL16.......32 A6
Hillside Way OL12.....4 C1
Hillside Wlk OL12....14 D4
Hills La BL9.........45 C2
Hillspring Rd OL4.....68 A6
Hill St
  Altrincham WA14......119 C8
  Ashton-u-L OL6, OL7...166 B2
  Bury BL8..........26 F4
  Dukinfield SK16......166 B3
  Heywood OL10.......29 C2
  Hindley WN2........56 D6
  Hyde SK14.........113 F8
  Leigh WN7.........75 E5
  Manchester M20......110 B7
  Middleton M24.......47 A3
  Oldham OL4.........67 A8
  Radcliffe M26.......43 F4
  Ramsbottom BL9......11 C3
  Rochdale OL16.......31 A7
  Romiley SK6.........113 B2
  Salford M7.........81 A8
  Shaw OL2..........149 C2
  Wigan WN6.........37 B1
Hillstone Ave OL12....14 D4
Hillstone Cl BL8.....10 F2
HILLTOP.........137 B8
Hilltop OL12........14 D4
HILL TOP.........60 D4
Hill Top
  Altrincham WA15......120 A1
  Bolton BL1.........143 A3
  Chadderton OL1......47 F2
  Little Lever BL3......43 A4
  Over Hulton M46......58 F5
  Romiley SK6.........113 B3
Hilltop Ave
  Cheadle SK8.........132 B8

Hill Top Ave continued
  Prestwich M25.......63 B4
  Stalybridge SK9......137 B8
Hill Top Com Specl Sch
  OL4...........50 A4
Hilltop Ct
  Manchester, Crumpsall
    M8............63 F2
  Manchester M14......98 D1
  Walkden M28........60 D4
Hill Top Ct SK8......123 B1
Hilltop Dr
  Bury BL8..........26 E6
  Haslingden BB4......1 C7
  Marple SK6.........125 C7
  Royton OL2.........48 E2
Hill Top Dr
  Altrincham WA15......120 A1
  Rochdale OL11.......30 F2
Hill Top Fold **1** WN2...56 E6
Hilltop Gr M45......63 B8
Hill Top La OL3......50 C4
Hilltop Rd SK13......104 B3
Hill Top Rd M28.....60 D4
Hillview OL15.......6 D1
Hill View
  Delph OL3.........50 F4
  Stalybridge SK15......102 E6
Hill View Cl OL11.....49 C2
Hillview Ct BL1......143 B4
Hill View Dr PR7.....19 D8
Hillview Rd BL1......143 B4
Hill View Wlk M34....100 A1
Hillwood Ave M8.....63 F3
Hillwood Dr SK13....116 F8
Hillyard **7** BL8......27 C3
Hilly Croft BL7......24 F8
Hilmarton Cl BL2.....25 E5
Hilrose Ave M41......95 F2
Hilson Ct **1** M43......84 A1
Hilton Arc OL1......153 C3
Hilton Ave
  Horwich BL6........22 A3
  Urmston M41........95 D2
Hilton Bank M28.....60 B3
Hilton Cl WN7.......76 A5
Hilton Cres
  Ashton-u-L OL6......85 C5
  Manchester M25......63 B2
  Worsley M28........78 B6
Hilton Ct SK3.......170 B4
Hilton Dr
  Ashton-u-L OL7......85 C5
  Irlam M44.........105 C5
  Manchester M25......63 B2
Hilton Fold La M24....47 B1
Hilton Gr
  Poynton SK12.......133 D4
  Walkden M28........60 B3
Hilton House.......39 A6
Hilton La
  Prestwich M25......63 B4
  Walkden M28........60 B2
Hilton La Prim Sch
  M28...........63 B2
Hilton Lo M25......63 B2
Hilton Park.......63 B2
Hilton Pl WN2......38 C6
Hilton Rd
  Bury BL9..........140 C2
  Disley SK12........135 B7
  Poynton SK12.......134 C5
  Stockport SK7......124 B1
  Wythenshawe M22....121 E5
Hilton St N M7......155 A2
Hilton St M7.......155 A1
Hiltons Cl OL8......153 B1
Hiltons Farm Cl M34...100 C6
Hilton Sq M27......62 A1
Hilton St
  Ashton-in-M WN4.....73 C3
  Bolton BL2.........148 C3
  Bury BL9..........140 C4
  Dukinfield SK16......101 F5
  Ince-in-M WN3.......151 B2
  Manchester M1.......159 B1
  Manchester M1, M4.....159 B2
  Salford M7.........155 A1
  Stockport SK3.......170 A4
  Walkden M28........60 A4
  Wigan WN1.........37 D1
Hilton Wlk M24.......64 C8
Himley Rd M11.......83 C3
Hincaster Wlk M18....165 C1
Hinchcombe Cl M38...60 A6
Hinchley Rd M9......65 B3
Hinchley Way M27....61 F2
Hinckley St M11......166 C4
Hindburn Cl M45.....45 B1
Hindburn Dr M28.....78 A8
Hindburn Wlk M45....45 B1
Hinde St M40.......83 A8
Hindhead Wlk M40....83 D4
Hind Hill St OL10....29 D1
Hindle Dr OL2......48 C3
Hindles Cl M46......58 A1
Hindle St
  Bacup OL13.........3 D8
  Radcliffe M26.......44 A3
Hindle Terr OL3......50 F4
HINDLEY.........56 E5
Hindley All Saints CE Prim
  Sch WN2.........56 E5
Hindley Ave M22.....121 B2
Hindley Bsns Ctr **10**
  WN2...........56 D5
Hindley Cl **2** OL7....84 F1
Hindley Com High Sch
  WN2...........56 F5

HINDLEY GREEN......57 B4
Hindley Green Bsns Pk
  WN2...........57 B2
Hindley Green Prim Sch
  WN2...........57 B3
Hindley Ho WN3.....150 A1
Hindley Jun & Inf Sch
  WN2...........56 E5
Hindley Mill La WN2...56 F7
Hindley Rd BL5, WN2...57 D5
Hindley St
  Ashton-u-L OL7......84 F1
  Stockport SK1.......170 C4
Hindley Sta WN2.....56 D7
Hindley Wlk **1** WN1...150 C4
Hind Rd WN5........54 D8
HINDSFORD.......58 D2
Hindsford CE Prim Sch
  M46...........58 E1
Hindsford Cl M23....108 C1
Hindsford St M46.....58 F1
Hind's Head Ave WN6...18 F6
Hinds La
  Bury BL8..........27 C1
  Radcliffe BL8, BL9....44 C7
Hinst St BL2........148 C3
Hinkler Ave BL3......147 B3
Hinstock Cres M18....99 D5
Hinton **1** OL12......139 B4
Hinton Cl OL11......29 E6
Hinton Gr SK14......114 A8
Hinton Mews SK1.....112 B1
Hinton St
  Manchester M4......159 B3
  Oldham OL8.........153 C1
Hipley Cl SK6.......113 A5
Hirons La OL4.......68 A5
Hirst Ave M28......60 C5
Hitchen Cl SK16......101 F7
Hitchen Dr SK16......101 F7
Hitchin Wlk M13.....163 C1
Hive St OL8.........66 B2
Hives The M17......96 C7
Hoade St WN4........56 E7
Hobart Cl SK7.......132 F4
Hobart St
  Bolton BL1.........143 A2
  Manchester M18......99 E5
Hobby Gr WN7.......76 B5
Hob Hey La WA3......91 D3
Hob Hill M35........85 F1
Hobkirk Cl SK16......101 F7
Hob La BL7.........9 C7
Hob Hill Mdws SK13...116 D7
Hobson Cres M34....100 C6
Hobson Ct M34......100 C6
Hobson Moor Rd
  SK14...........103 A7
Hobson St
  Droylsden M11......100 A7
  Failsworth M35......83 D4
  Oldham OL1........153 C2
  Reddish SK5........99 F2
Hockenhull Cl M22....121 E2
Hockerley Cl M33....107 D5
Hockery View WN5....56 C4
HOCKLEY.........134 A2
Hockley Cl SK12.....134 A3
Hockley Paddock
  SK12...........133 F3
Hockley Rd
  Poynton SK12.......134 A3
  8 Wythenshawe M23...120 F6
Hodder Ave
  Littleborough OL15....15 F6
  Platt Bridge WN2.....55 F2
Hodder Cl WN5.......54 D7
Hodder Way M45.....63 C8
Hoddesdon St M8.....156 B3
Hodge Clough Inf Sch
  OL1...........49 D3
Hodge Clough Jun Sch
  OL1...........49 D3
Hodge Clough Rd OL1..49 D3
HODGEFOLD.......114 F8
Hodge Fold SK14....114 F8
Hodge La
  Broadbottom SK14....114 F8
  Salford M5, M6......154 C1
Hodge Rd
  Oldham OL1........49 D3
  Walkden M28........60 D2
Hodges St WN6......37 A2
Hodge St M9.........64 F1
Hodgson Dr WA15....120 A8
Hodgson St
  Ashton-u-L OL6......166 A2
  Salford M8.........155 C1
Hodnet Dr WN4......73 C3
Hodnett Ave M41.....94 E1
Hodnet Wlk M34.....100 C1
Hodson Fold OL8.....67 A1
Hodson Rd M27......61 E2
Hodson St
  Salford M3.........158 B2
  Wigan WN5.........150 C3
Hogarth Rd
  Marple SK6.........126 B8
  Rochdale OL11.......30 F3
Hogarth Rise OL1.....49 D4
Hogarth Wlk M8......156 C2
Hoggs Bridge Cl M27...80 D8
Hoghton Ave OL13....4 A8
Holbeach Cl
  Bury BL8..........27 C5
  Hindley WN2........56 E4
Holbeck M29........77 B5

Hol–Hon 223

Holbeck Ave OL12 ....14 D4
Holbeck Cl BL6 ....39 D8
Holbeck Gr M14 ....98 E4
Holberton Cl M8 ....155 B1
Holbeton Cl SK7 ....124 A3
Holborn Ave
Failsworth M35 ....84 B7
Leigh WN7 ....75 F8
Radcliffe M26 ....43 D4
Wigan WN3 ....150 B1
Holborn Dr M8 ....156 B1
Holborn Gdns OL11 .....139 A1
Holborn Sq OL11 ....139 A1
Holborn St OL11 ....139 A1
Holbrook Ave M38 ....60 A6
Holbrook St M1 ....163 A4
HOLCOMBE 138 A2
Holcombe Ave
Bury BL8 ....27 B2
Golborne WA3 ....90 C8
HOLCOMBE BROOK 11 B2
Holcombe Brook Prim Sch
BL0 ....11 A2
Holcombe Cl
Altrincham WA14 ....119 B6
Kearsley BL4 ....61 A6
Oldham OL4 ....68 A7
Salford M6 ....81 A2
Holcombe Cres BL4 ....61 A6
Holcombe Ct BL0 ....10 F2
Holcombe Gdns M19 ......110 E5
Holcombe Lee BL0 ....11 A4
Holcombe Mews BL0 ....10 F3
Holcombe Old Rd
BL8 ....138 A1
Holcombe Prec BL0 ....10 F3
Holcombe Rd
Haslingden BB4 ....1 A6
Little Lever BL3 ....42 F3
Manchester M14 ....110 E7
Ramsbottom BL8 ....10 F2
Holcombe View Cl
OL4 ....49 D2
Holcombe Village
BL8 ....138 A2
Holcombe Wlk SK4 ....111 D7
Holcroft La WA3 ....92 D2
Holden Ave
Bolton BL1 ....24 E6
Bury BL9 ....28 E4
Manchester M16 ....97 E1
Ramsbottom BL0 ....138 A1
Holden Brook Cl WN7 .....76 B5
Holden Clough Com Prim
Sch OL6 ....85 D7
Holden Clough Dr OL7 ....85 B7
HOLDEN FOLD 48 C2
Holden Fold La OL1,
OL2 ....48 D3
Holden Lea BL5 ....39 E3
Holden Rd
Leigh WN7 ....76 B5
Manchester M7 ....63 D1
Holden St
Adlington PR7 ....20 F7
Ashton-u-L OL6 ....166 C4
Oldham OL8 ....66 F3
5 Rochdale OL12 ....15 A2
Holden Wlk WN5 ....54 E5
Holder Ave BL3 ....43 B5
Holderness Dr OL2 ....48 C2
Holdgate Cl M15 ....162 B1
Holding St WN2 ....56 D6
Holdsworth St M27 ....79 D7
Holebottom OL6 ....85 C6
Hole House Fold SK6 ....113 B2
Holford Ave M14 ....98 B2
Holford Ct M34 ....100 F3
Holford Way WA12 ....89 F3
Holford Wlk OL16 ....31 D7
Holgate Dr WN5 ....53 E6
Holgate St OL4 ....49 E1
Holhouse La BL8 ....10 F2
Holiday La SK2 ....124 F6
Holkar Mdws BL7 ....25 B8
Holker Cl
Manchester M13 ....164 A1
Poynton SK12 ....133 F4
Holker Way 21 M34 ......101 A1
Holkham Cl 6 M4 ....159 C2
Holland Ave SK15 ....86 A2
Holland Cl OL3 ....50 E4
Holland Ct
Manchester M8 ....63 F2
Poynton SK12 ....133 E3
Radcliffe M26 ....44 C4
Stockport SK1 ....124 A7
Holland Gr OL6 ....85 B6
Holland Rd
Bramhall SK7 ....132 E7
Dukinfield SK14 ....101 F5
Manchester M8 ....63 F2
Holland Rise 7 OL12 ....139 B4
Holland St E M34 ....100 E4
Holland St W M34 ....100 D4
Holland St
Bolton BL1 ....143 C4
Denton M34 ....100 D4
Heywood OL10 ....29 D2
Manchester M40 ....160 A3
Radcliffe M26 ....44 C4
Rochdale OL12 ....139 B4
Rochdale, Wuerdle OL16 ...15 D4
Salford M6 ....81 A5
Holland Wlk M6 ....81 A5
Hollies Ct M33 ....108 B4
Hollies Dr SK6 ....126 A5
Hollies La SK9 ....137 F7
Hollies The
10 Atherton M46 ....58 D3
Bolton BL2 ....42 F8
Gatley SK8 ....122 B5
Manchester, West Didsbury
M20 ....109 F3
Pendlebury M27 ....80 B7
Salford M6 ....80 B3
Stockport, Heaton Moor
SK4 ....168 B3
Wigan WN1 ....37 D3
Hollin Acre BL5 ....57 F7
Hollin Bank SK4 ....111 D7
Hollinbrook WN6 ....36 F2
Hollin Cres OL3 ....68 E5
Hollin Cross La SK13 ...116 C8
Hollin Dr M24 ....46 F4
Holliney Ave M22 ....121 F1
Holliney Rd M22 ....121 F2
HOLLINFARE 105 A3
Hollington Way WN3 ......54 C2
Hollingwood Cl WN4 ......73 A3
HOLLINGWORTH
Glossop 103 C6
Littleborough 16 A3
Hollingworth Ave M40 ....65 F2
Hollingworth Business &
Enterprise Coll OL16 ....32 A6
Hollingworth Cl 4
SK1 ....170 C4
Hollingworth Dr SK6 .....125 F3
Hollingworth La OL14 .....6 B8
Hollingworth Lake Ctry
Pk* OL15 ....16 B2
Hollingworth Lake Ctry Pk
Visitor Ctr* OL15 ....16 C3
Hollingworth Lake Water
Sports Ctr* OL15 ....16 B3
Hollingworth Prim Sch
SK14 ....103 C5
Hollingworth Rd
Littleborough OL15 ......16 B4
Romiley SK6 ....112 E4
Hollingworth St OL9 .....66 B3
Hollinhall St OL4 ....67 C7
Hollin Hey Cl WN5 ....71 D3
Hollin Hey Rd BL1 ....23 E3
Hollinhey Terr SK14 ....103 C5
Hollin Ho M24 ....47 A3
Hollinhurst Dr BL6 ......40 C7
Hollinhurst Rd M26 ......44 C1
Hollin La
Middleton M24, OL10 ......46 F4
Rochdale OL11 ....29 E6
Styal SK9 ....130 F5
Hollin Prim Sch M24 ....47 A3
HOLLINS
Middleton 47 A3
Oldham 66 D2
Radcliffe 45 A5
Hollins Ave
Hyde SK14 ....113 E7
Oldham OL4 ....67 F8
Hollins Bank 41 SK13 ...171 A2
Hollins Brook Cl BL9 ....45 B5
Hollins Brook Way BL9 ...45 B6
Hollins Brow BL9 ....44 F4
Hollins Cl
40 Gamesley SK13 ....171 A2
Garswood WN4 ....72 D4
Tyldesley M29 ....77 A8
Whitefield BL9 ....45 B4
Hollinsclough Cl M22 ...121 E5
Hollinscroft Ave
WA15 ....120 D5
Hollins Fold 43 SK13 ...171 A2
Hollins Gdns 45 SK13 ...171 A2
Hollins Gn M24 ....47 A3
Hollins Gr
42 Gamesley SK13 ....171 A2
Manchester M12 ....99 A3
Sale M33 ....108 A4
HOLLINS GREEN
Irlam 105 B2
Oldham 66 E2
Hollins Green Rd SK6 ...125 F6
Hollins Green St Helens
CE Prim Sch WA3 ....105 B2
Hollins Grundy Prim Sch
BL9 ....45 A5
Hollinshead M7 ....155 B2
Hollins Ind Pk SK13 ......104 B5
Hollins La
Edenfield BL0 ....1 E2
Marple, Marple Bridge
SK6 ....126 C8
Marple SK6 ....125 F6
Mossley OL5 ....68 D1
Uppermill OL3 ....69 D5
Whitefield BL9 ....45 B4
Hollins Mews
44 Gamesley SK13 ....171 A2
Whitefield BL9 ....45 C4
Hollinsmoor Rd SK6,
SK22 ....127 D7
Hollins Mount SK6 ......126 B8
Hollins Rd
Hindley WN2 ....57 A5
Oldham, Greenacres Fold
OL4 ....67 F8
Oldham, Hollins OL8 .....66 D2
Hollins Sq BL9 ....45 B3
Hollins St
Bolton BL2 ....148 B2
6 Oldham OL4 ....67 F6
Stalybridge SK15 ....101 F8
Walsden OL14 ....6 B8
Hollins Terr 2 SK6 .....125 F6
Hollins The 4 SK6 ......125 F6
HOLLINS VALE 45 B5
Hollins Way 45 SK13 ....171 A2
Hollins Wlk M22 ....121 D2
Hollinswood Rd
Bolton BL2 ....148 B2
Worsley M28 ....78 B6
Hollin Well Cl M24 ....46 F4
HOLLINWOOD 66 B1
Hollinwood Ave M40,
OL9 ....65 E2
Hollinwood Bsns Ctr
M35 ....66 B1
Hollinwood La SK6 ......126 B2
Hollinwood Rd SK12 .....135 D6
Hollinwood Sta OL9 ....66 A2
Holllins Ave 47 SK13 ...171 A2
Holloway Dr M27, M28 ....61 C1
Hollowbrook Way 4
OL12 ....14 D2
Hollowell La BL6 ....22 D1
Hollow End SK5 ....112 B7
Hollowfield OL11 ....13 D1
Hollowgate M28 ....79 B6
Hollow Mdws M26 ....61 C6
Hollows Ct SK14 ....167 B2
Hollowspell OL12 ....15 C3
Hollows The SK8 ....122 C1
Hollow The SK8 ....122 C1
Hollow Vale Dr
Reddish SK5 ....99 F1
Reddish SK5 ....112 A8
Holly Ave
Cheadle SK8 ....122 D5
Newton-le-W WA12 ....89 D3
Urmston M41 ....95 B2
Walkden M28 ....60 E2
Hollybank M43 ....84 C3
Holly Bank
Ashton-u-L OL6 ....85 D2
Entwistle BL7 ....9 B7
Failsworth M40 ....83 C7
Glossop SK13 ....116 E8
Hollingworth SK14 ......103 D5
2 Royton OL2 ....48 D4
Royton OL2 ....48 D6
Sale M33 ....108 C3
Holly Bank Cl M15 ......161 C2
Holly Bank Ct SK8 ......123 A1
Holly Bank Cvn Pk
WA3 ....105 A1
Hollybank Dr BL6 ....40 B7
Holly Bank Rd SK9 ......131 B1
Hollybank Rise SK16 ....101 F8
Hollybank St M26 ....43 F3
Hollybrook OL1 ....48 B3
Hollybrook Dene SK6 ....113 E2
Hollybush Sq WA3 ....74 E1
Hollybush St M18 ....99 E6
Holly Cl WA15 ....120 A6
Hollycroft Ave
Bolton BL2 ....42 E5
Wythenshawe M22 ....121 D6
Holly Ct
Bury BL9 ....141 A2
Hyde SK14 ....102 A2
1 Irlam M44 ....94 B3
8 Manchester M20 ....110 B6
Stockport SK3 ....170 B1
Hollydene WN2 ....38 B5
Holly Dene Dr BL6 ....40 B7
Holly Dr M33 ....108 A4
Hollyedge Dr M25 ....63 A2
Holly Fold M45 ....44 F1
Holly Gr
Bolton BL1 ....142 C1
Chadderton OL9 ....152 B4
Denton M34 ....101 A3
Dukinfield SK15 ....101 E8
Farnworth BL4 ....60 A8
Leigh WN7 ....75 E7
Oldham OL4 ....67 E7
Sale M33 ....108 D4
Holly Grange
Altrincham WA14 ....119 D2
Stockport SK7 ....123 F3
Holly Heath Dr WN1 ......37 B4
Hollyhedge Ave M22 .....121 D5
Hollyhedge Court Rd
M22 ....121 E5
Hollyhedge Ct M22 ......121 E4
Hollyhedge Rd M22,
M23 ....121 C5
Hollyhey Dr M23 ....109 C2
Holly Heys 4 M33 ....108 D4
Hollyhouse Dr SK6 ......113 A5
Holly House Dr M41 ......94 F2
Hollyhurst M28 ....79 B6
Holly La
Oldham OL8 ....66 C2
Wythenshawe SK9 ....130 E5
Holly Mill Cres BL1 ....143 C4
Hollymount
Failsworth M40 ....65 D3
Manchester M16 ....97 B4
Holly Mount
2 Glossop SK13 ....104 D1
Haslingden BB4 ....1 A7
Hollymount Ave SK2 .....124 C5
Hollymount Dr
Oldham OL4 ....49 E3
Stockport SK2 ....124 C5
Hollymount Gdns
SK2 ....124 D5
Holly Mount La BL8 ......10 E1
Holly Mount RC Prim Sch
BL8 ....10 D1
Hollymount Rd SK2 ......124 D5
Holly Oak Gdns OL10 .....29 C1
Holly Rd
Aspull WN2 ....38 B5
Bramhall SK7 ....132 E5
Golborne WA3 ....90 C8
High Lane SK6 ....134 F7
Lymm WA13 ....117 B5
Poynton SK12 ....133 E3
Reddish SK4 ....111 C5
Swinton M27 ....79 D6
Wigan WN5 ....54 E6
Holly Rd N SK9 ....137 B6
Holly Rd S SK9 ....137 B5
Holly Royde Cl M20 .....110 B6
Holly St
Bolton BL1 ....143 C4
Bury BL9 ....141 A2
Bury, Tottington BL8 .....26 F6
Droylsden M43 ....83 D2
Manchester M11 ....164 B4
Ramsbottom BL9 ....11 C3
Stockport SK1 ....112 B1
Wardle OL12 ....15 C6
Hollythorn Ave SK8 .....132 C7
Hollyville OL3 ....69 C5
Hollyway M22 ....121 E8
Holly Wlk M31 ....105 D3
Hollywood
Altrincham WA14 ....119 D2
Bolton BL1 ....142 B2
Hollywood Rd
Bolton BL1 ....142 B2
Marple SK6 ....126 F8
Hollywood Twrs SK3 .....170 A4
Hollywood Way SK3,
SK4 ....169 A1
Holmbrook M29 ....59 C1
Holmcroft Rd M18 ....99 D3
Holm Ct M6 ....81 A3
Holmdale Ave M19 ....110 E5
Holme Ave
Bury BL8 ....27 C5
Wigan WN1 ....37 C2
Holmebrook Dr
Horwich BL6 ....22 D1
Horwich BL6 ....39 D8
Holme Cres OL2 ....48 C2
Holme Ct 7 WN1 ....37 C2
Holmedale Ct 3 M33 .....108 C4
Holmefield M33 ....108 B4
Holme House St OL15 ......6 D1
Holme La
Haslingden BB4 ....1 D8
Rawtenstall BB4 ....1 E8
Holme Park Gdns M28 .....78 A5
Holme Park Way M35 ......84 B7
Holme Rd M20 ....110 A3
Holmes Cotts BL1 ....142 C3
Holmes Ct SK1 ....169 C1
Holmes House Ave
WN3 ....54 D3
Holmes Rd OL12 ....139 A3
Holmes St
Bolton BL3 ....42 A4
Cheadle SK8 ....122 E6
Rochdale, Greengate
OL12 ....15 C3
Rochdale, Spotland Bridge
OL12 ....139 A3
Stockport SK2 ....170 B3
Holme St
Bacup OL13 ....3 D8
Hyde SK14 ....167 A2
Holmes Way M34 ....112 F7
Holmeswood Cl SK9 ......137 C8
Holmeswood Pk BB4 ....1 E8
Holmeswood Rd BL3 ......147 A2
Holme Terr
Calderbrook OL15 ....6 D1
Haslingden BB4 ....1 D8
Wigan WN1 ....37 B3
Holme Vale BB4 ....1 A6
Holmfield Ave
Manchester, Harpurhey
M9 ....157 C3
Manchester, Sedgley Park
M25 ....63 C3
Holmfield Ave W M9 .....157 C3
Holmfield Cl SK4 ....169 A3
Holmfield Dr SK8 ....132 B8
Holmfield Gn BL3 ....40 F4
Holmfirth Rd
Diggle OL3 ....52 D1
Oldham OL3 ....70 A8
Holmfirth St M13 ....98 F4
Holmfoot Wlk 6 M9 ......157 A3
Holmlea Rd M43 ....83 E2
Holmleigh Ave M9 ....64 E1
Holmpark Rd M11 ....99 F7
Holmrook WA14 ....119 B5
Holmsfield Cl WN2 ....38 A2
Holmside Gdns M19 ......110 E4
Holmwood WA14 ....119 A3
Holmwood Cl WN4 ....73 A5
Holmwood Ct M20 ....110 B4
Holmwood Rd M20 ....110 B5
Holroyd St
Manchester M11 ....165 A4
Rochdale OL16 ....31 A7
Holset Dr WA14 ....119 B5
Holset Wlk SK7 ....124 A2
Holst Ave M8 ....156 A2
Holstein Ave OL12 ....14 D4
Holt Ave WN5 ....71 D4
Holtby St M9 ....64 E1
Holt Cres WN5 ....71 D4
Holt Ho M20 ....110 B2
Holthouse Rd BL8 ....26 F5
Holt La M35 ....84 B7
HOLT LANE END 84 A7
Holt Lane Mews M35 ......84 B7
Holt Mill Rd BB4 ....2 D8
Holton Way WN3 ....54 E1
HOLTS 67 E4
Holt St W BL0 ....138 B1
Holts La OL4 ....67 D4
Holt's La SK9 ....130 F3
Holt St
Altrincham WA14 ....119 C8
Ashton-u-L M34 ....100 E8
Bolton BL3 ....145 A1
Calderbrook OL15 ....6 D2
Eccles M30 ....95 C8
Hindley WN2 ....56 C5
Leigh WN7 ....75 E7
Manchester M40 ....157 C1
Milnrow OL16 ....32 A5
Oldham OL4 ....67 C8
Orrell WN5 ....53 D5
Ramsbottom BL0 ....11 D6
9 Rawtenstall BB4 ....2 E8
Stockport SK1 ....170 C4
Swinton M27 ....61 F2
Tyldesley M29 ....59 A1
Whitworth OL12 ....4 C1
Wigan, Scholes WN1 .....151 C4
Wigan, Springfield WN6 ...36 F2
Wigan, Worsley Mesnes
WN3 ....55 A4
Holt's Terr OL12 ....14 E2
Holtswell Cl WA3 ....74 E1
Holt Town M4, M40 ......160 B2
Holtwood Wlk SK5 ....112 C7
Holway Wlk M9 ....156 C3
Holwick Rd M23 ....108 F2
Holwood Dr M16 ....109 E8
Holybourne Wlk M23 .....120 D8
Holy Cross & All Saints RC
Prim Sch M30 ....95 D8
Holy Cross Coll BL9 ....44 E8
Holy Family RC Inf Sch
WN2 ....38 A2
Holy Family RC Prim Sch
Oldham OL8 ....84 D8
Platt Bridge WN2 ....56 A1
Rochdale OL11 ....31 A2
Sale M33 ....108 E4
Holy Family RC Sch
M28 ....77 E7
Holy Harbour St BL1 ....142 C2
Holyhurst Wlk 29 BL1 ...143 B2
Holy Inf & St Anthony RC
Prim Sch BL1 ....143 B4
Holy Name RC Prim Sch
M15 ....163 A1
Holyoake Rd M28 ....60 E2
Holyoake St M43 ....84 C2
Holyoak St M40 ....83 C6
Holyrood Cl
Leigh WN7 ....76 E7
Prestwich M25 ....63 C6
Holyrood Ct M25 ....63 C6
Holyrood Dr
Prestwich M25 ....63 C6
Swinton M27 ....79 D7
Holyrood Gr M25 ....63 C6
Holyrood Rd M25 ....63 C5
Holyrood St
Failsworth M40 ....83 E4
Oldham OL1 ....49 A1
Holy Rosary RC Jun & Inf
Sch OL8 ....66 F2
Holy St OL16 ....31 B2
Holy Trinity CE Dobcross
Prim Sch OL3 ....50 F2
Holy Trinity CE Prim Sch
Ashton-u-L OL6 ....166 A3
Littleborough OL15 ......16 B5
Manchester M9 ....157 B4
Holy Trinity Prim Sch
BL9 ....140 C1
Holy Trinity Stacksteads
CE Prim Sch OL13 ....3 C8
Holywood St 1 M14 ....98 B3
Homebeck Ho SK8 ....122 A5
Homebury Dr M11 ....83 B2
Home Dr M24 ....64 F7
Home Farm Ave SK14 .....102 F1
Homelands Cl M33 ....107 F2
Homelands Rd M33 ....107 F2
Homelands Wlk M9 ....157 A3
Homelaurel Ho M33 ......108 B2
Homer Dr SK6 ....126 B8
Homer St 5 M26 ....43 E3
Homerton Rd M40 ....83 B4
Homestead Cl M31 ....106 A4
Homestead Cres M19 .....110 D3
Homestead Gdns OL12 .....15 D4
Homestead Rd SK12 ......135 C6
Homestead The 3
M33 ....107 F5
Homewood Ave M22 ....109 D1
Homewood Rd M22 ....109 C1
Honduras St 1 OL4 ....67 B7
Hondwith Cl BL2 ....25 C5
Honeybourne Cl M29 ......59 C1
Honeycombe Cotts
SK8 ....122 E5
Honey Hill OL4 ....67 F5
Honey St M8 ....159 B4
Honeysuckle Ave WN6 .....36 F3
Honeysuckle Cl
Romiley SK6 ....113 A5

Honeysuckle Cl *continued*
Sale M23 . . . . .108 D1
Honeysuckle Dr SK15 . . . .86 C2
Honeysuckle Way
OL12 . . . . .14 D3
Honeysuckle Wlk
M33 . . . . .107 D6
Honeywell La OL8 . . . . . .66 F3
Honeywood Cl BL0 . . . . . .11 A3
Honford Rd M22 . . . . . . .121 C4
Hong Kong Ave M90 . . . .130 A8
Honister Dr M44 . . . . .46 F2
Honister Rd
Manchester M9 . . . . .157 C3
Wigan WN5 . . . . .54 B6
Honister Way OL11 . . . . . .30 B4
Honiton Ave SK14 . . . . . .102 D2
Honiton Cl
Chadderton OL9 . . . . .47 E1
Heywood OL10 . . . . .46 C8
Hindley WN7 . . . . .57 D2
Honiton Dr BL2 . . . . .43 A6
Honiton Gr M26 . . . . .43 D4
Honiton Way WA14 . . . . .119 B6
Honiton Wlk 3 SK14 . . . .102 D2
Honor St M13 . . . . .98 F3
Honsham Wlk M23 . . . . . .108 C1
Hood Cl M29 . . . . .59 D1
Hood Gr WN7 . . . . .76 B3
Hood Sq OL4 . . . . .68 A5
Hood St M4 . . . . .159 B2
Hood Wlk 3 M34 . . . . . . .113 A7
Hook St WN2 . . . . .151 C3
Hoole Cl SK8 . . . . .123 A5
HOOLEY BRIDGE 29 C4
Hooley Bridge Ind Est
OL10 . . . . .29 C4
HOOLEY BROW 29 D3
HOOLEY HILL 100 F6
Hooley Range SK4 . . . . . .168 B3
Hooper St
Manchester M12 . . . . .164 A4
8 Oldham OL4 . . . . .67 A6
Stockport SK1, SK4 . . . . . .169 B1
HOOTEN GARDENS 76 C3
Hooten La WN7 . . . . .76 C3
Hooton St
Bolton BL3 . . . . .146 C3
Manchester M40 . . . . .160 C3
Hooton Way 14 SK9 . . . .131 D5
Hopcroft Cl M9 . . . . .64 B6
Hope Ave
Bolton, Harwood Lee
BL2 . . . . .25 E5
Bolton, Springfield BL2 . . . .148 B2
Handforth SK9 . . . . .131 C3
Stretford M32 . . . . .96 B3
Walkden M38 . . . . .60 C4
Hope Carr La WN7 . . . . . .76 B2
Hope Carr Rd
Leigh WN7 . . . . .76 A3
Leigh WN7 . . . . .76 B3
Hope Carr Way WN7 . . . . .76 A3
Hopecourt Cl M6 . . . . .80 B4
Hope Cres WN6 . . . . .36 B6
Hope Ct 4 OL12 . . . . .139 C4
Hopedale Cl M11 . . . . . . .160 C1
Hopedale Rd SK5 . . . . . . .111 F6
Hope Ent Ctr WN5 . . . . . .36 E1
Hopefield Rd WA13 . . . . .117 B4
Hopefield St BL3 . . . . .147 A4
Hope Fold Ave M46 . . . . . .58 B2
Hopefold Dr M28 . . . . .60 E2
Hope Green Way
SK10 . . . . .133 D2
Hope Hey La M38 . . . . . . .59 F5
Hope High Sch M6 . . . . . .80 B3
Hope Hospl M6 . . . . .80 B3
Hope La
Leigh WA3, WN7 . . . . .76 E2
Midway SK10 . . . . .133 D1
Woodford SK10 . . . . .133 E1
Hopelea St M20 . . . . .110 B7
Hope Park Cl M25 . . . . . . .63 B3
Hope Park Rd M25 . . . . . . .63 B3
Hope Pl OL11 . . . . .30 C1
Hope Rd
Manchester M14 . . . . .98 D4
Prestwich M25 . . . . .63 A2
Sale M33 . . . . .108 B4
Hope St N BL6 . . . . .22 B5
Hopes Carr SK1 . . . . .169 C1
Hope Sch WN3 . . . . .54 F2
Hope St
Adlington PR6 . . . . .21 B8
Ashton-in-M WN4 . . . . .73 D5
Ashton-u-L OL6 . . . . .85 D4
Aspull WN2 . . . . .38 F3
Denton M34 . . . . .100 F5
Dukinfield SK16 . . . . .101 B8
Eccles M30 . . . . .79 F2
Glossop SK13 . . . . .104 E2
Hazel Grove SK7 . . . . .124 D3
Heywood OL10 . . . . .46 F8
Hindley WN2 . . . . .56 F6
Horwich BL6 . . . . .22 B4
Ince-in-M WN3 . . . . .55 E4
Leigh WN7 . . . . .75 F6
Manchester M1 . . . . .159 A1
Newton-le-W WA12 . . . . . . .89 B3
Oldham OL1 . . . . .67 B7
Pendlebury M27 . . . . .80 A8
Ramsbottom BL0 . . . . .138 B1
Rochdale OL12 . . . . .139 C4

Hope St *continued*
Salford, Higher Broughton
M7 . . . . .155 A3
Salford, New Windsor
M5 . . . . .81 C1
Scot Lane End BL6 . . . . . . .38 E8
Shaw OL2 . . . . .149 B3
Stockport SK4 . . . . .169 A1
Swinton M27 . . . . .79 D7
Tyldesley M29 . . . . .77 B5
Walkden M38 . . . . .60 A4
Wigan WN1 . . . . .150 C4
Hope Terr
Dukinfield SK16 . . . . .101 B8
Stockport SK3 . . . . .170 B4
Hopgarth Wlk M40 . . . . . .83 D5
Hopkin Ave OL1 . . . . .67 B8
Hopkin Mill OL4 . . . . .67 D4
Hopkins Bldgs OL5 . . . . . .68 E3
Hopkins Field WA14 . . . .119 B1
Hopkinson Ave M34 . . . .100 E5
Hopkinson Cl OL3 . . . . . . .69 B8
Hopkinson Rd M9 . . . . . . .64 D5
Hopkins St
Hyde SK14 . . . . .167 B4
Manchester M12 . . . . .99 A3
Hopkin St OL1 . . . . .153 C3
Hoppet La M43 . . . . .84 C2
Hopton Ave M22 . . . . . . .121 F3
Hopton Ct M15 . . . . .163 A2
HOPWOOD 29 E1
Hopwood Ave
Eccles M30 . . . . .79 D3
Heywood OL10 . . . . .46 D8
Horwich BL6 . . . . .22 C4
Hopwood Cl
5 Golborne WA3 . . . . .90 F8
Whitefield BL9 . . . . .44 F3
Hopwood Com Prim Sch
OL10 . . . . .46 E8
Hopwood Ct M24 . . . . .47 A4
Hopwood Ct Mews 5
OL10 . . . . .46 E8
Hopwood Hall Coll
M24 . . . . .47 A5
Hopwood Hall Coll
Rochdale Campus
OL12 . . . . .139 B3
Hopwood Rd M24 . . . . . . .47 A4
Hopwood St
Farnworth M40 . . . . .83 B6
Pendlebury M27 . . . . .80 A8
Horace Barnes Cl M14 . . .98 A3
Horace Gr SK4 . . . . .169 B4
Horace St BL1 . . . . .143 A2
Horatio St 4 M18 . . . . . . .99 F6
Horbury Ave M18 . . . . . . .99 D3
Horbury Dr BL8 . . . . .27 C2
Horden Wlk 9 OL2 . . . . . .48 E4
Hordern Cl SK13 . . . . . . .104 A8
Horeb St BL3 . . . . .145 A1
Horest La OL3 . . . . .50 B7
Horley Cl BL8 . . . . .27 C7
Hornbeam Cl
Altrincham WA15 . . . . .120 E5
Sale M33 . . . . .107 C5
Hornbeam Cres WN4 . . . . .73 B3
Hornbeam Ct M6 . . . . .81 A3
Hornbeam Rd M19 . . . . . . .99 B2
Hornby Ave M9 . . . . .64 E5
Hornby Dr BL3 . . . . .40 D3
Hornby Gr WN7 . . . . .76 D7
Hornby Lo M25 . . . . .63 B3
Hornby Rd M16, M32 . . . . .96 F4
Hornby St
Bury BL9 . . . . .140 C4
Heywood OL10 . . . . .29 D2
Manchester M8 . . . . .158 C4
Middleton M24 . . . . .65 A8
Oldham OL8 . . . . .153 A1
Wigan WN1 . . . . .37 C2
Horncastle Cl
Bury BL8 . . . . .27 D5
4 Golborne WA3 . . . . .90 F8
Horncastle Rd M40 . . . . . .65 B1
Hornchurch Ct
Heywood OL10 . . . . .46 E7
2 Manchester M15 . . . . . .162 C2
Hornchurch St M15 . . . . .162 B2
Horncliffe Cl BB4 . . . . .1 E8
Horncliffe View BB4 . . . . . .1 B8
Horne Dr M4 . . . . .159 C2
Horne Dr WN3 . . . . .54 F5
Horne St N BL9 . . . . .44 E8
Hornet Cl OL11 . . . . .31 A3
Horniman Ho M13 . . . . . .163 B1
Hornsea Cl
Bury BL8 . . . . .26 F2
Chadderton OL9 . . . . .47 F1
Hornsea Rd SK2 . . . . .125 A5
Hornsea Wlk M11 . . . . . . .83 A1
Hornsey Gr WN3 . . . . .54 D3
Horridge Ave WA12 . . . . . .89 C5
Horridge Fold BL7 . . . . .9 D7
Horridge Fold Ave BL5 . . . .40 F2
Horridge St BL8 . . . . .27 B4
Horrobin Fold BL7 . . . . .9 C2
Horrobin La BL7 . . . . .9 C2
Horrocks Fold BL1 . . . . . . .24 C7
Horrocks Fold Ave
BL1 . . . . .24 D6
Horrocks Rd BL7 . . . . .9 D6
Horrocks St
Leigh WN7 . . . . .75 A4
Radcliffe M26 . . . . .44 C4
Tyldesley M46 . . . . .58 E1
Horsa St 16 BL2 . . . . .25 B1
Horsedge St OL1 . . . . . . .153 C3

Horsefield Ave OL12 . . . . .14 C6
Horsefield Cl M21 . . . . . .109 E7
Horseshoe La
Alderley Edge SK9 . . . . . . .137 A2
Bolton BL7 . . . . .25 A8
Oldham OL9 . . . . .65 F6
Horsfield St BL3 . . . . .144 A1
Horsfield Way SK6 . . . . . .112 F6
Horsforth La OL3 . . . . .69 A4
Horsham Ave SK7 . . . . . .124 C1
Horsham Cl
Bury BL8 . . . . .27 C7
Westhoughton BL5 . . . . . . .57 F6
Horsham Gr WN2 . . . . .37 F2
Horsham St M6 . . . . .154 B2
Horstead Wlk 8 M19 . . . . .99 A2
Horton Ave BL1 . . . . .24 E6
Horton Mill Com Prim Sch
OL4 . . . . .67 B6
Horton Rd M14 . . . . .98 A2
Horton Sq OL2 . . . . .149 B2
Horton St
Stockport SK1 . . . . .124 A7
Wigan WN6 . . . . .36 E3
Hortree Rd M32 . . . . .96 E2
HORWICH 22 B2
Horwich Bsns Pk BL6 . . . . .22 B2
Horwich Heritage Ctr*
BL6 . . . . .22 C4
Horwich L Ctr* BL6 . . . . .22 C3
Horwich Parish CE Prim
Sch BL6 . . . . .22 C4
Horwich Parkway Sta
BL6 . . . . .39 C7
Horwood Cres M20 . . . . .110 D5
Hoscar Dr M19 . . . . .110 F7
Hoskers Nook BL5 . . . . . . .57 D7
HOSKER'S NOOK 57 D6
Hoskers The BL5 . . . . .57 D6
Hoskins Cl M12 . . . . .165 A1
Hospital Ave M30 . . . . . . .79 E2
Hospital Cotts M25 . . . . . .62 E5
Hospital Rd
Bolton BL7 . . . . .25 A8
Pendlebury M27 . . . . .80 B7
Hotel Rd M90 . . . . .130 C7
Hotel St
Bolton BL1 . . . . .145 C3
Newton-le-W WA12 . . . . . . .89 B3
Hothersall Rd 4 SK5 . . . .111 F8
Hothersall St M7 . . . . .158 B3
Hotspur Cl M14 . . . . .110 A8
HOUGH 137 D1
Hough Cl OL8 . . . . .67 A2
Hough End Ave M21 . . . . .109 C6
Houghend Cres M21 . . . .109 E8
Hough Fold Way BL2 . . . . .25 E4
Hough Gn WA15 . . . . .128 E5
Hough Hall Rd M40 . . . . . .157 C4
Hough Hill Rd SK15 . . . . .102 B8
Hough La
Alderley Edge SK9 . . . . . . .137 D3
Dukinfield SK14 . . . . .24 F7
Dukinfield SK14 . . . . .101 F6
Stake Hill M24 . . . . .47 F4
Tyldesley M29 . . . . .77 C8
Hough St
Bolton BL3 . . . . .146 A4
Tyldesley M29 . . . . .77 D8
Houghton Ave
Oldham OL8 . . . . .66 D2
Wigan WN5 . . . . .36 E2
Houghton Cl
Newton-le-W WA12 . . . . . . .89 B3
Rochdale OL16 . . . . .31 C6
Houghton La
Shevington WN6 . . . . .35 F6
Swinton M27 . . . . .79 D5
Houghton Rd M8 . . . . .64 A1
Houghton St
Bolton BL3 . . . . .145 B1
Bury BL9 . . . . .140 B1
Leigh WN7 . . . . .75 F6
Newton-le-W WA12 . . . . . . .89 B3
Pendlebury M27 . . . . .80 D6
Royton OL2 . . . . .48 E2
Tyldesley M46 . . . . .58 D3
Hough Wlk M7 . . . . .158 A3
Houghwood Grange
WN4 . . . . .72 F3
Houldsworth Ave
WA14 . . . . .119 E7
Houldsworth Mill Bsns &
Art Ctr SK4, SK5 . . . . . . .111 F7
Houldsworth Sq 2
SK5 . . . . .111 F7
Houldsworth St
Manchester M1 . . . . .159 B2
2 Radcliffe M26 . . . . .43 F5
Reddish SK5 . . . . .111 F7
Houseley Ave OL9 . . . . . . .66 A3
Houseman Gr WN6 . . . . . . .37 A2
Housley Cl WN3 . . . . .150 A1
Houson St OL8 . . . . .153 C1
Houston Pk M50 . . . . .154 C1
Hove Cl BL8 . . . . .10 F1
Hoveden St M8 . . . . .158 C4
Hove Dr M14 . . . . .110 E7
Hove St N 13 BL3 . . . . . .144 C1
Hove St BL3 . . . . .144 C1
Hovey Cl M8 . . . . .155 C3
Hovingham St OL16 . . . . . .31 B8
Hovington Gdns M19 . . . .110 E6
Hovis St M11 . . . . .165 C4
Howard Ave
Bolton BL3 . . . . .146 B4
Cheadle SK8 . . . . .123 A1
Eccles M30 . . . . .79 D3

Howard Ave *continued*
Kearsley BL4 . . . . .60 F7
Lymm WA13 . . . . .117 B4
Reddish SK4 . . . . .111 C6
Howard Cl
Glossop SK13 . . . . .104 B2
Romiley SK6 . . . . .113 A2
Howard Ct OL6 . . . . .166 C3
Howard Hill BL9 . . . . .45 A5
Howardian Cl OL8 . . . . . . .66 E2
Howard La M34 . . . . .100 F4
Howard Pl
Hyde SK14 . . . . .167 A2
Rochdale OL16 . . . . .139 C4
Howard Rd
Culcheth WA3 . . . . .92 A2
Wythenshawe M22 . . . . . .109 D1
Howards La WN5 . . . . .53 F7
Howard's La OL5 . . . . .68 F1
Howards Mdw SK13 . . . . .116 B7
Howard Spring Wlk
M8 . . . . .155 C4
Howard St
Ashton-u-L OL7 . . . . .166 A4
Bolton BL1 . . . . .143 C1
Denton M34 . . . . .100 E5
Glossop SK13 . . . . .104 C1
Oldham OL4 . . . . .49 E1
Radcliffe M26 . . . . .44 B3
Rochdale OL12 . . . . .139 C4
Salford M5 . . . . .161 A4
Shaw OL2 . . . . .149 A3
Stalybridge SK15 . . . . .86 D4
Stockport SK1 . . . . .169 C2
Stretford M32 . . . . .96 D2
Wigan WN5 . . . . .54 C5
Howard Way OL15 . . . . .6 C1
Howarth Ave M28 . . . . . . .79 C7
Howarth Cl M11 . . . . .83 A1
HOWARTH CROSS 15 C2
Howarth Cross St OL16 . . .15 B2
Howarth Ct SK6 . . . . .125 F5
Howarth Dr M44 . . . . .93 F1
Howarth Farm Way
OL12 . . . . .15 C3
Howarth Gn OL12 . . . . .15 C3
Howarth Sq OL16 . . . . .31 A8
Howarth St
Farnworth BL4 . . . . .60 D7
Leigh WN7 . . . . .76 B4
Littleborough OL15 . . . . . . .16 B6
Manchester M16 . . . . .97 C4
Westhoughton BL5 . . . . . . .57 F8
Howbridge Cl M28 . . . . . . .78 C8
Howbro Dr OL7 . . . . .84 E5
Howbrook Wlk 7
M15 . . . . .162 C2
How Clough Cl M28 . . . . . .60 F2
How Clough Dr M28 . . . . . .60 F2
Howcroft Cl BL1 . . . . .145 B4
Howcroft St BL3 . . . . .145 A1
Howden Cl SK5 . . . . .99 E2
Howden Dr WN3 . . . . .55 B4
Howden Rd
Manchester M9 . . . . .64 C5
New Mills SK22 . . . . .127 C1
HOWE BRIDGE 58 B1
Howe Bridge Cl M46 . . . . .58 A1
Howe Dr BL0 . . . . .11 B2
Howell Croft N 7
BL1 . . . . .145 C3
Howell Croft S BL1 . . . . . .145 C3
Howells Ave M33 . . . . .108 B5
Howell's Yd 6 BL1 . . . . . .145 C3
Howe St
Ashton-u-L OL7 . . . . .100 F8
Salford M7 . . . . .155 A3
Howgill Cres OL8 . . . . .66 E3
Howgill St M11 . . . . .83 D1
How Lea Dr BL9 . . . . .27 F6
Howley Cl M44 . . . . .94 B1
Howsin Ave BL2 . . . . .25 B4
Howton Cl M12 . . . . .99 A4
Howty Cl SK9 . . . . .131 D1
Hoxton Cl SK6 . . . . .113 A4
Hoy Dr M41 . . . . .95 D5
Hoylake Cl
Failsworth M40 . . . . .83 D8
Leigh WN7 . . . . .75 D2
Hoylake Rd
Stockport SK3 . . . . .123 B8
Wythenshawe M33 . . . . . .108 F2
Hoyland Cl M12 . . . . .164 C2
Hoyle Ave OL8 . . . . .153 B1
Hoyles Ct 3 M26 . . . . .44 C4
Hoyle St
Bacup OL13 . . . . .3 E8
3 Bolton BL1 . . . . .143 B4
Manchester M12 . . . . .163 C4
Middleton M24 . . . . .65 C6
Radcliffe M26 . . . . .44 C1
Wythenshawe OL3 . . . . .4 D3
Hoyle's Terr OL16 . . . . . . .31 E6
Hoyle Street Ind Est
M12 . . . . .163 C3
Hoyle Wlk M13 . . . . .164 D5
Hubert Worthington Ho 8
SK9 . . . . .137 A2
Hucclecote Ave M22 . . . .121 C2
Huckleberry Cl BL9 . . . . . .45 A2
Hucklow Bank 38
SK13 . . . . .171 A2
Hucklow Cl 33 SK13 . . . .171 A2
Hucklow Fold 34
SK13 . . . . .171 A2

Hucklow Lanes 53
SK13 . . . . .171 A2
Hudcar La BL9 . . . . .141 A4
Huddart Cl M5 . . . . .161 B4
Huddersfield Rd
Denshaw OL3 . . . . .33 E2
Diggle OL3 . . . . .51 C7
Diggle OL3 . . . . .51 D5
Newhey OL16, OL3 . . . . . . .32 D5
Oldham OL4 . . . . .67 D8
Stalybridge OL5, SK15 . . . . .86 E4
Hudson Gr 8 WA3 . . . . . . .90 E8
Hudson Rd
Bolton BL3 . . . . .146 B3
Hyde SK14 . . . . .113 E7
Hudsons Pas OL15 . . . . . . .16 C7
Hudson Sq OL1 . . . . .48 D1
Hudson St OL9 . . . . .66 A2
Hudsons Wlk OL11 . . . . . . .30 C7
Hudswell Cl M45 . . . . .62 E8
Hughendon Ct BL8 . . . . . . .26 F7
Hughes Ave BL6 . . . . .22 A4
Hughes Cl
Bury BL9 . . . . .141 A3
Failsworth M35 . . . . .83 E8
Hughes St
Bolton BL1 . . . . .142 C2
Bolton BL1 . . . . .143 A2
Manchester M11 . . . . .164 B4
Hughes Way M30 . . . . .79 A1
Hugh Fold OL4 . . . . .67 E5
Hughley Cl OL2 . . . . .49 A4
Hugh Lupus St BL1 . . . . . . .25 A5
HUGH MILL 2 F7
Hugh Oldham Dr M7 . . . . .81 C6
Hugh St
Glossop SK13 . . . . .104 B1
Rochdale OL16 . . . . .31 A8
Hughtrede St OL16 . . . . . . .31 B3
Hugo St
Farnworth BL4 . . . . .42 B2
Manchester M40 . . . . .83 A7
Rochdale OL11 . . . . .30 D2
Hulbert St
Bury BL8 . . . . .27 C1
Middleton M24 . . . . .47 B1
Hullet Cl WN6 . . . . .35 E8
Hull Mill La OL3 . . . . .50 F5
Hull Sq M3 . . . . .158 A2
Hully St 8 SK15 . . . . .85 F2
HULME 162 C2
Hulme Court Prep Sch
OL8 . . . . .66 D4
Hulme Ct M15 . . . . .162 B3
Hulme Dr WA15 . . . . .120 C7
Hulme Gr WN7 . . . . .75 C6
Hulme Gram Sch for Boys
OL8 . . . . .66 D4
Hulme Gram Sch for Girls
SK8 . . . . .123 A1
Hulme Hall Ave SK8 . . . . .132 B8
Hulme Hall Cl SK8 . . . . . .123 A1
Hulme Hall Cres SK8 . . . .132 A8
Hulme Hall Grammar Sch
SK8 . . . . .123 A1
Hulme Hall La M40 . . . . . .160 B4
Hulme Hall Rd
Cheadle SK8 . . . . .123 A1
Manchester M15 . . . . .162 A3
Hulme High St M15 . . . . .162 C1
Hulme Pl M5 . . . . .81 C2
Hulme Rd
Bolton BL2 . . . . .25 E5
Kearsley M26 . . . . .61 C7
Leigh WN7 . . . . .75 C6
Reddish, Dane Bank
M34 . . . . .100 B3
Reddish, Heaton Chapel
SK4 . . . . .111 D6
Sale M33 . . . . .108 D3
Hulmes Rd M35, M40 . . . . .83 E5
Hulme St
Ashton-u-L OL6 . . . . .85 D4
Bury BL8 . . . . .140 A3
Manchester M1, M15 . . . . .162 C3
Oldham OL8 . . . . .66 E4
Salford M5 . . . . .81 C1
Stockport SK1 . . . . .124 B7
Hulme's Terr BL2 . . . . .43 C8
Hulton Ave M28 . . . . .60 B3
Hulton Cl BL3 . . . . .146 A3
Hulton District Ctr
M28 . . . . .60 A4
Hulton Dr BL3 . . . . .146 A3
Hulton Hospl BL3 . . . . . . .146 A3
Hulton La BL3 . . . . .146 A3
HULTON LANE ENDS 59 A8
Hulton St
Denton M34 . . . . .100 E4
Failsworth M35 . . . . .83 E7
Manchester M16 . . . . .97 E4
Salford M5 . . . . .161 A3
Humber Dr BL9 . . . . .27 F7
Humber Pl WN5 . . . . .54 C7
Humber Rd
Milnrow OL16 . . . . .32 A6
Tyldesley M29 . . . . .77 C7
Humber St
Manchester M8 . . . . .156 B3
Salford M50 . . . . .154 A1
Humberstone Ave
M15 . . . . .162 C2
Hume St
Manchester M19 . . . . .111 B8
Rochdale OL16 . . . . .31 A5
Humphrey Booth Gdns
M6 . . . . .154 B3
Humphrey Cres M41 . . . . . .96 A2

Humphrey La M41 . . . . .96 A2
Humphrey Park Sta
M32 .96 A3
Humphrey Pk M41 . . . . .96 A2
Humphrey Rd M16 . . . . .161 B1
Humphrey St
Ince-in-M WN2 . . . . .56 A7
Salford M8 . . . . .155 C4
Humphries Ct M40 . . . . .159 C4
Huncoat Ave SK4 . . . . .111 D5
Huncote Dr M9 . . . . .64 E1
Hungerford Wlk **5**
M23 .120 D7
HUNGER HILL
Bolton 40 D3
Standish 18 F4
Hunger Hill Ave BL3 . . . . .40 E2
Hunger Hill La OL12 . . . . .13 F3
Hunmanby Ave M15 . . . . . . .162 C3
Hunstanton Dr BL8 . . . . .27 D5
Hunston Rd M33 . . . . .107 F2
Hunt Ave OL7 . . . . .85 B5
Hunter Dr M26 . . . . .44 A5
Hunter Rd WN5 . . . . .36 E1
Hunters Chase WN5 . . . . .53 E1
Hunters Cl
Handforth SK9 . . . . .131 F1
6 Romiley SK6 . . . . .112 F3
Hunters Ct
Dukinfield SK16 . . . . .101 F7
Stalybridge SK15 . . . . .102 D8
Hunters Gn BL0 . . . . .10 F3
Hunters Hill BL0 . . . . .45 B4
Hunters Hill La OL3 . . . . .51 C6
Hunters La SK13 . . . . .115 F8
Hunter's La
Oldham OL1 . . . . .153 C3
Rochdale OL2,OL16 . . . . .139 C4
Hunters Lo SK9 . . . . .131 F1
Hunters Mews
Sale M33 . . . . .108 A5
Wilmslow SK9 . . . . .137 C7
Hunterston Ave M30 . . . . .80 A2
Hunter's View SK9 . . . . .131 C3
Hunt Fold Dr BL8 . . . . .10 F1
Huntingdon Ave M13 . . . . . . .152 B1
Huntingdon Cres SK5 . . . . . . .112 C5
Huntingdon Way **7**
M34 .100 F1
Huntingdon Wlk **21**
BL1 . . . . .143 B2
Huntington Ave M20 . . . . . . .110 A7
Hunt La OL9 . . . . .152 A3
Huntley Mount Rd
BL9 .141 B3
Huntley Rd
Manchester M8 . . . . .63 E2
Stockport SK3 . . . . .123 B7
Huntley St BL9 . . . . .141 B3
Huntly Chase SK9 . . . . .137 C7
Huntly Wy OL10 . . . . .28 E1
Hunt Rd SK14 . . . . .102 A5
Huntroyde Ave **22** BL2 . . . . . .25 B1
Hunts Bank
Manchester M3 . . . . .158 C2
Westhoughton BL5 . . . . .57 F6
Huntsham Cl WA14 . . . . .119 B6
Huntsman Dr M44 . . . . .105 F7
Huntsman Rd M9 . . . . .157 C4
Huntspill Rd WA14 . . . . .119 C8
Hunts Rd **2** M6 . . . . .80 D5
Hunt St
Atherton M46 . . . . .58 D3
Manchester M9 . . . . .64 D1
Wigan WN1 . . . . .151 B3
Hurdlow Ave M7 . . . . .81 A7
Hurdlow Gn **10** SK13 . . . . . . .171 A1
Hurdlow Lea **11** SK13 . . . . . .171 A1
Hurdlow Mews SK13 . . . . . . .171 A1
Hurdlow Way **12**
SK13 . . . . .171 A1
Hurdlow Wlk M9 . . . . .157 A3
Hurdsfield Rd SK2 . . . . .124 D4
Hurford Ave M18 . . . . .99 D6
Hurlbote Cl SK9 . . . . .131 D5
Hurley Dr SK8 . . . . .122 E2
Hurlston Rd BL3 . . . . .147 A2
HURST 85 D5
Hurst Ave
Cheadle SK8 . . . . .132 C6
Sale M33 . . . . .107 C3
Hurstbank Ave M19 . . . . .110 D4
Hurst Bank Rd OL6 . . . . .85 E4
Hurstbourne Ave M11 . . . . . . .83 B2
HURST BROOK 166 C4
Hurstbrook Cl SK13 . . . . .104 F1
Hurst Brook Cl OL6 . . . . .166 C4
Hurstbrook Dr M32 . . . . .95 F2
Hurst Cl
Glossop SK13 . . . . .104 E1
Over Hulton BL5 . . . . .58 F7
Hurst Cres SK13 . . . . .116 E8
Hurst Cross OL6 . . . . .85 D5
Hurst Ct
Ashton-u-L OL6 . . . . .85 E5
Wythenshawe M23 . . . . .120 F4
Hurstead **2** OL12 . . . . .15 C4
Hurstead Cl M8 . . . . .156 A2
Hurstead Rd OL12 . . . . .15 B4
Hurstead Rd OL16 . . . . .31 F6
Hurstfield Ind Est SK4,
SK5 . . . . .15 C4
Hurstfield Rd M28 . . . . .78 B8
Hurstfold Ave M19 . . . . .110 D3
Hurst Gr OL6 . . . . .85 E5
Hurst Green Cl BL8 . . . . .43 F8
Hurst Hall Dr OL6 . . . . .85 E5

Hursthead Inf Sch
SK8 .132 C6
Hursthead Jun Sch
SK8 .132 C7
Hursthead Rd SK8 . . . . .132 B7
Hursthead Wlk M13 . . . . .163 B3
Hurst Hill Cres OL6 . . . . .85 D4
HURST KNOLL 85 C5
Hurst Knoll St James' CE
Prim Sch OL6 . . . . .166 C4
Hurst La WA3 . . . . .92 C7
Hurst Lea Ct SK9 . . . . .137 A2
Hurst Mdw
Ashton-u-L OL6 . . . . .85 D5
Rochdale OL16 . . . . .31 C3
Hurstmead Terr M20 . . . . . . .110 B2
Hurst Mill La WA3 . . . . .92 C8
HURST NOOK 85 E6
Hurst Rd SK13 . . . . .104 F1
Hurst St
Bolton BL3 . . . . .146 C3
Bury BL9 . . . . .141 A2
Hindley WN2 . . . . .56 C6
Leigh WN7 . . . . .76 B3
Oldham OL9 . . . . .153 A3
Reddish SK5 . . . . .111 E7
Rochdale OL11 . . . . .31 A5
Walkden M28 . . . . .60 D6
Hurstvale Ave SK8 . . . . .122 B1
Hurstville Rd M21 . . . . .109 B6
Hurstway Dr **33** M9 . . . . .64 E3
Hurst Wlk **4** M22 . . . . .121 A2
Hurstwood
Ashton-u-L OL6 . . . . .85 F6
Bolton BL1 . . . . .24 E5
Hurstwood Cl OL8 . . . . .67 C4
Hurstwood Ct
Bolton BL3 . . . . .42 C4
Leigh WN7 . . . . .76 B2
Hurstwood Rd SK2 . . . . .124 F6
Huskisson Way WA12 . . . . . . .89 B4
Hus St **1** M43 . . . . .100 A8
Husteads OL3 . . . . .50 E1
Husteads La OL3 . . . . .50 F1
Hutchins La OL4 . . . . .49 D1
Hutchinson Rd OL11 . . . . .13 D2
Hutchinson St
4 Radcliffe M26 . . . . .44 C4
Rochdale OL11 . . . . .30 C6
Hutchinson Way M26 . . . . . . .44 A3
Huttock End La OL13 . . . . .3 D8
Hutton Ave
Ashton-u-L OL6 . . . . .85 E3
Boothstown M28 . . . . .77 F6
Hutton Cl WA3 . . . . .91 E5
Hutton Lo M20 . . . . .110 C7
Hutton St WN1 . . . . .20 A3
Hutton Wlk **7** M13 . . . . .163 C2
Huxley Ave M8 . . . . .156 A2
Huxley Cl SK7 . . . . .132 E7
Huxley Dr SK7 . . . . .132 E7
Huxley Pl WN3 . . . . .150 A1
Huxley St
Altrincham WA14 . . . . .119 D7
Bolton BL1 . . . . .142 C2
6 Oldham OL4 . . . . .67 C6
Huxley Terr **4** WA14 . . . . . . .119 C1
Huxton Gn SK7 . . . . .124 A2
Huyton Rd BL6,PR7 . . . . .21 A6
Huyton Terr PR6 . . . . .21 A6
Hyacinth Cl SK3 . . . . .19 C3
Hyatt Cres WN6 . . . . .19 C3
HYDE 167 C2
Hyde Central Sta
SK14 . . . . .101 C2
Hyde Cl WN3 . . . . .150 A1
Hyde Clarendon Sixth
Form Coll SK14 . . . . .167 B4
Hyde Clarendon Sports H
SK14 . . . . .167 B3
Hyde Dr M28 . . . . .60 C2
Hyde Fold Cl M19 . . . . .110 F6
Hyde Gr
Manchester M13 . . . . .163 C1
Sale M33 . . . . .108 B4
Walkden M28 . . . . .60 C2
Hyde Ho SK4 . . . . .111 C5
Hyde Hospl SK14 . . . . .167 C1
Hyde North Sta SK14 . . . . . . .101 C5
Hyde Pl M13 . . . . .163 C1
Hyde Rd
Denton M34 . . . . .101 A3
Manchester, Gorton M12,
M18 . . . . .99 D4
Manchester, West Gorton
M12 .164 B2
Mottram in L SK14 . . . . .103 A4
Oldham M24 . . . . .65 E6
Romiley SK14,SK6 . . . . .113 B5
Walkden M28 . . . . .60 C2
HYDES 85 F1
Hyde's Cross M4 . . . . .159 A2
Hyde Sq M7 . . . . .46 E1
Hyde St
Bolton BL3 . . . . .146 C3
Droylsden M43 . . . . .84 C4
Dukinfield SK16 . . . . .101 D8
Hydes Terr **1** SK15 . . . . .86 B2
Hyde Tech Sch & Hearing
Impaired Resource Base
SK14 . . . . .167 A4
Hydon Brook Wlk
OL11 .30 C4
Hydra Cl M7 . . . . .81 C3
Hydrangea Cl M33 . . . . .107 C6
Hyldavale Ave SK8 . . . . .122 B6
Hylton Dr SK8 . . . . .132 C8

Hyman Goldstone Wlk **4**
M8 . . . . .155 C3
Hyndman Ct M5 . . . . .154 A1
Hypatia St BL2 . . . . .148 B3
Hythe Cl M14 . . . . .98 C3
Hythe Rd SK3 . . . . .123 B8
Hythe St BL3 . . . . .146 A4
Hythe Wlk OL9 . . . . .152 B2

Ibberton Wlk **8** M9 . . . . .64 F1
Ibsley **20** OL12 . . . . .139 B4
Ice House Cl M28 . . . . .59 F3
Iceland St M6 . . . . .154 C2
Idonia St BL1 . . . . .143 A3
Ifco Ctr M14 . . . . .98 C3
Ilex Gr M7 . . . . .155 A2
Ilford St M11 . . . . .83 A2
Ilfracombe Rd SK2 . . . . .124 D8
Ilfracombe St M40 . . . . .83 D6
Ilkeston Dr WN2 . . . . .38 F3
Ilkeston Wlk
5 Denton M34 . . . . .113 A8
4 Manchester M40 . . . . . . .83 A6
Ilkley Cl
Bolton BL2 . . . . .148 C3
Chadderton OL9 . . . . .152 B2
Ilkley Cres SK5 . . . . .111 E8
Ilkley Dr M41 . . . . .95 A4
Ilkley St M40 . . . . .83 A8
Ilk St M11 . . . . .83 B2
Illingworth Ave SK15 . . . . .86 C2
Illona Dr M7 . . . . .81 A8
Ilminster **7** M9 . . . . .139 B2
Ilminster Wlk **2** M9 . . . . .64 E5
Ilthorpe Wlk **7** M40 . . . . .83 A6
Imex Bsns Pk M13 . . . . .98 F3
Imogen Ct M5 . . . . .161 C4
Imperial Dr WN7 . . . . .76 D6
Imperial Point M50 . . . . .96 F7
Imperial Terr M33 . . . . .108 A4
Imperial War Mus*
M17 . . . . .96 E7
Ina Ave BL1 . . . . .23 F1
Ince CE Prim Sch WN2 . . . . . .56 A7
Ince Cl
Manchester M20 . . . . .110 B7
Stockport SK4 . . . . .169 B3
Ince Green La WN2,
WN3 .151 C2
Ince Hall Ave WN2 . . . . .151 C4
INCE-IN-MAKERFIELD
. . . . .151 B3
Ince St Mary's CE Prim
Sch WN3 . . . . .55 F4
Ince St SK4 . . . . .169 B3
Ince Sta WN3 . . . . .151 C2
Ince Wlk WN1 . . . . .150 C4
Inchcape Dr M9 . . . . .64 B4
Inchfield Cl OL11 . . . . .30 B4
Inchfield Rd
Manchester M40 . . . . .65 B1
Walsden OL14 . . . . .6 A8
Inchley Rd M13 . . . . .163 B3
Inchwood Mews OL4 . . . . .49 E4
Incline Rd OL8 . . . . .66 C2
Independent St BL3 . . . . .43 A3
India Ho M1 . . . . .163 A4
India St BL9 . . . . .11 C3
Indigo St M6 . . . . .80 F5
Indigo Wlk M6 . . . . .80 F5
Indus Pl M7 . . . . .81 C4
Industrial Cotts **10** BB4 . . . . . .2 F8
Industrial St
Ramsbottom BL0 . . . . .1 C1
14 Littleborough OL15 . . . . .16 B5
1 Rochdale OL11 . . . . .13 E1
Whitworth OL12 . . . . .4 D2
Infant St M25 . . . . .63 C4
Infirmary St **11** BL1 . . . . .145 C3
Ingham Ave WA12 . . . . .89 C1
Ingham Rd WA14 . . . . .107 D1
Inghams La OL15 . . . . .16 B5
Ingham St
Bury BL9 . . . . .141 A1
Failsworth M40 . . . . .83 E4
Leigh WN7 . . . . .75 E8
5 Manchester M11 . . . . . . .83 C1
Inghamwood Cl M7 . . . . .155 C3
Ingleby Ave M9 . . . . .64 F4
Ingleby Cl
Shaw OL2 . . . . .149 A4
Standish WN6 . . . . .19 D2
Westhoughton BL5 . . . . .40 A2
Ingleby Ct M32 . . . . .96 E1
Ingleby Way M9 . . . . .64 F4
Ingledene Ave M7 . . . . .63 E1
Ingledene Ct **6** M7 . . . . .63 E1
Ingledene Gr BL1 . . . . .142 A2
Inglehead Cl M34 . . . . .101 A2
Inglenook Rd M46 . . . . .76 A8
Ingle Rd SK8 . . . . .123 A6
Ingles Fold M28 . . . . .78 A6
Inglesham Cl
Leigh WN7 . . . . .75 E1
Wythenshawe M23 . . . . .121 B6
Ingleton Ave M8 . . . . .64 D3
Ingleton Cl
Bolton BL2 . . . . .25 D4

Ingleton Cl *continued*
Cheadle SK8 . . . . .122 C6
Newton-le-W WA12 . . . . .89 B4
Royton OL2 . . . . .48 D5
Ingleton Dr WA11 . . . . .71 B1
Ingleton Mews BL8 . . . . .27 B4
Ingleton Rd SK3 . . . . .123 C7
Inglewhite M m40 . . . . .37 C2
Inglewhite Cl BL9 . . . . .44 D7
Inglewhite Cres **1**
WN1 . . . . .37 C2
Inglewhite Pl **2** WN1 . . . . . . .37 C2
Inglewood WA14 . . . . .119 B3
Inglewood Ave WN1 . . . . .151 B3
Inglewood Cl
Ashton-u-L OL7 . . . . .84 F5
Bury BL9 . . . . .141 C4
Partington M31 . . . . .105 F4
Inglewood Cvn Pk
M31 .105 F4
Inglewood Hollow
SK15 . . . . .102 C8
Inglewood Rd M24 . . . . .47 E1
Inglewood Wlk M13 . . . . .163 C2
Inglis St OL15 . . . . .16 B6
Ingoe Cl OL10 . . . . .29 F3
Ingoldsby Ave M13 . . . . .98 D4
Ingram Ct SK4 . . . . .110 E3
Ingram St
Platt Bridge WN2 . . . . .56 A3
Wigan WN6 . . . . .36 F2
Ings Ave OL12 . . . . .14 B2
Ings La OL12 . . . . .14 C2
Inkerman St
Hyde SK14 . . . . .167 A4
Manchester M40 . . . . .157 A2
12 Rochdale OL12 . . . . .14 F1
Ink St OL16 . . . . .139 C3
Inman St
Bury BL9 . . . . .44 E8
Denton M34 . . . . .100 F3
Innes St OL12 . . . . .14 C1
Innes St M12 . . . . .99 B3
Innis Ave M40 . . . . .83 C5
Inscape House Salford
M28 . . . . .60 E1
Institute St BL1 . . . . .148 A3
Instow Cl
Chadderton OL9 . . . . .47 F1
Manchester M13 . . . . .164 A2
Intake La OL3 . . . . .69 B3
International App
M90 .130 C7
Invar Rd M27 . . . . .61 D1
Inverbeg Dr BL2 . . . . .43 A7
Invergarry Wlk **15** M11 . . . . . .83 C1
Inverlael Ave BL1 . . . . .144 B4
Inverness Ave M9 . . . . .65 A4
Inverness Cl WN2 . . . . .38 D5
Inverness Rd SK16 . . . . .101 C7
Inver Wlk **10** M40 . . . . .65 D2
Inward Dr WN6 . . . . .36 A5
Inwood Wlk M8 . . . . .156 C2
Inworth Cl BL5 . . . . .57 F6
Inworth Wlk **10** M8 . . . . .155 C3
Iona Pl BL2 . . . . .25 C2
Iona Way M41 . . . . .95 E5
Ionian Gdns **2** M7 . . . . .81 C5
Ipswich St M11 . . . . .139 C1
Ipswich Wlk
Denton M34 . . . . .101 A1
Manchester M12 . . . . .164 B1
Iqbal Cl M12 . . . . .165 A1
Irby Wlk SK8 . . . . .123 A4
Ireby Cl M24 . . . . .46 C2
Iredale Cres WN6 . . . . .36 F7
Iredine St M11 . . . . .83 C1
Irene Ave SK14 . . . . .101 E5
Iris Ave
Farnworth BL4 . . . . .42 A1
Kearsley BL4 . . . . .60 F5
Manchester M11 . . . . .99 D8
Iris St
Oldham OL8 . . . . .66 F3
Ramsbottom BL0 . . . . .138 B2
Iris Wlk **7** M31 . . . . .105 E7
Irk Vale Dr OL1,OL9 . . . . .47 E1
Irk Way M45 . . . . .45 B2
IRLAM 105 F7
Irlam Ave M30 . . . . .79 D1
Irlam & Cadishead Com
High Sch M44 . . . . .105 E7
Irlam Endowed Prim Sch
M44 . . . . .94 A2
Irlam Ind Est M44 . . . . .105 E7
Irlam Prim Sch M44 . . . . .94 A1
Irlam Rd
Sale M33 . . . . .108 C4
Urmston M41 . . . . .94 D2
IRLAMS O' TH' HEIGHT
. . . . .80 E5
Irlam Sq M6 . . . . .80 D5
Irlam St
Bolton BL1 . . . . .143 B3
Manchester M40 . . . . .157 B1
Manchester M44 . . . . .105 E7
Irlam Wharf Rd M44 . . . . .106 A6
Irmass Ind Est M17 . . . . .96 D6
Irma St BL1 . . . . .143 C3
IRON BROW 35 B7
Iron St
Horwich BL6 . . . . .22 C2
Manchester M40 . . . . .160 B3
Iron Works The OL9 . . . . .48 D3
Irvin Dr M22,SK8 . . . . .131 A8
Irvine Ave **6** M28 . . . . .78 A6
Irvine St WN7 . . . . .75 F6

Irving Cl SK2 . . . . .124 A3
Irving Ho **1** BL1 . . . . .143 B2
Irving St
Bolton BL1 . . . . .143 B2
Oldham OL8 . . . . .66 B2
Irvin St M40 . . . . .83 C6
Irwell Ave
Denton M34 . . . . .79 F1
Walkden M38 . . . . .60 B4
Irwell Cl M4 . . . . .44 B2
Irwell Gr M30 . . . . .79 F1
Irwell Ho **2** M7 . . . . .162 A3
Irwell Park High Sch
Eccles M30 . . . . .79 C2
Salford M6 . . . . .81 A5
Irwell Pl
Eccles M30 . . . . .79 F1
Kearsley M26 . . . . .61 B8
Salford M5 . . . . .81 C2
Wigan WN5 . . . . .54 C6
Irwell Rd WN5 . . . . .53 F7
Irwell St
Bury BL9 . . . . .140 B2
Kearsley M26 . . . . .61 B8
Manchester M3 . . . . .158 B1
Manchester, Strangeways M7,
M8 . . . . .158 B4
Radcliffe M26 . . . . .44 B2
Ramsbottom BL0 . . . . .138 C2
IRWELL VALE 1 C5
Irwell Vale Rd BB4,BL0 . . . . . . .1 C6
Irwell Vale Sta 1 C5
Irwell Wlk OL8 . . . . .66 C3
Irwin Ct SK8 . . . . .122 F3
Irwin Dr SK9 . . . . .131 C5
Irwin Rd WA14 . . . . .119 D8
Irwin St M34 . . . . .100 E3
Isaac Cl M5 . . . . .161 A4
Isaac St BL1 . . . . .144 C4
Isabella Cl M16 . . . . .97 C4
Isabella Sq WN1 . . . . .151 B4
Isabella St OL12 . . . . .15 A2
Isabel Wlk BL3 . . . . .145 A1
Isaiah St OL8 . . . . .66 F4
Isa St BL0 . . . . .11 A4
Isca St SM11 . . . . .160 C1
Isel Wlk M24 . . . . .46 D2
Isherwood Dr SK6 . . . . .125 D6
Isherwood Fold BL7 . . . . .9 D7
Isherwood Rd M31 . . . . .106 F6
Isherwood St
Heywood OL10 . . . . .29 E1
Leigh WN7 . . . . .75 E8
Rochdale OL11 . . . . .31 A6
Isis Cl M7 . . . . .81 A8
Island Cotts BL9 . . . . .11 C2
Island Row WN2 . . . . .56 B7
Islington Rd SK2 . . . . .124 C4
Islington St M3 . . . . .158 A1
Islington Way M3 . . . . .158 A1
Isobel Cl
Eccles M30 . . . . .79 B1
5 Manchester M16 . . . . . . .97 F4
Ivanhoe Ave WA3 . . . . .74 D1
Ivanhoe Ct BL3,BL4 . . . . .42 C2
Ivanhoe St
Farnworth BL3,BL4 . . . . .42 C2
Oldham OL1 . . . . .49 C1
Iveagh Ct **18** OL16 . . . . .31 B6
Iver Ho **11** M46 . . . . .154 C1
Ivor St M11 . . . . .30 B3
Ivy Ave WA12 . . . . .89 C2
Ivy Bank Cl BL1 . . . . .24 E5
Ivy Bank Rd BL1 . . . . .24 E5
Ivybridge Cl M13 . . . . .164 A1
Ivybridge Ho BL3 . . . . .144 C1
Ivy Cl
Droylsden M43 . . . . .83 F3
13 Rawtenstall BB4 . . . . .2 F8
Shaw OL2 . . . . .149 B3
Ivy Cotts
Denton M34 . . . . .113 A7
12 Rawtenstall BB4 . . . . .2 F8
Ivycroft SK13 . . . . .171 B4
Ivydale Dr WN7 . . . . .76 C5
Ivy Dr M24 . . . . .64 F6
Ivy Farm Gdns WA3 . . . . .91 D4
Ivy Gr
Farnworth BL4 . . . . .60 F7
Kearsley M26 . . . . .61 B8
Walkden M38 . . . . .59 F4
Ivygreen Dr OL4 . . . . .67 F6
Ivygreen Rd M21 . . . . .109 A8
Ivy Ho M27 . . . . .79 D6
Ivy House Rd WA3 . . . . .74 D1
Ivyleaf Sq M7 . . . . .155 B2
Ivylea Rd M19 . . . . .110 E4
Ivylodge Cl SK15 . . . . .86 E4
Ivy Rd
Bolton BL1 . . . . .142 B1
Bury BL8 . . . . .27 B2
Golborne WA3 . . . . .90 B8
Poynton SK12 . . . . .133 E3
Westhoughton BL5 . . . . .57 F7
Ivy St
Ashton-in-M WN4 . . . . .73 B3
Bolton BL3 . . . . .146 C4
Eccles M30 . . . . .79 D1
Manchester M40 . . . . .83 A8
Ramsbottom BL0 . . . . .10 F3
Wigan WN1 . . . . .150 B4
Ivy Terr OL15 . . . . .6 D2
Ivy Wlk M31 . . . . .105 D3

J

J2 Bsns Pk BL9 . . . . 141 C2
Jack Brady Cl M23. . . . . 120 E4
Jackdaw Rd BL8 . . . . .10 F2
Jackie Brown Wlk
M40 . . . . 157 A1
Jack La
Droylsden M43. . . . . .84 C2
Urmston M41. . . . . .95 E2
Jack McCann Ct 10
OL16. . . . . .31 A8
Jackman Ave OL10. . . . . .46 D7
Jack's La BL5 . . . . .57 A8
Jackson Ave
Culcheth WA3 . . . . .91 E3
8 Dukinfield SK16 . . . . 101 D8
Jackson Cl
Altrincham WA15. . . . . 120 C7
Bury BL8 . . . . .27 B3
Oldham OL8. . . . . 153 B1
Jackson Cres M15 . . . . 162 B3
Jackson Ct
Manchester M21 . . . . .96 F1
Urmston M41. . . . . .95 A3
Jackson Gdns M34 . . . . 100 D2
Jackson Mews OL4. . . . . .49 D1
Jackson Pit **1** OL1 . . . . 153 B2
Jackson Pl OL16. . . . . .31 B8
Jacksons Edge Rd
SK12. . . . . 135 B6
Jackson's La SK7. . . . . 133 C8
Jackson's Row M2. . . . . 158 C1
Jackson St
Ashton-u-L OL6 . . . . 166 B4
Cheadle SK8 . . . . 122 E6
Failsworth M35 . . . . .83 D6
Farnworth BL4. . . . . .60 D8
Glossop, Padfield SK13 . . . . 104 C5
Glossop SK13. . . . . 116 C7
Hyde SK14 . . . . 167 A2
Ince-in-M WN2 . . . . .56 A7
Kearsley BL4 . . . . .60 F7
Middleton M24. . . . . .65 B8
Mottram in L SK14. . . . . 103 A3
Oldham, County End OL4. . . .67 F6
Oldham, Greenacres Moor
OL4. . . . . .67 B7
Radcliffe M26 . . . . .44 B2
Rochdale OL16. . . . . .31 B6
Salit M3 . . . . 108 D5
Stretford M32. . . . . .96 C1
Walkden M28. . . . . .60 C4
Wardle OL12. . . . . .15 C6
Whitefield M45 . . . . .62 F7
Jackson Warehouse
M1 . . . . 159 B1
Jack St BL2 . . . . .25 C1
Jack Taylor Ct OL12. . . . . .15 B7
Jacob Brigth Mews **5**
OL12. . . . . .14 F2
Jacobite Cl M7 . . . . .63 C1
Jacobsen Ave SK14 . . . . 167 C4
Jacob St WN2 . . . . .56 D6
Jaffrey St **2** WN7 . . . . .75 E5
James Andrew St M24 . . . . . . .47 B1
James Bentley Wlk **4**
M40 . . . . .83 C5
James Brindley Basin
M1 . . . . 159 C1
James Brindley Com Prim
Sch M28 . . . . .60 C1
James Butterworth Ct **6**
OL16. . . . . .31 B6
James Butterworth St **9**
OL16. . . . . .31 B6
James Cl SK16 . . . . 101 E8
James Corbett Rd
M50 . . . . 154 A1
James Ct 10 M18 . . . . .99 D5
James Dr SK14 . . . . 167 B2
James Henry Ave M5 . . . . . . 161 B4
James Hill St 15 OL15. . . . . . .16 B5
James Leech St SK1,
SK3. . . . . 170 B4
James Leigh St M1 . . . . 163 A4
Jameson St OL11 . . . . .30 B2
James Pl
Coppull PR7 . . . . .19 E8
Standish WN6 . . . . .19 D2
James Rd OL2 . . . . 149 B3
James St N M26 . . . . .44 B2
James St S OL9 . . . . 152 A3
James Sq WN6 . . . . .19 D2
James St
Ashton-in-M WN4 . . . . .73 E7
3 Ashton-u-L M34 . . . . . . 100 E8
Bacup OL13 . . . . .3 B8
Bolton BL7. . . . . .8 D3
Bury BL9 . . . . 141 A1
Denton M34. . . . . 101 A4
Droylsden M43. . . . . .84 B2
Dukinfield SK15, SK16. . . . . 101 E8
Failsworth M35 . . . . .84 A7
7 Glossop SK13. . . . . 116 C8
Heywood OL10. . . . . .29 D3
Horwich BL6 . . . . .22 B2
Ince-in-M WN3 . . . . 151 A2
Kearsley BL4 . . . . .60 F8
Little Lever BL3 . . . . .43 B3
Manchester M40 . . . . 160 A3
Oldham OL4. . . . . .49 D1
Prestwich M25. . . . . .63 A5

James St continued
Radcliffe M26 . . . . .44 B2
Rochdale, Dearnley OL15 . . .15 A8
Rochdale, Hurstead
OL12. . . . . .15 C4
5 Rochdale, Newbold Brow
OL12 . . . . .31 A8
Romiley Sk6. . . . . 113 A5
Royton OL2 . . . . 149 A1
Sale M33 . . . . 108 D4
Salford M3. . . . . 158 A1
Stockport SK3 . . . . 170 B3
Tyldesley M29 . . . . .76 F8
Westhoughton BL5 . . . . .39 E2
Whitworth OL12. . . . . .4 D2
Jameston Rise 18 BL6 . . . . . .22 B4
Jamieson Cl M8 . . . . 155 B1
Jammy La OL9 . . . . 152 C2
Jane Barter Ho **1** BL4. . . . . .60 D8
Jane St
Chadderton OL9. . . . . 152 B2
Rochdale OL12. . . . . 139 B4
Whitworth OL12. . . . . .4 E5
Janus Dr OL1 . . . . .48 D1
Japan St M7 . . . . 155 C3
Jardine Way OL9 . . . . .65 F4
Jarvis Cl M34 . . . . 100 E2
Jarvis St
10 Oldham OL4. . . . . .67 A6
Rochdale OL12. . . . . .14 F1
Jasmine Ave M43. . . . . .84 C2
Jasmine Cl M23 . . . . 108 E1
Jasmine Ct BL3. . . . . 147 B3
Jasmine Rd WN5 . . . . .54 D7
Jasmine Wlk M31 . . . . 105 F2
Jauncey St BL3. . . . . 144 C1
Jaunces Ct WN1. . . . . 150 C4
Jayton Ave M20 . . . . 122 B8
Jean Ave WN7 . . . . .75 E5
Jean Cl M19 . . . . .99 A2
Jedburgh Ave BL1. . . . . 144 B4
Jefferson Way OL12 . . . . .14 F3
Jeffreys Dr SK16. . . . . 101 D8
Jeffrey St WN2 . . . . .56 A8
Jeffrey Wlk OL10 . . . . .29 A2
Jehlum Cl M8 . . . . 156 B3
Jellicoe Ave M44. . . . . 105 E6
Jenkinson St WN2. . . . . .56 D6
Jenkyn Wlk **5** M11. . . . . 160 C1
Jennet Hey WN4. . . . . .72 F6
Jennet's La WA3 . . . . .76 C1
Jennings Ave M5 . . . . 161 A4
Jennings Cl SK14 . . . . 102 B5
Jennings St SK3. . . . . 170 A3
Jennison Cl M18 . . . . 165 B2
Jenny Beck Gr BL3 . . . . 147 B4
Jenny La SK7. . . . . 132 E4
Jenny Lind Cl **8** BL4. . . . . . . .42 C2
Jenny St OL8 . . . . .66 C2
Jepheys St **17** OL12. . . . . .14 F1
Jepheys St OL12. . . . . .14 F1
Jepson St SK2. . . . . 124 A6
JERICHO 28 E4
Jericho Rd BL9 . . . . .28 E4
Jermyn St OL12. . . . . .28 A8
Jerrold St **2** OL15. . . . . .16 B5
Jersey Cl M19 . . . . 179 F7
Jersey Rd SK5. . . . . 169 C4
Jersey St
Ashton-u-L OL6 . . . . 166 B4
Manchester M4 . . . . 159 C2
Jerusalem Pl M2. . . . . 162 C4
Jesmond Ave M25. . . . . .63 B2
Jesmond Dr BL8. . . . . .27 C5
Jesmond Gr SK8. . . . . 132 B8
Jesmond Rd BL1. . . . . 142 B4
Jesmond Wlk M9. . . . . .64 D5
Jespersen St OL1 . . . . 153 C3
Jessamine Ave M7. . . . . 158 A4
Jessel Cl M13 . . . . 163 C2
Jessica Way WN7. . . . . .75 B4
Jessie St
Bolton BL3. . . . . 144 C1
Failsworth M40 . . . . .83 A6
Jessop Dr SK6. . . . . 125 F8
Jessop Forge BL3 . . . . .43 A3
Jessop St M18. . . . . .99 D5
Jethro St
Bolton, Bradshaw BL2 . . . . . .25 C4
Bolton, Tonge Fold BL2 . . . . 148 C4
Jetson St M18. . . . . .99 F6
Jewell Cl M41. . . . . .95 B2
Jewish Senior Boys Sch
M14. . . . . 110 D8
Jimmy McMullen Wlk **6**
M14. . . . . .98 A3
Jinnah Cl
Manchester M11 . . . . 165 C4
Oldham OL4. . . . . .67 C5
JJ Thomson Mews
M14. . . . . 110 D8
Joan St M40. . . . . .83 A7
Jobling St M11. . . . . 164 C4
Jocelyn St M40. . . . . 157 B1
Joddrell St M3 . . . . 162 B1
Joe Connolly Way **1**
M35. . . . . .83 E8
Joel La SK14 . . . . 113 F7
Johannesburg Gdns
M23. . . . . 120 C8
John Ashworth St
OL12. . . . . .14 F1
John Atkinson Ct M5 . . . . . . 154 A2
John Ave SK8 . . . . 122 A2
John Beeley Ave M11. . . . . . . .99 D8
John Booth St OL4. . . . . .67 F5
John Boste Ct BL4 . . . . .42 C5

John Brown St 13
BL1. . . . . 145 B4
John Clynes Ave M40. . . . . . 159 C3
John Cross St BL3. . . . . 147 B4
John Dalton St
Glossop SK13. . . . . 103 E5
Manchester M2. . . . . 158 C1
John Foran Cl M40. . . . . .83 B6
John Gilbert Way M17 . . . . . . .96 E5
John Henry St OL12 . . . . .4 D4
John Heywood St M11. . . . . . .83 B2
John Howarth Countryside
Visitor Ctr **1** M35. . . . . . . .84 E6
John Kemble Ct OL11. . . . . . . .30 D4
John Kennedy Gdn
SK14. . . . . 103 A3
John Kennedy Rd
SK14. 102 F3
John Knott St OL4. . . . . .67 F6
John Lee Fold M24. . . . . .47 A1
John Lloyd Ct M44. . . . . 105 F8
John Murray St OL4. . . . . . . 157 A1
John Roberts Cl OL11. . . . . 139 B1
John Robinson Wlk **3**
M40 . . . . .83 A7
John St E OL7. . . . . .84 F1
John St W OL7 . . . . 100 F8
Johns Cl M21 . . . . 109 B8
John Shepley St SK14. . . . . . 167 B2
John Smeaton Ct M1 . . . . . . 159 C1
Johnson Ave
Leigh WN2. . . . . .56 E1
Newton-le-W WA12. . . . . .89 B5
Oldham OL1. . . . . .49 E5
Johnsonbrook Rd SK14,
SK16. . . . . 101 D6
Johnson Cl WN7. . . . . .75 B4
JOHNSON FOLD 23 F3
Johnson Fold Ave BL1 . . . . . . .23 F3
Johnson Fold Com Prim
Sch BL1 . . . . .23 F3
Johnson Gr M24. . . . . .64 E8
Johnson's Sq M40 . . . . 160 A4
Johnson St
Atherton M46 . . . . .58 A1
Bolton BL1 . . . . 145 C2
Manchester M15 . . . . 162 A2
Pendlebury M27 . . . . .80 D6
Radcliffe M26 . . . . .44 B1
Salford M3. . . . . 158 B2
Tyldesley M29 . . . . .59 A1
11 Wigan WN5 . . . . .54 B6
Johnson Terr 28
SK16. . . . . 166 B1
John's Pl SK6 . . . . 113 C2
John St
Altrincham WA14. . . . . 119 D4
Ashton-in-M WN4 . . . . .73 D5
Ashton-u-L OL7 . . . . 166 A1
Bolton BL7. . . . . .25 A7
Bredbury SK6. . . . . 113 A4
Bury BL9 . . . . 140 C3
Compstall SK6. . . . . 114 B3
Denton M34. . . . . 100 F4
Droylsden M43. . . . . .83 F1
Eccles M30 . . . . .79 B1
Failsworth M35 . . . . .65 F1
Farnworth BL4. . . . . .60 E8
Glossop SK13. . . . . 116 C8
Golborne WA3 . . . . .90 A8
Hazel Grove SK7 . . . . 124 D3
Heywood OL10. . . . . .29 D2
Heywood OL10. . . . . .29 D2
Hindley WN2 . . . . .57 B3
Hyde SK14 . . . . 167 A3
Irlam M44 . . . . 105 E5
Leigh WN7 . . . . .75 F5
2 Littleborough OL15 . . . . .16 A5
12 Little Lever BL3 . . . . . . .43 B3
Manchester M4 . . . . 159 A2
Marple SK6. . . . . 126 A5
Middleton M25 . . . . .63 E8
Oldham, Bank Top OL8. . . . 153 B2
Oldham, County End OL4. . . .68 A6
Pendlebury M27 . . . . .80 A8
Rochdale OL16. . . . . .15 C3
Romiley Sk6. . . . . 113 C2
Royton OL2 . . . . .48 D4
Sale M33 . . . . 108 B5
Salford, Lower Broughton
M7. . . . . 158 A4
Salford M3. . . . . 158 B2
Shaw OL2. . . . . 149 A1
Stalybridge SK15. . . . . .86 C5
Stockport SK1 . . . . 169 C1
Stockport SK1 . . . . 170 C4
7 Tyldesley M29 . . . . .59 A1
Walkden M28. . . . . .60 D4
Whitworth OL12. . . . . .4 D2
4 Wigan, Pemberton
WN5. .54 D5
Wigan, Scholes WN1. . . . . . 151 A4
Johnston 21 OL12. . . . . 139 B4
Johnston Ave OL15. . . . . .15 F3
Johnstone Ct M32. . . . . .96 A3
John William St
Droylsden M11. . . . . .83 C1
Eccles M30. . . . . .79 F2
Joiner St
Manchester M4 . . . . 159 A1
Salford M5. . . . . .81 C1
Join Rd M33 . . . . 108 D4
Jolly Brows BL2 . . . . .25 D3
Jolly Tar La PR7 . . . . .20 B7
Jonas St
Manchester M9 . . . . 157 B4
Salford M3. . . . . 158 B3
Jonathan Cl BB4 . . . . .1 A8

Jones Sq SK1 . . . . 124 A7
Jones St
Bolton BL1. . . . . 145 C4
Glossop SK13. . . . . 104 A5
Horwich BL6 . . . . .22 B4
Oldham OL1. . . . . .67 A8
Radcliffe M26 . . . . .44 B4
Rochdale OL16. . . . . .31 A6
Royton OL2 . . . . .48 E2
Salford M6. . . . . 154 C2
Jonquil Dr M28. . . . . .59 F3
Jopson St M24 . . . . .47 B1
Jordan Ave OL2 . . . . .49 D8
Jordan St
Glossop SK13. . . . . 104 C1
Manchester M15 . . . . 162 B3
Joseph Adamson Ind Est
SK14. . . . . 101 C2
Joseph Dean Rd
M40 . . . . .83 A7
Josephine Dr **2** M27. . . . . . .80 A7
Joseph Jennings Ct
M22. . . . . 109 E1
Joseph Johnson Mews
M22. . . . . 109 C1
Joseph St
Eccles M30 . . . . .79 B1
Failsworth M35 . . . . .83 F8
1 Farnworth BL4. . . . . .42 D1
Littleborough OL15 . . . . .16 B6
Marple SK6 . . . . 126 A6
Middleton M24. . . . . .46 F1
Radcliffe M26 . . . . .44 B2
3 Rochdale OL12. . . . . .14 D2
Joshua La M24 . . . . .65 D7
Josslyn Rd M5 . . . . 154 A3
Jo St M5. . . . . .81 A1
Joule Cl M5 . . . . 161 A4
Joules Ct **2** SK1 . . . . 170 C4
Joule St M9 . . . . .64 E1
Jowett St
Oldham OL1. . . . . .49 C1
Reddish SK5 . . . . 169 C4
Jowett's Wlk OL7. . . . . 166 A2
Jowkin La OL11 . . . . .29 D6
Joyce St M40. . . . . .83 B7
Joynson Ave M7. . . . . 158 A4
Joynson St M33 . . . . 108 B5
Joy St **8** OL12. . . . . .14 F2
Joy St
Ramsbottom BL0 . . . . 138 B2
Rochdale OL12. . . . . .14 F2
JUBILEE .32 C2
Jubilee Cl M30 . . . . .32 C2
Jubilee Ave
Orrell WN5 . . . . .53 D4
Radcliffe M26 . . . . .44 C1
Stalybridge SK16. . . . . .85 E1
Jubilee Cl M30 . . . . .79 D3
Jubilee Cotts M28. . . . . .60 C3
Jubilee Ct
Golborne WA3 . . . . .74 A1
2 Handforth SK9 . . . . 131 E5
Manchester M16 . . . . .97 B4
Reddish SK5 . . . . .99 F2
Jubilee Ho BL1 . . . . 145 B2
Jubilee Rd M24. . . . . .47 B1
Jubilee St
3 Ashton-u-L OL7 . . . . .84 F1
Bolton BL3 . . . . 146 C3
Salford M6. . . . . 154 C2
Shaw OL2. . . . . 149 C2
Jubilee Terr M24 . . . . .47 B2
Jubilee Way BL9. . . . . 140 A2
Judith St OL12 . . . . .14 C3
Judson Ave M21 . . . . 109 C6
Julia Mews **4** BL6. . . . . .22 B4
Julian Ho OL1 . . . . 153 C3
Julia St
Horwich BL6 . . . . .22 B4
Manchester M3. . . . . 158 C3
Middleton M25 . . . . 139 B4
Julius St M19 . . . . 111 B8
Jumbles Beck BL7 . . . . .9 D4
Jumbles Ctry Pk* BL7 . . . . . . .9 D2
JUMBO. .65 C2
Junction 19 Ind Pk
OL10. . . . . .29 F1
Junction 22 Bsns Pk
OL9. . . . . .65 F1
Junction Alley OL16 . . . . 139 C3
Junction Ho M1. . . . . 159 B1
Junction La WA12 . . . . .89 B3
Junction Rd
Bolton BL3. . . . . 144 A1
Stockport SK1, SK2,
SK3. . . . . 170 C3
Junction Rd W BL6 . . . . .40 D5
Junction St
Dukinfield SK14 . . . . 101 C5
Oldham OL8. . . . . .66 E4
Junction Terr WN3. . . . . 151 B2
Junction Works M1. . . . . 159 B1
June Ave
Leigh WN7. . . . . .75 C6
Stockport SK4 . . . . 168 B2
June St OL7 . . . . .84 F2
Juniper Bank SK5 . . . . 112 A8
Juniper Cl
Bolton BL1. . . . . 143 B1
Oldham OL4. . . . . .49 F4
Sale M33 . . . . 108 A6
Juniper Cres M43. . . . . .99 E8
Juniper Dr
Hindley WN2 . . . . .57 A3
Milnrow OL16. . . . . .31 F6
Jupiter Gr WN3. . . . . .54 E2
Jupiter Wlk M40. . . . . .83 D2

Jura Cl SK16 . . . . 101 D8
Jura Dr M41. . . . . .95 E5
Jura Gr OL10 . . . . .29 B1
Jurby Ave M9 . . . . .64 D4
Jury St
Leigh WN7 . . . . .75 E7
Manchester M8 . . . . 158 C4
Justene Cl WA3 . . . . .74 A2
Justin Cl M13 . . . . 163 B3
Jutland Ave OL11. . . . . .30 C8
Jutland Gr BL5 . . . . .39 F1
Jutland Ho M1 . . . . 159 B1
Jutland St M1 . . . . 159 B1

K

Kale St M13 . . . . 163 B3
Kalima Gr M7 . . . . 155 A2
Kane Ct WA3 . . . . .75 A1
Kansas Ave M50 . . . . .96 E8
Kara St M6 . . . . 154 B2
Karen Rd WN1. . . . . 151 C4
Karmo End Rd OL11 . . . . 139 A2
Kaskenmoor Sch OL8. . . . . . . .66 B1
Kassim Darwish Gram Sch
for Boys M16 . . . . .97 C1
Kate St BL0 . . . . 138 B2
Kathan Cl OL16. . . . . .31 B7
Katherine Ct M16. . . . . 161 C1
Katherine Rd SK2. . . . . 124 C5
Katherine St OL6 . . . . 166 A2
Kathkin Ave M46 . . . . .64 B2
Kathleen Gr M14 . . . . .98 D2
Kathleen St OL12 . . . . 139 A3
Kay Ave SK6. . . . . 112 D3
Kay Brow
Heywood OL10. . . . . .29 B2
Ramsbottom BL0 . . . . 138 C2
Kay Cl WN1. . . . . 151 A4
Kayfields BL2. . . . . .25 E4
Kay Garden Sh Ctr
BL9. . . . . 140 B2
Kayley Ind Est OL7. . . . . .84 F3
Kay Lo M14 . . . . 110 C8
Kaymar Ct M4 . . . . 142 A1
Kays Gdns M3 . . . . 112 B1
Kays Gdns SK3 . . . . 158 A2
Kay St
Atherton M46 . . . . .58 D2
Bolton BL1 . . . . 145 B4
Bury BL9 . . . . 141 A3
Chapeltown BL7. . . . . .9 C4
Heywood OL10. . . . . .29 C2
Little Lever BL3 . . . . .43 A3
Manchester, Charlestown
M6 . . . . .80 F6
Manchester, West Gorton
M11 . . . . 164 C3
Ramsbottom BL9 . . . . .11 C3
Rochdale OL11 . . . . 139 B1
Kays Wood Rd SK6 . . . . 125 D6
Keadby Cl M30. . . . . .79 B8
Keal Dr M44 . . . . .94 B4
Keane Ct M8 . . . . 156 A3
Kean St WA3 . . . . 166 A3
Kean Pl M30 . . . . .79 D1
KEARSLEY 61 A6
Kearsley Dr BL3 . . . . .42 B3
Kearsley Hall Rd M26. . . . . . . .61 C7
Kearsley Mount St Prec
BL4. . . . . .61 B6
Kearsley Rd
Kearsley M26. . . . . .61 D8
Manchester M8 . . . . .64 A2
Kearsley St
Eccles M30 . . . . .79 B2
Leigh WN7 . . . . .75 D5
Kearsley Vale M26. . . . . .61 F8
Kearsley Vale BL4 . . . . .61 A7
Kearsley West Prim Sch
BL4. . . . . .60 E7
Kearton Dr M30. . . . . .80 A1
Keary Cl M18. . . . . .99 D6
Keaton Ave M22. . . . . 121 D4
Keadon Cl M6 . . . . 154 B4
Keats Ave
Denton M34. . . . . 113 A8
Droylsden M43. . . . . .84 A2
Longshaw WN5 . . . . .53 D1
Rochdale OL12. . . . . .14 A1
Wigan, Poolstock WN3 . . . . 150 B1
Wigan, Standish Lower
Ground WN6. . . . . .36 E3
Keats Cres M46 . . . . .58 E5
Keats Fold SK16. . . . . 102 B7
Keats Mews M23 . . . . 120 C8
Keats Rd
Eccles M30 . . . . .79 D1
Oldham OL1. . . . . .49 B1
Ramsbottom BL8. . . . . .10 F2
Keats St WN7 . . . . .75 D7
Keats Way M34. . . . . .56 B1
Keats Wlk M8 BL1. . . . . 143 B2
Keble Ave OL8. . . . . .66 C3
Keble Gr WN7 . . . . .75 D5
Keble St WN2. . . . . 151 C3
Kedington Cl M40 . . . . 160 C1
Kedleston Ave M14 . . . . .98 C4
Kedleston Gn SK2 . . . . 124 D7
Kedleston Wlk M34 . . . . 100 F1
Keele Cl SK2 . . . . 124 B6

Keele Wlk M40 .... 159 C3
Keeley Cl M40 .... 83 C4
Keepers Dr OL12 .... 13 E2
Keep The BL1 .... 40 F7
Keighley Ave M43 .... 84 A3
Keighley Cl BL8 .... 26 F2
Keighley St BL1 .... 142 C2
Keilder Mews BL1 .... 144 A3
Keith Dr SK3 .... 123 B7
Keith Wlk M40 .... 160 A3
Kelboro Ave M34 .... 100 D7
Kelbrook Ct SK2 .... 124 E5
Kelbrook Rd M11 .... 165 B4
Kelby Ave M23 .... 121 B7
Kelday Wlk M8 .... 156 C2
Keld Cl BL8 .... 27 B5
Keld Wlk M18 .... 165 C1
Kelfield Ave M23 .... 109 A2
Kelham Wlk **3** M40 .... 65 C1
Kellaton Cl WN3 .... 151 B2
Kellbank Rd WN3 .... 54 E3
Kellbrook Cres
  Manchester M7 .... 63 B1
  Salford M7 .... 81 A8
Kellett Cl WN5 .... 36 D1
Kellett St
  4 Bolton BL1 .... 24 F6
  Rochdale OL16 .... 31 B8
Kellet Wlk M11 .... 83 B2
Kelling Wlk M15 .... 162 A3
Kells Gr WN6 .... 37 A2
Kelmarsh Cl **7** M11 .... 99 D7
Kelmscott Lo M41 .... 95 B3
Kelsall Cres SK3 .... 170 A2
Kelsall Dr
  Altrincham WA15 .... 120 C6
  Droylsden M43 .... 83 F3
  Sale M33 SK8 .... 123 A5
Kelsall St
  Manchester M12 .... 164 C2
  Oldham OL9 .... 153 A2
  Rochdale OL16 .... 139 C4
  Sale M33 .... 108 B4
Kelsall Way **6** SK9 .... 131 D5
Kelsey Wlk **14** OL10 .... 29 C2
Kelsey Wlk M9 .... 64 B5
Kelso Cl OL8 .... 66 F1
Kelso Gr WN2 .... 56 D4
Kelson Ave OL7 .... 166 A4
Kelstern Ave M13 .... 98 E3
Kelstern Sq M13 .... 98 E3
Kelton Cl SK5 .... 111 F5
Kelverlow St OL4 .... 67 C6
Kelvin Ave
  Middleton M24 .... 64 B6
  Sale M33 .... 108 B4
Kelvin Cl WN4 .... 72 D4
Kelvindale Dr WA15 .... 120 C7
Kelvin Gr
  Manchester M8 .... 156 A2
  Wigan WN3 .... 54 F2
Kelvington Dr M9 .... 157 A2
Kelvin St
  Ashton-u-L OL7 .... 100 F8
  Manchester M4 .... 159 A2
Kelway Terr WN1 .... 37 C1
Kelwood Ave BL9 .... 28 D5
Kemball **3** M30 .... 79 F2
Kemble Ave M23 .... 109 C1
Kemble Cl BL6 .... 22 B5
Kemmel Ave M22 .... 121 E5
Kemnay Wlk **8** M11 .... 83 C1
Kemp Ave OL11 .... 139 A1
Kempley Cl M12 .... 164 C2
Kempnough Hall Rd
  M28 .... 78 F7
Kemp Rd SK6 .... 126 C7
Kempsey Ct OL9 .... 152 B3
Kempsey Wlk M40 .... 65 D1
Kempsford Cl M23 .... 121 B6
Kemp St
  Hyde SK14 .... 167 B4
  Middleton M24 .... 64 F8
Kempster St M7 .... 158 A4
Kempston Gdns **25**
  BL1 .... 143 B2
Kempton Ave
  Little Lever BL3 .... 43 A2
  Sale M33 .... 107 D3
Kempton Cl
  Droylsden M43 .... 84 C2
  Hazel Grove SK7 .... 125 A1
  Newton-le-W WA12 .... 89 D5
Kempton Rd M19 .... 111 A8
Kempton Way OL9 .... 152 C3
Kemsing Wlk M15 .... 81 A1
Kenchester Ave M11 .... 99 D8
Kendal Ave
  Ashton-u-L OL7 .... 84 F4
  Denton M34 .... 101 A1
  Dukinfield SK14 .... 101 C5
  Rochdale OL12 .... 13 E2
  Sale M33 .... 108 C3
  Urmston M41 .... 94 E4
Kendal Cl
  Altrincham WA15 .... 120 D5
  Heywood OL10 .... 46 E8
Kendal Ct
  Stalybridge SK15 .... 86 A3
  Wythenshawe M22 .... 121 E6
Kendal Dr
  Bramhall SK7 .... 132 C5
  Bury BL9 .... 44 D7
  Gatley SK8 .... 122 C4
  Shaw OL2 .... 49 D7
Kendal Gdns SK6 .... 113 B4
Kendal Gr
  Ashton-in-M WN4 .... 73 B4

Kendal Gr continued
  Leigh WN7 .... 75 D5
  Walkden M28 .... 60 F2
  Whitefield M45 .... 62 F8
Kendal Ho SK15 .... 86 A3
Kendall Rd M9 .... 63 F3
Kendal Rd
  Bolton BL1 .... 144 C4
  Boothstown M28 .... 77 E7
  Hindley WN2 .... 56 E5
  Ince-in-M WN2 .... 56 A7
  Ramsbottom BL0 .... 11 A2
  Salford M6 .... 80 C5
  Stretford M32 .... 96 D3
Kendal Rd W BL0 .... 10 F2
Kendal St WN6 .... 150 B4
Kendal Terr **4** SK16 .... 166 C1
Kendal Wlk M24 .... 46 E1
Kendon Gr M34 .... 100 E3
Kendrew Rd BL3 .... 146 A4
Kendrew Wlk M9 .... 64 E1
Kendrick Pl WN1 .... 151 B4
Kenford Dr WN3 .... 54 E2
Kenford Wlk M8 .... 155 C2
Kenhall Rd WN7 .... 76 C4
Kenilworth **4** OL11 .... 139 B2
Kenilworth Ave
  Chadderton OL9 .... 47 E1
  Cheadle SK8 .... 123 A3
  Handforth SK9 .... 131 D3
  Manchester M20 .... 109 F5
  Swinton M27 .... 62 B3
  Whitefield M45 .... 63 A7
Kenilworth Cl
  Marple SK6 .... 125 F8
  Oldham OL4 .... 67 F5
  Radcliffe M26 .... 43 F6
Kenilworth Dr
  Hazel Grove SK7 .... 133 D8
  Hindley WN2 .... 56 F4
  Leigh WN7 .... 76 E7
Kenilworth Gdns
  WA12 .... 89 C1
Kenilworth Gr M34 .... 100 C8
Kenilworth Rd
  Cheadle SK3 .... 122 F7
  Golborne WA3 .... 90 E7
  Royton OL16 .... 48 C8
  Sale M33 .... 107 E4
  Urmston M41 .... 94 C2
Kenion Rd OL11 .... 30 B6
Kenion St OL16 .... 139 C3
Kenley Dr OL10 .... 46 F7
Kenley Wlk M8 .... 156 C2
Kenmay Ave BL3 .... 40 F6
Kenmere Gr M40 .... 65 B1
Kenmor Ave BL8 .... 27 A1
Kenmore Cl M45 .... 63 B8
Kenmore Dr WA15 .... 120 B3
Kenmore Gr
  Garswood WN4 .... 72 D4
  Irlam M44 .... 105 D6
Kenmore Rd
  Sale M33 .... 107 C1
  Whitefield M45 .... 63 B8
  Wythenshawe M22 .... 121 D7
Kenmore Way M45 .... 63 B8
Kennard Cl M9 .... 64 F1
Kennard Pl WA14 .... 119 E6
Kennedy Cl WN6 .... 36 F8
Kennedy Dr
  Little Lever BL3 .... 43 C3
  Whitefield M45 .... 45 B2
Kennedy Rd
  Salford M5 .... 80 C2
  Tyldesley M28, M29 .... 77 D6
Kennedy Sq **3** SK14 .... 102 F3
Kennedy St
  Bolton BL2 .... 148 C3
  Manchester M2 .... 158 C1
  Oldham OL8 .... 153 B1
Kennedy Way
  Denton M34 .... 100 D2
  Stockport SK4 .... 168 C2
Kennerley Ct
  Stockport SK2 .... 124 A5
  Wilmslow SK9 .... 137 A7
Kennerley Lo SK3 .... 170 C1
Kennerley Rd SK2 .... 124 A5
Kennerley's La SK9 .... 137 A7
Kennet Cl WN7 .... 76 E4
Kennet **15** OL10 .... 29 C2
Kennet Cl
  Handforth SK9 .... 131 D2
  Westhoughton BL5 .... 39 E1
Kenneth Ave WN7 .... 75 D6
Kenneth Collis Ct
  M22 .... 121 C3
Kenneth Gr WN7 .... 75 D6
Kenneth Sq M7 .... 155 B2
Kennett Dr SK6 .... 112 F4
Kennett Rd M23 .... 121 A3
Kennet Way M7 .... 75 F7
Kenninghall Rd M22 .... 121 D3
Kennington Ave M40 .... 83 B4
Kennington Fold BL2 .... 147 A3
Kenny Cl OL4 .... 67 D5
Kenside St **3** M16 .... 97 F3
Kensington Ave
  Ashton-u-L OL6 .... 85 E4
  Chadderton OL9 .... 65 E8
  2 Hyde SK14 .... 167 B1
  Manchester M14 .... 98 D4
  Radcliffe M26 .... 43 D4
  Royton OL2 .... 48 C6
Kensington Cl
  Milnrow OL16 .... 32 A6
  Ramsbottom BL8 .... 11 A1

Kensington Ct
  Bolton BL1 .... 145 B3
  1 Hyde SK14 .... 167 B1
  Reddish M34 .... 100 B4
  Salford M7 .... 81 C8
  Wilmslow SK9 .... 137 A6
Kensington Dr
  Bury BL8 .... 44 A8
  Horwich BL6 .... 22 D3
  Leigh WN7 .... 76 E7
  Salford M5 .... 154 A3
Kensington Gdns
  Altrincham WA15 .... 119 F1
  Hyde SK14 .... 167 C1
Kensington Gr
  Altrincham WA14 .... 119 E8
  Reddish M34 .... 100 B4
  14 Stalybridge SK15 .... 86 A1
Kensington Rd
  Failsworth M35 .... 84 B8
  Manchester M21 .... 97 B2
  Oldham OL8 .... 66 D4
  Stockport SK3 .... 123 B7
  3 Wigan WN5 .... 54 D5
Kensington St
  Bolton BL1 .... 145 A3
  Hyde SK14 .... 167 B1
  Manchester M14 .... 98 A3
  Rochdale OL11 .... 139 B1
Kensington The M20 .... 110 B5
Kenslow Ave M8 .... 63 F2
Kensworth Cl
  6 Altrincham M23 .... 120 D6
  Bolton BL1 .... 143 A1
Kensworth Dr BL1 .... 143 A1
Kent Ave
  Chadderton OL9 .... 152 B2
  Cheadle SK8 .... 123 C5
  Droylsden M43 .... 83 E1
  Platt Bridge WN2 .... 56 A2
Kent Cl
  Diggle OL3 .... 51 C4
  Walkden M28 .... 60 B2
Kent Ct
  Bolton BL1 .... 145 B4
  Manchester M14 .... 98 B1
Kent Dr
  Bury BL9 .... 45 A8
  Kearsley BL4 .... 61 B6
Kentford Dr M40 .... 159 C4
Kentford Gr **6** BL4 .... 60 C8
Kentford Rd BL1 .... 143 C1
Kentmere Ave
  Billinge WA11 .... 71 C1
  Rochdale OL12 .... 15 B3
Kentmere Cl SK8 .... 122 B3
Kentmere Ct M9 .... 65 A3
Kentmere Dr
  Middleton M24 .... 46 E3
  Tyldesley M29 .... 77 B7
Kentmere Gr BL4 .... 59 F7
Kentmere Prim Sch
  OL12 .... 15 B3
Kentmere Rd
  Altrincham WA23,
  WA15 .... 120 D6
  Bolton BL2 .... 25 F1
Kentmore Cl
  Manchester, Heaton Mersey
  SK4 .... 110 E2
  Manchester, West Gorton
  M12 .... 165 A3
Kenton Ave M18 .... 99 C3
Kenton Cl
  Bolton BL1 .... 143 A1
  Denton M34 .... 100 D7
Kenton Rd OL2 .... 149 A3
Kenton St OL8 .... 67 B5
Kent Rd
  Atherton M46 .... 58 C4
  Glossop SK13 .... 104 D1
  Irlam M44 .... 105 E2
  Partington M31 .... 105 C2
  Reddish M34 .... 100 A2
  Stockport SK3 .... 123 B8
  Tyldesley M29 .... 59 A2
Kent Rd E M14 .... 98 D3
Kent Rd W M14 .... 98 D3
Kentsford Dr M26 .... 43 B5
Kent St
  Bolton BL1 .... 145 B4
  Leigh WN7 .... 76 E4
  11 Manchester M2 .... 158 C1
  Oldham OL8 .... 66 F4
  Rochdale OL11 .... 139 C2
  Salford M7 .... 158 A4
  Swinton M27 .... 62 A2
  Wigan WN1 .... 151 A3
Kentstone Ave SK4 .... 110 E3
Kentucky St OL4 .... 67 C6
Kent Way WA12 .... 89 C1
Kentwell Cl SK16 .... 101 B7
Kent Wlk
  Haslingden BB4 .... 1 A8
  Heywood OL10 .... 29 B2
Kenwick Dr M40 .... 65 E2
Kenwood Ave
  Altrincham WA15 .... 119 F2
  Bramhall SK7 .... 132 D5
  Gatley SK8 .... 122 A6
  Leigh WN7 .... 76 C5
  Manchester M19 .... 111 A8
Kenwood Cl
  Leigh WN7 .... 76 C4
  Stretford M32 .... 96 B2
Kenwood Ct M32 .... 96 E1

Kenwood La M28 .... 78 F5
Kenwood Rd
  Bolton BL1 .... 142 B3
  Oldham OL11 .... 48 C1
  Reddish SK5 .... 99 E2
  Stretford M32 .... 96 E1
Kenworthy Ave OL6 .... 85 E5
Kenworthy Cl SK14 .... 102 E2
Kenworthy Gdns OL3 .... 51 B1
Kenworthy La M22 .... 109 D1
Kenworthy St
  Rochdale OL16 .... 31 C7
  3 Stalybridge SK15 .... 86 A1
Kenworthy Terr OL16 .... 31 C7
Kenwright St M4 .... 159 A2
Kenwyn St M40 .... 160 B3
KENYON 90 F3
Kenyon Ave
  Dukinfield SK16 .... 101 E7
  Oldham OL8 .... 66 F3
  Sale M33 .... 108 E2
Kenyon Cl SK14 .... 101 F5
Kenyon Cres **6** BL9 .... 27 F6
Kenyon Fold OL11 .... 29 E5
Kenyon Gr M38 .... 59 E4
Kenyon La
  Culcheth WA3 .... 91 A4
  Kenyon WA3 .... 90 F3
  Manchester M40 .... 83 A8
  Middleton M24 .... 65 C8
  Prestwich M25 .... 63 C4
Kenyon Rd
  Little Lever BL2 .... 43 B5
  Standish WN6 .... 19 D2
  Wigan WN1 .... 37 C2
Kenyon St
  Ashton-u-L OL6 .... 166 B3
  Britannia OL13 .... 4 B8
  Bury BL9 .... 141 A3
  Droylsden M18 .... 99 F6
  Dukinfield SK16 .... 101 B8
  Heywood OL10 .... 29 C2
  Leigh WN7 .... 75 D8
  Radcliffe M26 .... 44 B3
  Ramsbottom BL0 .... 138 C2
  Warren Terr M38 .... 59 E3
Kenyon Way
  Bury BL8 .... 26 F5
  Walkden M38 .... 59 E4
Keppel Rd M21 .... 97 B1
Keppel St SK16 .... 166 C3
Kepplecove Mdw M28 .... 77 F5
Kepwick Dr M22 .... 121 E1
Kerans Dr BL5 .... 57 E6
Kerenhappuch St BL0 .... 138 B2
Kerfield Wlk **13** M13 .... 163 B3
Kerfoot Cl M22 .... 121 E8
Kerfoot St WN7 .... 76 C4
Kermishaw Nook M29 .... 77 B6
Kermoor Ave BL1 .... 24 E6
Kerne Gr M23 .... 109 A1
Kerrera Dr M5 .... 154 A1
Kerridge Dr SK6 .... 112 F4
Kerrier Cl M30 .... 80 A2
Kerris Cl M27 .... 121 E1
Kerry Gr BL2 .... 148 B4
Kerry Wlk M23 .... 120 F3
KERSAL 81 B8
Kersal Ave
  Pendlebury M27 .... 80 C8
  Walkden M38 .... 60 A6
Kersal Bank M7 .... 81 C8
Kersal Bar M7 .... 63 C1
Kersal Cell M7 .... 80 F8
Kersal Cl
  Manchester M25 .... 63 A1
  2 Prestwich M7 .... 63 C1
Kersal Crag M7 .... 63 C1
KERSAL DALE 120 C7
Kersal Dr WA15 .... 120 C7
Kersal Hall Ave M7 .... 81 A8
Kersal Rd M25, M7 .... 63 A1
Kersal Vale Ct M7 .... 81 A8
Kersal Vale Rd M7, M25 .... 80 F8
Kersal Way M7 .... 81 B7
Kerscott Rd M23 .... 108 F2
Kersh Ave M19 .... 111 B8
Kershaw Ave
  Little Lever BL3 .... 43 A4
  Prestwich M25 .... 62 F2
  Sale M33 .... 108 C2
Kershaw Bsns Ctr
  BL3 .... 145 A1
Kershaw Dr OL9 .... 65 D3
Kershaw Gr M34 .... 100 C8
Kershaw La M34 .... 100 D8
Kershaw Rd M35 .... 83 F7
Kershaw St E OL2 .... 149 B3
Kershaw St
  Ashton-u-L OL7 .... 100 F8
  Bolton BL1 .... 145 A1
  Bolton, Bradshaw BL2 .... 25 C5
  Bury BL9 .... 141 A2
  Droylsden M43 .... 84 A1
  Glossop SK13 .... 116 C8
  Heywood OL10 .... 29 B2
  2 Rochdale OL12 .... 139 C4
  Royton OL2 .... 48 D5
  Shaw OL2 .... 149 B3
  Tyldesley M29 .... 59 A1
  Wigan WN5 .... 54 B6
Kershaw Way WA12 .... 89 C5
Kershope Gr M5 .... 161 A4
Kersley St OL4 .... 67 B6
Kerswell Wlk M40 .... 83 A6
Kerwin Wlk M11 .... 165 A4

Kerwood Dr OL2 .... 48 E3
Kesteven Rd M9 .... 157 A3
Keston Ave
  Droylsden M43 .... 83 E1
  Manchester M9 .... 65 A3
Keston Cres SK5 .... 112 B6
Keston Rd **4** OL1 .... 49 C1
Kestor St BL2 .... 148 B3
Kestrel Ave
  Droylsden M43 .... 84 C1
  Farnworth BL4 .... 59 F7
  Oldham OL4 .... 67 C5
  Swinton M27 .... 62 B2
  Walkden M38 .... 60 A5
Kestrel Cl
  Hyde SK14 .... 167 B4
  Marple SK6 .... 126 A3
  Prestwich M25 .... 63 B6
Kestrel Dr
  Ashton-in-M WN4 .... 73 C6
  Bury BL9 .... 141 B4
  Irlam M44 .... 94 A3
Kestrel Rd M17 .... 95 F8
Kestrel St **3** BL1 .... 148 A4
Kestrel View SK13 .... 115 F8
Kestrel Wlk M12 .... 165 A2
Keswick Ave
  Ashton-u-L OL7 .... 84 F5
  Chadderton OL9 .... 152 A3
  Denton M34 .... 100 D4
  Dukinfield SK14 .... 101 C1
  Gatley SK8 .... 122 B4
  Oldham OL8 .... 67 A3
  Urmston M41 .... 94 E1
Keswick Cl
  Irlam M44 .... 105 C4
  Manchester M13 .... 164 A1
  Middleton M24 .... 46 D2
  Stalybridge SK15 .... 86 A4
Keswick Ct
  3 Middleton M24 .... 46 D2
  Wythenshawe M22 .... 121 E6
Keswick Dr
  Bramhall SK7 .... 132 C5
  Bury BL9 .... 44 D7
Keswick Gr M6 .... 154 C2
Keswick Pl WN3 .... 56 A7
Keswick Rd
  Altrincham WA15 .... 120 D6
  High Lane SK6 .... 134 E8
  Reddish SK4 .... 111 D7
  Stretford M32 .... 96 C3
  Walkden M28 .... 60 F2
Keswick St
  Bolton BL1 .... 143 C2
  Rochdale OL11 .... 30 B2
Ketley Wlk **1** M22 .... 121 F3
Kettering Rd M19 .... 99 B2
Kettleshulme Way
  SK12 .... 134 A3
Kettleshulme Wlk **4**
  SK9 .... 131 E1
Kettlewell Wlk M18 .... 165 C1
Ketton Cl M11 .... 99 E7
Kevin Ave OL2 .... 48 E2
Kevin St M19 .... 111 B8
Kew Ave SK14 .... 167 B1
Kew Dr
  Cheadle SK8 .... 122 E2
  Urmston M41 .... 95 A4
Kew Gdns M40 .... 65 A1
Kew Rd
  Failsworth M35 .... 84 A8
  Oldham OL4 .... 67 C6
  Rochdale OL11 .... 31 A3
Keyhaven Wlk M40 .... 157 A1
Keymer St M11 .... 160 B2
Keynsham Rd M11 .... 83 B3
Keystone Cl M6 .... 154 B4
Key West Cl M11 .... 160 C1
Keyworth Wlk M40 .... 160 B4
Khartoum St
  Droylsden M35 .... 83 D2
  Manchester M16 .... 97 D4
Kibbles Brow BL7 .... 25 B8
Kibboth Crew BL0 .... 138 B3
Kibworth Cl M45 .... 62 D8
Kibworth Wlk **7** M9 .... 64 E5
Kidacre Wlk **2** M40 .... 83 A7
Kidderminster Way
  OL9 .... 47 F1
Kidd Rd SK13 .... 116 E6
Kid Glove Rd WA3 .... 74 B1
Kidwall Wlk **9** M9 .... 64 F1
Kiel Cl M30 .... 95 E8
Kielder Cl WN4 .... 72 F7
Kielder Hill M24 .... 46 F4
Kielder Sq M5 .... 154 C1
Kiers Ct BL4 .... 59 E1
Kilbride Ave BL2 .... 42 F4
Kilburn Cl La WA11 .... 89 A8
Kilburn Ave
  Ashton-in-M WN4 .... 73 D4
  Manchester M9 .... 64 D5
Kilburn Cl
  Gatley SK8 .... 131 B7
  Leigh WN7 .... 57 D4
Kilburn Ct **3** M14 .... 98 D4
Kilburn Dr WN6 .... 36 A7
Kilburn Rd
  Orrell WN5 .... 53 C5
  Radcliffe M26 .... 43 E4

Kilburn Rd continued
Stockport SK3 . . . . 123 C7
Kilburn St 7 OL1 . . . . .49 D1
Kilcoby Ave M27 . . . . .80 D8
Kildale Cl BL3 . . . . .40 E4
Kildare Cres OL11 . . . . . . .30 F2
Kildare Grange WN2 . . . . .56 C5
Kildare Rd
Manchester M21 . . . . . . 109 D8
Swinton M27 . . . . .79 E6
Kildare St
Farnworth BL4 . . . . .60 C7
Hindley WN2 . . . . .56 C5
Wigan WN3, WN5 . . . . . . .54 F6
Kildonan Dr BL3 . . . . .40 F6
Killer St BL0 . . . . 138 C2
Killington Cl WN3 . . . . . . .55 B2
Killingworth Mews 4
BL6 . . . . .22 D1
Kilton St BL3 . . . . 141 A1
Kilmaine Dr BL3 . . . . .40 E5
Kilmarsh Wlk 7 M8 . . . . 155 C3
Kilmington Dr M8 . . . . . . 155 C2
Kilmory Dr BL2 . . . . .42 F6
Kilmory Fold SK13 . . . . . 104 E3
Kiln Bank OL12 . . . . .4 C2
Kiln Bank La OL12 . . . . . . .4 C2
Kilnbrook Cl OL4 . . . . .68 B4
Kiln Brow BL7 . . . . .25 C8
Kiln Croft SK6 . . . . 112 F1
Kiln Croft La SK9 . . . . . . 131 E4
Kilner Cl BL9 . . . . .45 B4
Kilnerdeyne Terr
OL16 . . . . 139 B2
Kilner Wlk M40 . . . . 159 C4
Kiln Field BL7 . . . . .24 F8
Kiln Hill Cl OL1 . . . . .47 F2
Kiln Hill La OL1 . . . . .47 F2
Kilnhurst Wlk 12 BL1 . . . 145 A4
Kiln La
Glossop SK13 . . . . 104 A5
Milnrow OL16 . . . . .31 F4
Kilnside Dr M9 . . . . 157 A3
Kilnsley Wlk M18 . . . . . . 165 C1
Kiln St
Little Lever BL3 . . . . .43 A3
Ramsbottom BL0 . . . . . . 138 B1
Kiln Terr 5 OL13 . . . . .3 D8
Kilnwick Cl M18 . . . . .99 B3
Kiln Wlk OL12 . . . . .14 E2
Kilphin The BL6 . . . . .40 B8
Kilrush Ave M30 . . . . .95 D8
Kilsby Cl
Bolton BL6 . . . . .40 D6
Farnworth BL4 . . . . .42 C2
Kilsby Wlk M40 . . . . 160 A4
Kilshaw St WN5 . . . . .54 C5
Kilton Wlk M40 . . . . 159 C4
Kilvert Dr M33 . . . . 107 F5
Kilworth Ave M33 . . . . . . 107 F3
Kilworth Dr BL6 . . . . .40 C6
Kilworth St OL11 . . . . . . 139 A1
Kimberley Ave SK6 . . . . . 113 C2
Kimberley Pl WN4 . . . . . . .73 C3
Kimberley Rd BL1 . . . . . . .24 E5
Kimberley St
Bacup OL13 . . . . .3 A7
Oldham OL8 . . . . .66 C3
Salford M7 . . . . 155 B3
Stockport SK3 . . . . 170 B3
Kimberley Wlk M15 . . . . . 162 A3
Kimberly St WN6 . . . . . . .37 A1
Kimble Cl BL8 . . . . .10 F2
Kimbolton Cl M12 . . . . . . 165 A2
Kinburn Rd M19 . . . . 110 D2
Kinbury Wlk M40 . . . . . . 159 C4
Kincardine Ct M13 . . . . . . 163 B2
Kincardine Rd M13 . . . . . 163 B2
Kincraig Cl
Bolton BL3 . . . . .40 C4
Droylsden M11 . . . . .83 C1
Kinder Ave
Ashton-u-L OL6 . . . . .86 A6
Oldham OL4 . . . . .67 D5
Kinder Cl SK13 . . . . 116 A8
Kinder Ct SK3 . . . . 170 B3
Kinder Dr SK6 . . . . 126 A6
Kinder Fold SK15 . . . . . . 102 D6
Kinder Gr
Ashton-in-M WN4 . . . . . .72 F6
Romiley SK6 . . . . 113 E2
Kinder Ho M5 . . . . 154 A3
Kinderlee Way SK13 . . . . 115 B5
Kinder Mews OL3 . . . . . . .69 B5
Kinders Cres OL3 . . . . . . .69 B5
Kinders Fold OL15 . . . . . .15 F7
Kinders La OL3 . . . . .69 B6
Kinder St
Stalybridge SK15 . . . . . . .86 A2
Stockport SK3 . . . . 170 B3
Kinderton Ave M20 . . . . . 110 B7
Kinder Way
Middleton M24. . . . . .46 F2
Mottram in L SK14 . . . . . 102 F3
King Albert St OL2 . . . . . 149 B3
King Charles Ct SK13 . . . 116 D7
Kingcombe Wlk 12
M9 . . . . 157 B4
King Cup Cl SK13 . . . . . . 116 E8
King David High Sch The
M8 . . . . .63 F1
King David Jun & Inf Schs
M8 . . . . .63 F1

King Edward Ave
SK13 . . . . 104 D1
King Edward Ct SK14 . . . 113 F8
King Edward Rd SK14 . . . 113 E8
King Edward's Bldgs
M7 . . . . 155 C4
King Edward St
Eccles M30 . . . . .79 C2
4 Manchester M19 . . . . .99 B1
Salford M5 . . . . 161 B4
Kingfisher Ave M34 . . . . . .84 C1
Kingfisher Cl M12 . . . . . . 164 B1
Kingfisher Com Specl Sch
The OL9 . . . . .65 F5
Kingfisher Ct
Ashton-in-M WN4 . . . . . .73 B6
Rochdale OL12 . . . . .15 C4
10 Wigan WN6 . . . . .37 A1
Kingfisher Ctr OL13 . . . . . .3 E8
Kingfisher Dr
Bury BL9 . . . . 141 B4
Farnworth BL4 . . . . .59 F7
Kingfisher Mews SK6 . . . 126 A6
Kingfisher Rd SK2 . . . . . 124 F5
Kingfisher Way SK13 . . . . 115 F8
King George Cl WN4 . . . . .73 B3
King George Rd
Haydock WA11 . . . . .89 A7
Hyde SK14 . . . . 113 E8
Kingham Dr M4 . . . . 159 C2
Kingholm Gdns BL1 . . . . 143 A1
King La
Oldham OL1 . . . . .49 E4
Oldham OL1 . . . . .49 E5
Kingmoor Ave M26 . . . . . .44 B4
King of Kings Sch
M4 . . . . 159 A3
King's Acre WA14 . . . . . . 119 A1
King St E
Rochdale OL11 . . . . 139 C2
Stockport SK1 . . . . 169 C2
King St S OL11 . . . . 139 B1
King St W
Manchester M3 . . . . 158 C1
Stockport SK3 . . . . 169 B1
8 Wigan WN1 . . . . 150 C4
Kings Ave
Gatley SK8 . . . . 122 A4
Manchester M8 . . . . 156 B4
Whitefield M45 . . . . .44 E2
King's Ave WA3 . . . . .90 F7
Kingsbridge Ave
Ainsworth BL2 . . . . .26 D1
Hattersley SK14 . . . . . . 102 E2
Kingsbridge Cl SK6 . . . . . 125 E7
Kingsbridge Ct M9 . . . . . 157 A3
Kingsbridge Dr SK16 . . . . 101 B7
Kingsbridge Ho BL3 . . . . 144 C1
Kingsbridge Rd
Manchester M9 . . . . 157 A3
5 Oldham OL8 . . . . .67 B5
Kingsbridge Wlk
SK14 . . . . 102 C2
Kingsbrook Ct M21 . . . . . 109 E8
Kingsbrook Rd M16,
M21 . . . . 109 E8
Kingsbury Ave BL1 . . . . . 142 A1
Kingsbury Cl BL8 . . . . . . .27 A6
Kingsbury Ct BL1 . . . . . . 142 A1
Kingsbury Ct Lo BL1 . . . . 142 A1
Kingsbury Dr 14 SK9 . . . 131 D1
Kingsbury Rd M11 . . . . . . .83 C2
Kings Cl
Prestwich M25 . . . . .63 C5
Wilmslow SK9 . . . . 137 A6
King's Cl
Droylsden M18 . . . . .99 F6
Stockport SK7 . . . . 123 F2
Kingscliffe St M9 . . . . . . 157 B4
Kingscourt Ave BL1 . . . . . 142 C2
Kings Cres M16 . . . . .97 B3
King's Cres M16 . . . . .76 E8
Kings Croft Ct WN1 . . . . . 151 A3
Kings Ct
5 Glossop SK13 . . . . . . 116 C8
Stockport SK5 . . . . 169 C3
11 Tyldesley M29 . . . . . .58 F1
Kingsdale Cl BL9 . . . . .45 A7
Kingsdale Rd M18 . . . . . . 100 A4
Kingsdown Cres WN1 . . . .37 C4
Kingsdown Dr BL1 . . . . . . 143 C1
Kingsdown Gdns 8
BL1 . . . . 143 C1
Kingsdown Rd
Abram Brow WN2 . . . . . .74 B7
Wythenshawe M22 . . . . 121 C1
Kingsdown Wlk SK5 . . . . 112 B5
Kings Dr SK8 . . . . 123 A3
King's Dr
Marple SK6 . . . . 125 E7
Middleton M24. . . . . .64 D8
Stockport SK4 . . . . 168 A3
Kingsfield Dr M20 . . . . . . 110 C2
Kingsfield Way M29 . . . . . .77 B8
Kings Fold M46 . . . . .58 E3
Kingsfold Ave M40 . . . . . 159 C4
Kingsford St M5 . . . . 154 A2
Kingsgate BL1 . . . . 145 B3
King's Gdns WN7 . . . . . . .76 C5
Kings Gr
Rochdale OL12 . . . . .15 C4
Stretford M32 . . . . .96 F7
Kingshill Ct WN6 . . . . . . .36 F7
Kingshill Rd M21 . . . . . . 109 A8
Kingshill Sch M29 . . . . . . .76 F8
Kingsholme Rd M22 . . . . 121 C2

Kings La M32. . . . . .96 F3
Kingsland Cl M40. . . . . . . 160 A3
Kingsland Rd
Cheadle SK3 . . . . 123 A7
Farnworth BL4 . . . . .42 A1
Rochdale OL11 . . . . .30 B3
Kingslea PR7 . . . . .20 F8
Kingslea Rd M20 . . . . 110 C5
Kingsleigh Rd SK4 . . . . . . 110 F4
Kingsley Ave
Handforth SK9 . . . . 131 C2
Manchester M9 . . . . 157 C3
Salford M7 . . . . .81 A7
Stockport SK4 . . . . 169 B4
Stretford M32 . . . . .96 F3
Urmston M41 . . . . .95 B2
Whitefield M45 . . . . .63 B8
Wigan WN3 . . . . .54 F3
Kingsley Cl
Ashton-u-L OL6 . . . . .86 A5
Denton M34 . . . . 100 D1
Kingsley Dr
Cheadle SK8 . . . . 123 A3
Oldham OL4 . . . . .67 E7
Kingsley Gr M34 . . . . 100 C8
Kingsley Ho M1 . . . . 159 B1
Kingsley Rd
Altrincham WA15 . . . . . . 120 B7
Hindley WN2 . . . . .56 F5
Middleton M24. . . . . .47 B2
Oldham OL4 . . . . .67 C6
Swinton M27 . . . . .61 D1
Walkden M28 . . . . .60 C4
Wythenshawe M22 . . . . 121 D8
Kingsley St
Bolton BL1 . . . . 143 A2
Bury BL8 . . . . .27 B2
Leigh WN7 . . . . .75 C7
King's Lynn Cl 5
M20 . . . . 110 B3
Kingsmead Mews M9 . . . . .64 C5
Kingsmede WN1 . . . . .37 D3
Kingsmere Ave M19 . . . . . .98 F1
Kingsmill Ave M19 . . . . . . 111 B8
Kingsmoor Fields
SK13 . . . . 104 D3
Kingsmoor Rd SK13 . . . . . 104 D2
Kingsnorth Cl 5 BL1 . . . . 143 C1
Kingsnorth Rd M41 . . . . . .94 E4
Kings Oak Cl WN1 . . . . . . 151 A4
Kings Pk
Leigh WN7 . . . . .76 A8
Stretford M17 . . . . .96 B4
King Sq SK3 . . . . 153 B2
King's Rd
Ashton-in-M WN4 . . . . . .73 A5
Ashton-u-L OL6 . . . . .85 E5
Manchester M25 . . . . . . .63 C2
Oldham OL8 . . . . 153 C1
Reddish M34 . . . . 100 A8
Rochdale OL16 . . . . .31 B5
Romiley SK6 . . . . 113 A3
Wilmslow SK9 . . . . 136 E8
Kings Reach Bsns Pk
SK4. . . . . 168 C1
Kings Road Prim Sch
M16 . . . . .97 A3
King St
Bolton BL1 . . . . 145 B3
Bolton, Bradshaw Chapel
BL2 . . . . .25 D5
5 Bolton, Cox Green
BL7 . . . . .24 F8
Broadbottom SK14 . . . . 115 A8
Delph OL3 . . . . .50 F4
Denton, Hooley Hill
M34 . . . . 100 F6
Denton M34 . . . . 100 F3
Droylsden M43. . . . . 100 A8
Dukinfield SK16 . . . . . . 101 C7
Eccles M30 . . . . .79 F1
Failsworth M35 . . . . .83 D6
Farnworth BL4 . . . . .60 D8
Glossop SK13 . . . . 116 C8
Hadfield SK13 . . . . .29 D1
Hindley WN2 . . . . .56 D6
Hollingworth SK14 . . . . 103 D5
Horwich BL6 . . . . .22 A4
Hyde SK14 . . . . 167 A3
Ince-in-M WN2 . . . . .56 A7
Leigh WN7 . . . . .75 F4
Manchester M2 . . . . 158 C1
Middleton M24. . . . . .64 F8
Mossley OL5 . . . . .68 D1
Newton-le-W WA12 . . . . .89 B3
Oldham OL8 . . . . 153 B2
Radcliffe M26 . . . . .44 B2
Ramsbottom BL0 . . . . . . 138 C2
Rawtenstall BB4 . . . . .2 E8
Rochdale OL16 . . . . 139 C3
17 Royton OL2 . . . . .48 D4
Salford, Higher Broughton
M7 . . . . 155 B3
Salford, Irlams o' th' Height
M6 . . . . .80 D5

King St continued
Salford M3 . . . . 158 B2
8 Stalybridge SK15 . . . . .86 A2
Stretford M32 . . . . .96 D1
Westhoughton BL5 . . . . . .39 F1
Whitworth OL12 . . . . .4 D3
Wigan WN1 . . . . 150 C3
Kings Terr M32 . . . . .96 F3
King's Terr 14 SK16 . . . . . 166 B1
KINGSTON 101 B3
Kingston Arc 6 SK14 . . . . 102 E2
Kingston Ave
Bolton BL2 . . . . .25 C1
Chadderton OL9 . . . . .66 A4
Manchester M20 . . . . . . 110 B1
5 Oldham OL1 . . . . .49 B1
Kingston Cl
Bury BL8 . . . . .44 B8
Hattersley SK14 . . . . . . 102 E2
Sale M33 . . . . 107 D2
Salford M7 . . . . 155 A4
Shaw OL2 . . . . 149 B4
Wigan WN3 . . . . .55 B3
Kingston Cres SK8 . . . . . . .1 A7
Kingston Ct
14 Handforth SK9 . . . . . 131 C1
Manchester M20 . . . . . . 110 B1
Kingston Dr
Royton OL2 . . . . .48 C6
Sale M33 . . . . 108 D5
Urmston M41 . . . . 107 B8
Kingston Gdns SK14 . . . . 101 B3
Kingston Gr M9 . . . . .64 F4
Kingston Hill SK8 . . . . . . 122 D4
Kingston Pl SK8 . . . . 122 E2
Kingston Rd
Failsworth M35 . . . . .84 B7
Handforth SK9 . . . . 131 D5
Manchester M20 . . . . . . 110 B1
Radcliffe M26 . . . . .44 C6
Stockton St SK3 . . . . . . 169 A1
Kingstreet SK7 . . . . 132 B1
Kingsway
Altrincham WA14 . . . . . . 119 D5
Cheadle M20, SK8 . . . . . 122 C5
Dukinfield SK16 . . . . . . 101 E7
Ince-in-M WN2 . . . . 151 C3
Kearsley BL4 . . . . .60 F6
Manchester M14, M19,
M20 . . . . 110 D4
Middleton M24. . . . . .65 B6
Newton-le-W WA12 . . . . .89 C2
Pendlebury M27 . . . . .80 C6
Rochdale OL16 . . . . .31 C5
Romiley SK6 . . . . 112 E3
Stockport SK7 . . . . 123 F2
Stretford M32 . . . . .96 C1
Walkden M28 . . . . .78 D8
Wigan WN1 . . . . .37 D2
Kingsway Ave M19 . . . . . . .98 F1
Kingsway Bldgs M19 . . . . 110 C5
Kingsway Cl OL8 . . . . 153 B1
Kingsway Cres M19 . . . . . 110 C5
Kingsway Pk M41 . . . . . . .95 D4
Kingsway Prim Sch
M41 . . . . .95 E4
Kingsway Sch The
SK8. . . . . 122 C4
Kingsway W Ind Pk
OL16 . . . . .31 B5
Kingswear Dr BL1 . . . . . . 142 C1
Kings Wlk M43 . . . . 100 A8
Kings' Wlk OL6 . . . . .85 E5
Kingswood Gr SK5 . . . . . . .99 F1
Kingswood Rd
Eccles M30 . . . . .79 B4
Manchester M14 . . . . . . 110 E8
Middleton M24. . . . . .46 F3
Prestwich M25 . . . . .62 F5
Kingthorpe Gdns BL3 . . . 147 C4
King William Ent Pk
M50 . . . . 161 A4
King William St
Eccles M30 . . . . .79 A3
Salford M50 . . . . 161 A4
11 Tyldesley M29 . . . . . .76 F8
Kingwood Ave BL1 . . . . . . .40 F8
Kingwood Cres WN5 . . . . .54 D6
Kinlay Rd BL4 . . . . 147 C1
Kinlet Rd WN3 . . . . .54 C4
Kinlett Wlk 11 M40 . . . . . .65 D2
Kinley Cl M12 . . . . 164 C2
Kinloch Dr BL1 . . . . 144 B3
Kinloch Gdns OL8 . . . . . . .67 A4
Kinloch St
Droylsden M11. . . . . .83 A2
Failsworth M35 . . . . .83 D6
Oldham OL8 . . . . .67 A4
Kinmel Ave SK5 . . . . 112 C4
Kinmel Wlk 4 M23 . . . . . 120 F6
Kinmount Wlk M9 . . . . . . 157 A2
Kinnaird Cres SK1 . . . . . . 124 B8
Kinnaird Rd M20 . . . . 110 C3
Kinnerly Gr M28 . . . . .60 A1
Kinniside Cl WN3 . . . . . . .55 A4
Kinross Ave
Garswood WN4 . . . . .72 C4
Oldham, Mumps OL1 . . . .67 A5
Stockport SK7 . . . . 124 A3
Kinross Cl BL3 . . . . .21 B2
Kinross Dr BL3 . . . . .40 F5
Kinross Rd M14 . . . . .98 E3
Kinsale Wlk M23 . . . . 120 F3
Kinsey Ave M23 . . . . 120 C5
Kinsley Dr M28 . . . . .60 C2
Kintbury St WN2 . . . . .73 F7
Kintore Ave SK7 . . . . 124 F3
Kintore Wlk 5 M40 . . . . . 156 C1

Kintyre Ave M5 . . . . 154 B1
Kintyre Cl 5 M11 . . . . .83 C1
Kintyre Dr BL3 . . . . .40 E5
Kinver Cl BL3 . . . . 146 C3
Kinver Rd M40 . . . . .65 C2
Kipling Ave
Denton M34 . . . . 113 A7
Droylsden M43. . . . . .84 A3
Wigan WN3 . . . . .55 A4
Kipling Cl SK2 . . . . 124 E7
Kipling Gr WN7 . . . . .75 D7
Kipling Rd OL1 . . . . .49 B2
Kipling St M7 . . . . 155 A2
Kippax St M14 . . . . .98 B3
Kirby Ave
Atherton M46 . . . . .58 C5
Failsworth OL9 . . . . .65 D3
Swinton M27 . . . . .79 D5
Kirby Rd WN7 . . . . .75 E5
Kirby Wlk
3 Manchester M4 . . . . . 159 C2
Shaw OL2 . . . . 149 B4
Kiribati Way WN7 . . . . . . .75 E6
Kirkbank St
Oldham OL9 . . . . 153 A4
Oldham OL9 . . . . 153 A4
Kirkbeck WN7 . . . . .76 C3
Kirkburn View BL8 . . . . . .27 C5
Kirkby Ave
Manchester M40 . . . . . . .83 B7
Sale M33 . . . . 108 C2
Kirkby Cl BL9 . . . . .44 E7
Kirkby Dr M33 . . . . 108 D2
Kirkby Rd
Bolton BL1 . . . . 144 B4
Culcheth WA3 . . . . .91 F3
Kirkdale Ave M40 . . . . . . .65 D2
Kirkdale Dr OL2 . . . . .48 C5
Kirkdale Gdns WN8 . . . . . .53 A7
Kirkebrook Rd BL3 . . . . . 146 A4
Kirkfell Dr
High Lane SK6 . . . . 134 E8
Tyldesley M29 . . . . .77 B7
Kirkfell Wlk OL1 . . . . .48 F1
Kirkgate Cl 5 M40 . . . . . 159 C3
Kirkhall La
Bolton BL1 . . . . 144 C4
Leigh WN7 . . . . .75 E7
Kirkhall Wkshps The
BL1. . . . . 144 C4
Kirkham Ave
Golborne WA3 . . . . .90 E6
Manchester M18 . . . . . . .99 D6
Kirkham Cl M34 . . . . 100 F3
Kirkham Rd
Gatley SK8 . . . . 131 C8
Leigh WN7 . . . . .75 D2
KIRKHAMS 63 B6
Kirkham St
Abram WN2 . . . . .74 B8
Bolton BL2 . . . . .25 C1
Oldham OL9 . . . . 153 B3
Salford M6 . . . . 154 B3
Walkden M38 . . . . .60 A5
Kirkhaven Sq M40 . . . . . . 160 B4
Kirkhill Grange BL5 . . . . . .40 A2
Kirkhill Wlk 12 M40 . . . . .65 D2
KIRKHOLT 30 F2
Kirkholt Wlk 11 M9 . . . . .64 E3
Kirkhope Dr BL1 . . . . 143 A1
Kirkhope Wlk BL1 . . . . . . 143 A1
Kirklands
Bolton BL2 . . . . .25 D2
Sale M33 . . . . 108 A2
Kirklee Ave OL9 . . . . .48 A1
Kirklee Rd OL11 . . . . .30 D2
Kirklees Cl BL8 . . . . .26 F7
Kirklees St
Bury BL8 . . . . .26 F7
Tottington BL8 . . . . 151 B4
Kirklees Wlk M45 . . . . . . .63 B8
Kirkless Ind Est WN2 . . . . .38 B1
Kirkless La WN2 . . . . .38 B1
Kirkless St WN2 . . . . .38 A3
Kirkless Villas WN2 . . . . . .38 A2
Kirkley St SK14 . . . . 167 B1
Kirklinton Dr M9 . . . . 157 A2
Kirkman Ave M30 . . . . . . .95 C8
Kirkmanshulme La M12,
M18. . . . . 165 B1
Kirkman St BL9 . . . . .44 F3
Kirkpatrick St WN2 . . . . . .57 B3
Kirk Rd M19 . . . . 111 B7
Kirk St M18 . . . . .99 D5
Kirkstall 27 OL12 . . . . . . 139 B4
Kirkstall Ave
Heywood OL10 . . . . .29 C3
Littleborough OL15 . . . . .16 A7
Kirkstall Cl SK12. . . . . 133 D4
Kirkstall Gdns 7 M26 . . . .43 E5
Kirkstall Rd
Middleton M24. . . . . .46 F1
Urmston M41. . . . . .95 E3
Kirkstead Cl M11 . . . . 165 A4
Kirkstead Rd SK8 . . . . . . 132 C6
Kirkstead Way WA3 . . . . . .90 A8
Kirkstile Cres WN3 . . . . . .54 E2
Kirkstile Pl M27 . . . . .61 E4
Kirkstone WN5 . . . . .54 C7
Kirkstone Ave M28 . . . . . . .60 F1
Kirkstone Cl OL1 . . . . .48 F1
Kirkstone Dr
Middleton M24. . . . . .46 E2
Royton OL2 . . . . .48 D6
Kirkstone Rd
Dukinfield SK14 . . . . . . 101 C5

Kirkstone Rd continued
Failsworth M40 . . . . .65 C2
Kirktown Wlk M11 . . . . .165 C6
Kirkwall Dr BL2 . . . . .148 B1
Kirkway
Manchester M9 . . . . .65 A4
Middleton M24 . . . . .65 A7
Rochdale OL11 . . . . .30 F2
Kirkwood Cl WN7 . . . . .30 F2
Kirkwood Dr M40 . . . . . . .159 C4
Kirtley Ave M30 . . . . .79 D3
Kirtlington Cl OL2 . . . . . . .149 A1
Kirton Lo M25 . . . . .63 C4
Kirton Wlk M9 . . . . .64 C5
Kitchener Ave M44 . . . . . . .105 C4
Kitchener St
Bolton BL3 . . . . .42 B3
Bury BL8 . . . . .27 B1
Kitchener Way BL4 . . . . . . .147 C1
Kitchen St OL16 . . . . .31 A8
Kite Gr WN7 . . . . .76 B5
Kitepool St M30 . . . . .79 A3
Kitter St OL12 . . . . .15 C3
KITT GREEN 54 C8
Kitt Green Rd WN5 . . . . .54 C8
Kittiwake Cl M29 . . . . .77 A7
Kittiwake Ct SK2 . . . . .124 F5
KITT'S MOSS 132 D6
Kitt's Moss La SK7 . . . . . . .132 D6
Kitty Wheeldon Gdns
M33 . . . . .108 A5
Kiveton Cl M28 . . . . .60 C2
Kiveton Dr WN4 . . . . .73 C2
Kiwi Pk M17 . . . . .96 C5
Knacks La OL12 . . . . .14 A5
Knaresborough Cl SK5 . . . . .99 E1
Knaresborough Rd
WN2 . . . . .56 E4
Knarr Barn La OL3 . . . . .50 D3
Knarr La OL3 . . . . .50 E2
Kneller Wlk OL1 . . . . .49 D4
Knight Cres M24 . . . . .46 D3
Knightley Wlk M40 . . . . . . .157 A1
Knightsbridge SK1 . . . . . . .169 C2
Knightsbridge Cl
13 Handforth SK9 . . . . .131 D1
Salford M7 . . . . .155 A4
Knightsbridge Mews
M20 . . . . .110 B4
Knight's Cl M25 . . . . .63 B5
Knightscliffe Cres
WN6 . . . . .35 D6
Knights Ct M45 . . . . .80 A2
Knightshill Cres WN6 . . . . . .37 A1
Knight St
Ashton-u-L OL7 . . . . .84 F2
Bolton BL1 . . . . .145 C4
Bury BL8 . . . . .27 C2
Hyde SK14 . . . . .167 B1
Manchester M20 . . . . .110 B4
Knightswood BL3 . . . . .40 F3
Knightswood Rd M8 . . . . . . .156 A3
Kniveton Rd M12 . . . . .164 C2
Knivton St SK14 . . . . .167 C3
Knob Hall Gdns M23 . . . . . .120 F3
Knole Ave SK12 . . . . .133 F4
Knoll St
Rochdale OL11 . . . . .30 C2
Salford M7 . . . . .155 A3
Knoll The
Mossley OL5 . . . . .68 B1
Shaw OL2 . . . . .149 C2
Knott Fold SK14 . . . . .167 A1
Knott Hill La OL3 . . . . .50 E3
Knott Hill St OL12 . . . . .4 E1
Knott La
Bolton BL1 . . . . .23 F2
Hyde SK14 . . . . .113 E8
Knott Lanes OL8 . . . . .84 F8
Knotts Brow BL7 . . . . .9 F4
Knott's Hos WN7 . . . . .91 B8
Knowe Ave 5 M22 . . . . .121 D1
Knowl St
Ramsbottom BL0 . . . . .11 C4
Reddish M34 . . . . .100 B2
Knowldale Way M12 . . . . . . .164 B1
Knowle Ave OL7 . . . . .85 C6
Knowle Ave SK14 . . . . .166 A4
Knowle Dr M25 . . . . .63 A2
Knowle Gn SK9 . . . . .131 C3
Knowle Pk SK9 . . . . .131 C3
Knowle Rd SK6 . . . . .126 D6
Knowles Ave WN3 . . . . .54 F4
Knowles Ct M6 . . . . .80 B3
Knowles Edge St BL1 . . . . . .142 C2
Knowles Pl
1 Manchester M15 . . . . .162 C2
Wigan WN1 . . . . .151 B4
Knowles St
Ince-in-M WN3 . . . . .151 A2
Radcliffe M26 . . . . .44 A4
Knowle Way 5 SK14 . . . . . . .102 F2
Knowl Hill Dr OL12 . . . . .13 E2
Knowl Hill View OL10 . . . . . . .29 A2
Knowl La OL12 . . . . .13 B5
Knowl Mdw BB4 . . . . .1 A6
Knowl Rd OL16 . . . . .31 D6
Knowls La OL4 . . . . .67 F5
Knowl St
Oldham OL8 . . . . .66 C2
Stalybridge SK15 . . . . .86 B2
Knowls The OL8 . . . . .66 C1
Knowl Syke St OL12 . . . . . . .15 C7
Knowl Top La OL3 . . . . .69 D7
Knowl View
Bury BL8 . . . . .27 A6
Littleborough OL15 . . . . .15 F2
Knowsley OL4 . . . . .68 A7

Knowsley Ave
Atherton M46 . . . . .58 C4
Golborne WA3 . . . . .74 B1
Oldham OL4 . . . . .68 A7
Salford M5 . . . . .161 B4
Urmston M41 . . . . .95 C4
Knowsley Cres
Stockport SK1 . . . . .124 B8
Whitworth OL12 . . . . .4 E6
Knowsley Dr
Leigh WN7 . . . . .75 E2
Oldham OL4 . . . . .68 A7
Swinton M27 . . . . .79 D5
Knowsley Gn
Oldham OL4 . . . . .68 A7
Salford M5 . . . . .161 B4
Knowsley Gr 5 BL6 . . . . .22 D1
Knowsley Grange BL1 . . . . . .40 D7
Knowsley Jun Sch OL4 . . . . .68 A7
Knowsley Park Way BB4 . . . .1 B8
Knowsley Rd
Ainsworth BL2 . . . . .26 C1
Bolton BL1 . . . . .142 B2
Haslingden BB4 . . . . .1 B8
Hazel Grove SK7 . . . . .133 F8
Stockport SK1 . . . . .124 B8
Whitefield M45 . . . . .62 F8
Wigan WN6 . . . . .37 A3
Knowsley Rd Ind Est
BB4 . . . . .1 B8
Knowsley St
Bolton BL1 . . . . .145 C3
Bury BL9 . . . . .140 B1
Leigh WN7 . . . . .75 D5
Manchester M8 . . . . .159 A4
Rochdale OL12 . . . . .139 B4
Knowsley Terr
Oldham OL4 . . . . .68 A7
Stockport SK1 . . . . .124 B8
Knutsford Ave
Manchester M16 . . . . .97 D3
Reddish SK4 . . . . .111 D7
Sale M33 . . . . .108 C4
Knutsford Rd
Manchester M18 . . . . .99 C4
Row-of-Trees SK9,
WA16 . . . . .136 D3
Knutsford St M6 . . . . .154 B2
Knutsford View
WA15 . . . . .129 C8
KNUTSHAW BRIDGE 40 E2
Knutshaw Cres BL3 . . . . .40 E2
Knypersley Ave SK2 . . . . . . .124 C7
Krester Ct M20 . . . . .110 A5
Krokus Sq OL9 . . . . .152 A3
Kyle Ct SK7 . . . . .124 F1
Kylemore Ave BL3 . . . . .144 B1
Kylemore Pl BL4 . . . . .60 C7
Kyle Rd SK7 . . . . .124 F1
Kynder St M34 . . . . .100 F3

L

Labrador Quay M50 . . . . .96 F7
Labtec St M27 . . . . .62 B1
Laburnum Ave
Ashton-u-L OL6 . . . . .85 C6
Atherton M46 . . . . .58 E3
Bury BL8 . . . . .26 F7
Chadderton OL9 . . . . .48 C1
Droylsden M34 . . . . .84 C1
Eccles M30 . . . . .95 A8
Failsworth M35 . . . . .83 F6
Hyde SK14 . . . . .113 D8
Ince-in-M WN3 . . . . .151 C2
Laburnum Cl 4
WA15 . . . . .120 B5
Laburnum Ct
Bury BL8 . . . . .26 F7
Lymm WA13 . . . . .117 B4
Laburnum Dr
Whitefield BL9 . . . . .45 A1
Wigan WN6 . . . . .37 A4
Laburnum Gr
Horwich BL6 . . . . .22 E1
Prestwich M25 . . . . .63 A5
Tyldesley M29 . . . . .59 D1
Laburnum La
Altrincham WA15 . . . . .128 E8
Newhey OL16 . . . . .32 A3
Laburnum Pk BL2 . . . . .25 B5
Laburnum Rd
Farnworth BL4 . . . . .60 B8
Golborne WA3 . . . . .90 F7
Haslingden BB4 . . . . .1 A1
Irlam M44 . . . . .105 D5
Manchester M18 . . . . .99 D4
Oldham OL8 . . . . .65 C8
Oldham OL8 . . . . .84 C8
Reddish M34 . . . . .99 F3
Urmston M41 . . . . .95 B4
Walkden M28 . . . . .60 E1
Laburnum St
Ashton-in-M WN4 . . . . .73 B2
Atherton M46 . . . . .58 E3
2 Bolton BL1 . . . . .145 A4
Salford M6 . . . . .154 C2
Laburnum Terr OL11 . . . . .30 E4
Laburnum Way
Littleborough OL15 . . . . .15 F5
Stockport SK3 . . . . .123 B8

Laburnum Wlk 1
M33 . . . . .107 C5
Lacerta Mews M7 . . . . .81 C3
Lacey Ave SK9 . . . . .131 B1
Lacey Ct SK9 . . . . .131 B1
Lacey Gn SK9 . . . . .131 B1
Lacey Gr SK9 . . . . .131 C1
LACEY GREEN 131 B1
Lacey Green Prim Sch
SK9 . . . . .131 B1
Lackford Dr M40 . . . . .159 C4
Lacrosse Ave M40 . . . . .66 C4
Lacy Gr M32 . . . . .96 E3
Lacy St
Stockport SK1 . . . . .170 C4
Stretford M32 . . . . .96 D1
Lacy Wlk M12 . . . . .164 B4
Ladbrooke Cl OL6 . . . . .166 C4
Ladbrooke Rd OL6 . . . . .85 C5
Ladcastle Rd OL3 . . . . .69 B5
Ladhill La OL3 . . . . .69 B5
Ladies La WN2 . . . . .56 D6
Ladybarn Ave WA3 . . . . .89 F7
Ladybarn Cres
Bramhall SK7 . . . . .132 F6
Manchester M14 . . . . .110 D7
Ladybarn Ho 1 M14 . . . . . . .110 D8
Lady Barn House Sch
SK8 . . . . .122 D3
Ladybarn La M14 . . . . .110 D8
Ladybarn Manor M7 . . . . . . .132 E8
Ladybarn Mews 2
M14 . . . . .110 D8
Ladybarn Prim Sch
M20 . . . . .110 D6
Ladybarn Rd M14 . . . . .110 D8
Ladybower SK8 . . . . .123 C4
Ladybower Ct SK13 . . . . .104 C1
Ladybower Ave M28 . . . . .78 C8
Lady Bridge Bow BL1 . . . . . . .40 F7
Ladybridge Com Prim Sch
BL3 . . . . .40 F4
Ladybridge High Sch
BL3 . . . . .40 F4
Lady Bridge La BL1 . . . . .40 F7
Ladybridge Prim Sch
SK8 . . . . .123 B4
Ladybridge Rd SK8 . . . . .123 B3
Ladybridge Rise SK8 . . . . . . .123 C3
Ladybrook Ave WA15 . . . . . . .120 B8
Ladybrook Gr 14 SK9 . . . . . .131 D2
Ladybrook Prim Sch
SK7 . . . . .132 F7
Ladybrook Rd SK7 . . . . .123 C1
Ladyburn Ct M14 . . . . .110 D7
Ladyfield St SK9 . . . . .137 B7
Ladyfield Terr SK9 . . . . .137 C7
Lady Harriet Wlk M28 . . . . . .60 C1
Ladyhill View M28 . . . . .78 C8
LADY HOUSE 31 E4
Ladyhouse Cl OL16 . . . . .32 A5
Ladyhouse La OL16 . . . . .32 A5
Lady Kelvin Rd WA14 . . . . . . .119 C6
Lady La
Culcheth WA3 . . . . .91 C1
Wigan WN3 . . . . .54 E3
Ladylands Ave 15 M11 . . . . . .83 C2
Lady Rd OL4 . . . . .67 E6
Ladys Cl SK12 . . . . .133 E4
Ladyshore Cl M6 . . . . .154 C1
Ladyshore Rd BL3 . . . . .43 C2
Ladysmith Ave
Ashton-in-M WN4 . . . . .73 C3
Bury BL9 . . . . .28 A5
Ladysmith Dr OL6 . . . . .85 F5
Ladysmith Rd
Ashton-u-L OL6 . . . . .85 F5
Manchester M20 . . . . .110 C3
Stalybridge SK15 . . . . .86 A4
Ladysmith Sh Ctr OL6 . . . . . .166 B3
Ladysmith St
Oldham OL8 . . . . .66 C3
Stockport SK3 . . . . .170 D3
Ladythorn Ave SK6 . . . . .126 A5
Ladythorn Cres SK7 . . . . . . .132 F6
Ladythorn Ct M25 . . . . .63 A2
Ladythorne Ave M25 . . . . . . .63 A2
Ladythorne Dr M25 . . . . .63 A2
Ladythorn Gr SK7 . . . . .132 F6
Ladythorn Rd SK7 . . . . .132 F6
Ladywell Ave M38 . . . . .60 A5
Ladywell Cl SK7 . . . . .124 A2
Ladywell Gr M38 . . . . .60 A6
Ladywell Sta M5 . . . . .80 A2
Ladywood Sch BL3 . . . . .43 B4
Lafford La WN8 . . . . .35 C2
Lagan Wlk M22 . . . . .121 E2
Lagos Cl M14 . . . . .98 A4
Laindon Rd M13,M14 . . . . .98 E4
Lainton Ct 3 SK3 . . . . .123 C8
LAITHWAITE 54 D8
Laithwaite Rd WN5 . . . . .54 E7
Lake Bank OL15 . . . . .16 A3
Lake Dr M24 . . . . .64 F8
Lakeland Ave WN4 . . . . .73 C4
Lakeland Cres BL9 . . . . .44 E6
Lakeland Ct 1 M24 . . . . .46 D2
Lakeland Dr OL2 . . . . .48 C8
Lakelands Dr BL3 . . . . .40 F4
Lakenheath Cl 10 BL1 . . . . . . .24 F6
Lakenheath Dr BL1 . . . . .25 A6
Lake Rd
Denton M34 . . . . .100 F4
Stalybridge SK15 . . . . .85 F4

Lake Rd continued
Stretford M17 . . . . .96 C7
Lakes Dr WN5 . . . . .53 E6
Lakeside
Gatley SK8 . . . . .122 C3
Prestwich M7 . . . . .63 D1
Lake Side
Bury BL9 . . . . .44 F5
Glossop SK13 . . . . .104 A6
Leigh WN7 . . . . .75 D6
Littleborough OL15 . . . . .16 A2
Lakeside Ave
Ashton-u-L OL7 . . . . .84 F4
Bolton BL3 . . . . .42 A2
Orrell WN5 . . . . .53 E3
Walkden M28 . . . . .60 D5
Lake Side OL18 . . . . .99 F6
Lake Side Cotts WN1 . . . . .20 C1
Lakeside Dr SK12 . . . . .133 E5
Lakeside Gn SK2 . . . . .124 C6
Lakeside Rise M9 . . . . .64 A3
Lakeside Way BL9 . . . . .140 C1
Lakes Rd
Dukinfield SK16 . . . . .101 C8
Marple SK6 . . . . .126 B6
Lakes Terr WN2 . . . . .56 A7
Lake View
Manchester M9 . . . . .65 A2
Stalybridge SK15 . . . . .85 F4
Lake Wk WN5 . . . . .54 D2
Lakin St M40 . . . . .83 A7
Laleham Gn SK7 . . . . .123 D3
Lamb Cl M12 . . . . .164 C1
Lamb Ct M3 . . . . .158 B2
LAMBERHEAD GREEN 54 B5
Lamberhead Ho WN5 . . . . .54 B6
Lamberhead Ind Est
WN5 . . . . .54 C5
Lambert Dr M33 . . . . .107 C6
Lamberton Dr M23 . . . . .120 E6
Lambert St OL7 . . . . .100 F8
Lamb La M3 . . . . .158 B2
Lamb St
Bolton BL3 . . . . .145 B1
Poynton SK12 . . . . .133 D4
Lambourne Cl M22 . . . . .121 B2
Lambourne Gr 4 OL16 . . . . . . .31 F7
Lambourn Cl
Bolton BL3 . . . . .145 B1
Wigan WN5 . . . . .54 C5
Lamburn Ave M40 . . . . .65 D2
Lamb Wlk 11 M34 . . . . .113 A1
Lamerton Way SK9 . . . . .131 E2
Lamorna Cl M7 . . . . .81 B7
Lamphey Cl BL1 . . . . .40 D8
Lamplight Way M27 . . . . .80 E7
Lamport Cl M1 . . . . .163 B3
Lamport Ct M1 . . . . .163 B3
Lampson St M8 . . . . .158 E4
Lamsholme Cl 7 M19 . . . . . . .99 A2
Lanark Ave M22 . . . . .121 E8
Lanark Cl
Hazel Grove SK7 . . . . .125 A2
Heywood OL10 . . . . .28 F1
Lanbury Dr M8 . . . . .155 C3
Lancashire Ct OL12 . . . . .152 C1
Lancashire Fusiliers
Regimental Mus*
BL8 . . . . .27 B1
LANCASHIRE HILL 169 B3
Lancashire Hill SK1, SK4,
SK5 . . . . .169 B3
Lancashire Mining Mus*
M5 . . . . .154 A3
Lancashire Rd M31 . . . . .105 E2
Lancaster Ave
Atherton M46 . . . . .58 E2
Failsworth M35 . . . . .83 E7
Golborne WA3 . . . . .90 C8
Haslingden BB4 . . . . .1 A1
Horwich BL6 . . . . .22 D2
Middleton M24 . . . . .65 C7
Ramsbottom BL0 . . . . .11 A4
Stalybridge SK15 . . . . .86 A3
Urmston M41 . . . . .95 A3
Whitefield M45 . . . . .63 A7
Lancaster Cl
Adlington PR6 . . . . .21 B7
Bolton BL2 . . . . .148 A3
Hazel Grove SK7 . . . . .133 D8
Romiley SK6 . . . . .113 A1

Lancaster Ct
Failsworth M40 . . . . .83 C4
4 Leigh WN7 . . . . .76 B4
3 Manchester M19 . . . . .110 F8
Lancaster Dr
Bury BL9 . . . . .27 F8
Little Lever BL3 . . . . .43 B4
Manchester M25 . . . . .63 C2
Lancaster Ho
Royton OL2 . . . . .48 D5
5 Stockport SK3 . . . . .170 B4
Lancastrian Sch
M20 . . . . .109 E4
Lancaster Pl PR6 . . . . .21 A8
Lancaster Rd
Denton M34 . . . . .100 F1
Droylsden M43 . . . . .83 F3
Handforth SK9 . . . . .131 E1
Hindley WN2 . . . . .56 A4
Irlam M44 . . . . .105 D5
Manchester M20 . . . . .110 A3
Salford M6 . . . . .80 B4
Wigan WN5 . . . . .53 C5
Lancaster Sq OL2 . . . . .48 D5
Lancaster St
Chadderton OL9 . . . . .66 A3
Ince-in-M WN3 . . . . .151 A2
Mossley OL5 . . . . .68 B1
2 Radcliffe M26 . . . . .43 E3
Stockport SK1 . . . . .112 A2
Lancaster Terr
24 Bolton BL1 . . . . .143 B2
Rochdale OL11 . . . . .13 C2
Lancaster Way BL5 . . . . .39 D2
Lancaster Wlk
22 Bolton BL1 . . . . .143 B2
Wigan WN5 . . . . .36 D1
Lancelot Rd M22 . . . . .121 F2
Lancelyn Dr SK9 . . . . .137 D8
Lance Wood Pl WN5 . . . . .36 F6
Lanchester Dr BL3 . . . . .145 A1
Lanchester St M40 . . . . .160 B3
Lancing Ave M20 . . . . .110 D3
Lancing Wlk OL9 . . . . .152 A2
Landau Dr M28 . . . . .59 F3
Landcross Rd M14 . . . . .98 C1
Landedmans BL5 . . . . .58 A7
Landells Wlk M40 . . . . .83 A5
Lander Gr M9 . . . . .64 F2
LAND GATE 73 A8
Land Gate Ct OL12 . . . . .4 F5
Landgate Ind Est WN4 . . . . . . .73 A8
Landgate La WN7 . . . . .73 B8
Landgate Sch WN4 . . . . .73 A7
Landkey Cl 1 M23 . . . . .108 F2
Land La SK9 . . . . .137 C6
Landmark Ct BL1 . . . . .23 F1
Landor Cl WA3 . . . . .90 E8
Landor Ct M34 . . . . .99 F3
Landore Cl M26 . . . . .44 B4
Landos Rd M40 . . . . .159 C3
Landrace Dr M28 . . . . .78 B6
Landsberg Rd M35 . . . . .84 B8
Landsberg Terr M35 . . . . .84 B8
Landseer Dr SK6 . . . . .126 B7
Landseer St OL4 . . . . .67 A5
Lands End Rd M24 . . . . .64 B7
LANDSIDE 75 F1
Landside WN7 . . . . .75 F2
Land St WN6 . . . . .150 B4
Lane Brow OL4 . . . . .68 B5
Lane Ct 1 M14 . . . . .98 D4
Lane End OL4 . . . . .68 B5
LANE END 46 F8
Lane End
Eccles M30 . . . . .79 F1
Heywood OL10 . . . . .29 B1
Lane End Cl M35 . . . . .84 A6
Lane End Prim Sch
SK8 . . . . .123 C2
Lane End Rd
Britannia OL13 . . . . .4 A8
Manchester M19, SK4 . . . . . .110 E4
LANE ENDS 114 D1
Lane Ends
Romiley SK6 . . . . .113 D3
5 Wigan WN5 . . . . .54 D5
Lanegate SK14 . . . . .113 D8
LANE HEAD 90 E6
Lane Head Ave WA3 . . . . .90 F8
Lane Head Rd
Mossley OL4, OL5 . . . . .68 A3
Oldham OL4 . . . . .68 A3
Lanesfield Wlk M8 . . . . .156 C4
Laneside Cl OL15 . . . . .16 A6
Laneside Dr SK7 . . . . .124 A1
Laneside Rd
Manchester M20 . . . . .122 C8
New Mills, Rowarth
SK22 . . . . .127 C6
Laneside Wlk OL16 . . . . .31 F7
Lane The BL1 . . . . .40 F8
Lanfield Dr M8 . . . . .155 F7
Langcliffe Cl WA3 . . . . .91 E3
Langcliffe Cl OL4 . . . . .68 A4
Langcliffe Wlk M18 . . . . .165 C1
Langcroft Dr 18 M40 . . . . .83 C5
Langdale Ave
Golborne WA3 . . . . .74 C1
Ince-in-M WN2 . . . . .56 B8
Manchester M19 . . . . .111 B8
Oldham OL8 . . . . .66 D4

Langdale Ave continued
Royton OL16 . . . . .48 C8
Wigan WN1 . . . . .37 B3
Langdale Cl
Altrincham WA15 . . . . .119 E5
Denton M34 . . . . .100 E1
Gatley SK8 . . . . .122 C3
High Lane SK6 . . . . .134 E8
Langdale Cres
Abram WN2 . . . . .74 B8
Wigan WN5 . . . . .54 B8
Langdale Dr
Middleton M24 . . . . .46 F3
Walkden M28 . . . . .60 F1
Whitefield BL9 . . . . .45 A3
Langdale Gr WN2 . . . . .56 B2
Langdale Mews 9 BL9 . . . .27 F5
Langdale Rd
Bramhall SK7 . . . . .132 C5
Hindley WN2 . . . . .56 E5
Manchester M14 . . . . .98 D4
Partington M31 . . . . .105 E3
Reddish SK4 . . . . .111 C6
Romiley SK6 . . . . .113 B4
Sale M33 . . . . .107 E1
Stretford M32 . . . . .96 C3
Wigan WN5 . . . . .54 B7
Langdale St
Bolton BL3 . . . . .147 B3
Farnworth BL4 . . . . .60 C7
Leigh WN7 . . . . .75 E5
Langdale Terr SK15 . . . . . .86 A4
Langden Cl
Culcheth WA3 . . . . .91 D4
Shaw OL2 . . . . .149 A4
Langdon Cl BL1 . . . . .143 A1
Langdon Coll M7 . . . . .63 F1
Langfield WA3 . . . . .90 E7
Langfield Ave M16 . . . . .97 D3
Langfield Cres M43 . . . . . . .84 C2
Langfield Wlk M5 . . . . .154 C2
Langford Dr
Irlam M44 . . . . .94 A1
Leigh WN7 . . . . .75 E2
Langford Gdns BL3 . . . . . .147 B4
Langford Rd
Manchester, Withington
M20 . . . . .110 A6
Stockport, Heaton Moor
SK4 . . . . .168 C4
Langford St M34 . . . . .100 F3
Langham Cl BL1 . . . . .25 A5
Langham Ct
Manchester M20 . . . . .109 F4
Manchester M32 . . . . .96 A4
Langham Gr WA15 . . . . . . .120 B8
Langham Ho SK4 . . . . .168 B2
Langham Rd
Altrincham WA14 . . . . .119 C2
Oldham OL8 . . . . .66 E4
Salford M6 . . . . .154 C2
Standish WN6 . . . . .19 D1
Stockport SK4 . . . . .168 B1
Langham St OL7 . . . . .85 A5
Langholm Dr BL2 . . . . .42 F6
Langholme Cl M15 . . . . . . .162 A3
Langholme Pl M30 . . . . .79 B2
Langholme Way OL10 . . . . .28 F1
Langholm Rd WN4 . . . . .72 C4
Langland Cl
Manchester, Charlestown
M9 .64 E4
Manchester, North Reddish
M19 . . . . .99 D2
Langland Dr M30 . . . . .95 C7
LANGLEY 46 D2
Langley Ave
Hazel Grove SK7 . . . . .124 B1
Middleton M24 . . . . .46 C4
Newton-le-W WA12 . . . . .89 C1
Oldham OL4 . . . . .68 B5
Prestwich M25 . . . . .63 B6
Langley Cl
Golborne WA3 . . . . .74 C1
Standish WN6 . . . . .19 E2
Urmston M41 . . . . .95 E2
Langley Cres M25 . . . . .63 B6
Langley Ct
Glossop SK13 . . . . .104 A3
13 Manchester M7 . . . . .63 E1
Langley Dr
3 Bolton BL3 . . . . .144 C1
Boothstown M28 . . . . .77 F6
Glossop SK13 . . . . .116 F8
Handforth SK9 . . . . .131 E3
Langley Gdns M25 . . . . .63 B6
Langley Gr M25 . . . . .63 B6
Langley Grange M25 . . . . . .63 B6
Langley Hall Rd M25 . . . . . .63 B6
Langley Ho M24 . . . . .47 A3
Langley La M24, OL10 . . . . .46 D4
Langley Platt La M29,
M46 . . . . .76 C8
Langley Prim Sch M24 . . . .46 E2
Langley Rd
Manchester, Charlestown
M6, M27 . . . . .80 F7
Manchester M14 . . . . .98 D1
Prestwich M25 . . . . .63 A5
Sale M33 . . . . .107 E4
Langley Rd S M6, M27 . . . . .81 A5
Langley St WN5 . . . . .54 D6
Langness St 2 M11 . . . . . . .83 C1

Lango St 1 M16 . . . . .97 C4
Langport Ave M12 . . . . .164 B2
Langroyd Wlk 11 M8 . . . . .155 C3
Langset Ave 2 WN2 . . . . . .56 D6
Langsett Ave
13 Gamesley SK13 . . . . . . .171 A1
Salford M6 . . . . .80 C3
Langsett Gn 15 SK13 . . . . .171 A1
Langsett Gr 14 SK13 . . . . .171 A1
Langsett La SK13 . . . . .171 A2
Langsett Lea 23 SK13 . . . .171 A1
Langsett Terr 24
SK13 . . . . .171 A1
Langshaw Rd BL3 . . . . .144 C1
Langshaw St
Manchester M16 . . . . .97 C4
Salford M5, M6 . . . . .154 C1
Langshaw Wlk BL3 . . . . . . .144 C1
Langside Ave M9 . . . . .64 E4
Langside Dr BL3 . . . . .40 E4
Langstone Cl BL6 . . . . .22 B3
Langston Gn SK7 . . . . .124 A1
Langston St M3 . . . . .158 C3
Langthorne St M19 . . . . . . .111 B8
Langthorne Wlk BL3 . . . . . .145 A1
Langton Ave WN6 . . . . .19 E1
Langton Cl
Newton-le-W WA12 . . . . .89 A4
Oldham M35 . . . . .84 C8
Langton Pl WN6 . . . . .19 E1
Langton St
Heywood OL10 . . . . .29 D3
Middleton M24 . . . . .65 A8
Salford M6 . . . . .154 B2
Langton Terr OL11 . . . . .30 E4
Langtree Cl M28 . . . . .78 B8
Langtree La WN6 . . . . .19 D3
Langworthy Ave M38 . . . . . .60 B4
Langworthy Rd
Manchester M40 . . . . .83 A7
Salford M6 . . . . .154 C3
Langworthy Road Prim
Sch M6 . . . . .154 C3
Langworthy Sta M5 . . . . . . .154 B1
Lanhill Dr M8 . . . . .156 C2
Lankro Way M30, M17 . . . . .79 F1
Lanreath Wlk M8 . . . . .156 B2
Lansbury Ho 2 M16 . . . . . . .97 D3
Lansbury St WN5 . . . . .54 A6
Lansdale Gdns M19 . . . . . .110 E5
Lansdale St
Eccles M30 . . . . .95 A8
Walkden M28 . . . . .60 D5
Lansdown Cl SK8 . . . . .132 C7
Lansdowne M43 . . . . .91 E2
Lansdowne Ave
Droylsden M34 . . . . .84 C1
Romiley SK6 . . . . .113 D2
Lansdowne Cl
5 Bolton BL2 . . . . .25 B1
Ramsbottom BL0 . . . . .138 B1
Lansdowne Ct OL9 . . . . . . .152 B2
Lansdowne Dr M28 . . . . .60 C1
Lansdowne Ho M20 . . . . . . .110 B2
Lansdowne Rd
Altrincham WA14 . . . . .119 D6
5 Bolton BL2 . . . . .25 B2
Chadderton OL9 . . . . .152 C2
Eccles M30 . . . . .79 D3
Flixton M41 . . . . .106 E8
Manchester M8 . . . . .64 A1
Over Hulton M46 . . . . .58 F5
Sale M33 . . . . .108 A6
Lansdowne Rd N M41 . . . . . .94 E1
Lansdowne St OL11 . . . . . . .30 C7
Lanstead Dr M40 . . . . .160 B2
Lantern View SK22 . . . . . . .127 B1
Lapwing Cl
Newton-le-W WA12 . . . . .89 C3
Rochdale OL11 . . . . .29 E7
Stalybridge SK15 . . . . .86 A4
Lapwing Ct 4 M20 . . . . . . .110 A5
Lapwing La
Brinnington SK5 . . . . .112 C6
Manchester M20 . . . . .110 A5
Larch Ave
Cheadle SK8 . . . . .123 A1
Newton-le-W WA12 . . . . .89 C2
Radcliffe M26 . . . . .44 B1
Stretford M32 . . . . .96 D1
Swinton M27 . . . . .79 C6
Wigan WN5 . . . . .54 D6
Larch Cl
Billinge WN5 . . . . .71 D5
Failsworth M35 . . . . .83 F6
Golborne WA3 . . . . .90 F6
Marple SK6 . . . . .125 E5
Poynton SK12 . . . . .133 F3
Rawtenstall BB4 . . . . .1 F8
Sale M33 . . . . .120 C8
Larches The OL5 . . . . .68 E1
Larch Gr
Atherton M46 . . . . .58 C4
Chadderton OL9 . . . . .152 B4
Oldham OL4 . . . . .67 E8
Swinton M27 . . . . .61 B2
Larchlea WA15 . . . . .119 F4
Larchway
Bramhall SK7 . . . . .132 C7

Larchway continued
High Lane SK6 . . . . .134 F7
Milnrow OL16 . . . . .31 D7
Larch Way SK13 . . . . .116 F8
Larchwood
Chadderton OL9 . . . . .65 E8
Cheadle SK8 . . . . .122 D6
Larchwood Ave M9 . . . . . . .157 C3
Larchwood Cl M33 . . . . .107 C4
Larchwood Dr
Wigan WN1 . . . . .37 B4
Wilmslow SK9 . . . . .137 E8
Larchwood St BL1 . . . . .143 C2
Larden Wlk 1 M8 . . . . .155 C2
Larel Trad Est OL2 . . . . .49 A2
Lark Hill East SK23 . . . . . . .183 C2
Larke Rise M20 . . . . .109 F3
Larkfield Ave
Walkden M38 . . . . .59 F5
Wigan WN1 . . . . .37 B4
Larkfield Cl
Bolton BL2 . . . . .148 B4
Walkden M38 . . . . .59 F5
Larkfield Mews M38 . . . . . . .59 F5
Larkhall Rise M22 . . . . .121 E5
LARK HILL 77 A5
Lark Hill
Farnworth BL4 . . . . .60 E7
Stalybridge SK15 . . . . .86 A4
Lark Hill WN6 . . . . .36 F8
Larkhill Cl WA15 . . . . .120 B6
Lark Hill Com Prim Sch
M6 .154 C2
Lark Hill Ct M24 . . . . .65 A8
Lark Hill La OL3 . . . . .51 A4
Lark Hill Pl OL12 . . . . .14 E1
Lark Hill Prim Sch
SK5 . . . . .123 C8
Larkhill Rd SK8 . . . . .123 C5
Lark Hill Rd
Stockport SK3 . . . . .123 C8
Uppermill OL3 . . . . .51 A3
Larkhill Wlk 2 M8 . . . . .156 B2
Larkside Ave M28 . . . . .60 E3
Larkspur Cl
Bolton BL1 . . . . .25 B3
Leigh WN7 . . . . .75 F3
Larks Rise M43 . . . . .84 D3
Lark St
Bolton BL1 . . . . .145 C4
Farnworth BL4 . . . . .60 D7
Oldham OL1 . . . . .49 D3
Larkswood Dr SK2 . . . . . . .124 F5
Larkwood Cl SK15 . . . . .86 E7
Larmuth Ave M21 . . . . .109 C6
Larne Ave
Stockport SK3 . . . . .123 B7
Stretford M32 . . . . .96 C2
Larne St M11 . . . . .165 A4
Larwood Ave SK4 . . . . .168 B1
Lascar Ave M5 . . . . .161 A4
Lashbrook Cl M40 . . . . .160 A4
Lassell Fold SK14 . . . . .102 B6
Lassell St M11 . . . . .99 F7
Last Drop Village The *
BL7 . . . . .9 A1
Lastingham St M40 . . . . .83 C6
Latchford St OL7 . . . . .166 A4
Latchmere Rd M14 . . . . . . .110 C8
Latham Ave WA12 . . . . .89 C4
Latham Cl SK6 . . . . .112 F5
Latham Ho WA12 . . . . .89 B4
Latham La WN5 . . . . .54 A8
Latham Rd BL6 . . . . .21 C3
Latham Row BL6 . . . . .22 F3
Latham St
Bolton BL1 . . . . .143 C2
Droylsden M11 . . . . .99 F7
Lathbury Rd M40, M9 . . . . .157 A2
Lathom Gr M33 . . . . .108 C3
Lathom Hall Ave OL4 . . . . . .68 A7
Lathom Rd
Irlam M44 . . . . .105 F8
Manchester M20 . . . . .110 D7
Lathom St 8 BL9 . . . . .141 A4
Latimer Cl 2 WN5 . . . . .53 F7
Latimer St OL4 . . . . .67 A6
Latrigg Cres M24 . . . . .46 C2
Latrobe St M43 . . . . .100 A8
Lauderdale Cres M13 . . . . .163 C2
Launceston Cl
Bramhall SK7 . . . . .132 F7
Oldham OL8 . . . . .67 C4
Launceston Rd
Hindley WN7 . . . . .57 C3
Radcliffe M26 . . . . .43 D5
Laundry St M6 . . . . .154 D1
Laura St BL9 . . . . .11 C2
Laureate's Pl OL4 . . . . .68 B7
Laureate Way M34 . . . . . . .113 A7
Laurel Ave
Bolton, Darcy Lever
BL3 . . . . .42 E5
Chadderton OL9 . . . . .65 E8
Cheadle SK8 . . . . .122 D5
Manchester M14 . . . . .98 A2
Newton-le-W WA12 . . . . .89 D3
Laurel Bank
Hyde SK14 . . . . .113 C8
Stalybridge SK15 . . . . .102 B8
Laurel Bank Gdns M9 . . . . .64 D3
Laurel Cres WN2 . . . . .57 A3
Laurel Ct
18 Rochdale OL16 . . . . .31 B6

Laurel Dr
Altrincham WA15 . . . . .120 B4
Walkden M38 . . . . .60 A4
Laurel End La SK4 . . . . .168 A3
Laurel Gn M34 . . . . .101 A2
Laurel Gr
Altrincham M WN4 . . . . .73 B4
Golborne WA3 . . . . .90 C8
Leigh WN7 . . . . .75 E8
Salford M5 . . . . .80 C2
Laurel Ho SK4 . . . . .168 B4
Laurels Dr OL15 . . . . .15 F2
Laurel St
Bolton BL1 . . . . .144 C3
Bury BL0 . . . . .141 B2
Bury, Tottington BL8 . . . . . . .26 F6
Middleton M24 . . . . .65 D8
6 Oldham OL4 . . . . .67 B6
Stockport SK4 . . . . .169 B2
Wigan WN5 . . . . .54 F7
Laurels The
2 Bolton BL1 . . . . .145 C4
High Lane SK6 . . . . .134 E8
Mossley OL5 . . . . .68 D1
Laurel Way SK8 . . . . .132 C8
Laurel Wlk M31 . . . . .105 E2
Laurence Cl M12 . . . . .165 B2
Laurence Lowry Ct 2
M27 .61 F1
Lauren Cl 13 OL4 . . . . .67 F6
Lauria Terr BL2 . . . . .26 D1
Lauria Pl 2 OL12 . . . . .14 F1
Laurieston Ct SK8 . . . . .122 C5
Lausanne Rd
Manchester M20 . . . . .110 B7
Stockport SK7 . . . . .123 E3
Lavender Cl
Altrincham M23 . . . . .108 C1
Sale M33 . . . . .107 C5
Lavender Hill BB4 . . . . .1 F8
Lavender Rd
Farnworth BL4 . . . . .42 A1
Oldham OL4 . . . . .67 E4
Wigan WN6 . . . . .36 F3
Lavenders Brow SK1 . . . . . .169 C1
Lavender St M26 . . . . .43 E1
Lavender Wlk
Partington M31 . . . . .105 E2
Lavenham Ave M11 . . . . .83 D1
Lavenham Bsns Ctr
OL9 . . . . .152 C2
Lavenham Cl
Hazel Grove SK7 . . . . .133 E8
Whitefield BL9 . . . . .44 F3
Laverton Cl BL9 . . . . .28 E1
Lavington Ave SK8 . . . . .123 A6
Lavington Gr M18 . . . . .99 D4
Lavinia St M30 . . . . .79 B2
Lavister Ave M19 . . . . .110 E4
Lawefield Cres M27 . . . . .61 D4
Lawers Ave OL9 . . . . .152 A4
Lawflat OL12 . . . . .15 C5
Lawler Ave M5 . . . . .161 B2
Lawnbank Cl M24 . . . . .46 E1
Lawn Cl OL8 . . . . .67 C3
Lawn Closes OL8 . . . . .67 C3
Lawndale Cl M26 . . . . .44 B2
Lawndale Dr M28 . . . . .78 B8
Lawn Dr
Altrincham WA15 . . . . .119 E6
Swinton M27 . . . . .79 E7
Lawnfield Cl SK7 . . . . .123 D2
Lawnfold SK13 . . . . .171 B4
Lawngreen Ave M21 . . . . . .109 A7
Lawnhurst Trad Est
SK3 . . . . .123 B5
Lawns Ave WN5 . . . . .53 C5
Lawnside Mews M20 . . . . . .110 A5
Lawn St BL1 . . . . .143 A1
Lawns The
Altrincham WA14 . . . . .119 C3
Hindley WN2 . . . . .56 D6
Wilmslow SK9 . . . . .136 E4
Lawnswood OL11 . . . . .30 C3
Lawnswood Dr
Pendlebury M27 . . . . .80 B6
Tyldesley M29 . . . . .59 D1
Lawnswood Park Rd
M27 .80 B6
Lawrence Cl OL12 . . . . .14 A1
Lawrence Ct 6 WN2 . . . . . . .56 B1
Lawrence Pl SK12 . . . . .133 D2
Lawrence Rd
Altrincham WA14 . . . . .119 C4
Hazel Grove SK7 . . . . .124 E3
Urmston M41 . . . . .94 D3
Lawrence St
Bury BL9 . . . . .44 F4
Lawrie Ave BL0 . . . . .138 B1
Lawson Ave
Gatley SK8 . . . . .122 B5
Horwich BL6 . . . . .22 C4
Leigh WN7 . . . . .57 E1
Lawson Cl
Middleton M24 . . . . .47 A4
Swinton M28 . . . . .79 C7
Lawson Dr WA15 . . . . .120 A6
Lawson Gr M33 . . . . .108 A6
Lawson Rd BL1 . . . . .142 C2
Lawson St
2 Bolton BL1 . . . . .143 B4
Manchester M40 . . . . .65 D2
Lawson Wlk M34 . . . . .112 F8
Law St
Rochdale OL11 . . . . .30 C4

Law St continued
Walsden OL14 . . . . .6 B7
Lawton Ave SK7 . . . . .132 E8
Lawton Cl
Culcheth WA3 . . . . .91 E3
Romiley SK6 . . . . .112 F1
Lawton Fold OL4 . . . . .68 B7
Lawton Moor Rd M23 . . . . .109 A1
Lawton Rd SK4 . . . . .168 C4
Lawton Sq OL3 . . . . .50 F4
Lawton St
Delph OL3 . . . . .50 F4
Droylsden M43 . . . . .84 B2
Hyde SK14 . . . . .167 B3
Mossley OL5 . . . . .90 D7
Rochdale OL12 . . . . .15 A1
2 Stalybridge SK15 . . . . . . .86 B1
Laxey Ave M46 . . . . .58 E2
Laxey Cres WN7 . . . . .75 C7
Laxey St M40 . . . . .83 B7
Laxfield Dr M41 . . . . .94 D3
Laxford St BL3 . . . . .40 E6
Laxley Cl OL9 . . . . .152 B1
Layard St OL6 . . . . .166 A3
Laycock Ave
Bolton BL2 . . . . .25 B3
Stalybridge SK15 . . . . .86 E4
Laycock Cres 4 M35 . . . . . .83 F7
Laycock Dr SK16 . . . . .102 A7
Laycock Gr M35 . . . . .83 F7
Laycock Way M34 . . . . .112 F8
Layfield Cl BL8 . . . . .26 D7
Layland Ave WA3 . . . . .91 E4
Laystall St M1 . . . . .159 B1
Layton Ave SK14 . . . . .101 C2
Layton Cl
Stockport SK1 . . . . .124 A8
2 Wigan WN5 . . . . .54 D5
Layton Dr
Kearsley BL4 . . . . .60 F6
Romiley SK6 . . . . .113 C3
Layton St M40 . . . . .160 A2
Lazenby Cres WN2 . . . . .38 F3
Lazonby Ave WN2 . . . . .38 F3
Lazonby Wlk 7 M13 . . . . . . .98 F4
Leabank St 8 M19 . . . . .99 A2
Leabrook Dr M40 . . . . .159 B8
Leaburn Dr M19 . . . . .110 E4
Leach Cl OL16 . . . . .15 C2
Leaches Rd BL0 . . . . .11 D8
Leach Mews M25 . . . . .62 F4
Leach St
Failsworth M35 . . . . .83 E7
Stockport SK4 . . . . .168 B4
Leadale Cl WN6 . . . . .19 D1
Leadale Rise OL4 . . . . .68 A6
Leader St
Wigan, Norley WN5 . . . . .54 C6
Wigan, Scholes WN1 . . . . . .151 B4
Leader Williams Rd
M44 .93 F1
Lea Dr M9 . . . . .64 F3
Leafield M29 . . . . .59 C1
Leafield Ave M20 . . . . .110 D4
Leafield Cl M26 . . . . .43 E3
Leafield Dr
Cheadle SK8 . . . . .131 F6
Worsley M28 . . . . .78 A6
Leafield Rd SK12 . . . . .135 C6
Leaford Ave M34 . . . . .100 D4
Leaford Cl M34 . . . . .100 D4
Leaf St
Bolton BL3 . . . . .148 C5
Manchester M15 . . . . .162 C2
Reddish SK5 . . . . .111 E7
Leagate M41 . . . . .95 E1
Lea Gate BL2 . . . . .25 D5
Lea Gate Cl
Bolton BL2 . . . . .25 D5
Wigan WN3 . . . . .54 E3
Leaholme Cl M40 . . . . .83 D5
Leak St 3 OL15 . . . . .16 B5
Leak St M16 . . . . .161 C2
Leal Holme Ave WN2 . . . . . .38 A3
Leamington Ave
Bury BL9 . . . . .27 E8
Manchester M20 . . . . .109 F4
Newton-le-W WA12 . . . . .89 C1
Leamington Ct 3
SK5 . . . . .111 F7
Leamington Ho M13 . . . . . .163 B1
Leamington Rd
Eccles M30 . . . . .79 B3
Reddish SK5 . . . . .111 E7
Urmston M41 . . . . .95 C3
Leamington St
Manchester M11 . . . . .99 D7
Oldham OL4 . . . . .67 D8
Rochdale OL12 . . . . .139 B4
Leamore Wlk 9 M9 . . . . .64 E3
Lea Mount Dr BL9 . . . . .28 D4
Leam St OL6 . . . . .85 D4

Leander Cl M9 ....64 E2
Leander Dr OL11 ....30 D1
Lean Town SK13 ....116 D6

Lea Rd
Gatley SK8 ....122 B1
Stockport SK4 ....168 C4
Leaside Ave OL1 ....48 B2
Leaside Cl OL12 ....14 D2
Leaside Dr M20 ....110 D5
Leaside Gr M28 ....60 E3
Leaside Way SK9 ......137 C6
Leas The WA15 ....120 C3
Leaton Ave M23 ....121 A6
Leavale Cl M38 ....59 F4
Leavengreave Ct OL12 ...4 D4

Lea View
Royton OL12 ....48 C3
Wigan WN1 ....37 F1

Leaway
Ince-in-M WN2 ....151 C3
Wardle OL15 ....15 C6
Le Bas Ho M20 ....109 F6
Lecester Rd M8 ....156 B2
Leckenby Cl M27 ......78 A6
Leconfield Dr M9 ......64 E4
Leconfield Rd M30 ....78 F4
Lecturers Ct BL3 ......145 C1
Ledbrooke Cl M5 ......161 B4
Ledburn Cl M15 ....162 A2
Ledburn Ct M15 ....162 A2
Ledbury Ave M41 .....95 C3
Ledbury Cl M24 ....65 A6
Ledbury Rd M35 ......83 E4
Ledbury St WN7 ......75 F6
Ledbury Wlk M9 ......64 C3
Ledge Ley SK8 ....131 E8
Ledmore Gr WN4 .....72 D3
Ledsham Ave M9 .....64 A5
Ledson Rd M23 ....120 F5
Ledward La WA14 ....119 B2

Lee Ave
Altrincham WA14 ....119 C7
Bolton BL3 ....147 A3
Leebangs Rd SK14 ...115 A8
Lee Bank BL5 ....58 B8
Leech Ave OL6 ....85 E5
Leech Brook Ave M34 ..100 E5
Leech Brook Cl M34 ...100 E6

Leech St
Hyde SK14 ....167 C2
Stalybridge SK15 .....86 A1
Lee Cl M44 ....93 F2
Lee Cres M32 ....96 E2
Lee Ct M22 ....121 E8
Lee Dale Cl M34 .....101 A2
Leedale St M12 ......99 A2
Leeds St BL9 ....45 B3
Leeds St WN3 ....150 B3

Leeds Street Ind Est
WN3 ....150 B3
Leefields Cl OL3 .....69 B8
Lee Fold M29 ....77 C7
Leegate Dr M9 ......64 F4
Leegate Gdns SK4 ...168 A4
Leegate Rd SK4 .....168 A4
Lee Gr BL4 ....59 F8
Leegrange Rd M9 ...64 E1
Lee Head SK13 ......115 C5
Lee Ho M22 ....121 E8
Leek St M26 ....43 E3

Lee La
Abram WN2 ....74 B8
Horwich BL6 ....22 B4
Leemans Hill St BL8 ..27 A5
Lee Mount SK13 .....116 C7
Lee Rd OL13 ....3 E8
LEES 67 E6
Lees Ave M34 ....100 E3
Lees Brook Pk OL4 ..67 D6
Lees Cotts BL7 ......9 C2
Leesfield OL6 ....166 B4
Lees Gr OL4 ....67 D5
Leeshall Cres M14 ..110 D8
Lees Hall Ct M14 ....110 D8
Leeside SK4 ....168 A1
Lee Side OL3 ....51 D4
Lees La WN8 ....35 B6
Lees New Rd OL4, OL6 ..67 D2
Lees Park Ave M43 ..84 C2
Lees Park Way M43 ..84 C2

Lees Rd
Adlington PR6 ....21 B8
Ashton-u-L OL6 .....85 D7
Bramhall SK7 ....132 D5
Oldham OL4 ....67 C6
Lees Row SK13 .....104 C5
Lees St E OL2 ......149 C3
Lees Sq OL6 ....166 C3

Lees St
Ashton-u-L OL6 .....166 B4
Droylsden M43 ......84 B2
Manchester M11, M18 ..99 E6
Middleton M24 ......65 D7
❷ Mossley OL5 ......68 C2
Oldham OL8 ....85 A8
Oldham OL2 ....149 B3
❸ Stalybridge SK15 ..86 A2
Swinton M27 ....61 F1
Lee's St OL13 ....4 C8

Lee St
Atherton M46 ......58 D2
Bury BL9 ....27 F8
Littleborough OL15 ..16 B6
Middleton M24 .....46 F3
Oldham OL8 ....153 B1
Stockport SK1 .....169 C1

Lee St *continued*
Uppermill OL3 ....69 B8
Leestone Rd M22 ...121 E6
Leesway OL4 ....67 E5
Leesway Dr M34 ....101 A2
Leeswood Ave M21 ..109 C6
Lee Vale Dr SK13 ...115 D7
Leewood M27 ......61 A6
Leewood St SK4 ....168 B3
Left Bank M3 ......158 B1
Le Gendre St BL2 ...25 B2
Legh Cl SK12 ....133 E4
Legh St M33 ....108 E3

Legh Dr
Droylsden M34 .....84 B1
Romiley SK6 ....113 B6
Leghorn Wlk [14] M11 ..160 C1

Legh Rd
High Lane SK12 ....135 A6
Sale M33 ....108 E3
Salford M7 ....155 A4

Legh St
Ashton-in-M WN4 ..73 B2
Eccles M30 ....79 C1
Golborne WA3 .....90 A8
Newton-le-W WA12 ..89 A3
Salford M7 ....155 A3
Legion Gr M7 ......155 B2
Legwood Ct M41 ...95 C2

Leicester Ave
Denton M34 ....100 F1
Droylsden M43 ....83 F3
Hindley WN2 ......56 F6
Horwich BL6 ......22 A3
Sale WA15 ....120 A8
Salford M7 ....155 C4
Leicester Ct M7 ...63 F1
Leicester Dr SK13 ..116 F8

Leicester Rd
Altrincham WA14 ..119 F2
Failsworth M35 ....84 A6
Sale M33 ....108 B5
Tyldesley M29 ....59 A2
Whitefield M45 ....44 D1

Leicester St
Ashton-u-L OL7 ...166 B4
Oldham OL4 ......67 E6
Reddish SK5 ......99 F2
Rochdale OL11 ....31 A5
Leicester Wlk M7 ..155 B2
LEIGH 75 E6
Leigh Arc [4] WN1 ..150 C4

Leigh Ave
Marple SK6 ....125 E6
Swinton M27 .....79 D5
Leighbrook Rd M14 ..110 B8
Leigh Bsns Pk WN7 ..75 F5
Leigh CE Inf Sch WN7 ..75 E5
Leigh CE Jun Sch WN7 ..75 F5

Leigh Central Prim Sch
WN7 ....75 F5
Leigh Cl BL8 ......26 F7
Leigh Comm BL5 ..39 E1

Leigh Commerce Pk
WN7 ....76 B2
Leigh Fold SK14 ..101 E5

Leigh High Appartments
SK14 ....167 B2
Leigh Infmy WN7 ..76 A6
Leigh La BL8 ......27 B3
Leigh Prim Sch SK14 ..167 C2

Leigh Rd
Altrincham WA15 ..119 E2
Atherton M46 .....58 B2
Hindley WN2 .....57 B2
Leigh WN7 ....75 F6
Westhoughton BL5 ..57 F6
Westhoughton BL5 ..57 F6
Wilmslow SK9 ....136 D5
Worsley M28 .....77 C5

Leigh St Peter's CE Jun
Sch WN7 ....75 C5
Leighs Cotts WA15 ..120 C4

Leigh St
Aspull WN2 ......38 F3
Bury BL8 ....26 F4
Farnworth BL4 ...60 D8
❶ Heywood OL10 ..29 C2
Hyde SK14 ......167 B2
Leigh WN2 ......57 B1
Milnrow OL16 ....31 F7
Westhoughton BL5 ..39 E1
Wigan WN1 .....151 A3

Leighton Ave
Atherton M46 ....58 B3
Bolton BL1 ......144 B4
Littleborough OL15 ..15 F2

Leighton Dr
Golborne WN7 ...75 B1
Marple SK6 .....126 C8
Leighton Rd M16 ..97 C4

Leighton St
Atherton M46 ....58 B3
Manchester M40 ..83 A8

Lena St
Bolton BL1 ....143 C2
Manchester M1 ...159 B1
Lench Rd M9 .....64 D4
Lench St [5] BB4 ...2 D8
Len Cox Wlk [3] M4 ..159 B2
Lenfield La OL1 ...48 E1
Lenham Ave M40 ..83 D5
Lenham Cl SK5 ...112 B6
Lenham Gdns BL2 ..42 E6
Lenham Twrs SK5 ..112 B6
Lenham Wlk M22 ..130 D8
Lennox Gdns BL3 ..40 F5
Lennox St OL6 ...166 C3
Lennox Wlk BL1 ...24 E5
Lenora St BL3 ....146 B4
Lenten Gr OL10 ...46 F8
Lenthall Wlk [20] M8 ..155 C3
Lentmead Dr M40 ..65 A1
Lenton Gdns M22 ..121 E5
Lentworth Dr M28 ..60 C5
Leominster Dr M22 ..121 F2
Leominster Rd M26 ..65 B6
Leonard Ct WN7 ..75 B4
Leonardin Cl OL12 ..14 B3

Leonard St
Bolton BL3 ......147 B3
Rochdale OL11 ...30 C1
Leonard Way OL12 ..48 F3
Leopold Ave M20 ..110 A5

Leopold St
Rochdale OL11 ...139 A3
Wigan WN5 .....54 C5
Lepp Cres BL8 ....27 C5
Leroy Dr M9 .....75 A4
Lerryn Dr SK7 ...123 D1
Lesley Rd M32 ...96 A1

Leslie Ave
Oldham OL9 .....66 B3
Whitefield BL9 ...44 F3
Leslie Gr WA15 ..120 A6
Leslie Hough Way M6 ..81 B4

Leslie St
Bolton BL2 ......25 B1
Manchester M14 ..98 B3
Lessingham Ave WN1 ..37 B3
Lester Rd M38 ...59 E5
Lester St M32 ...96 D2

Letchworth Ave [2]
OL11 ....31 A5
Letchworth St M14 ..98 B3
Letcombe Cl WN7 ..75 F7
Letham St OL8 ...66 F2
Letitia St BL6 ....22 A3
Levedale Rd M9 ..64 E4
Leven Cl BL4 .....61 C5
Levengreave Cl WN2 ..57 C3
Levenhurst Rd M8 ..155 C3
Levens Cl SK8 ...122 B4
Levens Dr BL2 ...25 E1
LEVENSHULME ..99 B1

Levenshulme High Sch
M19 ....111 A7
Levenshulme Rd M18 ..99 A1
Levenshulme Sta M19 ..99 A1

Levenshulme Terr [8]
M19 ....99 A1

Levenshulme Trad Est
M19 ....99 C2

Levens Pl
Ince-in-M WN2 ...56 A8
Wigan WN5 .....54 C7
Levens Rd SK7 ...124 C2

Levens St
Manchester M40 ..83 A7
Salford M6 ......81 B5

Levens Wlk
Chadderton OL9 ..152 A1
Wigan WN5 .....54 C7

Leven Wlk
Whitefield M45 ...44 E2
❷ Wythenshawe M23 ..121 A5
Lever Ave M27 ...62 B2
Lever Bridge Pl BL3 ..42 D5
Lever Cl M27 ....81 B8
Lever Dr BL3 ....147 C4
Lever Ct M7 .....81 B8
Lever Edge La BL3 ..147 B2
Leverett Cl WA14 ..119 A5
Lever Gr BL2 .....148 A1
Lever Hall Rd BL2 ..42 D7
Leverhulme Ave BL3 ..42 A3

Leverhulme Com Prim Sch
BL2 ....42 E7
Lever Park Ave BL6 ..22 B5
Lever Park Sch BL6 ..22 C3

Lever St
Bolton BL3 ......147 C4
Hazel Grove SK7 ..124 D3
Heywood OL10 ...29 D3
Little Lever BL3 ..43 A4
Manchester M1 ...159 B1
Middleton M24 ...47 A1
Radcliffe M26 ....43 F5
Ramsbottom BL0 ..138 C1
Tyldesley M29 ...58 F1
Westhoughton BL5 ..39 E3
Lever Wlk M24 ..64 F7
Levi St BL1 .....23 F1
Lewes Ave M34 ..100 F1

Lewis Ave
Manchester M9 ..64 E1

Lewis Ave *continued*
Urmston M41 ......95 D5

Lewis Cl
Adlington PR7 ....20 C1
Wigan WN3 ......150 A1
Lewis Ct OL10 ...28 F1
Lewisham Ave M40 ..83 B4
Lewisham Cl OL2 ..48 C6

Lewis Rd
Droylsden M43 ...83 E2
Reddish SK5 .....99 F1

Lewis St
Eccles M30 ......79 D1
Heywood OL10 ..29 E3
Manchester M40 ..160 A3
Shaw OL2 ......149 B1

Lewis Street Prim Sch
M30 ....79 D1
Lewtas St M30 ...79 E1
Lexton Ave M8 ..64 B2
Leybourne Ave M19 ..99 B2
Leybourne St BL1 ..143 B2
Leybrook Rd M22 ..121 C3

Leyburn Ave
Royton OL2 .....48 D4
Stretford M32 ...96 C3
Urmston M41 ...95 A1

Leyburn Cl
Whitefield M45 ..62 E8
Wigan WN1 .....151 C4

Leyburn Gr
❷ Farnworth BL4 ...42 D1
Romiley SK6 ....113 C2
Leyburn Ho [2] M13 ..98 E4
Leyburn Rd M40 ..65 C2
Leycett Dr M23 ..109 A1
Ley Cres M29 ...77 B6
Leycroft St M1 ...163 B4
Leyden Wlk M23 ..121 A4
Ley Dr OL10 .....46 E8
Leyfield Ave SK6 ..113 C2
Leyfield Rd OL16 ..31 E6
Leygate View SK22 ..127 B1
Ley Hey Ave SK6 ..125 F7
Ley Hey Ct SK6 ..125 F7
LEY HEY PARK ..125 F7
Ley Hey Rd SK6 ..125 F7
Ley La SK6 ......126 D8

Leyland Ave
Gatley SK8 ......122 B6
Hindley WN2 ....56 E3
Irlam M44 ......94 B4
Manchester M20 ..110 D3

Leyland Green Rd
WN4 ....72 C5

Leyland Mill Farm
WN1 ....37 D4
Leyland Mill La WN1 ..37 C3
Leylands La SK14 ..114 F7

Leyland St
Abram WN2 .....56 B1
Bury BL9 ....44 F4
Hindley WN2 ....56 C4
Stockport SK1 ...169 B1
Ley Rd M29 .....77 A7
Leyton Ave M8 ..83 B7
Leyton Cl BL4 ..147 C1
Leyton Dr BL9 ..44 F5
Leyton St [2] OL12 ..15 A2
Leywell Dr OL1 ..49 D3
Leywell Rd M9 ..157 C4
Library La OL9 ..153 A4

Library St
Westhoughton BL5 ..57 F8
Wigan WN1 ....150 C4
Libra St BL1 ....143 A2
Lichens Cres OL8 ..67 A3

Lichfield Ave
Altrincham WA15 ..120 C3
Ashton-u-L OL6 ...85 D8
Bolton BL2 .....25 B2
Golborne WA3 ...90 A8
Reddish SK5 ....111 E8
Tyldesley M29 ...77 C7

Lichfield Cl
Farnworth BL4 ...60 A8
Radcliffe M26 ...43 D5

Lichfield Dr
Bury BL8 ....140 A4
Chadderton OL9 ..48 A1
Manchester, Cheetham Hill
M8 ....156 B3
Manchester, Sedgley Park
M25 ....63 C2
Swinton M27 ...79 F6
Lichfield Gr WN4 ..73 C2

Lichfield Rd
Eccles M30 .....79 F4
Radcliffe M26 ...43 D5
Urmston M41 ...95 D3

Lichfield St
Salford M6 .....81 B5
Wigan WN5 ....54 C5
Lichfield Terr OL16 ..31 C4
Lichfield Wlk SK6 ..113 A1
Lidbrook Wlk M12 ..164 B1
Liddington Hall Dr BL0 ..11 B4
Lidgate Cl M43 ...54 D3

Lidgate Gr
❼ Farnworth BL4 ...60 C8
❹ Manchester M20 ..110 A3
Lidgett Cl M38 ...60 C5
Lidiard St M8 ....64 A3
Lido Ho OL4 .....68 A6
Lieutenant Wlk M5 ..161 B4
Liffey Ave M22 ..121 E3

Lea–Lim **231**

Lifton Ave M40 ...160 B4
Light Alders La SK12 ..135 A6
Lightborne Rd M33 ..107 E4
Lightbounds Rd BL1 ..23 F3

Lightbourne Ave [5]
M27 ....79 F7
LIGHT BOURNE GREEN
..............79 F6
Lightbowne Rd M40 ..65 C2
Lightburn Ave OL15 ..15 E4

Lightburne Ave
Bolton BL1 ......144 B3
Leigh WN7 .....75 E3
Lightfoot Wlk [6] M11 ..160 C1
Lighthorne Ave SK3 ..122 F7
Lighthorne Gr SK3 ..122 F7
Lighthorne Rd SK3 ..122 F7
Lighthouse OL15 ..6 C1

Light Oaks Inf & Jun Schs
M6 ....80 B4

Light Oaks Rd
Fowley Common WA3 ..92 C6
Salford M6 ......80 C4
Lightowlers La OL15 ..16 D7
Lightshaw La WA3 ..74 B4
Lightwood M26 ...78 B8
Lightwood [7] BL4 ..42 E1
Lignum Ave OL9 ..152 B2

Lilac Ave
Bury BL9 ....44 D7
Downall Green WN4 ..72 D5
Hyde SK14 .....113 D8
Leigh WN7 .....75 E7
Newhey OL16 ...32 A3
Pendlebury M27 ..80 A8
Wigan WN6 ....37 A3
Lilac Cl [3] M6 ...81 A2
Lilac Gdns WN3 ..55 F4

Lilac Gr
Billinge WN5 ....71 D4
Chadderton OL9 ..152 B4
Manchester M40 ..65 A1
Prestwich M25 ..63 A6
Lilac La OL8 ....66 D2

Lilac Rd
Altrincham WA15 ..120 A3
Golborne WA3 ...74 A1
Rochdale OL12 ..30 F2
Lilac St SK2 ....170 C2
Lilac Terr [2] OL13 ..3 D8
Lilac View Cl OL2 ..49 D6
Lilac Wlk M31 ..105 E3
Lila St M9 ......157 C3
Lilburn Cl BL0 ...11 C4
Liley St OL16 ...31 A7
Lilford Cl M12 ...165 A2

Lilford St
Atherton M46 ...58 B2
Leigh WN7 .....75 E4
Lilian Dr WN2 ...56 A1
Lilian Gr SK5 ...111 F8
Lillian St M16 ...97 D4

Lilly St
Bolton BL1 .....145 A4
Hyde SK14 .....113 F8
Lilmore Ave M40 ..83 C6
Lilstock Wlk [10] M9 ..64 E3

Lily Ave
Farnworth BL4 ...42 E2
Newton-le-W WA12 ..89 D2
Lily Cl SK3 .....170 A1
LILY HILL 44 E2
Lily Hill St M45 ..44 E2

Lily La
Ashton-in-M WN4 ..73 F5
Eccles M30 .....79 B1
Middleton M24 ...65 C8
Milnrow OL16 ...31 F6
Oldham OL1 ....48 E1
Royton OL2 ....48 E8

Lily Lane Jun & Inf Schs
M40 ....83 A8
LILY LANES 85 E8
Lily Lanes OL6 ..85 E8
Lily Pl WN4 ....73 C2

Lily St
Ashton-in-M WN4 ..73 E5
Eccles M30 .....79 B1
Middleton M24 ...65 C8
Milnrow OL16 ...31 F6
Oldham OL1 ....48 E1
Royton OL2 ....48 E8
Lily Thomas Ct [3] M11 ..99 D7
Lima St BL9 ....141 B3
Limbert Circ M8 ..64 C1

Lime Ave
Leigh WN7 .....75 E8
New Mills SK22 ..127 D1
Swinton M27 ...79 C6
Urmston M41 ...95 B2
Lime Bank St M12 ..164 A4
Limebrook Cl M11 ..99 E7

Lime Cl
Abram Brow WN2 ..74 C7
Dukinfield SK16 ..101 D6
Hollinfare WA3 ..105 A2
Salford M6 .....80 C4
Limecroft Rd M35 ..84 A8
LIMEFIELD 27 F7

Limefield
Middleton M24 ..64 E8
Milnrow OL16 ...31 E7
Mossley OL5 ....68 B2
❶ Wigan WN1 ...151 A4
LIME FIELD 64 E8
Limefield Ave BL4 ..42 D1

Limefield Brow BL9....27 F7
Limefield Cl BL1....142 B4
Limefield Ct M7....63 D1
Limefield Rd
Bolton BL1....142 B4
Bury BL9....27 F7
Manchester M7....63 D1
Radcliffe M26....43 E3
Limefield Terr M19....99 A1
LIME GATE....66 C1
Lime Gate OL8....66 C2
Lime Gdns
Dukinfield SK16....101 B8
Middleton M24....64 E8
Lime Gn OL8....66 D1
Lime Gr
Altrincham WA15....120 B7
Ashton-u-L OL6....85 C5
Bury BL9....27 F7
Cheadle SK8....122 D6
Denton M34....100 F4
Dukinfield SK15....101 E8
Golborne WA3....90 E6
Heywood OL10....29 C3
Hindley WN2....56 F3
Littleborough OL15....15 F6
Manchester M16....97 B4
Prestwich M25....63 A4
Ramsbottom BL0....11 D7
Royton OL2....48 D6
Walkden M28....60 D1
Lime Green Rd OL8....85 A6
LIMEHURST....85 A6
Limehurst WA14....119 C4
Limehurst Ave
8 Ashton-u-L OL7....85 A6
Manchester M20....109 F8
Limehurst Ct OL8....66 D1
Limehurst Jun & Inf Sch
OL8....84 D8
Limehurst Rd OL7....85 A6
Limekiln La M12....164 A4
Lime Kiln La SK6....126 A5
Lime La M35....84 C7
Lime Pl SK16....101 B8
Lime Rd M32....96 D1
Limers Gate OL12....14 F5
Limerston Dr M40....83 A5
Limes Ave WN6....37 B6
Limesdale Cl BL2....43 B5
LIME SIDE....66 D1
Limeside Jun & Inf Sch
OL8....66 D1
Limeside Rd OL8....66 C1
Lime St
Atherton M46....57 F3
Bury BL9....27 F6
Chadderton OL1....48 C1
Dukinfield SK16....101 B8
Eccles M30....79 D1
Farnworth BL4....60 E8
Rochdale OL11....30 C4
Romiley SK6....112 E4
Tyldesley M29....58 F1
Wigan WN1....151 A4
Limestead Ave M8....156 A4
Limes The
Culcheth WA3....91 D4
Golborne WA3....90 D6
Mossley, Micklehurst
OL5....68 E1
Mossley, Mossley Cross
OL5....68 B1
Standish WN6....37 A6
Stockport SK3....170 A3
Lime Tree Cl M41....95 E1
Lime Tree Gr M35....84 B7
Lime Tree Prim Sch
M33....108 E3
Limetrees Rd M24....64 F8
Lime Vale WN3....55 F4
Lime Vale Rd WN5....71 C3
Lime Wlk
8 Handforth SK9....131 D1
Partington M31....105 D3
Limewood Cl
Bridge End BB4....1 A7
Haslingden BB4....1 A7
Limewood Mdw M29....77 C6
Limley Gr M21....109 C7
Linacre Ave BL3....147 B2
Linacre Way SK13....116 F7
Linbeck Gr WA3....74 E1
Linby St M15....162 B3
Lincoln Ave
Denton M34....100 F1
Droylsden M43....84 A3
Gatley SK8....131 B7
Golborne WA3....74 D1
Irlam M44....105 C4
Little Lever BL3....43 A2
Manchester M19....99 B1
Urmston M32....95 F3
Lincoln Cl
Ashton-u-L OL6....85 D8
Golborne WN7....91 C8
Rochdale OL11....31 A6
Tyldesley M29....59 A2
Lincoln Close Ind Est 2
OL11....31 A6
Lincoln Ct
Failsworth M40....83 B4
14 Manchester M7....63 E1
Lincoln Dr
Altrincham WA15....120 B5

Lincoln Dr continued
Ashton-in-M WN4....73 D2
Aspull WN2....38 D5
7 Bury BL9....44 F8
Littleborough OL15....16 A3
Manchester M25....63 C2
Lincoln Gn SK5....112 C6
Lincoln Gr
Atherton M46....58 B3
Bolton BL2....25 F4
Manchester M13....163 C1
Sale M33....108 F4
Lincoln Leach Ct
OL11....139 C1
Lincoln Mill (Bolton Ent
Ctr) BL1....144 C2
Lincoln Minshull Cl 12
M23....158 C1
Lincoln Pl WN5....36 C1
Lincoln Rd
Bolton BL1....144 B4
Failsworth M35....84 A6
Handforth SK9....131 E1
Hindley WN2....56 E5
Middleton M24....65 C5
7 Swinton M27....79 F7
Lincoln Rise SK6....113 A1
Lincoln Sq M2....158 C1
Lincoln St
Eccles M30....79 C1
Manchester M13....98 F4
Oldham OL9....152 C1
Rochdale OL11....31 A6
Lincoln Way 5 SK13....116 F8
Lincoln Wlk OL10....29 A2
Lincombe Rd OL2....130 D8
Lincroft Rd WN2....57 A3
Linda Dr SK7....124 D2
Lindale SK14....101 C5
Lindale Ave
Bolton BL1....40 F8
Chadderton OL9....152 A2
Failsworth M40....65 D2
Royton OL2....48 C8
Urmston M41....94 F3
Whitefield BL9....45 A3
Lindale Cl M28....77 E7
Lindale Dr M24....46 E3
Lindale Rd M28....77 E7
Lindale Rise OL2....49 D7
Lindbury Ave SK2....124 C7
Linden Ave
Altrincham WA15....119 E5
Ashton-in-M WN4....72 F5
Atherton M46....58 B2
Denton M34....100 D7
Little Lever BL3....43 A5
Oldham OL4....67 D8
Orrell WN5....53 E6
Pendlebury M6....80 A6
Ramsbottom BL0....11 D6
Sale M33....107 F4
Swinton M27....79 D7
Linden Cl
Denton M34....101 A3
Edenfield BL0....1 D2
Lymm WA13....117 A4
Linden Cres BL8....26 F5
Linden St WN5....53 E6
Linden Dr WN5....161 A4
Linden Gr
Billinge WN5....71 C3
Bramhall SK7....132 D4
Leigh WN7....75 E7
Manchester M14....110 D8
Orrell WN5....53 E6
Stockport SK2....124 B4
Linden Lea
Ravenstall BB4....1 F8
Sale M33....108 B2
Linden Mews M28....77 F6
Linden Pk M19....111 A8
Linden Rd
Boothstown M28....77 F6
Cheadle SK8....123 A3
Denton M34....101 A3
Hindley WN2....56 E7
Manchester M20....110 A4
Stalybridge SK15....102 D7
Linden Road Prim Sch
M34....101 A3
Linden St WN5....54 C5
Linden Way
Droylsden M43....99 E8
High Lane SK6....135 A7
Linden Wlk
Bolton BL2....25 B5
Orrell WN5....53 E6
Lindenwood OL9....65 E8
Lindeth Ave M18....99 D4
Lindfield Dr BL1....143 B1
Lindfield Est N SK9....137 A6
Lindfield Est S SK9....136 F6
Lindfield Rd SK5....99 F1
Lindinis Ave M6....81 B2
Lindisfarne 17 OL12....139 B4
Lindisfarne Ave WA3....91 C8
Lindisfarne Cl M33....108 B2
Lindisfarne Dr SK12....133 D4
Lindisfarne Pl BL2....25 C2
Lindisfarne Rd OL7....84 E5
Lindley Ave WN5....53 C5
Lindley Gr SK3....170 A1
Lindley St
Kearsley BL4....61 B6
Little Lever BL3....43 B3
Lindleywood Rd M14....110 E8
Lindon Park Rd BB4....1 C7

Lindop Rd WA15....119 F1
Lindow Cl BL8....27 B6
Lindow Com Prim Sch
SK9....136 D3
Lindow Court Pk
WA16....136 A3
Lindow Ct
Romiley SK6....112 D3
4 Sale M33....108 F3
Wilmslow SK9....136 E8
LINDOW END....136 B2
Lindow Fold Dr SK9....136 D5
Lindow La SK9....136 E6
Lindow Par SK9....136 E6
Lindow Rd M16....97 C2
Lindow St
Leigh WN7....75 D6
Sale M33....108 F3
Lindrick Ave M45....62 D6
Lindrick Cl M40....83 C7
Lindrick Terr BL3....145 A1
Lindsay Ave
Bramhall SK8....123 B1
Manchester M19....98 F1
Swinton M27....79 E7
Lindsay St
Horwich BL6....22 D1
Stalybridge SK15....86 B1
Lindsay Terr WN2....38 B5
Lindsell Rd WA14....119 C8
Lindsgate Dr WA15....120 B7
Lindside Wlk 18 M9....64 E3
Lind St M40....160 B2
Lindum Ave M16....97 C4
Lindum Ct OL10....29 E2
Lindum St M14....98 B3
Lindwall Cl M23....109 B2
Linear View WA12....89 C1
Linehan Cl SK4....110 D2
Lineholme OL2....48 C2
Line Crt M43....158 A3
Lines Rd
Droylsden M43....84 B1
Irlam M44....105 F8
Linfield Cl BL2....25 D4
Linfield St M11....83 B1
Linford Ave M40....65 C2
Lingard Cl M34....100 C8
Lingard La SK6....112 D5
Lingard Rd M22....109 D1
Lingards Dr M29....77 A4
Lingards St M29....77 A4
Lingard St
Leigh WN7....76 B4
Reddish SK5....111 F8
Lingard Terr M34....100 C8
Lingcrest Rd M19....111 C7
Lingdale Rd SK8....123 B1
Lingdale Wlk M40....83 A7
Ling Dr M46....58 D2
Lingfield 2 M16....97 D3
Lingfield Ave
Hazel Grove SK7....124 F2
Sale M33....107 B2
Lingfield Cl
Bury BL8....27 C7
Farnworth BL4....60 C7
Lingfield Cres WN6....36 E3
Lingfield Rd M11....83 C2
Lingfield Wlk OL9....152 C3
Lingholme Dr M24....46 C2
Lingmell Ave WA11....71 C1
Lingmell Cl
Bolton BL1....40 F8
Middleton M24....46 D2
Urmston M41....95 A4
Lingmoor Cl
Middleton M24....46 C2
Wigan WN3....55 A1
Lingmoor Dr M29....77 B7
Lingmoor Rd BL1....23 F1
Lingmoor Wlk
1 Manchester M15....162 C1
3 Manchester M15....162 C2
Lings Wlk M22....121 E1
Linguard Bsns Pk 8
OL16....31 A6
Linhope Cl SK4....110 E3
Link 25 Bsns Pk WN4....72 F8
Link Ave M41....96 A1
Linkfield Dr M28....77 F6
Link La OL8....66 E2
Link Rd
Oldham OL4....67 F7
Sale M33....107 D2
Links Ave M35....83 F5
Links Cres M25....63 E2
Links Ct M27....61 F2
Links Dr BL6....40 B7
Linksfield M34....100 F5
Linkside Ave OL2....48 D5
Links Pl OL6....85 E6
Links Rd
Bolton, Harwood BL2....26 A3
Bolton, Lostock Junction
BL6....40 B7
Heywood OL10....46 D8
Marple SK6....125 F4
Romiley SK6....113 C2
Wilmslow SK9....136 E4
Links Rise M41....95 A4
Links The M40....83 C7
Links View
Manchester M25....63 A1
Rochdale OL16....30 B6
Linksview Ct M45....62 D7

Linksway
Gatley SK8....122 A4
Manchester M25....63 D2
Pendlebury M27....80 A6
Links Way OL9....152 C1
Linksway Cl SK4....111 A5
Linksway Dr BL9....45 B3
Link The
Brinnington SK5....112 C6
Handforth SK9....131 D3
Shaw OL2....48 E8
Linkway Ave WN4....73 E5
Linkway The BL6....39 D8
Link Wlk M31....105 D2
Linley Ave M26....44 E5
Linley Cl WN6....36 C4
Linley Dr OL4....67 D4
Linley Gr BL0....11 A2
Linley Rd
Cheadle SK8....132 B8
Sale M33....108 B5
Wigan WN5....54 E5
Linnell Dr OL11....29 E8
Linnet Cl
Droylsden M34....84 C1
Hazel Grove SK7....124 F5
Manchester M12....98 F4
Newton-le-W WA12....89 C3
Linnet Dr
Bury BL9....141 B4
Irlam M44....94 A3
Leigh WN7....76 B5
Linnet Hill OL11....30 C6
Linnet's Wood Mews
M28....60 E3
Linney La OL2....149 C3
Linney Rd SK7....123 D2
Linney Sq WN1....151 B4
Linn St M8....64 A1
Linnyshaw Cl M28....60 F3
LINNYSHAW....60 F3
Linnyshaw Ind Est M28....60 F3
Linslade Gdns BL3....145 B1
Linslade Ho M5....154 C1
Linslade Wlk 7 M9....157 A3
Linstead Dr M8....155 C2
Linstock Way M46....58 B3
Linthorpe Wlk BL3....146 B4
Linton Ave
Bury BL9....27 F5
Golborne WA3....73 F2
Reddish M34....100 A3
Linton Cl M4....164 A4
Linton Rd M33....108 C6
Linton Vale M26....61 B8
Linton Wlk M7....80 F8
Linwood Gr 9 WN2....56 D4
Linwood Gr M12....99 A2
Linwood St M35, M40....153 D6
Lion Brow M9....64 D3
Lion Fold La M9....64 D3
Lion La BL6....21 C2
Lions Dr M27....80 A7
Lion St M9....64 A1
Liptrot St WN5....54 F7
Lisbon St 17 OL12....14 C1
Lisburn Ave
Manchester M16, M21....97 C1
Sale M33....108 A3
Lisburne Ave SK2....124 D7
Lisburne Cl SK2....124 D6
Lisburne La SK2....124 D6
Lisburne Sch SK2....124 D6
Lisburn Rd M40....83 A8
Liscard Ave M14....98 B1
Liscard St M46....58 B3
Lisetto Ave 1 OL4....67 B6
Liskeard Ave OL2....48 F4
Liskeard Cl OL16....15 C1
Liskeard Dr SK7....132 F7
Lisle St 3 OL12....31 A8
Lismore WA15....119 F2
Lismore Ave
Bolton BL3....40 F5
6 Stockport SK3....123 B8
Lismore Way M41....95 E5
Lismore Wlk M22....130 E8
Lissadel St M6....81 B4
Lisson Gr WA15....119 E2
Lister Rd M24....64 B6
Lister St BL3....146 B3
Liston St SK16....101 C8
Litcham Cl M1....163 B3
Litchfield Cl OL3....33 C2
Litchfield Ct M40....64 C7
Litchfield Gr M28....79 A7
Litherland Ave M22....121 E2
Litherland Rd
Bolton BL3....147 B2
Sale M33....108 B3
Little 66 BL9....45 B7
Little Ancoats St M1,
M4....159 B2
Little Bank St 8 M9....64 F1
LITTLE BOLLINGTON....118 B2
Little Bollington CE Prim
Sch WA14....118 B2
LITTLE BOLTON....80 B1
Little Bolton Terr M5....80 C2
LITTLEBOROUGH....16 B5
Littleborough Coach
House & Heritage Ctr*
OL15....16 B7
Littleborough Com Prim
Sch OL15....16 B7
Littleborough Sta
OL15....16 B5

Littlebourne Wlk BL1....25 A6
Littlebrook Cl
Cheadle SK8....123 C4
Glossop SK13....104 A4
Little Brook Rd M33....107 C1
Little Brow BL7....25 A7
Little Church St 3
WN5....54 B6
LITTLE CLEGG....15 F2
Little Clegg Rd OL15....15 F2
Littledale St OL12....139 B4
Little David St M1....163 A4
Little Ees La M33....107 F7
Little Egerton St SK1....169 B2
Little Factory St M29....58 F1
Littlefields SK14....103 A4
Little Flatt OL12....58 F1
Littlegate BL5....57 E5
Littlegreen Gdns M6....154 C3
Littleham Wlk M18....165 C1
Little Harwood Lee
BL2....25 E3
Littlehaven Cl M12....164 B1
Little Heath La WA14....118 D5
Little Heaton CE Prim Sch
M24....64 C7
Little Hey St OL2....49 B4
Littlehills Cl M24....46 E1
Little Holme St M4....160 A1
Little Holme Wlk M4....147 C4
Little Howarth Way 1
OL12....15 C4
LITTLE HULTON....60 A4
Little John St M3....158 B1
Little La WN3, WN5....54 E4
LITTLE LEVER....43 C4
(Specialist Language
Coll) BL3....42 F3
Little Lever St
Manchester M1....159 B1
2 Manchester M1, M4....159 B2
Little London 8 WN1....37 C1
Little Mdws BL7....24 F7
Little Meadow Rd
WA14....119 B1
Little Moor Clough 8 B2
Littlemoor Cotts SK1....124 B8
Littlemoor Ct 3 SK13....116 C8
Littlemoor Ho 1 OL4....67 C8
Little Moor La OL4....51 B4
Little Moor La OL4....67 C8
Littlemoor Prim Sch
OL4....67 C8
Littlemoor Rd SK14....103 A2
LITTLEMOSS....84 C3
Littlemoss Bsns Pk
M43....84 C3
Littlemoss High Sch for
Boys M43....84 C4
Little Moss La M27....61 F2
Littlemoss Rd M43....84 C3
Little Nelson St 1
M4....159 A3
Little Oak Cl M4....67 E6
Little Pasture WN7....75 D7
Little Peter St M15....162 B3
Little Pitt St M1....159 B1
Little Quay St M3....158 B1
Littler Ave M21....109 C5
Littlers Point* M17....96 D5
LITTLE SCOTLAND....21 B2
Little Scotland BL6....21 B2
Little St SK1....124 B8
Little Stones Rd BL7....8 E2
Littleton Gr WN6....19 E2
Littleton Rd M6, M7,
M25....81 A6
LITTLE TOWN....91 C1
Little Town OL8....66 C4
Little Underbank SK1....169 C1
Littlewood OL2....49 A4
Littlewood Ave 1 BL9....27 F5
Littlewood Rd M22....121 E2
Littlewood St M6....154 B2
Litton Bank SK13....171 B1
Littondale Cl OL2....48 E5
Litton Fold 16 SK13....171 B1
Litton Gdns 17 SK13....171 B1
Litton Mews SK13....171 B1
Liverpool Cl SK5....111 E7
Liverpool Rd
Ashton-in-M WN4....73 A3
Eccles M30....79 C1
Garswood WA11, WN4....72 D2
Irlam, Cadishead M44....105 D4
Irlam M30, M44....94 D4
Manchester M3....162 B4
Platt Bridge WN2....56 C3
Liverpool St
7 Reddish SK5....111 E7
Salford M5....81 B1
Liverstudd Ave SK5....111 F8
Liverton Ct M9....64 D1
Livesey St
Manchester, Levenshulme
M19....111 B8
Manchester M4....159 C3
Oldham OL1....67 C8
Livingstone Ave M22....121 E2
Livingstone Pl M16....161 B1
Livingstone Prim Sch
OL5....68 C1
Livingstone St
2 Ashton-in-M WN4....73 A5
Oldham, County End OL4....68 A6

Livingstone St *continued*
Oldham, Lees OL4 . . . . .67 E5
Livsey La OL10 . . . . .29 A2
Livsey St
Rochdale OL16 . . . . .31 A7
Whitefield M45 . . . . .62 F8
Lizard St M1 . . . . .159 B1
Liza St WN7 . . . . .75 E8
Lizmar Terr M40, M9 . . . . . . .157 C4
Llanberis Rd SK8 . . . . .122 E1
Llanfair Rd 7 SK3 . . . . .123 C8
Lloyd Ave SK8 . . . . .122 A6
Lloyd Ct M12 . . . . .164 C2
Lloyd Gdns WA14 . . . . .119 D3
Lloyd Rd M19 . . . . .111 B7
Lloyd St N M14, M15 . . . . . .163 A1
Lloyd St S M14 . . . . .98 A2
Lloyd's Ct WA14 . . . . .119 D4
Lloyd Sq 7 WA14 . . . . .119 D4
Lloyd St
Altrincham WA14,
WA15 . . . . .119 D4
Heywood OL10 . . . . .29 D1
Manchester M2 . . . . .158 C1
Rochdale OL11 . . . . .30 D4
Stockport SK4 . . . . .169 A3
Whitworth OL12 . . . . .4 C1
Lloyd Wright Ave
M11 .164 B4
Lobden Cres OL12 . . . . .14 D8
Lobelia Ave BL4 . . . . .42 A1
Lobelia Wlk 6 M31 . . . . . . .105 E2
Lobley Cl OL12 . . . . .15 B2
Local Board St WN2 . . . . . . .151 C3
Lochawe Cl OL10 . . . . .29 A1
Lochinver Gr OL10 . . . . .29 A1
Lochmaddy Cl SK7 . . . . .124 F1
Loch St WN5 . . . . .54 B6
Lock Cl OL10 . . . . .46 E8
Locke Ind Est BL6 . . . . .22 B3
Lockerbie Pl WN3 . . . . .54 F4
Locker La WN4 . . . . .73 F4
Lockes Yd M1 . . . . .163 A3
Lockett Bsns Pk WN4 . . . . . .73 C5
Lockett Gdns M3 . . . . .158 A2
Lockett Rd WN4 . . . . .73 C6
Lockett St
Manchester M8 . . . . .158 B4
Salford M6 . . . . .81 A5
Lock Flight Bldgs WN3 . . . . .54 F7
Lockhart Cl M12 . . . . .165 A1
Lockhart St OL16 . . . . .31 B5
Lockingate St OL6 . . . . .85 B6
Locking Gate Rise OL4 . . . . .49 E1
Lock Keepers Mews
M27 . . . . .80 D8
Lock La
Bolton BL3, BL6 . . . . .40 D8
Partington M31 . . . . .105 E3
Locklands La M44 . . . . .94 A2
Lock Rd WA14 . . . . .119 C6
Lockside SK6 . . . . .126 A6
Lockside Mews WN1 . . . . . . .151 A3
Lockside View OL5 . . . . .68 E3
Locksley Cl SK4 . . . . .168 C2
Locks The M44 . . . . .94 B1
Locks View WN1 . . . . .151 C4
Lockton Cl
Manchester M1 . . . . .163 B3
Reddish SK5 . . . . .111 E6
Lockton Ct M1 . . . . .163 B3
Lock View M26 . . . . .61 B8
Lockwood St 7 M12 . . . . .99 B3
Locomotion Ind Est
BL6 . . . . .22 B2
Lodden Wlk 4 M9 . . . . .157 B4
Lodge Ave M41 . . . . .95 E2
Lodge Bank
Glossop SK13 . . . . .104 A6
Horwich BL6 . . . . .21 F2
Lodge Bank Rd BL6 . . . . .21 F3
Lodge Bank Est OL15 . . . . . .15 F3
Lodge Brow M26 . . . . .44 B2
Lodge Cl
Dukinfield SK16 . . . . .101 E7
Lymm WA13 . . . . .117 B4
Lodge Ct
Manchester SK4 . . . . .110 F2
Mottram in L SK14 . . . . .103 A4
Lodge Dr
Culcheth WA3 . . . . .91 F3
Tyldesley M29 . . . . .77 B6
Lodge Farm Cl SK7 . . . . .123 C2
Lodge Fold M43 . . . . .84 B2
Lodge Gn SK16 . . . . .101 E7
Lodge Gr M46 . . . . .58 E1
Lodge Hill La BL0 . . . . .12 A8
Lodge La
Delph OL3 . . . . .50 E5
Dukinfield SK16 . . . . .101 E8
Haydock WA11, WA12,
WA9 . . . . .89 B8
Hyde SK14 . . . . .167 A4
Leigh WN7 . . . . .76 E4
Tyldesley M46 . . . . .58 D1
Lodge Mews BL0 . . . . .138 C2
Lodge Mill La BL0 . . . . .2 A1
Lodgepole Cl M30 . . . . .94 F8
Lodge Rd
Orrell WN5 . . . . .53 E4
Radcliffe M26 . . . . .44 B2
Tyldesley M46 . . . . .58 E1
Lodgeside Cl M43 . . . . .84 B2
Lodge St
Ashton-u-L OL7 . . . . .84 F1
Dukinfield SK14 . . . . .101 E5
Littleborough OL15 . . . . .16 B5
Manchester M40 . . . . .157 B1

Lodge St *continued*
Middleton M24 . . . . .47 A1
Ramsbottom BL0 . . . . .138 C2
Ramsbottom, Shuttleworth
BL0 .11 E8
Wardle OL12 . . . . .15 C6
Lodge The SK13 . . . . .104 A6
Lodge View
Droylsden M43 . . . . .84 B2
Ramsbottom BL0 . . . . .12 A8
Lodge View Cvn Pk
BL2 .148 A4
Loeminster PI M27 . . . . .151 C3
Loen Cres BL1 . . . . .142 C3
Loganberry Ave M6 . . . . .81 A3
Logan St BL1 . . . . .24 E5
Logwood Ave
Bury BL8 . . . . .140 A3
Wigan WN5 . . . . .54 E7
Logwood Ho WN5 . . . . .54 E8
Logwood PI WN5 . . . . .54 E8
Loire Dr WN5 . . . . .54 F8
Loisine Cl OL11 . . . . .30 B3
Lok Fu Gdns M8 . . . . .155 B1
Lomas Cl M19 . . . . .110 E3
Lomas La BL2 . . . . .1 F8
Lomas St
Failsworth M35 . . . . .66 A1
Middleton M24 . . . . .47 B1
Stockport SK3 . . . . .170 A3
Lomax's Bldgs BL2 . . . . .145 C2
Lomax St
Bolton BL1 . . . . .143 B2
Bury BL9 . . . . .141 A3
7 Farnworth BL4 . . . . .42 C2
Manchester M1, M4 . . . . . . .159 F1
4 Platt Bridge WN2 . . . . . . .56 B2
Radcliffe M26 . . . . .44 A2
Ramsbottom BL8 . . . . .10 F1
Whitefield M45 . . . . .44 E2
Lombard Cl SK6 . . . . .112 F4
Lombard Gr M14 . . . . .110 C8
Lombard St
Atherton M46 . . . . .58 B3
Oldham OL1 . . . . .153 B3
Rochdale OL12 . . . . .139 A4
Lombardy Ct 9 M6 . . . . .81 A3
Lomond Ave
Altrincham WA15 . . . . .120 A3
Stretford M32 . . . . .96 D3
Lomond Cl SK2 . . . . .124 A3
Lomond Dr BL8 . . . . .27 B4
Lomond PI BL3 . . . . .40 E6
Lomond Rd M22, SK8 . . . . . .121 F2
Lomond Terr OL16 . . . . .31 C4
London Cl WN5 . . . . .54 E8
London Fields WN5 . . . . .71 E5
London PI SK1 . . . . .169 C1
London Rd
Alderley Edge SK9 . . . . .137 A1
Hazel Grove SK2, SK7 . . . . .124 D3
Manchester M1 . . . . .163 B4
Midway SK10, SK12 . . . . . . .133 C1
Oldham OL1 . . . . .49 B1
London Rd N SK12 . . . . .133 E5
London Rd S SK12 . . . . .133 D3
London Sq SK1 . . . . .169 C1
London St
Bolton BL3 . . . . .147 B4
Salford M6 . . . . .81 B4
Whitefield M45 . . . . .62 F7
Long Acres Dr OL12 . . . . .4 D2
Longacres St M, M45 . . . . . .159 C1
Longacres Rd WA15 . . . . . . .129 D7
Longacre St M1, M4 . . . . . . .159 C1
Longbow Ct M7 . . . . .155 A8
Longbridge Rd M17 . . . . .96 A6
Longbrook M9 . . . . .36 B7
Longbutt La WA13 . . . . .117 A2
Longcliffe Wlk 12
BL1 .143 C2
Long Clough OL2 . . . . .48 C2
Longclough Dr SK13 . . . . . . .116 A8
Longcrag Wlk 4 M15 . . . . . .163 A1
Longcroft M29 . . . . .76 E4
Longcroft Cotts BL9 . . . . .11 F1
Longcroft Dr WA14 . . . . .119 B4
Longcroft Gr
Droylsden M34 . . . . .100 B8
Wythenshawe M23 . . . . .120 F7
Long Croft La SK8 . . . . .122 F1
Long Cswy
Farnworth BL4 . . . . .60 D7
Leigh M46 . . . . .76 B8
Longdale Cl OL2 . . . . .48 C4
Longdale Dr SK14 . . . . .103 A3
Longdale Gdns SK14 . . . . . .103 A3
Longdell Wlk 4 M9 . . . . . . .157 B4
Longden Ave OL4 . . . . .49 E3
Longden Ct SK7 . . . . .132 E6
Longdendale
Language Coll SK14 . . . . . . .103 C5
Longdendale Recn Ctr
SK14 . . . . .102 F3
Longden Fold
Ashton-in-M WN4 . . . . .73 A3
Manchester M19 . . . . .99 B2
Longden St 11 BL1 . . . . .144 C4
Longfellow Ave BL3 . . . . . . .146 B3
Longfellow Cl WN3 . . . . .150 A1
Longfellow Cres OL1 . . . . . . .49 D4
Longfellow Wlk 5
M34 .113 A7
Longfield Ave
Altrincham WA15 . . . . .120 C6
Gatley SK8 . . . . .131 C4

Longfield Ave *continued*
Urmston M41 . . . . .95 C1
Longfield Cl SK14 . . . . .101 E6
Longfield Cres OL4 . . . . .67 D8
Longfield Dr M41 . . . . .95 B2
Longfield La 13 OL4 . . . . . . .49 D1
Longfield Pk OL2 . . . . .149 A2
Longfield Rd
Bolton BL3 . . . . .146 B3
Rochdale OL11 . . . . .30 C8
Shaw OL2 . . . . .149 A2
Wythenshawe M23 . . . . .120 F8
Longfield Sh Ctr M25 . . . . . . .63 A5
Longford Ave 7 WN2 . . . . . . .37 F2
Longford Ave
Bolton BL1 . . . . .142 C2
Stretford M32 . . . . .96 E2
Longford Cl M32 . . . . .96 F2
Longford Cotts M32 . . . . .96 F2
Longford Ho 4 M21 . . . . .96 F1
Longford Park Sch
M32 . . . . .96 F2
Longford PI M14 . . . . .98 E4
Longford Rd
Manchester M21 . . . . .97 A1
Reddish SK5 . . . . .99 F1
Stretford M32 . . . . .96 E3
Longford Rd W SK5 . . . . .99 F1
Longford St
Heywood OL10 . . . . .29 D2
Manchester M18 . . . . .99 D6
Longford Trad Est
M32 . . . . .96 D3
Longford Wharf 2
M32 . . . . .96 E2
Long Grain PI SK2 . . . . .124 D5
Longham Cl
Bramhall SK7 . . . . .123 D1
Manchester M11 . . . . .160 B1
Longhey Rd M22 . . . . .121 D5
Long Heys or Back La
WN8 .35 A6
Longhill Wlk 8 M40 . . . . .83 A6
Longhirst Cl BL1 . . . . .142 B3
Longhope Rd M22 . . . . .121 C2
Longhurst La SK6 . . . . .126 C6
Longhurst Rd
Hindley M67 . . . . .57 A4
Manchester M9 . . . . .64 B5
Long La
Bolton BL2, BL3 . . . . .42 E6
Broadbottom SK13 . . . . .115 C7
Bury BL9 . . . . .27 E7
Hindley WN2 . . . . .57 A4
Oldham OL9 . . . . .65 F3
Uppermill OL3 . . . . .51 A3
Westhoughton BL5 . . . . .39 D2
Longlands Dr SK14 . . . . .102 B3
Longlevens Rd M22 . . . . . . .121 C3
Longley Dr M28 . . . . .79 B6
Longley La M22 . . . . .121 E7
Longley Rd M28 . . . . .60 D2
Longley St
Oldham OL1 . . . . .153 C2
Shaw OL2 . . . . .149 B1
Long Marl Dr SK9 . . . . .131 F4
Long Mdw
Bolton BL7 . . . . .25 C7
Dukinfield SK14 . . . . .101 F6
Longmead Ave
Ashton-in-M WN4 . . . . .73 C4
Hazel Grove SK7 . . . . .124 D1
Longmeade Gdns
SK9 .137 C6
Longmeadow SK8 . . . . .132 C7
Longmeadow Gr M34 . . . . . .100 C2
Long Meadow Pas
SK14 . . . . .167 A3
Longmead Rd M6 . . . . .154 A4
Longmead Way M24 . . . . .47 B1
Longmere Ave M22 . . . . .121 D3
Long Millgate
Manchester M3 . . . . .158 C2
Manchester M3, M4 . . . . . . .159 A2
Longmoor Rd SK13 . . . . .116 A7
Longnor Gn 38 SK13 . . . . . . .171 A2
Longnor Mews 39
SK13 . . . . .171 A2
Longnor Rd
Gatley SK8 . . . . .131 D8
Hazel Grove SK7 . . . . .133 E7
Longnor Way 40 SK13 . . . . .171 A2
Longport Ave M20 . . . . .110 A7
Longridge BL7 . . . . .25 C8
Longridge Ave
Stalybridge SK15 . . . . .86 A4
Standish WN6 . . . . .36 F8
Longridge Cres BL1 . . . . .23 F7
Longridge Dr
Bury BL8 . . . . .44 A8
Heywood OL10 . . . . .28 F2
Long Row SK15 . . . . .86 F7
Long Rushes OL2 . . . . .48 F8
LONGSHAW 53 E1
Longshaw Ave
Billinge WN5 . . . . .71 E8
Longshaw WN5 . . . . .53 E1
Swinton M27 . . . . .79 B7
Longshaw Comm
Billinge WN5 . . . . .71 E8
Longshaw WN5 . . . . .53 E1
Longshaw Dr M28 . . . . .60 A4
Longshaw Ford Rd BL1 . . . . .23 F5
Longshaw Old Rd WN5 . . . . .37 E1
LONGSHOOT 37 E1

Longshoot Cl WN1 . . . . .37 D1
Longshut La SK1, SK2 . . . . . .170 C3
Longshut La W SK2 . . . . .170 C3
Longsides Rd WA15 . . . . .129 C7
LONGSIGHT 164 C1
Longsight BL2 . . . . .25 E5
LONG SIGHT 48 E2
Longsight Ind Est M12 . . . . . .98 F4
Longsight La
Bolton BL2 . . . . .25 D4
Cheadle SK8 . . . . .131 F6
Longsight Rd
Manchester M18 . . . . .99 B3
Ramsbottom BL0, BL8 . . . . . .11 A2
Longson St BL1 . . . . .25 A1
Longsons The SK5 . . . . .169 C3
Long St
Manchester M18 . . . . .99 E6
Middleton M24 . . . . .47 A1
Swinton M27 . . . . .79 F7
Longthwaite Cl 2
M24 . . . . .46 D2
Longton Ave
Bolton BL1 . . . . .90 C7
Manchester M20 . . . . .110 A5
Longton Rd
Manchester M9 . . . . .64 C4
Salford M6 . . . . .80 C5
Longton St
Bury BL9 . . . . .44 F4
Hindley WN2 . . . . .56 C4
Longtown Gdns 7
BL1 .143 B2
Longview Dr M27 . . . . .61 C1
Longwall Ave M28 . . . . .78 C8
Long Wlk M31 . . . . .105 D3
Longwood Ave SK2 . . . . .124 B6
Longwood Cl SK6 . . . . .113 E3
Longwood Rd M22 . . . . .121 E3
Long Wood Rd M17 . . . . .96 B6
Longworth Ave BL6 . . . . .21 C3
Longworth Cl M41 . . . . .94 E1
Longworth Clough BL7 . . . . . .8 D2
Longworth La BL7 . . . . .8 C2
Longworth Rd
Bolton BL7 . . . . .8 B3
Horwich BL6 . . . . .22 C4
Longworth St
Bolton BL3 . . . . .148 C3
Manchester M3 . . . . .162 B4
Lonsdale Ave
Leigh WN7 . . . . .75 D2
Reddish SK5 . . . . .99 F3
Rochdale OL16 . . . . .31 B5
Swinton M27 . . . . .79 D5
Urmston M41 . . . . .95 B4
Lonsdale Gr 5 BL4 . . . . .60 C8
Lonsdale Rd
Bolton BL1 . . . . .144 B4
Manchester M19 . . . . .99 B2
Oldham OL8 . . . . .66 B2
Lonsdale St
Bury BL9 . . . . .27 C2
Failsworth M40 . . . . .83 C6
Manchester M40 . . . . .95 A4
Lonsdale Wlk WN5 . . . . .54 B8
Loom St M4 . . . . .159 B2
Loomies Ct 1 SK1 . . . . .170 C4
Lord Ave
Bacup OL13 . . . . .3 C8
2 Tyldesley M46 . . . . .58 F1
Lord Byron Sq M50 . . . . .154 C1
Lord Derby Rd SK14 . . . . . . .113 E7
Lord Gr 1 M46 . . . . .58 F1
Lord Kitchener Ct
M33 .108 B5
Lord La M35 . . . . .83 F6
Lord Lane Mews M35 . . . . . . .83 F6
Lord Napier Dr M5 . . . . .161 B3
Lord North St M40 . . . . .160 C4
Lord St S WN7 . . . . .76 A5
Lord's Ave M5 . . . . .154 A2
Lords Coll SK12 . . . . .148 A2
Lordsfields Ave OL6 . . . . .166 B4
Lord Sheldon Way OL7 . . . . .84 E2
Lordship Cl M9 . . . . .64 F1
Lordsmead St M15 . . . . .162 A2
Lord's St M44 . . . . .105 C5
Lord's Stile La BL7 . . . . .25 B7
Lord St
Ashton-in-M WN4 . . . . .73 D4
Ashton-u-L OL6 . . . . .166 B3
Bury BL9 . . . . .140 E2
Bury, Heap Bridge BL9 . . . . .141 C1
Farnworth BL4 . . . . .60 E8
Glossop SK13 . . . . .104 D1
Hindley WN2 . . . . .56 D4
Hollingworth SK14 . . . . .171 A4
Horwich BL6 . . . . .22 B4
Ince-in-M WN2 . . . . .56 A7
Leigh WN7 . . . . .75 F5
Little Lever BL3 . . . . .43 B3
Manchester M3, M4 . . . . . . .159 A3
Middleton M24 . . . . .47 A2
Newton-le-W WA12 . . . . .89 A3
Oldham OL1 . . . . .153 C3
Radcliffe M26 . . . . .44 A3
Reddish M34 . . . . .100 A4
Salford M7 . . . . .81 C4
Stalybridge SK15, SK16 . . . .101 F8
Swinton, Gin Pit WN2 . . . . . .76 F6
Tyldesley, Hindsford
M46 .58 E1
Westhoughton BL5 . . . . .39 E1
Wigan WN1 . . . . .37 E1
Lord Street Prim Sch
BL6 . . . . .22 B4
Lordy Cl WN6 . . . . .37 B7

Loreto Coll M15 . . . . .162 B1
Loreto Gram Sch
WA14 . . . . .119 C5
Loreto Prep Sch
WA14 . . . . .119 C5
Loretto Rd M41 . . . . .95 F1
Lorgill Cl SK3 . . . . .123 F4
Loring St M40 . . . . .83 C5
Lorland Rd SK3 . . . . .123 B7
Lorna Gr SK8 . . . . .121 F6
Lorna Rd SK8 . . . . .123 B2
Lorna Way M44 . . . . .106 A8
Lorne Ave OL2 . . . . .48 B3
Lorne Gr
Stockport SK3 . . . . .170 B2
Urmston M41 . . . . .95 E2
Lorne Rd M14 . . . . .110 C8
Lorne St
Bolton BL1 . . . . .145 C3
Eccles M30 . . . . .95 B8
Farnworth BL3, BL4 . . . . .42 C2
Heywood OL10 . . . . .29 D1
Mossley OL5 . . . . .68 C1
Oldham OL4 . . . . .66 E4
Rochdale OL12 . . . . .15 B3
Wigan WN1 . . . . .151 B4
Lorne Way OL10 . . . . .28 F1
Lorraine Cl 3 OL10 . . . . .46 E8
Lorraine Rd WA15 . . . . .120 B5
Lorton Cl
Boothstown M28 . . . . .77 F6
Middleton M24 . . . . .46 C2
Lorton Gr BL2 . . . . .42 F8
LOSTOCK
Bolton 23 E3
Horwich 39 F8
Lostock Ave
Hazel Grove SK7 . . . . .124 B1
7 Manchester M19 . . . . .99 B1
Poynton SK12 . . . . .133 B4
Sale M33 . . . . .108 E4
Urmston M41 . . . . .95 B3
Lostock Cl
Billinge WN5 . . . . .71 E5
Heywood OL10 . . . . .29 B3
Lostock Coll M32 . . . . .96 A4
Lostock Ct M32 . . . . .95 F4
Lostock Dr BL2 . . . . .27 F6
Lostock Gr M32 . . . . .96 B3
Lostock Hall Prim Sch
SK12 . . . . .133 B3
Lostock Hall Rd SK12 . . . . . .133 B3
Lostock Junction La BL6 . . . .40 C6
LOSTOCK JUNCTION 40 D5
Lostock Junction La
BL6 . . . . .40 C7
Lostock La
Horwich BL5, BL6 . . . . .39 E6
Horwich BL6 . . . . .39 E8
Lostock Park Dr BL6 . . . . .40 A7
Lostock Prim Sch BL6 . . . . . .40 A6
Lostock Rd
Four Gates BL5 . . . . .39 C4
Poynton SK12 . . . . .133 D2
Salford M5 . . . . .154 B2
Urmston M41 . . . . .95 D4
Lostock St M40 . . . . .160 A3
Lostock Sta BL6 . . . . .40 C6
Lostock Way SK9 . . . . .131 D4
Lostock Wlk
Leigh WN7 . . . . .75 D6
Whitefield M45 . . . . .45 C1
Lothian Ave M30 . . . . .79 B3
Lottery Row BL1 . . . . .145 C3
Lottery St SK3 . . . . .169 A1
Lottie St M27 . . . . .80 A8
Loughborough Cl 2
M33 .107 D3
Loughfield M41 . . . . .95 A3
Loughrigg Ave
Billinge WA11 . . . . .71 B1
Royton OL2 . . . . .48 C8
Loughrigg Cl M29 . . . . .77 B7
Louisa St
Bolton BL1 . . . . .143 B2
Manchester M11 . . . . .99 D8
Walkden M28 . . . . .60 D4
Louis Ave BL9 . . . . .140 C4
Louise Cl OL12 . . . . .4 D1
Louise Gdns
Rochdale OL12 . . . . .15 C3
Westhoughton BL5 . . . . .57 F6
Louis St BL0 . . . . .1 D5
Louvaine Ave BL1 . . . . .23 F4
Louvaine Cl M18 . . . . .99 E5
Louvain St M35 . . . . .83 E7
Lovat Rd BL2 . . . . .43 A7
Lovatt Ct WA13 . . . . .117 B4
Love La
Edenfield BL0 . . . . .1 E1
Stockport SK4 . . . . .169 B2
Loveless Ho M46 . . . . .58 D4
Lovell Cl M8 . . . . .64 C4
Lovell Dr SK14 . . . . .167 C4
Lovers La
Atherton M46 . . . . .58 A1
Uppermill OL4 . . . . .68 C4
Lovett Wlk M22 . . . . .121 E8
Low Bank OL12 . . . . .15 C3
Low Bank Rd WN4 . . . . .72 F7
Lowbrook Ave M9 . . . . .65 B3
Low Comm WN7 . . . . .76 B2
Lowcroft Cres OL9 . . . . .65 F8

LOW CROMPTON 48 F6
Low Crompton Rd OL2...48 E6
Lowcross Rd M40........83 A6
Lowe Ave M46..........58 C5
Lowe Gn OL2...........48 E5
Lowe Mill La WN2......56 D5
Lower Albion St M1...163 B4
Lower Alma St SK16...166 B1
LOWER ARTHURS......69 B6
Lower Bamford Cl 7
　M24...............47 A2
Lowerbank M34.......100 F5
Lower Bank SK13......116 D8
Lower Bank Cl SK13...171 C3
Lower Bank St BL9.....140 B2
Lower Barn Rd SK13...171 B4
Lower Beechwood
　OL11............. 139 A1
Lower Bennett St
　SK14............. 101 C5
Lower Bents La SK6...112 F4
Lower Birches OL4.....67 F4
Lower Blue Bell Cotts
　BL5.............. 39 C4
LOWER BOARSGREAVE
　..................3 A6
LOWER BREDBURY...112 E2
Lower Bridgeman St
　BL2.............. 148 A2
Lower Broadacre
　SK15............. 102 E6
Lowerbrook Cl BL6.....22 D1
Lower Brook Farm BL5..58 F7
Lower Brook La M28....79 A5
Lower Brooklands Par 5
　M8............... 63 E2
LOWER BROUGHTON
　..................158 A4
Lower Broughton Rd
　Salford, Higher Broughton
　M7...............81 C6
　Salford, Lower Broughton
　M7...............158 A4
Lower Bury St SK4....169 A2
Lower Byrom St M3...162 B4
Lower Calderbrook
　OL15............. 6 C1
Lower Carr La OL3.....69 B6
Lower Carrs
　Ashton-u-L OL6.......85 D5
　Stockport SK1........169 C1
Lower Chatham St
　M1...............163 A3
Lower Chesham BL3...141 B3
Lower Clowes BB4.....1 E8
Lower Clowes Rd BB4...1 E8
Lower Count Hill OL4...49 E2
Lower Crimble OL11....29 F4
Lower Croft M45......62 C6
Lowercroft Bsns Pk
　BL8.............. 26 F3
Lowercroft Prim Sch
　BL8.............. 26 F2
Lowercroft Rd BL8.....26 F2
Lower Crossbank OL4...67 F8
Lower Darcy St BL2...148 C1
Lower Dingle OL1.....49 C4
LOWER DINTING.....104 B1
Lower Drake Fold BL5...57 E5
Lower Edge Ave OL4...153 B4
Lower Falinge OL12...139 B4
Lowerfield Dr SK2....124 F5
Lowerfields OL8.......67 B4
Lower Fields OL3......51 A1
Lower Fields Rise
　OL2.............. 149 B4
LOWER FOLD........14 C3
Lower Fold
　Bolton BL2..........25 F4
　Denton M34.........101 A2
　Marple SK6.........126 B8
Lower Fold Ave OL2....49 A4
Lowerfold Cl OL12.....14 C4
Lower Fold Cott SK6..134 D7
Lowerfold Cres OL12...14 C4
Lowerfold Dr OL12.....14 C4
Lowerfold Way OL12...14 C4
Lower Frenches Dr
　OL3.............. 69 A5
Lower Gates OL16....139 C3
Lower Gn
　Ashton-u-L OL6.....166 C4
　Middleton M9........64 F5
　3 Rochdale OL12....14 C1
Lower Goodwin Cl BL2..25 E2
LOWER GREEN........77 C3
Lower Green La M29....77 C3
Lower Greenshall La
　SK12............. 135 F6
LOWER HEALEY......14 E4
Lower Hey La OL5......68 E3
Lower Higham Visitor
　Ctr *SK14........114 A8
Lower Hillgate SK1...169 C1
LOWER HINDS.......44 D8
Lower House Dr BL6....40 C7
Lower House La OL12...15 B7
Lower House St 7
　OL1.............. 67 B8
Lower House Wlk BL7..25 A8
Lower Hyde Green Farm
　SK15............. 86 E4
LOWER INCE........151 B1
Lower Jowkin La OL11..29 D7

LOWER KERSAL 81 A7
Lower Kersall Com Prim
　Sch M7............81 B6
Lower Knoll Rd OL3....51 C5
Lower La OL16........31 D4
Lower Landedmans
　BL5.............. 57 F7
Lowerlea SK12.......135 C6
Lower Leigh Rd BL5....57 F5
Lower Lime Rd OL8....84 C7
Lower Longshoot
　WN1............. 151 A4
Lower Lyndon Ave
　WN6............. 36 A6
Lower Makinson Fold 1
　BL6.............. 22 D1
Lower Market St
　SK14............. 115 B8
Lower Marlands OL7...24 F8
Lower Mdw BL7........9 D6
Lower Mead BL7........8 F1
Lower Meadow Rd
　SK9.............. 131 E4
Lower Moat Cl SK4...169 B3
Lower Monton Rd M30..79 F2
LOWER MOOR........67 A8
Lower Mosley St M1,
　M2............... 162 C4
Lower Moss La
　Manchester M15.....162 A3
　Whitefield M45......62 F8
Lower New Row M28....60 A1
Lower Ormond St
　M15............. 163 A3
Lower Park Cres
　SK12............. 133 C6
Lower Park Prim Sch
　SK12............. 133 C4
Lower Park Rd
　Manchester M14......98 C3
　Poynton SK12.......133 B5
LOWER PLACE.......31 B4
Lowerplace Prim Sch
　OL16............. 31 B4
LOWER POOLS.......142 A2
Lower Rawson St BL4...42 E1
Lower Rd BL0.........11 E8
LOWER RUSHCROFT
　..................149 A4
Lower St Stephen St 13
　WN6............. 37 A1
Lower Seedley Rd
　M6............... 154 B3
Lower Sherriff St
　OL12............. 139 B4
Lower Southfield BL5...57 E7
Lower Sq SK13.......104 A7
Lower St
　Farnworth BL4.......60 C7
　18 Rochdale OL16....31 A4
Lower Stones OL3.....50 E3
Lower Strines Rd
　SK6.............. 126 A5
LOWER SUMMERSEAT
　..................11 C1
Lower Sutherland St
　M27............. 79 E8
Lower Tenterfield
　OL11............. 13 D2
Lower Tong BL7.......24 F7
Lower Turf La OL4.....68 B8
Lower Tweedale St
　OL11............. 139 C2
Lower Vickers St
　M40............. 160 A3
Lower Victoria St
　OL9.............. 152 B3
Lower Wharf St OL16..166 C2
Lower Wheat End
　OL16............. 31 B8
Lower Woodhill Rd
　BL8.............. 140 A3
Lowerwood La 12 BL2..25 B1
Lowerwood Wlk OL3...51 C3
Lowes Rd BL9........28 A6
Lowe St
　Denton M34.........101 B4
　Golborne WA3........90 A8
　Radcliffe M26........43 F4
　Stockport SK1.......169 C1
Lowestead Rd 8 M11...83 C2
Lowes The WA14.....119 B1
Lowestoft St M14.....98 B2
Loweswater Ave M29...77 A7
Loweswater Rd
　Farnworth BL4.......59 E7
　Gatley SK8..........131 A8
Loweswater Terr SK15..86 A4
Lowfell Wlk M18......99 D3
Lowfield Ave
　Ashton-u-L OL6.....85 F5
　Droylsden M43.......83 F3
Lowfield Gdns WA3....92 C7
Lowfield Gr SK8......123 A4
Lowfield Rd SK2, SK3..170 B3
Lowfield Wlk 7 M9....64 E3
Low Gate La OL3......34 A1
Lowgill Wlk 11 M18....99 D5
Low Gn M46..........58 F5
Low Grove La OL3.....68 E5
Low Hall Gdns WN2....56 B3
Low Hill OL12........15 C3
Lowhouse Cl OL16.....32 A7
Lowick Ave BL3.......42 A3
Lowick Cl SK7.......124 D2
Lowick Gn SK6.......112 F5
Lowland Gr OL7.......85 A6
Lowland Rd SK2......124 B4

Lowlands Cl M24......65 C5
Low Lea Rd SK6......126 B6
Low Mdws OL2........48 D6
Lowndes Cl SK2......124 B7
Lowndes La SK1, SK2..124 B7
Lowndes St BL1.......142 B1
Lowndes Wlk 5 M13..163 C2
Lownorth Rd M22....130 E8
Lowood Ave M41......94 F4
Lowood Cl OL16.......31 F6
Lowood St M40.......97 D5
Lowrey Wlk 11 M9...157 B3
Lowry Ct SK14.......103 A4
Lowry Dr
　Marple SK6.........126 B8
　Swinton M27.........61 F1
Lowry Gr SK14.......102 F3
Lowry Ho 4 M14....110 D8
Lowry Outlet Mall M50..96 F7
Lowry The 4 M14...110 C8
Lowry The *'M50.....96 E7
Lowry Wlk BL1......143 A1
LOW SIDE...........67 C4
Lowside Ave
　Bolton BL1..........40 C6
　Romiley SK6........113 C5
Lowside Dr OL4.......67 B5
Lowstern Cl BL7.......8 E1
Lows The OL4........48 D6
Lowther Ave
　Altrincham WA15....120 A6
　Culcheth WA3........91 F4
　Manchester M18......99 B3
　Royton OL2..........48 C8
Lowther Cl M25.......63 A3
Lowther Cres M24.....46 D1
Lowther Ct M25......62 F3
Lowther Dr WN7......76 E7
Lowther Gdns M41....94 D3
Lowther Rd
　Manchester M8.......64 A1
　Prestwich M25.......62 F3
　Rochdale OL11.......30 E4
Lowther St BL3.......42 A3
Lowther Terr WN6.....35 C8
Lowthorpe St M14.....98 A2
Lowton Ave M9.......157 C3
Lowton Bsns Pk WA3..91 A7
Lowton Com High Sch
　WA3............. 91 B4
LOWTON COMMON....91 A8
Lowton Gdns WA3....90 B5
LOWTON HEATH.....90 C6
Lowton Jun & Inf Sch
　WA3............. 91 A7
Lowton Rd
　Golborne WA3........74 C1
Lowton St 8 M26....107 D2
LOWTON ST MARY'S...90 F8
Lowton St Mary's CE Prim
　Sch WA3...........91 A8
Lowton St Marys Jun Sch
　WA3............. 90 D8
Lowton West Prim Sch
　WA3............. 90 C8
Low Wood Cl SK7....123 C1
Low Wood Rd M34...100 A4
Loxford Ct M15......162 C2
Loxford St M15......162 C2
Loxham St BL4.......42 D2
Loxley Wlk M40.....160 B4
Loxton Cres WN3.....55 B3
Loynd St BL0.........11 D6
Lubeck St M9........157 B4
Lucas St BL4.........60 A7
Lucas St
　Bury BL4............141 A3
　Oldham OL4..........67 B7
Lucerne Wlk M11....164 C4
Lucerne Cl OL9......152 C2
Lucerne Rd SK7......123 E3
Lucien Cl M12.......164 B1
Luciol Cl M29........59 D1
Lucknow St OL11....139 C1
Lucy St
　Bolton BL1..........142 A1
　Manchester M15.....162 A2
　Salford M7..........155 A1
　Stockport SK3.......170 B4
Ludford Gr M33.....107 F1
Ludgate Hill M4.....159 B3
Ludgate Rd
　Failsworth M40......83 C4
　Rochdale OL11.......31 A2
Ludgate St M4.......159 A3
Ludlow Ave
　Hindley WN2........57 A4
　Prestwich M25, M45..63 B6
　Swinton M27.........62 A2
Ludlow Dr WN7.......76 E7
Ludlow Pk 2 OL4.....67 D6
Ludlow Rd SK2......124 C8
Ludlow St WN6.......19 D3
Ludovic Terr WN1....54 A3
Ludwell Wlk 11 M8..156 A2
Ludworth Prim Sch
　SK6.............. 126 B8
Lugano Rd SK7......123 E3
Luke Kirby Ct M27....61 F1
Luke Rd M43.........84 B1
Luke St
　Ashton-in-M WN4....73 D5
　17 Bacup OL13......3 D8
Luke Wlk M8........156 B2
Lullington Cl SK2....124 C8
Lullington Rd M22....154 A4

Lulworth Ave M41.....94 F2
Lulworth Cl BL8......27 C6
Lulworth Cres M35....84 B8
Lulworth Dr WN2......57 A4
Lulworth Gdns M23..120 F8
Lulworth Rd
　Bolton BL3..........146 A3
　Eccles M30..........79 C3
　Middleton M24........47 A2
LUMB..............1 B4
Lumb Carr Ave BL0....11 A4
Lumb Carr Rd BL0, BL8..11 A4
Lumb Cl SK7.........132 E6
Lumb Cotts BL0.......1 B4
Lumber La M28.......78 E8
Lumb Flats BL0.......1 B4
Lumb Holes La BB4....2 E7
Lumb La
　Bramhall SK7.......132 E6
　Droylsden, Littlemoss M34,
　M43, OL7............84 D4
　Droylsden M34.......84 C1
　Droylsden M34.......100 C8
　Droylsden M43.......84 C1
Lum Head Prim Sch
　SK8.............. 122 B3
Lumiere Bldgs 9
　M15............. 162 C3
Lumley Cl M14.......98 B4
Lumn Hollow SK14...167 B2
Lumn Rd SK14.......167 B2
Lumn's La M27.......62 C1
Lumn St BL9..........27 F8
Lumsdale Rd M32.....96 A5
Lumsden St BL3.....145 B1
Lum St BL1..........148 A4
Lumwood BL1.......142 B3
Luna St M4..........159 B2
Lundale Wlk 13 M40..83 A6
Lund Ave M26........62 B8
Lund St M16.........161 C2
Lundy Ave M21......109 C5
Lune Cl M45.........45 A1
Lunedale 7 WN2.....56 B2
Lunedale Gn SK2....124 E6
Lune Dr M45.........63 A8
Lune Gr
　Heywood OL10.......29 B3
　Leigh WN7..........75 C5
Lunehurst 12 WA3....90 E8
Lune Rd WN2.........56 A2
Lune St
　Oldham OL8.........66 E4
　Tyldesley M29.......76 F8
Lune Way SK5.......111 F5
Lune Wlk
　Droylsden M43......100 B8
　Whitefield M45......63 A8
Lunn Ave M18........99 F6
Luntswood Gr WA12...89 A4
Lupin Ave BL4........42 A1
Lupin Cl OL1.........49 E3
Lupton St M34.......100 F4
Lurden Wlk 2 OL9.....66 B4
Lurdin La WN1, WN6...37 E7
Lurgan Ave M33.....108 C3
Lutener Ave WA14...119 C8
Luton Dr M23........121 A4
Luton Gr M46........58 B3
Luton Rd SK5........111 F8
Luton St
　Bolton BL3..........42 A4
　3 Bury BL8..........27 B1
Luxhall Wlk M40......83 A6
Luxor Gr M34........99 F3
LUZLEY.............86 B7
LUZLEY BROOK......48 F5
Luzley Brook Rd OL2..149 A1
Luzley Rd OL5, OL6....86 B7
Lyceum Pas 1 OL16..139 C3
Lyceum Pl M15......163 A3
Lychgate WN5.........54 E5
Lychgate Ct OL4......67 C4
Lychgate Mews
　1 Manchester, Chorlton-
　cum-Hardy M21.....109 A8
　Manchester, Heaton Mersey
　SK4.............. 110 E2
Lychwood 11 SK6....125 F6
Lydbrook Cl BL1.....145 B2
Lydden Ave M11......83 D3
Lydford OL11.......139 B2
Lydford Gdns BL2.....42 F6
Lydford Gn WN6......36 F8
Lydford St M6........81 B4
Lydford Wlk M13.....163 C2
LYDGATE...........68 D5
Lydgate Ave BL2......42 E8
Lydgate Cl
　Denton M34.........101 B1
　Mossley SK15........86 E6
　Whitefield M45.......45 A1
Lydgate Dr OL4.......67 D5
Lydgate Fold OL4.....68 C5
Lydgate Rd
　Droylsden M43.......83 E2
　Sale M33...........108 C2
Lydgate The OL15.....15 A4
Lydgate Wlk M45.....45 A1
Lydiate Cl BL3.......147 C2
Lydiat La SK9........137 A1
Lydney Ave SK8......131 C7
Lydney Rd M41.......94 D3
Lyefield Ave WN1.....37 F1
Lyefield Wlk 24 OL16..31 B6
Lymbridge Dr BL6.....21 D1
Lyme Ave SK9.......131 B1
Lyme Clough Way M24..46 F4

Lyme Ct
　Hazel Grove SK7....124 D3
　Hyde SK14..........167 B3
Lymefield Dr M28.....78 A7
Lymefield Dr SK2....124 B6
Lymefield Terr SK14...115 B8
Lymefield Visitor Ctr*
　SK14............. 115 B8
Lyme Gr
　Altrincham WA14....119 C4
　Droylsden M43.......99 F8
　Marple SK6.........125 F5
　Romiley SK6.........113 D2
Lyme Lea Cl SK8....132 B2
Lyme Park Ctry Pk*
　SK12............. 135 B2
Lyme Pk* SK12......135 B1
Lyme Rd
　Hazel Grove SK7....124 E1
　High Lane SK12......135 A6
　Poynton SK12........134 C3
Lyme St
　Hazel Grove SK7....124 D3
　Manchester SK4......110 F2
Lyme Terr 1 SK16....166 B1
Lymewood Dr
　Disley SK12.........135 C6
　Wilmslow SK9.......137 E8
Lymington Cl M24....65 E5
Lymington Dr M23...108 D1
LYMM............. 117 A3
Lymm Cl
　Stockport SK3.......170 A2
　Walkden M28........60 A3
Lymm High Sch
　WA13............. 117 B3
Lymm Rd WA14......118 B1
Lymm Wlk 5 SK8.....123 A5
Lynd St M6..........56 B3
Lynbridge Cl WN5.....53 E5
Lyncombe Cl SK8....132 B6
Lyndale Ave
　Reddish SK5.........99 F3
　Swinton M27.........79 D6
Lyndale Dr OL15......16 A6
Lyndene Ave M28.....79 A8
Lyndene Cl M28.......79 C3
Lyndene Ct OL9......29 C3
Lyndene Gdns SK8...122 B6
Lyndene Rd M22.....121 D5
Lyndhurst Ave
　Ashton-u-L OL6......85 B5
　Denton M34.........100 B5
　Hazel Grove SK7....124 C1
　Irlam M44...........94 B3
　Manchester M15......63 E3
　Oldham OL9..........65 F5
　Sale M33...........107 F3
　Trub OL11...........47 D8
　Urmston M41.........95 C4
Lyndhurst Cl SK9....136 D5
Lyndhurst Com Prim Sch
　SK16............. 166 C1
Lyndhurst Dr WA15...120 A2
Lyndhurst Prim Sch
　OL8.............. 66 D3
Lyndhurst Rd
　Manchester M20.....110 B5
　Oldham OL8.........66 F3
　Reddish SK5.........99 E2
　Stretford M32........96 B3
Lyndhurst St M6.....154 B2
Lyndhurst View SK16..166 C1
Lyndon Ave WN6......36 A7
Lyndon Cl
　Bury BL8............26 F6
　Oldham OL8.........68 B8
Lyndon Croft OL8.....66 C4
Lyndon Rd M44.......93 F2
Lyne Ave SK13......116 B8
Lyne Edge Cres SK16..101 F7
Lyne Edge Rd SK16...102 A7
Lyneham Wlk M7....155 F2
Lyne View M41.......101 F6
Lyngard Cl SK9......137 E8
Lyngarth Ho 1 WA14..119 E6
Lyngate Cl SK1......124 A8
Lyn Gr OL10.........29 A3
Lynham Dr OL10......46 D8
Lynmouth Ave
　Manchester M20.....110 A6
　Oldham OL8.........66 F3
　10 Reddish SK5.....111 E7
　Royton OL2..........48 C3
　Urmston M41.......107 B8
Lynmouth Cl
　Chadderton OL9.....47 C1
　Radcliffe M26........44 C4
　Wigan M27..........37 A2
Lynmouth Ct M25.....63 F3
Lynmouth Gr M25.....62 F3
Lynn Ave M33.......108 D6
Lynn Dr M43.........83 E2
Lynne Cl SK13.......116 F8
Lynn St OL9.........153 B6
Lynnwood Dr OL11....30 B8
Lynnwood Rd M19....110 D2
Lynroyle Way OL11....30 D3
Lynside Wlk M22....130 E8
Lynsted Ave BL3.....42 A3
Lynstock Way BL6....39 E6
Lynthorpe Ave M44...105 E6
Lynthorpe Rd M40....65 D2
Lynton Ave
　Hattersley SK14.....102 C3
　Irlam M44...........105 E6
　Oldham OL8.........66 C2

Lynton Ave *continued*
Rochdale OL11 ... 30 B3
Royton OL2 ... 48 C3
Swinton M27 ... 61 F1
Urmston M41 ... 94 C2
Wigan WN6 ... 37 A3
Lynton Cl OL9 ... 47 F1
Lynton Cres M28 ... 78 D8
Lynton Dr
High Lane SK6 ... 134 E8
Manchester M19 ... 110 F7
Prestwich M25 ... 63 C6
Lynton Gr WA15 ... 119 F5
Lynton La SK9 ... 137 A2
Lynton Lea M26 ... 44 C4
Lynton Mews SK9 ... 137 A2
Lynton Park Rd SK8 ... 131 F8
Lynton Rd
Bolton BL3 ... 146 C2
Cheadle SK8 ... 122 C5
Hindley WN2 ... 56 F6
Manchester, Chorlton-cum-Hardy M21 ... 97 A1
Manchester, Heaton Chapel SK4 ... 111 C5
Swinton M27 ... 61 F1
Tyldesley M29 ... 77 D8
Lynton St
Leigh WN7 ... 75 D5
Manchester M14 ... 98 B2
Lyntonvale Ave SK8 ... 122 B6
Lynton Wlk SK14 ... 102 C2
Lyntown Trad Est M30 ... 79 E2
Lynway Dr M20 ... 110 B5
Lynway Gr M24 ... 110 F4
Lynwell Rd M30 ... 79 D2
Lynwood
Altrincham WA15 ... 129 A8
Wilmslow SK9 ... 137 A6
Lynwood Ave
Bolton BL3 ... 42 B2
Eccles M30 ... 79 D2
Golborne WA3 ... 90 C8
Manchester M16 ... 97 C2
Lynwood Cl OL7 ... 85 A7
Lynwood Ct M8 ... 63 F7
Lynwood Dr OL4 ... 67 E8
Lynwood Gr
Atherton M46 ... 58 B3
Bolton BL2 ... 25 D4
Droylsden M34 ... 84 C1
Sale M33 ... 111 C6
Sale M33 ... 108 C5
Lyon Gr M28 ... 79 A8
Lyon Ind Est WA14 ... 119 B7
Lyon Rd
Altrincham WA14 ... 119 C7
Kearsley BL4 ... 60 E6
Wigan WN6 ... 37 A2
Lyon Road Ind Est M28 ... 60 F6
Lyons Dr BL8 ... 27 A1
Lyons Fold M33 ... 108 B6
Lyons Rd M17 ... 96 A7
Lyon St
Ashton-in-M WN4 ... 72 F7
Shaw OL2 ... 149 B3
Swinton M27 ... 79 E7
Wigan WN3 ... 150 B3
Lyra Pl M7 ... 81 C3
Lysander Cl M14 ... 110 B8
Lytham Ave M21 ... 109 C7
Lytham Cl OL6 ... 85 E6
Lytham Ct OL6 ... 85 E6
Lytham Dr
Bramhall SK7 ... 133 A7
Heywood OL10 ... 29 C1
Lytham Rd
Ashton-in-M WN4 ... 72 F5
Gatley SK8 ... 122 B1
Manchester M14, M19 ... 98 F1
Urmston M41 ... 94 C2
Lytham St
Rochdale OL12 ... 14 E3
Stockport SK3 ... 170 C2
Lytherton Ave M44 ... 105 D4
Lytton Ave M8 ... 156 A2
Lytton Rd M43 ... 84 A2
Lytton St BL1 ... 143 A2

M

Mabel Ave
Bolton BL3 ... 42 A3
Worsley M28 ... 79 A7
Mabel Rd M35 ... 66 A1
Mabel's Brow BL4 ... 60 E7
Mabel St
9 Bolton BL1 ... 144 C4
Failsworth M40 ... 83 D5
2 Rochdale OL12 ... 14 D2
Ravensdale BL5 ... 74 F8
Westhoughton BL5 ... 57 F6
Maberry Cl WN6 ... 35 D7
Mabfield Rd M14 ... 98 C1
Mableden Cl SK8 ... 131 D8
Mab's Cross Ho 5
WN1 ... 37 C1
Mab's Cross Prim Sch
WN1 ... 37 D1
Mabs Ct OL6 ... 85 D2
Macaulay St
Rochdale OL11 ... 30 D2
Royton OL2 ... 48 E4
Macauley Cl SK16 ... 102 A7
Macauley Pl WN3 ... 54 F4

Macauley Rd
Manchester M16 ... 97 B2
Reddish SK5 ... 99 E1
Macauley Way 7
M34 ... 113 A8
McCall Wlk M11 ... 43 B2
Macclesfield Cl WN2 ... 56 C5
Macclesfield Rd
Alderley Edge SK9 ... 137 B1
Hazel Grove SK7 ... 133 F8
Wilmslow SK9 ... 137 D6
McConnell Rd M40 ... 83 A7
McCormack Dr WN1 ... 151 A4
MCCready Dr M5 ... 161 B4
Macdonald Ave
Farnworth BL4 ... 60 B7
Wigan WN3 ... 55 A3
Macdonald Rd M44 ... 105 E8
Macdonald St
Oldham OL8 ... 66 F4
Wigan WN5 ... 54 B6
McDonna St BL1 ... 142 C4
Mcdonough Cl OL8 ... 67 A3
Macefin Ave M21 ... 109 D4
McEvoy St 6 BL1 ... 143 C2
MacFarren St M12 ... 99 A3
McGinty Pl M11 ... 163 A4
McKean St BL3 ... 42 A4
Mackenzie Ave WN3 ... 55 A3
Mackenzie Gr BL1 ... 24 D5
Mackenzie Ind Pk
SK3 ... 123 B6
Mackenzie Rd M7 ... 81 B6
Mackenzie St
Bolton BL1 ... 143 A4
Manchester M12 ... 99 A3
Mackenzie Wlk OL1 ... 49 E5
Mackeson Dr OL6 ... 85 E4
Mackeson Rd OL6 ... 85 E4
Mckie Cl OL10 ... 67 A3
Mackintosh Way M3 ... 153 C3
Mackworth St M15 ... 162 E3
McLaren Ct M21 ... 97 A1
Maclaren Dr M8 ... 63 E1
McLean Dr M44 ... 94 B4
Maclure Rd OL11 ... 139 C2
Macnair Ct SK6 ... 126 A5
Macnair Mews SK6 ... 126 A5
McNaught St 26 OL16 ... 31 B6
Madams Wood Rd
M28 ... 60 A3
Maddison Rd M43 ... 99 F8
Madeira Pl M10 ... 79 C2
Madeley Cl
Altrincham WA14 ... 128 E8
Wigan WN3 ... 54 E3
Madeley Dr OL9 ... 152 B2
Madeley Gdns
Bolton BL1 ... 143 B2
Maden's Sq 9 OL15 ... 16 B5
Maden St M29 ... 76 F6
Maden Wlk OL9 ... 152 B4
Madison Apartments
M16 ... 161 B1
Madison Ave
Cheadle SK8 ... 123 A2
Droylsden M34 ... 100 C8
Madison Gdns BL5 ... 40 A2
Madison Pk BL5 ... 40 A2
Madison St M18 ... 99 F6
Madras Rd SK3 ... 123 C7
Maesbrook Dr M29 ... 77 A8
Mafeking Ave BL9 ... 28 A5
Mafeking Pl WN4 ... 73 C3
Mafeking Rd BL2 ... 42 E7
Mafeking St OL8 ... 66 C3
Magdala St
Heywood OL10 ... 46 E8
Oldham OL1 ... 153 B4
Magdalen Dr WN4 ... 72 F4
Magda Rd SK2 ... 124 D5
Magenta Ave M44 ... 105 E6
Magna Carta Ct M6, M27 ... 58 A4
Magnolia Cl
6 Partington M31 ... 105 E2
Sale M33 ... 107 C6
Magnolia Ct
6 Sale M33 ... 107 C6
6 Salford M6 ... 81 A2
Magpie Cl M43 ... 84 C3
Magpie La OL4 ... 67 E4
Magpie Wlk 8 M11 ... 160 C1
Magpie Way SK13 ... 104 A6
Maher Gdns M15 ... 97 E4
Mahogany Wlk 11
M33 ... 107 C5
Mahood St SK3 ... 170 A3
Maida St M12 ... 99 B2
Maiden Cl
5 Ashton-u-L OL7 ... 85 A6
Bury BL9 ... 2 F8
Maiden Mews 4 M27 ... 79 F7
Maidford Cl
Manchester M4 ... 160 A1
Stretford M32 ... 96 E2
Maidstone Ave M21 ... 97 A1
Maidstone Cl WN7 ... 57 C2
Maidstone Mews 2
M21 ... 97 A1
Maidstone Rd SK4 ... 110 D3
Maidstone Wlk 5
M34 ... 101 A1
Main Ave M19 ... 110 C7
Main Dr OL1 ... 48 D1
Maine Rd M14 ... 98 A3
Mainhill Wlk M40 ... 83 C5

Main La WA3 ... 90 F3
Mainprice Cl M6 ... 154 C4
Main Rd
Oldham OL9 ... 152 C3
Swinton M27 ... 62 C3
Mains Ave WN2 ... 73 F7
Main St
Billinge WN5 ... 71 E5
Failsworth M35 ... 83 F8
Hyde SK14 ... 167 A4
Mainwaring Dr SK9 ... 137 D8
Mainwaring Terr
M23 ... 109 A2
Mainway M24 ... 64 F6
Mainway E M24 ... 65 C6
Mainwood Rd WA15 ... 120 C5
Maismore Rd M22 ... 121 B1
Maitland Ave M21 ... 109 D5
Maitland Cl
Rochdale OL12 ... 15 C3
Walsden OL12 ... 6 A8
Maitland St
Stockport SK1 ... 124 B7
Walsden OL12 ... 6 A8
Maitland Wlk OL9 ... 152 B4
Maizefield Cl SK8 ... 133 A8
Majestic Mews WN5 ... 53 D5
Major St
Manchester M1 ... 163 A4
Milnrow OL16 ... 31 F6
Ramsbottom BL0 ... 138 B2
Wigan WN5 ... 54 C6
Major Wlk M5 ... 161 B4
Makants Cl
Over Hulton M46 ... 58 F5
Tyldesley M29 ... 77 E8
Makepeace Wlk M8 ... 63 E2
Makerfield Dr WA12 ... 89 A5
Makerfield Way WN2 ... 56 B7
Makin Cl OL10 ... 29 D1
Makinson Arc 15
WN1 ... 150 C4
Makinson Ave
Hindley WN2 ... 56 E7
Horwich BL6 ... 22 E1
Makinson La BL6 ... 22 F4
Makin St M1 ... 163 A3
Makkah St M40 ... 83 A5
Malaga Ave M90 ... 130 B7
Malakoff St SK15 ... 85 E1
Malbern Ind Est M43 ... 100 D4
Malbrook Wlk 3
M13 ... 163 C2
Malby St OL1 ... 153 C4
Malcolm Ave M27 ... 62 A3
Malcolm Dr M27 ... 62 A2
Malcolm St OL11 ... 30 D3
Malden Gr M23 ... 121 A7
Maldon Cl
Hazel Grove SK2 ... 125 A6
Little Lever BL3 ... 40 A3
Wigan WN2 ... 37 F2
Maldon Cres M27 ... 79 F6
Maldon Dr M30 ... 79 E4
Maldon Rd WN6 ... 36 F8
Maldon St OL11 ... 139 C1
Maldwyn Ave
Bolton BL3 ... 146 C2
Manchester M8 ... 64 A2
Maleham St M7 ... 155 B2
Malgam Dr M20 ... 122 B8
Malham Ave WN3 ... 55 A2
Malham Cl
Leigh WN7 ... 75 C5
Royton OL2 ... 48 D4
Malham Ct SK2 ... 124 D6
Malham Dr M45 ... 63 A8
Malham Gdns 8 BL3 ... 146 C3
Malika Pl WN4 ... 72 C2
Malimson Bourne M7 ... 155 A2
Mallaig Wlk M11 ... 165 C4
Mallard Cl
Dukinfield SK16 ... 101 E7
Hazel Grove SK2 ... 125 A5
1 Oldham OL8 ... 66 D2
Mallard Cres SK12 ... 133 A4
Mallard Ct SK8 ... 131 B8
Mallard Dr BL6 ... 22 A3
Mallard Gn WA14 ... 119 B8
Mallards Reach SK6 ... 113 A2
Mallard St M1 ... 163 A3
Mallet Cres BL1 ... 23 F2
Malley Gdns OL5 ... 86 D8
Malling Rd M23 ... 121 A4
Mallison St BL1 ... 143 C3
Mallory Ave OL7 ... 85 B5
Mallory Dr WA14 ... 119 C3
Mallory Dr WN7 ... 76 C5
Mallory Rd SK14 ... 102 A4
Mallory Wlk M23 ... 120 D8
Mallow Croft OL16 ... 31 C4
Mallow Dr M9 ... 78 B8
Mallowdale Ave
M14 ... 110 B8
Mallowdale Cl BL1 ... 40 D7
Mallowdale Rd SK2 ... 124 E5
Mallow St M15 ... 97 E4
Mall The
Bury BL9 ... 140 C2
3 Eccles M30 ... 79 F2
Sale M33 ... 108 B5
Stalybridge SK15 ... 102 E6
Malmesbury Cl SK12 ... 133 A4
Malmesbury Rd SK8 ... 132 B6
Malpas Ave WN1 ... 37 E1

Malpas Cl
Cheadle SK8 ... 123 A4
Handforth SK9 ... 131 E1
Malpas Dr WA14 ... 107 E1
Malpas St
Manchester M12 ... 165 A2
Oldham OL1 ... 153 C3
Malpas Wlk M16 ... 162 A1
Malrae WA15 ... 137 E4
Malsham Rd M23 ... 108 F2
Malta St M4 ... 160 A1
Oldham OL4 ... 67 D6
Maltby Ct OL4 ... 67 F5
Maltby Dr BL3 ... 146 C3
Maltby Rd M23 ... 120 F6
Maltings La 7 OL11 ... 30 C2
Malton Ave
Bolton BL3 ... 146 A4
Golborne WA3 ... 90 E7
Manchester M21 ... 109 B8
Whitefield M45 ... 44 F2
Malton Cl
Chadderton OL9 ... 47 F1
Leigh WN7 ... 75 C6
6 Whitefield M45 ... 44 F2
Malton Dr
Altrincham WA14 ... 119 A6
Hazel Grove SK7 ... 133 D7
Malton Rd
Boothstown M28 ... 77 E7
Stockport SK4 ... 168 A4
Walton OL8 ... 113 B2
Malt St M15 ... 162 A3
Malus Ct M6 ... 81 A3
Malvern Ave
Ashton-u-L OL6 ... 85 C7
Atherton M46 ... 58 F5
Bolton BL1 ... 142 A1
Bury BL9 ... 27 F5
Droylsden M43 ... 84 A2
Hindley WN2 ... 57 A4
Urmston M41 ... 95 B2
Wythenshawe SK8 ... 121 F5
Malvern Cl
Ashton-in-M WN4 ... 73 B4
2 Farnworth BL4 ... 59 F8
Horwich BL6 ... 22 C5
Milnrow OL16 ... 32 A7
Pendlebury M27 ... 80 B6
Prestwich M25 ... 63 C5
Royton OL2 ... 48 C3
5 Shaw OL2 ... 48 F8
Stockport SK4 ... 169 A3
Wigan WN3 ... 54 C3
Malvern Cres WN3 ... 55 F4
Malvern Dr
Altrincham WA14 ... 119 B5
Mossley OL3, OL5, SK15 ... 68 C3
Oldham OL8 ... 66 C3
Pendlebury M27 ... 80 B7
Malvern Rd M24 ... 65 A5
Malvern Rise SK13 ... 104 A5
Malvern Row 1 M15 ... 162 A2
Malvern St E OL11 ... 30 C7
Malvern St W OL11 ... 30 C7
Malvern St
Manchester M15 ... 162 A2
Oldham OL8 ... 153 A1
Standish WN6 ... 19 D3
Malvern Terr WN7 ... 75 F3
Malvern Way BB4 ... 1 A7
Manby Rd M18 ... 99 B4
Mancentral Trad Est
M3 ... 158 A1
MANCHESTER ... 159 B3
Manchester Acad M15 ... 98 B4
Manchester Airport Sta
M90 ... 130 B7
Manchester Bsns Pk
M22 ... 130 D8
Manchester Bsns Sch
M15 ... 163 A2
Manchester CE Cath* M3 ... 158 C2
Manchester Chambers
OL1 ... 153 B3
Manchester City Art Gal* M1 ... 159 A1
Manchester Coll of Arts & Tech (Openshaw Campus) M11 ... 165 B3
Manchester Coll of Art & Tech Manchester Nti M40 ... 157 C2
Manchester Coll of Art & Tech (St John's Ctr) M3 ... 158 B1
Manchester Evening News Arena* M3 ... 158 C3
Manchester Fort Sh Pk M8 ... 156 B1
Manchester Gram Sch The M13 ... 98 C2
Manchester High Sch for Girls M14 ... 98 C1
Manchester Ind Pk M40 ... 157 C1
Manchester International Airport M90 ... 130 A7
Manchester Islamic High Sch for Girls M21 ... 109 A8

Manchester Jewish Mus* M8 ... 159 A4
Manchester Jun Girls Sch M7 ... 63 E1
Manchester Mesivta Sch M25 ... 63 B3
Manchester Met Univ, Didsbury Campus The M20 ... 110 B2
Manchester Met Univ, Elizabeth Gaskell Campus M13 ... 98 C4
Manchester Met Univ, Hollings Bldg M14 ... 98 D2
Manchester Met Univ The M1, M13, M15 ... 163 A3
Manchester Met Univ The (Aytoun Campus) M1 ... 163 B4
Manchester Muslim Prep Sch M20 ... 110 B6
Manchester Mus The* M13 ... 163 B2
Manchester New Rd
Middleton M24, M9 ... 64 F6
Partington M31 ... 105 F3
Manchester Old Rd
Bury BL9 ... 140 B1
Middleton M24 ... 64 D7
Manchester RC Cath* M3 ... 158 A2
Manchester Rd
Altrincham WA14 ... 119 D7
Ashton-u-L M34, M43, OL7 ... 84 E1
Bolton BL3 ... 42 B4
Bury BL9 ... 140 B2
Bury, Blackford Bridge BL9, M45 ... 44 F5
Carrington M31 ... 106 B6
Cheadle M20, SK8 ... 122 D7
Denton M34 ... 100 C3
Droylsden M34 ... 100 B8
Dukinfield SK14 ... 101 C3
Glossop SK13, SK14 ... 103 E7
Handforth SK9 ... 131 C2
Haslingden BB4 ... 1 D7
Heywood OL10 ... 46 D7
Hollinfare, Hollins Green WA3 ... 105 B3
Hollinfare WA3 ... 105 A2
Ince-in-M WN2, WN1 ... 56 A7
Kearsley BL4, M27 ... 61 D4
Leigh M29, WN7 ... 76 D4
Manchester M16, M21 ... 97 B1
Manchester M21 ... 109 A8
Mossley OL3, OL5, SK15 ... 68 D3
Oldham OL8 ... 66 C3
Pendlebury M27 ... 80 B7
Ramsbottom BL0, BL9 ... 11 E4
Reddish M34 ... 100 B4
Rochdale OL11 ... 30 C4
Scot Lane End BL6 ... 38 E8
Shaw OL2 ... 149 A1
Swinton M27, M28 ... 61 C2
Tyldesley M29 ... 77 C8
Walkden M28 ... 60 E2
Westhoughton BL5 ... 40 B1
Manchester Rd E M38 ... 60 B4
Manchester Rd N
M34 ... 100 D4
Manchester Rd S
M34 ... 100 D3
Manchester Rd W M38 ... 59 E5
Manchester Road Prim Sch M43 ... 83 E1
Manchester Royal Infmy M13 ... 163 C1
Manchester Science Pk M15 ... 163 A1
Manchester St
Heywood OL10 ... 29 E1
Manchester M16 ... 97 A1
Oldham OL8, OL9 ... 153 A2
Manchester United Mus* M32 ... 96 F5
Manchet St OL11 ... 30 B1
Mancroft Ave BL3 ... 147 A4
Mancroft Terr BL3 ... 147 A4
Mancroft Wlk 1 M1 ... 163 B3
Mancunian M41 ... 113 A8
Mancunian Way
Manchester M1, M12, M15 ... 163 B3
Manchester, St George's
Mandalay Gdns SK6 ... 125 D7
Mandarin Gn WA14 ... 119 B8
Mandarin Wlk 8 M6 ... 81 A3
Mandeville St M19 ... 111 B8
Mandeville Terr BL8 ... 10 B2
Mandley Ave M40 ... 65 D2
Mandley Cl BL3 ... 43 A5
Mandley Park Ave
M7 ... 155 B3
Mandon Cl M26 ... 43 E5
Manesty Cl M24 ... 46 C2
Manet Cl M7 ... 81 B8
Mangle St M1 ... 159 B1
Mango Pl M6 ... 81 A2
Manifold Dr SK6 ... 134 F6
Manifold St M6 ... 81 B5

Manilla Wlk 1 M11.....160 C1
Manipur St M11.....164 C4
Manley Ave
Golborne WA3.....73 F2
Swinton M27.....61 E4
Manley Cl
Leigh WN7.....75 D8
Ramsbottom BL9.....11 C2
Manley Cres BL5.....40 B1
Manley Gr
Bramhall SK7.....132 E6
Mottram in I SK14.....102 F3
Manley Park Jun Sch
M16.....97 C3
Manley Park Prim Sch
M16.....97 C3
Manley Rd
Manchester M16, M21.....97 D1
Oldham OL8.....66 E4
Rochdale OL11.....30 C3
Rochdale OL11.....30 C4
Sale M33.....107 F1
Manley St
Ince-in-M WN3.....151 B2
Salford M7.....155 A2
Manley Terr BL1.....143 B4
Manley Way SK14.....103 B3
Manning Ave M36.....37 A2
Manningham Rd BL3.....144 B3
Mannington Dr M9.....156 C3
Mannion Ho WN1.....153 A4
Mannock St OL8.....153 A2
Manns OL3.....68 F5
Manns The BL8.....68 F5
Manor Ave
Golborne WA3.....90 C8
Little Lever BL3.....43 C3
Manchester M16.....97 D2
Sale M33.....107 D4
Urmston M41.....95 D1
Manor Cl
Bramhall SK8.....123 C1
Chadderton OL9.....152 C4
Denton M34.....101 B2
Garswood WN4.....72 C3
Uppermill OL4.....68 E5
Wilmslow SK9.....136 F8
Manor Ct
Bury BL9.....27 E7
Golborne WA3.....90 C8
Sale M33.....107 D4
5 Stockport SK1.....112 A1
Stretford M32.....96 B1
Manordale Wlk M40.....156 C1
Manor Dr
Manchester M21.....109 D4
Royton OL2.....48 E3
Manor Farm Cl OL7.....84 F5
Manor Farm Rise OL4.....67 D7
Manorfield Cl BL1.....142 A1
Manor Gate Rd BL2.....43 A8
Manor Gdns SK9.....137 D7
Manor Gr
Aspull WN2.....38 B5
Leigh WN7.....76 C3
Wigan WN5.....54 B8
Manor Green Prim Sch
M34.....113 A8
Manor High Sch M33.....107 D5
Manor Hill Rd SK6.....125 F7
Manor Ho M36.....136 D3
Manor House Cl WA11.....71 B1
Manorial Dr M38.....59 E5
Manor La OL3.....51 E8
Manor Lo
Bramhall SK8.....123 C1
Pendlebury M27.....80 D8
Manor Mill Cl OL2.....15 D3
Manor Park Rd SK13.....104 C1
Manor Park View
SK13.....104 E2
Manor Pk M41.....95 D1
Manor Pl WN3.....151 C2
Manor Rd
Altrincham WA15.....119 E4
Bramhall SK7, SK8.....123 C1
Brinnington SK5.....112 C4
Denton M34.....101 B1
Droylsden, Fairfield
M34.....100 B7
Droylsden, Greenside
M43.....83 F1
Dukinfield SK14.....101 F5
Hindley WN2.....56 F5
Horwich BL6.....22 D4
Manchester M19.....99 B2
Marple SK6.....125 F7
Middleton M24.....65 A6
Oldham OL4.....67 C4
Romiley SK6.....113 B5
Sale M33.....108 B5
Salford M6.....154 A4
Shaw OL2.....149 A2
Shevington WN6.....36 A6
Stretford M32.....96 B2
Swinton M27.....79 F6
Tyldesley M29.....77 C6
Wilmslow SK9.....136 E8
Manor St
Bolton BL1.....145 C3
Bury BL9.....141 A2
Denton M34.....100 F7
Farnworth BL4.....60 C7
Glossop SK13.....104 D1
Golborne WA3.....74 B1

Manor St *continued*
Kearsley BL4.....61 B5
Manchester M12.....163 C3
Middleton M24.....47 A2
Mossley OL5.....68 C2
Oldham OL2.....49 A2
Ramsbottom BL0.....138 B3
Wigan WN1.....150 C4
Wigan, Worsley Hall
WN5.....54 F6
Manor View SK6.....113 B5
Manor Way PR7.....19 D8
Manor Wlk M34.....100 F7
Mansart Cl WN4.....73 D3
Manse Ave M6.....18 F5
Manse Gdns WA12.....89 D4
Mansell Way BL6.....39 D8
Manse The OL5.....86 C8
Mansfield Ave
Denton M34.....100 D5
Manchester M9.....64 D4
Ramsbottom BL0.....11 C2
Mansfield Cl
Ashton-u-L OL7.....84 F1
Denton M34.....100 D5
Mansfield Dr M9.....64 D4
Mansfield Gr BL1.....142 B1
Mansfield Grange
OL11.....30 C6
Mansfield Rd
Hyde SK14.....167 C1
Manchester M9.....64 E4
Mossley OL5.....68 E1
7 Oldham OL8.....67 B5
Rochdale OL11.....29 E7
Urmston M41.....95 B1
Mansfield St
Ashton-u-L OL7.....84 F1
Golborne WA3.....73 F1
Mansfield View OL5.....68 E1
Mansford Dr M40.....157 C1
Manshaw Cres M34.....100 A7
Manshaw Rd M11,
M34.....100 A7
Mansion Ave M45.....44 E3
Mansion The WA3.....91 D3
Manson Ave M15.....162 A3
Manstead Wlk M40.....160 B2
Manston Dr SK8.....123 A2
Manswood Dr M8.....156 A3
Mantell Wlk M40.....83 A5
Manthorpe Ave M28.....79 A7
Mantley La OL1, OL3.....50 A7
Manton Ave
Manchester M9.....65 B2
Reddish M34.....100 A3
Manton Cl M7.....155 A2
Manvers St SK5.....169 B3
Manwaring St M35.....83 E8
Manway Bsns Pk
WA14.....119 E8
Maple Ave
Altrincham WA15.....120 E5
Atherton M46.....58 B4
Bolton BL1.....142 B1
Bury BL9.....141 B2
Cheadle SK8.....122 F2
Denton M34.....100 E3
Droylsden M34.....84 B1
Eccles M30.....79 A4
Golborne WA3.....90 F7
Hindley WN2.....56 F3
Horwich BL6.....22 E1
Ince-in-M WN2.....155 F8
Manchester M21.....109 B8
Marple SK6.....125 F4
Newton-le-W WA12.....89 D2
Poynton SK12.....133 F3
Stalybridge SK15.....101 F8
Stretford M32.....96 D1
Whitefield M45.....62 F6
Maple Cl
Billinge WN5.....71 D5
Chadderton OL9.....48 B1
Kearsley BL4.....60 F5
Middleton M24.....65 D8
Sale M33.....107 C4
Salford M6.....154 C3
Shaw OL2.....48 F8
Stockport SK2.....124 B6
Maple Cres WN7.....75 F7
Maplecroft SK1.....124 B8
Maple Ct SK4.....168 C4
Mapledon Rd M9.....157 C4
Maple Dr WN2.....74 B7
Maplefield Dr M28.....78 B7
Maple Gr
Bury BL8.....27 A5
Failsworth, Holt Lane End
M35.....83 E5
Failsworth, New Moston
M40.....65 F2
Prestwich M25.....63 A6
Ramsbottom BL0.....11 D6
Walkden M28.....78 D8
Wigan WN6.....37 A3
Maple Lo M23.....120 C8
Maple Rd
Alderley Edge SK9.....137 B3
Bramhall SK7.....132 E6
Chadderton OL9.....48 B1
Farnworth BL4.....60 A8
Partington M31.....105 C3
Sale M23.....108 C1
Swinton M27.....79 F6

Maple Rd W M23.....120 C8
Maples SK9.....136 F6
Maple St
Ashton-in-M WN4.....73 A6
Bolton BL3.....145 A1
Bolton, Bradshaw BL2.....25 C5
Oldham OL8.....66 C3
Rochdale OL11.....139 A2
Walsden OL14.....6 A7
Maple Wlk
Bolton, Darcy Lever
BL3.....42 E5
Wythenshawe M23.....120 C8
Maplewood Cl
5 Manchester M9.....64 C2
Royton OL2.....48 C2
Maplewood Ct M7.....155 A3
Maplewood Gdns
BL1.....143 C2
Maplewood Gr SK15.....86 C3
Maplewood Ho BL1.....143 B1
Maplewood Rd SK9.....137 E8
Mapley Ave M22.....121 D8
Maplin Cl M13.....163 C3
Maplin Dr SK2.....125 A5
Maranatha Ct 6 M30.....95 D8
Marble St
Manchester M2.....159 A1
Oldham OL1.....67 B8
Marbury Ave M14.....98 B1
Marbury Cl
Cheadle SK3.....123 A7
Urmston M41.....94 D3
Marbury Dr WA14.....107 C1
Marbury Gr WN6.....36 E8
Marbury Rd
Handforth SK9.....131 B1
Reddish SK4.....111 D7
Marcer Rd M40.....160 A2
March Ave SK4.....168 B2
Marchbank WN2.....38 A2
Marchbank Dr SK8.....122 C6
March Dr BL8.....27 D5
Marchers Mews 7
M30.....79 B1
Marches Cl OL2.....49 B4
Marchioness St 6
M18.....99 F6
Marchmont Cl M13.....164 A2
March St OL2.....31 A7
Marchwood Ave M21.....97 D1
Marcliffe Dr
Reddish M19.....99 C1
Rochdale OL11.....30 B6
Marcliff Gr SK4.....168 B2
Marcroft Pl 8 OL11.....31 A4
Marcus Garvey Ct M16.....97 E2
Marcus Gr M14.....98 C3
Marcus St BL1.....142 B1
Mardale Ave
Manchester M20.....110 C5
Royton OL2.....48 C8
Swinton M27.....61 C2
Urmston M41.....94 F3
Mardale Cl
Atherton M46.....58 C5
Bolton BL2.....25 F1
Oldham OL4.....67 D8
Prestwich M25.....63 C7
Stalybridge SK15.....86 A3
Mardale Dr
1 Bolton BL2.....25 F1
Gatley SK8.....122 B6
Middleton M24.....46 E1
Mardyke OL12.....139 B4
Mardale Rd M27.....79 D6
Marden Rd M23.....121 A5
Marfield Ave OL9.....152 A1
Marford Cl M22.....121 D6
Marford Cres M33.....107 F2
Margaret Ashton Cl
M9.....157 C3
Margaret Ave
Rochdale OL16.....31 C7
Wigan WN6.....36 C4
Margaret Ho 5 OL6.....166 A2
Margaret Rd
Denton M34.....101 A4
Droylsden M43.....83 E2
Margaret Sands St 9
M15.....162 A2
Margaret St
Ashton-u-L OL6.....166 A2
Ashton-u-L OL6.....166 A1
1 Bury BL9.....140 C1
Heywood OL10.....29 B2
Hindley WN2.....56 D6
Oldham OL8.....66 B2
Reddish SK5.....111 E7
Shaw OL2.....149 B2
Wigan WN6.....37 A1
Margaret Terr OL6.....166 A2
Margate Ave M40.....83 B5
Margate Rd SK5.....111 F7
Margrove Chase BL6.....40 C5
Margrove Cl M35.....84 C7
Margrove Rd M6.....80 C4
Margroy Cl OL12.....15 A2
Marguerita Rd M40.....83 D4
Marham Cl M21.....109 E6
Marhill Cl SK1.....143 B2
Marie Cl M34.....100 F2
Marie St M7.....155 D5
Marigold St
Rochdale OL11.....139 C1
Wigan WN5.....54 D7
Marigold Terr M24.....65 D7

Mariman Dr M8.....64 A2
Marina Ave M34.....101 A1
Marina Cl SK9.....131 D5
Marina Cres M11.....83 B3
Marina Dr
Marple SK6.....125 C2
Wigan WN5.....54 D5
Marina Rd
Droylsden M43.....84 B2
Romiley SK6.....112 E4
Marine Ave M31.....105 D3
Marion Pl WN2.....73 F8
Marion St
Farnworth BL3.....42 C2
Oldham OL8.....66 F3
Maritime Cl WA12.....89 C5
Maritime Ct 5 M33.....107 E3
Marjorie Cl M18.....165 B2
Mark Ave M6.....81 B4
Markenfield Dr M2.....48 F7
Market App 3 WN4.....73 B3
Market Arc 2 SK13.....104 C1
Market Ave M6.....166 B3
Market Chambers
BL0.....138 C3
Marketgate Sh Ctr
WN1.....150 C4
Market Par BL1.....140 C2
Market Pl
Adlington PR7.....21 A7
Ashton-u-L OL6.....166 B3
13 Atherton M46.....58 D3
Bury BL9.....140 B2
Compstall SK6.....114 A2
Edenfield BL0.....1 D3
Farnworth BL4.....60 D8
Heywood OL10.....29 D2
Hyde SK14.....167 A2
Leigh WN7.....75 F5
Middleton M24.....47 A2
Mottram in I SK14.....103 A3
Oldham OL1.....153 B3
Ramsbottom BL0.....138 C3
11 Royton OL2.....48 E4
Standish WN6.....19 E1
Stockport SK1.....169 C2
Wigan WN1.....150 C4
Market Pl The BL1.....145 C4
Market Prec BL4.....60 D8
Market Sq OL2.....48 D4
Market St
Adlington PR7.....21 A6
Altrincham WA14.....119 D4
Ashton-u-L OL6.....166 B3
Atherton M46.....58 C3
Bolton BL1.....145 A3
Broadbottom SK14.....115 A8
Bury BL9.....140 C1
Bury, Gigg BL9.....44 F8
Bury, Tottington BL8.....26 F6
Denton M34.....100 F3
Disley SK12.....135 D6
Droylsden M43.....84 B1
Edenfield BL0.....1 D4
Farnworth BL4.....42 D1
Glossop SK13.....104 C1
Heywood OL10.....29 C2
Hindley WN2.....56 D5
Hollingworth SK14.....103 D5
Hyde SK14.....167 A2
Kearsley M26.....61 B8
Leigh WN7.....75 F5
Little Lever BL3.....43 B3
Manchester M1.....159 A1
Manchester M4.....158 C2
Marple SK6.....125 F6
5 Middleton M24.....46 F1
Mossley OL5.....68 C1
Mottram in L SK14.....103 A4
Newton-le-W WA12.....89 A3
11 Rawtenstall BL4.....2 E8
Shaw OL2.....149 B2
Stalybridge SK15.....86 A2
Standish WN6.....19 E1
Swinton M27.....62 A1
Tyldesley M29.....58 F1
Westhoughton BL5.....57 E8
Whitworth OL12, OL13.....4 D4
Wigan WN1.....150 C4
Market Street Sta M1....159 A1
Market Way
Rochdale OL16.....139 C4
Salford M6.....154 C3
Market Wlk M33.....108 B4
Markfield Ave M13.....164 A1
Markham Cl
Dukinfield SK14.....101 D6
Manchester M12.....164 B4
Markham St SK14.....101 D5
Markington St M14.....98 A3
Mark Jones Wlk M40.....83 B5
Mark La OL2.....49 D6
MARKLAND OL16.....150 A4
MARKLAND HILL.....40 E8
Markland Hill BL1.....40 E8
Markland Hill Cl BL1.....23 F1
Markland Hill La BL1.....23 F1
Markland Hill Prim Sch
BL1.....40 F8
Marklands Rd
Horwich BL6.....22 E5
Standish WN6.....19 A4
Markland St
6 Bolton BL3.....145 C2
Hyde SK14.....167 B1
Ramsbottom BL0.....138 C3
Wigan WN1.....151 B4
Markland Tops BL1.....23 F1

Marks St M26.....44 A3
Mark St
Bacup OL13.....3 C8
Boothstown M28.....77 F7
Oldham OL9.....153 A3
Rochdale OL12.....15 B1
Mark Wood Rd SL3.....50 F4
MARLAND.....30 A4
Marland Ave
Cheadle SK8.....122 F2
Oldham OL8.....67 A1
Rochdale OL11.....30 B4
Marland Cl OL11.....30 B5
Marland Cres SK5.....111 F8
Marland Fold OL11.....30 B5
Marland Fold La OL8.....66 F1
Marland Hill Com Prim
Sch OL11.....30 C5
Marland Hill Rd OL11.....30 C4
Marland Old Rd OL11.....30 C4
Marlands Sq 15 M29.....58 F1
Marland St OL9.....66 A3
Marland Way M32.....96 D3
Marlborough Ave
Alderley Edge SK9.....137 B2
Denton M34.....123 B2
Ince-in-M WN3.....55 F4
Manchester M16.....97 C2
Marlborough Cl
Ashton-u-L OL7.....100 E8
Denton M34.....100 F3
Marple SK6.....125 D7
Ramsbottom BL0.....11 C3
Whitworth OL12.....14 C7
Marlborough Ct BL1.....23 E2
Marlborough Dr
Failsworth M35.....83 E6
Reddish SK4.....169 A4
Marlborough Gdns 3
BL4.....59 F8
Marlborough Gr M43.....84 C2
Marlborough Rd
Altrincham WA14.....119 D2
Atherton M46.....58 F4
Hyde SK14.....113 E8
Irlam M44.....94 B3
Royton OL2.....48 E2
Sale M33.....108 B3
Salford, Ellesmere Park
M30.....80 A4
Salford, Higher Broughton
M7.....155 C3
Salford M7, M8.....155 C2
Stretford M32.....96 C3
Urmston M41.....94 F2
Marlborough Rd Prim Sch
M7.....155 C2
Marlborough St
5 Ashton-u-L OL7.....84 F1
Bolton BL1.....145 A4
Heywood OL10.....46 E8
Oldham OL4.....67 A6
4 Rochdale OL12.....14 C1
Marlborough St BL5.....57 E5
Marlbrook Wlk BL3.....147 E4
Marlcroft Ave SK4.....168 B2
Marlcroft Cl M23.....121 A7
Marle Ave OL5.....68 A1
Marle Croft M45.....62 C6
Marled Way BL7.....9 D5
Marle Rise OL5.....68 C1
Marler Rd SK14.....167 B4
Marley Cl WA15.....119 F7
Marley Dr M33.....108 A6
Marleyer Cl M40.....83 C7
Marleyer Rise SK6.....125 A8
Marley Rd
Manchester M19.....111 B8
Poynton SK12.....133 E2
Marlfield Ct M41.....94 E1
Marlfield Rd
Altrincham WA15.....129 C3
Shaw OL2.....48 E8
Marlfield St M9.....64 E1
Marl Gr WN5.....53 D4
Marlhill Cl SK2.....124 E5
Marlhill Ct SK2.....124 E5
Marlinford Dr M40.....83 C5
Marloes WA14.....119 B2
Marlor Ct OL10.....29 B2
Marlor St M34.....100 E4
Marlow Brow SK13.....104 A4
Marlow Dr
Altrincham WA14.....119 F6
Handforth SK9.....131 C5
Irlam M44.....94 A3
Swinton M27.....79 F7
Marlowe Cl WN3.....150 A1
Marlowe Dr M20.....110 A4
Marlowe Wlk 15 M34.....113 A7
Marlowes The WN5.....112 F2
Marlow Ho 9 M5.....154 C1
Marlow Rd M9.....64 F1
Marlow St SK13.....104 A5
Marlton Wlk M9.....64 E4
Marlwood Rd BL1.....23 D2
Marmion Cl WA3.....74 E1
Marmion Dr M21.....109 A4
Marne Ave
Ashton-u-L OL6.....85 F5

Marne Ave *continued*
Wythenshawe M22 . . . . 121 E5
Marne Cres OL11 . . . . 30 C7
Marnland Gr BL3 . . . . 40 E4
Marnock Cl WN2 . . . . 74 F8
Maroon Rd M22 . . . . 130 F7
MARPLE 125 D5
Marple Ave BL1 . . . . 25 A4
MARPLE BRIDGE 126 B8
Marple Cl
Oldham OL8 . . . . 66 D2
Shevington Moor WN6 . . . . . . 19 B2
Marple Ct SK1 . . . . 124 A7
Marple Gr M32 . . . . 96 C3
Marple Hall Dr SK6 . . . . . 125 D7
Marple Hall Sch SK6 . . . . 125 C7
Marple Old Rd SK2 . . . . . 125 A6
Marple Rd
Broadbottom SK13 . . . . 115 B5
Stockport SK2 . . . . 124 E6
MARPLERIDGE 126 A2
Marple St M15 . . . . 162 A1
Marple Sta SK6 . . . . 126 A7
Marquis Ave BL9 . . . . 140 B4
Marquis Dr SK8 . . . . 131 D7
Marquis St M19 . . . . 99 D1
Marrick Ave SK8 . . . . 122 C5
Marrick Cl WN3 . . . . 55 A2
Marriott St
Manchester M20 . . . . 110 B6
Stockport SK1 . . . . 170 C4
Marron Pl M2 . . . . 162 C4
Marryat Ct M12 . . . . 164 C2
Mars Ave BL3 . . . . 146 C3
Marsden Cl
Ashton-u-L OL7 . . . . 84 E5
Mossley OL5 . . . . 68 B1
Royton OL16 . . . . 48 C8
Marsden Dr WA15 . . . . . . 120 C6
Marsden Rd
Bolton BL1 . . . . 145 B3
Romiley SK6 . . . . 113 C3
Marsden St
Boothstown M28 . . . . 77 F6
Bury BL9 . . . . 140 C3
Eccles M30 . . . . 79 C3
Glossop SK13 . . . . 104 A4
Ince-in-M WN3 . . . . 55 F4
13 Manchester M2 . . . . 158 C1
2 Middleton M24 . . . . 65 C7
Walkden M28 . . . . 61 B2
Westhoughton BL5 . . . . 57 E8
Wigan WN1 . . . . 150 C4
Wigan, Worsley Hall
WN5 . . . . 54 F6
Marsett Cl OL12 . . . . 14 A1
Marsett Wlk 9 M23 . . . . . 108 F2
Marshall Ct
6 Ashton-u-L OL6 . . . . 85 D2
1 Oldham OL1 . . . . 153 B4
Marshall Rd M19 . . . . 99 A1
Marshall St
Leigh WN7 . . . . 75 E4
Manchester, Brunswick
M12 . . . . 163 C2
Manchester M4 . . . . 159 B2
Rochdale OL16 . . . . 31 C7
Marshall Stevens Way
M17 . . . . 96 B5
Marsham Cl
7 Manchester M13 . . . . 98 E4
Oldham OL4 . . . . 68 B5
Marsham Dr SK6 . . . . 126 A5
Marsham Rd
Hazel Grove SK7 . . . . 124 C1
Westhoughton BL5 . . . . 57 F6
Marshbank 16 BL5 . . . . 39 E1
Marshbrook Cl WN2 . . . . . . 57 A6
Marsh Brook Cl WA3 . . . . 105 A2
Marshbrook Dr M9 . . . . 64 C2
Marsh Brook Fold BL5 . . . . 57 A7
Marshbrook Rd 1
M41 . . . . 95 C3
Marsh Cl SK3 . . . . 170 A2
Marshdale WN7 . . . . 75 D6
Marshdale Rd BL1 . . . . 40 F8
Marshfield Rd WA15 . . . . 120 C6
Marshfield Wlk 10
M13 . . . . 163 C2
Marsh Fold La BL1 . . . . . . 144 C4
Marsh Gn WN5 . . . . 36 D1
MARSH GREEN 36 D1
Marsh Green Prim Sch
WN5 . . . . 54 D8
Marsh Hey Cl M38 . . . . 59 F6
Marsh La
Ashley WA16 . . . . 128 A4
Farnworth BL4 . . . . 60 A8
Little Lever BL3 . . . . 43 B4
Wigan WN1 . . . . 150 C4
Marsh Rd
Little Lever BL3 . . . . 43 B4
Walkden M38 . . . . 60 B4
Marsh Row WN2 . . . . 57 A4
Marsh St
12 Bolton BL1 . . . . 143 B2
Horwich BL6 . . . . 22 A4
Walkden M28 . . . . 60 F2
Westhoughton BL5 . . . . 39 E1
Marshway Dr WA12 . . . . 89 B5
Marsland Ave WA15 . . . . . 120 B8
Marsland Cl M34 . . . . 100 B3
Marsland Green La
M29 . . . . 76 E3
Marsland Rd
Altrincham WA15 . . . . 120 B6
Marple SK6 . . . . 125 D7
Sale M33 . . . . 108 B3
Marslands OL3 . . . . 51 B3
Marsland St N M7 . . . . . . 155 C3
Marsland St S M7 . . . . . . 155 C3
Marsland St
Hazel Grove SK7 . . . . 124 D2
Stockport SK1 . . . . 169 C3
Marsland Street Ind Ctr
SK7 . . . . 124 E2
Marsland Terr SK1 . . . . . . 124 B8
Mars St
Edgworth BL7 . . . . 9 E6
Oldham OL9 . . . . 152 C3
Marston Cl
Failsworth M35 . . . . 84 C6
Horwich BL6 . . . . 39 F8
Whitefield M45 . . . . 63 C8
Marston Dr M44 . . . . 94 B1
Marston Ho 8 M5 . . . . 154 C1
Marston Rd
Salford M7 . . . . 155 B4
Stretford M32 . . . . 96 F2
Marston St M40 . . . . 157 A1
Martens Rd M44 . . . . 105 E5
Marthall Dr M33 . . . . 108 E1
Marthall Way 8 SK9 . . . . 131 E5
Martham Dr SK2 . . . . 125 A6
Martha St
8 Bolton BL3 . . . . 147 A4
Oldham OL1 . . . . 153 A4
Martha's Terr OL16 . . . . . . 15 C3
Martin Ave
Farnworth BL4 . . . . 59 F7
Little Lever BL3 . . . . 43 C3
Newton-le-W WA12 . . . . 89 C5
8 Oldham OL4 . . . . 67 C6
Martin Cl
Denton M34 . . . . 100 F5
Hazel Grove SK2 . . . . 124 F5
Martindale Cl OL2 . . . . 48 E5
Martindale Cres
Manchester M12 . . . . 164 B1
Middleton M24 . . . . 46 D3
Wigan WN5 . . . . 54 F6
Martindale Gdns BL1 . . . . 143 B2
Martindale Rd WA11 . . . . . . 71 C2
Martin Dr M44 . . . . 94 A4
Martingale Cl M26 . . . . 44 A5
Martingale Ct M8 . . . . 156 A3
Martingale Way M43 . . . . . . 84 D2
Martin Gr BL4 . . . . 60 F7
Martin Ho M14 . . . . 98 D3
Martin La OL12 . . . . 14 B1
Martin Rd M27 . . . . 62 B2
Martinsclough BL6 . . . . 40 C6
Martinscroft Rd M23 . . . . . 121 B5
Martins Ct WN2 . . . . 57 A6
Martins Field OL12 . . . . 13 F1
Martin St
8 Atherton M46 . . . . 58 D3
Bury BL9 . . . . 28 D3
Denton M34 . . . . 100 F7
Edgworth BL7 . . . . 9 D4
Hyde SK14 . . . . 167 B2
Salford M5 . . . . 154 B2
Martland Ave
Golborne WA3 . . . . 90 E7
Shevington WN6 . . . . 35 F5
Martland Cres WN6 . . . . 36 E3
Martland Mill La WN5 . . . . 36 D2
Martland Pk WN5 . . . . 36 B2
Martlesham Wlk 5
M4 . . . . 159 A2
Martlet Ave
Disley SK12 . . . . 135 C6
Rochdale OL11 . . . . 29 F7
Martlet Cl M14 . . . . 98 B1
Martlew Dr M46 . . . . 58 F4
Martock Ave M22 . . . . 121 E3
Marton Ave
Bolton BL2 . . . . 148 C4
Manchester M20 . . . . 110 C2
Marton Cl WA3 . . . . 91 E4
Marton Dr M46 . . . . 58 E4
Marton Gn SK3 . . . . 170 A1
Marton Gr SK4 . . . . 111 E6
Marton Grange M25 . . . . 63 E3
Marton Pl M33 . . . . 108 A4
Marton St WN1 . . . . 37 C1
Marton Way 5 SK9 . . . . . . 131 E5
Marus Ave WN3 . . . . 54 F3
MARUS BRIDGE 54 F2
Marus Bridge Prim Sch
WN3 . . . . 54 E2
Marvic Ct M13 . . . . 98 E3
Marwick Cl WN6 . . . . 19 D2
Marwood Cl
Altrincham WA14 . . . . 119 B6
Kearsley M26 . . . . 61 A8
Marwood Dr M23 . . . . 120 F3
Maryfield Cl WA3 . . . . 90 A7
Mary France St M15 . . . . . 162 B2
Mary Hulton Ct BL5 . . . . . . 58 A8
Maryland Ave BL2 . . . . 42 D7
MARYLEBONE 37 D3
Marylebone Ct WN1 . . . . . . 37 D3
Marylebone Pl WN1 . . . . . . 37 D3
Marylon Dr M22 . . . . 121 E8
Maryport Dr WA15 . . . . . . 120 D7
Mary St E BL6 . . . . 22 B4
Mary St W BL6 . . . . 22 A4
Mary St
Cheadle SK8 . . . . 122 D6
Denton M34 . . . . 101 A4
Droylsden M43 . . . . 84 B1
Dukinfield SK16 . . . . 166 B1
Farnworth BL4 . . . . 60 D7
Heywood OL10 . . . . 29 C2
Hyde SK14 . . . . 167 A3
Mary St *continued*
Manchester M3 . . . . 158 C3
Ramsbottom BL0 . . . . 138 B1
Rochdale OL16 . . . . 15 D4
Stockport SK1 . . . . 112 A2
Tyldesley M29 . . . . 77 A8
Masboro St M8 . . . . 155 C3
Masbury Cl BL1 . . . . 24 E7
Masefield Ave
Leigh WN7 . . . . 75 D7
Prestwich M25 . . . . 62 F3
Radcliffe M26 . . . . 43 E4
Wigan WN5 . . . . 54 A6
Masefield Cl SK16 . . . . 102 B7
Masefield Cres 4 M43 . . . . 84 A1
Masefield Dr
Farnworth BL4 . . . . 60 B7
Stockport SK4 . . . . 168 A2
Wigan WN3 . . . . 54 F5
Masefield Gr SK5 . . . . 99 E1
Masefield Prim Sch
BL3 . . . . 43 B4
Masefield Rd
Droylsden M43 . . . . 84 A1
Little Lever BL3 . . . . 43 B4
Oldham OL1 . . . . 49 B2
Mason Cl WN4 . . . . 73 D4
Mason Gdns BL3 . . . . 145 B2
Mason La M46 . . . . 58 E2
Mason Row
Bolton BL7 . . . . 8 E2
Oldham OL4 . . . . 50 C1
Masons Gr SK13 . . . . 104 A6
Mason St
Abram WN2 . . . . 74 B8
10 Ashton-u-L OL7 . . . . 84 F1
Bolton BL7 . . . . 8 E1
Bury BL9 . . . . 141 A2
Heywood OL10 . . . . 29 B2
Horwich BL6 . . . . 22 B3
Manchester M4 . . . . 159 B2
Rochdale OL16 . . . . 139 C3
Wigan WN3 . . . . 150 B3
Mason Street Ind Est
WN3 . . . . 150 B3
Massey Ave
Ashton-u-L OL6 . . . . 85 C6
Failsworth M35 . . . . 84 B8
Massey Croft OL12 . . . . 14 C8
Massey Rd
Altrincham WA15 . . . . 119 E4
Sale M33 . . . . 108 E4
Massey St
6 Alderley Edge SK9 . . . . 137 A1
Bury BL9 . . . . 141 B3
Salford M5 . . . . 81 C1
Stockport SK1 . . . . 169 C1
Massey Wlk M22 . . . . 121 F1
Massie St SK8 . . . . 122 D6
Matchmoor La BL6 . . . . 23 A4
Matham Wlk M15 . . . . 163 A3
Mather Ave
Eccles M30 . . . . 79 E2
Golborne WA3 . . . . 90 E6
Manchester M25 . . . . 63 C1
Whitefield M45 . . . . 44 F1
Mather Cl M45 . . . . 44 F1
Mather Fold Rd M28 . . . . . . 60 B1
Mather La WN7 . . . . 76 A4
Mather Rd
Bury BL9 . . . . 27 F7
Eccles M30 . . . . 79 E2
Mather St
2 Atherton M46 . . . . 58 D3
Bolton BL3 . . . . 145 B2
Failsworth M35 . . . . 83 E7
Farnworth BL4 . . . . 60 E8
Radcliffe M26 . . . . 44 A3
Mather Street Prim Sch
M35 . . . . 83 D7
Mather Way 4 M6 . . . . 81 A3
Matheson Dr WN5 . . . . 54 E8
Matisse Way M7 . . . . 81 B8
MATLEY 102 D5
Matley Cl SK14 . . . . 102 B5
Matley Gn SK5 . . . . 112 C6
Matley La SK14, SK15 . . . . 102 D6
Matley Park La SK15 . . . . 102 D6
Matlock Ave
Ashton-u-L OL6 . . . . 85 F6
Denton M34 . . . . 113 A8
Manchester M20 . . . . 109 F6
Salford M7 . . . . 81 A7
Urmston M41 . . . . 107 B8
Matlock Bank 8
SK13 . . . . 171 B1
Matlock Cl
Atherton M46 . . . . 58 D2
Farnworth BL4 . . . . 42 E1
Sale M33 . . . . 108 C4
Matlock Ct BL6 . . . . 22 E4
Matlock Dr SK7 . . . . 133 E8
Matlock Gdns 5
SK13 . . . . 171 B1
Matlock La 7 SK13 . . . . . . 171 B1
Matlock Mews WA14 . . . . . 119 E5
Matlock Pl 6 SK13 . . . . . . 171 B1
Matlock Rd
Gatley SK8 . . . . 131 C7
Reddish SK5 . . . . 100 A1
Stretford M32 . . . . 96 A3
Matlock St M30 . . . . 95 C8
Matson Wlk 3 M22 . . . . . . 121 A2
Matt Busby Cl M27 . . . . 80 B7
Matterdale Terr SK15 . . . . . 86 A4
Matthew Cl
Glossop SK13 . . . . 103 F7
Oldham OL8 . . . . 67 C4
Matthew Moss High Sch
OL11 . . . . 30 B4
Matthew Moss La OL11 . . . 30 B4
Matthews Ave BL4 . . . . 60 F7
Matthews La M12, M19 . . . . 99 B2
Matthew's St M12 . . . . 164 C3
Matthias Ct M3 . . . . 158 A3
Mattison St M11 . . . . 99 E7
Maudsley St BL9 . . . . 140 B1
Maud St
Bolton BL2 . . . . 25 C5
Rochdale OL12 . . . . 15 A2
Mauldeth Cl SK4 . . . . 168 A3
Mauldeth Rd
Manchester, Burnage
M19 . . . . 110 F6
Manchester M14, M19,
M20 . . . . 110 D7
Stockport, Heaton Moor SK4,
M19 . . . . 168 A3
Stockport M19, SK4 . . . . . . 110 F4
Mauldeth Rd W
Manchester M20,
M21 . . . . 109 D8
Manchester, Withington
M20 . . . . 110 B8
Mauldeth Road Prim Sch
M14 . . . . 110 E7
Mauldeth Road Sta
M14 . . . . 110 E7
Maunby Gdns M38 . . . . 60 C3
Maureen Ave M8 . . . . 156 A4
Maureen St OL12 . . . . 15 A2
Maurice Cl SK16 . . . . 101 E8
Maurice Dr M6 . . . . 154 C4
Maurice Pariser Wlk
M8 . . . . 155 C3
Maurice St M6 . . . . 154 C4
Maveen Ct SK2 . . . . 124 A4
Maveen Gr SK2 . . . . 124 A4
Mavis Gr OL16 . . . . 32 A6
Mavis St OL11 . . . . 30 C1
Mawdsley Dr M8 . . . . 156 C4
Mawdsley St BL1 . . . . 145 C3
Maxton Ho BL4 . . . . 60 E8
Maxwell Ave SK2 . . . . 124 C5
Maxwell St
Bolton BL1 . . . . 143 B4
Bury BL9 . . . . 141 B3
Max Woosnam Wlk 3
M14 . . . . 98 A3
Mayall St E 8 OL4 . . . . 67 C7
Mayall St OL5 . . . . 68 C1
Mayan Ave M3 . . . . 158 A2
May Ave
Abram Brow WN2 . . . . 74 C7
Cheadle SK8 . . . . 132 B6
Leigh WN7 . . . . 75 D6
Stockport SK4 . . . . 168 C2
Maybank St BL3 . . . . 145 A1
Mayberth Ave M8 . . . . 64 A2
Maybreck Cl BL3 . . . . 144 C1
Maybrook Wlk 11 M9 . . . . 157 A4
Mayburn Cl M24 . . . . 65 C5
Maybury Cl BL0 . . . . 138 B1
Maybury St M18 . . . . 99 E6
Maycroft SK5 . . . . 112 B6
Maycroft Ave M20 . . . . 110 C5
May Ct 13 M16 . . . . 97 D3
May Dr M19 . . . . 110 F6
Mayer St SK2 . . . . 124 C7
Mayes Ct M14 . . . . 110 D7
Mayes Gdns M4 . . . . 160 A1
Mayes St M4 . . . . 159 A2
Mayfair
Horwich BL6 . . . . 22 D3
1 Manchester M7 . . . . 63 C1
Mayfair Ave
Radcliffe M26 . . . . 43 D4
Salford M6 . . . . 80 B3
Urmston M41 . . . . 95 B2
Whitefield M45 . . . . 62 F7
Mayfair Cl
Dukinfield SK16 . . . . 102 A8
Haslingden BB4 . . . . 1 A7
Poynton SK12 . . . . 133 E4
Stalybridge SK16 . . . . 101 F8
Mayfair Cotts WN1 . . . . 20 C1
Mayfair Cres M35 . . . . 84 B8
Mayfair Ct
Altrincham WA15 . . . . 120 B7
3 Manchester, Fallowfield
M14 . . . . 110 C8
Manchester, West Didsbury
M20 . . . . 109 F3
Mayfair Dr
Atherton M46 . . . . 58 F4
Irlam M44 . . . . 94 A2
Pennington Green WN2 . . . . 38 D2
Royton OL2 . . . . 48 D2
Sale M33 . . . . 107 E2
Wigan WN3 . . . . 54 F2
Mayfair Gdns
Rochdale OL11 . . . . 139 A1
Whitefield M45 . . . . 62 F7
Mayfair Gr M45 . . . . 62 F7
Mayfair Rd M22 . . . . 121 E4
Mayfair The M20 . . . . 110 B5
Mayfield
Bolton BL2 . . . . 25 D5
Radcliffe M26 . . . . 43 E2
Mayfield Ave
Adlington PR6 . . . . 21 A7
Bolton BL3 . . . . 42 B3
7 Denton M34 . . . . 113 A7
Farnworth BL4 . . . . 60 C7
Oldham OL4 . . . . 68 A7
Reddish SK5 . . . . 111 F5
Mayfield Ave *continued*
Sale M33 . . . . 108 E4
Stretford M32 . . . . 96 B1
Swinton M27 . . . . 79 C6
Walkden M28 . . . . 60 D3
Mayfield Cl
Altrincham WA15 . . . . 120 B6
Ramsbottom BL0 . . . . 11 A2
Mayfield Ct WN5 . . . . 54 B8
Mayfield Dr WN7 . . . . 91 C8
Mayfield Gr
Manchester M18 . . . . 99 F3
Reddish SK5 . . . . 111 F5
Wilmslow SK9 . . . . 136 E5
Mayfield Ind Est M44 . . . . . 94 C3
Mayfield Mans M16 . . . . 97 E3
Mayfield Prim Sch OL1 . . . 49 B1
Mayfield Rd
Altrincham WA15 . . . . 120 B6
Bramhall SK7 . . . . 132 E4
Manchester, Broughton Park
M7 . . . . 63 C1
Manchester, Whalley Range
M16 . . . . 97 E3
Marple SK6 . . . . 114 B1
Oldham OL1 . . . . 49 B1
Ramsbottom BL0 . . . . 11 A2
Up Holland WN8 . . . . 53 B7
Wigan WN5 . . . . 54 B8
Mayfield St
Ashton-in-M WN4 . . . . 73 A3
Atherton M46 . . . . 58 C2
Denton M34 . . . . 100 E5
Rochdale OL16 . . . . 15 B1
Mayfield Terr OL16 . . . . 15 B1
Mayflower Ave M5 . . . . 161 B4
Mayflower Cotts WN1 . . . . . 37 C8
Mayford Rd M19 . . . . 99 B2
Maygate OL9 . . . . 153 A4
May Gr M19 . . . . 111 B8
Mayhill Dr
Salford M6 . . . . 80 A4
Worsley M28 . . . . 79 A8
Mayhurst Ave M21 . . . . 109 D3
Mayorlowe Ave SK5 . . . . . 112 C4
Mayor's Rd WA15 . . . . 119 E4
Mayor St
Bolton BL1 . . . . 145 A2
Bury BL8 . . . . 27 C3
Chadderton OL9 . . . . 152 C3
Mayo St M12 . . . . 164 A4
May Pl 9 OL11 . . . . 31 A4
Maypool Dr SK5 . . . . 111 F6
May Rd
Cheadle SK8 . . . . 132 B6
Manchester M16 . . . . 97 D3
Pendlebury M27 . . . . 80 B6
Maysmith Mews 1
M7 . . . . 155 A2
May St
Bolton BL2 . . . . 148 A3
Eccles M30 . . . . 79 C4
Edgworth BL7 . . . . 9 E6
Failsworth M40 . . . . 83 C5
Golborne WA3 . . . . 74 B2
Heywood OL10 . . . . 46 E8
Leigh WN7 . . . . 75 C5
Oldham OL8 . . . . 66 C4
Radcliffe M26 . . . . 44 A3
Mayton St M11 . . . . 165 A4
Maytree Ct PR6 . . . . 20 F8
May Tree Dr WN1 . . . . 37 B4
Mayville Dr M20 . . . . 110 B5
May Wlk 2 M31 . . . . 105 E3
Maywood Ave M20 . . . . 122 B8
Maze St BL3 . . . . 42 D5
Meachin Ave M21 . . . . 109 C5
Meade Cl M41 . . . . 95 C2
Meade Gr M13 . . . . 98 F3
Meade Hill Rd M25, M8 . . . . 63 E3
Meade Hill Sch M8 . . . . 63 F4
Meade Manor M21 . . . . 109 B7
Meade The
Bolton BL3 . . . . 147 B2
Manchester M21 . . . . 109 B7
Wilmslow SK9 . . . . 137 C8
Meadfoot Ave M25 . . . . 63 C3
Meadfoot Rd M18 . . . . 99 D6
Meadland Gr BL1 . . . . 143 C4
Meadow Ave
Altrincham WA15 . . . . 120 B3
Swinton M27 . . . . 62 B1
Meadowbank OL7 . . . . 85 B6
Meadow Bank
Altrincham WA15 . . . . 120 A7
Glossop SK13 . . . . 115 F7
Hollingworth SK14 . . . . 103 D6
Manchester M21 . . . . 109 A7
Romiley SK6 . . . . 112 F3
Stockport SK4 . . . . 168 B2
Meadowbank Ave M46 . . . . . 58 E5
Meadowbank Cl M35 . . . . . . 84 A6
Meadow Bank Cl OL4 . . . . . 67 E4
Meadow Bank Ct M32 . . . . . 96 B1
Meadowbank Gdns
WA3 . . . . 92 C7
Meadowbank Prim Sch
Atherton M46 . . . . 58 D4
Cheadle SK8 . . . . 122 F5
Meadowbank Rd BL3 . . . . 146 B2
Meadowbrook Cl
Bolton BL6 . . . . 40 B3
Bury BL9 . . . . 141 C4
Meadow Brook Way
SK8 . . . . 123 B4

Meadow Brow SK9 . . . . . . **137** A2
Meadowburn Nook
M30 . . . . **79** B4
Meadow Cl
Altrincham WA15 . . . . **120** B3
Denton M34 . . . . **113** A7
Heywood OL10 . . . . **29** C2
High Lane SK6 . . . . **134** F8
Leigh WN7 . . . . **75** E2
Little Lever BL3 . . . . **43** B2
Mossley OL5 . . . . **68** E3
Newton-le-W WA12 . . . . . . **89** A3
Romiley SK6 . . . . **113** A5
Stretford M32 . . . . **96** E1
Wilmslow SK9 . . . . **136** E4
Meadow Cotts OL12 . . . . . **4** D3
Meadowcroft
Ashton-in-M WN4 . . . . **72** F6
Mottram in L SK14 . . . . . . **103** A4
Radcliffe M26 . . . . **43** F5
Westhoughton BL5 . . . . . . **57** F7
Meadow Croft
Hazel Grove SK7 . . . . **124** E4
Whitefield M45 . . . . **62** C6
Meadowcroft Ho OL11 . . . **29** F6
Meadowcroft La
1 Oldham OL1 . . . . **49** B1
Rochdale OL11 . . . . **29** F6
Meadowcroft Way
WN7 . . . . **76** B2
Meadow Ct
2 Altrincham WA15 . . . . **120** D6
Altrincham, Well Green
WA15 . . . . **120** C3
Salford M6 . . . . **80** B3
Stretford M21 . . . . **108** F8
7 Wigan WN6 . . . . **37** A1
Meadowfield
Bolton BL6 . . . . **40** C7
Rochdale OL16 . . . . **31** B3
1 Up Holland WN8 . . . . . **53** A7
Meadowfield Cl SK13 . . . . **171** C3
Meadowfield Ct SK14 . . . . **167** A4
Meadowfield Dr M28 . . . . . **78** B6
Meadow Fold OL3 . . . . **69** C8
Meadowgate
Urmston M41 . . . . **95** D1
Worsley M28 . . . . **78** F8
Meadowgate Rd M6 . . . . . **80** C3
Meadow Head Ave
OL12 . . . . **14** D6
Meadow Ind Est SK1 . . . . **169** C3
Meadow La
Bolton BL2 . . . . **43** A7
Denton M34 . . . . **113** A7
Disley SK12 . . . . **135** D6
Dukinfield SK16 . . . . **101** D8
Oldham OL8 . . . . **66** E2
Meadow Pit La WN2 . . . . . **37** F8
Meadow Pk BL0 . . . . **1** C4
Meadow Rd
Manchester M24 . . . . **64** E6
Salford M7 . . . . **81** C3
Urmston M41 . . . . **95** D1
Meadow Rise
Glossop SK13 . . . . **115** F7
Shaw OL2 . . . . **32** A1
Meadows Cl
Hazel Grove SK7 . . . . **124** E3
4 Hindley WN2 . . . . **56** D5
Meadowside
Bramhall SK7 . . . . **123** C2
Newhey OL16 . . . . **32** C3
Meadowside Ave
Ashton-in-M WN4 . . . . **73** A8
Bolton BL2 . . . . **148** C3
Bolton, Breightmet BL2 . . . **42** D8
Irlam M44 . . . . **94** A2
Walkden M28 . . . . **60** E4
Wythenshawe M22 . . . . . **121** E4
Meadowside Cl M26 . . . . . **44** A5
Meadowside Gr M28 . . . . . **60** E3
Meadowside Rd WN2 . . . . **57** A4
Meadows La BL2 . . . . **25** F3
Meadows Rd
Cheadle SK8 . . . . **131** F8
Gatley SK8 . . . . **122** F3
Reddish M19 . . . . **111** C6
Sale M33 . . . . **108** C6
Meadows Sch The M9 . . . . **64** F4
Meadows St WN6 . . . . **37** A1
Meadow St
Adlington PR7 . . . . **21** A6
Hyde SK14 . . . . **167** B1
Stockport SK2 . . . . **124** C5
Meadows The
Irlam M44 . . . . **105** C6
Middleton M24 . . . . **65** B6
Oldham OL4 . . . . **68** A6
Prestwich M25 . . . . **63** C3
Radcliffe M26 . . . . **43** E5
Rochdale OL12 . . . . **13** A4
Romiley SK6 . . . . **113** B4
Uppermill OL3 . . . . **69** B7
Whitefield M45 . . . . **62** C7
Whitworth OL12 . . . . **4** C1
Meadow The
Bolton BL6 . . . . **40** C7
Delph OL3 . . . . **50** F5
Meadowvale Dr WN5 . . . . . **54** C6
Meadow View
Adlington PR6 . . . . **20** F8
Rochdale OL12 . . . . **14** A1

Meadow Way
Altrincham WA15 . . . . **120** B3
Blackrod BL6 . . . . **21** E1
Bury BL8 . . . . **26** E6
Coppull PR7 . . . . **19** D8
Edgworth BL7 . . . . **9** E6
Manchester M40 . . . . **65** A1
Ramsbottom, Summerseat
BL9 . . . . **11** C2
Wilmslow SK9 . . . . **136** E4
Meadow Wlk
Farnworth BL4 . . . . **60** A8
Littleborough OL15 . . . . . . **15** F5
Partington M31 . . . . **105** C3
Romiley SK6 . . . . **112** F3
Tyldesley M29 . . . . **77** B4
Meadscroft Dr SK9 . . . . . . **136** F1
Meads Gr
Farnworth BL4 . . . . **59** E8
Tyldesley M29 . . . . **77** C6
Meads The OL9 . . . . **152** A2
Mead The M5 . . . . **154** A2
Meadway
Bramhall SK7 . . . . **132** C5
Bury BL9 . . . . **44** F6
Dukinfield SK16 . . . . **101** E7
Failsworth OL9 . . . . **65** E2
Golborne WA3 . . . . **90** D8
High Lane SK6 . . . . **134** F8
Ince-in-M WN2 . . . . **151** C3
Poynton SK12 . . . . **133** B4
Ramsbottom BL0 . . . . **1** C1
Rochdale OL11 . . . . **30** C4
Sale M33 . . . . **107** E2
Stalybridge SK15 . . . . **102** E8
Tyldesley M29 . . . . **59** D1
Mead Way M34 . . . . **112** F8
Meadway Cl
Horwich BL6 . . . . **22** D3
Sale M33 . . . . **107** E2
Meadway Rd SK8 . . . . **123** B3
Mealhouse Brow SK1 . . . . **169** C1
Mealhouse Ct M46 . . . . . . **58** C3
Mealhouse La
Atherton M46 . . . . **58** C3
Bolton BL1 . . . . **145** C3
Meal St SK4 . . . . **169** B3
Meanley Rd M29, WN7 . . . **76** F7
Meanley St M29 . . . . **59** A1
Meanwood Brow **15**
OL12 . . . . **14** C1
Meanwood Com Prim Sch
OL12 . . . . **14** C1
Meanwood Fold OL12 . . . . **139** A4
Measham Mews M1 . . . . . **163** A3
Meburn Wlk M14 . . . . **98** B4
Mechinoh Sch M7 . . . . . . **63** E1
Medina Cl SK8 . . . . **123** B4
Medlar Way WN4 . . . . **72** F5
Medley St OL12 . . . . **14** F1
Medlock Cl BL4 . . . . **60** B8
Medlock Ct M14 . . . . **165** B3
Medlock Dr OL8 . . . . **85** A8
Medlock Ho **1** M15 . . . . . **162** A3
Medlock Prim Sch
M13 . . . . **163** C3
Medlock Rd M35 . . . . **84** B5
Medlock St
Droylsden M43 . . . . **84** B2
Manchester M15 . . . . **162** C3
MEDLOCK VALE **84** A4
Medlock Vale *★* M35 . . . . . **84** A6
Medlock Valley Com Sch
OL8 . . . . **67** A2
Medlock Valley Visitor
Ctr *★* OL6 . . . . **67** A2
Medlock Way
Oldham OL4 . . . . **67** E6
Platt Bridge WN2 . . . . **56** A2
Whitefield M45 . . . . **63** C8
Medowell Wlk M8 . . . . **64** B2
Medway Cl
Ashton-in-M WN4 . . . . **72** F6
Golborne WN7 . . . . **91** C8
Handforth SK9 . . . . **131** D2
Oldham OL8 . . . . **66** C3
Salford M5 . . . . **154** A3
Medway Cres WA14 . . . . . **119** C6
Medway Dr
Horwich BL6 . . . . **22** D3
Kearsley BL4 . . . . **61** B5
Medway Pl WN5 . . . . **54** D7
Medway Rd
Culcheth WA3 . . . . **92** A2
Oldham OL8 . . . . **66** C3
Shaw OL2 . . . . **149** B4
Walkden M28 . . . . **78** B8
Medway The OL10 . . . . . . **29** B3
Medway Wlk
Manchester M40 . . . . **160** A3
Wigan WN5 . . . . **54** D7
Meech St M11 . . . . **165** C4
Meek St OL2 . . . . **48** A4
Meerbrook Rd SK3 . . . . . **123** A8
Mee's Sq M30 . . . . **95** D8
Megfield BL5 . . . . **57** E6
Megna Cl OL9 . . . . **153** A3
Melandra Castle Rd
SK13 . . . . **171** A2
Melandra Cres SK14 . . . . **102** E2
Melandra Rd SK13 . . . . . **171** B3
Melanie Cl M8 . . . . **116** A8
Melanie Dr SK5 . . . . **111** F8
Melba St M11 . . . . **99** E8
Melbecks Wlk **5** M23 . . . **108** F2
Melbourne Ave
Chadderton OL9 . . . . **152** B3
Stretford M32 . . . . **96** D2

Melbourne Ave *continued*
Wythenshawe M90 . . . . . **130** A8
Melbourne Cl
Horwich BL6 . . . . **22** C3
Rochdale OL11 . . . . **31** B2
Melbourne Gr BL6 . . . . . . **22** C3
Melbourne Mews
Chadderton OL9 . . . . **152** B3
Salford M7 . . . . **155** B1
Melbourne Rd
Bolton BL3 . . . . **144** B1
Bramhall SK7 . . . . **132** F5
Rochdale OL11 . . . . **31** A2
Melbourne St N OL6 . . . . **166** C4
Melbourne St S OL6 . . . . **166** C3
Melbourne St
Chadderton OL9 . . . . **152** B3
Denton M34 . . . . **100** E2
Manchester, Harpurhey
M9 . . . . **157** B4
Manchester M15 . . . . **162** B3
Pendlebury M27 . . . . **80** B8
Reddish SK5 . . . . **111** F8
Salford M7 . . . . **155** B1
Stalybridge SK15 . . . . **86** A1
Melbury Ave M20 . . . . . . **110** D4
Melbury Dr BL6 . . . . **39** F8
Melbury Rd SK6 . . . . **132** B6
Meldon Rd M13 . . . . **98** E2
Meldreth Dr M12 . . . . **98** F4
Meldrum St OL8 . . . . **66** F4
Melford Ave M40 . . . . **65** E1
Melford Dr
Ashton-in-M WN4 . . . . **73** A4
Orrell WN5 . . . . **53** D3
Melford Gr OL4 . . . . **67** D6
Melford Rd SK7 . . . . **124** F1
Melfort Ave WA3 . . . . **96** E1
Melia Ho M4 . . . . **159** A3
Meliden Cres
Bolton BL1 . . . . **142** B1
Wythenshawe M22 . . . . . **121** E3
Melksham Cl **4** M5 . . . . . **81** B2
Mellalieu St
Middleton M24 . . . . **46** F1
Royton OL2 . . . . **48** E2
Melland Ave M13 . . . . . . **109** C5
Melland High Sch M18 . . . **99** D2
Melland Rd M18 . . . . **99** C3
Meller Rd M13 . . . . **98** F2
Melling Ave
Chadderton OL9 . . . . **47** E1
Reddish SK4 . . . . **111** E6
Melling Cl
Adlington PR6 . . . . **21** B7
Leigh WN7 . . . . **75** F1
Melling Rd OL4 . . . . **67** C6
Mellings Ave WN5 . . . . . . **53** E1
Melling St
Manchester M12 . . . . **99** A4
Wigan WN5 . . . . **54** E5
Mellington Ave M20 . . . . **122** C8
Melling Way WN5 . . . . **54** D1
Mellodew Dr OL1 . . . . **49** D4
MELLOR **126** D5
Mellor Brook Dr WN2 . . . . **56** A2
Mellor Brow OL10 . . . . . . **29** C2
Mellor Cl
Ashton-u-L OL6 . . . . **85** E2
Standish WN6 . . . . **19** E2
Mellor Ct SK4 . . . . **124** E6
Mellor Dr
Bury BL9 . . . . **44** D7
Walkden M28 . . . . **60** C1
Mellor Gr BL1 . . . . **142** B1
Mellor Prim Sch SK6 . . . . **126** C6
Mellor Rd
Ashton-u-L, Higher Hurst
OL6 . . . . **85** F4
Ashton-u-L, Stamford Park
OL6 . . . . **85** E3
Cheadle SK8 . . . . **123** B1
New Mills SK, SK22 . . . . . **127** C3
Mellors Rd M17 . . . . **96** B7
Mellor St
Droylsden M43 . . . . **83** F1
Eccles M30 . . . . **79** D1
Failsworth M35 . . . . **83** D6
Manchester, Ardwick
M12 . . . . **163** C4
Manchester, Miles Platting
M40 . . . . **160** A3
Oldham, Lees OL4 . . . . . . **67** E6
6 Oldham, The Edge
OL8 . . . . **66** C2
Prestwich M25 . . . . **62** F4
2 Radcliffe M26 . . . . **44** B2
Rochdale OL11, OL12 . . . **139** A3
Royton OL2 . . . . **48** D5
Stretford M32 . . . . **96** E4
Mellor Way **1** OL9 . . . . . . **66** B4
Mellowstone Dr M21 . . . **109** F8
Melloy Pl M8 . . . . **159** A4
Melmerby Cl WN4 . . . . . . **72** F3
Melmerby Ct M5 . . . . **154** C1
Melon Pl **7** M6 . . . . **81** B2
Melrose **18** OL12 . . . . **139** B4
Melrose Apartments
M13 . . . . **98** C4
Melrose Ave
Bolton BL1 . . . . **142** A1
Bury BL9 . . . . **27** C3
Cheadle SK8 . . . . **122** F7
Eccles M30 . . . . **79** B4
Heywood OL10 . . . . **29** C3
Leigh WN7 . . . . **57** D1
Littleborough OL15 . . . . . . **16** A7
Manchester M20 . . . . **110** C3

Melrose Ave *continued*
Sale M33 . . . . **108** B4
Melrose Cl **6** M45 . . . . . . **44** F2
Melrose Cres
Altrincham WA15 . . . . **120** B1
Garswood WN4 . . . . **72** C3
Poynton SK12 . . . . **134** D5
Stockport SK3 . . . . **123** D4
Melrose Ct
Chadderton OL9 . . . . **66** A4
15 Handforth SK9 . . . . . **131** E1
Melrose Dr WN3 . . . . **54** D3
Melrose Gdns M26 . . . . . . **43** E5
Melrose Rd
Little Lever BL3 . . . . **42** F3
6 Radcliffe M26 . . . . **43** E5
Melrose St
Failsworth M40 . . . . **83** C5
3 Oldham OL1 . . . . **49** B1
Ramsbottom BL9 . . . . **11** B2
Rochdale OL11 . . . . **139** A3
Melsomby Rd M23 . . . . . **109** A2
Meltham Ave M20 . . . . . . **110** A6
Meltham Cl SK4 . . . . **110** A6
Meltham Pl **7** BL3 . . . . . . **147** A4
Meltham Rd SK4 . . . . **110** C1
Melton Ave
Reddish M34 . . . . **100** A3
Urmston M41 . . . . **94** D3
Melton Cl
Heywood OL10 . . . . **29** B1
Tyldesley M29 . . . . **77** B8
Walkden M28 . . . . **60** C2
Melton Dr BL9 . . . . **45** A5
Melton Rd M8 . . . . **64** B2
Melton Row M26 . . . . **43** F4
Melton St
Heywood OL10 . . . . **29** B1
Manchester M9 . . . . **64** F1
Radcliffe M26 . . . . **43** F4
Reddish SK5 . . . . **169** C4
Melton Way M26 . . . . **43** F4
Melton Wlk M26 . . . . **43** F4
Melverley Rd M9 . . . . **64** A5
Melverley St WN3 . . . . . . **150** A3
Melville Cl M11 . . . . **99** E7
Melville Ct **3** M20 . . . . . . **110** A2
Melville Rd
Irlam M44 . . . . **105** C5
Kearsley BL4 . . . . **60** F6
Stretford M32 . . . . **96** A3
Melville St
Ashton-u-L OL6 . . . . **166** B3
Bolton BL3 . . . . **42** A4
Oldham OL4 . . . . **67** E5
Rochdale OL11 . . . . **30** D1
Salford M3 . . . . **158** A2
Melvin Ave M22 . . . . **121** E4
Melyncourt Dr SK14 . . . . **102** E3
Memorial Rd M28 . . . . **60** D2
Menai Gr SK8 . . . . **123** A6
Menai Rd SK3 . . . . **170** B2
Menai St BL3 . . . . **146** B4
Mendip Ave
Wigan WN5 . . . . **54** C3
Wythenshawe M22 . . . . . **121** F4
Mendip Cl
Bolton BL2 . . . . **43** A7
Chadderton OL9 . . . . **152** A1
Gatley SK8 . . . . **131** B7
Horwich BL6 . . . . **22** C5
Royton OL2 . . . . **48** F8
Stockport SK4 . . . . **169** B3
Mendip Cres BL8 . . . . **27** B3
Mendip Ct SK4 . . . . **169** B3
Mendip Dr
Bolton BL3 . . . . **43** A6
Milnrow OL16 . . . . **32** A7
Mendip Rd OL8 . . . . **66** D3
Menston Ave M40 . . . . **65** E3
Mentmore Rd OL16 . . . . . **31** D8
Mentone Cres M22 . . . . . **121** E4
Mentone Rd SK4 . . . . **168** C3
Mentor St M13 . . . . **98** F3
Menzies Ct M21 . . . . **97** B1
Mercer Cres BB4 . . . . **1** A8
Mercer La OL11 . . . . **29** E8
Mercer Rd
Heywood OL10 . . . . **46** D7
Manchester M18 . . . . **99** D5
Mercer St
Droylsden M43 . . . . **84** B2
Manchester M19 . . . . **99** A2
Newton-le-W WA12 . . . . . . **89** D4
Merchants Cres WA3 . . . . **74** E1
Merchants Quay M50 . . . **161** A2
Mercian Mall **6** OL6 . . . . **166** B3
Mercian Way SK3 . . . . . . **170** B3
Mercia St BL3 . . . . **144** C1
Mercury Bldgs M1 . . . . . **159** B3
Mercury Pk M41 . . . . **95** F5
Mercury Way M41 . . . . **95** F6
Mere Ave
Droylsden M43 . . . . **99** E8
Leigh WN7 . . . . **57** D1
Middleton M24 . . . . **65** A6
Salford M6 . . . . **154** E2
Merebank Cl OL11 . . . . . . **29** E8
Mere Bank Cl M28 . . . . . . **60** C3
Merebrook Dr M28 . . . . . . **44** B1
Mere Cl
Reddish M34 . . . . **100** B3
Sale M33 . . . . **108** F3
Whitefield BL9 . . . . **45** B1
Mereclough Ave M28 . . . . **60** F1
Meredew Ave M27 . . . . . . **79** E6
Meredith Ct **6** M15 . . . . . **163** A2

Meredith St
Bolton BL3 . . . . **147** C3
Manchester M14 . . . . **110** D7
Mere Dr
Manchester M20 . . . . **110** B4
Swinton M27 . . . . **62** A2
Merefield Ave OL11 . . . . . **139** B1
Merefield Cl WN2 . . . . **56** E4
Merefield Rd WA15 . . . . . **120** C5
Merefield St OL11 . . . . . . **139** B1
Merefield Terr OL11 . . . . **139** B1
Merefold BL6 . . . . **21** F3
Mere Fold M28 . . . . **60** B3
Mere Gdns BL1 . . . . **145** B4
Mere Gr WA11 . . . . **71** A1
Merehall Cl BL1 . . . . **145** B4
Merehall Dr BL1 . . . . **145** B4
Merehall St BL1 . . . . **143** B1
Mere Ho SK4 . . . . **110** C1
Mere La OL11 . . . . **139** C1
Mereland Ave M20 . . . . . **110** C4
Mereland Cl WN5 . . . . **53** E6
Meremanor M28 . . . . **60** F1
Mere Rd
Ashton-in-M WN4 . . . . **73** C4
Newton-le-W WA12 . . . . . . **89** F4
Mereside SK15 . . . . **85** F4
Mereside Cl SK8 . . . . **122** F4
Mereside Gr M28 . . . . **60** E3
Mereside Wlk **15** M15 . . . **162** A2
Mere St
7 Leigh WN7 . . . . **75** D5
Rochdale OL11 . . . . **139** C2
Wigan WN5 . . . . **54** F6
Mere The
Ashton-u-L OL6 . . . . **85** E6
Cheadle SK8 . . . . **123** A4
Mere Wlk BL1 . . . . **145** B4
Merewood Ave M22 . . . . . **121** D6
Meriden Cl M26 . . . . **43** F6
Meriden Gr BL6 . . . . **40** D6
Meridian Pl M20 . . . . **110** A4
Merinall Cl OL16 . . . . **31** C7
Meriton Rd SK9 . . . . **131** D4
Meriton Wlk M18 . . . . **99** B4
Merlewood OL5 . . . . **1** B3
Merlewood Ave
6 Droylsden M34 . . . . . **84** B1
Reddish M19 . . . . **111** C7
Uppermill OL3 . . . . **69** B8
Merlewood Dr
Swinton M27 . . . . **79** C6
Tyldesley M29 . . . . **77** B8
Merlin Cl
Hazel Grove SK2 . . . . **125** A6
Littleborough OL15 . . . . . . **16** A2
Oldham OL8 . . . . **85** A8
Merlin Dr M27 . . . . **62** B2
Merlin Gr BL1 . . . . **142** B1
Merlin Ho **3** M19 . . . . . . **110** D4
Merlin Rd
Irlam M44 . . . . **94** A4
Milnrow OL16 . . . . **31** F6
Merlyn Ave
Denton M34 . . . . **100** A3
Manchester M20 . . . . **110** C4
Sale M33 . . . . **108** C6
Merrick Ave M22 . . . . **121** E4
Merrick St OL10 . . . . **29** E1
Merridale Rd **5** M40 . . . . **65** C1
Merridge Wlk **5** M8 . . . . **155** C2
Merrill St M4 . . . . **160** A1
Merriman St M16 . . . . **97** E4
Merrion St M4 . . . . **42** C2
Merridale Rd M40 . . . . . . **163** B3
Merrybent Cl SK2 . . . . . . **124** D4
Merrybower Rd M7 . . . . . **155** B4
Merrydale Ave M30 . . . . . . **79** E4
Merryman Hall OL16 . . . . **15** B2
Merseybank Ave M21 . . . **109** D4
Mersey Bank Rd
SK13 . . . . **171** C4
Mersey Cl
Hindley WN2 . . . . **57** C3
Whitefield M45 . . . . **45** B1
Mersey Cres M20 . . . . . . **109** D3
Mersey Dr
Partington M31 . . . . **106** A4
Whitefield M45 . . . . **45** B1
Mersey Drive Com Prim
Sch M45 . . . . **45** C2
Mersey Ind Est
Manchester SK4 . . . . **110** E1
Oldham M35 . . . . **66** B1
Mersey Mdws M20 . . . . . **109** F3
Mersey Rd
Manchester, Heaton Mersey
SK4 . . . . **110** F2
Manchester, West Didsbury
M20 . . . . **109** F3
Orrell WN5 . . . . **53** F7
Platt Bridge WN2 . . . . **55** F2
Sale M33 . . . . **108** B6
Mersey Rd N M35 . . . . . . **66** B1
Mersey Sh Ctr SK4 . . . . . **169** B1
Mersey Sq
Stockport SK1 . . . . **169** B1
Whitefield M45 . . . . **45** B1
Mersey St
Droylsden M11 . . . . **99** E7
Leigh WN7 . . . . **75** C5
Stockport SK1 . . . . **112** A2
Mersey Vale Prim Sch
SK4 . . . . **168** A1

Mersey Valley Visitor Ctr ★
M33 . . . . .108 F6
Merseyway SK1. . . . . .169 B2
Merston Dr M20 . . . . .122 C8
Merton Ave
  Hazel Grove SK7. . . . . .133 F8
  Oldham OL3 . . . . .66 D3
  Romiley SK6. . . . . .113 A4
Merton Cl BL3 . . . . .144 C1
Merton Dr M43 . . . . .83 E1
Merton Gr
  Altrincham WA15. . . . . .120 B6
  Failsworth OL9 . . . . .65 D3
  Tyldesley M29 . . . . .77 C6
Merton Rd
  Poynton SK12 . . . . .133 B4
  Prestwich M25. . . . . .63 C5
  Sale M33 . . . . .108 A6
  Stockport SK3 . . . . .123 B8
  Wigan WN3 . . . . .54 C4
Merton St BL8. . . . . .140 A3
Merton Wlk **14** M9. . . . . . . .157 B3
Merville Ave M40. . . . . .64 F1
Mervyn Pl WN3. . . . . .55 B4
Mervyn Rd M7. . . . . .81 B6
Merwell Rd M41. . . . . .94 E4
Merwood Ave SK8. . . . . .131 D8
Merwood Gr M14. . . . . .98 E4
Meshaw Cl M23 . . . . .108 E2
Mesnefield Rd M7. . . . . .81 A8
Mesne Lea Gr M28. . . . . .78 E8
Mesne Lea Prim Sch
  M28. . . . . .60 E1
Mesne Lea Rd M28. . . . . .60 E1
Mesnes Ave WN3. . . . . .150 A1
Mesnes Rd WN1. . . . . .37 C3
Mesnes St WN1. . . . . .150 C4
Mesnes Terr **12** WN1. . . . . . .37 C1
Metal Box Way BL5 . . . . .40 A2
Metcalfe Ct
  Romiley SK6. . . . . .113 B2
  Walkden M38. . . . . .59 F4
Metcalfe Dr SK6. . . . . .113 B2
Metcalf Mews OL3. . . . . .69 B8
Metcalf Terr BL2. . . . . .26 D1
Metfield Pl **8** BL1 . . . . .144 C4
Metfield Wlk **18** M40. . . . . . .65 D2
Methodist Cotts BL5. . . . . . . .39 D3
Methuen St **6** M12 . . . . .99 B3
Methwold St BL3 . . . . .146 C4
Mevagissey Wlk **3**
  OL4. . . . . .67 C8
Mews The
  Bolton BL1. . . . . .144 B4
  Gatley SK8. . . . . .122 B5
  12 Hindley WN2. . . . . .56 D5
  Leigh WN7 . . . . .76 A7
  Manchester M40 . . . . .160 B3
  Prestwich M25. . . . . .63 B3
  Sale M33 . . . . .108 C3
  Whitefield M45 . . . . .62 D8
  Wilmslow SK9. . . . . .130 D4
  Worsley M28 . . . . .78 E6
Mexborough St **7** OL4. . . . .67 D8
Meyer St SK2, SK3. . . . . .170 C2
Meynell Dr WN7 . . . . .75 F2
Meyrick Cl
  Newton-le-W WA12. . . . . . . .89 A3
  Wigan WN3 . . . . .54 C2
Meyrick Rd M6. . . . . .81 A3
Meyrick St WN6. . . . . .54 F6
Miall St OL13 . . . . .139 C2
Micawber Rd SK12. . . . . .133 E2
Michael Ct M19 . . . . .110 D2
Michaels Hey Par
  M23 . . . . .120 C8
Michael St **3** M24. . . . . . . .64 F8
Michael Wife La
  Edenfield BL0. . . . . .1 F2
  Edenfield BL0. . . . . .1 F3
Michigan Ave M50. . . . . .96 F8
Mickleby Wlk M40. . . . . .160 A3
MICKLEHURST. 68 F1
Micklehurst All Saints' CE
  Prim Sch OL5. . . . . .68 E1
Micklehurst Ave M20 . . . . . . .109 E4
Micklehurst Gn SK22. . . . . . . .124 E5
Micklehurst Rd OL5. . . . . .68 E1
Mickleton M46 . . . . .58 E4
Midbrook Wlk **8**
  M22. . . . . .121 B1
Middlebourne St M6. . . . . . . .154 B2
Middlebrook Dr BL6. . . . . .40 D6
Middlecot Cl **2** WN5 . . . . . .53 E5
Middlefield OL8 . . . . .85 A8
Middle Field OL11 . . . . .165 C1
Middlefields SK8 . . . . .123 B4
Middlegate M40 . . . . .65 D3
Middle Gate OL8 . . . . .66 E2
Middle Gn OL6 . . . . .166 C4
Middleham St M14 . . . . .98 A2
MIDDLE HEALEY 14 D4
Middle Hill OL12. . . . . .14 F4
Middle Hillgate SK1 . . . . .170 C4
MIDDLE HULTON 57 F8
Middle Newgate OL15. . . . . . .16 B8
Middlesex Dr **9** BL9. . . . . . .44 F8
Middlesex Rd
  Brinnington SK5. . . . . .112 C6
  Manchester M9 . . . . .64 D2
Middlesex Wlk OL9 . . . . .153 A2
Middle St OL12 . . . . .4 D1
Middlestone Dr M9. . . . . .157 A3
MIDDLETON 68 B8
Middleton Ave M35 . . . . .83 F7
Middleton Central Ind Est
  M24 . . . . .64 F8
Middleton Cl M26 . . . . .43 F7

Middleton Dr BL9. . . . . .44 F3
Middleton Gdns **9**
  M24. . . . . .64 F8
MIDDLETON JUNCTION
  .65 D6
Middleton Old Rd M24 . . . . . . .64 D2
Middleton Parish CE Prim
  Sch M24 . . . . .46 F2
Middleton Rd
  Chadderton, Chadderton
    Park OL9. . . . . .65 F8
  Chadderton, Westwood
    OL9. . . . . .152 B3
  Heywood OL10. . . . . .46 E7
  Manchester M8, M9 . . . . . . .63 A3
  Middleton M24. . . . . .64 C3
  Reddish SK5 . . . . .99 F2
  Royton OL2 . . . . .48 C3
Middleton Sh Ctr M24 . . . . . . .64 F8
Middleton Tech Sch
  M24 . . . . .65 C8
Middleton View M24. . . . . . . .65 B8
Middleton Way M24 . . . . .65 B8
Middle Turn BL7. . . . . .9 D7
Middleway OL4. . . . . .68 B5
Middlewich Wlk M18 . . . . .165 C1
MIDDLEWOOD 134 C5
Middlewood WA3. . . . . .90 E8
Middlewood Ct OL9. . . . . .152 A4
Middlewood Dr SK4 . . . . .168 A1
Middlewood Gn OL9. . . . . . . .152 A4
Middle Wood La OL15. . . . . . .15 E6
Middlewood Rd
  Hazel Grove SK7,
    SK12 . . . . .134 C7
  High Lane SK6 . . . . .134 C7
  Poynton SK12 . . . . .134 B4
Middlewood St M5 . . . . .158 A1
Middlewood Sta
  SK12 . . . . .134 D6
Middlewood View
  SK6. . . . . .134 D7
Middlewood Wlk M9. . . . . . . .157 A3
Midford Ave M30 . . . . .79 B2
Midford Dr BL1. . . . . .24 E7
Midford Wlk **18** M16. . . . . . .156 A2
Midge Hall Dr OL11. . . . . .30 A6
Midge Hill OL5 . . . . .68 D4
Midgley Ave M18. . . . . .99 C6
Midgley Cres OL6. . . . . .85 E4
Midgley Dr OL16. . . . . .31 C2
Midgley St M27. . . . . .79 D6
Midgrove OL3 . . . . .50 F4
Midgrove La OL3 . . . . .50 F4
Midhurst Ave M40 . . . . .83 B4
Midhurst Cl
  1 Bolton BL1. . . . . .143 B1
  Cheadle SK8 . . . . .131 F8
Midhurst St OL11 . . . . .139 C1
Midhurst Way **1**. 152 B2
Midland Cl WN7 . . . . .75 C6
Midland Rd
  Reddish SK5 . . . . .99 F2
  Stockport SK7 . . . . .123 E3
Midland St M12 . . . . .164 A3
Midland Wlk SK7 . . . . .123 E3
Midlothian St M11. . . . . .83 B2
Midmoor Wlk **5** M9. . . . . . .64 E3
Midville Rd M11. . . . . .83 C3
MIDWAY 133 D2
Midway SK8. . . . . .132 B5
Midway St M12 . . . . .99 A2
Milan St M7 . . . . .155 B3
Milbourne Rd BL9 . . . . .27 F6
Milburn Ave M23 . . . . .109 B2
Milburn Dr BL2. . . . . .42 F8
Milbury Dr OL15. . . . . .16 C2
Milden Cl M20. . . . . .110 C4
Mildred Ave
  Manchester M25. . . . . .63 C1
  Oldham OL8. . . . . .66 B5
  Royton OL2 . . . . .48 E5
Mildred St M7. . . . . .81 C5
MILE END 124 B5
Mile End La SK2. . . . . .124 B6
Mile La BL8 . . . . .26 F1
Miles Ave OL13 . . . . .3 D8
Miles La
  Appley Bridge WN6 . . . . .35 E6
  Shevington M6 . . . . .36 A4
MILES PLATTING 160 A3
Miles St
  4 Bolton BL1. . . . . .143 A2
  Farnworth BL4. . . . . .60 C8
  Hyde SK14. . . . . .167 C2
  Manchester M12 . . . . .165 A3
  Oldham OL1. . . . . .67 B8
Milford Ave **2** OL8. . . . . . . .66 C2
Milford Brow OL4. . . . . .67 E7
Milford Cres OL15. . . . . .16 B6
Milford Dr M19 . . . . .111 C7
Milford Gr SK2 . . . . .124 C7
Milford Rd
  Bolton, Harwood BL2. . . . . . .25 F4
  Bolton, Lever Edge BL3. . . . .147 B3
  4 Heywood OL10 . . . . .37 F2
Milford St
  Ince-in-M WN3 . . . . .151 B2
  Manchester M9 . . . . .64 B4
  6 Rochdale OL12. . . . . . . .14 F1
  Salford M6. . . . . .154 B2
Milking Green Ind Est
  OL4. . . . . .67 F5
Milk St
  Hyde SK14. . . . . .167 A2
  Manchester M2. . . . . .159 A1
  2 Oldham OL4. . . . . .67 C7
  Rochdale OL16. . . . . .15 C2
  Ramsbottom BL0. . . . . .138 B1

Milk St continued
  Rochdale OL11. . . . . .139 C2
  Tyldesley M29 . . . . .59 A1
  Wigan WN3 . . . . .150 C3
Milkstone Pl OL11 . . . . .139 C2
Milkstone Rd OL11. . . . . .139 C2
Milkwood Gr **2** M18. . . . . . .99 D4
Millais St M40. . . . . .83 A8
Millar Barn La
  M26 **10** Rawtenstall BB4. . . .2 E8
  Rawtenstall BB4 . . . . .2 E8
Millard St OL9. . . . . .152 A3
Mill Bank
  Appley Bridge WN6 . . . . .35 D7
  Radcliffe M26 . . . . .44 B2
Millbank Ct OL10 . . . . .29 B2
Millbank St
  Heywood OL10. . . . . .29 B2
  Manchester M1, M4 . . . . . . .159 C1
Millbeck Cl **4** M44. . . . . . . .46 D2
Millbeck Farm WN5 . . . . .54 D5
Millbeck Gr WA11 . . . . .71 B2
Mill Beck Gr BL3 . . . . .147 B4
Millbeck Rd M24. . . . . .46 D2
Millbeck St **5** M15 . . . . . . .163 A2
Millbrae Gdns OL2. . . . . .48 F7
Millbrook OL2. . . . . .86 D4
Millbrook SK14 . . . . .103 D6
Millbrook Ave
  Atherton M46 . . . . .58 E5
  Denton M34. . . . . .100 D1
Millbrook Bank OL11 . . . . . . .13 C1
Millbrook Cl
  Fowley Common WA3. . . . . . .92 C5
  Shaw OL2. . . . . .49 D6
Millbrook Fold SK7. . . . . .133 F8
Millbrook Gr **4** SK9 . . . . . .131 D1
Millbrook Ho
  Farnworth BL4. . . . . .60 E8
  Hollingworth SK14. . . . . . . .103 E6
Mill Brook Ind Est
  M23 . . . . .120 C6
Millbrook Prim Sch
  Mossley SK15. . . . . .86 E5
  Stevington WN6. . . . . .36 B6
Millbrook Rd M23. . . . . .121 A4
Millbrook St SK1 . . . . .170 C4
MILL BROW
  4 Broadbottom
    SK14 . . . . .115 A4
  Chadderton OL1. . . . . .48 A2
  Marple SK6 . . . . .126 D8
  Oldham OL6, OL8 . . . . .67 C2
  Worsley M28 . . . . .78 F6
Mill Brow Rd SK6. . . . . .126 E8
Mill Court Br M24 . . . . .61 B8
Millcrest Cl M28 . . . . .77 F5
Mill Croft
  Bolton BL1. . . . . .145 A4
  Shaw OL2. . . . . .149 C2
Millcroft Ave WN5. . . . . .53 D5
Mill Croft Cl OL12 . . . . .13 C2
Mill Croft La OL3 . . . . .51 A7
Mill Ct
  Glossop SK13. . . . . .104 C1
  Urmston M41. . . . . .95 C2
Milldale Cl
  Atherton M46 . . . . .58 C3
  Bolton BL6. . . . . .40 B7
Milldale Rd M47. . . . . .75 B1
Miller Meadow Cl
  OL2. . . . . .149 C4
Miller Rd OL8 . . . . .66 E3
Millers Brook Cl OL10. . . . . . .29 D3
Millers Cl M23. . . . . .109 A3
Millers Ct
  Salford M5. . . . . .80 A2
  5 Stalybridge SK15. . . . . .101 F8
Millersdale Ct **3**
  SK13. . . . . .104 F1
Millers La WA13 . . . . .117 B5
Miller St
  Ashton-u-L OL6 . . . . .166 C4
  Bolton BL1. . . . . .143 B4
  Heywood OL10. . . . . .29 D2
  Manchester M4 . . . . .159 A2
  Radcliffe M26 . . . . .43 F6
  Ramsbottom BL9 . . . . .11 C2
  Scot Lane End BL6. . . . . .38 E7
Millers Wharf SK15. . . . . .86 B2
Millet Terr **8** SK7. . . . . .28 E7
Millett St
  Bury M3 . . . . .140 A2
  Ramsbottom BL0. . . . . .11 D7
Millfield Ct WA15. . . . . .119 E2
Millfield Dr M28. . . . . .78 B6
Millfield Gr OL16 . . . . .31 B6
Millfield La WN4, WA11. . . . . .72 E1
Millfield Rd BL2 . . . . .43 A7
Millfield Wlk **2** M40. . . . . . .65 C2
Millfold OL12 . . . . .4 D1
Mill Fold Gdns OL15 . . . . .16 A4
Mill Fold Rd M24 . . . . .64 F8
Millford Ave M41 . . . . .94 E2
Millford Gdns M41. . . . . .94 E2
MILLGATE 4 D4
Millgate
  Bolton BL1. . . . . .8 D2
  Delph OL3 . . . . .50 F4
  Rochdale OL16. . . . . .15 C2
  Stockport SK1 . . . . .169 C2

Millgate continued
  Wigan WN1 . . . . .150 C4
Mill Gate OL8 . . . . .66 D2
Millgate La M20 . . . . .110 B1
Millgate Terr OL12. . . . . .4 E5
Millgreen Cl WN6. . . . . .53 A7
Mill Green Sch WA12. . . . . . . .89 E3
Mill Green St M12. . . . . .164 A4
Millhall Cl M15. . . . . .162 B1
Millhead Ave M40 . . . . .160 B2
MILL HILL 148 A4
Mill Hill M18 . . . . .59 E6
Mill Hill Ave SK12. . . . . .133 D7
Mill Hill Gr SK14. . . . . .102 F2
Mill Hill Hollow SK12. . . . . . .133 D7
Mill Hill St BL2. . . . . .148 A4
Mill Hill Way **3** SK14 . . . . .102 F2
Millhouse Ave M23 . . . . .121 A4
Mill House Cl OL12 . . . . .15 D4
Millhouse St BL0 . . . . .11 B8
Mill House View WN8 . . . . .53 C7
Milliner Ct SK2 . . . . .124 D7
Millingford Ave WA3 . . . . .73 F2
Millingford Gr WN4. . . . . .73 B3
Millingford Ind Est
  WA3. . . . . .90 A8
Milling St M1 . . . . .162 C4
Millington Wlk **12**
  M15 . . . . .162 A2
Mill La
  Altrincham WA15. . . . . .129 E4
  Appley Bridge WN6 . . . . .35 D7
  Ashton-u-L OL6 . . . . .166 B2
  Aspull WN2 . . . . .38 F3
  4 Bury BL8. . . . . .27 B4
  Cheadle Hulme SK8. . . . . . .123 B3
  Cheadle SK8 . . . . .122 D6
  Denton M34, SK14. . . . . . . .101 B2
  Failsworth M35 . . . . .83 C7
  Hazel Grove SK7 . . . . .133 F8
  Horwich BL6 . . . . .22 D4
  Leigh WN7 . . . . .76 B4
  Lymm WA13. . . . . .117 C4
  Marple SK6 . . . . .125 B7
  Mossley OL5 . . . . .68 C2
  Newton-le-W WA12. . . . . . . .89 E3
  Oldham OL9 . . . . .66 C4
  Reddish, North Reddish
    SK5. . . . . .99 F1
  Reddish, Reddish Vale
    SK5. . . . . .112 B8
  Romiley SK6. . . . . .113 A5
  Royton OL2 . . . . .48 C4
  Up Holland WN8 . . . . .53 A8
  Uppermill OL4 . . . . .50 D1
  Westhoughton BL5. . . . . .57 E5
  Wythenshawe M22 . . . . . . .109 E1
Mill Mdw WN7. . . . . .89 E3
Mill Nook OL2 . . . . .14 F3
Millom Ave M23 . . . . .109 B1
Millom Cl OL16 . . . . .15 C1
Millom Dr BL9 . . . . .45 A2
Millom Pl SK8 . . . . .122 B3
Millow St M4 . . . . .159 A3
Mill Point M1 . . . . .163 B4
Mill Pond Ave
  6 Bolton BL3. . . . . .42 A3
  New Mills SK22 . . . . .127 D1
Mill Pond Cl OL12 . . . . .149 B2
Millpool Wlk **1** M9. . . . . . . .157 A4
Mill Rd
  Bury M9. . . . . .27 F8
  Orrell WN5. . . . . .53 D5
  Wilmslow SK9 . . . . .137 B7
Millrise OL1 . . . . .153 B4
Mills Farm Cl OL8 . . . . .67 A1
Mills Hill Prim Sch
  OL9. . . . . .65 E8
Mills Hill Rd M24 . . . . .65 D8
Mills Hill Sta M24 . . . . .47 D1
Mills St
  Heywood OL10. . . . . .29 B2
  Whitworth OL12. . . . . .4 D1
Mill St
  Adlington PR6 . . . . .21 B8
  Altrincham WA14. . . . . .119 E5
  Ashton-in-M WN4. . . . . .73 C2
  8 Bolton, Cox Green
    BL7. . . . . .24 F8
  Bolton, Mill Hill BL1. . . . . . .148 A4
  Bury BL8 . . . . .26 F8
  Dukinfield SK14. . . . . .101 E5
  Failsworth M35. . . . . .83 D7
  Farnworth BL4. . . . . .60 C8
  Glossop SK13. . . . . .104 D1
  Golborne WA3. . . . . .90 A8
  Hazel Grove SK7 . . . . .124 D3
  Hindley WN2 . . . . .56 D5
  Leigh WN7 . . . . .76 A4
  Manchester M11. . . . . .165 A4
  Mossley SK15. . . . . .86 C8
  Radcliffe M26 . . . . .44 B2
  Ramsbottom BL0. . . . . .11 B8
  Royton OL2 . . . . .48 D4
  Salford M6. . . . . .81 A4
  Stalybridge SK15. . . . . .86 C1
  Tyldesley M46 . . . . .58 E1
  Uppermill OL3 . . . . .69 B8
  Westhoughton BL5. . . . . .57 F8
  Wigan WN3 . . . . .150 B3
  Wilmslow SK9 . . . . .137 B7
  Wigan, Marylebone WN1. . . . .37 C3
Millstone Cl
  Poynton SK12 . . . . .133 F5
  Romiley SK6. . . . . .113 A3
Millstone Rd BL1 . . . . .23 F1
Millstream La M40 . . . . .83 E4

Milltown 104 D1
Milltown Cl **3** M26. . . . . . . .44 B2
Milltown St M26. . . . . .44 B3
Mill View Ct OL8. . . . . .66 D3
Mill View La BL6. . . . . .22 E4
Millwall Cl M18. . . . . .99 D5
Millway WA15. . . . . .129 C2
Millway **5** BL1 . . . . .145 C3
Millwell La **5** BL1 . . . . .145 C3
Millwood
  Ashton-in-M WN4 . . . . .73 A5
  4 Cheadle SK8. . . . . .131 E8
Millwood Cl BL9. . . . . .44 F6
Millwood Prim Specl Sch
  BL9. . . . . .44 F6
Millwood Terr **3**
  SK14. . . . . .167 A2
Millwood View **6**
  SK15. . . . . .86 B2
Millwright St M40 . . . . .83 C5
Mill Yd BL9 . . . . .141 A3
Milne Cl M12. . . . . .165 A3
Milner Ave
  Altrincham WA14. . . . . .119 B7
  Bury BL9 . . . . .27 F5
Milner St
  Manchester M16 . . . . .97 D4
  Pendlebury M27 . . . . .80 A8
  Radcliffe M26 . . . . .43 E3
  Whitworth OL12. . . . . .4 C1
  Whitworth OL12. . . . . .14 C8
Milnes Ave WN7 . . . . .75 F2
Milne St
  Chadderton OL9. . . . . .48 C1
  Chadderton OL9. . . . . .152 B3
  Haslingden BL0 . . . . .1 C5
  Oldham, Higginshaw OL1. . . .49 A2
  Oldham OL9. . . . . .152 C1
  Rochdale OL11. . . . . .30 C2
  Shaw OL2. . . . . .149 B2
Milngate Cl OL16 . . . . .31 C3
Milnholme BL1. . . . . .142 B3
MILNROW 31 E4
Milnrow Cl M13 . . . . .163 B3
Milnrow Parish CE Prim
  Sch OL16 . . . . .31 F6
Milnrow Rd
  Littleborough OL15 . . . . .16 A2
  Rochdale OL16. . . . . .31 B7
  Shaw, Jubilee OL16, OL2. . . . .32 C2
  Shaw OL2. . . . . .149 B3
  Shaw, Small Brook OL2. . . . .149 C4
Milnrow Sta OL16 . . . . .31 F5
Milnthorpe Rd BL2 . . . . .42 E8
Milnthorpe St M6. . . . . .81 B5
Milnthorpe Way M12. . . . . . . .164 B2
Milo St M9 . . . . .64 D3
Milsom Ave **3** BL3 . . . . . . .146 C3
Milstead Wlk M40 . . . . .83 A5
Milston Wlk M8 . . . . .156 A2
Milton Ave
  Bolton BL3. . . . . .146 B4
  Droylsden M43 . . . . .84 A1
  Irlam M44. . . . . .105 E6
  Little Lever BL3 . . . . .43 B4
  Newton-le-W WA12. . . . . . . .89 B3
  Salford M5. . . . . .154 A2
  Stalybridge SK15. . . . . .86 E4
Milton Cl
  Atherton M46 . . . . .58 D5
  Dukinfield SK16. . . . . .102 B7
  Haslingden BB4 . . . . .1 A7
  Marple SK6 . . . . .125 F4
  Stretford M32 . . . . .96 E3
Milton Cres
  Cheadle SK8 . . . . .122 C5
  Farnworth BL4. . . . . .60 B6
Milton Ct
  Bramhall SK7. . . . . .132 F6
  3 Eccles M30. . . . . .79 D2
  5 Manchester, Broughton
    Park M7 . . . . .81 C5
  Manchester, Green End
    M19 . . . . .110 E4
Milton Dr
  Chadderton OL9. . . . . .152 A2
  Poynton SK12 . . . . .133 D4
  Sale, Brooklands WA15. . . . .108 A3
  Sale M33 . . . . .108 B6
Milton Gr
  Longshaw WN5. . . . . .53 D1
  Manchester M16 . . . . .97 C2
  Orrell WN5. . . . . .53 F6
  Sale M33 . . . . .108 A6
  Wigan, Marylebone WN1. . . . .37 C3
  Wigan, Redwood WN5. . . . . . .54 A6
Milton Ho Ct SK6 . . . . .112 F5
Milton Lo BL1. . . . . .143 F2
Milton Mount **1** M18 . . . . . .99 D4
Milton Pl M6 . . . . .81 B3
Milton Rd
  Bramhall SK7. . . . . .132 E7
  Coppull PR7 . . . . .19 E8
  Droylsden M34. . . . . .84 D1
  Golborne WA3. . . . . .90 D7
  Prestwich M25. . . . . .63 C5
  Radcliffe M26 . . . . .44 B3
  Stretford M32 . . . . .96 E3
  Swinton M27 . . . . .79 C6
Milton St John's CE Prim
  Sch OL5. . . . . .68 C2
Milton St
  Eccles M30. . . . . .79 D2
  Hyde SK14. . . . . .167 A4
  Leigh WN7 . . . . .75 E5

Milton St continued
Middleton M24. . . . . .46 F1
Mossley OL5 . . . . .68 C2
Ramsbottom BL0. . . . . . . .138 B2
Rochdale OL16. . . . . .139 C3
Royton OL2 . . . . .48 B4
Salford M7. . . . . .158 B4
Milton View OL5 . . . . .68 D2
Milverton Ave SK14 . . . . .102 C2
Milverton Cl BL6 . . . . .40 D5
Milverton Dr SK7. . . . . . .132 B5
Milverton Rd M14 . . . . . . .98 D3
Milverton Wlk SK14. . . . .102 C2
Milwain Dr SK4 . . . . .111 C6
Milwain Rd
Manchester M19 . . . . .111 A8
Stretford M32 . . . . .96 C1
Mimosa Dr M27 . . . . .61 F2
Mimosa Rd B2 OL9. . . . . . .65 F8
Mincing St B M4. . . . . . .159 A3
Minden Cl
Bury BL8 . . . . .27 B2
Manchester M20 . . . . .110 D4
Minden Par BL0 . . . . .140 C2
Minden St M6. . . . . .80 E6
Minehead Ave
Hindley WN7 . . . . .57 D2
Manchester M20 . . . . .109 F6
Urmston M41. . . . . .107 B8
Miners Mews The M28. . . .78 B7
Minerva Rd
Ashton-u-L OL6, SK16 . . . .166 C2
Farnworth BL4. . . . . .42 A2
Mine St OL10 . . . . .29 D4
Minford Cl M40. . . . . .83 B6
Minnie St
Bolton BL3 . . . . .146 B3
Whitworth OL12. . . . . .4 D2
Minoan Gdns M7 . . . . .81 C5
Minorca Ave M11. . . . . . . .83 D2
Minorca Cl M11. . . . . .29 E8
Minorca St BL3 . . . . .147 B4
Minor St
Failsworth M35 . . . . .66 A1
Oldham OL8 . . . . .153 B1
Rochdale OL11. . . . . .30 C1
Minshull S S M1. . . . . . . .163 B4
Minshull St M1. . . . . .159 A1
Minsmere Cl B M8. . . . . .156 A2
Minsmere Wlks SK2. . . . .124 F4
Minstead Cl SK14. . . . . . .102 A1
Minstead Wlk B M22. . . .121 B4
Minster Cl
Bolton BL2 . . . . .25 C2
Dukinfield SK16 . . . . .101 D6
Minster Dr
Altrincham WA14. . . . . . . .128 A8
Cheadle SK8 . . . . .123 A5
Urmston M41. . . . . .95 A3
Minster Gr M29. . . . . .77 B7
Minsterley Par M22. . . . .121 C1
Minster Rd
Bolton BL2 . . . . .25 C2
Manchester M9 . . . . .157 C4
Minster Way OL9 . . . . .48 A1
Minstrel Cl
Abram Brow WN2 . . . . .74 B7
Swinton M27 . . . . .79 D7
Minton St BL3 . . . . .146 A4
Minton St
Failsworth M40 . . . . .83 C8
Oldham OL4 . . . . .67 A5
Minto St OL7 . . . . .166 A4
Mintridge Cl B M11. . . . . .99 E7
Mirabel St BL0. . . . . .1 C2
Mirabel St M3. . . . . .158 C3
Miranda Cl M5 . . . . .161 C4
Mirfield Ave
Manchester M9 . . . . .64 D4
Oldham OL8 . . . . .66 E4
Stockport SK4 . . . . .168 B2
Mirfield Cl WA3 . . . . .90 D7
Mirfield Dr
Eccles M30 . . . . .79 D4
Middleton M24. . . . . .46 F1
Urmston M41. . . . . .95 C4
Mirfield Rd M9 . . . . .64 D4
Miriam Gr WN7. . . . . .76 A4
Miriam St
B Bolton BL3 . . . . .146 B4
Failsworth M35 . . . . .83 D5
Miry La
Westhoughton BL5 . . . . .57 E6
Wigan WN3, WN6 . . . . . . .150 A4
Missenden Ho B2 M5 . . .154 C1
Mission St OL10 . . . . .29 C2
Missouri Ave M50 . . . . . .154 B1
Mistletoe Gr M3. . . . . . . .158 A3
Mistral Ct M30 . . . . .79 E3
Mitcham Ave M9 . . . . .63 A3
Mitchell Cl SK8. . . . . .121 F6
Mitchell Fold SK6. . . . . . .134 D1
Mitchell Gdns M22 . . . . .121 E4
MITCHELL HEY 139 B3
Mitchell Hey OL12 . . . . . .139 B3
Mitchell Rd WN5 . . . . .71 E5
Mitchells Quay M35 . . . . .83 E7
Mitchell St
Ashton-in-M WN4 . . . . .73 C2
Bury BL8 . . . . .27 C4
Eccles M30 . . . . .79 C3
Failsworth M40 . . . . .83 B5
Golborne WA3 . . . . .90 A8
Ince-in-M WN2 . . . . .56 A7
Leigh WN7 . . . . .75 B5

Mitchell St continued
Manchester M11. . . . . . . .164 C4
Oldham OL1. . . . . .153 B4
Rochdale, Greengate
OL16. . . . . .15 C3
Rochdale, Spotland Bridge
OL12. . . . . .139 A4
Wigan WN5 . . . . .54 E6
Mitcheson Gdns M6 . . . . .154 C3
Mitford Cl M14 . . . . .110 C7
Mitford Rd M14 . . . . .110 C7
Mitford St M32 . . . . .96 C1
Mitre Rd M12, M13 . . . . . . .98 F4
Mitre St
Bolton BL1 . . . . .143 B4
Failsworth M35 . . . . .83 F8
Mitton Cl
Bury BL8 . . . . .26 F2
Culcheth WA3 . . . . .91 E5
Heywood OL10. . . . . .28 F2
Mizpah Gr BL8 . . . . .27 B2
Mizzy Rd OL12. . . . . .14 F1
Moadlock SK6. . . . . .113 C4
Moat Ave M22. . . . . .121 C5
Moat Gdns M22 . . . . .121 C4
Moat Hall Ave M30 . . . . . . .95 A8
Moat House St SK4 . . . . .169 B3
Moat House St WN2 . . . . . .56 A7
Moat Rd M22. . . . . .121 C4
Moat Wlk SK5 . . . . .112 C7
Mobberley Cl M19 . . . . . .110 E4
Mobberley Rd
Ashley WA14, WA15,
WA16 . . . . .128 E3
Bolton BL2 . . . . .42 E8
Wilmslow SK9 . . . . .130 D1
Mocha Par M7 . . . . .158 A3
Modbury Cl SK7 . . . . .124 A1
Modbury Wlk B M8 . . . . .156 A2
Mode Hill La M45. . . . . . . .45 C1
Mode Hill Wlk M45 . . . . . .63 C8
Mode Wheel Circ M17 . . . .96 C7
Mode Wheel Rd M5,
M50 . . . . .154 A1
Mode Wheel Rd S
Salford M50. . . . . .154 A1
Stretford M50. . . . . .96 D8
Modwen Rd M5 . . . . .161 B2
Moelfre Dr SK8 . . . . .132 C7
Moffat Cl BL2 . . . . .42 F6
Moffat St B SK16 . . . . . . .166 B1
Moggie La SK10 . . . . .133 F1
Moisant St BL3 . . . . .147 A3
Moison Ho SK2 . . . . .124 A6
Mold St
Bolton BL1 . . . . .143 B3
Oldham OL1. . . . . .153 B4
Molesworth St OL16. . . . . .31 A7
Mollets Wood M34. . . . . .101 A5
Mollington Rd M22 . . . . . .130 E8
Mollis Gr OL1 . . . . .49 E3
Molyneux Rd
Reddish M19 . . . . .99 C1
Westhoughton BL5 . . . . .40 B1
Molyneux St
Rochdale OL12. . . . . .139 A4
Wigan WN1 . . . . .151 A4
Mona Ave
Cheadle SK8 . . . . .122 D1
Stretford M32 . . . . .96 C3
Monaco Dr M22 . . . . .109 D2
Monarch Cl
Irlam M44 . . . . .105 E4
Royton OL2 . . . . .48 E2
Mona Rd OL9. . . . . .152 B1
Monart Rd M9. . . . . .64 E1
Mona St
Hyde SK14 . . . . .167 B2
Salford M6. . . . . .81 A4
Wigan WN1 . . . . .150 B4
Mona Way M44. . . . . .106 B8
Moncrieffe St
Bolton BL3 . . . . .145 C2
Bolton, Rose Hill BL4. . . . .148 A1
Monde Trad Est M17. . . . . .96 A6
Mond Rd M44 . . . . .94 B4
Money Ash Rd WA15. . . . .119 E3
Monfa Ave SK2 . . . . .124 A4
Monica Ave M8. . . . . .63 F2
Monica Gr M19 . . . . .110 F8
Monica Terr WN4 . . . . .73 B2
Monks La
Manchester M8 . . . . .64 B2
Milnrow OL16 . . . . .31 E6
Monks Ct M5. . . . . .80 B2
Monksdale Ave M41. . . . . .95 B2
Monks Hall Gr M30 . . . . . .79 F2
Monks La BL2 . . . . .25 D2
Monk's Rd SK13 . . . . .116 A4
Monkswood OL1. . . . . . . .153 B3
Monkton Ave M18 . . . . .99 C4
Monkwood Dr B M9. . . . .157 B4
Monmouth Ave
Bury BL9 . . . . .27 F5
Sale M33. . . . . .107 F5
Monmouth Cres WN4 . . . .73 D2
Monmouth Rd SK8. . . . . .123 B1
Monmouth St
B Manchester M18 . . . . . . .99 E6
Middleton M24. . . . . .65 C8
Oldham OL9. . . . . .152 C1
Rochdale OL11. . . . . .139 C2
Monroe Cl
Salford M6. . . . . .154 B4
Wigan WN3 . . . . .55 A3

Monsal Ave
Salford M7. . . . . .81 A7
Stockport SK2 . . . . .124 D7
Monsall Cl BL9 . . . . .45 A2
Monsall Rd M40, M9. . . . .157 B2
Monsall St
Manchester M40 . . . . .157 A1
Oldham OL8. . . . . .66 E3
Mons Ave OL11. . . . . .30 C8
Montague Ho SK3 . . . . . .170 A4
Montague Rd
Ashton-u-L OL6 . . . . .85 D3
Manchester M16 . . . . .161 A1
Sale M33. . . . . .108 B4
Montague St BL3. . . . . . .146 B3
Montague Way SK15. . . . . .86 A2
Montagu Rd SK2 . . . . . . .124 D8
Montagu St SK6 . . . . .114 B2
Montana Ho B M1 . . . . . .163 A3
Montana Sq M11. . . . . .99 E7
Montcliffe Cres M16. . . . . .97 F2
Monteagle St M9 . . . . .64 B4
Montford St M50 . . . . .96 F8
Montford St M40 . . . . .96 F8
Montfort Cl BL5 . . . . .57 D6
Montgomery OL11 . . . . . .139 B2
Montgomery Ho BL9. . . . . .45 B2
Montgomery Ho M13 . . . . .98 F2
Montgomery St
Oldham OL8. . . . . .66 B1
Rochdale OL11. . . . . .30 C4
Montgomery Way M26 . . . .43 C5
Montmano Dr M20 . . . . . .109 F6
MONTON 79 D4
Monton Ave M30 . . . . .79 D4
Monton Bridge Ct M30. . . .79 C4
Montondale M30 . . . . .79 C3
Montonfields Rd M30 . . . .79 C3
Monton Gn M30. . . . . .79 D4
Monton Green Prim Sch
M30 . . . . .79 E4
Monton Ho SK5. . . . . .112 B4
Monton La M30. . . . . .79 E2
Monton Lo M30 . . . . .79 E2
Monton Mews B WN1 . . . .37 B3
Montonmill Gdns M30 . . . .79 C3
Monton Rd
Brinnington SK5. . . . . .112 C4
Eccles M30 . . . . .79 D3
Monton St
Bolton BL3 . . . . .147 B3
Manchester M14 . . . . .98 A4
Radcliffe M26 . . . . .43 F3
Monton Village Sch
M30 . . . . .79 D3
Montpellier Mews B
M7 . . . . .63 E1
Montpellier Rd M22 . . . . .121 D2
Montreal St
Abram Brow WN7 . . . . .74 E4
B Manchester M19 . . . . . . .99 B1
Oldham OL8. . . . . .66 F4
Montrey Cres WN4. . . . . . .72 C3
Montrose B M30 . . . . .79 E2
Montrose Ave
Bolton BL2 . . . . .25 C1
Dukinfield SK14 . . . . .101 C7
Laithwaite WN5 . . . . .54 D8
B Manchester M20 . . . . . .110 A5
Ramsbottom BL0 . . . . .11 A2
Stockport SK2 . . . . .124 A3
Stretford M32 . . . . .96 B2
Wigan WN5 . . . . .54 D7
Montrose Cres B M19 . . . .99 A1
Montrose Dr BL7 . . . . .25 B7
Montrose Gdns OL2. . . . . .48 F4
Montrose St OL11 . . . . . . .30 C1
Montserrat Brow BL1. . . . .23 D2
Montserrat Rd BL1. . . . . . .23 E2
Monument Mans B
WN1. . . . . .37 C2
Monument Rd WN1. . . . . . .37 D2
Monyash Ct B2 SK13 . . . .171 A1
Monyash Gr B1 SK13 . . . .171 A1
Monyash Lea B SK13 . . . .171 A1
Monyash Mews B
SK13. . . . . .171 A1
Monyash Pl B2 SK13 . . . .171 A1
Monyash View WN7. . . . . .56 F3
Monyash Way B
SK13. . . . . .171 B1
Moody St WN6 . . . . .19 E1
Moon Gr M14 . . . . .98 D3
Moon St SK9 . . . . .152 C3
Moor Allerton Sch
M20 . . . . .109 F4
Moor Ave WN6 . . . . .35 E8
Moor Bank La OL16. . . . . .31 E3
Moorbottom Rd BL8 . . . . .10 E5
Moorby Ave M19 . . . . .110 E4
Moorby St B OL1 . . . . .67 A6
Moorby Wlk BL3. . . . . . . .145 C1
Moor Cl M26. . . . . .43 E5
MOORCLOSE 65 C8
Moorcock Ave M27 . . . . . .80 B8
Moorcot Ct M23 . . . . .120 F7
Moor Cres OL3 . . . . .51 B3
Moorcroft
Edenfield BL0. . . . . .1 D2
Rochdale OL11. . . . . .30 F3
Moorcroft Dr M19 . . . . . . .110 F4
Moorcroft Rd M23 . . . . . .108 F1
Moorcroft Sq SK14 . . . . . .101 E6
Moorcroft St
B Droylsden M43. . . . . .84 B1
Oldham OL8. . . . . .66 C2
Moorcroft Wlk M19. . . . . .110 F4

Moordale Ave OL4. . . . . . . .49 E1
Moordale St M20 . . . . . . .110 A5
Moordown Cl M8 . . . . . . .156 B2
Moor Edge Rd OL5,
SK15. . . . . .86 F8
Mooredge Terr OL2 . . . . . .48 E2
Moore Gr WA13 . . . . .117 B5
Moore Ho B M30. . . . . .95 D8
MOOREND 127 A6
Moor End M22 . . . . .121 D8
Moor End Ave M7 . . . . .81 C8
Moor End Ct M7. . . . . .81 C8
Moor End Rd SK6. . . . . . . .127 A8
Moore St E WN1. . . . . .37 E1
Moore's Ct B BL1 . . . . . . .144 C4
Moores La WN6 . . . . .19 C2
Moore St
Rochdale OL16. . . . . .139 C3
Wigan WN1 . . . . .37 E1
Moore Wlk B M34. . . . . . .113 A7
Moorfield
Boothstown M28 . . . . .77 F6
Edgworth BL7 . . . . .7 D6
Manchester M7 . . . . .81 C8
Radcliffe M26 . . . . .43 E4
Worsley M28 . . . . .78 F8
Moorfield Ave
Denton M34. . . . . .101 A2
Littleborough OL15 . . . . . . .16 A7
Manchester M20 . . . . .110 C7
Stalybridge SK15 . . . . .102 D7
Moorfield Chase BL4 . . . . .60 D7
Moorfield Cl
B Eccles M30. . . . . .79 D1
Irlam M44 . . . . .94 B3
Swinton M27 . . . . .79 D6
Moorfield Com Prim Sch
M44 . . . . .94 A3
Moorfield Cres WA3 . . . . . .91 A7
Moorfield Dr
Dukinfield SK14 . . . . .101 E5
Wilmslow SK9 . . . . .136 E5
Moorfield Gr
Bolton BL2 . . . . .25 B1
Sale M33. . . . . .108 D3
Stockport SK4 . . . . .168 B4
Moorfield Hamlet OL2 . . . .48 F7
Moorfield Hts SK15 . . . . . .86 E7
Moorfield Mews OL2. . . . . .48 F7
Moorfield Par M44 . . . . . . .94 B3
Moorfield Pl B OL12 . . . . .14 F1
Moorfield Prec SK14 . . . . .103 D5
Moorfield Prim Sch
SK7. . . . . .124 C1
Moorfield Rd
Irlam M44 . . . . .94 B3
Manchester M20 . . . . .109 F4
Moorfield Terr
Hollingworth SK14. . . . . . .103 D5
B Manchester M20 . . . . . .110 B7
Platt Bridge WN2. . . . . .56 B3
Moorfield Wlk M41 . . . . . . .95 D2
Moorgate BL9 . . . . .141 A3
Moor Gate BL2 . . . . .25 D5
Moorgate Ave
Manchester M20 . . . . .109 F6
Rochdale OL11. . . . . .30 A7
Moorgate Ct B2 BL2. . . . . .25 B1
Moorgate Dr
Mossley SK15 . . . . .86 E6
Tyldesley M29 . . . . .77 C5
Moor Gate La OL15 . . . . . .15 E7
Moorgate Mews SK15. . . . .86 E7
Moorgate Prim Sch
BL2. . . . . .148 B4
Moorgate Rd
Mossley SK15 . . . . .86 E7
Radcliffe M26 . . . . .43 F8
Moorgate St OL2 . . . . .48 F5
Moorhead St M4 . . . . .159 B3
MOORHEY 67 B6
Moorhey Rd M38 . . . . .59 F6
Moorhey St OL4 . . . . .67 B6
Moor Hill OL11 . . . . .29 F8
Moorhill Ct B M7 . . . . .63 C1
Moorhouse Farm OL16. . . .31 E6
Moorhouse Fold OL16 . . . .31 E6
Moorhouse Prim Sch
OL16. . . . . .31 E6
Moorings Cl WN1. . . . . . . .151 C4
Moorings Rd M17 . . . . .96 B8
Moorings The
Disley SK12 . . . . .135 E4
Mossley OL5 . . . . .68 E3
Worsley M28 . . . . .79 A5
Moor La
Bolton BL1, BL3. . . . . .145 B2
Bramhall SK7. . . . . .132 E3
Leigh WN7 . . . . .75 E8
Manchester M7 . . . . .63 C1
Rochdale OL12. . . . . .13 F3
Salford M7, M25 . . . . .81 B8
Uppermill OL3 . . . . .51 C2
Urmston M41. . . . . .94 A3
Wilmslow SK9 . . . . .136 C5
Wythenshawe M23 . . . . . .109 A2
Moorland Ave
Droylsden M43. . . . . .83 E1
Manchester M8 . . . . .63 F2
Milnrow OL16 . . . . .32 A6
Rochdale OL11. . . . . .29 F8

Moorland Ave continued
Sale M33. . . . . .108 C3
Uppermill OL3 . . . . .50 F2
Whitworth OL12. . . . . .14 C7
Moorland Cres OL12 . . . . .14 C7
Moorland Dr
Cheadle SK8 . . . . .131 F8
Horwich BL6 . . . . .22 F3
Walkden M38. . . . . .60 A6
Moorland Fold SK15 . . . . .102 E7
Moorland Gr BL1 . . . . .142 A2
Moorland Rd
Ashton-in-M WN4 . . . . .73 E5
Hindley M WN2 . . . . .56 C5
Manchester M20 . . . . .110 B3
Mossley SK15 . . . . .86 E5
Stockport SK2 . . . . .124 B4
Moorlands Ave
Leigh WN7 . . . . .75 F3
Urmston M41. . . . . .95 B3
Moorlands Cres OL5 . . . . .68 D1
Moorlands Dr OL5 . . . . . . .68 E3
Moorlands Home BL1. . . .142 B3
Moorlands Jun Sch
M33 . . . . .108 C3
Moorland St
Littleborough OL15 . . . . . . .16 C7
Rochdale OL12. . . . . .14 E1
Shaw OL2. . . . . .149 C3
Moorlands View
Bolton BL3 . . . . .146 A2
Edenfield BL0. . . . . .1 D5
Moorland Terr OL12. . . . . .14 A1
Moorlea M35 . . . . .83 F8
Moor Lo SK4 . . . . .168 B4
Moor Nook M33 . . . . .108 D3
Moor Park Ave OL11. . . . . .30 B2
Moor Park Rd M20 . . . . . .122 C8
Moor Platt M33. . . . . .108 B3
Moor Platt Cl BL6. . . . . . . .22 F3
Moor Rd
Calderbrook OL15 . . . . .6 C1
Haslingden BB4. . . . . .1 A5
Orrell WN5. . . . . .53 E6
Ramsbottom BL8 . . . . .138 A2
Wythenshawe M23 . . . . . .120 B8
Moorsbrook Gr B
SK9. . . . . .131 E1
Moorsholme Ave B
M40 . . . . .83 A7
MOORSIDE
49 E3
79 D7
Moorside
Littleborough OL15 . . . . . . .16 D6
Rochdale OL11. . . . . .30 F3
Moorside Ave
Ainsworth BL2 . . . . .26 D1
Bolton BL1. . . . . .142 A1
Droylsden M43. . . . . .84 C2
Farnworth BL4. . . . . .60 B7
Horwich BL6 . . . . .22 C4
Moorside Cl SK13. . . . . . .116 B7
Moorside Cres M43. . . . . . .84 C2
Moorside Ct
Denton M34. . . . . .101 A4
Sale M33. . . . . .108 B4
Moorside High Sch
M27. . . . . .79 D7
Moorside Ho WA15 . . . . . .120 C7
Moorside La M34. . . . . . . .101 A4
Moorside Lo M27. . . . . .79 D8
Moorside Prim Sch
Droylsden M43. . . . . .84 B1
Swinton M27 . . . . .79 D7
Moorside Rd
Bury BL8 . . . . .26 E5
Manchester M8 . . . . .64 A1
Mossley OL5 . . . . .68 E1
Salford M7. . . . . .81 C8
Stockport SK4 . . . . .168 A2
Swinton M27 . . . . .79 D8
Urmston M41. . . . . .94 A3
Moorside St M43 . . . . .84 C2
Moorside Sta M27 . . . . .61 C2
Moorside View
Bury BL8 . . . . .26 F6
Shaw OL2. . . . . .149 C4
Moorside Wlk WN5 . . . . . . .54 B8
Moorsley Dr M9 . . . . .64 F4
Moor St
Aspull WN2 . . . . .38 C5
Bury BL9 . . . . .140 C3
Eccles M30 . . . . .79 B1
Heywood OL10. . . . . .29 B2
Oldham OL1. . . . . .67 B7
Shaw OL2. . . . . .149 A2
Swinton M27 . . . . .79 F1
Moorsview BL0. . . . . .138 B2
Moorton Ave M19 . . . . . . .110 F7
Moorton Pk M19 . . . . .110 F7
Moortop Cl M9 . . . . .64 C6
Moor Top Pl SK4. . . . . . . .168 B3
Moor View
Bacup OL13 . . . . .3 B7
Rawtenstall BB4 . . . . .2 F6
Moor View Cl OL12 . . . . . .13 F2
Moorville Rd M6. . . . . .80 C5
Moor Way BL0. . . . . .10 C3
Moorway Dr M9 . . . . .65 A4
Moorwood Dr
Oldham OL3. . . . . .67 C4
Sale M33. . . . . .107 C3
Mora Ave OL9 . . . . .48 B1
Moran Cl SK9 . . . . .131 E2
Morano Dr WN2. . . . . .56 A3
Moran Wlk B M15. . . . . . .162 C2

Morar Dr BL2 .....43 A7
Morar Rd SK16 .....101 D7
Mora St M9 .....157 C4
Moravian Cl SK16 .....166 C1
Moravian Field 3
M43 .....100 A8
Moray Cl BL0 .....11 A4
Moray Rd OL9 .....66 A4
Morbourne Cl M12 .....164 B2
Morden Ave
Ashton-in-M WN4 .....73 B3
17 Droylsden M11 .....83 C2
Morecambe Cl M40 .....83 B6
Morelands The BL1 .....144 A3
Morely St OL4 .....49 E1
Moresby Dr WN7 .....75 D5
Moresby Dr M20 .....122 B8
Moreton Ave
Bramhall SK7 .....132 E5
Sale M33 .....107 F3
Stretford M32 .....96 D2
Whitefield M45 .....44 F1
Moreton Cl
Dukinfield SK16 .....101 D6
Golborne WA3 .....73 F1
Moreton Dr
Bury BL8 .....27 B3
Handforth SK9 .....131 E3
Leigh WN7 .....75 E1
Poynton SK12 .....133 F4
Moreton Ho M14 .....119 B4
Moreton La SK2 .....124 C7
Moreton St OL9 .....65 F8
Moreton Way SK14 .....102 F3
Moreton Wlk SK2 .....124 D7
Morgan Pl SK5 .....169 C4
Morgan St OL15 .....16 B5
Morgans Way WA3 .....91 A8
Morillon Rd M44 .....94 A4
Morland Rd M16 .....97 C4
MORLEY 130 C2
Morley Ave
Manchester M14 .....98 A1
Swinton M27 .....79 E6
MORLEY GREEN 130 C1
Morley Green Rd SK9 .....130 C1
Morley Ho M22 .....121 F7
Morley Rd 43 D4
Morley's La
Tyldesley M29 .....76 F3
Tyldesley M29 .....77 A3
Morley St
Atherton M46 .....58 C2
Bolton BL3 .....145 A2
Bury BL9 .....44 F8
Glossop SK13 .....116 D8
Rochdale OL16 .....15 B1
Whitefield M45 .....62 F8
Morley Way OL3 .....69 B5
Morna Wlk M12 .....164 A4
Morningside WA14 .....119 B5
Morningside Cl
Droylsden M43 .....100 A7
22 Rochdale OL16 .....31 B6
Morningside Dr M20 .....122 C8
Mornington Ave M28 .....122 D4
Mornington Cres
M14 .....110 B8
Mornington Ct 5
OL1 .....153 B4
Mornington Rd
Adlington PR6 .....21 B8
Bolton BL1 .....144 B4
Cheadle SK8 .....122 D4
Hindley WN2 .....56 F5
Over Hulton M46 .....58 F6
Rochdale OL11 .....31 A3
Sale M33 .....108 D5
Morpeth Cl
Ashton-u-L OL7 .....84 E4
Manchester M12 .....164 B1
Morpeth St M27 .....79 E6
Morrell Rd M22 .....121 E8
Morris Ct 4 M14 .....110 C8
Morris Fold Dr BL6 .....40 C6
Morris Gn BL3 .....146 C2
Morris Gr M41 .....95 B2
Morris Green Bsns Pk
BL3 .....146 C4
Morris Green La BL3 .....146 C2
Morris Green St BL3 .....146 C2
Morris Hall 8 M14 .....98 D4
Morris Ho WN1 .....151 A4
Morrison St BL3 .....147 B3
Morris Rd WN8 .....53 A7
Morris St
Bolton BL3 .....148 A3
1 Hindley WN2 .....56 D5
Ince-in-M WN3 .....55 E4
Manchester M20 .....110 B7
Oldham OL4 .....67 A5
Radcliffe M26 .....44 E5
Tyldesley M29 .....77 A3
Wigan WN1 .....151 A4
Morrowfield Ave M8 .....155 C3
Morse Rd M40 .....83 B5
Morston Cl M28 .....78 B8
Mortar St
Oldham OL4 .....67 C7
Oldham OL4 .....67 C8
Mortfield Gdns BL1 .....145 A4
Mortfield La BL1 .....145 A4
Mort Fold La BL5 .....60 A5
Mortimer Ave M40 .....64 E4
Mortimer Ho SK4 .....168 C2
Mortimer St OL1 .....67 A8
Mort La M28, M29, M38 .....59 E2

Mortlake Cl M28 .....59 F3
Mortlake Dr M40 .....83 B5
Morton Ave WN3 .....150 B1
Morton Cl WN3 .....54 C2
Morton St
Failsworth M35 .....83 C6
Middleton M24 .....47 A1
Radcliffe M26 .....44 B2
Stockport SK4 .....169 B4
Mortons The BL5 .....39 E2
Morton Terr
18 Denton M34 .....101 A1
Romiley SK6 .....113 B5
Mort St
Farnworth BL4 .....60 B8
Hindley WN2 .....57 A5
Horwich BL6 .....22 B7
Leigh WN6 .....75 B5
Wigan WN6 .....37 A1
Morven Ave SK7 .....124 F3
Morven Dr M23 .....121 A5
Morven Gr BL2 .....42 F7
Morville Dr WN3 .....55 B4
Morville Rd M21 .....97 D1
Moschatel Wlk M31 .....106 A3
Moscow Rd SK3 .....170 A3
Moscow Rd E SK3 .....170 A3
Mosedale Ave WA11 .....71 B1
Mosedale Cl
Tyldesley M29 .....77 C6
Wythenshawe M23 .....120 E6
Mosedale Rd M24 .....46 E2
Moseldene Rd SK2 .....124 D5
Moseley Ct
Cheadle SK8 .....122 F3
Manchester M19 .....98 F1
Moseley Grange SK8 .....122 F3
Moseley Rd
Cheadle SK8 .....122 F3
Manchester M14 .....110 E8
Moseley St SK3 .....170 B4
MOSES GATE 42 C2
Moses Gate Ctry Pk*
BL3 .....42 E3
Moses Gate Sta 4 M42 .....42 C2
Moses Gate Wkshps 2
BL3 .....42 D2
Mosley Ave
Bury BL9 .....27 F5
Ramsbottom BL0 .....11 B2
Mosley Cl WA15 .....119 F7
MOSLEY COMMON 77 F8
Mosley Common Rd M28,
M29 .....77 F7
Mosley Rd
Altrincham WA15 .....120 B6
Stretford M17 .....96 C6
Mosley St
Manchester M1, M2 .....159 A1
Radcliffe M26 .....44 B2
Mosley Street Sta M1 .....159 A1
MOSLEY VILLAGE 96 C5
Mossack Ave 4 M22 .....121 D1
Moss Ave
Leigh WN7 .....76 B5
Orrell WN5 .....53 D3
Rochdale OL16 .....31 C6
Moss Bank
Bramhall SK7 .....132 C5
Manchester M8 .....156 A4
Moss Bank Ave M43 .....84 C2
Mossbank Cl SK13 .....171 B4
Moss Bank Cl BL1 .....143 B4
Moss Bank Ct 84 C2
Mossbank Gr OL10 .....29 C3
Moss Bank Gr M27 .....61 D2
Moss Bank Ho BL1 .....142 A3
Moss Bank Rd
Billinge WN5 .....71 B2
Swinton M27 .....61 D2
Moss Bank Way
Bolton, Smithills BL1 .....142 B3
Doffcocker BL1 .....23 E1
Mossbray Ave M19 .....110 D4
Moss Bridge Rd OL16 .....31 B6
Mossbrook Ct M40 .....159 C4
Mossbrook Dr M38 .....59 E5
Moss Brook Rd M9 .....157 B3
MOSSBROW 117 E7
Moss Cl
Haslingden BB4 .....1 A8
Radcliffe M26 .....43 D5
Mossclough Ct M9 .....157 B3
Moss Colliery Rd M27 .....61 E4
Moscroft Wlk M13 .....163 B3
Moss Croft Cl WA11 .....94 E3
Mossdale Ave BL1 .....40 D7
Mossdale Rd
Ashton-in-M WN4 .....73 A8
Sale M33 .....107 F1
Wythenshawe M23 .....108 F1
Mossdown Rd OL2 .....49 A3
Moss Dr BL6 .....22 F3
Moss Farm Ct M24 .....65 B6
MOSSFIELD 96 B4
Mossfield Cl
Bury BL9 .....141 B4
Stockport SK4 .....168 B2
Tyldesley M29 .....77 A8
Mossfield Dr M9 .....65 A4
Mossfield Prim Sch
M27 .....61 F1
Mossfield Rd
Altrincham WA15 .....120 D6
Farnworth BL4 .....60 B8
Kearsley BL4 .....60 F5

Mossfield Rd continued
Swinton M27 .....61 F2
Mossfields WN6 .....18 F6
Moss Fold M29 .....77 C8
Moss Gate Rd OL2 .....32 A1
Moss Gn M31 .....106 F6
Moss Gr
Lymm WA13 .....117 B4
Shaw OL2 .....31 E1
Standish WN6 .....36 E8
Moss Grange Ave M16 .....97 D4
MOSS GROVE 66 E1
Moss Grove Ct 2 M15 .....97 E4
Mossgrove Rd WA15 .....119 F6
Mossgrove St 8 OL8 .....66 D2
Mosshall Cl M15 .....162 A2
Moss Hall Farm BL5 .....59 D7
Moss Hall Rd BL6 .....21 A4
MOSS HEY 149 C2
Moss Hey Dr M23 .....109 B1
Moss Hey Prim Sch
SK7 .....132 C5
Moss Hey St OL2 .....149 C2
Moss House La M28 .....78 A5
Moss House Terr M9 .....64 C1
Moss Ind Est
Golborne WN7 .....75 B1
Rochdale OL16 .....31 B5
Moss La
Alderley Edge SK9 .....137 B3
Altrincham WA15 .....119 F7
Altrincham WA15 .....120 A5
Appley Bridge WN6 .....18 E3
Ashton-u-L OL7 .....84 E2
Bolton BL1 .....142 B3
Bramhall SK7 .....132 D5
Broadbottom SK14 .....114 F8
Fowley Common WA3 .....92 D5
Hale WA14, WA15 .....119 E4
Horwich BL6 .....21 F2
Irlam M44 .....105 D5
Kearsley BL4 .....61 B5
Middleton M9 .....64 F5
Paddockhill WA16 .....136 A4
Partington M31 .....105 F3
Partington M31, WA13 .....106 A2
Platt Bridge WN2 .....56 A3
Rochdale OL16 .....31 A6
Royton OL2 .....49 A3
Sale M33 .....107 B3
Sale M33 .....108 A4
Swinton M27 .....61 D2
Town of Lowton WA3 .....90 B5
Tyldesley M29 .....77 C7
Urmston M41 .....95 D5
Walkden M28 .....60 D6
Whitefield M45 .....62 F8
Wythenshawe M23 .....108 F1
Moss La E M14, M16 .....98 A4
Mossland Cl OL10 .....46 D8
Mossland Gr BL3 .....40 D2
Moss La W M15, M16 .....97 E4
Moss Lea BL1 .....143 A4
Mosslee Ave M8 .....63 F3
MOSSLEY 68 C1
MOSSLEY BROW 68 C1
MOSSLEY CROSS 68 B1
Mossley Hollins High Sch
OL5 .....68 E1
Mossley Rd
Ashton-u-L, Higher Hurst
OL6 .....85 E4
Ashton-u-L OL6 .....166 C3
Uppermill OL4 .....45 E7
Mossley Sta OL5 .....68 C1
Moss Lodge La OL7 .....84 F2
Moss Manor M33 .....107 E3
Moss Mdw BL5 .....39 E2
Moss Meadow Rd M6 .....80 C4
Mossmere Rd SK8 .....123 A4
Moss Mill St OL16 .....31 B5
MOSS NOOK 130 F7
Moss Park Inf Sch M32 .....96 B2
Moss Park Jun Sch
M32 .....96 B2
Moss Park Rd M32 .....96 B2
Moss Pit Row WN2 .....38 B4
Moss Pl 3 BL9 .....44 E8
Moss (PRU) The BL2 .....42 F6
Moss Rd
Alderley Edge SK9 .....137 C2
Irlam M44 .....93 B1
Irlam M44 .....105 C7
Kearsley BL4 .....60 E5
Orrell WN5 .....53 D3
Sale M33 .....107 B3
Stretford M17 .....96 C6
Moss Rose SK9 .....137 B2
Moss Row
Bury BL9 .....140 C1
Rochdale OL11 .....13 D1
Moss St E OL6 .....166 B3
Moss Side Way M26 .....84 F2
MOSS SIDE 97 F4
Moss Side La
Hollinfare WA3 .....105 A2
Rochdale OL16 .....15 B2
Moss Side Rd M44 .....105 E6
Moss Side St OL12 .....4 E5
Moss St
Bury BL9 .....140 B2
Droylsden M43 .....84 B1
Droylsden M43 .....84 B2
2 Farnworth BL4 .....42 E1
6 Heywood OL10 .....29 C2
Hollingworth SK14 .....103 D5
Ince-in-M WN3 .....55 F3

Moss St continued
Oldham OL4 .....67 E8
Platt Bridge WN2 .....56 A3
Ramsbottom BL9 .....11 D2
Rochdale OL16 .....31 B6
Salford M7 .....155 A1
10 Wigan, Redwood
WN5 .....54 B6
Wigan, Springfield WN6 .....37 A1
Moss Terr
Ashton-u-L OL6 .....166 A2
Rochdale OL16 .....31 B6
3 Wigan WN5 .....54 B5
Wilmslow SK9 .....137 F8
Moss The M24 .....65 A2
Moss Vale Cres M32 .....95 F3
Moss Vale Rd M41 .....95 E2
Moss View Com Sch
M31 .....106 A3
Moss View Rd
Bolton BL2 .....42 E8
Partington M31 .....106 A3
Mossway M24, M9 .....64 F5
Moss Way M33 .....107 E4
Moss Way M33 .....136 C7
Mosswood Pk M20 .....122 B8
Mosswood Rd SK9 .....131 E1
MOSSY LEA 18 F6
Mossylea Cl M24 .....65 B5
Mossy Lea Fold WN6 .....19 A3
Mossy Lea Rd WN6 .....18 F5
MOSTON 65 B1
Moston Fields Prim Sch
M40 .....65 A1
Moston La
Manchester M9, M40 .....157 C4
Manchester, Moston
M40 .....65 B2
Moston La E M9 .....157 C3
Moston Lane Com Prim
Sch M9 .....157 C4
Moston Rd M24 .....65 D5
Moston St
Reddish SK5 .....111 F8
Salford M7 .....155 C3
Stockport SK4, M40 .....65 D2
Mostyn Ave
Bury BL9 .....27 F5
Cheadle SK8 .....122 E1
Manchester M14 .....110 E8
Mostyn Rd SK7 .....124 C1
Mostyn St SK15, SK16 .....101 F8
Motcombe Farm Rd
SK8 .....122 B1
Motcombe Gr SK8 .....122 A3
Motcombe Rd SK8 .....122 A2
Motherwell Ave 2
M19 .....111 A8
Mottershead Ave BL3 .....43 A4
Mottershead Rd M22 .....121 C4
Mottram Ave M21 .....109 C5
Mottram CE Prim Sch
SK14 .....103 A3
Mottram Cl SK8 .....123 A5
Mottram Dr
Altrincham WA15 .....120 A5
Wigan WN3 .....150 B1
Mottram Fold
Mottram in L SK14 .....103 A3
Stockport SK1 .....170 C4
MOTTRAM IN
LONGDENDALE 103 B4
Mottram Mews 6 BL6 .....22 B4
Mottram Moor SK14 .....103 B4
Mottram Old Rd
Compstall SK14 .....114 B8
Stalybridge SK15 .....102 D7
Mottram Rd
Alderley Edge SK9 .....137 D1
Broadbottom SK14 .....115 A8
Hattersley SK14 .....102 C3
Sale M33 .....108 F3
Stalybridge SK15 .....102 D7
MOTTRAM RISE 102 E7
Mottram St
Horwich BL6 .....22 B4
5 Stockport SK1 .....170 C4
Mough La OL9 .....65 E3
Mouldsworth Ave
Manchester M20 .....110 A2
Reddish SK4 .....111 D6
Moulton St Prec M8 .....158 D4
Moulton St M8 .....158 D4
Mouncey St M1 .....163 A3
Mountain Ash OL12 .....14 B3
Mountain Ash Cl
Rochdale OL12 .....14 B3
9 Sale M33 .....108 C1
Mountain Ash Cotts
OL3 .....33 D1
Mountain Gr M28 .....60 C4
Mountain Rd PR7 .....19 E3
Mountain St
Failsworth M40 .....83 D4
Mossley OL5 .....68 C1
Stockport SK1 .....112 A2
Walkden M28 .....60 C4
Mount Ave
Littleborough OL15 .....16 A7
Rawtenstall BB4 .....2 F8
Rochdale OL12 .....15 E4
Mountbatten Ave
SK16 .....101 F6
Mountbatten Cl BL9 .....45 C2
Mountbatten St M18 .....165 C1
Mount Carmel Cres
M5 .....161 C3

Mount Carmel Ct M5 .....161 C3
Mount Carmel RC Prim
Sch M9 .....64 D2
Mount Cres WN5 .....53 F6
Mount Dr
Marple SK6 .....125 F5
Urmston M41 .....95 F2
Mountfield M25 .....63 B4
Mountfield Ct WN5 .....53 F7
Mountfield Rd
Bramhall SK7 .....132 E5
Stockport SK3 .....123 C7
Mountfield Wlk
8 Bolton BL1 .....143 B1
11 Manchester M11 .....160 C1
Mountfold M24 .....65 B7
Mountford Ave M8 .....63 F2
Mount Gr SK8 .....121 F6
Mountheath Ind Pk
M25 .....63 B1
Mount La OL3 .....50 E1
Mountmorres Cl BL5 .....59 A7
Mount Pleasant
Adlington PR6 .....21 A8
18 Bacup OL13 .....3 C8
Bolton BL3 .....148 C1
Edgworth BL7 .....9 D5
Hazel Grove SK7 .....124 D3
Middleton, Rhodes M24 .....64 C8
Middleton, Simister M25 .....62 B8
Ramsbottom BL9 .....11 F3
Wilmslow SK9 .....137 B8
Mount Pleasant Bsns Ctr
OL4 .....67 B7
Mount Pleasant Rd
Denton M34 .....100 F2
Farnworth BL4 .....59 F8
Mount Pleasant St
Ashton-u-L OL6 .....166 C3
Denton M34 .....100 F7
2 Horwich BL6 .....22 D1
Oldham OL4 .....67 B7
Mount Pleasant Trad Est
OL6 .....166 C4
Mount Pleasant Wlk
M26 .....44 A4
Mount Rd
Compstall SK14 .....114 A6
Manchester M18, M19 .....99 C3
Middleton M24 .....65 A7
Prestwich M25 .....63 C6
Stockport SK4 .....168 C2
Mountroyal Cl SK14 .....102 A5
Mount St Joseph Business
& Enterprise Coll
BL4 .....42 A2
Mount St Joseph's Rd
BL3 .....144 B1
Mountside Cl OL12 .....14 F7
Mountside Cres M25 .....62 F4
Mount Sion Rd M26 .....43 E2
Mount Skip La M38 .....60 A4
Mount St
Bolton BL1 .....143 B1
Denton M34 .....101 B1
Eccles M30 .....95 C8
Glossop SK13 .....116 C8
Heywood OL10 .....29 D1
Horwich BL6 .....22 D2
Hyde SK14 .....167 B2
Leigh WN7 .....75 C4
Manchester M2 .....162 C4
Ramsbottom BL0 .....138 B2
Rochdale, Castleton
OL11 .....30 C1
Rochdale OL12 .....139 B4
Royton OL2 .....48 E3
Salford M3 .....158 A3
Swinton M27 .....79 F7
Mount Terr M43 .....83 C3
Mount The
Altrincham WA14 .....119 C5
Ashton-u-L OL6 .....85 D3
Brinnington SK5 .....112 B4
Hale WA15 .....129 C8
Mount View
Ince-in-M WN3 .....151 A1
Uppermill OL3 .....69 B8
Mount Zion Rd BL2 .....42 E6
Mount Zion Rd OL2 .....48 F5
Mousell St M8 .....159 A4
Mouselow Cl SK13 .....171 C3
Mowat St M14 .....110 D8
Mowbray Ave
Manchester M25 .....63 C1
Sale M33 .....108 C3
Mowbray St
Ashton-u-L OL7 .....166 A2
Bolton BL1 .....142 B1
5 Oldham OL1 .....153 C2
Rochdale OL16 .....30 B3
Stockport SK1 .....170 C4
Mowbray Wlk 4 OL10 .....46 E2
Mow Halls La OL3 .....51 A1
Moxley Rd M8 .....63 F1
Moxon Way WN4 .....73 C6
Moyse Ave BL8 .....26 F5
Mozart Cl M4 .....159 C2
MUDD 103 A2
Mudhurst La SK12 .....135 E3
Muirfield Ave SK6 .....113 A4
Muirfield Cl
Bolton BL3 .....40 F3
Failsworth M40 .....83 C7
Heywood OL10 .....29 D1

Muirfield Cl continued
Prestwich M25. . . . . .63 B5
Wilmslow SK9. . . . . .137 D8
Muirfield Dr M29. . . . . .77 C7
Muirhead Ct M6. . . . . .81 A5
Mulberry Ave WA3. . . . . . .90 F7
Mulberry Cl
Gatley SK8. . . . . .131 C7
Radcliffe M26 . . . . .44 A2
Rochdale OL11. . . . . .139 B1
Wigan WN5 . . . . .54 D6
Mulberry Ct
Altrincham WA14. . . . . . .119 D6
8 Horwich BL6. . . . . .22 D1
7 Salford M6. . . . . .81 A3
6 Urmston M41. . . . . .95 E2
Mulberry Mews SK4. . . . .169 B2
Mulberry Mount St
SK3. . . . . .170 B4
Mulberry Rd M6. . . . . .81 A3
Mulberry St
2 Ashton-u-L OL6. . . . . . .166 B2
Manchester M2. . . . . .158 C1
Mulberry Wlk
Droylsden M43. . . . . .99 E8
Sale M33 . . . . .107 D6
Mule St BL2. . . . . .148 A3
Mulgrave Rd M28. . . . . . . .79 A8
Mulgrave St
Bolton BL3. . . . . .146 C2
Swinton M27 . . . . .61 D1
Mulgrove Wlk **23** M9. . . . .64 E3
Mullacre Rd M22 . . . . . . .121 D6
Mull Ave M12 . . . . .164 C1
Mulliner St **1** BL1. . . . . . .143 C1
Mullineux St M28. . . . . . . .60 D2
Mullins Ave WA12. . . . . . . .89 C5
Mullion Cl M19. . . . . .99 D2
Mullion Dr WA15. . . . . . . .119 E6
Mullion Wlk M8. . . . . .156 B2
Mulmount Cl OL8. . . . . . . .66 C3
MUMPS 67 A7
Mumps OL1. . . . . .67 A7
Munday St M4. . . . . .160 A1
Municipal Cl **2** OL10 . . . .29 D2
Munn Rd M9 . . . . .64 C5
Munro Ave
Orrell WN5. . . . . .53 E6
Wythenshawe M22 . . . . . .121 F2
Munslow Wlk M9. . . . . .64 F3
Munster St M4 . . . . .159 A3
Muriel St
Heywood OL10. . . . . .29 E2
Rochdale OL16. . . . . .31 B5
Salford M7. . . . . .155 A1
Murieston Rd WA15. . . . . .119 E2
Murphy Cl WN3 . . . . .150 A1
Murrayfield OL11. . . . . .29 E6
Murray Rd BL9 . . . . .140 C2
Murray St
Atherton M46 . . . . .58 B2
Manchester M4 . . . . .159 C2
Salford M7. . . . . .155 A2
Murrow Wlk **3** M9. . . . . . .157 A4
Murton Terr BL1. . . . . . . .143 C4
Musbury Ave SK8. . . . . . . .123 B2
Musden Ave BL4 . . . . . . .1 A7
Musden Wlk SK4 . . . . . . .111 D7
**Museum of the
Manchesters The** *
OL6 . . . . .166 B3
Museum of Transport *
M8. . . . . .156 B2
Museum St M2. . . . . .162 C4
Musgrave Gdns BL1 . . . . .144 C4
Musgrave Rd
Bolton BL1. . . . . .144 C4
Wythenshawe M22 . . . . . .121 D3
Muslin St M5. . . . . .81 C1
Mus of Science & Ind *
M60, M3. . . . . .162 B4
**Mus of Science & Ind (Air
& Space Gal)** * M3 . . . . .162 B4
Mustard La WA3. . . . . .91 B1
Muter Ave M22 . . . . .121 F2
Mutual St OL10. . . . . .29 E3
Mycroft Cl WN7 . . . . .75 E8
Myerscroft Cl M40. . . . . . . .65 E1
Myrrh St BL1. . . . . .143 B2
Myrrh Wlk **7** BL1 . . . . . . .143 B3
Myrtle Ave
Ashton-in-M WN4 . . . . .72 F6
Leigh WN7 . . . . .75 E7
Newton-le-W WA12. . . . . . .89 C2
Myrtle Bank M25 . . . . .63 A1
Myrtle Cl OL8 . . . . .153 B1
Myrtle Gdns BL9. . . . . . . .141 B2
Myrtle Gr
Billinge WN5 . . . . .71 D4
Droylsden M43. . . . . .84 C2
Manchester M25. . . . . .63 B2
Reddish M34 . . . . .99 F3
Whitefield M45 . . . . .44 D2
Myrtleleaf Gr M5. . . . . . . .154 A2
Myrtle Pl M7 . . . . .81 C4
Myrtle St
Bolton BL1. . . . . .145 A4
Manchester, Beswick
M11 . . . . .164 C4

Myrtle St continued
3 Manchester, Old Trafford
M16 . . . . .97 C4
Stockport SK3 . . . . .123 B8
Wigan WN1 . . . . .150 B4
My St M5. . . . . .154 B1
Mytham Gdns BL3. . . . . . . .43 B2
Manchester, Prim Sch BL3. . .43 B3
Mytham Rd BL3. . . . . .43 B2
Mytholme Ave M44 . . . . . .105 C3
Mythorn Wlk M40. . . . . . . .83 B5
Mytton Rd BL1 . . . . .142 B4
Mytton St M15 . . . . .162 C1

N

Nabbs Fold BL8 . . . . .10 F3
Nabbs Way BL8 . . . . .11 A1
Nab La SK6. . . . . .125 E7
Naburn Cl SK5. . . . . .112 C6
Naburn Dr WN5 . . . . .53 E5
Naburn St M13 . . . . .98 D4
Nada Lo M8. . . . . .63 F1
Nada Rd M8. . . . . .63 F1
Naden Wlk M45. . . . . .63 A8
Nadine St M6. . . . . .154 B3
Nadin St **1** OL8. . . . . .66 E3
Nailgate OL16. . . . . .31 C2
Nairn Cl
Manchester M40 . . . . .160 B3
Standish WN6 . . . . .19 D1
Nall St
Manchester M19 . . . . .111 B7
Milnrow OL16. . . . . .31 E6
Nameplate Cl M30. . . . . . . .79 B2
Nancy St M15 . . . . .162 A2
Nandywell BL3. . . . . .43 B3
Nangreave Rd SK2. . . . . . .124 B6
NANGREAVES 11 F2
Nangreaves St WN7 . . . . . .75 C5
Nangreave St M5. . . . . . . .158 A1
Nan Nook Rd M23 . . . . . . .108 F1
Nansen Ave M30. . . . . .79 C3
Nansen Cl M32 . . . . .96 E4
Nansen Rd SK8. . . . . .122 A4
Nansen St
Salford M6. . . . . .154 B2
Stretford M32 . . . . .96 E4
Nansmoss La SK9. . . . . . .130 D1
Nantes Ct BL1. . . . . .143 A2
Nantwich Ave OL12 . . . . . . .14 F3
Nantwich Cl **3** SK8. . . . . .123 A5
Nantwich Rd M14. . . . . .98 A1
Nantwich Way **6** SK9. . . .131 E5
Nantwich Wlk BL3. . . . . . .147 B4
Napier Ct
Hyde SK14. . . . . .167 B1
Manchester, City Park
M15 . . . . .161 C2
Stockport, Heaton Moor
SK4 . . . . .168 B3
Napier Gn M5. . . . . .161 B3
Napier Ho OL14 . . . . .6 A8
Napier Rd
Eccles M30 . . . . .79 C3
Manchester, Chorlton-cum-
Hardy M21. . . . . .109 B8
Stockport, Heaton Moor
SK4 . . . . .168 B3
Napier St E OL8. . . . . .153 A1
Napier St W OL8. . . . . . . .153 A1
Napier St
Hazel Grove SK7. . . . . . . .124 D3
Hyde SK14. . . . . .167 B1
Shaw OL2. . . . . .149 B4
Swinton M27 . . . . .79 E4
Naples Rd SK3 . . . . .123 B7
Naples St M4. . . . . .159 A3
Narbonne Ave M30. . . . . . . .80 A4
Narborough Cl WN2 . . . . . .56 E4
Narbuth Dr M8 . . . . .155 C3
Narcissus Ave BL4. . . . . . .1 A8
Narcissus Wlk **6** M28. . . . .59 F3
Narrowgate Brow OL2. . . . .48 D7
Narrow La SK10 . . . . .134 A1
Narrows The WA14. . . . . . .119 C4
Naseby Ave M9. . . . . .64 F4
Naseby Ct M25 . . . . .63 C5
Naseby Pl M25 . . . . .63 C5
Naseby Rd SK5. . . . . .99 F1
Naseby Wlk M45. . . . . .63 C8
Nash Rd M17 . . . . .95 F8
Nash St M15 . . . . .162 A1
Nasmyth Ave M34 . . . . . . .101 A4
Nasmyth Bsns Ctr M30. . . . .79 C2
Nasmyth Rd M30 . . . . .95 C8
Nasmyth St
Horwich BL6. . . . . .22 C3
Manchester M8. . . . . .156 C1
Nately Rd M16. . . . . .97 A2
Nathan Dr M3. . . . . .158 B2
Nathaniel Ct M27 . . . . .56 B3
Nathans Rd M22 . . . . .121 C4
National Cycling Ctr *
M11. . . . . .83 A2
National Dr M5. . . . . .161 A4
National Squash Ctr
M11. . . . . .160 C2
National Trad Est
SK7. . . . . .124 C3
Naunton Ave WN7 . . . . . . .75 C5
Naunton Rd M24. . . . . .65 B7
Naunton Wlk **24** M9. . . . . .157 B4
Naval St M4. . . . . .159 C2
Navenby Ave M16. . . . . .97 C4
Navenby Rd WN3. . . . . .55 A2
Navigation Cl WN7 . . . . . . .75 E4

Navigation Ho
Leigh WN7 . . . . .76 A4
Manchester M1 . . . . .159 B1
Navigation Prim Sch
WA14. . . . . .119 D6
Navigation Rd WA14. . . . . .119 D6
Navigation Road Sta
WA14. . . . . .119 E6
Naylor Ave WA3. . . . . .90 B8
Naylor Ct **18** M40 . . . . . . .159 C3
Naylorfarm Ave WN6 . . . . .35 F5
Naylor St
Atherton M46 . . . . .58 C2
Manchester M40 . . . . .160 A3
Oldham OL1. . . . . .153 B3
Nazarene Ct BL5. . . . . .39 E2
Nazarene Theological Coll
The M20. . . . . .110 A3
Nazeby Wlk OL9 . . . . .152 C1
Naze Ct **3** OL1. . . . . .153 B4
Naze Wlk SK5. . . . . .112 C6
Neal Ave
Ashton-u-L OL6 . . . . .85 D3
Gatley SK8. . . . . .122 A1
Neale Ave OL3. . . . . .69 B5
Neale Rd M21. . . . . .109 B7
Neasden Ave M9 . . . . .64 A1
NEAR BARROWSHAW 49 E1
Near Birches Par OL7. . . . . .85 A4
Nearbrook Rd M22 . . . . . .121 C4
Nearcroft Rd M23. . . . . . . .121 B7
Near Hey Cl M26 . . . . .43 E3
Nearmaker Ave M22 . . . . .121 C4
Nearmaker Rd M22 . . . . . .121 C4
Neary Way M41. . . . . .95 C5
Neasden Gr **6** BL3 . . . . . .144 C1
Neath Ave M22 . . . . .121 D7
Neath Cl
Poynton SK12 . . . . .133 D5
Prestwich M45. . . . . .63 C7
Neath Fold BL3 . . . . .147 A3
Neath St OL9 . . . . .153 A3
Nebo St BL3. . . . . .147 A4
Nebraska St BL1. . . . . . . .165 B4
Neden Cl M11. . . . . .165 B4
Needham Ave M21. . . . . . .109 B8
Needwood Cl M40 . . . . . . .157 A1
Needwood Rd SK6. . . . . . . .113 C5
Neenton Sq M12. . . . . .165 A3
Neild Gdns WN7. . . . . .75 E4
Neild St
Manchester M1. . . . . .163 B4
Oldham OL8. . . . . .66 F4
Neill St M8. . . . . .158 B4
Neilson Cl M23. . . . . .65 C7
Neilson Cl M23. . . . . .121 A6
Neilston Ave M40. . . . . .83 B7
Neilston Rise BL1. . . . . .40 D7
Nellie St OL10. . . . . .29 B2
Nell La M20, M21. . . . . . . .109 D6
Nell St BL1. . . . . .143 C4
Nel Pan La WN7. . . . . .75 D8
Nelson Ave
Eccles M30 . . . . .79 D3
Poynton SK12 . . . . .134 A3
Nelson Bsns Ctr M34 . . . . .100 F4
Nelson Cl SK12 . . . . .134 A3
Nelson Ct
Manchester, Miles Platting
M40 . . . . .160 A4
Manchester, Old Trafford
M15 . . . . .97 E4
Nelson Dr
Droylsden M43. . . . . .83 E2
Ince-in-M WN2 . . . . .56 A8
Irlam M44 . . . . .105 E6
Nelson Fold M27 . . . . .62 A1
Nelson Mandela Ct **9**
M16 . . . . .97 E3
Nelson Rd M9 . . . . .64 D5
Nelson Sq M15 . . . . .145 C3
Nelson St
Atherton M46 . . . . .58 B3
Atherton M46 . . . . .58 B4
Bolton BL3. . . . . .148 A1
Britannia OL13. . . . . .4 F8
6 Bury BL9. . . . . .44 F8
Denton, Hooley Hill
M34 . . . . .100 F4
Denton M34. . . . . .100 F4
Eccles M30 . . . . .79 D2
Farnworth BL4. . . . . .60 E8
Hazel Grove SK7 . . . . .124 F4
Heywood OL10. . . . . .29 D1
8 Hindley WN2 . . . . .56 D6
Horwich BL6. . . . . .22 D3
Hyde SK14. . . . . .167 B2
7 Littleborough OL15. . . . .16 B5
5 Little Lever BL3 . . . . . . .43 B3
Manchester, Brunswick
M13 . . . . .163 B1
Manchester, Miles Platting
M40. . . . . .160 B4
Middleton M24. . . . . .46 F1
Newton-le-W WA12. . . . . . .89 A3
Oldham OL4. . . . . .67 C5
Rochdale OL16. . . . . .31 A5
Salford M7. . . . . .155 A1
Salford, Weaste M5. . . . . . .80 D1
Stretford M32 . . . . .96 D1
Tyldesley M29 . . . . .77 B8
Walsden OL14 . . . . .6 A8
New Barn
Haslingden BB4. . . . . .1 B6
Shaw OL3. . . . . .50 C6
Uppermill OL3. . . . . .69 C3
New Barn Ave WN4. . . . . . .73 C3
New Barn Cl OL2. . . . . . . .149 A3
New Barn La
Leigh WN7 . . . . .75 E2
Rawtenstall BB4. . . . . .2 A8

Nepaul Rd M9. . . . . .64 E1
Neptune Gdns **11** M7 . . . . .81 C4
Nesbit St **4** BL2. . . . . .25 B3
Nesfield Rd M23. . . . . .108 F2
Neston Ave
Bolton BL1. . . . . .24 F5
Manchester M20 . . . . .110 A6
Sale M33 . . . . .108 E2
Neston Cl OL2. . . . . .49 D7
Neston Gr SK3. . . . . .170 A1
Neston Rd
Bury BL8 . . . . .26 F5
Rochdale OL16. . . . . .31 C4
Neston St M11 . . . . .99 F7
Neston Way SK9. . . . . . . .131 D3
Neswick Wlk **4** M23. . . . . .108 F2
Netherbury Cl M18 . . . . .99 C3
Netherby Rd WN6 . . . . .37 A3
Nethercote Ave M23. . . . . .121 B6
Nethercott Ct M29 . . . . .58 E1
Nethercroft OL11. . . . . .13 E1
Nethercroft Rd WA15. . . . .120 C5
Netherfield Cl OL8. . . . . . . .66 C4
Netherfield Rd BL3. . . . . . .147 B2
Netherhey Cl M35 . . . . .75 D7
Netherhey La OL2. . . . . . . .48 C2
Nether Hey St OL8. . . . . . . .67 B4
Netherhouse Rd OL2. . . . . .149 A3
Netherland St M5 . . . . .161 A4
Netherlees OL4. . . . . .67 D5
NETHER LEES 67 D4
Netherley Rd PR7. . . . . . . .19 E8
Netherlow Ct SK14. . . . . . .167 B2
Nether St
Hyde SK14. . . . . .113 F8
Manchester M12 . . . . .163 C4
Netherton Gr BL4. . . . . . . .42 B2
Netherton Rd M14. . . . . . . .98 A1
Nethervale Dr M9 . . . . . . .157 B3
Netherwood M35 . . . . .84 B8
Netherwood Cl M16. . . . . . .97 B4
Netherwood Rd M22. . . . . .121 C7
Netherwood Way BL5. . . . . .40 A2
Netley Ave OL12 . . . . .14 F3
Netley Gdns **2** M26. . . . . . .43 E5
Netley Rd M23. . . . . .121 A4
Nettlebarn Rd M22 . . . . . .121 C5
Nettleford Rd M16. . . . . . .109 E8
Nettleton Gr M9. . . . . .64 F1
Network Ctr M27 . . . . .80 E7
Nevada St **3** BL1. . . . . . . .143 B1
Nevendon Dr M23 . . . . . . .121 A4
Nevern Cl BL1 . . . . .40 F8
Nevile Ct M7 . . . . .81 B8
Nevile Rd M7 . . . . .81 B8
Neville Cardus Wlk **12**
M14. . . . . .98 C3
Neville Cl BL1. . . . . .145 B4
Neville Dr M44 . . . . .94 A4
Neville St
Chadderton OL9. . . . . .152 C3
Hazel Grove SK7 . . . . .124 D3
Newton-le-W WA12. . . . . . .89 A3
Platt Bridge WN2. . . . . .56 A3
Nevill Rd SK7. . . . . .123 E2
Nevill Road Inf Sch
SK7. . . . . .123 E2
Nevill Road Jun Sch
SK7. . . . . .123 E2
Nevin Ave SK8. . . . . .122 E1
Nevin Cl SK7 . . . . .133 A7
Nevin Rd M40 . . . . .65 D1
Nevis Gr BL1 . . . . .24 D5
Nevis St OL11. . . . . .31 A2
Nevy Fold Ave BL6. . . . . . . .22 F3
New Acre Ct SK6 . . . . .113 B2
New Allen St M4, M40 . . . . .159 C3
Newall Gr WN7. . . . . .75 D5
NEWALL GREEN 121 A3
Newall Green High Sch
M23 . . . . .120 F3
Newall Green Prim Sch
M23 . . . . .121 B4
Newall Rd M23 . . . . .120 F3
Newall St
Littleborough OL15. . . . . . .16 B6
Oldham OL9. . . . . .66 B2
Walsden OL14 . . . . .6 A8
Newark Ave
Little Lever M26 . . . . .43 C5
3 Manchester M44. . . . . . .94 B3
Newark Park Way OL2. . . . .48 C6
Newark Rd
Hindley WN2 . . . . .56 C4
Reddish SK5 . . . . .111 F5
Rochdale OL12. . . . . .14 F3
Swinton M27 . . . . .62 B2
Newark Sq OL12 . . . . .14 F3
Newark St WN6 . . . . .36 F1
New Bailey St M3 . . . . . . .158 B1
Newbank Chase OL9. . . . .152 A4
Newbank Cl M24 . . . . .65 C7
New Bank Cl OL3 . . . . .50 F1
New Bank St
Hadfield SK13 . . . . .104 A5
Manchester M12 . . . . .164 C1
Tyldesley M29 . . . . .77 A8
Newbank Twrs M3 . . . . . . .158 B3

New Barn La continued
Rochdale OL11. . . . . .30 E4
New Barn Rd OL8. . . . . .67 A2
New Barns Ave M21. . . . . .109 D6
New Barn St
Bolton BL1. . . . . .142 B1
11 Rochdale OL16. . . . . . .31 A5
Shaw OL2. . . . . .149 A3
New Barton St M6. . . . . . . .80 E5
Newbeck Cl BL6. . . . . .22 D1
Newbeck St **2** M4. . . . . . .159 A2
New Beech Rd SK4. . . . . . .110 E2
New Beech St SK4. . . . . . .110 E2
New Belvedere Cl M32. . . . .96 D2
Newberry Gr SK3. . . . . . . .170 A1
NEWBOLD 31 C7
NEWBOLD BROW 31 B8
Newbold Moss OL16. . . . . . .31 B8
Newbold St
Bury BL8 . . . . .27 C2
Rochdale OL16. . . . . .31 C7
Newbold Wlk M15. . . . . . . .162 C2
Newboult Rd SK8. . . . . . . .122 E6
Newbourne Cl SK7 . . . . . . .124 D3
Newbreak Cl **2** OL4. . . . . . .67 D8
Newbreak St **3** OL4. . . . . . .67 D8
NEWBRIDGE 96 B8
Newbridge Cl WN4 . . . . . . .72 E3
Newbridge Gdns BL2. . . . . .25 F4
New Bridge Gdns M26 . . . . .44 E5
New Bridge La SK1. . . . . . .112 A2
New Bridge St M3. . . . . . . .158 C3
Newbridge View OL15. . . . . .16 B5
New Briggs Fold BL7. . . . . . .8 E2
**New Broadcasting House
(BBC)** M1. . . . . .163 A3
New Broad La OL16. . . . . . .31 C3
Newbrook Ave M21 . . . . . .109 E8
Newbrook Rd BL5, M46. . . . .58 F6
New Brunswick St BL6. . . . .22 B3
New Buildings Pl **4**
OL16. . . . . .139 C4
Newburn Ave M9 . . . . .64 F4
Newburn Cl WN3 . . . . .54 E1
NEW BURY 60 B7
Newbury Cl M33 . . . . .107 C4
Newbury Ct SK9. . . . . .132 A6
Newbury Dr
Eccles M30 . . . . .79 B3
Urmston M41 . . . . .95 C5
Newbury Gr OL10. . . . . .46 C8
Newbury Pl M7. . . . . .155 A3
Newbury Rd
Gatley SK8. . . . . .131 C7
Little Lever BL3 . . . . .42 F3
Newbury Wlk
Bolton BL1. . . . . .143 B1
Chadderton OL9. . . . . .152 C3
Manchester M9 . . . . .157 A2
Newby Cl BL9 . . . . .45 A7
Newby Dr
Altrincham WA14. . . . . . . .119 D6
Gatley SK8. . . . . .122 A6
Middleton M24. . . . . .46 F3
Sale M33 . . . . .108 E3
Newby Rd
Bolton BL2. . . . . .25 F2
Hazel Grove SK7 . . . . .124 D2
Stockport SK4 . . . . .168 C2
Newby Road Ind Est
SK7. . . . . .124 D2
Newby Sq WN5 . . . . .54 B5
Newcastle St **6** M15. . . . . .162 C3
Newcastle Wlk **2**
M34 . . . . .101 A1
New Cathedral St M1. . . . .158 C2
New Century Apartments
BL0. . . . . .138 C3
New Chapel La BL6. . . . . . . .22 F2
Newchurch OL8. . . . . .85 A8
Newchurch Com Prim Sch
WA3. . . . . .91 E2
Newchurch Ct **8** M26. . . . . .44 B3
New Church Ct M45 . . . . . . .62 F7
Newchurch La WA3. . . . . . . .91 F2
New Church Rd BL1. . . . . . .23 F7
Newchurch St
Rochdale OL11. . . . . .30 C1
Rochdale OL16. . . . . .31 D1
New Church St M26. . . . . . .44 B3
Newchurch Wlk **5**
M26. . . . . .44 B3
New City Rd M28. . . . . .78 A8
Newcliffe Rd M9 . . . . .64 F4
New Coin St OL2 . . . . .48 D3
New Collier's Row BL1. . . . .23 C6
Newcombe Cl M11 . . . . . . .160 C1
Newcombe Ct **3** M33. . . . .107 F4
Newcombe Dr M38 . . . . .59 F6
Newcombe Rd BL0 . . . . . . .11 B2
Newcombe St M3. . . . . . . .158 C3
New Copper Moss
WA15. . . . . .119 F4
New Court Dr BL7. . . . . .8 E3
Newcroft M35. . . . . .84 B6
Newcroft Cres M41. . . . . . . .95 F1
Newcroft Dr
Manchester M9. . . . . .64 C1
Stockport SK3 . . . . .170 A2
Stretford M32 . . . . .96 A1
Newcroft Rd M41. . . . . .95 F1
New Cross M4. . . . . .159 B2

New Cross St
Pendlebury M27 . . . . .80 A7
Salford M5 . . . . .80 C2
Newdale Rd M12 . . . . .99 B2
New Drake Gn BL5 . . . . . . .57 E5
Newearth Rd M28 . . . . .78 B8
New Earth St
Mossley OL5 . . . . .68 D2
Oldham OL4 . . . . .67 C5
New Ellesmere App
M28 . . . . .60 D4
New Elm Rd M3 . . . . .162 A4
Newenden Rd WN1 . . . . . . .37 B4
New Farm Cotts WA3 . . . .105 A7
New Field Cl
Radcliffe M26 . . . . .43 E3
Rochdale OL16 . . . . .31 B8
Newfield Ct WA13 . . . . . . .117 A5
Newfield Head La
OL16 . . . . .32 B5
Newfield View OL16 . . . . . .32 A6
New Fold WN5 . . . . .53 C4
New Forest Rd M23 . . . . . .120 C8
NEWGATE 53 A6
Newgate OL16 . . . . .139 C3
New Gate BL5 . . . . .146 A1
Newgate Ave WN6 . . . . . . .35 E8
Newgate Dr M38 . . . . .60 A6
Newgate Rd
Sale M33 . . . . .107 C1
Wilmslow SK9 . . . . .136 D7
New George St [8] BL8 . . . .27 C3
New Gn BL2 . . . . .25 E6
New Greenhall M46 . . . . . . .58 F4
Newhall Ave
Eccles M30 . . . . .95 A7
Little Lever BL2 . . . . .43 B6
New Hall Ave
Gatley SK8 . . . . .131 B7
Salford M7 . . . . .155 A4
Newhall Dr M23 . . . . .109 B2
New Hall La
Bolton BL1 . . . . .144 A4
Culcheth WA3 . . . . .92 A2
Culcheth, Wigshaw WA3 . . . .91 E1
New Hall Mews BL1 . . . . . . .23 D1
New Hall Pl BL1 . . . . .144 A4
Newhall Rd SK5 . . . . .100 A1
New Hall Rd
Bury BL9 . . . . .28 E4
Sale M33 . . . . .108 F4
Salford M7 . . . . .155 A4
Newham Ave M11 . . . . .83 B2
Newham Dr [7] BL8 . . . . . . .27 B1
Newhart Gr M28 . . . . .60 C2
Newhaven Ave
Droylsden M11 . . . . .99 F7
Leigh WN7 . . . . .75 F8
Newhaven Bsns Pk
M30 . . . . .79 E1
Newhaven Cl
Bramhall SK8 . . . . .123 C2
Bury BL8 . . . . .27 C7
Newhaven Wlk [4] BL2 . . . .25 E1
New Herbert St M6 . . . . . . .80 C5
NEWHEY 32 B4
Newhey Ave M22 . . . . .121 D5
Newhey Com Prim Sch
OL16 . . . . .32 A3
Newhey Rd
Milnrow OL16 . . . . .32 A5
Wythenshawe M22 . . . . . . .121 D5
New Hey Rd SK8 . . . . .122 E6
New Hey Sta OL16 . . . . .32 B4
New Heys Way BL2 . . . . . . .25 B3
New Ho OL4 . . . . .68 C8
New Holder St BL1 . . . . . . .145 B3
Newholme Ct
Manchester M20 . . . . .110 C6
Stretford M32 . . . . .96 E2
Newholme Gdns M20 . . . . . .60 C3
Newholme Rd M20 . . . . . . .109 F5
Newhouse Cl OL12 . . . . .15 C6
Newhouse Cres OL11 . . . . . .29 E8
Newhouse Dr WN3 . . . . .54 D1
Newhouse Rd OL10 . . . . . . .46 D8
NEW HOUSES 54 C1
Newhouse St OL12 . . . . .15 C6
Newick Wlk [6] M9 . . . . . . .64 E3
Newington Ave M8 . . . . .63 F3
Newington St WA14 . . . . . .119 B3
Newington Dr
Bolton BL1 . . . . .143 C1
Bury BL8 . . . . .27 A1
Newington Wlk [7]
BL1 . . . . .143 C1
New Islington Wharf M3 . . . . .159 C2
New Kings Head Yd
M3 . . . . .158 C2
New La
Bolton BL2 . . . . .25 E2
Eccles M30 . . . . .79 B1
Middleton M24 . . . . .47 A1
Royton OL2 . . . . .48 D4
Newland Ave WN5 . . . . .54 D5
Newland Dr BL5 . . . . .58 F8
Newland Mews WA3 . . . . . . .91 E5
Newlands M35 . . . . .83 E4
Newlands Ave
Bolton BL2 . . . . .25 F1
Bramhall SK7 . . . . .132 F8
Cheadle SK8 . . . . .132 A7
Eccles M30 . . . . .94 A2
Irlam M44 . . . . .94 A2
Rochdale OL12 . . . . .14 F3
Tyldesley M29 . . . . .77 A6
Whitefield M45 . . . . .44 E1

Newlands Cl
Cheadle SK8 . . . . .132 A7
Rochdale OL12 . . . . .14 F3
Newlands Dr
Glossop SK13 . . . . .171 C4
Golborne WA3 . . . . .90 D8
Manchester M20 . . . . .122 C8
Pendlebury M27 . . . . .80 C6
Prestwich M25 . . . . .63 A5
Scot Lane End BL6 . . . . .38 E7
Wilmslow SK9 . . . . .136 E5
Newlands Rd
Cheadle SK8 . . . . .132 A7
Leigh WN7 . . . . .75 F3
Wythenshawe M23 . . . . . . .120 F8
Newland St M8 . . . . .64 B1
Newlands Wlk M24 . . . . .46 E3
New Lane Ct BL2 . . . . .25 E2
NEW LANE END 91 A2
New Lane Rd WA3 . . . . .91 A2
New Lawns SK5 . . . . .100 A1
Newlea Cl BL1 . . . . .142 C2
New Lees St OL6 . . . . .85 D5
New Lester Cl M33 . . . . .59 F4
New Lester Way M38 . . . . . .59 E4
New Line OL13 . . . . .4 B8
New Lo WN1 . . . . .37 D2
Newlyn Ave SK15 . . . . .86 D3
Newlyn Cl SK7 . . . . .124 D1
Newlyn Dr
Ashton-in-M WN4 . . . . .73 B1
Romiley SK6 . . . . .113 A3
Sale M33 . . . . .108 C1
Newlyn St M14 . . . . .98 B2
Newman Ave WN5 . . . . .37 A2
NEW MANCHESTER 60 A1
Newman Cl WN2 . . . . .56 C6
Newman St
Ashton-u-L OL6 . . . . .166 A3
Hyde SK14 . . . . .167 B3
Rochdale OL16 . . . . .15 C3
Wigan WN1 . . . . .37 E2
New Market M2 . . . . .158 C1
Newmarket Cl M33 . . . . . . .107 B2
Newmarket Gr OL7 . . . . .84 E5
Newmarket Mews
M7 . . . . .155 A2
Newmarket Rd
Ashton-u-L OL7 . . . . .84 F5
Little Lever BL3 . . . . .43 A2
New Market St WN1 . . . . . .150 C4
New Mdw BL6 . . . . .40 C7
New Miles La WN6 . . . . .35 F5
NEW MILLS 127 D1
New Mills Rd SK13 . . . . . . .115 B4
New Mill St OL15 . . . . .16 A5
Newmill Wlk [2] M8 . . . . . .156 A2
New Moor La SK7 . . . . .124 D3
New Moss Rd M44 . . . . .105 D6
NEW MOSTON 65 E1
New Moston Prim Sch
M40 . . . . .65 E2
New Mount St [4] M4 . . . .159 A3
Newnham St BL1 . . . . .143 C4
New Oak Cl M35 . . . . .84 C8
New Park Rd M5 . . . . .161 B3
Newpark Wlk [5] M8 . . . . .156 A2
Newport Ave SK5 . . . . .111 F7
Newport Mews BL4 . . . . .60 D7
Newport Rd
Bolton BL3 . . . . .42 A3
Denton M34 . . . . .113 B8
Manchester M21 . . . . .97 A1
Newport St
Bolton BL1, BL3 . . . . .145 C2
Bury BL8 . . . . .27 A5
Farnworth BL4 . . . . .60 D7
Manchester M14 . . . . .98 B3
Middleton M24 . . . . .47 C1
Oldham OL4 . . . . .153 A1
Salford M6 . . . . .154 B2
Newquay Ave
Ainsworth BL2 . . . . .26 D1
Reddish SK5 . . . . .111 E7
Newquay Dr SK7 . . . . .132 F7
Newquay Ho [6] OL9 . . . . . .48 A1
New Quay St M3 . . . . .158 B1
New Radcliffe St OL1 . . . . .153 B3
New Rd
Adlington PR6 . . . . .21 D8
Aspull WN2 . . . . .38 A5
Glossop SK13 . . . . .103 F7
Littleborough OL15 . . . . .15 F5
Oldham OL8 . . . . .66 E4
Radcliffe M26 . . . . .4 B1
Whitworth OL12 . . . . .4 B1
New Ridd Rise SK14 . . . . . .113 D8
New Riven Ct BL3 . . . . .43 A3
New Rock St BL5 . . . . .57 F5
New Royd Ave OL4 . . . . .67 F8
Newry Rd M30 . . . . .95 E8
Newry St M9 . . . . .64 B3
Newry Wlk M9 . . . . .64 B3
Newsham Cl BL3 . . . . .145 A1
Newsham Rd SK3 . . . . .170 B2
Newsham Wlk
[2] Manchester M12 . . . . . . .99 B3
Wigan WN6 . . . . .36 F1
Newshaw La SK13 . . . . .171 C4
Newsholme Cl WA3 . . . . . . .91 F3
Newsholme St M8 . . . . .155 C3
New Smithfield Mkt
M18 . . . . .165 C3
NEW SPRINGS 38 A3
New Springs BL1 . . . . .142 B3
New St
Altrincham WA14 . . . . .119 D4
Ashton-in-M WN4 . . . . .73 C4

New St continued
Blackrod BL6 . . . . .21 D2
Bolton BL1 . . . . .145 B2
[5] Broadbottom SK14 . . . .115 A8
Bury BL8 . . . . .26 F6
Droylsden M43 . . . . .100 A8
Eccles M30 . . . . .79 C1
Littleborough OL15 . . . . .15 F4
Manchester M40 . . . . .160 E4
Milnrow OL16 . . . . .32 A5
Oldham OL4 . . . . .67 E6
Platt Bridge WN2 . . . . .56 A2
Radcliffe M26 . . . . .44 B2
Rochdale OL12 . . . . .14 E2
Stalybridge SK15 . . . . .102 A8
Swinton M27 . . . . .62 A1
Uppermill OL3 . . . . .69 B8
Wigan WN5 . . . . .54 B5
Wilmslow SK9 . . . . .136 E5
Newstead [14] OL12 . . . . . .139 B4
Newstead Ave
Ashton-u-L OL6 . . . . .85 C7
Manchester M20 . . . . .110 D5
Newstead Cl SK12 . . . . .133 D5
Newstead Dr BL3 . . . . .146 A2
Newstead Gr SK6 . . . . .112 F3
Newstead Rd
Urmston M41 . . . . .95 E3
Wigan WN3 . . . . .54 F3
Newstead Terr WA15 . . . . .119 F7
New Tame OL3 . . . . .50 C7
New Tempest Rd BL6 . . . . . .40 C4
New Terr SK14 . . . . .101 F5
New Thomas St M6 . . . . . . .81 A4
NEWTON 89 E4
Newton Ave
Manchester, Longsight
M12 . . . . .98 F4
Manchester, Withington
M20 . . . . .110 A6
Newton Bank Sch
WA12 . . . . .89 E4
Newton Bsns Pk
SK14 . . . . .102 A5
Newton Cl WN1 . . . . .37 D2
Newton Com Hospl
WA12 . . . . .89 B2
Newton Cres M24 . . . . .46 D3
Newtondale Ave OL2 . . . . . . .48 C4
Newton Dr BL8 . . . . .11 A1
New Tong Field BL7 . . . . . . .24 F7
Newton Gn SK14 . . . . .101 F5
Newton Hall Ct SK14 . . . . .101 F5
Newton Hall Rd SK14 . . . .101 F5
NEWTON HEATH 83 B5
Newton Ho M14 . . . . .110 D8
Newtonhurst M34 . . . . .102 A5
Newton La WA12 . . . . .89 E6
NEWTON-LE-WILLOWS 89 B2
Newton-le-Willows Com
High Sch WA12 . . . . .89 D5
Newton-le-Willows Prim
Sch WA12 . . . . .89 C3
Newton Moor Ind Est
SK14 . . . . .101 E5
Newtonmore Wlk M11 . . . . .83 B1
Newton Park Dr WA12 . . . . .89 F3
Newton Rd
Altrincham WA14 . . . . .119 E7
Billinge WN5 . . . . .71 F6
Failsworth M35 . . . . .83 E6
Golborne, Lowton Common
WA3, WN7 . . . . .91 A8
Handforth SK9 . . . . .131 A1
Manchester M24 . . . . .64 B6
Newton-le-W WA12 . . . . . . .89 F1
Town of Lowton WA3,
WA12 . . . . .90 D5
Urmston M41 . . . . .95 C2
Newton St
Ashton-u-L OL6 . . . . .166 C3
Bolton BL3 . . . . .143 B2
Bury BL9 . . . . .27 F6
Droylsden M43 . . . . .84 C3
Failsworth M40 . . . . .83 C6
Hyde SK14 . . . . .167 A4
Leigh WN7 . . . . .75 F5
Manchester M1 . . . . .159 A1
Rochdale OL16 . . . . .31 A5
[5] Stalybridge SK15 . . . . . .85 F2
Stockport SK3 . . . . .170 B4
Stretford M32 . . . . .96 D1
Newton Terr
[23] Bolton BL1 . . . . .143 B2
[20] Dukinfield SK16 . . . . .166 B1
Newton Westpark Prim
Sch WA12 . . . . .75 C8
Newton Wlk BL1 . . . . .143 B2
NEWTON WOOD 101 B6
Newton Wood Rd
SK16 . . . . .101 B6
NEWTOWN
Poynton 134 A3
Swinton 61 F1
Wigan 54 E6
Newtown Ave M34 . . . . . . .100 F2
Newtown Cl
Manchester M11 . . . . .165 B4
Swinton M27 . . . . .61 F2
Newtown Ct
Manchester M40 . . . . .159 C4
Prestwich M25 . . . . .63 C4

Newtown St
Prestwich M25 . . . . .63 C4
Shaw OL2 . . . . .149 B2
New Union St M4 . . . . .159 C2
New Vernon St [12]
BL9 . . . . .140 C4
New Viaduct St M11,
M40 . . . . .160 B2
Newville Dr M20 . . . . .110 D5
New Vine St M15 . . . . .162 C2
New Wakefield St
[2] Manchester M1 . . . . . . .162 C3
Manchester M1 . . . . .163 A3
New Way OL12 . . . . .4 C1
New Welcome St
M15 . . . . .162 C2
New William Cl M31 . . . . . .105 F4
NEW WINDSOR 81 B1
New York BL3 . . . . .40 F5
New York St OL10 . . . . .29 B2
New Zealand Rd SK3 . . . . .112 B2
Neyland Cl BL1 . . . . .40 F7
Ney St OL7 . . . . .84 F6
Niagara Ho SK12 . . . . .124 A6
Niagara St SK12 . . . . .124 A6
Nicholas Croft M4 . . . . .159 A2
Nicholas Ct M20 . . . . .110 A3
Nicholas Owen Cl
M11 . . . . .165 C4
Nicholas St
Bolton BL2 . . . . .148 A4
Manchester M1, M2 . . . . . .159 A1
Nicholas Varley Com Sch
M40 . . . . .160 B4
Nicholls St M12 . . . . .164 A3
Nicholson Rd SK14 . . . . . . .101 C5
Nicholson Sq SK16 . . . . . . .101 B8
Nicholson St
Oldham OL4 . . . . .67 E6
Rochdale OL11 . . . . .139 C1
Stockport SK4 . . . . .169 E2
Nichols St M6 . . . . .81 B3
Nickleby Rd SK12 . . . . .133 E3
Nicola St BL7 . . . . .24 E8
Nicolas Rd M21 . . . . .97 A1
Nicola St BL7 . . . . .24 E8
Nicol Mere Dr WN4 . . . . . . .73 A5
Nicol Rd WN4 . . . . .73 B5
Nield Rd M34 . . . . .100 F3
Nield's Brow WA14 . . . . . . .119 B1
Nield St OL5 . . . . .68 B2
Nields Way SK6 . . . . .126 D4
Nigel Rd M9 . . . . .64 D1
Nigher Moss Ave OL16 . . . .31 C6
Nightingale Cl SK9 . . . . . . .131 A1
Nightingale Ct [11] WN6 . . . .37 A1
Nightingale Dr M34 . . . . . . .84 C1
Nightingale Gdns
M23 . . . . .109 A1
Nightingale Rd BL6 . . . . .21 C3
Nightingale St [2] PR6 . . . . .21 A8
Nightingales Wlk [3]
BL3 . . . . .147 C3
Nile St
Ashton-u-L OL7 . . . . .100 F8
Bolton BL3 . . . . .145 C1
Dukinfield SK16 . . . . .101 B4
Rochdale OL16 . . . . .31 A8
Nile Terr M7 . . . . .155 A1
Nile The [12] M15 . . . . .162 C3
NIMBLE NOOK 152 A1
Nimble Nook OL9 . . . . .152 A1
Nina Dr M40 . . . . .65 C3
Nine Acre Ct M5 . . . . .161 B3
Nine Acre Dr M5 . . . . .161 B3
Ninehouse La BL3 . . . . .147 C4
Ninfield Rd M23 . . . . .121 B4
Ninian Ct [2] M24 . . . . .46 F1
Ninian Gdns M28 . . . . .60 D3
Ninth Ave OL8 . . . . .66 D1
Nipper La M45 . . . . .44 E2
Nisbet Ave M22 . . . . .121 E3
Niven St M12 . . . . .163 C3
Nixon Rd BL3 . . . . .146 C3
Nixon Rd S BL3 . . . . .146 C3
Nixon St
Failsworth M35 . . . . .83 E7
Rochdale OL11 . . . . .30 B3
Stockport SK3 . . . . .170 B4
No 2 Pas SK3 . . . . .169 A1
Noards Ark La WA16 . . . . .136 A1
NOB END 43 A2
Noble Mdw OL12 . . . . .15 D4
Noble St
Bolton BL3 . . . . .145 B1
[7] Leigh WN7 . . . . .76 A5
Oldham OL8 . . . . .66 F4
Noel Dr M33 . . . . .108 D4
Noel St BL1 . . . . .145 B7
Nolan St M9 . . . . .157 B4
Nona St M6 . . . . .154 B3
NOOK 112 A5
Nook Farm Ave OL12 . . . . .14 F3
Nook Fields BL2 . . . . .25 E3
Nook La
Ashton-u-L OL6 . . . . .85 E6
Golborne WA3 . . . . .90 B8
Tyldesley M29 . . . . .77 D2
Nook Terr [5] OL12 . . . . . . .14 F3
Nook The
Appley Bridge WN6 . . . . .35 E7
Bramhall SK7 . . . . .132 D5
Eccles M30 . . . . .79 A4
Uppermill OL3 . . . . .69 C4
Urmston M41 . . . . .95 D1
Worsley M28 . . . . .78 F8

New—Nor 243

Noon Ct WA12 . . . . .89 B1
Noon Sun Cl OL3 . . . . .69 A4
Noon Sun St OL12 . . . . .14 F1
Norbet Wlk [8] M9 . . . . . . .157 B3
Norbreck Ave
Cheadle SK8 . . . . .123 A6
Manchester M21 . . . . .109 B7
Norbreck Cres WN6 . . . . . . .37 C2
Norbreck Gdns BL2 . . . . . .148 C4
Norbreck St BL2 . . . . .148 C4
Norburn Rd M13 . . . . .98 F2
Norbury Ave
Billinge WN5 . . . . .71 D6
Hyde SK14 . . . . .167 A2
Marple SK6 . . . . .125 E6
Sale M33 . . . . .107 F4
[7] Salford M6 . . . . .80 D5
Uppermill OL4 . . . . .68 C6
Norbury Cl M40 . . . . .160 B4
Norbury Cres SK7 . . . . .124 D2
Norbury Dr Sr K6 . . . . .125 F6
Norbury Gr
Bolton BL1 . . . . .25 A4
Hazel Grove SK7 . . . . .124 E2
Swinton M27 . . . . .61 F1
Norbury Hall Prim Sch
SK7 . . . . .124 E1
Norbury Ho [4] OL4 . . . . . . .67 B5
Norbury Hollow Rd
SK7 . . . . .134 B8
Norbury La OL8 . . . . .67 D3
Norbury Mews SK6 . . . . . . .125 E6
NORBURY MOOR 124 E1
Norbury St
Leigh WN7 . . . . .75 D5
Rochdale OL16 . . . . .31 B4
Salford M7 . . . . .155 D3
Stockport SK1 . . . . .169 C1
Norbury Way [9] SK9 . . . . .131 D5
Norcliffe Wlk [18] M15 . . . .99 B4
Norcot Wlk [18] M15 . . . . .162 A2
Norcross Cl SK2 . . . . .124 D5
Nordale Pk OL12 . . . . .13 D2
Nordek Cl OL2 . . . . .48 D5
Nordek Dr OL2 . . . . .48 D5
NORDEN 13 E2
Norden Ave M20 . . . . .110 A6
Norden Ct OL11 . . . . .13 C2
Norden Com Prim Sch
OL12 . . . . .13 F2
Norden Ct BL3 . . . . .147 B4
Norden Lo OL11 . . . . .19 E8
Norden Rd OL11 . . . . .29 E6
Nordens Dr OL9 . . . . .47 F1
Nordens Rd [1] OL9 . . . . . . .65 F8
Nordens Dr OL9 . . . . .152 A4
Norden Way OL11 . . . . .13 C2
Noreen Ave M25 . . . . .63 C5
Norfield St SK16 . . . . .101 C8
Norfolk Ave
Droylsden M43 . . . . .83 F3
Heywood OL10 . . . . .29 A2
Manchester M18 . . . . .99 C4
Reddish, Denshaw M34 . . . .99 F3
Reddish, Heaton Chapel
SK4 . . . . .111 C6
Whitefield M45 . . . . .63 A8
Norfolk Cl
Calderbrook OL15 . . . . .6 C1
Hindley WN2 . . . . .57 A6
Irlam M44 . . . . .105 C5
Little Lever BL3 . . . . .43 B4
Shaw OL2 . . . . .48 F7
Norfolk Cres M35 . . . . .83 E6
Norfolk Dr BL4 . . . . .42 D1
Norfolk Gdns M41 . . . . .94 D3
Norfolk Ho
[3] Manchester M7 . . . . .63 E1
[1] Sale M33 . . . . .108 D4
Norfolk Rd
Atherton M46 . . . . .58 C5
Manchester M18 . . . . .53 E1
Manchester M18 . . . . .99 C4
Norfolk Sq [3] SK13 . . . . . .104 C1
Norfolk St
Glossop SK13 . . . . .104 D1
Hyde SK14 . . . . .167 A2
Manchester M2 . . . . .159 A1
Rochdale OL11 . . . . .139 C2
Salford M6 . . . . .81 A5
Walkden M28 . . . . .60 D6
Wigan, Springfield WN6 . . . .37 A2
[9] Wigan, Worsley Hall
WN5 . . . . .54 F4
Norfolk Way OL2 . . . . .48 D2
Norford Way OL11 . . . . .29 E7
Norgate St M20 . . . . .110 B3
Norlan Ave M34 . . . . .100 E7
Norland Wlk M40 . . . . .83 A5
Norleigh Rd M22 . . . . .121 D8
NORLEY 54 C6
Norley Ave M32 . . . . .96 F3
Norley Cl OL1 . . . . .48 B2
Norley Dr
Manchester M19 . . . . .99 C2
Sale M33 . . . . .108 E4
Norley Hall Ave WN5 . . . . . .54 C6
Norley Rd
Leigh WN7 . . . . .75 B4
Wigan WN5 . . . . .54 C7
Norman Ave
Haydock WA11 . . . . .89 A7
Hazel Grove SK7 . . . . .124 C3
Newton-le-W WA12 . . . . . . .89 E3

Normanby Chase
WA14...........................119 B4
Normanby Gr M27.........61 E1
Normanby Rd M28.........60 C1
Normanby St
Bolton BL3.....................146 C2
Manchester M14.............98 A4
Swinton M27...................61 E1
Wigan WN5.....................54 B6
Norman Cl M24...............47 C1
Normandale Ave BL1....142 A4
Normandy Cres M26......43 F3
Norman Gr
Manchester M12.............99 A4
Reddish SK5...................111 E7
Norman Rd
Altrincham WA14...........119 C6
Ashton-u-L OL6..............85 C6
Manchester M14.............98 D2
Rochdale OL11................139 A2
Sale M33..........................108 B3
Salford M7......................155 B3
Stalybridge SK15............85 F2
Stockport, Heaton Norris
SK4...................................168 B3
Norman Rd W M9...........157 C3
Norman's Pl WA14.........119 D4
Norman St
Bury BL9..........................141 B4
Failsworth M35...............66 A1
Hyde SK14.......................167 B2
Manchester M12.............165 B1
Middleton M24................47 B1
Oldham OL1....................153 A4
Radcliffe M26.................44 D4
Normanton Ave M6........80 C3
Normanton Cl WN6........36 E4
Normanton Dr M9...........64 E4
Normanton St BL3,
SK8...................................123 A6
Norman Weall Ct 5
M24..................................47 A2
Normington St 1 OL4....67 C7
Norreys Ave M41............94 E3
Norreys St OL16.............31 A8
Norris Ave SK4...............168 C1
Norris Bank Prim Sch
SK4...................................168 A3
Norris Bank Terr SK4....168 C1
Norris Hill Dr SK4..........168 C2
Norris Rd M33................108 D2
Norris St
Bolton BL3.......................145 B1
Farnworth BL4.................60 D7
Little Lever BL3...............43 A3
Tyldesley M29.................77 A8
Norris Twrs SK4.............169 B2
Nortex Bsns Ctr BL1.....145 A4
Northallerton Rd M7.....81 B6
Northam Cl WN6.............19 D1
Northampton Rd M40....157 C2
Northampton Way 1
M34..................................101 A1
NORTH ASHTON................72 E6
North Ave
Farnworth BL4.................60 B8
Golborne WN7................74 F4
Leigh WN7.......................76 C3
Manchester M19.............110 F7
Ramsbottom BL8............10 F1
Stalybridge SK15............86 A3
Uppermill OL3.................69 B5
Whitefield BL9................45 B4
Northaven Cl M30..........80 A1
North Back Rock BL9.....140 C2
Northbank Gdns M19....110 E6
Northbank Ind Pk
M44..................................105 F6
Northbank Wlk M20.......109 D3
North Blackfield La
M7....................................81 C8
Northbourne St M6.......154 B2
Northbrook Ave M8.......63 F4
North Brook Rd SK13....171 B4
North Broughton St
M3....................................158 B2
North Butts St WN7.......76 B3
North Cestrian Gram Sch
WA14................................119 C5
North Chadderton Sch
OL9...................................48 A2
North Chadderton Sch
(Lower) OL9....................152 A4
North Cheshire Jewish
Prim Sch SK8..................122 C2
North Circ M45...............163 A6
North City Ctr Mkt M9...157 B4
North Cl SK13.................103 F7
North Clifden La M7......155 B2
Northcliffe Rd SK2.........124 C8
Northcombe Rd SK3......170 B1
Northcote Ave M22........121 D4
Northcote Rd SK7...........132 F7
North Cres
Droylsden M11................83 D3
Failsworth M40................65 D3
Northcroft WN1..............37 F1
North Croft
Atherton M46...................58 B5
Oldham OL8.....................67 A3
Northdale Rd M9............64 B5
North Dean St M27.........62 A1
Northdene Dr OL11........29 F6
Northdown Ave
Manchester M15.............162 A2

Northdown Ave continued
Romiley SK6....................113 C5
Northdowns Rd OL2.......48 F8
North Downs Rd SK8.....122 F3
North Dr
Appley Bridge WN6........18 C2
Droylsden M34................84 C1
Pendlebury M27.............80 B7
North Edge WN7.............76 B6
NORTHENDEN.................121 D8
Northenden Com Sch
M22..................................109 D1
Northenden Rd
Gatley SK8.......................122 A6
Sale M33..........................108 C4
Northenden View
M20..................................110 B2
North End Rd SK15.........86 B2
North Gr M20..................109 F4
Northern Ave M27...........62 C3
Northern Gr BL1..............142 C1
NORTHERN MOOR...........109 A1
Northfield Ave M26.........65 F2
Northfield Ct WN3...........74 C1
Northfield Dr SK9............137 D8
Northfield Rd
Bury BL9...........................27 F6
Failsworth M40................65 F2
Northfield St BL3.............144 C1
Northfleet Rd M30..........94 F8
Northgate OL12...............14 C7
North Gate OL8...............66 E2
Northgate Cl BL6.............22 C1
Northgate La OL1............49 E3
Northgate Rd SK3...........123 C8
North George St M3.......158 A2
North Gr
Manchester M13..............164 A1
Urmston M41...................95 C2
Walkden M28...................60 C3
North Grecian Street Prim
Sch M7..............................81 C5
North Hill St M3...............158 A3
North La
Rochdale OL12.................139 C4
Tyldesley M29..................77 A6
Northland Rd
Bolton BL1........................24 F6
Manchester M9................65 A3
Northlands M26...............43 E5
Northleach Cl BL8...........27 B3
Northleigh Dr SK5...........62 D3
Northleigh Ho 1 M16.....97 B2
Northleigh Rd M16..........97 B3
North Lonsdale St M32..96 E4
North Manchester General
Hospl M8..........................64 B1
North Manchester High
Sch for Boys M9..............65 B3
North Manchester High
Sch for Girls M40............65 A1
North Manchester Sixth
Form Coll M9....................157 B4
North Meade M21............109 B7
NORTH MOOR...................153 A3
North Moor Rd M12........99 A3
North Nook OL4...............67 F8
Northolme Gdns M19.....110 E5
Northolt Ave WN7............75 F8
Northolt Cl M11................83 D2
Northolt Dr BL3...............147 C4
Northolt Fold OL10..........46 E7
Northolt Rd M23..............108 F1
North Par
20 Manchester M2...........158 C1
Newhey OL16...................32 C4
Sale M33...........................108 D2
North Park Rd SK7...........123 E3
North Pl SK1....................169 C1
North Quarry Bsns Pk
M46..................................18 D1
North Rd
Altrincham WA15.............129 A8
Atherton M46....................58 B5
Carrington M31...............106 C4
Droylsden, Clayton M11..83 C2
Droylsden M34.................84 D1
Glossop SK13...................104 C3
Prestwich M25.................62 F5
Stretford M17...................96 C5
North Reddish Inf Sch
SK5...................................99 F1
North Reddish Jun Sch
SK5...................................99 F1
North Ridge High Sch
M12...................................160 B1
Northridge Rd M9............64 D6
North Rise OL3................69 B5
Northside Ave M41..........94 F1
North St
Ashton-in-M WN4............73 D5
Ashton-u-L OL6...............166 A2
Heywood OL10.................29 B2
Leigh WN7........................76 B4
Manchester M8................159 A4
Middleton M24.................47 A2
Radcliffe M26...................44 C4
Ramsbottom BL0.............1 C2
Rochdale OL16.................31 A8
Royton OL2......................48 D3
1 Royton OL2....................48 F8
Whitworth OL12...............4 C1
North Stage M50.............96 F8
North Star Dr M3.............158 A1
Northstead Ave M34.......101 B2
North Trafford Coll of F
Ed M32..............................96 F4

Northumberland Ave
OL7...................................166 B4
Northumberland Cl
M16...................................161 C1
Northumberland Cres
M16...................................161 C1
Northumberland Rd
Brinnington SK5..............112 B6
Manchester M16..............161 C1
Partington M31................105 E2
Northumberland St
Salford M7.......................155 B3
Wigan WN1......................37 E1
Northumberland Way
M22...................................121 E6
Northumbria St 9
BL3...................................144 C1
Northurst Dr M8..............63 F3
North Vale Rd WA15.......119 F6
North Veiw M45...............44 E2
North View
Mossley OL5....................68 E1
Ramsbottom, Higher
Summerseat BL9.............11 B2
Ramsbottom, Strongstry
BL0...................................1 C2
North View Cl OL4...........68 C5
North Walkden Prim Sch
M28..................................60 C5
Northward Rd SK9..........136 F6
Northway
Altrincham WA14.............119 E6
Droylsden M43.................100 A8
4 Eccles M30...................79 F2
Wigan WN1......................37 C1
North Way
Bolton BL1........................25 B4
Brinnington SK5..............112 C6
Hyde SK14.......................167 B2
Northwell St 2 WN7.......75 E8
North Western St
Manchester, Ardwick
M12...................................164 A3
Manchester, Levenshulme
M19...................................111 A8
Manchester M1, M12......163 C4
Northwold Cl WN3...........54 D3
Northwold Dr
Bolton BL1........................40 E8
Manchester M9................65 B3
Northwood BL2................25 D4
Northwood Ave WA12.....89 F3
Northwood Cres BL3.......144 C1
Northwood Gr M33..........108 B4
North Woodley 6 M26....44 C1
Norton Ave
Manchester M12...............99 B3
Reddish M34....................100 A3
Sale M33...........................107 D6
Urmston M41....................95 D4
Norton Gr SK4.................168 B1
Norton Grange M25........63 D3
Norton Rd
Boothstown M28.............77 E7
Rochdale OL12.................14 F3
Norton St
Bolton BL1........................143 C3
Manchester M1................159 C1
Manchester M3................158 C2
Manchester, Miles Platting
M40...................................160 B4
Manchester, Old Trafford
M16...................................97 D4
Salford, Higher Broughton
M7....................................155 B3
Norview Dr M20...............122 B8
Norville Ave M40, M9.....65 D3
Norway Gr SK5................169 C4
Norway St
Bolton BL3........................143 A2
Salford M6........................154 B2
Stretford M32...................96 E3
Norweb Way WN7...........76 B3
Norwell Rd M22...............121 C5
Norwich Ave
Ashton-in-M WN4............73 D3
Chadderton OL9..............48 A1
Denton M34......................100 F1
Golborne WA3..................90 D8
Rochdale OL11.................30 B7
Norwich Cl
Ashton-u-L OL6...............85 D8
Dukinfield SK16...............102 A7
Norwich Dr BL8...............140 A3
Norwich Rd M32..............95 F3
Norwich St OL11.............31 A5
Norwick Cl BL3................40 E4
Norwood M25...................63 B2
Norwood Ave
Ashton-in-M WN4............72 F6
Bramhall SK7...................132 D5
Cheadle SK8....................123 A3
Golborne WA3..................90 F7
High Lane SK6.................134 D7
Manchester M20...............110 D4
Salford M7........................81 B8
Tyldesley M29..................77 B6
Wigan WN6......................37 A3
Norwood Cl
Adlington PR6..................21 A8
Shaw OL2.........................149 A4
Walkden M28....................78 E8
Norwood Cres OL2..........48 E2
Norwood Ct M22.............121 E6
Norwood Dr
Altrincham WA15.............120 D5
Swinton M27....................79 D7

Norwood Gr
Bolton BL1........................144 C4
Royton OL2......................48 E2
Norwood Ho 6
WA14................................119 D5
Norwood Lo M7...............81 B8
Norwood Pk WA14..........119 C5
Norwood Rd
Gatley SK8.......................122 B6
Stockport SK2.................124 B4
Stretford M32...................96 E2
Noseby Ct M25................63 C5
Nostell Rd WN4...............73 A5
Nottingham Ave SK5......112 C6
Nottingham Cl SK5.........112 C5
Nottingham Dr
Ashton-u-L OL6...............85 B7
Bolton BL1........................143 B1
Failsworth M35................84 A6
Nottingham Pl WN1........37 E1
Nottingham Way 3
M34..................................101 A1
Nowell Ct M24................47 A3
Nowell Ho M24...............47 A3
Nowell Rd M24...............47 A3
Nudger Cl OL3.................50 F2
Nudger Gn OL3................51 A2
Nuffield Cl BL1...............142 B1
Nuffield Rd M22..............121 E4
Nugent House Sch
WN5..................................71 D4
Nugent Rd BL3................147 B3
Nugget St OL4.................67 B6
Nuneaton Dr M40............160 A3
Nuneham Ave M20..........110 C1
Nunfield Cl M40..............65 B2
NUN HILLS.......................3 C7
Nunnery Rd BL3..............146 B4
Nunthorpe Dr M8...........156 C4
Nursery Ave WA15..........128 E8
Nursery Cl
4 Glossop SK13...............116 C8
Sale M33..........................108 C4
Stockport SK2.................124 D7
Nursery Dr SK12.............133 D4
Nursery Gdns OL16........31 C8
Nursery Gr M31..............105 F4
Nursery La
Cheadle SK3....................123 A7
Wilmslow SK9..................136 F5
Nursery Rd
Cheadle SK8....................123 A1
Dukinfield SK14...............101 C3
Failsworth M35................84 A7
Prestwich M25.................63 A6
Stockport SK4..................168 C2
Urmston M41....................95 A4
Nursery St
Manchester M16..............97 F3
Salford M6........................154 C3
Nuthatch Ave M28..........78 D8
Nuthurst Rd M40............65 D1
Nutsford Vale M12,
M18..................................99 B4
NUTTALL...........................11 C4
Nuttall Ave
Horwich BL6....................22 A3
Little Lever BL3...............43 C3
Whitefield M45.................62 F8
Nuttall Cl BL0..................138 C1
Nuttall Hall Cotts BL0....11 D5
Nuttall Hall Rd BL0.........11 D5
Nuttall La BL0..................138 B1
NUTTALL LANE................138 B1
Nuttall Mews M45...........62 F8
Nuttall Rd BL0.................11 D4
Nuttall Sq BL9.................44 F5
Nuttall St
Atherton M46...................58 E3
Bury BL9...........................141 A1
Irlam M44.........................105 E6
Manchester, City Park
M16...................................161 C1
Manchester M11...............165 A3
Oldham OL8.....................67 B4
Rochdale OL16.................31 A7
Nutt La M25......................63 E8
Nutt St WN1.....................37 E2
Nutwood Ct SK5..............111 E7

O

Oadby Cl M12..................99 A4
Oadby Pl 2 SK5..............99 F7
Oak Ave
Abram Brow WN2...........74 C7
Cheadle SK8....................123 A2
Golborne WA3..................90 B8
Hindley WN2....................57 A3
6 Horwich BL6................22 E1
Irlam M44.........................105 D5
Little Lever BL3...............43 B3
Manchester M21..............109 B8
Middleton M24.................65 A4
Newton-le-W WA12.........89 D3
Ramsbottom BL0.............11 A2
Romiley SK6.....................113 C2
Royton OL2......................48 D6
Standish WN6..................19 E2
Stockport, Heaton Norris
SK4...................................168 B2
Whitefield M45.................62 F7
Wilmslow SK9..................136 F5
Oakbank WN2.................56 B8
OAK BANK.......................63 A8
Oak Bank
Alderley Edge SK9..........137 A2

Oak Bank continued
Manchester M9................157 A4
Mossley, Carrbrook SK15..86 F7
Prestwich M25.................62 F1
Oakbank Ave OL9............65 F8
Oak Bank Ave M9............64 F1
Oak Bank Cl M45.............63 B8
Oakbank Dr BL1..............24 D6
Oakbarton BL6................40 C4
Oak Brow Cotts SK9.......130 E4
Oak Cl
Mottram in L SK14..........103 A4
Whitworth OL12...............4 D4
Wilmslow SK9..................136 F6
Oakcliffe Rd
Rochdale OL12................15 D4
Wythenshawe M23..........121 A7
Oak Coppice BL1............144 A3
Oak Cotts SK9.................130 E4
Oakcroft SK15.................102 E8
Oakcroft Way M22..........121 E6
Oak Ct SK6......................113 A5
Oakdale BL2....................25 E4
Oakdale Cl M45...............62 D8
Oakdale Ct
Altrincham WA14.............119 C5
Delph OL3........................50 E3
Stalybridge SK15............86 B2
Oakdale Dr
Gatley SK8.......................122 B2
Manchester M20..............110 C1
Tyldesley M29..................77 C6
Oakdale Sch SK16...........101 E6
Oakdene M27...................79 B6
Oak Dene OL3.................69 A4
Oakdene Ave
Gatley SK8.......................131 C7
Reddish SK4....................111 D5
Oakdene Cres SK6..........125 F7
Oakdene Ct SK9..............131 B1
Oakdene Gdns SK6.........125 F7
Oakdene Rd
Marple SK6......................125 F7
Middleton M24.................65 C8
Sale M15..........................120 B8
Oakdene St M9................157 C4
Oak Dr
Cheadle SK7....................132 C7
Marple SK6......................125 D6
Reddish M34....................100 A8
Oakenbottom Rd BL2.....42 D7
Oakenclough 1 OL1........153 B3
Oaken Clough 3 OL7......85 A6
Oakenclough Dr BL1.......131 D2
Oaken Clough Dr 1
OL7...................................85 A6
Oaken Clough Terr
OL7...................................84 F6
Oakenden Cl WN4...........73 A6
Oakengates WN6............19 F1
Oakenrod Hill OL11.........30 C6
Oakenshaw Ave OL12....14 C5
Oakenshaw View OL12...14 C5
Oaker Ave M20................109 E4
Oaker Pl M20...................109 E4
Oakes St BL4...................60 F7
Oakfield
Dukinfield SK16...............101 E6
Gatley SK8.......................122 C2
Manchester M25..............63 D3
Sale M33...........................108 A5
Oakfield Ave
Atherton M46...................58 C4
Cheadle SK8....................122 E6
Droylsden M43.................83 F1
Golborne WA3..................73 F1
Manchester, Firswood
M16...................................97 A3
Manchester, Whalley Range
M16...................................97 D3
Mossley SK15..................86 E6
Oakfield Cl
Alderley Edge SK9..........137 B3
Bramhall SK7...................132 E4
Horwich BL6....................22 F2
Oakfield Cres WN2.........38 C5
Oakfield Ct SK15.............119 F6
Oakfield Dr M38..............59 E5
Oakfield Gr
Farnworth BL4.................60 C6
Manchester M18..............99 D4
Oakfield Mews
1 Sale M33......................108 A4
Stockport SK3..................170 C1
Oakfield Prim Sch
SK14.................................101 E5
Oakfield Rd
Alderley Edge SK9..........137 B2
Altrincham WA15.............119 E4
Dukinfield SK14...............101 E5
Glossop SK13...................171 B3
Manchester M20..............110 A3
Poynton SK12...................133 F4
Stockport SK3..................170 C1
Oakfield St
Altrincham WA15.............119 E5
Manchester M8................156 A2
Oakfield Terr OL11..........30 C8
Oakfield Trad Est
WA15................................119 E5
Oakfold Ave OL6..............85 D6
Oakford Ave M40............159 C3
Oakford Cl SK13..............171 C4
Oakford Wlk BL3.............146 C4
Oak Gates BL7................8 E1

Oak Gr
Ashton-u-L OL6 . . . . .85 D6
Cheadle SK8 . . . . .122 E5
Eccles M30 . . . . .79 B1
Poynton SK12 . . . . .133 D4
Urmston M41 . . . . .95 E2
Oak Grove Sch SK8 . . . . .131 C7
Oakham Ave M20 . . . . . .110 A8
Oakham Cl BL8 . . . . .27 D5
Oakham Mews M7 . . . . . .63 D1
Oakham Rd M34 . . . . . . .101 A1
Oakhead WN7 . . . . .76 C3
Oak Hill OL15 . . . . .15 F5
Oakhill Cl BL2 . . . . .43 A7
Oak Hill Cl WN1 . . . . .37 B4
Oakhill Ct M7 . . . . .155 B3
Oakhill Trad Est M28 . . . .60 C6
Oakhill Way M8 . . . . .155 C3
Oak Ho M14 . . . . .98 D1
Oakhouse Dr M22 . . . . . .109 B7
Oakhurst Chase SK9 . . .137 A2
Oakhurst Dr SK3 . . . . . . .123 B5
Oakhurst Gdns M25 . . . .63 A4
Oakhurst Gr BL5 . . . . .57 C7
Oakington Ave 10 M14 . .98 B3
Oak La
Whitefield M45 . . . . .63 B8
Wilmslow SK9 . . . . .136 F6
Oakland Ave
Manchester M19 . . . . .110 E4
Salford M6 . . . . .80 B4
Stockport SK2 . . . . .124 D6
Oakland Ct SK12 . . . . . . .133 D4
Oakland Gr BL1 . . . . .142 A2
Oaklands BL1 . . . . .40 F7
Oaklands Ave
Cheadle SK8 . . . . .123 A2
Marple SK6 . . . . .126 C8
Oaklands Cl SK9 . . . . . . .131 E1
Oaklands Ct OL4 . . . . .68 F5
Oaklands Dene SK14 . . .102 A2
Oaklands Dr
Hazel Grove SK7 . . . . .124 E1
Hyde SK14 . . . . .102 A2
Prestwich M25 . . . . .63 B4
Sale M33 . . . . .108 A5
Oaklands Ho M14 . . . . . . .98 C1
Oaklands Hospl M6 . . . . .80 B4
Oaklands Inf Sch SK9 . . .131 E1
Oaklands Pk OL4 . . . . . . .68 F5
Oaklands Rd
Edenfield BL0 . . . . .1 D2
Golborne WA3 . . . . .90 F7
Royton OL2 . . . . .48 E2
Salford M7 . . . . .81 A8
Swinton M27 . . . . .79 D6
Uppermill OL4 . . . . .68 F5
Oaklea
1 Manchester M16 . . . . . . .97 C3
Shevington Moor WN6 . . .19 A2
Oak Lea Ave SK14 . . . . . .137 A5
Oaklea Rd M33 . . . . .107 E5
Oakleigh
4 Stockport, Davenport
SK3 . . . . .123 F4
Stockport, Heaton Moor
SK4 . . . . .168 B3
Oakleigh Ave
Altrincham WA15 . . . . . . .120 A7
Bolton BL3 . . . . .42 A2
1 Manchester M19 . . . . . .110 F7
Oakleigh Cl OL10 . . . . . . .46 E7
Oakleigh Rd SK8 . . . . . . .131 E8
Oakley Ave WN5 . . . . .71 E6
Oakley Cl
Failsworth M40 . . . . .83 C5
Radcliffe M26 . . . . .62 A8
Oakley Dr
Oldham OL1 . . . . .49 D4
Wigan WN5 . . . . .54 E6
Oakley Pk BL1 . . . . .40 F7
Oakley St OL15 . . . . .15 E4
Oakley Villas SK4 . . . . . .168 B3
Oaklings The WN2 . . . . . . .57 A3
Oak Lo SK7 . . . . .132 F7
Oakmere Ave M30 . . . . . .79 C4
Oakmere Cl M22 . . . . . . .121 D4
Oakmere Rd
Cheadle SK8 . . . . .122 F4
Handforth SK9 . . . . .131 D5
Oakmoor Dr M7 . . . . .81 B8
Oakmoor Rd M23 . . . . . . .121 A6
Oak Rd
Altrincham WA15 . . . . . . .119 E3
Cheadle SK8 . . . . .122 E5
Failsworth M35 . . . . .83 F6
Manchester M20 . . . . .110 B5
Oldham OL8 . . . . .66 D2
Paddockhill WA16 . . . . . .136 B5
Partington M31 . . . . .105 D2
Sale M33 . . . . .108 D4
Salford M7 . . . . .81 C5
Oakridge Wlk 3 M9 . . . .157 A3
Oaks Ave BL2 . . . . .25 C4
Oaks Bsns Pk The
M23 . . . . .120 E8
Oak Shaw Cl M9 . . . . .64 D2
Oakshaw Dr OL12 . . . . . . .14 A1
Oakside Cl SK8 . . . . .122 E6
Oaks La BL2 . . . . .25 B4
Oaks Prim Sch The
BL1 . . . . .24 F6
Oak St
Atherton M46 . . . . .58 A1
Denton M34 . . . . .100 F4
Eccles M30 . . . . .79 D1
Glossop SK13 . . . . .104 C1

Oak St continued
Hazel Grove SK7 . . . . .124 D3
Heywood OL10 . . . . .29 B3
Hyde SK14 . . . . .167 B4
Leigh WN7 . . . . .75 F3
Littleborough OL15 . . . . . .16 C5
Manchester M4 . . . . .159 A2
2 Manchester M4 . . . . . .159 B2
Middleton M24 . . . . .65 D7
Newhey OL16 . . . . .32 B4
Radcliffe M26 . . . . .44 C1
Ramsbottom BL0 . . . . . . .138 B1
Rochdale OL16 . . . . .139 C3
Shaw OL2 . . . . .149 C3
Stockport SK3 . . . . .123 B8
Swinton M27 . . . . .62 A1
Tyldesley M29 . . . . .59 A1
Whitworth OL12 . . . . .4 D5
Wigan WN1 . . . . .151 B3
Oaks The
Gatley SK8 . . . . .122 A2
Glossop SK13 . . . . .116 A7
Hyde SK14 . . . . .102 A3
Oak Terr BL8 . . . . .1 E8
Oak Tree Cl
Atherton M46 . . . . .58 A1
Hyde SK14 . . . . .102 A2
Stockport SK2 . . . . .124 D8
Oaktree Cotts SK14 . . . .122 F8
Oak Tree Cres SK15 . . . .102 B8
Oak Tree Ct SK8 . . . . . . .122 E5
Oak Tree Dr SK16 . . . . . .101 F7
Oak View
Oldham OL1 . . . . .48 D1
Whitworth OL12 . . . . .4 D4
Oak View Rd OL3 . . . . .69 B5
Oakville Dr M6 . . . . .80 A4
Oakville Terr 11 M40 . . . .64 F1
Oakway
Manchester M20 . . . . .122 C8
Middleton M24 . . . . .46 F4
Oakwell Dr
Manchester M7 . . . . .63 E1
Whitefield BL9 . . . . .45 B3
Oakwell Mans M7 . . . . . . .63 E1
Oak Wlk M34 . . . . .100 E6
OAKWOOD 86 E4
Oakwood
Chadderton OL9 . . . . .65 E7
Glossop SK13 . . . . .115 F8
Sale M33 . . . . .107 C4
Oakwood Ave
Ashton-in-M WN4 . . . . .73 A2
Denton M34 . . . . .100 E7
Failsworth M40 . . . . .65 D1
Gatley SK8 . . . . .122 B5
Shevington WN6 . . . . .35 F5
Swinton M27 . . . . .61 A4
Walkden M28 . . . . .60 F2
Wilmslow SK9 . . . . .136 E6
Oakwood Cl BL8 . . . . .27 B3
Oakwood Ct M14 . . . . . . .128 B8
Oakwood Dr
Bolton BL1 . . . . .40 F8
Leigh WN7 . . . . .75 E1
Salford M6 . . . . .80 B5
Walkden M28 . . . . .60 F2
Oakwood East Mt S 154 A1
Oakwood High Sch
Eccles M30 . . . . .79 F4
Salford M6 . . . . .80 C5
Oakwood La WA14 . . . . . .119 B1
Oakwood Mews M24 . . . . .65 C8
Oakwood Rd
Disley SK12 . . . . .135 D6
Romiley SK6 . . . . .113 C2
Oak Wood View OL5 . . . . .86 C6
Oakworth Croft OL4 . . . . .49 F4
Oakworth Dr BL1 . . . . .24 D5
Oakworth St M9 . . . . .64 C3
Oatlands Rd M22 . . . . . . .121 C2
Oat St SK1 . . . . .124 A7
Oban Ave
Failsworth M40 . . . . .83 A4
Oldham OL1 . . . . .49 B1
Oban Cres SK3 . . . . .123 D4
Oban Dr
Garswood WN4 . . . . .72 C4
Sale M33 . . . . .108 E3
Oban Gr BL1 . . . . .24 E5
Oban St BL1 . . . . .143 A3
Oban Way WN2 . . . . .38 D5
Oberlin St
Oldham OL4 . . . . .67 D7
Rochdale OL11 . . . . .139 A1
Oberon Cl 1 M30 . . . . . . .79 D2
Occlestone Cl M33 . . . . .108 E1
Ocean Ho M15 . . . . .163 A1
Ocean St WA14 . . . . .119 B1
Ocean Street Trad Est
WA14 . . . . .119 B6
Ocean Wlk 3 M15 . . . . . .162 C1
Ockendon Dr M9 . . . . . . .157 B3
Octavia Dr M40 . . . . .83 C4
Odell St M11 . . . . .165 B3
Odessa Ave M6 . . . . .80 B4
Odette St M18 . . . . .99 C4
OFFERTON 124 E6
Offerton Dr SK2 . . . . .124 D6
Offerton Fold SK2 . . . . . .124 C7
Offerton Gn SK2 . . . . . . .124 C6
OFFERTON GREEN 125 A6
Offerton High Sch
SK2 . . . . .124 E8
Offerton Ind Est SK1,
. . . . .124 C7
Offerton La SK1, SK2 . . . .124 C8
Offerton Rd SK2, SK7 . . . .125 A4

Offerton St
Horwich BL6 . . . . .22 A3
Stockport SK1 . . . . .112 B2
Off Grove Rd SK15 . . . . . .86 D4
Off Ridge Hill La 3
SK15 . . . . .85 F2
Off Stamford St SK15 . . .86 D4
Off Vaudrey La 4
M34 . . . . .101 A2
Ogbourne Wlk 8
M13 . . . . .163 C2
OGDEN 32 F5
Ogden Cl
Haslingden BB4 . . . . .1 A7
Heywood OL10 . . . . .29 A2
Whitefield M45 . . . . .45 A1
Ogden Ct SK14 . . . . .167 B2
Ogden Dr BB4 . . . . .1 A7
Ogden Gdns SK16 . . . . . .101 E8
Ogden Gr SK8 . . . . .121 F4
Ogden La
Manchester M11 . . . . .99 D7
Newhey OL16 . . . . .32 D5
Ogden Rd
Bramhall SK7 . . . . .132 D5
Failsworth M35 . . . . .83 F6
Ogden Sq SK16 . . . . .101 B8
Ogden St
Broadbottom SK14 . . . . . .115 B8
Chadderton OL9 . . . . .152 C4
4 Manchester M20 . . . . .110 B3
Middleton M24 . . . . .65 A8
9 Oldham OL4 . . . . .67 D6
Prestwich M25 . . . . .63 C4
Rochdale OL11 . . . . .30 C2
Swinton M27 . . . . .79 F7
Ogden Wlk M45 . . . . .63 A8
Ogmore Wlk M40 . . . . .65 C2
Ogwen Dr M25 . . . . .63 B5
Ohio Ave M50 . . . . .96 F8
O'Kane Ho 10 M30 . . . . . .79 D1
Okehampton Cres
M33 . . . . .107 D5
Okell Gr WN7 . . . . .75 D6
Okeover Rd M7 . . . . .155 A4
Olaf St 13 BL2 . . . . .25 B1
Olanyian Dr M8 . . . . .155 B1
Old Bank Cl SK6 . . . . .113 A3
Old Bank St M2 . . . . .158 C1
Old Bank View OL1 . . . . . .49 C4
Old Barn Pl BL7 . . . . .25 A8
Old Barton Rd M17,
M30 . . . . .95 C2
Old Bedions Sports Ctr
M20 . . . . .122 A8
Old Beechfield Gdns
WN6 . . . . .2 E1
Old Bent La OL12 . . . . .15 A7
Old Birley St M15 . . . . . .162 C1
OLD BIRTLE 28 E7
OLD BOSTON 89 A8
Old Boston WA11 . . . . .89 A7
Old Boston Trad Est
WA11 . . . . .89 B8
Oldbridge Dr WN2 . . . . . . .56 D6
Old Broadway M20 . . . . .110 B5
Old Brook Cl OL12 . . . . . . .49 D8
Oldbrook Fold WA15 . . . .120 B4
Old Brow OL6 . . . . .68 C1
Old Brow La OL16 . . . . . . .15 C3
Old Brown Ct OL5 . . . . . . .86 C8
Oldbury Cl
Heywood OL10 . . . . .46 D7
Manchester M40 . . . . .160 A3
Old Chapel St SK3 . . . . . .170 A3
Old Church Mews 2
SK16 . . . . .101 E4
Old Church St
Failsworth M40 . . . . .83 C6
Oldham OL1 . . . . .153 C3
Old Clay Dr OL12 . . . . .15 A4
Old Clough La M28 . . . . . .60 F1
Old Colliery Yd WN4 . . . . .72 C3
Oldcott Cl M28 . . . . .77 F2
Old Courthouse The
M3 . . . . .158 A2
Old Court St SK14 . . . . . .167 A2
Old Croft OL4 . . . . .68 A6
Old Croft Mews SK1 . . . .124 B7
Old Crofts Bank M41 . . . . .95 C3
Old Cross SK13 . . . . .104 E2
Old Cross St OL6 . . . . . . .166 C3
Old Ctyd The M22 . . . . . .121 F5
Old Dairy Mews
SK14 . . . . .101 C5
Old Delph Rd OL11 . . . . . .13 F1
Old Doctors St BL8 . . . . . .26 F7
Old Eagley Mews BL1 . . .24 F6
Old Edge La OL2 . . . . .48 E2
Old Elm St M12, M13 . . .163 C2
Old Engine Ho The
BL0 . . . . .138 C2
Old Engine La BL0 . . . . . .11 D6
Oldershaw Dr M9 . . . . . .157 A2
Old Farm Cres M43 . . . . . .99 F8
Old Farm Dr SK2 . . . . . . .124 F6
Old Farm Rd SK8 . . . . . .132 E6
OLDFIELD BROW 119 A5
Oldfield Brow Prim Sch
WA14 . . . . .119 A5
Oldfield Cl BL5 . . . . .57 F8
Oldfield Gr WA14 . . . . . . .119 C1
Oldfield Gr M33 . . . . .108 C5
Oldfield La WA14 . . . . . . .118 F4
Oldfield Mews WA14 . . . .119 C5

Oldfield Rd
Altrincham WA14 . . . . . . .119 B5
Prestwich M25 . . . . .63 C7
Sale M33 . . . . .108 C5
Salford M5 . . . . .161 C4
Oldfield St M11 . . . . .83 C1
Old Fold
Eccles M30 . . . . .79 C4
7 Wigan WN5 . . . . .54 B6
Old Fold Rd
Aspull WN2 . . . . .38 D5
Westhoughton BL5 . . . . . . .57 C7
Old Gardens St 3
SK1 . . . . .170 C4
Old Garden The
WA15 . . . . .120 B7
Oldgate Wlk 20 M15 . . . .162 A2
OLD GLOSSOP 104 E2
Old Gn
Bolton BL2 . . . . .25 E6
Ramsbottom BL8 . . . . .10 F1
Old Greenwood La
BL6 . . . . .22 D1
Old Ground St BL0 . . . . . .138 C2
Old Hall Cl
Bury BL8 . . . . .27 B7
Glossop SK13 . . . . .104 D2
Old Hall Clough BL6 . . . . .40 C7
Oldhall Cres SK9 . . . . . . .131 E3
Old Hall Ct
Sale M33 . . . . .108 E4
Whitefield M45 . . . . .62 C7
Old Hall Dr
Ashton-in-M WN4 . . . . .73 A2
Manchester M18 . . . . .99 D4
Stockport SK2 . . . . .124 E6
Old Hall Drive Prim Sch
M18 . . . . .99 D4
Old Hall Farm BL3 . . . . . . .42 E4
Old Hall La
Bolton BL6 . . . . .23 C1
Manchester M25 . . . . .64 A6
Manchester, Rusholme M13,
M14, M19 . . . . .98 E2
Marple SK6 . . . . .126 C5
Mottram in L SK14 . . . . . .103 A5
Westhoughton BL5 . . . . . . .57 E6
Whitefield M45 . . . . .62 C6
Woodford SK7 . . . . .132 D1
Worsley M28 . . . . .78 E7
Old Hall Mill La M46 . . . . .76 A8
Old Hall Prim Sch BL8 . . .27 B7
Old Hall Rd
Failsworth M40 . . . . .83 B7
Gatley SK8 . . . . .122 A6
Manchester M7 . . . . .63 D1
Sale M33 . . . . .108 E4
Stretford M32 . . . . .96 C7
Whitefield M45 . . . . .62 C7
Old Hall St N BL1 . . . . . . .145 C3
Old Hall St 5 SK13 . . . . .104 A5
Old Hall St
Dukinfield SK16 . . . . .101 A7
Farnworth BL4 . . . . .60 E7
Ince-in-M WN3 . . . . .151 B2
3 Manchester M11 . . . . . .99 F7
Oldham M24 . . . . .47 A1
Old Hall Terrs OL6 . . . . . . .85 E5
Old Hey La WA11 . . . . .89 C1
Old Heyes Rd WA15 . . . . .120 B8
Old Hey Wlk WA12 . . . . . . .89 C1
Old House Terrs OL6 . . . . .85 E5
Old Kiln OL3 . . . . .69 A7
Old Kiln La
Ashton-u-L OL6 . . . . .85 A5
Delph OL3, OL4 . . . . .50 D2
Failsworth M35, M40 . . . . .83 D6
Middleton M24 . . . . .65 A8
Royton OL1, OL16 . . . . . . .31 A3
Shaw OL1, OL4 . . . . .50 B7
Shaw, Shaw Side OL2 . . .149 B1
Uppermill OL3, OL3 . . . . . .68 D6
Oldknow Rd SK6 . . . . .126 A6
Old La
Bury BL9 . . . . .27 F8
Horwich BL6 . . . . .22 F7
Manchester M11 . . . . .99 D7

Old La continued
Oldham, Werneth OL9 . . . .66 B4
Oldham, Wood Brook
OL4 . . . . .68 A8
Shevington WN6 . . . . .36 B6
Uppermill, Lydgate OL4 . . .68 E6
Uppermill OL3 . . . . .51 B2
Walkden M38 . . . . .59 F6
Westhoughton BL5 . . . . . . .57 D8
Whitworth OL12, OL13 . . . .4 E6
Wigan WN1 . . . . .37 B4
Old Lansdowne Rd
M20 . . . . .110 A4
Old Lees St OL6 . . . . .85 D5
Old Links Cl BL1 . . . . .23 E2
Old Lord's Cres BL6 . . . . .22 B5
Old Manor Pk M46 . . . . . . .58 A2
Old Market Pl 4
WA14 . . . . .119 D5
Old Market St M9 . . . . .64 D2
Old Meadow Dr M34 . . . .100 F5
Old Meadow La WA15 . . .120 B3
Old Medlock St M3 . . . . .162 B4
Old Mill Cl
Lymm WA13 . . . . .117 C6
Pendlebury M27 . . . . .80 B8
Old Mill Ho OL4 . . . . .68 A5
Old Mill La
Hazel Grove SK7 . . . . .134 A8
Oldham OL4 . . . . .68 A5
Old Mills Hill M24 . . . . . . .47 D1
Oldmill St OL12 . . . . .139 C3
Old Mill St M4 . . . . .159 C1
Old Moat Com Prim Sch
M20 . . . . .110 A7
Old Moat La M20 . . . . . . .110 A7
Old Moor Rd SK6 . . . . . . .112 E5
Old Moss La WA3 . . . . .92 E6
Old Mount St M4 . . . . . . .159 B3
Old Nans La BL2 . . . . .25 F2
Old Nursery Fold BL2 . . . .25 E4
Old Oak Cl BL2 . . . . .43 B5
Old Oak Dr M34 . . . . .101 A3
Old Oake Cl M28 . . . . .60 E2
Old Oak St M20 . . . . .110 B3
Old Orch SK9 . . . . .137 A7
Old Orch The WA15 . . . . .120 B8
Old Packhorse Rd
OL15 . . . . .16 F6
Old Pack Horse Rd
OL3 . . . . .51 B6
Old Park La M17 . . . . .95 C6
Old Parrin La M30 . . . . . . .79 B3
Old Pasture Cl SK2 . . . . .124 F7
Old Pepper La WN6 . . . . . .19 B2
Old Quarry La BL7 . . . . .8 F1
Old Rake BL6 . . . . .22 B5
Old Rd
Ashton-in-M WN4 . . . . .73 A4
Ashton-u-L OL6 . . . . .86 A6
Bolton BL1 . . . . .143 B3
Cheadle SK8 . . . . .166 C1
Dukinfield SK16 . . . . .166 C1
Failsworth M35 . . . . .83 E8
Glossop SK13 . . . . .104 A7
Handforth SK9 . . . . .131 D3
Hyde SK14 . . . . .167 A4
Manchester M9 . . . . .64 D2
Mottram in L SK14 . . . . . .102 F5
Rochdale OL16 . . . . .15 E4
Stalybridge SK15 . . . . . . .102 C8
Stockport SK4 . . . . .169 B3
Wilmslow SK9 . . . . .137 B8
Old Rectory Gdns
SK8 . . . . .122 D5
Old River Cl M44 . . . . .94 A2
Old School Ct
Eccles M30 . . . . .79 D4
3 Manchester M9 . . . . . . .64 C2
Old School Dr M9 . . . . . . .64 C2
Old School House The
OL15 . . . . .15 F6
Old School La
Adlington PR7 . . . . .20 E5
Cheadle SK8 . . . . .132 A4
Old School Mews
12 Bacup OL13 . . . . .3 C8
1 Dukinfield SK15,
SK16 . . . . .101 E8
Old School Wlk M9 . . . . . . .73 A3
Old School Rooms The 2
BL1 . . . . .145 C2
Old Shaw St M5 . . . . .161 B4
Old Sirs BL5 . . . . .57 F5
Old Sq 8 OL6 . . . . .166 C3
Old St
Ashton-u-L OL6 . . . . .166 B3
Broadbottom SK14 . . . . . .115 A8
Oldham OL4 . . . . .67 D5
Stalybridge SK15 . . . . .86 A2
Old Stables The M34 . . . .100 F6
Old Station St 8 M30 . . . .79 C1
Oldstead Gr BL3 . . . . .40 F3
Oldstead Wlk M9 . . . . . . .157 A2
Old Swan Cl BL7 . . . . .8 E2
Old Swan Cotts BL7 . . . . . .8 E2
OLD TAME 50 B8
Old Tannery The
SK14 . . . . .113 C8
Old Thorn La OL3 . . . . .69 D6
Old Towns Cl BL8 . . . . .26 F7
OLD TRAFFORD 161 B1
Old Trafford Com Sch
M16 . . . . .161 C2
Old Trafford Sta M16 . . . . .97 A4

Old Vicarage BL5 . . . . .57 E5
Old Vicarage Gdns
M28 .60 D3
Old Vicarage Mews
BL5 .57 E5
Old Vicarage Rd BL6 . . . .22 F3
Old Wargrave Rd
WA12 . . . . .89 C3
Oldway Wlk M40 . . . . .83 B5
Old Wellington Rd
M30 .79 E2
Old Wells Cl M38 . . . . .60 A6
Old Well Wlk M33 . . . . . .107 C2
Old Will's La BL6 . . . . .22 B6
Oldwood Rd M23 . . . . . . .121 A3
Old Wool La SK8 . . . . .122 F4
Old York St M15 . . . . .162 B2
Oleo Terr M44 . . . . .94 C3
Olga St BL1 . . . . .143 A2
Olivant St BL9 . . . . .44 E8
Olive Bank BL8 . . . . .27 B4
Olive Gr WN6 . . . . .36 F3
Oliver Cl OL15 . . . . .15 F5
Oliver Rd M15 . . . . .120 A8
Oliver Fold Cl M28 . . . . . .77 E6
Oliver St
Atherton M46 . . . . .58 D3
[10] Bacup OL13 . . . . .3 C8
Manchester, Beswick
M11 . . . . .164 C4
Stockport SK1, SK3 . . . . .170 C4
Olive Shapley Ave
M20 . . . . .110 B3
Olive St
Bacup OL13 . . . . .3 E8
Bolton BL3 . . . . .147 A4
Bury BL8 . . . . .140 A2
Failsworth M35 . . . . .83 E8
Heywood OL10 . . . . .29 E2
Radcliffe M26 . . . . .44 C3
Rochdale OL11 . . . . .30 C1
Olive Terr SK14 . . . . .115 A8
Olive Wlk [5] M33 . . . . . .107 C6
Olivia Ct M5 . . . . .161 C4
Olivia Gr M14 . . . . .98 D3
Ollerbarrow Rd WA15 . . .119 E2
Ollerbrook Ct [1] BL1 . . .143 C2
Ollersett Ave SK22 . . . . . .127 D1
Ollersett La SK22 . . . . . . .127 E1
Ollerton [10] OL12 . . . . . .139 B4
Ollerton Ave
Manchester M16 . . . . . . .97 C3
Sale M33 . . . . .107 D5
Ollerton Cl
Wigan WN2 . . . . .38 A2
Wythenshawe M22 . . . . .109 E1
Ollerton Dr M35 . . . . .83 F6
Ollerton Rd SK9 . . . . .131 E5
Ollerton St
[1] Adlington PR6 . . . . . . .21 A8
Bolton BL1 . . . . .24 F6
Ollerton Terr BL1 . . . . . . .24 F6
Ollier Ave M12 . . . . .99 B2
Olney OL11 . . . . .139 B2
Olney Ave M22 . . . . .121 D6
Olney St M13 . . . . .98 D4
Olsberg Cl M26 . . . . .44 C4
Olwen Ave M12 . . . . .165 A1
Olwen Cres SK5 . . . . .111 F8
Olympia Ct [2] M44 . . . . . .94 A2
Olympic Ct M9 . . . . .96 F8
Omer Ave M13 . . . . .98 F2
Omer Dr M19 . . . . .110 E7
Onchan Ave OL4 . . . . .67 B6
One Ash Cl OL12 . . . . .14 F2
One Oak Ct SK7 . . . . .123 C2
One Oak La SK9 . . . . .137 F7
Ongar Wlk M9 . . . . .64 B3
Onslow Ave M40 . . . . .65 E1
Onslow Cl OL1 . . . . .153 B4
Onslow Rd SK3 . . . . .123 C8
Onslow St OL11 . . . . .30 C4
Onward St SK14 . . . . .167 A2
OOZEWOOD 48 B6
Oozewood Rd M2, OL2 . . .48 B5
Opal Ct [5] M14 . . . . .110 D8
Opal Gr WN7 . . . . .75 E4
Opal St M19 . . . . .111 B8
OPENSHAW 99 F1
Openshaw Fold Rd
BL9 . . . . .44 D8
Openshaw La M44 . . . . . .105 E6
Openshaw Pl BL4 . . . . . . .60 B8
Openshaw St M11 . . . . . .141 A1
Openshaw Wlk [15] M11 . .83 C1
Oracle Ct M28 . . . . .60 D2
Orama Ave M6 . . . . .80 A4
Oram St BL9 . . . . .141 A4
Orange Hill Rd M25 . . . . .63 C5
Orbital 24 Bsns Pk
M43 . . . . .100 D3
Orbital Way M34 . . . . .100 D3
Orchard Ave
Bolton BL1 . . . . .143 C4
Partington M31 . . . . . . .105 F4
Reddish M18 . . . . .99 E4
Worsley M28 . . . . .78 B7
Orchard Brow WA3 . . . . .105 A2
Orchard Cl
Cheadle SK8 . . . . .132 C7
Leigh WN7 . . . . .75 F7
Poynton SK12 . . . . .133 E3
Shevington WN6 . . . . . .36 A7
Wilmslow SK9 . . . . .136 F5

Orchard Ct
Orrell WN5 . . . . .53 D3
Stockport SK2 . . . . .124 D6
Orchard Dr
Altrincham WA15 . . . . . .120 A3
Gamesley SK13 . . . . . . .171 B1
Handforth SK9 . . . . .131 E2
Orchard Gdns
Bolton BL2 . . . . .25 F3
Mossy Lea WN6 . . . . .18 F6
Orchard Gn SK9 . . . . .137 B1
Orchard Gr
Manchester M20 . . . . . .109 F5
Shaw OL2 . . . . .149 A3
Orchard House Day Hospl
OL2 . . . . .48 E4
Orchard Ind Est M6 . . . . . .81 A5
Orchard La WN7 . . . . .76 A7
Orchard Pl
Poynton SK12 . . . . .133 D4
[4] Sale M33 . . . . .108 B5
Sale M33 . . . . .120 B7
Orchard Rd
Altrincham WA15 . . . . . .119 E5
Compstall SK6 . . . . .114 B2
Failsworth M35 . . . . .83 F7
Lymm WA13 . . . . .117 B5
Orchard Rd E M22 . . . . . .109 E2
Orchard Rd W M22 . . . . . .109 D2
Orchard Rise SK14 . . . . . .113 F7
Orchard St
Ashton-in-M WN4 . . . . . .73 C3
Heywood OL10 . . . . .29 E3
Hyde SK14 . . . . .167 B2
Manchester M40 . . . . . .109 F5
Salford M6 . . . . .81 A4
Stockport SK1 . . . . .169 C1
Wigan WN1 . . . . .151 A4
Orchards The
Heywood OL10 . . . . .29 E2
[3] Orrell WN5 . . . . .53 E5
Orchard The
Disley SK12 . . . . .135 D6
Oldham OL4 . . . . .67 C3
[4] Westhoughton BL5 . . .57 E5
Orchard Trad Est M6 . . . . .80 F5
Orchard Vale SK3 . . . . . . .123 C6
Orchard Wlk BL8 . . . . .10 F1
Orchid Ave BL4 . . . . .42 B1
Orchid Cl
Irlam M44 . . . . .105 E8
Oldham OL1 . . . . .48 D1
Up Holland WN8 . . . . . . .53 B6
Orchid Dr BL9 . . . . .45 A7
Orchid St M9 . . . . .157 A3
Orchid Way OL12 . . . . .14 D3
Ordell Wlk [1] M9 . . . . . . .64 E3
ORDSALL 161 B3
Ordsall Ave M38 . . . . .60 B4
Ordsall District Ctr
M5 . . . . .161 B4
Ordsall Dr M5 . . . . .161 B3
Ordsall Hall Mus* . . . .
M5 . . . . .161 B3
Ordsall La M5 . . . . .161 C4
Oregon Ave OL1 . . . . .48 C1
Oregon Cl M13 . . . . .163 C2
Orford Ave SK12 . . . . .135 D6
Orford Cl
Golborne WA3 . . . . .90 A7
High Lane SK6 . . . . .134 E7
Orford Ct WN7 . . . . .76 B2
Oriel Cl
Chadderton OL9 . . . . . . .152 A1
Stockport SK2 . . . . .124 B6
Oriel Ct [7] M33 . . . . .108 B5
Oriel Rd
Ashton-in-M WN4 . . . . . .72 F4
Manchester M20 . . . . . .110 A4
Oriel St
Bolton BL3 . . . . .144 C1
Rochdale OL11 . . . . .139 C1
Orient Ho M1 . . . . .163 A4
Orient Rd M6 . . . . .80 A4
Orient St M7 . . . . .155 C3
Oriole Cl M28 . . . . .78 B8
Oriole Ho [2] M19 . . . . . .110 D4
Orion Bsns Pk SK3 . . . . . .123 B5
Orion Pl M7 . . . . .81 C4
Orkney Cl
Radcliffe M26 . . . . .44 B4
Wythenshawe M23 . . . . .121 A4
Orkney Dr M41 . . . . .95 D5
Orlanda Ave M6 . . . . .80 B4
Orlanda Dr M7 . . . . .155 C2
Orlando St BL3 . . . . .148 A1
Orleans Way OL1 . . . . . . .153 B3
Orley Wlk OL1 . . . . .49 D4
Orme Ave
Middleton M24 . . . . .65 A2
Salford M6 . . . . .80 B4
Orme Cl
Manchester M11 . . . . . .160 B1
Urmston M41 . . . . .95 F2
Ormerod Ave OL2 . . . . . . .48 E3
Ormerod Cl SK6 . . . . .113 A1
Ormerod St OL10 . . . . .29 E1
Orme St
Alderley Edge SK9 . . . . .137 A1

Orme St continued
Oldham OL4 . . . . .67 A5
Ormonde Ave M6 . . . . . . .80 B4
Ormonde Ct OL6 . . . . . . .166 C4
Ormonde St OL6 . . . . . . .166 C4
Ormond St
Bolton BL3 . . . . .42 D5
Bury BL9 . . . . .141 A3
Ormrod Ct BL9 . . . . .141 A2
Ormrod St
Bolton BL3 . . . . .145 B2
Bolton, Hall i' th' Wood
BL2 . . . . .25 C4
Bury BL9 . . . . .141 A2
[7] Farnworth BL4 . . . . . .60 C8
Ormrods The BL9 . . . . .28 F5
Ormsby Ave M18 . . . . .99 B4
Ormsby Cl
Standish WN6 . . . . .19 E2
Stockport SK3 . . . . .123 E4
Orms Gill Pl SK2 . . . . .124 E6
Ormsgill St M15 . . . . .162 C2
Ormside Cl WN2 . . . . .57 C4
Ormskirk Ave M20 . . . . . .109 F6
Ormskirk Cl BL8 . . . . .44 A8
Ormskirk Rd
[2] Reddish SK5 . . . . . .111 F6
Up Holland WN8 . . . . . . .53 A7
Wigan WN5 . . . . .54 D6
Ormston Ave BL6 . . . . .22 C5
Ormston Gr WN7 . . . . .75 F7
Ornatus St BL1 . . . . .24 F5
Ornsay Wlk [1] M11 . . . . .83 C1
Oronsay Gr M5 . . . . .154 B1
Orphanage St SK4 . . . . . .169 B3
Orpington Dr BL8 . . . . .27 B1
Orpington Rd [2] M9 . . . .157 B3
Orpington St WN5 . . . . . . .54 C6
ORRELL 53 D6
Orrell Arc [3] WN1 . . . . . .150 C4
Orrell Gdns WN5 . . . . .53 F6
Orrell Hall Cl WN5 . . . . . . .54 B8
Orrell Holgate Prim Sch
WN5 . . . . .53 E5
Orrell Lamberhead Green
Com Prim Sch WN5 . . . .54 B6
Orrell Newfold Com Prim
Sch WN5 . . . . .53 D4
ORRELL POST 53 E7
Orrell Rd WN5 . . . . .53 E7
Orrell St
Bury BL8 . . . . .140 A3
Manchester M11 . . . . . . .99 D8
Wigan WN1 . . . . .151 A3
Orrell Sta WN5 . . . . .53 E4
Orrell Water Pk* WN5 . . . .53 E4
Orrel St M6 . . . . .154 B2
Orrishmere Prim Sch
SK8 . . . . .123 A3
Orrishmere Rd SK8 . . . . . .122 F3
Orron St OL15 . . . . .16 A5
Orsett Cl M40 . . . . .159 C3
Orthes Gr SK4 . . . . .111 D5
Orton Ave M23 . . . . .109 A1
Orton Rd M23 . . . . .109 A1
Orton Way WN4 . . . . .72 F3
Orvietto Ave M6 . . . . .80 B4
Orville Dr M19 . . . . .110 F7
Orwell Ave
Reddish M34 . . . . .100 A3
Wythenshawe M22 . . . . .121 D6
Orwell Cl
Bury BL8 . . . . .140 A4
Handforth SK9 . . . . .131 D2
Wigan WN6 . . . . .36 E3
Orwell Rd BL1 . . . . .142 B2
Osborne Cl BL8 . . . . .44 B8
Osborne Ct M46 . . . . .58 C3
Osborne Dr M27 . . . . .80 C7
Osborne Gr
Bolton BL1 . . . . .142 C1
Gatley SK8 . . . . .122 A3
Leigh WN7 . . . . .76 D6
Osborne Ho
Eccles M30 . . . . .79 C2
[7] Radcliffe M26 . . . . . .43 E3
Osborne Ind Est OL9 . . . .152 C4
Osborne Rd
Altrincham WA15 . . . . . .119 E5
Ashton-in-M WN4 . . . . . .73 A4
Denton M34 . . . . .100 F4
Golborne WA3 . . . . .90 E7
Hyde SK14 . . . . .167 B1
[3] Manchester, Harpurhey
M9 . . . . .157 B3
Manchester, Levenshulme
M19 . . . . .99 A1
Oldham OL8 . . . . .153 A1
Salford M6 . . . . .80 A2
Stockport SK2 . . . . .170 C3
Osborne St
Heywood OL10 . . . . .29 D1
Manchester, Didsbury
M20 . . . . .110 A3
Manchester M40 . . . . . .159 C4
Oldham OL9 . . . . .152 C4
Rochdale OL11 . . . . .139 C1
Romiley SK6 . . . . .112 D3
Salford M6 . . . . .154 C2
Shaw OL2 . . . . .149 B2
Osborne Terr
[10] Ashton-u-L OL6 . . . .166 C3
Bacup OL13 . . . . .3 D8
Osbourne Cl
Farnworth BL4 . . . . .42 D1
Wilmslow SK9 . . . . .137 D6

Osbourne Pl [9] WA14 . . .119 D4
Osbourne Wlk [8] M26 . . .43 E3
Oscar St
Bolton BL1 . . . . .142 C2
Manchester M40 . . . . . .83 A7
Oscott Ave M38 . . . . .60 A6
Oscroft Cl M8 . . . . .155 C2
Oscroft Wlk M14 . . . . . . .110 D7
Osmond St OL4 . . . . .67 C7
Osmund Ave M22 . . . . . . .42 D7
Osprey Ave BL5 . . . . .57 D6
Osprey Cl
Dukinfield SK16 . . . . . . .101 E7
Manchester M15 . . . . . .162 B1
Osprey Ct M15 . . . . .162 B1
Osprey Dr
Droylsden M43 . . . . .84 C3
Irlam M44 . . . . .94 C3
Wilmslow SK9 . . . . .137 C8
Ospreys The WN3 . . . . . . .54 C4
Ossington Ct M23 . . . . . .109 A3
Ossington Wlk M23 . . . . .109 A3
Ossory St M14 . . . . .98 B3
Osterley Rd M9 . . . . .65 E1
Ostlers Gate M43 . . . . .84 D2
Ostrich La M25 . . . . .63 C3
Oswald Cl M6 . . . . .81 A5
Oswald La M21 . . . . .97 B1
Oswald Rd M21 . . . . .97 B1
Oswald Road Prim Sch
M21 . . . . .97 A1
Oswald St
Bolton BL3 . . . . .146 C4
Manchester, Bradford
M4 . . . . .160 A1
Manchester M4 . . . . . . .159 A3
Oldham OL9 . . . . .153 A4
Reddish SK5 . . . . .99 F3
Rochdale OL16 . . . . .31 B8
Shaw OL2 . . . . .149 C4
Oswestry Cl BL8 . . . . .26 F8
Oswin St [2] OL4 . . . . .49 C1
Othello Dr [8] M30 . . . . . .79 D2
Otley Ave M6 . . . . .80 C3
Otley Cl OL9 . . . . .152 B2
Otley Gr SK3 . . . . .123 D4
Otmoor Way OL2 . . . . . . .49 A4
Otranto Ave M6 . . . . .80 B4
Otterburn Pl SK2 . . . . . . .124 E6
Otterbury Cl BL8 . . . . .26 F2
Otter Dr
Salford M8 . . . . .155 B1
Whitefield BL9 . . . . .45 B4
Otterham Wlk M40 . . . . . .83 D5
Otterspool Rd SK6 . . . . . .125 B8
Otterwood Sq WN5 . . . . . .36 C2
Ottery Wlk [6] M40 . . . . . .65 D2
Ottowa Cl M23 . . . . .120 F4
OUGHTRINGTON 117 C4
Oughtrington Com Prim
Sch WA13 . . . . .117 B4
Oughtrington Cres
WA13 . . . . .117 B4
Oughtrington La
WA13 . . . . .117 B3
Oughtrington View
WA13 . . . . .117 B4
Oulder Hill OL11 . . . . .30 B7
Oulder Hill Com Sch &
Language Coll OL11 . . . .30 B7
Oulder Hill Dr OL11 . . . . . .30 B7
Oldfield Cl [22] OL16 . . . .31 B6
Oulton Ave M33 . . . . .108 E5
Oulton Cl [5] WN7 . . . . . . .76 A4
Oulton St BL1 . . . . .25 A5
Oulton Wlk M40 . . . . .160 A3
Oundle Cl M14 . . . . .98 C3
Our Lady Immaculate RC
Prim Sch WN4 . . . . .72 E6
Our Lady & Lancashire
Martyrs RC Prim Sch
M28 . . . . .60 A3
Our Lady of Grace RC
Prim Sch M25 . . . . .63 A6
Our Lady of Lourdes RC
Prim Sch
Bury BL8 . . . . .27 C6
Farnworth BL4 . . . . .60 A8
Partington M31 . . . . . . .105 E3
Our Lady of Mount Carmel
RC Prim Sch OL6 . . . . . .85 D4
Our Lady of the Rosary RC
Prim Sch M41 . . . . .95 C4
Our Lady & St Anselm's
RC Prim Sch OL12 . . . . . .4 D2
Our Lady & St Paul's RC
Prim Sch OL10 . . . . .28 F1
Our Lady's RC High Sch
OL2 . . . . .48 D3
Our Lady's RC Prim Sch
Aspull WN2 . . . . .38 C5
Manchester M16 . . . . . .97 D3
Oldham OL4 . . . . .49 E3
Stockport SK3 . . . . .170 B4
Our Lady's RC Sports Coll
M9 . . . . .64 D5
Ouse St M50 . . . . .80 C3
Outram Cl SK6 . . . . .125 F4
Outram Ho M4 . . . . .159 C1
Outram Mews OL1 . . . . . .31 A6
Outram Rd SK14, SK16 . . .101 B6
Outram Sq M43 . . . . .100 A8
Outrington Dr M11 . . . . . .165 A4
Outterside St PR7 . . . . .21 A6
OUTWOOD 61 D4
Outwood Ave M27 . . . . . . .61 D4
Outwood Dr SK8 . . . . .131 A8
OUTWOOD GATE 62 B8

Outwood Gr BL1 . . . . .24 E5
Outwood La M90 . . . . . . .130 C7
Outwood La W M90 . . . . .130 B8
Outwood Prim Sch
SK8 . . . . .131 D7
Outwood Rd
Gatley SK8 . . . . .131 B7
Radcliffe M26 . . . . .44 A1
Oval Dr SK16 . . . . .101 B7
Oval The
Gatley SK8 . . . . .131 B8
Shevington WN6 . . . . . . .35 F5
Oval View SK6 . . . . .113 B5
Overbeck Cl WN6 . . . . . . .37 A4
Overbridge Rd M7,
M8 . . . . .158 B4
Overbrook Ave M40 . . . . .157 A1
Overbrook Dr M25 . . . . . . .63 B3
Overcombe Wlk [1]
M40 . . . . .156 C1
Overdale
[1] Marple SK6 . . . . . . .125 F6
Pendlebury M27 . . . . . . .80 A6
Overdale Cl OL1 . . . . .48 E1
Overdale Cres M41 . . . . . .94 F2
Overdale Dr
Bolton BL1 . . . . .144 A3
Glossop SK13 . . . . .116 B8
Overdale Rd
New Mills SK12 . . . . . . .135 F4
Romiley SK6 . . . . .125 A8
Wythenshawe M22 . . . . .121 D5
Overdell Dr OL12 . . . . .14 C4
Overdene Cl BL6 . . . . .40 C6
Overens St OL4 . . . . .67 B7
Overfield Way OL12 . . . . . .14 F2
Overgreen BL2 . . . . .25 E3
Overhill Dr SK9 . . . . .137 E7
Overhill La SK9 . . . . .137 E7
Overhill Rd
Chadderton OL9 . . . . . . .65 F8
Wilmslow SK9 . . . . .137 D7
Overhill Way WN3 . . . . . . .54 B3
Over Hos BL7 . . . . .9 B6
OVER HULTON 58 F7
Overlea Dr M19 . . . . .110 E5
Overlinks Dr M6 . . . . .80 B5
Overshores Rd BL7 . . . . . . .9 B8
Overstone Dr M8 . . . . . . .155 C3
Overton Ave M22 . . . . . . .121 D5
Overton Cl M26 . . . . .44 B1
Overton Cres
Hazel Grove SK7 . . . . . .124 E4
Sale M33 . . . . .107 D1
Overton Rd M22 . . . . .121 D5
Overton St WN7 . . . . .75 E4
Overton Way [2] SK9 . . . .131 D5
Over Town La
Rochdale OL12 . . . . .13 A3
Rochdale, Wolstenholme
OL12 . . . . .13 C3
Overt St OL11 . . . . .139 C1
Overwood Rd M22 . . . . . .121 C1
Ovington Wlk [6] M40 . . .156 C1
Owen Fold OL4 . . . . .67 F7
Owenington Gr M38 . . . . .60 A5
Owens Cl OL9 . . . . .65 E8
Owens Farm Dr SK2 . . . .124 E7
Owen's Row BL6 . . . . .22 C3
Owen St
Eccles M30 . . . . .79 B1
[2] Leigh WN7 . . . . .75 D5
Oldham OL1 . . . . .49 E3
Salford M6 . . . . .81 A5
Stockport SK3 . . . . .169 A1
OWLER BARROW 27 A3
Owlerbarrow Rd BL8 . . . . .27 A3
Owler La OL9 . . . . .65 C6
Owlsfield WA12 . . . . .89 E3
Owlwood Dr M38 . . . . .59 E3
Owlwood Dr M38 . . . . .59 E3
Owsten Ct BL6 . . . . .21 F3
Oxbow Way M45 . . . . .63 A8
Oxbridge Cl [3] M33 . . . .107 D3
Oxburgh Rd WN3 . . . . .55 F4
Oxendale Dr M24 . . . . .46 D1
Oxenhope Rd M41 . . . . . . .83 B3
Oxenholme Wlk [12]
M18 . . . . .99 D5
Oxenhurst Gn SK2 . . . . . .124 E5
Oxford Ave
Droylsden M43 . . . . .83 F3
Rochdale OL11 . . . . .30 A6
Sale M33 . . . . .107 D4
Whitefield M45 . . . . .63 A8
Oxford Cl BL4 . . . . .59 F8
Oxford Ct
Manchester, City Centre
M2 . . . . .162 C4
[3] Manchester, Hulme
M15 . . . . .162 C2
Manchester, Hulme
M15 . . . . .163 A2
Manchester, Old Trafford
M16 . . . . .162 A1
Wigan WN1 . . . . .37 D1
Oxford Dr
Middleton M24 . . . . .47 C2
Romiley SK6 . . . . .113 C4
Oxford Gr
Bolton BL1 . . . . .142 C1
Oxford Grove Prim Sch
BL1 . . . . .142 C1
Oxford Ho [1] OL1 . . . . . .152 C2
Oxford Pl
Manchester M14 . . . . . .98 C4
[14] Rochdale OL16 . . . . .31 A5

Oxford Rd
Altrincham WA14. . . . . . . 119 D3
Atherton M46. . . . . .58 B5
Dukinfield SK16. . . . . 101 D8
Horwich BL6. . . . . .39 B3
Hyde SK14. . . . . 113 E8
Little Lever BL3. . . . . .42 F3
Manchester M1, M13. . . . 163 B2
Orrell WN5. . . . . .53 F8
Salford M6. . . . . .80 B4
Oxford Road Sta M1. . . 163 A3
Oxford St E OL7. . . . . . . 166 A1
Oxford St W OL7. . . . . . 100 F8
Oxford St
Adlington PR7. . . . . .21 A4
Bolton BL1. . . . . 145 C3
Bury BL9. . . . . 141 A1
Eccles M30. . . . . .79 E1
Hindley WN2. . . . . .56 F7
Leigh WN7. . . . . .75 F6
Manchester, City Centre M1,
M60, M2. . . . . 163 A4
Manchester, Old Trafford
M16. . . . . 162 A1
Newton-le-W WA12. . . . . . .89 B3
Oldham OL9. . . . . 152 C1
Shaw OL2. . . . . 149 B3
Stalybridge, Copley SK15. .86 C1
Stalybridge, Millbrook
SK15. . . . . .86 B4
Oxford Way
Rochdale OL12. . . . . .14 E2
Stockport SK4. . . . . 169 A3
Oxford Wlk ⁴ M34. . . . . 101 A1
Ox Gate BL2. . . . . .25 D5
Ox Hey Cl
Horwich BL6. . . . . .39 E8
Ramsbottom BL0. . . . . . . 138 C3
Ox Hey La
Denshaw OL3. . . . . .33 E1
Horwich BL6. . . . . .39 F7
Oxhill Wlk ⁷ M40. . . . . . .65 D2
Oxhouse Rd WN5. . . . . . .53 D4
Oxlea Gr BL5. . . . . .57 E7
Oxney Rd M14. . . . . .98 C4
Ox St BL0. . . . . 138 B1
Oxted Wlk ⁸ M8. . . . . . . 156 A2
Oxton Ave M22. . . . . 121 C4
Oxton St M11. . . . . .99 F7
Oyy Lubavitch Girls Sch
M7. . . . . .63 D1
Ozanam Ct M7. . . . . 155 A3

P

Pacific Rd WA14. . . . . . . 119 A6
Pacific Way M50. . . . . . . .96 C8
Packer St
1 Bolton BL1. . . . . 142 C2
Rochdale OL16. . . . . 139 C3
Pack Horse Yd 6
OL16. . . . . 139 C3
Packwood Chase OL9. . . .65 F8
Padbury Cl M41. . . . . .94 D3
Padbury Ho 6 M6. . . . . . 154 C1
Padbury Way BL2. . . . . . .25 E1
Padbury Wlk M40. . . . . . 157 C1
Padden Brook SK6. . . . . 113 B2
Padden Brook Mews
SK6. . . . . 113 B2
Paddington Ave M40. . . . .83 B5
Paddington Cl M6. . . . . . . .81 A2
Paddison St M27. . . . . . . .79 E7
Paddock Chase SK12. . . 133 F6
Paddock Cl M46. . . . . .58 E5
PADDOCKHILL. 136 A4
Paddock Hill La
WA14. . . . . 136 A3
Paddock La
Failsworth M35. . . . . .83 F5
Lymm WA13. . . . . 117 C7
Partington WA13,
WA14. . . . . 118 B5
Paddock Rd SK14. . . . . . 113 D8
Paddock Rise M46. . . . . . .36 E3
Paddock St M12. . . . . 163 C3
Paddocks The SK3. . . . . 124 A4
Paddock The
Altrincham WA15. . . . . . . 120 B4
Ashton-in-M WN4. . . . . . . .72 F6
Bramhall SK7. . . . . 123 D1
Cheadle SK8. . . . . 122 E5
Handforth SK9. . . . . 131 D4
Hollingworth SK14. . . . . . 103 E5
Lymm WA13. . . . . 117 C4
Ramsbottom BL0. . . . . . . 138 B3
Uppermill OL3. . . . . .68 F4
Worsley M28. . . . . .78 E7
Paderborn Ct BL1. . . . . . 145 B2
PADFIELD. 104 C5
Padfield Com Prim Sch
SK13. . . . . 104 B5
Padfield Gate SK13. . . . 116 D7
Padfield Main Rd
SK13. . . . . 104 C5
Padiham Cl
Bury BL9. . . . . .44 D7
Leigh WN7. . . . . .76 A5
Padstow Cl SK14. . . . . . . 102 D3
Padstow Dr SK7. . . . . 132 F7
Padstow Pl 2 OL9. . . . . . .48 A1
Padstow St M40. . . . . 160 B3
Padstow Wlk SK14. . . . . 102 D3
Padworth M23. . . . . 120 D8
Pagan St OL16. . . . . 139 C4
Pagefield Cl 15 WN6. . . . .37 A1

Pagefield Ind Est
WN6. . . . . 150 A4
Pagefield St WN6. . . . . . . .37 A1
Paget St M40. . . . . 157 A1
Pagnall Ct OL9. . . . . 152 B1
Paignton Ave
Hattersley SK14. . . . . 102 D2
Manchester M19. . . . . 110 F8
Paignton Cl WN5. . . . . . . .71 E8
Paignton Dr M33. . . . . . . 107 D5
Paignton Gr SK5. . . . . . . 111 E7
Paignton Wlk SK14. . . . . 102 C2
Pailin Dr M43. . . . . .84 C2
Pailton Cl BL6. . . . . .40 D6
Painswick Rd M22. . . . . . 121 B1
Paisley Pk BL4. . . . . .42 D1
Paiton St BL1. . . . . 144 C3
Palace Arc 1 WN4. . . . . . .73 B3
Palace Ct 8 BL1. . . . . 145 C4
Palace Gdns OL1. . . . . . . .48 D2
Palace Gr WN7. . . . . .76 D6
Palace Rd
Ashton-u-L OL6. . . . . .85 E5
Sale M33. . . . . 108 A5
Palace St
Bolton BL1. . . . . 145 C4
5 Bury BL9. . . . . 141 A2
Oldham OL9. . . . . 152 C3
Palatine Ave
Manchester M20. . . . . 110 B6
Rochdale OL11. . . . . .30 A8
Palatine Cl
Irlam M44. . . . . .93 F1
Wigan WN3. . . . . .54 E4
Palatine Cres M20. . . . . . 110 B5
Palatine Dr BL9. . . . . .27 F8
Palatine Ho 4 SK3. . . . . . 170 B4
Palatine Mans M20. . . . . 110 A4
Palatine Rd
Manchester M20. . . . . 110 B6
Rochdale OL11. . . . . .30 A8
Wythenshawe M20,
M22. . . . . 109 E2
Palatine Sq WN7. . . . . . . .75 D5
Palatine St
4 Bolton BL1. . . . . 145 C3
Denton M34. . . . . 100 E4
Ramsbottom BL0. . . . . . . 138 C2
Rochdale OL16. . . . . .31 C7
Palatine Terr OL11. . . . . . .30 A8
Palewood Cl WN1. . . . . . . .37 E1
Paley St BL1. . . . . 145 C3
Palfrey Pl M12. . . . . 163 C3
Palgrave Ave M40. . . . . . 157 A1
Palin St WN2. . . . . .57 B3
Pall Mall M2. . . . . 158 C1
Pallotine Wlk OL11. . . . . 139 A1
Palma Ave M90. . . . . 130 B8
Palm Ave WN4. . . . . .72 D5
Palm Bsns Ctr OL9. . . . . 152 B3
Palm Cl M33. . . . . 107 D5
Palmer Ave SK8. . . . . 122 F6
Palmer Cl
Manchester M8. . . . . .64 B2
Oldham OL8. . . . . .66 F4
Palmer Gr WN7. . . . . .57 E1
Palmer St
Dukinfield SK16. . . . . 166 B1
6 Sale M33. . . . . 108 A4
Salford M7. . . . . .81 C5
Palmerston Ave M16. . . . . .97 D2
Palmerston Cl
Hindley WN2. . . . . .56 C4
Reddish M34. . . . . .11 C4
Reddish M34. . . . . 100 B3
Palmerstones Ct BL1. . . 144 A3
Palmerston Rd
Reddish M34. . . . . 100 B3
Stockport SK2. . . . . 124 B3
Palmerston St M12. . . . . 160 B1
Palm Gr
Chadderton OL9. . . . . 152 B4
Oldham OL9. . . . . .54 D6
Palm St
Bolton BL1. . . . . 143 C3
Droylsden M43. . . . . .83 E2
Manchester M13. . . . . .98 F3
Oldham OL4. . . . . .67 C8
Pandora St M20. . . . . 110 A5
Panfield Rd M22. . . . . 121 D4
Pangbourne Ave M41. . . . .95 E3
Pangbourne Cl SK3. . . . . 123 C6
Pankhurst Wlk 11 M14. . .98 B3
Panmure St OL8. . . . . .66 F4
Pansy Rd BL4. . . . . .60 A8
Panton St BL6. . . . . .22 D1
Paper Mill Rd BL7. . . . . . . .25 A7
Paprika Ct M11. . . . . .99 D7
Parade Rd M90. . . . . 130 C7
Parade The
1 Alderley Edge SK9. . . 137 A1
Culcheth WA3. . . . . .91 E3
Romiley SK6. . . . . 113 A1
Swinton M27. . . . . .79 F8
2 Whitefield M45. . . . . . .44 F2
Paradise St
Denton M34. . . . . 100 F7
Glossop SK13. . . . . 104 A5
Ramsbottom BL0. . . . . . . 138 C3
Paragon Bsns Pk BL6. . . .39 E8
Paragon Ind Est OL15. . . .15 F3
Paramel Ave M26. . . . . . . .43 B5
Parbold Ave M20. . . . . . . 110 A6
Parchments The WA12. . . .89 D4
Pardoners Ct M5. . . . . .80 B2
Pargate Chase OL11. . . . . .30 A8
Parham Wlk 4 M9. . . . . . .64 E3

Paris Ave
Salford M5. . . . . 161 B3
Wigan WN3. . . . . .54 C3
Parish Church CE Jun Sch
The OL1. . . . . 153 C4
Parish View M5. . . . . 161 B4
Parish Wlk BL2. . . . . .26 D1
Paris St BL3. . . . . 146 B4
Park Ave
Altrincham WA14. . . . . . . 119 E8
Bolton BL1. . . . . 143 B4
Bramhall SK7. . . . . 132 D5
Chadderton OL9. . . . . .48 B1
Cheadle, Cheadle Heath
SK3. . . . . 122 F7
Cheadle SK8. . . . . 122 F1
Failsworth M35. . . . . .83 D8
Golborne WA3. . . . . .73 F2
Hale WA15. . . . . 119 F1
Hyde SK14. . . . . 167 A4
Longshaw WN5. . . . . .53 E1
Manchester, Levenshulme
M19. . . . . .99 A1
Manchester, Old Trafford
M16. . . . . 161 C1
Pendlebury M27. . . . . .80 A7
Poynton SK12. . . . . 133 E4
Prestwich M25. . . . . .63 B4
Radcliffe M26. . . . . .44 D4
Ramsbottom M1. . . . . 138 D6
Romiley SK6. . . . . 113 C2
Sale M33. . . . . 108 A6
Salford M7. . . . . 155 C4
Shevington WN6. . . . . .36 B7
Urmston M41. . . . . .95 C2
Whitefield M45. . . . . .63 B7
Wilmslow SK9. . . . . 137 C8
Park Ave N WA12. . . . . . . .89 C2
Park Ave WA12. . . . . .89 C2
Park Bank M46. . . . . .58 F6
Park Bglws 4 SK6. . . . . . 125 F5
PARK BRIDGE. 67 C1
Park Bridge Rd
Oldham OL7. . . . . .85 A8
Oldham, Park Bridge OL6 . .67 B1
Park Brook La WN6. . . . . . .36 B7
Parkbrook Rd M23. . . . . . 121 B7
Park Brow CT M21. . . . . . 109 C7
Park Cl
Altrincham WA14. . . . . . . 119 E8
Chadderton OL9. . . . . .48 B1
Glossop SK13. . . . . 104 D3
Stalybridge SK15. . . . . .85 F3
Whitefield M45. . . . . .62 F6
Park Cotts
Shaw OL2. . . . . .48 F8
Uppermill OL3. . . . . .68 E5
Park Court Mews SK8. . . 122 E4
Park Cres
Ashton-u-L OL6. . . . . .85 C2
Bacup OL13. . . . . .3 F8
Chadderton OL9. . . . . .47 F1
Glossop SK13. . . . . 104 B3
Manchester M14. . . . . .98 C3
Sale WA15. . . . . 120 C7
Wigan WN1. . . . . .37 B1
Park Cres W WN1. . . . . . . .37 B1
Park Ct
Droylsden M11. . . . . .83 D2
Manchester M25. . . . . .63 D2
Rochdale OL11. . . . . 139 C2
Sale M33. . . . . 108 A5
Wythenshawe M22. . . . . . 121 D3
Parkdale
Chadderton OL9. . . . . .48 B1
Tyldesley M29. . . . . .77 B5
Parkdale Ave
Denton M34. . . . . 100 D7
Manchester M18. . . . . 165 C1
Parkdale Rd BL2. . . . . .25 D4
Parkdene Cl BL2. . . . . .25 D4
Park Dene Dr SK13. . . . . 104 C2
Park Dr
Altrincham, Timperley
WA15. . . . . 120 A7
Altrincham WA15. . . . . . . 119 F1
Eccles M30. . . . . .79 D4
Hyde SK14. . . . . 167 A4
Manchester M16. . . . . .97 C2
Stockport SK4. . . . . 168 B2
Park Edge BL5. . . . . .58 A7
Parkedge Cl WN7. . . . . . . .75 E3
Parkend Dr WN7. . . . . .75 D3
Parkend Rd M23. . . . . 121 A5
Parker St
Bury BL9. . . . . 141 A2
Manchester M1. . . . . 159 A1
Parkfield
Chadderton OL9. . . . . .48 B1
Droylsden M43. . . . . .84 A2
1 Middleton M24. . . . . . . .64 F8
Salford M5. . . . . 154 A2
Shevington WN6. . . . . .35 D7
Parkfield Ave
Farnworth BL4. . . . . .60 C7
Manchester M14. . . . . .98 B3
Manchester, Sedgley Park
M25. . . . . .63 D3
2 Oldham OL8. . . . . .66 B2
Tyldesley M29. . . . . .77 B6
Urmston M41. . . . . .95 B2
Parkfield Cl
Leigh WN7. . . . . .76 A7
Tyldesley M29. . . . . .77 B6
Parkfield Ct
Altrincham WA14. . . . . . . 119 C4

Parkfield Ct continued
Manchester M20. . . . . 110 A3
Parkfield Dr
Tyldesley M29. . . . . .59 D1
Parkfield Ind Est M24. . . .64 F8
Parkfield Lo M20. . . . . . . 110 A4
Parkfield Prim Sch
M24. . . . . .46 E1
Parkfield Rd
Altrincham WA14. . . . . . . 119 C4
Bolton BL3. . . . . 147 C3
Cheadle SK8. . . . . 122 F1
Uppermill OL4. . . . . .67 A5
Parkfield Rd N M40. . . . . . .65 F1
Parkfield Rd S M20. . . . . 110 A4
Parkfields
Abram Brow WN2. . . . . . . .74 B6
Stalybridge SK15. . . . . .86 D3
Parkfield St
Manchester M14. . . . . .98 B3
Manchester M14. . . . . .98 B4
Rochdale OL16. . . . . .31 B2
Parkgate
Altrincham WA14. . . . . . . 119 B4
Bury BL8. . . . . .26 F5
Chadderton OL9. . . . . .48 B1
Park Gate Ave M20. . . . . 110 B6
Parkgate Cl SK6. . . . . 112 C5
Parkgate Dr
Bolton BL1. . . . . .25 A5
Pendlebury M27. . . . . .80 A7
Stockport SK2. . . . . 124 B4
Parkgate Rd M26. . . . . . . .44 B4
Park Gate Rd WA14. . . . . 119 C8
Park Gates Ave SK8. . . . 123 C1
Park Gates Dr SK8. . . . . 123 C1
Parkgate Way
7 Handforth SK9. . . . . . . 131 D4
Shaw OL2. . . . . .49 D7
Park Gr
Manchester M19. . . . . .99 A2
Radcliffe M26. . . . . .43 F4
Stockport, Heaton Moor
SK4. . . . . 168 B4
Walkden M28. . . . . .78 D8
Park Grange WN2. . . . . . . .56 E4
Parkham Cl BL5. . . . . .57 F6
Park Hey Dr WN6. . . . . . . .35 E7
Park Hill
Manchester. 63 D2
21 Rochdale OL12. . . . . . .14 F1
Parkhill Ave M8. . . . . .64 B2
Parkhill Cl SK22. . . . . 127 C1
Park Hill Dr M45. . . . . .62 E8
Park Hill Rd WA15. . . . . . 120 A1
Parkhills Cl BL9. . . . . .44 F8
Parkhills Rd BL9. . . . . .44 F8
Park Hill St BL1. . . . . 145 A4
Park Ho
Droylsden M43. . . . . 100 A8
Manchester, Levenshulme
M19. . . . . .99 A1
Manchester M24. . . . . 110 A4
Sale WA15. . . . . 120 C7
Park House Bridge Est
M6. . . . . .80 F7
Park House Bridge Rd
M6. . . . . .80 E6
Parkhouse St M11. . . . . . 165 B4
Parkhurst Ave M40. . . . . . .65 E1
Parkin Cl SK16. . . . . 101 C8
Park Ind Est WN4. . . . . . . .72 E3
Parkinson St
Bolton BL3. . . . . 144 C1
Bury BL9. . . . . .27 F5
Parkin St M12. . . . . .99 A3
Park La
Altrincham WA15. . . . . . . 120 A1
Dukinfield SK16. . . . . 101 C8
Golborne WN2, WN7. . . . . .74 D6
Horwich BL6. . . . . .22 D3
Leigh WN7. . . . . .76 C4
Little Bollington WA14. . . 118 B2
Oldham OL8. . . . . .66 F2
Pendlebury M27. . . . . .80 D7
Poynton SK12. . . . . 133 F3
Rochdale OL16. . . . . 139 C4
Royton OL2. . . . . .48 D4
Royton OL2. . . . . .48 D5
Salford, Irlams o' th' Height
M6. . . . . .80 C5
Salford M7. . . . . 155 A4
Stockport SK1. . . . . 124 B8
Uppermill OL3. . . . . .69 C5
Whitefield M45. . . . . .62 D7
Parklake Ave M7. . . . . 155 B4
Parkland Ave SK22. . . . . 127 C1
Parklands
Romiley SK6. . . . . 113 C3
Royton OL2. . . . . .48 C7
Sale M33. . . . . 108 C5
Shaw OL2. . . . . .49 D8
Whitefield M45. . . . . .62 E6
Parklands Dr
Aspull WN2. . . . . .38 C6
Sale M33. . . . . 107 D2
Parklands High Sch
M22. . . . . 121 C3
Parklands Rd M23. . . . . . 120 F7
Parklands The
Horwich BL6. . . . . .39 D7
Kearsley M26. . . . . .61 B7
Stockport SK4. . . . . 169 B4
Parklands Way SK12. . . . 133 E4
PARK LANE. 62 D7
Park Lane Ct
Salford M7. . . . . 155 A4

Park Lane Ct continued
Whitefield M45. . . . . .62 D7
Park La W M27. . . . . .80 D7
Parklea Ct 6 M7. . . . . .63 E1
Parklee Com Sch M46. . . .58 C2
Parkleigh Dr M40. . . . . . . .65 E2
Park Lo
Manchester, Heaton Moor
SK4. . . . . 111 B5
1 Manchester, Levenshulme
M19. . . . . .99 A1
Manchester, Whalley Range
M16. . . . . .97 E2
Park Lodge Cl SK8. . . . . . 122 E4
Park Lodge Ind Hospl
SK6. . . . . 113 D3
Park Mdw BL5. . . . . .58 A8
Park Mews M16. . . . . .97 C2
Park Mill Ind Est OL5. . . .68 D3
Park Mount SK8. . . . . 122 A5
Parkmount Rd M9. . . . . . . .64 E1
Park Par
Ashton-u-L OL6. . . . . 166 C1
Shaw OL2. . . . . .32 C1
Park Par Ind Est OL6. . . . 166 A2
Park Pl
Manchester SK4. . . . . 110 F2
Manchester, Strangeways
M4. . . . . 159 A3
Prestwich M25. . . . . .63 C5
Salford M6. . . . . .80 A3
Park Range M14. . . . . .98 D3
Park Rd
Adlington PR7. . . . . .20 F6
Altrincham, Ashley Heath
WA15. . . . . 119 F1
Altrincham, Bowdon
WA14. . . . . 119 A2
Altrincham, Timperley
WA15. . . . . 120 A7
Bolton BL1. . . . . 144 C3
Bramhall SK8. . . . . 123 C1
Bury BL9. . . . . 140 E6
Cheadle SK8. . . . . 122 E2
Denton M34. . . . . 100 E3
Droylsden M34. . . . . 100 D8
Eccles M30. . . . . .79 D4
Edgworth BL7. . . . . .9 E5
Glossop SK13. . . . . 104 A4
Golborne WA3. . . . . .90 A7
High Lane SK12. . . . . 135 A6
Hindley WN2. . . . . .56 E3
Hyde SK14. . . . . 167 A4
Little Lever BL3. . . . . .42 F4
Longshaw WN5. . . . . .53 F1
Manchester, Heaton Moor
SK4. . . . . 111 B5
Manchester M45, M8. . . . . .63 E2
Middleton M24. . . . . .65 A8
Oldham, Glodwick OL4,
OL8. . . . . .67 A5
Oldham OL8. . . . . 153 C1
Partington M31. . . . . 106 A3
Partington, Warburton
WA13. . . . . 117 C8
Ramsbottom BL0. . . . . .10 F3
Rochdale OL12. . . . . .15 A1
Romiley SK6. . . . . 113 C3
Sale, Ashton upon Mersey
M33. . . . . 108 A6
Sale, Timperley WA15. . . . 120 B7
Salford M6. . . . . .80 A3
Stalybridge SK15, SK16. . . .85 D1
Standish WN6. . . . . .36 E8
Stretford M17, M32. . . . . . .96 C3
Walkden M28. . . . . .60 D1
Westhoughton BL5. . . . . . . .58 A8
Wigan, Redwood WN5. . . . .54 B6
Wigan, Springfield WN6. . . .37 A1
Wilmslow SK9. . . . . 136 F7
Wythenshawe SK8. . . . . . 121 F5
Park Rd N
Newton-le-W WA12. . . . . . .89 C4
Urmston M41. . . . . .95 C2
Park Rd S
Newton-le-W WA12. . . . . . .89 D2
Urmston M41. . . . . .95 C2
Park Rise
Romiley SK6. . . . . 113 C3
Stalybridge SK15. . . . . .85 F3
Park Road Prim Sch
Altrincham WA14. . . . . . . 119 E6
Sale M33. . . . . 108 A6
Park Row
8 Bolton BL1. . . . . .24 F6
Manchester SK4. . . . . 110 F2
Park Seventeen M45. . . . .44 F1
Parkside
Hindley WN2. . . . . .56 E6
Manchester M14. . . . . .98 C1
Middleton M24. . . . . .64 F6
Whitworth OL12. . . . . .4 D2
Parkside Ave
Ashton-in-M WN4. . . . . . . .72 F8
Eccles M30. . . . . .79 C1
Failsworth M35. . . . . .83 F5
Salford M7. . . . . 155 B4
Walkden M28. . . . . .60 D1
Park Side Ave OL2. . . . . . 149 C4
Parkside Bsns Pk WA3. . . .90 A8
Parkside Cl
High Lane SK6. . . . . 134 D8
Radcliffe M26. . . . . .44 D4
Parkside Cres WN5. . . . . . .53 F6
Parkside Ind Est OL2. . . . .48 E4

Parkside La SK6 . . . . 126 C6
Parkside Mews M45 . . . . . . 44 F1
Parkside Rd
  Golborne WA12, WA2 . . . . .90 B2
  Manchester M14 . . . . .98 A2
  Sale M33 . . . . 108 D3
Parkside St BL2 . . . . .25 C1
Parkside Wlk
  Bury BL9 . . . . 140 C1
  Stockport SK7 . . . . 123 E3
Parks Nook BL4 . . . . .60 C7
Park Sq
  Ashton-u-l OL6 . . . . .85 E4
  Manchester M16 . . . . .97 A2
Park St
  Ashton-u-l OL7 . . . . 166 A2
  Ashton-u-l OL7 . . . . 166 B2
  Atherton M46 . . . . .58 E4
  Bolton BL1 . . . . 145 A4
  Denton M34 . . . . 100 D3
  Droylsden M43. . . . . .84 C2
  Farnworth BL4. . . . . .42 D1
  Heywood OL10. . . . . .46 E8
  Manchester M3 . . . . 158 C3
  Mossley OL5 . . . . .86 C8
  Oldham OL8 . . . . 153 B2
  Pendlebury M27 . . . . .80 A7
  Prestwich M25. . . . . .63 C4
  Radcliffe M26 . . . . .44 C4
  Rochdale OL16. . . . . 139 C2
  Romiley SK6. . . . . 112 F3
  Royton OL2 . . . . .48 E4
  Salford, Kersal Dale
    M7 . . . . 155 A4
  Salford M3 . . . . 158 A1
  Shaw OL2. . . . . 149 C3
  Stalybridge SK15. . . . . . . .86 B1
  Stockport SK1 . . . . 169 C2
  1 Tyldesley M29 . . . . . . .59 A1
  Wigan WN3 . . . . 150 B2
Parkstead Dr M9 . . . . 157 A2
Parks The WA12 . . . . .73 B1
Parkstone Ave
  Droylsden M18. . . . . .99 F6
  Whitefield M45 . . . . .62 D6
Parkstone Cl BL8 . . . . .26 F2
Parkstone Dr M27 . . . . .80 B6
Parkstone La M28 . . . . .78 F4
Parkstone Rd M44 . . . . .94 A3
Parkway
  Manchester, Higher Blackley
    M9 . . . . .64 B6
  Manchester, Sedgley Park
    M25 . . . . .63 C2
  Pendlebury M27 . . . . .80 C6
Parks Yd BL9 . . . . 140 B2
Park Terr
  Heywood OL10. . . . . .29 D3
  Mossley OL5 . . . . .86 C8
  Westhoughton BL5. . . . . . .39 F1
  Whitefield M45 . . . . .62 D7
Park The
  Stretford M32 . . . . .96 E4
  Uppermill, Lydgate OL4 . . . .68 D6
  Uppermill OL3 . . . . .69 C5
Park View
  Abram WN2 . . . . .56 B1
  Ashton-in-M WN4 . . . . .73 B2
  2 Bolton BL1 . . . . .24 F6
  Chadderton OL9. . . . . .48 B1
  Cheadle SK3 . . . . 122 F7
  Droylsden M34. . . . . 100 D8
  Farnworth BL4. . . . . .42 D1
  Gatley SK8. . . . . 122 A6
  Hazel Grove SK7 . . . . 134 B8
  Ince-in-M WN2 . . . . .56 B7
  Kearsley BL4 . . . . .60 F7
  Little Bollington WA14. . . . 118 B2
  Littleborough OL15 . . . . . . .16 B6
  Manchester, Burnage
    M14 . . . . 110 E7
  Manchester, Collyhurst
    M9 . . . . 156 C2
  7 Manchester M9 . . . . . .96 F1
  Manchester, Moss Side
    M14 . . . . .98 A4
  Newton-le-W WA12. . . . . . .89 E3
  Romiley SK6. . . . . 112 C3
  Stalybridge OL6. . . . . .85 F4
  Stockport SK1 . . . . 124 B7
Parkview Ct BL2 . . . . .96 E1
Park View Ct
  Poynton SK12 . . . . 133 E4
  Prestwich M25. . . . . .63 B3
  Romiley SK6. . . . . 113 C2
Parkview Pk WA13 . . . . 117 D1
Park View Prim Sch
  M25 . . . . .63 B3
Park View Rd
  Bolton BL3. . . . . 146 C4
  Prestwich M25. . . . . .63 B3
Park View Rise SK22 . . . . . 127 C1
Parkville Rd
  Manchester M20. . . . . 110 C5
  Prestwich M25. . . . . .63 C6
Parkway
  Chadderton OL9. . . . . .48 A1
  Cheadle SK3 . . . . 122 F7
  Denton M34 . . . . 100 C3
  New Mills SK22 . . . . 127 C1
  Rochdale OL11. . . . . .30 B8
  Shevington Moor WN6. . . . .19 A2
  Stockport SK7 . . . . 123 E2
  Walkden M38. . . . . .59 F4
  Westhoughton BL5. . . . . . .57 D6

Parkway continued
  Wilmslow SK9 . . . . 137 B6
Park Way
  Eccles M17, M41. . . . . .96 A6
  Urmston M32, M41. . . . . . . .95 F5
Parkway Bsns Ctr M14. . . . .97 F2
Parkway Circ M17 . . . . .96 A6
Parkway Four Ind Est
  M17 . . . . .96 A6
Parkway Gr M38. . . . . .59 E4
Parkway Ind Est M17 . . . . . .96 A6
Parkway Trad Est M32 . . . . .96 A5
Parkwood BL7 . . . . .8 D2
Parkwood Cl WN3 . . . . 151 B2
Parkwood Dr BL5. . . . . .58 F7
Parkwood Rd M23 . . . . 121 C7
Parliament Pl BL9 . . . . 140 B1
Parliament St
  Bury BL9 . . . . 140 B1
  Ince-in-M WN3 . . . . 151 A2
  Up Holland WN8 . . . . .53 C7
Parndon Dr SK2 . . . . 124 C7
Parnell Ave M22 . . . . 121 D8
Parnell Cl M27 . . . . .77 B5
Parnham Cl M26. . . . . .43 B5
Parrot St
  Bolton BL3. . . . . 145 B1
  Droylsden M11. . . . . .83 C1
Parrs Ct M44 . . . . .93 F2
Parrs Mount Mews
  SK4. . . . . 110 F2
Parr St
  Droylsden M11. . . . . .99 F7
  Eccles M30 . . . . .79 D1
  Tyldesley M29 . . . . .76 F8
Parrs Wood Ave M20 . . . . . 110 C2
Parrs Wood Entertainment
  Ctr M20. . . . . 110 D1
Parrs Wood High Sch
  M20 . . . . 110 D1
Parrs Wood La M19,
  M20 . . . . 110 D2
Parrs Wood Rd
  Manchester, Burnage
    M20 . . . . 110 D4
  Manchester, East Didsbury
    M20 . . . . 122 B8
Parry Mead SK6 . . . . 113 A4
Parry Rd M12 . . . . .99 A4
Parry Wlk **12** EG OL6 . . . .85 D4
Parslow Ave M8 . . . . 156 A4
Parsonage M38 . . . . 158 C1
Parsonage Brow WN8. . . . . .53 A8
Parsonage Cl
  Bury BL9 . . . . 141 A3
  Salford M5. . . . . 161 C4
  Up Holland WN8 . . . . .53 A7
Parsonage Ct
  5 Manchester, Withington
    M20 . . . . 110 B6
  Stockport, Heaton Moor
    SK4. . . . . 168 B4
Parsonage Dr M28. . . . . . . .78 C7
Parsonage Gdns SK6. . . . . 126 A4
Parsonage Gn SK9. . . . . . . 137 B7
Parsonage La M29 . . . . 158 C2
Parsonage Rd
  Kearsley M26. . . . . .61 C7
  Manchester, Withington
    M20 . . . . 110 C7
  Stockport, Heaton Moor
    SK4. . . . . 168 C4
  Urmston M41. . . . . .94 E1
  Walkden M28. . . . . .60 C2
Parsonage Ret Pk
  WN7. . . . . .75 C5
Parsonage St
  Bury BL9 . . . . 141 A3
  Hyde SK14. . . . . 167 A1
  Manchester, Crumpsall
    M8 . . . . .63 F1
  Manchester, Hulme
    M15 . . . . 162 B1
  Radcliffe M26 . . . . .44 A3
  Stockport SK4 . . . . 169 B2
Parsonage Way
  Cheadle SK8 . . . . 123 B5
  Leigh WN7 . . . . .75 E6
Parsonage Wlk OL16. . . . . .31 F7
Parsons Dr M24 . . . . .46 F2
Parsons Field M6. . . . . .81 A5
Parson's La BL9 . . . . 140 C3
PARSON'S MEADOW
  . . . . 150 A2
Parsons St OL9 . . . . 152 C2
Parsons Way M9 . . . . 157 B3
Parson's Wlk WN1. . . . . . . .37 B1
Parth St BL9 . . . . .28 C1
PARTINGTON 105 F4
Partington Cl
  Farnworth BL4. . . . . .42 C1
  2 Glossop SK13. . . . . . 104 F1
Partington La M27. . . . . . . .79 E7

Partington Pk
  Glossop SK13. . . . . 104 C3
  Trub OL11 . . . . .47 C8
Partington Pl **3** M33 . . . 108 B5
Partington Prim Sch
  M31 . . . . 105 F3
Partington St
  Bolton BL3. . . . . 146 C2
  Eccles M30 . . . . .79 D3
  Failsworth M35 . . . . .83 F7
  Heywood OL10. . . . . .29 A2
  Manchester M40 . . . . 157 C1
  4 Oldham OL1 . . . . .67 A7
  Rochdale OL11. . . . . .30 B2
  Swinton M28 . . . . .79 C8
  Wigan WN5 . . . . .54 E8
Partridge Ave M23. . . . . . . 121 C6
Partridge Cl
  Irlam M44 . . . . .94 A4
  Rochdale OL11. . . . . .29 F7
Partridge Ct SK2 . . . . 124 B5
Partridge Rd M35. . . . . .84 C6
Partridge Rise M43. . . . . . . .84 D3
Partridge St M32 . . . . .96 F5
Partridge Way OL9 . . . . . . .65 E8
Part St BL5. . . . . .39 E2
Parvet Ave M43. . . . . .83 F3
Pascal St M19 . . . . 111 A8
PASSMONDS 14 B1
Passmonds Cres OL11,
  OL12. . . . . .14 B1
Passmonds Way OL11. . . . . .30 B8
Pass St OL9 . . . . 153 A2
Pass The OL16. . . . . .31 A8
Paston Rd M22 . . . . 121 D7
Pasture Cl
  Ashton-in-M WN4 . . . . .72 E6
  Heywood OL10. . . . . .29 B1
Pasturefield Cl **1**
  M33 . . . . 108 F3
Pasture Field Rd M22. . . . . 121 F1
Pasturegreen Way
  M44 . . . . .94 B3
Pastures La OL4 . . . . .68 B8
Patch Croft Rd M22. . . . . . 121 F1
Patchett St
  Manchester M12 . . . . 164 C2
  9 Tyldesley M29 . . . . . .59 A1
Patch La SK7 . . . . 132 D5
Pateley Sq **2** WN6 . . . . . .37 B3
Patey St M12 . . . . .99 A3
Pathfield Wlk **2** M9 . . . . . 157 A4
Patience St **11** OL12 . . . . .14 C1
Patmos St BL3 . . . . .11 D6
Paton Ave BL3. . . . . .42 A3
Paton Ct M7 . . . . .81 C4
Paton Mews **5** BL3. . . . . .42 A3
Paton St
  Manchester M1 . . . . 159 B1
  Rochdale OL12. . . . . .14 D3
Patricia Dr M28 . . . . .60 E2
Patrick Roddy Ct
  M18. . . . . 165 C1
PATRICROFT 79 D2
Patricroft Rd M30 . . . . 151 C2
Patricroft Sta M30. . . . . . . .79 C2
Patten St M20 . . . . 110 B6
Patterdale Ave
  Ashton-u-l OL7 . . . . .84 F5
  Urmston M41. . . . . .95 B4
Patterdale Cl
  Oldham OL1. . . . . .49 A1
  Rochdale OL11. . . . . .30 B3
  Stalybridge SK15. . . . . . . .86 A3
Patterdale Dr
  Bury M45 . . . . .44 E7
  Middleton M24. . . . . .46 E2
Patterdale Pl WN2. . . . . . . .56 A7
Patterdale Rd
  Ashton-in-M WN4 . . . . .73 A8
  Ashton-u-l OL7 . . . . .84 F5
  Bolton BL2. . . . . .25 F4
  Leigh WN7 . . . . .76 C4
  Partington M31 . . . . 105 E3
  Romiley SK6. . . . . 113 B4
  Stockport SK1 . . . . 124 B7
  Wythenshawe M22 . . . . . . 121 E8
Patterdale Wlk WA15 . . . . 120 D5
Patterson Ave M21 . . . . . . .97 A1
Patterson St
  Bolton BL3. . . . . 146 A4
  Denton M34 . . . . 100 F4
  Newton-le-W WA12. . . . . . .89 B3
  Westhoughton BL5. . . . . . .57 B7
Patting Cl M44 . . . . .94 C3
Pattishall Cl M4 . . . . 162 F8
Pattison Cl OL12. . . . . .14 D3
Patton Cl BL9 . . . . .45 B2
Paul Ct **6** SK1 . . . . 112 A1
Paulden Ave
  Oldham OL4. . . . . .49 E1
  Wythenshawe M23 . . . . . . 121 B6
Paulden Dr M35 . . . . .84 B1
Paulette St BL1 . . . . 143 B2
Paulhan Rd M20 . . . . 110 D4
Paulhan St BL3 . . . . 147 B3
Pauline St WN2 . . . . .57 B1
Paul Row OL15 . . . . .6 D1
Pavilion Cl **2** OL12 . . . . . .14 F2
Pavilion Dr OL6 . . . . .85 D5
Pavilion Ho M20. . . . . 110 A4
Pavilion Sq BL5 . . . . .57 E8
Pavilions The SK8 . . . . 122 D4
Pavilion Wlk M26 . . . . .43 F3
Paxford PI SK9 . . . . 137 A5
Paxton Pl M11. . . . . 164 B4
Paythorne Cl WA3 . . . . .91 F3
Paythorne Gn SK2 . . . . 124 E5

Peabody St BL3 . . . . 147 B4
Peacefield SK6 . . . . 125 E5
Peacefield Prim Sch
  SK6. . . . . 125 E5
Peacehaven Ave **12**
  M11 . . . . .83 C2
Peace St
  Atherton M46 . . . . .58 E3
  Bolton BL3. . . . . 145 A1
  3 Failsworth M35 . . . . . .83 F7
  Tyldesley M29 . . . . .76 F7
Peaceville Rd M19 . . . . .98 F1
Peach Bank M24 . . . . .65 A8
Peach Bank Ho M24 . . . . . .65 A8
Peach Ct OL4. . . . . .49 D1
Peach St M25 . . . . .63 C5
Peach Tree Cl M24 . . . . . . 155 C2
Peach Tree Cl **1** M6. . . . . .81 A2
Peacock Ave **2** M6 . . . . . .80 D5
Peacock Cl
  Glossop SK13. . . . . 171 B4
  Manchester M18 . . . . 165 C2
Peacock Dr SK8 . . . . 131 B6
Peacock Fold WN7 . . . . .75 D6
Peacock Gr M18 . . . . .99 D4
Peacock La OL14 . . . . .6 B6
Peacock Way **5** SK9 . . . . 131 D5
Peak Ave M46. . . . . .58 D5
Peak Bank SK6 . . . . 113 B2
Peak Cl OL4 . . . . .49 F4
Peakdale Ave
  Gatley SK8. . . . . 122 B1
  Manchester M8 . . . . 156 B4
Peakdale Rd
  Droylsden M43. . . . . .83 E3
  Glossop SK13. . . . . 171 B3
  Marple SK6 . . . . 126 A4
Peak Ho SK13 . . . . 104 A5
Peaknaze Cl
  Glossop SK13. . . . . 116 B8
  Pendlebury M27 . . . . .80 B8
Peak St
  Bolton BL1. . . . . 143 A2
  Manchester M1 . . . . 159 B1
  Oldham OL9 . . . . 152 C2
  Stockport SK1 . . . . 112 A2
Peak View SK13 . . . . 171 C4
Pear Ave M4 . . . . 141 C3
Pear Cl M24 . . . . .65 B6
Peardale Cl M30. . . . . .95 C8
Pear Ind Est SK6 . . . . 112 C2
Pearl Ave M7. . . . . .63 E1
Pearl Brook Ind Est
  BL6. . . . . .22 B3
Pearl Mill Cl OL8 . . . . .67 B4
Pearl St
  Denton M34 . . . . 100 E3
  Hazel Grove SK7 . . . . 124 E4
  Rochdale OL11. . . . . .30 C8
  Wigan WN6 . . . . .37 B3
Pearl Way SK14. . . . . 103 A2
Pearly Bank OL11. . . . . .30 B8
Pearn Ave M19 . . . . 110 F5
Pearn Rd M19 . . . . 110 F5
Pearson Cl
  Milnrow OL16. . . . . .31 F7
  Partington M31 . . . . 106 A3
Pearson Gr **7** M46 . . . . . .67 E6
Pearson Ho **6** M30 . . . . . .95 D8
Pearson Mews SK16 . . . . . 101 C6
Pearson St
  Bury BL9 . . . . 141 B3
  Dukinfield SK16. . . . . 101 C6
  Reddish SK5 . . . . 169 C3
  Rochdale OL16. . . . . .31 C8
Peart Ave SK6 . . . . 113 C6
Pear Tree Cl
  Glossop SK13. . . . . 171 B4
  Marple SK6 . . . . 126 B8
  Salford M6. . . . . .81 A2
Pear Tree Ct
  Aspull WN2 . . . . .38 C6
  3 Salford M6. . . . . .81 A2
Pear Tree Dr
  Farnworth BL4. . . . . .60 A7
  Stalybridge SK15. . . . . . . .86 B2
Pear Tree Fl **2** M29 . . . . . .59 E1
Pear Tree PI BL4 . . . . .60 A7
Peartree Wlk M22 . . . . 121 B4
Pear Tree Wlk **10**
  M33 . . . . 107 C5
Peart St M34 . . . . 100 E3
Peary St M4 . . . . 159 B3
Peaslake Cl SK6 . . . . 113 D2
Peatfield Ave M27 . . . . .61 E2
Peatfield Wlk M5 . . . . 162 C1
Pebble Cl SK15. . . . . .86 A4
Pebworth Cl M24, M9 . . . . .64 F5
Peckford Dr M40 . . . . .83 A5
Peckforton Cl SK8 . . . . 122 A5
Peckforton Wlk **11**
  SK9. . . . . 131 E1
Peckmill Cl SK9 . . . . 131 E2
Pedder St BL1 . . . . 142 C1
Pedder Brow La OL12 . . . . .13 E6
Pedley Wlk M13 . . . . 163 B3
Peebles Dr M40 . . . . .83 D4
Peebles St WN4 . . . . .72 C4
Peebles Dr M40 . . . . .83 D4
PEEL 59 F4
Peel Ave
  Altrincham WA14. . . . . 119 D2
  Ramsbottom BL0 . . . . 138 A1
PEEL BROW 11 D7
Peel Brow Sch BL0 . . . . . . .11 D6
Peel Cl M46. . . . . .58 C3
Peel Cnr M29 . . . . .77 B8
Peel Cross Rd M5 . . . . .81 A1

Peel Ct SK2 . . . . 124 A6
Peel Ctr The SK1 . . . . 112 A2
Peel Dr
  Sale M33 . . . . 108 E4
  Walkden M38. . . . . .59 F4
Peele The M29. . . . . 121 D4
Peelgate Dr SK8. . . . . 122 A2
Peel Gr
  Manchester M12 . . . . .99 A4
  Worsley M28 . . . . .78 F8
PEEL GREEN 95 A8
Peel Green Rd M30 . . . . . . .95 C8
Peel Green Trad Est
  M30. . . . . .95 B8
PEEL HALL 121 F2
Peel Hall Ave M29 . . . . .59 B1
Peel Hall Prim Sch
  Walkden M38. . . . . .59 F3
  Wythenshawe M22 . . . . . . 121 F3
Peel Hall Rd
  Ramsbottom BL0, BL9 . . . . .11 B2
  Wythenshawe M22 . . . . . . 121 F2
Peel House Cl M38 . . . . . . .59 F3
Peel House Ct Ind Est BL9. 140 B3
Peel La
  Heywood OL10. . . . . .29 B3
  Manchester M8 . . . . 159 B4
  Tyldesley M29 . . . . .77 C4
  Walkden M28, M38 . . . . . . .59 F3
Peel Moat Ct SK4. . . . . 111 E5
Peel Moat Rd SK4 . . . . 111 B5
Peel Moat Sports Ctr
  SK4. . . . . 111 B5
Peel Mount
  Ramsbottom BL0 . . . . .11 A4
  Salford BL5. . . . . .81 B3
Peel Park Cres M38 . . . . . . .59 F4
Peel Park Wlk M45 . . . . 119 C3
Peels Ave OL4 . . . . .68 A7
Peel Sq M18 . . . . .99 D5
Peel St
  Adlington PR6 . . . . .21 B8
  Ashton-u-l OL6 . . . . 166 B3
  Chadderton OL9. . . . . 152 B3
  Denton, Audenshaw
    M34. . . . . 100 E6
  Denton M34 . . . . 100 E4
  Droylsden M43. . . . . .99 F8
  Dukinfield SK16. . . . . 166 C1
  Eccles M30 . . . . .79 F2
  Failsworth M35 . . . . .83 D6
  Farnworth BL4. . . . . .60 E8
  Glossop SK13. . . . . 104 C5
  Heywood OL10. . . . . .29 B2
  Hyde SK14. . . . . 167 C1
  Leigh WN7 . . . . .75 E5
  Littleborough OL15 . . . . . . .16 B5
  Newton-le-W WA12. . . . . . .89 A3
  Platt Bridge WN2. . . . . . . .56 A2
  1 Radcliffe M26. . . . . . . .44 B2
  Rochdale OL12. . . . . 139 E4
  Shaw OL2. . . . . 149 A3
  Stalybridge SK15. . . . . . . .85 F1
  Stockport SK2 . . . . 124 A6
  Stockport SK2 . . . . 170 C2
  Westhoughton BL5 . . . . . . .39 E1
Peel Terr
  19 Dukinfield SK16. . . . . 166 B1
  Whitefield BL8. . . . . .39 E2
Peel Twr **4** BL8 . . . . .10 F5
Peel View BL8. . . . . .27 A6
Peel Way **3** M9 . . . . 140 B2
Peelwood Ave M38 . . . . . . .60 A4
Peelwood Gr M46 . . . . .58 E2
Peerglow Pk Est
  WA14. . . . . 119 E8
Peers Cl M41. . . . . .94 D4
Peers St BL8 . . . . .27 C2
Pegamoid St BL2 . . . . .25 B1
Pegasus Ct
  Rochdale OL16. . . . . .30 C6
  Sale M33 . . . . 108 D5
Pegasus Sq M7 . . . . .81 C3
Pegwell Dr M7 . . . . 155 B1
Pekin St OL6 . . . . 166 C4
Pelham Gr WN2 . . . . .56 D4
Pelham PI M8 . . . . .64 B2
Pelham St
  Ashton-u-l OL7 . . . . .84 C1
  Bolton BL3. . . . . 146 C3
  Oldham OL8 . . . . .66 F2
Pellowe Rd **3** OL8. . . . . . .66 E4
Pelton Ave M27 . . . . .61 D2
Pelton Wlk M40 . . . . 157 A1
PEMBEC at Kingsdown
  High Sch WN5 . . . . .54 C7
Pemberlei Rd WN2 . . . . . . .38 D2
PEMBERTON 54 C5
Pemberton Ho OL2 . . . . . . 149 B4
Pemberton Rd WN3,
  WN5. . . . . .54 B2
Pemberton St
  Bolton BL1. . . . . 143 B4
  Manchester M16. . . . . .97 C4
  Rochdale OL11. . . . . .30 C2
  Walkden M38. . . . . .60 B6
Pemberton Sta WN3. . . . . . .54 D4
Pemberton Way OL2 . . . . . 149 B4
Pembridge Fold M24 . . . . . .65 D2
Pembridge Rd M9 . . . . .64 F4
Pembroke Ave
  Eccles M30 . . . . .79 D2
  Sale M33 . . . . 107 F5
Pembroke Cl
  Horwich BL6 . . . . .22 A4
  Manchester M13 . . . . 164 A2
Pembroke Ct
  Hazel Grove SK7 . . . . 124 E2

Pembroke Ct continued
Pendlebury M27 ....80 B8
14 Rochdale OL12 ......14 F1
Romiley SK6...............112 F2
Pembroke Dr
Bury BL9 ....44 E7
Oldham OL4 ....49 E4
Pembroke Gr M44 ......105 C6
Pembroke Ho 3 SK3 ..170 B4
Pembroke Rd
Hindley WN2 ....57 C3
Wigan WN5 ....36 D1
Pembroke St
Bolton BL1 ....145 A4
Littleborough OL15 .....16 B6
Oldham OL8 ....153 A2
Salford, Higher Broughton
M7 ....155 B2
Salford, Seedley M6....154 B1
Pembroke Way 6
M34 ....101 A1
Pembry Cl SK5 ....112 B5
Pembury Cl M22 ....121 C3
Penarth Rd
Bolton BL3 ....146 B4
Wythenshawe M22 ....121 D8
Penbury Rd WN1 ....37 B5
Pencarrow Cl M20 .....109 F3
Pencombe Cl M12 .....165 A1
Pencroft Way M15 .....163 A1
Pendeen Cl
Tyldesley M29 ....77 A7
Wythenshawe M22 ....121 E1
Pendennis 2 OL11 ...139 B2
Pendennis Ave BL6 ....40 D5
Pendennis Cl M26 ......43 C5
Pendennis Cres WN2 ...57 A3
Pendennis Rd SK4 ....168 C3
Pendle Ave BL1...........24 E6
PENDLEBURY 80 C8
Pendlebury Cl M25 .....62 F2
Pendlebury Ct SK3 ....124 A4
Pendlebury Fold BL3 ...40 D2
Pendlebury La WN1,
.............................37 D6
Pendlebury Rd
Gatley SK8 ....122 B6
Swinton M27 ....79 F8
Pendlebury St BL1 ....143 C3
Pendlebury Twrs SK5 169 C3
Pendle Cl
Bury BL8 ....27 B3
Oldham OL4 ....67 D5
Wigan WN5 ....54 D5
Pendlecroft Ave M27 ...80 C7
Pendle Ct
Bolton BL3 ....143 A4
Leigh WN7 ....76 B4
Pendle Dr BL6 ....22 C5
Pendle Gdns WA3 ......91 E2
Pendle Gr OL2 ....48 C3
Pendle Rd
Denton M34 ....100 F2
Golborne WA3 ....74 C1
PENDLETON 81 A3
Pendleton Coll M6 ....154 A4
Pendleton Gn 3 M6 ..154 C3
Pendleton Way M6 ....154 C3
Pendleway M27 ....62 A1
Pendle Wlk SK5 ....112 A4
Pendragon Pl M35.......84 A7
Pendrell Wlk 32 M9 ....64 E3
Penelope Rd 4 M6 .....80 D5
Penerly Dr M9 ....157 A2
Penfair Cl M11 ....83 A1
Penfield Cl M1 ....163 B3
Penfold Wlk M12 ......164 C2
Pengarth Rd BL6 ....22 E2
Pengham Wlk M23 ....109 A1
Pengwern Ave 8 BL3..146 B4
Penhale Mews M4.....132 F7
Penhall Wlk M40 ....83 A5
Peninsula M7 ....81 B7
Penistone Ave
Manchester M9 ....65 A3
Rochdale OL16 ....31 C6
Salford M6................80 C3
Penketh Ave
Manchester M18 ....99 B4
Tyldesley M29 ....77 B6
Penketh St WN6 ....37 B2
Penleach Ave WN7 .....76 B5
Penmere Gr M33 ......107 E1
Penmoor Chase SK7 ..124 B1
Penmore Cl OL2 ....49 D7
Pennant Dr M25.........63 A5
Pennant St OL1 ....67 B8
Pennant Street Ind Est 9
OL1........................67 B8
Pennell Dr WN3 ....54 F5
Pennell St M11 ....83 D1
Penn Gn SK8 ....123 B1
Penn House Cl SK7 ...132 E8
Pennine Ave
Chadderton OL9.........152 A1
Wigan WN5 ....54 C2
Pennine Bsns Pk OL10..46 B8
Pennine Cl
Bury BL8 ....27 B3
Horwich BL6 ....22 C5
Manchester M9 ....64 F4
Pennine Ct
Stalybridge SK15 ....86 D3
Swinton M27 ....62 A1
Pennine Dr
Altrincham WA14 ....119 B5
Ashton-u-l OL6 ....85 E4

Pennine Dr continued
Milnrow OL16 ....32 A6
Wardle OL12 ....15 C6
Pennine Gr
Ashton-u-l OL6 ....85 E6
Leigh WN7 ....75 C8
Pennine La WA3 ....74 C1
Pennine Prec 3 OL16...31 F5
Pennine Rd
Glossop SK13............116 A8
Horwich BL6 ....22 C5
Romiley SK6.............113 C6
Stockport SK7 ....124 B1
Pennine Sq OL1 ....48 D1
Pennine Terr 2 SK16 .166 C1
Pennine Vale OL2 .....149 C4
Pennine View
Denton M34 ....100 E5
Mossley OL5 ....68 D1
Royton OL2 ....48 D1
Stalybridge SK15 ....86 C4
Pennine Wlk WN2 ....48 D1
PENNINGTON 75 E3
Pennington Ave WN7 ...75 E3
Pennington Cl
Pennington Green
WN2 ....38 E2
Walkden M38.............59 E4
Pennington Ct WN7 ....75 B1
Pennington Dr WA12 ..89 E3
Pennington Flash Ctry
Pk * WN7 ....75 B3
Pennington Gdns WN5..75 E3
PENNINGTON GREEN ..38 E1
Pennington Green La
WN2 ....38 E2
Pennington La
Ince-in-M WN2 ....56 A8
Standish WN2 ....37 E8
Pennington Mews
WN7.......................75 E2
Pennington Rd
Bolton BL3 ....147 C3
Leigh WN7 ....75 F3
Pennington St
Bury BL8 ....26 F4
7 Hindley WN2 ....56 D6
Manchester M12 ....99 A2
Oldham OL9...............66 B3
1 Walkden M28 ....60 E2
Pennistone Cl 5 M44 ..94 B3
Pennon Cl M7............155 D2
Penn St
Farnworth BL4............60 C8
Heywood OL10 ....29 D1
Horwich BL6 ....22 C3
Manchester M40 ......157 C4
Oldham OL8 ....153 A1
Rochdale OL16 ....139 C4
Penny Black Chambers
M28 ....78 F5
Penny Bridge La M41...95 A2
Penny Gate Cl WN2 ....56 D6
Pennyhurst St WN3 ...150 B3
Penny La
Haydock WA11...........89 B7
Stockport SK5 ....169 C3
Penny Mdw OL6 ......166 C3
Pennymoor Dr WA14..119 B6
Penrhos Ave SK8 ......121 F4
Penrhyn Ave
Cheadle SK8 ....122 E1
Middleton M24............65 A7
Penrhyn Cres SK7 ....133 C8
Penrhyn Dr
Hazel Grove SK7 ....124 D1
Prestwich M25...........63 B4
Penrhyn Gr M46 ....58 C5
Penrhyn Rd SK3 ....123 C8
Penrice Cl M26...........43 D5
Penrice Fold M28 ....78 B7
Penrith Ave
Ashton-u-l OL7 ....84 F5
Bolton BL1 ....142 A1
Droylsden M11..........83 B3
Oldham OL8...............66 C4
Prestwich M45...........63 B7
Reddish SK5 ....99 F1
Sale M33 ....108 C2
Walkden M28.............60 F2
Penrith Cl M31..........105 E4
Penrith Cres WN4 ......73 B4
Penrith St OL11 ....139 C1
Penrod Pl M6.............81 B4
Penrose Cl M8 ....156 A2
Penrose Gdns M24 .....47 B1
Penrose St BL2 ....148 C3
Penrose Wlk M24.......47 A4
Penroy Ave M20 ....109 D3
Penroyson Cl M12 ....164 C2
Penruddock Wlk 4
M13 ....98 F4
Penry Ave M44 ....105 E6
Penryn Ave
Royton OL2 ....48 F3
Sale M33 ....108 C1
Penryn Ct M7............63 D1
Pensarn Ave M14 .....110 E8
Pensarn Gr SK5 ....169 C4
Pensby Cl M27 ....80 C7
Pensby Wlk M40........157 A1
Pensford Ct BL2 ....25 E6
Pensford Rd M23 ......120 F3
Penshaw Ave WN5 .....55 B3
Penshurst Rd SK5 ....112 B6

Penshurst Wlk 20
M34 ....101 A1
Penson St WN1...........37 D2
Penswick Rd WN2 ......57 C3
Penthorpe Dr OL2 ......48 F3
Pentland Ave M40 ......65 C2
Pentland Cl SK7 ....124 B1
Pentlands Ave M7 .....155 A1
Pentlands The 4 ....48 F8
Pentland Terr BL1 ....143 B1
Pentland Way SK14 ...102 B6
Pentwyn Gr M23 ....121 B7
Penwell Fold OL1........48 C1
Penydarren View 9
BL4........................42 C2
Penzance Pl 3 OL9.....48 A1
Penzance St M40 .....160 B3
Peoples History Mus *
M3 ....158 B1
People's History Mus
(Archive & Study Ctr) *
M1 ....163 A4
Peover Ave M33 ....108 C4
Peover Rd SK9 ....131 E5
Peover Wlk 4 SK8 ....123 A5
Pepler Ave M23 ....109 B2
Peploe Wlk M40 ....157 A6
Pepper Cl WN6 ....19 B3
Pepper Mill La WN1 ...151 A3
Peppermint Cl OL16 ...32 C4
Pepper Rd SK7 ....124 B2
Pepper St WA16 ....128 F1
Pepperwood Dr WN3 ...54 C2
Pepys Pl WN3 ....55 A4
Percival Way WN2 ......56 D4
Perch St 4 WN1 ....37 E1
Percival Rd M8 ....155 C2
Percival Rd M43..........84 B1
Percival Wlk OL2 ....48 E3
Percy Dr M5 ....161 B3
Percy Rd M34 ....100 E2
Percy St
Bolton BL1 ....143 C2
Bury BL9 ....141 B3
Farnworth BL4............60 E7
Oldham OL4 ....67 C7
Ramsbottom BL0 ......138 B1
Rochdale OL16 ....31 B5
Stalybridge SK15 ....86 B2
Stockport SK1 ....169 D2
Peregrine Cres M43 ...84 C3
Peregrine Dr M44 ......94 A3
Peregrine Rd SK2 .....125 A4
M16 ....162 C1
Perendale Rise BL1 ...143 B4
Periton St 8 M9..........64 E3
Perivale Dr OL8 ....67 B4
Perkins Ave M7 ....155 B1
Pernham St OL4 ....67 C7
Perrin St SK14...........167 A2
Perry Ave SK14 ....102 A4
Perrybrook Wlk WN4 ...73 D4
Perry Cl OL11 ....139 A1
Perrygate Ave M20 ...110 A6
Perrymead M25 ....63 C6
Perrymead Dr WA14..119 B6
Perry Rd WA15 ....120 B6
Pershore 8 OL12 ......139 B4
Pershore Rd M24........47 A3
Perth 4 M30 ....79 E2
Perth Ave
Chadderton OL9.........66 A4
Ince-in-M WN2 ....56 A8
Perth Cl SK7 ....132 F5
Perth Rd OL11 ....31 B2
Perth St
Bolton BL3 ....146 C3
Royton OL2 ....49 A4
Swinton M27 ....79 D7
Peru St M3 ....158 A2
Peterborough Cl OL6...85 B6
Peterborough Dr BL1 143 B1
Peterborough St 1
M18 ....99 F6
Peterborough Wlk 10
BL1........................143 C1
Peterchurch Wlk
M11 ....165 C4
Peterhead Cl BL3 .....145 D6
Peterhead Wlk 4 M5...81 A1
Peterhouse Gdns SK6.113 C4
Peterhouse Wlk WH4..72 F4
Peterloo Ct 5 M6 .....154 B2
Peterloo Terr 8 M24 ...47 A1
Peter Martin St 3 BL6...22 B4
Peter Moss Way M19 ...99 C1
Petersburg Rd SK3 ...170 A2
Peters Ct WA15.........120 D5
Petersfield Dr M23 ...120 D7
Petersfield Gdns WA3 151 B4
Petersfield Wlk 1
BL1........................145 B4
Peter St
Altrincham WA14 ....119 D3
Ashton-in-M WN4 ....73 C3
Bury BL9 ....140 C3
Denton M34 ....101 A3
Eccles M30 ....79 C7
Golborne WA3 ....90 A8
Hazel Grove SK7 ....124 D3
Hindley WN2 ....56 D5
Leigh WN7 ....76 B4

Peter St continued
Manchester M2, M3 ...162 C4
Oldham OL1 ....153 C2
Stockport SK1 ....112 A2
14 Tyldesley M29 ....58 F1
Westhoughton BL5 .....57 A7
Wigan WN5 ....54 B8
Peterswood 22 M22 ..121 B3
Peterwood Gdns M32...96 A1
Petherbridge Dr 3
M22 ....121 B1
Petrel Ave SK12 ....133 B4
Petrel Cl
Droylsden M43...........84 C3
Rochdale OL11 ....29 F7
Stockport SK3 ....170 A2
Tyldesley M29 ....77 A8
Petrie Ct M6 ....81 B4
Petrie St OL12 ....139 C4
Petrock Wlk 6 M40 ....83 C5
Petticoat La WN2 ....56 B7
Petts Cres OL15 ....16 A6
Petunia Wlk 8 M28 ....59 F3
Petworth Ave WN3 ....54 D2
Petworth Cl M22 ......121 E5
Petworth Rd OL9 ......152 B2
Pevensey Ct M7.........63 D2
Pevensey Rd M6.........80 E5
Pevensey Wlk M16 ....152 B2
Peveril Ave SK22 ......127 C1
Peveril Cl M45 ....63 C7
Peveril Cres 1 SK13 ..116 F8
Peveril Dr SK7 ....133 F8
Peveril Rd
Altrincham WA14 ....119 C7
Oldham OL1 ....49 C1
Salford M5................154 A2
Peveril St BL3 ....146 C3
Peveril Terr SK14 .....113 F8
PEWFOLD 72 C1
Pewfist Gn BL5 ....57 E6
Pewfist Spinney The
BL5........................57 D7
Pewit The BL5 ....57 E7
Pewsey Rd M22 ....121 F3
Pexhill Ct SK4 ....168 A2
Pexwood OL4.............47 E1
Phaeton Cl M46 ....58 A1
Pheasant Cl M28........78 B6
Pheasant Dr M21 .....109 D7
Pheasant Rise WA14..119 D1
Phelan Cl M40...........156 C1
Phethean St
Bolton BL2 ....148 A3
Farnworth BL4............42 C2
Philip Ave M34 ....100 E5
Philip Cl 6 WN5 ....54 D5
Philip Godlee Lo M20..110 B1
Philip Howard Ct 2
BL4........................60 C8
Philip Howard Rd
SK13 ....116 C8
Philips Ave M45 ....60 D7
Philips Ct 5 M14 ....98 D4
Philips Dr M45 ....62 D6
Philips High Sch M45...62 E8
PHILIPS PARK 83 A3
Philips Park Rd
Manchester M11 ....160 B2
Whitefield M45 ....62 F6
Whitefield, Park Lane
M45 ....62 D6
Philip St
Bolton BL3 ....145 A1
Eccles M30 ....79 D1
Oldham OL4 ....67 C8
Phillimore St OL4 ....67 E5
Phillips Pl M45 ....62 F7
Phillips St WN7 ....75 E8
Phillip Way 1 SK14 ...102 E1
Phipps St M28 ....60 C4
Phoebe St
5 Bolton BL3 ....146 C4
Salford M5...............161 B4
Phoenix Cl OL10.........29 E1
Phoenix Close Ind Est
OL10......................29 E1
Phoenix Ct SK4 ....111 E5
Phoenix Ind Est M35...84 A8
Phoenix Pl OL4 ....67 F7
Phoenix St
Bolton BL3 ....148 A4
Bury BL9 ....140 B2
Farnworth BL4............60 D7
Littleborough OL15 .....16 B6
Manchester M2 ....159 A1
Oldham, County End OL4...67 F7
Oldham OL1 ....153 C2
Rochdale OL12 ....14 C1
Phoenix Way
Ince-in-M WN3 ....151 B1
Urmston M41............44 A2
Phyllis St
Middleton M24............65 C7
Rochdale OL12 ....14 B1
Piccadilly WN5 ....71 E5
Piccadilly
Manchester M1 ....159 B1
Stockport SK1 ....169 C1
Piccadilly Gdns M1 ...159 A1
Piccadilly Gdns Sta
M1 ....159 A1
Piccadilly Lofts M1 ...159 B1
Piccadilly Plaza M1...159 A1

Piccadilly Sta M1........163 B4
Piccadilly Trad Est
M1 ....163 C4
Pickering Cl
Altrincham WA15........119 A8
Bury BL8 ....27 B5
Kearsley M26.............61 A8
Urmston M41.............95 B2
Pickering St M15 ......162 B1
Pickford Ave BL3 ....43 C3
Pickford Ct
Dukinfield SK16 ....101 C8
Manchester M15 ....162 B1
Pickford La SK16 ......101 C8
Pickford Mews 5
SK16 ....101 C8
Pickford's Brow SK1 ..169 C1
Pickford St M4 ....159 B2
Pickford Wlk OL2........48 E3
Pickhill La OL3 ....69 B8
Pickhill Mews OL3 ......69 B8
Pickley Gn WN7 ....57 E1
PICKLEY GREEN 57 E1
Pickmere Ave M20....110 B8
Pickmere Cl
4 Droylsden M43........84 B1
Stockport SK3 ....123 C6
Wythenshawe M33 ...108 C4
Pickmere Ct 10 SK9 ..131 D5
Pickmere Gdns SK8 ..122 F4
Pickmere Mews OL3 ...69 B8
Pickmere Rd SK9 .....131 D5
Pickmere Terr 2
SK16 ....166 B1
Picksley St WN7 ....76 B4
Pickthorn Cl WN2 ......56 B3
Pickup St
Ince-in-M WN2 ....151 C3
Rochdale OL16 ....31 A7
Pickwick Rd SK12 ....133 D3
Picton Cl M3 ....158 B2
Picton Dr SK9 ....131 E2
Picton Sq 8 OL4 ....67 A6
Picton St
Ashton-u-l OL7 ....85 A6
Salford M7 ....81 C1
Picton Wlk 5 M16......97 F3
Pictor Sch M45 ....120 A7
Pierce St OL1 ....49 C1
Piercy Ave M7 ....158 A4
Piercy St
Failsworth M35 ....83 E7
Manchester M4 ....160 A2
Piethorne Cl OL16......32 C4
Pigeon St M1 ....159 B1
Pigginshaw SK9 ....136 E8
Piggott St 4 BL4..........60 C7
Pigot St 2 WN5 ....54 B6
Pike Ave
Atherton M46 ....58 A2
Failsworth M35 ....84 C6
Pike Fold La 2
M9 ....64 C3
Pike Rd BL3 ....145 A1
Pike's La SK13 ....116 B8
Pikes Lane Prim Sch
BL3........................145 A2
Pike St OL11 ....139 C1
Pike View BL6 ....22 D4
Pike View Dr OL4 ....67 B5
Pilgrim Dr M11 ....160 C1
Pilgrims Way WN4 .....37 A7
Pilgrim Way OL1 ....49 D3
Pilkington Dr M45 ......45 B2
Pilkington Rd
Kearsley BL4 ....60 F6
Manchester M9 ....65 A3
Radcliffe M26 ....43 F4
Pilkington St
Bolton BL3 ....145 B1
Hindley WN2 ....56 D6
Middleton M24............47 C1
Ramsbottom BL0 ......138 B1
Pilkington Way M26 ...44 A2
Pilling Field BL7 ....8 E1
Pilling St
Bury BL9 ....27 C3
Denton M34 ....100 F3
Leigh WN7 ....75 D5
3 Rawtenstall BB4 ......2 F8
Rochdale OL12 ....139 A4
Pilling Wlk OL9 ....152 A2
Pilning St BL3 ....42 A4
Pilot Ind Est BL3 ....42 B4
Pilot St BL9 ....140 C1
Pilsley Cl WN5 ....36 A1
Pilsworth Cotts BL9....45 C5
Pilsworth Rd
Bury BL9, OL10 ....45 D7
Heywood OL10 ....46 A8
Whitefield BL9 ....45 A6
Pilsworth WAY BL9.....45 A6
Pimblett St
Golborne WA3 ....90 A7
Manchester M3 ....158 C3
Pimbo La WN8 ....35 A3
PIMHOLE 141 A1
Pimhole Bsns Pk BL9...141 A1
Pimhole Rd BL9 ....141 A1
Pimlico Cl M7............155 A2

Pimlott Gr
Dukinfield SK14 . . . . **101** D5
Prestwich M25 . . . . **62** F2
Pimlott Rd BL1 . . . . **25** B3
Pimmcroft Way M33 . . . . . **109** A3
Pincher Wlk 14 M11 . . . . . . **83** C1
Pinder Wlk 5 M15 . . . . **162** C2
Pineapple St SK7 . . . . **124** E2
Pine Ave
Newton-le-W WA12 . . . . **89** D2
Whitefield M45 . . . . **62** F6
Pine Cl
Denton M34 . . . . **100** E6
Marple SK6 . . . . **125** E4
Pine Ct
Manchester M20 . . . . **110** A4
Stockport SK7 . . . . **123** D2
Pine Gr
Denton M34 . . . . **101** A3
Eccles M30 . . . . **79** E4
Farnworth BL4 . . . . **60** B8
Golborne WA3 . . . . **90** C8
Manchester M13, M14 . . . **98** E4
Prestwich M45 . . . . **63** A6
Royton OL2 . . . . **48** D6
Sale M33 . . . . **107** D6
Stalybridge SK16 . . . . **101** F8
Swinton M27 . . . . **79** D7
Westhoughton BL5 . . . . **57** E7
Worsley M28 . . . . **79** D7
Pinehurst Rd M40 . . . . **157** B1
Pinelea WA15 . . . . **119** F4
Pine Lo SK7 . . . . **132** F7
Pine Mdw M26 . . . . **61** C6
Pine Rd
Bramhall SK7 . . . . **132** F8
Dukinfield SK15 . . . . **101** E8
Manchester M20 . . . . **110** B4
Poynton SK12 . . . . **133** F3
Wigan WN5 . . . . **54** E6
Pine St N BL9 . . . . **141** B3
Pine St S BL9 . . . . **141** B2
Pine St
Ashton-u-L OL6 . . . . **166** B4
Bolton BL1 . . . . **143** C2
Bury BL9 . . . . **141** B2
Chadderton OL9 . . . . **152** A4
Dukinfield SK14 . . . . **101** D5
Heywood OL10 . . . . **29** D2
Littleborough OL15 . . . . **16** B6
Manchester M1 . . . . **159** A1
Middleton M24 . . . . **65** C7
Newhey OL16 . . . . **32** B4
Radcliffe M26 . . . . **44** B4
Rochdale OL16 . . . . **31** B7
Romiley SK6 . . . . **113** B5
5 Tyldesley M29 . . . . **59** A1
Pines The
Leigh WN7 . . . . **75** F3
Sale M33 . . . . **108** B2
Pinetop Cl M21 . . . . **109** D7
Pine Tree Rd OL8 . . . . **66** D1
Pinetree St M18 . . . . **165** C1
Pinevale WN6 . . . . **37** A7
Pine View WN3 . . . . **54** B1
Pine Way OL4 . . . . **67** F6
Pine Wlk 1 M31 . . . . **105** E3
Pinewood
Altrincham WA14 . . . . **119** A2
Ashton-in-M WN4 . . . . **73** A2
Chadderton OL9 . . . . **65** E7
Sale M33 . . . . **107** D4
Pinewood Cl
Abram Brow WN2 . . . . **74** C7
30 Bolton BL1 . . . . **143** B2
Dukinfield SK16 . . . . **166** C1
Stockport SK4 . . . . **168** A3
Pinewood Cres
Ince-in-M WN3 . . . . **151** C2
Orrell WN5 . . . . **53** E6
Ramsbottom BL0 . . . . **11** B2
Pinewood Ct
Altrincham WA14 . . . . **119** E1
Westhoughton BL5 . . . . **57** D5
Pinfold Cl
Altrincham WA15 . . . . **129** D7
Westhoughton BL5 . . . . **57** D5
Pinfold Ct
4 Stretford M32 . . . . **96** C1
Whitefield M45 . . . . **62** E8
Pinfold Dr
Cheadle SK8 . . . . **123** A1
Prestwich M25 . . . . **62** F5
Pinfold La
Romiley SK6 . . . . **113** E4
Whitefield M45 . . . . **62** F8
Wythenshawe M90,
WA15 . . . . **129** F6
Pinfold Prim Sch
SK14 . . . . **102** E1
Pinfold Rd M28 . . . . **60** C1
Pinfold St WN7 . . . . **75** D4
Pingate Dr SK8 . . . . **132** A6
Pingate La SK8 . . . . **132** A6
Pingate La S SK8 . . . . **132** A6
Pingle La OL3 . . . . **50** E5
Pingot OL2 . . . . **32** B6
Pingot Ave M23 . . . . **109** B1
Pingot Ct 6 WN7 . . . . **75** D5
Pingot Rd WN5 . . . . **71** E5

Pingot The
Irlam M44 . . . . **94** B3
Leigh WN7 . . . . **75** D5
Pingot La SK13 . . . . **104** A5
Pinhigh Pl M6 . . . . **80** B6
Pink Bank La M12 . . . . **99** A4
Pin Mill Brow M12 . . . . . . **164** A4
Pinnacle Bsns Ctr
SK4 . . . . **169** B3
Pinnacle Dr BL7 . . . . **8** E2
Pinner Fold SK15 . . . . **86** D3
Pinner Pl M19 . . . . **111** A6
Pinners Cl BL0 . . . . **138** B3
Pinnington La M32 . . . . **96** D2
Pinnington Rd M18 . . . . **99** D6
Pintail Ave SK3 . . . . **170** A2
Pintail Cl 5 OL12 . . . . **14** B2
Pinwood Ct 13 SK9 . . . . . . **131** E1
Pioneer Cl BL6 . . . . **22** C4
Pioneer Ct OL7 . . . . **166** A1
Pioneer Ind Est WN5 . . . . . **54** E6
Pioneer Rd M27 . . . . **62** D2
Pioneers St 4 OL11 . . . . . . **31** A6
Pioneer St
Droylsden M11 . . . . **83** B2
Horwich BL6 . . . . **22** C4
4 Littleborough OL15 . . . . . **16** B5
Walsden OL14 . . . . **6** A7
Pioneers Villa OL16 . . . . . . **32** E4
Piperhill Ave M22 . . . . **109** D2
Piper Hill High Sch
M23 . . . . **109** B2
Pipers Cl OL11 . . . . **29** D8
Pipers Ct M44 . . . . **94** C3
Pipers The WA3 . . . . **90** F8
Pipewell Ave M18 . . . . **165** C1
Pipit Ave WA12 . . . . **89** C3
Pipit Cl M34 . . . . **84** C2
Pirie Wlk 4 M40 . . . . **83** C6
Pitcairn Ho 12 M30 . . . . . . **79** D1
Pitchcombe Rd M22 . . . . . **121** B2
Pitcombe Cl BL1 . . . . **24** D7
Pitfield Gdns M23 . . . . **120** F7
Pitfield St BL2 . . . . **25** F4
Pitfield St BL2 . . . . **148** B3
Pit La OL16, OL2 . . . . **31** D1
Pitman Cl M11 . . . . **165** A4
Pitmore Wlk 3 M40 . . . . . . **65** D2
PITSES **67** D4
Pits Farm Ave OL11 . . . . . . **30** C7
Pitsford Rd M40 . . . . **157** B1
Pitshouse OL12 . . . . **13** E2
Pitshouse La OL12 . . . . **13** E2
Pit St
Denton M34 . . . . **100** F3
Oldham OL9 . . . . **66** B4
Pittbrook St M12 . . . . **164** A3
Pitt St E OL4 . . . . **67** B5
Pitt St
Denton M34 . . . . **100** F6
Heywood OL10 . . . . **29** C2
Hyde SK14 . . . . **167** A3
Ince-in-M WN3 . . . . **151** A2
Oldham OL4 . . . . **67** A5
Radcliffe M26 . . . . **43** E3
Rochdale OL12 . . . . **139** C4
Stockport SK3 . . . . **170** A4
Wigan WN3 . . . . **150** B3
Pixmore Ave BL1 . . . . **25** B4
Place Rd WA14 . . . . **119** C6
Place The M1 . . . . **159** B1
Plain Pit St SK14 . . . . **101** C5
Plainsfield St 8 M16 . . . . . . **97** E4
Plane Ave WN5 . . . . **54** E7
Plane Ct 4 M6 . . . . **81** A2
Plane St OL4 . . . . **67** C7
Plane Tree Cl SK6 . . . . **125** D5
Plane Tree Gr WA11 . . . . . . **89** A7
Planetree Rd WA15 . . . . . . **120** A2
Plane Tree Rd M31 . . . . . . **105** D3
Planetree Wlk M23 . . . . . . **120** C8
Planet Way M34 . . . . **100** E5
Plank La WN7 . . . . **75** B4
PLANK LANE **75** B4
Plantagenet Wlk M40 . . . . . **83** D4
Plantation Ave M28 . . . . **60** C4
Plantation Gates WN1 . . . . **37** E2
Plantation Gr BL9 . . . . **45** C4
Plantation Ind Est OL6 . . . . **85** D2
Plantation Rd BL7 . . . . **9** F7
Plantation St
Ashton-u-L OL6 . . . . **85** D2
Bacup OL13 . . . . **3** C8
Manchester M18 . . . . **99** E5
Plant Cl M33 . . . . **108** A5
Plant Hill Arts Coll M9 . . . . . . **64** D4
Plant Hill Rd M9 . . . . **64** D4
Plasden Ct M23 . . . . **121** A5
Plate St OL1 . . . . **153** C3
Plato St OL9 . . . . **153** A3
Platt Ave OL6 . . . . **85** C6
PLATT BRIDGE **56** A2
Plattbrook Cl M14 . . . . **98** B1
Platt Cl OL16 . . . . **32** A5
Platt Croft WN7 . . . . **76** C4
Platt Ct M14 . . . . **98** C2
Platt Fold Rd WN7 . . . . **76** A6
Platt Fold St WN7 . . . . **76** A5
Platt Hill Ave BL3 . . . . **146** A4
Platting Gr OL7 . . . . **84** F5
Platting La OL11 . . . . **31** A4
Platting Rd OL4 . . . . **67** F7
Platt La
Hindley WN2 . . . . **56** D5
Manchester M14 . . . . **98** B2
Standish WN1 . . . . **20** B3

Platt La continued
Uppermill OL3 . . . . **50** F2
Westhoughton BL5 . . . . **58** B7
Wigan WN1 . . . . **37** E1
Platts Dr M44 . . . . **94** A2
Platt St
Cheadle SK8 . . . . **122** E6
Dukinfield SK16 . . . . **101** A7
Glossop SK13 . . . . **104** B5
Leigh WN7 . . . . **75** F6
8 Oldham OL4 . . . . **67** F6
Platt Bridge WN2 . . . . **56** A2
Platt Wlk M34 . . . . **100** E1
Plattwood Wlk 19
M15 . . . . **162** A2
Playfair Cl OL10 . . . . **46** E7
Playfair St
Bolton BL1 . . . . **24** F6
Manchester M14 . . . . **98** B4
Plaza The **3** SK1 . . . . **169** B1
Pleachway SK4 . . . . **110** F2
Pleasance Way WA12 . . . . . . **89** D4
Pleasant Ct 5 OL11 . . . . . . **30** C2
Pleasant Gdns BL1 . . . . . . **145** B4
Pleasant Rd M30 . . . . **79** E1
Pleasant St
Bury BL8 . . . . **26** F4
Heywood OL10 . . . . **29** C4
Manchester M9 . . . . **157** A3
Rochdale OL11 . . . . **30** C2
Pleasant Terr 6
SK16 . . . . **166** C1
PLEASANT VIEW **31** C2
Pleasant View
Bacup OL13 . . . . **3** C7
Compstall SK6 . . . . **114** B3
Manchester M9 . . . . **64** B4
Radcliffe M26 . . . . **62** B8
Pleasant Way SK8 . . . . **132** C6
Pleasington Dr
Bury BL8 . . . . **26** E2
Failsworth M40 . . . . **65** C2
Plevna St BL2 . . . . **148** A3
Plodder La BL4, BL5 . . . . . . **59** D8
Plodder La Prim Sch
BL4 . . . . **60** B8
Ploughbank Dr M21 . . . . . . **109** D7
Plough Cl M41 . . . . **94** C1
Ploughfields BL5 . . . . **39** E3
Plough Fields M28 . . . . **78** A5
Plough St 6 SK16 . . . . **101** D8
Plover Cl
Glossop SK13 . . . . **116** F8
Newton-le-W WA12 . . . . **89** C3
Rochdale OL11 . . . . **29** F1
Plover Dr
Altrincham WA14 . . . . **119** B8
Bury BL9 . . . . **141** B4
Irlam M44 . . . . **94** A4
Plover Terr M21 . . . . **109** D7
Plover Way WA3 . . . . **90** E8
Plowden Ave BL3 . . . . **146** C3
Plowden Rd M22 . . . . **121** B2
Plowley Cl M20 . . . . **110** B2
Plucksbridge Rd SK6 . . . . . **126** B3
Plumbley Dr M16 . . . . **97** C3
Plumbley St 11 M11 . . . . **99** E7
Plumley Cl SK3 . . . . **170** C1
Plumley Rd SK9 . . . . **131** D5
Plummer Ave M21 . . . . **109** B6
Plumpton Cl OL1, OL2 . . . . . **48** E1
Plumpton Dr BL9 . . . . **27** E6
Plumpton Rd OL11 . . . . **48** C8
Plumpton Wlk 6 M13 . . . . . . **98** F4
Plum St OL8 . . . . **153** A1
Plum Tree Cl M30 . . . . **79** E2
Plum Tree Ct 2 M5 . . . . **81** A2
Plunge Rd BL0 . . . . **1** E3
Pluto Cl M6 . . . . **81** C4
Plymouth Ave M13 . . . . . . **164** B1
Plymouth Cl WA11 . . . . **89** A6
Plymouth Dr
Bramhall SK7 . . . . **132** F7
11 Farnworth BL4 . . . . **59** F8
Plymouth Gr
Manchester M13 . . . . **164** A1
Radcliffe M26 . . . . **43** D5
Standish WN6 . . . . **37** A7
Stockport SK3 . . . . **123** B7
Plymouth Grove Prim Sch
M13 . . . . **164** B1
Plymouth Gr W M13 . . . . . . **164** B1
Plymouth Ho M13 . . . . **163** C2
Plymouth Rd M33 . . . . **107** D5
Plymouth St OL8 . . . . **66** F4
Plymouth View M13 . . . . . **163** C2
Plymouth Village
M12 . . . . **164** A1
Plymtree Cl M8 . . . . **63** E2
Pobgreen La OL3 . . . . **51** D1
Pochard Dr
Altrincham WA14 . . . . **119** B7
Poynton SK12 . . . . **133** A4
Pochin St M40 . . . . **160** B3
POCKET **132** A5
Pocket Nook BL6 . . . . **40** B3
Pocket Nook La WA3 . . . . . . **91** B7
Pocket Nook Rd BL6 . . . . . . **40** B3
Pocket Wkshps The
BL3 . . . . **144** C2
Pocklington Dr M23 . . . . . . **120** F7
Podnor La SK6 . . . . **127** A6
Podsmead Rd M22 . . . . . . **121** B2
Poffley La WN2 . . . . **56** C3
Point Ret Pk The OL16 . . . . . . **31** A7
Poise Brook Dr SK2 . . . . . **124** F5
Poise Brook Rd SK2 . . . . . **124** F5
Poise Cl SK7 . . . . **125** A3

Poke St 1 WN5 . . . . **54** B6
Poland St
1 Ashton-u-L M34 . . . . . **100** E8
Manchester M4 . . . . **159** C2
Poland Street Ind Est
M4 . . . . **159** C2
Polden Ct 5 OL8 . . . . **66** E3
Polden Wlk 1 M9 . . . . **64** F1
Polding St WN3 . . . . **55** E4
Poleacre La SK6 . . . . **113** C6
Polebrook Ave M12 . . . . . . **164** A2
Polefield App M25 . . . . **63** B6
Polefield Circ M25 . . . . **63** B6
Polefield Gdns M25 . . . . . . **63** B6
Polefield Gr M25 . . . . **63** B6
Polefield Grange M25 . . . . **63** B6
Polefield Hall Rd M25 . . . . **63** B6
Polefield Rd
Manchester M9 . . . . **64** E2
Prestwich M25 . . . . **63** C6
Polegate Dr M27 . . . . **57** D2
Pole La
Failsworth M35 . . . . **83** F8
New Mills SK22, SK6 . . . . . **127** B4
Whitefield M45 . . . . **45** D1
Whitefield, Unsworth BL9,
M45 . . . . **45** C2
Pole Lane Ct BL9 . . . . **45** C3
Pole St
Ashton-u-L OL7 . . . . **166** B4
Bolton BL2 . . . . **25** B1
Standish WN6 . . . . **19** E1
Polesworth Cl M12 . . . . . . **165** A2
Police St
1 Altrincham WA14 . . . . . **119** D5
Eccles M30 . . . . **79** C2
Manchester M2 . . . . **158** C1
Pollard Cl 4 OL1 . . . . **153** B4
Pollard Gr OL15 . . . . **16** C8
Pollard Ho BL3 . . . . **146** B2
Pollard St E M4, M40 . . . . . **160** A2
Pollards La BL9 . . . . **11** C2
Pollard Sq M31 . . . . **106** A3
Pollen Cl M33 . . . . **108** D2
Pollen Rd WA14 . . . . **119** C6
Polletts Ave SK5 . . . . **112** C6
Pollit Croft SK6 . . . . **112** F1
Pollitt Ave OL6 . . . . **85** C5
Pollitt Cl M12 . . . . **164** C2
Pollitts Cl M30 . . . . **79** B2
Polly Gn OL12 . . . . **14** F3
Polonia Ct OL8 . . . . **66** C3
Polperro Cl OL2 . . . . **49** A4
Polperro Wlk SK14 . . . . **102** D3
Polruan Rd M21 . . . . **97** A2
Polruan Wlk SK14 . . . . **102** E3
Polworth Rd M9 . . . . **64** E1
Polygon Ave M12,
M13 . . . . **163** C2
Polygon Rd M8 . . . . **63** F1
Polygon St M13 . . . . **163** C2
Polygon The
Eccles M30 . . . . **80** A2
Salford M7 . . . . **81** C5
Pomfret St
Manchester M12 . . . . **165** A2
Salford M6 . . . . **80** C5
Pomona Cres M5 . . . . **161** B3
Pomona Cl OL11 . . . . **139** C1
Pomona Sta M5, M16 . . . . . **161** B2
Pomona Strand M16,
M5 . . . . **161** B2
Ponds Cl M21 . . . . **97** B1
Pond St WA3 . . . . **91** A8
Pondwater Cl M28 . . . . **60** A3
Ponsford Ave M9 . . . . **65** A3
Ponsonby Rd M32 . . . . **96** D3
Pontefract Cl M27 . . . . **80** B7
Poolbank Cl WN2 . . . . **57** C3
Pool Bank St M24 . . . . **64** B7
Poolcroft M33 . . . . **108** F3
Poole Cl SK7 . . . . **123** D1
Pooley Cl M24 . . . . **46** B1
Poolfield Cl M26 . . . . **43** E3
Pool Fold
Bolton BL1 . . . . **142** A2
Failsworth M35 . . . . **84** A6
Pool House Rd SK12 . . . . . **134** D5
Pool Pl BL1 . . . . **142** A2
Pool Rd WA3 . . . . **105** A3
Pool St
Bolton BL3 . . . . **145** B3
Bolton BL1 . . . . **145** B4
Hindley WN2 . . . . **56** D4
Oldham OL8 . . . . **66** F4
Wigan WN3 . . . . **150** B2
POOLSTOCK **150** B2
Poolstock WN3 . . . . **150** B2
Poolstock La WN3 . . . . **55** A4
Pool Terr BL1 . . . . **142** A2
Poolton Rd M9 . . . . **64** B4
Poot Hall OL12 . . . . **14** F3
Pope Way 8 M34 . . . . **113** A8
Poplar Ave
Altrincham WA14 . . . . **119** E6
Bolton, Astley Bridge BL1 . . . **24** F5
Bolton, Bradshaw BL2 . . . . . **25** C6
Bury BL9 . . . . **141** B3
Culcheth WA3 . . . . **91** F3
Dowall Green WN4 . . . . **72** D5
Horwich BL6 . . . . **22** E1
Manchester M19 . . . . **111** B7
New Mills SK22 . . . . **127** D1
Newton-le-W WA12 . . . . **89** D3

Poplar Ave continued
Oldham OL8 . . . . **66** D2
4 Rochdale OL12 . . . . **14** C1
Uppermill OL4 . . . . **68** C4
Wigan WN5 . . . . **54** E6
Wilmslow SK9 . . . . **136** F5
Poplar Cl SK8 . . . . **122** B5
Poplar Ct
Denton M34 . . . . **100** F7
Manchester M14 . . . . **98** D1
Poplar Dr M25 . . . . **63** A2
Poplar Gr
Ashton-u-L OL6 . . . . **85** C5
Hindley WN2 . . . . **57** B3
Irlam M44 . . . . **105** D6
Manchester M18 . . . . **99** D4
Ramsbottom BL0 . . . . **11** D7
Sale M33 . . . . **108** B3
Stockport SK2 . . . . **124** C4
Tyldesley M29 . . . . **77** B4
Urmston M41 . . . . **95** C2
Westhoughton BL5 . . . . **57** E8
Poplar Rd
Dukinfield SK16 . . . . **101** F7
Eccles M30 . . . . **79** E4
Manchester M19 . . . . **110** D3
Stretford M32 . . . . **108** C8
Swinton M27 . . . . **79** D7
Walkden M28 . . . . **60** C1
Poplar St Prim Sch
M34 . . . . **100** E6
Poplars Rd SK15 . . . . **86** D3
Poplar St
Denton M34 . . . . **100** F7
Failsworth M35 . . . . **83** D6
Golborne WA3 . . . . **74** B1
Leigh WN7 . . . . **75** F4
Manchester SK4 . . . . **110** F2
Middleton M24 . . . . **65** D7
Poplars The
Adlington PR7 . . . . **20** F6
Golborne, Bank Heath
WA3 . . . . **74** B1
Golborne WN7 . . . . **91** C8
Mossley OL5 . . . . **68** E1
Poplar Way SK6 . . . . **135** A7
Poplar Wlk
Chadderton OL9 . . . . **152** B4
Partington M31 . . . . **105** D3
Poplin Dr M3 . . . . **158** B3
Poppy Cl
Chadderton OL9 . . . . **65** E7
Sale M33 . . . . **108** C1
Poppyfield Ho 4 OL9 . . . . . . **65** F8
Poppyfield View OL11 . . . . . **29** E8
Poppythorn La M25 . . . . **63** A5
Popular St M29 . . . . **59** A1
Porchester Dr M26 . . . . **43** C5
Porchfield Sq M3 . . . . **162** B4
Porlock Ave
Droylsden M34 . . . . **100** C8
Hattersley SK14 . . . . **102** C2
Porlock Cl
Platt Bridge WN2 . . . . **56** A1
Stockport SK1 . . . . **124** C8
Porlock Rd
Urmston M41 . . . . **107** B8
Wythenshawe M23 . . . . **121** B6
Porlock Wlk SK14 . . . . **102** C2
Porritt Cl OL11 . . . . **29** E6
Porritt St
Bury BL9 . . . . **141** A4
Bury BL9 . . . . **141** B4
Porritt Way BL0 . . . . **138** C3
Portal Ct M24 . . . . **65** C8
Portal Gr M34 . . . . **101** B1
Portal Ho 9 M9 . . . . **157** A4
Porter Ave WA12 . . . . **89** C5
Porter Dr M40 . . . . **157** A2
Porterfield Dr M29 . . . . **77** A8
Porter St
Bury BL9 . . . . **140** C4
Oldham OL9 . . . . **153** B1
Portfield Cl BL1 . . . . **40** F8
Portfield Wlk 18 M40 . . . . . **83** A6
Portgate Wlk M13 . . . . **98** F4
Porthleven Cres M29 . . . . . . **77** C8
Porthleven Dr M23 . . . . . . **120** E6
Porthtowan Wlk SK14 . . . . **102** E3
Portinscale Cl BL8 . . . . **27** B3
Portland Basin Mus*
OL7 . . . . **166** A1
Portland Chmbrs 3
SK15 . . . . **86** B2
Portland Cl
Abram WN2 . . . . **74** A8
Hazel Grove SK7 . . . . **124** B1
Platt Bridge WN2 . . . . **56** A1
Portland Cres M13 . . . . . . **164** A1
Portland Ct M20 . . . . **110** B3
Portland Gr SK4 . . . . **168** B4
Portland Ho
3 Ashton-u-L OL6 . . . . . . **166** A2
Marple SK6 . . . . **125** C5
Salford M6 . . . . **80** A3
Portland Ind Est BL9 . . . . . . **141** A4
Portland Pl
Ashton-u-L OL7 . . . . **166** A2
Horwich BL6 . . . . **22** C3
Portland Rd
Altrincham WA14 . . . . **119** D3
Manchester M13 . . . . **98** F3
Pendlebury M27 . . . . **80** B7
Salford M30 . . . . **80** A4
Stretford M32 . . . . **96** E4
Walkden M28 . . . . **60** C5

Portland St N OL6 . . . . . . 166 A3
Portland St S OL6,
OL7 . . . . 166 A2
Portland St
Bolton BL1 . . . . 143 B2
Bury BL9 . . . . 141 A4
5 Leigh WN7 . . . . 75 F5
Manchester M1 . . . . 159 A1
Rochdale OL16 . . . . 139 C4
Wigan WN3 . . . . 54 E6
Portland Terr OL6 . . . . 166 A2
Portland The **10** M14 . . . 110 D8
Portloe Rd SK8 . . . . 131 B7
Portman Rd M16 . . . . 97 E3
Portman St OL5 . . . . 68 C1
Porton Wlk **1** M22 . . . . 121 B1
Portrea Cl SK3 . . . . 170 C1
Portree Cl M30 . . . . 79 B2
Portree Ct OL10 . . . . 46 A8
Portrush Rd M22 . . . . 121 E2
Portside Cl M28 . . . . 78 B5
Portslade Wlk M23 . . . . . . 120 F4
Portsmouth Cl M7 . . . . 155 A1
Portsmouth St M13 . . . . . . 163 B1
Port Soderick Ave M5 . . . . 81 A1
Port St
Manchester M1 . . . . 159 B1
Oldham OL8 . . . . 66 F4
Stockport SK1 . . . . 169 B2
Portstone Cl **11** M16 . . . . 97 E4
Portugal Rd M25 . . . . 63 B2
Portugal St E M1 . . . . 163 C4
Portugal St
Ashton-u-L OL7 . . . . 84 F1
Bolton BL2 . . . . 148 B3
Manchester M4 . . . . 159 C3
8 Manchester M4 . . . . . 159 C3
Portville Rd M19 . . . . 99 A2
Portway M22 . . . . 121 C1
PORTWOOD 112 A2
Portwood Ct SK1 . . . . 112 A2
Portwood Ind Est
SK1. . . . . 112 B2
Portwood Pl SK1 . . . . 169 C2
Portwood Wlk M9 . . . . . . 157 A3
Posnett St SK3 . . . . 123 C8
Postal St M1 . . . . 159 B1
Postbridge Cl M13 . . . . . . 163 C2
Post Office St WA14 . . . . . 119 D5
Post St SK13 . . . . 104 B5
Potato Wharf M3 . . . . 162 A4
Pot Gn BL0 . . . . 11 A3
Pot Hill OL6 . . . . 166 C4
Pot Hill Sq OL6 . . . . 166 C4
Potterdale Cl OL1 . . . . 49 A1
Potter Ho OL8 . . . . 153 C1
Potter Rd SK13 . . . . 171 B3
Potters La M9 . . . . 157 C3
Potter St
Bury BL9 . . . . 141 A3
Radcliffe M26 . . . . 44 D4
Pottery La M11, M12 . . . . . 165 A3
Pottery Rd WN3 . . . . 150 B3
Pottery Terr WN3 . . . . 150 B3
Pottinger St
Ashton-u-L OL7 . . . . 84 F1
Ashton-u-L OL7 . . . . 100 F8
Pott St
1 Altrincham WA14 . . . . 119 D4
Swinton M27 . . . . 61 F2
Poulton Ave BL2 . . . . 42 E7
Poulton Dr **8** WN4 . . . . . 72 F5
Poulton St M11 . . . . 99 E7
Poundswick La M22 . . . . . 121 D3
Powder Mill Cl M44 . . . . . . 94 B1
Powell Ave WA14 . . . . 167 B3
Powell Ct **8** BL9 . . . . . . 140 C3
Powell Dr WN5 . . . . 71 D3
Powell Ho **9** BL9 . . . . . . 140 C3
Powell St
Abram WN2 . . . . 56 B1
Bury BL8 . . . . 27 B1
Droylsden M11 . . . . 83 D2
Manchester M16 . . . . 97 C4
13 Wigan WN1 . . . . 37 C1
Powicke Dr SK6 . . . . 112 F1
Powicke Wlk SK6 . . . . 113 A1
Powys Rd M41 . . . . 94 C1
Pownall Ave
Bramhall SK7. . . . . 132 F7
4 Manchester M20 . . . . 110 A8
Pownall Ct SK9 . . . . 136 E8
POWNALL GREEN 132 E6
Pownall Green Prim Sch
SK7. . . . . 132 E7
Pownall Hall Sch SK9 . . . . 136 F8
POWNALL PARK 136 F7
Pownall Pl **7** SK7 . . . . . 132 E7
Pownall Rd
Altrincham WA14 . . . . 119 D3
Cheadle SK8 . . . . 123 A1
Wilmslow SK9 . . . . 136 F8
Pownall St
Hazel Grove SK7 . . . . 124 D3
7 Manchester M7 . . . . . . 76 A5
Powys St M46 . . . . 58 E1
Poynings Dr M22 . . . . 121 C1
Poynt Chase M28 . . . . 78 B6
Poynter St M40 . . . . 65 C1
Poynter Wlk OL1 . . . . 49 D4
POYNTON 133 E4
Poynton High Sch
SK12. . . . . 133 F2
Poynton Ind Est SK12 . . . 133 D1
Poynton St
Bury BL9 . . . . 141 A1
Manchester M15 . . . . 162 C2
Poynton Sta SK12. . . . . . . 133 C4

Praed Rd M17 . . . . 96 C6
Pratt Wlk **1** M11 . . . . . . 160 C1
Precinct The
2 Cheadle SK8 . . . . 123 A2
Rochdale OL11. . . . . 29 E7
Stockport SK2 . . . . 124 D6
Preece Cl SK14 . . . . 102 A4
Preesall Ave SK8 . . . . 131 B8
Preesall Cl BL8 . . . . 26 F1
Prefect Pl WN5 . . . . 54 C8
Premier Rd M8 . . . . 158 C4
Premier St M16 . . . . 97 D4
Prentice Wlk M11 . . . . 83 A1
Prenton St M11 . . . . 99 E8
Prenton Way OL8 . . . . 26 F5
Presall St **2** BL2 . . . . . . 148 C4
Presbury Ct **1** M8 . . . . . . 63 B5
Presbyterian Fold 6
WN2 . . . . 56 D6
Prescot Ave
Atherton M46 . . . . 58 E5
Tyldesley M29 . . . . 59 D1
Prescot Cl BL9 . . . . 141 A1
Prescot Rd
Altrincham WA15 . . . . 119 F2
Manchester M9 . . . . 157 A3
Prescott Ave WA3 . . . . 73 F2
Prescott La WN5 . . . . 54 B8
Prescott St SK14 . . . . 131 B1
Prescott St
Bolton BL3 . . . . 146 C4
Golborne WA3 . . . . 74 A1
Hindley WN2 . . . . 56 D5
Leigh WN7 . . . . 75 F6
Rochdale OL16 . . . . 15 C2
Walkden M28 . . . . 60 B3
Wigan WN3, WN1,
WN6 . . . . 150 B4
Prescott Wlk M34 . . . . 101 B1
Press St M11 . . . . 99 D7
Prestage St
Manchester, Levenshulme
M12 . . . . 99 B2
Manchester, Old Trafford
M16 . . . . 97 D4
Salford M16. . . . . 161 C1
Prestbury Ave
Altrincham WA15 . . . . 119 E6
Manchester M14 . . . . 97 F1
Wigan WN3 . . . . 54 E2
Prestbury Cl
Bury BL9 . . . . 141 A1
Stockport SK2 . . . . 124 C7
Prestbury Ct **1** M28 . . . . 60 D2
Prestbury Dr
Oldham OL1 . . . . 48 D1
Romiley SK6. . . . . 112 F3
Prestbury Rd
Bolton BL1. . . . . 25 A5
Wilmslow SK9 . . . . 137 E5
Prestfield Rd M45 . . . . 63 A7
Presto Gdns BL3. . . . . 146 B4
PRESTOLEE 61 A8
Prestolee Ct M27 . . . . 80 E8
Prestolee Prim Sch
M26 . . . . 61 B8
Prestolee Rd
Kearsley M26. . . . . 43 B1
Little Lever BL3 . . . . 43 A1
Preston Ave
Irlam M44 . . . . 105 F7
Salford M30. . . . . 80 A3
Preston Cl M30. . . . . 80 A3
Preston Rd
Manchester M19 . . . . 111 A8
Standish PR7, WN6 . . . . . . 19 D5
Preston St
2 Bolton BL3 . . . . 42 B4
Manchester M18 . . . . 165 C2
Middleton M24 . . . . 65 A8
Oldham OL4 . . . . 67 B8
16 Rochdale OL12 . . . . . . 14 C1
Presto St
Bolton BL3 . . . . 146 B4
Farnworth BL4. . . . . 60 E8
PRESTWICH 63 A4
Prestwich Arts Coll
M25 . . . . 63 B5
Prestwich Cl
Culcheth WA3 . . . . 91 E3
Leigh WN7 . . . . 76 B5
Prestwich Cl SK4 . . . . 124 B7
Prestwich Forest Pk*
M25 . . . . 62 E3
Prestwich Hills M25 . . . . . . 63 A2
Prestwich Hospl M25 . . . . 62 F5
Prestwich Ind Est M46 . . . 58 B4
PRESTWICH PARK 63 A3
Prestwich Park Rd S
M25 . . . . 63 A3
Prestwich Prep Sch
M25 . . . . 63 C5
Prestwich Sta M46. . . . . . . 58 B3
Prestwich Sta M25 . . . . . . 63 A5
Prestwich Wlk **1** M40 . . . 65 C2
Prestwood Cl BL1 . . . . 143 A1
Prestwood Dr BL1 . . . . 143 A1
Prestwood Rd
Farnworth BL4. . . . . 42 A1
Salford M6. . . . . 80 C4
Pretoria Rd
Ashton-in-M WN4 . . . . 73 B4
Bolton BL2 . . . . 42 E8
Oldham OL8 . . . . 66 C3
Pretoria St **2** OL12 . . . . . 14 C1
PRETTYWOOD 28 E2
Price St
Bury BL9 . . . . 141 A1

Price St continued
Dukinfield SK16. . . . . 101 C8
Farnworth BL4. . . . . 42 D1
Prichard St M32 . . . . 96 D2
Prickshaw OL12 . . . . 14 B6
Prickshaw La OL12 . . . . . . 14 B6
Pride Cl WA12. . . . . 89 E2
Pridmouth Rd M20 . . . . . . 110 C6
Priest Ave SK8 . . . . 122 A4
Priestfields WN7 . . . . 76 B5
Priest Hill **6** OL1. . . . . . 153 B3
Priestley Rd M27, M28. . . . 79 C8
Priestley Way OL2 . . . . 49 D7
Priestnall Cl SK4 . . . . 110 F3
Priestnall Rd SK4 . . . . 110 F3
Priestnall Sch SK4 . . . . . . 110 F3
Priestners Way WN7 . . . . . 75 E6
Priest St
Oldham OL4 . . . . 66 B4
Stockport SK1 . . . . 170 C3
Priestwood Ave OL4 . . . . . 49 F4
Primary Cl M44. . . . . 105 D5
Primley Wlk **8** M9 . . . . 157 B4
Primrose Ave
Farnworth BL4. . . . . 42 A1
Hyde SK14 . . . . 113 D8
Marple SK6 . . . . 125 E6
Uppermill OL3 . . . . 51 C1
Urmston M41. . . . . 95 D2
Walkden M28. . . . . 60 B2
Primrose Bank
2 Altrincham WA14 . . . . 119 C1
1 Bacup OL13 . . . . 3 C8
Bury BL8 . . . . 26 F7
Oldham OL8 . . . . 153 B1
Oldham OL3 . . . . 69 B5
Walkden M28. . . . . 60 B2
Primrose Cl
Bolton BL2 . . . . 26 A4
Salford M6. . . . . 154 C2
Primrose Cotts 1
WA14 . . . . 119 C1
Primrose Cres
1 Glossop SK13 . . . . . . 116 B8
Hyde SK14 . . . . 113 D8
Primrose Dr
Bury BL9 . . . . 28 D4
Droylsden M43. . . . . 84 C3
Primrose Gr WN5. . . . . 54 E7
Primrose Hill SK13 . . . . 116 B8
Primrose Hill Ct 7
OL2 . . . . 48 F8
Primrose La
Glossop SK13 . . . . 116 B8
Marple SK6 . . . . 127 A4
Standish WN6. . . . . 19 D2
Primrose St N M29 . . . . 59 A1
Primrose St S M29 . . . . 77 A8
Primrose St
9 Bacup OL13 . . . . 3 C8
Bolton BL1 . . . . 143 C4
2 Farnworth BL4. . . . . . . 60 E7
4 Leigh WN7 . . . . 75 D5
Manchester M4 . . . . 159 B2
Rochdale OL12. . . . . 139 A4
Tyldesley M29 . . . . 59 A1
Primrose Terr
1 Glossop SK13 . . . . . . 116 B8
Urmston M41. . . . . 95 C6
Primrose View WN4 . . . . . . 73 C2
Primrose Wlk
Marple SK6 . . . . 125 E6
Oldham OL8 . . . . 153 B1
Primula Dr WA3 . . . . 90 D8
Primula St BL1 . . . . 24 F5
Prince Albert Ave **4**
M19 . . . . 99 A2
Prince Charlie St OL1 . . . . 67 C8
Princedom St M9. . . . . 157 B4
Prince Edward Ave
Denton M34. . . . . 100 F2
2 Oldham OL4 . . . . 67 C7
Prince George St **3**
OL1. . . . . 49 C1
Prince Mead Pl M17. . . . . . 96 B5
Prince of Wales Bsns Pk
6 OL1. . . . . 153 B8
Prince Rd SK12. . . . . 134 C5
Princes Ave M44 . . . . 94 C3
Prince's Ave
Little Lever BL3 . . . . 43 B4
Manchester M20 . . . . 110 C4
Romiley SK6. . . . . 113 A3
Tyldesley M29 . . . . 77 B6
Princes Ct
Manchester M20 . . . . 110 B5
Ramsbottom BL0 . . . . 138 C2
Princes Dr M33. . . . . 108 D3
Prince's Dr SK6 . . . . 125 E7
Princes Gdns WN7 . . . . . . 76 C5
Prince's Pk WN6 . . . . 35 F4
Princes Rd
Altrincham WA14 . . . . 119 D6
Sale M33 . . . . 108 D3
Sale M33 . . . . 108 D5
Swinton M27 . . . . 79 E8
Up Holland WN8 . . . . 53 C7
Wilmslow SK9 . . . . 136 E8
Princess Ave
Ashton-in-M WN4 . . . . 73 C3
Atherton M46 . . . . 58 C5
Cheadle SK8 . . . . 123 A3
Denton M34. . . . . 100 E3
Haydock WA11. . . . . 89 A7
Kearsley BL4 . . . . 60 F6
Manchester M25 . . . . 63 C2
Rochdale OL12. . . . . 15 C4
Princess Christian Coll
M14 . . . . 98 C1

Princess Cl
Dukinfield SK16. . . . . 101 D8
Heywood OL10. . . . . 29 D1
Mossley OL5 . . . . 86 E8
Princess Ct M15. . . . . 162 A2
Princess Dr M24. . . . . 64 E8
Princess Gr BL4 . . . . 60 D8
Princess Ho **5** M1 . . . . 163 A3
Princess Par
Bury BL9 . . . . 140 C2
Manchester M41 . . . . 109 H8
Princess Parkway M20, M22,
M23 . . . . 109 C2
Princess Rd
Adlington PR6 . . . . 21 B8
Ashton-in-M WN4 . . . . 73 C3
Bolton BL6 . . . . 40 B8
Failsworth OL9 . . . . 65 E3
Manchester, Moss Side M14,
M16 . . . . 97 F4
Manchester, West Didsbury
M14, M20, M21, M15 . . . 109 E6
Milnrow OL16 . . . . 31 D7
Prestwich M25. . . . . 63 C4
Shaw OL2. . . . . 149 A2
Urmston M41. . . . . 95 B2
Wigan WN6 . . . . 36 C4
Wilmslow SK9 . . . . 136 F5
Princess St
Altrincham WA14 . . . . 119 C8
Ashton-u-L OL6 . . . . 85 D4
Bolton BL1. . . . . 145 C3
Eccles M30 . . . . 79 C2
Failsworth M35 . . . . 83 E7
Glossop SK13. . . . . 116 C8
Hindley WN2 . . . . 56 C5
Hyde SK14 . . . . 167 B2
5 Leigh WN7 . . . . 76 A5
Manchester M1, M60,
M2 . . . . 163 A4
Manchester, St George's
M15 . . . . 162 A2
Oldham OL4 . . . . 67 E6
Pendlebury M27 . . . . 80 A7
1 Radcliffe M26 . . . . 43 E3
Rochdale OL12. . . . . 14 F1
Salford M6. . . . . 81 A4
Whitworth OL12. . . . . 14 C8
Wigan WN3 . . . . 150 C3
Princes St WA12. . . . . 89 B3
Prince's St SK1. . . . . 169 B2
Princess Wlk SK7 . . . . 133 A7
Prince St
Ashton-in-M WN4 . . . . 73 A5
Bolton BL1. . . . . 145 B4
Britannia OL13. . . . . 4 D7
Heywood OL10. . . . . 29 D2
6 Oldham OL1 . . . . 67 A7
Ramsbottom BL0 . . . . 138 C2
Rochdale OL16. . . . . 31 B5
Princethorpe Cl BL6 . . . . . 40 D6
Princeton Cl **1** M6. . . . . . 81 A3
Prince Way OL2. . . . . 48 C6
Prinknash Rd M22 . . . . . . 121 D1
Printers Cl M19 . . . . 110 D2
Printers Dr SK15 . . . . 87 A6
Printers Fold SK14. . . . . . 103 D5
Printers La BL2, BL7. . . . . . 25 C6
Printers Pk SK14 . . . . 103 E5
Printer St
Droylsden M11. . . . . 99 D8
Oldham OL1 . . . . 153 C2
Printon Ave M9. . . . . 64 B3
Printshop La M46. . . . . 58 E1
Printworks La M19 . . . . 99 C1
Printworks Rd SK15 . . . . . . 86 C3
Printworks The M4 . . . . . . 159 A2
Priorsleigh SK4 . . . . 110 F2
Prior St OL8. . . . . 67 B5
Priory Ave
Leigh WN7 . . . . 57 D1
Manchester M21 . . . . 109 B8
Salford M7. . . . . 81 C6
Priory Cl
5 Altrincham WA14 . . . . 119 C1
Eccles M30 . . . . 79 E2
Reddish SK5 . . . . 111 E8
Priory La SK5 . . . . 111 E8
Priory Nook WN8. . . . . 53 C7
Priory Pl BL2 . . . . 25 C2
Priory Rd
Altrincham WA14 . . . . 128 B8
Ashton-in-M WN4 . . . . 72 F5
Cheadle SK8 . . . . 122 C1
Sale M33 . . . . 108 D5
Swinton M27 . . . . 79 E8
Up Holland WN8 . . . . 53 C7
Wilmslow SK9 . . . . 136 E8
Priory St M41 . . . . 119 C1
Priory The M7. . . . . 81 C6
Pritchard St M1 . . . . 163 A3
Private La BB4 . . . . 1 C8
Privet St OL4 . . . . 49 F4
Proctor Cl WN5 . . . . 36 E1
Proctor St BL8. . . . . 27 C1
Proctor Way M30 . . . . 94 F7
Prodesse Ct WN2. . . . . 56 D6
Proe's Ct WN1 . . . . 150 B4
Progress Ave M34 . . . . . . 100 F6

Por–Pyt 251

Progress St
Ashton-u-L OL6 . . . . 166 A3
Bolton BL1. . . . . 143 C1
Hindley WN2 . . . . 56 D5
Rochdale OL11. . . . . 30 C1
Promenade St OL10. . . . . . 29 E2
Props Hall Dr M35. . . . . . . 83 E6
Props Jun & Inf Sch
M35 . . . . 83 E6
Prospect Ave
Bolton BL2 . . . . 26 A3
Farnworth BL4. . . . . 42 A4
Irlam M44 . . . . 105 E6
Prospect Cotts WN2 . . . . 56 B4
Prospect Ct BL8 . . . . 26 F7
Prospect Dr
Altrincham WA15 . . . . 129 D8
Failsworth M35 . . . . 83 F5
Prospect Hill BL2 . . . . 25 F4
Prospect Ho
Manchester M9 . . . . 157 B3
Standish WN6 . . . . 36 E8
Prospect Ind Ctr **18**
 . . . . 56 D5
Prospect Pl
Ashton-u-L OL6 . . . . 85 D5
Farnworth BL4. . . . . 60 C7
Heywood OL10. . . . . 29 D3
Prospect Rd
Ashton-u-L OL6 . . . . 85 E5
Dukinfield SK16. . . . . 101 D8
Irlam M44 . . . . 105 E6
Oldham OL9 . . . . 152 C3
Standish WN6. . . . . 36 E8
Prospect St
Bolton BL3 . . . . 143 C1
Heywood OL10. . . . . 46 E8
Hindley WN2 . . . . 56 D5
Littleborough OL15 . . . . . . 16 B6
Rochdale OL11. . . . . 30 E4
Tyldesley M29 . . . . 58 F1
Prospect Terr
Bacup OL13 . . . . 3 E7
Bury BL8 . . . . 140 A4
Prospect Vale SK8 . . . . . . 122 B1
Prospect Vale Prim Sch
SK8. . . . . 122 B1
Prospect View M27 . . . . . . 80 A7
Prospect Villas **3** M9 . . . 64 F1
Prosser Ave M46 . . . . 58 A2
Protector Way M44 . . . . . . 105 F8
Prout St M12 . . . . 99 A3
Providence Ho OL4 . . . . . . 67 E8
Providence St
4 Ashton-u-L OL6 . . . . . . 85 D4
Bolton BL3, BL11. . . . . 145 C1
Denton M34. . . . . 100 F7
Manchester M4 . . . . 160 A1
Walsden OL14 . . . . 6 A7
Provident Ave M19 . . . . 99 C1
Provident St OL2 . . . . 149 B8
Provident Way WA15 . . . . 120 A7
Provis Rd M21 . . . . 109 B7
Prubella Ave M34. . . . . . . 100 E5
Pryce Sq WN2 . . . . 151 C3
Pryce St BL1 . . . . 143 A1
Pryme St M15 . . . . 162 B3
Pudding La SK14 . . . . 102 C3
Puffin Ave SK12 . . . . 133 B4
Puffingate Cl SK15. . . . . . . 86 E7
Pugin Wlk M9 . . . . 157 A2
Pulborough Cl BL8 . . . . 27 B7
Pulford Ave M21. . . . . 109 C4
Pulford Rd M33. . . . . 108 D2
Pullman Cl M19 . . . . 111 B8
Pullman Dr M32 . . . . 95 F3
Pullman St OL11 . . . . 139 C1
Pulman Ct BL3 . . . . 148 A1
Pump St
10 Hindley WN2 . . . . 56 D5
9 Oldham OL9 . . . . 66 B2
Punch La BL3 . . . . 40 D2
Punch St BL3. . . . . 145 A2
Pungle The BL5. . . . . 57 D5
Purbeck Cl M22 . . . . 121 C1
Purbeck Dr
Bury BL8 . . . . 27 C6
Horwich BL6 . . . . 39 F8
Purbeck Way M29 . . . . 77 B7
Purcell Cl M11 . . . . 143 A1
Purcell St M12 . . . . 99 A3
Purdon St **2** BL2. . . . . . . 42 F6
Purdy Ho OL8 . . . . 153 B1
Puritan Wlk **7** M40. . . . . 156 C1
Purley Ave M23. . . . . 121 B6
Purley Dr M44 . . . . 105 C4
Purple St BL1 . . . . 143 C4
Purslow Cl M12 . . . . 160 B1
Putney Cl OL8 . . . . 153 B3
Putney St **1** OL6. . . . . . . 48 E1
Puzzletree Ct SK2 . . . . . . 124 C7
Pye Cl WA11 . . . . 89 B8
Pyegreave Cl M16 . . . . . . 104 F1
Pyegreave Rd SK13 . . . . . 104 A1
Pyke St WN1 . . . . 37 D1
Pymgate Dr SK8. . . . . 122 F1
Pym St
Eccles M30 . . . . 79 D2
Heywood OL10. . . . . 29 D2
Manchester M40 . . . . 157 C4
Pyramid Ct M7 . . . . 155 A8
Pyrus Cl M30 . . . . 94 F8
Pytha Fold Rd M20 . . . . . . 110 D5

252 Qua–Ran

Q

Quadrant The
 Droylsden M43 83 F1
 Manchester M9 65 A3
 Romiley SK6 113 A2
 Stockport SK1 112 B1
Quail Dr M44 94 A3
Quail St OL4 67 C6
Quainton Ho 5 M5 154 C1
Quakerfields BL5 57 D7
Quakers Field BL8 26 F8
Quakers' Pl WN6 19 E1
Quakers Terr WN6 19 D3
Quantock Cl
 Stockport SK4 169 B2
 Wigan WN3 54 C2
Quantock Dr OL8 66 F3
Quantock St 7 M16 97 E4
Quarlton Dr BL8 10 B3
Quarmby Rd M18 99 F4
Quarry Bank Mill*
 SK9 130 F2
Quarry Bank Rd SK9 130 F3
Quarry Cl SK13 104 D1
Quarry Clough SK15 102 D8
Quarry Hill OL12 14 E3
Quarry Hts 4 SK15 101 F8
Quarry Pl WN1 151 B4
Quarry Pond Rd M28 59 F3
Quarry Rd
 Hayfield SK22 127 F2
 Kearsley BL4 61 A7
 Romiley SK6 113 B2
Quarry Rise
 Romiley SK6 113 B3
 Stalybridge SK15, SK16 101 F8
Quarry St
 Radcliffe M26 44 B3
 Ramsbottom BL0 11 D6
 Rochdale OL12 14 E1
 Romiley SK6 113 B5
 Stalybridge SK15 85 F1
 Whitworth OL12 4 E6
Quarry Wlk 17 M11 160 C1
Quay 5 M5 161 B3
Quayside WN7 75 E4
Quayside Cl M28 78 B5
Quays Reach M50 154 B1
Quay St
 Heywood OL10 29 E1
 Salford M3 158 B2
Quays The M50 96 E7
Quay View M5 161 A4
Quebec Pl BL3 145 A1
Quebec St
 Abram Brow WN2,
 WN7 74 E5
 Bolton BL3 145 A1
 Denton M34 100 E4
 Oldham OL9 153 A4
Queen Alexandra Cl
 M5 161 C4
Queen Ann Cl BL9 45 C4
Queen Ann Dr M28 78 B7
Queen Anne Ct SK9 137 C6
Queen Elizabeth Sch The
 M24 46 F4
Queenhill Dr SK14 102 A5
Queenhill Rd M22 109 E1
Queen St W M20 110 B7
Queens Ave
 Manchester M18 165 B1
 Rochdale OL12 15 C4
Queen's Ave
 Ashton-in-M WN4 73 B3
 Atherton M46 58 C5
 Bolton BL7 25 A7
 Glazebury WA3 92 C7
 Little Lever BL3 43 A4
 Romiley SK6 113 A3
Queensbridge Prim Sch
 BL4 60 C8
Queensbrook BL1 145 B3
Queensbury Cl
 Bolton BL1 24 D5
 15 Handforth SK9 131 D1
 Wilmslow SK9 137 D8
Queensbury Ct M40 160 B3
Queensbury Par M40 160 B3
Queens Cl
 Boothstown M28 77 F7
 Hyde SK14 113 E7
 Stockport SK4 168 A2
Queen's Cl M28 60 D3
Queenscroft 2 M30 79 F3
Queens Ct
 Manchester, Collyhurst
 M40 157 A1
 Stockport SK4 168 A3
 Urmston M41 94 E2
Queen's Ct
 3 Manchester M21 97 B2
 Manchester, Withington
 M20 110 A4
Queen's Ct SK6 126 A6
Queens Dr
 Cheadle SK8 123 A2
 Golborne WA3 90 C8
 Hyde SK14 113 F7
 Newton-le-W WA12 89 C5
 Rochdale OL11 30 E3
Queen's Dr
 Glossop SK13 104 F1
 Manchester, Sedgley Park
 M25 63 C2
 Stockport SK4 168 A2
Queensferry St M40 83 C6
Queensgate
 Bolton BL1 144 C4
 Bramhall SK7 132 E5
Queensgate Dr OL2 48 C6
Queensgate Prim Sch
 SK7 132 E4
Queens Gdns WN7 76 C5
Queen's Gdns SK8 122 E6
Queen's Gr M12 99 A4
Queensland Rd M18 165 B1
Queen's Park Rd OL10 29 D3
Queens Pl BL9 11 C2
Queen Sq OL6 85 D3
Queens Rd
 Bolton BL3 146 B4
 Chadderton OL9 152 A3
 Haydock WA11 89 A7
 Manchester, Cheetham Hill
 M8, M9 156 B2
 Manchester, Collyhurst M40,
 M9 157 A1
 Oldham OL8 67 A5
 Orrell WN5 53 C5
 Sale M33 107 F5
Queen's Rd
 Altrincham WA15 119 F3
 Ashton-in-M WN4 73 B4
 Ashton-u-L OL6 85 D5
 Cheadle SK8 122 F4
 Cheadle SK8 123 A3
 Hazel Grove SK7 124 E3
 12 Littleborough OL15 16 B5
 Romiley SK6 113 A3
 Urmston M41 95 D1
 Wilmslow SK9 137 A6
Queens Road Prim Sch
 SK8 123 A3
Queen St
 Ashton-u-L OL6 166 C3
 5 Bacup OL13 3 C8
 Bolton BL1 145 B3
 Bury, Pimhole BL9 141 A2
 Bury, Tottington BL8 27 A5
 Cheadle SK8 122 F6
 Denton, Hooley Hill
 M34 100 F6
 Dukinfield SK16 166 B1
 Failsworth M35 83 E7
 Farnworth BL4 60 D8
 Glossop SK13 116 B8
 Golborne WA3 90 B8
 Hadfield SK13 104 A4
 Heywood OL10 29 D2
 5 Hindley WN2 56 D6
 Horwich BL6 22 B3
 Hyde SK14 167 B1
 Leigh WN7 76 A5
 Littleborough OL15 16 B5
 Manchester M2 158 C1
 Marple SK6 126 A6
 Middleton M24 65 C8
 Mossley OL5 68 C1
 Newton-le-W WA12 89 B3
 10 Oldham, County End
 OL4 67 F6
 Oldham OL1 153 C2
 Platt Bridge WN2 56 A2
 Radcliffe M26 44 C2
 Ramsbottom BL0 138 B2
 Rochdale OL12 139 C4
 Royton OL2 48 D4
 Salford, Irlams o' th' Height
 M6 80 D5
 Salford M3 158 B2
 Shaw OL2 149 B2
 Stalybridge SK15 86 A2
 Walkden M38 60 B3
 Westhoughton BL5 57 E8
 Wigan, Norley WN5 54 B6
 Wigan, Pemberton WN5 54 D5
 Wigan WN3 150 C3
Queens Terr SK9 131 D3
Queen's Terr
 8 Bacup OL13 3 E8
 7 Dukinfield SK16 166 B1
Queenston Rd M20 110 A4
Queens View OL15 16 A3
Queensway
 Dukinfield SK16 101 F7
 Gatley SK8 131 C8
 Ince-in-M WN2 56 A8
 Irlam M44 93 F2
 Kearsley BL4 60 F5
 Leigh WN7 76 D6
 Manchester M19 110 D2
 Mossley OL5 86 D8
 Partington M31 105 F4
 Poynton SK12 133 D3
 Rochdale OL11 30 E3
 Shevington WN6 35 F4
 Swinton M27 62 A2
 Uppermill OL3 69 B6
 Urmston M41 95 E4
 Walkden M28 78 C8
 Wigan WN1 37 B2
Queens Wlk M43 84 A1
Queen Victoria St
 Eccles M30 79 C2
 Rochdale OL11 31 A4
Quenby St M15 162 A3
Quendon Ave M7 158 B4
QUICK 68 D4
Quick Edge La OL4 68 B4
Quickedge Rd OL4, OL5 68 C3
Quickmere Ct 7 OL5 68 C2
Quick Rd OL4, OL5 68 D4
Quick View OL5 68 E3
QUICKWOOD 68 D3
Quickwood OL5 68 D2
Quill Ct M44 105 E6
Quilter Gr M9 64 C2
Quinney Cres M16 97 F4
Quinn St M11 83 A1
Quinton 10 OL12 139 B4
Quinton Wlk M13 163 B2
Quintrell Brow BL7 25 A8

R

Raby St M14, M16 97 F4
Racecourse Pk SK9 136 F6
Racecourse Rd SK9 136 E6
Racecourse Wlk M26 43 F4
Racefield Hamlet OL2 48 A4
Racefield Rd WA14 119 C4
Race The SK9 131 D2
Rachel Ho BL9 141 C3
Rachel Rosing Wlk
 M8 155 C4
Rachel St M12 163 C4
Rack House Prim Sch
 M23 109 A1
Rackhouse Rd M23 109 B1
Radbourne Cl M12 165 A2
Radbourne Gr BL3 40 F4
RADCLIFFE 44 C3
Radcliffe Ave WA3 91 E3
Radcliffe Gr WN7 75 F7
Radcliffe Hall CE/Meth
 Prim Sch M26 44 D4
Radcliffe Moor Rd BL2,
 M26 43 C5
Radcliffe New Rd M45,
 M26 44 D2
Radcliffe Park Cres
 M6 80 C5
Radcliffe Park Rd M6 80 C5
Radcliffe Prim Sch
 M26 43 E4
Radcliffe Rd
 Bolton, Darcy Lever BL2,
 BL3 42 D5
 Bolton, Springfield BL2 148 B3
 Bury BL9 44 E7
 Oldham OL4 49 D2
Radcliffe Riverside Sch
 Radcliffe M26 44 A3
 Radcliffe M26 44 B4
Radcliffe St
 Oldham, Cold Hurst
 OL1 153 C4
 Oldham, Grotton OL4 68 A6
 Royton OL2 48 E4
Radcliffe Sta M26 44 B3
Radclyffe Prim Sch
 M5 161 A3
Radclyffe Sch The
 OL9 152 A2
Radclyffe Sch (Upper) The
 OL9 65 F7
Radclyffe St
 Chadderton OL9 152 C4
 Middleton M24 47 A2
Radelan Gr M26 43 D4
Radford Cl SK2 124 E7
Radford Dr
 Irlam M44 94 A3
 2 Manchester M9 157 B4
Radford Ho SK2 124 E7
Radford St M7 81 C8
Radium St M4 159 C2
Radlet Dr WA15 120 A8
Radlett Wlk 3 M13 163 C1
Radley Cl
 Bolton BL1 142 A1
 7 Sale M33 107 D3
Radley St
 Droylsden M43 99 E8
 Manchester M16 97 F3
Radnor Ave M34 100 B3
Radnor Cl WN2 57 A3
Radnor Dr WN7 75 C5
Radnormere Dr SK8 123 A4
Radnor St
 Manchester, Gorton
 M18 99 C4
 Manchester, Moss Side
 M15 97 F4
 Oldham OL9 152 C1
 Stretford M32 96 D1
Radstock Cl
 Bolton BL1 24 E7
 Manchester M14 98 B1
Radstock Rd M32 96 C2
Radway M29 59 C1
Raeburn Dr SK6 126 B8
Rae St SK3 123 C8
Raglan Ave
 Prestwich M25, M45 63 B7
 Swinton M27 62 B2
Raglan Cl M11 160 C1
Raglan Dr WA14 119 E8
Raglan Rd
 Sale M33 108 A3
 Stretford M32 96 B3
Raglan St
 Bolton BL1 143 A2
 Hyde SK14 101 C2
 Rochdale OL11 30 C1
Raglan Wlk 6 M15 162 C2
Ragley Cl SK12 133 F4
Raikes Clough Ind Est
 BL3 42 C4
Raikes La BL3 42 B4
Raikes Lane Ind Est
 BL3 42 C4
Raikes Rd BL3 42 D5
Raikes Way BL3 42 D5
Railgate OL13 4 C8
Rail Pl 8 M15 163 A2
Railside Terr M30 80 A2
Railton Ave M16 97 D3
Railton Terr M9 157 C3
Railway App 4 OL11 30 C2
Railway Bank SK14 101 C2
Railway Brow OL11 30 C1
Railway Cotts
 Hollinfare WA3 105 B5
 Romiley SK6 112 F4
Railway Rd
 Adlington PR6, PR7 21 A7
 Golborne WA3 74 B1
 Leigh WN7 75 E5
 Oldham, Factory Fold
 OL9 66 A2
 Oldham OL9 153 A2
 Stockport SK1, SK3 170 B4
 Stretford M32 96 F5
 Urmston M41 95 E2
Railway St
 Altrincham WA14 119 D4
 Atherton M46 58 B4
 Bacup OL13 3 B8
 Dukinfield SK16 166 B1
 Farnworth BL4 42 E1
 Glossop SK13 104 C1
 Hadfield SK13 104 A5
 Heywood OL10 29 E1
 Hindley WN2 56 E7
 Hyde SK14 167 A2
 Littleborough OL15 16 B5
 Manchester M18 99 D6
 Newhey OL16 32 B4
 Newton-le-W WA12 89 B3
 Radcliffe M26 44 A3
 Ramsbottom BL0 138 C2
 Ramsbottom, Summerseat
 BL9 11 C2
 Rochdale OL16 31 A6
 Stockport SK4 169 B2
 Wigan WN6 37 A1
Railway Street Ind Est
 M18 99 D6
Railway Terr
 Bury BL8 27 C1
 Disley SK12 135 D6
 Entwistle BL7 9 B8
 5 Manchester M21 97 B2
Railway View
 3 Oldham OL4 67 F6
 Shaw OL2 149 C4
Raimond St BL1 142 C3
Rainbow Cl M21 109 B7
Rainbow Dr M46 58 D5
Raincliff Ave M13 98 F2
Raines Crest OL16 32 A6
Rainford Ave
 Altrincham WA15 120 A6
 Manchester M20 110 A8
Rainford Ho 4 BL1 145 C4
Rainford Rd WA11,
 WN5 71 C5
Rainford St BL2 25 C6
Rainforth St M13 98 F3
Rainham Dr
 Bolton BL1 143 B1
 Manchester M8 156 A3
Rainham Gr 2 BL1 143 B1
Rainham Way
 Brinnington SK5 112 B6
 Chadderton OL9 152 B2
Rainhill Wlk M40 83 D4
Rainow Ave M43 83 E1
Rainow Dr SK12 134 A2
Rainow Rd SK3 123 C6
Rainow Way 10 SK9 131 E1
Rainshaw St
 Bolton BL1 143 C4
 1 Oldham OL4 67 D8
 Royton OL2 48 D4
RAINSOUGH 63 A1
Rainsough Ave M25 63 A1
Rainsough Brow M25 62 F1
Rainsough Cl M25 63 A1
Rainton Wlk 2 M40 65 D2
Rainwood OL9 65 E8
Raithby Dr WN3 55 A3
Raja Cl M8 156 B3
Rake
 Ramsbottom BL0 138 B2
 Rochdale OL11 29 D8
Rake Fold BL8 138 A2
RAKE HEAD 3 A7
Rake Head Barn La
 OL14 6 A8
Rake Head La OL13 3 B8
Rakehead Wlk 4
 M15 162 C1
Rake La M27 62 B2
Rake St BL9 140 C4
Rake Terr OL15 16 C6
Rakewood Dr OL4 49 E4
Rakewood Rd OL15 16 C2
Raleigh Cl
 Manchester M20 110 A5
 Oldham OL1 153 C4
Raleigh Gdns OL15 6 C1
Raleigh St
 Reddish SK5 169 B4
 Stretford M32 96 E2
Ralli Courts M3 158 B1
Ralph Ave SK14 113 E7
Ralph Green St OL9 66 B3
Ralph Sherwin Ct
 OL12 15 D4
Ralphs La SK16 101 C7
Ralph St
 Bolton BL1 143 A2
 Droylsden M11 83 D1
 Rochdale OL12 15 A1
Ralston Cl M7 155 C4
Ralstone Ave OL8 66 F4
Ramage Wlk M12 160 B1
Ramillies Ave SK8 123 C1
Ramillies Hall Sch
 SK8 123 C2
Ramp Rd E M90 130 C7
Ramp Rd S M90 130 C7
Ramp Rd W M90 130 B7
Ramsay Ave BL4 60 B7
Ramsay Pl OL16 31 A8
Ramsay St
 Bolton BL1 143 B4
 Rochdale OL16 31 A8
Ramsay Terr 10 OL16 31 A8
RAMSBOTTOM 138 C1
Ramsbottom Cottage
 Hospl BL0 138 C1
Ramsbottom Heritage Ctr
 Mus* BL0 138 C2
Ramsbottom La BL0 138 C3
Ramsbottom Rd
 Hawkshaw BL8, BL7 10 A3
 Horwich BL6 22 C3
Ramsbottom Sta*
 BL0 138 C2
Ramsbury Dr M40 65 D2
Ramsdale Rd SK7 132 E8
Ramsdale St OL9 152 A3
Ramsden Cl
 Glossop SK13 104 D2
 Oldham OL1 153 B3
 Wigan WN3 150 A1
Ramsden Cres OL1 153 B4
Ramsden Fold M27 61 F2
Ramsden La OL14 5 F7
Ramsden Rd
 Calderbrook OL12 5 C1
 Wardle OL12 15 C6
Ramsden St
 Ashton-u-L OL6 166 B4
 Bolton BL3 42 D5
 Oldham OL1 153 B3
 Walsden OL14 6 A7
Ramsden Wood Rd
 OL14 6 A7
Ramsey Ave M19 99 D1
Ramsey Cl
 Ashton-in-M WN4 73 B2
 Atherton M46 58 E2
Ramsey Gr BL8 27 B2
Ramsey St
 Chadderton OL9 152 B1
 3 Leigh WN7 76 A4
 Manchester M40 83 B7
 Oldham OL1 67 B8
Ramsgate Rd
 Failsworth M40 83 C4
 Reddish SK5 111 F7
Ramsgate St M7, M8 155 B1
Ramsgill Cl M23 108 F1
Ramsgreave Cl BL9 44 D7
Ram St M38 59 F5
Ramwell Gdns BL3 145 A1
Ramwells Brow BL7 25 A8
Ramwells Ct BL7 25 B8
Ranby Ave M9 64 F4
Randale Dr BL9 45 A2
Randall Ave WN6 36 A5
Randall Cl WA12 89 B4
Randall Wlk 22 M11 160 C1
Randal St BL3 146 C4
Randerson St M12 163 C3
Randlesham St M25 63 C4
Randle St 1 WN2 56 D6
Randolph Pl SK3 170 B3
Randolph Rd BL4 60 F7
Randolph St
 Bolton BL3 145 A2
 Manchester M19 99 B2
 Oldham OL8 66 C2
Rands Clough Dr M28 78 B6
Rand St 6 OL1 49 D1
Ranelagh Rd M27 80 C7
Ranelagh St M11 83 B2
Raneley Gr OL11 31 A2
Ranford Rd M19 111 A8
Range Dr SK6 113 C6
Range Hall Ct 7 SK1 112 A1
Range La OL3 33 D1
Rangemore Ave M22 121 D8
Range Rd
 Dukinfield SK16 102 B7
 Manchester M16 97 E3
 Stalybridge SK15 102 B8
 Stockport SK3 170 B3
Range St
 Bolton BL3 147 A4
 Manchester M11 165 C4
Ranicar St WN2 57 C3
Rankine Terr BL3 145 A1
Ranmore Ave
 Garswood WN4 72 D4
 Manchester M11 99 D8
Rannoch Rd BL2 43 A7

Ransfield Rd M21. . . . . .97 B1
Ranulph Ct 🏠 M6 . . . . .80 D5
Ranworth Ave SK4 . . . . . . .110 F2
Ranworth Cl
  Bolton BL1. . . . . .25 A6
  Manchester M11 . . . . .165 A4
Raper St OL4 . . . . .67 C8
Rapes Highway OL3 . . . . . .33 F5
Raphael St BL1 . . . . .143 A2
Rappax Rd WA15 . . . . .129 A8
Rasbottom St BL3 . . . . .145 B1
Raspberry La M44 . . . . .94 A5
Rassbottom Brow 🖸
  SK15. . . . . .85 F2
Rassbottom Ind Est
  SK15. . . . . .85 F2
Rassbottom St SK15. . . . . . .85 F2
Rassey Cl WN6 . . . . .37 A7
Rastell Wlk 🟦 M9 . . . . .64 E3
Ratcliffe Ave M44 . . . . .94 A2
Ratcliffe Rd WN2 . . . . .38 C5
Ratcliffe St
  Leigh WN7 . . . . .75 F6
  Manchester M19 . . . . .99 B1
  🖸 Stockport SK1 . . . . . . .170 C4
  Wigan WN6 . . . . .37 A1
Ratcliffe Terr OL5. . . . . .86 C8
Rathan Rd M41. . . . . .95 C4
Rathbone St OL16 . . . . .31 C7
Rathbourne Ave M9 . . . . . . .64 D4
Rathen Ave M20 . . . . .56 A8
Rathen Rd M20 . . . . .110 C5
Rathmell Cl M43 . . . . .91 E3
Rathmell Rd M23. . . . . .108 F2
Rathmore Ave M40 . . . . . . .157 B1
Rathvale Dr M22. . . . . .130 C8
Rath Wlk M40 . . . . .83 C5
Rathybank Cl 🟦 BL1. . . . . .142 C2
Rattenbury Ct M6 . . . . .80 C5
Raveden Cl BL1. . . . . .142 C3
Raveley Ave M14 . . . . .110 D8
Ravelston Dr M9 . . . . .157 A3
Raven Ave
  Chadderton OL9. . . . . .152 A1
  Haslingden BB4. . . . . .1 A7
Raven Cl M43 . . . . .84 C3
Raven Croft BB4. . . . . .1 B8
Raven Ct M15 . . . . .162 B1
Raven Dr M44 . . . . .109 D5
Ravenfield Gr 🟦 BL1. . . . . .145 A4
Ravenhead Cl 🟦 M41. . . . .110 D8
Ravenhead Dr M8 . . . . .53 A7
Ravenhead Sq SK15. . . . . . .86 E5
Raven Ho M6. . . . . .81 A5
Ravenhurst 🟦 M7 . . . . .63 C1
Ravenhurst Dr BL1. . . . . . . .40 D6
Ravenna Ave M23. . . . . . . .120 D7
Ravenoak Ave M19 . . . . . . .111 C8
Ravenoak Dr M35. . . . . .84 A8
Ravenoak Park Rd
  SK8. . . . . .132 B8
Ravenoak Rd
  Cheadle SK8 . . . . .132 B8
  Stockport SK2 . . . . .124 A4
Raven Rd BB4 . . . . .1 B8
Raven Rd
  Bolton BL3. . . . . .146 A4
  Sale WA15. . . . . .108 B1
Ravensbury Com Sch
  M11. . . . . .83 B2
Ravensbury St M11. . . . . . . .83 B2
Ravenscar Cres M22 . . . . . .130 D8
Ravenscar Wlk BL4 . . . . .60 D7
Ravens Cl
  Glossop SK13. . . . . .115 F8
  Manchester M25 . . . . .63 E2
Ravenscraig Rd M38. . . . . . .60 B6
Ravensdale Gdns M30 . . . . .79 E3
Ravensdale Rd BL1. . . . . . . .40 D7
Ravensdale St M14 . . . . .98 C3
Ravensfield Ind Est
  SK16. . . . . .166 B1
Ravens Holme BL1. . . . . .40 E7
Ravenside Pk OL9 . . . . .152 A1
Ravensmede Ret Pk
  BL2. . . . . .148 A2
Raven St
  Bury BL9 . . . . .140 C4
  Manchester M12. . . . . .163 C4
  Rochdale OL11. . . . . .13 E1
Ravenstonedale Dr
  OL2. . . . . .48 E5
Ravenstone Dr M33. . . . . . .108 E5
Ravenstons Dr OL3 . . . . .51 C3
Ravensway M25 . . . . .63 D2
Ravenswood M20. . . . . .109 F4
Ravens Wood BL1 . . . . .40 E7
Ravenswood Ave
  Stockport SK4 . . . . .168 A1
  Wigan WN3 . . . . .54 D3
Ravenswood Ct 🟦
  SK3. . . . . .123 F4
Ravenswood Dr
  Bolton BL1. . . . . .40 E7
  Cheadle SK8 . . . . .132 B8
  Hindley WN2 . . . . .56 E7
  Manchester M9 . . . . .64 E3
Ravenswood Rd
  Stretford M32 . . . . .96 F4
  Wilmslow SK9. . . . . .136 E4
Raven Terr 🟦 SK16. . . . . . .166 C1
Raven Way
  Salford M6. . . . . .154 C3
  🟦 Salford, Pendleton
  M6 .81 A3
Ravenwood OL9. . . . . .65 D7

Ravenwood Dr
  Altrincham WA15. . . . . . . .129 D7
  Denton M34. . . . . .100 E6
Ravine Ave M9 . . . . .157 C3
Rawcliffe Ave BL2 . . . . .42 F7
Rawcliffe St M14 . . . . .98 B3
Rawdon Cl 🖸 M40 . . . . .99 B1
Rawkin Cl M15 . . . . .162 B1
Rawlinson St 🟦 BL6. . . . . . .22 B4
Rawlyn Rd BL1 . . . . .142 A2
Rawpool Gdns M23 . . . . . . .121 A7
Rawson Ave BL4. . . . . .42 E1
Rawson Rd BL1. . . . . .142 C1
Rawsons Rake BL0,
  BL8. . . . . .138 A2
Rawson St BL4 . . . . .42 E1
Rawsthorne Ave
  Edenfield BL0. . . . . .1 D2
  Manchester M18 . . . . .99 D2
Rawsthorne St
  Bolton BL1. . . . . .143 B2
  Tyldesley M29 . . . . .77 D8
Rawstron St OL12. . . . . .4 C1
RAWTENSTALL 2 E7
Rawtrey Pl M22. . . . . .55 F2
Raycroft Ave M9. . . . . .65 A2
Raydale Cl M43 . . . . .74 E1
Rayden Cres BL5 . . . . .57 E6
Raydon Ave M40. . . . . .157 A1
Raylees BL0 . . . . .11 C4
Rayleigh Ave M11 . . . . .99 F2
Raymond Ave
  Bury BL9 . . . . .27 F5
  Oldham OL9 . . . . .66 B4
Raymond Rd M23. . . . . .109 B2
Raymond St M27 . . . . .61 F1
Rayner La
  Ashton-u-L M27 . . . . .84 F3
  Droylsden M34, M43,
  OL7. . . . . .84 D2
Rayners Cl SK15. . . . . .85 F1
Raynham Ave M20. . . . . . . .110 B3
Raynham St OL6. . . . . .166 C3
Rayson Hill Dr M9 . . . . .64 C2
Reabrook Ave M12. . . . . . . .164 C2
Reach The M28. . . . . .60 E2
Read Cl
  Bury BL9 . . . . .44 D7
  Shaw OL2. . . . . .149 B2
Reade Ave WN4 . . . . .94 F1
Reade Ho M41. . . . . .94 F1
Reading Cl M11. . . . . .165 C4
Reading Dr M33. . . . . .107 D4
Reading St M6 . . . . .81 B5
Reading Wlk 🟦 M34 . . . . . .100 F1
Readitt Wlk M11. . . . . .83 B2
Read St W SK14. . . . . .101 C3
Read St SK14. . . . . .101 C3
Reamey Wlk M12. . . . . .165 A2
Reather Wlk M40 . . . . .159 C3
Rebecca St M8 . . . . .156 A4
Recreation Ave WN4 . . . . . .73 D4
Recreation Dr WN5. . . . . . . .71 E5
Recreation Rd M35 . . . . .66 B1
Recreation St
  Bolton BL3. . . . . .147 B4
  Bolton, Harwood Lee BL2. . .25 E5
Rectory Ave
  Golborne WA3 . . . . .90 C8
  Manchester M8 . . . . .64 A1
  Prestwich M25. . . . . .63 B4
Rectory CE Prim Sch
  WN4. . . . . .72 D5
Rectory Cl
  Denton M34. . . . . .101 A2
  Radcliffe M26 . . . . .44 D4
Rectory Ct 🖸 SK6 . . . . .125 F5
Rectory Fields SK1 . . . . . . .112 A1
Rectory Gdns
  Prestwich M25. . . . . .63 B4
  Westhoughton BL5 . . . . . . .57 E5
Rectory Gn
  Prestwich M25. . . . . .63 B4
  Manchester M12. . . . . .99 A4
Rectory Gr M25 . . . . .112 A1
Rectory Gr M25 . . . . .63 B3
Rectory Hill BL9 . . . . .28 D4
Rectory La
  Prestwich M25. . . . . .28 D4
  Prestwich M25. . . . . .63 A4
  Radcliffe M26 . . . . .44 B3
  Standish WN1, WN6. . . . . . .20 A1
Rectory Rd
  Dowhall Green WN4 . . . . . .72 D5
  Manchester M8 . . . . .63 F1
Rectory St M24. . . . . .46 F1
Redacre SK12 . . . . .133 F6
Redacre Rd M18. . . . . .99 E5
Red Bank
  Bury BL9 . . . . .28 E6
  Manchester M4, M8 . . . . . .159 A3
Red Bank Ave WA14. . . . . . .89 F1
Red Bank Rd M26. . . . . .43 F5
Redbarn Cl SK6 . . . . .112 F4
Red Barn Rd M9 . . . . .71 C6
Redbourne Dr M41. . . . . . . .94 F4
Redbrick Cl 🟦 OL7 . . . . . . .166 A1
Red Bridge BL2 . . . . .26 A1
Redbridge Gr 🟦 M21. . . . . .109 A8
Redbrook Ave M40. . . . . . . .157 B1
Redbrook Cl 🟦 BL4. . . . . . . .42 E1
Redbrook Gr 🟦 SK9 . . . . . .131 D1
Redbrook Rd
  Altrincham WA15. . . . . . . .120 D5
  Ince-in-M WN3 . . . . .151 B2
  Partington M31. . . . . .105 E2
Red Brook St OL11 . . . . . . .139 A3

Redbrow Hollow SK6 . . . . .114 A2
Redburn Cl WN3. . . . . .150 B2
Redburn Rd M23 . . . . .121 B7
Redby St M11 . . . . .165 B3
Redcar Ave
  Manchester M20. . . . . .110 B6
  Urmston M41. . . . . .95 A4
Redcar Cl
  Hazel Grove SK7 . . . . .125 A1
  Oldham OL1 . . . . .49 B1
Redcar Rd
  Bolton BL1. . . . . .142 B4
  Little Lever BL3. . . . . .43 A3
  Pendlebury M27 . . . . .80 C7
Redcar St OL12. . . . . .139 B4
Red Cedar Pk BL2. . . . . .42 D5
Redcliffe Ct M25. . . . . .63 B2
Redclyffe Ave M14. . . . . .98 C3
Redclyffe Rd
  Eccles M41. . . . . .95 D7
  Manchester M20 . . . . .110 A5
Redcot Ct M45 . . . . .62 C7
Redcote St M40. . . . . .83 A8
Redcourt Ave M20 . . . . .110 C5
Redcroft Gdns 🟦
  M19 . . . . .110 E4
Redcroft Rd M33 . . . . .107 E6
Redcross St N OL12. . . . . . .14 F1
Redcross St
  Rochdale OL12. . . . . .14 F1
  Rochdale, Town Head
  OL12. . . . . .139 C4
Redditch Gr M6 . . . . .81 A5
REDDISH 111 D8
Reddish Cl 🟦 BL2 . . . . .25 E6
REDDISH GREEN 111 F7
Reddish La
  Lymm WA13. . . . . .117 A5
  Reddish M18, SK5. . . . . . . .99 E4
Reddish North Sta SK5. . . . .99 F2
Reddish Rd SK5. . . . . .111 F5
Reddish South Sta
  SK5. . . . . .111 F7
REDDISH VALE 112 A7
Reddish Vale Ctry Pk*
  SK5 . . . . .112 B7
Reddish Vale Ctry Pk
  Visitor Ctr*●SK5. . . . . . . .112 B7
Reddish Vale Sch SK5. . . . .112 A7
Reddish Vale Tech Coll
  SK5. . . . . .111 F7
Reddy La WN14. . . . . .118 B1
Reddyshore Brow
  OL15. . . . . .16 C8
Reddyshore Scout Gate
  OL14. . . . . .16 A8
Redesmere Cl
  Altrincham WA15. . . . . . . .120 B6
  Droylsden M43. . . . . .84 B1
Redesmere Dr
  Alderley Edge SK9 . . . . . . .137 A1
  Cheadle SK8 . . . . .122 F4
Redesmere Pk M41. . . . . . .109 B8
Redesmere Rd SK9 . . . . . . .131 D5
Redfern Wood OL12 . . . . . . .14 B2
Redfern Ave M33 . . . . .108 E3
Redfern Cl SK13. . . . . .104 A6
Redfern Cotts OL12 . . . . . . .13 D1
Redfern Ho SK6 . . . . .113 A2
Redfern St M4 . . . . .159 A2
Redfern Way OL11. . . . . .13 D1
Redfield Cl M11 . . . . .160 C1
Redfield Croft WN7. . . . . . . .76 A5
Redford Cl WN7 . . . . .76 A5
Redford Dr SK7. . . . . .124 A2
Redford Rd M8. . . . . .63 F4
Redford St BL8 . . . . .27 C3
Red Gables SK13 . . . . .104 A4
Redgate
  Glossop SK13. . . . . .104 C4
  Hyde SK14. . . . . .113 D8
Redgate La
  Manchester, Longsight
  M12 . . . . .164 C1
  Manchester M12 . . . . .99 A4
Redgate Rd WN4 . . . . .73 B6
Redgate Way BL4. . . . . .147 C1
Redgrave Pas OL4 . . . . .67 D8
Redgrave Rise WN3. . . . . . . .54 D3
Redgrave St OL4 . . . . .67 D8
Redgrave Wlk M19 . . . . .99 C1
Red Hall St OL4 . . . . .67 C6
Redhill Dr SK6 . . . . .112 E3
Redhill Gr BL1. . . . . .143 B1
Redhill St M4 . . . . .159 C2
Red Hill Way WN2 . . . . .56 D6
Redhouse La
  Disley SK12 . . . . .135 E7
  Romiley SK6. . . . . .113 A4
Red House La WA14. . . . . . .118 C8
Redington Cl BL0 . . . . .10 F3
Redisher Cl BL0 . . . . .10 F3
Redisher Croft BL0. . . . . . . .10 F3
Redisher La BL8. . . . . .10 E3
Red La
  Bolton BL2. . . . . .42 F8
  Disley SK12 . . . . .135 C5
  Rochdale OL12. . . . . .15 A6
Redland Ave SK5 . . . . .111 F5
Redland Cl OL15. . . . . .16 B6
Redland Cres M21 . . . . .109 B6
Redland Ct WN2. . . . . .56 B4
Red Lane Prim Sch
  BL2. . . . . .25 F1
Red Lion St M4. . . . . .159 A2
Red Lo SK12 . . . . .135 A6
Red Lumb St OL12. . . . . . . .14 A1
Redlynch Wlk M8. . . . . .156 A4

Redmain Gr WA3 . . . . .90 E8
Redmans Cl M30 . . . . .79 B1
Redmayne Dr WA12. . . . . . .89 B4
Redmere Dr M14 . . . . .110 C8
Redmire Mews SK14 . . . . . .101 F7
Redmires Ct 🟦 M5 . . . . .81 A1
Redmond Cl M34 . . . . .100 E7
Redmoor Sq 🟦 M13. . . . . . .163 B3
Redmoss Row M27 . . . . .80 D8
Rednal Wlk WN3 . . . . .150 B2
Red Pike Wlk 🟦 OL1. . . . . . .67 A8
Redpol Ave WN7. . . . . .76 B5
Redpoll Cl M28 . . . . .78 B7
Red Rock Rd WN1. . . . . .37 C8
RED ROCK 37 D8
Red Rock La
  Kearsley M26. . . . . .61 E6
  Standish WN1, WN2. . . . . . .37 D8
Red Rose Cres M19 . . . . . . .111 C7
Red Rose La M33 . . . . .108 B6
Red Rose Stad M6. . . . . .60 A4
Red Rose Wks OL2 . . . . .48 F4
Red Row WN7. . . . . .134 B8
Redruth St M14 . . . . .98 B2
Redruth Wlk 🟦 OL9 . . . . . . .48 A1
Redscar Wlk M24. . . . . .46 E1
Redshank Cl WA12. . . . . . . .89 C4
Redshank Gr WN7. . . . . .76 A6
Redshaw Ave BL2 . . . . .25 B6
Redshaw Cl M14. . . . . .98 C3
Redstart Cl 🟦 WA3 . . . . .90 E8
Redstart Gr M28. . . . . .78 D8
Redstock Cl BL5. . . . . .40 B1
Redstone Rd M19. . . . . .110 D3
Redthorn Ave 🟦 M19 . . . . .110 F7
Redthorpe Cl 🟦 BL2. . . . . . .25 B1
Redvale Rd M7 . . . . .155 B2
REDVALES 44 E6
Redvales Rd BL9. . . . . .44 C5
Redvers St OL1. . . . . .153 A4
Redwater Cl 🟦 M28 . . . . . . .78 A6
Red Waters WN7. . . . . .76 A6
Redwing Ctr M17 . . . . .96 C6
Redwing Rd BL8. . . . . .10 F2
REDWOOD 54 A5
Redwood
  Chadderton OL9. . . . . .65 D7
  Sale M33. . . . . .107 C4
  Shevington WN6 . . . . .36 B6
  Westhoughton BL5 . . . . . . .57 D6
Redwood Ave
  Wigan, Beech Hill WN6 . . . .36 F3
  Wigan WN5 . . . . .54 A6
Redwood Cl
  Bolton, Darcy Lever
  BL2. . . . . .42 E5
  Cheadle SK8 . . . . .123 B8
  Rochdale OL12. . . . . .14 B3
Redwood Dr
  Denton M34. . . . . .100 E6
  Manchester M8 . . . . .156 B1
  Rawtenstall BB4 . . . . .1 F8
  Romiley SK6. . . . . .112 F3
Redwood Ho M22. . . . . .109 C1
Redwood La OL4 . . . . .67 E7
Redwood Park Gr
  OL16. . . . . .31 D7
Redwood Rd OL3 . . . . .69 C7
Redwood St M6 . . . . .81 A4
Reebok Stad (Bolton
  Wanderers FC) BL6. . . . . . .39 D7
Reece Ct 🟦 SK16. . . . . .101 D8
Reece Gordon Gdns BL1 . . .144 A2
Reedbank M26 . . . . .62 A8
Reed Cl WN3. . . . . .55 A4
Reed Ct 🟦 OL1 . . . . .153 E4
Reedham Cl BL1 . . . . .144 C4
Reedham Wlk
  Manchester M40 . . . . .160 A4
  Oldham OL9 . . . . .66 C4
Reed Hill OL16 . . . . .139 C4
Redler Dr M28 . . . . .78 C8
Reedmace Cl M28 . . . . .60 E1
Reedmaker Pl M27 . . . . .79 D8
Reedshaw Bank SK2 . . . . . .124 D5
Reedshaw Rd M9 . . . . .156 C2
Reedsmere Cl WN5 . . . . .54 F6
Reed St
  Manchester M18 . . . . .99 D6
  🟦 Oldham OL1. . . . . .67 A7
Reecham Ave M35. . . . . . . .113 A4
Reecman Cl SK9. . . . . .131 B2
Reeman Ct SK4 . . . . .168 A1
Reepham Cl WN3. . . . . .54 D3
Reeve Cl SK2. . . . . .124 F5
Reeve St M5 . . . . .80 A2
Reeves Rd M21. . . . . .109 B7
Reeves St WN7 . . . . .75 F6
Reeve St WA3 . . . . .91 B8
Reeve Way SK7 . . . . .124 C2
Reform St OL12 . . . . .139 C4
Reform Wlk M11 . . . . .165 B4
Refuge St OL2. . . . . .149 B2
Regaby Gr WN2. . . . . .57 A5
Regal Cl WN2 . . . . .56 B4
Regal Fold OL12. . . . . .15 A4
Regal Wlk 🟦 M40 . . . . .83 C5
Regan Ave M21. . . . . .109 D7
Regan St
  Bolton BL1. . . . . .143 A3
  🖸 Radcliffe M26. . . . . .44 B2
Regatta Cl M7 . . . . .81 B7
Regatta St M6. . . . . .80 F6
Regency Chambers
  BL9. . . . . .140 B2
Regency Cl
  🖸 Glossop SK13. . . . . . . .104 D1

Regency Cl continued
  Manchester M40 . . . . .157 A1
  Oldham OL6. . . . . .66 F4
Regency Ct
  Altrincham WA15. . . . . . . .120 C3
  🖸 Cheadle SK8. . . . . .123 A2
  🟦 Manchester M21 . . . . . . .97 A1
  Rochdale OL11. . . . . .29 F7
  Sale M33. . . . . .107 F4
  Stockport SK2 . . . . .124 A6
  Wigan WN1 . . . . .151 A4
Regency Gdns
  Cheadle SK8 . . . . .131 E8
  Hyde SK14. . . . . .167 C4
Regency Ho 🟦 M1. . . . . . . .163 A4
Regency La M25. . . . . .63 A3
Regency Pk SK9 . . . . .136 F5
Regency Wharf WN7. . . . . . .76 C4
Regent Ave
  Ashton-in-M WN4 . . . . .72 F5
  Manchester M40 . . . . .98 A2
  Walkden M38. . . . . .60 C7
Regent Bank SK9 . . . . .136 F5
Regent Cl
  Bramhall SK7. . . . . .132 D4
  Cheadle SK8 . . . . .123 C4
  Heywood OL10. . . . . .29 B1
  Wilmslow SK9 . . . . .136 F5
Regent Cres
  Failsworth M35. . . . . .83 E6
  Royton OL1, OL2. . . . . .48 D2
Regent Ct
  Altrincham WA15. . . . . . . .119 D4
  Hale WA15. . . . . .129 C8
  Manchester, Broughton Park
  M7 .63 D1
  Manchester SK4 . . . . .111 C5
Regent Cvn Pk M6 . . . . .154 C4
Regent Dr
  Bolton BL6. . . . . .40 B7
  Denton M34. . . . . .100 D1
  Leigh WN7 . . . . .76 D7
  Mossley OL5 . . . . .86 D8
Regent Ho M14. . . . . .98 D3
Regent Pl M14 . . . . .98 C4
Regent Rd
  Altrincham WA14. . . . . . . .119 D4
  Bolton BL6. . . . . .40 B6
  Platt Bridge WN2. . . . . .56 A3
  Salford M5. . . . . .81 A1
  Stockport SK2 . . . . .124 A6
Regents Hill BL6. . . . . .40 C6
Regent Sq M5 . . . . .161 B1
Regent St
  Bury BL9 . . . . .140 C4
  Eccles M30 . . . . .79 F2
  Failsworth M40 . . . . .83 D5
  Glossop, Padfield SK13 . . .104 B5
  Glossop SK13 . . . . .104 D1
  Heywood OL10. . . . . .29 B2
  🟦 Hindley WN2 . . . . .56 D5
  Littleborough OL15 . . . . . . .16 B5
  Middleton M24. . . . . .46 F2
  Newton-le-W WA12. . . . . . .89 A3
  Oldham OL1. . . . . .67 A7
  Ramsbottom BL0. . . . . .11 A4
  Rochdale OL12, OL16 . . . . .15 A1
  Shaw OL2. . . . . .149 B3
  Tyldesley M46. . . . . .74 C8
Regents The SK9. . . . . .137 C8
Regent Trad Est M5. . . . . . .158 B3
Regent Wlk BL4 . . . . .60 D8
Regina Ave SK15 . . . . .86 A2
Regina Cres M9. . . . . .76 E6
Regina Ct M6. . . . . .80 A3
Reginald Latham Ct
  M40 . . . . .160 A3
Reginald St
  Bolton BL3. . . . . .146 A2
  🟦 Droylsden M11. . . . . .99 F7
  Eccles M30 . . . . .95 A8
  Swinton M27 . . . . .61 D1
Reid Cl M34 . . . . .113 A8
Reigate Cl BL8 . . . . .27 B1
Reigate Rd M41 . . . . .106 E8
Reilly St M15. . . . . .162 C2
Reins Lee Ave OL8. . . . . .67 A2
Reins Lee Rd OL7. . . . . .85 A6
Reliance St M40 . . . . .83 C4
Reliance Street Ent Pk 🟦
  M40 . . . . .83 C6
Reliance Trad Est M40 . . . . . .83 C6
Rembrandt Wlk OL11 . . . . . .49 D4
Rena Cl SK4. . . . . .169 A3
Rena Ct SK4. . . . . .169 A3
Rendel Cl
  Newton-le-W WA12. . . . . . .89 D2
  Stretford M32 . . . . .96 D2
Renfrew Cl WN3. . . . . .55 A3
Renfrew Dr BL3 . . . . .40 F3
Renfrew Rd WN2 . . . . .38 D5
Rennie Cl M32. . . . . .96 E2
Renshaw Ave M30 . . . . .79 C1
Renshaw Dr BL9. . . . . .141 C3
Renshaw St
  Altrincham WA14. . . . . . . .119 E5
  Eccles M30 . . . . .79 D1
Renton Rd
  Bolton BL3. . . . . .146 B3
  Stretford M32 . . . . .96 E3
  Wythenshawe M22 . . . . . .121 D4
Renwick Gr BL3 . . . . .146 C3
Renwick Sq WN4 . . . . .72 F3
Repton Ave
  Droylsden M43. . . . . .83 D3

Repton Ave continued
Failsworth M40 . . . . .65 E1
Hyde SK14 . . . . .167 B3
Ince-in-M WN3 . . . . .55 F4
Oldham OL8 . . . . .66 D3
Reddish M34 . . . . .100 A3
Urmston M41. . . . . .94 D2
Repton Cl 6 M33. . . . . .107 D3
Reservoir Gdns M28 . . . . . . .60 D4
Reservoir Rd SK3. . . . . .170 A8
Reservoir St
Aspull WN2 . . . . .38 F3
Ince-in-M WN2 . . . . .56 A8
Rochdale OL16. . . . . .15 C1
Salford M3. . . . . .158 B3
Salford, Seedley M6 . . . . . .154 C2
Residences The WN2 . . . . . .38 D5
Restormel Ave WN2 . . . . . . .38 D5
Retford Ave OL16 . . . . .31 B4
Retford Cl BL8 . . . . .27 C4
Retford St OL4 . . . . .67 B5
Retiro St OL1. . . . . .153 C2
Retreat The
Romiley SK6. . . . . .113 C1
Worsley SK6. . . . . .78 F8
Reuben St M34 . . . . .169 B4
Revers St BL8 . . . . .140 A3
Reveton Gn SK7 . . . . .124 A2
Rex Bldgs SK9. . . . . .137 B6
Reynard Ct 5 M14. . . . . . . .98 E4
Reynard Rd M21. . . . . .109 B7
Reynard St SK14 . . . . .167 A3
Reynell Rd M13. . . . . .98 F2
Reyner St
Ashton-u-L OL6 . . . . .85 E2
Manchester M1 . . . . .163 A4
Reynolds St BL5 . . . . .58 F6
Reynolds Dr
Manchester M18 . . . . .99 D6
Marple SK6 . . . . .126 B8
Over Hulton BL5 . . . . .58 F7
Reynolds Mews SK9 . . . . . .137 E8
Reynolds Rd M16. . . . . .97 C4
Reynold St SK14 . . . . .167 A2
Rhine Cl BL8 . . . . .26 F7
Rhine Dr M8 . . . . .155 B1
Rhine The 11 M15. . . . . . . .162 C3
Rhiwlas Dr BL9 . . . . .44 F8
Rhode Hos SK6. . . . . .125 F3
RHODES 64 B7
Rhodes Ave
Haslingden BB4 . . . . .1 A7
Oldham OL4 . . . . .67 F5
Uppermill OL3 . . . . .51 C1
Rhodes Bank OL1. . . . . .67 A6
Rhodes Bsns Pk M24 . . . . . .64 C7
Rhodes Dr BL9 . . . . .30 F3
Rhodes Dr BL9 . . . . .45 A2
Rhodes Gn M24 . . . . .64 B8
Rhodes Hill OL4 . . . . .67 F5
Rhodes St N SK14 . . . . . . .101 C3
Rhodes St
Dukinfield SK14. . . . . .101 C3
Glossop SK13. . . . . .104 B5
Oldham, County End OL4 . . . .67 F7
Rochdale OL12. . . . . .15 B3
Royton OL2 . . . . .49 A3
Rhode St BL8. . . . . .26 F6
Rhodeswood Dr SK13. . . . .104 A6
Rhos Ave
Cheadle SK8 . . . . .122 E1
Manchester M14 . . . . .110 E8
Middleton M24. . . . . .65 A7
Rhos Dr SK7. . . . . .124 D1
Rhosleigh Ave BL1. . . . . . .143 B4
Rhyddings The BL9 . . . . . . .28 E7
Rialto Gdns M7. . . . . .155 B2
Ribbesford Rd WN3. . . . . . .54 C4
Ribble Ave
Bolton BL2 . . . . .42 E7
Chadderton OL9. . . . . .47 F1
Littleborough OL15 . . . . .15 F6
Ribble Cl WA3. . . . . .91 F2
Ribble Cres WN5 . . . . .71 C3
Ribble Dr
Boothstown M28 . . . . .77 F6
Bury BL9 . . . . .27 F8
Kearsley BL4 . . . . .61 B5
Whitefield M45 . . . . .45 A1
Wigan WN5 . . . . .54 C2
Ribble Drive Com Prim
Sch M45 . . . . .45 A1
Ribble Gr
Heywood OL10. . . . . .29 A3
Leigh WN7 . . . . .75 C5
Ribblehead Ct M26 . . . . . . .61 C8
Ribble Rd
Oldham OL8 . . . . .66 C3
Platt Bridge WN2 . . . . .56 A2
Shevington Moor WN6 . . . . . .19 B2
Ribblesdale Cl OL10 . . . . . . .46 E7
Ribblesdale Dr M40 . . . . . .156 C1
Ribblesdale Rd BL3. . . . . . .147 A4
Ribble St
Britannia OL13. . . . . .4 A8
Rochdale OL11. . . . . .30 E4
Ribbleton Cl BL8 . . . . .26 F1
Ribble Wlk M43 . . . . .100 A8
Ribchester Dr BL9 . . . . .44 D7
Ribchester Gdns WA3. . . . . .92 A3
Ribchester Gr BL2. . . . . .25 E1
Riber Bank 14 SK13 . . . . . .171 B1
Riber Cl 20 SK13 . . . . .171 B1
Riber Fold 18 SK13 . . . . . .171 B1

Riber Gn 19 SK13 . . . . .171 B1
Ribston St M15. . . . . .162 B2
Rice St M3 . . . . .162 B4
Richard Burch St 3
BL9. . . . . .140 C3
Richard Gwyn Cl BL5 . . . . .57 D6
Richard Reynolds Ct
M44 . . . . .105 E6
Richards Cl M34. . . . . .100 F6
Richardson Cl M45 . . . . . . .44 F1
Richardson Rd M30. . . . . . .79 E2
Richardson St
8 Manchester M11 . . . . . . .99 E7
Stockport SK1. . . . . .124 A7
Richards Rd M36. . . . . .19 B3
Richard St
Failsworth M35 . . . . .83 F7
Ince-in-M WN3 . . . . .151 A2
Radcliffe M26 . . . . .43 F3
Ramsbottom BL0 . . . . .11 E7
Rochdale OL11. . . . . .139 C2
Stockport SK1. . . . . .169 C2
Richbell Cl M44. . . . . .105 E7
Richborough Cl M7. . . . . . .155 B1
Richelieus St BL3. . . . . .42 A4
Richmond Ave
Chadderton OL9. . . . . .66 A4
Handforth SK9 . . . . .131 D4
Manchester M25 . . . . .63 C1
Royton OL2 . . . . .48 D4
Urmston M41. . . . . .95 E2
Richmond Cl
Bury BL8 . . . . .26 F6
Culcheth WA3 . . . . .91 D4
Dukinfield SK16. . . . . .101 D6
Glossop SK13. . . . . .104 A5
Lymm WA13. . . . . .117 B4
Mossley OL5 . . . . .86 E8
Rochdale OL16. . . . . .31 C3
Sale M33 . . . . .108 F3
Shaw OL2. . . . . .149 B1
Stalybridge SK15. . . . . .86 A1
Standish WN1. . . . . .37 B7
Whitefield M45 . . . . .62 D7
Richmond Cres OL5. . . . . . .86 E8
Richmond Ct
Altrincham WA14. . . . . .119 B2
Cheadle SK8 . . . . .122 C5
Denton M34. . . . . .100 E6
1 Manchester M13 . . . . . . .98 C4
Salford M3. . . . . .158 A2
Stockport SK2. . . . . .124 D5
Richmond Dr
Leigh WN7 . . . . .76 D7
Lymm WA13. . . . . .117 B4
Swinton M27 . . . . .79 C8
Richmond Gdns
Bolton BL3 . . . . .42 B3
Newton-le-W WA12. . . . . . . .89 C2
Richmond Gn WA14. . . . . .119 B2
Richmond Gr
Bramhall SK7. . . . . .132 F6
Cheadle SK8 . . . . .122 F1
Eccles M30 . . . . .79 E3
Farnworth BL4. . . . . .42 A1
Leigh WN7 . . . . .76 E6
Manchester M13 . . . . .98 C4
Richmond Gr E M12 . . . . . .164 B1
Richmond Hill
Hyde SK14 . . . . .167 C1
Wigan WN5 . . . . .54 C6
Richmond Hill Rd
SK8. . . . . .122 C6
Richmond Ho 7 SK15 . . . . .86 A1
Richmond Pk M14 . . . . .98 D1
Richmond Prim Sch
OL9. . . . . .153 A2
Richmond Rd
Altrincham, Rosehill
WA14 . . . . .119 C2
Altrincham WA14 . . . . .119 D5
Ashton-in-M WN4 . . . . .72 F5
Boothstown M28 . . . . .77 E7
Dukinfield SK16. . . . . .101 D6
Eccles M17 . . . . .96 A7
Failsworth M35. . . . . .84 B8
Hindley WN2 . . . . .57 A3
Manchester, Heaton Mersey
SK4 . . . . .110 F2
Manchester M14 . . . . .110 D8
Reddish M34 . . . . .100 A3
Romiley SK6. . . . . .113 C3
Richmond St
Ashton-u-L OL7 . . . . .84 F3
Atherton M46 . . . . .58 C2
Bury BL9 . . . . .44 E8
Denton M34. . . . . .100 F6
Droylsden M43. . . . . .84 C2
Horwich BL6 . . . . .22 B3
Hyde SK14 . . . . .167 B2
Manchester M1 . . . . .163 A4
Salford M3. . . . . .158 B3
Stalybridge SK15. . . . . .86 C2
Wigan WN1 . . . . .150 B4
Wigan, Worsley Mesnes
WN3 . . . . .150 A1
Richmond Terr SK6. . . . . . .126 B1
Richmond Wlk
Oldham OL9 . . . . .153 A2
Radcliffe M26 . . . . .43 E6
Ricroft Rd SK6 . . . . .114 B3
Riddell Ct M5 . . . . .80 C2
Ridding Ave M22 . . . . .121 E3
Ridding Cl SK2 . . . . .124 D6
Riddings Ct WA15 . . . . . . .119 F8
Riddings Rd
Altrincham WA15. . . . . .119 F2
Sale WA15 . . . . .120 A8

Riders Gate BL9 . . . . .28 F4
Ridge Ave
Altrincham WA15. . . . . .129 D6
Marple SK6 . . . . .126 A4
Standish WN1 . . . . .37 B7
Ridge Cl
Glossop SK13. . . . . .171 B3
Romiley SK6. . . . . .113 F2
Ridge Cres
Marple SK6 . . . . .126 A3
Whitefield M45 . . . . .63 B8
Ridgecroft OL7 . . . . .85 B6
Ridgedale Ctr 3 SK6 . . . .125 F6
Ridgedales The OL11. . . . . .49 E4
Ridgefield Fold SK6 . . . . . .126 A2
Ridgefield M2 . . . . .158 C1
Ridgefield St M35 . . . . .83 E6
Ridge Gr M45 . . . . .63 B8
Ridgegreen M28. . . . . .78 A5
RIDGE HILL 86 A4
Ridge Hill La SK15. . . . . . . .86 A3
Ridge Hill Prim Sch
SK15. . . . . .85 F3
Ridge La OL3 . . . . .51 D5
Ridgemont Ave SK4 . . . . . .168 B2
Ridgemont Wlk 10
M23 . . . . .108 F2
Ridge Pk SK7. . . . . .132 D6
Ridge Rd SK6 . . . . .126 A3
Ridge The SK6. . . . . .126 A3
Ridgeway
Golborne WA3 . . . . .90 E7
Swinton M27 . . . . .62 B2
Wilmslow SK9 . . . . .137 F7
Ridgeway Gates 3
BL1. . . . . .145 C3
Ridgeway Rd WA15 . . . . . .120 C5
Ridgewell Ave 4 WA3 . . . .90 D8
Ridge Wlk M9 . . . . .64 D3
Ridgewood Ave
Chadderton OL9. . . . . .65 E8
Manchester M40 . . . . .157 A1
Ridgewood Cl WN2. . . . . . . .57 C3
Ridgmont Cl BL6 . . . . .22 F7
Ridgmont Dr
Boothstown M28 . . . . .77 F6
Horwich BL6 . . . . .22 F3
Ridgmont Rd SK7. . . . . . . .132 E5
Ridgway BL6 . . . . .21 C2
Ridgway St M40 . . . . .160 A2
Ridgway The
Disley SK12. . . . . .135 C6
Romiley SK6. . . . . .113 A1
Riding Cl
Sale M33 . . . . .108 F4
Tyldesley M29 . . . . .77 D7
Riding Fold M43. . . . . .84 D3
Riding Fold La M28 . . . . . . .79 A5
Riding Gate BL2 . . . . .25 E6
Riding Gate Mews BL2 . . . .25 E6
Riding Head La BL0. . . . . . .11 F8
Riding La WN4 . . . . .73 F5
Ridings Ct BL3 . . . . .51 A2
Ridings Rd SK13. . . . . .103 F5
Ridings St
Manchester M40 . . . . .157 C1
Manchester, Openshaw
M11 . . . . .165 B4
Riding St M3. . . . . .158 B1
Ridings The SK9 . . . . .136 D4
Ridings Way OL9 . . . . .152 B2
Ridley Dr WA14. . . . . .107 E1
Ridley Gr M33 . . . . .108 F3
Ridley St OL4 . . . . .67 A6
Riding Wlk SK14. . . . . .163 A1
Ridling La SK14 . . . . .167 B2
Ridsdale Ave M20 . . . . . . .110 A6
Ridsdale Wlk M6 . . . . .81 A5
Ridyard St
Platt Bridge WN2 . . . . .56 B3
Walkden M38. . . . . .60 C4
Wigan WN5 . . . . .54 E7
Riefield BL1. . . . . .142 B3
Rifle Rd M21, M33. . . . . . . .108 F5
Rifle St OL1 . . . . .153 A7
Riga Rd M14 . . . . .98 C1
Riga St M3 . . . . .159 A2
Rigby Ave
Blackrod BL6 . . . . .21 C2
Radcliffe M26 . . . . .44 C5
Rigby Ct
Bolton BL3 . . . . .147 C4
Rochdale OL12. . . . . .13 E2
Rigby Gr M38 . . . . .59 E4
Rigby La BL2 . . . . .25 C5
Rigby St
Altrincham WA14 . . . . .119 D3
Ashton-in-M WN4 . . . . .73 A3
Bolton BL3. . . . . .147 C4
Golborne WA3 . . . . .90 A8
Hindley WN2 . . . . .56 F6
Salford M7. . . . . .155 A2
Rigby's Yd 6 BL8. . . . . . . .54 B6
Rigby Wlk M7 . . . . .155 B2
Rigel St M40 . . . . .159 C3
Rigton Cl M12 . . . . .165 A1
Riley Cl M33. . . . . .107 B1
Riley Ct 3 BL1. . . . . .143 C1
Riley La WN2 . . . . .38 B7
Riley St WN3 . . . . .151 A4
Riley St M46 . . . . .58 A1
Rileywood Cl SK6. . . . . . . .112 F1
Rilldene Wlk OL11 . . . . .29 D8
Rilston Ave WA3 . . . . .91 D3
Rimington Ave WA3 . . . . . . .74 C1
Rimington Cl WA3 . . . . .91 E3
Rimington Fold M24 . . . . . .46 D3
Rimmer Cl M11 . . . . .160 B1

Rimmington Cl M9 . . . . .65 A2
Rimsdale Cl SK8 . . . . .122 A3
Rimsdale Wlk BL3 . . . . .40 E5
Rimworth Dr M40 . . . . .159 C4
Rindle Rd M29 . . . . .93 C8
Ringcroft Gdns M40 . . . . . .65 B1
Ringford Wlk M40 . . . . . . .157 B1
RINGLEY 61 D7
Ringley Ave WA3 . . . . .73 F1
Ringley Chase M45 . . . . . . .62 E8
Ringley Cl M45. . . . . .62 E8
Ringley Ct M27 . . . . .80 E8
Ringley Dr M45 . . . . .62 D7
RINGLEY FOLD 61 D6
Ringley Gr BL1 . . . . .24 E5
Ringley Hey M45 . . . . .62 D8
Ringley Mdws M26 . . . . . . .61 C7
Ringley Old Brow M26 . . . .61 C7
Ringley Pk M45 . . . . .62 D8
Ringley Rd
Kearsley, Ringley M26 . . . . . .61 D8
Kearsley, Stoneclough
M26 . . . . .61 C8
Whitefield M45 . . . . .62 C7
Ringley Rd W M26 . . . . . . .61 E8
Ringley St M9 . . . . .157 A4
Ringlow Ave M27 . . . . .79 C7
Ringlow Park Rd M27 . . . . .79 C7
Ring Lows La OL12 . . . . . . .15 A4
Ringmer Dr 4 M22 . . . . . .121 C1
Ringmere Ct 7 OL1 . . . . . .153 B4
Ringmore Rd SK7. . . . . . . .124 A2
Ring-o-Bells La SK12. . . . .135 D6
Rings Cl M35 . . . . .83 F6
Ringstead Cl SK9 . . . . .131 D1
Ringstead Dr
Handforth SK9 . . . . .131 D1
Manchester M40 . . . . .159 C3
Ringstone Cl M25. . . . . .63 A3
Ringway Ave WN7 . . . . .75 F8
Ringway Gr M33 . . . . .108 E2
Ringway Prim Sch
M22 . . . . .130 D8
Ringway Rd M22, M90 . . . .130 D7
Ringway Rd W M22,
M90 . . . . .130 D8
Ringway Trad Est
M22 . . . . .130 E8
Ringwood Ave
Compstall SK14 . . . . .114 A8
Droylsden M34. . . . . .84 C1
Hazel Grove SK7 . . . . .124 B1
Hyde SK14 . . . . .102 A1
Manchester M12 . . . . .99 B3
Radcliffe M26 . . . . .44 B3
Ramsbottom BL0 . . . . .11 A4
Ringwood Way OL9 . . . . . .152 C4
Rink St M14 . . . . .110 D7
Ripley Ave
Cheadle SK8 . . . . .132 B5
Stockport SK2. . . . . .124 B4
Ripley Cl
Hazel Grove SK7 . . . . .133 E8
Manchester M4 . . . . .164 A4
Ripley Cres M41 . . . . .94 F5
Ripley Dr
Altrincham WA15. . . . . .75 F6
Wigan WN3 . . . . .54 C4
Ripley St BL2 . . . . .25 B4
Ripley Way M34 . . . . .112 F8
Ripon Ave
Bolton BL1. . . . . .23 F1
Golborne WA3 . . . . .90 D8
1 Manchester M9 . . . . .37 B3
Ripon Cl
Altrincham WA15. . . . . .120 C1
Chadderton OL9. . . . . .152 B2
Little Lever BL3 . . . . .42 F3
Newton-le-W WA12. . . . . . . .89 D5
Radcliffe M26 . . . . .44 D5
Stockport SK1. . . . . .170 C4
5 Whitefield M45. . . . . .44 F1
Ripon Cres M32 . . . . .95 F3
Ripon Dr
Ashton-in-M WN4 . . . . .73 D2
Bolton BL1. . . . . .23 F1
Ripon Gr M33 . . . . .107 F6
Ripon Hall Ave BL0 . . . . . . .11 A4
Ripon Ho M14 . . . . .98 E4
Ripon Rd M32 . . . . .95 F3
Ripon St
Ashton-u-L OL6 . . . . .166 C3
Manchester M15 . . . . .163 A1
Oldham OL1. . . . . .153 A4
Ripon Wlk SK6 . . . . .113 A1
Rippenden Ave M21 . . . . . .97 A2
Rippingham Rd M20 . . . . . .110 B7
Rippleton Rd M22 . . . . . . .121 E4
Ripponden Rd
Denshaw OL3. . . . . .33 D3
Oldham OL1, OL4 . . . . .49 C3
Ripponden St 11 OL1 . . . . .49 C1
Ripton Wlk M9 . . . . .64 D3
Risbury Wlk 8 M40. . . . . . .83 C6
Rises The SK3 . . . . .103 F5
Rise The
Oldham OL4 . . . . .67 F7
Wigan WN6 . . . . .36 C3
Rishton Ave BL3 . . . . .147 C2
Rishton La BL3 . . . . .147 C3
Rishworth Cl SK2 . . . . .124 D5
Rishworth Dr M40 . . . . .83 E8
Rishworth Rise OL2. . . . . . .32 A1
Rising La OL8 . . . . .66 E2
Rising Lane Cl OL8 . . . . . . .66 E2
Risings The SK22 . . . . .127 B1
Risley Ave M9 . . . . .64 D1
Risley St OL11 . . . . .153 C4

Rissington Ave M23. . . . . .121 B6
Rita Ave 4 M14 . . . . .98 B3
Ritson Cl M18 . . . . .165 B2
Riva Rd M19. . . . . .110 D2
Riverbank OL3. . . . . .50 F1
Riverbank Dr BL8. . . . . . . .140 A3
Riverbank Gdn BL8 . . . . . .140 A3
Riverbank Lawns M3 . . . . .158 B3
Riverbanks BL2. . . . . .148 C1
Riverbank The M26. . . . . . . .61 A8
Riverbank Twr M3 . . . . . . .158 B3
Riverbank Wlk SK13. . . . . .116 F7
Riverbank Wlk M26. . . . . . .109 C4
Riverbend Ave M40 . . . . . .107 C1
Riverdale Cl M36. . . . . .36 D4
Riverdale Rd M9. . . . . .64 B3
River La M31. . . . . .105 F4
Rivermead OL16 . . . . .32 B3
Rivermead Ave WA15 . . . .129 C7
Rivermead Ct M34 . . . . . . .113 A7
Rivermead Rd M34 . . . . . .113 B7
Rivermead Way M45. . . . . . .63 A8
Riverpark Rd M40 . . . . .83 A3
River Pl
Manchester M15 . . . . .162 B3
Milnrow OL16 . . . . .31 F6
Riversdale M25 . . . . .63 A3
Riversdale Dr OL8 . . . . .67 A1
Riversdale Rd SK8 . . . . . . .122 C5
Riversdale View SK6 . . . . .113 A5
Rivers Edge The OL12. . . . . .4 C1
Rivershill M33. . . . . .108 A6
Rivershill Dr OL10 . . . . .29 B1
Rivershill Gdns WA15 . . . .129 D6
Riverside
Bolton BL1. . . . . .25 A2
Chadderton OL1. . . . . .47 E1
Dukinfield SK16. . . . . .166 C1
Salford M7 . . . . .158 A3
Riverside Ave
Irlam M44 . . . . .94 B1
Manchester M21 . . . . .109 D3
Wigan WN1 . . . . .37 D1
Riverside Bsns Pk
SK9. . . . . .137 B7
Riverside Cl SK13. . . . . . . .104 D1
Riverside Ct
Manchester M20 . . . . .109 F3
Whitworth OL12. . . . . .4 D4
Riverside Dr
Kearsley M26. . . . . .61 B8
Ramsbottom BL9 . . . . .11 B2
Rochdale OL16. . . . . .15 C2
Urmston M41. . . . . .107 B8
Riverside Gdns M33 . . . . .108 A6
Riverside Ho OL3 . . . . .69 B8
Riverside Lo M20 . . . . .109 F3
Riverside Mews M15 . . . . .162 B3
Riverside Rd M26 . . . . .44 D4
Riverside Wlk B8m 1 A7
Riverside Works BL2. . . . .148 B4
Rivers La M41. . . . . .95 C5
Riverslegil Cl BL1. . . . . .23 F7
Riversmeade
Bolton BL7. . . . . .25 C7
Leigh WN7 . . . . .76 A6
Rivers St WN5. . . . . .53 E6
River St
Bolton BL2. . . . . .148 A2
Heywood OL10. . . . . .29 D3
Manchester, Ardwick
M12 . . . . .163 C4
Manchester M15 . . . . .162 C3
Radcliffe M26 . . . . .44 B2
Ramsbottom BL0 . . . . .138 C2
Rochdale OL16. . . . . .139 C3
Stockport SK1. . . . . .112 B3
Wilmslow SK9 . . . . .137 B8
Riverstone Bridge
OL15. . . . . .16 B5
Riverstone Dr M23. . . . . . .120 D7
Riverton Rd M20 . . . . .122 B8
Riverview SK4. . . . . .110 F1
River View SK5 . . . . .112 A7
River View Cl M25 . . . . .62 F2
Riverview Cotts 2
SK13. . . . . .116 C7
Riverview Ct
Oldham OL5 . . . . .68 C1
Salford M7 . . . . .81 C8
Riverview Wlk BL1. . . . . . .145 A2
River Way WN1. . . . . .150 C4
Riviera Cl OL12 . . . . .13 C2
Rivington M6. . . . . .80 C4
Rivington Ave
Adlington PR6 . . . . .21 B7
Golborne WA3 . . . . .74 C1
Pendlebury M27 . . . . .80 C8
Platt Bridge WN2. . . . . .56 A3
Wigan WN1 . . . . .37 B2
Rivington & Blackrod High
Sch BL6 . . . . .22 B6
Rivington & Blackrod High
Sch (Annexe) BL6 . . . . . . .22 A7
Rivington Cres M27. . . . . . .80 C7
Rivington Ct M45 . . . . .62 C7
Rivington Ctry Pk*
BL6. . . . . .22 A8
Rivington Dr
Bickershaw WN2 . . . . .74 F8
Bury BL8 . . . . .27 A1
Shaw OL2. . . . . .49 D7
Up Holland WN8 . . . . .53 C7
Rivington Gr
Droylsden M34. . . . . .100 C8
Irlam M44 . . . . .105 C6
Rivington Hall Cl BL0 . . . . .11 C4

Rivington La
Adlington PR6 . . . . .21 D6
Horwich BL6 . . . . .22 A7
Rivington Pl PR7 . . . . . . .19 D6
Rivington Rd
Altrincham WA15. . . . . . . .119 F2
Oldham OL4 . . . . .68 A7
Salford M6. . . . . .80 C4
Rivington St
Atherton M46 . . . . .58 B2
Blackrod BL6 . . . . .21 D2
Oldham OL1 . . . . .48 F1
Rochdale OL12. . . . . .14 F1
Rivington Way WN6. . . . . . .36 F8
Rivington Wlk M12 . . . . .164 C1
Rixson St OL4 . . . . .49 D2
Rix St BL1. . . . . .143 B2
Rixton Cl M16 . . . . .97 B3
Rixton Dr M29. . . . . .77 B8
Rixtonleys Dr M44 . . . . . .59 E1
RL Hughes Prim Sch
. . . . .73 A3
Roach Bank Rd BL9. . . . . .45 B7
Roach Ct M40 . . . . .159 C4
ROACHES 68 D3
Roaches Ind Est OL5. . . . . .68 E4
Roaches Mews OL5. . . . . .68 D3
Roaches Way OL5 . . . . . . .68 E3
Roach Gn WN1 . . . . .37 E1
Roachill Cl WA14 . . . . . . .119 B5
Roach Pl OL16. . . . . .31 A8
Roach St
Bury, Blackford Bridge
BL9 . . . . .44 F4
Bury, Heap Bridge BL9. . . .141 C2
Roach Vale OL16. . . . . . . .15 C2
Roachwood Cl OL9 . . . . . .65 E7
Roading Brook Rd BL2. . . .26 B3
Road Knowl OL2. . . . . . .149 C2
Road La OL12 . . . . .14 C4
Roads Ford Ave OL16 . . . .31 F7
Roadside Ct WA3 . . . . . . .90 C8
Roaring Gate La
WA15 . . . . .120 E2
Robert Hall St M5 . . . . . .161 B4
Robert Harrison Ave
M20 . . . . .109 F6
Robert Lawrence Ct
M41 . . . . .95 A1
Robert Malcolm Cl
M40 . . . . .157 A1
Robert Owen Gdns
M22 . . . . .121 D8
Robert Owen St M43. . . . .84 C2
Robert Salt Ct WA14 . . . .119 E6
Roberts Ave M14. . . . . . . .98 B4
Robert Saville Ct OL11 . . .30 C6
Robertscroft Cl M22. . . . .121 C3
Robertshaw Ave M21 . . . .109 B6
Robertshaw St WN7 . . . . .75 E7
Robertson St M26 . . . . . . .44 A4
Roberts St M30. . . . . .79 D1
Robert St
Bolton BL2. . . . . .25 E5
Bury BL8 . . . . .27 C3
Dukinfield, Kingston
SK14. . . . . .101 C3
Dukinfield SK16. . . . . .101 B8
6 Failsworth M35 . . . . . . .66 A1
2 Heywood OL10. . . . . . . .46 E8
Manchester M3 . . . . .158 C3
Oldham OL8. . . . . .66 B3
Platt Bridge WN2. . . . . .56 A3
Prestwich M25. . . . . .63 C4
Radcliffe M26 . . . . .44 C3
Ramsbottom BL0 . . . . .1 C1
15 Rochdale OL16. . . . . . .31 A8
Sale M33 . . . . .108 E4
Tyldesley M46 . . . . .58 A4
Robeson Way M22,
SK8. . . . . .121 F6
Robe Wlk 5 M18. . . . . . . .99 D6
Robin Cl BL4 . . . . .59 F7
Robin Croft SK6 . . . . . . .112 D3
Robin Dr M44 . . . . .94 A3
Robin Hill Dr WN6 . . . . . . .19 B2
Robin Hill La WN6 . . . . . . .19 C3
ROBIN HOOD 18 C4
Robin Hood Ave M19 . . . . .18 B3
Robin Hood St M8 . . . . . .155 C4
Robinia Cl M30. . . . . .54 F7
Robin Park Rd WN5 . . . . . .54 F8
Robin Pk WN5. . . . . .54 F8
Robin Rd
Ramsbottom BL9 . . . . .11 B2
Sale WA14 . . . . .107 C1
Robinsbay Rd M22. . . . . .130 E8
Robins Cl
Bramhall SK7. . . . . .132 E7
Droylsden M43. . . . . .84 C3
Robins La WA3 . . . . .91 D2
Robin's La
Billinge WA11 . . . . .71 A8
Bramhall SK7. . . . . .132 D7
Robinson Pk SK15 . . . . . . .85 E1
Robinson's St OL6 . . . . . .166 B4
Robinson St
Chadderton OL9. . . . . .152 B2
Dukinfield SK15. . . . . .101 E8
16 Horwich BL6. . . . . .22 B4
Hyde SK14. . . . . .167 C3
Leigh WN7 . . . . .76 A4
Rochdale OL16. . . . . .15 A1
Stockport SK3 . . . . .170 A3
13 Tyldesley M29 . . . . . . .59 A1
Robin St OL1 . . . . .153 B4
Robinsway WA14 . . . . . . .119 C1
Robinswood Rd M22 . . . . .121 D2

Robinwood Lo 30
SK13. . . . . .171 B1
Rob La WA12 . . . . .89 E5
Robson Ave M41. . . . . . . .95 E7
Robson Pl WN2. . . . . .74 B8
Robson St OL1 . . . . .153 C2
Robson Way 3 WA3. . . . . .90 F8
Roby Ct M1 . . . . .159 B1
ROBY MILL 35 B3
Roby Mill WN8 . . . . .35 B3
Roby Rd M30. . . . . .95 C8
Roby St M1 . . . . .159 B1
Roby Well Way WN5 . . . . .71 D5
Roch Ave OL10 . . . . .29 A2
Roch Bank M9 . . . . .63 F3
Rochbury Cl OL11 . . . . . . .29 F6
Roch Cl M45 . . . . .45 B1
Roch Cres M45 . . . . .45 C1
ROCHDALE 30 D7
. . . . .139 A3
Rochdale AFC (Spotland
Stadium) OL11 . . . . .30 C8
Rochdale Exchange Sh Ctr
OL16. . . . . .139 C3
Rochdale Ho M15. . . . . . .162 B3
Rochdale Infmy OL12 . . . .14 F1
Rochdale La
Heywood OL10. . . . . .29 D2
Royton OL2 . . . . .48 D5
Rochdale Old Rd BL9 . . . . .28 D4
**Rochdale Pioneers Mus*
OL12 . . . . .139 C4
Rochdale Rd
Britannia OL13. . . . . .4 B8
Bury BL9 . . . . .141 B2
Denshaw OL3. . . . . .33 B3
Edenfield BL0. . . . . .1 F2
Heywood OL10. . . . . .29 D2
Littleborough OL15, HX6. . . .7 E1
Manchester, Collyhurst M40,
M8, M9 . . . . .159 C2
Manchester M9 . . . . .64 D3
Middleton M24, OL11 . . . . .47 C4
Milnrow OL16 . . . . .31 E7
Oldham, Cold Hurst
OL1 . . . . .153 B4
Oldham OL1 . . . . .48 E1
Ramsbottom BL0 . . . . .12 B7
Royton OL2 . . . . .48 D6
Shaw, High Crompton OL2,
OL16. . . . . .48 F8
Shaw OL2. . . . . .149 B3
Walsden OL14 . . . . .6 B6
Rochdale Rd E OL10 . . . . .29 E3
Rochdale Sta OL11 . . . . .139 C2
Roche Gdns SK8. . . . . . . .132 B6
Roche Rd BL0 . . . . .50 E5
Rochester Ave
Bolton BL2. . . . . .25 E1
Manchester M21 . . . . .109 D6
Manchester, Sedgley Park
M25 . . . . .63 C2
Walkden M28. . . . . .60 C1
Rochester Cl
Ashton-u-L SK14. . . . . .85 C7
Dukinfield SK16. . . . . .102 A7
Golborne WA3 . . . . .90 A8
Rochester Dr WA14 . . . . .107 E1
Rochester Gr SK7. . . . . . .124 E3
Rochester Rd M41. . . . . . .95 D4
Rochester Way OL9. . . . .152 B2
Rochford Ave M45 . . . . . . .62 D7
Rochford Cl M45 . . . . .62 D7
Rochford Ho M34. . . . . . .100 E6
Rochford Rd M30. . . . . . . .94 F8
Roch Mills Cres OL11 . . . .30 C5
Roch Mills Gdns
OL11. . . . . .139 A1
Roch Pl WN2. . . . . .55 F2
Roch St OL16. . . . . .15 B1
Roch Vale Cvn Pk
OL16. . . . . .31 A7
Roch Valley Way OL11. . . .30 C5
Roch Way M45 . . . . .45 B1
Roch Wlk M45 . . . . .45 B1
Rockall Wlk M11 . . . . . . .160 C1
Rock Ave BL1 . . . . .142 C2
Rockbourne Cl 7
. . . . .56 D4
Rockdove Ave M15 . . . . . .162 C3
Rocket Way M3. . . . . . . .158 A1
Rockfield Dr 6 M9 . . . . . .157 B4
Rock Fold BL7. . . . . .8 F1
Rock Nook OL15. . . . . .6 D1
Rock Rd
Urmston M41. . . . . .95 C2
Warmley M28. . . . . .78 B2
Rock St
Ashton-u-L OL7 . . . . .85 A5
Droylsden M11. . . . . .99 E8
Golborne WA3 . . . . .74 A2
3 Heywood OL10. . . . . . . .29 E1
Horwich BL6 . . . . .22 C4
Hyde SK14 . . . . .113 E7

Rock St continued
Oldham OL1 . . . . .153 C3
Radcliffe M26 . . . . .44 B2
Ramsbottom BL0 . . . . .11 E7
Salford M7. . . . . .155 A2
Rock Terr
Bolton BL1 . . . . .8 F1
Mossley OL5 . . . . .68 D3
Rock The
Bury BL9 . . . . .140 C3
Bury BL9 . . . . .140 C3
Rocky Bank Terr
. . . . .151 B1
Rocky La M27, M30. . . . . .79 D4
Roda St M9 . . . . .157 C3
Rodborough Rd M23. . . . .121 A3
Rodeheath Cl SK9 . . . . . .137 D7
Rodenhurst Dr 15 M40. . . .83 A7
Rodepool Cl SK9 . . . . . . .131 D2
Rodgers Cl BL5. . . . . .57 E6
Rodgers Way BL5. . . . . . . .57 E6
Rodmell Ave M40. . . . . . .157 A1
Rodmell Cl BL7. . . . . .24 F7
Rodmill Ct M14. . . . . .98 C1
Rodmill Dr SK8. . . . . .122 A4
Rodney Ct 7 M4. . . . . . . .159 C3
Rodney Dr SK6. . . . . .113 A5
Rodney St
Ashton-u-L OL6 . . . . .85 D4
Atherton M46 . . . . .58 C2
Manchester M4 . . . . .159 C2
Rochdale OL11. . . . . .30 B1
Salford M3. . . . . .158 A1
Wigan WN1 . . . . .150 C3
Roeacre Bsns Pk OL10. . . .29 E2
Roeacre St OL10. . . . . . . .29 E2
Roebuck Gdns 6
M33 . . . . .108 A4
Roebuck La
Oldham OL4 . . . . .50 A3
Sale M33 . . . . .108 A4
Roebuck Low OL4 . . . . . . .50 A3
Roebuck St WN7 . . . . .57 C3
Roeburn Wlk M45 . . . . . . .63 C8
Roecliffe Cl WN3. . . . . . .150 B2
Roe Cross Gn SK14 . . . . .102 F5
Roe Cross Ind Est
SK14. . . . . .103 A5
Roe Cross Rd SK14,
SK15. . . . . .103 A5
Roedean Gdns M41. . . . . . .94 D2
Roefield Terr OL12 . . . . . .30 C8
Roe Gn M28 . . . . .79 A8
ROE GREEN 79 A8
Roe Green Ave M28. . . . . .79 A8
Roe La OL4 . . . . .67 D5
Roe St
Manchester M4 . . . . .159 C3
Rochdale OL12. . . . . .14 C1
Rogate Dr M23 . . . . .121 A3
Roger Byrne Cl M40 . . . . . .83 B5
Roger Cl SK6. . . . . .112 F2
Roger Hay 6 SK8 . . . . . .123 A2
Rogerson Cl WA15. . . . . .120 C7
Roger St M8 . . . . .159 A3
Rogerstead BL3 . . . . .144 C2
Rogerton Cl WN7. . . . . . . .76 B4
Rokeby Ave
Golborne WA3 . . . . .74 D1
Stretford M32 . . . . .96 D1
Rokeden WA12. . . . . .89 D4
Roker Ave M13 . . . . .98 F2
Roker Ind Est OL1 . . . . . . .67 B7
Roker Park Ave M34 . . . .100 D7
Roland Rd
2 Bolton BL3. . . . . .146 C4
Reddish SK5. . . . . .111 F7
Rolla St M3 . . . . .158 B2
Rollesby Cl BL8. . . . . .27 D5
Rolleston Ave M40. . . . . .160 A2
Rollins La SK6. . . . . .114 A1
Rolls Cres M15 . . . . .162 B1
Rollswood Dr M40. . . . . . .83 A6
Romana Sq WA14. . . . . . .119 E8
Roman Cl
Newton-le-W WA12. . . . . . .89 C2
Wigan WN3 . . . . .53 F4
Roman Rd
Ashton-in-M WN4 . . . . .73 A5
Manchester M25 . . . . .63 A1
Oldham M35, OL8 . . . . .66 B1
Royton OL2 . . . . .48 E3
Stockport SK4 . . . . .169 B2
Roman St
Ashton-u-L OL7 . . . . .166 A1
Manchester M4 . . . . .159 A1
Mossley OL5 . . . . .68 D3
8 Radcliffe M26. . . . . .43 E3
Romer Ave 3 M40. . . . . . .65 E1
Rome Rd M40 . . . . .159 C3
Romer St BL2 . . . . .148 C3
Romford Ave
Denton M34. . . . . .101 A4
Leigh WN7 . . . . .75 F6
Romford Cl OL9 . . . . .153 B1
Romford Pl WN2 . . . . .56 E5
Romford Rd M33 . . . . . . .107 E6
Romford St WN2 . . . . .56 E5
Romford Wlk M9 . . . . .64 A3
ROMILEY 113 D2
Romiley Cres BL2. . . . . . . .42 D8
Romiley Dr BL2. . . . . .42 D8
Romiley Prec SK6 . . . . . .113 C3
Romiley Prim Sch
SK6. . . . . .113 C2
Romiley Sq WN6. . . . . . . .36 E8

Romiley St
Salford M6. . . . . .80 D5
Stockport SK1 . . . . .112 B3
Romiley Sta SK6. . . . . . . .113 C2
Romiley Rd M41. . . . . .95 D4
Romney Chase BL1 . . . . .143 B4
Romney Rd BL1 . . . . .23 E2
Romney St
Ashton-u-L OL6 . . . . .166 C3
Manchester M40 . . . . .83 A8
Salford M6. . . . . .81 B5
Romney Twrs SK5. . . . . . .112 B6
Romney Way
Brinnington SK5. . . . . .112 B6
Wigan WN1 . . . . .37 B3
Romney Wlk OL9 . . . . . . .152 B2
Romney 9 OL12 . . . . .139 B4
Romsey Ave M24 . . . . .46 F3
Romsey Dr SK8 . . . . .132 C6
Romsey Gdns M23. . . . . .121 A6
Romsey Gr WN3 . . . . .54 D2
Romsley Cl M12. . . . . . . .165 A2
Romsley Dr BL3 . . . . .146 C3
Rona Cl M12 . . . . .164 C1
Ronald St
Droylsden M11, M43. . . . . .83 D1
Oldham OL4 . . . . .67 C7
Rochdale OL11. . . . . .30 C1
Ronan Ct SK4. . . . . .168 B4
Rondin Cl M12 . . . . .164 B3
Rondin Rd M12. . . . . .164 B4
Ronnis Mount OL7. . . . . . .85 A7
Ronton Wlk M8. . . . . . . .156 C4
Roocroft Ct BL1 . . . . .143 A1
Roocroft St BL5 . . . . .57 D6
Rooden Ct M25. . . . . .63 C4
Roods La OL11 . . . . .13 C1
Rookery Ave
Appley Bridge WN6 . . . . . . .35 E8
Ashton-in-M WN4 . . . . .73 B2
Droylsden M18. . . . . .99 F6
Rookery Cl SK15. . . . . . . .102 E7
Rookerypool Cl SK9 . . . . .131 D2
Rookery The M40 . . . . . . .89 D4
Rookfield M33. . . . . .108 C5
Rookfield Ave M33. . . . . .108 C5
Rookley Wlk 11 M14 . . . . .98 C3
Rook St
Manchester M14. . . . . . . .162 B1
Oldham OL4 . . . . .67 C5
Ramsbottom BL0 . . . . .138 C2
Rookswood Dr OL11 . . . . . .30 B3
Rookway M24 . . . . .65 A7
Rookwood OL1, OL9 . . . . . .47 E1
Rookwood Ave M23. . . . . .120 F7
Rookwood Hill SK7 . . . . . .123 E1
Rooley Moor Rd
Bacup OL12, OL13 . . . . .3 C4
Rochdale OL12. . . . . .14 A3
Rooley St OL12. . . . . .14 C1
Roosevelt Rd BL4. . . . . . . .60 F7
Rooth St SK4 . . . . .169 A2
Ropefield Way OL12 . . . . .14 E3
Rope Ct OL12 . . . . .139 C4
Rope Wlk M3. . . . . .158 B3
Ropeworks The 13
M15 . . . . .162 C3
Ropley Wlk 4 M9 . . . . . . .64 F1
Rosa Gr M7 . . . . .155 A2
Rosalind Ct M5. . . . . . . .161 C4
Rosamond Dr M3. . . . . . .158 A2
Rosamond St W M13,
M15 . . . . .163 A2
Rosamond St BL3. . . . . . .146 C4
Rosary Cl OL8 . . . . .67 A1
Rosary Rd OL8 . . . . .67 A1
Roscoe Ave WA12 . . . . . . .89 E3
Roscoe Ct BL5. . . . . .57 F7
Roscoe Lowe Brow
PR6 . . . . .21 D7
Roscoe Rd M44. . . . . .93 E1
Roscoe St
Oldham OL1 . . . . .67 A6
Stockport SK3 . . . . .170 A4
Wigan WN1 . . . . .151 B3
Roscow Ave BL2 . . . . .42 E8
Roscow Rd BL4. . . . . .61 A7
Rose Acre M28 . . . . .78 B7
Roseacre Ct B2. . . . . . . .148 C4
Roseacre Dr SK8 . . . . . . .122 C1
Rose Ave
Abram Brow WN2. . . . . . . .74 B7
Farnworth BL4. . . . . .42 C1
Irlam M44 . . . . .93 F1
Littleborough OL15 . . . . . . .15 F3
Rochdale OL15. . . . . .13 D2
Wigan WN6 . . . . .37 B4
Rosebank
Bolton BL6. . . . . .40 C7
Edenfield BL0. . . . . .1 D1
Rosebank Cl BL2. . . . . . . .26 A6
Rose Bank Cl
Hollingworth SK14. . . . . . .103 D5
Wigan WN1 . . . . .37 B4
Rosebank Rd
Failsworth M40 . . . . .83 B4
Irlam M44 . . . . .105 C4
Rosebay Cl OL2 . . . . .49 B1
Roseberry Ave 4 OL6 . . . .85 E1
Roseberry Cl BL0 . . . . . . .11 C3
Roseberry Rd WN4 . . . . . . .73 A1
Roseberry St
Bolton BL3 . . . . .146 C4

Roseberry St continued
Oldham OL8. . . . . .153 A2
Stockport SK2 . . . . .124 D4
Rosebery St
Manchester M14 . . . . .97 F3
Westhoughton BL5 . . . . . . .57 F8
ROSE BRIDGE 151 C4
Rosebridge Ct WN1 . . . . .151 C4
Rose Bridge High Sch
WN1. . . . . .151 C4
Rosebridge Way
WN1. . . . . .151 C4
Rosebury Ave WN7 . . . . . .76 B5
Rose Cottage Rd M14,
M20 . . . . .110 B8
Rose Cotts 14 M14. . . . . .110 D8
Rose Cres WN3 . . . . .93 F1
Rosecroft Cl SK3 . . . . . . .123 E4
Rose Ct WN1 . . . . .151 C4
Rosedale Ave
Atherton M46 . . . . .58 D3
Bolton BL1. . . . . .24 E5
Golborne WA3 . . . . .90 C7
Rosedale Cl OL11 . . . . . . .48 B1
Rosedale Ct M34 . . . . . . .100 E3
Rosedale Dr WN7. . . . . . . .76 C5
Rosedale Rd
Manchester M14 . . . . .98 A2
Reddish SK4 . . . . .111 D5
Reddish SK4 . . . . .169 A4
Rosedale Way SK16. . . . .101 C6
Rosefield Cl SK3. . . . . . . .170 B1
Rosefield Cres OL16 . . . . .31 C7
Rosegarth Ave M20 . . . . .109 D4
Rose Gr
Bury BL8 . . . . .27 A2
Kearsley BL4 . . . . .60 F7
Rosehay Ave M34. . . . . . .100 F2
Rose Hey La M35 . . . . . . .83 E4
ROSEHILL 119 C2
ROSE HILL
Ashton-in-Makerfield. 72 F7
Bolton 148 A1
Rose Hill
Bolton BL1. . . . . .148 A1
Delph OL3. . . . . .50 F4
Denton M34. . . . . .100 E3
Ramsbottom BL0 . . . . .138 B2
Stalybridge SK15. . . . . . . .102 A8
Rose Hill Ave
Failsworth M40 . . . . .83 B4
Wigan WN5. . . . . .54 C6
Rosehill Cl M6 . . . . .154 C2
Rose Hill Cl
Ashton-u-L. 85 F5
Rose Hill Cres OL6. . . . . . .85 F5
Rosehill Ct
Oldham OL4 . . . . .67 B8
Salford M6. . . . . .154 C2
Rose Hill Dr BL2. . . . . .25 A7
Rose Hill Marple Sta
SK6. . . . . .125 E6
Rosehill Methodist Com
Prim Sch OL6. . . . . .85 F6
Rose Hill Rd M27. . . . . . . .61 F2
Rose Hill St OL6 . . . . .85 F5
Rose Hill St OL10 . . . . . . .29 B2
Rose Hill View WN4 . . . . . .72 F7
Rose La SK6. . . . . .125 E6
Roseland Ave M20 . . . . . .110 B8
Roseland Dr M25 . . . . . . .63 C6
Roselands Ave M33. . . . . .107 F2
Rose Lea BL2. . . . . .25 E4
Roseleigh Ave M19 . . . . .110 F7
Rose Leigh M41. . . . . .95 D2
Rose Mount M24. . . . . . . .46 F2
Rosemount Cres
SK14. . . . . .101 D5
Roseneath SK7 . . . . .123 D1
Roseneath Ave M19. . . . . .99 C1
Roseneath Gr BL3 . . . . . .147 A3
Roseneath Rd
Bolton BL3 . . . . .147 A3
Urmston M41. . . . . .95 C2
Rosen Sq OL9 . . . . .152 B3
Rose St
Bolton BL2. . . . . .148 A1
Chadderton OL9. . . . . .66 A3
Hindley WN2 . . . . .56 D5
Middleton M24. . . . . .65 D8
Reddish SK5. . . . . .169 C3
Wigan WN1 . . . . .151 C4
Rose Terr WN5. . . . . .86 A1
Rose Thorns 5 M24 . . . . . .46 F4
Rose Vale WN7. . . . . .76 C5
Rose Vale Sch SK8 . . . . . .122 B1
Rosevale Ave M19 . . . . . .110 E5
Roseville Mews M33. . . . .108 B4
Roseway SK7. . . . . .123 F2

Rosewell Cl M40........ 160 A4
Rose Wlk
  Marple SK6...........125 E6
  5 Partington M31 .....105 E3
Rosewood
  Rochdale OL11........13 E1
  Westhoughton BL5 .....57 D6
Rose Wood M34 ....100 D3
Rosewood Ave
  Bury BL8 ....27 A6
  Droylsden M43.......84 C3
  Stockport SK4 ....168 A1
Rosewood Cl
  Abram Brow WN2 .....74 B7
  Dukinfield SK16.......101 D6
Rosewood Cres OL9 .....48 B1
Rosewood Ct SK2.......124 C5
Rosewood Gdns
  6 Sale M33..........108 F3
  Wythenshawe SK8....121 F6
Rosewood Rd M9........64 E5
Rosewood Wlk M23.....120 C8
Rosford Ave M14 ......98 B2
Rosgill Cl M14........110 E2
Rosgill Dr M24 ....46 D1
Rosgill Wlk M18 .....165 C1
Rosina Cl M11........72 F6
Rosina St M11........99 F7
Rosley Rd M9.........55 B3
Roslin Gdns BL1......142 C3
Roslin St M11........83 D2
Roslyn Ave M41......94 E1
Roslyn Rd SK3.......170 B1
Rossall Ave
  5 Radcliffe M26.......44 C1
  Stretford M32 ....96 C3
Rossall Cl BL2........148 C4
Rossall Cres WN7.....76 A3
Rossall Dr SK7.......132 E6
Rossall Dr SK7.......132 E6
Rossall Rd
  Bolton BL2...........148 C4
  Rochdale OL12........15 A2
Rossall St 1 BL2......148 C4
Rossall Way M6.......81 A3
Ross Ave
  Manchester M19 ....98 F1
  Oldham OL9...........65 F4
  Stockport SK3 ....170 B1
  Whitefield M45 ....62 F6
Ross Cl
  Billinge WN5 ....71 E6
  Wigan WN2 ....37 F2
Rossdale Gr WN6.......37 A7
Ross Dr M27 ....61 E4
Rossenclough Rd
  SK9................131 D1
Rossendale Ave 6 M9...64 F1
Rossendale Cl OL2......49 D7
Rossendale Rd SK8.....131 C8
  Rossendale Sch BL0 ....12 A7
Rossendale Way OL2....149 B4
Rossett Ave
  Sale WA15 ....120 A8
  1 Wythenshawe M22...120 D8
Rossett Cl M33........54 D2
Rossett Dr M41.......95 A4
Rossetti Wlk 4 M34...113 A7
Ross Gr M41 ....95 C2
Rosshill Wlk 20 M15...162 A2
Rossington St M40......83 D5
Rossini St BL1........143 A3
Rosslare Rd M22.......121 E2
Ross Lave La M34......100 C1
Rosslave Wlk SK5......112 C7
Rosslyn Gr WA15......120 A6
Rosslyn Rd
  Cheadle SK8..........122 D1
  Manchester M16 ....97 A2
  Manchester, Moston
    M40................65 A1
Rossmere Ave OL11.....30 C6
Rossmill La WA15......129 B7
Ross St OL8...........153 A1
Rostherne Ave
  Golborne WA3 ....90 D8
  High Lane SK6........134 E8
  Manchester, Fallowfield
    M14................98 A1
  Manchester, Old Trafford
    M16................97 C3
Rostherne Ct 3
  WA14................119 D3
Rostherne Gdns BL3....146 B4
Rostherne Rd
  Sale M33............108 F3
  Stockport SK3 ....170 B1
  Wilmslow SK9........136 F4
Rostherne St
  1 Altrincham WA14 ...119 D3
  1 Salford M6........154 B1
Rosthernmere Rd
  SK8................122 F4
Rosthwaite Cl
  Middleton M24........46 C1
  Wigan WN3 ....55 A2
Rosthwaite Gr WA11....71 B1
Roston Ct M7.........155 B4
Roston Rd M7.........155 B4
Rostrevor Rd SK3......170 B1
Rostron Ave M12......164 B2
Rostron Rd BL0.......138 B2
Rostron St 8 M19......99 B1
Rothay Cl
  Bolton BL2...........25 F1

Rothay Cl continued
  Prestwich M45........63 C8
Rothay Dr
  Middleton M24........46 E3
  Reddish SK5.........111 F8
Rothay St WN7.......76 B4
Rothbury Ave OL7.....84 C5
Rothbury Cl BL8.......26 F2
Rothbury Ct BL3......146 B3
Rotherby Rd M22.....121 E5
Rotherdale Ave
  WA15...............120 D5
Rotherhead Cl BL6.....21 F2
Rothermere Wlk 5
  M23................120 E7
Rotherwood Ave M32...96 E3
Rotherwood Rd SK9...136 D6
Rothesay Ave SK16.....101 C7
Rothesay Cres M33....107 C2
Rothesay Rd
  Bolton BL3...........146 B3
  Manchester M8 ....63 E2
  Oldham OL1..........49 C1
  Pendlebury M27.......80 C7
Rothesay Terr OL16.....31 C4
Rothiemay Rd M41.....94 E2
Rothman Cl M22.......121 D5
Rothman Cl M40.......83 C6
Rothwell Cres M38......59 E5
Rothwell La M38.......59 E5
Rothwell Rd
  Adlington PR6.........21 B7
  Golborne WA3 ....74 C1
Rothwell St
  Bolton BL3...........145 B1
  Failsworth M35.......83 F7
  Failsworth, Newton Heath
    M40................83 C6
  Ramsbottom BL0......138 B2
  Rochdale OL12........15 B1
  Royton OL2..........48 D3
  Walkden M28.........60 F3
Rottingdene Dr 3
  M22................121 C1
Roughey Gdns M22.....121 D4
Rough Hill La BL9......28 E4
Roughlea Ave WA3.....91 D4
Roughlee Ave M27.....79 D7
Roughtown Rd OL5......68 D2
Roundcroft SK6.......113 E3
Roundham Wlk 27
  M9.................157 B4
Roundhey SK8........131 C8
Round Hey OL5........86 C8
Round Hill Cl SK13.....171 C3
Roundhill Way OL4.....49 E1
Round House Ave WN1...37 F1
Roundmoor Rd WN6....37 A7
ROUNDTHORN 120 E5
  Roundthorn Bsns Pk
    M23................120 E5
  Roundthorn Com Prim Sch
    OL4................67 C5
Roundthorn Ct M23....120 F7
  Roundthorn Ind Est
    M23................120 E6
Roundthorn La BL5.....57 E7
Roundthorn Rd
  Middleton M24........65 B7
  Oldham OL4..........67 C5
  Wythenshawe M23....120 F6
Roundthorn Wlk 6
  M23................120 F6
Roundway SK7........132 D6
Roundwood Rd M22....121 D7
Rousdon Cl M40.......157 A1
Rouse Cl M11.........160 C1
Rouse St OL11........30 C4
Routledge Wlk M9.....157 B4
Roving Bridge Rise
  M27................80 D8
Rowan Ave
  Golborne WA3 ....90 F7
  2 Horwich BL6.......22 E1
  Manchester M16 ....97 D3
  Sale M33............108 C2
  Urmston M41.........95 D3
  Wigan WN6 ....36 F3
Rowan Cl
  Failsworth M35.......83 F6
  Rochdale OL12........14 B3
Rowan Cres SK16......101 F7
Rowan Ct
  Hyde SK14...........167 B1
  Manchester M14 ....110 D7
  Wilmslow SK9.........137 B7
Rowan Dr
  Bury BL9 ....141 B3
  Cheadle SK8..........132 C8
Rowanhill WN1........37 D1
Rowan Lo WN7........132 F7
Rowan Pl M25.........63 B3
Rowans OL SK15......86 C3
Rowanside Dr SK9......137 E8
Rowans St BL3.......27 C4
Rowan St SK14........167 C1
Rowans The
  6 Adlington PR6.....21 A8
  Bolton BL3...........40 F7
  Mossley OL5..........68 D1
Rowanswood Dr
  SK14...............102 A3
Rowan Tree Dr M33....108 B1
Rowan Tree Rd
  Oldham OL4..........66 D1
  Paddockhill WA16 .....136 B5
Rowan Way M7........155 A3

Rowan Wlk
  Glossop SK13.........171 B4
  Partington M31 ....105 E2
Rowanwood OL9.......65 E7
Rowantree Rd M33.....108 A1
Rowany Cl M25........63 A3
ROWARTH............127 E7
Rowarth Ave
  Denton M34..........113 A8
  13 Gamesley SK13...171 A2
Rowarth Bank 9
  SK13...............171 A2
Rowarth Cl 10 SK13...171 A2
Rowarth Fold 12
  SK13...............171 A2
Rowarth Rd M23......121 A2
Rowarth Way 11
  SK13...............171 A2
Rowbottom St SK14....113 E8
Rowbottom Sq WN1....150 C4
Rowbottom Wlk OL8....153 B1
Rowcon Cl M34........100 E4
Rowdell Wlk M23......109 B2
Rowden Rd OL4........67 E4
Rowe Gn M34.........100 F2
Rowena St BL3........42 C2
Rowendale St M1......162 C4
Rowe St M29..........77 B8
Rowfield Dr M23.......120 F3
Rowland Ave M41......95 E3
Rowland Ct 17 OL16....31 B6
ROWLANDS...........11 D2
Rowland St N M46......58 D3
Rowland St S M46......58 D2
Rowlands Rd BL9.......11 D2
Rowland St
  16 Rochdale OL16.....31 B6
  Salford M5...........161 A4
Rowlandsway M22.....121 D2
Rowland Way OL4......67 E7
Rowley Rd SK7........133 E8
Rowley St OL6.........85 D6
ROW-OF-TREES.......136 D3
Rowood Ave
  Manchester M8 ....156 B2
  Reddish SK5..........111 F8
Rowrah Cres M24......46 C1
Rowsley Ave
  Bolton BL1...........142 A1
  Manchester M20 ......109 E4
Rowsley Cl 22 SK13...171 B2
Rowsley Gn 24 SK13...171 B2
Rowsley Mews SK13...171 B2
Rowsley Rd
  Eccles M30 ....95 C8
  Stretford M32 ....96 A3
Rowsley St
  Manchester M11 ......160 C1
  Salford M6...........81 A3
Rowsley Wlk 23 SK13...171 B2
Rowson Dr M44.......105 D6
Rowton Rise WN1.....37 B8
Rowton St 3 BL2......25 B3
Roxalina St BL3.......40 F7
Roxburgh St 5 M18....99 D5
ROXBURY............67 D5
Roxbury Ave OL4......67 D5
Roxby Wlk 6 M40......65 D2
Roxholme Wlk M22....130 C8
Roxton Cl BL6.........22 E1
Roxton Rd SK4........111 C6
Roxwell Wlk 8 M9.....157 A4
Royal Albert Edward Infmy
  WN1................37 C2
Royal Arc 5 WN1......150 C4
Royal Ave
  Bury BL9 ....27 F5
  Droylsden M43........84 B2
  Heywood OL10........29 D1
  Manchester M21.......109 A8
  Urmston M41.........95 D2
Royal Bolton Hospl
  BL4................147 C1
Royal Court Dr BL1.....145 A4
Royal Cres SK8........122 C2
Royal Dr WN7........76 E6
Royal Exchange 23
  M2.................158 C1
Royal Exchange Sh Ctr
  M2.................158 C2
Royal Eye Hospl M13...163 B1
Royal Gdns
  Altrincham WA14 .....118 F2
  Ramsbottom BL0......11 A1
Royal George Cotts
  OL3................68 E5
Royal George Mills
  OL3................68 E5
Royal George St SK1,
  SK3................170 C4
Royal Ho OL1.........143 A2
Royal Manchester
  Children's Hospl
  M27................80 C7
Royal Northern Coll of
  Music M13...........163 A2
Royal Oak Ind Est
  SK1................170 C3
Royal Oak Rd M23.....121 A7
Royal Oak Yd SK1......169 C1
Royal Oldham Hospl The
  OL1................48 D1
Royal Par OL1.........48 E1
Royal Rd SK12........135 D5

Royal Schools for The
  Deaf & Communication
  Disorders SK8.......131 D6
Royal St OL16.........15 C3
Royal The M3.........158 A2
Royalthorn Ave M22...121 D6
Royalthorn Dr M22....121 C6
Royalthorn Rd M22....121 D6
Royce Ave WA15......119 C5
Royce Cres Prim Sch
  SK3................162 B1
Royce Ct 15 M15......162 A2
Royce Rd M15.........162 B2
Royce Trad Est M17....95 F7
Roydale St M40.......160 B3
Royden Ave
  Irlam M44............105 E4
  Manchester M9 ....64 D5
  Wigan WN3 ....55 A2
Royden Cres WN5......71 E5
Royden Rd WN5.......71 E5
Roydes St M24........47 B2
Royds Cl
  Bury BL8 ....27 A5
  Manchester M13 ......164 A1
Royds Pl 15 OL16......31 A5
Royds Rd OL13 ....3 A7
Royds St W OL16......31 A5
Royds St
  Bury, Tottington BL8 ..26 F7
  Bury, Woodgate Hill BL9 ..28 D4
  Littleborough OL15 ...16 C5
  Milnrow OL16........32 A5
  Rochdale OL16.......31 B5
Royd St OL8...........66 C4
Roy Grainger Ct 8
  M16................97 E3
Roy Ho OL2...........48 D6
Royland Ave BL3.......42 A3
Royland Ct BL3........147 C3
Royle Ave SK13........104 D1
Royle Barn Rd OL11....30 C3
Royle Cl
  Oldham OL8..........66 F3
  Stockport SK2 ....124 A5
Royle Ct M14.........110 D7
Royle Green Rd M22....121 B2
Royle Higginson Ct
  M41................95 C1
Roylelands Bglws
  OL11...............30 C3
Royle Pennine Trad Est
  OL16...............30 D3
Royle Rd OL11........30 D3
Royles Sq 2 SK9......137 A1
Royle St
  Denton M34..........100 F5
  Manchester M14 ......110 D7
  Salford M6...........154 C1
  Stockport SK1 ....170 C3
  Walkden M28.........60 D2
ROYLEY.............48 C3
  Royley Carr Flats SK6...113 A3
Royley Cres OL2.......48 C3
Royley Ho OL2........48 C3
Royley Way OL2.......48 C3
Roynton Rd BL6.......22 B7
Royon Dr SK3.........123 B7
Roy St
  Bolton BL3...........146 B4
  Royton OL2..........48 D4
Royston Ave
  Bolton BL3...........148 C4
  Manchester M16 ......97 D3
  Reddish M34 ....100 A3
Royston Cl
  2 Golborne WA3 .....90 E8
  Ramsbottom BL8......10 F1
Royston Ct 5 M16......97 D3
Royston Rd
  Manchester M16 ......97 B3
  Urmston M41.........95 E3
ROYTON.............48 E4
Royton Ave M33......108 E2
Royton & Crompton Sch
  OL2................49 A4
Royton Hall Wlk OL2...48 E4
ROYTON MOSS.......49 B3
Rozel Sq M3..........162 B4
Ruabon Cres WN2......57 A4
Ruabon Rd M20.......110 C2
Rubens Cl SK6.........126 C8
Ruby St
  Bolton BL3...........143 C3
  Denton M34..........100 E3
  Manchester M15......163 A2
  Ramsbottom BL9......11 C3
Rudcroft Cl M13.......163 B2
Rudding St OL2.......49 A2
Ruddpark Rd M22.....121 D1
Rudd St M40..........83 A7
Rudford Gdns BL3......147 C4
Rudgwick Dr BL8......27 C7
Rudheath Ave M20.....110 A7
Rudman Dr M5........161 C4
Rudman St OL12.......14 E2
Rudolph St BL3........147 C3
Rudston Ave M40......65 B2
Rudyard Ave
  Middleton M24........47 C3
  Standish WN6........19 E2
Rudyard Gr
  Reddish SK4.........111 D6
  Rochdale OL11........30 E2
  Sale M33............107 E2

Rudyard Rd M6........80 C5
Rudyard St M7........155 A2
Ruecroft Cl WN6.......35 D8
Rufford Ave
  Hyde SK14...........167 C2
  Rochdale OL11........30 D4
Rufford Cl
  Ashton-u-L OL6.......85 C7
  Shaw OL2...........48 F7
  Whitefield M45.......45 A4
Rufford Dr BL3........147 A2
Rufford Gr BL3........147 A2
Rufford Pl
  Reddish M18 ....99 F4
  Tyldesley M29........76 F4
Rufford Rd M16.......97 D3
Rufford St 4 WN4.....72 F5
Rufus St M14.........110 C7
Rugby Cl WN5.........53 E5
Rugby Dr
  Orrell WN5...........53 F8
  Sale M33............108 A2
Rugby Rd
  Leigh WN7...........75 F3
  Rochdale OL12, OL16...15 A1
  Salford M6...........80 A2
  Rugby Rd Ind Est OL12...15 A1
Rugby St M7, M8......158 B4
Rugeley St M6.........81 B5
Ruins La BL2..........25 E4
Ruislip Ave M40.......157 B1
Ruislip Cl OL8.........67 B4
Rumbles La OL3........50 F4
Rumbold St 6 M18.....99 E6
Rumworth Rd BL6......40 C6
Rumworth St BL3......147 A4
Runcorn St M15.......161 C3
Runger La M90, WA15 ...129 F8
Runhall Cl M12........165 A2
Running Hill Farm OL3...51 D2
Running Hill Gate OL3...51 D1
Running Hill La OL3....51 D2
Runnymede M6, M27....80 B5
Runnymede Cl SK3.....123 C6
Runnymede Ct
  Bolton BL3...........145 A1
  Royton OL2..........48 E4
  Stockport SK3 ....123 C6
Runshaw Ave WN6.....35 E8
Rupert St
  Bolton BL3...........147 C3
  Failsworth M40.......83 E4
  Radcliffe M26.........44 B1
  Reddish SK5..........111 E7
  Rochdale OL12........14 C1
  Wigan WN1 ....151 B3
Rupert Terr 5 SK5......111 E7
Ruscombe Fold M24....46 D3
Rush Acre Cl M26.....43 E3
Rush Bank OL2........48 F8
Rushbrooke Ave 1
  M11................83 C2
Rushbury Dr OL2......49 A4
Rushcroft Ct M9.......65 A2
Rushcroft Prim Sch
  OL2................149 B4
Rushcroft Rd OL2......48 F8
Rushdene VN3.........56 B4
Rushden Rd M19......99 B2
Rushen St 4 M11......83 C1
Rushes Mdw WA13....117 B5
Rushes The SK13......171 C4
Rushey Ave M22......121 C6
Rushey Cl WA15......129 D7
Rushey Field 5
  BL7................24 F8
Rushey Fold Ct 23
  BL1................143 A2
Rushey Fold La BL1....143 A2
Rusheylea Cl BL1......142 C2
Rushey Rd M22........121 C6
Rushfield Dr M13......98 F3
Rushfield Rd SK8......132 A6
Rushford Ct 1 M19....99 A2
Rushford Gr BL1.......142 C4
Rushford St M12......99 A3
Rush Gdns WA13......117 A4
RUSHGREEN.........117 A4
Rushgreen Rd WA13...117 A4
Rushgrove OL3........69 B7
Rush Hill Rd OL3......69 B7
Rush Hill Terr OL3.....69 B7
Rushlake Gdns OL11...29 E8
Rushley Ave M7.......81 B7
Rushmere
  Ashton-u-L OL6.......85 C6
  Glossop SK13........116 E8
Rushmere Ave M19....99 B1
Rushmere Dr BL8......27 C5
Rushmere Wlk M16....162 A1
Rushmoor Cl M44.....94 A2
Rush Mount OL2.......48 F8
RUSHOLME...........98 E2
Rusholme Gdns 3
  M14................98 C2
Rusholme Gr M14......98 C3
Rusholme Pl M14......98 D3
Rushside Rd SK8......132 A6
Rush St SK16.........101 F8
Rushton Ave
  Leigh WN7...........75 D8
  Newton-le-W WA12....89 B4

Rushton Dr
Marple SK6 . . . . 125 F5
Romiley SK6 . . . . 113 C3
Stockport SK7 . . . . 123 D3
Rushton Gdns SK7 . . . . 123 D2
Rushton Gr
Manchester M11 . . . . 99 E7
Oldham OL4 . . . . 49 E3
Rushton Rd
Bolton BL1 . . . . 142 B1
Cheadle SK8 . . . . 132 A6
Stockport SK3 . . . . 123 B7
Rushton St
5 Bacup OL13 . . . . 3 E8
Manchester M20 . . . . 110 B2
Walkden M28 . . . . 60 D2
Rushway Ave M9 . . . . . . 65 B2
Rushwick Ave M40 . . . . 157 B1
Rushworth Bldgs OL13 . . 3 E8
Rushworth St SK4 . . . . 111 C5
Rushycroft SK14 . . . . . . 103 A4
Rushyfield Cres SK6 . . . 113 D3
Rushy Hill View 18
OL12 . . . . 14 C1
Rushy View WA12 . . . . . 89 A4
Ruskin Ave
Denton M34 . . . . 100 E1
Droylsden M34 . . . . 100 C7
Kearsley BL4 . . . . 60 F7
Manchester M14 . . . . 98 B4
Newton-le-W WA12 . . . . . 89 C4
Oldham OL9 . . . . 65 F3
Wigan WN3 . . . . 54 F3
Ruskin Cres
Abram WN2 . . . . 56 B1
Prestwich M25 . . . . 62 F3
Ruskin Dr M33 . . . . 107 D4
Ruskin Gdns SK6 . . . . . 113 A3
Ruskin Gr SK6 . . . . 113 A3
Ruskington Dr M9 . . . . . 157 A3
Ruskin Rd
Droylsden M43 . . . . 84 A2
Little Lever BL3 . . . . 43 B4
Manchester M16 . . . . 97 C3
Prestwich M25 . . . . 62 F3
Reddish SK5 . . . . 99 E1
Rochdale OL11 . . . . 30 F2
Ruskin St
Oldham OL1 . . . . 153 A4
Radcliffe M26 . . . . 44 C4
Rusland Ct
Manchester M9 . . . . 65 A3
Sale M33 . . . . 108 A5
Rusland Dr BL2 . . . . 25 E2
Rusland Wlk 8 M22 . . . 121 C2
Russeldene Rd WN3 . . . 54 E3
Russell Ave
High Lane SK6 . . . . 134 E7
Manchester M16 . . . . 97 D2
Sale M33 . . . . 108 D5
Russell Cl BL1 . . . . 144 C4
Russell Ct
Farnworth BL4 . . . . 60 E7
Manchester M16 . . . . 97 C3
Walkden M38 . . . . 60 C3
Russell Dr M44 . . . . 94 A2
Russell Gdns SK4 . . . . . 168 B1
Russell Pl 1 M33 . . . . . 108 B5
Russell Rd
Manchester M16 . . . . 97 D3
Partington M31 . . . . 106 A3
Salford M6 . . . . 80 B5
Russell Scott Prim Sch
M34 . . . . 100 E4
Russell St
6 Ashton-u-L OL6 . . . . . . 85 D4
Atherton M46 . . . . 58 C3
Bolton BL1 . . . . 145 A4
5 Bury BL9 . . . . 140 C4
Chadderton OL9 . . . . 152 B3
Compstall SK6 . . . . 114 B3
Dukinfield SK16 . . . . 101 C8
Eccles M30 . . . . 79 F2
Farnworth BL4 . . . . 60 E8
Heywood OL10 . . . . 29 E2
Hindley WN2 . . . . 57 C2
Hyde SK14 . . . . 167 A3
Ince-in-M WN2 . . . . 56 A8
Manchester, Moss Side
M16 . . . . 97 F3
Prestwich M25 . . . . 63 C4
Rochdale OL11 . . . . 139 B1
Stockport SK2 . . . . 124 A6
Walkden M38 . . . . 60 C3
Russet Rd M9 . . . . 64 D1
Russet Way SK9 . . . . . . 136 E3
Russet Wlk BL1 . . . . . . 143 B4
Rustons Wlk 2 M40 . . . . 65 E1
Ruthen La M16 . . . . 97 B4
Rutherford Ave 2 M14 . . 98 B3
Rutherford Cl SK14 . . . . 167 A2
Rutherford Dr BL5 . . . . . 58 F7
Rutherford Way SK14 . . 167 A2
Rutherglade Cl M40 . . . . 156 C2
Rutherglen Dr BL3 . . . . . 40 F6
Rutherglen Wlk M40 . . . 157 B1
Ruthin Ave
Cheadle SK8 . . . . 122 E2
Manchester M9 . . . . 64 C5
Middleton M24 . . . . 46 F1
Ruth St
Bolton BL1 . . . . 145 B4
10 Bury BL9 . . . . 140 C4
Edenfield BL0 . . . . 1 D2
Manchester M18 . . . . 99 D3

Ruth St continued
Oldham OL1 . . . . 153 C4
Whitworth OL12 . . . . 4 D1
Rutland OL11 . . . . 139 B2
Rutland Ave
Denton M34 . . . . 101 B2
Golborne WA3 . . . . 90 D7
Manchester, Firswood
M16 . . . . 97 A3
Manchester, Withington
M20 . . . . 110 A6
Over Hulton M46 . . . . 58 F5
Swinton M27 . . . . 61 F2
Urmston M41 . . . . 95 E3
Rutland Cl
8 Ashton-u-L OL6 . . . . . . 85 D2
Gatley SK8 . . . . 122 B6
Little Lever BL3 . . . . 43 B4
Rutland Cres SK5 . . . . . 112 D6
Rutland Ct
Manchester M20 . . . . 110 B5
Stockport, Heaviley
SK2 . . . . 124 B7
Stockport SK2 . . . . 124 A5
Rutland Dr
Ashton-in-M WN4 . . . . . . 73 C4
Bury BL9 . . . . 45 A8
Manchester M7 . . . . 63 D1
Rutland Gr
Bolton BL1 . . . . 142 C1
Farnworth BL4 . . . . 60 C7
Rutland La M33 . . . . 108 F4
Rutland Rd
Altrincham WA14 . . . . . . 119 D6
Droylsden M43 . . . . 83 E2
Eccles M30 . . . . 79 F3
Hazel Grove SK7 . . . . . . 133 E8
Hindley WN2 . . . . 56 F6
Irlam M44 . . . . 105 D5
Partington M31 . . . . 105 E2
Tyldesley M29 . . . . 58 F2
Wigan WN3 . . . . 60 D1
Rutland St
Ashton-u-L OL6 . . . . 85 D2
Bolton BL3 . . . . 147 A4
Dukinfield SK14 . . . . 101 D5
Failsworth M35 . . . . 83 F8
Heywood OL10 . . . . 29 D3
Leigh WN7 . . . . 76 E4
4 Manchester M18 . . . . . . 99 E6
Oldham OL9 . . . . 152 C1
Swinton M27 . . . . 61 E1
Rutland Way OL2 . . . . . . 149 C3
Rutland Wlk BB4 . . . . 1 A8
Rutter's La SK7 . . . . . . 124 C2
Ryall Ave M5 . . . . 161 B4
Ryall Ave S M5 . . . . . . 161 B4
Ryan St M11 . . . . 99 E7
Ryburn Sq OL11 . . . . 29 E6
Rydal Ave
Chadderton OL9 . . . . 47 F1
Droylsden M43 . . . . 83 E1
Dukinfield SK14 . . . . 101 C5
Eccles M30 . . . . 79 B4
Hazel Grove SK7 . . . . . . 124 C3
High Lane SK6 . . . . 134 E8
Hindley WN2 . . . . 56 E5
Middleton M24 . . . . 64 F6
Orrell WN5 . . . . 53 F7
Royton OL2 . . . . 48 C8
Sale M33 . . . . 107 F5
Urmston M41 . . . . 107 A8
Rydal Cl
Ashton-in-M WN4 . . . . . . 73 C4
Blackrod BL6 . . . . 21 C3
Bury BL9 . . . . 44 E7
Gatley SK8 . . . . 122 B4
Reddish M34 . . . . 100 B2
Tyldesley M29 . . . . 77 A3
Rydal Cres
Swinton M27 . . . . 79 F7
Walkden M28 . . . . 60 E1
Rydal Dr WA15 . . . . . . 129 D8
Rydal Gr
Ashton-u-L OL7 . . . . . . 166 A4
Farnworth BL4 . . . . 59 F7
Heywood OL10 . . . . 46 D8
Whitefield M45 . . . . 63 A8
Rydal Ho 4 M28 . . . . . . 60 E2
Rydal Mount 4 SK5 . . . . 99 F2
Rydal Pl
Abram WN2 . . . . 74 B8
Ince-in-M WN2 . . . . 56 B8
Rydal Rd
Bolton BL1 . . . . 144 A4
Haslingden BB4 . . . . 1 C8
Little Lever BL3 . . . . 43 A3
Stretford M32 . . . . 96 D3
Rydal Wlk
Leigh WN7 . . . . 75 E5
Newton-le-W WA12 . . . . . 89 C3
Rydal Wlk
Oldham OL4 . . . . 67 D7
Stalybridge SK15 . . . . . . 86 A3
Wigan WN5 . . . . 54 C7
Ryde Ave
Denton M34 . . . . 113 B8
Stockport SK4 . . . . 168 B2
Ryder Ave WA14 . . . . . . 119 E7
Ryder Brow M18 . . . . . . 99 D4
Ryderbrow Rd M18 . . . . 99 D4
Ryder Brow Sta M18 . . . 99 D4
Ryder Gr WN7 . . . . 76 C2
Ryder St
Bolton BL1 . . . . 142 C2
Heywood OL10 . . . . 29 D2
Manchester M40 . . . . 160 A4

Ryde St
Bolton BL3 . . . . 146 A4
Wigan WN5 . . . . 54 E6
Rydings La OL12 . . . . . . 15 A5
Rydings Rd OL12 . . . . . . 15 B4
Rydings Specl Sch
OL12 . . . . 15 B4
Rydley St BL2 . . . . 148 B2
Ryebank Gr OL6 . . . . . . 85 D5
Ryebank Mews 3 M21 . . 96 F1
Ryebank Rd M21 . . . . . . 96 F1
Rye Bank Rd M16 . . . . . 97 B3
Ryeburn Ave M22 . . . . . 121 D3
Ryeburn Dr BL2 . . . . 25 B5
Ryeburne St OL4 . . . . . . 67 C7
Ryeburn Wlk M41 . . . . . 94 F4
Rye Croft M45 . . . . 62 C7
Ryecroft Ave
Bury BL8 . . . . 26 F6
Golborne WA3 . . . . 74 E1
Heywood OL10 . . . . 29 E2
Rye Croft Ave M20 . . . . 80 C3
Ryecroft Bsns Pk 12
OL7 . . . . 84 F1
Ryecroft Cl OL9 . . . . 65 F3
Ryecroft Dr BL5 . . . . 39 D3
Ryecroft Gr M23 . . . . . . 121 A7
Ryecroft Ho OL7 . . . . . . 166 A1
Ryecroft La
Denton M34 . . . . 100 F7
Eccles M30 . . . . 78 F4
Ryecroft Rd M32 . . . . . . 96 C1
Ryecroft St OL7 . . . . 84 F1
Ryecroft View M14 . . . . 100 C8
Ryedale Ave M40 . . . . . 157 A1
Ryedale Cl SK4 . . . . 168 B3
Ryefield
14 Ashton-u-L OL7 . . . . . . 84 F1
Pendlebury M6 . . . . 80 D6
Ryefield Cl WA15 . . . . . 120 C5
Ryefield Rd M33 . . . . . . 107 C2
Ryefields
4 Rochdale, Hurstead
OL12 . . . . 15 D4
Rochdale OL11 . . . . 30 A6
Ryefields Dr OL3 . . . . . . 51 B1
Ryefield St BL1 . . . . 25 A1
Ryeford Cl WN3 . . . . . . 151 C2
Rye Hill BL5 . . . . 57 F8
Ryeland Cl OL16 . . . . . . 31 B4
Ryelands BL5 . . . . 57 F8
Ryelands Ct BL5 . . . . . . 57 F8
Rye St OL10 . . . . 29 E3
Rye Wlk
Chadderton OL9 . . . . 152 A2
Manchester M13 . . . . 163 C1
Rygate Wlk 3 M8 . . . . . 155 C2
Rylance Rd WN3 . . . . . . 54 D1
Rylance St M11 . . . . 164 B4
Ryland Cl SK5 . . . . 99 F1
Ryland Ho 1 M21 . . . . . 109 A8
Rylands Cl 8 M15 . . . . . 162 A2
Rylands Ho 7 M14 . . . . . 110 D8
Rylands St WN6 . . . . . . 37 A2
Rylane Wlk M40 . . . . . . 157 A1
Rylatt St 1 M33 . . . . . . 107 F5
Ryley St SK9 . . . . 136 F1
Ryleys Farm SK9 . . . . . . 136 F1
Ryleys La SK9 . . . . 136 F1
Ryleys Sch The SK9 . . . 136 F1
Ryley St 4 BL3 . . . . 144 C2
Rylstone Ave M21 . . . . . 109 D3
Ryther Gr WN6 . . . . 64 B5
Ryton Ave M18 . . . . 99 C3
Ryton Cl WN3 . . . . 150 B2

S

Sabden Cl
Bury BL9 . . . . 27 F7
Heywood OL10 . . . . 29 A2
Manchester M40 . . . . 160 B3
Sabden Rd BL1 . . . . 23 E2
Sabrina St M8 . . . . 155 B1
Sack St 4 SK14 . . . . . . 101 D5
Sackville Cl OL2 . . . . . . 32 A1
Sackville St
Ashton-u-L OL6 . . . . . . 166 B3
2 Bolton BL2 . . . . 148 C3
Manchester M1 . . . . 163 A4
6 Rochdale OL11 . . . . . . 15 C4
Salford M3 . . . . 158 B2
Sacred Heart RC Jun & Inf
Sch OL1 . . . . 49 C2
Sacred Heart RC Prim Sch
Hindley WN2 . . . . 57 B3
Leigh WN7 . . . . 75 E5
Manchester M18 . . . . 99 C4
Rochdale OL16 . . . . 31 C6
Westhoughton BL5 . . . . . 58 E1
Wigan WN6 . . . . 36 F2
Wythenshawe M23 . . . . 120 F6
Saddleback Cl 3 M28 . . 78 B6
Saddleback Cres WN5 . . 54 B7
Saddleback Rd WN5 . . . 54 B7
Saddle Cote M28 . . . . . . 79 A4
Saddlecote Cl M8 . . . . . 156 B4
Saddle Ct 3 WN5 . . . . . 54 D6
Saddle Gr M43 . . . . 84 D3
Saddle St BL2 . . . . 25 B2
Saddlewood Ave M19 . . 110 D2
Saddleworth Bsns Ctr
OL3 . . . . 50 F4
Saddleworth Bsns Pk
OL3 . . . . 69 B8
Saddleworth Fold OL3 . . 51 C1

Saddleworth Mus & Art
Gall *10 OL3 . . . . 69 B8
Saddleworth Prep Sch
OL4 . . . . 68 C8
Saddleworth Sch OL3 . . 51 B1
Sadie Ave M32 . . . . 96 A4
Sadler Ct M15 . . . . 162 B1
Sadler St
Bolton BL3 . . . . 42 A4
Middleton M24 . . . . 46 F1
Safflower Ave M27 . . . . 79 D8
Saffron Cl WA3 . . . . 90 E8
Saffron Dr OL4 . . . . 49 D2
Saffron Wlk
Partington M31 . . . . 105 F2
8 Wythenshawe M22 . . . 121 D1
Safton Ct 9 BL9 . . . . . . 27 B6
Sagars Rd
Handforth SK9 . . . . 131 C3
Styal SK9 . . . . 131 B4
Sagar St M8 . . . . 158 C4
St Aelred's RC Tech Coll
M33 . . . . 89 D4
St Agnes CE Prim Sch
Manchester M13 . . . . 98 F3
Oldham OL4 . . . . 68 A4
St Agnes Rd M13 . . . . . 98 F2
St Agnes St SK5 . . . . . . 99 F3
St Aidan & St Oswald's RC
Sch OL2 . . . . 48 E3
St Aidan's CE Com Prim
Sch WN5 . . . . 71 E5
St Aidan's Cl
Billinge WN5 . . . . 71 E6
Rochdale OL11 . . . . 139 A1
St Aidans RC Prim Sch
M23 . . . . 109 B1
St Aidan's RC Prim Sch
WN3 . . . . 54 E1
St Aidan's Ct M26 . . . . . 44 A1
St Albans Ave
Ashton-u-L OL6 . . . . 85 C7
Failsworth M40 . . . . 83 B5
St Alban's Ave SK4 . . . . 111 C5
St Albans Cl
Haydock WA11 . . . . 89 A7
Oldham OL8 . . . . 66 F4
St Albans Cres WA14 . . 119 C8
St Alban's St OL11 . . . . 139 B2
St Alban's St OL16 . . . . 139 B2
St Alban's Terr
Rochdale OL11 . . . . 139 B2
Salford M8 . . . . 155 C1
St Aldates SK6 . . . . 112 F2
St Aldwyn's Rd M20 . . . 110 B5
St Alphonsus RC Prim Sch
M16 . . . . 162 A1
St Ambrose Barlow RC
High Sch M27 . . . . 79 F7
St Ambrose Barlow RC
Prim Sch M29 . . . . 77 A5
St Ambrose Coll
WA15 . . . . 129 B8
St Ambrose Gdns M6 . . 154 C2
St Ambrose RC Prim Sch
Manchester M21 . . . . . . 109 D4
Stockport SK3 . . . . 170 B1
St Ambrose Rd
Oldham OL11 . . . . 49 C1
Tyldesley M29 . . . . 77 A5
St Andrews Ave M30 . . . 79 E1
St Andrew's Ave
Altrincham WA15 . . . . . . 119 F7
Droylsden M43 . . . . 83 E1
St Andrew's CE Jun Sch
SK13 . . . . 171 C4
St Andrews CE Prim Sch
Eccles M30 . . . . 79 E1
Manchester M19 . . . . . . 111 B8
Radcliffe M26 . . . . 43 F6
Ramsbottom BL0 . . . . . . 138 B1
Wigan WN6 . . . . 36 F2
St Andrew's CE Sch
Dearnley OL12 . . . . 15 B5
M28 . . . . 78 A6
St Andrews Cl
Rochdale OL15 . . . . 15 C4
Sale M33 . . . . 107 C1
Stockport SK4 . . . . 168 B4
St Andrew's Cl
Ramsbottom BL0 . . . . . . 138 C1
Romiley SK6 . . . . 113 B1
St Andrew's Cres WN2 . . 56 D5
St Andrews
Altrincham WA15 . . . . . . 119 F3
Glossop SK13 . . . . 104 A4
Stockport SK1 . . . . 112 A1
St Andrew's Dr
Heywood OL10 . . . . 46 D8
Leigh WN7 . . . . 76 C5
St Andrew's Dr
Heywood OL10 . . . . 29 D1
Wigan WN6 . . . . 36 F2
St Andrews Ho M38 . . . 60 B3
St Andrew's Rd
Bolton BL6 . . . . 40 B7
Gatley SK8 . . . . 122 C1
Stockport SK4 . . . . 168 B4
St Andrew's Rd
Radcliffe M26 . . . . 43 F6
Stretford M32 . . . . 96 B2
St Andrew's Sq M1 . . . . 163 C4

St Andrew's St
Manchester M1 . . . . 163 C4
Radcliffe M26 . . . . 43 F6
St Andrew's View M26 . . 43 F6
St Anne's Ave
Denton M34 . . . . 48 E3
Salford M6 . . . . 154 B3
Tyldesley M46 . . . . 58 E1
St Anne's CE Jun & Inf
Sch OL2 . . . . 48 E3
St Anne's CE Lydgate Prim
Sch OL4 . . . . 68 C6
St Anne's CE Prim Sch
Sale M33 . . . . 108 D4
Wigan WN6 . . . . 36 D3
St Anne's Cres OL4 . . . . 68 D5
St Anne's Ct
Denton M34 . . . . 100 E6
Sale M33 . . . . 108 C4
Shevington WN6 . . . . 35 F5
St Anne's Dr
Denton M34 . . . . 101 A4
Shevington WN6 . . . . 36 A5
St Anne's Fulshaw CE
Prim Sch SK9 . . . . 136 F6
St Anne's Gdns OL10 . . . 29 F2
St Anne's Hospl
WA14 . . . . 119 C3
St Annes Mdw BL8 . . . . 26 F7
St Anne's RC High Sch
SK4 . . . . 169 A4
St Anne's RC Prim Sch
Droylsden M34 . . . . 100 A7
Manchester, Bradford
M4 . . . . 160 A1
Manchester, Cheetham Hill
M8 . . . . 156 A4
Oldham OL4 . . . . 67 C7
St Annes Rd
Denton M34 . . . . 100 F6
Horwich BL6 . . . . 22 C4
Manchester M21 . . . . . . 109 B7
St Anne's Rd M34 . . . . . 101 A4
St Annes Sq OL3 . . . . . . 50 F4
St Anne's St 6 SK14 . . . 115 A8
St Anne's St BL9 . . . . . . 140 C4
St Anne's Churchyard 22
M2 . . . . 158 C1
St Anns Ct M25 . . . . 63 A3
St Ann's Pas M2 . . . . . . 158 C1
St Ann's RC Prim Sch
M32 . . . . 96 D2
St Ann's Rd
Hazel Grove SK7 . . . . . . 124 C1
Prestwich M25 . . . . 63 A3
Rochdale OL16 . . . . 31 D8
St Ann's Rd N SK8 . . . . 122 B2
St Ann's Rd S SK8 . . . . 131 C8
St Ann's Sq
Gatley SK8 . . . . 131 C8
Manchester M2 . . . . 158 C1
Sale M33 . . . . 108 F3
St Ann's St M27 . . . . . . 79 E8
St Ann St
Bolton BL1 . . . . 143 B1
Manchester M2 . . . . 158 C1
St Anthonys Dr OL5 . . . 68 D2
St Anthony's Prim Sch
M22 . . . . 121 D1
St Antony's RC Coll
M41 . . . . 95 F2
St Asaphs Dr OL15 . . . . 85 B6
St Asaph's Dr M7 . . . . . 155 C4
St Aubin's Rd BL2 . . . . . 148 B2
St Aubyn's Rd WN1 . . . . 37 C4
St Augustine of
Canterbury RC High Sch
OL8 . . . . 66 D3
St Augustine's CE Prim
Sch
Manchester M40 . . . . . . 157 B1
Pendlebury M27 . . . . 80 B8
St Augustine's Ct 27
BL2 . . . . 25 B1
St Augustine's Rd
SK3 . . . . 123 B8
St Augustine St
Bolton BL1 . . . . 143 A2
Manchester M40 . . . . . . 157 B1
St Austell Ave M29 . . . . 77 C8
St Austell Dr
Gatley SK8 . . . . 131 B8
Ramsbottom BL8 . . . . 10 F2
St Austell Ho M16 . . . . . 97 F1
St Austell Pl OL9 . . . . . . 48 B1
St Austell Rd M16 . . . . . 97 F1
St Austells Dr M25 . . . . 63 B5
St Austell's Rd M27 . . . 80 C7
St Barnabas' CE Prim Sch
M11 . . . . 165 B4
St Barnabas's Dr OL15 . . 16 A6
St Barnabas Sq M11 . . . 165 B4
St Bartholomew's CE Prim
Sch OL12 . . . . 14 C8
St Bartholomew's Dr
M5 . . . . 161 C4
St Bartholomew St 4
BL3 . . . . 42 A4
St Bede CE Prim Sch
BL3 . . . . 146 B2
St Bede's Ave BL3 . . . . . 146 B2
St Bede's Coll M16 . . . . 97 E3

St Bees Cl
Gatley SK8. . . . .**122** B3
Manchester M14 . . . .**98** A4
St Bees Rd BL2. . . . .**25** C2
St Bees Wlk 9 M24 . . . . . .**46** E2
St Benedict's Ave
M12 . . . .**164** C2
St Benedicts RC Prim Sch
WN2. . . . .**56** C6
St Benedict's RC Prim Sch
SK9. . . . .**131** E3
St Bernadette's RC Prim Sch
Brinnington SK5. . . . .**112** B4
Whitefield M45 . . . .**44** F2
St Bernadett's RC Prim Sch WN6 . . . .**36** A6
St Bernard's Ave 1
M6 . . . .**81** C5
St Bernard's Cl M6 . . . .**81** B5
St Bernard's RC Prim Sch
Bolton BL3. . . . .**40** E5
Manchester M19 . . . .**110** F6
St Boniface RC Prim Sch
M7 . . . .**81** C6
St Brannocks Rd SK8 . . . .**132** B7
St Brannock's Rd M21 . . . .**97** C1
St Brelades Dr M7 . . . .**155** C4
St Brendan's RC Prim Sch
BL2. . . . .**25** E4
St Brendan's Rd M20 . . . .**110** B7
St Brendan's Rd N
M20 . . . .**110** B7
St Brides Cl BL6. . . . .**22** A4
St Brides Way M16 . . . . . .**162** A1
St Brigid's RC Prim Sch
M11 . . . .**165** A4
St Catherine's CE Prim Sch
Horwich BL6 . . . .**22** A3
Wigan WN1 . . . .**151** B4
St Catherines Ct BL6. . . . . .**22** B3
St Catherines Dr BL4 . . . . .**59** F8
St Catherines Prep Sch
SK6. . . . .**126** B7
St Catherine's RC Prim Sch
Golborne WA3 . . . .**90** E7
Manchester M20 . . . .**110** C3
St Catherine's Rd
M20 . . . .**110** B7
St Chad's Ave SK6 . . . .**113** C2
St Chad's CE Prim Sch
OL3. . . . .**51** C1
St Chad's Cl OL16 . . . .**139** C3
St Chad's Cres OL3. . . . . . .**69** C8
St Chad's Ct OL16 . . . .**139** C3
St Chad's Gr SK6 . . . .**113** C2
St Chad's RC Prim Sch
M8 . . . .**156** A1
St Chad's Rd M20 . . . .**110** D7
St Chad's St M4, M8 . . . . .**159** A4
St Charles Cl SK13. . . . . . .**103** F5
St Charles' RC Prim Sch
M27 . . . .**79** D8
St Charles's RC Prim Sch
SK13. . . . .**103** E5
St Christopher Ho WN6. . .**36** C4
St Christopher's Ave
OL6. . . . .**85** E6
St Christophers Cl
M20 . . . .**109** F6
St Christopher's Dr
SK6. . . . .**113** A2
St Christopher's RC Prim Sch
Ashton-u-L OL6 . . . .**85** E6
Romiley SK6. . . . .**113** A2
St Christopher's Rd
OL6. . . . .**85** E6
St Chrysostom's CE Prim Sch M13 . . . .**164** A1
St Clair Rd BL8. . . . .**10** F3
St Clare's RC Prim Sch
M9 . . . .**64** C5
St Clare Terr BL6 . . . .**39** F8
St Clement St M41 . . . .**95** D1
St Clement's Ct OL11. . . . . .**30** C8
St Clement's Ct
2 Irlam M44 . . . .**94** B3
Oldham OL8 . . . .**153** C1
Prestwich M25. . . . .**63** C4
Wigan WN3 . . . .**150** A1
St Clement's Dr M5. . . . . .**161** B3
St Clement's Egerton CE Prim Sch M41 . . . .**161** B3
St Clements Fold M41 . . . . .**95** E2
St Clement's Rd
Manchester M21 . . . .**109** A8
Wigan WN1 . . . .**37** C4
St Clement's St WN3 . . . . .**55** F4
St Columba's RC Prim Sch
BL2. . . . .**25** B4
Saint Cuthberts Fold
OL8. . . . .**67** A1
St Cuthbert's Rd Prim Sch
OL16. . . . .**31** B1
St Cuthbert's RC Prim Sch
Manchester M20 . . . .**110** B7
Wigan WN5 . . . .**54** D6
St Damian's RC Science College OL6 . . . .**85** E7

St David Haigh & Aspull CE Prim Sch WN2. . . . . . .**38** B7
St David's Ave SK6 . . . . . .**113** B2
St Davids Cl M33 . . . .**108** A3
St David's Cl OL6 . . . .**85** D7
St David's Cres WN2 . . . . . .**38** B5
St David's Ct M8 . . . .**156** A1
St Davids Rd SK8 . . . .**123** A6
St David's Rd SK7 . . . .**124** C1
St Davids Wlk M32 . . . .**96** A2
St Domingo St OL9 . . . . . .**153** B2
St Dominics Mews
BL3. . . . .**146** C3
St Dominics Way M24 . . . . .**65** A7
St Dominic's RC Prim Sch
M40 . . . .**83** A8
St Dunstan Wlk 14
M40 . . . .**83** A6
St Edmund Arrowsmith RC High Sch WN4 . . . .**73** B2
St Edmund Hall Cl BL0. . . . .**11** C4
St Edmunds RC Prim Sch
M40 . . . .**157** B2
St Edmund's RC Prim Sch
M38 . . . .**60** A4
St Edmund's Rd M40 . . . . .**157** B2
St Edmund St BL1 . . . .**145** B3
St Edwards CE Prim Sch
OL11. . . . .**30** C2
St Edward's RC Prim Sch
Manchester M14 . . . .**98** B2
Oldham OL4 . . . .**67** E7
St Elisabeth's CE Prim Sch
SK5. . . . .**111** E8
St Elisabeth's Way
SK5. . . . .**111** E8
St Elizabeth's RC Prim Sch
M22 . . . .**121** E2
St Elizabeth's Rd WN2 . . . .**38** B5
St Elmo Ave SK2 . . . .**124** D7
St Elmo Pk SK12. . . . .**134** C4
SS Osmund & Andrew RC Prim Sch BL2 . . . .**42** E7
SS Simon & Jude's CE Prim Sch BL3 . . . .**42** A3
St Ethelbert's Ave
BL3. . . . .**144** B1
St Ethelbert's RC Prim Sch
BL3. . . . .**144** B1
St Francis RC Prim Sch
M12 . . . .**165** B2
St Gabriel Cl WN8 . . . .**35** C3
St Gabriel's CE Prim Sch
M24 . . . .**65** D7
St Gabriel's Cl OL11 . . . .**30** D1
St Gabriels Mews 4
M24 . . . .**65** C7
St Gabriel's RC High Sch
BL9 . . . .**140** A1
St Gabriel's RC Prim Sch
Leigh WN7 . . . .**76** E7
Rochdale OL11. . . . .**30** D1
ST GEORGE'S. **162** A3
St George's Ave
Manchester M15 . . . .**162** A3
Sale WA15 . . . .**120** A8
Westhoughton BL5 . . . .**57** E6
St Georges CE Prim Sch
BL5. . . . .**57** D7
St George's Cl
Atherton M46 . . . .**58** C4
Hyde SK14 . . . .**167** A1
Mossley OL5 . . . .**68** B1
Salford M6. . . . .**81** A5
Stockport SK2 . . . .**170** C2
St George's Cres
Sale WA15 . . . .**120** B8
Salford M6. . . . .**80** A3
Walkden M28. . . . .**60** D2
St Georges Ct
Hyde SK14 . . . .**167** B2
Manchester M15 . . . .**162** A3
Tyldesley M29 . . . .**76** F8
St George's Ct
Altrincham WA14 . . . .**119** B7
15 Bolton BL1 . . . .**145** B4
10 Bolton BL1 . . . .**145** C4
Eccles M30 . . . .**79** F1
3 Stretford M32 . . . .**96** C1
Whitefield BL9. . . . .**44** E2
St Georges Dr SK14. . . . . .**167** A1
St George's Dr M40. . . . . . .**83** F3
St George's Gdns
M34 . . . .**101** A1
St George's Pl
Atherton M46 . . . .**58** B4
Salford M6. . . . .**81** A5
St George's RC High Sch
M28 . . . .**60** C2
St Georges Rd
Stretford M32 . . . .**96** C1
Whitefield BL9 . . . .**45** C4
St George's Rd
Bolton BL1 . . . .**145** B4
Carrington M31. . . . .**106** D6
Droylsden M43. . . . .**83** F3
Manchester M14 . . . .**110** E7
Rochdale OL11. . . . .**29** F8
St George's Sq
9 Bolton BL1 . . . .**145** C4
Failsworth OL9 . . . .**65** E3
St George's St
Bolton BL1 . . . .**145** C4
Stalybridge SK15. . . . .**86** A3
Tyldesley M29 . . . .**76** F8
St George's Terr BB4. . . . . . .**3** A6
St George's Way M6. . . . . . .**81** A4
St Germain St BL4. . . . .**60** C8

St Gilbert's RC Prim Sch
M30 . . . .**79** B2
St Giles Dr SK14. . . . .**167** C2
St Gregorys Cl BL4 . . . .**60** C8
St Gregory's RC Prim Sch
BL4. . . . .**60** C8
St Helena Rd BL1. . . . .**145** B3
St Helens Cl WA3. . . . .**105** B3
St Helens Coll Newton Campus WA12 . . . .**89** B4
St Helens Rd
Bolton BL3, BL5. . . . .**146** B3
Leigh WN7. . . . .**75** C2
St Helier's Dr M7 . . . .**155** C4
St Helier Sq M19 . . . .**110** F5
St Heliers St BL3 . . . .**147** A4
St Herberts Ct OL9 . . . . . .**152** B3
St Herberts RC Prim Sch
OL9. . . . .**152** A3
St Hilda's CE Prim Sch
Manchester M16 . . . .**97** B2
Oldham OL1. . . . .**153** A4
Prestwich M25. . . . .**63** C4
St Hilda's Cl M22 . . . .**109** E1
St Hilda's Dr OL1 . . . .**153** A4
St Hilda's Rd
Denton M34. . . . .**100** F6
Manchester M16 . . . .**161** C1
Wythenshawe M22 . . . . . .**109** D1
St Hilda's View M40. . . . . . .**83** C5
St Hugh of Lincoln RC Prim Sch M32. . . . .**95** F3
St Hugh's Cl WA14. . . . . . .**119** E8
St Hugh's Ct
OL4. . . . .**67** E3
St Hugh's RC Prim Sch
WA15. . . . .**119** F8
St Ignatius Wlk M5 . . . . . .**161** B4
St Ives Ave SK8. . . . .**123** A6
St Ives Cres M33 . . . .**108** A1
St Ives Rd M14 . . . .**98** B2
St Ives Way OL2 . . . .**49** A4
St James' Ave BL2 . . . .**42** E7
St James' Ave BL8 . . . .**27** B4
St James CE Prim Sch
Farnworth BL4. . . . .**60** C7
Glossop SK13. . . . .**116** B8
Wardle OL12 . . . .**15** C6
St James' CE Prim Sch
Ashton-u-L OL6 . . . .**166** C3
Manchester M18 . . . .**99** D5
St James' Cl
M14 . . . .**98** D2
St James' CE Prim Sch
WN3. . . . .**54** F5
St James CE Prim Sch
Daisy Hill BL5. . . . .**57** F5
St James Cl
Glossop SK13. . . . .**116** C7
Oldham OL1. . . . .**80** B3
St James Cres WN2. . . . . . .**74** F8
St James Ct
Altrincham WA15. . . . . . .**119** E4
10 Bury BL8. . . . .**27** B4
Cheadle SK8 . . . .**131** F6
Manchester M20 . . . .**122** B8
4 Oldham OL4 . . . .**67** C8
Standish WN6. . . . .**19** D2
St James' Ct
1 Hattersley SK14. . . . . . .**102** D2
Salford M6. . . . .**80** B3
St James Dr M33 . . . .**108** A3
St James' Dr SK9 . . . .**137** A6
St James's Dr M33 . . . .**150** B2
St James' Gr 4 OL10 . . . . .**29** C2
St James Lo SK3 . . . .**124** A4
St James' RC High Sch
SK8. . . . .**131** F6
St James Rd
Hattersley SK14. . . . .**102** D2
Orrell WN5. . . . .**53** D4
St James Rd
Manchester SK4 . . . .**111** B5
Salford M7 . . . .**155** B2
St James' Rd WN5. . . . .**53** D4
St James's CE Sch & Sports Coll BL4 . . . .**60** A8
St James's Gr WA14 . . . . . .**107** F1
St James's RC Prim Sch
M6. . . . .**154** C3
St James's Sq 8 M2 . . . . .**158** C1
St James's St OL1 . . . .**67** B7
St James St
Ashton-u-L OL6 . . . .**85** D2
Eccles M30 . . . .**79** E2
Farnworth BL4. . . . .**60** B7
Heywood OL10 . . . .**29** C2
Manchester M1 . . . .**163** A4
Milnrow OL16 . . . .**31** A6
Shaw OL2. . . . .**149** B3
Westhoughton BL5 . . . .**57** F5
St James' St BB4. . . . .**2** E8
St James' Terr OL10 . . . .**29** C2
St James' Way SK8 . . . . . .**131** F6
St John Bosco RC Prim Sch M9 . . . .**65** A3
St John Fisher RC High Sch WN6. . . . .**36** F2
St John Fisher RC Prim Sch
Denton M34. . . . .**101** B1
Middleton M24. . . . .**47** B3
Wythenshawe M22 . . . . . .**121** D4
St John Rigby RC Sixth Form Coll WN5 . . . .**35** F2

St John's Ave
Droylsden M43. . . . .**84** B2
Westhoughton BL5 . . . .**39** D3
St John's CE Inf Sch
Failsworth M35 . . . .**83** F8
Leigh WN7 . . . .**75** F6
St John's CE Jun Sch
M35 . . . .**84** A7
St John's CE Prim Sch
Dukinfield SK16 . . . .**101** E8
Farnworth BL4. . . . .**60** E8
Hindley WN2 . . . .**57** B3
Manchester, Heaton Mersey SK4. . . . .**110** E2
Manchester M13 . . . .**98** E4
Radcliffe M26 . . . .**44** B1
St John's CE Prim Sch
M27 . . . .**80** C6
St John's CE Prim Sch
Slattocks M24 . . . .**47** E6
Wigan WN5 . . . .**54** B6
St John's CE Prim Sch
Mosley Comm M28. . . . . . .**77** F7
St John's Cl
Dukinfield SK16 . . . .**101** E8
Romiley SK6. . . . .**113** B2
St John's Ct
Oldham OL4 . . . .**67** F7
Ramsbottom BL0 . . . .**138** C2
Westhoughton BL5 . . . .**39** E3
St John's Ct
6 Abram WN2 . . . .**56** B1
Altrincham WA14 . . . .**119** D3
Hyde SK14. . . . .**167** C3
Radcliffe M26 . . . .**44** C2
4 Rochdale OL16 . . . .**31** B6
Salford M7. . . . .**155** A2
St John's Dr
Hyde SK14. . . . .**167** C3
3 Rochdale OL16 . . . .**31** B6
St John's Gdns OL5. . . . . . .**68** D2
St John's Ind Est OL4 . . . . .**67** F6
St John's Mews BL8 . . . .**26** F7
St John's Pass M3. . . . . . .**162** B4
St John's Pl SK4. . . . .**110** E2
St John's RC Prim Sch
Manchester M21 . . . .**97** A1
Rochdale OL11. . . . .**139** C2
St John's Rd
Altrincham WA14 . . . .**119** D3
Aspull WN2 . . . .**38** B5
Bolton BL6. . . . .**40** B4
Boothstown M28. . . . .**77** F7
Denton M34. . . . .**100** F5
Hazel Grove SK7 . . . .**124** B1
Manchester, Heaton Mersey SK4. . . . .**110** E2
Manchester, Longsight M13 . . . .**98** F4
Manchester, Old Trafford M16 . . . .**97** C4
Wilmslow SK9 . . . .**136** E3
St Johns Sq M3 . . . .**158** A2
St John's St
Abram WN2 . . . .**74** B8
Farnworth BL4. . . . .**60** E8
Radcliffe M26 . . . .**44** B2
Rawtenstall BB4 . . . .**2** F8
Salford M7. . . . .**155** A2
St John St
Atherton M46 . . . .**58** D3
Dukinfield SK16 . . . .**101** E8
1 Eccles M30. . . . .**79** D1
Horwich BL6 . . . .**22** B3
Irlam M44 . . . .**94** A2
Manchester M3 . . . .**162** B4
Newton-le-W WA12 . . . . . .**89** A3
6 Oldham OL4 . . . .**67** E6
Pendlebury M27 . . . .**80** D6
Walkden M28. . . . .**60** D4
Wigan WN5. . . . .**54** B6
St John's Wlk 3 SK3. . . . . .**123** B8
St John's Wlk OL9 . . . .**152** C2
St John Wood BL6 . . . .**40** B4
St John the Evangelist RC Prim Sch BL7 . . . .**24** F8
St John Vianney Lower Sch SK4 . . . .**168** B2
St John Vianney Upper Sch M16. . . . .**97** B2
St John with St Mark CE Prim Sch BL9 . . . .**140** C4
St John with St Michael CE Prim Sch OL2 . . . . . .**4** E5
St Joseph & St Bede RC Prim Sch BL9 . . . .**141** B4
St Josephs Ave M45 . . . .**63** C7
St Josephs Cl OL2 . . . .**149** C4
St Joseph's Con Ctr
M38 . . . .**35** B2
St Joseph's Dr
Rochdale OL16. . . . .**31** B4
Salford M5. . . . .**161** B4
St Joseph's RC High Sch
OL10. . . . .**29** C1
St Joseph's RC High Sch & Sports Coll BL6 . . . .**22** E1
St Joseph's RC Inf Sch
SK5. . . . .**111** D8
St Joseph's RC Jun & Inf Sch OL2 . . . .**149** B1
St Joseph's RC Jun Sch
SK5. . . . .**111** D8
St Joseph's RC Prim Sch
Bacup OL13 . . . .**3** D8
Bolton BL1 . . . .**142** C1
Heywood OL10 . . . .**29** C1

St Joseph's RC Prim Sch
continued
Leigh WN7 . . . .**76** A4
Manchester M13 . . . .**98** E4
Mossley OL5 . . . .**68** C1
Ramsbottom BL0 . . . .**138** B2
Sale M33 . . . .**108** B4
Salford M5. . . . .**161** B4
Shevington Moor WN6. . . . .**19** A3
Stockport SK1 . . . .**169** C1
Walkden M38. . . . .**60** A5
St Joseph St 11 BL1 . . . . .**143** A2
St Joseph's The Worker RC Prim Sch M44 . . . .**94** A3
St Jude's RC Prim Sch
WN3. . . . .**54** F5
St Katherines Dr BL6 . . . . . .**21** C3
St Kentigern's RC Prim Sch M14 . . . .**98** A1
St Kilda Ave BL4 . . . .**60** F6
St Kilda's Ave M43. . . . .**83** F3
St Kilda's Dr M7 . . . .**155** C4
St Lawrence Quay M50 . . . . .**96** F7
St Lawrence Rd M34. . . . . .**101** A3
St Lawrence St 10
M15 . . . .**162** A2
St Leonard's Ave BL6 . . . . . .**22** F1
St Leonard's Ct 4
M33 . . . .**108** A4
St Leonards Dr WA15 . . . . .**119** F6
St Leonard's Rd SK4 . . . . . .**111** D5
St Leonard's Sq 3
M24 . . . .**47** A1
St Leonard's St M24 . . . . . .**47** A1
St Lesmo Ct SK3. . . . .**123** C7
St Lesmo Rd SK3 . . . .**123** C7
St Lewis RC Prim Sch
WA3 . . . .**91** B1
St Luke's Ave WA3. . . . .**90** D8
St Lukes CE Prim Sch
OL9. . . . .**152** A3
St Luke's Cl
Bury BL9 . . . .**44** F8
Glossop SK13. . . . .**104** C1
Golborne WA3 . . . .**90** E7
Heywood OL10. . . . .**29** D3
Manchester M12 . . . .**164** B1
Salford M5. . . . .**154** A1
St Luke's Cres SK16. . . . . .**101** C8
St Lukes Ct
Bolton BL1. . . . .**144** C4
Chadderton OL9. . . . .**152** A3
St Luke's Dr WN5. . . . .**53** E4
St Lukes Ho WN4 . . . .**73** D4
St Luke's RC Prim Sch
M6 . . . .**80** C5
St Luke's Rd M6. . . . .**154** B2
St Luke St OL11 . . . .**139** C1
St Lukes Wlk 16 M40. . . . . .**83** A6
St Malachy's RC Prim Sch
M40 . . . .**156** C1
St Malo Rd WN1. . . . .**37** C4
St Margaret Mary's RC Prim Sch M40 . . . .**65** D3
St Margaret's Ave
M19 . . . .**110** F6
St Margaret's CE Jun & Inf Sch OL8 . . . .**66** B2
St Margaret's CE Prim Sch
Heywood OL10. . . . .**29** A1
Manchester M16 . . . .**97** D2
Prestwich M25. . . . .**63** D7
St Margaret's Cl
Altrincham WA14 . . . .**119** C4
Bolton BL1. . . . .**144** B4
Prestwich M25. . . . .**63** C6
St Margaret's Gdns
OL8. . . . .**66** C3
St Margaret's RC Prim Sch
SK13. . . . .**115** D8
St Margaret's Rd
Altrincham WA14 . . . .**119** C4
Bolton BL1. . . . .**144** B4
Cheadle SK8 . . . .**123** A6
Prestwich M25. . . . .**63** C6
St Margaret Ward RC Prim Sch M33 . . . .**107** C2
St Marie's RC Prim Sch
BL9. . . . .**140** C1
St Marie's RC Prim Sch
WN6. . . . .**19** E2
St Mark's Ave
Altrincham WA14 . . . .**119** A5
Royton OL2 . . . .**49** A4
Wigan WN5 . . . .**54** F7
St Marks CE Prim Sch
WN5. . . . .**54** F7
St Mark's CE Prim Sch
Manchester M40 . . . .**160** A4
Romiley SK6. . . . .**113** A4
Worsley M28. . . . .**78** F6
St Mark's Cl OL2 . . . .**49** A4
St Mark's Cres M28 . . . .**60** D1
St Mark's La M7, M8 . . . . .**155** B4
St Mark's RC Prim Sch
M27 . . . .**62** A2
St Mark's Sq 11 BL9 . . . . .**140** C4
St Mark's St
Bolton BL3 . . . .**145** C1
Reddish M19 . . . .**99** C1
Romiley SK6. . . . .**113** A4
St Mark St SK16. . . . .**166** B1
St Mark's View BL3 . . . . . .**145** C1
St Mark's Wlk BL3. . . . .**147** A4
St Martin's Ave SK4. . . . . .**168** C2

St Martin's CE Jun & Inf
Sch OL8 . . . . .67 B2
St Martin's Cl
Droylsden M43. . . . . .83 F3
Hyde SK14 . . . . .167 C2
St Martin's Dr M7 . . . . . .155 C4
St Martins Rd M33. . . . . .107 E6
St Martin's Rd
Marple SK6 . . . . .126 A6
Oldham OL8 . . . . .67 B2
St Martin's St OL11 . . . . .30 D1
St Maryis Ct SK14 . . . . . .103 C5
St Mary & St John RC
Prim Sch WN1 . . . . .37 D1
St Mary's Ave
Billinge WN5 . . . . .71 C4
Bolton BL3 . . . . .144 B1
Denton M34 . . . . .113 A8
St Mary's CE Jun & Inf Sch
M16 . . . . .97 E4
St Mary's CE Prim Sch
Bolton BL3 . . . . .146 A4
Droylsden M43. . . . . .84 B1
Failsworth M40 . . . . .65 C1
Hawkshaw BL8 . . . . .10 C2
Irlam M44 . . . . .105 C5
Prestwich M25. . . . . .63 A4
Reddish SK5 . . . . .112 A6
Rochdale OL11. . . . . .31 A4
Sale M33 . . . . .108 A4
Urmston M41. . . . . .95 B4
St Mary's CE Prim Sch
High Crompton OL2 . . . .48 F8
St Marys Cl M25 . . . . . . .63 A4
St Mary's Cl
Aspull WN2 . . . . .38 B5
Atherton M46 . . . . .58 E2
Rochdale OL16. . . . . .31 B4
Stockport SK1 . . . . .112 A1
St Mary's Crest OL3 . . . .69 C5
St Marys Ct ❷ M19 . . . . .99 A1
St Mary's Ct
Failsworth M40 . . . . .83 B8
Golborne WA3 . . . . .91 B8
Manchester M8 . . . . .63 F1
Partington M31 . . . . . . .105 F4
Prestwich M25. . . . . .63 A4
St Mary's Dr
Cheadle SK8 . . . . .122 F6
Reddish SK5 . . . . .111 F6
Uppermill OL3 . . . . .69 C5
St Mary's Gate
Manchester M3 . . . . .158 C2
Rochdale OL12, OL16 . . .139 B4
Shaw OL2. . . . . .149 B3
Uppermill OL3 . . . . .69 B8
St Mary's Hall Rd M8 . . .63 F1
St Mary's Hospl M13. . . . .98 C4
St Marys Ind Pk
SK14. . . . . .102 A6
St Mary's Parsonage
M3 . . . . .158 C1
St Mary's Pk M25. . . . . . .63 A4
St Mary's Pl BL9. . . . . . .140 B2
St Mary's RC High Sch
M29 . . . . .77 A4
St Mary's RC Inf Sch
WA12. . . . . .89 C4
St Mary's RC Jun Sch
WA12. . . . . .89 B3
St Mary's RC Prim Sch
Denton M34. . . . . .100 E3
Dukinfield SK16 . . . . . . .101 E6
Eccles M30 . . . . .79 E1
Failsworth M35 . . . . .83 E6
Horwich BL6 . . . . .22 D2
Littleborough OL15. . . . . .16 A5
Manchester M19 . . . . . .111 A8
Marple SK6 . . . . .126 B7
Middleton M24. . . . . .46 E2
Radcliffe M26 . . . . .44 A4
Stockport SK4. . . . . .169 B2
Swinton M27 . . . . .79 F8
Saint Mary's RC Prim Sch
SK13. . . . . .116 D8
St Mary's Rd
Altrincham WA14. . . . . . .119 C3
Aspull WN2 . . . . .38 C5
Disley SK12 . . . . .135 D5
Dukinfield SK14 . . . . . . .101 F5
❶ Eccles M30. . . . . .79 F2
Failsworth M40 . . . . .83 B7
Glossop SK13. . . . . .104 B5
Prestwich M25. . . . . .63 B4
Sale M33. . . . . .107 F5
Walkden M28. . . . . .60 C5
St Marys St OL1 . . . . . .153 C4
St Mary's St
Manchester, Hulme
M15 . . . . .162 B1
Manchester M3 . . . . . . .158 C1
St Marys View ❸
SK14. . . . . .101 F5
St Mary's Way
❷ Leigh WN7 . . . . .75 F5
Oldham OL1. . . . . .153 C3
Stockport SK1 . . . . .112 A2
St Matthew's CE Inf Sch
M24 . . . . .47 F2
St Matthew's CE Prim Sch
M32 . . . . .108 C8
St Matthew's CE Prim Sch
Bolton BL1. . . . . .143 B1
Little Lever BL3 . . . . .43 A3
Stockport SK3 . . . . .170 B4
St Matthew's Cl WN3 . . . .54 C4
St Matthews Ct ❾
M32 . . . . .96 C1

St Matthew's Dr OL1. . . . .48 A2
St Matthews Grange
BL1. . . . . .143 B1
St Matthew's RC High Sch
M40 . . . . .65 C2
St Matthew's Rd SK3 . . .170 A4
St Matthew's Terr
❽ Bolton BL1. . . . . .143 B1
Stockport SK3 . . . . .170 A4
St Matthew's Wlk
BL1. . . . . .143 B1
St Mawes Ct M26. . . . . . .43 C5
St Maxentius CE Prim Sch
BL2. . . . . .25 D5
St Michael's Ave
Atherton M46 . . . . .58 A1
Bolton BL2. . . . . .42 B2
Bramhall SK7. . . . . .132 E8
St Michael's Bamford CE
Prim Sch OL10 . . . . .29 D5
St Michael's CE Prim Sch
Ashton M46 . . . . .58 B2
Bolton BL3. . . . . .42 C3
Middleton M24. . . . . .48 A1
Urmston M41. . . . . .94 F1
St Michaels Cl BL8 . . . . . .43 F8
St Michael's Ct M33. . . .107 E6
St Michael's Ct
Eccles M30 . . . . .95 A8
❻ Wigan WN1 . . . . .37 C2
St Michaels Gdns M45 . . .45 B1
St Michael's RC Prim Sch
M45. . . . . .45 B1
St Michael's Rd SK14 . . .102 A2
St Michael's Sq
❻ Ashton-u-L OL6 . . . .166 C3
❸ Manchester M4 . . . .159 A3
St Modwen Rd M32. . . . . .96 A5
St Monica's RC High Sch
M25 . . . . .63 C3
St Monica's RC Prim Sch
M41. . . . . .94 E2
St Nicholas Rd
Golborne WA3 . . . . .75 A1
Manchester M15 . . . . . .162 B2
St Osmund's Dr BL2 . . . . .42 E7
St Osmund's Gr BL2 . . . . .42 E7
St Oswalds Ct PR7. . . . . .19 E8
St Oswald's RC Prim Sch
Ashton-in-M WN4 . . . . . .73 B3
Coppull PR7. . . . . .19 D8
St Oswalds Rd M34 . . . . .73 A2
St Oswald's Rd M19 . . . . .99 B2
St Ouen Ctr M28. . . . . . . .60 D3
St Patrick's RC High Sch &
Arts Coll M30 . . . . .79 B1
Manchester M4 . . . . . . .159 C3
Oldham OL8. . . . . .153 A2
Rochdale OL12. . . . . .15 A1
St Patrick St WN1 . . . . .151 A4
St Patricks Way WN1 . . .151 A3
St Paul's Ave WN3 . . . . . .54 F4
St Pauls CE Prim Sch
Salford M5. . . . . .81 B1
Walkden M28 . . . . .60 E3
St Paul's CE Prim Sch
Bolton BL1. . . . . .143 C3
Brinnington SK5. . . . . . .112 B4
Bury BL9 . . . . .141 B4
Royton OL2 . . . . .48 C3
Salford M7 . . . . .81 B8
Stalybridge SK15. . . . . . .86 C2
Walkden M28. . . . . .60 F2
Wigan WN3 . . . . .54 F3
St Paul's Cl
Adlington PR6 . . . . .21 A8
Stalybridge SK15. . . . . . .86 C2
St Pauls Ct
❸ Manchester M7 . . . . .63 C1
Stalybridge SK15. . . . . . .86 C2
❷ Walkden M28 . . . . . . .60 D2
St Paul's Gdns M26 . . . . .44 A1
St Paul's Gdns ❻ M7. . . .63 C1
St Paul's Gdns SK14 . . .167 B3
St Paul's Hill Rd
Hyde SK14. . . . . .102 A2
Hyde SK14 . . . . .167 C2
St Pauls Ho ❾ OL2 . . . . .48 D4
St Paul's Peel CE Prim Sch
M38 . . . . .59 F5
St Paul's RC High Sch
M23 . . . . .121 B4
St Paul's RC Prim Sch
Hyde SK14 . . . . .167 C4
Poynton SK12 . . . . .133 E2
St Pauls Rd M28. . . . . . . .60 E2
St Paul's Rd
Manchester, Sedgley Park
M7 . . . . .63 C1
Manchester, Withington
M20 . . . . .110 C6
Stockport, Heaton Moor
SK4. . . . . .168 B4
St Paul's Rise ❹ M7. . . . .63 C1
St Paul's St
Bury BL9 . . . . .141 A3
Hyde SK14 . . . . .167 B3
Ramsbottom BL0. . . . . . .138 C2
Stockport SK1 . . . . .112 A3
St Pauls Trad Est SK15. . .86 C2
St Paul's Villas BL3 . . . .147 A3
St Peter & St John RC
Prim Sch M3. . . . . .158 A2

St Peter & St Paul RC
Prim Sch BL3 . . . . .145 B1
St Peter's Ave BL1. . . . . .142 A2
St Peter's CE Inf Sch
WN7. . . . . .75 C5
St Peter's CE Prim Sch
Ashton-u-L OL7 . . . . . . .166 A1
Bury BL9 . . . . .44 E6
Farnworth BL4. . . . . .60 D7
Hindley WN2 . . . . .56 C5
Newton-le-W WA12. . . . . .89 E4
Rochdale OL16. . . . . .31 B5
Swinton M27 . . . . .79 E8
St Peters Cl OL7. . . . . . . .84 F2
St Peter's Cl ❼ WA13 . . .117 A4
St Peter's Ct ❶ M32. . . . .96 E3
St Peter's Dr SK14. . . . .167 C2
St Petersgate SK1 . . . . .169 C1
St Peter's Gate OL14. . . . .6 B8
St Peter's Ho BL2. . . . . .148 B2
St Peter's RC High Sch
M12 . . . . .99 A4
St Peter's RC High Sch
Visual Arts Coll WN5 . . . .53 F7
St Peter's RC Prim Sch
Hazel Grove SK7 . . . . . .124 D1
Middleton M24. . . . . .65 A7
Stalybridge SK15. . . . . . .86 A1
Wythenshawe M23 . . . . .121 A3
St Peter's Rd
Bury BL9 . . . . .44 F6
Swinton M27 . . . . .79 E8
St Peter's Smithills Dean
CE Prim Sch BL1. . . . . .142 B4
St Peter's Sq
Manchester M1 . . . . . . .162 C4
Stockport SK1 . . . . .169 C1
St Peter's Sq
❻ Ashton-u-L OL6 . . . .166 A2
Rochdale OL16. . . . . .31 B6
St Peter's Terr M14 . . . . .60 D7
St Peter's Way
Bolton, Burnden BL1, BL2,
BL3, BL4 . . . . .145 A4
Bolton, Mill Hill BL1. . . .145 C4
Saint Philip Howard Comp
Sch SK13 . . . . .104 B1
St Philip Howard RC Comp
Sch SK13 . . . . .116 B8
St Philip's Ave BL2 . . . . . .147 A4
St Philips CE Prim Sch
M15 . . . . .162 C2
St Philip's CE Prim Sch
Atherton M46 . . . . .58 E3
Salford M3. . . . . .158 A1
St Philip's Pl M3 . . . . . .158 A2
St Philip's RC Prim Sch
Manchester M7 . . . . .63 E1
Stockport SK2 . . . . .124 E6
St Philip's Rd M18. . . . . . .99 D4
St Philips Sq M3 . . . . . .158 A2
St Phillip's Dr OL1, OL2. . .48 E1
St Raphael's RC Prim Sch
SK15. . . . . .86 A5
St Richard's Cl M46. . . . . .58 C4
St Richard's RC Jun & Inf
Sch M46. . . . . .58 C4
St Richard's RC Prim Sch
M12 . . . . .99 B3
St Saviour CE Prim Sch
M26 . . . . .61 C7
St Saviour's Com Prim
Sch OL13 . . . . .4 A8
St Saviour's Rd SK2 . . . .124 C5
Saintsbridge Rd M22 . . .121 C2
St Sebastian's RC Prim
Sch M6. . . . . .81 A5
St Simons Cl SK2. . . . . .124 C8
St Simon's RC Prim Sch
SK7. . . . . .124 C8
St Simon St M3 . . . . . . .158 B3
St Stephen & All Martyrs
CE Inf Sch OL1. . . . . . .153 C4
St Stephen & All Martyrs'
CE Sch BL2 . . . . .148 C1
St Stephen's Ave
Ashton-u-L M34 . . . . . . .100 E8
Wigan WN1 . . . . .37 E2
St Stephen's CE Prim Sch
Ashton-u-L M34 . . . . . . .100 E8
Bury BL8 . . . . .27 B4
Hazel Grove SK2 . . . . . .124 F4
Kearsley BL4 . . . . .61 A6
Tyldesley M29 . . . . .77 B6
St Stephens Cl M29. . . . . .77 A5
St Stephen's Cl
Bolton BL2. . . . . .148 C1
Manchester M13 . . . . . .166 A1
St Stephen's Gdns
Kearsley BL4 . . . . .61 A6
❿ Middleton M24. . . . . . .47 A2
St Stephen's RC Prim Sch
M43 . . . . .84 B3
St Stephen's Rd WN6. . . . .19 C1
St Stephen St
❻ Oldham OL1. . . . . . . .67 A8
Salford M3. . . . . .158 A1
St Stephens View M43 . . .84 A2
St Teresa's RC Prim Sch
Irlam M44 . . . . .105 E8
Little Lever BL3. . . . . . . .43 A3
Manchester M19 . . . . . . .98 C1
Up Holland WN8 . . . . . . .35 B1
St Teresa's Rd M16 . . . . .97 A3
St Thomas Aquinas RC
High Sch (Upper Sch)
M21 . . . . .109 D7

St Thomas CE Jun & Inf
Sch WA14 . . . . .74 B1
St Thomas CE Prim Sch
Ashton-in-M WN4 . . . . . .73 C3
Leigh WN7 . . . . .76 B4
Oldham OL8. . . . . .153 A1
Westhoughton BL5 . . . . . .40 B1
St Thomas' CE Prim Sch
Newhey OL16. . . . . .32 B4
Reddish SK4 . . . . .111 C6
Stockport SK1 . . . . .170 C4
St Thomas Cl BB4. . . . . . . .1 A7
St Thomas' Cl BL9. . . . . .141 A3
St Thomas Com Prim Sch
M46 . . . . .156 C4
St Thomas Ct BL8 . . . . . .27 A1
St Thomas Hospl SK3. . .170 B4
St Thomas' Leesfield CE
Prim Sch OL4 . . . . .67 E5
St Thomas Moorside CE
Prim Sch OL1 . . . . .49 E4
St Thomas More RC High
Sch
Denton M34. . . . . .100 F2
Wigan WN5. . . . . .54 F7
St Thomas More RC Prim
Sch M24 . . . . .65 A5
St Thomas of Canterbury
Prim Sch M7. . . . . .155 B2
St Thomas of Canterbury
RC Sch BL1 . . . . .144 A4
St Thomas Par OL4 . . . . .67 E6
St Thomas' Pl M8 . . . . . .159 A4
St Thomas St N OL8 . . . .153 A1
St Thomas St S OL8 . . . .153 B1
St Thomas's CE Prim Sch
Bolton BL1. . . . . .143 A2
Bury BL9 . . . . .140 E2
St Thomas's Circ OL8 . . .153 A1
St Thomas's Ct WN8 . . . . .53 C7
St Thomas's PI SK1 . . . .170 C4
St Thomas St
Bolton BL3. . . . . .143 A2
Wigan WN3 . . . . .150 C3
St Thomas the Martyr CE
Prim Sch WN8 . . . . .53 B7
St Veronica's RC Prim Sch
BB4 . . . . .1 B7
St Vincent RC Prim Sch
OL12. . . . . .14 A1
St Vincent's RC Inf Sch
WA15. . . . . .119 E5
St Vincent's RC Jun Sch
WA15. . . . . .119 E5
St Vincent St M4 . . . . . .159 C2
St Werburgh's Rd M21,
M16. . . . . .109 C8
St Wilfrid's Dr OL12 . . . . .14 D4
St Wilfrid's CE Jun & Inf
Sch M40. . . . . .83 D5
St Wilfrids CE Prim Sch
M22 . . . . .121 E8
St Wilfrid's Ent Ctr
M15 . . . . .162 B2
St Wilfrid's Rd WN4. . . . . .73 D4
St Wilfrid's Rd WN6 . . . . .19 F1
St Wilfrids St M15 . . . . . .162 B2
St Wilfrid's Way WN6 . . . .19 E1
St William of York RC
Prim Sch BL3 . . . . .147 B3
St Williams Ave BL3 . . . .147 B3
St William's RC Prim Sch
M27 . . . . .151 C3
St Willibrord's RC Prim
Sch M11 . . . . .83 C3
St Winifred's Pl ❷
SK16. . . . . .85 F2
St Winifred's RC Prim Sch
SK4. . . . . .168 A2
Salcombe Ave BL2. . . . . .26 D1
Salcombe Cl
Sale M33. . . . . .107 F5
Wigan WN1 . . . . .37 E2
Salcombe Gr BL2. . . . . . .42 F6
Salcombe Rd
Droylsden M11, M43. . . . .99 D8
Stockport SK2 . . . . .124 C8
Salco Sq WA14 . . . . . . .119 D6
Salcot Wlk ❷ M40. . . . . .159 C3
SALE 108 C3
Sale Gram Sch M33. . . .108 C4
Sale Heys Rd M33. . . . . .107 F3
Sale High Sch M33 . . . .108 C2
Sale La M29 . . . . .77 D8
SALEM 67 C6
Salem Gr OL4 . . . . .67 C6
Sale Rd M23 . . . . .109 B2
Sales's Ave WN3 . . . . . . .55 A3
Sale's La BL9 . . . . .12 B3
Sale St OL15 . . . . .16 B6
Sale Sta M33 . . . . .108 C4
Sale Water Pk* M33. . . .108 E7
SALFORD 81 A2
Salford App M3 . . . . . . .158 C2
Salford Art Gallery &
Mus* M6 . . . . .81 C2
Salford Central Sta
M3 . . . . .158 C2
Salford City Acad M30 . . .78 F1
Salford Coll (Worsley
Campus) M28 . . . . .60 D1
Salford Crescent Sta
M6. . . . . .81 B2
Salford Foyer M6 . . . . . .154 C3

Salford Quays Sta
M50 . . . . .161 A3
Salford Rd BL5 . . . . .59 C7
Salford St
Bury BL9 . . . . .141 A4
Oldham OL4. . . . . .67 C5
Salik Gdns OL11 . . . . . .139 C1
Salisbury Ave
Heywood OL10 . . . . .46 C8
Hindley WN2 . . . . .56 E6
Salisbury Cres OL6 . . . . .85 D7
Salisbury Dr
Dukinfield SK16. . . . . . .102 A7
Manchester M25 . . . . . . .63 C2
Salisbury Ho M3. . . . . . .158 B2
Salisbury Rd
Altrincham WA14. . . . . . .119 D7
❶ Ashton-in-M WN4 . . . .73 A5
Horwich BL6 . . . . .22 F1
Manchester M21 . . . . . . .97 C1
Radcliffe M26 . . . . .43 E5
Salford M30. . . . . .80 A4
Swinton M27 . . . . .79 E7
Urmston M41. . . . . .95 C4
Salisbury St
Bolton BL3. . . . . .145 A2
Glossop SK13. . . . . .104 A5
Golborne WA3 . . . . .90 A8
Manchester M14 . . . . . . .98 A4
Middleton M24. . . . . .47 B1
Reddish SK5 . . . . .111 F8
Shaw OL2. . . . . .48 F8
Whitefield M45 . . . . .62 F8
Salisbury Terr BL3 . . . . . .43 C3
Salisbury Way M29 . . . . .77 B8
Salix Ct M6 . . . . .81 A3
Salkeld Ave WN4 . . . . . . .72 F3
Salkeld St OL11 . . . . . . .139 C1
Salley St OL15 . . . . .6 C2
Sallowfields WN5. . . . . . .53 D5
Sally Barn Cotts BB4. . . . .1 B8
Salmon Fields OL2. . . . . .48 F3
Salmon Fields Bsns
Village OL2 . . . . .48 F3
Salmon St
Manchester M4 . . . . . . .159 A2
❶ Wigan WN1 . . . . .37 E1
Salop St
Bolton BL2. . . . . .148 A2
Salford M6 . . . . .81 A4
Saltash Ct M22 . . . . . . .121 D1
Saltburn Wlk ❷ M9 . . . .157 B4
Saltdene Rd M22 . . . . . .121 C1
Saltergate Cl BL3. . . . . . .40 F4
Saltergate News M5. . . . .81 A1
Salter Rake Gate OL14 . . . .6 B8
Salters Ct M46 . . . . .58 D3
Salterton Dr BL3 . . . . . . .40 F2
Salterton Wlk ❿ M40. . . .83 A7
Saltersgate WN3 . . . . . . .79 A1
Saltford Ave M4 . . . . . . .159 C2
Saltford Ct M4 . . . . .160 A2
Salthill Ave OL10 . . . . . . .46 E7
Salthill Dr M22 . . . . .121 E2
Saltire Gdns M7 . . . . . . .155 B4
Saltney Ave M20 . . . . . .109 F7
Saltram Cl M26 . . . . .43 C5
Saltram Rd WN3. . . . . . . .54 C4
Saltrush Rd M22. . . . . . .121 D1
Salts Dr OL15 . . . . .16 A6
Salts St OL2 . . . . .149 B3
Saltwood Gr BL1 . . . . . . .143 C1
Salutation St ❿ M15. . . .162 C2
Salvin Cl WN4 . . . . .73 D3
Salvin Wlk ❷ M9 . . . . . . .64 E3
Salwick Cl WN3 . . . . .54 E4
Sam Cowan Cl M14 . . . . .98 A3
Saman Gdns M7 . . . . . . .81 C5
Samlesbury
Manchester M20 . . . . . .109 F3
Shaw OL2. . . . . .48 F7
Sammy Cookson Cl
M14 . . . . .98 A3
Samouth Cl M40. . . . . . .160 A3
Sampson Sq M14 . . . . . . .98 A4
Sam Rd OL3 . . . . .69 C5
Samson St OL16 . . . . . . .31 C8
Sam Swire St M15 . . . . .162 C1
Samuel Laycock Sch
SK15. . . . . .85 F4
Samuel Ogden St M1 . . .163 A4
Samuel St
Bury BL9 . . . . .141 A3
Failsworth SK14. . . . . . .103 C4
Hollingworth SK14. . . . . .103 C4
Manchester M19 . . . . . .111 B8
Middleton M24. . . . . .47 A2
Rochdale OL11. . . . . .30 C2
Stockport SK4 . . . . .169 A3
Tyldesley M46 . . . . .58 F1
Samwoods Ho WN4. . . . . .73 A5
Sanby Ave M18. . . . . .99 C4
Sanby Rd M18 . . . . .99 C4
Sanctuary Cl M15. . . . . .163 B1
Sanctuary The M15 . . . .162 B2
Sandacre Rd M23. . . . . .121 B7
Sandal St M40 . . . . .160 B3
Sandbach Rd SK5. . . . . . .57 C6
Sandalwood Dr WN6. . . . .36 F3
Sandbach Ave M14 . . . .109 F8

Sandbach Rd
Reddish SK5 . . . . .99 C3
Sale M33 . . . . .108 F3
Sandbach Wlk SK8 . . . .123 A4
Sandbank Gdns OL12 . . . .4 C2
Sand Banks BL1 . . . . . . .24 F6
Sandbed La
Delph OL3 . . . . .51 A5
Mossley OL5 . . . . .68 C2
Sand Beds La BL0, BB4 . . .2 B5
Sandbrook Com Prim Sch
OL11 . . . . .30 F3
Sandbrook Gdns WN5 . . .53 D5
Sandbrook Rd WN5 . . . .53 C5
Sandbrook Way
Denton M34 . . . . .101 A5
Rochdale OL11 . . . . .30 E4
Sandby Dr SK6 . . . . .126 B8
Sandering Dr M8 . . . . . .155 B1
Sandering Cl BL5 . . . . . .57 D6
Sandering Dr WN7 . . . . .76 A6
Sandering Rd
Hazel Grove SK2 . . . . . . .125 A4
Newton-le-W WA12 . . . . . .89 C4
Sanderson Cl M28 . . . . .79 A7
Sanderson Cl M40 . . . . .157 B1
Sanderson La PR7 . . . . .18 A8
Sanderson's Croft
WN7 . . . . .76 C4
Sanderson St
Bury BL9 . . . . .141 A3
Leigh WN7 . . . . .75 D5
Manchester M40 . . . . . . .157 B1
Sanderstead Dr M9 . . . .64 E3
Sandfield Cl 3 WA3 . . . .90 E8
Sandfield Cres WA3 . . . .92 C7
Sandfield Dr BL6 . . . . . .40 C6
Sandfield Rd OL16 . . . . .31 B5
Sandfold SK5 . . . . .99 C6
Sandford Ave 3 M18 . . .99 D6
Sandford Cl BL2 . . . . . . .25 E4
Sandford La SK5 . . . . . .99 D2
Sandford Rd
Orrell WN5 . . . . .53 C5
Sale M33 . . . . .108 F3
Sandford St M26 . . . . . .44 D4
Sandgate Ave
Droylsden M11 . . . . .83 D2
Kearsley M26 . . . . .61 C7
Sandgate Cl WN7 . . . . . .75 F6
Sandgate Dr M41 . . . . . .95 C4
Sandgate Rd
Chadderton OL9 . . . . . . .152 B2
Prestwich M45 . . . . .63 B7
Sandham St BL3 . . . . . .147 C4
Sandham Wlk BL3 . . . . .147 C4
Sandheys M34 . . . . .100 F5
Sandheys Gr M18 . . . . . .99 F4
Sandhill Cl BL3 . . . . . . .147 C4
Sandhill La
Broadbottom SK6 . . . . . .115 A4
Marple SK6 . . . . .114 E1
Sandhill St SK14 . . . . . .167 C4
Sandhole La OL11 . . . . . .29 E5
Sand Hole La OL11 . . . . .30 F1
Sand Hole Rd BL4 . . . . .61 A6
Sandhurst Ave M20 . . . .110 A6
Sandhurst Cl BL8 . . . . . .27 B3
Sandhurst Ct BL2 . . . . . .42 E6
Sandhurst Dr
Bolton BL2 . . . . .42 E6
2 Wilmslow SK9 . . . . .137 C8
Sandhurst Rd
Manchester M20 . . . . . . .110 B2
Stockport SK2 . . . . .124 C7
Sandhutton Rd M9 . . . . .64 D1
Sandiacre WN6 . . . . .36 E8
Sandilands Prim Sch
M23 . . . . .120 E2
Sandilands Rd M23 . . . .120 D7
Sandilea Ct M7 . . . . .63 A1
Sandileigh Ave
Altrincham WA15 . . . . . . .119 F3
Brinnington SK5 . . . . . . .112 B4
Cheadle SK8 . . . . .123 A6
Manchester M20 . . . . . . .110 B5
Sandileigh Dr
Altrincham WA15 . . . . . . .119 F3
Bolton BL1 . . . . .25 B3
Sandinmoss Ct 1 M33 . .107 F4
Sandiway
Glossop SK13 . . . . .116 F7
Heywood OL10 . . . . .29 E2
Irlam M44 . . . . .94 A2
Romiley SK6 . . . . .112 F3
Stockport SK7 . . . . .123 E2
Sandiway Cl SK6 . . . . . .125 F8
Sandiway Dr M20 . . . . . .110 A3
Sandiway Pl WA14 . . . . .119 D5
Sandiway Rd
Altrincham WA14 . . . . . . .119 D6
Handforth SK9 . . . . .131 D5
Sale M33 . . . . .107 F4
Sandling Dr WA3 . . . . . .74 E2
Sandmere Wlk 25 M9 . . .64 E3
Sandon St BL3 . . . . .147 A4
Sandown Ave M6 . . . . . .154 B2
Sandown Cl
Culcheth WA3 . . . . .91 F4
6 Oldham OL1 . . . . .49 A1
Wilmslow SK9 . . . . .137 D8
Sandown Cres
Little Lever BL3 . . . . .43 A2
Manchester M18 . . . . . . .99 D3

Sandown Dr
Altrincham WA15 . . . . . . .129 D6
Denton M34 . . . . .113 B8
Sale M33 . . . . .107 E3
Sandown Gdns M41 . . . .95 A4
Sandown Rd
Bolton BL5 . . . . .25 E3
Hazel Grove SK7 . . . . . . .125 A2
Stockport SK3 . . . . .123 B8
Whitefield BL9 . . . . .45 A2
Wigan WN6 . . . . .36 E3
Sandown St M18 . . . . . . .99 F6
Sandpiper Cl
Dukinfield SK16 . . . . . . .101 E7
Farnworth BL4 . . . . .59 F7
Newton-le-W WA12 . . . . . .89 C7
Rochdale OL11 . . . . .29 F7
Sandpiper Dr SK3 . . . . .170 A2
Sandpiper Rd WN3 . . . . .54 B4
Sandpits Bsns Pk
SK14 . . . . .102 C3
Sandra Dr WA12 . . . . . . .89 E3
Sandray Cl BL3 . . . . .40 F5
Sandray Gr M5 . . . . .154 B1
Sandridge Cl M41 . . . . . .60 E8
Sandridge Wlk M12 . . . .164 B2
Sandringham Ave
Denton M34 . . . . .100 D6
Reddish M34 . . . . .100 A3
Stalybridge SK15 . . . . . . .86 A3
Sandringham Cl
Adlington PR7 . . . . .20 E6
Altrincham WA14 . . . . . . .118 F1
Wigan WN3 . . . . .54 E5
Sandringham Ct
Golborne WA3 . . . . .90 E7
5 Wilmslow SK9 . . . . .137 A6
Sandringham Dr
Dukinfield SK16 . . . . . . .101 F7
Leigh WN7 . . . . .76 E7
Milnrow OL16 . . . . .32 A6
Poynton SK12 . . . . .133 D3
Ramsbottom BL8 . . . . . . .11 A1
Stockport SK4 . . . . .168 A1
Sandringham Grange
M25 . . . . .63 E3
Sandringham Rd
Cheadle SK8 . . . . .123 A3
Hazel Grove SK7 . . . . . . .124 F2
Hindley WN2 . . . . .56 F4
Horwich BL6 . . . . .22 E2
Hyde SK14 . . . . .113 E7
Romiley SK6 . . . . .112 D3
Worsley M28 . . . . .78 A6
Sandringham St M18 . . .99 C4
Sandringham Way
Royton OL2 . . . . .48 C6
4 Wilmslow SK9 . . . . .137 A6
Sands Ave
Chadderton OL9 . . . . .47 D1
Chadderton OL9 . . . . .65 E8
Sands Cl SK14 . . . . .102 D1
Sandsend Cl M8 . . . . . . .155 B1
Sandsend Rd M41 . . . . . .95 C3
Sand St
Manchester M40 . . . . . . .159 C4
Stalybridge SK15 . . . . . . .101 F8
Sandstone Rd
Milnrow OL16 . . . . .31 F7
Wigan WN3 . . . . .54 E2
Sandstone Way M21 . . .109 D6
Sands Wlk SK14 . . . . . . .102 D1
Sandway WN6 . . . . .36 F2
Sandwich St M33 . . . . . .108 B6
Sandwich Rd M30 . . . . . .79 F3
Sandwich St M28 . . . . . .60 D2
Sandwick Cres BL1 . . . . .145 A1
Sandwith Cl WN3 . . . . . .55 B2
Sandy Acre M8 . . . . .40 E6
Sandy Acre OL5 . . . . .86 C8
Sandycroft Ave BL1 . . . . .59 A6
Sandy Bank OL2 . . . . . . .48 F8
Sandy Bank Ave SK14 . .102 C1
Sandybank Cl SK13 . . . .171 B4
Sandy Bank Rd
Edgworth BL7 . . . . .9 D5
Salford M8 . . . . .155 C4
Sandybrook Cl BL8 . . . . .26 F6
Sandybrook Dr M9 . . . . .64 C2
Sandy Brow M9 . . . . .64 D2
Sandy Brow La WA3 . . . .90 E2
Sandy Cl BL9 . . . . .44 F4
Sandycroft Ave
1 Wigan WN1 . . . . .37 C1
Wythenshawe M22 . . . . . .121 D3
Sandygate Cl WN7 . . . . .75 A1
Sandygate Cl M27 . . . . .79 E7
Sandy Gr
Dukinfield SK16 . . . . . . .101 D8
Salford M6 . . . . .154 B3
Swinton M27 . . . . .79 F8
Sandy Haven Cl SK14 . .102 D1
Sandy Haven Wlk
SK14 . . . . .102 D1
Sandyhill Rd M9 . . . . . . .64 B3
Sandyhills BL3 . . . . .147 B4
Sandy La
Adlington PR7 . . . . .20 F6
Broadbottom SK13 . . . . .115 A4
Culcheth WA3 . . . . .91 F4
Droylsden M43 . . . . .84 C2
Dukinfield SK16 . . . . . . .101 D8
Golborne, Aspull Common
WA3 . . . . .75 A1
Golborne WA3 . . . . .89 F8
Irlam M44 . . . . .94 A2
Lymm WA13 . . . . .117 B4

Sandy La continued
Altrincham M21 . . . . .109 C8
Middleton M24 . . . . .65 C8
Orrell WN5 . . . . .53 D4
Prestwich M25 . . . . .63 A2
Reddish SK4, SK5 . . . . . .169 B3
Rochdale OL11 . . . . .30 C7
Romiley SK6 . . . . .113 D3
Royton OL2 . . . . .48 D4
Salford M40 . . . . .154 B3
Stretford M32 . . . . .96 C1
Tyldesley M29 . . . . .77 B1
Tyldesley, Town Lane
M29 . . . . .77 A4
Uppermill OL3 . . . . .51 B7
Wilmslow SK9 . . . . .136 E8
Wythenshawe M23 . . . . .120 C7
Sandylands Dr M25 . . . .63 A1
Sandy Meade M25 . . . . .63 A3
Sandy Pk WN2 . . . . .57 A6
Sandyshot Wlk 4
M22 . . . . .121 F3
Sandy Vale SK16 . . . . . . .85 E1
Sandywarps M44 . . . . . .106 A8
Sandyway M25 . . . . .63 A3
Sandy Way WN2 . . . . . . .56 F6
Sandywell Cl BL5 . . . . . .57 D8
Sandywell St M11 . . . . . .99 D7
Sandywell St M11 . . . . . .99 D8
Sandy Wlk 4 OL2 . . . . . .48 D4
Sandy Wood M6 . . . . . . .154 B3
Sanfold La M19 . . . . .99 C2
Sangster Ct M5 . . . . . . .161 A4
Sankey Gr M9 . . . . .64 B3
Sankey St
Bury BL9 . . . . .140 A2
Golborne WA3 . . . . .90 A8
Newton-le-W WA12 . . . . . .89 A3
Sankey Valley Ind Est
WA12 . . . . .89 A2
Santiago St M14 . . . . . . .98 B3
Santley St M12 . . . . .99 A3
Santon Ave M14 . . . . . . .110 E8
Santon Dr WA3 . . . . .90 E8
Sapling Gr M33 . . . . .107 D2
Sapling Rd
Bolton BL3 . . . . .146 C2
Swinton M27 . . . . .79 D5
Sarah Butterworth Ct 11
OL16 . . . . .31 B6
Sarah Butterworth St 10
OL16 . . . . .31 B6
Sarah St
Britannia OL13 . . . . .4 C8
1 Eccles M30 . . . . .79 B1
Edenfield BL0 . . . . .1 E3
Hindley WN2 . . . . .57 B2
Manchester M11 . . . . . . .164 C4
Middleton M24 . . . . .64 F8
2 Oldham OL8 . . . . .64 D2
6 Rochdale OL11 . . . . . .31 A6
Shaw OL2 . . . . .149 A1
Sargent Dr M16 . . . . .97 E4
Sargent Rd SK6 . . . . . . .112 D2
Sark Rd M21 . . . . .97 A2
Sarn Ave M22 . . . . .121 D4
Sarnesfield Cl M12 . . . . .99 F4
Sarsfield Ave 1 WA3 . . . .90 D8
Satinwood Cl WA3 . . . . .72 F2
Satinwood Wlk M3 . . . . .158 B3
Saturn Gr M6 . . . . .81 C4
Saunton Ave M11 . . . . . .99 D8
Saunton Rd M11 . . . . . . .99 D8
Sautridge Cl OL11 . . . . . .47 D7
Savernake Rd SK6 . . . . .113 C5
Savick Ave BL2 . . . . .42 F7
Saville Rd
Gatley SK8 . . . . .122 B6
Radcliffe BL8 . . . . .43 F7
Saville St
Bolton BL3 . . . . .148 A2
Middleton M24 . . . . .65 D7
Saviour CE Prim Sch
M40 . . . . .156 C1
Saviours Terr BL3 . . . . . .144 C1
Savio Way M24 . . . . .65 A7
Savoy Ct M45 . . . . .44 E2
Savoy Dr OL2 . . . . .48 D2
Savoy St
Oldham OL4 . . . . .67 B5
Rochdale OL11 . . . . .30 C8
Sawley Ave
Golborne WA3 . . . . .74 D1
Littleborough OL15 . . . . . .16 A7
Oldham OL4 . . . . .67 D4
Whitefield M45 . . . . .44 F2
Wigan WN6 . . . . .36 F2
Sawley Cl WA3 . . . . .92 A2
Sawley Dr SK8 . . . . .132 C6
Sawley Rd M40 . . . . .160 B4
Sawmill The BL9 . . . . . .140 C1
Saw Mill Way 5 OL15 . . .16 A5
Sawpit St WA13,
WA14 . . . . .118 A6
Saw St BL1 . . . . .143 B2
Sawston Wlk M40 . . . . . .65 C3
Sawyer Brow SK14 . . . . .167 C4
Sawyer Dr WN4 . . . . .73 D3
Sawyer St
Bury BL8 . . . . .27 B4
6 Rochdale OL12 . . . . . .14 F1
Saxby Ave BL7 . . . . .24 F8
Saxby St M6 . . . . .80 C5
Saxelby Dr M8 . . . . .156 B3
Saxfield Dr M23 . . . . . . .121 C6

Saxholme Wlk 5
M22 . . . . .121 C2
Saxon Ave
Dukinfield SK16 . . . . . . .101 C8
Manchester M8 . . . . .64 A2
Saxon Cl BL8 . . . . .27 B2
Saxon Dr
Chadderton OL9 . . . . .65 E8
Denton M34 . . . . .100 E7
Droylsden M43 . . . . .84 B2
Saxon Ho 8 M16 . . . . . . .97 D3
Saxonholme Rd OL11 . . .47 C7
Saxon Rd OL5 . . . . .68 D3
Saxon St
Denton M34 . . . . .100 F3
Droylsden M43 . . . . .84 B2
Manchester M40 . . . . . . .160 B3
Middleton M24 . . . . .64 F8
Oldham OL4 . . . . .67 C2
Radcliffe M26 . . . . .43 F3
Saxons The BL3 . . . . . . .146 A2
Saxthorpe Cl
8 Sale M33 . . . . .107 D5
Wigan WN3 . . . . .54 D3
Saxthorpe Wlk M12 . . . .164 B1
Saxwood Ave M9 . . . . . .64 D1
Saxwood Cl OL12 . . . . . .13 F1
Scafell Ave OL7 . . . . .84 F4
Scafell Cl
High Lane SK6 . . . . .134 E8
Oldham OL1 . . . . .48 F1
Scafell Dr WN5 . . . . .54 B6
Scafell Gr WN7 . . . . .56 B2
Scalby Wlk 2 M22 . . . . .121 D1
Scale St M5 . . . . .81 A1
Scarborough St M40 . . . .83 A8
Scarcroft Rd M12 . . . . . .165 A1
Scarfield Dr OL11 . . . . . .13 E1
Scargill Cl 1 M14 . . . . . .110 C8
Scargill Rd BL3 . . . . .146 A3
Scarisbrick Ave M20 . . . .110 D3
Scarisbrick Rd M19 . . . . .110 F8
Scarisbrick St 3 WN1 . . .37 C1
Scarr Ave M26 . . . . .44 C2
Scarr Dr OL12 . . . . .14 F3
Scarr La OL2 . . . . .49 D7
Scarr Terr OL12 . . . . .14 F2
Scarsdale Ave BL1 . . . . .142 A1
Scarsdale Rd M14 . . . . . .98 E4
Scarsdale St M6 . . . . . . .81 B3
Scarthwood Cl BL2 . . . . .25 E5
Scawfell Ave BL2 . . . . . . .25 F5
Scawton Wlk M9 . . . . . . .64 B5
Sceptre Cl WA12 . . . . . . .89 A3
Schofield Cl M24 . . . . . . .47 A3
Schofield Gdns WN7 . . . .75 E3
Schofield Hall Rd
OL15 . . . . .16 C1
Schofield La BL6 . . . . . . .57 F3
Schofield Pl OL15 . . . . . . .6 D2
Schofield Rd
Droylsden M43 . . . . .84 B1
Eccles M30 . . . . .79 A1
Schofield St
Calderbrook OL15 . . . . . . .6 D2
Droylsden M11 . . . . .83 C2
Failsworth M35 . . . . .83 F8
Haslingden BB4 . . . . .1 A6
Heywood OL10 . . . . .29 D1
Leigh WN7 . . . . .75 E4
Littleborough OL15 . . . . . .16 C1
Milnrow OL16 . . . . .32 A5
Oldham OL8 . . . . .66 F3
Radcliffe M26 . . . . .44 B4
Scholfield St
Ashton-u-L OL6 . . . . .85 D6
Stretford M32 . . . . .96 F3
Wigan WN1 . . . . .37 D4
School Brow
Billinge WN5 . . . . .71 E5
Bury BL9 . . . . .140 B3
Romiley SK6 . . . . .113 A2
Worsley M28 . . . . .78 F6
School Cl SK12 . . . . .133 F3
School Cres SK15 . . . . . .86 A4
School Ct
Bolton BL3 . . . . .8 E2
Edenfield BL0 . . . . .1 E3
Manchester M4 . . . . .159 C2

School Ct continued
Stockport SK3 . . . . .170 C2
School Dr
Billinge WN5 . . . . .71 E5
Dukinfield SK16 . . . . . . .101 E6
School Gr
Manchester M20 . . . . . . .110 D6
Prestwich M25 . . . . .63 A2
School Hill BL1 . . . . .145 B4
School Ho The 3 BL7 . . .24 F7
Schoolhouse M17 . . . . . .96 D5
School La
Aspull WN2 . . . . .37 E7
Bury BL9 . . . . .27 E8
Carrington M31 . . . . .106 C6
Compstall SK6 . . . . .114 B4
Edgworth BL7 . . . . .9 D8
Garswood WN4 . . . . .72 C3
Hollinfare WA3 . . . . .105 A3
Hyde SK14 . . . . .113 E7
Irlam, Cadishead M44 . . .105 D3
Manchester, Didsbury M19,
M20 . . . . .110 C3
Manchester M9 . . . . .64 C2
Mossley SK15 . . . . .86 E7
Partington WA14 . . . . . . .118 D5
Poynton SK12 . . . . .133 F4
Reddish SK4 . . . . .111 C5
Rochdale, Bagslate Moor
OL11 . . . . .29 C8
Rochdale OL16 . . . . .139 C3
Standish WN6 . . . . .19 D1
Up Holland, Roby Mill
WN8 . . . . .35 B3
Up Holland WN5, WN8 . . .53 C7
Wigan WN1 . . . . .151 A4
School Mews
Bramhall SK7 . . . . .132 E7
Rochdale OL16 . . . . .32 B4
School Rd
Altrincham WA15 . . . . . . .119 F3
Eccles M30 . . . . .95 C8
Failsworth M35 . . . . .83 F7
Handforth SK9 . . . . .131 D4
Oldham OL8 . . . . .66 B2
Sale M33 . . . . .108 B5
Stretford M32 . . . . .108 B5
School Side SK8 . . . . . . .122 D3
Schoolside Cl M8 . . . . . .156 A2
Schoolside La M24 . . . . .64 C7
Schools Rd M18 . . . . .99 E5
School St
Ashton-in-M WN4 . . . . . . .73 D5
Atherton M46 . . . . .58 B2
Bacup OL13 . . . . .3 B8
Bury BL9 . . . . .141 B1
Eccles M30 . . . . .79 B3
Golborne WA3 . . . . .90 A8
Hazel Grove SK7 . . . . . . .124 E2
Heywood OL10 . . . . .29 C2
Horwich BL6 . . . . .22 C3
Ince-in-M WN2 . . . . .151 C3
Leigh WN7 . . . . .75 C8
Littleborough OL15 . . . . . .15 E5
Little Lever BL3 . . . . .43 B3
Manchester M4 . . . . .159 B3
Newton-le-W WA12 . . . . . .89 B3
Oldham, Grotton OL4 . . . .68 A6
Oldham OL8 . . . . .153 A1
Radcliffe M26 . . . . .44 A3
Ramsbottom BL8 . . . . . . .138 B1
Rochdale OL12 . . . . .139 C4
Tyldesley, Gin Pit M29 . . .76 F7
Tyldesley M29 . . . . .76 F8
Uppermill OL3 . . . . .69 B8
Westhoughton BL5 . . . . . .57 F8
Wigan WN1 . . . . .151 A4
School Street Ind Est
SK7 . . . . .124 C2
School Terr
Golborne WA3 . . . . .90 A8
Whitworth OL12 . . . . .4 C1
School View BL7 . . . . .9 D8
School Way WN5 . . . . . . .54 C6
School Wlk M16 . . . . . . .162 A1
Schuster Rd M14 . . . . . . .98 D3
Schwabe St M24 . . . . . . .64 C8
Scobell St BL8 . . . . .27 A5
Scoltock Way OL1 . . . . .153 F2
Score St M11 . . . . .83 A1
Scorton Ave BL2 . . . . . . .42 F7
Scorton St BL1 . . . . .144 C4
Scorton Wlk 22 M40 . . . .65 D2
Scotforth Cl M15 . . . . . .162 B3
Scotia Wlk 1 WA3 . . . . . .90 F8
Scot La
Aspull BL6, WN2 . . . . . . .38 E6
Wigan, Marsh Green WN5,
WN6 . . . . .36 E1
Wigan, Worsley Hall
WN5 . . . . .54 F7
Scotland M44 . . . . .159 A3
Scotland Hall Rd M40 . . .83 C4
Scotland La BL9 . . . . .28 D8
Scotland Pl BL2 . . . . . . .138 C2
Scotland St
Ashton-u-L OL6 . . . . . . .166 C2
Failsworth M40 . . . . .83 C5
SCOT LANE END 38 F7
Scot Lane End CE Prim
Sch BL16 . . . . .38 E7
Scotta Rd M30 . . . . .95 C8
Scott Ave
Bury BL9 . . . . .44 F6

Scott Ave *continued*
Eccles M30 ....79 C3
Hindley WN2 ....56 E6
Manchester M21 ....97 B2
Scott Cl SK5.............169 C4
Scott Court Appts M27...80 D8
Scott Dr
Altrincham WA15.......119 F4
Marple SK6............126 B8
Scottield Ol8...........153 C1
Scottfield Rd OL8.......153 C1
Scott Gate M34.........100 F7
Scott Ho
Manchester M19 ....99 A2
Walsden OL14 ....6 A8
Scott Rd
Denton M34............100 E1
Droylsden M43.........84 A1
Golborne WA3..........74 D2
Prestwich M25..........62 F3
Scotts Ind Est OL16.....31 A6
Scott St
Kearsley M26...........61 D7
Leigh WN7.............75 D5
Oldham OL8............153 C1
Tyldesley M29..........77 C4
Walsden OL14 ....6 A8
Westhoughton BL5......39 E2
Wigan WN6.............37 B1
Scott Wlk WA12.........89 C1
Scotty Brook Cres
SK13................116 B8
Scout Dr M23...........120 F4
Scout Gn M24...........47 A3
Scout Rd
Bolton BL1, BL7........24 B7
Edenfield BL0...........2 A2
Scout View BL8..........27 A6
Scovell St M7...........155 A2
Scowcroft La OL2........149 A2
Scowcroft St [31] BL2....25 B1
Scroggins La WN3.......105 F4
Scropton St M40........157 A2
Seabright Wlk [12]
M11.................160 C1
Seabrook Cres M41......95 D4
Seabrook Rd M40........83 C4
Seacombe Ave M14......98 A1
Seacombe Gr SK3.......123 B8
Seaford Rd
Bolton BL2.............25 E6
Salford M6.............81 B4
Seaford Wlk
Chadderton OL9........152 B2
Manchester M9 ....64 C3
Seaforth Ave M14.......58 C4
Seaforth Rd BL1.........24 E5
Seaham Dr BL8..........27 C5
Seaham Wlk [5] M44....98 B3
Sealand Cl OL8..........108 E2
Sealand Dr M30.........95 A8
Sealand Ho M25.........63 C5
Sealand Rd M23.........108 F2
Sealand Way [2] SK9....131 D4
Seale Ave M34..........100 D7
Sealey Wlk M40.........160 B4
Seal Rd SK7.............133 A7
Seaman Way WN2........56 A6
Seamon's Dr WA14......119 A6
Seamon's Rd WA14......119 A6
Seamons Wlk WA14.....119 B5
Searby Rd M18..........99 B4
Searness Rd M24........46 D2
Seascale Ave M11.......83 B3
Seascale Cres WN1......37 C3
Seascale Wlk [3] M24...46 E2
Seathwaite Cl
Middleton M24.........46 D2
Tyldesley M29..........77 A7
Seathwaite Rd BL4......59 F7
Seathwaite Wlk M11....165 C1
Seatoller Cl OL2.........48 E4
Seatoller Dr M24........46 C1
Seatoller Pl WN5........54 B7
Seaton Cl SK1...........124 D1
Seaton Mews OL7........84 F4
Seaton Rd BL1..........142 C2
Seaton Way M14........98 A4
Sebastian Cl SK6........126 B7
Second Ave
Atherton M46..........58 D4
Bolton BL1............144 B3
Bury BL9..............28 D4
Droylsden M43.........83 D2
Little Lever BL3........42 B3
Mossley SK15..........86 E5
Oldham OL8............66 D1
Poynton SK12..........133 D1
Stretford M17..........96 D5
Swinton M27...........79 D5
Tyldesley M29..........77 B4
Wigan WN6.............37 A2
Second St BL1...........23 F4
Section St [8] BL3.......145 C2
Sedan Cl M5.............81 A1
Sedburgh Cl M33........107 D3
Sedbury Cl M23.........108 F1
Seddon Ave
Manchester M18........99 D6
Radcliffe M26..........44 D5
Seddon Cl
Atherton M46..........58 C3
Radcliffe M26..........44 A4
Seddon Gdns M26.......61 A8
Seddon House Dr WN6...36 E3
Seddon La M26..........61 A8
Seddon St WA14........119 D2
Seddons Ave BL8........44 A8

Seddon St
[7] Little Lever BL3.....43 B3
Manchester M12........99 B2
Radcliffe M26..........44 A3
Walkden M38...........59 F5
Westhoughton BL5......39 E3
Sedgeborough Rd M16...97 E3
Sedge Cl SK5............112 A8
Sedgefield Cl M5........81 A2
Sedgefield Dr
Bolton BL1............142 B3
Wigan WN6............36 E3
Sedgefield Pk [1] OL4...67 D6
Sedgefield Rd M26......62 A8
Sedgefield Wlk [8]
M23.................108 F2
Sedgeford Cl SK4........131 D1
Sedgeford Rd M40.......157 A1
Sedgely WN6............37 A7
Sedgemoor St M40......123 B2
Sedgemoor Vale BL2....25 F2
Sedgemoor Way OL1....153 B3
Sedgley Ave
Manchester M25........25 C2
Prestwich M25.........62 C5
Rochdale OL16.........31 B4
Sedgley Bldgs M43......100 A8
Sedgley Cl M24..........65 C7
Sedgley Dr BL5..........57 E5
SEDGLEY PARK..........63 C2
Sedgley Park Com Prim
Sch M25...............63 D2
Sedgley Park Rd M25....63 C2
Sedgley Park Trad Est
M25.................63 B1
Sedgley Rd M8..........156 A4
Sedgley St M24.........65 C7
Sedgwick Cl
Atherton M46..........58 E3
Westhoughton BL5......57 F6
Sedwyn St [7] WN1.....37 E1
SEEDFIELD.............27 F5
Seedfield Rd BL9.......27 F5
SEEDLEY..............154 B3
Seedley Ave M38........60 B4
Seedley Park Rd M6.....154 B2
Seedley Prim Sch M6....154 B2
Seedley Rd M6..........154 C3
Seedley St M14.........98 B3
Seedley Terr M6........154 B3
Seedley View Rd M6.....154 B2
Seel St BL1.............144 C3
Seel St OL5.............68 B1
Sefton Ave
Atherton M46..........58 C5
Orrell WN5.............53 D5
Sefton Cl
Manchester M13........163 B2
Middleton M24.........64 E8
Oldham OL1............49 D4
Orrell WN5.............53 D5
Sefton Cres M33........108 B6
Sefton Ct
[8] Bolton BL1.........145 B4
[4] Bolton BL9.........27 F6
Sefton Dr
Bury BL9..............28 A6
Handforth SK9.........131 C2
Swinton M27...........79 D6
Worsley M28...........79 A6
Sefton Fold Dr WN5.....71 D5
Sefton Fold Gdns WN5..71 D5
Sefton La BL6...........22 E1
Sefton Rd
Ashton-in-M WN4......72 F6
Bolton BL1............142 B2
Manchester M21........109 B8
Middleton M24.........64 E8
Orrell WN5.............53 D5
Sale M33..............108 B5
Swinton M27...........61 F1
Wigan WN3.............54 F4
Sefton St
Bury BL9..............27 F6
Glossop SK13..........116 C8
Heywood OL10.........29 E1
Leigh WN7.............75 F5
Manchester M8.........156 A4
Oldham OL9............66 B2
Radcliffe M26..........44 C1
Rochdale OL11.........139 C1
Whitefield M45........67 F7
Sefton View WN5........53 D5
Segal Cl M7............155 A3
Selborne Rd M21........97 B1
Selbourne Cl
Reddish SK5...........99 E2
Westhoughton BL5......40 A1
Selbourne St
Leigh WN7.............75 F7
Oldham OL8............67 A1
Selby Ave
Chadderton OL9........47 F1
Whitefield M45........44 F2
Selby Cl
Milnrow OL16.........31 E6
Poynton SK12..........133 D5
Radcliffe M26..........44 D5
Stretford M32..........96 A3
Selby Dr
Salford M6.............80 B3
Salford M6.............141 A1
Swinton M41...........94 F5
Selby Gdns SK8.........132 C6
Selby Rd
Middleton M24.........46 F3
Stretford M32..........96 A3

Selby St
Manchester M11........165 A4
Reddish SK4...........169 A4
Rochdale OL16.........31 B8
Selby Wlk BL8...........26 C1
Selden St OL8...........153 A1
Selham Wlk M13.........163 C3
Selhurst Ave M11.......83 C2
Selkirk Ave
Garswood WN4.........72 D4
Oldham OL8............66 D4
Selkirk Dr M9...........64 F3
Selkirk Gr WN5..........54 C8
Selkirk Pl OL10..........29 A1
Selkirk Rd
Chadderton OL9........66 A4
Manchester SK4........100 A8
Sellars Sq M43...........100 A8
Sellers Way OL9.........66 A3
Selsby Ave M30..........79 B2
Selsey Ave
Cheadle SK3...........122 F7
Sale M33..............107 F3
Selsey Dr M20..........122 C8
Selside WN3.............55 B2
Selside Cl M26..........61 B8
Selside Wlk [1] M14.....110 C8
Selstead Rd M22........121 C1
Selston Rd M9..........64 B4
Selworth Ave M33.......108 A3
Selworth Cl [5] WA15...119 E6
Selworthy Rd M16......97 E4
Selwyn Ave M9..........64 D1
Selwyn Cl [3] OL8.......153 E6
Selwyn Dr SK8..........132 C7
Selwyn St
Bolton BL2............148 A2
Leigh WN7.............75 F4
Oldham OL8............153 B1
Semple Way OL9........65 F3
Senator Cl WN2........38 B2
Senecar Cl WN14.......110 E7
Senior Ave M14........110 D5
Senior Rd M30..........95 A8
Senior St M3...........158 B3
Sennicar La
Aspull WN2............37 E6
Wigan WN1............37 C5
Sepal Cl SK5...........100 A1
Sephton Ave WA3.......91 E3
Sephton St WN3........151 C2
Sepia Gr M24...........46 F1
Sequoia St M9..........157 B4
Sergeants La M45.......62 C7
Serin Cl
Hazel Grove SK2.......124 F5
Newton-le-W WA12.....89 C3
Service St SK3..........123 B8
Sesame Gdns M44.......94 C3
Setantii - Tales of
Tameside (Mus)*
OL6................166 B3
Set St SK15.............85 F1
Settle Cl BL8...........26 F2
Settle St
Bolton BL2............147 B3
Little Lever BL3........43 C3
Setstones La OL3.......51 D1
Seven Acres OL3........50 F5
Seven Acres La OL12....13 E2
Seven Oaks WN7........76 A6
Sevenoaks Ave
Manchester SK4........111 A5
Urmston M41...........95 D4
Sevenoaks Dr
Bolton BL3............147 B3
Pendlebury M27........80 A6
Sevenoaks Rd SK8......122 B6
Sevenoaks Wlk [1]
M13.................163 C1
Seven Stars Rd WN3....150 A3
Seven Stiles Dr SK6....125 E7
Seventh Ave OL8........66 D1
Severn Cl
Altrincham WA14......119 C6
Billinge WN5..........71 D3
Bury BL9..............27 F7
Severn Dr
Bramhall SK7..........132 C6
Hindley WN2...........21 A6
Milnrow OL16.........32 A6
Wigan WN5.............53 C8
Severn Rd
Ashton-in-M WN4......73 E5
Chadderton OL9........65 F8
Culcheth WA3..........91 F2
Heywood OL10.........29 A3
Oldham OL8............66 C1
Severnside Trad Est
M17................96 B5
Severn St WN7..........76 B4
Severn Way
Kearsley BL4...........61 B6
Reddish SK5...........111 F5
Seville's Bldgs OL5.....68 C2
Seville St
Royton OL2............48 E2
Shaw OL2.............149 A1
Sewell Way M38.........59 F3
Sewerby St M16.........97 F4
Sexa St M11............99 D8
Seymon St
Glossop SK13..........103 F7
Heywood OL10.........29 C7
Seymour Ave M11.......83 D2
Seymour Cl M16.........161 C1
Seymour Ct
Manchester SK4........110 E2

Seymour Ct *continued*
[2] Radcliffe M26......44 B3
Salford M7.............155 C4
Seymour Dr BL2.........25 C6
Seymour Gr
Altrincham WA15.......120 A5
Farnworth BL4..........42 A1
Manchester M16.......97 B4
Marple SK6............125 E6
Rochdale OL16.........31 B3
Sale M33..............108 A4
Seymour Ho [16] SK9...131 C1
Seymour Park Prim Sch
M16................97 B4
Seymour Rd
Bolton BL1............143 C3
Cheadle SK8..........132 A8
Manchester M7, M8....63 F1
Stockport SK2.........124 B5
Seymour Rd S M11......83 D2
Seymour St
Bolton BL2............25 C6
Denton M34...........100 D4
Heywood OL10.........29 C1
Manchester M18........99 D6
Radcliffe M26.........44 B3
Seymour Wlk [2] M26...44 B3
Shackleton Cl M40......83 C4
Shackleton Gr BL1......23 E2
Shackleton St M30......79 C3
Shackliffe Rd M40......65 B2
Shaddock Ave OL12.....13 F1
Shade Ave OL4.........67 F5
Shade Terr M14.........134 F7
Shadowbrook Ave
M23................121 A4
Shadowbrook Cl OL11...48 E1
Shadowmoss Rd M22...130 E8
Shadows La OL5........68 E4
Shadows Mews OL5....68 B8
Shadwell Gr WN7.......75 C8
Shadwell St E OL10.....29 E3
Shadwell St W OL10.....29 D3
Shadworth Cl OL5.......68 E4
Shadworth Ho OL3, OL5..68 E5
Shady La
Bolton BL7............120 D7
Shady Oak Rd SK2.....124 F6
Shaftesbury Ave
Altrincham WA15.......120 C6
Bramhall SK8..........123 C1
Eccles M30............95 C8
Horwich BL6...........39 F8
Littleborough OL15.....15 F3
Shaftesbury Cl BL6......39 F8
Shaftesbury Dr OL12....15 D6
Shaftesbury Gdns M41...94 D2
Shaftesbury Rd
Cheadle SK8..........123 B6
Manchester M8.........156 A3
Swinton M27...........79 F7
Shafton Wlk [22] M40...65 D2
Shaftsbury Cl BL1......143 B1
Shaftsbury Ct [1]
M15................120 D6
Shaftsbury Dr OL10.....46 C8
Shaftsbury Rd WN5.....54 A8
Shaftsbury Rd WN6.....36 F3
SHAKERLEY............59 A2
Shakerley CE Prim Sch
M29................59 F4
Shakerley La M46, M29..58 F4
Shakerley Rd M29......58 F1
Shakespeare Ave
Bury BL9..............44 F6
Denton M34...........112 F8
Radcliffe M26.........43 E4
Stalybridge SK15......86 E4
Shakespeare Cl OL15....6 C1
Shakespeare Cres
Droylsden M43.........84 A2
Eccles M30............79 D2
Shakespeare Dr SK8....122 F6
Shakespeare Gr WN3....55 A4
Shakespeare Rd
Droylsden M43.........84 A2
Oldham OL1............49 C2
Prestwich M25.........62 F3
Romiley SK6...........112 F2
Swinton M27...........79 E8
Shakespeare Wlk
M13................163 C2
Shakleton Ave M9.......65 A3
Shalbourne Rd M28.....60 C3
Shaldon Dr M40........83 E4
Shalebrook Cl M46......58 A2
Shalemere Ct M46......58 A2
Shalfleet Cl BL2........25 E5
Shambrook Ave M22....109 D1
Shandon Ave M22.......121 E4
Shap Ave WA15.........120 D5
Shap Cres M28..........60 F1
Shap Dr M28............60 F1
Shap Gate WN5.........54 B7
Shapwick Cl [5] M9.....157 A4
Sharcott Cl [7] M16.....97 F4
Shardlow Cl M40.......160 A4

Shared St WN1.........151 A3
Shargate Cl SK9........131 C2
Sharman St BL3.........148 B1
Sharnbrook Wlk
[3] Bolton BL2.........25 B1
[4] Manchester M8.....63 E2
Sharnford Cl BL2.......148 B2
Sharnford Sq M12.......165 A2
Sharon Ave OL4.........68 E5
Sharon Cl OL7...........84 E1
Sharon Sq WN2..........73 F8
SHARPLES.............143 B4
Sharples Ave BL1........24 E6
Sharples Dr BL8.........27 A3
Sharples Gn BL7..........9 D6
Sharples Hall [8] BL1....24 F6
Sharples Hall Dr BL1....24 F6
Sharples Hall Fold BL1..24 F5
Sharples Hall Mews
BL1.................24 F6
Sharples Hall St OL4....67 D8
Sharples Mdw BL7.......9 D6
Sharples Pk [1] BL1.....143 A4
Sharples Prim Sch
BL1.................25 A5
Sharples Sch BL1........24 F5
Sharples St SK4.........169 B3
Sharp St
Bury BL8..............27 B4
Ince-in-M WN3........151 B2
Manchester M4.........159 B3
Middleton M24........65 A8
Prestwich M25.........63 A4
Walkden M28...........60 E3
Sharrington Dr M23....120 E6
Sharrow Wlk M9........157 A3
SHARSTON.............121 D5
Sharston Ind Area
M22................121 E2
Sharston Rd M22.......121 E7
Shaving La M28.........60 D1
SHAW..................149 B3
Shaw Ave SK14.........113 F8
Shawbrook Ave M28....78 B8
Shawbrook Rd M19.....111 A5
Shawbury Cl BL6........21 D1
Shawbury Gr M33.......107 F2
Shawbury Rd M23......121 B4
Shawbury St M24.......65 C7
SHAWCLOUGH...........14 C2
Shawclough Cl OL12....14 D3
Shawclough Com Prim
Sch OL12..............14 E3
Shawclough Dr OL12....14 D3
Shawclough Rd OL12....14 D3
Shawclough Way OL12...14 D3
Shawcroft Cl OL2.......149 A1
Shaw & Crompton Sta
OL2................149 C2
Shawcross Fold SK1....169 C2
Shawcross La M22......121 E8
Shawcross St
Hyde SK14............113 F8
Salford M6............154 C1
Stockport SK1.........124 A8
Shawdene Rd M22......121 D8
Shawe Hall Ave M41....107 A8
Shawe Hall Cres M41...107 A8
Shawe Rd M41..........95 A2
Shawes Dr PR6.........21 C7
Shawe View M41........95 A2
SHAWFIELD............110 A8
Shawfield Cl M14.......110 A8
Shawfield Ct SK2........124 D5
Shawfield Gr OL12......13 F2
Shawfield La
Rochdale, Norden OL12..13 F2
Rochdale OL12.........14 A2
Shawfield Rd SK13......171 C3
Shawfields SK15........86 D3
Shawfold OL2...........149 B3
Shawford Cres M40.....65 C2
Shawford Rd M40.......65 C2
SHAWFORTH...........4 D6
Shawgreen Cl M15......162 A2
Shaw Hall [7] M14......98 D4
Shaw Hall Ave SK14....102 B5
Shaw Hall Bank Rd
OL3.................68 F5
Shaw Head Dr M35......83 F6
SHAW HEATH..........170 B3
Shaw Heath SK2, SK3...170 B3
Shawheath Cl M15......162 A2
Shawhill Wlk M40......160 B2
Shaw Ho
Atherton M46..........58 D4
Farnworth BL4.........60 D7
Shaw La
Glossop SK13..........171 C3
Littleborough OL15,
OL16...............16 A1
Shawlea Ave M19.......110 E6
Shaw Moor Ave SK15...86 C1
Shaw Rd
Horwich BL6...........22 B5
Oldham OL16...........32 B3
Oldham OL1............67 A8
Royton, Buersil Head
OL16...............31 B1
Royton OL2.............48 F4
Stockport SK4..........168 B4
Shaw Rd S SK3..........170 B2
Shaws OL3..............69 C7
Shaws Fold SK9.........131 F3

SHAW SIDE ...149 B1
Shaws La OL3 ...69 C7
Shaw's Rd WA14...119 D4
Shaw St
Ashton-in-M WN4 ...73 B5
Ashton-u-L OL6 ...85 D3
Bolton BL3...141 B3
Bury BL9 ...141 B3
Culcheth WA3 ...92 A3
Farnworth BL4...42 D2
Glossop SK13...116 C8
Manchester M3 ...158 C3
Mottram in L SK14...103 A4
Oldham, Grotton OL4...68 A6
Oldham OL1...153 C4
Rochdale OL12...15 B2
Royton OL2...48 E4
Uppermill OL3 ...69 B6
Wigan WN1 ...37 C1
Shaw Terr 5 SK16 ...166 C1
Shaw The SK13 ...171 C3
Shay Ave WA15...120 E1
Shayfield Ave
Chadderton OL9...65 E8
Wythenshawe M22 ...121 D5
Shayfield Dr M22...121 D6
Shayfield Rd M22...121 D5
Shay La WA15 ...120 D1
Sheader Dr M5...80 C2
Sheaf Field Wlk M26...44 A4
Sheard Ave OL6 ...85 D6
Sheardhall Ave SK12...135 E5
Shearer Way M27...80 D7
Shearing Ave OL12...13 F1
Shearsby Cl M15...162 B1
Shearwater Ave M29...77 A8
Shearwater Dr
Walkden M28...60 C3
Westhoughton BL5 ...57 D6
Shearwater Gdns M30 ...95 A8
Shearwater Ho 1
M19 ...110 D4
Shearwater Rd SK2 ...125 A5
Sheddings The BL3 ...42 A4
Shed St OL12...4 D1
Sheepfoot La
Manchester M25, M8...63 E3
Oldham OL1...48 D1
Sheepfoot Wlk OL1...48 D1
Sheep Gap OL12...14 B1
Sheep Gate Dr BL8 ...26 E5
Sheerness St M18 ...99 D5
Sheffield Rd
Glossop SK13...104 F1
Hyde, Godley SK14 ...102 A3
Hyde SK14...167 C4
Sheffield St
Manchester M1...163 C4
Stockport SK4 ...169 B3
Shefford Cl M11 ...164 C4
Shefford Cres WN3 ...54 C2
Sheiling Ct WA14 ...119 C4
Sheilings The WA3...90 F8
Shelbourne Ave BL1...142 B1
Shelburne Dr WN2 ...56 C4
Shelden Cl 4 SK13 ...171 A1
Shelden Fold 3 SK13...171 A1
Shelden Mews SK13 ...171 A1
Shelden Pl 5 SK13 ...171 A1
Shelderton Cl 6 M40...83 A7
Sheldon Ave
Standish WN6 ...19 E2
Urmston M41...95 B2
Sheldon Cl
Partington M31...105 F3
Sheldon Ct OL7...85 B5
Sheldon Rd
Hazel Grove SK7...133 E8
Poynton SK12 ...134 C2
Sheldon St M11 ...83 B2
Sheldrake Cl SK16...101 E7
Sheldrake Rd WA14...119 B8
Sheldwich Dr WN7...75 F3
Shelfield Cl OL11 ...13 F1
Shelfield Cl OL11...13 F1
Shelfield La OL11...13 F1
Shelford Ave M18...99 B4
Shellbrook Gr 3 SK9 ...131 D1
Shelley Ave M24...47 B3
Shelley Cl SK7 ...19 F8
Shelley Ct SK8...123 A1
Shelley Dr
Abram WN2 ...56 B1
Wigan WN5 ...54 A6
Shelley Gr
Droylsden M43...84 A1
Dukinfield SK14 ...101 D5
Stalybridge SK15...86 E4
Shelley Rd
9 Oldham, Broadbent
OL1...49 C1
Oldham OL9 ...65 F3
Prestwich M25...62 F3
Reddish SK5 ...99 E1
Swinton M27 ...79 E8
Walkden M38...60 A5
Shelley Rise SK16...102 B7
Shelley St
Failsworth M40 ...83 C8
Leigh WN7 ...75 D7
Shelley Way M34 ...112 F8
Shelley Wlk
Atherton M46 ...58 D5
Bolton BL1...143 A1

Shellingford Cl WN6 ...35 D7
Shelmerdine Cl 1
SK14...102 F2
Shelmerdine Gdns M6 ...80 C4
Shelton Ave M33 ...107 D4
Shenfield Wlk M40 ...160 A3
Shenhurst Cl SK9...136 E4
Shentonfield Rd M22 ...121 E6
Shenton Park Ave
M33 ...107 C2
Shenton St SK14 ...101 C4
Shepherd Cross St Ind Est
BL1...143 A2
Shepherd Cross St
BL1...142 C1
Shepherd Ct 1 OL16...31 B6
Shepherd's Brow
WA14...119 A3
Shepherds Cl
Blackrod BL6...21 C3
Ramsbottom BL8...10 F1
Shepherd's Dr BL6...23 A3
Shepherds Gn OL3...69 D5
Shepherd St
Bury BL9 ...140 C1
Bury, Greenmount BL8...26 F8
Heywood OL10...29 C2
Manchester M9 ...64 E1
Rochdale, Norden OL11...13 D1
Rochdale, Town Head
OL12...139 C4
Royton OL2...48 E3
Royton OL2...48 E4
Shepherds Way OL16 ...31 F5
Shepherd Wlk M34 ...112 F8
Shepley Ave BL3...144 C1
Shepley Cl
2 Dukinfield SK16 ...101 D8
Hazel Grove SK7 ...133 D8
Shepley Dr SK7...124 E1
Shepley La
Marple SK6 ...125 F3
Marple SK6 ...125 F4
Shepley Lane Ind Est
SK6...125 F3
Shepley North Ind Est
M34 ...101 A7
Shepley South Ind Est
M34 ...101 A6
Shepley St
Denton M34...100 F7
Failsworth M35 ...66 A1
Glossop, Brookfield
SK13 ...171 B3
Glossop, Old Glossop
SK13...104 F2
Hyde SK14...167 B2
4 Oldham OL4...67 E6
Stalybridge SK15...86 A2
Shepton Ave WN2 ...56 A1
Shepton Cl BL1...24 D7
Shepton Dr M23 ...121 A2
Shepway Ct M30...79 B2
Sheraton Cl WN5 ...36 B1
Sheraton Rd OL8 ...66 E4
Sherborne Ave WN2 ...57 A5
Sherborne Ho M24 ...47 A3
Sherborne Rd
Cheadle SK3 ...123 A7
Urmston M41...95 E3
Wigan WN5 ...54 A8
Sherborne St W M3 ...158 B3
Sherborne St M3, M8...158 C4
Sherborne Trad Est
M8 ...156 A1
Sherbourne Cl
Cheadle SK8 ...132 B6
Oldham OL8...147 F2
Radcliffe M26 ...43 D5
Sherbourne Ct M25...63 A4
Sherbourne Dr OL10...29 A3
Sherbourne Pl WN3 ...151 B1
Sherbourne Rd
Bolton BL1 ...142 A1
Middleton M24...47 A3
Sherbourne St M25 ...63 A4
Sherbrook Cl M33 ...107 F3
Sherbrooke Ave OL3...51 C1
Sherbrooke Rd SK13...135 D6
Sherbrook Rise SK9 ...137 C6
Sherdley Ct M8 ...64 A1
Sherdley Rd M8 ...64 A1
Sherford Cl SK7...124 A2
Sheridan Ave WA3...90 D7
Sheridan Ct M40 ...157 B1
Sheridan Way
Chadderton OL9...65 E8
Denton M34...112 F8
Sheri Dr WA12...89 E2
Sheriffs Dr M29 ...59 D1
Sheriff St
Bolton BL2...25 B1
Milnrow OL16 ...32 A5
Rochdale OL12...14 E1
Rochdale OL12...139 B4
Sheringham Dr
Bury BL8...27 D5
Hyde SK14...102 A3
Swinton M27 ...79 F6
Sheringham Pl BL3 ...145 A1
Sheringham Rd M14 ...110 D7
Sherlock St M14 ...110 D7
Sherratt St M4 ...159 B2
Sherrington St M12...99 A3
Sherway Dr WA15 ...120 C6
Sherwell Rd M9 ...64 B3
Sherwin Way OL11...30 D1

Sherwood Ave
Ashton-in-M WN4 ...73 C4
Cheadle SK8 ...122 F2
Droylsden M43...84 C2
Manchester M14...110 C8
Radcliffe M26 ...43 F8
Sale M33 ...108 D5
Salford M7...81 B7
Stockport SK4 ...168 A1
Wigan M29 ...77 A6
Sherwood Bsns Pk
OL11...30 D2
Sherwood Cl
Ashton-u-L OL6 ...85 C7
Bury BL8 ...26 F7
Marple SK6 ...125 F4
Salford M5...154 A3
Sherwood Cres
Platt Bridge WN2...56 A2
Wigan WN5 ...54 D7
Sherwood Dr
Pendlebury M27 ...80 B7
Wigan WN5 ...54 D6
Sherwood Fold SK13...115 D7
Sherwood Gr
Leigh WN7 ...76 B2
Wigan WN5 ...54 D7
Sherwood Ind Pk OL11...30 D2
Sherwood Rd
Reddish M34 ...100 B3
Romiley SK6...113 B5
Sherwood St
Bolton BL1...143 C3
Manchester M14...110 C8
Oldham OL1...153 A4
Rochdale OL11...30 D2
Sherwood Way OL2...48 E8
Shetland Rd M40 ...160 A3
Shetland Way
Radcliffe M26 ...44 A5
Urmston M41...95 D5
SHEVINGTON...35 F6
Shevington Com Prim Sch
WN6...35 F6
Shevington Gdns
M23 ...109 B1
Shevington High Sch
WN6...36 B7
Shevington La WN6...36 B7
SHEVINGTON MOOR...19 A2
Shevington Moor WN6...19 A2
SHEVINGTON VALE...35 E7
Shevington Vale Prim Sch
WN6...35 E8
Shieldborn Dr M9 ...157 B3
Shield Cl OL8...153 B2
Shield Dr M28...79 C8
Shield St SK3...170 B4
Shiel St M28 ...60 D3
Shiers Dr SK8 ...122 E4
Shiffnall St BL2...148 A2
Shildon Cl WN7 ...77 A2
Shilford Dr M4 ...159 C3
Shillingford Rd BL4...60 C8
Shillingstone Cl BL2...26 A3
Shillington Cl 1 M28...59 F3
Shiloh La OL4 ...68 A5
Shiloh Rd SK22, SK6...127 B6
Shilton Gdns BL3...145 B1
Shilton St BL0...138 B1
Shilton Wlk M8 4 M40 ...65 D2
Ship Canal Ho M15...162 B4
Shipham Cl WN7 ...75 D8
Ship La OL3, OL4 ...50 B5
Shipla Cl OL9...153 B3
Shipley Ave M6...80 C3
Shipley View M41...94 F5
Shipper Bottom La
BL6...11 D5
Shippey St M14...110 D7
Shipston Cl BL8 ...27 B3
Shipton St BL1 ...142 B1
Shirburn BL0 OL11...139 B2
Shirebrook Dr
Glossop SK13...116 F8
Glossop, Whitfield
SK13...116 E8
Radcliffe M26 ...44 B4
Shireburn Ave BL2...148 C4
Shiredale Cl SK8 ...123 B4
Shiredale Dr M9...157 A3
Shire Gdns M26 ...43 F4
Shiregreen M40 ...156 C1
Shire Hill Hospl SK13 ...104 E3
Shirehills M25...63 A3
Shireoak Rd M20 ...110 D7
Shires Cl WN2...56 E4
Shires The
Droylsden M43...84 D3
Radcliffe M26 ...44 A5
Shire Way SK13...104 E3
Shirewell Rd WN5...53 E5
Shirley Ave
Droylsden M34...100 C8
Dukinfield SK14 ...101 D5
Eccles M30 ...95 C8
Failsworth OL9 ...65 E2
Gatley SK8 ...131 C6
Marple SK6 ...125 E6
Pendlebury M27 ...80 C7
Reddish M34 ...99 F3
Salford M7...81 A7
Stretford M32 ...96 F3
Shirley Cl SK7 ...124 A2
Shirley Ct SK13 ...108 C4
Shirley Gr SK3...170 B1
Shirley Rd M8 ...156 A3
Shirley St OL11...30 C2

Shoecroft Ave M34 ...100 E2
Shoemaker Gdns WN2 ...38 C5
SHOLVER...49 D4
Sholver Hey La OL1...49 E4
Sholver Hill Cl OL1...49 E4
Sholver La OL1...49 D4
Shone Ave M22...121 F2
Shopping City M6 ...154 C3
SHORE...15 F6
Shore Ave OL2 ...32 C1
Shoreditch Cl SK4 ...111 B5
SHORE EDGE...49 E8
Shorefield Cl OL16 ...31 F7
Shorefield Mount BL7...24 E8
Shore Fold OL15...15 F6
Shore Gn M23 ...121 A3
Shoreham Cl 5 M16...97 E4
Shoreham Wlk M19 ...152 A2
Shore Hill OL15...16 C6
Shore Lea OL15...15 F6
Shore Mount OL15...15 F6
Shore Rd OL15...15 F7
Shore St
Milnrow OL16 ...31 F6
Oldham OL1...67 A7
Shoreswood BL1...24 D5
Shorland St M27 ...79 C7
Shorrocks St BL8 ...26 F3
Short Ave M43 ...99 F8
Shortcroft St M15 ...162 C3
Shortland Cres M19 ...110 D3
Shortland Pl WN2 ...75 A8
Shortlands Ave BL9 ...44 F8
Short St E SK4 ...169 B3
Short St
Bacup OL13 ...3 B8
Golborne WA3 ...74 B1
Hazel Grove SK7 ...124 D3
Heywood OL10...29 B1
Manchester M1 ...159 A1
Salford M7 ...158 B3
Stockport SK4 ...169 B3
1 Tyldesley M46 ...58 F1
12 Wigan WN5 ...54 E6
Shortwood Cl 11 M40...83 A8
Shortry Wilks SK6...112 F3
Shotton Wlk M14 ...98 C3
Shottwood Fold OL15...16 C8
Shrewsbury Cl WN2 ...56 D6
Shrewsbury Ct M16 ...162 A1
Shrewsbury Gdns
SK8...132 C6
Shrewsbury Rd
Bolton BL1...144 B4
Droylsden M43...84 A3
Prestwich M25...63 A3
Sale M33 ...108 A2
Shrewsbury St
Glossop SK13...104 C1
Manchester M16...97 D4
Manchester M16 ...162 A1
Oldham OL4...68 A6
Shrewsbury Way 7
M34 ...101 A1
Shrigley Cl SK9 ...131 D1
Shrigley Rd N SK12 ...134 C3
Shrigley Rd S SK10,
SK12...134 C2
Shrivenham Wlk M23 ...120 F7
Shropshire Ave SK5...112 C6
Shropshire Cl SK13...116 F8
Shropshire Rd M35...84 A6
Shropshire Sq M12 ...164 C2
Shrowbridge Wlk
M12 ...165 A2
Shrubbery The BL6 ...40 C7
Shrub St BL3 ...146 C2
Shudehill M4 ...159 A2
Shudehill Rd M28 ...60 A1
Shudehill Sta M4 ...159 A2
Shurdington Rd BL5,
M46...58 F6
Shurmer St BL3 ...146 C4
Shutt La OL3 ...50 F2
Shuttle Hillock Rd
WN2...74 F7
Shuttle St
8 Eccles M30...79 F2
Ince-in-M WN2 ...56 E6
Radcliffe M26 ...44 C1
Tyldesley M29 ...59 A1
SHUTTLEWORTH...11 B1
Shuttleworth Cl M21...109 E8
Shutts La SK15 ...102 D8
Siam St M11 ...164 C4
Sibley Ave WN4 ...73 D4
Sibley Rd SK4 ...168 A3
Sibley St M18 ...99 D5
Sibles Wlk 7 M22 ...121 B1
Sibson Cl 3 M21...97 A1
Sibson Rd
Manchester M21...97 A1
Sale M33 ...108 B4
Sickle St
Manchester M1, M2 ...159 A1
Oldham OL4...67 A5
Sidbrook St WN2 ...56 C5
Sidbury Rd M21 ...109 C8
Sidcup Rd M23 ...120 F5
Siddall St
Heywood OL10...46 E8
Manchester M12...99 A2
Oldham OL1...153 C4
2 Radcliffe M26 ...44 C2
Shaw OL2 ...149 B3
Siddal Moor Sports Coll
OL10...46 D6
Siddeley St WN7...75 D5

Siddington Ave
Manchester M20 ...110 A7
Stockport SK3 ...170 A2
Siddington Rd
Handforth SK9...131 D5
Poynton SK12 ...133 F2
Siddow Comm WN7 ...76 A4
SIDDOW COMMON...76 A3
Side Ave WA14 ...119 C1
Sidebottom St
Droylsden M43...83 F1
Oldham OL4...67 E8
Stalybridge SK15...86 A2
Side St
Droylsden M11...83 B2
Oldham OL8...66 C2
Sidford Cl BL3...42 D5
Siding St OL13 ...3 C8
Sidings The
Britannia OL13...4 A8
Bury BL9 ...140 B1
Worsley M28...79 A5
Sidlaw Cl OL8 ...66 F2
Sidley Ave M9...64 F4
Sidley Pl SK14 ...167 C3
Sidley St SK14...167 C3
Sidmouth Ave M41 ...94 E3
Sidmouth Dr M9...64 D2
Sidmouth Gr
Cheadle SK8 ...131 F7
Wigan WN3 ...54 E3
Sidmouth Rd M33 ...107 D5
Sidmouth St
Denton M34 ...100 D7
Oldham OL9...152 B1
Sidney Rd M9 ...64 D1
Sidney St
Bolton BL3...145 C1
Leigh WN7 ...76 A5
Manchester M1 ...163 A3
6 Manchester M3 ...158 C1
Oldham OL1...49 A1
Salford M3...158 A2
Sidwell Wlk M4 ...160 A1
Siemens Rd
Irlam M44 ...105 E5
Manchester M20 ...109 E5
Siemens St BL6...22 C2
Sienna Cl M44...105 E6
Sighthill Wlk M9 ...157 A4
Signal Cl M30 ...79 B2
Signal Dr M40 ...157 A2
Signet Wlk M4 ...156 B1
Silas St OL6 ...85 D5
Silburn Way M24, M9...64 D7
Silbury Wlk M8...155 C1
Silchester Dr M40 ...157 A2
Silchester Way SK22...25 E1
Silchester Wlk 3
OL1...153 C3
Silcock St WA3 ...74 A1
Silfield Cl M11 ...160 B1
Silkhey Gr M28...79 B8
Silkin Cl M13...163 B3
Silkin Ct M13...163 B3
Silk Mill SK12 ...133 C4
Silk Mill Way 11 M24 ...64 F8
Silk St
Eccles M30...79 F1
Failsworth M40 ...83 C6
Glossop SK13...104 E1
Manchester M4...159 C2
Middleton M24...64 F8
Rochdale OL11...30 D4
Salford M3...158 A3
Westhoughton BL5 ...39 E1
Silkstone St M11 ...165 C3
Sillavan Way M3...158 B2
Silliloe Dr WN6...37 A1
Silsbury Gr WN6...37 A8
Silsden Ave
Golborne WA3 ...91 B8
Manchester M9 ...64 B5
Silsden Wlk M7 ...80 F8
Silton St M9...157 C4
Silverbirch Cl M33 ...107 D2
Silver Birch Gr
Ashton-in-M WN4 ...73 A5
Pendlebury M27 ...80 B6
Silver Birch Mews
SK16...101 E7
Silverbirch Way 3
M35...83 F7
Silver Cl SK16...101 E7
Silvercroft St M15 ...162 B3
Silver Ct 3 M45...44 E1
Silverdale
Altrincham WA14...119 C4
5 Romiley SK6...112 F3
Swinton M27 ...62 A2
Wigan WN1 ...37 C2
Silverdale Ave
Chadderton OL9...152 A2
Leigh WN7 ...76 A5
Ince-in-M WN2 ...56 A8
Irlam M44 ...94 B3
Walkden M38...60 A5
Silverdale Cl
Bury BL9 ...45 A8
High Lane SK6...134 E8
Silverdale Ct WN1 ...151 A4
Silverdale Dr
Oldham OL4...67 F6
Wilmslow SK9 ...137 A4

Silverdale Rd
Bolton BL1 . . . . 144 C3
Farnworth BL4 . . . . 42 A1
Gatley SK8 . . . . 122 B4
Hindley WN2 . . . . 56 F5
Manchester M21 . . . . 97 C1
Newton-le-W WA12 . . . . 89 B4
Stockport SK4 . . . . 168 C4
Wigan WN5 . . . . 54 B8
Silverdale St M11 . . . . 99 F8
Silver Hill OL16 . . . . 31 F7
Silver Hill Rd SK14 . . . . 167 B1
Silver Jubilee Wlk 4
M4 . . . . 159 B2
Silverlea Dr M9 . . . . 64 C2
Silvermere OL6 . . . . 85 E6
Silvermere Cl BL0 . . . . 138 B1
Silver Spring SK14 . . . . 113 F8
Silver St
Bury BL9 . . . . 140 B2
Irlam M44 . . . . 94 B3
Manchester M1 . . . . 159 A1
Manchester M1 . . . . 163 A4
Oldham OL1 . . . . 153 B2
5 Platt Bridge WN2 . . . . 56 B2
Ramsbottom BL0 . . . . 138 C2
Rochdale OL12 . . . . 139 A4
Walsden OL14 . . . . 6 A7
Whitefield M45 . . . . 44 E1
Silverstone Dr M40 . . . . 83 D4
Silver Terr WN1 . . . . 151 A3
Silverthorne Cl 12
SK15 . . . . 86 A1
Silverton Cl SK14 . . . . 102 E2
Silverton Gr
Bolton BL1 . . . . 143 C4
Middleton M24 . . . . 46 D4
Silverton Ho M6 . . . . 80 A3
Silverwell La BL1, BL2 . . . . 145 C3
Silverwell St
Bolton BL1 . . . . 145 C3
Failsworth M40 . . . . 83 D5
Horwich BL6 . . . . 22 D2
Silverwood Ave M21 . . . . . . 109 B8
Silvington Way WN2 . . . . . . 38 A2
Simeon St
Manchester M4 . . . . 159 B3
Milnrow OL16 . . . . 31 F6
Walsden OL14 . . . . 6 A8
Simfield Cl WN6 . . . . 19 D1
SIMISTER 63 E8
Simister Dr BL9 . . . . 45 A2
Simister Gn M25 . . . . 63 E8
Simister La
Middleton, Bowlee M24,
M25 . . . . 46 A1
Middleton, Simister M25 . . . . . 63 E8
Simister Rd M35 . . . . 83 F7
Simister St 10 M9 . . . . 157 B4
SIMMONDLEY 116 A7
Simmondley Gr SK13 . . . . . 116 A8
Simmondley La SK13 . . . . . 116 A8
Simmondley New Rd
SK13 . . . . 116 A8
Simmondley Prim Sch
SK13 . . . . 116 A8
Simms Cl M3 . . . . 158 A2
SIMM'S LANE END 72 B5
Simm's Sq WN2 . . . . 38 D4
Simonbury Cl BL8 . . . . 26 F2
Simon Freeman Cl
M19 . . . . 111 C6
Simon La M24 . . . . 46 A2
Simons Cl
Glossop SK13 . . . . 116 A7
Sale M33 . . . . 108 A3
Simonsway M22, SK8 . . . . . 121 D2
Simons Wlk SK13 . . . . 116 A8
Simpkin St WN2 . . . . 56 B1
Simpson Ave M27 . . . . 62 C2
SIMPSON CLOUGH 29 C5
Simpson Gr M28 . . . . 78 A6
Simpson Hill Cl OL10 . . . . . . 29 F3
Simpson Rd M28 . . . . 78 A6
Simpson Sq OL9 . . . . 66 C3
Simpson St
Droylsden M11 . . . . 83 A1
Hyde SK14 . . . . 167 A2
Manchester M4 . . . . 159 B3
Oldham OL9 . . . . 66 B4
Wilmslow SK9 . . . . 136 F6
Sinclair Ave M8 . . . . 63 F1
Sinclair St WN5 . . . . 54 E8
Sinclair St OL11 . . . . 30 D3
SINDERLAND GREEN 106 C1
Sinderland La WA14 . . . . . . 106 D1
Sinderland Rd
Altrincham WA14 . . . . 119 C8
Partington M31, WA14 . . . . . 106 C2
Sindsley Ct M27 . . . . 61 D1
Sindsley Gr BL3 . . . . 147 B3
Sindsley Rd M27 . . . . 61 D2
Singapore Ave M90 . . . . 130 A8
Singleton Ave
Bolton BL2 . . . . 42 F7
Horwich BL6 . . . . 22 C5
Singleton Cl M7 . . . . 63 C1
Singleton Gr BL5 . . . . 40 B1
Singleton Lo M7 . . . . 63 D1
Singleton Rd
Manchester M7 . . . . 63 D1
Stockport, Heaton Moor
SK4 . . . . 168 B4
Singleton St M26 . . . . 43 D4
Sion St M26 . . . . 44 A2
Sirdar St M11 . . . . 99 F8

Sirius Pl M7 . . . . 158 A3
Sir Matt Busby Way
M17 . . . . 96 F5
Sir Richard Fairey Rd
SK4 . . . . 111 B7
Sir Williams Ct M23 . . . . 121 B6
Siskin Cl
Leigh WN7 . . . . 76 B5
Newton-le-W WA12 . . . . 89 C3
Siskin Rd SK2 . . . . 124 F5
Sisley Cl M7 . . . . 81 B8
Sisson St M35 . . . . 83 F7
Sisters' St M43 . . . . 100 A8
Sitch La SK22 . . . . 127 F3
Sittingbourne Rd WN1 . . . . . 37 C4
Sixpools Gr 6 M28 . . . . 78 C8
Sixth Ave
Bolton BL1 . . . . 144 B3
Bury BL9 . . . . 28 D4
Little Lever BL3 . . . . 42 F4
Oldham OL8 . . . . 66 C1
Sixth St M17 . . . . 96 D5
Size House Pl 7 WN7 . . . . . . 76 A4
Size St OL12 . . . . 4 D1
Skagen Cl BL3 . . . . 143 B1
Skaife Rd M33 . . . . 108 E4
Skarratt Cl M12 . . . . 164 C2
Skegness Cl BL3 . . . . 27 D5
Skellorn Green La
SK10 . . . . 133 F1
Skelton Gr
Bolton BL2 . . . . 42 F8
Manchester M13 . . . . 98 F2
Skelton Rd
Altrincham WA14 . . . . 119 E7
Stretford M32 . . . . 96 D3
Skelton St WN4 . . . . 72 F6
Skelwith Ave BL3 . . . . 147 C2
Skelwith Cl M41 . . . . 95 A4
Skerry Cl M13 . . . . 163 B3
Skerton Rd M16 . . . . 97 B4
Skiddaw Cl M24 . . . . 46 D3
Skiddaw Pl WN5 . . . . 54 C6
Skilgate Wlk 10 M40 . . . . 83 C6
Skip Pl M3, M4 . . . . 159 A3
Skipton Ave
Chadderton OL9 . . . . 47 F1
Failsworth M40 . . . . 65 D1
Hindley WN2 . . . . 57 A4
Skipton Cl
Bury BL8 . . . . 26 F2
Hazel Grove SK7 . . . . 133 C8
Reddish SK5 . . . . 111 E8
Skipton Dr M41 . . . . 94 F5
Skipton St
Bolton BL2 . . . . 148 C4
Oldham OL8 . . . . 67 B4
Skipton Wlk BL2 . . . . 148 C3
Skull House La WN6 . . . . 35 D8
Skull House Mews
WN6 . . . . 35 C8
Skye Cl OL10 . . . . 28 F1
Skye Rd M41 . . . . 95 D5
Skyes Cres WN3 . . . . 54 C1
Skyes Ct 8 OL16 . . . . 31 B6
Skye Wlk M23 . . . . 121 A4
SLACKCOTE 50 B7
Slackcote OL3 . . . . 50 C7
Slackcote La OL3 . . . . 50 C7
Slackey Brow BL4 . . . . 61 C6
Slackey Fold WN2 . . . . 57 B1
Slack Fold La BL4 . . . . 147 A1
Slack Gate OL12 . . . . 14 F8
Slack Gate La OL3 . . . . 50 D8
Slack Hall OL4 . . . . 67 F8
Slack La
Bolton BL2 . . . . 25 E7
Delph OL3 . . . . 50 D6
Swinton M27 . . . . 62 A1
Westhoughton BL5 . . . . 39 F3
Slack Rd M9 . . . . 64 D1
Slack St
Hyde SK14 . . . . 167 C4
Rochdale OL16 . . . . 139 C3
Slade Gr M13 . . . . 98 F2
Slade Hall Rd M12 . . . . 99 A2
Slade La M13, M19 . . . . 98 F2
Slade Mount M19 . . . . 110 F8
Sladen Fold OL15 . . . . 16 D8
Sladen St OL12 . . . . 14 F1
Slade St BL3 . . . . 43 A3
Slades View Cl OL3 . . . . 51 C5
Slag La WA3 . . . . 74 F2
Slaidburn Ave BL2 . . . . 42 F6
Slaidburn Cl
6 Milnrow OL16 . . . . 31 F5
Wigan WN3 . . . . 55 A3
Slaidburn Cres WA3 . . . . 73 F2
Slaidburn Dr BL8 . . . . 26 F3
Slaithwaite Dr 5 M11 . . . . . . 83 C2
Slant Cl SK13 . . . . 116 E8
Slateacre Rd SK14 . . . . 113 F7
Slate Ave M4 . . . . 159 C1
Slate La
Ashton-u-L OL7 . . . . 84 E1
Ashton-u-L OL7 . . . . 100 E8
Droylsden M34 . . . . 100 C8
Slatelands Ave SK13 . . . . . . 116 B8
Slatelands Rd SK13 . . . . . . 116 B8
Slater Ave BL6 . . . . 22 C4
Slaterfield BL3 . . . . 145 B1
Slater La BL1 . . . . 25 A1
Slater St N WN7 . . . . 75 D5
Slater's Nook 10 BL5 . . . . . . 39 E1
Slater St
Bolton BL1 . . . . 143 C1
Eccles M30 . . . . 79 B2
Failsworth M35 . . . . 65 F1

Slater St continued
Farnworth BL4 . . . . 60 D8
Oldham OL9 . . . . 153 B2
Slater Way 2 SK14 . . . . 102 E2
Slate Wharf M15 . . . . 162 A3
SLATTOCKS 47 D6
Slaunt Bank OL12 . . . . 13 D2
Slawson Way OL10 . . . . 29 F3
Sleaford Cl
Bury BL8 . . . . 27 D5
Manchester M40 . . . . 160 A3
Sledbrook St WN5 . . . . 54 C5
Sleddale Cl SK2 . . . . 124 D5
Sledmere Cl
Bolton BL1 . . . . 143 C2
Droylsden M11 . . . . 83 A1
Sledmoor Rd M23 . . . . 108 F1
Slimbridge Cl BL2 . . . . 26 A1
Sloane Ave OL4 . . . . 67 F8
Sloane St
5 Ashton-u-L OL6 . . . . 166 C3
Bolton BL3 . . . . 146 B3
Slough Ind Ctr M5 . . . . 161 C4
SMALLBRIDGE 15 D2
Smallbridge Cl 5 M28 . . . . . 78 C8
SMALL BROOK 149 C4
Smallbrook La WN7 . . . . 76 B3
Smallbrook Rd OL2 . . . . 32 C1
Smalldale Ave M16 . . . . 97 F3
Smalley St
Rochdale OL11 . . . . 30 C2
Standish WN6 . . . . 19 E1
Smallfield Dr M9 . . . . 157 A4
Smallridge Cl M40 . . . . 160 A3
SMALLSHAW 85 C5
Smallshaw Cl WN4 . . . . 73 A2
Smallshaw Fold OL6 . . . . 85 B5
Smallshaw La OL6 . . . . 85 C5
Smallshaw Rd OL12 . . . . 14 A4
Smallshaw Sq OL6 . . . . 85 B5
Smallwood St M40 . . . . 83 C6
Smart St M12 . . . . 99 A3
Smeaton Cl M32 . . . . 96 E2
Smeaton St
Horwich BL6 . . . . 22 C2
Manchester M8 . . . . 156 C2
Smedley Ave
Bolton BL3 . . . . 42 A3
Manchester M8 . . . . 156 C2
Smedley La
Manchester M8 . . . . 156 B2
Manchester M8, M9 . . . . 156 C3
Smedley Pl SK13 . . . . 104 C2
Smedley Rd M40, M8 . . . . . 156 B2
Smedley St M8 . . . . 156 B2
Smethurst Hall Pk
WN5 . . . . 53 C2
Smethurst Hall Rd BL9 . . . . 28 F4
Smethurst La
Bolton BL3, BL4 . . . . 146 B2
Wigan WN5 . . . . 54 C5
Smethurst Rd WN5 . . . . 53 C2
Smethurst St
Heywood OL10 . . . . 29 C3
Manchester M9 . . . . 64 D1
Middleton M24 . . . . 65 D7
Smith Ave WN5 . . . . 54 B8
Smith Brow BL6 . . . . 21 C3
Smith Fold La M28 . . . . 60 A3
Smith Hill OL16 . . . . 32 A6
Smithies Ave M24 . . . . 47 A2
Smithies St OL10 . . . . 29 C2
SMITHILLS 24 B5
Smithills Country Pk★
BL1 . . . . 24 B5
Smithills Croft Rd
BL1 . . . . 142 B3
Smithills Dean Rd
BL1 . . . . 142 A3
Smithills Dr BL1 . . . . 23 F2
Smithills Hall Cl BL0 . . . . . . 138 C1
Smithills' Hall (Mus)★
BL1 . . . . 142 B4
Smithills Open Farm★
BL1 . . . . 24 C5
Smithills Sch BL1 . . . . 142 C4
Smith La BL7 . . . . 8 F1
Smith's La WN2 . . . . 75 B8
Smiths Lawn SK9 . . . . 137 A7
Smith's Pl 11 M46 . . . . 58 D3
Smith's Rd BL3 . . . . 42 D3
Smith St
Adlington PR7 . . . . 20 F6
Ashton-u-L OL7 . . . . 84 F1
Aspull WN2 . . . . 38 C5
Atherton M46 . . . . 58 C3
Bury BL9 . . . . 141 A3
Cheadle SK8 . . . . 122 F6
Denton M34 . . . . 100 F7
Dukinfield SK14 . . . . 101 D5
Dukinfield SK16 . . . . 101 A8
5 Heywood OL10 . . . . 29 D2
2 Leigh WN7 . . . . 76 A5
6 Littleborough OL15 . . . . . 16 B5
Manchester M16 . . . . 161 C2
Mossley OL5 . . . . 68 B2
Oldham OL4 . . . . 67 E8
Ramsbottom BL0 . . . . 138 B1
Rochdale OL16 . . . . 31 A8
Walkden M28 . . . . 60 D3
Smithwood Ave WN2 . . . . . . 56 F6
SMITHY BRIDGE 15 F4
Smithy Bridge Prim Sch
OL15 . . . . 15 F3
Smithy Bridge Rd OL15,
OL16 . . . . 15 F3

Smithy Bridge Sta
OL15 . . . . 15 F3
Smithy Brow WN6 . . . . 18 C8
Smithy Cl SK13 . . . . 104 D1
Smithy Croft BL7 . . . . 24 F8
Smithy Fold
Glossop SK13 . . . . 104 D1
Rochdale OL12 . . . . 14 C1
Smithy Fold Rd 3
SK13 . . . . 167 B1
Smithy Glen Dr WN5 . . . . . . 53 E4
Smithy Gn
Cheadle SK8 . . . . 132 A8
Ince-in-M WN2 . . . . 151 C3
Newhey OL16 . . . . 32 E4
Romiley SK6 . . . . 113 B5
Smithy Gr OL6 . . . . 166 C4
SMITHY GREEN 132 B7
Smithy Hill BL3 . . . . 146 A4
Smithy La
Altrincham WA14 . . . . 118 D3
Hyde SK14 . . . . 167 B1
4 Manchester M3 . . . . 158 E1
Marple SK6 . . . . 126 A3
Partington M31 . . . . 105 F3
Uppermill OL3 . . . . 69 B8
Smithy Nook OL15 . . . . 6 C1
Smithy St
Hazel Grove SK7 . . . . 124 D3
Leigh WN7 . . . . 75 F4
Ramsbottom BL0 . . . . 138 C2
Westhoughton BL5 . . . . 39 E3
Wigan WN4 . . . . 72 C4
Smyrna St
Heywood OL10 . . . . 29 C1
7 Oldham OL4 . . . . 67 C6
Radcliffe M26 . . . . 43 F4
Salford M5 . . . . 154 B1
Smyrna Wlk M26 . . . . 43 F4
Snapebrook Gr 6
SK9 . . . . 131 E1
Snape St M26 . . . . 43 F6
Snell St M4 . . . . 160 A1
Snipe Ave OL11 . . . . 29 F7
Snipe Cl SK12 . . . . 133 A4
Snipe Rd OL8 . . . . 67 B2
Snipe Ret Pk OL7 . . . . 100 D8
Snipe St BL3 . . . . 147 C4
Snipe Way OL7 . . . . 100 D8
Snowberry Wlk M31 . . . . . . 105 E3
Snowden Ave
Urmston M41 . . . . 107 B8
Wigan WN3 . . . . 55 A4
Snowden St
Bolton BL3 . . . . 145 B4
Heywood OL10 . . . . 46 E8
1 Oldham OL4 . . . . 67 C6
Snowdon Wlk 4 M40 . . . . . . 65 C2
Snowdon Dr BL6 . . . . 22 C5
Snowdon Rd M30 . . . . 80 A3
Snowdon St OL11 . . . . 31 A2
Snowdrop Cl BB4 . . . . 1 A8
Snowdrop Wlk M7 . . . . 155 A2
Snow Hill Rd BL3 . . . . 42 D5
Snowshill Dr WN3 . . . . 54 C4
Snydale Cl BL5 . . . . 40 A8
Snydale Way BL3, BL5 . . . . . 40 C1
Soane Cl WN4 . . . . 73 D3
Soap St M4 . . . . 159 A2
Soapstone Way M44 . . . . . . 106 A8
Society St OL2 . . . . 149 B3
Sofa St BL1 . . . . 142 B1
Soham Cl WN2 . . . . 56 E4
Soho St
Bolton BL3 . . . . 145 C2
Oldham OL4 . . . . 67 B7
Wigan WN5 . . . . 54 F7
Solent Ave M8 . . . . 64 A2
Solent Dr BL3 . . . . 42 D5
Sole St WN1 . . . . 37 E1
Solness St BL9 . . . . 27 F6
Soloman Rd WA14 . . . . 107 C1
Solway Cl
Ashton-in-M WN4 . . . . 73 A4
Bolton BL3 . . . . 147 A3
Oldham OL8 . . . . 153 B1
Swinton M27 . . . . 61 E4
Solway Rd M22 . . . . 121 E4
Somerby Dr M22 . . . . 121 C1
Somerdale Ave BL1 . . . . 144 A3
Somerfield Rd M9 . . . . 64 C3
Somerford Ave M20 . . . . . . 110 A8
Somerford Ho M12 . . . . 133 E4
Somerford Rd SK5 . . . . 99 F2
Somerford Way 3
SK9 . . . . 131 E5
Somersby Ct SK7 . . . . 123 E1
Somersby Dr BL7 . . . . 24 F8
Somersby Wlk BL3 . . . . 145 C1
Somerset Ave
Shaw OL2 . . . . 48 F7
Tyldesley M29 . . . . 58 F3
Somerset Cl
Brinnington SK5 . . . . 112 C4
Irlam M44 . . . . 105 D6
Somerset Dr BL9 . . . . 44 F8
Somerset Gr OL11 . . . . 30 A8
Somerset Pl M33 . . . . 108 B6
Somerset Rd
Altrincham WA14 . . . . 119 D6
Atherton M46 . . . . 58 C5
Bolton BL1 . . . . 144 B4
Droylsden M43 . . . . 84 A3
Failsworth M35 . . . . 83 E6
Salford M30 . . . . 80 A4
Wigan WN5 . . . . 54 C7
Somerset St OL4 . . . . 67 C6
Somerset Wlk BB4 . . . . 1 B8

Somers Rd SK5 . . . . 99 F1
Somers Wlk M9 . . . . 64 B3
Somerton Ave
Sale M33 . . . . 108 C3
Wythenshawe M22 . . . . 121 C3
Somerton Cl WN6 . . . . 19 D1
Somerton Ct M9 . . . . 65 A3
Somerton Rd BL2 . . . . 43 A6
Somerton Wlk 8 OL9 . . . . . . 48 A1
Somerville Gdns
WA15 . . . . 119 F7
Somerville Rd WN1 . . . . 37 C3
Somerville Sq BL1 . . . . 142 C3
Somerville St BL1 . . . . 142 C3
Somerwood Wlk M12 . . . . . . 164 C2
Sommerville Ct M7 . . . . 155 A4
Sonning Dr BL3 . . . . 146 A2
Sonning Wlk M8 . . . . 156 B2
Sopwith Dr M14 . . . . 98 B1
Sorby Rd M44 . . . . 106 A7
Sorrel Bank M6 . . . . 154 C4
Sorrel Dr OL15 . . . . 15 F6
Sorrel St M15 . . . . 162 B2
Sorrel Way OL4 . . . . 49 E2
Sorting Ho The M1 . . . . 159 B2
Sorton St M1 . . . . 163 A3
Soudan Rd SK2 . . . . 124 A6
Soudan St M24 . . . . 47 C1
Sougher's La WN4 . . . . 72 F7
Sougher's Lane End
WN4 . . . . 72 E6
Sound The OL3 . . . . 50 F4
SOURACRE 86 C3
Souracre Fold SK15 . . . . 86 B3
Southall St M3 . . . . 158 C4
Southampton Cl M7 . . . . . . 155 A1
Southam St M7 . . . . 155 C3
South Ave
Golborne WN7 . . . . 74 F4
Heywood OL10 . . . . 29 B2
Kearsley BL4 . . . . 60 F6
Leigh WN7 . . . . 76 C3
Manchester M19 . . . . 97 D7
Swinton M27 . . . . 79 D5
Uppermill OL3 . . . . 69 B6
Whitefield M45 . . . . 44 E1
South Back Rock 1
BL9 . . . . 140 C2
South Bank Cl SK9 . . . . 137 B2
Southbank Rd M19 . . . . 110 D5
South Bank Rd BL0 . . . . 140 B1
Southbourne Ave M41 . . . . . 95 F2
Southbourne St M6 . . . . 154 B2
Southcliffe Rd SK5 . . . . 140 D1
Southcombe Wlk M15 . . . . . 97 F4
Southcourt WN7 . . . . 76 B6
South Cres
Droylsden M11 . . . . 83 D2
Failsworth M40 . . . . 65 D3
South Croft OL8 . . . . 67 B3
Southcross Rd M18 . . . . 99 D3
South Cross St
Bury BL9 . . . . 140 C2
Bury BL9 . . . . 141 A1
South Croston St M16 . . . . . 97 D4
South Ct OL16 . . . . 31 A8
Southdene Ave M20 . . . . . . 109 E4
Southdown Cl
Rochdale OL11 . . . . 30 C5
Stockport SK4 . . . . 169 B2
Southdown Cres
Cheadle SK8 . . . . 131 F8
Manchester M9 . . . . 65 A2
Southdown Dr M28 . . . . 77 F6
South Downs Cl 2
OL2 . . . . 48 F8
South Downs Dr
WA14 . . . . 119 D1
South Downs Rd
WA14 . . . . 119 D1
South Dr
Altrincham WA15 . . . . 120 A7
Appley Bridge WN6 . . . . 18 C2
Bolton BL2 . . . . 25 E3
Gatley SK8 . . . . 122 A4
Manchester M21 . . . . 109 B6
Wilmslow SK9 . . . . 137 B6
Southend Ave M15 . . . . 162 A2
Southend St BL3 . . . . 146 C3
Southern App M27 . . . . 62 C2
Southern Cl 9 M13 . . . . 98 F4
Southern Cl
Denton M34 . . . . 112 F8
Stockport SK7 . . . . 123 F1
Southern Cres SK7 . . . . 123 F1
Southern Cross Sch
M21 . . . . 109 C5
Southern Ho M11 . . . . 143 A1
Southern Ind Est M28 . . . . . 60 D5
Southern Rd M33 . . . . 108 A6
Southern's Fold WN2 . . . . . . 38 A3

Southern St
Manchester M3 . . . .**162** B4
Salford M6 . . . .**154** B2
Walkden M28 . . . .**60** D5
Wigan WN5 . . . .**54** D5
Southery Ave WN3 . . . .**54** C3
Southey CI OL15 . . . .**15** F2
Southey Ct 14 M34 . . . .**113** A8
Southey Wlk 5 M34 . . . .**113** A7
South Failsworth Com
Prim Sch M35 . . . .**83** F5
Southfield M22 . . . .**56** B2
Southfield Ave BL9 . . . .**27** F6
Southfield CI
Dukinfield SK16 . . . .**101** D6
Handforth SK9 . . . .**131** C3
Southfield Dr BL5 . . . .**57** E7
Southfield Ind Est M17 . . . . . .**96** C6
Southfield Rd BL0 . . . .**1** A2
Southfields WA14 . . . .**119** C2
Southfields Ave 2
M11 . . . .**83** C2
Southfields Dr WA15 . . . .**120** B7
Southfield St 15 BL3 . . . .**42** A4
Southgarth Rd M6 . . . .**154** B3
Southgate
Bolton BL2 . . . .**25** E4
Manchester, Chorlton-cum-
Hardy M21 . . . .**109** B7
Manchester, Heaton Chapel
SK4 . . . .**111** C5
Manchester M3 . . . .**158** C1
Uppermill OL3 . . . .**51** A2
Urmston M41 . . . .**107** B8
Wilmslow SK9 . . . .**14** C7
Southgate Ave M40 . . . .**83** A4
Southgate Ct BL3 . . . .**108** C5
Southgate Ind Pk OL10 . . . .**29** E1
Southgate Mews SK4 . . . .**111** C5
Southgate Rd
Failsworth OL9 . . . .**65** E3
Whitefield BL9 . . . .**44** F3
Southgate St OL1 . . . .**153** C2
Southgate Way 11
OL7 . . . .**166** A1
South Gr
3 Alderley Edge SK9 . . . .**137** A1
Manchester M13 . . . .**164** A1
Sale M33 . . . .**108** B3
Walkden M28 . . . .**60** D5
Southgrove Ave BL1 . . . .**24** E6
South Hall St M5 . . . .**161** C4
South Hey WN4 . . . .**75** C5
South Hill OL4 . . . .**67** F5
South Hill St OL4 . . . .**67** A6
South King St
Eccles M30 . . . .**79** B2
Manchester M2 . . . .**158** C1
South La M29 . . . .**77** A5
South Lancashire Ind Est
WN4 . . . .**73** B6
Southlands Ave
Eccles M30 . . . .**95** A8
Standish WN6 . . . .**36** E8
South Langworthy Rd
M50 . . . .**154** C1
Southlea CI M19,
M20 . . . .**110** D5
Southleigh Dr BL2 . . . .**43** A6
Southlink OL4 . . . .**67** A6
Southlink Bsns Pk OL4 . . . .**67** A6
Southlink Wkshps OL4 . . . .**67** A6
South Lonsdale St
M32 . . . .**96** C3
South Marlow St
SK13 . . . .**104** A4
South Mead SK12 . . . .**133** B5
South Meade
Altrincham WA15 . . . .**120** A7
Manchester M21 . . . .**109** B7
Manchester, Sedgley Park
M25 . . . .**63** D2
Swinton M27 . . . .**79** E6
South Meadway SK6 . . . .**134** F7
Southmere CI 2 M40 . . . .**65** C3
South Mesnefield Rd
M7 . . . .**81** A8
Southmill St M2 . . . .**162** C4
Southmoor M23 . . . .**120** F7
Southmoor Pk M23 . . . .**120** E7
Southmoor Rd
Wythenshawe M23 . . . .**120** F5
Wythenshawe M23 . . . .**120** F6
Southolme WIk BL3 . . . .**145** B1
South Oak La SK9 . . . .**136** F5
Southolme Gdns M19 . . . .**110** E4
Southover BL5 . . . .**57** E6
South Par
Rochdale OL16 . . . .**139** C3
Stockport SK7 . . . .**123** F2
South Park Dr SK12 . . . .**133** E5
South Park Rd SK8 . . . .**122** C5
South PI 11 OL16 . . . .**31** A8
Southpoint SK4 . . . .**168** A2
Southpool CI SK7 . . . .**124** A2
South Pump St M1 . . . .**163** A8
South Radford St M7 . . . .**81** A7
South Rd
Altrincham, Ashley Heath
WA14 . . . .**128** E8
Altrincham, Rosehill
WA14 . . . .**119** C2
Manchester M20 . . . .**110** B2
Swinton M27 . . . .**62** D2

SOUTH REDDISH **111** E5
South Ridge M34 . . . .**100** F5
South Row M25 . . . .**62** F1
South Royd St BL8 . . . .**26** F7
Southsea St M11 . . . .**99** D7
Southside SK6 . . . .**112** E6
South Side SK14 . . . .**113** F8
South St
Alderley Edge SK9 . . . .**137** A1
Ashton-u-L OL7 . . . .**100** E8
Bolton BL3 . . . .**147** B3
Heywood OL10 . . . .**29** B2
Manchester, Longsight
M12 . . . .**164** B1
Manchester M11 . . . .**165** C3
Oldham OL8 . . . .**66** B2
Ramsbottom BL0 . . . .**11** D6
Rochdale OL16 . . . .**31** A8
Tyldesley M46 . . . .**58** E1
South Stage M50 . . . .**96** F8
South Terr
2 Alderley Edge SK9 . . . . . .**137** A1
Bury BL9 . . . .**44** D7
Ramsbottom BL0 . . . .**1** C2
South Terrace Ct 12
OL16 . . . .**31** A5
South Trafford Coll
WA14 . . . .**119** D8
South Vale Cres
WA15 . . . .**119** F5
South View
Atherton M46 . . . .**58** C3
2 Manchester M14 . . . .**98** C2
Mossley SK15 . . . .**86** F6
Reddish SK5 . . . .**99** F3
Rochdale OL16 . . . .**29** E6
Romiley SK6 . . . .**113** C6
South View Gdns SK8 . . . .**122** C3
South View Rd
Glossop SK13 . . . .**116** F7
Rochdale OL12 . . . .**15** E3
South View Terr OL16 . . . .**15** E4
Southview Wlk OL4 . . . .**49** E1
South Villa Ct WN6 . . . .**36** E8
Southward Rd WA11 . . . .**89** A7
Southward Dr SK16 . . . .**101** D6
Southway
Altrincham WA14 . . . .**119** C6
Ashton-u-L OL7 . . . .**85** B6
Droylsden M43 . . . .**100** A8
2 Eccles M30 . . . .**79** F2
Failsworth OL9 . . . .**65** F2
Oldham OL8 . . . .**66** E2
Southwell CI
13 Bolton BL1 . . . .**145** A4
Golborne WA3 . . . .**90** C8
Romiley SK6 . . . .**113** A1
Southwell Ct 8 M32 . . . .**96** C1
Southwell Gdns OL6 . . . .**85** B7
Southwell Rd M23 . . . .**109** A2
South William St M3 . . . .**158** A1
South Wlk 11 SK15 . . . .**86** D4
Southwold CI M19 . . . .**99** C1
Southwood CI BL3 . . . .**147** C3
Southwood Dr M9 . . . .**64** A5
Southwood Rd SK2 . . . .**124** B4
Southworth St M3 . . . .**158** A2
Southworth Rd WA12 . . . .**89** F4
Southyard St M19 . . . .**111** B8
Sovereign Bsns Pk
WN1 . . . .**151** A3
Sovereign Ent Pk
M50 . . . .**161** A3
Sovereign Fold Rd
WN7 . . . .**57** E1
Sovereign Hall Cvn Pk
OL5 . . . .**68** B1
Sovereign Rd WN1 . . . .**151** A3
Sovereign St M6 . . . .**81** A4
Sowerby CI BL8 . . . .**26** F2
Sowerby Wlk M9 . . . .**64** B4
Spa CI SK5 . . . .**111** E8
Spa Cres M38 . . . .**60** A6
Spa Gr M38 . . . .**60** A6
Spa La
Oldham OL4 . . . .**67** E5
Walkden M38 . . . .**60** A6
Spalding Dr M23 . . . .**121** A2
Spa Rd
Atherton M46 . . . .**58** D5
Bolton BL1 . . . .**145** A3
Sparkford Ave M23 . . . .**108** D1
Sparkle St M1 . . . .**163** B4
Spark Rd M23 . . . .**120** F7
Sparrow CI SK5 . . . .**99** E2
Sparrowfield CI SK15 . . . .**86** E7
Sparrow Hill
Appley Bridge WN6,
WN8 . . . .**18** A2
Rochdale OL16 . . . .**139** C3
Sparrow St OL2 . . . .**48** E2
Sparta Ave M28 . . . .**60** D2
Sparta Wlk M11 . . . .**165** A4
Sparth Bottoms Rd
OL11 . . . .**139** A2
Sparth Ct SK4 . . . .**169** A3
Sparthfield Ave OL11 . . . .**139** B1
Sparthfield Rd SK4 . . . .**169** A3
Sparth Hall SK4 . . . .**169** A3
Sparth La SK4 . . . .**169** A3
Sparth Rd M40 . . . .**83** D5
Spa St M13, M15 . . . .**163** B1
Spathfield Ct SK4 . . . .**169** A3
Spath Bottoms Rd
Spath Holme 8 M20 . . . .**110** A3
Spath La SK8 . . . .**131** F5
Spath La E SK8 . . . .**132** B5

Spath Rd M20 . . . .**110** A3
Spath Wlk SK8 . . . .**132** B5
Spawell CI WA3 . . . .**90** E8
Spaw St M3 . . . .**158** B2
Speakman Ave
Leigh WN7 . . . .**76** B5
Newton-le-W WA12 . . . .**89** C5
Speakmans Dr WN6 . . . .**35** C6
Spean Wlk 8 M11 . . . .**83** C1
Spear St M1, M4 . . . .**159** B2
Specialist Learning Ctr
The M35 . . . .**83** D7
Spectator St M4 . . . .**160** A2
Specton Wlk 5 M12 . . . .**99** B3
Spectrum Bsns Pk
SK3 . . . .**123** B6
Speedwell SK13 . . . .**103** F7
Speedwell CI
Glossop SK13 . . . .**103** F7
11 Golborne WA3 . . . .**90** E8
Spelding Dr WN6 . . . .**36** E4
Spencer Ave
1 Dukinfield SK14 . . . .**101** D5
Little Lever BL3 . . . .**43** C3
Manchester M16 . . . .**97** C2
Whitefield M45 . . . .**44** E2
Spencer La OL11 . . . .**29** E5
Spencer Rd WN6 . . . .**37** A3
Spencer's La WN5 . . . .**53** D7
Spencer St
Bury BL8 . . . .**27** C3
1 Dukinfield SK16 . . . .**101** C8
Eccles M30 . . . .**79** C1
Littleborough OL15 . . . .**16** C6
Mossley OL5 . . . .**68** B1
Oldham, Lower Moor
OL1 . . . .**67** A8
Oldham OL9 . . . .**66** C4
Radcliffe M26 . . . .**44** C4
Ramsbottom BL0 . . . .**138** B1
Reddish SK5 . . . .**111** F8
Spender Ave M8 . . . .**156** A2
Spendmore La PR7 . . . .**19** D8
Spen Fold
Bury BL8 . . . .**44** A8
Littleborough OL15 . . . .**16** A4
Spenleach La BL8 . . . .**10** D3
Spenlow WN7 . . . .**76** C3
Spenlow CI SK12 . . . .**133** E1
Spennithorne Rd M41 . . . .**95** B2
Spenser Ave
Denton M34 . . . .**113** A8
Radcliffe M26 . . . .**43** E4
Spenwood Rd OL15 . . . .**15** F5
Spey CI
Altrincham WA14 . . . .**119** C6
Standish WN6 . . . .**19** D1
Spey Ho 7 SK5 . . . .**99** F2
Speyside CI M45 . . . .**63** A8
Spilsby Sq WN3 . . . .**55** A2
Spindle Ave SK15 . . . .**86** C3
Spindle Croft BL4 . . . .**60** D8
Spindle Ct OL2 . . . .**48** E4
Spindle Hillock WN4 . . . .**72** D4
SPINDLE POINT **86** C3
Spindlepoint Dr 4
M28 . . . .**78** C8
Spindle Point Prim Sch
BL4 . . . .**61** B5
Spindles Sh Ctr The
OL1 . . . .**153** B2
Spindles The OL5 . . . .**86** D8
Spindle Wlk BL5 . . . .**39** F2
Spindlewood CI SK15 . . . .**86** D2
Spindlewood Rd
WN3 . . . .**151** C2
Spiningdale M38 . . . .**59** D6
Spinks St OL4 . . . .**67** B5
Spinnerbottom SK22 . . . .**127** F2
Spinnerette CI WN7 . . . .**76** A5
Spinners Gdns OL12 . . . .**15** C4
Spinners Gn OL12 . . . .**14** F2
Spinners La SK12 . . . .**133** C4
Spinners Mews BL1 . . . .**145** B4
Spinners Way OL4 . . . .**49** E4
Spinney Apts WN8 . . . .**35** C1
Spinney CI
Glossop SK13 . . . .**104** C2
Handforth SK9 . . . .**131** C3
Spinney Dr
Bury BL9 . . . .**27** E6
Sale M33 . . . .**107** D2
Spinney Gr M34 . . . .**100** F5
Spinney Nook BL2 . . . .**25** D2
Spinney Rd M23 . . . .**121** B7
Spinney The
Bolton BL1 . . . .**144** B3
Chapeltown BL7 . . . .**9** C2
Cheadle SK8 . . . .**122** E3
Oldham OL4 . . . .**68** A8
Rochdale OL12 . . . .**14** A2
Urmston M41 . . . .**95** A2
Whitefield M45 . . . .**62** E8
Wigan WN5 . . . .**54** E5
Spinningfields BL1 . . . .**145** A4
Spinningfield Way
OL10 . . . .**46** D7
Spinning Gate Sh Ctr
WN7 . . . .**75** F4
Spinning Jenny Way
WN7 . . . .**75** F4
Spinning Jenny Wlk 2
M4 . . . .**159** C2
Spinnings Mdw BL1 . . . .**145** A4
Spinnings The BL9 . . . .**11** C3
Spion Kop WN4 . . . .**73** A3

Spiredale Brow WN6 . . . .**19** F2
Spire Hollin SK13 . . . .**104** C2
Spire Hollin Ho SK13 . . . .**104** C2
Spires Croft WN7 . . . .**76** B5
Spire Wlk M12 . . . .**164** A4
Spirewood Gdns SK6 . . . .**113** A2
Spodden Cotts OL12 . . . .**4** D2
Spodden Fold OL12 . . . .**14** C8
Spodden St OL12 . . . .**139** A4
Spodden Wlk M45 . . . .**45** C1
Spodegreen La WA14 . . . .**118** C1
Spod Rd OL12 . . . .**14** B1
Spokeshave Way OL16 . . . .**15** C2
Spooner Rd 8 M30 . . . .**79** C1
Sportside Ave M28 . . . .**60** E4
Sportside CI M28 . . . .**60** E4
Sportside Gr M28 . . . .**60** E4
Sportsmans Dr OL8 . . . .**67** A3
Sportsman St WN7 . . . .**75** D5
SPOTLAND BRIDGE **139** A4
Spotland Bridge Ind Ctr
OL11 . . . .**30** C8
SPOTLAND FOLD **14** C1
Spotland Prim Sch
OL12 . . . .**139** A4
Spotland Rd OL12 . . . .**139** B4
Spotland Tops OL12 . . . .**14** B1
Spreadbury St 7 M40 . . . .**83** A7
Spring Ave
Hyde SK14 . . . .**113** F8
Whitefield M45 . . . .**44** E2
Springbank
Chadderton OL9 . . . .**152** A3
Glossop SK13 . . . .**103** F5
Uppermill OL3 . . . .**69** B8
SPRING BANK **54** D6
Spring Bank
Altrincham WA14 . . . .**119** D3
Appley Bridge WN6 . . . .**35** C8
Salford M6 . . . .**154** B3
Stalybridge SK15 . . . .**102** B8
Whitworth, Broadley
OL12 . . . .**14** D4
Whitworth OL12 . . . .**4** D1
Spring Bank Ave
Ashton-u-L OL6 . . . .**85** B5
Denton M34 . . . .**100** D7
4 Eccles M30 . . . .**79** C1
Springbank CI
Manchester M8 . . . .**63** F1
Romiley SK6 . . . .**113** B5
Springbank Gdns
WA13 . . . .**117** B5
Springbank Ind Est
WN2 . . . .**56** C5
Spring Bank La
Rochdale OL11 . . . .**29** E8
Stalybridge SK15 . . . .**86** C5
Springbank PI SK1 . . . .**170** B4
Springbank Rd SK6 . . . .**113** C6
Spring Bank St OL8 . . . .**66** C4
Spring Bank Terr
M34 . . . .**100** C7
Spring Bottom OL14 . . . .**5** F7
Springbourne WN6 . . . .**36** F2
Springbridge Rd M16 . . . .**97** F1
Spring Brook Specl Sch
OL8 . . . .**67** A1
Springburn CI
Horwich BL6 . . . .**22** D1
1 Worsley M28 . . . .**78** A6
Springburn Way OL3 . . . .**69** B7
Spring CI
Ashton-u-L OL6 . . . .**85** A6
Bury BL8 . . . .**26** E6
Oldham OL4 . . . .**67** D5
Ramsbottom BL0 . . . .**138** B2
Spring Clough M28 . . . .**79** B6
Spring Clough Ave
M28 . . . .**60** F2
Spring Clough Dr
Oldham OL8 . . . .**67** C4
Walkden M28 . . . .**60** F2
Spring Cotts 8 OL5 . . . .**68** C2
Spring Ct Mews SK14 . . . . . .**103** D5
Springdale Gdns M20 . . . .**110** A3
SPRINGFIELD **148** B2
Springfield
Broadbottom SK13 . . . .**115** C6
Nelson M46 . . . .**61** C6
1 Urmston M41 . . . .**95** C2
SPRINGFIELD **37** A2
Springfield Ave
Golborne WA3 . . . .**89** F8
Hazel Grove SK7 . . . .**124** D3
Littleborough OL15 . . . .**16** A7
Lymm WA13 . . . .**117** B5
Manchester M8 . . . .**156** B4
9 Marple SK6 . . . .**125** F6
Reddish SK5 . . . .**111** F7
Springfield CI
Failsworth M35 . . . .**83** F8
Glossop SK13 . . . .**171** A4
5 Heywood OL10 . . . .**29** E1
Springfield Dr SK9 . . . .**136** D5
Springfield Gdns BL4 . . . .**61** A6
Springfield Ind Est
M35 . . . .**83** E8
Springfield La
Irlam M44 . . . .**93** F2
Rochdale OL12 . . . .**15** B4
Royton OL2 . . . .**48** C7
Salford M3 . . . .**158** B2
Springfield Prim Sch
M33 . . . .**108** A2
Springfield Rd
Adlington PR6 . . . .**21** A8

Springfield Rd *continued*
Altrincham WA14 . . . .**119** D5
Atherton M46 . . . .**58** E4
Bolton BL1 . . . .**24** E7
Coppull PR7 . . . .**19** E8
Droylsden M43 . . . .**83** E2
Farnworth BL4 . . . .**42** A1
Gatley SK8 . . . .**122** B5
Hindley WN2 . . . .**56** C6
Horwich BL6 . . . .**22** E1
Kearsley BL4 . . . .**60** F6
Middleton M24 . . . .**46** F2
Ramsbottom BL0 . . . .**11** A2
Sale M33 . . . .**108** B4
Wigan WN1 . . . .**37** A2
Springfield Rd N PR7 . . . .**19** E8
Springfield St
Ashton-u-L OL7 . . . .**85** E5
13 Bolton BL3 . . . .**42** A4
Denton M34 . . . .**100** F6
Heywood OL10 . . . .**29** A2
Wigan WN1 . . . .**37** D2
Spring Gardens St 4
BB4 . . . .**2** F8
Spring Garden St
12 Royton OL2 . . . .**48** D4
11 Royton OL2 . . . .**48** D4
Spring Gdns
Altrincham WA15 . . . .**120** C5
11 Atherton M46 . . . .**58** D3
Bolton BL2 . . . .**25** F4
Glossop SK13 . . . .**104** A5
Hazel Grove SK7 . . . .**124** D3
12 Horwich BL6 . . . .**22** B4
Hyde SK14 . . . .**167** A4
Manchester M1, M2 . . . .**159** A1
Middleton M24 . . . .**47** A1
Rawtenstall BB4 . . . .**2** F6
Royton OL2 . . . .**48** D4
Salford M6 . . . .**154** C3
Stockport SK1 . . . .**112** A1
Wigan WN1 . . . .**150** B4
Spring Gr
Uppermill OL3 . . . .**69** B5
Whitefield M45 . . . .**44** E2
Wigan WN1 . . . .**151** A3
Spring Hall Rise OL4 . . . .**49** F4
Springhead Ave
Manchester M20 . . . .**110** A7
Oldham OL4 . . . .**68** A5
Springhead Inf Sch
OL4 . . . .**68** A6
Springhill OL2 . . . .**48** D4
SPRING HILL **67** D8
Springhill Ave OL13 . . . .**3** D8
Spring Hill St 5 OL4 . . . .**67** D8
Springhill High Sch
OL16 . . . .**31** B5
Springhill Villas OL13 . . . .**3** D8
Spring La
Lymm WA13 . . . .**117** F3
Oldham OL4 . . . .**67** E5
Radcliffe M26 . . . .**44** B3
Springlawn BL1 . . . .**40** F8
Springlees Ct 7 OL4 . . . .**67** F6
Springmeadow SK13 . . . .**115** D7
Spring Meadow La
OL3 . . . .**69** C8
Spring Mill OL3 . . . .**69** B8
Spring Mill CI 4 BL3 . . . .**147** B4
Spring Mill Wlk OL16 . . . .**15** C2
Springmount WA3 . . . .**90** E7
Spring PI OL12 . . . .**4** D3
Springpool WN3 . . . .**54** B2
Spring Rd
Altrincham WA14 . . . .**119** D2
9 Cheadle SK3 . . . .**123** C8
Orrell WN5 . . . .**53** F8
Poynton SK12 . . . .**133** F2
Wigan WN5 . . . .**36** A1
Spring Rise
Glossop SK13 . . . .**115** F7
Shaw OL2 . . . .**32** A1
Stalybridge SK15 . . . .**85** F3
Springside SK4 . . . .**111** D7
Spring Side
Rawtenstall BB4 . . . .**2** F6
Whitworth OL12 . . . .**4** D4
Springside Ave M28 . . . .**60** E3
Springside CI M28 . . . .**60** E3
Spring Side Cotts 8 BL8 . . . . . .**27** C7
Spring Side Cotts BL7 . . . .**8** A2
Springside Gr M28 . . . .**60** E3
Springside Prim Sch
BL9 . . . .**27** E7
Springside Rd BL9 . . . .**27** E8
Springside View BL8 . . . .**27** C7
Springside Wlk 26
M15 . . . .**162** A2
Springs La SK15 . . . .**85** F3
Springs Rd M24 . . . .**65** C6
Spring St
Bolton BL3 . . . .**145** C1
Broadbottom SK14 . . . .**115** A8
Bury BL9 . . . .**140** C1
Bury, Tottington BL8 . . . .**26** F7
Bury, Walshaw BL8 . . . .**26** F4
Farnworth BL4 . . . .**42** D1
Hadfield SK13 . . . .**104** A5
Hollinworth SK14 . . . .**103** C5
Horwich BL6 . . . .**22** B4
Ince-in-M WN3 . . . .**55** E4
Manchester M12 . . . .**99** A2
Mossley OL5 . . . .**68** C2
Oldham, County End OL4 . . . . .**68** A6
Oldham OL4 . . . .**67** C8
Ramsbottom, Bank La
BL0 . . . .**11** D7

Spring St continued
Ramsbottom, Tanners
BL0 ....138 B2
Stalybridge SK15 ....86 A2
Uppermill OL3 ....69 B8
Wigan WN1 ....151 A3
Wilmslow SK9 ....137 A7
Springs The
Altrincham WA14 ....119 B2
Rochdale OL11 ....29 E7
Spring Terr
4 Bacup OL13 ....3 D8
Bury BL8 ....26 F7
Chadderton OL9 ....152 A3
Newhey OL16 ....32 B3
Rochdale OL11 ....14 A1
Spring Thyme Fold
OL15 ....16 A5
Spring Vale
Hazel Grove SK7 ....124 E2
Middleton M24 ....47 B1
Prestwich M25 ....63 A2
Springvale CI OL7 ....84 F5
Springvale CI M24 ....65 B8
Spring Vale Dr BL8 ....26 E6
Spring Vale St BL8 ....26 E6
Spring Vale Terr OL15 ....16 B5
Spring Vale Way OL2 ....149 A1
SPRING VIEW 55 F4
Springville Ave M9 ....157 C3
Springwater Ave BL0 ....11 A3
Springwater CI BL2 ....25 E3
Spring Water Dr
SK13 ....171 B3
Springwater La WN5 ....44 E2
Springwell CI 1 M6 ....154 B2
Springwell Gdns
SK14 ....102 E1
Springwell Way 2
SK14 ....102 E1
Springwood
Delph SK13 ....50 E5
Glossop SK13 ....115 F8
Springwood Ave
Chadderton OL9 ....47 E1
Pendlebury M27 ....80 B6
Springwood Cres OL15 ......113 E2
Springwood Hall OL7 ....85 A7
Springwood Hall Rd
OL8 ....67 A2
Springwood La WN5 ....113 F3
Springwood Prim Sch
M27 ....80 A7
Spring Wood St OL3 ....138 B3
Springwood Way OL7 ....85 A6
Sprodley Dr WN6 ....18 B2
Spruce Ave BL9 ....141 B2
Spruce CI WA3 ....90 E7
Spruce Cres 2 BL9 ....27 F7
Spruce Ct 1 M6 ....81 B2
Spruce Lo SK8 ....122 D6
Spruce Rd WN6 ....36 F3
Spruce St
Manchester M15 ....162 B2
Ramsbottom BL0 ....138 B1
Rochdale OL16 ....31 B6
Spruce Wlk
7 Sale M33 ....107 C6
Walsden OL14 ....6 A8
Sprucewood OL9 ....65 D8
Spurs La OL3 ....51 B4
Spurstow Mews SK8 ....132 C8
Spur The OL8 ....67 A3
Spur Wlk M8 ....155 C3
Square Rd M8 ....155 C3
Squires Ct M5 ....80 A2
Squires La M46 ....76 E8
Squirrel La WA14 ....119 C8
Squirrel's Jump SK9 ....137 C1
Stableford OL5 ....86 C8
Stable Fold
Eccles M28 ....79 A5
Radcliffe M26 ....44 A4
Stableford Ave M30 ....79 C4
Stable St OL9 ....66 A2
Stables The
Culcheth WA3 ....91 D3
Droylsden M43 ....84 D3
Leigh WN7 ....76 A7
Prestwich M25 ....63 C3
4 Sale M33 ....108 A4
Whitworth OL12 ....4 C1
Stablings The SK9 ....137 A5
Stack La OL13 ....4 B8
STACKSTEADS 3 B8
Stadium Way
Wigan, Marsh Green
WN5 ....36 E1
Wigan, Wallgate WN5,
M46 ....150 A3
Stafford CI 6 SK13 ....116 F8
Stafford Ct 2 OL16 ....15 E4
Stafford Rd
Eccles M30 ....79 E3
Failsworth M35 ....84 A5

Stafford Rd continued
Swinton M27 ....79 F8
Walkden M28 ....60 C1
Stafford St
Bury BL8 ....140 A4
Hindley WN2 ....56 C5
Leigh WN7 ....76 D4
New Mills SK22 ....127 C1
Oldham OL9 ....66 A4
Stafford Wlk 12 M34 ....101 A1
Stage La WA13 ....117 C4
Stag Ind Est WA14 ....119 B6
Stag Pasture Rd OL8 ....66 D1
Stainburn CI WN6 ....35 E6
Stainburn Rd M11 ....165 B4
Staindale OL4 ....67 D6
Stainer CI WA12 ....89 B5
Stainer St M12 ....99 A3
Stainforth CI
Bury BL8 ....26 F3
Culcheth WA3 ....91 D4
Stainforth St M11 ....164 C4
Stainmoor Ct SK2 ....124 D6
Stainmore Ave SK8 ....85 D7
Stainsbury St BL3 ....146 C4
Stainton Ave M18 ....99 E4
Stainton CI M26 ....43 F5
Stainton Dr M24 ....46 D3
Stainton Rd M26 ....43 F5
Stairgate WN1 ....150 C4
Staithes Rd M22 ....130 D8
Stakeford Dr M8 ....156 C4
STAKE HILL 47 E5
Stakehill Ind Est M24 ....47 E6
Stakehill La M24 ....47 E5
Staley CI SK15 ....86 C2
Staley Hall Cres SK15 ....86 C3
Staley Hall Rd SK15 ....86 C2
Staley Rd SK15 ....86 E8
Staley St
Oldham, Moorhey OL4 ....67 B6
8 Oldham OL4 ....67 F6
Stalham CI M40 ....160 A3
Stalmine Ave SK8 ....131 B8
STALYBRIDGE 86 B3
Stalybridge Ctry Pk*
SK15 ....87 A2
Stalybridge Sta SK15 ....85 F7
Stalyhill Dr SK15 ....102 E7
Stalyhill Inf Sch SK15 ....102 E7
Stalyhill Jun Sch
SK15 ....102 D7
Staly Ind Est 7 SK15 ....86 B2
Stamford Ave 7 OL6 ....166 C3
Stamford Ave
Altrincham WA14 ....119 A5
Ashton-u-L SK15 ....85 A2
Stamford Ct
8 Ashton-u-L OL6 ....85 D2
Manchester M13 ....98 F3
Stamford Dr
Failsworth M35 ....84 B6
Stalybridge SK15 ....85 F2
Stamford Gr SK15 ....85 F2
Stamford Grange 1
OL6 ....85 A4
Stamford High Sch
OL6 ....85 A4
Stamford New Rd
WA14 ....119 D4
STAMFORD PARK 85 E2
Stamford Park Inf Sch
WA15 ....119 E3
Stamford Park Jun Sch
WA15 ....119 E3
Stamford Park Rd
WA15 ....119 E3
Stamford Pl M33 ....108 C4
Stamford Rd
Alderley Edge SK9 ....137 B1
Altrincham WA14 ....119 C2
Carrington M31 ....106 D7
Denton M34 ....100 E6
Handforth SK9 ....131 A1
Little Bollington WA14 ....118 B2
Manchester M13 ....98 F3
Oldham OL4 ....67 F7
Salford M7 ....81 B6
Urmston M41 ....95 B2
Stamford St Central
OL6 ....166 B2
Stamford St Ctrl OL6 ....166 C3
Stamford St E OL6 ....85 D2
Stamford St W OL6 ....166 A2
Stamford St
Altrincham WA14 ....119 D5
Ashton-u-L OL6 ....85 D2
Stamford St
Altrincham WA14 ....119 D5
Atherton M46 ....58 E4
Heywood OL10 ....29 E1
Manchester M16 ....97 D4
Manchester, Old Trafford
M16 ....161 C1
Mossley OL5 ....68 B1
10 Oldham OL4 ....67 E6
Rochdale OL16 ....31 B6
Sale M33 ....108 A6
Stalybridge, Millbrook
SK15 ....86 D4
Stalybridge OL6, SK15 ....85 F2
Swinton M27 ....62 A1
Stamford Way 2
WA14 ....119 D5
Stampstone St OL1 ....67 B8

Stanage Ave M9 ....64 F4
Stanbank St SK4 ....169 A4
Stanbourne Dr BL1 ....143 C4
Stanbridge CI M40 ....169 B2
Stanbrook St M19 ....111 C8
Stanbury CI BL9 ....28 D1
Stanbury Dr SK16 ....101 D8
Stanbury Wlk M40 ....160 A3
Stancliffe Gr WN2 ....38 C6
Stancliffe Rd M22 ....121 E5
Stancross Rd M23 ....120 C8
STAND 62 C8
Standall Wlk M9 ....64 E1
Stand Ave M45 ....44 E1
Stand CI M45 ....44 E1
Standedge Foot Rd
OL3 ....51 D8
Standedge Rd OL3 ....51 C5
Standedge Wlk SK15 ....86 E6
Standfield Ctr 8 M28 ....78 A6
Standfield Dr M28 ....78 A7
Standish Ave WN5 ....71 E5
STANDISH 19 F2
Standish Com High Sch
WN6 ....19 C2
Standish Gallery 13
WN1 ....150 C4
Standishgate WN1 ....150 C4
Standish Ho SK14 ....167 B2
STANDISH LOWER
GROUND 36 E4
Standish Rd M14 ....110 D8
Standish St Wilfred's CE
Prim Sch WN6 ....19 F1
Standish St M29 ....77 A8
Standish Wlk M34 ....100 E1
Standish Wood La
Standish WN6 ....36 E7
Wigan, Beech Hill WN6 ....36 E5
Stand La
Radcliffe M26, M45 ....44 C1
Whitefield M26, M45 ....62 C8
Standmoor Ct M45 ....62 D7
Standmoor Rd M45 ....62 D7
Standon Wlk M40 ....65 D2
Standrick Hill Rise
SK15 ....86 E5
Standring Ave BL8 ....44 A8
Stand Rise M26 ....62 B8
Stanedge CI BL0 ....11 C4
Stanedge Gr WN3 ....55 B2
Stanford CI M26 ....61 C7
Stanford Hall Cres BL0 ....11 B4
Stanhope Ave
Denton M34 ....100 E5
Prestwich M25 ....63 A5
Stanhope CI
Denton M34 ....100 E5
Wilmslow SK9 ....137 D8
Stanhope Rd
Altrincham WA14 ....119 A2
Salford M6 ....80 E5
Stanhope St
Ashton-u-L OL6 ....85 D4
Denton M34 ....100 E5
Leigh WN7 ....75 D6
Manchester M19 ....99 B1
Mossley OL5 ....86 C8
Reddish SK5 ....111 E7
Rochdale OL11 ....139 C1
Stanhope Way M35 ....83 E8
Stanhorne Ave M8 ....64 A2
Stanier Ave M30 ....79 D3
Stanier Pl BL6 ....22 C2
Stanier St M9 ....157 B4
Stan Jolly Wlk M11 ....165 C4
Stanlaw M30 ....79 E1
Stanley Ave
Hazel Grove SK7 ....124 D3
Hyde SK14 ....167 B4
Manchester M14 ....98 B3
Marple SK6 ....125 D7
Stanley Ave N M25 ....63 A6
Stanley Ave S M25 ....63 A6
Stanley CI
Manchester M16 ....161 C1
Westhoughton BL5 ....57 F7
Whitefield M45 ....44 F1
Stanley Ct M16 ....161 C1
Stanley Dr
Altrincham WA15 ....120 A5
Gatley SK8, SK9 ....131 D6
Leigh WN7 ....75 D8
Whitefield M45 ....62 F6
Stanley Gr
Horwich BL6 ....22 D1
Manchester, Belle Vue M12,
M18 ....99 B4
8 Manchester M21 ....97 B1
Stockport, Heaton Moor
SK4 ....168 B4
Urmston M41 ....95 D2
STANLEY GREEN 131 E6
Stanley Green Ind Est
SK8 ....131 E5
Stanley Green Ret Pk
SK8 ....131 F6
Stanley Grove Com Prim
Sch M12 ....99 A4
Stanley Hall La SK12 ....135 C6
Stanley Ho M16 ....161 C1
Stanley La WN2 ....38 C7
Stanley Mews BL2 ....42 D7
Stanley Mount M33 ....108 A3
Stanley Park Wlk BL2 ....148 C4

Stanley Pl
Rochdale OL12 ....139 B4
Wigan WN1 ....151 B4
Stanley Rd
Aspull WN2 ....38 C6
Bolton BL1 ....142 B1
Eccles M30 ....95 C8
Farnworth BL4 ....60 E8
Handforth SK8, SK9 ....131 E6
Manchester, Old Trafford
M16 ....161 C1
Manchester, Whalley Range
M16 ....97 C4
Oldham OL9 ....66 B4
Pendlebury M27 ....80 A8
Platt Bridge WN2 ....56 A3
Radcliffe M26 ....43 E6
Reddish M34 ....100 B3
Salford M7 ....155 B4
Stockport SK4 ....168 B3
Up Holland WN8 ....53 B7
Walkden M28 ....60 D8
Whitefield M45 ....44 F1
Stanley Road Prim Sch
OL9 ....66 B4
Stanley Sq SK15 ....85 F1
Stanley St
Atherton M46 ....58 C3
Chadderton OL9 ....152 B4
Heywood OL10 ....29 D1
Manchester M3 ....158 B1
Manchester M11 ....99 E7
Manchester M40 ....157 C1
Manchester, Stangeways
M8 ....159 A3
Newton-le-W WA12 ....89 A3
Oldham, Nether Lees
OL4 ....67 E5
Oldham M11 ....99 E7
Prestwich M25 ....63 C4
Ramsbottom BL0 ....138 B1
Rochdale OL12 ....139 B4
3 Stalybridge SK15 ....85 F1
Stockport SK1 ....112 A2
Tyldesley M29 ....59 A1
Whitefield M45 ....44 F1
Wigan WN5 ....54 F6
Stanmere CI BL8 ....10 B3
Stanmoor Dr WN2 ....38 D6
Stanmore Rd M22 ....96 B2
Stanmore Dr BL3 ....144 C1
Stannard Rd M30 ....79 A1
Stanneybrook CI OL16 ....31 E8
Stanney CI OL16 ....31 E5
Stanneylands CI SK9 ....131 B2
Stanneylands Dr SK9 ....131 B2
Stanney Rd OL16 ....31 B8
Stannybrook Rd M35,
OL8 ....84 D6
Stanrose CI BL7 ....8 E1
Stansbury Pl SK2 ....124 E6
Stansby Gdns M12 ....164 B2
Stansfield Dr OL11 ....13 F1
Stansfield Hall CE/Free
Church Prim Sch
OL15 ....16 B8
Stansfield Rd
Bolton BL2 ....148 B4
Failsworth M35 ....84 A8
Hyde SK14 ....167 B4
Rawtenstall BB4 ....2 B1
Stansfield St
2 Bacup OL13 ....3 C8
Chadderton OL9 ....152 B1
Droylsden M11 ....99 D8
Failsworth M40 ....83 D4
Oldham M11 ....153 B4
Stanstead CI WN2 ....37 F2
Stansted Wlk M23 ....108 D1
Stanthorne Ave M20 ....110 A7
Stanton Ave
Manchester M20 ....109 E4
Salford M7 ....81 B7
Stanton CI WN3 ....55 B3
Stanton Ct M32 ....96 C4
Stanton Gdns
Manchester M20 ....109 E4
Stockport SK4 ....168 B1
Stanton St
Droylsden M11 ....83 C2
Oldham M11 ....99 E8
Stretford M32 ....96 C4
Stanway Ave 8 BL3 ....145 A2
Stanway CI
6 Bolton BL3 ....145 A2
Middleton M24 ....65 B6
Stanway Dr M15, M16 ....119 F3
Stanway Rd M45 ....63 B8
Stanway St
Manchester M9 ....157 B4
Stretford M32 ....96 D4
Stanwell Rd
Failsworth M40 ....65 C1
Swinton M27 ....79 F7
Stanwick Ave M9 ....64 A4
Stanworth Ave BL2 ....42 E6
Stanworth CI 6 M16 ....97 E3
Stanyard Ct M5 ....161 A4
STANYCLIFFE 47 B3
Stanycliffe La M24 ....47 B3
Stanyforth St SK13 ....104 A4
Stapleford CI
Over Hulton BL5 ....59 A6
Sale M33 ....108 E5

Stapleford CI continued
Wythenshawe M23 ....120 F4
Stapleford Gr BL8 ....27 A2
Stapleford Wlk M34 ....100 E1
Staplehurst Rd M40 ....157 C2
Staplehurst Rd M40 ....83 A4
Staplers Wlk 9 M14 ....98 C3
Stapleton Ave BL1 ....40 E8
Stapleton St
Platt Bridge WN2 ....56 A2
Salford M6 ....80 C5
Star Bank OL13 ....3 D7
Starbeck Cl BL8 ....26 F2
Starcliffe St BL3, BL4 ....42 D2
Starcross Wlk M40 ....83 B6
Starfield Ave OL15 ....15 F2
Star Gr M7 ....155 B2
Star Ind Est OL8 ....153 C1
Starkey St OL10 ....29 D3
Starkie Rd BL2 ....25 B1
Starkies BL9 ....44 E7
Starkie St M28 ....79 A8
Star La BL6 ....21 F3
STARLING 26 E1
Starling CI
Droylsden M43 ....84 D3
Wythenshawe M22 ....121 C6
Starling Dr BL4 ....59 F7
Starling Rd M26 ....43 E8
Starmount CI BL2 ....42 A6
Starmount CI BL2 ....43 B6
Starring La OL15 ....15 C5
Starring Rd OL15 ....15 C5
Starring Way OL15 ....15 F5
Startham Ave WN5 ....71 D3
Starting Chair OL4 ....68 C8
Stash Gr M23 ....121 B7
Statham CI M34 ....101 A3
Statham Fold SK14 ....102 A4
Statham St M6 ....81 B2
Statham Wlk 2 M13 ....163 B3
Station App
Delph SK13 ....50 F3
Manchester, East Didsbury
M20 ....110 C1
Manchester M1 ....163 A4
Manchester M1 ....163 B4
Station Approach Bsns Ctr
OL11 ....139 C2
Station Ave
Leigh WN2 ....56 D1
Orrell WN5 ....53 D5
Station Bridge M41 ....95 D2
Station CI 1 SK14 ....167 A2
Station Cotts SK8 ....123 B2
Stationers Entry 4
OL16 ....139 C3
Station La
Oldham OL4 ....68 B5
Uppermill OL3 ....69 A5
Station Lofts OL7 ....166 B2
Station Mews WN4 ....72 D3
Station Rd
Adlington PR7 ....21 A6
Blackrod BL6 ....21 E1
Chapeltown BL7 ....9 C4
Cheadle SK8 ....123 B1
Diggle SK13 ....51 D5
Eccles M30 ....79 D1
Garswood WN4 ....72 C3
Glossop SK13 ....104 A5
Handforth SK9 ....131 D3
Haslingden BB4 ....1 A7
Hyde SK14 ....102 B2
Irlam M44 ....105 C4
Kearsley BL4 ....61 A7
15 Littleborough OL15 ....16 B5
Manchester, Crumpsall
M8 ....64 A1
Manchester SK4 ....110 E1
Marple SK6 ....125 F6
Marple, Strines SK6,
SK22 ....126 D1
Milnrow OL16 ....31 F5
Mossley OL5 ....68 D1
Oldham OL4 ....68 A5
Partington WA14 ....118 B5
Ramsbottom BL8 ....10 F1
Reddish SK5 ....99 E2
Rochdale OL11 ....139 C2
Romiley SK6 ....113 B5
Stockport SK1 ....169 B1
Stretford M32 ....96 B3
Styal SK9 ....131 A4
Swinton M27 ....61 F1
Uppermill OL3 ....69 B8
Urmston M41 ....95 D2
Whitworth, Broadley
OL12 ....14 C5
Whitworth OL12 ....4 D3
Wigan WN1 ....150 C4
Wilmslow SK9 ....137 B7
Station St
Bolton BL3 ....145 C2
Dukinfield SK16 ....166 B1
Glossop SK13 ....104 D1
Hazel Grove SK7 ....124 D4
Oldham OL4 ....67 F6
Station View M43 ....100 A7
Staton Ave BL2 ....148 C4
Staton St M11 ....165 C4
Statter St 9 BL5 ....45 A4
Staveleigh Mall OL6 ....166 B3
Staveley Ave
Bolton BL1 ....24 E6

Staveley Ave *continued*
 Stalybridge SK15 . . . . .86 A3
Staveley Cl
 Middleton M24 . . . . .46 E2
 Shaw OL2 . . . . .49 D6
Stavely Wlk ⑧ OL2 . . . . . .48 E4
Staverton Cl M13 . . . . .163 C3
Stavesacre WN7 . . . . .75 F3
Staveton Cl SK7 . . . . .124 A3
Stavordale ⑪ OL12 . . . . . .139 B4
Staycott St M16 . . . . .97 F4
Stayley Dr SK15 . . . . .86 C2
Stayley Rd OL5 . . . . .86 D8
Stead St BL0 . . . . .138 C2
Steadway OL3 . . . . .69 C5
Stedman Cl M11 . . . . .160 B1
Steele Gdns BL2 . . . . .42 E5
Steeles Ave SK14 . . . . .167 B3
Steeple Cl M8 . . . . .155 C1
Steeple Dr M5 . . . . .161 A4
Steeple View OL2 . . . . .48 D4
Stein Ave WA3 . . . . .90 E8
Stelfox Ave
 Manchester M14 . . . . .98 A1
 Sale WA15 . . . . .120 C7
Stelfox La M34 . . . . .100 E7
Stelfox St M30 . . . . .95 B8
Stella Maris RC Jun Sch
 SK4 . . . . .110 E2
Stella St M9 . . . . .64 B4
Stelling St M18 . . . . .99 D5
Stenbury Cl M14 . . . . .98 C3
Stenner La M20 . . . . .110 B1
Stenson Sq ⓫ M11 . . . . .99 D7
Stephen Cl ⑦ BL8 . . . . .27 C2
Stephen Lowry Wlk ⓫
 M40 . . . . .83 A7
Stephen St S BL8 . . . . .27 C1
Stephenson Ave M43 . . . . . .84 A1
Stephenson Rd
 Newton-le-W WA12 . . . . .89 D2
 Stretford M32 . . . . .96 E2
Stephenson St
 Abram WN2 . . . . .74 B8
 Failsworth M35 . . . . .66 A1
 Horwich BL6 . . . . .22 B2
 ⑷ Oldham OL4 . . . . .67 D8
Stephens Rd
 Manchester M20 . . . . .110 D6
 Stalybridge SK15 . . . . .85 F4
Stephens St BL2 . . . . .42 D8
Stephen St
 Bury BL8 . . . . .27 C2
 Manchester M3 . . . . .158 C4
 Platt Bridge WN2 . . . . .56 A2
 Stockport SK1 . . . . .124 B8
 Urmston M41 . . . . .95 E2
Stephens Terr ⑥
 M20 . . . . .110 B3
Stephen's Way WN3 . . . . . . .54 E5
Stephen Wlk SK1 . . . . .124 D4
STEPPING HILL 124 D4
Stepping Hill Hospl
 SK2 . . . . .124 C4
Steps Mdw OL12 . . . . .15 D4
Steptoe Dr OL1 . . . . .48 D1
Sterling Pl OL10 . . . . .28 F1
Stern Ave M5 . . . . .161 A4
Sterndale Ave WN6 . . . . . . .19 E2
Sterndale Rd
 Boothstown M28 . . . . .77 F6
 Romiley SK6 . . . . .113 B1
 Stockport SK3 . . . . .170 B1
Sterratt St BL1 . . . . .145 A2
Stetchworth Dr M28 . . . . . .78 B7
Steven Cl M21 . . . . .109 C8
Stevenson Cl WN3 . . . . . . .150 B1
Stevenson Ct BL4 . . . . .60 E7
Stevenson Dr OL1 . . . . .49 E4
Stevenson Pl M1 . . . . .159 B1
Stevenson Rd M27 . . . . .61 E1
Stevenson Sq
 Manchester M1 . . . . .159 B1
 Rochdale OL12 . . . . .15 C3
Stevenson St
 Salford M3 . . . . .158 A1
 Walkden M28 . . . . .60 B3
Stevens St SK9 . . . . .137 A1
Stewart Ave BL4 . . . . .60 B7
Stewart Ho BL1 . . . . .143 B1
Stewart Rd WN3 . . . . .55 A3
Stewart St
 Ashton-u-L OL7 . . . . .84 F2
 Bolton BL1 . . . . .143 B2
 Bury BL8 . . . . .27 B3
 Bury BL8 . . . . .27 C4
 Newhey OL16 . . . . .32 B3
Stewerton Cl WA3 . . . . .73 F2
Steynton Cl BL1 . . . . .40 F8
Stickens Lock La ⑶
 M44 . . . . .94 A1
Stile Cl M41 . . . . .94 C2
Stiles Ave SK6 . . . . .125 F7
Stiles Cl SK13 . . . . .103 E5
Stillwater Dr M11 . . . . .83 A2
Stilton Dr M11 . . . . .165 A4
Stirling ⑹ M30 . . . . .79 E2
Stirling Ave
 Hazel Grove SK7 . . . . .124 D1
 Ince-in-M WN2 . . . . .56 A8
 Manchester M20 . . . . .109 F8
 ⑹ Marple SK6 . . . . .125 F5
Stirling Cl
 Leigh WN7 . . . . .76 D6
 Stockport SK3 . . . . .123 C6

Stirling Dr
 Garswood WN4 . . . . .72 D4
 Stalybridge SK15 . . . . .86 A3
Stirling Gr M45 . . . . .63 A8
Stirling Ind Est BL6 . . . . . . .22 C2
Stirling Rd
 Bolton BL1 . . . . .24 E5
 Hindley WN2 . . . . .56 F4
 Oldham OL9 . . . . .65 F4
Stirling St
 Oldham OL9 . . . . .152 C3
 Wigan WN1 . . . . .37 C2
Stirrup Brook Gr M28 . . . . .77 F5
Stirrup Gate M28 . . . . .79 A5
Stitch La SK4 . . . . .169 A3
Stitch-Mi-Lane BL2 . . . . . . .25 F2
Stiups La OL16 . . . . .31 B4
Stobart Ave M25 . . . . .63 C2
STOCK BROOK 152 B3
Stockburn Dr M35 . . . . .84 C7
Stockbury Gr ⑻ BL1 . . . . .143 C1
Stock Cl OL12 . . . . .14 E2
Stockdale Ave SK3 . . . . . . .170 C1
Stockdale Gr BL2 . . . . .25 F2
Stockdale Rd M9 . . . . .64 E4
Stockfield Mount OL9 . . . . .152 B2
Stockfield Rd OL9 . . . . .152 B3
Stock Gr OL16 . . . . .31 F7
Stockholm Rd SK3 . . . . . . .170 B2
Stockholm St M11 . . . . .83 B2
Stock La OL9 . . . . .152 B2
Stockland Cl M13 . . . . .163 B3
Stockley Ave BL2 . . . . .25 E2
Stockley Dr WN6 . . . . .35 E8
Stockley Wlk ❷ M15 . . . . .162 A2
Stockmar Grange BL1 . . . . . .40 E8
STOCKPORT 169 A1
Stockport Air Raid
 Shelters Mus * SK1 . . . . . .169 B1
Stockport Coll SK1 . . . . . . .170 C4
Stockport Coll Heaton
 Moor Campus SK4 . . . . . . .111 B5
Stockport Gram Sch
 SK2 . . . . .124 A5
STOCKPORT GREAT MOOR
 . . . . .124 C5
STOCKPORT LITTLE MOOR
 . . . . .124 D8
Stockport Rd
 Altrincham, Timperley
  WA15 . . . . .120 B6
 Ashton-u-L OL7 . . . . .119 F5
 Ashton-u-L OL7 . . . . .100 F8
 Broadbottom SK14 . . . . .114 D8
 Cheadle SK8 . . . . .122 E6
 Denton M34 . . . . .100 F2
 Hattersley SK14 . . . . .102 E2
 Hyde SK14 . . . . .113 D7
 Manchester M12, M13,
  M19 .164 A1
 Marple SK6 . . . . .125 E6
 Mossley OL5 . . . . .68 C2
 Romiley SK6 . . . . .113 B2
 Uppermill OL3 . . . . .68 C5
Stockport Rd E SK6 . . . . . .112 F4
Stockport Rd W SK6 . . . . .112 D3
Stockport St
 ⑶ Manchester M9 . . . . .64 E3
 Walkden M38 . . . . .59 F5
Stocksgate OL12 . . . . .14 B2
Stocks Gdns SK15 . . . . .86 C1
Stocks Ho M41 . . . . .94 F1
Stocks Ind Est M30 . . . . .79 E2
Stocks La SK15 . . . . .86 C1
Stocks Park Dr BL6 . . . . .22 C3
Stocks St E M4, M8 . . . . . . .159 A4
Stocks St
 Manchester M4, M8 . . . . . . .159 A4
 Rochdale OL11 . . . . .30 B2
Stock St BL8 . . . . .27 E5
Stocks The SK13 . . . . .104 A7
Stockton Ave ⑷ SK3 . . . . .123 B8
Stockton Dr BL8 . . . . .27 B5
Stockton Pk OL4 . . . . .67 D6
Stockton Rd
 Manchester M21 . . . . .109 A8
 Wilmslow SK9 . . . . .136 F4
Stockton St
 Farnworth BL4 . . . . .42 C2
 Littleborough OL15 . . . . .15 F4
 ⑷ Manchester M16 . . . . . . .97 E4
 ⑶ Swinton M27 . . . . .79 E7
Stockwell Cl WN3 . . . . .54 D3
Stockwood Wlk M9 . . . . . . .157 A3
Stoke Abbott Cl SK7 . . . . .132 E7
Stokesay Cl
 Bury BL9 . . . . .44 F5
 Royton OL2 . . . . .49 A4
Stokesay Dr SK7 . . . . .124 C1
Stokesay Rd M33 . . . . .107 E5
Stokesby Gdns SK6 . . . . .40 B8
Stokesley Wlk BL3 . . . . . . .147 B3
Stokes Mill ⑸ SK15 . . . . . . .86 B2
Stokes St M11 . . . . .83 D1
Stokoe Ave WA14 . . . . .119 A6
Stonall Ave M15 . . . . .162 A3
Stoneacre BL6 . . . . .39 F8
Stoneacre Ct M27 . . . . .79 F7
Stoneacre Rd M22 . . . . .121 C2
Stonebeck Ct BL5 . . . . .58 F8
Stonebeck Rd M23 . . . . . . .120 F5
Stonebreaks Rd OL4 . . . . . . .68 B7

Stonebridge Cl BL6 . . . . .40 C6
Stonebridge Mews
 M29 . . . . .77 A5
Stonechat Cl
 Droylsden M43 . . . . .84 C3
 ⑩ Golborne WA3 . . . . .90 E8
 Walkden M28 . . . . .78 B8
Stonechurch BL3 . . . . .145 A1
Stone Cl BL0 . . . . .11 A4
Stonecliffe Ave SK15 . . . . . .86 A2
Stonecliffe Terr SK15 . . . . .86 A3
STONECLOUGH 60 F6
Stoneclough Rd BL4,
 M26 . . . . .61 A7
Stoneclough Rise M26 . . . . .61 B8
Stonecroft ⑵ OL1 . . . . .153 B3
Stonecroft Ct M20 . . . . .110 A4
Stonecrop WN6 . . . . .18 D1
Stone Cross La N WA3 . . . . .90 C7
Stone Cross La S WA3 . . . . .90 C6
Stone Cross Pk WA3 . . . . . . .90 B7
Stonedelph Cl BL2 . . . . .26 D1
Stonefield M29 . . . . .59 C1
Stonefield Dr M8 . . . . .155 B1
Stonefield St ⓫ OL16 . . . . .31 F5
Stoneflat Ct OL12 . . . . .139 A4
Stone Gdns WN7 . . . . .76 A5
Stone Hall La WN8 . . . . .35 A5
Stonehaven BL3 . . . . .40 F3
Stone Haven WN3 . . . . .54 D2
Stonehead St M9 . . . . .157 C3
Stonehewer St M26 . . . . .44 B2
Stonehill Cres OL12 . . . . . . .14 A3
Stonehill Dr OL12 . . . . .14 B3
Stone Hill Ind Est BL4 . . . . .60 D6
Stone Hill La OL12 . . . . .14 A2
Stonehill Rd OL12 . . . . .14 B3
Stone Hill Rd BL4 . . . . .60 D6
Stonehouse BL7 . . . . .25 B7
Stonehouse WN5 . . . . .36 D2
Stonehouse Wlk ⑶
 M23 . . . . .120 E7
Stonehurst Cl M12 . . . . .165 A2
Stonelands Way OL4 . . . . . . .68 A4
Stone Lea Way M46 . . . . .58 A2
Stoneleigh M14 . . . . .98 C1
Stoneleigh Ave M33 . . . . . .107 E5
Stoneleigh Dr M26 . . . . .61 B7
Stoneleigh Mews
 SK4 . . . . .111 C5
Stoneleigh Prim Sch
 OL1 . . . . .49 B2
Stoneleigh Rd OL1 . . . . .49 B2
Stoneleigh St OL1 . . . . .67 B8
Stonelow Cl M15 . . . . .162 C2
Stonemead Cl OL4 . . . . .6 A7
Stonemead SK6 . . . . .113 E3
Stone Mead Ave
 WA15 .129 C7
Stonemead Dr M9 . . . . .64 D4
Stonemead M3 . . . . .147 C4
Stone Mill Cotts BL7 . . . . . . .9 D4
Stonemill Terr SK5 . . . . . . .169 C3
Stonepail Cl SK8 . . . . .121 F5
Stonepail Rd SK8 . . . . .122 A5
Stone Pale M45 . . . . .62 F7
Stone Pit Cl WA3 . . . . .74 F1
Stone Pit La WA3 . . . . .90 F2
Stone Pits BL0 . . . . .1 E3
Stone Pl M14 . . . . .98 C3
Stoneridge SK13 . . . . .103 F5
Stone Row
 Marple SK6 . . . . .126 A6
 Wigan WN2 . . . . .38 A3
Stoner Rd PR7 . . . . .20 F7
Stones Bank Rd BL7 . . . . .8 B5
Stonesby Cl M16 . . . . .97 D4
Stonesdale Cl OL2 . . . . .48 D2
Stones Meadow Cvn Pk
 M31 . . . . .106 E7
Stone St
 Bolton BL1 . . . . .25 B1
 Manchester M3 . . . . .162 B4
 Milnrow OL16 . . . . .31 F5
 Rawtenstall BL4 . . . . .2 F8
Stonesteads Dr BL7 . . . . . . .25 A8
Stonesteads Way BL7 . . . . .25 A8
Stoneswood Dr OL5 . . . . .68 E1
Stoneswood Rd OL3 . . . . . . .50 F4
Stonethwaite Cl WN3 . . . . . .55 A2
Stoney Bank M26 . . . . .61 C7
Stoney Bridge La
 WA15 .120 A7
Stoney Brow WN8 . . . . .35 B1
Stoneycroft Ave BL6 . . . . . . .22 D4
Stoneycroft Cl BL6 . . . . .22 D5
STONEYFIELD 139 C1
Stoneyfield SK15 . . . . .86 A4
Stoneyfield Cl M16 . . . . .97 F2
Stoneygate La WN6 . . . . .18 B2
Stoneygate Wlk M11 . . . . . . .99 D7
Stoneyhurst Cres WA3 . . . . .91 D5
Stoney Knoll M7 . . . . .155 A2
Stoney La
 Adlington PR7 . . . . .20 E4
 Delph OL3 . . . . .50 D7
 Wilmslow SK9 . . . . .136 F5
Stoney Royd OL12 . . . . .4 D1
Stoneyside Ave M28 . . . . . . .60 E4
Stoneyside Gr M28 . . . . .60 E4
Stoneyvale Ct OL11 . . . . .30 F4
Stonie Heyes Ave OL12 . . . .15 B2
Stonyford Rd M33 . . . . .108 D4
Stonyhurst Ave
 Bolton BL1 . . . . .24 F5
 Ince-in-M WN3 . . . . .151 A2
Stopes Rd BL3, M26 . . . . . . .43 C3
Stopford Ave OL15 . . . . .15 E4

Stopford St
 Droylsden M11 . . . . .99 F7
 Ince-in-M WN2 . . . . .151 C3
 Stockport SK3 . . . . .170 A4
Stopford Wlk M34 . . . . .100 F3
Stopforth St WN6 . . . . .37 A1
Stopley Wlk M11 . . . . .165 A4
Stores Rd M90 . . . . .130 A6
Stores St M25 . . . . .63 C4
Store St
 Ashton-u-L OL7 . . . . .85 A6
 Horwich BL6 . . . . .22 C4
 Manchester, Ancoats M1,
  M4 . . . . .159 C1
 Manchester, Openshaw
  M11 .165 B3
 Radcliffe M26 . . . . .44 D4
 ⑵ Rochdale OL11 . . . . .13 E1
 Shaw OL2 . . . . .149 C4
 Stockport SK2 . . . . .124 C4
Storeton Cl M22 . . . . .121 E2
Stortford Dr M23 . . . . .109 B2
Storth Bank SK13 . . . . .115 F7
Storth Meadow Rd
 SK13 . . . . .115 F7
Storwood WN5 . . . . .53 E5
Stothard Rd M32 . . . . .96 C1
Stott Dr M41 . . . . .94 D1
Stottfield OL2 . . . . .48 D1
Stott Ho OL8 . . . . .153 B1
Stott La
 Bolton BL2 . . . . .25 B1
 Middleton M24, OL10 . . . . .46 F5
 Salford M6, M5 . . . . .80 B2
 Stott Milne St OL9 . . . . .152 B1
Stott Rd
 Failsworth OL9 . . . . .65 E3
 Swinton M27 . . . . .79 D6
Stott's La M11 . . . . .83 D6
Stott St
 Failsworth M35 . . . . .83 D6
 Milnrow OL16 . . . . .31 F4
 ⑺ Rochdale, Hurstead
  OL16 .15 D4
 Rochdale OL12 . . . . .14 F1
Stott Wharf WN7 . . . . .76 B4
Stourbridge Ave M38 . . . . . .60 A6
Stour Cl WA14 . . . . .119 C6
Stourport Cl SK6 . . . . .113 A1
Stourport St OL1 . . . . .67 A8
Stour Rd M29 . . . . .77 B7
Stout St WN7 . . . . .75 C5
Stovell Ave M12 . . . . .99 A2
Stovell Rd M40 . . . . .83 A8
Stow Cl BL8 . . . . .27 D5
Stowell Cl BL1 . . . . .143 B1
Stowell Ho ⑺ M15 . . . . . . .154 B1
Stowell St
 Bolton BL1 . . . . .143 B1
 Salford M5 . . . . .154 B1
Stowell Tech Ctr
 Salford M5 . . . . .161 A4
 Stretford M50 . . . . .96 F8
Stowfield Cl M9 . . . . .64 B4
Stow Gdns M20 . . . . .110 A6
Stracey St M40 . . . . .160 B3
Stradbroke Cl
 Golborne WA3 . . . . .91 A7
 Manchester M18 . . . . .165 C1
Strain Ave M9 . . . . .64 C4
Straits The M29 . . . . .77 C6
Strand Ave WN4 . . . . .73 B6
Strand Ct M33 . . . . .108 C8
Strand The
 Ashton-in-M WN4 . . . . .73 B4
 Horwich BL6 . . . . .22 D3
 Rochdale OL16 . . . . .30 F2
Strand Way OL1, OL2 . . . . . . .48 D2
Strange Rd WN4 . . . . .72 D3
Strange St WN7 . . . . .75 B4
STRANGEWAYS 158 C4
Strangford St M26 . . . . .43 D4
Strang St BL0 . . . . .138 C2
Stranraer Rd WN5 . . . . .36 D1
Stranton Dr M28 . . . . .79 C8
Stratfield Ave M23 . . . . .108 D1
Stratford Ave
 Bolton BL1 . . . . .142 A1
 Bury BL9 . . . . .27 E8
 Eccles M30 . . . . .95 C8
 Manchester M20 . . . . .109 F5
 Oldham OL8 . . . . .66 F3
 Rochdale OL11 . . . . .139 B1
Stratford Cl BL4 . . . . .147 C1
Stratford Gdns SK6 . . . . . . .112 F3
Stratford Rd M24 . . . . .65 B5
Stratford Sq SK8 . . . . .123 B1
Stratford St WN6 . . . . .37 A1
Strathaven Pl OL10 . . . . .28 F1
Strathblane Cl ⑶
 M20 . . . . .110 B6
Strathdale Dr ⑻ M11 . . . . .83 C2
Strathmere Ave BL3 . . . . . . .32 F8
Strathmore Ave
 Ashton-in-M WN4 . . . . .73 A5
 Denton M34 . . . . .101 B2
 ⑷ Manchester M16 . . . . . . .97 B2
Strathmore Cl BL0 . . . . .11 C4
Strathmore Rd BL2 . . . . .25 E1
Stratton Dr WN2 . . . . .55 F1
Stratton Gr BL6 . . . . .22 B5
Stratton Rd
 Manchester M16 . . . . .97 B2
 Stockport SK2 . . . . .124 C8
 Swinton M27 . . . . .61 E1
Strawberry Bank M6 . . . . . . .81 B3
Strawberry Cl WA14 . . . . . .119 B7
Strawberry Hill M6 . . . . .81 B3

Strawberry Hill Rd
 BL2 . . . . .148 B1
Strawberry La
 Uppermill OL5 . . . . .68 C4
 Wilmslow SK9 . . . . .136 E6
Strawberry Rd M6 . . . . .81 B3
Stray St M11 . . . . .99 E8
Stray The BL1 . . . . .25 B4
Streamside Cl WA15 . . . . . .120 B4
Stream Terr SK1 . . . . .112 B1
Street Bridge Rd OL1,
 OL2 . . . . .48 A2
STREET END 84 B8
Streetgate M38 . . . . .59 F5
Streethouse La OL3 . . . . .50 F1
Street La M26 . . . . .43 F8
Street Lo OL11 . . . . .30 B1
STRETFORD 96 C2
Stretford Gram Sch
 M32 . . . . .96 E1
Stretford High Sch Com
 Language Coll M32 . . . . .96 F4
Stretford Ho ⑺ M32 . . . . . .96 C1
Stretford Meml Hospl
 M16 . . . . .97 B3
Stretford Motorway Est
 M32 . . . . .96 A5
Stretford Rd
 Manchester M15,
  M16 .162 B2
 Urmston M41 . . . . .95 E1
Stretford Sta M32 . . . . .96 D1
Stretton Ave
 Billinge WN5 . . . . .71 E5
 Golborne WA3 . . . . .90 E7
 Manchester M20 . . . . .110 C3
 Sale M33 . . . . .107 E4
 Stretford M32 . . . . .96 A3
Stretton Cl
 Manchester M40 . . . . .157 A1
 Standish WN6 . . . . .36 E3
Stretton Rd
 Bolton BL3 . . . . .146 B4
 Ramsbottom BL0 . . . . .11 A2
Stretton Way ⑻ SK9 . . . . .131 D5
Striding Edge Wlk ⓫
 OL1 . . . . .49 A1
STRINES 126 C2
Strines Cl WN2 . . . . .56 D6
Strines Ct SK14 . . . . .167 E4
Strines Rd
 Marple SK6 . . . . .126 B4
 New Mills SK6 . . . . .135 D8
 Strines St OL16 . . . . .6 A7
 Strines Sta SK6 . . . . .126 D1
Stringer Ave SK14 . . . . .102 F2
Stringer Cl SK14 . . . . .102 F2
Stringer St
 Leigh WN7 . . . . .75 F5
 Stockport SK1 . . . . .112 A2
Stringer Way SK14 . . . . . . .102 F2
Stroma Gdns M41 . . . . .95 C5
Stromness Gr OL10 . . . . .28 F1
Strong St M7 . . . . .158 B4
STRONGSTRY 1 C2
Strongstry Rd BL0 . . . . .1 C1
Strontian Wlk ⑼ M11 . . . . .83 C1
Stroud Ave M28 . . . . .79 B3
Stroud Cl
 Middleton M24 . . . . .65 A5
 Wigan WN2 . . . . .37 F2
Stuart Ave
 Bacup OL13 . . . . .3 D8
 Hindley WN2 . . . . .57 C3
 Irlam M44 . . . . .93 F2
 Marple SK6 . . . . .125 C7
Stuart Cl WN2 . . . . .55 F2
Stuart Cres WN5 . . . . .71 E5
Stuart Rd M43 . . . . .100 A8
Stuart Rd
 Altrincham WA14 . . . . .119 B7
 Brinnington SK6 . . . . .112 D6
 Stretford M32 . . . . .96 D3
 Stuart St E M11 . . . . .83 A2
Stuart St
 Droylsden M11 . . . . .83 A2
 Middleton M24 . . . . .65 C8
 Oldham OL8 . . . . .153 B1
 Rochdale OL16 . . . . .15 B8
 Rochdale OL16 . . . . .31 B6
 Stuart Wlk M24 . . . . .64 F7
STUBBINS 1 B1
Stubbins Cl M23 . . . . .108 E1
Stubbins La BL0 . . . . .138 C4
Stubbins Prim Sch BL0 . . . . .1 C1
Stubbins St BL0 . . . . .1 C1
Stubbins Vale Rd BL0 . . . . . .1 C1
Stubbins Vale Terr BL0 . . . . .1 B1
Stubbs Cl M7 . . . . .81 B8
Stubbylee La OL13 . . . . .3 F8
STUBLEY 15 E5
Stubley Gdns ⑺ OL15 . . . . .16 A5
Stubley La OL15 . . . . .15 F4
Stubley Mill Rd
 Littleborough, Dearnley
  OL15 . . . . .15 F4
 Littleborough OL15 . . . . .16 A5
STUBSHAW CROSS 73 D5
Student Village M1 . . . . . . .163 A3
Studforth Wlk ⑶
 M15 . . . . .163 A1
Studland Rd M22 . . . . .121 F3
Studley Cl OL2 . . . . .49 A4
Studley Ct M29 . . . . .58 F1
Sturton Ave WN3 . . . . .54 E3
STYAL 130 F4
Styal Ave
 Reddish SK5 . . . . .111 F6

Styal Ave *continued*
Stretford M32 ... 96 A3
Styal Cross SK9 ... 130 E4
Styal Ctry Pk* SK9 ... 130 E3
Styal Gn SK9 ... 130 F3
Styal Gr SK8 ... 122 A3
STYAL GREEN ... 131 A3
Styal Ho M22 ... 121 F7
Styal Prim Sch SK9 ... 130 E4
Styal Rd
Gatley M22, SK8, SK9 ... 122 A3
Wilmslow SK9 ... 137 B8
Wythenshawe M22 ... 130 F7
Styal St BL1 ... 144 B4
Styal Sta SK9 ... 131 A4
Styal View SK9 ... 131 B2
Styhead Dr M24 ... 46 D3
Style St M4 ... 159 A3
Styperson Way SK12 ... 133 E3
Sudbrook Cl WA3 ... 90 E8
Sudbury Cl
Manchester M16 ... 161 C1
Wigan WN3 ... 55 B2
Sudbury Dr
Bolton BL6 ... 40 C6
Gatley SK8 ... 131 C8
Sudbury Rd SK7 ... 133 E8
SUDDEN ... 30 D4
Sudden St OL11 ... 30 C4
Sudell St M4, M40 ... 159 B3
Sudell Street Ind Est
M4 ... 159 B3
Sudley Rd OL11 ... 139 A1
Sudlow St OL16 ... 15 B2
Sudren St BL8 ... 26 F3
Sue Patterson Wlk
M40 ... 157 A1
Suez St WA12 ... 89 B3
Suffield St M24 ... 65 A8
Suffield Wlk 1 M22 ... 121 D1
Suffolk Ave M43 ... 84 A3
Suffolk Cl
Little Lever BL3 ... 43 B5
Standish WN1 ... 37 B8
Suffolk Dr
Brinnington SK5 ... 112 C6
Handforth SK9 ... 131 C1
Suffolk Gr WN7 ... 75 C5
Suffolk Rd WA14 ... 119 B5
Suffolk St
Oldham OL9 ... 66 B4
Rochdale OL11 ... 139 C2
Salford M6 ... 81 A5
Sugar La OL3 ... 51 A2
Sugar Mill Sq M5 ... 154 A1
Sugden Sports Ctr
M1 ... 163 A3
Sugden St OL6 ... 85 D3
Sulby Ave M32 ... 96 E2
Sulby St
Kearsley M26 ... 61 B7
Manchester M40 ... 83 A8
Sulgrave Ave SK12 ... 133 F4
Sullivan St M12 ... 99 A3
Sullivan Way WN1 ... 37 D1
Sultan St BL9 ... 44 F8
Sulway Cl M27 ... 80 A7
Sumac St M11 ... 83 D2
Sumbland Ho M27 ... 62 B2
Summer Ave M41 ... 95 E2
Summerbottom 1
SK14 ... 115 A8
Summer Castle OL16 ... 31 A7
Summercroft OL9 ... 66 B4
Summercroft Cl WA3 ... 90 A7
Summer Ct M33 ... 107 C2
Summerdale Dr BL0 ... 11 B2
Summerfield Ave M43 ... 83 E3
Summerfield Ct 2
M21 ... 96 F1
Summerfield Dr
Middleton M24 ... 47 C1
Tyldesley M29 ... 77 B8
Summerfield Pl SK9 ... 137 A5
Summerfield Rd
Bolton BL3 ... 42 B4
Worsley M28 ... 79 A8
Wythenshawe M22 ... 121 C2
Summerfields PR7 ... 19 F7
Summerfields Ctr 10
SK9 ... 131 D1
Summerfield View
OL8 ... 67 C3
Summerhill View OL3 ... 33 D1
Summerlea SK8 ... 132 B8
Summer Pl 1 M14 ... 98 C2
Summersales Ind Est
WN3 ... 54 C4
Summers Ave SK15 ... 86 C2
SUMMERSEAT ... 11 C2
Summerseat Cl
Oldham OL4 ... 68 A7
Salford M5 ... 161 A4
Summerseat La BL0 ... 11 A2
Summerseat Meth Prim
Sch BL9 ... 11 D2
Summerseat Sta BL9 ... 11 C2
Summersgill Cl OL10 ... 29 E1
Summershades La OL4 ... 68 D6
Summershades Rise
OL4 ... 68 D6
Summers St OL9 ... 152 C3
Summer St
Horwich BL6 ... 22 B4
Rochdale OL16 ... 31 A7
Summerton Ho 3 M5 ... 81 A1
Summerville Ave M9 ... 157 C3
Summerville Prim Sch
M6 ... 80 D5
Summerville Rd M6 ... 80 D5
SUMMIT
Calderbrook ... 6 D1
Heywood ... 29 A2
Royton ... 48 C7
Summit Cl BL9 ... 28 F4
Summit St OL10 ... 28 F3
Sumner Ave BL2 ... 26 D1
Sumner Rd M6 ... 80 D5
Sumners Pl SK13 ... 104 B1
Sumner St
Aspull WN2 ... 38 D5
Atherton M46 ... 58 C3
Bolton BL3 ... 146 B2
Glossop SK13 ... 116 C8
Shaw OL2 ... 149 B1
Sumner Way M41 ... 95 D2
Sunadale Cl BL3 ... 144 B1
Sunbank Cl OL12 ... 14 D2
Sunbank La WA15 ... 129 E6
Sunbeam St WA12 ... 89 C3
Sunbeam Wlk 10 M11 ... 160 C1
Sunbury Cl
Handforth SK9 ... 131 E2
Stalybridge SK16 ... 101 F8
Sunbury Dr M40 ... 83 D4
Sundance Ct M50 ... 96 E8
Sunderland Ave OL6 ... 166 C4
Sunderland Pl WN5 ... 36 D1
Sundew Pl M24 ... 65 D7
Sundial Cl SK14 ... 102 D3
Sundial Rd SK2 ... 124 D7
Sundial Wlk SK14 ... 102 D3
Sundridge Cl BL3 ... 146 A3
Sunfield SK6 ... 113 C3
Sunfield Ave OL4 ... 49 E4
Sunfield Cres OL2 ... 48 E3
Sunfield Dr OL2 ... 48 F3
Sunfield Est OL3 ... 51 C4
Sunfield La OL3 ... 51 C4
Sunfield Rd OL1 ... 153 B4
Sunfield Way OL4 ... 67 E7
Sunflower Gr 3 OL9 ... 65 F8
Sunflower Mdw M44 ... 94 B3
Sun Gate OL15 ... 15 F1
Sunhill Cl OL16 ... 31 B2
Sun Inn Mews OL3 ... 33 D3
Sunk La M24 ... 65 A7
Sunlaws Ct SK13 ... 116 B8
Sunlaws St SK13 ... 116 B8
Sunleigh Rd WN2 ... 56 E6
Sunlight Rd BL1 ... 144 C3
Sunningdale Ave
Droylsden M11 ... 83 B2
Radcliffe M26 ... 43 D4
Sale M33 ... 108 E3
Whitefield M45 ... 62 C7
Sunningdale Cl
Bury BL8 ... 44 A8
Dukinfield SK14 ... 101 F5
Sunningdale Ct
Reddish M34 ... 100 B4
Sale M33 ... 108 E3
Sunningdale Dr
Bramhall SK7 ... 133 A7
Glossop SK13 ... 104 E1
Heywood OL10 ... 46 D8
Irlam M44 ... 93 F3
Prestwich M25 ... 63 B5
Salford M6 ... 80 B5
Sunningdale Gr WN7 ... 76 D7
Sunningdale Rd
Cheadle SK8 ... 132 A7
Denton M34 ... 101 B1
Urmston M41 ... 95 B1
Sunningdale Wlk 1
BL3 ... 145 A1
Sunninghey Ct SK9 ... 136 F2
Sunning Hill Prim Sch
BL3 ... 147 A4
Sunning Hill St 13
BL3 ... 147 A4
Sunny Ave BL9 ... 27 F5
SUNNY BANK ... 45 A4
Sunny Bank
Kearsley M26 ... 61 A8
Oldham OL4 ... 67 E5
Wilmslow, Fulshaw Park
SK9 ... 137 B6
Wilmslow SK9 ... 136 D4
Sunnybank Ave
Droylsden M43 ... 83 F1
Eccles M30 ... 79 F3
Manchester SK4 ... 110 F4
Sunnybank Cl WA12 ... 89 C4
Sunny Bank Cl BB4 ... 1 A6
Sunny Bank Prim Sch
BL9 ... 45 A3
Sunnybank Rd
Bolton BL1 ... 142 C2
Droylsden M43 ... 83 F1
Tyldesley M29 ... 77 B6
Sunny Bank Rd
Altrincham WA14 ... 128 C8
Haslingden BB4 ... 1 A6
Manchester M13 ... 98 E3
Whitefield BL9 ... 45 A3
Sunny Banks 3 SK13 ... 116 B8
Sunny Bower St BL8 ... 26 F6
Sunny Brow Rd
Manchester M18 ... 99 C4
Middleton M24 ... 64 E8
Sunny Dr
Orrell WN5 ... 53 F6
Prestwich M25 ... 62 F4
Sunnyfield Rd
Manchester SK4 ... 110 F3
Prestwich M25 ... 63 C7
Sunnyfields WN3 ... 54 C2
Sunny Garth BL5 ... 57 E8
Sunnylea Ave M19 ... 110 E5
Sunny Lea Mews SK9 ... 137 A6
Sunnymead Ave BL1 ... 143 C4
Sunnymede Vale BL0 ... 11 A3
Sunnyside OL7 ... 84 F5
Sunny Side M32 ... 96 F2
Sunnyside Ave M43 ... 83 F4
Sunny Side Cotts OL12 ... 13 B2
Sunnyside Cres 8 OL6 ... 85 D2
Sunnyside Ct
Droylsden M43 ... 83 F3
Manchester M20 ... 110 C3
Sunnyside Gr OL6 ... 85 D2
Sunnyside Rd
Ashton-in-M WN4 ... 72 F7
Bolton BL1 ... 142 C2
Droylsden M43 ... 84 A3
Sunnywood Cl BL8 ... 27 A6
Sunnywood Dr BL8 ... 27 A6
Sunnywood La BL8 ... 27 A6
Sunset Ave M22 ... 109 D2
Sun St
Mossley OL5 ... 68 C1
Ramsbottom BL0 ... 138 B3
Sun Vale Ave OL14 ... 6 B7
Sun View OL2 ... 49 A3
Sunwell Terr SK6 ... 125 F3
Surbiton Rd M40 ... 83 B4
Surma Cl
Oldham OL9 ... 153 A3
Rochdale OL16 ... 31 B5
Surrey Ave
Droylsden M43 ... 83 F3
Leigh WN7 ... 76 E4
Shaw OL2 ... 48 F7
Surrey Cl BL3 ... 43 B4
Surrey Dr BL9 ... 44 F8
Surrey Park Cl OL2 ... 149 B4
Surrey Rd M9 ... 64 D2
Surrey St
Ashton-u-L OL6 ... 85 D5
Glossop SK13 ... 104 C1
Manchester M9 ... 64 C2
Oldham OL9 ... 152 C1
Surrey Way SK5 ... 112 C4
Surtees Rd M23 ... 109 A2
Sussex Ave
Heywood OL10 ... 28 E1
Manchester M20 ... 110 B4
Sussex Cl
Chadderton OL9 ... 152 B2
Hindley WN2 ... 57 A5
Standish WN1 ... 20 B1
Swinton M27 ... 62 A2
Sussex Dr
Bury BL9 ... 44 F8
Droylsden M43 ... 84 A3
Haslingden BB4 ... 1 B8
Sussex Pl SK14 ... 101 F5
Sussex Rd
Irlam M44 ... 105 C6
Partington M31 ... 105 E2
Stockport SK3 ... 123 B8
Sussex St
Leigh WN7 ... 76 E4
12 Manchester M2 ... 158 C1
Rochdale OL11 ... 139 C2
Salford M7 ... 158 A4
Sutch La WA13 ... 117 A3
Sutcliffe Ave M12 ... 99 B2
Sutcliffes Pl 3 OL11 ... 31 A4
Sutcliffe St
Ashton-u-L OL7 ... 84 F1
Bolton BL1 ... 143 B2
Britannia OL13 ... 4 C8
Littleborough OL15 ... 16 B6
Middleton M24 ... 65 C8
Oldham OL8 ... 153 B1
Royton OL2 ... 49 A3
Sutherland Cl OL8 ... 66 F1
Sutherland Gr BL4 ... 60 C8
Sutherland Rd
Bolton BL1 ... 142 A1
Heywood OL10 ... 28 F1
Manchester M16 ... 97 A3
Wigan WN3 ... 55 A3
Sutherland St
Ashton-u-L OL6 ... 85 E3
Eccles M30 ... 79 B3
3 Farnworth BL4 ... 60 C8
Hindley WN2 ... 56 C5
Swinton M27 ... 61 E1
1 Wigan WN5 ... 54 F6
Suthers St
Oldham OL9 ... 152 C2
Radcliffe M26 ... 44 C1
Sutton Ave WA3 ... 91 F4
Sutton Cl BL8 ... 44 B8
Sutton Dr M43 ... 83 E3
Sutton La PR6 ... 21 B8
Sutton Manor 1 M21 ... 97 A1
Sutton Rd
Alderley Edge SK9 ... 136 F2
Bolton BL3 ... 40 F4
Manchester M18 ... 99 C3
Poynton SK12 ... 134 A2
Stockport, Heaton Norris
SK4 ... 168 C3
Suttons La SK6 ... 126 A5
Sutton Way
Glossop SK13 ... 104 A5
1 Handforth SK9 ... 131 E5
Salford M6 ... 154 C3
Swailes St 3 OL4 ... 67 B6
Swaindrod La OL15 ... 16 F7
Swaine St SK3 ... 169 B1
Swain St OL12 ... 14 E1
Swainsthorpe Dr 15
M9 ... 157 B4
Swale Cl SK9 ... 131 E2
Swalecliff Ave M23 ... 108 D1
Swaledale Cl OL2 ... 48 E5
Swale Dr WA14 ... 119 C6
Swallow Bank Dr OL11 ... 30 B3
Swallow Cl SK15 ... 86 F7
Swallow Ct
Handforth SK9 ... 131 B1
Stockport SK1 ... 169 B4
Swallow Dr
Bury BL9 ... 141 B4
Irlam M44 ... 94 A3
Rochdale OL11 ... 29 F7
Swallowfield WN7 ... 76 A5
Swallow Fold SK13 ... 115 F8
Swallow La SK15 ... 86 F6
Swallow St
Manchester, Bradford
M11 ... 160 C1
Manchester M12 ... 99 A2
Oldham OL8 ... 66 D2
Stockport SK1 ... 170 C3
Swanage Ave
Sale M23 ... 108 D1
Stockport SK2 ... 124 D6
Swanage Cl BL8 ... 27 C6
Swanage Rd M30 ... 79 B3
Swanbourne Gdns
SK3 ... 123 C6
Swan Bsns Ctr BL3 ... 147 A4
Swan Cl SK12 ... 133 B4
Swan Ct OL2 ... 149 B2
Swanfield Wlk WA3 ... 73 F2
Swanhill Cl 2 M18 ... 99 F6
Swan La
Bolton BL3 ... 147 A4
Hindley WN2 ... 57 B4
Swanley Ave M40 ... 157 B1
Swan Meadow Ind Est
WN3 ... 150 B3
Swan Meadow Rd
WN3 ... 150 B3
Swann Gr SK8 ... 123 B1
Swann La SK8 ... 123 B1
Swann St WN3 ... 150 B3
Swan Rd
Ramsbottom BL8 ... 10 F2
Sale WA15 ... 108 A1
Swansea St OL8 ... 67 B4
Swan St
Ashton-u-L OL6 ... 166 C3
Manchester M4 ... 159 B2
Wilmslow SK9 ... 137 B7
Swanton Wlk 17 M8 ... 155 C2
Swarbrick Dr M25 ... 62 F2
Swayfield Ave M13 ... 98 F3
Swaylands Dr M33 ... 108 B1
Sweetbriar Cl OL2 ... 149 B3
Sweet Briar Cl OL12 ... 14 E2
Sweet Briar La OL12 ... 14 E2
Sweetloves Gr BL1 ... 24 E5
Sweetloves La BL1 ... 24 E5
Sweetnam Dr M11 ... 83 B2
Swettenham Rd SK9 ... 131 D5
Swift Bank SK13 ... 115 F8
Swift Cl SK6 ... 113 C5
Swift Rd
Oldham OL1 ... 49 E5
Rochdale OL11 ... 29 F7
Swift St
Ashton-u-L OL6 ... 85 D5
Wigan WN5 ... 150 A3
Swiftsure Ave M3 ... 158 A1
Swift Wlk 2 M40 ... 83 C5
Swinbourne Gr M20 ... 110 C7
Swinburne Ave M43 ... 84 A3
Swinburne Gn SK5 ... 99 D1
Swinburne Way 12
M34 ... 113 A7
Swinburn Gr WN5 ... 53 D1
Swinburn St 2 M9 ... 64 F1
Swindells St SK14 ... 101 E5
Swindell's St 6 M11 ... 99 E7
Swindon Cl M18 ... 99 D5
Swinfield Ave M21 ... 108 F8
Swinford Gr OL2 ... 149 A1
Swinford Wlk 14 M9 ... 64 E3
Swinhoe Pl WA3 ... 91 D3
SWINLEY ... 37 C2
Swinley Chase SK9 ... 131 F1
Swinley La WN1 ... 37 C2
Swinley Rd WN1 ... 37 C2
Swinley St WN1 ... 37 C2
Swinside WN1 ... 37 F1
Swinside Cl M24 ... 46 C2
Swinside Rd BL2 ... 42 F8
Swinstead Ave M40 ... 157 B1
SWINTON ... 79 F8
Swinton Cres BL9 ... 45 A1
Swinton Gr M13 ... 163 C1
Swinton Hall Rd M27 ... 80 A8
Swinton High Sch The
M27 ... 61 F1
SWINTON PARK ... 80 B6
Swinton Park Rd M6 ... 80 B5
Swinton St
Bolton BL2 ... 42 E7
Oldham OL4 ... 67 C5
Swinton Sta M27 ... 61 F1
Swiss Cott SK9 ... 137 C1
Swiss Hill SK9 ... 137 B1
Swithemby St BL6 ... 22 A4
Swithin Rd M22 ... 130 E8
Swithland Rd WA14 ... 107 C1
Swithun Wells Ct M38 ... 60 A5
Swythamley Ct SK3 ... 123 A8
Swythamley Rd SK3 ... 123 A8
Sybil St OL15 ... 16 A6
Sycamore Ave
Altrincham WA14 ... 119 A5
Denton M34 ... 100 F2
Golborne WA3 ... 74 A1
Heywood OL10 ... 46 E8
Hindley WN2 ... 56 F3
Newhey OL16 ... 32 A3
Newton-le-W WA12 ... 89 C3
Oldham, Greenacres
OL4 ... 67 D8
Oldham, White Gate OL9 ... 65 F3
Radcliffe M26 ... 61 F8
Tyldesley M29 ... 59 D1
Wigan WN6 ... 36 F3
Sycamore Cl
Ashton-u-L OL6 ... 85 E2
Handforth SK9 ... 131 B2
Littleborough OL15 ... 15 F5
Manchester M20 ... 110 C7
New Mills SK22 ... 127 E1
Stalybridge SK16 ... 101 F8
Sycamore Cotts OL3 ... 50 F1
Sycamore Cres
Ashton-u-L OL6 ... 85 C5
Hollinfare WA3 ... 105 B2
Sycamore Ct
11 Manchester M16 ... 97 D3
Manchester, Miles Platting
M40 ... 160 B3
3 Sale M33 ... 107 C6
8 Salford M6 ... 81 A3
Sycamore Dr
3 Bury BL9 ... 27 F7
Radcliffe M26 ... 44 A5
Wigan WN3 ... 54 C2
Sycamore Gr M35 ... 84 B7
Sycamore Lo SK7 ... 132 F7
Sycamore Pl M45 ... 62 F6
Sycamore Rd
Atherton M46 ... 58 E3
Bury BL8 ... 26 F5
Eccles M30 ... 79 A4
Hayfield SK22 ... 127 F2
Paddockhill WA16 ... 136 B5
Partington M31 ... 105 E3
Romiley SK6 ... 113 A4
Sycamore St
Sale M33 ... 108 E4
Stockport SK3 ... 123 B8
Sycamores The
Glossop SK13 ... 171 C3
Kearsley M26 ... 61 B6
Mossley OL5 ... 68 E1
Oldham OL4 ... 67 E8
Stalybridge SK15 ... 102 B8
Sycamore Wlk
Cheadle SK8 ... 122 D6
1 Horwich BL6 ... 22 E1
Sydall St M34 ... 100 F3
Syddal Cl SK7 ... 132 D5
Syddal Cres SK7 ... 132 D4
Syddal Gn SK7 ... 132 D5
Syddall Ave SK8 ... 131 D8
Syddall St SK14 ... 167 A2
Syddal Rd SK7 ... 132 D5
Sydenham St 2 OL1 ... 49 B1
Sydenham Terr OL12 ... 14 D3
Syderstone Cl WN2 ... 56 E4
Sydney Ave
Eccles M30 ... 79 D2
Leigh WN7 ... 75 D2
Wythenshawe M90 ... 130 A8
Sydney Barnes Cl OL11 ... 30 B2
Sydney Gdns OL15 ... 6 C1
Sydney Jones Ct M40 ... 65 C1
Sydney Rd SK7 ... 132 F5
Sydney St
Failsworth M35 ... 83 E7
Mossley OL5 ... 86 D8
Platt Bridge WN2 ... 56 A3
Salford M6 ... 154 B2
Stockport SK2 ... 124 C7
Stretford M32 ... 96 D2
Swinton M27 ... 79 D7
SYKE ... 14 F4
Syke Croft SK6 ... 113 D3
Sykefield Cl WN2 ... 57 C3
Syke La OL12 ... 14 F4
Syke Rd OL15 ... 16 C2
Sykes Ave BL9 ... 45 B4
Sykes Cl OL3 ... 69 B5
Sykes Mdw SK3 ... 170 A2
Sykes Rd OL12 ... 15 A3
Sykes St
Hyde SK14 ... 167 C1
Newhey OL16 ... 32 A4
Reddish SK5 ... 111 F8
7 Rochdale OL16 ... 31 B6
Sykes Wlk 2 SK5 ... 111 F8
Sylvan Ave
Altrincham WA15 ... 119 F8
Failsworth M35 ... 83 E5
Manchester M16 ... 97 D3
Sale M33 ... 108 C3
Urmston M41 ... 95 D3
Wilmslow SK9 ... 136 F5
Sylvan Cl M24 ... 46 D2
Sylvandale Ave M19 ... 99 A1
Sylvan Gr WA14 ... 119 D5

Sylvan St OL9 . . . . 152 C3
Sylvester Ave SK1,
SK2 . . . . 124 B7
Sylvester Cl SK14 . . . . 102 E2
Sylvester Way
🔟 Denton M34 . . . . 113 A7
🔟 Hattersley SK14 . . . . . . 102 E2
Sylvia Gr 🟨 SK5 . . . . 111 E7
Symond Rd M9 . . . . 64 E5
Symons Rd M33 . . . . 108 B5
Symons St M7 . . . . 155 B3
Syndall Ave M12 . . . . 164 A2
Syndall St M12 . . . . 164 A2
Synergy Ho M15 . . . . 163 A1
Syresham St 🔟 WN2 . . . . . .56 B2

T

Taberner Cl WN6 . . . . .19 F1
Taberner St 🟨 WN2 . . . . . . .56 B2
Tabley Ave M14 . . . . .98 B2
Tabley Gdns
🟨 Droylsden M43 . . . . . . .84 B1
Marple SK6 . . . . 126 A4
Tabley Gr
Manchester M13 . . . . .98 F2
Reddish SK5 . . . . 111 E7
Sale WA15 . . . . 120 A8
Tabley Mere Gdns
SK8 . . . . 122 F3
Tabley Mews 🟨
WA14 . . . . 119 D5
Tabley Rd
Bolton BL3 . . . . 146 B4
Handforth SK9 . . . . 131 D5
Sale M33 . . . . 108 E2
Tabley St
Dukinfield SK16 . . . . 101 E8
Mossley OL5 . . . . .86 D8
Salford M6 . . . . .81 B5
Tabor St M24 . . . . .46 F2
Tackler Cl M27 . . . . .79 F7
Tadcaster Dr M40 . . . . 157 A2
Tadcaster Wlk OL1 . . . . . . 153 C3
Taddington Pl 🟨
SK13 . . . . 171 B1
Tadman Gr WA14 . . . . 119 A6
Tadmor Cl M38 . . . . .59 F4
TAGG WOOD 138 A1
Tagg Wood View BL0 . . . . . .18 A1
Tagore Cl M13 . . . . .98 E4
Tahir Cl M8 . . . . 156 B3
Tait Mews SK4 . . . . 110 F2
Talavera St M7 . . . . 155 A1
Talbenny Cl BL1 . . . . .40 F8
Talbot Ave BL3 . . . . .43 A4
Talbot Cl
Oldham OL4 . . . . .67 C8
Rawtenstall BB4 . . . . 1 E8
Talbot Ct
Bolton BL1 . . . . 143 C4
🟨 Stretford M32 . . . . .96 E3
Talbot Gr BL9 . . . . .28 A6
Talbot Pl M16 . . . . 161 B1
Talbot Rd
Alderley Edge SK9 . . . . . . 137 B1
Altrincham WA14 . . . . 119 B2
Dukinfield SK14 . . . . 101 F5
Glossop SK13 . . . . 104 C2
Manchester M14 . . . . 110 E7
Sale M33 . . . . 108 E4
Stretford M16, M32, M15 . . .96 F3
Talbot St
Ashton-u-L OL6 . . . . 166 A3
Eccles M30 . . . . .79 E1
Glossop SK13 . . . . 104 C1
Golborne WA3 . . . . .90 A8
Hazel Grove SK7 . . . . 124 E4
Middleton M24 . . . . .47 A2
Rochdale OL11 . . . . 139 C2
Stockport SK1, SK4 . . . . . 169 B1
Talford Gr M20 . . . . 110 A6
Talgarth Rd M40 . . . . 159 C4
Talkin Dr M24 . . . . .46 E3
Tallarn Cl M20 . . . . 110 C7
Tallis St M12 . . . . .99 A3
Tallow Way M44 . . . . 106 A8
Tall Trees M7 . . . . .63 D1
Tall Trees Cl OL2 . . . . .48 C4
Tall Trees Pl SK2 . . . . 124 C6
Tallyman Way M27 . . . . .80 F7
Talman Gr WN4 . . . . .73 D3
Talmud Torah Chinuch
Norim Sch M7 . . . . 155 A3
Tamar Cl
Kearsley BL4 . . . . .61 B5
Whitefield M45 . . . . .63 A8
Tamar Ct 🟨 M15 . . . . 162 E7
Tamar Dr M23 . . . . 121 A4
Tamarin Cl M27 . . . . .61 C1
Tamar Way OL10 . . . . .29 A3
Tamebank OL5 . . . . .68 D3
Tame Barn Cl OL16 . . . . . . .32 A6
Tame Cl SK15 . . . . .86 C3
Tame Ct 🟨 SK15 . . . . .86 B2
Tame La OL3 . . . . .50 D7
TAMER LANE END 75 C8
Tamerton Dr M8 . . . . 156 A2
Tameside Bsns
Development Ctr
M34 . . . . 100 D3
Tameside Coll OL6 . . . . . . .85 D3

Tameside Coll (The Hyde
Ctr) SK14 . . . . 113 D7
Tameside Coll (Union
Street Ctr) SK14 . . . . . . 167 B2
Tameside Ct
Dukinfield SK16 . . . . 101 B8
🟨 Hattersley SK14 . . . . . 102 E2
Tameside General Hospl
OL6 . . . . .85 E4
Tameside Hippodrome
(Theatre) * OL6 . . . . 166 B3
Tameside Work Ctr 🔟
OL7 . . . . .84 F1
Tame St
Denton, Guide Bridge
M34 . . . . 100 F7
Denton M34 . . . . 100 F4
Manchester M4 . . . . 160 A1
Mossley OL5 . . . . .68 C3
Stalybridge SK15, SK16 . . .85 E1
Uppermill OL3 . . . . .69 B8
Tame Valley Cl OL5 . . . . . . .68 E3
Tame Valley Prim Sch
SK5 . . . . 112 C7
Tame View OL5 . . . . .68 C2
Tame Water Villas OL3 . . . . .50 F1
Tame Wlk 🟨 SK9 . . . . 131 D2
Tamworth Ave
Prestwich M45 . . . . .63 B7
Salford M5 . . . . 161 B4
Tamworth Ave W M5 . . . . . 161 A4
Tamworth Cl
Hazel Grove SK7 . . . . 133 D8
Manchester M15 . . . . 162 B1
Tamworth Ct M15 . . . . 162 B1
Tamworth Dr
Bury BL8 . . . . .27 C5
Wigan WN2 . . . . .37 F2
Tamworth Gn SK1 . . . . 112 B2
Tamworth St
Manchester M15 . . . . .97 E4
Newton-le-W WA12 . . . . . . .89 A3
Oldham OL9 . . . . 152 C1
Stockport SK1 . . . . 112 B2
Tandis Ct M6 . . . . .80 A4
Tandle Hill Ctry Pk*
OL2 . . . . .48 A6
Tandle Hill Rd OL2 . . . . . . .48 B6
Tandlewood Mews 🟨
M40 . . . . .83 C5
Tandlewood Pk OL2 . . . . . . .48 B6
Tanfield Dr M26 . . . . .61 B7
Tanfield Rd M20 . . . . 122 B8
TANG 113 B2
Tangmere Ave OL10 . . . . . . .46 E7
Tangmere Cl M40 . . . . .65 C3
Tangmere Ct M16 . . . . .97 D3
Tang The SK6 . . . . 113 B1
Tanhill Cl SK2 . . . . 124 E6
Tanhill La OL8 . . . . .67 A2
Tanhouse Ave M29 . . . . .77 D7
Tan House Dr WN3 . . . . .54 C2
Tan House La WN3 . . . . .54 C2
Tanhouse Rd M41 . . . . .94 D3
Tanner Brook Cl BL3 . . . . . 147 B4
TANNERS 138 B2
Tanners Croft BL0 . . . . 138 B2
Tanners Fold OL8 . . . . .67 A3
Tanners Gn 🟨 M6 . . . . . . 154 C3
Tanner's La WA3 . . . . .90 B8
Tanners St
Droylsden M18 . . . . .99 E5
Ramsbottom BL0 . . . . 138 B2
Tanner St SK14 . . . . 167 A3
Tannery Way
Altrincham WA14 . . . . 119 E7
Manchester M18 . . . . .99 E5
Tannock Ct SK7 . . . . 124 F1
Tannock Rd SK7 . . . . 124 F1
Tan Pit Cotts WN8 . . . . .35 C4
Tan Pits Cl M29 . . . . .77 C7
Tanpits Rd BL9 . . . . 140 B3
Tanpit Wlk 🟨 M22 . . . . . . 121 C2
Tansey Gr M7 . . . . 155 C3
Tansley Ave PR7 . . . . 19 D8
Tansley Cl BL6 . . . . .22 C2
Tansley Rd M8 . . . . .64 B2
Tansley Sq WN5 . . . . .54 D5
Tanworth Wlk 🟨 BL1 . . . . 143 B2
Tan Yard Brow M18 . . . . . . .99 E5
Tanyard Dr WA15 . . . . 129 C6
Tanyard Gn SK5 . . . . 111 F5
Tanyard La WA15 . . . . 129 A6
Taper St BL0 . . . . 138 B2
Tape St BL0 . . . . 138 B2
Tapley Ave SK12 . . . . 133 E2
Taplin Dr M18 . . . . 165 C1
Taplow Gr SK8 . . . . 122 F2
Taplow Wlk M14 . . . . .98 E3
Tarbet Dr BL2 . . . . .42 F7
Tarbet Rd SK16 . . . . 101 A8
Tarbet Wlk M8 . . . . 155 C2
Tarbolton Cres WA15 . . . . 120 C3
Tariff St M1 . . . . 159 B1
Tarland Wlk 🟨 M11 . . . . . .83 C1
Tarleton Ave M46 . . . . .58 B5
Tarleton Cl BL8 . . . . .26 F1
Tarleton Ho 🟨 M6 . . . . . . .80 C4
Tarleton Pl BL3 . . . . 146 A3
Tarleton Wlk M13 . . . . 164 A2
Tarnbrook Cl M45 . . . . .63 C8
Tarnbrook Dr WN2 . . . . .38 B5
Tarnbrook Wlk M13 . . . . . . 163 A1
Tarn Cl WN4 . . . . .73 B5
Tarn Dr BL9 . . . . .44 E6
Tarn Gr M28 . . . . .60 F1
Tarnrigg Cl WN3 . . . . .54 E3

Tarnside Cl
Hazel Grove SK2 . . . . 124 F6
Rochdale OL16 . . . . .15 C3
Tarnside Fold SK13 . . . . . . 116 A7
Tarnside Rd WN5 . . . . .53 E6
Tarns The SK8 . . . . 122 B3
Tarnway WA3 . . . . .90 F7
Tarporley Ave M14 . . . . 110 A8
Tarporley Cl SK3 . . . . 170 A1
Tarporley Wlk SK9 . . . . 131 E2
Tarran Gr M34 . . . . 101 B1
Tarran Pl WA14 . . . . 119 E6
Tarrant Cl WN3 . . . . 54 C5
Tarrington Cl M12 . . . . 165 A1
Tartan St M11 . . . . 83 B2
Tarves Wlk M11 . . . . .83 B1
Tarvin Ave
Manchester M20 . . . . 110 A7
Reddish SK4 . . . . 111 D7
Tarvin Cl WA3 . . . . .90 E7
Tarvin Dr SK6 . . . . 112 E4
Tarvington Cl M40 . . . . 156 C2
Tarvin Rd SK8 . . . . 123 A4
Tarvin Way 🟨 SK9 . . . . . . 131 D5
Tarvin Wlk BL1 . . . . 143 B2
Tashbar Sch M7 . . . . .63 E1
Tasle Alley M2 . . . . 158 C1
Tatchbury Rd M35 . . . . .84 A7
Tate St OL8 . . . . .67 B5
Tatham Cl 🟨 M13 . . . . .98 F3
Tatham Gr WN3 . . . . .54 D1
Tatham St OL16 . . . . .31 A7
Tatland Dr M22 . . . . 121 F3
Tatlock Cl WN5 . . . . .71 E5
Tattenhall Wlk 🟨
M14 . . . . 110 D8
Tattersall Ave BL1 . . . . .23 E2
Tattersall St OL9 . . . . 153 A2
Tatton Cl
Handforth SK9 . . . . 131 E5
🟨 Manchester M14 . . . . . 110 D8
Stockport SK4 . . . . 168 C4
Tatton Dr WN4 . . . . .72 F4
Tatton Gdns SK6 . . . . 113 D5
Tatton Ho M20 . . . . 110 B6
Tatton Ho BL1 . . . . 144 C3
Tatton Mere Dr M43 . . . . . . .84 B1
Tattomere Gdns
SK8 . . . . 123 A4
Tatton Pl
Manchester M13 . . . . .98 E4
Sale M33 . . . . 108 B5
Tatton Rd
Denton M34 . . . . 101 A1
Handforth SK9 . . . . 131 E5
Sale M33 . . . . 108 B5
Tatton Rd N SK4 . . . . 168 C4
Tatton Rd S SK4 . . . . 168 C4
Tatton St
Hyde SK14 . . . . 113 E7
Manchester M15 . . . . 162 A3
Salford M5 . . . . 161 B4
Stalybridge SK15 . . . . 86 B1
Stockport SK1 . . . . 169 C1
Tatton Terr 🟨 SK16 . . . . . 166 B1
Tatton View 🟨 M20 . . . . . 110 B6
TAUNTON 84 E5
Taunton Ave
Ashton-u-L OL7 . . . . 166 A4
Brinnington SK5 . . . . 112 C5
Eccles M30 . . . . .79 B3
Hindley WN7 . . . . .57 D2
Urmston M41 . . . . 107 B8
Taunton Brook La OL7 . . . . .84 E5
Taunton Cl
Bolton BL1 . . . . 142 C1
Hazel Grove SK7 . . . . 125 A2
Taunton Dr BL4 . . . . 147 C1
Taunton Gn OL7 . . . . .84 F5
Taunton Gr M25, M45 . . . . .63 A6
Taunton Hall Cl OL7 . . . . . . .84 F5
Taunton Lawns OL7 . . . . . . .85 A5
Taunton Pl OL7 . . . . .84 F5
Taunton Rd
Ashton-u-L OL7 . . . . 166 A4
Chadderton OL9 . . . . .48 A1
Sale M33 . . . . 107 D4
Taunton St M18 . . . . .99 E6
Taunton Wlk 🟨 M34 . . . . . 101 A1
Taurus St OL4 . . . . .67 C8
Tavern Court Ave M35 . . . . .84 B7
Tavern Ct M35 . . . . .84 B7
Tavern Rd SK13 . . . . 171 B3
Tavery Cl 🟨 M4 . . . . 159 C2
Tavistock Cl SK14 . . . . 102 E2
Tavistock Dr OL9 . . . . .47 F1
Tavistock Rd
Bolton BL1 . . . . 145 A2
Hindley WN2 . . . . .57 A4
Rochdale OL11 . . . . .30 D7
Sale M33 . . . . 107 D5
Tavistock Sq M9 . . . . 157 A3
Tavistock St M46 . . . . .58 B4
Tawton Ave SK14 . . . . 102 A3
Taxi Rd M90 . . . . 130 B7
Tay Cl OL8 . . . . 153 B1
Tayfield Rd M22 . . . . 121 C2
Tayleur Terr WA12 . . . . .89 D2
Taylor Ave OL11 . . . . .29 F8
Taylor Bldgs BL4 . . . . .61 B6
Taylor Bsns Pk WA3 . . . . . . .91 F1
Taylor Gr WN2 . . . . .57 C3
Taylor Green Way OL4 . . . . .67 F7
Taylor Ho BL8 . . . . .27 C5

Taylor Holme Ind Est
OL13 . . . . 3 B8
Taylor La M34 . . . . 100 D4
Taylor Rd
Altrincham WA14 . . . . 119 A5
Hindley WN2 . . . . .57 C3
Urmston M41 . . . . .95 E7
Taylor's La
Ainsworth BL2 . . . . .43 B7
Ince-in-M WN3 . . . . .55 F3
Taylorson St S M5 . . . . 161 A2
Taylorson St M5 . . . . 161 B3
Taylors Pl 🔟 OL12 . . . . . . .14 F1
Taylor's Rd M32 . . . . .96 E3
Taylor St
🟨 Bolton BL3 . . . . 145 C2
Bury BL9 . . . . 141 A3
Chadderton OL9 . . . . 152 A4
Denton M34 . . . . 100 F4
Droylsden M43 . . . . .84 A1
Golborne WN3 . . . . .74 C1
Heywood OL10 . . . . .29 C2
Hollingworth SK14 . . . . . . 171 A4
Horwich BL6 . . . . .22 B3
Hyde SK14 . . . . 167 C3
Leigh WN7 . . . . .75 D8
Manchester, Belle Vue
M18 . . . . 165 C2
Manchester, Rusholme
M14 . . . . .98 C2
Middleton M24 . . . . .65 A8
🔟 Oldham, Lees OL4 . . . .67 E6
Oldham OL1 . . . . .67 C8
Prestwich M25 . . . . .63 C4
Radcliffe M26 . . . . .44 A3
Stalybridge SK15 . . . . .86 B1
Whitworth OL12 . . . . .14 D8
Wigan WN3 . . . . 150 B4
Taylor Terr 🔟 SK16 . . . . . 166 B1
Tayton Cl M29 . . . . .59 C1
Taywood Rd BL3 . . . . .40 D2
Teak Dr BL4 . . . . .61 A8
Teak St 🟨 BL9 . . . . 141 B2
Teal Ave SK12 . . . . 133 A4
Tealby Ave M16 . . . . .97 C4
Tealby Ct 🟨 M21 . . . . .97 C1
Tealby Rd M18 . . . . .99 B4
Teal Cl
Altrincham WA14 . . . . 119 B8
Hazel Grove SK2 . . . . 124 F5
Wigan WN3 . . . . .54 B4
Teal Ct OL11 . . . . .29 F7
Teal St BL3 . . . . 147 C4
Teasdale Cl OL9 . . . . .65 E3
Teasdale St M40 . . . . 159 B3
Tebbutt St M4 . . . . 159 B3
Tebworth Dr WN2 . . . . .56 A3
Tedburn Wlk 🔟 M40 . . . . . .65 D2
Tedder Dr M22 . . . . 130 F7
Teddington Rd M40 . . . . . . .65 C1
Tedder St 🟨 BL9 . . . . .45 B2
Ted Jackson Wlk
M11 . . . . 164 C4
Teer St M4 . . . . 160 A2
Teesdale Ave M41 . . . . .95 A4
Teesdale Cl SK2 . . . . 124 E6
Teesdale Dr WN7 . . . . .76 C5
Teesdale Wlk 🟨 M9 . . . . . . .64 E3
Tees St OL16 . . . . .31 B6
Tees Wlk OL8 . . . . 153 B1
Teignmouth Ave M40 . . . . . 159 C4
Teignmouth St M40 . . . . . . 159 C4
Telfer Ave M13 . . . . .98 E2
Telfer Rd M13 . . . . .98 E2
Telford Cl M34 . . . . 100 E7
Telford Cres WN7 . . . . .75 D8
Telford Mews OL3 . . . . .69 B8
Telford Rd SK6 . . . . 126 A4
Telford St
Atherton M46 . . . . .58 A2
Horwich BL6 . . . . .22 D2
Manchester M8 . . . . 156 C1
Telford Way OL11 . . . . .31 A2
Telford Wlk M16 . . . . .97 D4
Telham Wlk M23 . . . . 121 A5
Telkers Cl M46 . . . . .58 D3
Tellson Cl M6 . . . . .80 D6
Tellson Cres M6 . . . . .80 D6
Tell St OL12 . . . . 139 A3
Telryn Wlk M8 . . . . 156 C4
Temperance Sq SK14 . . . . 103 A4
Temperance St
Bolton BL3 . . . . 145 B1
🟨 Broadbottom SK14 . . . 115 A8
Manchester, Ardwick
M12 . . . . 164 D3
Manchester M1, M12 . . . . 163 C4
Tempest Chase BL6 . . . . . . .40 C4
Tempest Dr
Alderley Edge SK9 . . . . . . 137 C1
Bolton BL6 . . . . .40 C3
Temple Ave SK13 . . . . 104 C5
Temple Cl OL4 . . . . .67 E8
Templecombe Dr BL1 . . . . . .24 E7
Temple Dr
Bolton BL1 . . . . 142 C3
Pendlebury M27 . . . . .80 B7
Templegate Cl WN6 . . . . . . .19 F2
Temple La OL15 . . . . 6 D1
Temple Moor Inf Sch
M33 . . . . 108 A6
Temple Prim Sch M8 . . . . . 156 B2
Temple Rd
Bolton BL1 . . . . 142 C3
Sale M33 . . . . 108 A6
Temple Sq M8 . . . . 156 B2

Temple St
Glossop SK13 . . . . 104 C5
Heywood OL10 . . . . .29 D2
Middleton M24 . . . . .47 B1
Oldham OL1 . . . . .67 B7
Templeton Cl
Altrincham WA14 . . . . 119 B6
Westhoughton BL5 . . . . . . .57 E8
Templeton Rd WN2 . . . . .56 B2
Ten Acre Ct M45 . . . . .62 D7
Ten Acre Dr M45 . . . . .62 D7
Ten Acres La M40 . . . . .83 A4
Tenax Circ M17 . . . . .96 B8
Tenax Rd M17 . . . . .96 B7
Tenby Ave M14 . . . . 154 C3
Tenby Dr
Ashton-in-M WN4 . . . . .73 A4
Manchester M20 . . . . .65 A5
Tenby Ave
Bolton BL1 . . . . 142 A1
Manchester M20 . . . . 110 B6
Stretford M32 . . . . .96 E4
Tenby Ct M15 . . . . 161 C2
Tenby Dr
Cheadle SK8 . . . . 123 B1
Pendlebury M6 . . . . .80 D5
Tenby Gr 🟨 OL12 . . . . .14 C1
Tenby Rd
Oldham OL8 . . . . .66 B2
Stockport SK3 . . . . 123 B7
Tenby St OL12 . . . . .14 C1
Tenement La SK7,
SK8 . . . . 123 C3
Tenement St WN2 . . . . .56 B1
Teneriffe St M7 . . . . 155 A2
Ten Foot Cl SK13 . . . . 104 B2
Tenham Wlk 🟨 M9 . . . . . . .64 E3
Ten Ho M9 . . . . .67 C2
Tennis St
Bolton BL1 . . . . 143 A3
Manchester M16 . . . . .97 B4
Tennyson Ave
Bury BL9 . . . . .44 F6
Denton M34 . . . . 113 A7
Dukinfield SK16 . . . . 102 A7
Leigh WN7 . . . . .75 C8
Radcliffe M26 . . . . .43 E4
Tennyson Cl SK4 . . . . 168 B2
Tennyson Dr
Longshaw WN5 . . . . .53 D1
Wigan WN1 . . . . .37 C3
Tennyson Gdns M25 . . . . . . .62 F3
Tennyson Rd
Cheadle SK8 . . . . 122 F6
Droylsden M43 . . . . .84 A2
Farnworth BL4 . . . . .60 B6
Middleton M24 . . . . .47 B2
Reddish SK5 . . . . .99 D1
Swinton M27 . . . . .79 D8
Tennyson St
Bolton BL1 . . . . 143 A1
Manchester M13 . . . . 163 C1
Oldham OL1 . . . . .49 C1
🔟 Rochdale OL11 . . . . . . .31 A5
Tennyson Wlk 🟨 BL1 . . . . 143 B2
Tensing Ave
Ashton-u-L OL7 . . . . .85 B5
Atherton M46 . . . . .58 C5
Tensing St OL8 . . . . .85 A8
Tentercroft
OL16 . . . . 153 B3
Tenterden St BL9 . . . . 140 E2
Tenterden Wlk M22 . . . . . . 121 C3
Tenter Dr WN6 . . . . .37 B7
Tenterfield St 🟨 BB4 . . . . . 2 F8
Tenterheads BB4 . . . . 1 D7
Tenterhill La OL12 . . . . 13 C2
TENTERSFIELD 140 A2
Tenters St BL9 . . . . 140 A2
Tenth St M17 . . . . .96 B6
Terence St M40 . . . . .83 D5
Terminal Rd E M90 . . . . . . 130 C7
Terminal Rd N M90 . . . . . . 130 B7
Terminal Rd S M90 . . . . . . 130 B7
Terminal Rd BL4 . . . . .59 F8
Tern Cl
Altrincham WA14 . . . . 119 B8
Dukinfield SK16 . . . . 101 E7
Rochdale OL11 . . . . .29 F7
Tern Dr SK12 . . . . 133 B4
Ternhill Ct BL4 . . . . .60 D8
Terrace St OL4 . . . . .67 B7
Terrace The M25 . . . . .63 B3
Terrington Cl M21 . . . . 109 E7
Tetbury Cl WN5 . . . . .36 D1
Tetbury Dr BL2 . . . . .43 A8
Tetbury Rd M22 . . . . 121 B1
Tetlow Gr M30 . . . . .79 C1
Tetlow La M7 . . . . 155 B4
Tetlow St
Dukinfield SK14 . . . . 101 E5
Failsworth M40 . . . . .83 D5
Middleton M24 . . . . .65 A8
Oldham OL9 . . . . 153 A2
Tetsworth Wlk 🔟 M40 . . . . .65 D2
Teviot St 🟨 M13 . . . . .98 E4
Tewkesbury Ave
Altrincham WA15 . . . . 120 C3
Ashton-u-L OL6 . . . . .85 C7
Chadderton OL9 . . . . .48 A2
Droylsden M43 . . . . .84 A3
Middleton M24 . . . . .46 F3
Urmston M41 . . . . .95 D4
Tewkesbury Cl
Cheadle SK8 . . . . 132 B6
Poynton SK12 . . . . 133 D4
Tewkesbury Dr M25 . . . . . . .63 C2

Tewkesbury Rd
Cheadle SK3 123 B6
Golborne WA3 90 B8
Manchester M40 160 A3
Texas St OL6 166 C2
Textile St M12 165 A3
Textilose Rd M17 96 B5
Teynham Wlk 5 M22 121 C1
Thackeray Cl M8 156 A2
Thackeray Gr M43 84 A2
Thackeray Pl WN3 150 A1
Thackeray Rd OL1 49 C1
Thames Ave WN7 75 F1
Thames Cl
Bury BL9 27 F7
Manchester M11 165 B4
Thames Ct 2 M15 162 A2
Thames Dr WN5 53 F7
Thames Ind Est M12 164 A3
Thames Rd
Culcheth WA3 92 A2
Milnrow OL16 32 B6
Thames St
Oldham OL1 67 A8
Rochdale OL16 31 B6
Thames Trad Ctr M44 105 F7
Thanet Cl M7 155 B1
Thanet Gr WN7 76 A5
Thankerton Ave M34 84 D1
Thatcher Cl WA14 119 C1
Thatcher St OL8 67 A4
THATCH LEACH 65 F5
Thatch Leach OL9 65 F5
Thatch Leach La M45 63 A7
Thaxmead Dr M40 83 D4
Thaxted Dr SK2 125 A5
Thaxted Pl BL1 144 C4
Thaxted Wlk M22 130 C8
Theatre St OL1 153 C3
THE BANKS 126 E3
THE BELL 54 A8
THE EDGE 66 C2
THE HOLLINS 57 A5
Thekla St OL9 153 A4
Thelma St BL0 138 B2
Thelwall Ave
Bolton BL2 42 D8
Manchester M14 110 A8
Thelwall Cl
3 Altrincham WA15 119 E6
Leigh WN7 75 B4
Thelwall Ct M14 110 A8
Thelwall Rd M33 108 E3
Theobald Rd WA14 119 D1
THE PUNGLE 57 D5
Theta Cl M11 83 B2
Thetford 12 OL12 139 B4
Thetford Cl
Bury BL8 27 D5
Hindley WN2 56 E4
Thetford Dr M8 156 B3
THE VILLAGE 94 F1
THICKETFORD BROW 25 C1
Thicketford Brow BL2 25 D1
Thicketford Cl BL2 25 C2
Thicketford Rd BL2 25 C1
Thicknesse Ave WN6 36 F3
Thimble Cl OL12 15 D4
Thimbles The OL12 15 D4
Third Ave
Bolton BL1 144 B3
Bury BL9 28 D4
Droylsden M11 83 C3
Little Lever BL3 42 F4
Mossley SK15 86 E6
Oldham OL8 66 D1
Poynton SK12 133 D1
Stretford M17 96 D6
Swinton M27 79 E5
Tyldesley M29 77 B4
Wigan WN6 37 A2
Third St BL1 23 F4
Thirkhill Pl 2 M30 79 F2
Thirlby Dr M22 121 D1
Thirlemere Rd SK1 124 B7
Thirlmere Ave
Abram WN2 74 B8
Ashton-in-M WN4 73 C4
Ashton-u-L OL7 84 F4
Haslingden BB4 1 C8
Horwich BL6 22 C2
Ince-in-M WN2 56 B7
1 Orrell WN5 53 F7
Pendlebury M27 80 A7
Standish WN6 37 A7
Stretford M32 96 C3
Tyldesley M29 77 A7
Up Holland WN8 53 B7
Thirlmere Cl
Adlington PR6 21 B8
Alderley Edge SK9 136 F1
Stalybridge SK15 86 A4
Thirlmere Dr
Bury BL9 44 E7
Middleton M24 46 E2
Walkden M38 60 A5
Thirlmere Gr
Farnworth BL4 59 E8
Royton OL2 48 D6
Thirlmere Mews M24 46 E2
Thirlmere Rd
Blackrod BL6 21 C3
Golborne WA3 74 C1
Hindley WN2 56 E5
Over Hulton BL5 58 F7
Partington M31 105 E4
Rochdale OL11 30 B4
Urmston M41 94 E3
Thirlmere Rd *continued*
Wigan WN5 54 C7
Wythenshawe M22 121 B2
Thirlmere St WN7 75 E5
Thirlspot Cl BL1 24 E6
Thirlstone Ave OL4 49 F4
Thirsfield Dr 6 M11 83 C2
Thirsk Ave
Chadderton OL9 47 F1
Sale M33 107 C3
Thirsk Cl BL8 27 B5
Thirsk Mews M7 155 A2
Thirsk Rd BL3 43 A2
Thirsk St M12 163 C3
Thistle Bank Cl M9 64 C1
Thistle Cl SK15 102 E7
Thistledown Cl
Eccles M30 95 D8
Wigan WN6 37 A2
Thistle Gn OL16 31 E7
Thistle Sq M31 105 E2
Thistleton Rd BL3 40 F3
Thistle Way OL4 49 D2
Thistle Wlk 4 M31 105 E2
Thistlewood Dr SK9 137 D8
Thistley Fields SK14 113 C8
Thomas Chambers 3
SK13 116 C7
Thomas Cl M34 101 A4
Thomas Ct
Bolton BL7 25 A7
Manchester M15 162 A3
Thomas Dr BL3 145 A1
Thomas Garnet Ct 1
BL4 60 C8
Thomas Gibbon Cl 5
M32 96 C1
Thomas Henshaw Ct
OL11 30 C4
Thomas Ho 1 OL2 48 E4
Thomas Holden St
BL1 145 B4
Thomas Johnson Cl 4
M30 79 C1
Thomas More Cl BL4 60 F6
Thomason Fold BL7 9 D6
Thomas Regan Ct 4
M18 99 D6
Thomas St W SK1,
SK2 170 C3
Thomasson Cl 7 BL1 143 B1
Thomasson Ct BL1 144 B3
Thomasson Meml Sch
BL1 144 B4
Thomas St
Altrincham WA15 119 E4
Aspull WN2 38 B6
Atherton M46 58 D3
Bolton BL3 145 A1
Compstall SK6 114 B2
Farnworth BL4 60 E7
Farnworth BL4 60 E8
Glossop SK13 104 E1
Golborne WA3 90 A8
Hindley WN2 57 B3
Manchester M4 159 A2
Oldham OL4 67 E5
Radcliffe M26 44 B3
Rochdale, Dearnley OL15 15 E4
8 Rochdale OL16 31 A8
Romiley SK6 113 A3
Royton OL2 49 A3
Salford M8 155 C4
Shaw OL2 149 C2
Stockport SK1 170 C3
Stretford M32 96 D3
Westhoughton BL5 39 E3
Whitworth OL12 4 D2
Thomas Telford Basin
M1 159 C1
Thompson Ave
Ainsworth BL2 26 D1
Culcheth WA3 91 E3
Whitefield M45 63 A7
Thompson Cl
Newton-le-W WA12 89 C1
Reddish M34 100 B3
Thompson Court
Apartments M27 80 E8
Thompson Ct
Reddish M34 100 B3
Stalybridge SK15 85 F2
Thompson Dr BL9 141 C3
Thompson Fold SK15 85 F2
Thompson Ho M46 58 C3
Thompson La OL9 66 A4
Thompson Rd
Bolton BL1 142 B1
Reddish M34 100 B3
Urmston M17 95 E8
Thompson St
Ashton-in-M WN4 73 D4
Bolton BL3 145 C1
Horwich BL6 22 A3
Leigh WN7 75 B5
Manchester M4 159 B2
Manchester, Newton Heath
M40 157 C1
Manchester, Strangeways
M3 158 C3
Wigan, Longshoot WN1 37 E1
Wigan, Worsley Mesnes
WN3 55 A4
Thomson Rd M18 99 C4
Thomson St
Manchester M13 163 C2
Stockport SK3 170 B4
Thoralby Cl M12 165 A1
Thorburn Dr OL12 14 B7
Thorburn Ho WN5 54 C7
Thorburn La WN5 54 D8
Thorburn Rd WN5 54 D6
Thoresby Cl
Little Lever M26 43 C5
Wigan WN3 54 E3
Thoresway Rd
Manchester M13 98 E3
Wilmslow SK9 136 F5
Thorgill Wlk 10 M40 83 A7
Thor Gr M5 161 C4
Thoriby Rd WA3 91 F3
Thorley Cl OL9 65 E2
Thorley Dr
Altrincham WA15 120 B5
Urmston M41 95 D2
Thorley La
Altrincham WA15 120 B4
Wythenshawe M22,
WA15 121 A1
Thorley Mews SK7 132 F7
Thorley St M35 83 F8
Thornaby Wlk M9 157 A2
Thornage Dr M40 159 C4
Thorn Ave M35 83 F6
Thornbank
Bolton BL3 144 C2
Eccles M30 79 E3
Thorn Bank SK15 86 F7
Thornbank Cl OL10 46 E7
Thornbeck Dr BL1 23 F1
Thornbeck Rd BL1 23 F1
Thornbridge Ave M21 109 B8
Thornbury 9 OL11 139 B2
Thornbury Ave
Golborne WA3 90 E7
Hattersley SK14 102 E2
Thornbury Cl
3 Bolton BL1 145 B4
Bramhall SK8 123 C1
Thornbury Rd M32 96 E4
Thornbury Way M18 165 C1
Thornbush Cl WA3 74 E1
Thornbush Way OL16 31 C8
Thornby Wlk 8 M23 121 A5
Thorn Cl OL10 29 B3
Thorncliff Ave OL8 66 E3
Thorncliffe Ave
Dukinfield SK16 101 C7
Royton OL2 48 C6
Thorncliffe Gr M19 99 C1
Thorncliffe Pk OL2 48 C6
Thorncliffe Rd
Bolton BL1 24 E5
Glossop SK13 171 C4
Thorncombe Rd 1
M16 97 E3
Thorncross Cl M15 161 C3
Thorn Ct
2 Salford M6 81 B2
15 Stalybridge SK15 86 A2
Thorndale Cl OL2 48 E5
Thorndale Ct M9 64 C2
Thorndale Gr WA15 120 A5
Thornden Rd M40 160 A4
Thorn Dr M22 131 A8
Thorndyke Gdns M25 63 B3
Thorne Ave M41 95 A3
Thornecliffewood
SK14 103 D5
Thorne Ho M14 98 D2
Thorneside M34 100 F5
Thorne St BL4 42 C1
Thorneycroft WN7 76 C5
Thorneycroft Ave
M21 109 C5
Thorneycroft Cl
WA15 120 B5
Thorneycroft Rd
WA15 120 B5
Thorney Dr SK8 132 C6
Thorney Hill Cl 9 OL4 67 A6
Thorneyholme Cl BL6 40 C6
Thorneylea OL12 4 D1
Thornfield SK9 137 A4
Thornfield Ave 8 BB4 2 F8
Thornfield Cl WA3 90 C8
Thornfield Cres M38 59 F5
Thornfield Ct SK4 168 A3
Thornfield Dr 4 M27 79 E7
Thornfield Gr
Cheadle SK8 123 A2
Walkden M38 59 F5
Thornfield Hey SK9 137 E8
Thornfield Rd
Bury BL8 26 E7
Manchester, Green End
M19 110 E5
Stockport SK4 168 A3
Thornfield St M5 154 A1
Thornfield Terr OL6 166 C2
Thornford Wlk 14 M40 65 D2
Thorngate Rd M8 156 A1
Thorn Gr
Altrincham WA15 119 E3
Cheadle SK8 132 A7
Manchester M14 110 D8
Sale M33 108 B4
Thorngrove Ave 1
M23 120 D7
Thorngrove Dr SK9 137 C6
Thorngrove Hill SK9 137 C6
Thorngrove Ho 4
M23 120 D7
Thorn Grove Prim Sch
SK8 132 A7
Thorngrove Rd SK9 137 C6
Thornham Cl BL8 27 C6
Thornham Ct OL16 48 C8
Thornham Dr BL1 25 A6
Thornham La
Royton OL16, OL2 48 C8
Slattocks M24, OL11,
OL2 47 E6
Thornham New Rd OL11,
OL16 47 E8
Thornham Old Rd M24,
OL2 48 B7
Thornham Rd
Sale M33 107 F3
Shaw OL2 48 E8
Thornham St James CE
Prim Sch OL2 48 C8
Thornhill Cl
Bolton BL1 142 C3
Reddish M34 100 A2
Thornhill Dr M28 60 E1
Thornhill Rd
Droylsden M43 84 B2
Garswood WN4 72 C4
Manchester SK4 110 F2
Ramsbottom BL0 11 A1
Thorn Ho 14 SK15 86 A2
Thornholme Cl M18 99 B3
Thornholme Rd SK6 125 F4
Thorniley Brow M4 159 A2
Thornlea
Altrincham WA15 119 F4
Droylsden M43 83 E1
Thorn Lea
Atherton M46 58 E2
Bolton BL2 25 D4
Thornlea Ave
Oldham OL8 66 C1
Swinton M27 79 D6
Thorn Lea Cl BL1 40 F7
Thornlea Dr OL12 14 B2
Thornlee Ct OL4 68 B5
Thornleigh Rd M14 98 B1
Thornleigh Salesian Coll
BL1 143 A4
Thornley Ave BL1 142 C2
Thornley Cl OL4 68 A5
Thornley Cres
Oldham OL4 68 A5
Romiley SK6 113 A4
Thornley La OL4 68 A5
Thornley La N M34, SK5 99 F3
Thornley La S M34,
SK5 100 A2
Thornley Mews BL1 142 C2
Thornley Park Rd OL4 68 A5
Thornley Rd
Denton M34 101 A4
Prestwich M25 63 C7
Thornley St
Hyde SK14 167 B1
Middleton M24 47 B1
Radcliffe M26 44 B2
Thornmere Cl M27 61 C2
Thorn Rd
Bramhall SK7 132 E5
Oldham OL8 67 C3
Swinton M27 79 E6
Thorns Ave BL1 143 A3
Thorns Cl BL1 143 A3
Thorns Clough OL3 51 C5
THORNSETT 127 F3
Thornsett SK22 127 E2
Thornsett Cl 11 M9 157 B4
Thornsett Prim Sch
SK22 127 E3
Thornsett Trad Est
SK22 127 E2
THORNS GREEN 129 C5
Thornsgreen Rd M22 130 D8
Thorns Rd BL1 143 A3
Thorn St
Bolton BL1 143 C2
13 Hindley WN2 56 D4
Ramsbottom BL9 11 C3
Thorns The M21 109 B7
Thorns Villa Gdns M28 78 A5
Thornton Ave
Bolton BL1 23 F1
Droylsden M34 100 C8
Urmston M41 95 A2
Thornton Cl
Ashton-in-M WN4 72 F4
Boothstown M28 77 E7
Farnworth BL4 60 B7
Golborne WA3 75 A1
Leigh WN7 75 F1
Little Lever BL3 43 C3
Thornton Cres M25 62 F5
Thornton Ct M16 161 C1
Thornton Dr SK9 131 D3
Thornton Gate SK8 122 A6
Thornton Pl SK4 168 B4
Thornton Rd
Boothstown M28 77 E7
Gatley SK8 131 C8
Manchester M14 98 A2
Thornton St N M40 157 A1
Thornton St
1 Bolton BL2 148 A3
Manchester M40 160 A4
Oldham OL4 153 C1
Rochdale OL11 139 C1
Thorntree Cl M9 157 B3
Thorntree Pl 2 OL12 139 B4
Thornvale WN2 74 C7
Thorn View BL9 141 C3
Thornway
Bramhall SK8 132 C7
Thornway *continued*
High Lane SK6 134 F7
Walkden M28 78 A8
Thornway Dr OL7 84 F2
Thorn Well BL5 57 E7
Thorn Wlk M31 105 E2
Thornwood Ave M18 99 E4
Thornydyke Ave BL1 24 E5
Thorold Gr M33 108 E4
THORP 48 C5
Thorpe Ave
Radcliffe M26 44 D5
Swinton M27 61 E1
Thorpebrook Rd M40 83 A6
Thorpe Cl
Altrincham WA15 120 C7
Denton M34 100 F4
Oldham OL4 68 A8
Thorpe Gr SK4 111 D6
Thorpe Hall Gr SK14 101 F6
Thorpe La
Denton M34 100 F5
Oldham OL4 68 A8
Thorpeness Sq M18 99 D6
Thorpe St
Bolton BL1 143 A2
Glossop SK13 104 E2
Manchester M16 97 C4
Middleton M24 64 C7
Ramsbottom BL0 138 B1
Walkden M28 60 D4
Thorp Prim Sch OL2 48 C5
Thorp Rd
Manchester M40 83 A6
Royton OL2 48 D4
Thorp St
Eccles M30 95 B8
Whitefield M45 44 E1
Thorp View OL2 48 C6
Thorsby Ave SK14 167 C2
Thorsby Cl
Bolton BL7 24 F8
Droylsden M18 99 E5
Thorsby Rd WA15 119 E5
Thorsby Way 16 M34 101 A1
Thorverton Sq M40 83 C8
Thrapston Ave M34 84 D1
Threadfold Way BL7 24 F7
Threadmill La M27 79 D8
Threaphurst La SK7 125 C1
Threapwood Rd M22 121 E1
Three Acre Ave OL2 49 A4
Three Acre La SK8 131 E7
Three Acres Dr SK5 111 E5
Three Counties Rd
OL5 68 D1
Three Lane Ends OL10 45 F7
Three Sisters Rd WN4 73 B7
Three Sisters Recn Area*
WN4 73 C7
Threlkeld Cl M24 46 C1
Threlkeld Rd
Bolton BL1 24 D6
Middleton M24 46 C1
Thresher Cl 3 M33 108 F3
Threshfield Cl BL9 27 F7
Threshfield Dr WA15 120 C7
Threxton Pl BL3 40 F3
Throstle Bank St
SK14 101 C4
Throstle Ct 3 OL2 48 D4
Throstle Gr
Bury BL8 27 C5
Marple SK6 125 E5
Throstle Hall Ct 1
M24 46 F1
Throstle Nest Ave
WN6 37 A2
Throstles Cl M43 84 C3
Throstle St OL14 6 B6
Thrum Fold OL12 14 D3
Thrum Hall La
Rochdale OL12 14 D3
Rochdale OL12 14 E3
Thrush Ave BL4 59 F8
Thrush Dr BL9 141 B4
Thrush Ho M6 81 A5
Thrush St OL12 14 C1
Thruxton Cl 4 M16 97 E3
Thurcaston Rd WA14 107 C1
Thurland Rd OL4 67 C6
Thurland St OL9 65 E8
Thurlby Ave M9 64 E5
Thurlby Cl WN4 73 D4
Thurlby St M13 98 D4
Thurleigh Rd M20 110 B4
Thurlestone Ave BL2 26 D1
Thurlestone Dr
Stockport SK7 124 B2
3 Urmston M41 95 C3
Thurlestone Rd WA14 119 B6
Thurloe St M14 98 C3
Thurlow WA3 90 E7
Thurlow St M50 154 C1
Thurlston Cres M8 156 B3
Thurlwood Ave M20 110 A7
Thurnham St BL3 146 C3
Thursby Ave M20 110 A6
Thursby Ho WN5 54 C7
Thursby Wlk M24 46 C2
Thursfield St M6 81 B5
Thursford Gr BL6 21 D1
Thurstane St BL1 142 C2
Thurstan St WN3 55 E4
Thurston Ave WN3 55 B3

Thurston Cl BL9 . . . . .45 A2
Thurston Clough Rd OL3,
 OL4. . . . . .50 D2
Thurston Gn SK9 . . . . . .137 A1
Thurstons OL3. . . . . .51 D6
Thynne St
 Bolton BL3 . . . . .145 C1
 Farnworth BL4 . . . . .42 C2
Tiber Ave OL8 . . . . .66 C1
Tib La M2 . . . . .158 C1
Tib St
 Denton M34 . . . . .101 A2
 Manchester M1, M4 . . . .159 A2
 Ramsbottom BL0. . . . . . .138 B1
Tideswell Ave
 Manchester M40 . . . . . .160 A3
 Wigan WN5 . . . . .36 A1
Tideswell Bank 15
 SK13. . . . . .171 B1
Tideswell Cl SK8 . . . . . .131 D8
Tideswell Rd
 Droylsden M43. . . . . .83 E3
 Hazel Grove SK7 . . . . . .133 E8
Tideswell Way M34 . . . .113 A8
Tideswell Wlk 13
 SK13. . . . . .171 B1
Tideway Cl M7 . . . . .80 F8
Tidworth Ave M40 . . . . . .160 A2
Tiefield Wlk M21 . . . . . .109 E6
Tiernan Lo 12 WN6 . . . . .37 A1
Tiffin St OL12. . . . . .139 B4
Tig Fold Rd BL4 . . . . .59 E8
Tilbury Gr WN6. . . . . .35 D7
Tilbury St OL1. . . . . .153 B4
Tilby Cl M41. . . . . .94 E2
Tildsley St BL3 . . . . .147 B4
Tilehurst Ct M7 . . . . .81 B7
Tile St BL9 . . . . .140 C3
Tilgate Wlk 17 M9 . . . . . .64 E3
Tillard Ave SK3. . . . . . . .123 B8
Tillerman Cl M27. . . . . . .80 D8
Tillhey Rd M22 . . . . .121 D2
Tillington cl 6 BL1. . . . .143 B3
Tilney Ave M32 . . . . .96 E1
Tilshead Wlk M13 . . . . . .163 C2
Tilside Gr BL6 . . . . .40 B7
Tilson Rd M23. . . . . .120 F5
Tilstock Wlk M23. . . . . . .120 E8
Tilston Wlk 5 SK9. . . . . .131 E1
Tilton St OL1. . . . . .49 C1
Timberbottom BL2. . . . . .25 C4
Timbercliffe OL15 . . . . . . .6 D1
Timberhurst BL9 . . . . . . .28 D2
Timbersbrook Gr 5
 SK9. . . . . .131 D2
Times Ret Pk OL10 . . . . .29 C2
Times St M24 . . . . .65 B8
Timothy Cl M6 . . . . .80 B3
TIMPERLEY 120 B7
Timperley Cl OL8. . . . . . .67 B2
Timperley Fold OL6. . . . .85 C6
Timperley La WN7 . . . . . .76 B2
Timperley Rd OL6 . . . . . .85 C6
Timperley Sta WA15 . .119 F8
Timpson Rd M23 . . . . . .120 E7
Timsbury Cl BL2 . . . . . . .42 F5
Timson St 2 M35 . . . . . .83 F7
Tindall St
 Eccles M30 . . . . .95 B8
 Reddish SK5 . . . . .99 F3
Tindle St M28 . . . . .60 F3
Tinkerfield WN7 . . . . .75 D7
Tinline St BL9 . . . . .141 A2
Tinningham St 7 M11 . . .99 E7
Tinsdale Wlk M24 . . . . . .46 C1
Tinshill Cl M12 . . . . .165 A1
Tinsley Cl M40 . . . . .160 B2
Tinsley Gr BL2. . . . . .148 B4
Tin St BL3. . . . . .145 B1
Tintagel Ct
 Little Lever M26 . . . . . . .43 C5
 Stalybridge SK15. . . . . .85 F2
Tintagel Rd WN2 . . . . . . .57 A4
Tintagel Wlk SK14 . . . . .102 E3
Tintern Ave
 Ashton-in-M WN4 . . . . . .73 D3
 Bolton BL2. . . . . .25 B2
 Heywood OL10. . . . . .29 C4
 Littleborough OL15 . . . .16 A7
 Manchester M20 . . . . . .109 F5
 Rochdale OL12. . . . . . . .14 D5
 Tyldesley M29 . . . . .77 C7
 Urmston M41. . . . . .107 A8
 Whitefield M45 . . . . .44 F1
Tintern Cl SK12. . . . . . . .133 D5
Tintern Ct M20 . . . . .109 F5
Tintern Dr WA15. . . . . . .120 C2
Tintern Gr SK1 . . . . .112 B1
Tintern Pl OL10. . . . . . . .29 C4
Tintern Rd
 Cheadle SK8 . . . . .132 B6
 Middleton M24. . . . . . . .47 A4
Tintern St M14 . . . . .98 B2
TINTWISTLE 104 F8
Tintwistle CE Prim Sch
 SK13 . . . . .103 F6
Glossop SK13. . . . . .103 F6
Glossop SK13. . . . . .103 F6
Tinwald Pl WN1. . . . . . . .37 F1
Tipperary St SK15 . . . . . .86 E5
Tipping St
 Altrincham WA14. . . . . .119 D3
 Wigan WN3 . . . . .150 B2
Tipton Cl
 Cheadle SK8 . . . . .123 B4

Tipton Cl continued
 Radcliffe M26 . . . . .43 D5
Tipton Dr M23. . . . . .109 B2
Tiptree Wlk 18 M9. . . . . .157 B4
Tiree Cl SK7. . . . . .124 F1
Tirza Ave M19 . . . . .110 F8
Tissington Bank 27
 SK13. . . . . .171 A1
Tissington Gn 28
 SK13. . . . . .171 A1
Tissington Terr 28
 SK13. . . . . .171 A1
Titchfield Rd OL8. . . . . . .67 C4
Tithe Barn Cl OL12 . . . . .15 D4
Tithe Barn Cres BL1 . . . .25 B4
Tithe Barn St SK4 . . . . . .110 F4
Tithe Barn Prim Sch
 SK4. . . . . .168 A3
Tithebarn Rd
 Altrincham WA15. . . . . .129 C8
 Garswood WN4 . . . . . . .72 D2
Tithe Barn Rd SK4. . . . . .110 F4
Tithebarn St
 3 Bury BL9. . . . . .140 C2
 Radcliffe M26 . . . . .44 D4
 Up Holland WN8 . . . . . .53 B7
Tithe Barn St 6 BL5. . . .39 E1
Titian Rise OL3 . . . . .49 D5
Titterington Ave M21 . . .97 B2
Tiverton Ave
 Hindley WN7 . . . . .57 D2
 Sale M33. . . . . .107 F3
Tiverton Cl
 Little Lever M26 . . . . . . .43 C5
 Tyldesley M29 . . . . .77 D7
Tiverton Dr
 Handforth SK9 . . . . .131 D1
 Sale M33. . . . . .107 F3
Tiverton Ho M6 . . . . .80 A3
Tiverton Pl OL7. . . . . . . .85 A5
Tiverton Rd M41. . . . . . . .95 E3
Tiverton Wlk BL1 . . . . . .142 C1
Tiviot Dale SK1 . . . . .169 C2
Tiviot Way SK1, SK5 . . .169 C3
Tivoli St M3 . . . . .158 B1
Tixall Wlk 9 M8. . . . . . . .63 C2
Toad La OL12 . . . . .139 C4
Toad Pond Cl M27 . . . . . .79 C6
Tobermory Cl M11. . . . . .83 D1
Tobermory Rd SK8. . . . .122 C1
Toddington La WN2. . . . .38 B8
Todd's Pl M9 . . . . .64 C1
Todd St
 Bury BL9 . . . . .140 C4
 Glossop SK13. . . . . . . .116 D8
 Heywood OL10. . . . . . . .29 A2
 Manchester M3 . . . . . . .159 A2
 Salford M7. . . . . .155 A2
Todmorden Rd
 Calderbrook OL15 . . . . . .6 D2
 Littleborough OL15 . . . .16 C7
Toft Rd M18 . . . . .99 C4
Toft Way SK9. . . . . .131 E4
Toledo St M11. . . . . .83 D1
Tolland La WA15. . . . . . .128 F8
Tollard Ave M40 . . . . . . .157 A1
Tollard Cl SK8. . . . . .132 B6
Toll Bar Bsns Pk 11
 OL3. . . . . .3 D8
Tollbar St SK1 . . . . .170 C4
Toll Bar St M12. . . . . . . .164 B2
Tollemache Cl SK14. . . .103 A5
Tollemache Rd SK14 . . .103 A5
Tollesbury Cl M40 . . . . .160 A4
Toll Gate Cl M13. . . . . . .98 E4
Tollgate Way OL16. . . . . .31 C8
Toll Green Cl M40. . . . . .156 D7
Toll St
 Platt Bridge WN2. . . . . .56 A1
 Radcliffe M26 . . . . .43 D4
Tolworth Dr M8 . . . . . . .156 B3
Tomcroft La M34 . . . . . .100 D2
Tomlinson Cl OL8. . . . . .153 B1
Tomlinson St
 Horwich BL6 . . . . .22 B3
 Manchester, Hulme
  M15 . . . . .162 B2
 Manchester M40 . . . . . .65 C3
 Rochdale OL11. . . . . . . .30 C4
Tomlin Sq 7 BL2. . . . . . .148 C3
Tom Lomas Wlk M11. . . .83 B2
Tommy Browell Cl 8
 M14 . . . . .98 A3
Tommy Johnson Wlk 7
 M14 . . . . .98 A3
Tommy La BL2. . . . . .26 C1
Tommy Taylor Cl 1
 M40 . . . . .83 C5
Tom Shepley St SK14 . . .167 B2
Tomwood Rise SK13 . . . .115 C6
TONACLIFFE 14 C6
Tonacliffe Prim Sch
 OL12. . . . . .14 C6
Tonacliffe Rd OL12 . . . . .14 C6
Tonacliffe Terr OL12 . . . .14 C7
Tonacliffe Way OL12 . . . .14 C6
Tonbridge Cl BL8 . . . . . .27 C7
Tonbridge Pl 8 BL2. . . . .25 B1
Tonbridge Rd
 Manchester M19 . . . . . .111 B8
 Reddish SK5 . . . . .111 F8
Tonge Bridge Way
 BL2. . . . . .148 B4
Tonge Cl M45. . . . . .45 B1
Tonge Clough BL7. . . . . .24 F8
Tonge Ct M24 . . . . .65 B8
TONGE FOLD 148 C3

Tonge Fold Rd BL2 . . . .148 C3
Tonge Gn SK15 . . . . . . .102 E6
Tonge Hall Cl M24 . . . . .65 B8
Tonge Mdw M24. . . . . . .65 B8
TONGE MOOR 25 A1
Tonge Moor Prim Sch
 BL2. . . . . .25 B1
Tonge Moor Rd BL2 . . . .25 B2
TONG END 4 C2
Tong End OL12 . . . . .4 C2
Tonge Old Rd BL2 . . . . .148 C3
Tonge Park Ave BL2 . . . .25 C1
Tonge Roughs M24 . . . . .65 D8
Tonge St
 Heywood OL10. . . . . . . .29 D2
 Manchester M12 . . . . . .164 A3
 Rochdale OL16. . . . . . . .31 A6
Tongfields BL7 . . . . .24 F8
Tong Head Ave BL1 . . . .25 B4
Tong La
 Britannia OL13. . . . . .4 C8
 Whitworth OL12. . . . . . . .4 D1
Tongley Wlk 13 M40 . . . .65 D2
Tong Rd BL3 . . . . .140 C2
Tong St BL4 . . . . .61 C5
Tonman St M3. . . . . .162 B4
TONTINE 53 D5
Tontine WN5 . . . . .53 C5
Tontine Rd WN5, WN8 . . .53 C6
Toogood La WN6 . . . . . . .18 D6
Tooley Ho M30 . . . . .95 D8
Toon Cres SK8 . . . . .27 C6
Tootal Dr M5, M6 . . . . . .80 C3
Tootal Drive Prim Sch
 M6 . . . . .80 C3
Tootal Gr M5. . . . . .80 C2
Tootal Rd M5. . . . . .154 A2
Toothill Cl M14 . . . . .73 B5
Topcliffe Rd M9 . . . . . . .65 B3
Topcliffe St WN2. . . . . . .56 F6
Topcroft Cl M22 . . . . . . .121 E8
Topfield Rd M22. . . . . . .121 C4
Topfields G M7 . . . . . . .155 A3
Topgate Brow M27. . . . . .80 D8
Topham St M9 . . . . .45 A8
Topley St M40 . . . . .157 A2
TOP LOCK 38 B2
TOP OF HEAP 29 A1
Top Of Heap OL10 . . . . .28 F2
TOP OF HEBERS 46 F3
Top of Wallsuches BL6. .22 F4
TOP O'TH' BROW 25 D2
Top o' th' Brow Prim Sch
 BL2. . . . . .25 E2
Top o'Th' Close Rd
 OL14. . . . . .6 C6
Top o'The Fields M45 . . .62 F7
Top o'th' Gn OL9. . . . . . .66 C4
Top o'th' La BL2 . . . . . . .42 D5
TOP O'TH' MEADOWS
 . . . . .50 A1
Top o'th' Meadows La
 OL4. . . . . .50 A1
Topphome Ct BL4. . . . . .60 E7
TOPPING FOLD 28 D3
Topping Fold Rd BL9 . .141 C3
Topping Ho BL1 . . . . . . .143 B1
TOPPINGS 25 B8
Toppings Gn BL2 . . . . . .25 A7
Topping St
 Bolton BL3 . . . . .143 B1
 Bury BL9 . . . . .141 A3
Toppings The SK6. . . . . .113 A3
Topp St BL4 . . . . .60 E7
Topp Way BL1 . . . . .145 B4
Top Schwabe St M24 . . .64 C8
Topsham Wlk M40 . . . . . .83 D5
Topside OL1. . . . . .48 E1
Top St
 Middleton M24. . . . . . . .46 F1
 Oldham OL4 . . . . .67 D8
 Todmorden OL14 . . . . . .5 F7
Torah St M8. . . . . .159 A4
Tor Ave BL8 . . . . .10 F2
Torbay Cl 1 BL2 . . . . . .144 C1
Torbay Dr SK2. . . . . .124 B7
Torbay Rd
 Manchester M21 . . . . . .109 C8
 Urmston M41. . . . . .95 E1
Torbrook Gr 1 SK9. . . . .131 D2
Torcross Rd M9 . . . . . . .64 B5
Tor End Rd BB4 . . . . .1 A6
Tor Hey Mews BL8. . . . . .10 F2
TORKINGTON 125 A2
Torkington Ave M27 . . . .61 F1
Torkington Ho SK7 . . . .124 F2
Torkington La SK6,
 SK7. . . . . .125 C3
Torkington Manor
 SK7. . . . . .125 B3
TORKINGTON PARK . . .124 F2
Torkington Prim Sch
 SK7. . . . . .125 A2
Torkington Rd
 Gatley SK8. . . . . .122 B5
 Hazel Grove SK7. . . . . .125 B3
 Hazel Grove, Torkington Park
  SK7. . . . . .124 F2
 Wilmslow SK9 . . . . . . .137 D6
Torkington St SK3 . . . . .170 B4
Torksey Wlk M9 . . . . . . .64 C5
Torness Wlk M11. . . . . . .83 B1
Toronto Ave M90 . . . . . .130 B7
Toronto Rd SK2. . . . . . . .124 A6
Toronto St BL2 . . . . .42 E8
Torpoint Wlk 2 M40. . . . .65 C1
Torquay Cl M13. . . . . . . .164 A2
Torquay Dr WN5. . . . . . . .71 E8

Torquay Gr SK2. . . . . . . .124 B4
Torra Barn Cl BL7 . . . . . .8 E3
Torrax Cl M6. . . . . .80 B6
Torre Cl M44 . . . . .47 A3
Torrens St M6. . . . . .80 D5
Torridon Cl M6. . . . . . . .37 B7
Torridon Rd BL2. . . . . . .42 F7
Torridon Wlk 1 M22 . . .121 C1
Torrin Cl SK3. . . . . .170 C1
Torrington Ave
 Bolton BL1. . . . . .143 B3
 Manchester M9 . . . . . . .65 A2
Torrington Dr SK14 . . . .102 E2
Torrington Rd M27 . . . . .80 B6
Torrington St OL10 . . . . .46 E8
Torrisdale Cl BL3 . . . . . .144 B1
Torside Cl BL3 . . . . .144 B1
Torside Mews SK13 . . . .104 A6
Torside Way
 Glossop SK13. . . . . . . .104 A5
 Swinton M27 . . . . .61 F2
Torver Cl WN3. . . . . .55 A2
Torver Dr
 Bolton BL2. . . . . .42 F8
 Middleton M24. . . . . . . .46 D2
Torver Wlk 1 M22. . . . .121 B2
Tor View Sch BB4 . . . . . .1 D8
Torwood Rd OL9. . . . . . .47 E1
Totland Cl M12 . . . . .99 B3
Totley Ave 43 SK13. . . .171 A1
Totley Cl 44 SK13. . . . .171 A1
Totley Gdns 46 SK13 . .171 A1
Totley Lanes 45 SK13 . .171 A1
Totley Lanes 48 SK13 . .171 A1
Totley Mews 45 SK13 . .171 A1
Totley Pl 45 SK13 . . . . .171 A1
Totnes Ave
 Chadderton OL9. . . . . . .47 F1
 Stockport SK7 . . . . . . .124 A2
Totnes Rd
 Manchester M21 . . . . . .109 C8
 Sale M33. . . . . .107 D5
Totridge Cl SK2 . . . . . . .124 D5
Tottenham Dr M23. . . . .120 E7
TOTTINGTON 26 E6
Tottington Ave OL4 . . . . .67 F7
Tottington High Sch
 BL8. . . . . .26 F6
Tottington La M25 . . . . . .62 F5
Tottington Prim Sch
 BL8. . . . . .26 F6
Tottington Rd
 Bolton BL7, BL8. . . . . . . .9 F2
 Bolton, Harwood Lee BL2 .25 B8
 Bury BL8 . . . . .27 C4
Tottington St 18 M11 . . .83 C2
Totton Rd M35 . . . . .83 F7
Touchet Hall Rd M24 . . .47 C4
Touchstones * OL16 . . .139 B3
Toulston Rd M6 . . . . . . .36 F2
Tours Ave M23 . . . . .109 A2
Towcester Cl M4 . . . . . .160 A1
Tower Ave BL0 . . . . .138 A1
Tower Ct
 Bury BL8 . . . . .27 A8
 Chapeltown BL7. . . . . . . .9 C4
Tower Gr WN7. . . . . .76 D6
Tower Grange M7 . . . . . .155 A4
Tower Hill Rd WN8 . . . . .53 B6
Tower Nook WN8 . . . . . . .53 A5
Towers Ave BL3 . . . . . . .146 A4
Towers Bsns Pk M20. . .110 B1
Towers Cl SK12. . . . . . . .133 F5
Tower Sq M13 . . . . .163 C2
Towers Rd SK12 . . . . . . .133 F5
Towers St 2
 Chapeltown BL7. . . . . . . .9 C4
 Heywood OL10. . . . . . . .29 C2
 Hyde SK14. . . . . .167 A1
 Radcliffe M26 . . . . .44 D4
 Stalybridge SK16. . . . . .85 D1
Towers Yard Barns
 SK12. . . . . .133 F5
Tower View BL6. . . . . . . .21 C3
Towey Cl M18 . . . . .99 C6
Towncliffe Wlk 21
 M15 . . . . .162 E2
Towncroft M34 . . . . .101 A4
Towncroft Ave M24 . . . . .46 F2
Towncroft La BL1. . . . . . .40 E8
Townend St SK14 . . . . . .167 B2
Townfield M41 . . . . .95 B1
Townfield Ave WN4 . . . . .73 B2
Townfield Gdns
 WA14 . . . . .119 C5
Townfield La WA13 . . . .117 B7
Townfield Rd WA14 . . . .119 D5
Townfields WN4 . . . . . . .73 A3
Town Fields Cl BL9 . . . .140 C1
Townfield St 9 OL4 . . . .67 B7
Townfield Wlk 13
 M15 . . . . .162 A2
Town Fold SK6 . . . . .126 B7
Towngate Bsns Ctr
 M38 . . . . .59 E5
Town Gate Dr M41. . . . . .94 C2
TOWN GREEN 73 C4
Town Hall La 1 M2 . . . .158 C1
Town Hall Sq OL16 . . . . .31 B6
TOWN HEAD 139 C4
Town House Rd OL15 . . .16 B6
Town La
 Broadbottom SK13 . . . .115 D6
 Coppull PR7 . . . . .19 D8
 Denton M34. . . . . .100 E2
 Dukinfield SK16. . . . . . .101 C8
TOWN LANE 77 B4

Town Lane Ct M34. . . . .100 E2
Townley Fold SK14. . . . .102 B6
Townley Rd OL16 . . . . . .32 A6
Townley St
 Manchester, Beswick
  M11 . . . . .164 C4
 Middleton M24. . . . . . . .65 A8
 Salford M8. . . . . .155 C1
Town Mill Brow OL12 . .139 B3
TOWN OF LOWTON 90 B5
Townrow St OL10 . . . . . .29 E2
Townscliffe La SK6 . . . .126 C6
TOWNSEND FOLD 1 E8
Townsend Rd M27 . . . . .61 F1
Townsend St
 Bolton BL4. . . . . .2 F8
Townsfield Rd BL5. . . . .57 F7
TOWNS GATE 94 C2
Townsgate Way M44 . . . .94 B1
Townside Row BL9. . . . .140 C1
Townsley Gr OL6. . . . . . .85 E5
Townson Dr WN7 . . . . . .75 F1
Town Sq M33. . . . . .108 B4
Town Square Sh Ctr
 OL1. . . . . .153 C2
Town St SK6. . . . . .126 B7
Town's View SK15. . . . . .36 B1
Town St M9 . . . . .157 B4
Towyn Ave M5 . . . . .81 A2
Toxhead Cl BL6. . . . . . . .22 A3
Toxteth St M11. . . . . . . .99 F7
Tracey St M8 . . . . .64 A1
Tracks La WN5 . . . . .53 D3
Tracy Dr WA12 . . . . .89 E3
Traders Ave M41. . . . . . .95 E6
Trafalgar Ave
 Droylsden M34. . . . . . .100 C7
 Poynton SK12 . . . . . . .134 A3
Trafalgar Bsns Pk M8. .158 B4
Trafalgar Cl
 Bury BL9 . . . . .140 B1
 Manchester M16 . . . . . .97 E2
Trafalgar Gr M7 . . . . . . .155 A1
Trafalgar Ho M34 . . . . . .100 C7
Trafalgar Pl M20. . . . . . .110 A4
Trafalgar Rd
 Hindley WN2 . . . . .56 D5
 Sale M33. . . . . .108 C4
 Salford M6. . . . . .80 A3
 Wigan WN1 . . . . .37 C1
Trafalgar Sq 6 OL7. . . . .84 F1
Trafalgar St
 Ashton-u-L OL7 . . . . . . .84 F1
 Oldham OL1. . . . . .153 B4
 Rochdale OL16. . . . . . . .31 A8
Trafalgar St 5 M7. . . . . .155 B1
Trafalgar Wlk
 Manchester, Beswick
  M11 . . . . .165 A4
 Manchester, Old Trafford
  M15 . . . . .162 B1
Trafford Ave M41 . . . . . .95 C3
Trafford Bank Rd
 M16 . . . . .161 C1
Trafford Bar Sta M16 . .161 B1
Trafford Ct 7 M15. . . . . .162 A2
Trafford Ctr The M17. . . .95 E6
Trafford Dr
 Sale WA15. . . . . .120 B8
 Walkden M38. . . . . .60 B5
Trafford General Hospl
 M41 . . . . .95 A3
Trafford Gr
 Farnworth BL4. . . . . .42 E1
 Stretford M32 . . . . .96 C1
Trafford Mans 22 M16. . .97 B2
TRAFFORD PARK 96 D6
Trafford Park Rd M17. . .96 D6
Trafford Pk Rd M17. . . .161 A4
Trafford Pl
 Manchester M15 . . . . . .162 A4
 Wilmslow SK9 . . . . . . .137 D6
Trafford Rd
 Alderley Edge SK9 . . . .137 B1
 Eccles M30 . . . . .79 D1
 Handforth SK9 . . . . . . .131 B1
 Hindley WN2 . . . . .56 C5
 Salford M5, M16, M17 . .161 A3
 Trafford Ret Pk M41. . . .95 C5
Trafford St
 Farnworth BL4. . . . . .42 D1
 Manchester M1, M3 . . .162 C4
 Oldham OL8. . . . . .153 B1
 Rochdale OL11. . . . . . . .139 B1
Trafford Wharf Est
 M17 . . . . .96 D7
Trafford Wharf Rd
 M17 . . . . .96 C6
Tragan Cl SK2. . . . . .124 D6
Tragan Dr SK2. . . . . .124 D6
Trail St M6. . . . . .154 B2
Trail View SK13. . . . . . . .104 A6
Trajan Ho OL1 . . . . .153 C3
Tramore Wlk M22 . . . . . .121 C2
Tram St
 Manchester M11 . . . . . .165 C6
 Platt Bridge WN2. . . . . .56 A1
Tramway Dr
 Ashton-u-L OL6 . . . . . .166 C3
 Irlam M44 . . . . .105 F7
Tranby Cl M22 . . . . .121 F4
Tranmere Cl M18 . . . . . .165 B1
Tranmere Dr SK9 . . . . . .131 E2
Tranmere Rd 1 SK3. . . .123 B8
Transpennine Trad Est
 OL11. . . . . .30 D3
Transvaal St M11. . . . . . .83 D1

Travers St BL6 22 D1
Travis Brow SK4 169 A1
Travis Ct OL2 48 E4
Travis Ho OL14 6 A7
Travis St
Hyde SK14 167 B2
Manchester M1 163 C4
Newhey OL16 32 B4
Shaw OL2 149 C3
Trawden Ave BL1 142 C2
Trawden Dr BL9 27 E8
Trawden Gn SK2 124 D4
Traylen Way OL12 14 A1
Traynor Cl M24 46 F1
Trecastell Cl WN1 37 F1
Tredcroft St SK13 116 B8
Tredgold St BL6 22 C2
Tree Ave M43 84 A3
Tree Ct M14 98 D1
Tree House Ave 2
OL7 85 A6
Treelands Wlk M5 161 B2
Treen Rd M29 77 C8
Tree Tops BL7 25 C6
Treetops Ave BL0 11 A3
Treetops Cl
Marple SK6 125 E7
Uppermill OL3 50 F1
Tree Wlk M32 96 C1
Trefoil Way OL15 15 F6
Tregaer Fold M24 65 C8
Tregaron Gr WN2 57 A3
Tremain Wlk 10 M9 157 A3
Trenam Pl M5 81 B2
Trenant Rd M6 154 A4
Trenchard Ct M11, M43 83 D2
Trenchard Dr M22 130 F7
Trencherbone M26 43 E5
Trengrove St 7 OL12 14 C1
Trent Ave
Chadderton OL9 65 E8
Heywood OL10 29 A3
Milnrow OL16 32 A6
Trent Bridge Wlk M16 97 A3
Trent Cl
Bramhall SK7 132 C6
Brinnington SK5 112 C5
Culcheth WA3 92 A2
Trent Ct
Manchester M15 162 A2
Stockport SK3 170 A3
Trent Dr
Bury BL9 27 F8
Hindley WN2 57 C3
Walkden M28 60 B2
Trent Gr WN7 75 C4
Trentham Ave
Farnworth BL4 42 C1
Manchester SK4 110 F4
Trentham Cl BL4 42 C1
Trentham Gr M40 65 A1
Trentham Lawns M6 81 B4
Trentham Rd M16 97 A3
Trentham St
Farnworth BL4 42 C1
Salford M15 161 C3
Swinton M27 61 E1
Trent Ind Est OL2 149 B4
Trent Rd
Ashton-in-M WN4 73 E5
Billinge WN5 71 D3
Shaw OL2 149 A4
Wigan WN5 54 C7
Trent St OL16 31 B6
Trent Way BL4 61 B5
Tresco Ave M32 96 E1
Trescott Mews WN6 36 F8
Treswell Cl WN2 56 E2
Trevarrick Ct
Horwich BL6 22 E2
2 Oldham OL4 67 C8
Trevelyan Dr WN5 53 D1
Trevelyan St M30 80 A2
Trevor Ave
Bolton BL3 147 A3
Sale M33 107 F2
Trevor Dr M40 65 E2
Trevore Dr WN1 20 B1
Trevor Gr SK1 124 A8
Trevor Rd
Eccles M30 79 B3
Swinton M27 79 E6
Urmston M41 95 A2
Trevor St
Manchester M11 99 E7
Rochdale OL11 30 B3
Triangle The WA15 120 B7
Tribune Ave WA14 119 B7
Trident Rd M30 94 F7
Trillo Ave BL2 148 B2
Trimdon Cl M11 83 B2
Trimingham Dr BL8 27 D5
Trimley Ave M40 157 B1
Tring Wlk M9 64 B3
Trinity Ave M33 108 D4
Trinity Bldgs OL5 68 D2
Trinity CE High Sch
M15 163 A2
Trinity Cl SK16 101 E8
Trinity Cres M28 60 E3
Trinity Ct
Ashton-u-L OL6 166 A3
Salford M3 158 A2
Trinity Gdns
Ashton-in-M WN4 72 F4
Salford M3 158 A2
Stockport SK3 123 F3
Trinity Gn BL0 11 B2
Trinity Ho OL1 153 B4
Trinity Rd M33 108 D4
Trinity Ret Pk BL2 148 A2
Trinity Sch SK15 85 F1
Trinity St
15 Bacup OL13 3 C8
Bolton BL3 145 C2
Bury BL9 140 C1
Marple SK6 125 F6
2 Middleton M24 64 F8
Oldham OL1 153 B4
Rochdale OL12 13 E2
Stalybridge SK15 86 A1
Trinity Way M3 158 B2
Trinity Wlk 13 M14 98 B3
Trippier Rd M30 94 F8
Tripps Mews M20 109 F4
Triscombe Way M16 97 E3
Tristam Cl M13 163 C3
Trojan Gdns 7 M7 81 C5
Trongate Wlk 15 M9 157 B3
Troon Cl
Bolton BL3 40 F3
Bramhall SK7 133 A7
Troon Dr SK8 122 C1
Troon Rd M23 120 F6
TROUGH GATE 4 D8
Trough Gate OL8 66 D2
Troutbeck Ave M4 160 A2
Troutbeck Cl BL8 10 B2
Troutbeck Dr
Ramsbottom BL0 138 C3
Tyldesley M29 77 A7
Troutbeck Gr WA11 71 B2
Troutbeck Rd
Altrincham WA15 120 D5
Ashton-in-M WN4 73 C5
Gatley SK8 122 B3
Troutbeck Rise WN5 54 B6
Troutbeck Way OL11 30 B4
Troutbeck Wlk 5 OL2 48 E4
Trowbridge Dr M40 65 C1
Trowbridge Rd M34 101 A1
Trows La OL11 30 D1
Trowtree Ave M12 164 B2
Troydale Dr M40 83 B6
Troy Wlk M5 161 B3
TRUB 47 D8
Trumpet St M1 162 C4
Truro Ave
Ashton-u-L OL6 85 D7
Brinnington SK5 112 C5
Stretford M32 96 E2
Truro Cl
Bramhall SK7 132 F7
Bury BL8 140 A3
Truro Dr M33 107 D4
Truro Rd
Chadderton OL9 48 A1
Tyldesley M29 77 C8
Truro Wlk M34 100 F1
Trust Rd M18 99 C3
Tucana Ave M7 81 C3
Tucker's Hill Brow
WN2 21 B1
Tudbury Way M3 158 A2
Tudor Ave
Bolton BL1 144 B3
Failsworth OL9 65 D3
Farnworth BL4 60 B7
Manchester M9 64 E1
Stalybridge SK15 86 D3
Tudor Cl
Mossley OL5 68 E1
Reddish SK5 111 E7
Tudor Ct
Bolton BL1 145 B4
Leigh WN7 76 C5
Manchester, Old Trafford
M16 161 C1
Manchester, Sedgley Park
M25 63 C3
Rochdale OL12 15 B1
Tudor Gn SK9 131 E1
Tudor Gr
Middleton M24 46 D3
Wigan WN3 54 E2
Tudor Hall St OL11 30 C2
Tudor Ho M21 109 F8
Tudor Ind Est SK16 101 A7
Tudor Rd
Altrincham WA14 119 B7
Handforth SK9 131 E1
Tudor St
9 Bolton BL3 146 C4
Middleton M24 65 B8
Oldham OL8 153 A1
Oldham OL8 153 B1
Shaw OL2 149 B3
Tuer St M13 163 A2
Tuffley Rd M23 121 A3
Tufton Wlk M9 157 A3
Tugford Cl 9 M16 97 E4
Tuley St M11 164 C3
Tulip Ave
Farnworth BL4 42 A1
Kearsley BL4 60 F5
Tulip Cl
Chadderton OL9 65 E7
Sale M33 107 C4
Stockport SK3 170 A1
Tulip Dr
Altrincham WA15 119 F6
Wigan WN6 36 F3
Tulip Gr OL12 14 E3
Tulip Rd M31 105 E2
Tulip Wlk M7 158 A4
Tulketh Street Ind Est
M40 83 A8
Tulle Ct M25 63 A4
Tully St S M7 155 B2
Tully St M7 155 B3
Tulpen Sq OL9 152 B3
Tulworth Rd SK12 133 D4
Tumblewood Dr SK8 122 E4
Tumbling Bank M9 64 D3
Tumbling Bank Terr
OL4 67 F5
Tunbridge Sq M5 81 A2
Tunicliffe's New Row
WN7 75 C5
Tunley La WN6 18 E5
Tunley Moss WN6 18 E4
TUNSHILL 32 D7
Tunshill Gr OL16 32 A6
Tunshill La OL16 32 C7
Tunshill Rd M23 108 E1
Tuns Rd OL8 67 B2
Tunstall Cl BL9 45 A7
Tunstall La WN5 54 D5
Tunstall Rd OL4 67 C6
Tunstall St
2 Manchester M11 99 E7
Stockport SK4 169 B2
TUNSTEAD 69 D5
Tunstead Ave M20 109 F6
Tunstead La OL3 69 D5
Tunstead Mill Terr 3
OL13 3 B8
Tunstead Rd OL13 3 C8
Turbary Wlk OL16 31 D6
Turf Cl OL2 48 E3
TURF HILL 31 C4
Turf Hill Rd OL16 31 C4
Turf House Cl OL15 15 F7
Turf La
Chadderton OL9 66 A3
Royton OL2 48 F3
Turfland Ave OL2 48 F3
Turf Lea Rd SK6 126 B1
Turf Park Rd OL2 48 F3
Turf Pit La OL4 49 F4
Turf St M26 43 F3
Turf Terr OL15 16 A6
Turfton Rd OL2 48 F3
Turks Rd M26 43 E5
Turk St 6 BL1 144 C4
Turley St M8 156 B2
TURN 2 A1
Turnberry BL3 40 F3
Turnberry Cl M29 77 C8
Turnberry Dr SK9 137 D8
Turnberry Rd SK8 122 C1
Turnberry Wlk M8 156 C4
Turnbull Ave M25 63 C7
Turnbull Rd
Altrincham WA14 119 C8
Manchester M13 98 F2
Reddish M18 99 F4
Turnbury Cl M33 108 B6
Turnbury Rd M22 121 E5
Turncliff Cres SK6 125 D7
Turncroft La SK1 112 B1
Turncroft Way M28 77 F7
Turnditch Cl WN6 37 A4
Turnell Way M28 79 A5
Turner Ave
Failsworth M35 83 E6
Irlam M44 94 A3
Leigh WN2 56 E1
Turner Bridge Rd
BL2 148 C4
Turner Dr M41 95 F2
Turnerford Cl BL7 8 E1
Turner Gdns SK14 167 B4
Turner La
Ashton-u-L OL6 166 B4
Brinnington SK6 112 F6
Hyde SK14 167 C4
Turner Rd SK6 125 F5
Turner's Pl OL12 14 E3
Turner St
Ashton-u-L OL6 166 B4
3 Bacup OL13 3 C8
Bolton BL1 148 A4
Denton M34 100 E5
Droylsden M11 83 C1
Leigh WN7 76 A4
Manchester, Gorton M18 99 D5
Manchester M4 159 A2
Manchester, Old Trafford
M16 161 C2
Oldham OL4 67 E8
Rochdale OL12 14 E1
Salford M7 155 B3
Stockport SK1 169 C2
Westhoughton BL5 57 E5
Wigan WN1 37 D1
Turnfield Cl OL16 15 D3
Turnfield Ho SK8 122 D3
Turnfield Rd SK8 122 D3
Turnhill Rd OL16 31 B3
Turnill Dr WN4 73 B2
Turnlee Cl SK13 116 C7
Turnlee Dr SK13 116 C7
Turnlee Rd SK13 116 C7
Turn Moss Rd M21,
M32 96 F1
Turnough Rd OL16 31 F7
Turnpike Cl OL3 51 C5
Turnpike Gn 1 M6 154 C3
Turnpike The SK6 125 D7
Turnpike Wlk M11 160 C1
Turn Rd BL0 11 E8
Turn St OL6 85 D4
Turnstone Ave WA12 89 C4
Turnstone Cl WN7 76 A6
Turnstone Rd
2 Bolton BL2 148 A2
Hazel Grove SK2 125 A5
Turret Hall Dr 1 WA3 90 E8
Turriff Gr WN2 56 A8
Turton Ave BL3 43 A4
TURTON BOTTOMS 9 D4
Turton Cl
Bury BL8 44 A8
Heywood OL10 29 A2
Turton Ct 1 BL1 148 A4
Turton & Edgworth CE
Prim Sch BL7 9 D5
Turton High Sch Media
Arts Coll BL7 25 B7
Turton Hts BL2 25 B6
Turton La M25 62 F5
Turton Rd
Bolton BL2, BL7 25 C5
Bury BL8 26 D8
Turton St
Bolton BL1 148 A4
Golborne WA3 90 A8
Manchester M11 99 D7
Turton Twr* BL7 9 C3
Turves Rd SK8 122 F1
Turville Ho SK9 131 D2
Turvin Rd OL15 7 D2
Tuscan Rd M20 122 B8
Tuscany Ho 2 M1 163 A4
Tuscany View M7 81 B8
Tutbury St M4 160 A1
Tutor Bank Dr WA12 89 D3
Tuxford Wlk M40 157 A1
Tweedale Ave M9 64 C4
Tweedale St OL11 139 B2
Tweedale Way M35,
OL9 66 A1
Tweed Cl
Altrincham WA14 119 C6
Oldham OL8 153 B1
Tweedle Hill Rd M9 64 C4
Tweedsdale Cl M45 45 B1
Tweed St WN7 76 B4
Tweenbrook Ave
M23 121 A3
Twelve Apostles RC Prim
Sch WN7 75 D8
Twelve Yards Rd M44 93 D4
Twigworth Rd M22 121 C2
Twillbrook Dr M3 158 B3
Twinegate OL12 14 E3
Twine Valley Country Pk*
BL0 12 A8
Twingates Cl OL2 149 B2
Twining Brook Rd
SK8 123 B3
Twining Rd M17 95 E8
Twinnies Rd SK9 131 B1
Twin St OL10 29 E1
Twirl Hill Rd OL6 85 E8
Twisse Rd BL2 42 F7
TWISS GREEN 91 E4
Twiss Green Com Prim
Sch WA3 91 E4
Twiss Green Dr WA3 91 E4
Twiss Green La WA3 91 E4
Twist Ave WA3 90 C8
Twist La WN7 75 E5
Two Acre Ave M22 121 C5
Two Acre Dr OL2 48 F7
Two Acre La OL4 50 B3
Two Bridges Rd OL16 32 C3
Two Brooks La BL8 10 B2
Two Porches Sch M46 58 D4
Two Trees La M34 101 A1
Two Trees Sports Coll
M34 101 A1
Twyford Cl M20 109 F3
Tybyrne Cl M28 77 F7
Tydden St OL8 66 F3
Tydeman Wlk OL16 32 A5
Tyersall Cl M30 79 E4
TYLDESLEY 59 A1
Tyldesley Arc 11 WN1 150 C4
Tyldesley Old Rd M46 58 E2
Tyldesley Pas 5 M29 58 F1
Tyldesley Prim Sch
M29 77 B7
Tyldesley Rd M46 58 E2
Tyldesley St George's
Central CE Prim Sch
M29 59 A1
Tyldesley St M14 98 A3
Tyler St SK9 137 A1
Tyler Wlk 2 WA3 90 F8
Tymm St M40 83 C8
Tyndall Ave M40 65 A1
Tyndall St OL4 67 C6
Tyne Ct M28 60 C3
Tynedale Cl SK5 111 F5
Tynesbank M28 60 C3
Tynesbank Cotts M28 60 C3
Tyne St 9 OL4 67 C7
Tyntesfield Prim Sch
M33 107 E1
Tynwald St OL4 67 C7
Tynwell Wlk 2 M40 156 C1
Tyrer Ave WN3 54 F5
Tyrer Rd WA12 89 C1
Tyrol Wlk M11 164 C4
Tyrone Cl M23 120 D8
Tyrone Dr OL11 29 F5
Tyro St OL8 66 F3
Tyrrell Gr SK14 102 A1
Tyrrel Rd SK5 99 F1
Tysoe Gdns M3 158 A2
Tyson St M8 155 C4
Tytherington Dr M19 99 D1

U

Uganda St BL3 146 C2
Ukraine Rd M7 81 B6
Uldale Dr M24 46 E1
Ullesthorpe 13 OL12 139 B4
Ulleswater Cl BL3 42 F3
Ulleswater St BL1 143 C2
Ullock Wlk M24 46 D2
Ullswater Ave
Ashton-in-M WN4 73 B5
Ashton-u-L OL7 166 A4
Orrell WN5 53 F7
Rochdale OL12 14 C1
Royton OL2 48 D7
Ullswater Ct WA3 74 C1
Ullswater Dr
Bury BL9 44 E7
Farnworth BL4 59 E7
Ince-in-M WN2 56 B7
Middleton M24 46 F2
Ullswater Gr OL10 46 D8
Ullswater Rd
Golborne WA3 74 C1
Handforth SK9 131 C4
Stockport SK1 124 B7
Tyldesley M29 77 B6
Urmston M41 94 E3
Wythenshawe M22 121 B2
Ullswater St WN7 75 E5
Ullswater Terr SK15 86 A4
Ullswater Wlk 26 M9 64 E3
Ulster Ave OL11 139 B1
Ulundi St M26 44 A3
Ulverston Ave
Chadderton OL9 152 A2
Manchester M20 109 F7
Ulverston Rd WN3 54 F3
Umberton Rd BL5 58 F7
Uncouth Rd OL16 31 E7
Underhill SK6 113 C2
Underhill Rd OL1 48 E1
Underhill Wlk M40 83 B4
Under La
Oldham, Factory Fold
OL9 66 B3
Oldham OL4, OL5 68 B4
Underwood OL12 139 B3
Underwood Cl M18 99 F6
Underwood Court
Apartments M27 80 E8
Underwood Rd
Alderley Edge SK9 137 C1
Hattersley SK14 102 D2
Underwood St SK16 101 B8
Underwood Terr 16
M29 59 A1
Underwood Villas
OL15 15 E4
Underwood Way OL2 49 D8
Underwood Wlk 2
SK14 102 D2
Undsworth Ct 5 OL10 29 D2
Unicorn St M30 95 B8
Union Arc BL9 140 C2
Union Bldgs BL2 145 C2
Union Cl WN5 53 E5
Union Ct 13 OL13 3 C8
Union Rd
Ashton-u-L OL6 166 C4
Bolton BL2 25 A1
Marple SK6 125 F6
Rochdale OL12 15 E4
Union St W OL8 153 B2
Union St
Ashton-u-L OL6 166 C3
Bacup OL13 3 C8
Bolton BL7 8 D2
Bury BL9 140 C2
Glossop SK13 116 C8
Hyde SK14 167 B2
Ince-in-M WN2 56 A8
Leigh WN7 75 F5
Manchester, Abbey Hey
M18 99 E6
Manchester, Ardwick
M12 163 C3
Manchester M4 159 A2
Manchester M14 98 B3
Middleton M24 47 A1
Oldham, County End OL4 67 E6
Oldham, Mumps OL1 67 A7
Oldham OL1 153 C2
Oldham, Werneth OL9 66 B4
Ramsbottom BL0 138 C2
Rochdale OL12, OL16 139 C4
Royton OL2 48 D3
Salford M6 81 A4
Stockport SK1 170 C4
Swinton M27 62 A1
Swinton M27 79 E8
Tyldesley M29 58 F1
Whitworth OL12 14 C8
Union Terr M7 155 C4
United Rd M17 96 F5
United Trad Est M17 96 F5
Unity Cl OL10 29 B1
Unity Cres OL10 29 B1
Unity Dr M7 155 C2

Unity St
Heywood OL10 . . . . 29 B1
Walsden OL14 . . . . 6 A8
Unity Way SK1 . . . . 124 A8
Unity Wlk SK13 . . . . . . 116 C7
University Rd M5, M6 . . . 81 B7
University Rd W M5 . . . . 81 B2
Univ of Bolton (Deane
Campus) BL3 . . . . 145 B2
Univ of Manchester (Sch
of Mechanical Aerospace
& Civil Engineering)
M30 . . . . 94 D6
Univ of Manchester The
Manchester M1 . . . . 163 B4
Manchester, University
M13 . . . . 163 B2
Univ of Manchester The
(McDougall Ctr)
M15 . . . . 163 A1
Univ of Salford
Salford M3 . . . . 158 A2
Salford M6 . . . . 81 C3
Univ of Salford, Irwell
Valley Campus M6 . . . . . . 81 B4
UNSWORTH 45 C2
Unsworth Ave
Golborne WA3 . . . . 74 E1
Tyldesley M29 . . . . 77 B8
Unsworth Prim Sch
BL9 . . . . 45 A2
Unsworth St
Bacup OL13 . . . . 3 D7
2 Hindley WN2 . . . . 56 D4
Leigh WN7 . . . . 75 E7
Radcliffe M26 . . . . 43 F4
Tyldesley M29 . . . . 59 B1
Unsworth Way OL1 . . . . 153 B4
Unwin Ave M18 . . . . 99 D4
Unwin Ct M6 . . . . 154 C2
Upavon Ct M7 . . . . 155 C2
Upavon Rd M22 . . . . 121 F3
Upcast La SK9 . . . . 136 E3
UP HOLLAND 53 B6
Up Holland High Sch
WN5 . . . . 53 C4
Upholland Rd WN8 . . . . . 53 D2
Upholland Roby Mill CE
Prim Sch WN8 . . . . 35 B3
Upland Dr
Ashton-in-M WN4 . . . . . . 73 D4
Walkden M38 . . . . 59 F6
Upland Rd OL8 . . . . 66 E4
Uplands M26 . . . . 65 A7
Uplands Ave M26 . . . . . . 44 C2
Uplands Rd
Compstall SK14 . . . . 114 A6
Flixton M41 . . . . 106 E8
Glossop SK13 . . . . 116 D8
Uplands The OL5 . . . . . . 68 D1
Upper Brook St
Manchester M13 . . . . 163 B2
Stockport SK1 . . . . 112 A1
Upper Broom Way BL5 . . 40 A2
Upper Campfield Mkt
M3 . . . . 162 B4
Upper Camp St M7 . . . . . 155 A1
Upper Chorlton Rd
M16 . . . . 97 C3
Upper Cliff Hill OL2 . . . . 32 C1
Upper Conran St M9 . . . 157 B4
Upper Cyrus St M40 . . . 160 B2
Upper Dicconson St
WN1 . . . . 37 C1
Upper Downs WA14 . . . . 119 C3
Upper George St
23 Rochdale OL12 . . . . . 14 F1
Tyldesley M29 . . . . 77 A8
Upper Gloucester St
M6 . . . . 81 A3
Upper Hayes Cl OL16 . . . 31 C8
Upper Helena St M40 . . 160 B2
Upper Hibbert La SK6 . . 125 F4
Upper Kent Rd M14 . . . . . 98 E3
Upper Lees Dr BL5 . . . . . 40 A1
Upper Lloyd St M14 . . . . 98 A3
Upper Mead BL7 . . . . 8 F1
Upper Medlock St
M15 . . . . 162 C4
UPPERMILL 69 A8
Uppermill Dr M19 . . . . . 110 E3
Upper Monsall St
M40 . . . . 157 B2
Upper Moss La M15 . . . . 162 B2
Upper Park Rd
Manchester, Broughton Park
M7 . . . . 63 C1
Manchester M14 . . . . 98 C4
Upper Passmonds Gr
OL11 . . . . 30 B8
Upper St Stephen St
WN6 . . . . 150 B4
Upper Stone St OL16 . . . 31 D6
Upper West Gr M13 . . . . 164 A1
Upper Wharf St M5 . . . . . 81 C1
Upper Wilton St M25 . . . 164 A1
Uppingham Dr BL0 . . . . 138 B3
Upton OL11 . . . . 139 B2
Upton Ave
Cheadle SK8 . . . . 132 A8
Manchester SK4 . . . . 110 E4
Upton Cl
Golborne WA3 . . . . 90 D8
Middleton M24 . . . . 65 A5

Upton Dr WA14 . . . . 119 E8
Upton La M29 . . . . 77 C8
Upton Rd M46 . . . . 58 E4
Upton Way
Bury BL8 . . . . 26 F5
12 Handforth SK9 . . . . 131 D5
Upton Wlk 10 OL7 . . . . 166 A1
Upwood Rd WA3 . . . . 90 D7
Upwood Wlk 31 M9 . . . . 64 E3
Urban Ave WA15 . . . . . . 119 E4
Urban Dr WA15 . . . . 119 E4
Urban Rd
Altrincham WA15 . . . . . . 119 E4
Sale M33 . . . . 108 A4
Urbis*1 M4 . . . . 159 A2
Urmston St OL8 . . . . 66 F3
URMSTON 95 D1
Urmston Ave WA12 . . . . . 89 B5
Urmston Gram Sch
M41 . . . . 95 C2
Urmston Inf Sch M41 . . . 95 C2
Urmston Jun Sch M41 . . . 95 C2
Urmston La M32, M41 . . . 96 B1
Urmston Pk M41 . . . . 95 E2
Urmston St WN7 . . . . 75 D5
Urmston Sta M41 . . . . . . 95 D2
Urwick Rd SK6 . . . . 113 B2
Usk Cl M45 . . . . 63 C7
Uttley St
Bolton BL1 . . . . 143 A2
Rochdale OL11 . . . . 30 C4
Uvedale Rd 11 M30 . . . . 79 D1
Uxbridge Ave 16 M11 . . 83 C2
Uxbridge St OL6 . . . . . . 166 A3

V

Vaal St OL8 . . . . 66 C3
Valance Cl M12 . . . . 165 A2
Valdene Cl BL4 . . . . 60 D7
Valdene Dr
Farnworth BL4 . . . . 60 D7
Walkden M28 . . . . 78 D8
Vale Ave
Bury BL9 . . . . 44 D7
Horwich BL6 . . . . 22 A3
Hyde SK14 . . . . 102 A3
Kearsley M26 . . . . 61 C7
Sale M33 . . . . 108 E5
Swinton M27 . . . . 62 A1
Urmston M41 . . . . 94 E1
Vale Cl
Appley Bridge WN6 . . . . . 35 E8
Hazel Grove SK7 . . . . . . 124 E4
Manchester SK4 . . . . 110 F2
Romiley SK6 . . . . 113 F2
Vale Coppice
Horwich BL6 . . . . 22 A3
Ramsbottom BL0 . . . . 11 C3
Vale Cotts
Dukinfield SK14 . . . . 101 C4
Horwich BL6 . . . . 21 F2
Littleborough OL15 . . . . . 16 A5
Vale Cres SK8 . . . . 122 F2
Vale Croft WN8 . . . . 53 A6
Vale Dr
Oldham OL9 . . . . 153 A2
Prestwich M25 . . . . 63 A2
Vale Edge M26 . . . . 44 A5
Vale Head SK9 . . . . 131 D2
Vale House Dr SK13 . . . 104 A5
Vale La M35 . . . . 84 A4
Valemount SK13 . . . . 104 A5
Valencia Rd M7 . . . . 81 B6
Valentia Rd M9 . . . . 64 D4
Valentines Rd M46 . . . . . 58 A1
Valentine St
Failsworth M35 . . . . 83 E7
Oldham OL4 . . . . 67 C6
Vale Park Ind Est M8 . . 156 C3
Vale Park Way M8 . . . . . 156 C3
Vale Rd
Altrincham, Rosehill
WA14 . . . . 119 B1
Altrincham WA15 . . . . . . 120 B5
Droylsden M43 . . . . 84 B3
Manchester SK4 . . . . 110 F1
Mossley SK15 . . . . 86 E6
Romiley SK6 . . . . 125 B8
Shaw OL2 . . . . 49 D6
Wilmslow SK9 . . . . 136 E8
Valerie Wlk 7 M15 . . . . 162 C3
Vale Side OL5 . . . . 86 C8
Vale St
Ashton-u-L OL7 . . . . 85 A6
Bolton BL2 . . . . 43 A7
Droylsden M11 . . . . 83 C2
Heywood OL10 . . . . 29 E2
Middleton M24 . . . . 65 B8
Vale The
Appley Bridge WN6 . . . . . 35 E8
Vale Top Ave M9 . . . . . . 157 C3
Valetta Cl M14 . . . . 110 B8
Valewood Ave SK4 . . . . 168 A1
Vale Works M4 . . . . 159 A3
Valiant Rd WN5 . . . . 54 D8
Valiant Wlk 1 M40 . . . . 65 E1
Valletts La BL1 . . . . 142 C1
Valletts S BL1 . . . . 142 C1
Valley Ave BL8 . . . . 27 B4
Valley Cl
Cheadle SK8 . . . . 122 E3
Mossley OL5 . . . . 68 B2

Valley Com Prim Sch The
BL1 . . . . 143 C2
Valley Cotts OL3 . . . . . . 69 C4
Valley Dr SK9 . . . . 131 C3
Valley Gdns SK14 . . . . . 114 E8
Valley Gr M34 . . . . 101 B2
Valley Mews OL3 . . . . . . 69 C4
Valley Mill La BL9 . . . . 141 A1
Valley New Rd OL2 . . . . 48 E3
Valley Park Rd M25 . . . . 62 F5
Valley Rd
Bramhall SK7 . . . . 123 F1
Broadbottom SK14 . . . . . 114 E8
Cheadle SK8 . . . . 122 E3
Glossop SK13 . . . . 115 F8
Middleton M24 . . . . 47 B2
Romiley SK6 . . . . 112 D4
Royton OL2 . . . . 48 E3
Stockport SK4 . . . . 168 A1
Urmston M41 . . . . 94 D4
Wigan WN5 . . . . 54 D5
Valley Rd S M41 . . . . 94 C2
Valley Rise OL2 . . . . 32 A1
Valley Sch SK7 . . . . 132 C5
Valley View
Bolton BL7 . . . . 25 A7
Dukinfield SK14 . . . . 102 A4
Newton-le-W WA12 . . . . . 89 B1
Whitworth OL12 . . . . 4 D4
Valley Way SK15 . . . . . . 86 C1
Valley Wlk M11 . . . . 160 C1
Valpy Ave BL2 . . . . 25 B3
Vanbrugh Gr M91 . . . . . . 36 B1
Vancouver Quay M50 . . . 96 F7
Vandyke Ave M6 . . . . 80 B3
Vandyke St 5 OL12 . . . . 13 F1
Vane St M30 . . . . 79 D2
Vanguard Cl M30 . . . . . . 94 F7
Vannes Gr SK14 . . . . 102 F3
Vantage Quay M1 . . . . . 159 B1
Vantomme St BL1 . . . . . 143 B4
Vant St OL8 . . . . 67 C4
Varden Gr SK3 . . . . 170 A1
Varden Rd SK12 . . . . 133 E3
Varden Dr SK9 . . . . 137 D6
Varey St M18 . . . . 99 D5
Varley Rd BL3 . . . . 146 A4
Varley St M40 . . . . 160 A3
Varna St M11 . . . . 99 D7
Varna Street Prim Sch
M11 . . . . 99 D6
Vasser Rd M18 . . . . 165 B1
Vauban Dr M6 . . . . 80 B3
Vaudrey Dr
Cheadle SK8 . . . . 123 A2
Hazel Grove SK7 . . . . . . 124 E2
Sale WA15 . . . . 120 A8
Vaudrey La M34 . . . . 101 A2
Vaudrey Rd SK6 . . . . 113 A5
Vaudrey St 15 SK15 . . . . 86 A1
Vaughan Ave M40 . . . . . . 83 A8
Vaughan Gr OL4 . . . . 67 E6
Vaughan Rd
Manchester, Chorlton-cum-
Hardy M21 . . . . 109 D8
Sale WA14 . . . . 107 C1
Stockport SK4 . . . . 169 A3
Vaughan St
Eccles M30 . . . . 79 B3
Manchester M12 . . . . 164 C3
Royton OL2 . . . . 48 E3
Vauxhall Cl M40 . . . . . . 159 C4
Vauxhall Ind Est SK5 . . 111 E6
Vauxhall Rd WN1 . . . . . . 151 A4
Vauxhall St M40 . . . . . . 159 B4
Vauze Ave BL6 . . . . 21 D1
Vauze House Cl BL6 . . . . 21 D2
Vavasour Ct 6 OL16 . . . 31 B6
Vavasour St OL16 . . . . . . 31 B6
Vawdrey Dr 6 M23 . . . . 108 F2
Vaynor 15 OL12 . . . . . . 139 B4
Vega St M8 . . . . 158 B4
Vela Wlk M7 . . . . 81 C3
Velmere Ave M9 . . . . 64 A5
Velour Cl M3 . . . . 158 A3
Velvet Ct M1 . . . . 163 A4
Vendale Ave M27 . . . . . . 79 D6
Venesta Ave M6 . . . . 80 B4
Venetia St M40 . . . . 83 C5
Venice St
Bolton BL3 . . . . 146 C4
Manchester M1 . . . . 163 A4
Venlow Gdns SK8 . . . . . . 123 B1
Ventnor Ave
Bolton BL1 . . . . 143 C3
Manchester M19 . . . . 111 C8
Sale M33 . . . . 108 B6
Whitefield BL9 . . . . 45 A3
Ventnor Cl M34 . . . . 113 B8
Ventnor Rd
Manchester, Didsbury
M20 . . . . 110 C3
Manchester M19 . . . . 110 C3
Ventnor St
Manchester M9 . . . . 157 A4
Rochdale OL11 . . . . 139 C1
Salford M6 . . . . 81 B4
Ventura Cl M14 . . . . 98 A1
Ventura St SK22 . . . . . . 127 D1
Venture Scout Way
M8 . . . . 155 C2
Venture Way SK12 . . . . 133 F3
Venwood Rd M25 . . . . . . 62 F2
Verbena Ave BL4 . . . . . . 42 A1
Verbena Cl M31 . . . . 105 F3
Verdant La M30 . . . . 94 F8

Verdant Way OL16 . . . . . 31 C3
Verda St WN2 . . . . 74 B8
Verdun Ave M6 . . . . 80 B3
Verdun Cres OL11 . . . . . 30 C8
Verdun Rd M30 . . . . 79 B4
Verdure Ave
Bolton BL1 . . . . 40 E8
Sale M33 . . . . 108 C1
Verdure Cl M35 . . . . 84 B7
Vere St M50 . . . . 154 C1
Verity Cl
Manchester M20 . . . . 110 C6
Royton OL2 . . . . 48 D3
Verity Wlk M9 . . . . 64 B3
Vermont Gdns SK7 . . . . 132 B5
Vermont St BL1 . . . . 145 A4
Verna St BL0 . . . . 138 C2
Verne Ave M27 . . . . 79 E8
Verne Dr OL1 . . . . 49 E5
Verne Wlk WN4 . . . . 73 D3
Verney Rd OL2 . . . . 48 E2
Vernham Wlk BL3 . . . . . 147 B4
Vernon Ave
Eccles M30 . . . . 79 F2
Stockport SK1 . . . . 112 B2
Stretford M32 . . . . 96 D1
Vernon Cl
Cheadle SK8 . . . . 122 E1
Poynton SK12 . . . . 133 D2
Vernon Ct 8 M7 . . . . . . 63 C1
Vernon Dr
Marple SK6 . . . . 125 D7
Prestwich M25 . . . . 63 A2
Vernon Gr M33 . . . . 108 E4
Vernon Inf Sch SK12 . . 133 E3
Vernon Jun Sch SK12 . . 133 E3
Vernon Park Prim Sch
SK1 . . . . 112 A1
Vernon Pk WA15 . . . . . . 120 A7
Vernon Rd
Droylsden M43 . . . . 83 E2
Manchester M7 . . . . 63 C1
Poynton SK12 . . . . 133 E2
Ramsbottom BL8 . . . . 11 A1
Romiley SK6 . . . . 112 E3
Vernon St
Ashton-u-L OL6 . . . . 166 C4
Bolton BL1 . . . . 145 B4
Bury BL9 . . . . 140 C4
Farnworth BL4 . . . . 42 E1
Hazel Grove SK7 . . . . . . 124 D3
Hyde SK14 . . . . 167 B2
Leigh WN7 . . . . 75 E4
Manchester, Harpurhey
M9 . . . . 157 B3
Manchester M16 . . . . 162 A1
Mossley OL5 . . . . 68 C2
Salford M7 . . . . 155 A1
Stockport SK1 . . . . 169 C2
Vernon Wlk
8 Bolton BL1 . . . . 145 B4
Stockport SK1 . . . . 169 B1
Verona Dr M40 . . . . 83 C4
Veronica Rd M20 . . . . . . 110 C3
Verrill Ave M23 . . . . 109 C1
Verwood Wlk 9 M23 . . . 121 A5
Vesper St M35 . . . . 84 A8
Vesta St
Manchester M4 . . . . 159 C1
Ramsbottom BL0 . . . . 138 B2
Vestris Dr M6 . . . . 80 B3
Vetch Cl CI WA3 . . . . . . 105 B5
Viaduct Rd WA14 . . . . . 119 D7
Viaduct St
Manchester, Ardwick
M12 . . . . 164 B4
Manchester M3 . . . . 158 C2
Newton-le-W WA12 . . . . . 89 A3
Stockport SK3 . . . . 169 B1
Vicarage Ave SK8 . . . . . 132 B7
Vicarage Cl
Adlington PR6 . . . . 21 A8
Bury BL9 . . . . 27 E8
Dukinfield SK16 . . . . 101 E8
Oldham OL4 . . . . 67 F7
Platt Bridge WN2 . . . . . . 56 A2
Salford M6 . . . . 80 B3
Vicarage Cres OL6 . . . . . 85 D5
Vicarage Ct
8 Altrincham M23 . . . . 120 D6
Hyde SK14 . . . . 167 A1
Vicarage Dr
Dukinfield SK16 . . . . 101 E8
Rochdale OL12, OL16 . . . 15 C3
Vicarage Gdns
Hyde SK14 . . . . 167 C2
Stockport SK3 . . . . 170 A4
Vicarage Gr M30 . . . . 79 F2
Vicarage La
Altrincham WA14 . . . . . . 119 C1
Middleton M24 . . . . 65 D7
Poynton SK12 . . . . 133 E5
Shevington WN6 . . . . 36 A5
Vicarage Rd
Abram WN2 . . . . 56 B1
Ashton-in-M WN4 . . . . . . 73 B2
Ashton-u-L OL7 . . . . 85 B5
Blackrod BL6 . . . . 21 D4
Irlam M44 . . . . 94 A2
Orrell WN5 . . . . 53 D4
Stockport SK3 . . . . 170 B2
Swinton M27 . . . . 79 E8
Urmston M41 . . . . 95 D2
Walkden M28 . . . . 60 C4
Vicarage Rd N OL11 . . . . 30 D1
Vicarage Rd S OL11 . . . . 30 C1
Vicarage Rd W BL6 . . . . . 21 C2

Vicarage Sq WN7 . . . . . . 75 F5
Vicarage St
Bolton BL3 . . . . 145 A1
Oldham OL8 . . . . 66 C3
1 Radcliffe M26 . . . . . . 44 A3
Shaw OL2 . . . . 149 B3
Vicarage View OL11 . . . . 30 D1
Vicarage Way OL2 . . . . . 149 A2
Vicar's Dr OL16 . . . . 139 C2
Vicar's Gate OL16 . . . . . 139 C3
Vicars Hall Gdns M28 . . 77 F5
Vicars Hall La M28 . . . . . 77 F4
Vicars Rd M21 . . . . 109 A8
Vicars St M30 . . . . 79 F2
Viceroy Ct M20 . . . . 110 B2
Vicker Cl M27 . . . . 61 F2
Vicker Gr M20 . . . . 109 F5
Vickerman St BL1 . . . . . 143 A4
Vickers Row BL4 . . . . 60 B8
Vickers St
Bolton BL3 . . . . 145 B1
Manchester M40 . . . . 160 B4
Vickery Court Appts
M7 . . . . 80 D8
Victor Ave BL9 . . . . 140 B4
Victor Cl WN5 . . . . 54 D8
Victoria Ave
Bolton BL3 . . . . 145 B1
1 Eccles M30 . . . . 79 F3
Glossop SK13 . . . . 104 A5
Hazel Grove SK7 . . . . . . 124 E3
Leigh WN2 . . . . 56 E1
Manchester, Didsbury
M20 . . . . 110 A3
Manchester, Higher Blackley
M9 . . . . 64 C5
Manchester, Levenshulme
M19 . . . . 111 A8
Pendlebury M27 . . . . 80 A8
1 Romiley SK6 . . . . . . 112 F3
Whitefield M45 . . . . 63 A8
Wigan WN6 . . . . 37 A1
Victoria Ave E M24, M40,
M9 . . . . 65 B4
Victoria Avenue Com Prim
Sch M9 . . . . 64 D5
Victoria Bridge St
M3 . . . . 158 C2
Victoria Cl
Aspull WN2 . . . . 38 B6
Bramhall SK7 . . . . 132 D6
Stockport SK3 . . . . 170 B3
1 Worsley M28 . . . . . . 78 A6
Victoria Cres
Eccles M30 . . . . 79 F3
Standish WN6 . . . . 36 E8
Victoria Ct
5 Ashton-u-L OL7 . . . 166 A1
Bury BL8 . . . . 26 F6
Farnworth BL4 . . . . 42 C2
5 Glossop SK13 . . . . . 116 C8
Horwich BL6 . . . . 22 C3
7 Manchester M20 . . . 110 A3
Manchester, Openshaw
M11 . . . . 165 C4
Platt Bridge WN2 . . . . . . 56 A3
Stretford M32 . . . . 96 C2
Whitefield M45 . . . . 62 F7
Victoria Dr M33 . . . . 108 D3
Victoria Gdns
Hyde SK14 . . . . 167 C4
Shaw OL2 . . . . 149 B3
Victoria Gr
Bolton BL1 . . . . 142 C1
Manchester M14 . . . . 110 C7
Reddish SK4 . . . . 111 D5
Victoria Grange M20 . . . 110 A4
Victoria Ho
Manchester M11 . . . . 165 C4
Salford M6 . . . . 80 A4
Victoria Ind Est WN7 . . . 75 E7
Victoria La
Swinton M27 . . . . 79 D8
Whitefield M45 . . . . 62 F7
Victoria Lo M7 . . . . 81 C5
Victoria Mews
1 Dukinfield SK16 . . . 101 C6
2 Glossop SK13 . . . . . 116 C8
Whitefield BL9 . . . . 45 B2
Victoria Mill M40 . . . . . 160 A3
Victoria Mkt SK15 . . . . . 86 A1
Victoria Par
7 Rawtenstall BB4 . . . . . 2 E8
Urmston M41 . . . . 95 D2
Victoria Park Inf Sch
M32 . . . . 96 D2
Victoria Park Jun Sch
M32 . . . . 96 D2
Victoria Pl SK1 . . . . 124 B8
Victoria Pl M28 . . . . 60 D4
Victoria Rd
Altrincham, Timperley
WA15 . . . . 120 A6
Altrincham WA15 . . . . . . 119 D3
Bolton BL1 . . . . 142 B8
Dukinfield SK16 . . . . 101 C6
Eccles M30 . . . . 79 E3
Garswood WN4 . . . . 72 D4
Horwich BL6 . . . . 22 C2
Irlam M44 . . . . 93 F1
Kearsley BL4 . . . . 61 A6
Manchester, Fallowfield
M14 . . . . 110 B8
Manchester M19 . . . . 98 F1
Manchester, Whalley Range
M16 . . . . 97 D2
Newton-le-W WA12 . . . . . 89 C3

Victoria Rd continued
Platt Bridge WN2.........56 A2
Sale M33..............108 D3
Salford M6............80 A4
Stockport SK1.........112 B1
Stretford M32.........96 D2
Urmston M41...........95 B2
Wilmslow SK9.........137 A6
Wythenshawe M22......121 D8
Victoria St E OL7....166 A2
Victoria Sq
Bolton BL1............145 C3
Manchester M4.........159 B2
Walkden M28...........60 D3
Whitefield M45........62 F7
Victoria St
Ainsworth BL2.........26 C1
Altrincham WA14......119 D5
Ashton-u-L OL7........166 A1
Bacup OL13............3 D8
Blackrod BL6..........21 D2
Bury BL8..............140 A2
Bury BL8..............140 A3
Bury, Tottington BL8..26 F7
Chadderton OL9.......152 C4
Denton M34...........100 F3
Dukinfield, Newton
SK14.................102 A5
Dukinfield SK16.......101 D8
Failsworth M35........83 D6
4 Farnworth BL4.....42 B2
Glossop SK13.........116 C8
Heywood OL10.........29 E1
Leigh WN7............75 E6
Littleborough OL15....16 B5
Manchester M3........158 C2
Manchester, Openshaw
M11..................165 C4
Middleton M24.........67 E6
Oldham, Lees OL4.....67 E6
Oldham, Mumps OL4...67 A6
Oldham OL8...........84 F8
Platt Bridge WN2......56 A2
Radcliffe M26.........44 A3
Ramsbottom BL0......138 B2
Rawtenstall BB4.......2 E8
22 Rochdale OL12....14 F1
Shaw OL2.............149 B3
Stalybridge, Millbrook
SK15.................86 D4
1 Stalybridge, Stamford Park
SK15.................85 F2
Westhoughton BL5......57 F8
Whitworth OL12.......14 C8
Wigan WN5............54 F6
Worsley M28...........78 A6
Victoria Sta M3......159 A3
Victoria Station App
M3....................159 A2
Victoria Terr
Bickershaw WN2.......74 F8
Heywood OL10.........29 C4
Manchester, Longsight
M12..................98 F4
Manchester M13........98 C4
Salford M3............32 A5
Victoria The M50.....96 F7
Victoria Trad Est OL9..66 B3
Victoria Way
Bramhall SK7.........132 D6
Leigh WN7............75 E7
Royton OL2...........48 C6
Victoria Wlk OL9......48 C1
Victoria Works Ind Est
M8....................58 B4
Victor Mann St M11....100 A7
Victor St
7 Heywood OL10......46 E8
Manchester M40........159 C4
Salford M3............158 A2
VICTORY.............144 C4
Victory Gr M34.......100 C7
Victory Rd
Irlam M44............105 C4
Little Lever BL3.......43 B4
Victory St
Bolton BL1............144 C4
Manchester M14.......98 C3
Victory Trad Est BL3...148 A1
Vienna Rd SK3........170 A2
Vienna Rd E SK3......170 B2
Viewfield Wlk M9....157 B3
Vievlands Dr WN9....131 D2
View St BL3..........145 A1
Vigo Ave BL3.........146 B3
Vigo St
Heywood OL10.........29 E1
Oldham OL4...........67 D5
1 Wigan WN2........37 F2
Viking Cl M11........160 C1
Viking St
Bolton BL3............42 A4
Rochdale OL11.........30 C8
Villa Ave WN6........37 A4
Village Circ M17......96 D6
Village Ct
8 Handforth SK9.....131 D1
Stretford M32.........96 C6
Whitworth OL12.......4 C1
Village Gn OL3........69 B8
Village Manor OL3.....51 B1
Village St M7.........81 C5
Village The M41......106 F8
Village View
Billinge WN5..........71 E5
2 Leigh WN7.........76 B4
Village Way
11 Handforth SK9.....131 D1

Village Way continued
Manchester M4.........159 A2
Village Way (Ashburton
Rd E) M17...........96 C6
Village Wlk 13 M11....83 C1
Villa Rd OL8..........66 F4
Villa The SK14........103 A5
Villdale Ave SK2......124 C7
Villiers Ct M45.......63 A6
Villiers Dr OL8.......153 B1
Villiers Ind Est M6....154 C4
Villiers St
Ashton-u-L OL6........85 D2
Bury BL8..............141 A3
Hyde SK14............167 C2
Vinca Gr M7..........155 A2
Vincent Ave
Eccles M30............79 D4
Manchester M21.......97 A1
Oldham OL4...........67 C8
Vincent Ct BL3.......147 B3
Vincent St
Bolton BL1............145 A2
Hyde SK14............113 F8
Littleborough OL15....16 A6
Manchester M11.......165 C4
Middleton M24.........47 A2
17 Rochdale OL16.....31 A5
Salford M7............155 B3
Vincent Way WN5.....54 D8
Vine Cl
Sale M33.............107 C5
Shaw OL2.............149 B3
Vine Ct
Rochdale OL16.........31 B6
Stretford M32.........96 D1
Vine Fold M40........65 F1
Vine Gr
Stockport SK2.........124 C6
Wigan WN3............150 C3
Vine Pl OL11.........139 C1
Vinery Gr M34........100 E3
Vine St
Eccles M30............79 C1
Hazel Grove SK7......124 E3
Hindley WN2...........56 D6
Manchester M11, M18..96 B3
Oldham OL9............66 B3
Prestwich M25.........63 C5
Ramsbottom BL0.......11 A4
Salford M7............81 C8
Wigan WN1............37 D1
Vineyard Cl OL12......15 C7
Vineyard St OL4.......67 B7
Viola Cl WN6..........19 D2
Viola St
Bolton BL1............143 B3
Droylsden M11.........83 D2
Violet Ave BL4........42 A1
Violet Ct M22........121 D3
Violet Hill Ct OL4....67 E8
Violet St
Ashton-in-M WN4.......73 B2
Droylsden M18.........99 F6
Ince-in-M WN3........151 B2
Stockport SK2.........170 C2
Violet Way M24.......65 D7
Vip Centre Ind Est OL1..49 C1
Virgil St M15........162 A2
Virginia Chase SK8...131 F8
Virginia Cl M23.......120 D7
Virginia St
Bolton BL3............146 B4
Rochdale OL11.........30 E4
Virginia Way WN5.....54 C8
Viscount Dr
Gatley SK8...........131 D7
Wythenshawe M90......129 F7
Viscount Rd WN5......54 D8
Viscount St M14......98 C3
Vista Ave WN4........89 A4
Vista Rd WA11, WA12..89 A6
Vista The M44........105 C4
Vista Way WA12.......89 A4
Vivian Pl 9 M14......98 E4
Vivian St OL11.......139 B1
Vixen Cl M40.........109 E2
Voewood Ho SK1.......124 B8
Voltaire Ave M6......80 B3
Vorlich Dr OL9........65 F8
Vulcan Cl WA12.......89 C1
Vulcan Dr WN1........151 A3
Vulcan Ind Est WA12...89 D1
Vulcan Rd WN5........54 D8
Vulcan St OL1........49 B1
Vyner Gr M33.........107 F6

W

Wadcroft Wlk 19 M9...157 B4
Waddicor Ave OL6.....85 E6
Waddington Cl
Bury BL8..............26 E2
Golborne WA3.........90 F8
Waddington Fold OL16..31 C7
Waddington Rd BL1....142 A1
Waddington St OL9....152 C4
Wade Bank BL5........57 F8
Wadebridge Ave M23..120 D7
Wadebridge Cl 3 BL2..25 B1
Wadebrook Gr 4
SK9..................131 D1
Wadeford Cl M4.......159 C3
Wade Hill La OL3......48 E8
Wade Ho M30..........79 D1
Wade Row OL3.........69 B8

Wadesmill Wlk M13....163 B3
Wadeson Rd M13......163 C3
Wade St
7 Bolton BL3........147 C3
Middleton M24.........65 D6
Wade Wlk M11........165 A4
Wadham Gdns SK6.....113 C5
Wadham Way WA15....119 F1
Wadhurst Wlk 2
M13..................163 C1
Wadlow Cl M3.........158 B3
Wadsworth Cl SK9....131 E3
Wadsworth Dr WN6....36 F2
Wadsworth Ind Pk
BL3..................147 B4
Wadsworth Mews WN3..61 C6
Waggoners 2 M27.....79 F7
Waggon Rd
Bolton BL2............42 D8
Mossley OL5..........86 C8
Wagner St BL1........143 A3
Wagstaffe Dr M35....83 F7
Wagstaffe St M24.....47 A2
Wagtail Cl M28........78 D8
Wain Cl M30..........79 B2
Waincliffe Ave M20,
M21..................109 D4
Wainfleet Cl WN3.....54 E2
Waingap Cres OL12....14 D8
Waingap Rise OL12....14 F4
Waingap View OL12....14 D7
Wainman St M6.......81 B5
Wainscot Cl M29......77 B7
Wain Stones Gn SK2...124 E6
Wainwright Ave M34...99 F3
Wainwright Cl
Oldham OL4...........68 A7
Stockport SK2.........124 A7
Wainwright Rd WA14...119 C5
Wainwright St
Oldham OL8...........153 B1
Stalybridge SK16.......85 D1
Waithlands Rd OL16....31 B6
Wakefield Cres
Romiley SK6...........113 A2
Standish WN6..........37 A6
Wakefield Dr
Chadderton OL1.......48 C1
Swinton M27...........61 D4
Wakefield Mews BL7....24 F7
Wakefield Rd SK15.....86 B3
Wakefield St
Chadderton OL1.......48 C1
Golborne WA3.........90 A7
2 Manchester M1.....163 A3
Manchester, Whalley Range
M16..................97 E3
Wakeling Rd M34.....112 E8
Walcot Pl WN3........54 F2
Walcott Cl M13.......164 B1
Wald Ave M14........110 E7
Waldeck St 1 BL1....145 A4
Waldeck Wlk 4 M9....64 E3
Walden 18 OL10......29 C2
Walden Ave OL4.......49 D2
Walden Cl M14........110 A8
Walden Cres SK7......124 C3
Walderton Ave M40....83 A7
Waldon Ave SK8.......122 D5
Waldon Cl
Bolton BL3............146 C4
Hindley WN2...........56 F4
Waldorf St M3........54 D2
Wales St OL1.........49 C1
Walford Rd WN4.......73 C3
Walford St M16.......97 E4
Walkdale Brow SK13...116 A7
WALKDEN.............60 E4
Walkden Ave WN1.....37 B2
Walkden Ave E WN1....37 C2
Walkden Ct M28.......60 C4
Walkden High Sch
M28..................60 E1
Walkden Market Pl 1
M28..................60 D3
Walkden Rd
Walkden M28..........60 D1
Worsley M28..........78 E7
Walkdens Ave M46....58 A2
Walker Ave
Bolton BL3............147 C3
Failsworth M35........84 B6
Prestwich M25, M45...63 A6
Stalybridge SK15......86 D2
Walker Cl
Hyde SK14............167 C2
Ince-in-M WN3........61 A6
Walker Fold SK14.....167 C2
Walker Fold Rd BL1....23 D4
Walker Gn M30........79 B5
Walker Ho 9 M30.....79 D1
Walker La SK14.......167 C2
Walker St
Bolton BL1............145 A2

Walker St continued
3 Bury BL9..........44 E8
Denton M34...........100 E4
Glossop SK13.........104 A4
Heywood OL10.........29 C1
Middleton M24.........64 C7
Oldham OL8...........153 A2
4 Radcliffe M26.....44 C1
Rochdale OL16.........31 A7
Stockport SK1........169 B1
Westhoughton BL5......57 E8
Walkerwood Dr SK15...86 D2
Walkmill OL3..........50 F1
Walk Mill Cl OL12.....15 D4
Walk The
Atherton M46.........58 D3
5 Rochdale OL16.....139 C3
Walkway The BL3......40 F5
Wallace Ave M14.....98 D3
Wallace La WN1.......37 E1
Wallbank Dr OL12.....14 C7
Wallbrook Ave WN5....53 D1
Wallbrook Cres M38...60 B6
Wallbrook Dr M9......64 C1
Walleach Farm Cvn Pk
BL7...................9 E6
Walled Gdn The
Manchester M16.......97 E2
Swinton M27...........79 D6
Waller Ave M14......110 C8
Walley St BL1........143 B3
Wallgarth Cl WN3.....54 E2
WALLGATE............150 A4
Wallgate WN3........150 B3
Wallhead Rd OL16.....31 D7
WALL HILL...........50 E1
Wall Hill Rd OL3......50 E2
Wallingford Rd
Handforth SK9........131 C5
Urmston M41..........95 E3
Wallis St
Chadderton OL9.......66 A4
Failsworth M40........83 C5
2 Manchester M1.....163 A3
Wallshaw Pl OL1......67 A7
Wallshaw St OL1......67 A7
Walls St WN2.........57 C2
Wall St
Oldham OL8...........153 C1
Salford M6............154 C2
Wigan WN6............36 F1
Wallsuches BL6.......22 F4
Wall Way M18........99 E4
Wallwork Cl OL11.....13 E1
Wallwork Rd M29......77 D6
Wallwork St
Droylsden M11.........99 E8
Radcliffe M26.........44 A4
Reddish SK5...........99 F2
Wallworth Ave M18....99 D5
Wallworth Terr SK9...136 E8
Wally Sq M7..........155 B2
Walmer Dr SK7.......124 A1
Walmer Rd WN2.......57 A5
Walmer St E M14......98 C3
Walmer St
Manchester M14.......98 C3
Reddish M18...........99 D5
Walmersley Ct 8 SK6..125 F6
Walmersley Old Rd
BL9...................27 F7
Walmersley Rd
Bury BL9.............27 F6
Failsworth M40........65 E1
Walmer St
Manchester, Abbey Hey
M18..................99 E6
Manchester M14.......98 C3
Walmesley Dr WN2....56 B7
Walmesley Rd WN7....75 E5
Walmesley St WN1....151 A3
Walmley Gr BL3.......146 C3
Walmsley Ave OL15....15 F3
Walmsley Gr M41......95 D2
Walmsley St
1 Bury BL8..........27 B4
Newton-le-W WA12.....89 D4
Reddish SK5..........169 C3
Stalybridge SK15......102 A8
Walney Rd
Wigan WN3............54 D2
Wythenshawe M22.....121 D4
Walnut Ave
Bury BL9.............141 C3
Oldham OL4...........67 D8
Wigan WN1............37 D2
Walnut Cl
Hyde SK14............102 A2
Swinton M27...........61 D4
Wrightington WN6......137 E8
Walnut Gr
Leigh WN7............75 F8
Sale M33.............108 A4
Walnut Rd
Eccles M30............79 A4
Partington M31........105 D3
Walnut St
Bolton BL1............143 C2
Manchester M18.......99 D5
Walnut Tree Rd SK3...123 A8
Walnut Wlk 2 M32....96 C1
Walpole Ave WN3.....54 F3

Walpole St OL16......31 A7
Walsall St M6........81 A5
WALSDEN..............6 B7
Walsden Est OL14.......6 B7
Walsh Ave M9........64 C2
WALSHAW.............26 E4
Walshaw Brook Cl BL8..26 F4
Walshaw Dr M27........79 F7
Walshaw La BL8........26 F4
Walshaw Rd BL8........27 B4
Walshaw Wlk BL8.......26 F5
Walsh Cl WA12........89 C5
Walshe St BL9........140 A2
Walsh Fold BL7........9 D2
Walsh Ho M46.........58 D4
Walsh St
Chadderton OL9.......152 B2
Horwich BL6..........22 B4
Walsingham Ave
Manchester M20.......109 F4
Middleton M24.........65 A5
Walter Leigh Way
WN7...................75 B1
Walter St
Ashton-in-M WN4.......73 D4
Droylsden M18.........99 E6
Leigh WN7............75 B5
Manchester, Harpurhey
M9....................157 A4
Manchester, Old Trafford
M16...................97 C4
3 Oldham OL1........153 C2
Prestwich M25.........62 F4
Radcliffe M26.........43 F6
Walkden M28..........60 D2
Wigan WN5............54 D6
Waltham Ave
Glazebury WA3.........92 C7
Wigan WN6............36 F2
Waltham Dr SK8......132 B6
Waltham Gdns
Leigh WN7............76 C3
Radcliffe M26.........43 E5
Waltham Rd M16......97 E1
Walthall St OL4.......67 C4
WALTHEW GREEN.......35 C3
Walthew House La
Wigan, Marsh Green
WN5..................36 D2
Wigan WN5............36 B1
Walthew La
Platt Bridge WN2......56 A2
Wigan WN5............36 D2
Walton Cl
Heywood OL10.........46 D8
Middleton M24.........46 C1
Walton Ct BL3........147 C4
Walton Dr
Bury BL9.............27 E8
Marple SK6...........125 D7
Walton Hall Dr M19...99 D1
Walton Ho M35.......83 F8
Walton Pl BL4........60 E7
Walton Rd
Altrincham WA14......119 B5
Culcheth WA3.........91 F3
Manchester M9........64 D5
Sale M33.............107 F2
Walton St
Adlington PR7.........21 A4
Ashton-u-L OL7........84 F5
Atherton M46.........58 E4
Heywood OL10.........29 D1
1 Middleton M24.....47 A2
Stockport SK1.........170 C3
Walton Way M34......101 B1
Walworth Cl M26......61 C7
Walwyn Cl M32.......96 E1
Wanborough Cl WN7...75 F7
Wandsworth Ave M11..83 D2
Wanley Wlk 12 M9....64 E3
Wansbeck Cl M32.....96 E1
Wansbeck Lo M32.....96 E1
Wansfell Wlk M4......160 A2
Wansford St M14......98 A3
Wanstead Ave M9.....65 B3
Wapping St BL1......143 A2
Warbeck Cl
Hindley WN2...........56 E3
Reddish SK5..........100 A2
Warbeck Rd M40......65 D2
Warbreck Dr M41......95 C1
Warbreck Gr M33.....108 D3
WARBURTON..........117 C8
Warburton Bridge Rd
WA13, WA3...........105 A1
Warburton Cl
Altrincham WA15......129 D6
Lymm WA13...........117 A4
Romiley SK6..........113 A1
Warburton Dr WA15...129 D6
WARBURTON GREEN.....129 D6
Warburton Pl 12 M46..58 D3
Warburton Rd SK9....131 D4

Warburton St
Bolton BL1 . . . . 143 C2
Eccles M30 . . . . .79 E1
3 Manchester M20 . . . . . . .110 B3
Salford M5 . . . . .161 B2
Warburton View WA3 . . .105 A2
Warburton Way
WA15 . . . . .120 C7
Warcock Rd OL4 . . . . .67 C7
Wardend Cl M38 . . . . .60 A6
Warden La M40 . . . . .83 B6
Wardens Bank BL5 . . . . .57 E5
Warden St M40 . . . . .83 B6
Warde St M15 . . . . .162 B2
Wardham Cl BL5 . . . . .57 F5
Ward La
Diggle OL3 . . . . .51 D3
Disley SK12 . . . . .135 F4
WARDLE 15 D6
Wardle Brook Ave
SK14 . . . . .102 D3
Wardle Brook Wlk
SK14 . . . . .102 D3
Wardle Cl
Radcliffe M26 . . . . .43 E5
Stretford M32 . . . . .96 E2
Wardle Ct M33 . . . . .108 C4
Wardle Edge OL12 . . . . .15 B4
WARDLE FOLD 15 C7
Wardle Fold OL12 . . . . .15 C7
Wardle Gdns OL12 . . . . .15 C3
Wardle High Sch OL12 . . . .15 D5
Wardle Rd
Rochdale OL12 . . . . .15 C4
Sale M33 . . . . .108 C4
Wardle St
Bacup OL13 . . . . .3 D8
Bolton BL2 . . . . .148 C1
Littleborough OL15 . . . . .16 A6
Manchester M40 . . . . .160 B3
WARDLEY 61 C2
Wardley Ave
Manchester M16 . . . . .97 E1
Walkden M28 . . . . .60 B3
Wardley CE Prim Sch
M27 .61 E2
Wardley Gr BL1 . . . . .144 A3
Wardley Hall Ct M27 . . . . . . .61 C2
Wardley Hall La M28 . . . . . .79 A8
Wardley Hall Rd M27,
M28 .61 C2
Wardley Ho **1** M6 . . . . .80 C4
Wardley Ind Est M28 . . . . . . .61 C1
Wardley Rd M29 . . . . .77 D8
Wardley Sq M27 . . . . .77 D8
Wardley St
Swinton M27 . . . . .79 F8
Wigan WN5 . . . . .54 B6
Wardlow Ave
17 Gamesley SK13 . . . . . . .171 A1
Wigan WN5 . . . . .36 A1
Wardlow Fold 21
SK13 . . . . .171 A1
Wardlow Gdns 18
SK13 . . . . .171 A1
Wardlow Gr **22** SK13 . . . . .171 A1
Wardlow Mews
18 Gamesley SK13 . . . . . . .171 A1
23 Gamesley SK13 . . . . . . .171 A1
Wardlow St BL3 . . . . .146 B4
Wardlow Wlk
20 Gamesley SK13 . . . . . . .171 A1
24 Gamesley SK13 . . . . . . .171 A1
Wardour St
Atherton M46 . . . . .58 C2
Atherton M46 . . . . .58 D2
Ward Rd M43 . . . . .84 B1
WARDSEND 134 A1
Wardsend Wlk **18**
M15 .162 A2
Wards Pl **3** WN7 . . . . .76 B4
Ward St
Chadderton OL9 . . . . .152 C3
Failsworth M35 . . . . .83 E8
Hindley WN2 . . . . .56 E7
Hyde SK14 . . . . .167 B2
11 Manchester, Didsbury
M20 . . . . .110 B3
Manchester, Lower Broughton
M40 . . . . .157 C4
Manchester M9 . . . . .64 C2
Oldham OL1 . . . . .153 A4
Romiley SK6 . . . . .112 F3
Stockport SK1 . . . . .124 A7
Ware Cl WN4 . . . . .73 D4
Wareham Gr M30 . . . . .79 C3
Wareham St
Manchester M8 . . . . .64 B1
Wilmslow SK9 . . . . .137 B7
Wareing St M29 . . . . .76 F8
Wareings Yd **5** OL11 . . . . . .31 A4
Wareing Way BL3 . . . . .145 B2
Warfield Wlk **30** M9 . . . . . . .64 E3
Warford Ave M14 . . . . .134 A2
Warford La M46 . . . . .136 B1
Warford St M4 . . . . .159 B4
Warford Terr WA16 . . . . . . .136 B2
WARGRAVE 89 D3
Wargrave CE Prim Sch
WA12 . . . . .89 C1
Wargrave Mews WA12 . . . . .89 C1
Wargrave Rd WA12 . . . . .89 D1
WARHILL 103 A3
Warhurst Fold **2**
SK13 . . . . .104 A5

Warke The M28 . . . . .78 F6
WARLAND 6 D5
Warland End Gate OL14 . . . .6 C7
Warley Cl SK8 . . . . .122 E6
Warley Gr SK16 . . . . .101 C8
Warley Rd M16 . . . . .97 A3
Warley St OL15 . . . . .16 B2
Warlingham Cl BL8 . . . . .27 B1
Warlow Crest OL3 . . . . .69 A4
Warlow Dr
Leigh WN7 . . . . .57 D1
Uppermill OL3 . . . . .69 A4
Warmco Ind Pk OL5 . . . . . . .68 D2
Warmington Dr M12 . . . . . . .164 B2
Warminster Gr WN3 . . . . .54 D2
Warmley Rd M23 . . . . .120 D8
Warncliffe St **7** WN5 . . . . . . .54 D5
Warne Ave M43 . . . . .84 C2
Warner Wlk **9** M11 . . . . . . .160 C1
Warnford Cl M40 . . . . .83 D4
Warnford St **3** WN1 . . . . .37 C2
War Office Rd OL11 . . . . .29 E6
Warren Ave SK8 . . . . .122 D5
2 Manchester M46 . . . . . . .64 D3
Warren Bacup Rd M17 . . . . .96 D6
Warren Cl
Atherton M46 . . . . .58 E5
Denton M34 . . . . .100 D2
Middleton M24 . . . . .46 F1
Poynton SK12 . . . . .133 B4
Stockport SK7 . . . . .123 D2
Warren Dr
Altrincham WA15 . . . . .129 D7
Britannia OL13 . . . . .4 C8
Newton-le-W WA12 . . . . .89 F4
Swinton M27 . . . . .79 D5
Warrener St M33 . . . . .108 D4
Warren Hey SK9 . . . . .137 E8
Warren La OL8 . . . . .67 B4
Warren Lea
Compstall SK6 . . . . .114 B2
Poynton SK12 . . . . .133 E5
Warren Rd
Cheadle SK8 . . . . .123 B2
Stockport SK3 . . . . .170 B2
Stretford M17 . . . . .96 B6
Walkden M28 . . . . .60 E3
Warren St
2 Bury BL8 . . . . .27 B1
Manchester M9 . . . . .64 C2
Salford M7 . . . . .155 C4
Stockport SK1 . . . . .169 C2
Warren The WA12 . . . . .89 A3
Warren Wood Prim Sch
SK2 .125 A6
Warre St OL6 . . . . .166 B3
Warrington La
Lymm WA13 . . . . .117 E2
Wigan WN1 . . . . .151 A3
Warrington Rd
Abram Brow WN2 . . . . .74 B7
Ashton-in-M WN4 . . . . .73 B2
Fowley Common WA3 . . . . . . .92 C5
Golborne WA3, WA12 . . . . . . .90 A6
Ince-in-M WN3 . . . . .151 B2
Leigh WN7 . . . . .76 B3
Manchester M9 . . . . .64 C4
Platt Bridge WN2 . . . . .56 A1
Wigan WN3, WN5 . . . . .54 F3
Warrington St
Ashton-u-L OL6 . . . . .166 B3
9 Oldham OL4 . . . . .67 E6
Stalybridge SK15 . . . . .86 B1
Warsall Rd M22 . . . . .121 E7
Warslow Dr M33 . . . . .108 E1
Warsop Ave M22 . . . . .121 E5
Warth Fold Rd M26 . . . . .44 C6
Warth Ind Pk BL9 . . . . .44 D7
Warth La BB4 . . . . .2 D8
Warth Rd BL9 . . . . .44 D7
Warton Cl
Bramhall SK7 . . . . .133 A7
2 Bury BL8 . . . . .26 F1
Warton Dr M23 . . . . .121 A5
Warwick Ave
Ashton-in-M WN4 . . . . .73 D2
Denton M34 . . . . .100 F1
Manchester M20 . . . . .109 F4
Newton-le-W WA12 . . . . .89 C2
Prestwich M45 . . . . .63 B7
Swinton M27 . . . . .61 D2
Warwick Cl
Bury BL8 . . . . .27 B4
Cheadle SK8 . . . . .123 A4
Dukinfield SK16 . . . . .101 C6
Glossop SK13 . . . . .116 F8
Middleton M24 . . . . .65 A5
Prestwich M45 . . . . .63 A7
Ramsbottom BL8 . . . . .11 A1
Shaw OL2 . . . . .48 F7
Stockport SK4 . . . . .169 A4
Warwick Ct
12 Denton M34 . . . . .113 A8
Manchester, Firswood
M16 .97 A3
Stockport SK4 . . . . .169 A4
Warwick Dr
Altrincham WA15 . . . . .119 F1
Hazel Grove SK7 . . . . .124 D1
Hindley WN2 . . . . .56 F6
Sale M33 . . . . .108 D4
Urmston M41 . . . . .95 B3
Warwickgate Ho M16 . . . . . .97 A4
Warwick Gdns BL3 . . . . .146 B2
Warwick Gr M34 . . . . .100 C8
Warwick Ho
2 Manchester M19 . . . . . . .99 A2
2 Sale M33 . . . . .108 D4

Warwick Mall SK8 . . . . .122 D6
Warwick Rd
Altrincham WA15 . . . . .119 E1
Ashton-u-L OL6 . . . . .85 C5
Aspull WN2 . . . . .38 C5
Atherton M46 . . . . .58 C5
Failsworth M35 . . . . .84 A5
Irlam M44 . . . . .105 D8
Manchester, Firswood M16,
M17 .97 A4
Manchester M21 . . . . .97 B1
Middleton M24 . . . . .65 B6
Radcliffe M26 . . . . .43 F6
Romiley SK6 . . . . .113 A2
Stockport, Heaton Norris
SK4 . . . . .168 C3
Tyldesley M29 . . . . .59 A2
Walkden M28 . . . . .60 C1
Warwick Rd S M16 . . . . .97 A3
Warwick St
Adlington PR7 . . . . .20 F6
Bolton BL1 . . . . .143 B4
Leigh WN7 . . . . .76 E3
Manchester, Hulme
M15 . . . . .162 C1
Oldham OL9 . . . . .66 C4
Oldham OL9 . . . . .152 C1
Rochdale OL12 . . . . .15 B2
Swinton M27 . . . . .61 F1
Warwick Terr **18**
SK16 . . . . .166 B1
Wasdale Ave
Bolton BL2 . . . . .25 F1
Urmston M41 . . . . .95 B3
Wasdale Dr
Gatley SK8 . . . . .122 B3
Middleton M24 . . . . .46 E2
Wasdale Rd WN4 . . . . .73 A8
Wasdale St OL11 . . . . .30 C1
Wasdale Terr SK15 . . . . .86 A4
Wasdale Wlk **8** OL1 . . . . . .48 E8
Washacre BL5 . . . . .57 F7
Washacre Cl BL5 . . . . .57 F7
Washacre Prim Sch
BL5. .57 F7
Washbrook OL9 . . . . .66 B4
Washbrook Ave M28 . . . . . . .60 B1
Washbrook Ct **3** OL9 . . . . .66 B4
Washbrook Dr M32 . . . . .96 B2
Washburn Cl BL5 . . . . .39 F2
WASH END 91 C8
Wash Fold BL8 . . . . .27 B5
Washford Dr M23 . . . . .120 D8
Washington Cl SK8 . . . . .131 F8
Washington Ct **6**
BL9. . . . . .140 C3
Washington Ctr The
M50 .96 E8
Washington St
3 Bolton BL3 . . . . .144 C2
Oldham OL9 . . . . .152 C3
Wash La
Bury BL9 . . . . .141 B2
Leigh WN7 . . . . .76 C5
Wash Terr BL8 . . . . .27 B5
Washway Rd M33 . . . . .107 F2
Washwood Cl M38 . . . . .60 B6
Wasnidge Wlk **8**
M15 .162 C1
Wasp Ave OL11 . . . . .31 A3
Wasp Mill Dr OL12 . . . . .15 C6
Wastdale Ave BL9 . . . . .45 A3
Wastdale Rd M23 . . . . .121 A4
Waste St **2** OL6 . . . . .67 A7
Wastwater St **5** OL1 . . . . . .48 E8
Watburn Rd SK7 . . . . .124 A2
Watchgate Cl M24 . . . . .46 D3
WATERBARN 3 A8
Waterbarn La OL13 . . . . .3 B8
Waterbeck Cl WN1 . . . . .37 F1
Waterbridge M28 . . . . .79 A5
Watercroft OL11 . . . . .13 D1
Waterdale Cl M28 . . . . .78 B4
Waterdale Dr M45 . . . . .63 A8
Water Dr WN6 . . . . .37 B7
Wateredge Cl WN7 . . . . .75 D3
Waterfield Cl BL9 . . . . .27 F7
Waterfield Way M35 . . . . .84 A6
Waterfold Bsns Pk
BL9. . . . . .141 B1
Waterfold La BL9 . . . . .141 C1
WATERFOOT 2 E8
Waterfoot Cotts SK14 . . . . .103 A4
Waterfoot Prim Sch
BB4 . . . . .2 F8
Waterford Ave
Manchester M20 . . . . .109 D3
Romiley SK6 . . . . .113 F2
Waterford Cl WN2 . . . . .56 A3
Waterford Ct BL4 . . . . .42 E1
Waterford Pl SK8 . . . . .131 B8
Waterfront Quay M50 . . . . . .161 A3
Waterfront The M11 . . . . .83 A2
Watergate M34 . . . . .100 C8
Water Gate OL3 . . . . .69 B8
Watergate Dr BL5 . . . . .59 C7
Watergate La BL4, BL5 . . . . .59 C7
Watergate Milne Ct **6**
OL4. .67 D8
Water Grove Rd SK16 . . . . .101 F7
WATER HEYES 37 D1
Waterhouse Cl OL12 . . . . . . .15 C6
Waterhouse Nook BL6,
PR7 .21 A5
Waterhouse Rd M18 . . . . . . .99 E4
Waterhouse Rd OL12 . . . . . .139 C4

Water La
Droylsden M43. . . . . .83 E1
Edenfield BL0. . . . . .1 D2
Farnworth BL4. . . . . .60 E7
Hollingworth SK14. . . . . .103 D5
Milnrow OL16. . . . . .32 A5
Radcliffe M26 . . . . .43 F3
Wigan WN5 . . . . .137 A7
Water Lane St M26 . . . . .43 F3
WATERLOO 85 A5
Waterloo Ct
Bury BL9 . . . . .44 E8
3 Manchester M20 . . . . . .110 A5
4 Stalybridge SK15 . . . . . . .86 A2
Waterloo Gdns OL6 . . . . . . .85 E5
Waterloo Ind Pk BL1. . . . . . .25 A1
Waterloo Pk **1** SK1. . . . . . .112 A1
Waterloo Prim Sch
OL7. .85 A5
Waterloo Rd
Ashton-u-L OL6 . . . . .85 B5
Bramhall SK7. . . . . .132 F8
Poynton SK12 . . . . .134 A2
Romiley SK6. . . . . .113 E2
Salford M8. . . . . .155 C2
Stalybridge SK15. . . . . .86 A2
Stockport SK1 . . . . .169 C1
Waterloo St
Ashton-u-L OL6 . . . . .85 D4
Bolton BL1 . . . . .143 C1
Bury BL8 . . . . .140 A2
Manchester, Blackley
M9 . . . . .64 C1
Manchester, Blackley M8,
M9 . . . . .64 C1
Manchester M1 . . . . .163 A4
Oldham OL4 . . . . .67 A6
3 Wigan WN6 . . . . .37 A1
Watermans Cl
Horwich BL6 . . . . .22 C4
Manchester M9 . . . . .157 C4
Waterman View OL16 . . . . . . .31 C8
Watermead M33. . . . . .108 A1
Watermead Cl SK3. . . . . .123 E4
Watermede WN5 . . . . .53 E3
Watermeetings La
SK6. . . . . .113 F1
Watermill Cl OL16 . . . . .31 D6
Water Mill Clough OL2. . . . . .48 C2
Watermill Ct SK15 . . . . .85 A5
Watermill Ct SK15 . . . . .85 A5
Water park Hall M7. . . . . . . .163 E1
Waterpark Rd M7. . . . . .155 B4
Waters Edge
Ashton-u-L OL6 . . . . .85 E5
Marple SK6. . . . . .126 A8
Uppermill OL3 . . . . .69 A5
Walkden M28. . . . . .60 F2
Water's Edge BL4 . . . . .42 A2
Watersedge Cl SK8 . . . . . . .123 B3
Waters Edge Fold OL1 . . . . . .49 C4
Watersfield Cl SK8. . . . . .131 F8
WATERSHEDDINGS 49 D1
Watersheddings Prim Sch
OL1. .49 C1
Watersheddings St **9**
OL4. .49 D1
Watersheddings Way **11**
OL4. .49 D1
Waterside
Disley SK13 . . . . .135 E7
Glossop SK13. . . . . .104 A6
Hattersley SK14. . . . . .102 D2
Marple SK6 . . . . .125 F5
Sale M33 . . . . .108 C5
Stretford M17 . . . . .96 F6
Uppermill OL3 . . . . .69 A4
Waterside Ave SK6. . . . . .125 F5
Waterside Bsns Pk
SK13. . . . . .103 F6
Waterside Cl
Hattersley SK14 . . . . .102 D1
Manchester M21 . . . . .109 D4
Oldham OL1. . . . . .49 C4
Radcliffe M26 . . . . .44 D4
Waterside Cotts OL3. . . . . . . .69 C4
Waterside Dr WN3. . . . . .150 B3
Waterside Ind Est BL3 . . . . . .42 D4
Waterside La OL16 . . . . .31 B8
Waterside Mill OL3 . . . . .69 C4
Waterside Plaza **8**
M33. . . . . .108 B5
Waterside Rd
Disley SK12, SK22 . . . . .135 E7
Ramsbottom BL9. . . . . .11 C3
Waterside Trad Est **1**
WN7. . . . . .76 B4
Waterside View Wlk **4**
SK14. . . . . .102 D2
Waterslea
Eccles M30 . . . . .79 C2
Waterslea Dr BL1 . . . . .40 F8
Watersmead Cl BL1 . . . . . . .143 C2
Watersmeet M32 . . . . .96 D4
Waters Meeting Rd
Bolton BL1. . . . . .25 A2
Bolton BL1. . . . . .143 C1
Bolton BL1. . . . . .143 C3
Water's Nook Rd BL5 . . . . . . .58 A8
Waterson Ave M40. . . . . .83 A7
Waters Reach
High Lane SK6 . . . . .134 E7
Mossley OL5 . . . . .68 E4
Poynton SK12 . . . . .133 F5
Wigan WN1 . . . . .151 C4
Water's Reach M17. . . . . .96 F6

Water St
Adlington PR7 . . . . .21 A6
Ashton-u-L OL6 . . . . .166 B3
Atherton M46 . . . . .58 D3
Bolton BL1 . . . . .145 C3
Bolton, Egerton BL7. . . . . .8 D2
Denton M34. . . . . .100 F7
Glossop SK13. . . . . .104 E2
Hyde SK14. . . . . .167 A2
Manchester, Ardwick
M12 . . . . .163 C4
Manchester, Harpurhey
M9 .157 A4
Manchester M3 . . . . .162 A4
4 Middleton M24. . . . . .46 F1
Newton-le-W WA12. . . . . .89 C4
Radcliffe M26 . . . . .44 A3
Ramsbottom BL0. . . . . .138 B1
Rochdale OL16. . . . . .31 A7
Royton OL2. . . . . .49 A4
Stalybridge SK15. . . . . .86 A2
Stockport SK1 . . . . .169 C3
Whitworth OL12. . . . . .14 C8
Wigan WN1 . . . . .150 C4
Waterton Ave OL5 . . . . .68 B2
Waterton La OL5. . . . . .68 B2
Waterview Cl OL16. . . . . .32 B3
Waterview Pk WN7. . . . . .75 E4
Waterworks Rd
Delph OL3. . . . . .51 A4
Oldham OL4. . . . . .49 E1
Watfield Wlk **5** M9. . . . . . . .157 A3
Watford Ave M14 . . . . .98 B2
Watford Bridge Ind Est
SK22. . . . . .127 D1
Watford Bridge Rd
SK22. . . . . .127 D1
Watford Cl **16** BL1 . . . . . . .143 B2
Watford La SK22. . . . . .127 C2
Watford Lo SK22 . . . . .127 C1
Watford Rd
Manchester M19 . . . . .111 A6
New Mills SK22. . . . . .127 C2
Watkin Ave SK13 . . . . .171 B4
Watkin M13 . . . . .163 C2
Watkins Dr M25 . . . . .63 F3
Watkin St
Dukinfield SK14 . . . . .102 A5
Rochdale OL16. . . . . .31 B4
Salford M3. . . . . .158 A3
Watling St
Bolton BL8. . . . . .26 B7
Bury BL8. . . . . .26 F1
Littleborough OL15 . . . . .15 F5
Watlington Ct OL1 . . . . .49 D3
Watson Ave
Ashton-in-M WN4 . . . . .73 C3
Golborne WA3 . . . . .73 F1
Watson Gdns OL12. . . . . .14 D2
Watson Rd BL4 . . . . .59 F8
Watson Sq SK1 . . . . .169 C1
Watson St
Denton M34. . . . . .101 B3
Eccles M30 . . . . .79 C2
Manchester M2, M3 . . . . . . .162 C4
Oldham OL4. . . . . .67 C8
Radcliffe M26 . . . . .44 A4
Swinton M27 . . . . .79 F8
Watton Cl M27. . . . . .61 F2
Watts St
Chadderton OL9. . . . . .152 B3
Horwich BL6. . . . . .22 C2
Manchester M19 . . . . .111 B8
Oldham OL10. . . . . .66 D2
1 Rochdale OL12. . . . . .31 A8
Waugh Ave M35 . . . . .83 F7
Wavell Dr BL9 . . . . .45 A1
Wavell Rd M22 . . . . .121 D2
Waveney Dr
Altrincham WA14. . . . . .119 C6
Handforth SK9. . . . . .131 D2
Waveney Rd
Shaw OL2. . . . . .149 A4
Wythenshawe M22 . . . . .121 E4
Waverley
17 Heywood OL10. . . . . .29 C2
2 Rochdale SK14. . . . . .139 B4
Waverley Ave
Kearsley BL4 . . . . .60 F6
Stretford M32 . . . . .96 F3
Waverley Cres M43. . . . . .84 A3
Waverley Ct WN3. . . . . .54 D3
Waverley Dr SK8. . . . . .132 B7
Waverley Gr WN7 . . . . .76 D6
Waverley Rd
Bolton BL1. . . . . .143 B3
Golborne WA3. . . . . .74 D1
Hindley WN2. . . . . .56 C5
Hyde SK14 . . . . .113 D8
Manchester M9 . . . . .157 C3
Middleton M24 . . . . .47 A3
Pendlebury M27 . . . . .80 C7
Sale M33. . . . . .108 C6
Stockport SK3 . . . . .123 C7
Walkden M28. . . . . .60 B1
Waverley Rd W **9** M9 . . . . .157 C3
Waverley Sq BL4 . . . . .60 C6
Waverley St
Oldham OL1. . . . . .49 C1
Rochdale OL11. . . . . .30 C1
Waverton Ave SK4 . . . . .11 C8
Waverton Rd M14 . . . . .98 A1
Wavertree Ave M46 . . . . .58 C4
Wavertree Ct **6** BL1. . . . . . .145 B4
Waybridge Ind Pk M50. . . . . .96 C3
Wayfarers Dr
Newton-le-W WA12. . . . . .89 E2

Wayfarers Dr continued
Tyldesley M29 . . . . .77 A8
Wayfarers Way M27. . . . . .79 F7
Wayfaring BL5. . . . . .39 F2
Wayford Wlk M9. . . . . . . .156 C3
Wayland Rd M18. . . . . .99 E4
Wayland Rd S M18. . . . . . .99 D3
Wayne Cl M43. . . . . .84 C4
Wayne St M11. . . . . .99 E6
Wayoh Croft BL7 . . . . .9 D6
Wayside Dr SK12 . . . . . . .133 C4
Wayside Gdns SK7. . . . . .125 A2
Wayside Gr M28. . . . . .60 E4
Weald Cl M13 . . . . .163 C2
Wealdstone Gr BL2. . . . . .25 B2
Weardale Rd M9. . . . . .64 B5
Wearhead Cl M43. . . . . . . .89 F7
Wearhead Row M5 . . . . .154 C1
Wearish La BL5. . . . . .57 C6
WEASTE 154 B1
Weaste Ave M38. . . . . .60 B4
Weaste Dr M5. . . . . .154 A3
Weaste La M5, M6. . . . . .154 A3
Weaste Rd M5. . . . . .154 A2
Weaste Sta M5. . . . . .154 A1
Weatherall St N M7. . . . .155 C3
Weatherley Cl M15 . . . . . .67 A1
Weatherley Dr SK6. . . . . .125 D6
Weaver Ave M28. . . . . .60 A2
Weaver Cl WA14. . . . . . . .119 C1
Weaver Ct M15. . . . . .162 A2
Weaver Dr BL9 . . . . .27 F8
Weaver Gr WN7 . . . . .75 C4
Weaverham Cl 2 M13 . . .98 F3
Weaverham Way SK9 . . .131 E4
Weaverham Wlk M33 . . .108 E3
Weaver Ho 5 M7. . . . . . . .81 C5
Weaver Rd WA3 . . . . .92 A2
Weavers Ct
Bolton BL3. . . . . .145 B1
10 Middleton M24. . . . . . .46 F1
Mottram in L SK14. . . . .103 A4
Weavers Gn BL4. . . . . .60 D8
Weavers La SK7 . . . . .132 D6
Weaver Rd M24. . . . . .46 F1
Weaver Wlk 5 M11. . . . . .99 D7
Webb Cl SK14 . . . . .102 F1
Webb La SK1. . . . . .124 A8
Webb St
Bury BL8 . . . . .140 A3
Horwich BL6 . . . . .22 C3
Webb Wlk SK14. . . . . . . .102 F1
Webdale Dr M40. . . . . .83 A7
Weber Dr BL3 . . . . .145 A1
Webster Gr M25. . . . . .62 F2
Webster Prim Sch
M15. . . . . .98 A4
Webster's St WN2 . . . . . . .56 A3
Webster St
Bolton BL3. . . . . .148 B1
8 Mossley OL5. . . . . .68 C2
Oldham OL8. . . . . .153 C1
Wedgewood Dr WN6. . . . .36 D3
Wedgewood St M40 . . . .160 C4
Wedgwood Rd M27. . . . . .62 C2
Wedhurst St OL4 . . . . .67 C7
Wednesshough SK14. . . .103 C5
Weedall Ave M5. . . . . . . .161 A2
Weeder Sq OL2 . . . . .49 E8
Weedon Ave WA12. . . . . . .89 B5
Weedon St OL16. . . . . .31 B8
Weeton Ave BL2. . . . . .42 F7
Weighbridge Ct M44. . . . .94 C3
Weint The WA3 . . . . .105 B3
Weir Rd OL16. . . . . .31 E7
Weir St
Failsworth M35 . . . . .83 E7
Manchester M15. . . . . . .162 B1
Welbeck Ave
Failsworth OL9 . . . . .65 D3
Littleborough OL15 . . . . . .16 A6
Newton-le-W WA12. . . . . .89 D2
Urmston M41. . . . . .95 F3
Welbeck Cl
Milnrow OL16. . . . . .31 E6
Whitefield M45 . . . . .44 F7
Welbeck Gr M7. . . . . .155 B3
Welbeck Ho 4 OL6 . . . . .166 A2
Welbeck Rd
Ashton-in-M WN4 . . . . . . .73 C4
Bolton BL1 . . . . .144 A4
Eccles M30 . . . . .79 E4
Hyde SK14. . . . . .167 C2
1 Reddish SK5. . . . . . . .111 F8
Rochdale OL16. . . . . .31 B4
Swinton M28. . . . . .79 B6
Wigan WN3 . . . . .54 E3
Welbeck St N OL6. . . . . . .166 A2
Welbeck St S OL6,
OL7. . . . . .166 A2
Welbeck St M18. . . . . .99 E6
Welbeck Terr OL6. . . . . . .166 A2
Welburn Ave M22. . . . . . .121 E3
Welburn Cl WN5. . . . . .53 E5
Welburn St OL11. . . . . . . .139 C1
Welbury Rd M23. . . . . . . .108 F1
Welby St M13. . . . . .98 D4
Welch Hill St WN7. . . . . . .75 E4
Welch Rd SK14 . . . . .167 C4
Welcomb Cl SK6. . . . . . . .112 F4
Welcomb St M11. . . . . . . .160 B8
Welcomb Wlk M45. . . . . . .62 F7
Welcome Par OL8. . . . . . . .67 D3
Welcroft St SK1 . . . . .170 C4
Weldon Ave BL2. . . . . . . .146 A2
Weldon Cres SK3 . . . . . . .123 E4
Weldon Dr M9. . . . . .64 D5

Weldon Gr WN1 . . . . .37 E2
Weldon Rd WA14. . . . . . .119 D6
Weld Rd M20. . . . . .110 D7
Welfold Ho 3 OL4. . . . . . .67 B5
Welford Ave WA3. . . . . . . .90 C7
Welford Cl SK9. . . . . .137 E8
Welford Gn SK5. . . . . . . .111 F5
Welford Rd M9. . . . . .63 F3
Welford St M6. . . . . .81 B4
Welkin Rd M6. . . . . .112 C3
Welkin Rd Ind Est
SK6. . . . . .112 C3
Wellacre Ave M41. . . . . . . .94 D2
Wellacre Tech Coll
M41. . . . . .154 D1
Welland Ave OL10 . . . . . . .29 A3
Welland Cl M15. . . . . .162 A2
Welland Cl 4 M15. . . . . . .162 A2
Welland Rd
Ashton-in-M WN4 . . . . . . .73 C5
Handforth SK9. . . . . .131 E2
Shaw OL2. . . . . .149 A4
Welland St
Droylsden M11. . . . . .99 D8
Reddish SK5. . . . . .99 F1
Reddish SK5 . . . . .99 F1
Welland The BL6. . . . . .57 E8
Wellbank SK15 . . . . .102 D8
Wellbank Ave OL6 . . . . . . .85 E6
Wellbank Cl
Little Lever BL3 . . . . .43 B3
Oldham OL8. . . . . .67 A4
Wellbank Ct BL8. . . . . .26 F6
Wellbank St BL8. . . . . .26 F6
Wellbank View OL12 . . . . .13 F2
Wellbrooke Cl WN4 . . . . . .73 C3
Wellbrow Terr OL12. . . . . .14 D2
Wellbrow Wlk M9. . . . . . . .64 E3
Wellburn Cl BL3. . . . . .40 F2
Wellcross Rd WN8. . . . . . .53 B6
Well Cl M9. . . . . .19 E1
Welldale Mews M33 . . . .108 E5
Wellens Way M24. . . . . . . .64 C7
Weller Ave
Manchester M21. . . . . . .109 D7
Poynton SK12 . . . . .133 D2
Weller Cl SK12 . . . . .133 D2
Weller Ct M16. . . . . .97 E2
Weller Gdns M21 . . . . . . .109 D7
Wellesbourne Dr M23. . .120 F7
Wellesley Ave M19. . . . . . .99 D6
Wellesley Cl
Newton-le-W WA12. . . . . .89 B5
Wigan WN5 . . . . .54 E8
Wellfield SK6. . . . . .113 C4
Wellfield Cl BL9 . . . . .44 E6
Wellfield Gdns WA15. . . .120 C3
Wellfield Inf Sch M33. . .107 F6
Wellfield Jun Sch
M33. . . . . .107 F6
Wellfield Rd
Bolton BL3. . . . . .144 C1
Culcheth WA3 . . . . .91 F4
Hindley WN2 . . . . .57 A4
Manchester M8. . . . . . . .156 A4
Stockport SK2 . . . . .124 C6
Wigan WN6 . . . . .37 A3
Wythenshawe M23 . . . . .121 A7
Wellfield St OL11. . . . . . . .31 A5
Well Gate SK13. . . . . .104 E2
Wellgate Ave M19 . . . . . .111 B8
Well Gr M45. . . . . .44 E2
WELL GREEN 120 C3
Wellgreen Cl WA15 . . . . .120 C3
Wellgreen Lo WA15. . . . .120 C3
Well Green Prim Sch
WA15. . . . . .120 C2
Wellham Rd WN3 . . . . .55 B3
Wellhead Cl M15 . . . . . . .162 C1
Wellhouse Dr 3 M40 . . . .65 C3
Well-i-Hole Rd OL3. . . . . .68 F4
Welling Rd M40 . . . . .83 E8
Welling St 20 BL2. . . . . . .25 B1
Wellington Ave M16 . . . . .97 D2
Wellington Cl
Newton-le-W WA12. . . . . .89 A3
Sale M33 . . . . .108 C6
Wellington Clough 4
OL7. . . . . .85 A6
Wellington Cres M16 . . . . .97 C3
Wellington Ct
9 Ashton-u-L OL6 . . . . .166 C3
6 Bury BL8. . . . . .27 B1
Oldham OL8. . . . . .66 D4
Wellington Ctr OL6 . . . . .166 C2
Wellington Dr M29 . . . . . .59 E1
Wellington Gdns
Bury BL8 . . . . .27 B1
Newton-le-W WA12. . . . . .89 A3
Wellington Gr
Ince-in-M WN3 . . . . .151 A1
Manchester M15 . . . . . . .162 A2
Stockport SK2 . . . . .170 C3
Wellington Ho
Altrincham WA15. . . . . . .119 F5
Manchester M20 . . . . . . .110 C7
Wellington Lo OL15. . . . . .16 B6
Wellington Mews BL7. . . . .9 D4
Wellington Mill SK4 . . . . .169 B1
Wellington Par SK16. . . .166 B1
Wellington Pl
Altrincham WA14 . . . . . .119 D4
Manchester M3. . . . . . . .162 B4
13 Rochdale OL16. . . . . . .31 A8
Wellington Rd
Altrincham WA14 . . . . . .119 F6
Ashton-u-L OL6 . . . . . . .166 B3

Wellington Rd continued
Bury BL9 . . . . .140 C1
Chapeltown BL7. . . . . .9 D4
Eccles M30 . . . . .79 F2
Hazel Grove SK7 . . . . . . .134 B8
Manchester, Fallowfield M14,
M20. . . . . .110 C8
Manchester M8. . . . . . . .156 B4
Manchester, Whalley range
M16. . . . . .97 E2
Oldham OL8. . . . . .153 B1
Over Hulton M46. . . . . . . .58 F5
Swinton M27 . . . . .79 F8
Uppermill OL3. . . . . .69 B6
Wellington Rd N M19, SK3,
SK4. . . . . .169 A3
Wellington Rd S SK1,
SK2. . . . . .170 B2
Wellington St E M7. . . . . .155 B3
Wellington St W M7 . . . . .155 A2
Wellington Sch WA15. . . .119 F6
Wellington Sq 5 BL8 . . . . .27 B1
Wellington St
Ashton-u-L OL6 . . . . .166 B2
Bolton BL3. . . . . .145 B2
Bury BL8 . . . . .140 A1
Chadderton OL9. . . . . . . .152 B4
Denton M34. . . . . .100 F6
Dukinfield SK16 . . . . .101 C3
2 Failsworth M35 . . . . . . .66 A1
Farnworth BL4. . . . . .60 D8
Hazel Grove SK7 . . . . . . .124 F3
1 Littleborough OL15. . . .16 B5
Manchester M18 . . . . .99 D5
Milnrow OL16. . . . . .32 A6
Newton-le-W WA12. . . . . .89 A3
Oldham OL4, OL8 . . . . . .153 C2
6 Radcliffe M26. . . . . .44 C4
Rochdale OL12. . . . . .14 F1
Salford M3. . . . . .158 A2
Stockport SK1 . . . . .169 C1
Stretford M32. . . . . .96 C1
Westhoughton BL5. . . . . . .39 E2
Wigan WN1. . . . . .151 A4
Wellington Terr
13 Dukinfield SK16 . . . . .166 B1
Salford M5. . . . . .154 A2
Wellington Wlk BL3 . . . . .145 B2
Well i' th' La OL11 . . . . . . .31 A5
Well La M45. . . . . .44 F2
Well Mdw SK14. . . . . .167 A4
Well Mead SK6. . . . . .112 E3
Wellmead Ct M8. . . . . . . .155 C1
Well Meadow Ct
SK14. . . . . .167 A4
Wellmeadow La M33 . . . .108 C4
Wellpark Wlk 21 M40 . . . .83 C5
Well Rd WN7 . . . . .57 D1
Well Row SK14 . . . . .115 A8
Well St N BL0. . . . . .1 C2
Well St W BL0. . . . . .138 B1
Wells Ave
Billinge WN5 . . . . .71 D6
Chadderton OL9. . . . . .48 A1
Manchester M25 . . . . .63 C2
Wells Cl
Droylsden M43. . . . . .99 F8
Gatley SK8. . . . . .131 C7
Middleton M24. . . . . .64 C7
Tyldesley M29 . . . . .59 E3
Wells Ct SK16 . . . . .101 C6
Wells Dr
Dukinfield SK16 . . . . .101 C6
Manchester SK4 . . . . .110 E2
Wigan WN2 . . . . .37 F2
Wellside Wlk 7 M8. . . . . .156 A2
Wells Pl WN1. . . . . .151 B4
Wells Rd OL1. . . . . .49 E5
Wells St BL9. . . . . .140 B1
Well St
Ainsworth BL2. . . . . .26 C1
Bolton BL1 . . . . .148 A3
Heywood OL10. . . . . .29 E1
Manchester M4 . . . . .159 A2
6 Rochdale OL11. . . . . . . .31 A5
Uppermill OL3 . . . . .77 A8
Wellstock La M38. . . . . . . .59 F6
Wellwood Dr 11 M40. . . . .83 A7
Wellyhole St OL4. . . . . . . .67 D6
Welman Way WA15. . . . . .119 F4
Welney Rd M16. . . . . .97 B3
Welshpool Cl M23 . . . . . .109 B2
Welshpool Way 9
M34. . . . . .101 A1
Welton Ave M20. . . . . . . .110 C2
Welton Cl
Leigh WN7 . . . . .76 C5
Wilmslow SK9 . . . . .136 F4
Welton Dr SK9. . . . . .136 E4
Welton Gr SK9. . . . . .136 E4
Welwyn Cl M41. . . . . .95 B5
Welwyn Dr M6. . . . . .80 A5
Welwyn Wlk M40 . . . . . . .160 A2
Wembley Cl SK3 . . . . .170 A1
Wembley Gr M14 . . . . . . .110 C8
Wembley Rd M18 . . . . .99 C3
Wembury St N M9. . . . . . .157 E4
Wembury St M9. . . . . .157 E4
Wembury Wlk SK14 . . . . .102 E3
Wemsley Gr 10 BL2. . . . . .25 B1
Wem St OL9 . . . . .66 A4
Wemyss Ave SK5 . . . . .99 F1
Wendlebury Cl WN7. . . . . .75 D8
Wendlebury Gn OL2 . . . .149 A1
Wendon Rd M23. . . . . . . .121 B5
Wendover Dr BL3. . . . . . . .40 E5
Wendover Rd
Urmston M41. . . . . .95 C2

Wendover Rd continued
Wythenshawe M23 . . . . .120 D5
Wenfield Dr M9. . . . . .65 B3
Wenlock Ave OL6. . . . . . . .85 B5
Wenlock Cl
Hazel Grove SK2 . . . . . . .125 A6
Horwich BL6 . . . . .22 C6
Wenlock Ct M12. . . . . . . .164 C2
Wenlock Gr 4 WN2 . . . . . .56 D4
Wenlock Rd
Hindley WN7. . . . . .56 D5
Leigh WN7 . . . . .75 E2
Sale M33 . . . . .108 A2
Wenlock St
9 Hindley WN2 . . . . .56 D5
Swinton M27 . . . . .79 D8
Wigan WN4 M12. . . . . . .164 C2
Wenlock Way M12. . . . . . .165 A1
Wenning Cl M45 . . . . .45 C1
Wensley Cl M7. . . . . .63 A1
Wensleydale Ave SK8 . . .122 C6
Wensleydale Cl
Royton OL2 . . . . .48 C5
Whitefield BL9. . . . . .45 A3
Wythenshawe M23 . . . . .120 F3
Wensleydale Rd WN7 . . . .76 C5
Wensley Dr
Hazel Grove SK7 . . . . . . .133 D7
Manchester M20 . . . . . . .110 B5
Wensley Rd
Cheadle SK8 . . . . .122 C6
Golborne WA3 . . . . .90 E7
Manchester M7. . . . . .63 A1
Reddish SK5. . . . . .169 C4
Wensley Way OL16. . . . . . .31 C6
Wentbridge Rd BL1. . . . . .145 A4
Wentworth Ave
Altrincham WA15. . . . . . .120 A6
8 Bury BL8. . . . . .27 B4
Farnworth BL4. . . . . .60 C7
Heywood OL10. . . . . .46 D8
Irlam M44. . . . . .94 A3
8 Manchester M18 . . . . . .99 C6
Salford M6. . . . . .80 C3
Urmston M41. . . . . .95 B1
Whitefield M45 . . . . .62 D7
Wentworth Cl
Marple SK6. . . . . .125 F8
Middleton M24. . . . . .64 E8
Radcliffe M26 . . . . .43 D4
Wentworth Ct
Failsworth M35 . . . . .83 F6
Whitefield M45 . . . . .62 E8
Wentworth Dr
Bramhall SK7. . . . . .133 A7
Sale M33 . . . . .107 F5
Wentworth High Sch
M30. . . . . .79 F4
Wentworth Rd
Reddish SK5. . . . . .99 F1
Salford M30. . . . . .80 A4
Swinton M27 . . . . .79 D6
Wentworth Wlk 2
SK14. . . . . .101 F5
Werburgh Cl WA13 . . . . .117 C8
WERNETH 152 C1
Werneth Ave
Hyde SK14. . . . . .113 F8
Manchester M14 . . . . .98 B2
Werneth Cl
Denton M34. . . . . .100 F2
Hazel Grove SK7 . . . . . . .124 E4
Werneth Cres SK14 . . . . . .66 C4
Werneth Ct SK14. . . . . . . .167 B1
Werneth Hall Rd OL8 . . . .153 A1
Werneth Ho SK14 . . . . . . .167 B1
Werneth Hollow SK6. . . . .113 B6
Werneth Inf Sch OL8. . . .153 B1
Werneth Jun Sch
OL8. . . . . .153 B1
Werneth Low Ctry Pk*
SK14. . . . . .114 A7
Werneth Low Rd
Compstall SK14 . . . . .114 B6
Hyde SK14, SK6. . . . . . . .113 C5
Werneth Rd
Glossop SK13. . . . . .116 A7
Hyde SK14. . . . . .167 C2
Romiley SK6. . . . . .113 C5
Werneth Rise SK14 . . . . .113 F7
Werneth Sch SK6. . . . . . .113 A2
Werneth St
Denton M34. . . . . .100 F5
Stockport SK1 . . . . .112 B3
Werneth Wlk M34 . . . . . . .100 F2
Wescoe Cl WN5. . . . . .53 E5
Wesley Cl
Rochdale OL12. . . . . .15 C3
Westhoughton BL5 . . . . . .39 E2
Wesley Ct
Bury BL8 . . . . .26 E7
Manchester SK4 . . . . .110 F2
Walkden M28. . . . . .60 D4
Westhoughton BL5 . . . . . .39 E2
Wesley Dr
Ashton-u-L OL6 . . . . .85 C6
Worsley M28. . . . . .79 B7
Wesley Mews 4 BL2. . . . .148 B3
Wesley Sq M41. . . . . .95 A2
Wesley St
Atherton M46. . . . . .58 E3
Bolton BL3. . . . . .145 B1
Bolton, Toppings BL7 . . . .25 A8
Bury BL8 . . . . .26 E7
Eccles M30 . . . . .79 C2
Failsworth M35 . . . . .66 A1
Farnworth BL4. . . . . .60 E7

Wesley St continued
Glossop SK13. . . . . .104 E2
Hadfield SK13 . . . . .104 A5
Hazel Grove SK7 . . . . . . .124 E3
Heywood OL16. . . . . .29 C2
Manchester M11 . . . . . . .165 A4
Milnrow OL16. . . . . .31 E6
1 Rochdale OL12. . . . . . . .15 B3
Royton OL2. . . . . .48 E3
Stockport SK1 . . . . .169 C1
Stretford M32. . . . . .96 E3
Swinton M27 . . . . .79 F8
Westhoughton BL5 . . . . . .39 E2
Wigan WN5. . . . . .54 D5
Wesleys The 4 BL4. . . . . .59 F8
Wessenden Bank E
SK2. . . . . .124 D5
Wessenden Bank W
SK2. . . . . .124 D5
Wessex Cl WN1. . . . . .20 B1
Wessex Park Cl OL2 . . . . .149 B4
Wessex Rd WN5 . . . . .36 D1
Wessington Bank 7
SK13. . . . . .171 B2
Wessington Fold 12
SK13. . . . . .171 B2
Wessington Gn 11
SK13. . . . . .171 B2
Wessington Mews
SK13. . . . . .171 B2
Westage Gdns M23 . . . . .121 A7
West Ashton St M50 . . . .154 C1
West Ave
Altrincham WA14 . . . . . .119 A5
Droylsden M18. . . . . .99 F5
Failsworth M40 . . . . .65 D1
Farnworth BL4. . . . . .60 B8
Gatley SK8. . . . . .122 C1
Golborne WA3 . . . . .74 B1
Leigh WN7 . . . . .76 C3
Manchester M19 . . . . . . .110 F7
Rochdale OL12. . . . . .15 C3
Stalybridge SK15. . . . . . . .86 A3
Walkden M28. . . . . .60 E2
Whitefield M45 . . . . .44 E2
West Bank M11. . . . . .100 E4
Westbank Rd
Bolton BL6. . . . . .40 D6
Manchester M20 . . . . . . .110 D5
West Bank St
Salford M5. . . . . .161 C4
Tyldesley M46. . . . . .58 E1
Westbourne BL4. . . . . .1 A8
Westbourne Ave
Bolton BL3. . . . . .42 B3
Leigh WN7 . . . . .75 E7
Swinton M27 . . . . .61 D5
Whitefield M45 . . . . .44 D1
Westbourne Dr
Ashton-u-L OL7 . . . . .166 A4
16 Handforth SK9. . . . . . .131 D1
Westbourne Gr
Manchester M9. . . . . . . .157 A4
Manchester, Withington
M20. . . . . .110 A6
Reddish SK5. . . . . .111 F8
Sale M33 . . . . .108 A4
Westbourne Pk M41 . . . . . .95 D2
Westbourne Range
M18. . . . . .99 F4
Westbourne Rd
Denton M34. . . . . .100 C3
Eccles M30 . . . . .79 B4
Manchester M14 . . . . . . .110 D8
Urmston M41. . . . . .95 D2
Westbourne St OL9. . . . . .153 A2
Westbridge Mews
WN1. . . . . .150 C3
West Bridgewater St
WN7. . . . . .75 F4
Westbrook Cl OL11 . . . . . .47 D8
Westbrook Ct BL2. . . . . . .148 A2
Westbrook Rd
Stretford M17. . . . . .96 D7
Swinton M27 . . . . .79 F2
Westbrook Sq M12 . . . . . .165 A2
Westbrook St BL2. . . . . . .148 A2
Westbrook Trad Est
M17. . . . . .96 D7
Westbrook Wlk 3
M20. . . . . .110 A8
Westbury Cl
Bury BL8 . . . . .27 A1
Westhoughton BL5 . . . . . .40 A1
Westbury Dr SK6. . . . . . . .125 E6
Westbury Rd M8. . . . . .64 B1
Westbury St
Ashton-u-L OL6 . . . . .166 C3
Dukinfield SK14 . . . . .101 C5
Westbury Street Ind Est
SK14. . . . . .101 C5
Westbury Way OL1,
OL2. . . . . .48 D2
Westby Cl SK7 . . . . .133 A7
Westby Gr BL2 . . . . .148 C4
West Central Dr M27 . . . . .80 B7
Westchapel Mews BL5 . . .39 E3
West Charles St 6 . . . . . . .81 B1
West Church St 9
OL10. . . . . .29 C2
West Cl M46. . . . . .58 E1

Westcliffe Ho **3** OL12....15 D4
Westcliffe Rd BL1 ....24 F6
Westcombe Dr BL8 ......27 C5
Westcott Ave M20 ......110 A6
Westcott Cl BL2 ....25 E5
Westcott Ct M15........162 A3
Westcott Dr WN3......54 C4
Westcott Gr OL2........149 A1
West Cotts OL3 ....68 F5
Westcourt Rd
Bolton BL3.............147 A3
Sale M33 ....108 A6
Westcraig Ave M40 ....65 C3
West Craven St M5 ......161 B3
West Cres M24 ....64 F7
West Croft Ind Est
M24.....................64 C7
Westcroft Rd M19,
M20 ....110 D4
West Crown Ave M5 ......161 B4
Westdale Gdns M19.....111 A5
Westdean Cres M19 .....110 F5
West Dean St M5........81 C1
WEST DIDSBURY 109 E4
Westdown Gdns **1**
OL2.......................48 F8
West Downs Rd SK8 ....122 F3
West Dr
Bury BL9 ....27 E5
Droylsden M43.........83 F1
Gatley SK8.............122 A4
Glossop SK13...........103 E7
Pendlebury, Irlams o' th'
Height M6.............80 E6
Pendlebury, Swinton Park
M27 ....80 B7
West Duke St M5 ......158 A1
West Egerton St M5 .....81 B1
West End SK14 ....114 F8
West End Ave SK8 ......122 A6
Westend St BL4 ....60 B8
West End St OL9........153 A3
Westerdale **1** OL4.....67 C6
Westerdale Cl M29......77 B8
Westerdale Dr
Bolton BL3.............144 A1
Royton OL2 ....48 C5
Westerham Ave M5.......81 A1
Westerham Cl BL8.......27 C7
Wester Hill OL7.........85 B8
Wester Hill Rd OL8 ......67 A1
Westerling Way M16.....97 E3
Western Ave M27 ......62 D2
Western Circ M19 ......110 F6
Western Ct OL13........3 B8
Western Rd
Bacup OL13 ....3 C8
Urmston M41...........94 E1
Western St
Manchester M18 ....99 E6
Salford M6.............154 B3
Westerton Ct BL3......145 A1
Westfield
Altrincham WA14.......119 C3
Salford M6.............154 B4
Westfield Ave
Ashton-in-M WN4 ......73 A4
Middleton M24.........65 A7
Westfield Cl OL11.......13 F1
Westfield Com Sch
WN5.....................54 D7
Westfield Dr
Romiley SK6............113 C5
Uppermill OL4 ....86 D2
Westfield Gr
Denton M34............100 E5
Wigan WN1 ....37 B3
Westfield Rd
Bolton BL3.............146 B2
Cheadle SK8 ....131 F8
Droylsden M43.........83 E2
Manchester M21........97 B1
Tyldesley M46 ....128 E1
Westfields WA15........128 F8
Westfield St
Chadderton OL9........152 C4
Manchester M7.........63 D1
Westgate
Altrincham WA15.......119 E2
Sale M33 ....108 A4
Urmston M41...........95 B1
Whitworth OL12........14 F7
Wilmslow SK9 ....137 A5
Westgate Ave
Bolton BL1.............144 C3
Bury BL9 ....140 B1
2 Manchester M9 ......64 C2
Ramsbottom BL0 ....11 A2
Westgate Cl OL12.......14 B7
Westgate Dr
Orrell WN5.............53 D5
Swinton M27 ....79 F6
Tyldesley M29 ....77 C6
Westgate Ho **4** OL8...66 D2
Westgate Rd M6........80 C4
Westgate St OL7.......166 A1
West Gdns **1** OL13 ....3 B8
West Gn M24...........64 B7
WEST GORTON 164 C3
West Gr
Manchester M13 ....164 A1
1 Mossley OL5..........68 C1
Sale M33 ....108 B3
Westhoughton BL5......57 E6

Westgrove Ave BL1 ....24 E6
Westhead Ave WA3 ......74 E1
Westhide Wlk M9 ....64 F1
West High St M5 ....81 A2
West Hill OL11..........139 B2
West Hill Cl SK15.......85 F2
West Hill Sch SK15......85 F2
Westholm Ave SK4......111 B7
Westholme Ct SK9......137 A2
Westholme Rd
Manchester M20 ....110 B5
Prestwich M25.........60 D1
West Hope St M5........81 B1
Westhorne Fold **1** M8..63 F2
WESTHOUGHTON 57 C8
Westhoughton High Sch
BL5.......................57 F8
Westhoughton Parochial
CE Prim Sch BL5........57 C8
Westhoughton Prim Sch
BL5.......................39 F1
Westhoughton Rd PR6,
PR7 ....20 F8
Westhoughton Sta BL5...39 C2
WEST HULME 48 D1
Westhulme Ave OL1 .....48 D1
Westhulme St OL1 ......48 D1
Westhulme Way OL1 ....48 C1
Westinghouse Cl
M16.....................150 A4
Westinghouse Ind Est
M17 ....96 C5
Westinghouse Rd M17...96 B5
West King St M3 ....158 B2
Westlake Gr WN2......57 B4
Westlake St M11........165 C3
Westland Ave
Bolton BL1.............142 A1
Farnworth BL4.........60 C6
Stockport SK1.........112 B1
Westland Dr M9........64 D4
Westlands M45.........62 F6
Westlands The M27 .....80 C6
West Lea M34 ....101 A2
Westlea Dr M18 ....99 D3
WESTLEIGH 75 E7
Westleigh Dr M25 ......63 D3
Westleigh High Sch
WN7.....................57 D1
Westleigh La WN7......57 D1
Westleigh St Paul's CE
Prim Sch WN7 ....75 E8
Westleigh St M9.........64 F1
Westleigh View WN7....75 E8
Westlock WN3 ....67 A1
West Malling Cl OL10....46 F7
Westmarsh Cl **4** BL1...143 B1
West Marwood St M7...155 B2
West Mdw SK5 ....100 A1
Westmead WN6.........36 E8
Westmead Dr WA15....120 B7
West Meade
Bolton BL3.............147 A2
Manchester, Chorlton-cum-
Hardy M21............109 A7
Manchester, Sedgley Park
M25 ....63 D2
Swinton M27 ....79 E6
Westmeade Rd M28 ....60 C5
Westmere Dr M9 ......156 C2
Westminster Ave
Ashton-u-L OL6 ....85 D7
Farnworth BL4.........60 C8
Manchester M16 ....97 C2
Radcliffe M26 ....43 D4
Reddish SK5 ....111 E7
Royton OL2 ....48 C6
Whitefield M45 ....62 F8
Westminster Cl
Marple SK6............125 D7
Sale M33 ....107 D3
Shaw OL2...............149 B4
Westminster Dr
Cheadle SK8 ....132 B6
Leigh WN7.............76 E7
Wilmslow SK9 ....137 A4
Westminster Ho M3 ....158 B3
Westminster Rd
Altrincham WA15.......120 A2
Bolton BL1.............24 E5
Eccles M30 ....79 F3
Failsworth M35........84 B8
Urmston M41...........95 E4
Walkden M28..........60 D6
Westminster St
Bury BL9 ....140 B1
Farnworth BL4.........60 C8
5 Manchester M19 ......99 B1
Oldham OL1............139 E4
Rochdale OL11.........13 A1
Salford M15...........161 C3
Swinton M27 ....61 E1
Wigan WN5 ....54 F6
Westminster Way
SK16....................101 D6
Westminster Wlk **4**
BL4.......................60 C8
Westmoor Gables
SK4.....................168 A4
Westmoorland St 3
WN1.....................37 C1
Westmoreland Cl
Altrincham WA14.......128 B8
Bury BL9 ....44 E6
Westmorland Ave
Ashton-u-L OL7........166 A4
Dukinfield SK16........101 E8
Westmorland Cl SK5....112 C6

Westmorland Dr
Brinnington SK5........112 C6
Wardle OL12 ....15 D6
Westmorland Prim Sch
SK5.....................112 C6
Westmorland Rd
Manchester M20 ....110 A2
Partington M31 ....105 E2
Sale M33 ....108 C2
Stockport SK3.........80 A4
Tyldesley M29 ....59 A2
Urmston M41...........95 C1
Westmorland Wlk **2**
OL2.......................48 E4
West Mosley St M2.....159 A1
West Mount
Orrell WN5.............53 F6
Wigan WN1 ....37 D2
Westmount Cl M40 ....156 C2
West Oak Pl SK8 ......122 F1
Weston Ave
Failsworth M40 ....65 E1
Rochdale OL16.........31 B4
Swinton M27 ....61 F4
Urmston M41...........95 B1
Westonby St WN4 ......73 D3
Weston Ct M14 ....98 D2
Weston Dr
Denton M34............101 A3
Stockport SK8 ....123 D4
West One Ret Pk M50...80 A1
Weston Gr
Reddish SK4 ....111 C6
Wythenshawe M22 .....121 E8
Weston Pk WN6 ....36 D3
Weston Rd
4 Irlam M44 ....94 A2
Wilmslow SK9 ....137 E6
Weston St
Atherton M46 ....58 E4
Bolton BL3.............42 A4
Manchester M40 ....160 A2
Milnrow OL16 ....31 E6
Oldham OL8...........67 C4
Reddish SK5 ....169 B4
Westover SK6 ....113 A1
Westover Rd M41.......95 C3
Westover St M27 ......60 B1
West Par M13 ....107 C3
Westpark BL1 ....144 C3
West Park Ave
Denton M34............101 B2
Poynton SK12 ....133 A4
West Park Rd
Stockport, Bramhall Park
SK7 ....123 D2
Stockport, Portwood
SK1.....................112 B2
West Park St M5 ......161 B3
West Pk SK14 ....113 E6
West Pl M19............110 F7
Westpoint Ent Pk M17...95 F7
West Point Lo **1** M19...110 F8
Westray Cres M5 ......154 B1
Westray Rd M13.......98 E2
West Rd
Altrincham WA14.......119 C2
Prestwich M25.........62 F5
Urmston M41...........95 F7
Westrees WN7.........76 A7
Westridge Chase OL2...48 D5
West Row M25.........62 F1
West St
Alderley Edge SK9......137 A1
Ashton-u-L OL6 ....166 B3
Bolton BL1.............144 C3
Droylsden M11.........83 B2
Dukinfield SK14........101 D5
Dukinfield SK16........166 B1
Failsworth M35........83 F7
Glossop SK13.........103 E7
Heywood OL10.........29 D2
Hindley WN2...........57 B3
Ince-in-M WN2.........56 A8
Littleborough OL15.....16 C5
Middleton M24.........47 A2
Milnrow OL16 ....31 D7
Oldham, Nether Lees
OL4 ....67 E5
Oldham OL1............153 B3
Oldham OL9...........153 A2
2 Radcliffe M26.........44 A3
Ramsbottom BL0 ......138 B1
Rawtenstall BB4 ....2 E8
Rochdale OL16.........31 A8
Stalybridge SK15......85 F2
Stockport SK3.........169 A1
Tyldesley M46 ....58 D3
Wigan WN6 ....37 B1
West Starkey St OL10...29 C3
West Thorpe WA14.....119 B2
West Towers Mews
SK6.....................126 A4
West Towers St M6 ....154 C1
West Vale M26.........44 A5
West Vale Rd WA15....119 F6
West View
Bacup OL13 ....3 B8
Denton M34............100 E7
Haslingden BB4 ....1 A7
Littleborough OL15.....16 C5
Ramsbottom BL0 ......1 C2
Shaw OL3..............50 C6
West View Ct M22.....121 F8
West View Gr M45 .....44 D1
West View Rd M22.....121 E8
Westville Gdns M19....110 E5

Westward Ho OL16......31 F6
Westward Rd SK9.......136 F6
Westway
Droylsden M43.........100 A8
Manchester M9 ....64 B6
Oldham OL4...........67 E5
Shaw OL2..............149 B2
West Way
Bolton BL1.............25 B3
Walkden M38..........60 A5
Westwell Gdns **4**
BL1.....................143 C1
Westwell Gr **3** WN7...75 E8
Westwell St WN7 ......75 E8
Westwick Terr **11** BL1...143 B2
West Wlk BL7 ....8 D2
WESTWOOD 152 C3
Westwood WA14........119 B4
Westwood Ave
Altrincham WA15.......119 F7
Failsworth M40 ....65 E1
Hyde SK14.............102 B3
Salford M7.............155 B4
Urmston M41...........95 F1
Walkden M28..........60 A3
Westwood Bsns Ctr
OL9.....................153 A2
Westwood Cl BL4 ......60 D8
Westwood Cotts **6**
M16.....................97 F4
Westwood Cres M30....79 B4
Westwood Dr
Oldham OL9...........153 A3
Pendlebury M27 ....80 C6
Sale M33 ....108 B2
Westwood Ho **8** BL4...60 D8
Westwood Ind Est
OL9.....................152 C3
Westwood La WN5 .....151 A1
Westwood Lo M15......119 F2
WESTWOOD PARK 79 B4
Westwood Park Com Prim
Sch M30...............79 B3
Westwood Pk WN3 ....150 C2
Westwood Prim Sch
OL9.....................153 A3
Westwood Rd
Bolton BL1.............144 C4
Gatley SK8.............131 B8
Stockport SK2.........124 B4
Stretford M32 ....96 B2
Wigan WN3 ....150 C2
Westwood St M14 .....97 F4
Westwood Terr WN3 ...151 B1
Westwood Trad Est
SK6.....................125 E5
Westwood Way OL1....48 D1
West Works Rd M17,
M32.....................96 C5
Westworth Cl **11** BL1...145 A4
Wet Earth Gn M27.....80 D8
Wet Gate La WA3......117 E4
Wetheral Cl WN2 ......57 C3
Wetherall St BL4........147 B3
Wetherall St M19 ......99 B1
Wetherby Cl WA12.....89 C5
Wetherby Dr
Hazel Grove SK7 ......125 A2
Royton OL2 ....48 D5
Wetherby St M11......99 E7
Wexford Wlk M22......121 E2
Wexham Gdns WN2....56 A3
Weybourne Ave M9.....65 A2
Weybourne Dr
Romiley SK6............112 F4
Wigan WN3 ....54 E3
Weybourne Gr BL2.....25 B4
Weybridge Cl **4** BL1...145 B4
Weybridge Rd M4 .....159 C2
Weybrook Rd M19 .....111 C7
Weycroft Cl BL2 ....43 A6
Weydale Gr WN2 ......56 E4
Weygates Dr WA15 ....129 C7
Weyhill Rd M23........121 A5
Weylands Gr M6.......80 B5
Weymouth Dr WN2.....57 A4
Weymouth Ho **6** OL9...48 A1
Weymouth Rd
Ashton-u-L OL6 ....85 F6
Eccles M30 ....79 B3
Weymouth St BL1......143 B2
Weythorne Dr
Bolton BL1.............143 C4
Bury BL9 ....28 F4
Whalley Ave
Bolton BL1.............23 F3
Glazebury WA3 ....92 C7
Littleborough OL15.....16 A6
Manchester, Chorlton-cum-
Hardy M21............109 C7
Manchester, Levenshulme
M19 ....99 B2
Manchester, Whalley Range
M16.....................97 D3
Sale M33 ....108 C5
Urmston M41...........95 E3
Whalley Cl
Altrincham WA15.......119 F8
Milnrow OL16 ....31 E6
Whitefield M45 ....44 A1
Wigan WN3 ....55 A2
Whalley Dr BL8........26 F2
Whalley Gdns OL12....14 B1
Whalley Gr
Ashton-u-L OL6 ....85 C7
Leigh WN7.............57 D1
Manchester M16 ....97 D2
WHALLEY RANGE 97 E2

Whalley Range High Sch
M16.....................109 F8
Whalley Rd
Altrincham WA15.......120 A2
Heywood OL10.........29 A2
Manchester M16 ....97 D3
Middleton M24.........46 F3
Ramsbottom BL0 ......11 E7
Rochdale OL12.........14 B1
Stockport SK2.........124 C7
Whitefield M45 ....44 F1
Wham Bar Dr OL10 ....29 B3
Wham Bottom La OL12...14 D4
Wham La OL3..........33 D1
Wham St OL10.........29 B2
Wharf Cl
Altrincham WA14.......119 D7
Manchester M1........159 B1
Wharf Cotts OL5.......68 D1
Wharfdale **2** WN7.....76 A4
Wharfedale BL5 ....39 F2
Wharfedale Rd M40....65 A1
Wharfedale Rd M40 ....65 A1
Wharf End M17........161 A2
Wharf Rd
Altrincham WA14.......119 D7
Sale M33 ....108 C3
WHARFSIDE 97 A3
Wharfside Ave **11** M30...95 D8
Wharfside Bsns Ctr
M17 ....96 F6
Wharfside Bsns Pk
M44.....................106 A7
Wharfside Way (Trafford
Park Rd) M17..........96 E6
Wharf St
Dukinfield SK16........166 C1
Oldham OL10...........66 B3
Stockport SK4, SK5...169 B3
Wharf The OL3 ....51 B2
Wharmton Rise OL4 ....68 E6
Wharmton School Cotts
OL3.......................50 F1
Wharmton View
Mossley OL5...........68 E3
Uppermill OL3..........69 B4
Wharncliffe Cl SK13 ...171 B4
Wharncliffe St **8** WN2...56 D5
Wharton Ave M21 .....109 D7
Wharton Hall Cl M29 ...59 B1
Wharton La M38........59 D4
Wharton Lo M30.......79 E3
Wharton Prim Sch
M38.......................59 E6
Wheat Cl M13 ....163 C1
Wheatcroft SK13 ......171 A4
Wheat Croft SK3 ......170 C1
Wheater's St M7 ......158 A4
Wheater's Terr M7.....158 A4
Wheatfield SK15........102 E7
Wheatfield Cl
Bury BL9 ....27 F7
Romiley SK6............113 A4
Wheatfield Cres OL2...48 C3
Wheatfield Ho OL12....48 D3
Wheatfield St BL2 .....148 C1
Wheathill St M41.......31 A4
Wheatlea Ind Est WN3...54 F1
Wheatlea Rd WN3......54 F2
Wheatley Ave WA12....89 C5
Wheatley Rd M27......61 D2
Wheatley Wlk M12.....165 A2
Wheatsheaf Ctr The
OL16.....................139 C4
Wheatsheaf Ind Est
M27 ....62 D1
Wheatsheaf Wlk WN6...19 D1
Wheeldale OL4 ....67 D6
Wheeldale Cl BL1......143 B2
Wheel Forge Way
Stretford M17..........96 A6
Trafford M17..........95 F6
Wheelock Cl SK9 ......131 D1
Wheelton Cl BL8.......27 A1
Wheelwright Cl
Marple SK6............125 F8
Rochdale OL11.........30 B4
Wheelwright Dr OL16...15 C3
Whelan Ave BL9 ....44 E7
Whelan Cl BL9 ....44 E7
Wheler St M11, M43...99 E8
WHELLEY 37 E2
Whelley WN1, WN2.....37 E2
Whelley Hospl (General)
WN1.......................37 F2
Whernside Ave
Ashton-u-L OL6 ....85 C7
Manchester M40 ....65 A1
Whernside Cl SK4......169 B3
Whetmorhurst La
SK6.....................126 E4
Whetstone Hill Cl OL16...49 E2
Whetstone Hill La
Oldham OL1............49 C1
6 Oldham OL1..........49 D1
Whetstone Hill Rd OL1...49 B1
Whewell Ave M26 .....44 F8
Whewell St **8** M29 ....59 A1
Whickham Cl M14 .....98 B3
Whiley St M13..........98 F4
Whimberry Cl M5......161 C3
Whimberry Dr SK15....86 B3
Whimberry Way M20...110 D6
Whimbrel Ave WA12...89 C3
Whimbrel Rd
Hazel Grove SK2 ......125 A5
Tyldesley M29 ....77 C7
Whinberry Rd WA14...119 B7

Whinberry Way OL4 . . . . . .49 F4
Whinchat Ave WA12 . . . . . .89 C4
Whinchat Cl
  Golborne WA3 . . . . .90 E7
  Hazel Grove SK2 . . . . . . .125 A4
Whinfell Dr M24 . . . . .46 C1
Whinfield Cl WN6 . . . . . . .150 A4
Whingroves Wlk 3
  M40 . . . . .83 A6
Whinmoor Wlk M40 . . . . . .83 B7
Whins Ave BL4 . . . . .59 E8
Whins Crest BL6 . . . . .40 C7
Whinslee Ct BL6 . . . . .40 C7
Whinslee Dr BL6 . . . . .40 C7
Whinstone Way OL1
  OL9 . . . . .47 E1
Whipney La BL8 . . . . .10 E1
Whipp St OL10 . . . . .29 B3
Whirley Cl SK4 . . . . .111 D5
Whistlecroft Ct WN2 . . . . .151 C2
Whistley St WN3 . . . . .56 B3
Whiston Dr BL2 . . . . .148 C2
Whiston Rd M8 . . . . .64 A1
Whitaker St M24 . . . . .64 F8
Whitbeam Gr M22 . . . . . . .56 E2
Whitbrook Way M24 . . . . . .47 C5
Whitburn Ave M13 . . . . . . .98 E2
Whitburn Cl
  Bolton BL3 . . . . .40 E4
  Garswood WN4 . . . . .72 D4
Whitburn Dr BL8 . . . . .27 C5
Whitburn Rd M23 . . . . . . .121 A4
Whitby Ave
  Heywood OL10 . . . . .29 C3
  Manchester M14 . . . . . . .110 E8
  Manchester, Whalley Range
  M16 . . . . .97 D3
  Salford M6 . . . . .80 C3
  Urmston M41 . . . . .95 E2
Whitby Cl
  Bury BL8 . . . . .26 F2
  Cheadle SK8 . . . . .122 C6
  Poynton SK12 . . . . .133 D4
Whitby Rd
  Manchester M14 . . . . . . .110 E8
  Oldham OL8 . . . . .67 C4
Whitby St
  Middleton M24 . . . . .47 C1
  Rochdale OL11 . . . . .31 A5
Whitchurch Dr M16 . . . . . .162 A1
Whitchurch Gdns 8
  BL1 . . . . .143 B2
Whitchurch Rd M20 . . . . . .110 A7
Whiteacre WN6 . . . . .19 A2
Whiteacre Rd OL6 . . . . .85 D4
Whiteacres M27 . . . . .79 D7
Whiteanchor Wlk M15 . . . .162 B1
White Bank Ave SK5 . . . . .112 C4
White Bank Rd OL8 . . . . . .66 E1
Whitebeam Cl
  Altrincham WA15 . . . . . . .120 E5
  Newhey OL16 . . . . .32 A3
  Salford M6 . . . . .81 A3
Whitebeam Ct M6 . . . . .81 A3
Whitebeam Wlk
  1 Sale M33 . . . . .107 D5
  Westhoughton BL5 . . . . . .39 F2
Whitebeck Ct M9 . . . . .65 A4
White Birk Cl BL8 . . . . .10 F2
White Brook La
  Uppermill OL3 . . . . .69 C8
  Uppermill, Tunstead OL3 . .69 D6
Whitebrook Rd M14 . . . . . .98 B1
White Broom WA13 . . . . . .117 B4
Whitecar Ave M40 . . . . . . .65 C1
Whitecarr La M23,
  WA15 . . . . .120 E3
White Carr La BL9 . . . . .12 A1
Whitechapel Cl BL2 . . . . . .42 E7
Whitechapel St M20 . . . . .110 B3
White City Ret Pk
  M16 . . . . .161 A1
White City Way M16 . . . . .161 A1
Whitecliff Cl M14 . . . . .98 C3
Whitecroft Ave
  Golborne WA3 . . . . .74 E1
  Shaw OL2 . . . . .49 D7
Whitecroft Dr BL8 . . . . .27 C5
Whitecroft Gdns 3
  M19 . . . . .110 E4
Whitecroft Rd
  Bolton BL1 . . . . .142 A1
  Marple SK6 . . . . .126 C1
  Wigan WN3 . . . . .55 B2
Whitecroft St 12 OL1, OL4 . .
Whitecroft Villas M31 . . . .105 E2
WHITEFIELD 62 E7
Whitefield
  Lymm WA13 . . . . .117 A4
  Pendlebury M6 . . . . .80 D6
  Stockport SK4 . . . . .169 A3
Whitefield Ave
  Newton-le-W WA12 . . . . . .89 E2
  Rochdale OL11 . . . . .29 F8
Whitefield Cl
  Golborne WA3 . . . . .90 A8
  Lymm WA13 . . . . .117 A5
Whitefield Com Prim Sch
  M45 . . . . .62 E7
Whitefield Ct WA3 . . . . .91 F2
Whitefield Gr WA13 . . . . . .117 A4
Whitefield Rd
  Bury BL9 . . . . .44 D7
  Romiley SK6 . . . . .112 E4
  Sale M33 . . . . .108 A5
Whitefield Sta M45 . . . . . .44 F1
Whitefriar Ct M3 . . . . .158 B3

Whitefriars Wlk 2
  M22 . . . . .130 D8
Whitegate
  Bolton BL3 . . . . .40 C2
  Rochdale OL15 . . . . .15 E4
WHITE GATE 65 F4
Whitegate Ave
  Culcheth WA3 . . . . .91 F2
  Oldham OL9 . . . . .65 F4
Whitegate Cl M40 . . . . .65 E1
Whitegate Dr
  Bolton, Astley Bridge
  BL1 . . . . .24 F5
  Bolton BL1 . . . . .143 C4
  Salford M5 . . . . .154 A2
  Swinton M27 . . . . .62 B2
WHITE GATE END 65 E3
Whitegate End Prim Sch
  OL9 . . . . .65 E4
Whitegate La 1 OL9 . . . . . .66 A4
Whitegate Pk M41 . . . . .94 E2
Whitegate Rd OL9 . . . . .65 E3
Whitegates
  Cheadle SK8 . . . . .122 D5
  Mottram in L SK14 . . . . . .103 A1
Whitegates Cl WA15 . . . . .120 B5
Whitegates La OL4 . . . . .50 B2
Whitegates Rd
  Cheadle SK8 . . . . .122 D5
  Middleton M24 . . . . .47 C4
Whitehall Ave WN6 . . . . . . .35 E8
Whitehall Ct SK9 . . . . .137 A5
Whitehall La
  Blackrod BL6 . . . . .21 D3
  Bolton BL1 . . . . .24 D6
  Oldham OL4 . . . . .49 F4
Whitehall Rd
  Manchester M20 . . . . . . .110 C3
  Sale M33 . . . . .108 B3
Whitehall St
  Ince-in-M WN3 . . . . .151 B2
  Oldham OL1 . . . . .153 C4
  Rochdale OL12 . . . . .14 F1
White Hart Mdw 2
  M20 . . . . .47 A2
White Hart St SK14 . . . . . .167 A4
Whitehaven Gdns
  M20 . . . . .110 A2
Whitehaven Pl SK14 . . . . .101 C5
Whitehaven Rd SK7 . . . . . .132 C5
Whitehead Cl OL3 . . . . .68 E5
Whitehead Cres
  Bury BL8 . . . . .27 C5
  Kearsley M26 . . . . .61 C7
Whitehead Rd
  Stretford M21 . . . . .108 F8
  Swinton M27 . . . . .62 B2
Whiteheads Pl OL4 . . . . . . .67 F7
Whitehead St
  Denton M34 . . . . .100 F7
  Middleton M24 . . . . .47 C1
  Milnrow OL16 . . . . .31 E6
  Shaw OL2 . . . . .48 F8
  Walkden M28 . . . . .60 D4
White Hill Cl OL12 . . . . .14 C4
Whitehill Cotts BL1 . . . . . .24 D6
Whitehill Dr M40 . . . . .83 A7
Whitehill Ind Est SK4,
  SK5 . . . . .111 E5
Whitehill St W SK4 . . . . . .169 B4
Whitehill St SK5 . . . . .111 E5
Whiteholme Ave M21 . . . . .109 D4
White Horse Gdns 2
  M27 . . . . .61 F8
White Horse Gr BL5 . . . . . .40 A2
White Horse Mdws
  OL16 . . . . .31 C2
Whitehouse Ave 4
  OL4 . . . . .67 C6
White House Ave M8 . . . . . .63 F3
White House Cl OL10 . . . . . .46 D7
Whitehouse Dr
  Altrincham WA14 . . . . . . .128 B8
  Wythenshawe M23 . . . . . .121 A5
Whitehouse La WA14 . . . . .118 D8
Whitehurst Rd SK4 . . . . . .110 F4
Whitekirk Cl M13 . . . . .163 B2
White Lady Cl 2 M28 . . . . . .59 F3
Whitelake Ave M41 . . . . . . .94 F2
Whitelake View M41 . . . . . .94 F3
Whiteland Ave BL3 . . . . . .144 C1
Whitelands Rd OL6,
  SK15 . . . . .85 D2
Whitelands Terr OL6 . . . . .166 C2
Whiteledge St M3 . . . . . . .170 A1
White Lee Croft M46 . . . . . .58 B3
Whitelees Rd OL15 . . . . . . .16 A5
Whitelegge St BL8 . . . . .27 B4
Whiteley Dr M24 . . . . .65 C7
Whiteley Pl WA14 . . . . . . .119 D6
Whiteley's Fly 6 OL12 . . . .139 B4
Whiteley St
  Droylsden M11 . . . . .83 C2
  Oldham OL9 . . . . .66 B4
White Lion Brow BL1 . . . . .145 B3
White Lodge Dr WN4 . . . . . .73 D4
Whitelow Rd
  Manchester M21 . . . . . . .109 A8
  Ramsbottom BL0 . . . . .11 E5
  Stockport, Heaton Moor
  SK4 . . . . .168 A3
Whitemoss OL12 . . . . .14 B2
White Moss Ave M21 . . . . .109 D8

White Moss Gdns M9 . . . . .65 A2
White Moss Rd M9 . . . . . . .64 E3
Whiteoak Cl SK6 . . . . .125 E7
Whiteoak Ct M14 . . . . .110 C8
Whiteoak Rd M14 . . . . . . .110 C8
Whiteoak View M13 . . . . . .42 D5
White Rd SK22 . . . . .127 C2
Whites Croft M27 . . . . .79 F8
Whiteside Ave
  Hindley WN2 . . . . .56 E7
  2 Wigan WN2 . . . . .37 A1
Whiteside Cl M5 . . . . .154 A2
Whiteside Fold OL12 . . . . . .14 A1
White Slack Gate OL14 . . . . .6 A6
Whitesmead Cl SK12 . . . . .135 D5
White St
  Bury M6 . . . . .27 C1
  Leigh WN7 . . . . .76 C4
  Manchester M15 . . . . . . .162 A2
  Salford M6 . . . . .154 B1
  5 Wigan WN5 . . . . .54 B6
Whitestar Ct 3 M44 . . . . . .94 A2
Whitestone Cl BL6 . . . . .40 C4
Whitestone Ho 10
  OL1 . . . . .153 B4
Whitestone Wlk M13 . . . . .164 A1
White Swallows Rd
  M27 . . . . .80 B6
White Swan Ind Est 5
  OL1 . . . . .67 C8
Whitethorn Ave
  3 Manchester M19 . . . .110 F7
  1 Manchester, Whalley
  Range M16 . . . . .97 D3
Whitethorn Cl SK6 . . . . . . .125 E7
Whitewater Dr M7 . . . . . . .80 F8
Whiteway St M9 . . . . .157 B3
Whitewell Cl
  Bury BL9 . . . . .44 D7
  Rochdale OL16 . . . . .31 C8
Whitewillow Cl M35 . . . . . .84 A6
Whitewood Cl WN4 . . . . . . .73 A6
WHITFIELD 116 D8
Whitfield Ave SK13 . . . . . .116 C7
Whitfield Brows OL15 . . . . .16 C7
Whitfield Cres OL16 . . . . . .32 B3
Whitfield Cross SK13 . . . . .116 D7
Whitfield Dr OL16 . . . . .31 E5
Whitfield Pk SK13 . . . . . . .116 C7
Whitfield Rise OL2 . . . . . . .32 A3
Whitfield St
  Leigh WN7 . . . . .76 C4
  Manchester M3 . . . . .159 A4
Whitfield Wells SK13 . . . . .116 D7
Whitford Wlk M40 . . . . . . .160 A3
Whiting Gr BL3 . . . . .40 E6
Whitinlea Cl WN2 . . . . .57 C3
Whit La
  Manchester M6 . . . . .80 F6
  Salford M6 . . . . .81 A5
Whitland Ave BL1 . . . . .40 F8
Whitland Dr OL8 . . . . .66 B2
White Bank Rd SK22 . . . . .127 B2
Whitledge Gn WN4 . . . . . . .73 A5
Whitledge Rd WN4 . . . . . . .73 A5
White Rd SK22 . . . . .127 C1
WHITLEY 37 C3
Whitley Cres
  Abram Brow WN2 . . . . . . .74 B7
  Wigan WN1 . . . . .37 C4
Whitley Gdns WA15 . . . . . .120 C7
Whitley Pl WA15 . . . . .120 C7
Whitley Rd
  Manchester M40 . . . . . . .159 C4
  Stockport, Heaton Moor
  SK4 . . . . .168 B3
  Up Holland WN8 . . . . .35 D3
Whitley St BL4 . . . . .42 D2
Whitley Wlk SK13 . . . . . . .115 F8
Whitlow Ave
  Altrincham WA14 . . . . . . .119 B8
  Golborne WA3 . . . . .73 F1
Whitman St M40, M9 . . . . .157 C4
Whitmore Rd M14 . . . . .98 B1
Whitnall St
  Dukinfield SK14 . . . . .101 D5
  Manchester M16 . . . . .97 E4
Whitsand Rd M22 . . . . . . .121 E5
Whitsbury Ave
  Hindley WN2 . . . . .56 D4
  Manchester M18 . . . . .99 D3
Whitstable Cl OL9 . . . . . . .152 B2
Whitstable Rd M40 . . . . . . .65 C1
Whitsters Hollow BL1 . . . .142 B3
Whitsundale BL5 . . . . .39 F2
Whitswood Cl 2 M16 . . . . .97 E3
Whittaker Dr OL15 . . . . . . .15 F2
Whittaker La
  Littleborough OL15 . . . . . .16 E4
  Prestwich M25 . . . . .63 C4
  Rochdale OL11 . . . . .13 D1
Whittaker Moss Prim Sch
  OL11 . . . . .13 D1
Whittaker St
  Ashton-u-L OL6 . . . . .85 D5
  Manchester M40 . . . . .83 A8
  Radcliffe M26 . . . . .44 B4
  6 Rochdale OL11 . . . . . . .13 E1
  Royton OL2 . . . . .48 D4
Whittingham Dr BL0 . . . . . .11 C3
Whittingham Gr OL1 . . . . .153 E8
Whittington St OL7 . . . . . .166 A1
WHITTLE BROOK 60 E2
Whittlebrook Gr OL10 . . . . .46 E7
Whittle Dr
  Shaw OL2 . . . . .49 D8
  Walkden M28 . . . . .60 D5

Whittle Gr
  Bolton BL1 . . . . .142 B1
  Walkden M28 . . . . .60 E3
Whittle Hill BL7 . . . . .8 E3
Whittle La OL10 . . . . .46 B4
Whittles Ave M34 . . . . . . .101 A2
Whittle's Croft M1 . . . . . . .159 B1
Whittle's Croft Wharf
  M1 . . . . .159 B1
Whittles St OL13 . . . . .4 B8
Whittle St
  Bury BL8 . . . . .27 C3
  Littleborough OL15 . . . . . .15 F5
  Manchester M4 . . . . .159 B2
  Swinton M27 . . . . .79 E7
  Walkden M28 . . . . .60 E3
Whittles Terr OL16 . . . . . . .32 C4
Whittles Wlk M34 . . . . . . .101 A2
Whitwell Bank 5
  SK13 . . . . .171 A2
Whitwell Cl
  4 Gamesley SK13 . . . . .171 A2
  Standish WN6 . . . . .19 D2
Whitwell Fold 1
  SK13 . . . . .171 A2
Whitwell Gdns SK6 . . . . . . .22 B5
Whitwell Gn 2 SK13 . . . . .171 A2
Whitwell Lea 3 SK13 . . . .171 A2
Whitwell Way M18 . . . . . . .165 C1
Whitworth Ave M13 . . . . . .98 E4
Whitworth Cl 6 SK13 . . . .171 A2
WHITWORTH 14 D8
Whitworth Art Gall ★
  M15 . . . . .98 B4
Whitworth Cl OL10 . . . . . .166 C4
Whitworth Com High Sch
  OL12 . . . . .14 D8
Whitworth Heritage Mus ★
  OL12 . . . . .4 C2
Whitworth La M14 . . . . . . .98 D3
Whitworth Park Mans
  M14 . . . . .98 A4
Whitworth Rake OL12 . . . . .14 D8
Whitworth Rd OL12 . . . . . .14 A7
Whitworth St E M11 . . . . . .165 C3
Whitworth St W M1,
  M3 . . . . .162 C4
Whitworth Sq OL12 . . . . . .14 D8
Whitworth St
  Horwich BL6 . . . . .22 C2
  Manchester, City Centre
  M1 . . . . .163 A4
  Manchester, Openshaw
  M11 . . . . .165 B3
  Milnrow OL16 . . . . .31 F6
  Rochdale OL16 . . . . .15 A1
Whitworth Water Ski Ctr ★
  OL12 . . . . .4 C2
Whixhall Ave M12 . . . . . . .164 B2
Whoolden St BL4 . . . . .42 C1
Whowell Fold BL1 . . . . . . .142 A2
Whowell St BL3 . . . . .145 B2
Wibbersley Pk M41 . . . . . . .94 F2
Wibsey Cotts OL3 . . . . .33 D2
Wichbrook Rd 13 M28 . . . . .59 F3
Wicheaves Cres M28 . . . . . .60 A3
Wicheries The M28 . . . . . . .59 F3
Wicken Bank OL10 . . . . . . .46 E7
Wickenby Dr M33 . . . . . . .108 A4
Wicken St SK2 . . . . .124 B6
Wickentree Holt OL12 . . . . .14 A1
Wickentree La M35 . . . . . . .66 A1
Wicker La WA15 . . . . .129 C8
Wicket Gr M27 . . . . .61 E8
Wickham Terr 11 M24 . . . . .47 A2
Wickliffe St 10 BL1 . . . . . .145 B4
Wicklow Ave SK3 . . . . .123 B8
Wicklow Dr M22 . . . . .121 E2
Wicklow Gr 3 OL8 . . . . . . .66 E3
Wickmere Wlk M8 . . . . . . .155 C2
Widcombe Dr BL2 . . . . .42 F5
Widdop St OL9 . . . . .153 A3
Widdow's St WN7 . . . . .76 B4
Widdrington Rd WN1 . . . . . .37 D2
Widecombe Cl M41 . . . . . . .95 B4
Widford Wlk BL6 . . . . .21 E1
Widgeon Cl
  Manchester M14 . . . . . . .110 B8
  Poynton SK12 . . . . .133 B4
Widgeon Rd WA14 . . . . . . .119 B8
Widnes St M11 . . . . .165 C3
Wiend WN1 . . . . .150 C4
WIGAN 150 B4
Wigan Athletic FC &
  Wigan Warriors RLFC
  (JJB Stad) WN5 . . . . .54 F8
Wigan Ent Pk WN2 . . . . . . .56 A6
Wigan Gallery 2
  WN1 . . . . .150 C4
Wigan History Shop ★
  WN1 . . . . .150 C4
Wigan La
  Adlington PR7, WN1 . . . . .20 D7
  Wigan WN1 . . . . .37 C4
Wigan & Leigh Coll (Leigh
  Sixth Form Coll)
  WN7 . . . . .75 E3
Wigan & Leigh Coll
  (Linacre Bldg) WN1 . . . . .37 B1
Wigan & Leigh Coll
  (Pagefield Bldg)
  WN1 . . . . .37 B2
Wigan & Leigh Coll
  (Parsons Wlk) WN1 . . . . .150 B4
Wigan & Leigh Coll
  (Railway Road Bldg)
  WN7 . . . . .75 E5

Wigan & Leigh Coll (The
  Image Ctr) WN7 . . . . .75 E5
Wigan Little Theatre
  WN1 . . . . .151 A4
Wigan Lower Rd WN6 . . . . .36 C3
Wigan North Western Sta
  WN3 . . . . .150 C3
Wigan Pier ★ WN3 . . . . . .150 B3
Wigan Rd
  Ashton-in-M WN4 . . . . . . .73 A5
  Aspull WN2 . . . . .38 B4
  Atherton M46 . . . . .58 B3
  Billinge WN5 . . . . .71 F7
  Bolton, Knutshaw Bridge
  BL3 . . . . .40 C2
  Bolton, Willows BL3 . . . . .144 B1
  Golborne WA3 . . . . .74 B3
  Leigh WN7 . . . . .75 D7
  Shevington WN6 . . . . .36 B5
  Standish WN6 . . . . .37 A6
  Westhoughton BL5 . . . . . .57 C7
Wigan Sq WN1 . . . . .150 C4
Wigan St WN2 . . . . .56 A1
Wigan Wallgate Sta
  WN1 . . . . .150 C4
Wiggins Wlk 13 M14 . . . . . .98 C3
Wightman Ave WA12 . . . . . .89 C5
Wighurst Wlk 6 M22 . . . . .121 D1
Wigley St M12 . . . . .164 B3
Wigmore Rd M8 . . . . .156 B3
Wigmore St 15 OL6 . . . . . .85 D4
Wigsby Ave M40 . . . . .65 C2
Wigsey La WA13 . . . . .117 A7
WIGSHAW 91 D2
Wigshaw Cl WN7 . . . . .75 F1
Wigshaw La WA3 . . . . .91 D2
Wigwam Cl SK12 . . . . .133 C4
Wike St BL8 . . . . .140 A3
Wilberforce Cl M15 . . . . . .162 C1
Wilbraham Prim Sch
  M14 . . . . .98 A1
Wilbraham Rd
  Manchester M14, M16,
  M21 . . . . .97 C1
  Walkden M28 . . . . .60 E3
Wilbraham St
  Leigh WN7 . . . . .75 C5
  Westhoughton BL5 . . . . . .57 C8
Wilburn St M5 . . . . .162 A4
Wilby Ave BL3 . . . . .43 B5
Wilby Cl BL8 . . . . .27 D5
Wilby St M8 . . . . .156 B2
Wilcock Rd WA11 . . . . .89 B8
Wilcockson Ho 4 BL4 . . . . .60 D8
Wilcock St
  Manchester M16 . . . . .97 E4
  Wigan WN3 . . . . .150 A3
Wilcott Dr
  Sale M33 . . . . .107 E5
  Wilmslow SK9 . . . . .136 F4
Wilcott Rd SK8 . . . . .122 A5
Wild Arum Cl 8 WA3 . . . . . .90 E8
Wildbank Chase SK15 . . . .102 E7
Wild Bank Com Sch
  SK15 . . . . .86 D2
Wildbrook Cl M38 . . . . .59 E3
Wildbrook Cres OL8 . . . . . .67 A2
Wildbrook Gr M38 . . . . .59 E3
Wildbrook Rd M38 . . . . .59 E3
Wildbrook Terr OL8 . . . . . .67 A2
Wild Clough SK14 . . . . . . .167 C1
Wildcroft Ave M40 . . . . . . .65 A1
Wilders Moor Cl 3
  M28 . . . . .78 C8
Wilderswood Ave BL6 . . . . .22 C4
Wilderswood Cl M20 . . . . .110 C5
Wilderswood Ct BL6 . . . . . .22 D4
Wilde St M34 . . . . .100 F3
Wild Ho OL8 . . . . .153 C1
Wildhouse La OL16 . . . . . . .31 F8
Wilding St WN3 . . . . .151 B2
Wildman La BL4 . . . . .59 F8
Wildmoor Ave OL4 . . . . . . .67 E4
Wild Moor Wood Cl
  SK15 . . . . .86 D5
Wild's Pas WN7 . . . . .75 F4
Wilds Pl BL0 . . . . .138 B1
Wild's Sq 8 OL5 . . . . .68 C2
Wild St
  Dukinfield SK16 . . . . .101 D8
  Hazel Grove SK7 . . . . . . .124 E2
  Heywood OL10 . . . . .29 E2
  Oldham, Mumps OL1 . . . . .67 A7
  Oldham OL4 . . . . .67 E6
  Radcliffe M26 . . . . .44 D4
  Romiley SK6 . . . . .112 F3
  Shaw OL2 . . . . .149 C2
  Stockport SK2 . . . . .124 A6
Wildwood Cl
  Ramsbottom BL0 . . . . .11 A4
  Stockport SK2 . . . . .124 A5
Wilford Ave M33 . . . . .108 A2
Wilford Dr BL9 . . . . .141 B4
Wilford Rd
  Eccles M30 . . . . .95 A8
  Walkden M28 . . . . .60 D2
Wilford St
  Bolton BL7 . . . . .25 A7
  Manchester M40 . . . . .83 A4
  Oldham OL4 . . . . .67 B6
  Salford M7 . . . . .158 B4
  Wigan WN5 . . . . .54 F7
Wilfrid's Pl WN6 . . . . .19 F1
Wilfrid St M27 . . . . .61 F1
Wilham Ave 7 M30 . . . . . . .79 D1

Wilkesley Ave WN6 ....36 C8
Wilkes St OL1 ....49 D3
Wilkin Croft SK8............122 E1
Wilkins La SK9 ....130 E5
Wilkinson Ave BL3...........43 A5
Wilkinson Rd BL1...........24 D5
Wilkinson St
  Ashton-u-L OL6 ....166 A2
  Leigh WN7 ....75 E5
  3 Sale M33 ....108 D4
  Stockport SK4...........169 B2
Wilks Ave M22..............121 F3
Willand Cl BL2 ....43 A6
Willand Dr BL2 ....43 A6
Willan Ent Ctr
  Chadderton OL9..........152 B3
  Stretford M17............96 C6
Willan Ind Est M50 ....154 C1
Willan Rd
  Eccles M30 ....79 E2
  Manchester M9 ....64 C4
Willard Ave WN5 ....53 D3
Willard St SK7.............124 D3
Willaston Cl M21 ....109 A7
Willaston Way **8**
  SK9....................131 D5
Willbutts La OL11..........30 C8
Willdale Cl M11 ....83 A2
Willdor Gr SK3 ....123 B6
Willenhall Rd M23 ....109 C2
Willerby Rd M7............155 B1
Willesden Ave M13 ....98 E3
Will Griffith Wlk M11 .....164 B4
William Chadwick Cl **1**
  M40 ....159 C3
William Cl M41.............95 C2
William Coates Ct **8**
  M16 ....97 D3
William Fairburn Way **11**
  M4 ....159 A2
William Greenwood Cl
  OL10...................29 C2
William Henry St **2**
  OL11...................31 A4
William Hulme's Gram Sch
  M16 ....97 F1
William Jessop Ct
  M1 ....159 C1
William Kay Cl M16........97 E4
William Lister Cl M40......83 D4
Williams Ave WA12.........89 C5
Williams Cres OL9 ....65 F3
Williams Ct **4** M14 ....98 D4
Williamson Ave
  Radcliffe M26 ....43 F6
  Romiley SK6............113 A4
Williamson La M43 ....100 B8
Williamson St
  Ashton-u-L OL6 ....166 B3
  Manchester M4 ....159 B3
  Reddish SK5.............111 F7
Williamson's Yd **6**
  OL1....................67 B7
Williams Rd
  Failsworth M40 ....83 C7
  Manchester M18 ....165 C1
Williams St
  Little Lever BL3 ....43 B3
  Manchester M18 ....165 C1
William St
  Ashton-u-L OL7 ....84 F2
  Ashton-u-L OL7 ....166 A1
  Britannia OL13...........4 C8
  Failsworth M35...........66 A1
  Hindley WN2 ....56 E5
  Horwich BL6 ....22 A3
  Ince-in-M WN3 ....151 A2
  8 Leigh WN7 ....76 A5
  Leigh WN7 ....76 A5
  Littleborough OL15 .....16 A5
  Manchester, Ardwick
    M12 ....164 A4
  Manchester, Didsbury
    M20 ....110 B3
  Middleton M24..........65 B8
  Radcliffe M26 ....44 B4
  Ramsbottom BL0 ....1 C1
  Rochdale OL11.........139 C2
  Rochdale, Wuerdle OL16 ...13 D4
  Salford M3.............158 B2
  Whitworth OL12...........4 C1
William Way WN7 ....75 B1
Willingdon Cl BL8 ....27 C7
Willingdon Dr M25 ....63 B5
Willis Rd SK3 ....170 B2
Willis St BL3 ....146 C4
Williton Wlk **6** M22 ......121 F3
Willock St M7 ....155 C2
Willoughby Ave M20 ......110 C4
Willoughby Cl M33 ....108 A5
Willow Ave
  Cheadle SK8 ....122 F2
  Middleton M24..........65 C8
  Newton-le-W WA12......89 E4
  Reddish SK5............169 C4
  Tyldesley M29 ....77 A6
  Urmston M41............95 E2
Willowbank M26............61 F8
Willow Bank
  Altrincham WA15........120 A6
  Cheadle SK8 ....132 A6
  Manchester, Fallowfield
    M14 ....110 C8

Willow Bank *continued*
  1 Manchester, Harpurhey
    M9 ....157 B3
  Oldham OL4.............54 A4
Willowbank Ave BL2 ......148 B2
Willow Bank Cl SK2......124 D7
Willow Bank Ct M20 .....122 B8
Willow Bank Est WA12....89 F4
Willowbrook Ave M40.....83 A7
Willowbrook Dr WN6 ......36 B7
Willowbrook Gdns
  M22 ....121 C4
Willow Cl
  Adlington PR6 ....21 B8
  Bolton BL3.............146 B4
  Dukinfield SK16.........101 F7
  Paddockhill WA16.......136 B5
  Poynton SK12 ....133 E3
  Whitefield BL9 ....45 B3
Willow Cres WN4.........137 F8
Willowcroft Ave WN2 .....38 F3
Willow Ct
  Gatley SK8.............122 A6
  Manchester, Fallowfield
    M14 ....110 C8
  Manchester M14 ....98 D1
  Marple SK6.............125 F5
  Sale M33 ....108 E5
  Standish WN6 ....19 E2
Willowdale WA12 ....89 E3
Willowdale Ave SK8 .....122 B2
Willowdene Cl
  Bolton BL7 ....24 F8
  3 Manchester M40 ...156 C1
Willow Dr
  Handforth SK9 ....131 D3
  Hindley WN2 ....56 F3
  Sale M33 ....107 E2
  Whitefield BL9 ....45 B2
Willowfield Gr WN4 ......73 A2
Willowfield Rd OL4 ......49 D2
Willow Fold M41.........100 B8
Willow Gr
  Ashton-in-M WN4 ....73 E5
  Chadderton OL9.........152 B4
  Denton M34............100 E3
  Golborne WA3 ....74 A1
  Manchester M18 ....99 E4
  Marple SK6.............125 F5
Willow Hey BL7..........8 E2
Willow Hill Rd M8 ....64 A1
Willow Lawn SK8........123 A2
Willow Lo **1** WN2 ....56 B1
Willow Mead SK6 ....123 F1
Willowmead Way OL12....14 A2
Willowmoss Cl M28......60 E1
Willow Pk
  Manchester M14 ....110 C8
  Stockport SK2..........124 C7
Willow Rd
  Eccles M30 ....79 A4
  High Lane SK6..........134 F7
  Newton-le-W WA12......89 E4
  Partition M31..........105 E2
  Prestwich M25, M45 .....63 A6
  Uppermill OL3 ....69 C7
Willow Rise OL15 ....15 F3
WILLOWS 144 C1
Willows Cl SK9 ....136 F6
Willows Cotts OL16 ......31 E6
Willows Dr M35 ....83 F5
Willows End SK15........86 D3
Willows La
  Bolton BL3 ....146 C4
  Milnrow OL16...........31 E6
Willows Prim Sch
  WA15..................120 A6
Willows Prim Sch The
  M22 ....121 C2
Willows Rd M5 ....154 A2
Willow St
  2 Abram WN2 ....56 B1
  Atherton M46...........58 C4
  Bury BL9 ....141 B3
  Droylsden M11..........83 A1
  Heywood OL10..........29 D2
  Manchester M8 ....158 B4
  Oldham OL1 ....67 A7
  Rawtenstall BL8 ....2 E8
  Swinton, Chorlton Fold
    M27 ....79 D5
  Swinton, Parkhurst M28 ...79 C7
Willows The
  5 Atherton M46.......58 D3
  Coppull PR7 ....19 E8
  Little Lever BL3 ....43 A5
  Manchester, Barlow Moor
    M21 ....109 A7
  Mossley OL5 ....68 E1
  Partington M31.........105 F3
  Sale M33 ....107 D2
  Stockport SK4..........168 A3
  Whitworth OL12.........14 C5
Willow Tree Cl WN1......37 B4
Willow Tree Ct
  1 Eccles M30........79 C1
  Sale M33 ....108 B3
Willow Tree Mews
  SK8....................122 B1
Willow Tree Rd
  WA14..................119 D3
Willow Way
  Bramhall SK7...........132 D7
  Manchester M20 ....110 C3
Willow Wood Cl OL6......85 E3
Wilma Ave M90 ....64 C4
Wilmans Wlk SK13 ......104 A6

Wilmcote Cl BL6...........40 D6
Wilmcote Gdns **2**
  SK6....................112 F3
Wilmington Rd M32 ....96 B2
Wilmot Dr WA3...........89 F7
Wilmot St BL1...........142 C3
Wilmott St
  Manchester M15 ....162 C3
  Manchester M15 ....163 A2
WILMSLOW 137 C5
Wilmslow Ave BL1........24 E5
Wilmslow Ct SK9 ....131 D3
Wilmslow Grange Prim
  Sch SK9 ....131 C4
Wilmslow High Sch
  SK9....................137 B6
Wilmslow Old Rd
  M90 ....130 A6
WILMSLOW PARK 137 D7
Wilmslow Pk N SK9.....137 D7
Wilmslow Pk S SK9......137 C7
Wilmslow Prep Sch
  SK9....................137 B7
Wilmslow Rd
  Alderley Edge SK9......137 A2
  Cheadle SK8 ....122 D3
  Cheadle SK8 ....122 D5
  Gatley SK8, SK9........131 C6
  Handforth SK9 ....131 D4
  Manchester, Didsbury
    M20 ....110 B1
  Manchester, East Didsbury
    M20 ....110 C1
  Manchester, Rusholme
    M14 ....98 C2
  Manchester, Withington M14,
    M20 ....110 B5
  Woodford SK7 ....132 C1
  Wythenshawe M90, SK9,
    WA15 ....129 F5
Wilmslow Sta SK9 ....137 C7
Wilmur Ave
  Salford M7 ....155 B2
  Whitefield M45 ....63 A7
Wilpshire Ave **6** M12...99 B3
Wilsford Cl WA3 ....74 B1
Wilsham Rd WN5 ....53 E5
Wilshaw Gr OL7 ....85 B6
Wilshaw La OL7 ....85 A5
Wilson Ave
  Heywood OL10..........29 A2
  Swinton M27 ....62 B2
  Wigan WN6 ....37 B2
Wilson Cres OL6.........85 E4
Wilson Fold Ave BL6....39 F8
Wilson Rd
  Manchester, Blackley
    M9 ....64 D1
  Stockport, Heaton Moor
    SK4.................168 B4
Wilsons Pk M40 ....157 B1
Wilson St
  8 Bolton BL3 ....145 C2
  Bury BL9 ....141 A1
  Farnworth BL4 ....60 E8
  Horwich BL6 ....22 A4
  Hyde SK14.............167 B2
  Manchester, Brunswick M12,
    M13 ....163 C2
  Manchester M11 ....165 A4
  Oldham OL8 ....66 E4
  Radcliffe M26 ....43 F4
  Rochdale OL12..........139 C4
  2 Sale M33 ....108 B5
  Stretford M32..........96 E4
  Swinton M27 ....79 D4
Wilson's Terr SK13.....116 B8
Wilson Way OL1.........153 C4
Wilstrope Cl M19.......111 C7
Wilton Ave
  Gatley SK8.............131 C7
  Manchester, Firswood
    M16 ....97 A3
  Manchester, Sedgley Park
    M25 ....63 D2
  Pendlebury M27 ....80 C7
  Wigan WN2 ....37 F2
Wilton Cotts WA3.........75 A2
Wilton Cres SK9 ....136 F2
Wilton Ct
  Middleton M25..........63 E8
  Reddish M34 ....100 A4
Wilton Dr
  Altrincham WA15........129 C8
  Whitefield BL9 ....45 A5
Wilton Gdns M26 ....44 C5
Wilton Gr
  Heywood OL10..........29 D1
  Reddish M34 ....100 A4
Wilton La WA3 ....91 B5
Wilton Paddock M34...100 A4
Wilton Pl M3 ....158 A2
Wilton Rd
  Bolton BL1 ....24 E5
  Manchester, Crumpsall
    M8 ....64 A2
  Manchester M21 ....109 B8
  Salford M6 ....80 B4
  Shevington WN6 ....36 A6
Wilton St
  Bolton BL1 ....143 C3
  Heywood OL10..........29 C2
  Middleton M24..........64 B7
  Oldham OL9 ....66 B3
  Prestwich M25 ....63 C4
  Reddish SK5 ....99 F2
  Whitefield M45 ....62 F7
  Wigan WN1 ....151 A3

Wilton Terr OL12..........139 B4
Wiltshire Ave SK5 ....112 C4
Wiltshire Cl BL9 ....45 A8
Wiltshire Dr
  Glossop SK13...........116 F8
  Haslingden BB4 ....1 B8
Wiltshire Pl WN5 ....54 C6
Wiltshire Rd
  Chadderton OL9.........152 B1
  Failsworth M35..........84 A6
  Partington M31.........105 E2
Wiltshire St M7..........155 B2
Wimberry Cl **2** OL3 ....69 B5
Wimberry Hill Rd BL5...39 D3
Wimbledon Dr
  Rochdale OL11..........139 A1
  Stockport SK3..........123 C2
Wimbledon Rd M35.......84 B8
Wimborne Ave
  Chadderton OL9.........48 A1
  Urmston M41............95 D3
Wimborne Cl
  Cheadle SK8 ....123 C4
  Horwich BL6 ....22 A4
Wimborne Rd WN5 ....54 A8
Wimpey Ho OL8..........153 B1
Wimpole St
  Ashton-u-L OL6 ....166 C3
  4 Oldham OL1 ....49 A1
Wimpory St M11..........99 D7
Winbolt St SK2 ....124 C4
Winby St **1** OL11.......31 A4
Wincanton Ave M23 .....120 D8
Wincanton Dr BL1........24 D7
Wincanton Pk OL4.......67 D6
Wince Cl M24 ....65 C6
Wincham Cl **24** M15...162 A2
Wincham Rd M33........107 E2
Winchcombe Cl WN7.....75 E1
Winchester Ave
  Ashton-u-L WN4 ....73 A3
  Ashton-u-L OL6 ....85 D8
  Chadderton OL9.........47 F1
  Denton M34............100 F1
  Heywood OL10..........46 C8
  Manchester M25 ....63 C2
  Tyldesley M29 ....77 C7
Winchester Cl
  Bury BL8 ....27 C7
  4 Orrell WN5 ....53 F7
  Rochdale OL11..........30 A7
  Winslow SK9 ....136 E5
Winchester Dr
  Sale M33 ....107 D4
  Stockport SK4..........168 B2
Winchester Gr WN3....151 A2
Winchester Pk M20 .....109 F3
Winchester Rd
  Altrincham WA15........120 C1
  Ashton-in-M WN4 ....72 E1
  Dukinfield SK16.........102 A7
  Longshaw WN5 ....53 D2
  Radcliffe M26 ....43 D5
  Salford M6 ....80 C4
  Urmston M41............95 E3
Winchester Way BL2....25 D1
Wincle Ave SK12.........133 F2
Wincombe St M14 ....98 B2
Windale M26 ....60 B3
Windcroft Cl M11........56 B4
Winder Dr M4 ....159 C2
Windermere Ave
  Atherton M46...........58 D5
  Little Lever BL3 ....43 A4
  Pendlebury M27 ....80 A7
  Reddish M34 ....100 B2
  Sale M33 ....108 D2
Windermere Cl
  Manchester M11 ....165 A4
  Prestwich M25..........62 F5
  Stretford M32..........96 C3
Windermere Cres OL7...84 F4
Windermere Ct WN7....75 E5
Windermere Dr
  Adlington PR6 ....21 B8
  Alderley Edge SK9......136 F1
  Bury BL9 ....44 E7
  Ramsbottom BL0 ....138 C3
Windermere Gr WN7....75 E6
Windermere Ho **3**
  M28 ....46 E3
Windermere Mews
  M24 ....46 E3
Windermere Rd
  Abram WN2 ....74 B8
  Dukinfield SK14.........101 C5
  Farnworth BL4..........59 E7
  Handforth SK9 ....131 C4
  High Lane SK6..........134 E8
  Hindley WN2 ....56 E5
  Ince-in-M WN3 ....56 B7
  Leigh WN7 ....75 E5
  Middleton M24..........46 D3
  Orrell WN5 ....53 F8
  Royton OL2 ....48 D6
  Stalybridge SK15........86 A4
  Stockport SK1..........124 B7
  Urmston M41............95 C1
Windermere St
  Bolton BL1 ....143 C2
  3 Rochdale OL12.....14 F7
  5 Wigan WN1 ....37 E1
Windermere Wlk **5**
  OL4....................67 C7
Winder St BL1...........145 C4
Winders Way M6 ....81 B4
Windfields Cl SK8 ......123 B3

Windgate Rise SK15 .....86 D5
Windham St OL16 ....15 C3
Windle Ave M9 ....63 F3
Windle Ct SK2...........124 E5
WINDLEHURST 125 E1
Windlehurst Ct SK6....134 D7
Windlehurst Dr M28 ....78 B7
Windlehurst Hall SK6...125 F1
Windlehurst Old Rd
  SK6....................125 F2
Windlehurst Rd SK6...125 E2
Windleshaw St WN3 ...151 B2
Windley St BL2 ....148 A4
Windmill Ave M5 ....161 B3
Windmill Cl
  Reddish M34 ....100 C2
  Walkden M28...........60 C5
  Wigan WN1 ....151 A4
Windmill Ct **21** OL16 ...31 B6
Windmill Hts WN8......53 A8
Windmill La
  Denton M34 ....100 C2
  Reddish SK5 ....100 A1
  Tyldesley M29 ....76 F4
Windmill Lane Ind Est
  M34 ....100 C2
Windmill Rd
  Sale M33 ....108 B3
  Walkden M28...........60 C5
Windmill St
  Manchester M2 ....162 C4
  20 Rochdale OL16....31 B6
Windmill Trad Est
  M34 ....100 D3
Windover Cl BL5.........59 A7
Windover St **1** BL3...146 A4
Windrush Ave BL0 ....11 A2
Windrush Dr
  Manchester M9 ....157 A3
  Westhoughton BL5 ......39 F1
Windrush Millennium Ctr
  12 M16 ....97 E4
Windrush The OL12....14 C4
Windsor Ave
  Poynton SK12 ....133 D4
  Ramsbottom BL8 ....11 A1
Windsor Cres
  Aspull WN2 ....38 D5
  Manchester M25 ....63 E3
Windsor Ct
  Bolton BL3 ....147 A2
  1 Denton M34 ....113 A8
  2 Sale M33 ....107 F5
Windsor Dr
  Altrincham, Bowdon
    WA14 ....118 F1
  Altrincham, Timperley
    WA14 ....119 F8
  Ashton-u-L OL7 ....84 F4
  Bury BL8 ....44 B8
  Droylsden M34..........84 D1
  Dukinfield SK14.........101 C5
  Haydock WA11..........89 A7
  Horwich BL6 ....22 E2
  Marple SK6.............125 E5
  Romiley SK6............112 C3
  Stalybridge SK15........86 A3
Windsor Gr
  Ashton-u-L OL6 ....85 C7
  Bolton BL1 ....142 C1
  Cheadle SK8 ....131 F8
  Hindley WN2 ....57 B3
  Kearsley M26...........61 B7
  Romiley SK6............113 E2
Windsor Ho M21 ....109 F8
Windsor Pl
  Ashton-in-M WN4 ....73 C1
  Billinge WN5 ....71 F5
  Bolton BL7 ....20 A7
  Droylsden M43..........83 E1
  Failsworth M40..........83 E4
  Golborne WA3 ....90 C8
  Hazel Grove SK7........124 F2
  Hyde SK14.............113 E7
  Leigh WN7 ....76 E6
  Manchester, Harpurhey
    M9 ....157 B3
  Manchester, Levenshulme
    M19 ....99 A1
  Manchester M25 ....63 E3
  Oldham OL8 ....66 D4
  Reddish M34 ....100 A3
  Up Holland WN8 ....53 A8
Windsor St
  Ashton-u-L, Holt Lane End
    M35 ....84 A8
  Failsworth M40..........83 E4
  Manchester M18 ....99 C4
  Oldham OL1 ....49 A1
  Rochdale OL11..........31 A5
  Salford M5.............81 B1

Windsor St *continued*
  Stockport SK2 124 A6
  Tyldesley M46 58 E2
  Wigan WN1 37 D1
Windsor Terr
  Milnrow OL16 31 E6
  Rochdale OL16 31 C7
  Stockport SK2 124 A6
Windsor Wlk SK2 170 C2
WINDY ARBOUR 72 B8
Windybank M9 64 C5
Windy Bank Ave WA3 90 E8
Windy Harbour La BL7 25 B8
Windyhill Dr BL3 146 A3
Winfell Dr M40 160 A3
Winfield Ave M20 110 D6
Winfield Dr M18 99 D6
Winfield Gr SK6 114 B1
Winfield St SK14 167 C2
Winford St M9 157 B4
Wingate Ave BL8 27 B2
Wingate Dr
  Altrincham WA15 120 B5
  Manchester M20 110 C2
  Whitefield M45 44 E1
Wingate Rd
  Stockport SK4 168 C4
  Walkden M38 60 B4
WINGATES 39 E2
Wingates Gr BL5 39 D3
Wingates Ind Est BL5 39 D2
Wingates La M46 39 E5
Wingates Rd WN1 37 C4
Wingates Sq BL5 39 D3
Wingate St OL11 13 E1
Wingfield Ave SK9 136 E6
Wingfield Cl WN6 37 A4
Wingfield Dr
  Pendlebury M27 80 A6
  Wilmslow SK9 136 E6
Wingfield Gr SK13 116 F7
Wingfield St M32 96 D4
Wingfield Villas OL15 16 C7
Wingrave Ho [8] M6 154 C2
Wings Gr OL10 46 D7
Winhill Rd SK22 127 C1
Winifred Ave BL9 28 F4
Winifred Rd
  Failsworth M40 83 B7
  Farnworth BL4 42 A1
  Manchester M10 157 A4
  Stockport SK2 124 A6
  Urmston M41 95 D2
Winifred St
  [2] Eccles M30 79 B1
  Hyde SK14 113 E7
  Ince-in-M WN3 151 B2
  Ramsbottom BL0 138 B1
  Rochdale OL12 14 E1
Winmarith Dr WA15 129 D7
Winmarleigh Cl BL8 26 F1
Winmarleigh Gdns
  WN7 75 E3
Winnall Wlk [3] M40 83 C6
Winnard St WA3 74 B2
Winnats Cl SK13 116 F8
Winnie St M40 83 A8
Winning Hill Cl M18 99 D4
Winnington Gn SK2 124 D6
Winnington Rd SK6 125 F7
Winnipeg Quay M50 96 F7
Winnows The M34 100 D3
Winscar Rd WN2 56 D6
Winscombe Dr M40 159 C4
Winser St M1 163 A4
Winsfield Rd SK7 133 E8
Winsford Dr OL11 29 E5
Winsford Gr BL3 40 F5
Winsford Rd M14 98 A1
Winskill Rd M44 106 A8
Winslade Cl
  Oldham OL4 49 D1
  Stockport SK7 124 A2
Winslade Mews BL4 42 D1
Winsley Rd M23 108 F2
Winslow Ave SK14 103 A2
Winslow Pl M19 110 F6
Winslow Rd BL3 40 D3
Winslow St M11 165 A4
Winsmoor Dr WN2 56 E4
Winson Cl BL3 147 B4
WINSTANLEY 54 C3
Winstanley Cl [6] M6 80 D5
Winstanley Coll WN5 53 F3
Winstanley Com Prim Sch
  WN3 54 C2
WINSTANLEY PARK 54 B2
Winstanley Pl WN3 151 B2
Winstanley Rd
  Ashton-in-M WN2 73 F8
  Garswood WN4, WN5 72 B6
  Manchester M40 160 A3
  Orrell WN5 53 F3
  Sale M33 108 C5
Winstanley St WN5 54 F6
Winster Ave
  Manchester M20 109 E4
  Salford M7 81 B6
  Stretford M32 96 A3
Winster Cl
  Bolton BL2 25 F1
  Whitefield M45 63 B8
Winster Dr
  Bolton BL2 25 F1
  [6] Middleton M24 46 E2
Winster Gn M30 95 B8
Winster Gr SK2 124 A6

Winster Mews SK13 171 B2
Winster Rd M30 95 B8
Winston Ave
  Little Lever BL3 43 C3
  Newton-le-W WA12 89 C3
  Rochdale OL11 29 E6
Winston Cl
  Marple SK6 125 D7
  Radcliffe M26 43 E5
  Sale M33 107 F5
Winston Rd
  Manchester M9 64 F1
  Manchester M40, M9 157 C4
Winswell Cl M11 83 B2
Winterbottom Gr
  SK14 102 F2
Winterbottom St OL9 153 A3
Winterbottom Wlk [4]
  SK14 102 F2
Winterburn Ave
  Bolton BL2 25 B6
  Manchester M21 109 D4
Winterburn Gn SK2 124 E5
Winterdyne St M9 157 B3
Winterfield Dr BL3 146 A3
Winterford Ave M13 164 A1
Winterford Rd
  Mossley OL5 68 E1
  Salford M7, M8 155 C3
Wintergreen Wlk [3]
  M31 105 F3
Winter Hey La BL6 22 B3
Wintermans Rd M21 109 E7
Winterslow Ave M23 108 D1
Winter St BL1 143 A3
Winterton Cl BL1 40 A1
Winterton Rd SK5 100 A1
Winthrop Ave M40 157 A1
WINTON 79 B3
Winton Ave
  Denton M34 100 D7
  Failsworth M40 65 D1
  Wigan WN5 54 D5
Winton Cl SK7 123 D1
Winton Ct WA14 119 C2
Winton Gn BL6 22 F1
Winton Gr M23 108 E4
Winton Rd
  Altrincham WA14 119 C2
  Golborne WA3 90 E6
  Pendlebury M6 80 D5
Winton St
  Ashton-u-L OL6 166 B3
  Littleborough OL15 16 B5
  [3] Stalybridge SK15 86 B1
Winward St
  Bolton BL3 146 A4
  Leigh WN7 75 B5
  [14] Westhoughton BL5 57 E6
Winwick La WA3 90 E3
Winwick Rd WA12 89 F1
Winwood Dr M24 47 B1
Winwood Fold M24 46 F4
Winwood Rd M20 122 C8
Wirral Cl
  Culcheth WA3 91 E4
  Swinton M27 62 A2
Wirral Cres SK3 123 A8
Wirral Dr WN3 54 C2
Wisbech Dr M23 108 F1
Wisbeck Rd BL2 148 C4
Wiseley St M11 164 B4
Wiseman Terr M25 63 C4
Wishaw Sq M21 109 E7
Wisley Cl SK5 112 A8
Wistaria Rd M18 99 D5
Witham Ave M22 121 E5
Witham Cl
  Heywood OL10 29 A3
  Standish WN6 19 D1
Witham St OL6 85 E4
Withenfield Rd M23 120 F8
Withens Gn SK2 124 E6
Withern [16] OL10 29 F2
Withill Wlk [4] WN4 73 A5
WITHINGTON 110 B6
Withington Ave WA3 92 A3
Withington Cl M46 58 B4
Withington Com Hospl
  M20 109 F5
Withington Dr M29 77 C7
Withington Girls Sch
  M14 110 C8
Withington Gn M24 47 A4
Withington Hospl
  M20 109 F5
Withington La WA3 38 C2
Withington Rd M16, M21 97 D2
Withington St OL10 46 E8
Withinlea Cl BL5 40 A2
Withins Ave M26 44 C5
Withins Cl BL2 42 E8
Withins Dr BL2 42 E8
Withins Gr BL2 42 E8
Withins Hall Rd M35 84 B6
Withins La
  Bolton BL2 42 E8
  Radcliffe M26 44 C5
Withins Rd
  Culcheth WA3 91 F3
  Oldham OL8 66 B2
Withins Sch BL2 25 E2
Withins Sports Ctr BL2 25 E2
Withins St M26 44 C4
Withnell Cl WN6 37 A2
Withnell Dr BL8 27 A1
Withnell Rd M19 110 D3

Withycombe Pl M6 81 A5
Withy Gr M4 159 A2
Withypool Dr SK2 124 C5
Withy Tree Gr [1]
  M34 101 A2
Witley Dr M33 107 D6
Witley Rd OL16 31 B7
Witney Cl [15] BL1 143 B2
Wittenbury Rd SK4 168 B2
Wittenham Ho SK9 131 D2
Witterage Cl M12 164 C2
Witton Wlk M8 155 C2
Woburn Ave
  Bolton BL2 25 C3
  Leigh WN7 57 D1
  Newton-le-W WA12 89 D2
Woburn Cl OL16 31 E6
Woburn Ct SK12 133 F4
Woburn Dr
  Altrincham WA15 120 B2
  Bury BL9 44 F5
Woburn Rd M16 97 A2
Woburn St [3] M16 97 F3
Woden's Ave M5 161 C3
Woden St M5 161 C3
Woking Rd SK8 132 A7
Woking Terr BL1 143 B1
Wolfenden Gn BB4 2 F8
Wolfenden St BL1 143 B2
Wolfenden Terr [26]
  BL1 143 B2
Wolf Grange WA15 119 E1
Wolford Dr M29 59 C1
Wolfreton Cres M27 62 A3
Wolfson Sq WN4 72 F4
Wollaton Wlk M34 100 E1
Wolmer St WN4 73 A4
Wolseley Ho M33 108 C6
Wolseley Pl M20 110 B5
Wolseley Rd M33 108 C6
Wolseley St
  [1] Bury BL8 27 B1
  Newhey OL16 32 B4
Wolsey Cl
  Ashton-in-M WN4 73 A2
  Radcliffe M26 44 A3
Wolsey Dr WN4 73 A2
Wolsey St
  Heywood OL10 29 C1
  Radcliffe M26 44 A3
WOLSTENHOLME 13 C2
Wolstenholme Ave BL9 27 F6
Wolstenholme Coalpit La
  OL11, OL12 13 B2
Wolstenholme La OL11,
  OL12 13 C2
Wolstenvale Cl M24 47 B1
Wolver Cl M38 60 B6
Wolverton Ave OL8 66 D3
Wolverton Dr SK9 131 D1
Wolvesey OL11 139 B2
Wolveton St M11 164 C3
Woodacre M16 97 E1
Woodacre Cl M33 108 A3
Woodacres Ct SK9 136 F6
Woodall Cl M33 108 D4
Woodark Cl OL4 67 F5
Woodbank
  Alderley Edge SK9 137 A4
  Bolton BL2 25 D2
  Stockport SK1 112 B1
Woodbank Ave
  Romiley SK6 112 E3
  Stockport SK1 124 C8
Woodbank Ct M8 63 C4
Woodbank Ct BL8 27 C4
Woodbank Prim Sch
  BL8 140 A4
Wood Bank Rd OL15 16 A3
Wood Bank Terr OL5 68 D2
Woodbank Rd
  SK1 112 B1
Woodbine Ave M44 105 D4
Woodbine Cres SK2 170 C3
Woodbine Rd
  Bolton BL3 146 C3
  Lymm WA13 117 B4
Woodbine St E OL16 31 B5
Woodbine St
  Manchester M14 98 B3
  Rochdale OL16 31 A5
Woodbine Terr [1] M44 94 A2
Woodbourne Ct M33 108 B2
Woodbourne Rd
  Manchester SK4 111 C6
  Sale M33 108 A2
Woodbray Ave M19 110 E7
Woodbridge Ave M34 100 E5
Woodbridge Dr BL2 25 B1
Woodbridge Gdns
  OL12 14 C2
Woodbridge Gr M23 109 A1
Woodbridge Rd M41 94 D3
WOOD BROOK 68 B8
Woodbrook Ave
  Hyde SK14 167 C2
  Oldham OL4 68 B7
Woodbrook Dr WN3 54 D4
Woodbrook Rd
  Alderley Edge SK9 137 C1
  Oldham OL4 68 B7
Woodburn Dr BL1 142 B8
Woodburn Rd M22 121 D8
Woodburn Row WN7 77 C3
Woodbury Cres SK16 101 B7
Woodbury Rd SK3 123 B7
Woodchurch WN7 37 F1

Woodchurch Cl [3]
  BL1 143 B1
Woodchurch Wlk
  Chadderton OL9 152 B2
  [7] Sale M33 108 F3
Woodcock Cl
  Droylsden M43 84 C3
  Rochdale OL11 29 F7
Woodcock Dr WN2 56 B2
Woodcock Gr SK13 104 E1
Woodcock Ho WN1 151 A4
Woodcote Ave SK7 123 C2
Woodcote Rd
  Sale M14, M31 107 A2
  Sale WA14 107 D1
Woodcote View SK9 131 F1
Woodcote Wlk M8 156 C4
Wood Cottage Cl [4]
  M28 59 F3
Woodcott Bank BL1 143 B4
Woodcourt Cl [3] SK9 131 E1
Wood Cotts SK6 113 A6
Woodcourt
  Wigan WN3 150 B2
  Wythenshawe M23 120 C8
Wood Cres OL4 67 E3
Woodcroft
  Appley Bridge WN6 35 E5
  Stockport SK2 124 D6
Woodcroft Ave M19 110 E4
Wooddagger Cl M29 56 F5
Wooeaton Cl OL2 49 A4
Wooded Cl BL2 27 F5
Woodedge WN4 73 A3
Wood Edge Cl BL4 42 C2
WOODEND
  Mossley 68 E2
  New Mills 135 E8
Woodend
  Denton M34 100 A7
  Whitefield M45 62 D6
WOODFORD 132 E2
Woodford Aerodrome
  SK7 133 A4
Woodford Ave
  Denton M34 101 A4
  Eccles M30 79 B2
  Golborne WA3 90 D7
  Shaw OL2 49 D7
Woodford Ct
  Droylsden M43 100 B8
  [3] Hindley WN2 56 E6
Woodford Dr M27 61 E2
Woodford Gdns M20 110 A2
Woodford Gr BL3 146 C4
Woodford Lo SK12 133 C4
Woodford Mews SK9 131 D4
Woodford Rd
  Bramhall SK7 132 C4
  Failsworth M35 84 A7
  Poynton SK12 133 B6
Woodford St
  [4] Hindley WN2 56 E6
  [3] Wigan WN5 54 B6
Woodgarth WN7 75 C5
Woodgarth Ave M40 83 D5
Woodgarth Dr M27 79 E6
Woodgarth La M28 78 F5
Woodgate Ave
  Bury BL9 28 D4
  Rochdale OL11 30 A6
Woodgate Cl SK6 112 F3
Woodgate Dr M25 63 C6
WOODGATE HILL 28 D4
Woodgate Hill Rd
  Bury, Fern Grove BL9 141 C4
  Bury, Woodgate Hill BL9 28 D4
Woodgate Rd M16 97 E1
Woodgate St BL3 42 A3
Wood Gdns SK9 137 B2
Wood Gr
  Denton M34 100 F4
  Romiley SK6 113 A5
  Whitefield M45 44 F3
Woodgrange Cl [2]
  M6 154 B2
Woodgreen Dr M26 62 A8
Woodhall Ave
  Manchester M20 110 A7
  Whitefield M45 62 D6
Woodhall Cl
  Bolton BL2 25 C3
  Bramhall SK7 132 E3
  Bury BL8 27 D5
Woodhall Cres SK5 112 A4
Woodhall Rd SK5 169 C4
Woodhall St M35 83 F8
Woodhalt Rd M8 156 A4
Woodham Rd M23 108 F1
Woodham Wlk BL3 145 A1
Woodhays M6 154 C2
Woodhead Cl
  Oldham OL4 67 E7
  Ramsbottom BL0 11 C4
Woodhead Dr WA15 119 F1
Woodhead Gr WN3 55 B2
Woodhead Rd
  Altrincham WA15 119 F1
  Glossop SK13 104 D5
  Tintwistle SK13 104 B8
Woodhead St [6] M16 97 E4
WOODHEY 11 B3
Wood Hey Cl M26 43 D3
Woodhey Ct M33 107 E1
Wood Hey Gr
  [2] Denton M34 101 A2
Woodhey High Sch
  BL0 11 A3
Woodhey Rd BL0 11 A3
Woodheys SK4 110 F3
Woodheys Dr M33 107 D1
Woodheys Prim Sch
  M33 107 E1
Woodheys Rd OL15 16 A2
Woodheys St [1] M5 154 C1
WOODHILL 140 A4
Woodhill Cl
  Manchester M12 99 B4
  Middleton M24 46 F2
Woodhill Dr M25 63 B3
WOODHILL FOLD 140 A3
Woodhill Fold BL8 140 A3
Woodhill Gr M25 63 B3
Woodhill Rd BL8 140 A4
Woodhill St BL8 140 A4
Woodhill Vale BL8 140 A3
Woodhill Works BL8 140 A4
Woodhouse Dr WN6 36 E2
Woodhouse Farm Cotts
  OL12 13 D2
Woodhouse Knowl
  OL3 50 F4
Woodhouse La
  Partington WA14 118 C4
  Rochdale OL12 13 E3
  Sale M33 107 C2
  Sale M33 107 D2
  Wigan, Standish Lower
    Ground WN6 36 E3
  Wigan WN6 36 F2
  Wigan WN1 37 A1
  Wythenshawe, Benchill
    M22 121 D4
  Wythenshawe M90 130 D7
Woodhouse La E
  WA15 108 A1
WOODHOUSE PARK 121 D1
Woodhouse Prim Sch
  M41 95 A4
Woodhouse Rd
  Shaw OL2 32 C1
  Urmston M41 94 F4
  Wythenshawe M22 130 D8
WOODHOUSES 84 B6

Woodhouses Prim Sch
M35 . . . . .84 C6
Woodhouse St
Atherton M46 . . . . .58 D2
Manchester M18 . . . . .99 E5
Woodhurst Dr WN6 . . . . .19 C1
Wooding Cl M31 . . . . . . .106 A4
Wood La
Altrincham WA15 . . . . . . .120 B5
Ashton-u-L OL6, OL7 . . . . .85 B5
Edenfield BL0 . . . . .1 D2
Marple SK6 . . . . .125 E5
Middleton M24 . . . . .65 B7
Partington M31 . . . . .105 D3
Wilmslow WA16 . . . . .129 D1
Wrightington Bar WN6,
PR7 . . . . .18 E8
Woodlake Ave M21 . . . . .109 C4
Wood La N SK10 . . . . . . .134 B1
Woodland Ave
Bolton BL3 . . . . .42 B2
Hazel Grove SK7 . . . . . . .124 E1
Hindley WN2 . . . . .57 A3
Lymm WA13 . . . . .117 A2
Newton-le-W WA12 . . . . . .89 F3
Reddish M18 . . . . .99 E4
Woodland Com Prim Sch
OL10 . . . . .29 B1
Woodland Cres M25 . . . . .63 B2
Woodland Ct M29 . . . . . . .77 E8
Woodland Dr
Ashton-in-M WN4 . . . . . . .73 B5
Lymm WA13 . . . . .117 A2
Standish WN6 . . . . .19 E2
Woodland Gr
Bolton BL7 . . . . .8 D2
Wigan WN1 . . . . .37 D2
Woodland Pk OL2 . . . . . . .48 B6
Woodland Rd
Heywood OL10 . . . . .29 E3
Manchester M19 . . . . . . .111 A7
Reddish M18 . . . . .99 E4
Rochdale OL12 . . . . .14 C2
Tyldesley M29 . . . . .77 B7
Woodlands M35 . . . . .83 E4
WOODLANDS
Stalybridge 102 D7
Urmston 94 D1
Woodlands 5 M41 . . . . . .95 C3
Woodlands Ave
Cheadle SK8 . . . . .123 A2
Eccles M30 . . . . .95 A8
Ince-in-M WN3 . . . . .151 A8
Irlam M44 . . . . .94 A3
Leigh WN7 . . . . .75 F3
Rochdale OL11 . . . . .30 A6
Romiley SK6 . . . . .113 A5
Stretford M32 . . . . .96 D2
Swinton M27 . . . . .79 D6
Urmston M41 . . . . .94 C2
Whitefield M45 . . . . .44 E1
Woodlands Cl
Broadbottom SK14 . . . . . .102 F1
Cheadle SK8 . . . . .132 A8
Glossop SK13 . . . . .103 F6
Stalybridge SK15 . . . . . . .102 D7
Worsley M28 . . . . .78 E7
Woodlands Ct
Altrincham WA15 . . . . . . .119 E5
Stockport SK2 . . . . .124 D8
Woodlands Dr
Over Hulton M46 . . . . .58 F5
Romiley SK6 . . . . .113 A5
Sale M23, M33 . . . . .108 C1
Shevington WN6 . . . . .35 F4
Stockport SK2 . . . . .124 D8
Woodlands Gr
Broadbottom SK14 . . . . . .102 F1
Bury BL8 . . . . .27 B3
Woodlands Hospl M28 . . . .59 F4
Woodlands Ind Est
WA12 . . . . .89 C6
Woodlands La WA15 . . . .119 E5
Woodlands Park Cl
WN1 . . . . .37 C5
Woodlands Park Rd
SK2 . . . . .124 D8
Woodlands Parkway
WA15 . . . . .119 E6
Woodlands Rd
Altrincham WA14,
WA15 . . . . .119 E5
Ashton-u-L OL6 . . . . .85 E6
Edenfield BL0 . . . . .1 D2
Handforth SK9 . . . . .131 E3
High Lane SK12 . . . . .135 A6
Manchester, Cheetham Hill
M8 . . . . .156 B3
Manchester, Heaton Mersey
SK4 . . . . .110 D2
Manchester, Whalley Range
M21 . . . . .97 E1
Sale M33 . . . . .108 C4
Stalybridge SK15 . . . . . . .102 D7
Wilmslow SK9 . . . . .130 F1
Worsley M28 . . . . .78 F7
Woodlands Road Sta
M8 . . . . .156 B3
Woodlands St M8 . . . . . .156 A4
Woodland St
Heywood OL10 . . . . .29 D2
Manchester M12 . . . . . . .165 B1
Rochdale OL12 . . . . .15 C1

Woodlands The
Bolton BL6 . . . . .40 C8
Bury BL8 . . . . .140 A4
Droylsden M43 . . . . .83 E3
Heywood OL10 . . . . .46 E8
Pendlebury M27 . . . . .80 B7
Prestwich M25 . . . . .62 F1
Wigan WN1 . . . . .37 D3
Woodlands View OL16 . . . .31 C8
Woodlands Way M24 . . . . .64 F6
Woodland View
Bolton BL7 . . . . .25 B8
Hyde SK14 . . . . .167 C3
Woodlark Cl M3 . . . . .158 A1
Wood La W SK10 . . . . . . .133 F1
Woodlawn Ct M16 . . . . . . .97 C3
Woodlea
Altrincham WA15 . . . . . . .119 F4
Oldham OL9 . . . . .65 D7
Worsley M28 . . . . .78 E8
Woodlea Ave M19 . . . . . .110 E6
Wood Lea Bank 4 BB4 . . . .2 F8
Woodlea Chase M27 . . . . .61 D5
Woodlea Rd SK13 . . . . . .116 B7
Wood Lea Rd BB4 . . . . .2 F8
Woodleigh WA14 . . . . . . .119 A5
Woodleigh Ct
Alderley Edge SK9 . . . . . .137 A2
Bury BL8 . . . . .27 B5
Woodleigh Dr M43 . . . . . .84 C4
Woodleigh Rd OL4 . . . . . .68 A7
Woodleigh St M9 . . . . . . .64 F1
Woodleighs M30 . . . . .79 C4
WOODLEY 113 C6
Woodley Ave M26 . . . . . . .44 B1
Woodley Cl SK2 . . . . .124 D7
Woodley Gr WN7 . . . . .75 D5
Woodley Prec SK14 . . . . .113 A5
Woodley Prim Sch
SK6 . . . . .113 C5
Woodley St BL9 . . . . .44 F8
Woodley Sta SK6 . . . . . . .113 B6
Woodliffe St M16 . . . . . . .161 C1
Woodlinn Wlk M9 . . . . . . .157 A3
Woodman Dr BL9 . . . . .27 E6
Woodman St SK1 . . . . . . .169 B2
Woodmeadow Ct 11
OL5 . . . . .68 C2
Woodmere Dr M9 . . . . . . .64 E3
Wood Mount M45 . . . . . . .120 B5
Woodmount Cl SK6 . . . . . .113 F2
Woodnewton Cl M18 . . . . .99 C4
Woodnook Rd WN6 . . . . . .35 E8
Woodpark Cl OL8 . . . . .67 A3
Woodpecker Pl M28 . . . . .78 D8
Wood Rd
Manchester M16 . . . . .97 D3
Sale WA15 . . . . .108 B1
Wood Rd N M16 . . . . .97 C3
Woodridings WA14 . . . . . .119 B3
WOOD ROAD 11 B1
Wood Road La
Bury BL8, BL9 . . . . .27 B8
Ramsbottom BL9 . . . . .11 C1
Woodrow Way M44 . . . . .105 F8
Woodrow Wlk M12 . . . . . .164 C2
Woodroyd Cl SK7 . . . . . . .123 D1
Woodroyd Dr BL9 . . . . . . .141 C3
Woodruffe Gdns SK6 . . . . .126 E8
Woodruff Wlk 7 M31 . . . .105 F3
Woodrush Rd WN6 . . . . . . .36 D3
Woods Ct
Manchester M24 . . . . .64 C7
Newton-le-W WA12 . . . . . .89 A3
Woodseats La SK13 . . . . . .115 B6
Woodseaves Cl 1 M44 . . . .94 B1
WOODS END 94 E4
Woods End M20 . . . . .109 F4
Woodsend Circ M41 . . . . .94 D3
Woodsend Crescent Rd
M41 . . . . .94 D3
Woodsend Gn M41 . . . . . . .94 D3
Woodsend Rd M41 . . . . . .94 E3
Woodsend Rd S M41 . . . . .94 E1
Woods Gr SK8 . . . . .132 B7
Woodshaw Gr 2 M28 . . . .78 C8
Wood's Hospl SK13 . . . . .104 C3
Woodside
Manchester SK4 . . . . .110 F1
Newhey OL16 . . . . .32 B5
Poynton SK12 . . . . .133 F4
Shaw OL2 . . . . .49 D8
Woodside Ave
Ashton-in-M WN4 . . . . .73 A8
Manchester M19 . . . . . . .110 F5
Walkden M28 . . . . .60 F2
Woodside Cl
Oldham OL4 . . . . .67 E6
Up Holland WN8 . . . . .53 C8
Woodside Dr
High Lane SK6 . . . . .134 F7
Hyde SK14 . . . . .167 B1
Ramsbottom BL0 . . . . . . .138 A1
2 Salford M6 . . . . .80 C3
Woodside La
Lymm WA13 . . . . .117 B1
Poynton SK12 . . . . .133 E4
Woodside Mews SK3 . . . .123 C2
Woodside Pl BL2 . . . . . . .148 C1
Woodside Rd M16 . . . . . . .97 B2
Woodside Sq BL2 . . . . . . .148 C1
Woodside St SK15 . . . . . . .86 E6
Woods La
Cheadle SK8 . . . . .132 B7
Uppermill OL3 . . . . .51 A2
Wood's La WN4 . . . . .73 C5
Woods Lea BL1 . . . . .40 F7

Woodsleigh Coppice
BL1 . . . . .40 F7
Woodsley Rd BL1 . . . . .23 F2
WOODS MOOR 124 B4
Woodsmoor La SK2 . . . . .124 A4
Woodsmoor Rd M27 . . . . .79 D7
Woodsmoor Sta SK2 . . . .124 B4
Wood Sorrel Way WA3 . . . .90 E8
Wood Sq
Droylsden M43 . . . . .100 A8
Uppermill OL3 . . . . .69 B6
Woods Rd
Aspull WN2 . . . . .38 C4
Irlam M44 . . . . .105 F8
Wood's St WN3 . . . . .150 C3
Wood St
Altrincham WA14 . . . . . . .119 D4
Ashton-u-L OL6 . . . . .166 B2
Atherton M46 . . . . .58 B4
Bolton BL1 . . . . .145 C3
Bury BL8 . . . . .27 C3
Cheadle SK8 . . . . .122 D6
Denton M34 . . . . .100 F4
Dukinfield SK16 . . . . .101 C6
Eccles M30 . . . . .79 F1
Glossop SK13 . . . . .116 C8
Golborne WA3 . . . . .90 B8
Hindley WN2 . . . . .57 A4
Hollingworth SK14 . . . . . .103 D5
Horwich BL6 . . . . .22 C3
Hyde SK14 . . . . .167 B2
Littleborough OL15 . . . . . . .16 B5
Manchester, City Centre
M3 . . . . .158 C1
Manchester, Openshaw
M11 . . . . .165 B4
Middleton M24 . . . . .64 F8
Newhey OL16 . . . . .32 C4
Oldham OL8 . . . . .67 B8
Radcliffe M26 . . . . .61 E8
Ramsbottom BL0 . . . . . . .138 B1
Rochdale OL16 . . . . .31 A6
Shaw OL2 . . . . .48 F8
7 Stalybridge SK15 . . . . .85 F2
Stockport SK3 . . . . .169 A1
Tyldesley M29 . . . . .77 B8
Westhoughton BL5 . . . . . . .57 E8
Wigan, Parson's Meadow
WN5 . . . . .54 F7
Wigan WN3 . . . . .150 C3
Woods The
4 Altrincham WA14 . . . . .119 E6
Oldham OL4 . . . . .68 B6
Rochdale OL11 . . . . .30 C3
Woodstock Ave
Cheadle SK8 . . . . .132 A7
Newton-le-W WA12 . . . . . .89 D2
Reddish SK5 . . . . .111 F5
Woodstock Cl
Heywood OL10 . . . . .29 E2
Leigh WN7 . . . . .75 E1
Woodstock Cres SK6 . . . .113 A5
Woodstock Dr
Bolton BL1 . . . . .142 A1
Bury BL8 . . . . .26 D7
Pendlebury M27 . . . . .80 B6
Worsley M28 . . . . .79 A6
Woodstock Gn
Oldham OL8 . . . . .67 A3
Reddish SK5 . . . . .112 A5
Woodstock Rd
Altrincham WA14 . . . . . . .119 C8
Failsworth M40 . . . . .65 C1
Manchester M16 . . . . .97 B3
Romiley SK6 . . . . .113 A5
Woodstock St
Oldham OL4 . . . . .153 C2
12 Rochdale OL12 . . . . . .14 C1
Wood Terr BL2 . . . . .26 D1
Woodthorpe Ct M25 . . . . . .63 D2
Woodthorpe Dr SK8 . . . . .123 A2
Woodthorpe Grange
M25 . . . . .63 D2
Wood Top Ave SK4 . . . . . .29 F5
Wood Top Cl SK2 . . . . . . .124 E7
Woodvale
Altrincham WA14 . . . . . . .119 C8
Failsworth M40 . . . . .65 C1
Middleton M24 . . . . .47 A4
Woodvale Ave
Aspull WN2 . . . . .38 F3
Atherton M46 . . . . .58 B5
Bolton BL3 . . . . .147 A2
Woodvale Dr
Bolton BL3 . . . . .147 A2
Golborne WA3 . . . . .74 E1
Woodvale Gdns BL3 . . . . .147 A2
Woodvale Gr BL3 . . . . . . .147 A2
Woodvale Rd M26 . . . . . . .44 B2
Woodvale Wlk 18
M11 . . . . .160 C1
Wood View
Heywood OL10 . . . . .29 C4
Shevington WN6 . . . . .36 B5
Wythenshawe M22 . . . . . .109 D1
Woodview Ave M19 . . . . .110 F5
Woodville Dr
Marple SK6 . . . . .125 E4
Sale M33 . . . . .108 A5
Stalybridge SK15 . . . . . . .86 D3
Woodville Rd
Altrincham WA14 . . . . . . .119 C3
Ince-in-M WN3 . . . . .55 F4
Sale M33 . . . . .108 A5
Woodville Terr 10 M40 . . .64 F1
Woodward Cl BL9 . . . . . . .27 F5
Woodward Ct M4 . . . . . . .160 A2
Woodward Pl M4 . . . . . . .159 C2

Woodward Rd M25 . . . . . . .62 F2
Woodwards Rd BL5 . . . . . .57 F6
Woodward St M4 . . . . . . .159 C2
Woodwise La M23 . . . . . .108 E1
Woodyates St WN5 . . . . . .54 F6
Wooden Rd WA4,
WA3 . . . . .105 B8
Woolden St
Eccles M30 . . . . .79 B3
6 Wigan WN5 . . . . .54 F6
Wooler Gr WN2 . . . . .56 D2
Woolfall Cl M12 . . . . .164 C2
WOOLFOLD 27 B4
Woolfold Trad Est 6 BL8 . .27 B4
WOOLFORD 27 A4
Woollacott St 2 OL1 . . . .153 C2
Woollam Pl M3 . . . . .162 A4
Woolley Ave SK12 . . . . . .133 D2
Woolley Bridge Rd
SK13 . . . . .103 F5
Woolley Cl SK14 . . . . . . .171 A4
Woolley La
Hollingworth SK14 . . . . . .103 D6
Hollingworth SK14 . . . . . .171 A4
Woolley Mill La SK13 . . . .103 E7
Woolley St M8 . . . . .158 C4
Woolley Terr 3 SK16 . . . .166 B1
Woolmore Ave SK14 . . . . .48 E1
Woolpack Gn 2 M6 . . . . .154 C3
Wool Rd OL3 . . . . .51 B2
Woolston Dr M9 . . . . .77 C8
Woolston Ho 3 M6 . . . . . .80 C4
Woolton Cl
Ashton-in-M WN4 . . . . . . .72 F5
3 Failsworth M40 . . . . . . .65 C2
Wootton St SK14 . . . . . . .167 A4
Worcester Ave
Brinnington SK5 . . . . .112 C5
Denton M34 . . . . .101 A1
Golborne WA3 . . . . .90 B8
Hindley WN2 . . . . .56 F6
Worcester Cl
Ashton-u-L OL6 . . . . .85 D8
Bury BL9 . . . . .45 A8
Romiley SK6 . . . . .113 A1
Salford M6 . . . . .80 C4
Worcester Gr SK13 . . . . . .116 F8
Worcester Rd
Cheadle SK8 . . . . .123 A4
Little Lever BL3 . . . . .42 F3
Middleton M24 . . . . .64 F5
Sale M33 . . . . .107 D3
Salford M6 . . . . .80 C4
Swinton M27 . . . . .61 D2
Worcester St
4 Bolton BL1 . . . . .143 B1
Bury BL8 . . . . .140 A4
Oldham OL1 . . . . .152 B1
Rochdale OL11 . . . . .30 E4
Salford M7 . . . . .81 C4
Wordsworth Ave
Atherton M46 . . . . .58 E5
Bury BL9 . . . . .44 F6
Droylsden M43 . . . . .84 A2
Farnworth BL4 . . . . .60 B7
Leigh WN7 . . . . .75 D7
Longshaw WN5 . . . . .53 D1
Manchester M8 . . . . .156 A2
Orrell WN5 . . . . .53 F6
Radcliffe M26 . . . . .43 E4
Wigan WN1 . . . . .37 C3
Wordsworth Cl SK16 . . . .102 A7
Wordsworth Cres
Ashton-u-L OL7 . . . . .84 E5
Littleborough OL15 . . . . . . .15 F7
Wordsworth Rd M25 . . . . .62 F3
Wordsworth Ind Est
BL1 . . . . .143 A2
Wordsworth Rd
Denton M34 . . . . .113 A7
Manchester M16 . . . . .97 B2
Middleton M24 . . . . .47 B2
Oldham OL1 . . . . .49 B1
Reddish SK5 . . . . .99 D1
Swinton M27 . . . . .61 E1
Walkden M38 . . . . .60 B5
Wordsworth St BL1 . . . . .143 A2
Wordsworth Way OL11 . . . .29 E6
Workesleigh St 9
M40 . . . . .83 C5
Works Bsns Ctr The
M12 . . . . .163 C4
World Freight Ctr M16 . . . .96 E5
World Freight Terminal
M90 . . . . .129 F7
World Way M90 . . . . .130 B8
Worrall St
Failsworth M40 . . . . .83 A6
1 Rochdale OL12 . . . . . . .14 C2
Salford M5 . . . . .161 C3
Stockport SK3 . . . . .170 B3
Worrell Cl M26 . . . . .43 F4
Worsbrough Ave M28 . . . . .60 C2
Worsefold St M40 . . . . . . .83 A8
Worsel St BL3 . . . . .146 C4
WORSLEY 78 E6
Worsley Ave
Manchester M40 . . . . .83 A1
Walkden M28 . . . . .60 A2
Worsley Brow M28 . . . . . . .77 F8
Worsley Cl WN5 . . . . .54 C5
Worsley Cres 5 SK2 . . . .124 B7
Worsley Gdns M28 . . . . . .60 C4

Worsley Gn WN5 . . . . .54 B5
Worsley Gr
Manchester M19 . . . . .99 A1
Walkden M28 . . . . .60 A2
WORSLEY HALL 54 E7
WORSLEY MESNES 55 A4
Worsley Mesnes Com
Prim Sch WN3 . . . . .55 A4
Worsley Mesnes Dr
WN3 . . . . .150 A1
Worsley Pl
Rochdale OL16 . . . . .31 B7
Oldham OL2 . . . . .149 A2
Worsley Rd
Bolton BL3 . . . . .146 A4
Eccles M30 . . . . .79 B3
Farnworth BL4 . . . . .60 D7
Swinton M27, M28 . . . . . .79 C6
Worsley Rd N M28 . . . . . .60 D5
Worsley St
Bolton BL3 . . . . .145 B1
Bury BL8 . . . . .26 E7
Golborne WA3 . . . . .90 A8
Manchester, St George's
M15 . . . . .162 A3
Oldham OL8 . . . . .67 B5
Pendlebury M27 . . . . .80 A7
Rochdale OL16 . . . . .31 B7
Salford M3 . . . . .158 B2
Swinton M27 . . . . .61 A1
Wigan WN5 . . . . .54 B5
Worsley Terr WN1 . . . . . . .37 C1
Worsley Trad Est M38 . . . .59 E5
Worston Ave BL1 . . . . .23 F3
Worth St SK12 . . . . .133 D2
Worthenbury Wlk M13 . . . .98 E3
Worthing Cl SK2 . . . . . . .124 D6
Worthing Gr M46 . . . . .58 B3
Worthing St M14 . . . . .98 B2
Worthington Ave
Heywood OL10 . . . . .46 E7
9 Partington M31 . . . . . .105 F3
Worthington Cl
Ashton-u-L OL7 . . . . .85 A5
7 Hattersley SK14 . . . . .102 E3
Worthington Dr SK13 . . . .108 E4
Worthington Dr M7 . . . . . .63 D1
Worthington Fold M46 . . . .58 B3
Worthington Prim Sch
M33 . . . . .108 F4
Worthington Rd
Denton M34 . . . . .101 B0
Sale M33 . . . . .108 F4
Worthington St
Ashton-u-L OL7 . . . . .85 A5
4 Bolton BL3 . . . . .146 C3
Failsworth M40 . . . . .83 C8
Hindley WN2 . . . . .56 D6
Manchester M16 . . . . .97 C4
Stalybridge SK15 . . . . . . .85 F1
Worthington Way
Denton M34 . . . . .100 E4
Wigan WN3 . . . . .54 F2
Worth Prim Sch SK12 . . . .133 F2
Worth's La M40 . . . . .84 A3
Worthy Ave M46 . . . . .80 C3
Wotton Dr WN4 . . . . .73 D3
Wragby Cl BL8 . . . . .27 D5
Wrath Cl BL2 . . . . .25 B5
Wraxhall Cres WN7 . . . . . .75 D7
Wray Cl M22 . . . . .121 D4
Wray Gdns M19 . . . . .111 C8
Wray Pl OL16 . . . . .31 C6
Wraysbury Wlk 10 M40 . . .83 A7
Wray St WN1 . . . . .151 B4
Wrayton Lo M33 . . . . . . .108 B3
Wrekin Ave M23 . . . . .121 A3
Wren Ave M27 . . . . .62 B2
Wrenbury Ave M20 . . . . . .109 F7
Wrenbury Cl 5 WN5 . . . . .54 B5
Wrenbury Cres SK3 . . . . .123 C6
Wrenbury Dr
3 Bolton BL7 . . . . .24 F6
Cheadle SK8 . . . . .122 E6
Rochdale OL16 . . . . .31 C4
Wrenbury Wlk M33 . . . . .108 E3
Wren Cl
Droylsden M34 . . . . .84 C1
Farnworth BL4 . . . . .59 F8
Hazel Grove SK2 . . . . . . .124 F5
Wigan WN3 . . . . .36 B1
Wren Dr
Bury BL9 . . . . .141 B4
Irlam M44 . . . . .94 A4
Wren Gdns M24 . . . . .46 F1
Wren Gn OL16 . . . . .31 B6
Wren Nest Cl SK13 . . . . .116 B8
Wren Nest Rd SK13 . . . . .116 A8
Wren Nest Terr SK13 . . . .104 C1
Wren's Nest Ave OL2 . . . .149 C4
Wren St OL4 . . . . .67 C6
Wrenswood Dr M28 . . . . . .78 C8
Wren Way M11 . . . . .164 B4
Wrexham Cl OL8 . . . . .66 B2
Wrigglesworth Cl BL8 . . . .26 F3
WRIGHTINGTON BAR 18 F7
WRIGHTINGTON Hospl
WN6 . . . . .18 D2
Wrightington Mossy Lea
Prim Sch WN6 . . . . .18 F6
Wrightington St WN1 . . . . .37 C1
Wright Robinson Cl
M11 . . . . .164 B4
Wright Robinson Sports
Coll M18 . . . . .99 F6
Wright St W 3 BL6 . . . . . .22 B4

Wrights Bank N SK2 124 E5
Wrights Bank S SK2 124 E5
Wright St
Abram Brow WN2 74 B7
Ashton-in-M WN4 73 A6
Ashton-u-L, Guide Bridge M34 100 E8
14 Ashton-u-L OL6 85 D4
Chadderton OL9 152 B1
Failsworth M35 83 F8
Horwich BL6 22 B4
Manchester M16 161 C2
12 Oldham OL1 67 A7
Platt Bridge WN2 56 A3
Radcliffe M26 43 F3
6 Wigan WN1 37 E1
Wright Tree Villas M44 105 D5
Wrigley Cres M35 83 F7
Wrigley Fold M24 46 D3
Wrigley Head M35 83 F8
Wrigley Head Cres M35 83 F8
Wrigley Pl OL15 15 F3
Wrigley Sq 1 OL4 67 F6
Wrigley St
Ashton-u-L OL6 166 B4
Oldham, County End OL4 67 F6
Oldham, Greenacres Moor OL4 67 B7
Oldham, Wood Brook OL4 68 B8
Wrington Cl WN7 75 D8
Wroe St
11 Oldham OL4 67 F6
Salford M3 158 A2
Swinton M27 61 F3
Wroe Terr M27 61 F3
Wrotham Cl 2 M5 81 A1
Wroxeter Wlk M12 164 C2
Wroxham Ave
Reddish M34 100 A3
Urmston M41 95 B3
Wroxham Cl BL8 27 D5
Wroxham Rd M9 64 B3
WUERDLE 15 E3
Wuerdle Cl OL16 15 E4
Wuerdle Farm Way 3 OL16 15 E4
Wuerdle Pl OL16 15 E4
Wuerdle St 1 OL16 15 E4
Wyatt Ave M5 161 C3
Wyatt Gr WN4 73 D3
Wyatt St
4 Dukinfield SK16 101 C8
Stockport SK4 169 B2
Wybersley Rd SK6 135 A8
Wychbury St M6 154 B2
Wychelm Rd M31 105 F3
Wycherley Rd OL12 14 B2
Wych Fold SK14 113 E7
Wych St OL6 166 B2
Wychwood WA14 119 B1
Wychwood Cl M24 65 B7
Wycliffe Ave SK9 137 A7
Wycliffe Ct M41 95 C2
Wycliffe Rd M41 95 C2
Wycliffe St
Eccles M30 79 C2
Stockport SK4 169 A2
Wycombe Ave M18 99 E6
Wycombe Cl M41 95 C5
Wycombe Dr M29 77 B7
Wye Ave M35 83 F7
Wyecroft Cl SK6 113 B5
Wye St OL8 153 A1
Wykeham Cl WN3 151 C2
Wykeham Gr OL12 14 B1
Wykeham Mews BL1 144 A3
Wykeham St M14 98 A3
Wyke Pk OL4 67 D6
Wylam Wlk 4 M12 99 B3
Wylde The BL9 140 B2
Wynard Ave WN1 37 D1
Wynchgate Rd SK7 125 A3
Wyndale Dr M35 83 F5
Wyndale Rd OL8 66 F3
Wyndcliff Dr M41 94 E1
Wyndham Ave
Bolton BL3 146 A3
Swinton M27 61 F3
Wyndham Cl SK7 132 E7
Wyne Cl SK7 125 A3
Wynfield Ave M22 130 F7
Wynford Sq M50 154 C1
Wyngate Rd
Altrincham WA15 128 F8
Cheadle SK8 122 F1
Wynne Ave M27 62 A3
Wynne Cl
Denton M34 100 F1
Manchester M11 164 C4
Wynne Gr M34 100 F1
Wynne St
Bolton BL1 143 B2
Salford M6 81 B3
Tyldesley M29 58 F1
Walkden M38 60 A4
Wynnstay Gr M14 110 C8
Wynnstay Rd M33 108 B5
Wynton Cl WN7 75 E2
Wynyard Cl M33 108 D2
Wynyard Rd M22 121 C3
Wyre Ave WN2 56 A2
Wyre Cl M45 45 B1
Wyre Dr M28 78 B7
Wyresdale Rd BL1 144 C4
Wyre St
Manchester M1 163 B4
Mossley OL5 68 B1
Wyrevale Gr WN4 73 C3
Wythall Ave M38 60 A6
Wythburn Ave
Bolton BL1 142 A1
Manchester M8 156 C2
Urmston M41 95 B3
Wythburn Rd
Middleton M24 46 E3
Stockport SK1 124 B7
Wythburn St M6 154 B2
WYTHENSHAWE 121 B6
Wythenshawe Ctr M22 121 D2
Wythenshawe Hall (Art Gall & Mus)* M23 121 B8
Wythenshawe Hospl M23 120 F5
Wythenshawe Rd
Sale M33 108 F4
Wythenshawe M23 109 B1
Wythens Rd SK8 131 B8
Wythop Gdns M5 81 A1
Wyvern Ave SK5 111 E5
Wyverne Rd M21 109 D8
Wyville Cl SK7 125 A3
Wyville Dr
Manchester M9 64 B6
Salford M6 154 C3
Swinton M27 79 E6
Wyvis Cl OL9 48 A1

X

Xaverian Coll M14 98 C3

Y

Yale Rd M18 165 B1
Yale St BL7 9 D4
Yarburgh St M16 97 E3
Yardley Ave M32 96 A2
Yardley Cl M32 96 A2
Yard The 4 SK13 104 C1
Yare St 7 BB4 2 F8
Yarmouth Dr M23 109 B1
Yarn Croft M29 77 B8
Yarnton Cl OL2 149 A1
Yarn Wlk M4 159 C1
Yarrow Cl OL11 139 C1
Yarrow Gr BL6 22 B4
Yarrow Pl BL1 143 B1
Yarrow St WN2 56 C4
Yarrow Wlk M45 45 C1
Yarwell 25 OL12 139 B4
Yarwood Ave M23 120 F7
Yarwood Cl OL10 29 E3
Yarwood St
Altrincham WA14 119 D3
Bury BL9 141 A2
Yasmin Gdns OL1 48 D1
Yates Dr M28 60 A3
Yates Gr WN6 36 F4
Yates St
Bolton BL2 25 A1
Leigh WN7 75 E7
Middleton M24 64 C7
Oldham OL1 49 B1
Stockport SK1 112 B3
Wigan WN3 150 A3
Yattendon Ave M23 120 D8
Yeadon Rd M18 99 D3
Yea Fold OL15 15 E3
Yealand Ave SK4 169 A3
Yealand Cl OL11 30 B6
Yealand Gr WN2 57 A5
Yeardsley Cl SK7 123 E3
Yeargate Ind Est BL9 28 D2
Yellow Brook Cl WN2 38 C6
Yellow Lodge Dr BL5 40 B1
Yelverton Wlk M13 163 C2
Yeoford Dr WA14 119 B6
Yeoman Cl SK7 124 D3
Yeomanry Ct 3 M16 97 D3
Yeoman's Cl OL16 31 F7
Yeoman Wlk M11 160 C1
Yeovil St M16 97 F3
Yesoiday Hatorah Sch M25 63 B2
Yewbarrow Cl M29 77 B7
Yewbarrow Rd 1 OL1 67 A8
Yew Cl BL3 146 B4
Yew Cres OL4 67 D8
Yew Ct OL12 15 B2
Yewdale
Shevington WN6 36 B6
Swinton M27 62 B1
Yewdale Ave
Billinge WA11 71 B1
Bolton BL2 25 F2
Yewdale Cres 3 WN1 37 B3
Yewdale Dr
Failsworth M35 84 C8
Middleton M24 46 E1
Yewdale Gdns BL2 25 F2
Yew Dale Gdns OL11 30 B4
Yewdale Rd
Ashton-in-M WN4 73 A7
Stockport SK1 124 B7
Yew Gr WN6 36 F4
Yewlands Ave M9 64 D5
Yew St
Bury BL9 141 C3
Denton M34 100 F5
Heywood OL10 29 B2
Manchester M15 162 B1
Salford M7 81 C6
Stockport SK4 168 C1
YEW TREE 101 E7
Yewtree Ave M46 58 C4
Yew Tree Ave
Hazel Grove SK7 124 F1
7 Manchester, Levenshulme M19 99 A1
Manchester M14 98 A2
Newton-le-W WA12 89 A4
Wythenshawe M22 109 D1
Yew Tree Cl
Ashton-u-L OL7 85 A6
Marple SK6 125 E5
Wilmslow SK9 137 D7
Yew Tree Com Prim Sch SK16 101 E6
Yew Tree Com Sch OL9 66 A4
Yew Tree Cres M14 98 B1
Yew Tree Ct OL14 6 A8
Yew Tree Dr
Bolton BL6 40 B6
Chadderton OL9 65 D7
Prestwich M25 63 B4
Romiley SK6 112 D3
Sale M33 108 E4
Urmston M41 94 F4
Wythenshawe M22 109 D1
Yew Tree Farm Trad Est WA11 89 A8
Yew Tree Gr
Gatley SK8 122 A3
Rawtenstall BB4 1 F8
Yew Tree La
Bolton BL1 25 A4
Dukinfield SK16 101 F7
Poynton SK12 133 F3
Wythenshawe M23 109 B2
Yew Tree Park Rd SK8 132 B6
Yew Tree Rd
Denton M34 100 E1
Manchester M14 98 B2
Stockport SK3 123 F3
Wardsend SK10 134 B1
Yew Tree Way WA3 90 B7
Yew Wlk 1 M31 105 E2
York Ave
Culcheth WA3 91 F2
Haslingden BB4 1 B8
Little Lever BL3 43 A3
Manchester M16 97 C2
Manchester, Sedgley Park M25 63 D2
Oldham OL8 66 D4
Rochdale OL11 30 A6
Sale M33 108 B5
Swinton M27 61 D2
Tyldesley M29 59 A2
Urmston M41 95 E3
York Cl
Cheadle SK8 123 A5
Denton M34 100 F4
York Cres SK9 137 D8
Yorkdale OL4 67 D6
York Dr
Altrincham WA14 119 D1
Hazel Grove SK7 125 A2
Ramsbottom BL0 11 A4
Wythenshawe M90 129 F7
York Pl
Adlington PR6 21 A8
Ashton-u-L OL6 166 A2
Manchester M13 98 C4
York Rd
Altrincham WA14 119 C1
Ashton-in-M WN4 73 C3
Chadderton OL9 65 F8
Denton M34 100 F4
Droylsden M43 83 F3
Hindley WN2 56 F6
Hyde SK14 113 E8
Irlam M44 105 D5
Manchester, Heaton Moor SK4 111 B5
Manchester M21 109 B8
Sale M33 108 A5
York Rd E M24 65 C5
York Rd S WN4 73 C2
York Rd W M24 65 C5
Yorkshire Rd M31 105 E2
Yorkshire St
Ashton-u-L OL6 166 B3
Oldham OL1 153 C3
Rochdale OL12, OL16 31 A8
Rochdale OL16 139 C4
Salford M3 158 B2
Yorkshire Way SK13 116 F8
York Sq 6 OL2 48 D4
York St
Altrincham WA15 119 E3
Ashton-u-L M34 100 E8
Atherton M46 58 D3
Bury BL9 141 A2
Farnworth BL4 60 E8
Glossop SK13 104 E1
Golborne WA3 74 A1
Heywood OL10 29 D2
Leigh WN7 76 D4
Manchester, Didsbury M20 110 B3
Manchester, Harpurhey M9 157 B4
York St *continued*
Manchester, Hulme M15 162 B3
Manchester, Levenshulme M19 111 A8
Manchester M1 163 A4
Manchester M1, M2 159 A1
Manchester, University M1, M13 163 A3
Oldham OL9 153 B2
Radcliffe M26 44 D5
Rochdale OL16 31 B6
Stockport SK3 170 B4
Whitefield M45 62 F8
Wigan WN3 150 B4
York Terr
19 Bolton BL1 143 B2
Glossop SK13 116 C8
Sale M33 108 A4
Youd St WN7 75 F5
Youlgreave Cres SK13 171 A1
Young St
Farnworth BL4 60 E7
Leigh WN7 76 E4
Manchester M3 158 B1
Radcliffe M26 43 F5
Ramsbottom BL0 138 B2
Yulan Dr M33 107 C4
Yule St SK3 170 A4
Yvonne Cl WN4 73 D5

Z

Zama St BL0 11 A4
Zealand St OL4 67 C8
Zedburgh 22 OL12 139 B4
Zeta St M9 157 C3
Zetland Ave BL3 146 B2
Zetland Ave N BL3 146 B2
Zetland Rd M21 109 B8
Zetland St SK16 166 B1
Zinda Dil OL8 153 B1
Zinnia Dr M44 105 E8
Zion Terr OL12 13 E2
Zulu St BL2 148 B3
Zurich Gdns SK7 123 E3
Zyburn Ct M6 80 A3

Addresses

Name and Address	Telephone	Page	Grid reference

Name and Address	Telephone	Page	Grid reference

Addresses

Name and Address	Telephone	Page	Grid reference